# Statutes on the Conflict of La

CW00671318

*Statutes on the Conflict of Laws* provides students with the pr
legislation encountered in the study of private international law
volume. The legislation is not annotated, enabling the book to be used in examinations. It
has been structured and designed so that students can find the material they need quickly
and efficiently, with a table of contents organised chronologically by source type, and
alphabetical index.

# Statutes on the Conflict of Laws

Edited by

**Martin George and Andrew Dickinson**

·HART·
PUBLISHING

OXFORD AND PORTLAND, OREGON
2015

Published in the United Kingdom by Hart Publishing Ltd
16C Worcester Place, Oxford, OX1 2JW
Telephone: +44 (0)1865 517530
Fax: +44 (0)1865 510710
E-mail: mail@hartpub.co.uk
Website: http://www.hartpub.co.uk

Published in North America (US and Canada) by
Hart Publishing
c/o International Specialized Book Services
920 NE 58th Avenue, Suite 300
Portland, OR 97213-3786
USA
Tel: +1 503 287 3093 or toll-free: (1) 800 944 6190
Fax: +1 503 280 8832
E-mail: orders@isbs.com
Website: http://www.isbs.com

British Library Cataloguing in Publication Data
Data Available

ISBN: 978-1-84946-343-0

Typeset by Forewords, Oxon
Printed and bound in Great Britain by
CPI Group (UK) Ltd, Croydon CR0 4YY

# Preface

Twenty years ago a statute book on the conflict of laws would have been smaller, and perhaps more straightforward to compile. Now, however, the need for such a book seems more obvious. With the proliferation of European and international instruments, as well as domestic legislation on private international law, not only have the materials become more voluminous, but there is undoubtedly an additional layer of complexity in the subject that university students must seek to penetrate. Our hope is that in collecting the key primary sources in one manageable and accessible volume, we facilitate that task, and provide assistance to others undertaking research in the area.

The overarching purpose of the book is to deliver the material in a way that enables students to locate the relevant source quickly, whether in class or in an examination setting. This is reflected in the structure divided into four Parts: European Union materials (Part I); United Kingdom statutes (Part II); United Kingdom statutory instruments (Part III); and rules of procedure (Part IV). Other features, including grey-scaled tabs on the edges of each page marking out the sections, will hopefully provide further assistance (see the User Guide on p xi).

Our focus is on the general aspects of the subject, and on their application to the areas of commercial law, family law, wills and succession and property, as well as related aspects of civil procedure. Inevitably, we have not been able to include everything that might appear on the reading list in a university course on the conflict of laws. To attempt to do so would not only increase the size and weight of the volume, but also hinder the accessibility of the key materials. Accordingly, we have taken editorial decisions to exclude material that we consider to be of a specialist nature or as being of only peripheral relevance. In the former category, we have omitted (for example) the EU Insolvency Regulation, and other legislation in the insolvency field, as well as materials relating to arbitration. We have also been strict in drawing the line at legislation on the conflict of laws. Sources like the EU Charter of Fundamental Rights, the European Convention on Human Rights and the Human Rights Act 1998 are, no doubt, important in their interaction with rules of private international law (most obviously, in shaping public policy), but to include these sources would open the floodgates on what, in our view, is already a book full to the brim.

That said, we hope that this first edition will not be the last, and we would very much welcome suggestions from colleagues and students for inclusion or omission or for changes to the formatting in future editions.

We have sought to present the material as in force (including amendments) at 1 July 2015, although we have been able to include changes to the Civil Procedure Rules (including, importantly, to the grounds for service set out in Practice Direction 6B) due to enter into force on 1 October 2015. We have also included extracts from the Consumer Rights Act 2015, also expected to enter into force on that date.

The statutory materials relate to England and Wales, and provisions relating to Scotland or Northern Ireland only have been omitted.

We would like to thank the production team at Hart, in particular Tom Adams, for their assistance in putting this statute book together, and Jane Wright at the Ministry of Justice for help in updating the Civil Procedure Rules.

*Martin George*
*University of Leicester*
*Andrew Dickinson*
*St Catherine's College, Oxford*
*July 2015*
*martin.george@le.ac.uk*
*andrew.dickinson@law.ox.ac.uk*

# Contents

Preface                                                                                           v

User Guide                                                                                        xi

I.    **European Union Materials**
A.    **Treaties**
(1)   Treaty on the Functioning of the European Union                                             1

B.    **Regulations**
(2)   Council Regulation (EC) No 1206/2001 of 28 May 2001 on cooperation between the courts of
      the Member States in the taking of evidence in civil or commercial matters                  3
(3)   Council Regulation (EC) No 2201/2003 of 27 November 2003 concerning jurisdiction and the
      recognition and enforcement of judgments in matrimonial matters and the matters of parental
      responsibility, repealing Regulation (EC) No 1347/2000                                       13
(4)   Regulation (EC) No 805/2004 of the European Parliament and of the Council of 21 April 2004
      creating a European Enforcement Order for uncontested claims                                 37
(5)   Regulation (EC) No 1896/2006 of the European Parliament and of the Council of 12 December
      2006 creating a European order for payment procedure                                         49
(6)   Regulation (EC) No 861/2007 of the European Parliament and of the Council of 11 July 2007
      establishing a European Small Claims Procedure                                               61
(7)   Regulation (EC) No 864/2007 of the European Parliament and of the Council of 11 July 2007
      on the law applicable to non-contractual obligations (Rome II)                               73
(8)   Regulation (EC) No 1393/2007 of the European Parliament and of the Council of 13 November
      2007 on the service in the Member States of judicial and extrajudicial documents in civil or
      commercial matters (service of documents), and repealing Council Regulation (EC) No
      1348/2000                                                                                     85
(9)   Regulation (EC) No 593/2008 of the European Parliament and of the Council of 17 June
      2008 on the law applicable to contractual obligations (Rome I)                               95
(10)  Council Regulation (EC) No 4/2009 of 18 December 2008 on jurisdiction, applicable law,
      recognition and enforcement of decisions and cooperation in matters relating to maintenance
      obligations                                                                                  111
(11)  Regulation (EU) No 1215/2012 of the European Parliament and of the Council of 12 December
      2012 on jurisdiction and the recognition and enforcement of judgments in civil and
      commercial matters (recast)                                                                  139
(12)  Regulation (EU) No 606/2013 of the European Parliament and of the Council of 12 June 2013
      on mutual recognition of protection measures in civil matters                                165

C.    **Directives**
(13)  Council Directive 93/13/EEC of 5 April 1993 on unfair terms in consumer contracts           175
(14)  Council Directive 2003/8/EC of 27 January 2003 to improve access to justice in cross-border
      disputes by establishing minimum common rules relating to legal aid for such disputes        177
(15)  Directive 2008/52/EC of the European Parliament and of the Council of 21 May 2008 on
      certain aspects of mediation in civil and commercial matters                                 187

D.   Decisions

(16) Council Decision of 28 May 2001 establishing a European Judicial Network in civil and
commercial matters (2001/470/EC)                                                       193

E.   Conventions to which the EU is a party

(17) EC-Denmark Agreement (jurisdiction and judgments)

    Decision 2005/790/EC (signature)                                                   205

    Agreement                                                                          206

    Decision 2006/325/EC (conclusion)                                                  212

    Amending Agreement                                                                 213

    Amending Agreement                                                                 214

(18) EC-Denmark Agreement (service)

    Decision 2005/794/EC (signature)                                                   215

    Agreement                                                                          216

    Decision 2006/326/EC (conclusion)                                                  221

    Amending Agreement                                                                 222

(19) 2007 Lugano Convention (jurisdiction and judgments)

    Decision 2007/712/EC (signature)                                                   223

    Convention and Protocols                                                           224

    Decision 2009/430/EC (conclusion)                                                  247

(20) Hague Choice of Court Convention

    Decision 2009/397/EC (signature) incorporating Convention (Annex I)                251

    Decision 2014/887/EU (approval)                                                    262

(21) Hague Convention on the International Recovery of Child Support etc

    Decision 2011/220/EU (signature)                                                   265

    Decision 2011/432/EU (approval)                                                    266

    Convention                                                                         270

II.   United Kingdom Statutes

(22) Colonial Probates Act 1892                                                          293

(23) Administration of Justice Act 1920                                                  295

(24) Maintenance Orders (Facilities for Enforcement) Act 1920                            299

(25) Foreign Judgments (Reciprocal Enforcement) Act 1933                                 305

(26) Maintenance Orders Act 1950                                                         311

(27) Marriage (Enabling) Act 1960                                                        317

(28) Wills Act 1963                                                                      319

(29) Administration of Estates Act 1971                                                  321

(30) Civil Evidence Act 1972                                                             325

(31) Maintenance Orders (Reciprocal Enforcement) Act 1972                                327

(32) Domicile and Matrimonial Proceedings Act 1973                                       351

(33) Matrimonial Causes Act 1973                                                         359

(34) Evidence (Proceedings in Other Jurisdictions) Act 1975                              363

(35) Legitimacy Act 1976                                                                 367

(36) Unfair Contract Terms Act 1977                                                      369

(37) Protection of Trading Interests Act 1980 — 371

(38) Senior Courts Act 1981 — 373

(39) Civil Jurisdiction and Judgments Act 1982 — 375

(40) Foreign Limitation Periods Act 1984 — 399

(41) Matrimonial and Family Proceedings Act 1984 — 403

(42) Child Abduction and Custody Act 1985 — 411

(43) Family Law Act 1986 — 429

(44) Marriage (Prohibited Degrees of Relationship) Act 1986 — 449

(45) Recognition of Trusts Act 1987 — 451

(46) Foreign Corporations Act 1991 — 455

(47) Private International Law (Miscellaneous Provisions) Act 1995 — 457

(48) Employment Rights Act 1996 — 461

(49) Late Payment of Commercial Debts (Interest) Act 1998 — 463

(50) Adoption (Intercountry Aspects) Act 1999 — 465

(51) Adoption and Children Act 2002 — 475

(52) Civil Partnership Act 2004 — 481

(53) Mental Capacity Act 2005 — 493

(54) Companies Act 2006 — 501

(55) Defamation Act 2013 — 505

(56) Marriage (Same Sex Couples) Act 2013 — 507

(57) Consumer Rights Act 2015 — 513

## III. United Kingdom Statutory Instruments

(58) Civil Jurisdiction and Judgments Act 1982 (Interim Relief) Order SI 1997/302 — 517

(59) Unfair Terms in Consumer Contracts Regulations SI 1999/2083 — 519

(60) Civil Jurisdiction and Judgments (Authentic Instruments and Court Settlements) Order SI 2001/3928 — 521

(61) Civil Jurisdiction and Judgments Order SI 2001/3929 — 523

(62) Adoptions with a Foreign Element Regulations SI 2005/392 — 527

(63) Civil Partnership (Jurisdiction and Recognition of Judgments) Regulations SI 2005/3334 — 547

(64) Overseas Companies (Execution of Documents and Registration of Charges) Regulations SI 2009/1917 — 551

(65) Parental Responsibility and Measures for the Protection of Children (International Obligations) (England and Wales and Northern Ireland) Regulations SI 2010/1898 — 555

(66) Civil Jurisdiction and Judgments (Maintenance) (Rules of Court) Regulations SI 2011/1215 — 561

(67) Civil Jurisdiction and Judgments (Maintenance) Regulations SI 2011/1484 — 563

(68) International Recovery of Maintenance (Hague Convention 2007 etc) Regulations SI 2012/2814 — 573

(69) Marriage (Same Sex Couples) (Jurisdiction and Recognition of Judgments) Regulations SI 2014/543 — 579

(70) Consular Marriages and Marriages under Foreign Law (No. 2) Order SI 2014/3265 — 583

(71) Civil Jurisdiction and Judgments (Protection Measures) Regulations SI 2014/3298 — 589

## IV. Rules of Procedure

(72) Civil Procedure Rules SI 1998/3132     591

(73) Court of Protection Rules SI 2007/1744     659

(74) Family Procedure Rules SI 2010/2955     667

Alphabetical Index     755

# Statutes on the Conflict of Laws
## User Guide

Part I   European Union Materials
Treaties
Regulations
Directives
Decisions
Conventions to which the EU is a party

Part II   United Kingdom Statutes

Part III  United Kingdom Statutory Instruments

Part IV  Rules of Procedure

European Union Materials

UK Statutes

UK Statutory Instruments

Rules of Procedure

---

## Notes

For ease of access:

1. Each Part is marked by a greyscale box on the odd numbered (right hand side) pages (see examples to the right).

2. Page numbering is shown in the top corner of each page.

3. The first page of each source is marked in the black box in the top corner of the first odd numbered (right side) page on which that source appears (see example above).

## Key

| | |
|---|---|
| . . . | Provision(s) or words omitted from this collection |
| [. . .] | Provision(s) or words repealed or deleted by subsequent legislation |
| [Text] | Provision or words added by subsequent legislation |

# Treaty on the Functioning of the European Union

[2012] OJ C326/47

TITLE V

## AREA OF FREEDOM, SECURITY AND JUSTICE

CHAPTER 1

### GENERAL PROVISIONS

*Article 67*

**(ex Article 61 TEC and ex Article 29 TEU)**

1. The Union shall constitute an area of freedom, security and justice with respect for fundamental rights and the different legal systems and traditions of the Member States.

. . .

4. The Union shall facilitate access to justice, in particular through the principle of mutual recognition of judicial and extrajudicial decisions in civil matters.

*Article 68*

The European Council shall define the strategic guidelines for legislative and operational planning within the area of freedom, security and justice.

*Article 69*

National Parliaments ensure that the proposals and legislative initiatives submitted under Chapters 4 and 5 comply with the principle of subsidiarity, in accordance with the arrangements laid down by the Protocol on the application of the principles of subsidiarity and proportionality.

. . .

CHAPTER 3

### JUDICIAL COOPERATION IN CIVIL MATTERS

*Article 81*

**(ex Article 65 TEC)**

1. The Union shall develop judicial cooperation in civil matters having cross-border implications, based on the principle of mutual recognition of judgments and of decisions in extrajudicial cases. Such cooperation may include the adoption of measures for the approximation of the laws and regulations of the Member States.

2. For the purposes of paragraph 1, the European Parliament and the Council, acting in accordance with the ordinary legislative procedure, shall adopt measures, particularly when necessary for the proper functioning of the internal market, aimed at ensuring:

(a) the mutual recognition and enforcement between Member States of judgments and of decisions in extrajudicial cases;

(b) the cross-border service of judicial and extrajudicial documents;

(c) the compatibility of the rules applicable in the Member States concerning conflict of laws and of jurisdiction;

(d) cooperation in the taking of evidence;

(e)  effective access to justice;

(f)  the elimination of obstacles to the proper functioning of civil proceedings, if necessary by promoting the compatibility of the rules on civil procedure applicable in the Member States;

(g)  the development of alternative methods of dispute settlement;

(h)  support for the training of the judiciary and judicial staff.

3.  Notwithstanding paragraph 2, measures concerning family law with cross-border implications shall be established by the Council, acting in accordance with a special legislative procedure. The Council shall act unanimously after consulting the European Parliament.

The Council, on a proposal from the Commission, may adopt a decision determining those aspects of family law with cross-border implications which may be the subject of acts adopted by the ordinary legislative procedure. The Council shall act unanimously after consulting the European Parliament.

The proposal referred to in the second subparagraph shall be notified to the national Parliaments. If a national Parliament makes known its opposition within six months of the date of such notification, the decision shall not be adopted. In the absence of opposition, the Council may adopt the decision.

. . .

# Council Regulation (EC) No 1206/2001 of 28 May 2001 on cooperation between the courts of the Member States in the taking of evidence in civil or commercial matters

[2001] OJ L 174/1

THE COUNCIL OF THE EUROPEAN UNION,

Having regard to the Treaty establishing the European Community, and in particular Article 61(c) and Article 67(1) thereof,

Having regard to the initiative of the Federal Republic of Germany,

Having regard to the opinion of the European Parliament,

Having regard to the opinion of the Economic and Social Committee,

Whereas:

(1) The European Union has set itself the objective of maintaining and developing the European Union as an area of freedom, security and justice in which the free movement of persons is ensured. For the gradual establishment of such an area, the Community is to adopt, among others, the measures relating to judicial cooperation in civil matters needed for the proper functioning of the internal market.

(2) For the purpose of the proper functioning of the internal market, cooperation between courts in the taking of evidence should be improved, and in particular simplified and accelerated.

(3) At its meeting in Tampere on 15 and 16 October 1999, the European Council recalled that new procedural legislation in cross-border cases, in particular on the taking of evidence, should be prepared.

(4) This area falls within the scope of Article 65 of the Treaty.

(5) The objectives of the proposed action, namely the improvement of cooperation between the courts on the taking of evidence in civil or commercial matters, cannot be sufficiently achieved by the Member States and can therefore be better achieved at Community level. The Community may adopt measures in accordance with the principle of subsidiarity as set out in Article 5 of the Treaty. In accordance with the principle of proportionality, as set out in that Article, this Regulation does not go beyond what is necessary to achieve those objectives.

(6) To date, there is no binding instrument between all the Member States concerning the taking of evidence. The Hague Convention of 18 March 1970 on the taking of evidence abroad in civil or commercial matters applies between only 11 Member States of the European Union.

(7) As it is often essential for a decision in a civil or commercial matter pending before a court in a Member State to take evidence in another Member State, the Community's activity cannot be limited to the field of transmission of judicial and extrajudicial documents in civil or commercial matters which falls within the scope of Council Regulation (EC) No 1348/2000 of 29 May 2000 on the serving in the Member States of judicial and extrajudicial documents in civil or commercial matters. It is therefore necessary to continue the improvement of cooperation between courts of Member States in the field of taking of evidence.

(8) The efficiency of judicial procedures in civil or commercial matters requires that the transmission and execution of requests for the performance of taking of evidence is to be made directly and by the most rapid means possible between Member States' courts.

(9) Speed in transmission of requests for the performance of taking of evidence warrants the use of all appropriate means, provided that certain conditions as to the legibility and reliability of the document received are observed. So as to ensure the utmost clarity and legal certainty the request for the performance of taking of evidence must be transmitted on a form to be completed in the language of the Member State of the requested court or in another language accepted by that State. For the same reasons, forms should also be used as far as possible for further communication between the relevant courts.

(10) A request for the performance of the taking of evidence should be executed expeditiously. If it is not possible for the request to be executed within 90 days of receipt by the requested court, the latter should inform the requesting court accordingly, stating the reasons which prevent the request from being executed swiftly.

(11) To secure the effectiveness of this Regulation, the possibility of refusing to execute the request for the performance of taking of evidence should be confined to strictly limited exceptional situations.

(12) The requested court should execute the request in accordance with the law of its Member State.

(13) The parties and, if any, their representatives, should be able to be present at the performance of the taking of evidence, if that is provided for by the law of the Member State of the requesting court, in order to be able to follow the proceedings in a comparable way as if evidence were taken in the Member State of the requesting court. They should also have the right to request to participate in order to have a more active role in the performance of the taking of evidence. However, the conditions under which they may participate should be determined by the requested court in accordance with the law of its Member State.

(14) The representatives of the requesting court should be able to be present at the performance of the taking of evidence, if that is compatible with the law of the Member State of the requesting court, in order to have an improved possibility of evaluation of evidence. They should also have the right to request to participate, under the conditions laid down by the requested court in accordance with the law of its Member State, in order to have a more active role in the performance of the taking of evidence.

(15) In order to facilitate the taking of evidence it should be possible for a court in a Member State, in accordance with the law of its Member State, to take evidence directly in another Member State, if accepted by the latter, and under the conditions determined by the central body or competent authority of the requested Member State.

(16) The execution of the request, according to Article 10, should not give rise to a claim for any reimbursement of taxes or costs. Nevertheless, if the requested court requires reimbursement, the fees paid to experts and interpreters, as well as the costs occasioned by the application of Article 10(3) and (4), should not be borne by that court. In such a case, the requesting court is to take the necessary measures to ensure reimbursement without delay. Where the opinion of an expert is required, the requested court may, before executing the request, ask the requesting court for an adequate deposit or advance towards the costs.

(17) This Regulation should prevail over the provisions applying to its field of application, contained in international conventions concluded by the Member States. Member States should be free to adopt agreements or arrangements to further facilitate cooperation in the taking of evidence.

(18) The information transmitted pursuant to this Regulation should enjoy protection. Since Directive 95/46/EC of the European Parliament and of the Council of 24 October 1995 on the protection of individuals with regard to the processing of personal data and on the free movement of such data, and Directive 97/66/EC of the European Parliament and of the Council of 15 December 1997 concerning the processing of personal data and the protection of privacy in the telecommunications sector, are applicable, there is no need for specific provisions on data protection in this Regulation.

(19) The measures necessary for the implementation of this Regulation should be adopted in accordance with Council Decision 1999/468/EC of 28 June 1999 laying down the procedures for the exercise of implementing powers conferred on the Commission.

(20) For the proper functioning of this Regulation, the Commission should review its application and propose such amendments as may appear necessary.

(21) The United Kingdom and Ireland, in accordance with Article 3 of the Protocol on the position of the United Kingdom and Ireland annexed to the Treaty on the European Union and to the Treaty establishing the European Community, have given notice of their wish to take part in the adoption and application of this Regulation.

(22) Denmark, in accordance with Articles 1 and 2 of the Protocol on the position of Denmark annexed to the Treaty on European Union and to the Treaty establishing the European Community,

is not participating in the adoption of this Regulation, and is therefore not bound by it nor subject to its application,

HAS ADOPTED THIS REGULATION:

## CHAPTER I

## GENERAL PROVISIONS

*Article 1*

**Scope**

1. This Regulation shall apply in civil or commercial matters where the court of a Member State, in accordance with the provisions of the law of that State, requests:

(a)   the competent court of another Member State to take evidence; or

(b)   to take evidence directly in another Member State.

2. A request shall not be made to obtain evidence which is not intended for use in judicial proceedings, commenced or contemplated.

3. In this Regulation, the term 'Member State' shall mean Member States with the exception of Denmark.

*Article 2*

**Direct transmission between the courts**

1. Requests pursuant to Article 1(1)(a), hereinafter referred to as 'requests', shall be transmitted by the court before which the proceedings are commenced or contemplated, hereinafter referred to as the 'requesting court', directly to the competent court of another Member State, hereinafter referred to as the 'requested court', for the performance of the taking of evidence.

2. Each Member State shall draw up a list of the courts competent for the performance of taking of evidence according to this Regulation. The list shall also indicate the territorial and, where appropriate, the special jurisdiction of those courts.

*Article 3*

**Central body**

1. Each Member State shall designate a central body responsible for:

(a)   supplying information to the courts;

(b)   seeking solutions to any difficulties which may arise in respect of a request;

(c)   forwarding, in exceptional cases, at the request of a requesting court, a request to the competent court.

2. A federal State, a State in which several legal systems apply or a State with autonomous territorial entities shall be free to designate more than one central body.

3. Each Member State shall also designate the central body referred to in paragraph 1 or one or several competent authority(ies) to be responsible for taking decisions on requests pursuant to Article 17.

European Union Materials

## CHAPTER II

## TRANSMISSION AND EXECUTION OF REQUESTS

### SECTION 1

### Transmission of the request

*Article 4*

#### Form and content of the request

1. The request shall be made using form A or, where appropriate, form I in the Annex. It shall contain the following details:

(a) the requesting and, where appropriate, the requested court;

(b) the names and addresses of the parties to the proceedings and their representatives, if any;

(c) the nature and subject matter of the case and a brief statement of the facts;

(d) a description of the taking of evidence to be performed;

(e) where the request is for the examination of a person:

— the name(s) and address(es) of the person(s) to be examined,

— the questions to be put to the person(s) to be examined or a statement of the facts about which he is (they are) to be examined,

— where appropriate, a reference to a right to refuse to testify under the law of the Member State of the requesting court,

— any requirement that the examination is to be carried out under oath or affirmation in lieu thereof, and any special form to be used,

— where appropriate, any other information that the requesting court deems necessary;

(f) where the request is for any other form of taking of evidence, the documents or other objects to be inspected;

(g) where appropriate, any request pursuant to Article 10(3) and (4), and Articles 11 and 12 and any information necessary for the application thereof.

2. The request and all documents accompanying the request shall be exempted from authentication or any equivalent formality.

3. Documents which the requesting court deems it necessary to enclose for the execution of the request shall be accompanied by a translation into the language in which the request was written.

*Article 5*

### Language

The request and communications pursuant to this Regulation shall be drawn up in the official language of the requested Member State or, if there are several official languages in that Member State, in the official language or one of the official languages of the place where the requested taking of evidence is to be performed, or in another language which the requested Member State has indicated it can accept. Each Member State shall indicate the official language or languages of the institutions of the European Community other than its own which is or are acceptable to it for completion of the forms.

*Article 6*

#### Transmission of requests and other communications

Requests and communications pursuant to this Regulation shall be transmitted by the swiftest possible means, which the requested Member State has indicated it can accept. The transmission may be carried out by any appropriate means, provided that the document received accurately reflects the content of the document forwarded and that all information in it is legible.

# SECTION 2

## Receipt of request

### *Article 7*

### Receipt of request

1. Within seven days of receipt of the request, the requested competent court shall send an acknowledgement of receipt to the requesting court using form B in the Annex. Where the request does not comply with the conditions laid down in Articles 5 and 6, the requested court shall enter a note to that effect in the acknowledgement of receipt.

2. Where the execution of a request made using form A in the Annex, which complies with the conditions laid down in Article 5, does not fall within the jurisdiction of the court to which it was transmitted, the latter shall forward the request to the competent court of its Member State and shall inform the requesting court thereof using form A in the Annex.

### *Article 8*

### Incomplete request

1. If a request cannot be executed because it does not contain all of the necessary information pursuant to Article 4, the requested court shall inform the requesting court thereof without delay and, at the latest, within 30 days of receipt of the request using form C in the Annex, and shall request it to send the missing information, which should be indicated as precisely as possible.

2. If a request cannot be executed because a deposit or advance is necessary in accordance with Article 18(3), the requested court shall inform the requesting court thereof without delay and, at the latest, within 30 days of receipt of the request using form C in the Annex and inform the requesting court how the deposit or advance should be made. The requested Court shall acknowledge receipt of the deposit or advance without delay, at the latest within 10 days of receipt of the deposit or the advance using form D.

### *Article 9*

### Completion of the request

1. If the requested court has noted on the acknowledgement of receipt pursuant to Article 7(1) that the request does not comply with the conditions laid down in Articles 5 and 6 or has informed the requesting court pursuant to Article 8 that the request cannot be executed because it does not contain all of the necessary information pursuant to Article 4, the time limit pursuant to Article 10 shall begin to run when the requested court received the request duly completed.

2. Where the requested court has asked for a deposit or advance in accordance with Article 18(3), this time limit shall begin to run when the deposit or the advance is made.

# SECTION 3

## Taking of evidence by the requested court

### *Article 10*

### General provisions on the execution of the request

1. The requested court shall execute the request without delay and, at the latest, within 90 days of receipt of the request.

2. The requested court shall execute the request in accordance with the law of its Member State.

3. The requesting court may call for the request to be executed in accordance with a special procedure provided for by the law of its Member State, using form A in the Annex. The requested court shall comply with such a requirement unless this procedure is incompatible with the law of the Member State of the requested court or by reason of major practical difficulties. If the requested court does not comply with the requirement for one of these reasons it shall inform the requesting court using form E in the Annex.

4. The requesting court may ask the requested court to use communications technology at the performance of the taking of evidence, in particular by using videoconference and teleconference.

The requested court shall comply with such a requirement unless this is incompatible with the law of the Member State of the requested court or by reason of major practical difficulties.

If the requested court does not comply with the requirement for one of these reasons, it shall inform the requesting court, using form E in the Annex.

If there is no access to the technical means referred to above in the requesting or in the requested court, such means may be made available by the courts by mutual agreement.

*Article 11*

**Performance with the presence and participation of the parties**

1. If it is provided for by the law of the Member State of the requesting court, the parties and, if any, their representatives, have the right to be present at the performance of the taking of evidence by the requested court.

2. The requesting court shall, in its request, inform the requested court that the parties and, if any, their representatives, will be present and, where appropriate, that their participation is requested, using form A in the Annex. This information may also be given at any other appropriate time.

3. If the participation of the parties and, if any, their representatives, is requested at the performance of the taking of evidence, the requested court shall determine, in accordance with Article 10, the conditions under which they may participate.

4. The requested court shall notify the parties and, if any, their representatives, of the time when, the place where, the proceedings will take place, and, where appropriate, the conditions under which they may participate, using form F in the Annex.

5. Paragraphs 1 to 4 shall not affect the possibility for the requested court of asking the parties and, if any their representatives, to be present at or to participate in the performance of the taking of evidence if that possibility is provided for by the law of its Member State.

*Article 12*

**Performance with the presence and participation of representatives of the requesting court**

1. If it is compatible with the law of the Member State of the requesting court, representatives of the requesting court have the right to be present in the performance of the taking of evidence by the requested court.

2. For the purpose of this Article, the term 'representative' shall include members of the judicial personnel designated by the requesting court, in accordance with the law of its Member State. The requesting court may also designate, in accordance with the law of its Member State, any other person, such as an expert.

3. The requesting court shall, in its request, inform the requested court that its representatives will be present and, where appropriate, that their participation is requested, using form A in the Annex. This information may also be given at any other appropriate time.

4. If the participation of the representatives of the requesting court is requested in the performance of the taking of evidence, the requested court shall determine, in accordance with Article 10, the conditions under which they may participate.

5. The requested court shall notify the requesting court, of the time when, and the place where, the proceedings will take place, and, where appropriate, the conditions under which the representatives may participate, using form F in the Annex.

*Article 13*

**Coercive measures**

Where necessary, in executing a request the requested court shall apply the appropriate coercive measures in the instances and to the extent as are provided for by the law of the Member State of the requested court for the execution of a request made for the same purpose by its national authorities or one of the parties concerned.

## Article 14

**Refusal to execute**

1. A request for the hearing of a person shall not be executed when the person concerned claims the right to refuse to give evidence or to be prohibited from giving evidence,

(a)   under the law of the Member State of the requested court; or

(b)   under the law of the Member State of the requesting court, and such right has been specified in the request, or, if need be, at the instance of the requested court, has been confirmed by the requesting court.

2. In addition to the grounds referred to in paragraph 1, the execution of a request may be refused only if:

(a)   the request does not fall within the scope of this Regulation as set out in Article 1; or

(b)   the execution of the request under the law of the Member State of the requested court does not fall within the functions of the judiciary; or

(c)   the requesting court does not comply with the request of the requested court to complete the request pursuant to Article 8 within 30 days after the requested court asked it to do so; or

(d)   a deposit or advance asked for in accordance with Article 18(3) is not made within 60 days after the requested court asked for such a deposit or advance.

3. Execution may not be refused by the requested court solely on the ground that under the law of its Member State a court of that Member State has exclusive jurisdiction over the subject matter of the action or that the law of that Member State would not admit the right of action on it.

4. If execution of the request is refused on one of the grounds referred to in paragraph 2, the requested court shall notify the requesting court thereof within 60 days of receipt of the request by the requested court using form H in the Annex.

## Article 15

**Notification of delay**

If the requested court is not in a position to execute the request within 90 days of receipt, it shall inform the requesting court thereof, using form G in the Annex. When it does so, the grounds for the delay shall be given as well as the estimated time that the requested court expects it will need to execute the request.

## Article 16

**Procedure after execution of the request**

The requested court shall send without delay to the requesting court the documents establishing the execution of the request and, where appropriate, return the documents received from the requesting court. The documents shall be accompanied by a confirmation of execution using form H in the Annex.

## SECTION 4

**Direct taking of evidence by the requesting court**

## Article 17

1. Where a court requests to take evidence directly in another Member State, it shall submit a request to the central body or the competent authority referred to in Article 3(3) in that State, using form I in the Annex.

2. Direct taking of evidence may only take place if it can be performed on a voluntary basis without the need for coercive measures.

Where the direct taking of evidence implies that a person shall be heard, the requesting court shall inform that person that the performance shall take place on a voluntary basis.

3. The taking of evidence shall be performed by a member of the judicial personnel or by any other person such as an expert, who will be designated, in accordance with the law of the Member State of the requesting court.

4. Within 30 days of receiving the request, the central body or the competent authority of the requested Member State shall inform the requesting court if the request is accepted and, if necessary, under what conditions according to the law of its Member State such performance is to be carried out, using form J.

In particular, the central body or the competent authority may assign a court of its Member State to take part in the performance of the taking of evidence in order to ensure the proper application of this Article and the conditions that have been set out.

The central body or the competent authority shall encourage the use of communications technology, such as videoconferences and teleconferences.

5. The central body or the competent authority may refuse direct taking of evidence only if:

(a)   the request does not fall within the scope of this Regulation as set out in Article 1;

(b)   the request does not contain all of the necessary information pursuant to Article 4; or

(c)   the direct taking of evidence requested is contrary to fundamental principles of law in its Member State.

6. Without prejudice to the conditions laid down in accordance with paragraph 4, the requesting court shall execute the request in accordance with the law of its Member State.

## SECTION 5

### Costs

*Article 18*

1. The execution of the request, in accordance with Article 10, shall not give rise to a claim for any reimbursement of taxes or costs.

2. Nevertheless, if the requested court so requires, the requesting court shall ensure the reimbursement, without delay, of:

   — the fees paid to experts and interpreters, and

   — the costs occasioned by the application of Article 10(3) and(4).

The duty for the parties to bear these fees or costs shall be governed by the law of the Member State of the requesting court.

3. Where the opinion of an expert is required, the requested court may, before executing the request, ask the requesting court for an adequate deposit or advance towards the requested costs. In all other cases, a deposit or advance shall not be a condition for the execution of a request.

The deposit or advance shall be made by the parties if that is provided for by the law of the Member State of the requesting court.

## CHAPTER III

### FINAL PROVISIONS

*Article 19*

### Implementing rules

1. The Commission shall draw up and regularly update a manual, which shall also be available electronically, containing the information provided by the Member States in accordance with Article 22 and the agreements or arrangements in force, according to Article 21.

[2. The updating or making of technical amendments to the standard forms set out in the Annex shall be carried out by the Commission. Those measures, designed to amend non-essential elements of this Regulation, shall be adopted in accordance with the regulatory procedure with scrutiny referred to in Article 20(2).]

[*Article 20*

1. The Commission shall be assisted by a committee.

2. Where reference is made to this paragraph, Article 5a(1) to (4) and Article 7 of Decision 1999/468/EC shall apply, having regard to the provisions of Article 8 thereof.]

*Article 21*

**Relationship with existing or future agreements or arrangements between Member States**

1. This Regulation shall, in relation to matters to which it applies, prevail over other provisions contained in bilateral or multilateral agreements or arrangements concluded by the Member States and in particular the Hague Convention of 1 March 1954 on Civil Procedure and the Hague Convention of 18 March 1970 on the Taking of Evidence Abroad in Civil or Commercial Matters, in relations between the Member States party thereto.

2. This Regulation shall not preclude Member States from maintaining or concluding agreements or arrangements between two or more of them to further facilitate the taking of evidence, provided that they are compatible with this Regulation.

3. Member States shall send to the Commission:

(a) by 1 July 2003, a copy of the agreements or arrangements maintained between the Member States referred to in paragraph 2;

(b) a copy of the agreements or arrangements concluded between the Member States referred to in paragraph 2 as well as drafts of such agreements or arrangements which they intend to adopt; and

(c) any denunciation of, or amendments to, these agreements or arrangements.

*Article 22*

**Communication**

By 1 July 2003 each Member State shall communicate to the Commission the following:

(a) the list pursuant to Article 2(2) indicating the territorial and, where appropriate, the special jurisdiction of the courts;

(b) the names and addresses of the central bodies and competent authorities pursuant to Article 3, indicating their territorial jurisdiction;

(c) the technical means for the receipt of requests available to the courts on the list pursuant to Article 2(2);

(d) the languages accepted for the requests as referred to in Article 5.

Member States shall inform the Commission of any subsequent changes to this information.

*Article 23*

**Review**

No later than 1 January 2007, and every five years thereafter, the Commission shall present to the European Parliament, the Council and the Economic and Social Committee a report on the application of this Regulation, paying special attention to the practical application of Article 3(1)(c) and 3, and Articles 17 and 18.

*Article 24*

**Entry into force**

1. This Regulation shall enter into force on 1 July 2001.

2. This Regulation shall apply from 1 January 2004, except for Articles 19, 21 and 22, which shall apply from 1 July 2001.

This Regulation shall be binding in its entirety and directly applicable in the Member States in accordance with the Treaty establishing the European Community.

*[Annex omitted]*

# Council Regulation (EC) No 2201/2003 of 27 November 2003 concerning jurisdiction and the recognition and enforcement of judgments in matrimonial matters and the matters of parental responsibility, repealing Regulation (EC) No 1347/2000

[2003] OJ L 338/1

THE COUNCIL OF THE EUROPEAN UNION,

Having regard to the Treaty establishing the European Community, and in particular Article 61(c) and Article 67(1) thereof,

Having regard to the proposal from the Commission,

Having regard to the opinion of the European Parliament,

Having regard to the opinion of the European Economic and Social Committee,

Whereas:

(1) The European Community has set the objective of creating an area of freedom, security and justice, in which the free movement of persons is ensured. To this end, the Community is to adopt, among others, measures in the field of judicial cooperation in civil matters that are necessary for the proper functioning of the internal market.

(2) The Tampere European Council endorsed the principle of mutual recognition of judicial decisions as the cornerstone for the creation of a genuine judicial area, and identified visiting rights as a priority.

(3) Council Regulation (EC) No 1347/2000 sets out rules on jurisdiction, recognition and enforcement of judgments in matrimonial matters and matters of parental responsibility for the children of both spouses rendered on the occasion of the matrimonial proceedings. The content of this Regulation was substantially taken over from the Convention of 28 May 1998 on the same subject matter .

(4) On 3 July 2000 France presented an initiative for a Council Regulation on the mutual enforcement of judgments on rights of access to children.

(5) In order to ensure equality for all children, this Regulation covers all decisions on parental responsibility, including measures for the protection of the child, independently of any link with a matrimonial proceeding.

(6) Since the application of the rules on parental responsibility often arises in the context of matrimonial proceedings, it is more appropriate to have a single instrument for matters of divorce and parental responsibility.

(7) The scope of this Regulation covers civil matters, whatever the nature of the court or tribunal.

(8) As regards judgments on divorce, legal separation or marriage annulment, this Regulation should apply only to the dissolution of matrimonial ties and should not deal with issues such as the grounds for divorce, property consequences of the marriage or any other ancillary measures.

(9) As regards the property of the child, this Regulation should apply only to measures for the protection of the child, i.e. (i) the designation and functions of a person or body having charge of the child's property, representing or assisting the child, and (ii) the administration, conservation or disposal of the child's property. In this context, this Regulation should, for instance, apply in cases where the parents are in dispute as regards the administration of the child's property. Measures relating to the child's property which do not concern the protection of the child should continue to be governed by Council Regulation (EC) No 44/2001 of 22 December 2000 on jurisdiction and the recognition and enforcement of judgments in civil and commercial matters.

(10) This Regulation is not intended to apply to matters relating to social security, public measures of a general nature in matters of education or health or to decisions on the right of asylum and on immigration. In addition it does not apply to the establishment of parenthood, since this is a different

matter from the attribution of parental responsibility, nor to other questions linked to the status of persons. Moreover, it does not apply to measures taken as a result of criminal offences committed by children.

(11) Maintenance obligations are excluded from the scope of this Regulation as these are already covered by Council Regulation No 44/2001. The courts having jurisdiction under this Regulation will generally have jurisdiction to rule on maintenance obligations by application of Article 5(2) of Council Regulation No 44/2001.

(12) The grounds of jurisdiction in matters of parental responsibility established in the present Regulation are shaped in the light of the best interests of the child, in particular on the criterion of proximity. This means that jurisdiction should lie in the first place with the Member State of the child's habitual residence, except for certain cases of a change in the child's residence or pursuant to an agreement between the holders of parental responsibility.

(13) In the interest of the child, this Regulation allows, by way of exception and under certain conditions, that the court having jurisdiction may transfer a case to a court of another Member State if this court is better placed to hear the case. However, in this case the second court should not be allowed to transfer the case to a third court.

(14) This Regulation should have effect without prejudice to the application of public international law concerning diplomatic immunities. Where jurisdiction under this Regulation cannot be exercised by reason of the existence of diplomatic immunity in accordance with international law, jurisdiction should be exercised in accordance with national law in a Member State in which the person concerned does not enjoy such immunity.

(15) Council Regulation (EC) No 1348/2000 of 29 May 2000 on the service in the Member States of judicial and extrajudicial documents in civil or commercial matters should apply to the service of documents in proceedings instituted pursuant to this Regulation.

(16) This Regulation should not prevent the courts of a Member State from taking provisional, including protective measures, in urgent cases, with regard to persons or property situated in that State.

(17) In cases of wrongful removal or retention of a child, the return of the child should be obtained without delay, and to this end the Hague Convention of 25 October 1980 would continue to apply as complemented by the provisions of this Regulation, in particular Article 11. The courts of the Member State to or in which the child has been wrongfully removed or retained should be able to oppose his or her return in specific, duly justified cases. However, such a decision could be replaced by a subsequent decision by the court of the Member State of habitual residence of the child prior to the wrongful removal or retention. Should that judgment entail the return of the child, the return should take place without any special procedure being required for recognition and enforcement of that judgment in the Member State to or in which the child has been removed or retained.

(18) Where a court has decided not to return a child on the basis of Article 13 of the 1980 Hague Convention, it should inform the court having jurisdiction or central authority in the Member State where the child was habitually resident prior to the wrongful removal or retention. Unless the court in the latter Member State has been seised, this court or the central authority should notify the parties. This obligation should not prevent the central authority from also notifying the relevant public authorities in accordance with national law.

(19) The hearing of the child plays an important role in the application of this Regulation, although this instrument is not intended to modify national procedures applicable.

(20) The hearing of a child in another Member State may take place under the arrangements laid down in Council Regulation (EC) No 1206/2001 of 28 May 2001 on cooperation between the courts of the Member States in the taking of evidence in civil or commercial matters .

(21) The recognition and enforcement of judgments given in a Member State should be based on the principle of mutual trust and the grounds for non-recognition should be kept to the minimum required.

(22) Authentic instruments and agreements between parties that are enforceable in one Member

State should be treated as equivalent to 'judgments' for the purpose of the application of the rules on recognition and enforcement.

(23) The Tampere European Council considered in its conclusions (point 34) that judgments in the field of family litigation should be 'automatically recognised throughout the Union without any intermediate proceedings or grounds for refusal of enforcement'. This is why judgments on rights of access and judgments on return that have been certified in the Member State of origin in accordance with the provisions of this Regulation should be recognised and enforceable in all other Member States without any further procedure being required. Arrangements for the enforcement of such judgments continue to be governed by national law.

(24) The certificate issued to facilitate enforcement of the judgment should not be subject to appeal. It should be rectified only where there is a material error, i.e. where it does not correctly reflect the judgment.

(25) Central authorities should cooperate both in general matter and in specific cases, including for purposes of promoting the amicable resolution of family disputes, in matters of parental responsibility. To this end central authorities shall participate in the European Judicial Network in civil and commercial matters created by Council Decision 2001/470/EC of 28 May 2001 establishing a European Judicial Network in civil and commercial matters.

(26) The Commission should make publicly available and update the lists of courts and redress procedures communicated by the Member States.

(27) The measures necessary for the implementation of this Regulation should be adopted in accordance with Council Decision 1999/468/EC of 28 June 1999 laying down the procedures for the exercise of implementing powers conferred on the Commission.

(28) This Regulation replaces Regulation (EC) No 1347/2000 which is consequently repealed.

(29) For the proper functioning of this Regulation, the Commission should review its application and propose such amendments as may appear necessary.

(30) The United Kingdom and Ireland, in accordance with Article 3 of the Protocol on the position of the United Kingdom and Ireland annexed to the Treaty on European Union and the Treaty establishing the European Community, have given notice of their wish to take part in the adoption and application of this Regulation.

(31) Denmark, in accordance with Articles 1 and 2 of the Protocol on the position of Denmark annexed to the Treaty on European Union and the Treaty establishing the European Community, is not participating in the adoption of this Regulation and is therefore not bound by it nor subject to its application.

(32) Since the objectives of this Regulation cannot be sufficiently achieved by the Member States and can therefore be better achieved at Community level, the Community may adopt measures, in accordance with the principle of subsidiarity as set out in Article 5 of the Treaty. In accordance with the principle of proportionality, as set out in that Article, this Regulation does not go beyond what is necessary in order to achieve those objectives.

(33) This Regulation recognises the fundamental rights and observes the principles of the Charter of Fundamental Rights of the European Union. In particular, it seeks to ensure respect for the fundamental rights of the child as set out in Article 24 of the Charter of Fundamental Rights of the European Union,

HAS ADOPTED THE PRESENT REGULATION:

# CHAPTER I

## SCOPE AND DEFINITIONS

*Article 1*

### Scope

1. This Regulation shall apply, whatever the nature of the court or tribunal, in civil matters relating to:

(a)  divorce, legal separation or marriage annulment;

(b)  the attribution, exercise, delegation, restriction or termination of parental responsibility.

2.  The matters referred to in paragraph 1(b) may, in particular, deal with:

(a)  rights of custody and rights of access;

(b)  guardianship, curatorship and similar institutions;

(c)  the designation and functions of any person or body having charge of the child's person or property, representing or assisting the child;

(d)  the placement of the child in a foster family or in institutional care;

(e)  measures for the protection of the child relating to the administration, conservation or disposal of the child's property.

3.  This Regulation shall not apply to:

(a)  the establishment or contesting of a parent-child relationship;

(b)  decisions on adoption, measures preparatory to adoption, or the annulment or revocation of adoption;

(c)  the name and forenames of the child;

(d)  emancipation;

(e)  maintenance obligations;

(f)  trusts or succession;

(g)  measures taken as a result of criminal offences committed by children.

*Article 2*

**Definitions**

For the purposes of this Regulation:

1.  the term 'court' shall cover all the authorities in the Member States with jurisdiction in the matters falling within the scope of this Regulation pursuant to Article 1;

2.  the term 'judge' shall mean the judge or an official having powers equivalent to those of a judge in the matters falling within the scope of the Regulation;

3.  the term 'Member State' shall mean all Member States with the exception of Denmark;

4.  the term 'judgment' shall mean a divorce, legal separation or marriage annulment, as well as a judgment relating to parental responsibility, pronounced by a court of a Member State, whatever the judgment may be called, including a decree, order or decision;

5.  the term 'Member State of origin' shall mean the Member State where the judgment to be enforced was issued;

6.  the term 'Member State of enforcement' shall mean the Member State where enforcement of the judgment is sought;

7.  the term 'parental responsibility' shall mean all rights and duties relating to the person or the property of a child which are given to a natural or legal person by judgment, by operation of law or by an agreement having legal effect. The term shall include rights of custody and rights of access;

8.  the term 'holder of parental responsibility' shall mean any person having parental responsibility over a child;

9.  the term 'rights of custody' shall include rights and duties relating to the care of the person of a child, and in particular the right to determine the child's place of residence;

10.  the term 'rights of access' shall include in particular the right to take a child to a place other than his or her habitual residence for a limited period of time;

11.  the term 'wrongful removal or retention' shall mean a child's removal or retention where:

(a)  it is in breach of rights of custody acquired by judgment or by operation of law or by an agreement having legal effect under the law of the Member State where the child was habitually resident immediately before the removal or retention;

and

(b) provided that, at the time of removal or retention, the rights of custody were actually exercised, either jointly or alone, or would have been so exercised but for the removal or retention. Custody shall be considered to be exercised jointly when, pursuant to a judgment or by operation of law, one holder of parental responsibility cannot decide on the child's place of residence without the consent of another holder of parental responsibility.

## CHAPTER II

## JURISDICTION

### SECTION 1

### Divorce, legal separation and marriage annulment

*Article 3*

### General jurisdiction

1. In matters relating to divorce, legal separation or marriage annulment, jurisdiction shall lie with the courts of the Member State

(a) in whose territory:

— the spouses are habitually resident, or

— the spouses were last habitually resident, insofar as one of them still resides there, or

— the respondent is habitually resident, or

— in the event of a joint application, either of the spouses is habitually resident, or

— the applicant is habitually resident if he or she resided there for at least a year immediately before the application was made, or

— the applicant is habitually resident if he or she resided there for at least six months immediately before the application was made and is either a national of the Member State in question or, in the case of the United Kingdom and Ireland, has his or her 'domicile' there;

(b) of the nationality of both spouses or, in the case of the United Kingdom and Ireland, of the 'domicile' of both spouses.

2. For the purpose of this Regulation, 'domicile' shall have the same meaning as it has under the legal systems of the United Kingdom and Ireland.

*Article 4*

### Counterclaim

The court in which proceedings are pending on the basis of Article 3 shall also have jurisdiction to examine a counterclaim, insofar as the latter comes within the scope of this Regulation.

*Article 5*

### Conversion of legal separation into divorce

Without prejudice to Article 3, a court of a Member State that has given a judgment on a legal separation shall also have jurisdiction for converting that judgment into a divorce, if the law of that Member State so provides.

*Article 6*

### Exclusive nature of jurisdiction under Articles 3, 4 and 5

A spouse who:

(a)  is habitually resident in the territory of a Member State; or

(b)  is a national of a Member State, or, in the case of the United Kingdom and Ireland, has his or her 'domicile' in the territory of one of the latter Member States,

may be sued in another Member State only in accordance with Articles 3, 4 and 5.

*Article 7*

**Residual jurisdiction**

1. Where no court of a Member State has jurisdiction pursuant to Articles 3, 4 and 5, jurisdiction shall be determined, in each Member State, by the laws of that State.

2. As against a respondent who is not habitually resident and is not either a national of a Member State or, in the case of the United Kingdom and Ireland, does not have his 'domicile' within the territory of one of the latter Member States, any national of a Member State who is habitually resident within the territory of another Member State may, like the nationals of that State, avail himself of the rules of jurisdiction applicable in that State.

SECTION 2

**Parental responsibility**

*Article 8*

**General jurisdiction**

1. The courts of a Member State shall have jurisdiction in matters of parental responsibility over a child who is habitually resident in that Member State at the time the court is seised.

2. Paragraph 1 shall be subject to the provisions of Articles 9, 10 and 12.

*Article 9*

**Continuing jurisdiction of the child's former habitual residence**

1. Where a child moves lawfully from one Member State to another and acquires a new habitual residence there, the courts of the Member State of the child's former habitual residence shall, by way of exception to Article 8, retain jurisdiction during a three-month period following the move for the purpose of modifying a judgment on access rights issued in that Member State before the child moved, where the holder of access rights pursuant to the judgment on access rights continues to have his or her habitual residence in the Member State of the child's former habitual residence.

2. Paragraph 1 shall not apply if the holder of access rights referred to in paragraph 1 has accepted the jurisdiction of the courts of the Member State of the child's new habitual residence by participating in proceedings before those courts without contesting their jurisdiction.

*Article 10*

**Jurisdiction in cases of child abduction**

In case of wrongful removal or retention of the child, the courts of the Member State where the child was habitually resident immediately before the wrongful removal or retention shall retain their jurisdiction until the child has acquired a habitual residence in another Member State and:

(a)  each person, institution or other body having rights of custody has acquiesced in the removal or retention;

or

(b)  the child has resided in that other Member State for a period of at least one year after the person, institution or other body having rights of custody has had or should have had knowledge of the whereabouts of the child and the child is settled in his or her new environment and at least one of the following conditions is met:

   (i)  within one year after the holder of rights of custody has had or should have had knowledge of the whereabouts of the child, no request for return has been lodged before the competent authorities of the Member State where the child has been removed or is being retained;

(ii) a request for return lodged by the holder of rights of custody has been withdrawn and no new request has been lodged within the time limit set in paragraph (i);

(iii) a case before the court in the Member State where the child was habitually resident immediately before the wrongful removal or retention has been closed pursuant to Article 11(7);

(iv) a judgment on custody that does not entail the return of the child has been issued by the courts of the Member State where the child was habitually resident immediately before the wrongful removal or retention.

*Article 11*

**Return of the child**

1. Where a person, institution or other body having rights of custody applies to the competent authorities in a Member State to deliver a judgment on the basis of the Hague Convention of 25 October 1980 on the Civil Aspects of International Child Abduction (hereinafter 'the 1980 Hague Convention'), in order to obtain the return of a child that has been wrongfully removed or retained in a Member State other than the Member State where the child was habitually resident immediately before the wrongful removal or retention, paragraphs 2 to 8 shall apply.

2. When applying Articles 12 and 13 of the 1980 Hague Convention, it shall be ensured that the child is given the opportunity to be heard during the proceedings unless this appears inappropriate having regard to his or her age or degree of maturity.

3. A court to which an application for return of a child is made as mentioned in paragraph 1 shall act expeditiously in proceedings on the application, using the most expeditious procedures available in national law.

Without prejudice to the first subparagraph, the court shall, except where exceptional circumstances make this impossible, issue its judgment no later than six weeks after the application is lodged.

4. A court cannot refuse to return a child on the basis of Article 13b of the 1980 Hague Convention if it is established that adequate arrangements have been made to secure the protection of the child after his or her return.

5. A court cannot refuse to return a child unless the person who requested the return of the child has been given an opportunity to be heard.

6. If a court has issued an order on non-return pursuant to Article 13 of the 1980 Hague Convention, the court must immediately either directly or through its central authority, transmit a copy of the court order on non-return and of the relevant documents, in particular a transcript of the hearings before the court, to the court with jurisdiction or central authority in the Member State where the child was habitually resident immediately before the wrongful removal or retention, as determined by national law. The court shall receive all the mentioned documents within one month of the date of the non-return order.

7. Unless the courts in the Member State where the child was habitually resident immediately before the wrongful removal or retention have already been seised by one of the parties, the court or central authority that receives the information mentioned in paragraph 6 must notify it to the parties and invite them to make submissions to the court, in accordance with national law, within three months of the date of notification so that the court can examine the question of custody of the child.

Without prejudice to the rules on jurisdiction contained in this Regulation, the court shall close the case if no submissions have been received by the court within the time limit.

8. Notwithstanding a judgment of non-return pursuant to Article 13 of the 1980 Hague Convention, any subsequent judgment which requires the return of the child issued by a court having jurisdiction under this Regulation shall be enforceable in accordance with Section 4 of Chapter III below in order to secure the return of the child.

*Article 12*

**Prorogation of jurisdiction**

1. The courts of a Member State exercising jurisdiction by virtue of Article 3 on an application for divorce, legal separation or marriage annulment shall have jurisdiction in any matter relating to parental responsibility connected with that application where:

(a)  at least one of the spouses has parental responsibility in relation to the child;

and

(b)  the jurisdiction of the courts has been accepted expressly or otherwise in an unequivocal manner by the spouses and by the holders of parental responsibility, at the time the court is seised, and is in the superior interests of the child.

2. The jurisdiction conferred in paragraph 1 shall cease as soon as:

(a)  the judgment allowing or refusing the application for divorce, legal separation or marriage annulment has become final;

(b)  in those cases where proceedings in relation to parental responsibility are still pending on the date referred to in (a), a judgment in these proceedings has become final;

(c)  the proceedings referred to in (a) and (b) have come to an end for another reason.

3. The courts of a Member State shall also have jurisdiction in relation to parental responsibility in proceedings other than those referred to in paragraph 1 where:

(a)  the child has a substantial connection with that Member State, in particular by virtue of the fact that one of the holders of parental responsibility is habitually resident in that Member State or that the child is a national of that Member State;

and

(b)  the jurisdiction of the courts has been accepted expressly or otherwise in an unequivocal manner by all the parties to the proceedings at the time the court is seised and is in the best interests of the child.

4. Where the child has his or her habitual residence in the territory of a third State which is not a contracting party to the Hague Convention of 19 October 1996 on jurisdiction, applicable law, recognition, enforcement and cooperation in respect of parental responsibility and measures for the protection of children, jurisdiction under this Article shall be deemed to be in the child's interest, in particular if it is found impossible to hold proceedings in the third State in question.

*Article 13*

**Jurisdiction based on the child's presence**

1. Where a child's habitual residence cannot be established and jurisdiction cannot be determined on the basis of Article 12, the courts of the Member State where the child is present shall have jurisdiction.

2. Paragraph 1 shall also apply to refugee children or children internationally displaced because of disturbances occurring in their country.

*Article 14*

**Residual jurisdiction**

Where no court of a Member State has jurisdiction pursuant to Articles 8 to 13, jurisdiction shall be determined, in each Member State, by the laws of that State.

*Article 15*

**Transfer to a court better placed to hear the case**

1. By way of exception, the courts of a Member State having jurisdiction as to the substance of the matter may, if they consider that a court of another Member State, with which the child has a particular connection, would be better placed to hear the case, or a specific part thereof, and where this is in the best interests of the child:

(a) stay the case or the part thereof in question and invite the parties to introduce a request before the court of that other Member State in accordance with paragraph 4; or

(b) request a court of another Member State to assume jurisdiction in accordance with paragraph 5.

2. Paragraph 1 shall apply:

(a) upon application from a party; or

(b) of the court's own motion; or

(c) upon application from a court of another Member State with which the child has a particular connection, in accordance with paragraph 3.

A transfer made of the court's own motion or by application of a court of another Member State must be accepted by at least one of the parties.

3. The child shall be considered to have a particular connection to a Member State as mentioned in paragraph 1, if that Member State:

(a) has become the habitual residence of the child after the court referred to in paragraph 1 was seised; or

(b) is the former habitual residence of the child; or

(c) is the place of the child's nationality; or

(d) is the habitual residence of a holder of parental responsibility; or

(e) is the place where property of the child is located and the case concerns measures for the protection of the child relating to the administration, conservation or disposal of this property.

4. The court of the Member State having jurisdiction as to the substance of the matter shall set a time limit by which the courts of that other Member State shall be seised in accordance with paragraph 1.

If the courts are not seised by that time, the court which has been seised shall continue to exercise jurisdiction in accordance with Articles 8 to 14.

5. The courts of that other Member State may, where due to the specific circumstances of the case, this is in the best interests of the child, accept jurisdiction within six weeks of their seisure in accordance with paragraph 1(a) or 1(b). In this case, the court first seised shall decline jurisdiction. Otherwise, the court first seised shall continue to exercise jurisdiction in accordance with Articles 8 to 14.

6. The courts shall cooperate for the purposes of this Article, either directly or through the central authorities designated pursuant to Article 53.

## SECTION 3

### Common provisions

*Article 16*

### Seising of a Court

1. A court shall be deemed to be seised:

(a) at the time when the document instituting the proceedings or an equivalent document is lodged with the court, provided that the applicant has not subsequently failed to take the steps he was required to take to have service effected on the respondent;

or

(b) if the document has to be served before being lodged with the court, at the time when it is received by the authority responsible for service, provided that the applicant has not subsequently failed to take the steps he was required to take to have the document lodged with the court.

*Article 17*

### Examination as to jurisdiction

Where a court of a Member State is seised of a case over which it has no jurisdiction under this

Regulation and over which a court of another Member State has jurisdiction by virtue of this Regulation, it shall declare of its own motion that it has no jurisdiction.

### Article 18

**Examination as to admissibility**

1. Where a respondent habitually resident in a State other than the Member State where the action was brought does not enter an appearance, the court with jurisdiction shall stay the proceedings so long as it is not shown that the respondent has been able to receive the document instituting the proceedings or an equivalent document in sufficient time to enable him to arrange for his defence, or that all necessary steps have been taken to this end.

2. Article 19 of Regulation (EC) No 1348/2000 shall apply instead of the provisions of paragraph 1 of this Article if the document instituting the proceedings or an equivalent document had to be transmitted from one Member State to another pursuant to that Regulation.

3. Where the provisions of Regulation (EC) No 1348/2000 are not applicable, Article 15 of the Hague Convention of 15 November 1965 on the service abroad of judicial and extrajudicial documents in civil or commercial matters shall apply if the document instituting the proceedings or an equivalent document had to be transmitted abroad pursuant to that Convention.

### Article 19

**Lis pendens and dependent actions**

1. Where proceedings relating to divorce, legal separation or marriage annulment between the same parties are brought before courts of different Member States, the court second seised shall of its own motion stay its proceedings until such time as the jurisdiction of the court first seised is established.

2. Where proceedings relating to parental responsibility relating to the same child and involving the same cause of action are brought before courts of different Member States, the court second seised shall of its own motion stay its proceedings until such time as the jurisdiction of the court first seised is established.

3. Where the jurisdiction of the court first seised is established, the court second seised shall decline jurisdiction in favour of that court.

In that case, the party who brought the relevant action before the court second seised may bring that action before the court first seised.

### Article 20

**Provisional, including protective, measures**

1. In urgent cases, the provisions of this Regulation shall not prevent the courts of a Member State from taking such provisional, including protective, measures in respect of persons or assets in that State as may be available under the law of that Member State, even if, under this Regulation, the court of another Member State has jurisdiction as to the substance of the matter.

2. The measures referred to in paragraph 1 shall cease to apply when the court of the Member State having jurisdiction under this Regulation as to the substance of the matter has taken the measures it considers appropriate.

CHAPTER III

# RECOGNITION AND ENFORCEMENT

SECTION 1

## Recognition

*Article 21*

### Recognition of a judgment

1. A judgment given in a Member State shall be recognised in the other Member States without any special procedure being required.

2. In particular, and without prejudice to paragraph 3, no special procedure shall be required for updating the civil-status records of a Member State on the basis of a judgment relating to divorce, legal separation or marriage annulment given in another Member State, and against which no further appeal lies under the law of that Member State.

3. Without prejudice to Section 4 of this Chapter, any interested party may, in accordance with the procedures provided for in Section 2 of this Chapter, apply for a decision that the judgment be or not be recognised.

The local jurisdiction of the court appearing in the list notified by each Member State to the Commission pursuant to Article 68 shall be determined by the internal law of the Member State in which proceedings for recognition or non-recognition are brought.

4. Where the recognition of a judgment is raised as an incidental question in a court of a Member State, that court may determine that issue.

*Article 22*

### Grounds of non-recognition for judgments relating to divorce, legal separation or marriage annulment

A judgment relating to a divorce, legal separation or marriage annulment shall not be recognised:

(a)  if such recognition is manifestly contrary to the public policy of the Member State in which recognition is sought;

(b)  where it was given in default of appearance, if the respondent was not served with the document which instituted the proceedings or with an equivalent document in sufficient time and in such a way as to enable the respondent to arrange for his or her defence unless it is determined that the respondent has accepted the judgment unequivocally;

(c)  if it is irreconcilable with a judgment given in proceedings between the same parties in the Member State in which recognition is sought; or

(d)  if it is irreconcilable with an earlier judgment given in another Member State or in a non-Member State between the same parties, provided that the earlier judgment fulfils the conditions necessary for its recognition in the Member State in which recognition is sought.

*Article 23*

### Grounds of non-recognition for judgments relating to parental responsibility

A judgment relating to parental responsibility shall not be recognised:

(a)  if such recognition is manifestly contrary to the public policy of the Member State in which recognition is sought taking into account the best interests of the child;

(b)  if it was given, except in case of urgency, without the child having been given an opportunity to be heard, in violation of fundamental principles of procedure of the Member State in which recognition is sought;

(c)  where it was given in default of appearance if the person in default was not served with the document which instituted the proceedings or with an equivalent document in sufficient time and in such a way as to enable that person to arrange for his or her defence unless it is determined that such person has accepted the judgment unequivocally;

(d)    on the request of any person claiming that the judgment infringes his or her parental responsibility, if it was given without such person having been given an opportunity to be heard;

(e)    if it is irreconcilable with a later judgment relating to parental responsibility given in the Member State in which recognition is sought;

(f)    if it is irreconcilable with a later judgment relating to parental responsibility given in another Member State or in the non-Member State of the habitual residence of the child provided that the later judgment fulfils the conditions necessary for its recognition in the Member State in which recognition is sought.

or

(g)    if the procedure laid down in Article 56 has not been complied with.

*Article 24*

**Prohibition of review of jurisdiction of the court of origin**

The jurisdiction of the court of the Member State of origin may not be reviewed. The test of public policy referred to in Articles 22(a) and 23(a) may not be applied to the rules relating to jurisdiction set out in Articles 3 to 14.

*Article 25*

**Differences in applicable law**

The recognition of a judgment may not be refused because the law of the Member State in which such recognition is sought would not allow divorce, legal separation or marriage annulment on the same facts.

*Article 26*

**Non-review as to substance**

Under no circumstances may a judgment be reviewed as to its substance.

*Article 27*

**Stay of proceedings**

1. A court of a Member State in which recognition is sought of a judgment given in another Member State may stay the proceedings if an ordinary appeal against the judgment has been lodged.

2. A court of a Member State in which recognition is sought of a judgment given in Ireland or the United Kingdom may stay the proceedings if enforcement is suspended in the Member State of origin by reason of an appeal.

SECTION 2

**Application for a declaration of enforceability**

*Article 28*

**Enforceable judgments**

1. A judgment on the exercise of parental responsibility in respect of a child given in a Member State which is enforceable in that Member State and has been served shall be enforced in another Member State when, on the application of any interested party, it has been declared enforceable there.

2. However, in the United Kingdom, such a judgment shall be enforced in England and Wales, in Scotland or in Northern Ireland only when, on the application of any interested party, it has been registered for enforcement in that part of the United Kingdom.

*Article 29*

**Jurisdiction of local courts**

1. An application for a declaration of enforceability shall be submitted to the court appearing in the list notified by each Member State to the Commission pursuant to Article 68.

2. The local jurisdiction shall be determined by reference to the place of habitual residence of the person against whom enforcement is sought or by reference to the habitual residence of any child to whom the application relates.

Where neither of the places referred to in the first subparagraph can be found in the Member State of enforcement, the local jurisdiction shall be determined by reference to the place of enforcement.

*Article 30*

**Procedure**

1. The procedure for making the application shall be governed by the law of the Member State of enforcement.

2. The applicant must give an address for service within the area of jurisdiction of the court applied to. However, if the law of the Member State of enforcement does not provide for the furnishing of such an address, the applicant shall appoint a representative ad litem.

3. The documents referred to in Articles 37 and 39 shall be attached to the application.

*Article 31*

**Decision of the court**

1. The court applied to shall give its decision without delay. Neither the person against whom enforcement is sought, nor the child shall, at this stage of the proceedings, be entitled to make any submissions on the application.

2. The application may be refused only for one of the reasons specified in Articles 22, 23 and 24.

3. Under no circumstances may a judgment be reviewed as to its substance.

*Article 32*

**Notice of the decision**

The appropriate officer of the court shall without delay bring to the notice of the applicant the decision given on the application in accordance with the procedure laid down by the law of the Member State of enforcement.

*Article 33*

**Appeal against the decision**

1. The decision on the application for a declaration of enforceability may be appealed against by either party.

2. The appeal shall be lodged with the court appearing in the list notified by each Member State to the Commission pursuant to Article 68.

3. The appeal shall be dealt with in accordance with the rules governing procedure in contradictory matters.

4. If the appeal is brought by the applicant for a declaration of enforceability, the party against whom enforcement is sought shall be summoned to appear before the appellate court. If such person fails to appear, the provisions of Article 18 shall apply.

5. An appeal against a declaration of enforceability must be lodged within one month of service thereof. If the party against whom enforcement is sought is habitually resident in a Member State other than that in which the declaration of enforceability was given, the time for appealing shall be two months and shall run from the date of service, either on him or at his residence. No extension of time may be granted on account of distance.

*Article 34*

**Courts of appeal and means of contest**

The judgment given on appeal may be contested only by the proceedings referred to in the list notified by each Member State to the Commission pursuant to Article 68.

*Article 35*

**Stay of proceedings**

1. The court with which the appeal is lodged under Articles 33 or 34 may, on the application of the party against whom enforcement is sought, stay the proceedings if an ordinary appeal has been lodged in the Member State of origin, or if the time for such appeal has not yet expired. In the latter case, the court may specify the time within which an appeal is to be lodged.

2. Where the judgment was given in Ireland or the United Kingdom, any form of appeal available in the Member State of origin shall be treated as an ordinary appeal for the purposes of paragraph 1.

*Article 36*

**Partial enforcement**

1. Where a judgment has been given in respect of several matters and enforcement cannot be authorised for all of them, the court shall authorise enforcement for one or more of them.

2. An applicant may request partial enforcement of a judgment.

SECTION 3

**Provisions common to Sections 1 and 2**

*Article 37*

**Documents**

1. A party seeking or contesting recognition or applying for a declaration of enforceability shall produce:

(a) a copy of the judgment which satisfies the conditions necessary to establish its authenticity;

and

(b) the certificate referred to in Article 39.

2. In addition, in the case of a judgment given in default, the party seeking recognition or applying for a declaration of enforceability shall produce:

(a) the original or certified true copy of the document which establishes that the defaulting party was served with the document instituting the proceedings or with an equivalent document;

or

(b) any document indicating that the defendant has accepted the judgment unequivocally.

*Article 38*

**Absence of documents**

1. If the documents specified in Article 37(1)(b) or (2) are not produced, the court may specify a time for their production, accept equivalent documents or, if it considers that it has sufficient information before it, dispense with their production.

2. If the court so requires, a translation of such documents shall be furnished. The translation shall be certified by a person qualified to do so in one of the Member States.

European Union Materials

*Article 39*

**Certificate concerning judgments in matrimonial matters and certificate concerning judgments on parental responsibility**

The competent court or authority of a Member State of origin shall, at the request of any interested party, issue a certificate using the standard form set out in Annex I (judgments in matrimonial matters) or in Annex II (judgments on parental responsibility).

## SECTION 4

**Enforceability of certain judgments concerning rights of access and of certain judgments which require the return of the child**

*Article 40*

**Scope**

1. This Section shall apply to:

(a)   rights of access;

and

(b)   the return of a child entailed by a judgment given pursuant to Article 11(8).

2. The provisions of this Section shall not prevent a holder of parental responsibility from seeking recognition and enforcement of a judgment in accordance with the provisions in Sections 1 and 2 of this Chapter.

*Article 41*

**Rights of access**

1. The rights of access referred to in Article 40(1)(a) granted in an enforceable judgment given in a Member State shall be recognised and enforceable in another Member State without the need for a declaration of enforceability and without any possibility of opposing its recognition if the judgment has been certified in the Member State of origin in accordance with paragraph 2.

Even if national law does not provide for enforceability by operation of law of a judgment granting access rights, the court of origin may declare that the judgment shall be enforceable, notwithstanding any appeal.

2. The judge of origin shall issue the certificate referred to in paragraph 1 using the standard form in Annex III (certificate concerning rights of access) only if:

(a)   where the judgment was given in default, the person defaulting was served with the document which instituted the proceedings or with an equivalent document in sufficient time and in such a way as to enable that person to arrange for his or her defense, or, the person has been served with the document but not in compliance with these conditions, it is nevertheless established that he or she accepted the decision unequivocally;

(b)   all parties concerned were given an opportunity to be heard;

and

(c)   the child was given an opportunity to be heard, unless a hearing was considered inappropriate having regard to his or her age or degree of maturity.

The certificate shall be completed in the language of the judgment.

3. Where the rights of access involve a cross-border situation at the time of the delivery of the judgment, the certificate shall be issued ex officio when the judgment becomes enforceable, even if only provisionally. If the situation subsequently acquires a cross-border character, the certificate shall be issued at the request of one of the parties.

*Article 42*

**Return of the child**

1. The return of a child referred to in Article 40(1)(b) entailed by an enforceable judgment given in a Member State shall be recognised and enforceable in another Member State without the need for a declaration of enforceability and without any possibility of opposing its recognition if the judgment has been certified in the Member State of origin in accordance with paragraph 2.

Even if national law does not provide for enforceability by operation of law, notwithstanding any appeal, of a judgment requiring the return of the child mentioned in Article 11(b)(8), the court of origin may declare the judgment enforceable.

2. The judge of origin who delivered the judgment referred to in Article 40(1)(b) shall issue the certificate referred to in paragraph 1 only if:

(a) the child was given an opportunity to be heard, unless a hearing was considered inappropriate having regard to his or her age or degree of maturity;

(b) the parties were given an opportunity to be heard; and

(c) the court has taken into account in issuing its judgment the reasons for and evidence underlying the order issued pursuant to Article 13 of the 1980 Hague Convention.

In the event that the court or any other authority takes measures to ensure the protection of the child after its return to the State of habitual residence, the certificate shall contain details of such measures.

The judge of origin shall of his or her own motion issue that certificate using the standard form in Annex IV (certificate concerning return of the child(ren)).

The certificate shall be completed in the language of the judgment.

*Article 43*

**Rectification of the certificate**

1. The law of the Member State of origin shall be applicable to any rectification of the certificate.

2. No appeal shall lie against the issuing of a certificate pursuant to Articles 41(1) or 42(1).

*Article 44*

**Effects of the certificate**

The certificate shall take effect only within the limits of the enforceability of the judgment.

*Article 45*

**Documents**

1. A party seeking enforcement of a judgment shall produce:

(a) a copy of the judgment which satisfies the conditions necessary to establish its authenticity; and

(b) the certificate referred to in Article 41(1) or Article 42(1).

2. For the purposes of this Article,

— the certificate referred to in Article 41(1) shall be accompanied by a translation of point 12 relating to the arrangements for exercising right of access,

— the certificate referred to in Article 42(1) shall be accompanied by a translation of its point 14 relating to the arrangements for implementing the measures taken to ensure the child's return.

The translation shall be into the official language or one of the official languages of the Member State of enforcement or any other language that the Member State of enforcement expressly accepts. The translation shall be certified by a person qualified to do so in one of the Member States.

## SECTION 5

## Authentic instruments and agreements

*Article 46*

Documents which have been formally drawn up or registered as authentic instruments and are enforceable in one Member State and also agreements between the parties that are enforceable in the Member State in which they were concluded shall be recognised and declared enforceable under the same conditions as judgments.

## SECTION 6

## Other provisions

*Article 47*

### Enforcement procedure

1. The enforcement procedure is governed by the law of the Member State of enforcement.

2. Any judgment delivered by a court of another Member State and declared to be enforceable in accordance with Section 2 or certified in accordance with Article 41(1) or Article 42(1) shall be enforced in the Member State of enforcement in the same conditions as if it had been delivered in that Member State.

In particular, a judgment which has been certified according to Article 41(1) or Article 42(1) cannot be enforced if it is irreconcilable with a subsequent enforceable judgment.

*Article 48*

### Practical arrangements for the exercise of rights of access

1. The courts of the Member State of enforcement may make practical arrangements for organising the exercise of rights of access, if the necessary arrangements have not or have not sufficiently been made in the judgment delivered by the courts of the Member State having jurisdiction as to the substance of the matter and provided the essential elements of this judgment are respected.

2. The practical arrangements made pursuant to paragraph 1 shall cease to apply pursuant to a later judgment by the courts of the Member State having jurisdiction as to the substance of the matter.

*Article 49*

### Costs

The provisions of this Chapter, with the exception of Section 4, shall also apply to the determination of the amount of costs and expenses of proceedings under this Regulation and to the enforcement of any order concerning such costs and expenses.

*Article 50*

### Legal aid

An applicant who, in the Member State of origin, has benefited from complete or partial legal aid or exemption from costs or expenses shall be entitled, in the procedures provided for in Articles 21, 28, 41, 42 and 48 to benefit from the most favourable legal aid or the most extensive exemption from costs and expenses provided for by the law of the Member State of enforcement.

*Article 51*

### Security, bond or deposit

No security, bond or deposit, however described, shall be required of a party who in one Member State applies for enforcement of a judgment given in another Member State on the following grounds:

(a)   that he or she is not habitually resident in the Member State in which enforcement is sought; or

(b) that he or she is either a foreign national or, where enforcement is sought in either the United Kingdom or Ireland, does not have his or her 'domicile' in either of those Member States.

*Article 52*

**Legalisation or other similar formality**

No legalisation or other similar formality shall be required in respect of the documents referred to in Articles 37, 38 and 45 or in respect of a document appointing a representative ad litem.

## CHAPTER IV

## COOPERATION BETWEEN CENTRAL AUTHORITIES IN MATTERS OF PARENTAL RESPONSIBILITY

*Article 53*

**Designation**

Each Member State shall designate one or more central authorities to assist with the application of this Regulation and shall specify the geographical or functional jurisdiction of each. Where a Member State has designated more than one central authority, communications shall normally be sent direct to the relevant central authority with jurisdiction. Where a communication is sent to a central authority without jurisdiction, the latter shall be responsible for forwarding it to the central authority with jurisdiction and informing the sender accordingly.

*Article 54*

**General functions**

The central authorities shall communicate information on national laws and procedures and take measures to improve the application of this Regulation and strengthening their cooperation. For this purpose the European Judicial Network in civil and commercial matters created by Decision No 2001/470/EC shall be used.

*Article 55*

**Cooperation on cases specific to parental responsibility**

The central authorities shall, upon request from a central authority of another Member State or from a holder of parental responsibility, cooperate on specific cases to achieve the purposes of this Regulation. To this end, they shall, acting directly or through public authorities or other bodies, take all appropriate steps in accordance with the law of that Member State in matters of personal data protection to:

(a) collect and exchange information:

    (i) on the situation of the child;

    (ii) on any procedures under way; or

    (iii) on decisions taken concerning the child;

(b) provide information and assistance to holders of parental responsibility seeking the recognition and enforcement of decisions on their territory, in particular concerning rights of access and the return of the child;

(c) facilitate communications between courts, in particular for the application of Article 11(6) and (7) and Article 15;

(d) provide such information and assistance as is needed by courts to apply Article 56; and

(e) facilitate agreement between holders of parental responsibility through mediation or other means, and facilitate cross-border cooperation to this end.

European Union Materials

## Article 56

### Placement of a child in another Member State

1. Where a court having jurisdiction under Articles 8 to 15 contemplates the placement of a child in institutional care or with a foster family and where such placement is to take place in another Member State, it shall first consult the central authority or other authority having jurisdiction in the latter State where public authority intervention in that Member State is required for domestic cases of child placement.

2. The judgment on placement referred to in paragraph 1 may be made in the requesting State only if the competent authority of the requested State has consented to the placement.

3. The procedures for consultation or consent referred to in paragraphs 1 and 2 shall be governed by the national law of the requested State.

4. Where the authority having jurisdiction under Articles 8 to 15 decides to place the child in a foster family, and where such placement is to take place in another Member State and where no public authority intervention is required in the latter Member State for domestic cases of child placement, it shall so inform the central authority or other authority having jurisdiction in the latter State.

## Article 57

### Working method

1. Any holder of parental responsibility may submit, to the central authority of the Member State of his or her habitual residence or to the central authority of the Member State where the child is habitually resident or present, a request for assistance as mentioned in Article 55. In general, the request shall include all available information of relevance to its enforcement. Where the request for assistance concerns the recognition or enforcement of a judgment on parental responsibility that falls within the scope of this Regulation, the holder of parental responsibility shall attach the relevant certificates provided for in Articles 39, 41(1) or 42(1).

2. Member States shall communicate to the Commission the official language or languages of the Community institutions other than their own in which communications to the central authorities can be accepted.

3. The assistance provided by the central authorities pursuant to Article 55 shall be free of charge.

4. Each central authority shall bear its own costs.

## Article 58

### Meetings

1. In order to facilitate the application of this Regulation, central authorities shall meet regularly.

2. These meetings shall be convened in compliance with Decision No 2001/470/EC establishing a European Judicial Network in civil and commercial matters.

## CHAPTER V

## RELATIONS WITH OTHER INSTRUMENTS

## Article 59

### Relation with other instruments

1. Subject to the provisions of Articles 60, 63, 64 and paragraph 2 of this Article, this Regulation shall, for the Member States, supersede conventions existing at the time of entry into force of this Regulation which have been concluded between two or more Member States and relate to matters governed by this Regulation.

2.

(a) Finland and Sweden shall have the option of declaring that the Convention of 6 February 1931 between Denmark, Finland, Iceland, Norway and Sweden comprising international private law provisions on marriage, adoption and guardianship, together with the Final Protocol thereto, will apply, in whole or in part, in their mutual relations, in place of the rules of this Regulation. Such declarations shall be annexed to this Regulation and published in the Official Journal of the European Union. They may be withdrawn, in whole or in part, at any moment by the said Member States.

(b) The principle of non-discrimination on the grounds of nationality between citizens of the Union shall be respected.

(c) The rules of jurisdiction in any future agreement to be concluded between the Member States referred to in subparagraph (a) which relate to matters governed by this Regulation shall be in line with those laid down in this Regulation.

(d) Judgments handed down in any of the Nordic States which have made the declaration provided for in subparagraph (a) under a forum of jurisdiction corresponding to one of those laid down in Chapter II of this Regulation, shall be recognised and enforced in the other Member States under the rules laid down in Chapter III of this Regulation.

3. Member States shall send to the Commission:

(a) a copy of the agreements and uniform laws implementing these agreements referred to in paragraph 2(a) and (c);

(b) any denunciations of, or amendments to, those agreements or uniform laws.

*Article 60*

**Relations with certain multilateral conventions**

In relations between Member States, this Regulation shall take precedence over the following Conventions in so far as they concern matters governed by this Regulation:

(a) the Hague Convention of 5 October 1961 concerning the Powers of Authorities and the Law Applicable in respect of the Protection of Minors;

(b) the Luxembourg Convention of 8 September 1967 on the Recognition of Decisions Relating to the Validity of Marriages;

(c) the Hague Convention of 1 June 1970 on the Recognition of Divorces and Legal Separations;

(d) the European Convention of 20 May 1980 on Recognition and Enforcement of Decisions concerning Custody of Children and on Restoration of Custody of Children;

and

(e) the Hague Convention of 25 October 1980 on the Civil Aspects of International Child Abduction.

*Article 61*

**Relation with the Hague Convention of 19 October 1996 on Jurisdiction, Applicable law, Recognition, Enforcement and Cooperation in Respect of Parental Responsibility and Measures for the Protection of Children**

As concerns the relation with the Hague Convention of 19 October 1996 on Jurisdiction, Applicable law, Recognition, Enforcement and Cooperation in Respect of Parental Responsibility and Measures for the Protection of Children, this Regulation shall apply:

(a) where the child concerned has his or her habitual residence on the territory of a Member State;

(b) as concerns the recognition and enforcement of a judgment given in a court of a Member State on the territory of another Member State, even if the child concerned has his or her habitual residence on the territory of a third State which is a contracting Party to the said Convention.

*Article 62*

**Scope of effects**

1. The agreements and conventions referred to in Articles 59(1), 60 and 61 shall continue to have effect in relation to matters not governed by this Regulation.

2. The conventions mentioned in Article 60, in particular the 1980 Hague Convention, continue to produce effects between the Member States which are party thereto, in compliance with Article 60.

## Article 63

**Treaties with the Holy See**

1. This Regulation shall apply without prejudice to the International Treaty (Concordat) between the Holy See and Portugal, signed at the Vatican City on 7 May 1940.

2. Any decision as to the invalidity of a marriage taken under the Treaty referred to in paragraph 1 shall be recognised in the Member States on the conditions laid down in Chapter III, Section 1.

3. The provisions laid down in paragraphs 1 and 2 shall also apply to the following international treaties (Concordats) with the Holy See:

(a) 'Concordato lateranense' of 11 February 1929 between Italy and the Holy See, modified by the agreement, with additional Protocol signed in Rome on 18 February 1984;

(b) Agreement between the Holy See and Spain on legal affairs of 3 January 1979;

[(c) Agreement between the Holy See and Malta on the recognition of civil effects to canonical marriages and to decisions of ecclesiastical authorities and tribunals on those marriages of 3 February 1993, including the Protocol of application of the same date, with the second Additional Protocol of 6 January 1995.]

[4. Recognition of the decisions provided for in paragraph 2 may, in Spain, Italy or Malta, be subject to the same procedures and the same checks as are applicable to decisions of the ecclesiastical courts handed down in accordance with the international treaties concluded with the Holy See referred to in paragraph 3.]

5. Member States shall send to the Commission:

(a) a copy of the Treaties referred to in paragraphs 1 and 3;

(b) any denunciations of or amendments to those Treaties.

## CHAPTER VI

## TRANSITIONAL PROVISIONS

### Article 64

1. The provisions of this Regulation shall apply only to legal proceedings instituted, to documents formally drawn up or registered as authentic instruments and to agreements concluded between the parties after its date of application in accordance with Article 72.

2. Judgments given after the date of application of this Regulation in proceedings instituted before that date but after the date of entry into force of Regulation (EC) No 1347/2000 shall be recognised and enforced in accordance with the provisions of Chapter III of this Regulation if jurisdiction was founded on rules which accorded with those provided for either in Chapter II or in Regulation (EC) No 1347/2000 or in a convention concluded between the Member State of origin and the Member State addressed which was in force when the proceedings were instituted.

3. Judgments given before the date of application of this Regulation in proceedings instituted after the entry into force of Regulation (EC) No 1347/2000 shall be recognised and enforced in accordance with the provisions of Chapter III of this Regulation provided they relate to divorce, legal separation or marriage annulment or parental responsibility for the children of both spouses on the occasion of these matrimonial proceedings.

4. Judgments given before the date of application of this Regulation but after the date of entry into force of Regulation (EC) No 1347/2000 in proceedings instituted before the date of entry into force of Regulation (EC) No 1347/2000 shall be recognised and enforced in accordance with the provisions of Chapter III of this Regulation provided they relate to divorce, legal separation or marriage annulment or parental responsibility for the children of both spouses on the occasion of these matrimonial proceedings and that jurisdiction was founded on rules which accorded with those provided for either

in Chapter II of this Regulation or in Regulation (EC) No 1347/2000 or in a convention concluded between the Member State of origin and the Member State addressed which was in force when the proceedings were instituted.

## CHAPTER VII

## FINAL PROVISIONS

*Article 65*

Review

No later than 1 January 2012, and every five years thereafter, the Commission shall present to the European Parliament, to the Council and to the European Economic and Social Committee a report on the application of this Regulation on the basis of information supplied by the Member States. The report shall be accompanied if need be by proposals for adaptations.

*Article 66*

Member States with two or more legal systems

With regard to a Member State in which two or more systems of law or sets of rules concerning matters governed by this Regulation apply in different territorial units:

(a) any reference to habitual residence in that Member State shall refer to habitual residence in a territorial unit;

(b) any reference to nationality, or in the case of the United Kingdom 'domicile', shall refer to the territorial unit designated by the law of that State;

(c) any reference to the authority of a Member State shall refer to the authority of a territorial unit within that State which is concerned;

(d) any reference to the rules of the requested Member State shall refer to the rules of the territorial unit in which jurisdiction, recognition or enforcement is invoked.

*Article 67*

Information on central authorities and languages accepted

The Member States shall communicate to the Commission within three months following the entry into force of this Regulation:

(a) the names, addresses and means of communication for the central authorities designated pursuant to Article 53;

(b) the languages accepted for communications to central authorities pursuant to Article 57(2); and

(c) the languages accepted for the certificate concerning rights of access pursuant to Article 45(2).

The Member States shall communicate to the Commission any changes to this information.

The Commission shall make this information publicly available.

*Article 68*

Information relating to courts and redress procedures

The Member States shall notify to the Commission the lists of courts and redress procedures referred to in Articles 21, 29, 33 and 34 and any amendments thereto.

The Commission shall update this information and make it publicly available through the publication in the Official Journal of the European Union and any other appropriate means.

## Article 69

**Amendments to the Annexes**

Any amendments to the standard forms in Annexes I to IV shall be adopted in accordance with the consultative procedure set out in Article 70(2).

## Article 70

**Committee**

1. The Commission shall be assisted by a committee (committee).

2. Where reference is made to this paragraph, Articles 3 and 7 of Decision 1999/468/EC shall apply.

3. The committee shall adopt its rules of procedure.

## Article 71

**Repeal of Regulation (EC) No 1347/2000**

1. Regulation (EC) No 1347/2000 shall be repealed as from the date of application of this Regulation.

2. Any reference to Regulation (EC) No 1347/2000 shall be construed as a reference to this Regulation according to the comparative table in Annex V.

## Article 72

**Entry into force**

This Regulation shall enter into force on 1 August 2004.

The Regulation shall apply from 1 March 2005, with the exception of Articles 67, 68, 69 and 70, which shall apply from 1 August 2004.

This Regulation shall be binding in its entirety and directly applicable in the Member States in accordance with the Treaty establishing the European Community.

*[Annexes I–V omitted]*

# Regulation (EC) No 805/2004 of the European Parliament and of the Council of 21 April 2004 creating a European Enforcement Order for uncontested claims

[2004] OJ L143/15

THE EUROPEAN PARLIAMENT AND THE COUNCIL OF THE EUROPEAN UNION,

Having regard to the Treaty establishing the European Community, and in particular Articles 61(c) and the second indent of Article 67(5) thereof,

Having regard to the proposal from the Commission,

Having regard to the Opinion of the European Economic and Social Committee,

Acting in accordance with the procedure laid down in Article 251 of the Treaty,

Whereas:

(1) The Community has set itself the objective of maintaining and developing an area of freedom, security and justice, in which the free movement of persons is ensured. To this end, the Community is to adopt, inter alia, measures in the field of judicial cooperation in civil matters that are necessary for the proper functioning of the internal market.

(2) On 3 December 1998, the Council adopted an Action Plan of the Council and the Commission on how best to implement the provisions of the Treaty of Amsterdam on an area of freedom, security and justice (the Vienna Action Plan).

(3) The European Council meeting in Tampere on 15 and 16 October 1999 endorsed the principle of mutual recognition of judicial decisions as the cornerstone for the creation of a genuine judicial area.

(4) On 30 November 2000, the Council adopted a programme of measures for implementation of the principle of mutual recognition of decisions in civil and commercial matters. This programme includes in its first stage the abolition of exequatur, that is to say, the creation of a European Enforcement Order for uncontested claims.

(5) The concept of 'uncontested claims' should cover all situations in which a creditor, given the verified absence of any dispute by the debtor as to the nature or extent of a pecuniary claim, has obtained either a court decision against that debtor or an enforceable document that requires the debtor's express consent, be it a court settlement or an authentic instrument.

(6) The absence of objections from the debtor as stipulated in Article 3(1)(b) can take the shape of default of appearance at a court hearing or of failure to comply with an invitation by the court to give written notice of an intention to defend the case.

(7) This Regulation should apply to judgments, court settlements and authentic instruments on uncontested claims and to decisions delivered following challenges to judgments, court settlements and authentic instruments certified as European Enforcement Orders.

(8) In its Tampere conclusions, the European Council considered that access to enforcement in a Member State other than that in which the judgment has been given should be accelerated and simplified by dispensing with any intermediate measures to be taken prior to enforcement in the Member State in which enforcement is sought. A judgment that has been certified as a European Enforcement Order by the court of origin should, for enforcement purposes, be treated as if it had been delivered in the Member State in which enforcement is sought. In the United Kingdom, for example, the registration of a certified foreign judgment will therefore follow the same rules as the registration of a judgment from another part of the United Kingdom and is not to imply a review as to the substance of the foreign judgment. Arrangements for the enforcement of judgments should continue to be governed by national law.

(9) Such a procedure should offer significant advantages as compared with the exequatur procedure provided for in Council Regulation (EC) No 44/2001 of 22 December 2000 on jurisdiction and the

recognition and enforcement of judgments in civil and commercial matters , in that there is no need for approval by the judiciary in a second Member State with the delays and expenses that this entails.

(10) Where a court in a Member State has given judgment on an uncontested claim in the absence of participation of the debtor in the proceedings, the abolition of any checks in the Member State of enforcement is inextricably linked to and dependent upon the existence of a sufficient guarantee of observance of the rights of the defence.

(11) This Regulation seeks to promote the fundamental rights and takes into account the principles recognised in particular by the Charter of Fundamental Rights of the European Union. In particular, it seeks to ensure full respect for the right to a fair trial as recognised in Article 47 of the Charter.

(12) Minimum standards should be established for the proceedings leading to the judgment in order to ensure that the debtor is informed about the court action against him, the requirements for his active participation in the proceedings to contest the claim and the consequences of his non-participation in sufficient time and in such a way as to enable him to arrange for his defence.

(13) Due to differences between the Member States as regards the rules of civil procedure and especially those governing the service of documents, it is necessary to lay down a specific and detailed definition of those minimum standards. In particular, any method of service that is based on a legal fiction as regards the fulfilment of those minimum standards cannot be considered sufficient for the certification of a judgment as a European Enforcement Order.

(14) All the methods of service listed in Articles 13 and 14 are characterised by either full certainty (Article 13) or a very high degree of likelihood (Article 14) that the document served has reached its addressee. In the second category, a judgment should only be certified as a European Enforcement Order if the Member State of origin has an appropriate mechanism in place enabling the debtor to apply for a full review of the judgment under the conditions set out in Article 19 in those exceptional cases where, in spite of compliance with Article 14, the document has not reached the addressee.

(15) Personal service on certain persons other than the debtor himself pursuant to Article 14(1)(a) and (b) should be understood to meet the requirements of those provisions only if those persons actually accepted/received the document in question.

(16) Article 15 should apply to situations where the debtor cannot represent himself in court, as in the case of a legal person, and where a person to represent him is determined by law as well as situations where the debtor has authorised another person, in particular a lawyer, to represent him in the specific court proceedings at issue.

(17) The courts competent for scrutinising full compliance with the minimum procedural standards should, if satisfied, issue a standardised European Enforcement Order certificate that makes that scrutiny and its result transparent.

(18) Mutual trust in the administration of justice in the Member States justifies the assessment by the court of one Member State that all conditions for certification as a European Enforcement Order are fulfilled to enable a judgment to be enforced in all other Member States without judicial review of the proper application of the minimum procedural standards in the Member State where the judgment is to be enforced.

(19) This Regulation does not imply an obligation for the Member States to adapt their national legislation to the minimum procedural standards set out herein. It provides an incentive to that end by making available a more efficient and rapid enforceability of judgments in other Member States only if those minimum standards are met.

(20) Application for certification as a European Enforcement Order for uncontested claims should be optional for the creditor, who may instead choose the system of recognition and enforcement under Regulation (EC) No 44/2001 or other Community instruments.

(21) When a document has to be sent from one Member State to another for service there, this Regulation and in particular the rules on service set out herein should apply together with Council Regulation (EC) No 1348/2000 of 29 May 2000 on the service in the Member States of judicial and extrajudicial documents in civil or commercial matters, and in particular Article 14 thereof in conjunction with Member States declarations made under Article 23 thereof.

(22) Since the objectives of the proposed action cannot be sufficiently achieved by the Member States and can therefore, by reason of the scale or effects of the action, be better achieved at Community level, the Community may adopt measures, in accordance with the principle of subsidiarity as set out in Article 5 of the Treaty. In accordance with the principle of proportionality, as set out in that Article, this Regulation does not go beyond what is necessary in order to achieve those objectives.

(23) The measures necessary for the implementation of this Regulation should be adopted in accordance with Council Decision 1999/468/EC of 28 June 1999 laying down the procedures for the exercise of implementing powers conferred on the Commission.

(24) In accordance with Article 3 of the Protocol on the position of the United Kingdom and Ireland annexed to the Treaty on European Union and the Treaty establishing the European Community, the United Kingdom and Ireland have notified their wish to take part in the adoption and application of this Regulation.

(25) In accordance with Articles 1 and 2 of the Protocol on the position of Denmark annexed to the Treaty on European Union and the Treaty establishing the European Community, Denmark does not take part in the adoption of this Regulation, and is therefore not bound by it or subject to its application.

(26) Pursuant to the second indent of Article 67(5) of the Treaty, the codecision procedure is applicable from 1 February 2003 for the measures laid down in this Regulation,

HAVE ADOPTED THIS REGULATION:

## CHAPTER I

## SUBJECT MATTER, SCOPE AND DEFINITIONS

*Article 1*

**Subject matter**

The purpose of this Regulation is to create a European Enforcement Order for uncontested claims to permit, by laying down minimum standards, the free circulation of judgments, court settlements and authentic instruments throughout all Member States without any intermediate proceedings needing to be brought in the Member State of enforcement prior to recognition and enforcement.

*Article 2*

**Scope**

1. This Regulation shall apply in civil and commercial matters, whatever the nature of the court or tribunal. It shall not extend, in particular, to revenue, customs or administrative matters or the liability of the State for acts and omissions in the exercise of State authority ('*acta iure imperii*').

2. This Regulation shall not apply to:

(a) the status or legal capacity of natural persons, rights in property arising out of a matrimonial relationship, wills and succession;

(b) bankruptcy, proceedings relating to the winding-up of insolvent companies or other legal persons, judicial arrangements, compositions and analogous proceedings;

(c) social security;

(d) arbitration.

3. In this Regulation, the term 'Member State' shall mean Member States with the exception of Denmark.

*Article 3*

**Enforcement titles to be certified as a European Enforcement Order**

1. This Regulation shall apply to judgments, court settlements and authentic instruments on uncontested claims.

A claim shall be regarded as uncontested if:

(a) the debtor has expressly agreed to it by admission or by means of a settlement which has been approved by a court or concluded before a court in the course of proceedings; or

(b) the debtor has never objected to it, in compliance with the relevant procedural requirements under the law of the Member State of origin, in the course of the court proceedings; or

(c) the debtor has not appeared or been represented at a court hearing regarding that claim after having initially objected to the claim in the course of the court proceedings, provided that such conduct amounts to a tacit admission of the claim or of the facts alleged by the creditor under the law of the Member State of origin; or

(d) the debtor has expressly agreed to it in an authentic instrument.

2. This Regulation shall also apply to decisions delivered following challenges to judgments, court settlements or authentic instruments certified as European Enforcement Orders.

*Article 4*

**Definitions**

For the purposes of this Regulation, the following definitions shall apply:

1. 'judgment': any judgment given by a court or tribunal of a Member State, whatever the judgment may be called, including a decree, order, decision or writ of execution, as well as the determination of costs or expenses by an officer of the court;

2. 'claim': a claim for payment of a specific sum of money that has fallen due or for which the due date is indicated in the judgment, court settlement or authentic instrument;

3. 'authentic instrument':

(a) a document which has been formally drawn up or registered as an authentic instrument, and the authenticity of which:

   (i) relates to the signature and the content of the instrument; and

   (ii) has been established by a public authority or other authority empowered for that purpose by the Member State in which it originates;

or

(b) an arrangement relating to maintenance obligations concluded with administrative authorities or authenticated by them;

4. 'Member State of origin': the Member State in which the judgment has been given, the court settlement has been approved or concluded or the authentic instrument has been drawn up or registered, and is to be certified as a European Enforcement Order;

5. 'Member State of enforcement': the Member State in which enforcement of the judgment, court settlement or authentic instrument certified as a European Enforcement Order is sought;

6. 'court of origin': the court or tribunal seised of the proceedings at the time of fulfilment of the conditions set out in Article 3(1)(a), (b) or (c);

7. in Sweden, in summary proceedings concerning orders to pay (betalningsföreläggande), the expression 'court' includes the Swedish enforcement service (kronofogdemyndighet).

CHAPTER II

**EUROPEAN ENFORCEMENT ORDER**

*Article 5*

**Abolition of exequatur**

A judgment which has been certified as a European Enforcement Order in the Member State of origin shall be recognised and enforced in the other Member States without the need for a declaration of enforceability and without any possibility of opposing its recognition.

*Article 6*

**Requirements for certification as a European Enforcement Order**

1. A judgment on an uncontested claim delivered in a Member State shall, upon application at any time to the court of origin, be certified as a European Enforcement Order if:

(a)  the judgment is enforceable in the Member State of origin; and

(b)  the judgment does not conflict with the rules on jurisdiction as laid down in sections 3 and 6 of Chapter II of Regulation (EC) No 44/2001; and

(c)  the court proceedings in the Member State of origin met the requirements as set out in Chapter III where a claim is uncontested within the meaning of Article 3(1)(b) or (c); and

(d)  the judgment was given in the Member State of the debtor's domicile within the meaning of Article 59 of Regulation (EC) No 44/2001, in cases where

— a claim is uncontested within the meaning of Article 3(1)(b) or (c); and

— it relates to a contract concluded by a person, the consumer, for a purpose which can be regarded as being outside his trade or profession; and

— the debtor is the consumer.

2. Where a judgment certified as a European Enforcement Order has ceased to be enforceable or its enforceability has been suspended or limited, a certificate indicating the lack or limitation of enforceability shall, upon application at any time to the court of origin, be issued, using the standard form in Annex IV.

3. Without prejudice to Article 12(2), where a decision has been delivered following a challenge to a judgment certified as a European Enforcement Order in accordance with paragraph 1 of this Article, a replacement certificate shall, upon application at any time, be issued, using the standard form in Annex V, if that decision on the challenge is enforceable in the Member State of origin.

*Article 7*

**Costs related to court proceedings**

Where a judgment includes an enforceable decision on the amount of costs related to the court proceedings, including the interest rates, it shall be certified as a European Enforcement Order also with regard to the costs unless the debtor has specifically objected to his obligation to bear such costs in the course of the court proceedings, in accordance with the law of the Member State of origin.

*Article 8*

**Partial European Enforcement Order certificate**

If only parts of the judgment meet the requirements of this Regulation, a partial European Enforcement Order certificate shall be issued for those parts.

*Article 9*

**Issue of the European Enforcement Order certificate**

1. The European Enforcement Order certificate shall be issued using the standard form in Annex I.

2. The European Enforcement Order certificate shall be issued in the language of the judgment.

*Article 10*

**Rectification or withdrawal of the European Enforcement Order certificate**

1. The European Enforcement Order certificate shall, upon application to the court of origin, be

(a)  rectified where, due to a material error, there is a discrepancy between the judgment and the certificate;

(b)  withdrawn where it was clearly wrongly granted, having regard to the requirements laid down in this Regulation.

2. The law of the Member State of origin shall apply to the rectification or withdrawal of the European Enforcement Order certificate.

3. An application for the rectification or withdrawal of a European Enforcement Order certificate may be made using the standard form in Annex VI.

4. No appeal shall lie against the issuing of a European Enforcement Order certificate.

## Article 11

### Effect of the European Enforcement Order certificate

The European Enforcement Order certificate shall take effect only within the limits of the enforceability of the judgment.

## CHAPTER III

## MINIMUM STANDARDS FOR UNCONTESTED CLAIMS PROCEDURES

### Article 12

### Scope of application of minimum standards

1. A judgment on a claim that is uncontested within the meaning of Article 3(1)(b) or (c) can be certified as a European Enforcement Order only if the court proceedings in the Member State of origin met the procedural requirements as set out in this Chapter.

2. The same requirements shall apply to the issuing of a European Enforcement Order certificate or a replacement certificate within the meaning of Article 6(3) for a decision following a challenge to a judgment where, at the time of that decision, the conditions of Article 3(1)(b) or (c) are fulfilled.

### Article 13

### Service with proof of receipt by the debtor

1. The document instituting the proceedings or an equivalent document may have been served on the debtor by one of the following methods:

(a) personal service attested by an acknowledgement of receipt, including the date of receipt, which is signed by the debtor;

(b) personal service attested by a document signed by the competent person who effected the service stating that the debtor has received the document or refused to receive it without any legal justification, and the date of the service;

(c) postal service attested by an acknowledgement of receipt including the date of receipt, which is signed and returned by the debtor;

(d) service by electronic means such as fax or e-mail, attested by an acknowledgement of receipt including the date of receipt, which is signed and returned by the debtor.

2. Any summons to a court hearing may have been served on the debtor in compliance with paragraph 1 or orally in a previous court hearing on the same claim and stated in the minutes of that previous court hearing.

### Article 14

### Service without proof of receipt by the debtor

1. Service of the document instituting the proceedings or an equivalent document and any summons to a court hearing on the debtor may also have been effected by one of the following methods:

(a) personal service at the debtor's personal address on persons who are living in the same household as the debtor or are employed there;

(b) in the case of a self-employed debtor or a legal person, personal service at the debtor's business premises on persons who are employed by the debtor;

(c) deposit of the document in the debtor's mailbox;

(d) deposit of the document at a post office or with competent public authorities and the placing in the debtor's mailbox of written notification of that deposit, provided that the written notification clearly states the character of the document as a court document or the legal effect of the notification as effecting service and setting in motion the running of time for the purposes of time limits;

(e) postal service without proof pursuant to paragraph 3 where the debtor has his address in the Member State of origin;

(f) electronic means attested by an automatic confirmation of delivery, provided that the debtor has expressly accepted this method of service in advance.

2. For the purposes of this Regulation, service under paragraph 1 is not admissible if the debtor's address is not known with certainty.

3. Service pursuant to paragraph 1, (a) to (d), shall be attested by:

(a) a document signed by the competent person who effected the service, indicating:

   (i) the method of service used; and

   (ii) the date of service; and

   (iii) where the document has been served on a person other than the debtor, the name of that person and his relation to the debtor,

or

(b) an acknowledgement of receipt by the person served, for the purposes of paragraphs 1(a) and (b).

## Article 15

### Service on the debtor's representatives

Service pursuant to Articles 13 or 14 may also have been effected on a debtor's representative.

## Article 16

### Provision to the debtor of due information about the claim

In order to ensure that the debtor was provided with due information about the claim, the document instituting the proceedings or the equivalent document must have contained the following:

(a) the names and the addresses of the parties;

(b) the amount of the claim;

(c) if interest on the claim is sought, the interest rate and the period for which interest is sought unless statutory interest is automatically added to the principal under the law of the Member State of origin;

(d) a statement of the reason for the claim.

## Article 17

### Provision to the debtor of due information about the procedural steps necessary to contest the claim

The following must have been clearly stated in or together with the document instituting the proceedings, the equivalent document or any summons to a court hearing:

(a) the procedural requirements for contesting the claim, including the time limit for contesting the claim in writing or the time for the court hearing, as applicable, the name and the address of the institution to which to respond or before which to appear, as applicable, and whether it is mandatory to be represented by a lawyer;

(b) the consequences of an absence of objection or default of appearance, in particular, where applicable, the possibility that a judgment may be given or enforced against the debtor and the liability for costs related to the court proceedings.

*Article 18*

**Cure of non-compliance with minimum standards**

1. If the proceedings in the Member State of origin did not meet the procedural requirements as set out in Articles 13 to 17, such non-compliance shall be cured and a judgment may be certified as a European Enforcement Order if:

(a) the judgment has been served on the debtor in compliance with the requirements pursuant to Article 13 or Article 14; and

(b) it was possible for the debtor to challenge the judgment by means of a full review and the debtor has been duly informed in or together with the judgment about the procedural requirements for such a challenge, including the name and address of the institution with which it must be lodged and, where applicable, the time limit for so doing; and

(c) the debtor has failed to challenge the judgment in compliance with the relevant procedural requirements.

2. If the proceedings in the Member State of origin did not comply with the procedural requirements as set out in Article 13 or Article 14, such non-compliance shall be cured if it is proved by the conduct of the debtor in the court proceedings that he has personally received the document to be served in sufficient time to arrange for his defence.

*Article 19*

**Minimum standards for review in exceptional cases**

1. Further to Articles 13 to 18, a judgment can only be certified as a European Enforcement Order if the debtor is entitled, under the law of the Member State of origin, to apply for a review of the judgment where:

(a)

   (i) the document instituting the proceedings or an equivalent document or, where applicable, the summons to a court hearing, was served by one of the methods provided for in Article 14; and

   (ii) service was not effected in sufficient time to enable him to arrange for his defence, without any fault on his part;

or

(b) the debtor was prevented from objecting to the claim by reason of force majeure, or due to extraordinary circumstances without any fault on his part,

provided in either case that he acts promptly.

2. This Article is without prejudice to the possibility for Member States to grant access to a review of the judgment under more generous conditions than those mentioned in paragraph 1.

## CHAPTER IV

## ENFORCEMENT

*Article 20*

**Enforcement procedure**

1. Without prejudice to the provisions of this Chapter, the enforcement procedures shall be governed by the law of the Member State of enforcement.

A judgment certified as a European Enforcement Order shall be enforced under the same conditions as a judgment handed down in the Member State of enforcement.

2. The creditor shall be required to provide the competent enforcement authorities of the Member State of enforcement with:

(a) a copy of the judgment which satisfies the conditions necessary to establish its authenticity; and

(b) a copy of the European Enforcement Order certificate which satisfies the conditions necessary to establish its authenticity; and

(c) where necessary, a transcription of the European Enforcement Order certificate or a translation thereof into the official language of the Member State of enforcement or, if there are several official languages in that Member State, the official language or one of the official languages of court proceedings of the place where enforcement is sought, in conformity with the law of that Member State, or into another language that the Member State of enforcement has indicated it can accept. Each Member State may indicate the official language or languages of the institutions of the European Community other than its own which it can accept for the completion of the certificate. The translation shall be certified by a person qualified to do so in one of the Member States.

3. No security, bond or deposit, however described, shall be required of a party who in one Member State applies for enforcement of a judgment certified as a European Enforcement Order in another Member State on the ground that he is a foreign national or that he is not domiciled or resident in the Member State of enforcement.

## Article 21

**Refusal of enforcement**

1. Enforcement shall, upon application by the debtor, be refused by the competent court in the Member State of enforcement if the judgment certified as a European Enforcement Order is irreconcilable with an earlier judgment given in any Member State or in a third country, provided that:

(a) the earlier judgment involved the same cause of action and was between the same parties; and

(b) the earlier judgment was given in the Member State of enforcement or fulfils the conditions necessary for its recognition in the Member State of enforcement; and

(c) the irreconcilability was not and could not have been raised as an objection in the court proceedings in the Member State of origin.

2. Under no circumstances may the judgment or its certification as a European Enforcement Order be reviewed as to their substance in the Member State of enforcement.

## Article 22

**Agreements with third countries**

This Regulation shall not affect agreements by which Member States undertook, prior to the entry into force of Regulation (EC) No 44/2001, pursuant to Article 59 of the Brussels Convention on jurisdiction and the enforcement of judgments in civil and commercial matters, not to recognise judgments given, in particular in other Contracting States to that Convention, against defendants domiciled or habitually resident in a third country where, in cases provided for in Article 4 of that Convention, the judgment could only be founded on a ground of jurisdiction specified in the second paragraph of Article 3 of that Convention.

## Article 23

**Stay or limitation of enforcement**

Where the debtor has

— challenged a judgment certified as a European Enforcement Order, including an application for review within the meaning of Article 19, or

— applied for the rectification or withdrawal of a European Enforcement Order certificate in accordance with Article 10,

the competent court or authority in the Member State of enforcement may, upon application by the debtor:

(a) limit the enforcement proceedings to protective measures; or

(b) make enforcement conditional on the provision of such security as it shall determine; or

(c) under exceptional circumstances, stay the enforcement proceedings.

European Union Materials

CHAPTER V

## COURT SETTLEMENTS AND AUTHENTIC INSTRUMENTS

*Article 24*

**Court settlements**

1. A settlement concerning a claim within the meaning of Article 4(2) which has been approved by a court or concluded before a court in the course of proceedings and is enforceable in the Member State in which it was approved or concluded shall, upon application to the court that approved it or before which it was concluded, be certified as a European Enforcement Order using the standard form in Annex II.

2. A settlement which has been certified as a European Enforcement Order in the Member State of origin shall be enforced in the other Member States without the need for a declaration of enforceability and without any possibility of opposing its enforceability.

3. The provisions of Chapter II, with the exception of Articles 5, 6(1) and 9(1), and of Chapter IV, with the exception of Articles 21(1) and 22, shall apply as appropriate.

*Article 25*

**Authentic instruments**

1. An authentic instrument concerning a claim within the meaning of Article 4(2) which is enforceable in one Member State shall, upon application to the authority designated by the Member State of origin, be certified as a European Enforcement Order, using the standard form in Annex III.

2. An authentic instrument which has been certified as a European Enforcement Order in the Member State of origin shall be enforced in the other Member States without the need for a declaration of enforceability and without any possibility of opposing its enforceability.

3. The provisions of Chapter II, with the exception of Articles 5, 6(1) and 9(1), and of Chapter IV, with the exception of Articles 21(1) and 22, shall apply as appropriate.

CHAPTER VI

## TRANSITIONAL PROVISION

*Article 26*

**Transitional provision**

This Regulation shall apply only to judgments given, to court settlements approved or concluded and to documents formally drawn up or registered as authentic instruments after the entry into force of this Regulation.

CHAPTER VII

## RELATIONSHIP WITH OTHER COMMUNITY INSTRUMENTS

*Article 27*

**Relationship with Regulation (EC) No 44/2001**

This Regulation shall not affect the possibility of seeking recognition and enforcement, in accordance with Regulation (EC) No 44/2001, of a judgment, a court settlement or an authentic instrument on an uncontested claim.

*Article 28*

**Relationship with Regulation (EC) No 1348/2000**

This Regulation shall not affect the application of Regulation (EC) No 1348/2000.

CHAPTER VIII

## GENERAL AND FINAL PROVISIONS

*Article 29*

### Information on enforcement procedures and authorities

The Member States shall cooperate to provide the general public and professional circles with information on:

(a)   the methods and procedures of enforcement in the Member States; and

(b)   the competent authorities for enforcement in the Member States,

in particular via the European Judicial Network in civil and commercial matters established in accordance with Decision 2001/470/EC.

*Article 30*

### Information relating to redress procedures, languages and authorities

1. The Member States shall notify the Commission of:

(a)   the procedures for rectification and withdrawal referred to in Article 10(2) and for review referred to in Article 19(1);

(b)   the languages accepted pursuant to Article 20(2)(c);

(c)   the lists of the authorities referred to in Article 25;

and any subsequent changes thereof.

2. The Commission shall make the information notified in accordance with paragraph 1 publicly available through publication in the Official Journal of the European Union and through any other appropriate means.

*[Article 31*

### Amendments to the Annexes

The Commission shall amend the standard forms set out in the Annexes. Those measures, designed to amend non-essential elements of this Regulation, shall be adopted in accordance with the regulatory procedure with scrutiny referred to in Article 32(2).]

*[Article 32*

### Committee

1. The Commission shall be assisted by the committee referred to in Article 75 of Regulation (EC) No 44/2001.

2. Where reference is made to this paragraph, Article 5a(1) to (4) and Article 7 of Decision 1999/468/ EC shall apply, having regard to the provisions of Article 8 thereof.]

*Article 33*

### Entry into force

[This Regulation shall enter into force on 21 January 2005.]

It shall apply from 21 October 2005, with the exception of Articles 30, 31 and 32, which shall apply from 21 January 2005.

This Regulation shall be binding in its entirety and directly applicable in the Member States in accordance with the Treaty establishing the European Community.

*[Annexes I–VI omitted]*

# Regulation (EC) No 1896/2006 of the European Parliament and of the Council of 12 December 2006 creating a European order for payment procedure

[2006] OJ L399/1

THE EUROPEAN PARLIAMENT AND THE COUNCIL OF THE EUROPEAN UNION,

Having regard to the Treaty establishing the European Community, and in particular Article 61(c) thereof,

Having regard to the proposal from the Commission,

Having regard to the Opinion of the European Economic and Social Committee,

Acting in accordance with the procedure laid down in Article 251 of the Treaty,

Whereas:

(1) The Community has set itself the objective of maintaining and developing an area of freedom, security and justice in which the free movement of persons is ensured. For the gradual establishment of such an area, the Community is to adopt, inter alia, measures in the field of judicial cooperation in civil matters having cross-border implications and needed for the proper functioning of the internal market.

(2) According to Article 65(c) of the Treaty, these measures are to include measures eliminating obstacles to the good functioning of civil proceedings, if necessary by promoting the compatibility of the rules on civil procedure applicable in the Member States.

(3) The European Council meeting in Tampere on 15 and 16 October 1999 invited the Council and the Commission to prepare new legislation on issues that are instrumental to smooth judicial cooperation and to enhanced access to law and specifically made reference, in that context, to orders for money payment.

(4) On 30 November 2000, the Council adopted a joint Commission and Council programme of measures for implementation of the principle of mutual recognition of decisions in civil and commercial matters. The programme envisages the possibility of a specific, uniform or harmonised procedure laid down within the Community to obtain a judicial decision in specific areas including that of uncontested claims. This was taken forward by the Hague Programme, adopted by the European Council on 5 November 2004, which called for work to be actively pursued on the European order for payment.

(5) The Commission adopted a Green Paper on a European order for payment procedure and on measures to simplify and speed up small claims litigation on 20 December 2002. The Green Paper launched consultations on the possible objectives and features of a uniform or harmonised European procedure for the recovery of uncontested claims.

(6) The swift and efficient recovery of outstanding debts over which no legal controversy exists is of paramount importance for economic operators in the European Union, as late payments constitute a major reason for insolvency threatening the survival of businesses, particularly small and medium-sized enterprises, and resulting in numerous job losses.

(7) All Member States are trying to tackle the issue of mass recovery of uncontested claims, in the majority of States by means of a simplified order for payment procedure, but both the content of national legislation and the performance of domestic procedures vary substantially. Furthermore, the procedures currently in existence are frequently either inadmissible or impracticable in cross-border cases.

(8) The resulting impediments to access to efficient justice in cross-border cases and the distortion of competition within the internal market due to imbalances in the functioning of procedural means afforded to creditors in different Member States necessitate Community legislation guaranteeing a level playing field for creditors and debtors throughout the European Union.

(9) The purpose of this Regulation is to simplify, speed up and reduce the costs of litigation in cross-

border cases concerning uncontested pecuniary claims by creating a European order for payment procedure, and to permit the free circulation of European orders for payment throughout the Member States by laying down minimum standards, compliance with which renders unnecessary any intermediate proceedings in the Member State of enforcement prior to recognition and enforcement.

(10) The procedure established by this Regulation should serve as an additional and optional means for the claimant, who remains free to resort to a procedure provided for by national law. Accordingly, this Regulation neither replaces nor harmonises the existing mechanisms for the recovery of uncontested claims under national law.

(11) The procedure should be based, to the largest extent possible, on the use of standard forms in any communication between the court and the parties in order to facilitate its administration and enable the use of automatic data processing.

(12) When deciding which courts are to have jurisdiction to issue a European order for payment, Member States should take due account of the need to ensure access to justice.

(13) In the application for a European order for payment, the claimant should be obliged to provide information that is sufficient to clearly identify and support the claim in order to place the defendant in a position to make a well-informed choice either to oppose the claim or to leave it uncontested.

(14) In that context, it should be compulsory for the claimant to include a description of evidence supporting the claim. For that purpose the application form should include as exhaustive a list as possible of types of evidence that are usually produced in support of pecuniary claims.

(15) The lodging of an application for a European order for payment should entail the payment of any applicable court fees.

(16) The court should examine the application, including the issue of jurisdiction and the description of evidence, on the basis of the information provided in the application form. This would allow the court to examine prima facie the merits of the claim and inter alia to exclude clearly unfounded claims or inadmissible applications. The examination should not need to be carried out by a judge.

(17) There is to be no right of appeal against the rejection of the application. This does not preclude, however, a possible review of the decision rejecting the application at the same level of jurisdiction in accordance with national law.

(18) The European order for payment should apprise the defendant of his options to pay the amount awarded to the claimant or to send a statement of opposition within a time limit of 30 days if he wishes to contest the claim. In addition to being provided with full information concerning the claim as supplied by the claimant, the defendant should be advised of the legal significance of the European order for payment and in particular of the consequences of leaving the claim uncontested.

(19) Due to differences between Member States' rules of civil procedure and especially those governing the service of documents, it is necessary to lay down a specific and detailed definition of minimum standards that should apply in the context of the European order for payment procedure. In particular, as regards the fulfilment of those standards, any method based on legal fiction should not be considered sufficient for the service of the European order for payment.

(20) All the methods of service listed in Articles 13 and 14 are characterised by either complete certainty (Article 13) or a very high degree of likelihood (Article 14) that the document served has reached its addressee.

(21) Personal service on certain persons other than the defendant himself pursuant to Article 14(1)(a) and (b) should be deemed to meet the requirements of those provisions only if those persons actually accepted/received the European order for payment.

(22) Article 15 should apply to situations where the defendant cannot represent himself in court, as in the case of a legal person, and where a person authorised to represent him is determined by law, as well as to situations where the defendant has authorised another person, in particular a lawyer, to represent him in the specific court proceedings at issue.

(23) The defendant may submit his statement of opposition using the standard form set out in this Regulation. However, the courts should take into account any other written form of opposition if it is expressed in a clear manner.

(24) A statement of opposition filed within the time limit should terminate the European order for payment procedure and should lead to an automatic transfer of the case to ordinary civil proceedings unless the claimant has explicitly requested that the proceedings be terminated in that event. For the purposes of this Regulation the concept of ordinary civil proceedings should not necessarily be interpreted within the meaning of national law.

(25) After the expiry of the time limit for submitting the statement of opposition, in certain exceptional cases the defendant should be entitled to apply for a review of the European order for payment. Review in exceptional cases should not mean that the defendant is given a second opportunity to oppose the claim. During the review procedure the merits of the claim should not be evaluated beyond the grounds resulting from the exceptional circumstances invoked by the defendant. The other exceptional circumstances could include a situation where the European order for payment was based on false information provided in the application form.

(26) Court fees covered by Article 25 should not include for example lawyers' fees or costs of service of documents by an entity other than a court.

(27) A European order for payment issued in one Member State which has become enforceable should be regarded for the purposes of enforcement as if it had been issued in the Member State in which enforcement is sought. Mutual trust in the administration of justice in the Member States justifies the assessment by the court of one Member State that all conditions for issuing a European order for payment are fulfilled to enable the order to be enforced in all other Member States without judicial review of the proper application of minimum procedural standards in the Member State where the order is to be enforced. Without prejudice to the provisions of this Regulation, in particular the minimum standards laid down in Article 22(1) and (2) and Article 23, the procedures for the enforcement of the European order for payment should continue to be governed by national law.

(28) For the purposes of calculating time limits, Regulation (EEC, Euratom) No 1182/71 of the Council of 3 June 1971 determining the rules applicable to periods, dates and time limits should apply. The defendant should be advised of this and should be informed that account will be taken of the public holidays of the Member State in which the court issuing the European order for payment is situated.

(29) Since the objective of this Regulation, namely to establish a uniform rapid and efficient mechanism for the recovery of uncontested pecuniary claims throughout the European Union, cannot be sufficiently achieved by the Member States and can therefore, by reason of the scale and effects of the Regulation, be better achieved at Community level, the Community may adopt measures in accordance with the principle of subsidiarity as set out in Article 5 of the Treaty. In accordance with the principle of proportionality as set out in that Article, this Regulation does not go beyond what is necessary in order to achieve that objective.

(30) The measures necessary for the implementation of this Regulation should be adopted in accordance with Council Decision 1999/468/EC of 28 June 1999 laying down the procedures for the exercise of implementing powers conferred on the Commission.

(31) The United Kingdom and Ireland, in accordance with Article 3 of the Protocol on the position of the United Kingdom and Ireland annexed to the Treaty on European Union and the Treaty establishing the European Community, have given notice of their wish to take part in the adoption and application of this Regulation.

(32) In accordance with Articles 1 and 2 of the Protocol on the position of Denmark annexed to the Treaty on European Union and the Treaty establishing the European Community, Denmark does not take part in the adoption of this Regulation, and is not bound by it or subject to its application,

HAVE ADOPTED THIS REGULATION:

## Article 1

**Subject matter**

1. The purpose of this Regulation is:

(a) to simplify, speed up and reduce the costs of litigation in cross-border cases concerning uncontested pecuniary claims by creating a European order for payment procedure;

and

(b) to permit the free circulation of European orders for payment throughout the Member States by laying down minimum standards, compliance with which renders unnecessary any intermediate proceedings in the Member State of enforcement prior to recognition and enforcement.

2. This Regulation shall not prevent a claimant from pursuing a claim within the meaning of Article 4 by making use of another procedure available under the law of a Member State or under Community law.

*Article 2*

**Scope**

1. This Regulation shall apply to civil and commercial matters in cross-border cases, whatever the nature of the court or tribunal. It shall not extend, in particular, to revenue, customs or administrative matters or the liability of the State for acts and omissions in the exercise of State authority ('acta iure imperii').

2. This Regulation shall not apply to:

(a) rights in property arising out of a matrimonial relationship, wills and succession;

(b) bankruptcy, proceedings relating to the winding-up of insolvent companies or other legal persons, judicial arrangements, compositions and analogous proceedings;

(c) social security;

(d) claims arising from non-contractual obligations, unless:

(i) they have been the subject of an agreement between the parties or there has been an admission of debt,

or

(ii) they relate to liquidated debts arising from joint ownership of property.

3. In this Regulation, the term 'Member State' shall mean Member States with the exception of Denmark.

*Article 3*

**Cross-border cases**

1. For the purposes of this Regulation, a cross-border case is one in which at least one of the parties is domiciled or habitually resident in a Member State other than the Member State of the court seised.

2. Domicile shall be determined in accordance with Articles 59 and 60 of Council Regulation (EC) No 44/2001 of 22 December 2000 on jurisdiction and the recognition and enforcement of judgments in civil and commercial matters.

3. The relevant moment for determining whether there is a cross-border case shall be the time when the application for a European order for payment is submitted in accordance with this Regulation.

*Article 4*

**European order for payment procedure**

The European order for payment procedure shall be established for the collection of pecuniary claims for a specific amount that have fallen due at the time when the application for a European order for payment is submitted.

*Article 5*

**Definitions**

For the purposes of this Regulation, the following definitions shall apply:

1) 'Member State of origin' means the Member State in which a European order for payment is issued;

2) 'Member State of enforcement' means the Member State in which enforcement of a European order for payment is sought;

3)   'court' means any authority in a Member State with competence regarding European orders for payment or any other related matters;

4)   'court of origin' means the court which issues a European order for payment.

## Article 6

### Jurisdiction

1. For the purposes of applying this Regulation, jurisdiction shall be determined in accordance with the relevant rules of Community law, in particular Regulation (EC) No 44/2001.

2. However, if the claim relates to a contract concluded by a person, the consumer, for a purpose which can be regarded as being outside his trade or profession, and if the defendant is the consumer, only the courts in the Member State in which the defendant is domiciled, within the meaning of Article 59 of Regulation (EC) No 44/2001, shall have jurisdiction.

## Article 7

### Application for a European order for payment

1. An application for a European order for payment shall be made using standard form A as set out in Annex I.

2. The application shall state:

(a)   the names and addresses of the parties, and, where applicable, their representatives, and of the court to which the application is made;

(b)   the amount of the claim, including the principal and, where applicable, interest, contractual penalties and costs;

(c)   if interest on the claim is demanded, the interest rate and the period of time for which that interest is demanded unless statutory interest is automatically added to the principal under the law of the Member State of origin;

(d)   the cause of the action, including a description of the circumstances invoked as the basis of the claim and, where applicable, of the interest demanded;

(e)   a description of evidence supporting the claim;

(f)   the grounds for jurisdiction;

and

(g)   the cross-border nature of the case within the meaning of Article 3.

3. In the application, the claimant shall declare that the information provided is true to the best of his knowledge and belief and shall acknowledge that any deliberate false statement could lead to appropriate penalties under the law of the Member State of origin.

4. In an Appendix to the application the claimant may indicate to the court that he opposes a transfer to ordinary civil proceedings within the meaning of Article 17 in the event of opposition by the defendant. This does not prevent the claimant from informing the court thereof subsequently, but in any event before the order is issued.

5. The application shall be submitted in paper form or by any other means of communication, including electronic, accepted by the Member State of origin and available to the court of origin.

6. The application shall be signed by the claimant or, where applicable, by his representative. Where the application is submitted in electronic form in accordance with paragraph 5, it shall be signed in accordance with Article 2(2) of Directive 1999/93/EC of the European Parliament and of the Council of 13 December 1999 on a Community framework for electronic signatures. The signature shall be recognised in the Member State of origin and may not be made subject to additional requirements.

6. However, such electronic signature shall not be required if and to the extent that an alternative electronic communications system exists in the courts of the Member State of origin which is available to a certain group of pre-registered authenticated users and which permits the identification of those

users in a secure manner. Member States shall inform the Commission of such communications systems.

*Article 8*

**Examination of the application**

The court seised of an application for a European order for payment shall examine, as soon as possible and on the basis of the application form, whether the requirements set out in Articles 2, 3, 4, 6 and 7 are met and whether the claim appears to be founded. This examination may take the form of an automated procedure.

*Article 9*

**Completion and rectification**

1. If the requirements set out in Article 7 are not met and unless the claim is clearly unfounded or the application is inadmissible, the court shall give the claimant the opportunity to complete or rectify the application. The court shall use standard form B as set out in Annex II.

2. Where the court requests the claimant to complete or rectify the application, it shall specify a time limit it deems appropriate in the circumstances. The court may at its discretion extend that time limit.

*Article 10*

**Modification of the application**

1. If the requirements referred to in Article 8 are met for only part of the claim, the court shall inform the claimant to that effect, using standard form C as set out in Annex III. The claimant shall be invited to accept or refuse a proposal for a European order for payment for the amount specified by the court and shall be informed of the consequences of his decision. The claimant shall reply by returning standard form C sent by the court within a time limit specified by the court in accordance with Article 9(2).

2. If the claimant accepts the court's proposal, the court shall issue a European order for payment, in accordance with Article 12, for that part of the claim accepted by the claimant. The consequences with respect to the remaining part of the initial claim shall be governed by national law.

3. If the claimant fails to send his reply within the time limit specified by the court or refuses the court's proposal, the court shall reject the application for a European order for payment in its entirety.

*Article 11*

**Rejection of the application**

1. The court shall reject the application if:

(a)   the requirements set out in Articles 2, 3, 4, 6 and 7 are not met;

or

(b)   the claim is clearly unfounded;

or

(c)   the claimant fails to send his reply within the time limit specified by the court under Article 9(2);

or

(d)   the claimant fails to send his reply within the time limit specified by the court or refuses the court's proposal, in accordance with Article 10.

The claimant shall be informed of the grounds for the rejection by means of standard form D as set out in Annex IV.

2. There shall be no right of appeal against the rejection of the application.

3. The rejection of the application shall not prevent the claimant from pursuing the claim by means of a new application for a European order for payment or of any other procedure available under the law of a Member State.

*Article 12*

### Issue of a European order for payment

1. If the requirements referred to in Article 8 are met, the court shall issue, as soon as possible and normally within 30 days of the lodging of the application, a European order for payment using standard form E as set out in Annex V.

The 30-day period shall not include the time taken by the claimant to complete, rectify or modify the application.

2. The European order for payment shall be issued together with a copy of the application form. It shall not comprise the information provided by the claimant in Appendices 1 and 2 to form A.

3. In the European order for payment, the defendant shall be advised of his options to:

(a)  pay the amount indicated in the order to the claimant;

or

(b)  oppose the order by lodging with the court of origin a statement of opposition, to be sent within 30 days of service of the order on him.

4. In the European order for payment, the defendant shall be informed that:

(a)  the order was issued solely on the basis of the information which was provided by the claimant and was not verified by the court;

(b)  the order will become enforceable unless a statement of opposition has been lodged with the court in accordance with Article 16;

(c)  where a statement of opposition is lodged, the proceedings shall continue before the competent courts of the Member State of origin in accordance with the rules of ordinary civil procedure unless the claimant has explicitly requested that the proceedings be terminated in that event.

5. The court shall ensure that the order is served on the defendant in accordance with national law by a method that shall meet the minimum standards laid down in Articles 13, 14 and 15.

*Article 13*

### Service with proof of receipt by the defendant

The European order for payment may be served on the defendant in accordance with the national law of the State in which the service is to be effected, by one of the following methods:

(a)  personal service attested by an acknowledgement of receipt, including the date of receipt, which is signed by the defendant;

(b)  personal service attested by a document signed by the competent person who effected the service stating that the defendant has received the document or refused to receive it without any legal justification, and the date of service;

(c)  postal service attested by an acknowledgement of receipt, including the date of receipt, which is signed and returned by the defendant;

(d)  service by electronic means such as fax or e-mail, attested by an acknowledgement of receipt, including the date of receipt, which is signed and returned by the defendant.

*Article 14*

### Service without proof of receipt by the defendant

1. The European order for payment may also be served on the defendant in accordance with the national law of the State in which service is to be effected, by one of the following methods:

(a)  personal service at the defendant's personal address on persons who are living in the same household as the defendant or are employed there;

(b)  in the case of a self-employed defendant or a legal person, personal service at the defendant's business premises on persons who are employed by the defendant;

(c)  deposit of the order in the defendant's mailbox;

(d) deposit of the order at a post office or with competent public authorities and the placing in the defendant's mailbox of written notification of that deposit, provided that the written notification clearly states the character of the document as a court document or the legal effect of the notification as effecting service and setting in motion the running of time for the purposes of time limits;

(e) postal service without proof pursuant to paragraph 3 where the defendant has his address in the Member State of origin;

(f) electronic means attested by an automatic confirmation of delivery, provided that the defendant has expressly accepted this method of service in advance.

2. For the purposes of this Regulation, service under paragraph 1 is not admissible if the defendant's address is not known with certainty.

3. Service pursuant to paragraph 1(a), (b), (c) and (d) shall be attested by:

(a) a document signed by the competent person who effected the service, indicating:

  (i) the method of service used;

    and

  (ii) the date of service;

    and

  (iii) where the order has been served on a person other than the defendant, the name of that person and his relation to the defendant;

or

(b) an acknowledgement of receipt by the person served, for the purposes of paragraphs (1)(a) and (b).

## Article 15

**Service on a representative**

Service pursuant to Articles 13 or 14 may also be effected on a defendant's representative.

## Article 16

**Opposition to the European order for payment**

1. The defendant may lodge a statement of opposition to the European order for payment with the court of origin using standard form F as set out in Annex VI, which shall be supplied to him together with the European order for payment.

2. The statement of opposition shall be sent within 30 days of service of the order on the defendant.

3. The defendant shall indicate in the statement of opposition that he contests the claim, without having to specify the reasons for this.

4. The statement of opposition shall be submitted in paper form or by any other means of communication, including electronic, accepted by the Member State of origin and available to the court of origin.

5. The statement of opposition shall be signed by the defendant or, where applicable, by his representative. Where the statement of opposition is submitted in electronic form in accordance with paragraph 4, it shall be signed in accordance with Article 2(2) of Directive 1999/93/EC. The signature shall be recognised in the Member State of origin and may not be made subject to additional requirements.

However, such electronic signature shall not be required if and to the extent that an alternative electronic communications system exists in the courts of the Member State of origin which is available to a certain group of pre-registered authenticated users and which permits the identification of those users in a secure manner. Member States shall inform the Commission of such communications systems.

*Article 17*

**Effects of the lodging of a statement of opposition**

1. If a statement of opposition is entered within the time limit laid down in Article 16(2), the proceedings shall continue before the competent courts of the Member State of origin in accordance with the rules of ordinary civil procedure unless the claimant has explicitly requested that the proceedings be terminated in that event.

Where the claimant has pursued his claim through the European order for payment procedure, nothing under national law shall prejudice his position in subsequent ordinary civil proceedings.

2. The transfer to ordinary civil proceedings within the meaning of paragraph 1 shall be governed by the law of the Member State of origin.

3. The claimant shall be informed whether the defendant has lodged a statement of opposition and of any transfer to ordinary civil proceedings.

*Article 18*

**Enforceability**

1. If within the time limit laid down in Article 16(2), taking into account an appropriate period of time to allow a statement to arrive, no statement of opposition has been lodged with the court of origin, the court of origin shall without delay declare the European order for payment enforceable using standard form G as set out in Annex VII. The court shall verify the date of service.

2. Without prejudice to paragraph 1, the formal requirements for enforceability shall be governed by the law of the Member State of origin.

3. The court shall send the enforceable European order for payment to the claimant.

*Article 19*

**Abolition of exequatur**

A European order for payment which has become enforceable in the Member State of origin shall be recognised and enforced in the other Member States without the need for a declaration of enforceability and without any possibility of opposing its recognition.

*Article 20*

**Review in exceptional cases**

1. After the expiry of the time limit laid down in Article 16(2) the defendant shall be entitled to apply for a review of the European order for payment before the competent court in the Member State of origin where:

(a)

    (i)   the order for payment was served by one of the methods provided for in Article 14,

and

    (ii)   service was not effected in sufficient time to enable him to arrange for his defence, without any fault on his part,

or

(b)   the defendant was prevented from objecting to the claim by reason of force majeure or due to extraordinary circumstances without any fault on his part,

provided in either case that he acts promptly.

2. After expiry of the time limit laid down in Article 16(2) the defendant shall also be entitled to apply for a review of the European order for payment before the competent court in the Member State of origin where the order for payment was clearly wrongly issued, having regard to the requirements laid down in this Regulation, or due to other exceptional circumstances.

3. If the court rejects the defendant's application on the basis that none of the grounds for review referred to in paragraphs 1 and 2 apply, the European order for payment shall remain in force.

If the court decides that the review is justified for one of the reasons laid down in paragraphs 1 and 2, the European order for payment shall be null and void.

## Article 21

**Enforcement**

1. Without prejudice to the provisions of this Regulation, enforcement procedures shall be governed by the law of the Member State of enforcement.

A European order for payment which has become enforceable shall be enforced under the same conditions as an enforceable decision issued in the Member State of enforcement.

2. For enforcement in another Member State, the claimant shall provide the competent enforcement authorities of that Member State with:

(a) a copy of the European order for payment, as declared enforceable by the court of origin, which satisfies the conditions necessary to establish its authenticity;

and

(b) where necessary, a translation of the European order for payment into the official language of the Member State of enforcement or, if there are several official languages in that Member State, the official language or one of the official languages of court proceedings of the place where enforcement is sought, in conformity with the law of that Member State, or into another language that the Member State of enforcement has indicated it can accept. Each Member State may indicate the official language or languages of the institutions of the European Union other than its own which it can accept for the European order for payment. The translation shall be certified by a person qualified to do so in one of the Member States.

3. No security, bond or deposit, however described, shall be required of a claimant who in one Member State applies for enforcement of a European order for payment issued in another Member State on the ground that he is a foreign national or that he is not domiciled or resident in the Member State of enforcement.

## Article 22

**Refusal of enforcement**

1. Enforcement shall, upon application by the defendant, be refused by the competent court in the Member State of enforcement if the European order for payment is irreconcilable with an earlier decision or order previously given in any Member State or in a third country, provided that:

(a) the earlier decision or order involved the same cause of action between the same parties;

and

(b) the earlier decision or order fulfils the conditions necessary for its recognition in the Member State of enforcement;

and

(c) the irreconcilability could not have been raised as an objection in the court proceedings in the Member State of origin.

2. Enforcement shall, upon application, also be refused if and to the extent that the defendant has paid the claimant the amount awarded in the European order for payment.

3. Under no circumstances may the European order for payment be reviewed as to its substance in the Member State of enforcement.

## Article 23

**Stay or limitation of enforcement**

Where the defendant has applied for a review in accordance with Article 20, the competent court in the Member State of enforcement may, upon application by the defendant:

(a) limit the enforcement proceedings to protective measures;

or

(b)   make enforcement conditional on the provision of such security as it shall determine;

or

(c)   under exceptional circumstances, stay the enforcement proceedings.

## Article 24

### Legal representation

Representation by a lawyer or another legal professional shall not be mandatory:

(a)   for the claimant in respect of the application for a European order for payment;

(b)   for the defendant in respect of the statement of opposition to a European order for payment.

## Article 25

### Court fees

1. The combined court fees of a European order for payment procedure and of the ordinary civil proceedings that ensue in the event of a statement of opposition to a European order for payment in a Member State shall not exceed the court fees of ordinary civil proceedings without a preceding European order for payment procedure in that Member State.

2. For the purposes of this Regulation, court fees shall comprise fees and charges to be paid to the court, the amount of which is fixed in accordance with national law.

## Article 26

### Relationship with national procedural law

All procedural issues not specifically dealt with in this Regulation shall be governed by national law.

## Article 27

### Relationship with Regulation (EC) No 1348/2000

This Regulation shall not affect the application of Council Regulation (EC) No 1348/2000 of 29 May 2000 on the service in the Member States of judicial and extrajudicial documents in civil and commercial matters .

## Article 28

### Information relating to service costs and enforcement

Member States shall cooperate to provide the general public and professional circles with information on:

(a)   costs of service of documents;

and

(b)   which authorities have competence with respect to enforcement for the purposes of applying Articles 21, 22 and 23,

in particular via the European Judicial Network in civil and commercial matters established in accordance with Council Decision 2001/470/EC.

## Article 29

### Information relating to jurisdiction, review procedures, means of communication and languages

1. By 12 June 2008, Member States shall communicate to the Commission:

(a)   which courts have jurisdiction to issue a European order for payment;

(b)   the review procedure and the competent courts for the purposes of the application of Article 20;

(c)   the means of communication accepted for the purposes of the European order for payment procedure and available to the courts;

(d)   languages accepted pursuant to Article 21(2)(b).

Member States shall apprise the Commission of any subsequent changes to this information.

2. The Commission shall make the information notified in accordance with paragraph 1 publicly available through publication in the Official Journal of the European Union and through any other appropriate means.

### Article 30

**Amendments to the Annexes**

The standard forms set out in the Annexes shall be updated or technically adjusted, ensuring full conformity with the provisions of this Regulation, in accordance with the procedure referred to in Article 31(2).

### Article 31

**Committee**

1. The Commission shall be assisted by the committee established by Article 75 of Regulation (EC) No 44/2001.

2. Where reference is made to this paragraph, Article 5a(1)-(4) and Article 7 of Decision 1999/468/EC shall apply, having regard to the provisions of Article 8 thereof.

3. The Committee shall adopt its Rules of Procedure.

### Article 32

**Review**

By 12 December 2013, the Commission shall present to the European Parliament, the Council and the European Economic and Social Committee a detailed report reviewing the operation of the European order for payment procedure. That report shall contain an assessment of the procedure as it has operated and an extended impact assessment for each Member State.

To that end, and in order to ensure that best practice in the European Union is duly taken into account and reflects the principles of better legislation, Member States shall provide the Commission with information relating to the cross-border operation of the European order for payment. This information shall cover court fees, speed of the procedure, efficiency, ease of use and the internal payment order procedures of the Member States.

The Commission's report shall be accompanied, if appropriate, by proposals for adaptation.

### Article 33

**Entry into force**

This Regulation shall enter into force on the day following the date of its publication in the Official Journal of the European Union.

It shall apply from 12 December 2008, with the exception of Articles 28, 29, 30 and 31 which shall apply from 12 June 2008.

This Regulation shall be binding in its entirety and directly applicable in the Member States in accordance with the Treaty establishing the European Community.

*[Annexes I–VI omitted]*

# Regulation (EC) No 861/2007 of the European Parliament and of The Council of 11 July 2007 establishing a European Small Claims Procedure

[2007] OJ L199/1

THE EUROPEAN PARLIAMENT AND THE COUNCIL OF THE EUROPEAN UNION,

Having regard to the Treaty establishing the European Community, and in particular Article 61(c) and Article 67 thereof,

Having regard to the proposal from the Commission,

Having regard to the opinion of the European Economic and Social Committee,

Acting in accordance with the procedure laid down in Article 251 of the Treaty,

Whereas:

(1) The Community has set itself the objective of maintaining and developing an area of freedom, security and justice in which the free movement of persons is ensured. For the gradual establishment of such an area, the Community is to adopt, inter alia, measures in the field of judicial cooperation in civil matters having cross-border implications and needed for the proper functioning of the internal market.

(2) According to Article 65(c) of the Treaty, those measures are to include those eliminating obstacles to the good functioning of civil proceedings, if necessary by promoting the compatibility of the rules on civil procedure applicable in the Member States.

(3) In this respect, the Community has, among other measures, already adopted Council Regulation (EC) No 1348/2000 of 29 May 2000 on the service in the Member States of judicial and extrajudicial documents in civil or commercial matters, Council Regulation (EC) No 44/2001 of 22 December 2000 on jurisdiction and the recognition and enforcement of judgments in civil and commercial matters, Council Decision 2001/470/EC of 28 May 2001 establishing a European Judicial Network in civil and commercial matters, Regulation (EC) No 805/2004 of the European Parliament and of the Council of 21 April 2004 creating a European Enforcement Order for uncontested claims and Regulation (EC) No 1896/2006 of the European Parliament and of the Council of 12 December 2006 creating a European order for payment procedure.

(4) The European Council meeting in Tampere on 15 and 16 October 1999 invited the Council and the Commission to establish common procedural rules for simplified and accelerated cross-border litigation on small consumer and commercial claims.

(5) On 30 November 2000, the Council adopted a joint programme of the Commission and the Council of measures for the implementation of the principle of mutual recognition of decisions in civil and commercial matters. The programme refers to simplifying and speeding up the settlement of cross-border litigation on small claims. This was taken forward by the Hague Programme, adopted by the European Council on 5 November 2004, which called for work on small claims to be actively pursued.

(6) On 20 December 2002, the Commission adopted a Green Paper on a European order for payment procedure and on measures to simplify and speed up small claims litigation. The Green Paper launched a consultation on measures concerning the simplification and the speeding up of small claims litigation.

(7) Many Member States have introduced simplified civil procedures for small claims since costs, delays and complexities connected with litigation do not necessarily decrease proportionally with the value of the claim. The obstacles to obtaining a fast and inexpensive judgment are exacerbated in cross-border cases. It is therefore necessary to establish a European procedure for small claims (European Small Claims Procedure). The objective of such a procedure should be to facilitate access to justice. The distortion of competition within the internal market due to imbalances with regard to the functioning of the procedural means afforded to creditors in different Member States entails the need for Community legislation that guarantees a level playing-field for creditors and debtors

throughout the European Union. It should be necessary to have regard to the principles of simplicity, speed and proportionality when setting the costs of dealing with a claim under the European Small Claims Procedure. It is appropriate that details of the costs to be charged be made public, and that the means of setting any such costs be transparent.

(8) The European Small Claims Procedure should simplify and speed up litigation concerning small claims in cross-border cases, whilst reducing costs, by offering an optional tool in addition to the possibilities existing under the laws of the Member States, which will remain unaffected. This Regulation should also make it simpler to obtain the recognition and enforcement of a judgment given in the European Small Claims Procedure in another Member State.

(9) This Regulation seeks to promote fundamental rights and takes into account, in particular, the principles recognised by the Charter of Fundamental Rights of the European Union. The court or tribunal should respect the right to a fair trial and the principle of an adversarial process, in particular when deciding on the necessity of an oral hearing and on the means of taking evidence and the extent to which evidence is to be taken.

(10) For the purposes of facilitating calculation of the value of a claim, all interest, expenses and disbursements should be disregarded. This should affect neither the power of the court or tribunal to award these in its judgment nor the national rules on the calculation of interest.

(11) In order to facilitate the commencement of the European Small Claims Procedure, the claimant should make an application by filling in a standard claim form and lodging it with the court or tribunal. The claim form should be submitted only to a court or tribunal that has jurisdiction.

(12) The claim form should be accompanied, where appropriate, by any relevant supporting documents. However, this does not prevent the claimant from submitting, where appropriate, further evidence during the procedure. The same principle should apply to the response by the defendant.

(13) The concepts of 'clearly unfounded' in the context of the dismissal of a claim and of 'inadmissible' in the context of the dismissal of an application should be determined in accordance with national law.

(14) The European Small Claims Procedure should be a written procedure, unless an oral hearing is considered necessary by the court or tribunal or a party so requests. The court or tribunal may refuse such a request. Such refusal may not be contested separately.

(15) The parties should not be obliged to be represented by a lawyer or another legal professional.

(16) The concept of 'counterclaim' should be interpreted within the meaning of Article 6(3) of Regulation (EC) No 44/2001 as arising from the same contract or facts on which the original claim was based. Articles 2 and 4 as well as Article 5(3), (4) and (5) should apply, mutatis mutandis, to counterclaims.

(17) In cases where the defendant invokes a right of set-off during the proceedings, such claim should not constitute a counterclaim for the purposes of this Regulation. Therefore, the defendant should not be obliged to use standard Form A, as set out in Annex I, for invoking such a right.

(18) The Member State addressed for the purposes of the application of Article 6 is the Member State where service is to be effected or to where the document is to be dispatched. In order to reduce costs and delays, documents should be served on the parties primarily by postal service attested by an acknowledgment of receipt, including the date of receipt.

(19) A party may refuse to accept a document at the time of service or by returning the document within one week if it is not written in, or accompanied by a translation into, the official language of the Member State addressed (or, if there are several official languages in that Member State, the official language or one of the official languages of the place where service is to be effected or to where the document is to be dispatched) or a language which the addressee understands.

(20) In the context of oral hearings and the taking of evidence, the Member States should encourage the use of modern communication technology subject to the national law of the Member State where the court or tribunal is situated. The court or tribunal should use the simplest and least costly method of taking evidence.

(21) The practical assistance to be made available to the parties should include technical information concerning the availability and the filling in of the forms.

(22) The information about procedural questions can also be given by the court or tribunal staff in accordance with national law.

(23) As the objective of this Regulation is to simplify and speed up litigation concerning small claims in cross-border cases, the court or tribunal should act as soon as possible even when this Regulation does not prescribe any time limit for a specific phase of the procedure.

(24) For the purposes of calculating time limits as provided for in this Regulation, Regulation (EEC, Euratom) No 1182/71 of the Council of 3 June 1971 determining the rules applicable to periods, dates and time limits should apply.

(25) In order to speed up the recovery of small claims, the judgment should be enforceable notwithstanding any possible appeal and without the condition of the provision of a security except as provided for in this Regulation.

(26) Any reference in this Regulation to an appeal should include any possible means of appeal available under national law.

(27) The court or tribunal must include a person qualified to serve as a judge in accordance with national law.

(28) Whenever the court or tribunal is required to set a time limit, the party concerned should be informed of the consequences of not complying with it.

(29) The unsuccessful party should bear the costs of the proceedings. The costs of the proceedings should be determined in accordance with national law. Having regard to the objectives of simplicity and cost-effectiveness, the court or tribunal should order that an unsuccessful party be obliged to pay only the costs of the proceedings, including for example any costs resulting from the fact that the other party was represented by a lawyer or another legal professional, or any costs arising from the service or translation of documents, which are proportionate to the value of the claim or which were necessarily incurred.

(30) In order to facilitate recognition and enforcement, a judgment given in a Member State in the European Small Claims Procedure should be recognised and enforceable in another Member State without the need for a declaration of enforceability and without any possibility of opposing its recognition.

(31) There should be minimum standards for the review of a judgment in situations where the defendant was not able to contest the claim.

(32) Having regard to the objectives of simplicity and cost-effectiveness, the party seeking enforcement shall not be required to have an authorised representative or a postal address in the Member State of enforcement, other than with agents having competence for the enforcement procedure in accordance with the national law of that Member State.

(33) Chapter III of this Regulation should also apply to the determination of costs and expenses made by officers of the court or tribunal due to a judgment given pursuant to the procedure specified in this Regulation.

(34) The measures necessary for the implementation of this Regulation should be adopted in accordance with Council Decision 1999/468/EC of 28 June 1999 laying down the procedures for the exercise of implementing powers conferred on the Commission.

(35) In particular, power should be conferred on the Commission to adopt measures necessary to update or make technical amendments to the forms set out in the Annexes. Since those measures are of general scope and are designed to amend non-essential elements of this Regulation and/or to supplement this Regulation by the addition of new non-essential elements, they should be adopted in accordance with the regulatory procedure with scrutiny provided for in Article 5a of Decision 1999/468/EC.

(36) Since the objectives of this Regulation, namely, the establishment of a procedure to simplify and speed up litigation concerning small claims in cross-border cases, and to reduce costs, cannot be sufficiently achieved by the Member States and can therefore, by reason of the scale and effects of this Regulation, be better achieved at Community level, the Community may adopt measures in accordance with the principle of subsidiarity as set out in Article 5 of the Treaty. In accordance with the principle

of proportionality, as set out in that Article, this Regulation does not go beyond what is necessary to achieve those objectives.

(37) In accordance with Article 3 of the Protocol on the position of the United Kingdom and Ireland annexed to the Treaty on European Union and to the Treaty establishing the European Community, the United Kingdom and Ireland have given notice of their wish to take part in the adoption and application of this Regulation.

(38) In accordance with Articles 1 and 2 of the Protocol on the position of Denmark annexed to the Treaty on European Union and to the Treaty establishing the European Community, Denmark does not take part in the adoption of this Regulation and is not bound by it or subject to its application,

HAVE ADOPTED THIS REGULATION:

# CHAPTER I

## SUBJECT MATTER AND SCOPE

*Article 1*

### Subject matter

This Regulation establishes a European procedure for small claims (hereinafter referred to as the European Small Claims Procedure), intended to simplify and speed up litigation concerning small claims in cross-border cases, and to reduce costs. The European Small Claims Procedure shall be available to litigants as an alternative to the procedures existing under the laws of the Member States.

This Regulation also eliminates the intermediate proceedings necessary to enable recognition and enforcement, in other Member States, of judgments given in one Member State in the European Small Claims Procedure.

*Article 2*

### Scope

1. This Regulation shall apply, in cross-border cases, to civil and commercial matters, whatever the nature of the court or tribunal, where the value of a claim does not exceed EUR 2 000 at the time when the claim form is received by the court or tribunal with jurisdiction, excluding all interest, expenses and disbursements. It shall not extend, in particular, to revenue, customs or administrative matters or to the liability of the State for acts and omissions in the exercise of State authority (acta jure imperii).

2. This Regulation shall not apply to matters concerning:

(a) the status or legal capacity of natural persons;

(b) rights in property arising out of a matrimonial relationship, maintenance obligations, wills and succession;

(c) bankruptcy, proceedings relating to the winding-up of insolvent companies or other legal persons, judicial arrangements, compositions and analogous proceedings;

(d) social security;

(e) arbitration;

(f) employment law;

(g) tenancies of immovable property, with the exception of actions on monetary claims; or

(h) violations of privacy and of rights relating to personality, including defamation.

3. In this Regulation, the term 'Member State' shall mean Member States with the exception of Denmark.

*Article 3*

### Cross-border cases

1. For the purposes of this Regulation, a cross-border case is one in which at least one of the parties

is domiciled or habitually resident in a Member State other than the Member State of the court or tribunal seised.

2. Domicile shall be determined in accordance with Articles 59 and 60 of Regulation (EC) No 44/2001.

3. The relevant moment for determining whether there is a cross-border case is the date on which the claim form is received by the court or tribunal with jurisdiction.

## CHAPTER II

## THE EUROPEAN SMALL CLAIMS PROCEDURE

### Article 4

#### Commencement of the Procedure

1. The claimant shall commence the European Small Claims Procedure by filling in standard claim Form A, as set out in Annex I, and lodging it with the court or tribunal with jurisdiction directly, by post or by any other means of communication, such as fax or e-mail, acceptable to the Member State in which the procedure is commenced. The claim form shall include a description of evidence supporting the claim and be accompanied, where appropriate, by any relevant supporting documents.

2. Member States shall inform the Commission which means of communication are acceptable to them. The Commission shall make such information publicly available.

3. Where a claim is outside the scope of this Regulation, the court or tribunal shall inform the claimant to that effect. Unless the claimant withdraws the claim, the court or tribunal shall proceed with it in accordance with the relevant procedural law applicable in the Member State in which the procedure is conducted.

4. Where the court or tribunal considers the information provided by the claimant to be inadequate or insufficiently clear or if the claim form is not filled in properly, it shall, unless the claim appears to be clearly unfounded or the application inadmissible, give the claimant the opportunity to complete or rectify the claim form or to supply supplementary information or documents or to withdraw the claim, within such period as it specifies. The court or tribunal shall use standard Form B, as set out in Annex II, for this purpose.

Where the claim appears to be clearly unfounded or the application inadmissible or where the claimant fails to complete or rectify the claim form within the time specified, the application shall be dismissed.

5. Member States shall ensure that the claim form is available at all courts and tribunals at which the European Small Claims Procedure can be commenced.

### Article 5

#### Conduct of the Procedure

1. The European Small Claims Procedure shall be a written procedure. The court or tribunal shall hold an oral hearing if it considers this to be necessary or if a party so requests. The court or tribunal may refuse such a request if it considers that with regard to the circumstances of the case, an oral hearing is obviously not necessary for the fair conduct of the proceedings. The reasons for refusal shall be given in writing. The refusal may not be contested separately.

2. After receiving the properly filled in claim form, the court or tribunal shall fill in Part I of the standard answer Form C, as set out in Annex III.

A copy of the claim form, and, where applicable, of the supporting documents, together with the answer form thus filled in, shall be served on the defendant in accordance with Article 13. These documents shall be dispatched within 14 days of receiving the properly filled in claim form.

3. The defendant shall submit his response within 30 days of service of the claim form and answer form, by filling in Part II of standard answer Form C, accompanied, where appropriate, by any relevant supporting documents, and returning it to the court or tribunal, or in any other appropriate way not using the answer form.

4. Within 14 days of receipt of the response from the defendant, the court or tribunal shall dispatch a copy thereof, together with any relevant supporting documents to the claimant.

5. If, in his response, the defendant claims that the value of a non-monetary claim exceeds the limit set out in Article 2(1), the court or tribunal shall decide within 30 days of dispatching the response to the claimant, whether the claim is within the scope of this Regulation. Such decision may not be contested separately.

6. Any counterclaim, to be submitted using standard Form A, and any relevant supporting documents shall be served on the claimant in accordance with Article 13. Those documents shall be dispatched within 14 days of receipt.

The claimant shall have 30 days from service to respond to any counterclaim.

7. If the counterclaim exceeds the limit set out in Article 2(1), the claim and counterclaim shall not proceed in the European Small Claims Procedure but shall be dealt with in accordance with the relevant procedural law applicable in the Member State in which the procedure is conducted.

Articles 2 and 4 as well as paragraphs 3, 4 and 5 of this Article shall apply, mutatis mutandis, to counterclaims.

*Article 6*

**Languages**

1. The claim form, the response, any counterclaim, any response to a counterclaim and any description of relevant supporting documents shall be submitted in the language or one of the languages of the court or tribunal.

2. If any other document received by the court or tribunal is not in the language in which the proceedings are conducted, the court or tribunal may require a translation of that document only if the translation appears to be necessary for giving the judgment.

3. Where a party has refused to accept a document because it is not in either of the following languages:

(a) the official language of the Member State addressed, or, if there are several official languages in that Member State, the official language or one of the official languages of the place where service is to be effected or to where the document is to be dispatched; or

(b) a language which the addressee understands,

the court or tribunal shall so inform the other party with a view to that party providing a translation of the document.

*Article 7*

**Conclusion of the Procedure**

1. Within 30 days of receipt of the response from the defendant or the claimant within the time limits laid down in Article 5(3) or (6), the court or tribunal shall give a judgment, or:

(a) demand further details concerning the claim from the parties within a specified period of time, not exceeding 30 days;

(b) take evidence in accordance with Article 9; or

(c) summon the parties to an oral hearing to be held within 30 days of the summons.

2. The court or tribunal shall give the judgment either within 30 days of any oral hearing or after having received all information necessary for giving the judgment. The judgment shall be served on the parties in accordance with Article 13.

3. If the court or tribunal has not received an answer from the relevant party within the time limits laid down in Article 5(3) or (6), it shall give a judgment on the claim or counterclaim.

European Union Materials

## Article 8

### Oral hearing

The court or tribunal may hold an oral hearing through video conference or other communication technology if the technical means are available.

## Article 9

### Taking of evidence

1. The court or tribunal shall determine the means of taking evidence and the extent of the evidence necessary for its judgment under the rules applicable to the admissibility of evidence. The court or tribunal may admit the taking of evidence through written statements of witnesses, experts or parties. It may also admit the taking of evidence through video conference or other communication technology if the technical means are available.

2. The court or tribunal may take expert evidence or oral testimony only if it is necessary for giving the judgment. In making its decision, the court or tribunal shall take costs into account.

3. The court or tribunal shall use the simplest and least burdensome method of taking evidence.

## Article 10

### Representation of parties

Representation by a lawyer or another legal professional shall not be mandatory.

## Article 11

### Assistance for the parties

The Member States shall ensure that the parties can receive practical assistance in filling in the forms.

## Article 12

### Remit of the court or tribunal

1. The court or tribunal shall not require the parties to make any legal assessment of the claim.

2. If necessary, the court or tribunal shall inform the parties about procedural questions.

3. Whenever appropriate, the court or tribunal shall seek to reach a settlement between the parties.

## Article 13

### Service of documents

1. Documents shall be served by postal service attested by an acknowledgement of receipt including the date of receipt.

2. If service in accordance with paragraph 1 is not possible, service may be effected by any of the methods provided for in Articles 13 or 14 of Regulation (EC) No 805/2004.

## Article 14

### Time limits

1. Where the court or tribunal sets a time limit, the party concerned shall be informed of the consequences of not complying with it.

2. The court or tribunal may extend the time limits provided for in Article 4(4), Article 5(3) and (6) and Article 7(1), in exceptional circumstances, if necessary in order to safeguard the rights of the parties.

3. If, in exceptional circumstances, it is not possible for the court or tribunal to respect the time limits provided for in Article 5(2) to (6) and Article 7, it shall take the steps required by those provisions as soon as possible.

*Article 15*

**Enforceability of the judgment**

1. The judgment shall be enforceable notwithstanding any possible appeal. The provision of a security shall not be required.

2. Article 23 shall also apply in the event that the judgment is to be enforced in the Member State where the judgment was given.

*Article 16*

**Costs**

The unsuccessful party shall bear the costs of the proceedings. However, the court or tribunal shall not award costs to the successful party to the extent that they were unnecessarily incurred or are disproportionate to the claim.

*Article 17*

**Appeal**

1. Member States shall inform the Commission whether an appeal is available under their procedural law against a judgment given in the European Small Claims Procedure and within what time limit such appeal shall be lodged. The Commission shall make that information publicly available.

2. Article 16 shall apply to any appeal.

*Article 18*

**Minimum standards for review of the judgment**

1. The defendant shall be entitled to apply for a review of the judgment given in the European Small Claims Procedure before the court or tribunal with jurisdiction of the Member State where the judgment was given where:

(a)

    (i)   the claim form or the summons to an oral hearing were served by a method without proof of receipt by him personally, as provided for in Article 14 of Regulation (EC) No 805/2004; and

    (ii)  service was not effected in sufficient time to enable him to arrange for his defence without any fault on his part,

or

(b)   the defendant was prevented from objecting to the claim by reason of force majeure, or due to extraordinary circumstances without any fault on his part,

provided in either case that he acts promptly.

2. If the court or tribunal rejects the review on the basis that none of the grounds referred to in paragraph 1 apply, the judgment shall remain in force.

If the court or tribunal decides that the review is justified for one of the reasons laid down in paragraph 1, the judgment given in the European Small Claims Procedure shall be null and void.

*Article 19*

**Applicable procedural law**

Subject to the provisions of this Regulation, the European Small Claims Procedure shall be governed by the procedural law of the Member State in which the procedure is conducted.

CHAPTER III

## RECOGNITION AND ENFORCEMENT IN ANOTHER MEMBER STATE

*Article 20*

**Recognition and enforcement**

1. A judgment given in a Member State in the European Small Claims Procedure shall be recognised and enforced in another Member State without the need for a declaration of enforceability and without any possibility of opposing its recognition.

2. At the request of one of the parties, the court or tribunal shall issue a certificate concerning a judgment in the European Small Claims Procedure using standard Form D, as set out in Annex IV, at no extra cost.

*Article 21*

**Enforcement procedure**

1. Without prejudice to the provisions of this Chapter, the enforcement procedures shall be governed by the law of the Member State of enforcement.

Any judgment given in the European Small Claims Procedure shall be enforced under the same conditions as a judgment given in the Member State of enforcement.

2. The party seeking enforcement shall produce:

(a)  a copy of the judgment which satisfies the conditions necessary to establish its authenticity; and

(b)  a copy of the certificate referred to in Article 20(2) and, where necessary, the translation thereof into the official language of the Member State of enforcement or, if there are several official languages in that Member State, the official language or one of the official languages of court or tribunal proceedings of the place where enforcement is sought in conformity with the law of that Member State, or into another language that the Member State of enforcement has indicated it can accept. Each Member State may indicate the official language or languages of the institutions of the European Union other than its own which it can accept for the European Small Claims Procedure. The content of Form D shall be translated by a person qualified to make translations in one of the Member States.

3. The party seeking the enforcement of a judgment given in the European Small Claims Procedure in another Member State shall not be required to have:

(a)  an authorised representative; or

(b)  a postal address

in the Member State of enforcement, other than with agents having competence for the enforcement procedure.

4. No security, bond or deposit, however described, shall be required of a party who in one Member State applies for enforcement of a judgment given in the European Small Claims Procedure in another Member State on the ground that he is a foreign national or that he is not domiciled or resident in the Member State of enforcement.

*Article 22*

**Refusal of enforcement**

1. Enforcement shall, upon application by the person against whom enforcement is sought, be refused by the court or tribunal with jurisdiction in the Member State of enforcement if the judgment given in the European Small Claims Procedure is irreconcilable with an earlier judgment given in any Member State or in a third country, provided that:

(a)  the earlier judgment involved the same cause of action and was between the same parties;

(b)  the earlier judgment was given in the Member State of enforcement or fulfils the conditions necessary for its recognition in the Member State of enforcement; and

European Union Materials

(c) the irreconcilability was not and could not have been raised as an objection in the court or tribunal proceedings in the Member State where the judgment in the European Small Claims Procedure was given.

2. Under no circumstances may a judgment given in the European Small Claims Procedure be reviewed as to its substance in the Member State of enforcement.

## Article 23

### Stay or limitation of enforcement

Where a party has challenged a judgment given in the European Small Claims Procedure or where such a challenge is still possible, or where a party has made an application for review within the meaning of Article 18, the court or tribunal with jurisdiction or the competent authority in the Member State of enforcement may, upon application by the party against whom enforcement is sought:

(a) limit the enforcement proceedings to protective measures;

(b) make enforcement conditional on the provision of such security as it shall determine; or

(c) under exceptional circumstances, stay the enforcement proceedings.

## CHAPTER IV

## FINAL PROVISIONS

## Article 24

### Information

The Member States shall cooperate to provide the general public and professional circles with information on the European Small Claims Procedure, including costs, in particular by way of the European Judicial Network in Civil and Commercial Matters established in accordance with Decision 2001/470/EC.

## Article 25

### Information relating to jurisdiction, means of communication and appeals

1. By 1 January 2008 the Member States shall communicate to the Commission:

(a) which courts or tribunals have jurisdiction to give a judgment in the European Small Claims Procedure;

(b) which means of communication are accepted for the purposes of the European Small Claims Procedure and available to the courts or tribunals in accordance with Article 4(1);

(c) whether an appeal is available under their procedural law in accordance with Article 17 and with which court or tribunal this may be lodged;

(d) which languages are accepted pursuant to Article 21(2)(b); and

(e) which authorities have competence with respect to enforcement and which authorities have competence for the purposes of the application of Article 23.

Member States shall apprise the Commission of any subsequent changes to this information.

2. The Commission shall make the information notified in accordance with paragraph 1 publicly available through publication in the Official Journal of the European Union and through any other appropriate means.

## Article 26

### Implementing measures

The measures designed to amend non-essential elements of this Regulation, including by supplementing it, relating to updates or technical amendments to the forms in the Annexes shall be adopted in accordance with the regulatory procedure with scrutiny referred to in Article 27(2).

*Article 27*

**Committee**

1. The Commission shall be assisted by a Committee.

2. Where reference is made to this paragraph, Article 5a(1) to (4), and Article 7 of Decision 1999/468/EC shall apply, having regard to the provisions of Article 8 thereof.

*Article 28*

**Review**

By 1 January 2014, the Commission shall present to the European Parliament, the Council and the European Economic and Social Committee a detailed report reviewing the operation of the European Small Claims Procedure, including the limit of the value of the claim referred to in Article 2(1). That report shall contain an assessment of the procedure as it has operated and an extended impact assessment for each Member State.

To that end and in order to ensure that best practice in the European Union is duly taken into account and reflects the principles of better legislation, Member States shall provide the Commission with information relating to the cross-border operation of the European Small Claims Procedure. This information shall cover court fees, speed of the procedure, efficiency, ease of use and the internal small claims procedures of the Member States.

The Commission's report shall be accompanied, if appropriate, by proposals for adaptation.

*Article 29*

**Entry into force**

This Regulation shall enter into force on the day following its publication in the Official Journal of the European Union.

It shall apply from 1 January 2009, with the exception of Article 25, which shall apply from 1 January 2008.

This Regulation shall be binding in its entirety and directly applicable in the Member States in accordance with the Treaty establishing the European Community.

*[Annexes I–IV omitted]*

# Regulation (EC) No 864/2007 of the European Parliament and of the Council of 11 July 2007 on the law applicable to non-contractual obligations (Rome II)

[2007] OJ L199/40

THE EUROPEAN PARLIAMENT AND THE COUNCIL OF THE EUROPEAN UNION,

Having regard to the Treaty establishing the European Community, and in particular Articles 61(c) and 67 thereof,

Having regard to the proposal from the Commission,

Having regard to the opinion of the European Economic and Social Committee,

Acting in accordance with the procedure laid down in Article 251 of the Treaty in the light of the joint text approved by the Conciliation Committee on 25 June 2007,

Whereas:

(1) The Community has set itself the objective of maintaining and developing an area of freedom, security and justice. For the progressive establishment of such an area, the Community is to adopt measures relating to judicial cooperation in civil matters with a cross-border impact to the extent necessary for the proper functioning of the internal market.

(2) According to Article 65(b) of the Treaty, these measures are to include those promoting the compatibility of the rules applicable in the Member States concerning the conflict of laws and of jurisdiction.

(3) The European Council meeting in Tampere on 15 and 16 October 1999 endorsed the principle of mutual recognition of judgments and other decisions of judicial authorities as the cornerstone of judicial cooperation in civil matters and invited the Council and the Commission to adopt a programme of measures to implement the principle of mutual recognition.

(4) On 30 November 2000, the Council adopted a joint Commission and Council programme of measures for implementation of the principle of mutual recognition of decisions in civil and commercial matters. The programme identifies measures relating to the harmonisation of conflict-of-law rules as those facilitating the mutual recognition of judgments.

(5) The Hague Programme, adopted by the European Council on 5 November 2004, called for work to be pursued actively on the rules of conflict of laws regarding non-contractual obligations (Rome II).

(6) The proper functioning of the internal market creates a need, in order to improve the predictability of the outcome of litigation, certainty as to the law applicable and the free movement of judgments, for the conflict-of-law rules in the Member States to designate the same national law irrespective of the country of the court in which an action is brought.

(7) The substantive scope and the provisions of this Regulation should be consistent with Council Regulation (EC) No 44/2001 of 22 December 2000 on jurisdiction and the recognition and enforcement of judgments in civil and commercial matters (Brussels I) and the instruments dealing with the law applicable to contractual obligations.

(8) This Regulation should apply irrespective of the nature of the court or tribunal seised.

(9) Claims arising out of acta iure imperii should include claims against officials who act on behalf of the State and liability for acts of public authorities, including liability of publicly appointed office-holders. Therefore, these matters should be excluded from the scope of this Regulation.

(10) Family relationships should cover parentage, marriage, affinity and collateral relatives. The reference in Article 1(2) to relationships having comparable effects to marriage and other family relationships should be interpreted in accordance with the law of the Member State in which the court is seised.

(11) The concept of a non-contractual obligation varies from one Member State to another. Therefore for the purposes of this Regulation non-contractual obligation should be understood as an autonomous concept. The conflict-of-law rules set out in this Regulation should also cover non-contractual obligations arising out of strict liability.

(12) The law applicable should also govern the question of the capacity to incur liability in tort/delict.

(13) Uniform rules applied irrespective of the law they designate may avert the risk of distortions of competition between Community litigants.

(14) The requirement of legal certainty and the need to do justice in individual cases are essential elements of an area of justice. This Regulation provides for the connecting factors which are the most appropriate to achieve these objectives. Therefore, this Regulation provides for a general rule but also for specific rules and, in certain provisions, for an 'escape clause' which allows a departure from these rules where it is clear from all the circumstances of the case that the tort/delict is manifestly more closely connected with another country. This set of rules thus creates a flexible framework of conflict-of-law rules. Equally, it enables the court seised to treat individual cases in an appropriate manner.

(15) The principle of the *lex loci delicti commissi* is the basic solution for non-contractual obligations in virtually all the Member States, but the practical application of the principle where the component factors of the case are spread over several countries varies. This situation engenders uncertainty as to the law applicable.

(16) Uniform rules should enhance the foreseeability of court decisions and ensure a reasonable balance between the interests of the person claimed to be liable and the person who has sustained damage. A connection with the country where the direct damage occurred (lex loci damni) strikes a fair balance between the interests of the person claimed to be liable and the person sustaining the damage, and also reflects the modern approach to civil liability and the development of systems of strict liability.

(17) The law applicable should be determined on the basis of where the damage occurs, regardless of the country or countries in which the indirect consequences could occur. Accordingly, in cases of personal injury or damage to property, the country in which the damage occurs should be the country where the injury was sustained or the property was damaged respectively.

(18) The general rule in this Regulation should be the lex loci damni provided for in Article 4(1). Article 4(2) should be seen as an exception to this general principle, creating a special connection where the parties have their habitual residence in the same country. Article 4(3) should be understood as an 'escape clause' from Article 4(1) and (2), where it is clear from all the circumstances of the case that the tort/delict is manifestly more closely connected with another country.

(19) Specific rules should be laid down for special torts/delicts where the general rule does not allow a reasonable balance to be struck between the interests at stake.

(20) The conflict-of-law rule in matters of product liability should meet the objectives of fairly spreading the risks inherent in a modern high-technology society, protecting consumers' health, stimulating innovation, securing undistorted competition and facilitating trade. Creation of a cascade system of connecting factors, together with a foreseeability clause, is a balanced solution in regard to these objectives. The first element to be taken into account is the law of the country in which the person sustaining the damage had his or her habitual residence when the damage occurred, if the product was marketed in that country. The other elements of the cascade are triggered if the product was not marketed in that country, without prejudice to Article 4(2) and to the possibility of a manifestly closer connection to another country.

(21) The special rule in Article 6 is not an exception to the general rule in Article 4(1) but rather a clarification of it. In matters of unfair competition, the conflict-of-law rule should protect competitors, consumers and the general public and ensure that the market economy functions properly. The connection to the law of the country where competitive relations or the collective interests of consumers are, or are likely to be, affected generally satisfies these objectives.

(22) The non-contractual obligations arising out of restrictions of competition in Article 6(3) should cover infringements of both national and Community competition law. The law applicable to such non-contractual obligations should be the law of the country where the market is, or is likely to be, affected. In cases where the market is, or is likely to be, affected in more than one country, the

claimant should be able in certain circumstances to choose to base his or her claim on the law of the court seised.

(23) For the purposes of this Regulation, the concept of restriction of competition should cover prohibitions on agreements between undertakings, decisions by associations of undertakings and concerted practices which have as their object or effect the prevention, restriction or distortion of competition within a Member State or within the internal market, as well as prohibitions on the abuse of a dominant position within a Member State or within the internal market, where such agreements, decisions, concerted practices or abuses are prohibited by Articles 81 and 82 of the Treaty or by the law of a Member State.

(24) 'Environmental damage' should be understood as meaning adverse change in a natural resource, such as water, land or air, impairment of a function performed by that resource for the benefit of another natural resource or the public, or impairment of the variability among living organisms.

(25) Regarding environmental damage, Article 174 of the Treaty, which provides that there should be a high level of protection based on the precautionary principle and the principle that preventive action should be taken, the principle of priority for corrective action at source and the principle that the polluter pays, fully justifies the use of the principle of discriminating in favour of the person sustaining the damage. The question of when the person seeking compensation can make the choice of the law applicable should be determined in accordance with the law of the Member State in which the court is seised.

(26) Regarding infringements of intellectual property rights, the universally acknowledged principle of the *lex loci protectionis* should be preserved. For the purposes of this Regulation, the term 'intellectual property rights' should be interpreted as meaning, for instance, copyright, related rights, the *sui generis* right for the protection of databases and industrial property rights.

(27) The exact concept of industrial action, such as strike action or lock-out, varies from one Member State to another and is governed by each Member State's internal rules. Therefore, this Regulation assumes as a general principle that the law of the country where the industrial action was taken should apply, with the aim of protecting the rights and obligations of workers and employers.

(28) The special rule on industrial action in Article 9 is without prejudice to the conditions relating to the exercise of such action in accordance with national law and without prejudice to the legal status of trade unions or of the representative organisations of workers as provided for in the law of the Member States.

(29) Provision should be made for special rules where damage is caused by an act other than a tort/delict, such as unjust enrichment, *negotiorum gestio* and *culpa in contrahendo*.

(30) *Culpa in contrahendo* for the purposes of this Regulation is an autonomous concept and should not necessarily be interpreted within the meaning of national law. It should include the violation of the duty of disclosure and the breakdown of contractual negotiations. Article 12 covers only non-contractual obligations presenting a direct link with the dealings prior to the conclusion of a contract. This means that if, while a contract is being negotiated, a person suffers personal injury, Article 4 or other relevant provisions of this Regulation should apply.

(31) To respect the principle of party autonomy and to enhance legal certainty, the parties should be allowed to make a choice as to the law applicable to a non-contractual obligation. This choice should be expressed or demonstrated with reasonable certainty by the circumstances of the case. Where establishing the existence of the agreement, the court has to respect the intentions of the parties. Protection should be given to weaker parties by imposing certain conditions on the choice.

(32) Considerations of public interest justify giving the courts of the Member States the possibility, in exceptional circumstances, of applying exceptions based on public policy and overriding mandatory provisions. In particular, the application of a provision of the law designated by this Regulation which would have the effect of causing non-compensatory exemplary or punitive damages of an excessive nature to be awarded may, depending on the circumstances of the case and the legal order of the Member State of the court seised, be regarded as being contrary to the public policy (*ordre public*) of the forum.

(33) According to the current national rules on compensation awarded to victims of road traffic

accidents, when quantifying damages for personal injury in cases in which the accident takes place in a State other than that of the habitual residence of the victim, the court seised should take into account all the relevant actual circumstances of the specific victim, including in particular the actual losses and costs of after-care and medical attention.

(34) In order to strike a reasonable balance between the parties, account must be taken, in so far as appropriate, of the rules of safety and conduct in operation in the country in which the harmful act was committed, even where the non-contractual obligation is governed by the law of another country. The term 'rules of safety and conduct' should be interpreted as referring to all regulations having any relation to safety and conduct, including, for example, road safety rules in the case of an accident.

(35) A situation where conflict-of-law rules are dispersed among several instruments and where there are differences between those rules should be avoided. This Regulation, however, does not exclude the possibility of inclusion of conflict-of-law rules relating to non-contractual obligations in provisions of Community law with regard to particular matters.

This Regulation should not prejudice the application of other instruments laying down provisions designed to contribute to the proper functioning of the internal market in so far as they cannot be applied in conjunction with the law designated by the rules of this Regulation. The application of provisions of the applicable law designated by the rules of this Regulation should not restrict the free movement of goods and services as regulated by Community instruments, such as Directive 2000/31/EC of the European Parliament and of the Council of 8 June 2000 on certain legal aspects of information society services, in particular electronic commerce, in the Internal Market (Directive on electronic commerce).

(36) Respect for international commitments entered into by the Member States means that this Regulation should not affect international conventions to which one or more Member States are parties at the time this Regulation is adopted. To make the rules more accessible, the Commission should publish the list of the relevant conventions in the Official Journal of the European Union on the basis of information supplied by the Member States.

(37) The Commission will make a proposal to the European Parliament and the Council concerning the procedures and conditions according to which Member States would be entitled to negotiate and conclude on their own behalf agreements with third countries in individual and exceptional cases, concerning sectoral matters, containing provisions on the law applicable to non-contractual obligations.

(38) Since the objective of this Regulation cannot be sufficiently achieved by the Member States, and can therefore, by reason of the scale and effects of this Regulation, be better achieved at Community level, the Community may adopt measures, in accordance with the principle of subsidiarity set out in Article 5 of the Treaty. In accordance with the principle of proportionality set out in that Article, this Regulation does not go beyond what is necessary to attain that objective.

(39) In accordance with Article 3 of the Protocol on the position of the United Kingdom and Ireland annexed to the Treaty on European Union and to the Treaty establishing the European Community, the United Kingdom and Ireland are taking part in the adoption and application of this Regulation.

(40) In accordance with Articles 1 and 2 of the Protocol on the position of Denmark, annexed to the Treaty on European Union and to the Treaty establishing the European Community, Denmark does not take part in the adoption of this Regulation, and is not bound by it or subject to its application,

HAVE ADOPTED THIS REGULATION:

CHAPTER I

SCOPE

*Article 1*

Scope

1. This Regulation shall apply, in situations involving a conflict of laws, to non-contractual obligations in civil and commercial matters. It shall not apply, in particular, to revenue, customs or administrative

matters or to the liability of the State for acts and omissions in the exercise of State authority (*acta iure imperii*).

2. The following shall be excluded from the scope of this Regulation:

(a)  non-contractual obligations arising out of family relationships and relationships deemed by the law applicable to such relationships to have comparable effects including maintenance obligations;

(b)  non-contractual obligations arising out of matrimonial property regimes, property regimes of relationships deemed by the law applicable to such relationships to have comparable effects to marriage, and wills and succession;

(c)  non-contractual obligations arising under bills of exchange, cheques and promissory notes and other negotiable instruments to the extent that the obligations under such other negotiable instruments arise out of their negotiable character;

(d)  non-contractual obligations arising out of the law of companies and other bodies corporate or unincorporated regarding matters such as the creation, by registration or otherwise, legal capacity, internal organisation or winding-up of companies and other bodies corporate or unincorporated, the personal liability of officers and members as such for the obligations of the company or body and the personal liability of auditors to a company or to its members in the statutory audits of accounting documents;

(e)  non-contractual obligations arising out of the relations between the settlors, trustees and beneficiaries of a trust created voluntarily;

(f)  non-contractual obligations arising out of nuclear damage;

(g)  non-contractual obligations arising out of violations of privacy and rights relating to personality, including defamation.

3. This Regulation shall not apply to evidence and procedure, without prejudice to Articles 21 and 22.

4. For the purposes of this Regulation, 'Member State' shall mean any Member State other than Denmark.

*Article 2*

**Non-contractual obligations**

1. For the purposes of this Regulation, damage shall cover any consequence arising out of tort/delict, unjust enrichment, *negotiorum gestio* or *culpa in contrahendo*.

2. This Regulation shall apply also to non-contractual obligations that are likely to arise.

3. Any reference in this Regulation to:

(a)  an event giving rise to damage shall include events giving rise to damage that are likely to occur; and

(b)  damage shall include damage that is likely to occur.

*Article 3*

**Universal application**

Any law specified by this Regulation shall be applied whether or not it is the law of a Member State.

## CHAPTER II

## TORTS/DELICTS

*Article 4*

**General rule**

1. Unless otherwise provided for in this Regulation, the law applicable to a non-contractual obligation arising out of a tort/delict shall be the law of the country in which the damage occurs irrespective of the country in which the event giving rise to the damage occurred and irrespective of the country or countries in which the indirect consequences of that event occur.

2. However, where the person claimed to be liable and the person sustaining damage both have their habitual residence in the same country at the time when the damage occurs, the law of that country shall apply.

3. Where it is clear from all the circumstances of the case that the tort/delict is manifestly more closely connected with a country other than that indicated in paragraphs 1 or 2, the law of that other country shall apply. A manifestly closer connection with another country might be based in particular on a pre-existing relationship between the parties, such as a contract, that is closely connected with the tort/delict in question.

*Article 5*

**Product liability**

1. Without prejudice to Article 4(2), the law applicable to a non-contractual obligation arising out of damage caused by a product shall be:

(a)  the law of the country in which the person sustaining the damage had his or her habitual residence when the damage occurred, if the product was marketed in that country; or, failing that,

(b)  the law of the country in which the product was acquired, if the product was marketed in that country; or, failing that,

(c)  the law of the country in which the damage occurred, if the product was marketed in that country.

However, the law applicable shall be the law of the country in which the person claimed to be liable is habitually resident if he or she could not reasonably foresee the marketing of the product, or a product of the same type, in the country the law of which is applicable under (a), (b) or (c).

2. Where it is clear from all the circumstances of the case that the tort/delict is manifestly more closely connected with a country other than that indicated in paragraph 1, the law of that other country shall apply. A manifestly closer connection with another country might be based in particular on a pre-existing relationship between the parties, such as a contract, that is closely connected with the tort/delict in question.

*Article 6*

**Unfair competition and acts restricting free competition**

1. The law applicable to a non-contractual obligation arising out of an act of unfair competition shall be the law of the country where competitive relations or the collective interests of consumers are, or are likely to be, affected.

2. Where an act of unfair competition affects exclusively the interests of a specific competitor, Article 4 shall apply.

3.

(a)  The law applicable to a non-contractual obligation arising out of a restriction of competition shall be the law of the country where the market is, or is likely to be, affected.

(b)  When the market is, or is likely to be, affected in more than one country, the person seeking compensation for damage who sues in the court of the domicile of the defendant, may instead choose to base his or her claim on the law of the court seised, provided that the market in that Member State is amongst those directly and substantially affected by the restriction of competition out of which the non-contractual obligation on which the claim is based arises; where the claimant sues, in accordance with the applicable rules on jurisdiction, more than one defendant in that court, he or she can only choose to base his or her claim on the law of that court if the restriction of competition on which the claim against each of these defendants relies directly and substantially affects also the market in the Member State of that court.

4. The law applicable under this Article may not be derogated from by an agreement pursuant to Article 14.

*Article 7*

**Environmental damage**

The law applicable to a non-contractual obligation arising out of environmental damage or damage sustained by persons or property as a result of such damage shall be the law determined pursuant to Article 4(1), unless the person seeking compensation for damage chooses to base his or her claim on the law of the country in which the event giving rise to the damage occurred.

*Article 8*

**Infringement of intellectual property rights**

1. The law applicable to a non-contractual obligation arising from an infringement of an intellectual property right shall be the law of the country for which protection is claimed.

2. In the case of a non-contractual obligation arising from an infringement of a unitary Community intellectual property right, the law applicable shall, for any question that is not governed by the relevant Community instrument, be the law of the country in which the act of infringement was committed.

3. The law applicable under this Article may not be derogated from by an agreement pursuant to Article 14.

*Article 9*

**Industrial action**

Without prejudice to Article 4(2), the law applicable to a non-contractual obligation in respect of the liability of a person in the capacity of a worker or an employer or the organisations representing their professional interests for damages caused by an industrial action, pending or carried out, shall be the law of the country where the action is to be, or has been, taken.

## CHAPTER III

## UNJUST ENRICHMENT, *NEGOTIORUM GESTIO AND CULPA IN CONTRAHENDO*

*Article 10*

**Unjust enrichment**

1. If a non-contractual obligation arising out of unjust enrichment, including payment of amounts wrongly received, concerns a relationship existing between the parties, such as one arising out of a contract or a tort/delict, that is closely connected with that unjust enrichment, it shall be governed by the law that governs that relationship.

2. Where the law applicable cannot be determined on the basis of paragraph 1 and the parties have their habitual residence in the same country when the event giving rise to unjust enrichment occurs, the law of that country shall apply.

3. Where the law applicable cannot be determined on the basis of paragraphs 1 or 2, it shall be the law of the country in which the unjust enrichment took place.

4. Where it is clear from all the circumstances of the case that the non-contractual obligation arising out of unjust enrichment is manifestly more closely connected with a country other than that indicated in paragraphs 1, 2 and 3, the law of that other country shall apply.

*Article 11*

**Negotiorum gestio**

1. If a non-contractual obligation arising out of an act performed without due authority in connection with the affairs of another person concerns a relationship existing between the parties, such as one arising out of a contract or a tort/delict, that is closely connected with that non-contractual obligation, it shall be governed by the law that governs that relationship.

2. Where the law applicable cannot be determined on the basis of paragraph 1, and the parties have

their habitual residence in the same country when the event giving rise to the damage occurs, the law of that country shall apply.

3. Where the law applicable cannot be determined on the basis of paragraphs 1 or 2, it shall be the law of the country in which the act was performed.

4. Where it is clear from all the circumstances of the case that the non-contractual obligation arising out of an act performed without due authority in connection with the affairs of another person is manifestly more closely connected with a country other than that indicated in paragraphs 1, 2 and 3, the law of that other country shall apply.

*Article 12*

**Culpa in contrahendo**

1. The law applicable to a non-contractual obligation arising out of dealings prior to the conclusion of a contract, regardless of whether the contract was actually concluded or not, shall be the law that applies to the contract or that would have been applicable to it had it been entered into.

2. Where the law applicable cannot be determined on the basis of paragraph 1, it shall be:

(a) the law of the country in which the damage occurs, irrespective of the country in which the event giving rise to the damage occurred and irrespective of the country or countries in which the indirect consequences of that event occurred; or

(b) where the parties have their habitual residence in the same country at the time when the event giving rise to the damage occurs, the law of that country; or

(c) where it is clear from all the circumstances of the case that the non-contractual obligation arising out of dealings prior to the conclusion of a contract is manifestly more closely connected with a country other than that indicated in points (a) and (b), the law of that other country.

*Article 13*

**Applicability of Article 8**

For the purposes of this Chapter, Article 8 shall apply to non-contractual obligations arising from an infringement of an intellectual property right.

CHAPTER IV

**FREEDOM OF CHOICE**

*Article 14*

**Freedom of choice**

1. The parties may agree to submit non-contractual obligations to the law of their choice:

(a) by an agreement entered into after the event giving rise to the damage occurred;

or

(b) where all the parties are pursuing a commercial activity, also by an agreement freely negotiated before the event giving rise to the damage occurred.

The choice shall be expressed or demonstrated with reasonable certainty by the circumstances of the case and shall not prejudice the rights of third parties.

2. Where all the elements relevant to the situation at the time when the event giving rise to the damage occurs are located in a country other than the country whose law has been chosen, the choice of the parties shall not prejudice the application of provisions of the law of that other country which cannot be derogated from by agreement.

3. Where all the elements relevant to the situation at the time when the event giving rise to the damage occurs are located in one or more of the Member States, the parties' choice of the law applicable other than that of a Member State shall not prejudice the application of provisions of Community law, where

European Union Materials

appropriate as implemented in the Member State of the forum, which cannot be derogated from by agreement.

## CHAPTER V

## COMMON RULES

*Article 15*

### Scope of the law applicable

The law applicable to non-contractual obligations under this Regulation shall govern in particular:

(a)  the basis and extent of liability, including the determination of persons who may be held liable for acts performed by them;

(b)  the grounds for exemption from liability, any limitation of liability and any division of liability;

(c)  the existence, the nature and the assessment of damage or the remedy claimed;

(d)  within the limits of powers conferred on the court by its procedural law, the measures which a court may take to prevent or terminate injury or damage or to ensure the provision of compensation;

(e)  the question whether a right to claim damages or a remedy may be transferred, including by inheritance;

(f)  persons entitled to compensation for damage sustained personally;

(g)  liability for the acts of another person;

(h)  the manner in which an obligation may be extinguished and rules of prescription and limitation, including rules relating to the commencement, interruption and suspension of a period of prescription or limitation.

*Article 16*

### Overriding mandatory provisions

Nothing in this Regulation shall restrict the application of the provisions of the law of the forum in a situation where they are mandatory irrespective of the law otherwise applicable to the non-contractual obligation.

*Article 17*

### Rules of safety and conduct

In assessing the conduct of the person claimed to be liable, account shall be taken, as a matter of fact and in so far as is appropriate, of the rules of safety and conduct which were in force at the place and time of the event giving rise to the liability.

*Article 18*

### Direct action against the insurer of the person liable

The person having suffered damage may bring his or her claim directly against the insurer of the person liable to provide compensation if the law applicable to the non-contractual obligation or the law applicable to the insurance contract so provides.

*Article 19*

### Subrogation

Where a person (the creditor) has a non-contractual claim upon another (the debtor), and a third person has a duty to satisfy the creditor, or has in fact satisfied the creditor in discharge of that duty, the law which governs the third person's duty to satisfy the creditor shall determine whether, and the extent to which, the third person is entitled to exercise against the debtor the rights which the creditor had against the debtor under the law governing their relationship.

*Article 20*

**Multiple liability**

If a creditor has a claim against several debtors who are liable for the same claim, and one of the debtors has already satisfied the claim in whole or in part, the question of that debtor's right to demand compensation from the other debtors shall be governed by the law applicable to that debtor's non-contractual obligation towards the creditor.

*Article 21*

**Formal validity**

A unilateral act intended to have legal effect and relating to a non-contractual obligation shall be formally valid if it satisfies the formal requirements of the law governing the non-contractual obligation in question or the law of the country in which the act is performed.

*Article 22*

**Burden of proof**

1. The law governing a non-contractual obligation under this Regulation shall apply to the extent that, in matters of non-contractual obligations, it contains rules which raise presumptions of law or determine the burden of proof.

2. Acts intended to have legal effect may be proved by any mode of proof recognised by the law of the forum or by any of the laws referred to in Article 21 under which that act is formally valid, provided that such mode of proof can be administered by the forum.

## CHAPTER VI

## OTHER PROVISIONS

*Article 23*

**Habitual residence**

1. For the purposes of this Regulation, the habitual residence of companies and other bodies, corporate or unincorporated, shall be the place of central administration.

Where the event giving rise to the damage occurs, or the damage arises, in the course of operation of a branch, agency or any other establishment, the place where the branch, agency or any other establishment is located shall be treated as the place of habitual residence.

2. For the purposes of this Regulation, the habitual residence of a natural person acting in the course of his or her business activity shall be his or her principal place of business.

*Article 24*

**Exclusion of renvoi**

The application of the law of any country specified by this Regulation means the application of the rules of law in force in that country other than its rules of private international law.

*Article 25*

**States with more than one legal system**

1. Where a State comprises several territorial units, each of which has its own rules of law in respect of non-contractual obligations, each territorial unit shall be considered as a country for the purposes of identifying the law applicable under this Regulation.

2. A Member State within which different territorial units have their own rules of law in respect of non-contractual obligations shall not be required to apply this Regulation to conflicts solely between the laws of such units.

*Article 26*

**Public policy of the forum**

The application of a provision of the law of any country specified by this Regulation may be refused only if such application is manifestly incompatible with the public policy (ordre public) of the forum.

*Article 27*

**Relationship with other provisions of Community law**

This Regulation shall not prejudice the application of provisions of Community law which, in relation to particular matters, lay down conflict-of-law rules relating to non-contractual obligations.

*Article 28*

**Relationship with existing international conventions**

1. This Regulation shall not prejudice the application of international conventions to which one or more Member States are parties at the time when this Regulation is adopted and which lay down conflict-of-law rules relating to non-contractual obligations.

2. However, this Regulation shall, as between Member States, take precedence over conventions concluded exclusively between two or more of them in so far as such conventions concern matters governed by this Regulation.

## CHAPTER VII

## FINAL PROVISIONS

*Article 29*

**List of conventions**

1. By 11 July 2008, Member States shall notify the Commission of the conventions referred to in Article 28(1). After that date, Member States shall notify the Commission of all denunciations of such conventions.

2. The Commission shall publish in the Official Journal of the European Union within six months of receipt:

    (i)   a list of the conventions referred to in paragraph 1;

    (ii)  the denunciations referred to in paragraph 1.

*Article 30*

**Review clause**

1. Not later than 20 August 2011, the Commission shall submit to the European Parliament, the Council and the European Economic and Social Committee a report on the application of this Regulation. If necessary, the report shall be accompanied by proposals to adapt this Regulation. The report shall include:

    (i)   a study on the effects of the way in which foreign law is treated in the different jurisdictions and on the extent to which courts in the Member States apply foreign law in practice pursuant to this Regulation;

    (ii)  a study on the effects of Article 28 of this Regulation with respect to the Hague Convention of 4 May 1971 on the law applicable to traffic accidents.

2. Not later than 31 December 2008, the Commission shall submit to the European Parliament, the Council and the European Economic and Social Committee a study on the situation in the field of the law applicable to non-contractual obligations arising out of violations of privacy and rights relating to personality, taking into account rules relating to freedom of the press and freedom of expression in the media, and conflict-of-law issues related to Directive 95/46/EC of the European Parliament and of the

Council of 24 October 1995 on the protection of individuals with regard to the processing of personal data and on the free movement of such data.

*Article 31*

**Application in time**

This Regulation shall apply to events giving rise to damage which occur after its entry into force.

*Article 32*

**Date of application**

This Regulation shall apply from 11 January 2009, except for Article 29, which shall apply from 11 July 2008.

This Regulation shall be binding in its entirety and directly applicable in the Member States in accordance with the Treaty establishing the European Community.

# Regulation (EC) No 1393/2007 of the European Parliament and of the Council of 13 November 2007 on the service in the Member States of judicial and extrajudicial documents in civil or commercial matters (service of documents), and repealing Council Regulation (EC) No 1348/2000

[2007] OJ L324/79

THE EUROPEAN PARLIAMENT AND THE COUNCIL OF THE EUROPEAN UNION,

Having regard to the Treaty establishing the European Community, and in particular Article 61(c) and Article 67(5), second indent, thereof,

Having regard to the proposal from the Commission,

Having regard to the opinion of the European Economic and Social Committee,

Acting in accordance with the procedure laid down in Article 251 of the Treaty,

Whereas:

(1) The Union has set itself the objective of maintaining and developing the Union as an area of freedom, security and justice, in which the free movement of persons is assured. To establish such an area, the Community is to adopt, among others, the measures relating to judicial cooperation in civil matters needed for the proper functioning of the internal market.

(2) The proper functioning of the internal market entails the need to improve and expedite the transmission of judicial and extrajudicial documents in civil or commercial matters for service between the Member States.

(3) The Council, by an Act dated 26 May 1997, drew up a Convention on the service in the Member States of the European Union of judicial and extrajudicial documents in civil or commercial matters and recommended it for adoption by the Member States in accordance with their respective constitutional rules. That Convention has not entered into force. Continuity in the results of the negotiations for conclusion of the Convention should be ensured.

(4) On 29 May 2000 the Council adopted Regulation (EC) No 1348/2000 on the service in the Member States of judicial and extrajudicial documents in civil or commercial matters . The main content of that Regulation is based on the Convention.

(5) On 1 October 2004 the Commission adopted a report on the application of Regulation (EC) No 1348/2000. The report concludes that the application of Regulation (EC) No 1348/2000 has generally improved and expedited the transmission and the service of documents between Member States since its entry into force in 2001, but that nevertheless the application of certain provisions is not fully satisfactory.

(6) Efficiency and speed in judicial procedures in civil matters require that judicial and extrajudicial documents be transmitted directly and by rapid means between local bodies designated by the Member States. Member States may indicate their intention to designate only one transmitting or receiving agency or one agency to perform both functions, for a period of five years. This designation may, however, be renewed every five years.

(7) Speed in transmission warrants the use of all appropriate means, provided that certain conditions as to the legibility and reliability of the document received are observed. Security in transmission requires that the document to be transmitted be accompanied by a standard form, to be completed in the official language or one of the official languages of the place where service is to be effected, or in another language accepted by the Member State in question.

(8) This Regulation should not apply to service of a document on the party's authorised representative

in the Member State where the proceedings are taking place regardless of the place of residence of that party.

(9) The service of a document should be effected as soon as possible, and in any event within one month of receipt by the receiving agency.

(10) To secure the effectiveness of this Regulation, the possibility of refusing service of documents should be confined to exceptional situations.

(11) In order to facilitate the transmission and service of documents between Member States, the standard forms set out in the Annexes to this Regulation should be used.

(12) The receiving agency should inform the addressee in writing using the standard form that he may refuse to accept the document to be served at the time of service or by returning the document to the receiving agency within one week if it is not either in a language which he understands or in the official language or one of the official languages of the place of service. This rule should also apply to the subsequent service once the addressee has exercised his right of refusal. These rules on refusal should also apply to service by diplomatic or consular agents, service by postal services and direct service. It should be established that the service of the refused document can be remedied through the service on the addressee of a translation of the document.

(13) Speed in transmission warrants documents being served within days of receipt of the document. However, if service has not been effected after one month has elapsed, the receiving agency should inform the transmitting agency. The expiry of this period should not imply that the request be returned to the transmitting agency where it is clear that service is feasible within a reasonable period.

(14) The receiving agency should continue to take all necessary steps to effect the service of the document also in cases where it has not been possible to effect service within the month, for example, because the defendant has been away from his home on holiday or away from his office on business. However, in order to avoid an open-ended obligation for the receiving agency to take steps to effect the service of a document, the transmitting agency should be able to specify a time limit in the standard form after which service is no longer required.

(15) Given the differences between the Member States as regards their rules of procedure, the material date for the purposes of service varies from one Member State to another. Having regard to such situations and the possible difficulties that may arise, this Regulation should provide for a system where it is the law of the Member State addressed which determines the date of service. However, where according to the law of a Member State a document has to be served within a particular period, the date to be taken into account with respect to the applicant should be that determined by the law of that Member State. This double date system exists only in a limited number of Member States. Those Member States which apply this system should communicate this to the Commission, which should publish the information in the Official Journal of the European Union and make it available through the European Judicial Network in Civil and Commercial Matters established by Council Decision 2001/470/EC.

(16) In order to facilitate access to justice, costs occasioned by recourse to a judicial officer or a person competent under the law of the Member State addressed should correspond to a single fixed fee laid down by that Member State in advance which respects the principles of proportionality and non-discrimination. The requirement of a single fixed fee should not preclude the possibility for Member States to set different fees for different types of service as long as they respect these principles.

(17) Each Member State should be free to effect service of documents directly by postal services on persons residing in another Member State by registered letter with acknowledgement of receipt or equivalent.

(18) It should be possible for any person interested in a judicial proceeding to effect service of documents directly through the judicial officers, officials or other competent persons of the Member State addressed, where such direct service is permitted under the law of that Member State.

(19) The Commission should draw up a manual containing information relevant for the proper application of this Regulation, which should be made available through the European Judicial Network in Civil and Commercial Matters. The Commission and the Member States should do their utmost to

ensure that this information is up to date and complete especially as regards contact details of receiving and transmitting agencies.

(20) In calculating the periods and time limits provided for in this Regulation, Regulation (EEC, Euratom) No 1182/71 of the Council of 3 June 1971 determining the rules applicable to periods, dates and time limits should apply.

(21) The measures necessary for the implementation of this Regulation should be adopted in accordance with Council Decision 1999/468/EC of 28 June 1999 laying down the procedures for the exercise of implementing powers conferred on the Commission.

(22) In particular, power should be conferred on the Commission to update or make technical amendments to the standard forms set out in the Annexes. Since those measures are of general scope and are designed to amend/delete non-essential elements of this Regulation, they must be adopted in accordance with the regulatory procedure with scrutiny provided for in Article 5a of Decision 1999/468/EC.

(23) This Regulation prevails over the provisions contained in bilateral or multilateral agreements or arrangements having the same scope, concluded by the Member States, and in particular the Protocol annexed to the Brussels Convention of 27 September 1968 and the Hague Convention of 15 November 1965 in relations between the Member States party thereto. This Regulation does not preclude Member States from maintaining or concluding agreements or arrangements to expedite or simplify the transmission of documents, provided that they are compatible with this Regulation.

(24) The information transmitted pursuant to this Regulation should enjoy suitable protection. This matter falls within the scope of Directive 95/46/EC of the European Parliament and of the Council of 24 October 1995 on the protection of individuals with regard to the processing of personal data and on the free movement of such data, and of Directive 2002/58/EC of the European Parliament and of the Council of 12 July 2002 concerning the processing of personal data and the protection of privacy in the electronic communications sector (Directive on privacy and electronic communications).

(25) No later than 1 June 2011 and every five years thereafter, the Commission should review the application of this Regulation and propose such amendments as may appear necessary.

(26) Since the objectives of this Regulation cannot be sufficiently achieved by the Member States and can therefore, by reason of the scale or effects of the action, be better achieved at Community level, the Community may adopt measures, in accordance with the principle of subsidiarity as set out in Article 5 of the Treaty. In accordance with the principle of proportionality, as set out in that Article, this Regulation does not go beyond what is necessary in order to achieve those objectives.

(27) In order to make the provisions more easily accessible and readable, Regulation (EC) No 1348/2000 should be repealed and replaced by this Regulation.

(28) In accordance with Article 3 of the Protocol on the position of the United Kingdom and Ireland, annexed to the Treaty on European Union and to the Treaty establishing the European Community, the United Kingdom and Ireland are taking part in the adoption and application of this Regulation.

(29) In accordance with Articles 1 and 2 of the Protocol on the position of Denmark, annexed to the Treaty on European Union and to the Treaty establishing the European Community, Denmark does not take part in the adoption of this Regulation and is not bound by it or subject to its application,

HAVE ADOPTED THIS REGULATION:

# CHAPTER I

## GENERAL PROVISIONS

*Article 1*

### Scope

1. This Regulation shall apply in civil and commercial matters where a judicial or extrajudicial document has to be transmitted from one Member State to another for service there. It shall not

extend in particular to revenue, customs or administrative matters or to liability of the State for actions or omissions in the exercise of state authority (acta iure imperii).

2. This Regulation shall not apply where the address of the person to be served with the document is not known.

3. In this Regulation, the term 'Member State' shall mean the Member States with the exception of Denmark.

*Article 2*

**Transmitting and receiving agencies**

1. Each Member State shall designate the public officers, authorities or other persons, hereinafter referred to as 'transmitting agencies', competent for the transmission of judicial or extrajudicial documents to be served in another Member State.

2. Each Member State shall designate the public officers, authorities or other persons, hereinafter referred to as 'receiving agencies', competent for the receipt of judicial or extrajudicial documents from another Member State.

3. A Member State may designate one transmitting agency and one receiving agency, or one agency to perform both functions. A federal State, a State in which several legal systems apply or a State with autonomous territorial units shall be free to designate more than one such agency. The designation shall have effect for a period of five years and may be renewed at five-year intervals.

4. Each Member State shall provide the Commission with the following information:

(a)  the names and addresses of the receiving agencies referred to in paragraphs 2 and 3;

(b)  the geographical areas in which they have jurisdiction;

(c)  the means of receipt of documents available to them; and

(d)  the languages that may be used for the completion of the standard form set out in Annex I.

Member States shall notify the Commission of any subsequent modification of such information.

*Article 3*

**Central body**

Each Member State shall designate a central body responsible for:

(a)  supplying information to the transmitting agencies;

(b)  seeking solutions to any difficulties which may arise during transmission of documents for service;

(c)  forwarding, in exceptional cases, at the request of a transmitting agency, a request for service to the competent receiving agency.

A federal State, a State in which several legal systems apply or a State with autonomous territorial units shall be free to designate more than one central body.

# CHAPTER II

## JUDICIAL DOCUMENTS

### SECTION 1

**Transmission and service of judicial documents**

*Article 4*

**Transmission of documents**

1. Judicial documents shall be transmitted directly and as soon as possible between the agencies designated pursuant to Article 2.

2. The transmission of documents, requests, confirmations, receipts, certificates and any other papers between transmitting agencies and receiving agencies may be carried out by any appropriate means,

provided that the content of the document received is true and faithful to that of the document forwarded and that all information in it is easily legible.

3. The document to be transmitted shall be accompanied by a request drawn up using the standard form set out in Annex I. The form shall be completed in the official language of the Member State addressed or, if there are several official languages in that Member State, the official language or one of the official languages of the place where service is to be effected, or in another language which that Member State has indicated it can accept. Each Member State shall indicate the official language or languages of the institutions of the European Union other than its own which is or are acceptable to it for completion of the form.

4. The documents and all papers that are transmitted shall be exempted from legalisation or any equivalent formality.

5. When the transmitting agency wishes a copy of the document to be returned together with the certificate referred to in Article 10, it shall send the document in duplicate.

## Article 5

### Translation of documents

1. The applicant shall be advised by the transmitting agency to which he forwards the document for transmission that the addressee may refuse to accept it if it is not in one of the languages provided for in Article 8.

2. The applicant shall bear any costs of translation prior to the transmission of the document, without prejudice to any possible subsequent decision by the court or competent authority on liability for such costs.

## Article 6

### Receipt of documents by receiving agency

1. On receipt of a document, a receiving agency shall, as soon as possible and in any event within seven days of receipt, send a receipt to the transmitting agency by the swiftest possible means of transmission using the standard form set out in Annex I.

2. Where the request for service cannot be fulfilled on the basis of the information or documents transmitted, the receiving agency shall contact the transmitting agency by the swiftest possible means in order to secure the missing information or documents.

3. If the request for service is manifestly outside the scope of this Regulation or if non-compliance with the formal conditions required makes service impossible, the request and the documents transmitted shall be returned, on receipt, to the transmitting agency, together with the notice of return using the standard form set out in Annex I.

4. A receiving agency receiving a document for service but not having territorial jurisdiction to serve it shall forward it, as well as the request, to the receiving agency having territorial jurisdiction in the same Member State if the request complies with the conditions laid down in Article 4(3) and shall inform the transmitting agency accordingly using the standard form set out in Annex I. That receiving agency shall inform the transmitting agency when it receives the document, in the manner provided for in paragraph 1.

## Article 7

### Service of documents

1. The receiving agency shall itself serve the document or have it served, either in accordance with the law of the Member State addressed or by a particular method requested by the transmitting agency, unless that method is incompatible with the law of that Member State.

2. The receiving agency shall take all necessary steps to effect the service of the document as soon as possible, and in any event within one month of receipt. If it has not been possible to effect service within one month of receipt, the receiving agency shall:

(a) immediately inform the transmitting agency by means of the certificate in the standard form set out in Annex I, which shall be drawn up under the conditions referred to in Article 10(2); and

(b) continue to take all necessary steps to effect the service of the document, unless indicated otherwise by the transmitting agency, where service seems to be possible within a reasonable period of time.

*Article 8*

**Refusal to accept a document**

1. The receiving agency shall inform the addressee, using the standard form set out in Annex II, that he may refuse to accept the document to be served at the time of service or by returning the document to the receiving agency within one week if it is not written in, or accompanied by a translation into, either of the following languages:

(a) a language which the addressee understands;

or

(b) the official language of the Member State addressed or, if there are several official languages in that Member State, the official language or one of the official languages of the place where service is to be effected.

2. Where the receiving agency is informed that the addressee refuses to accept the document in accordance with paragraph 1, it shall immediately inform the transmitting agency by means of the certificate provided for in Article 10 and return the request and the documents of which a translation is requested.

3. If the addressee has refused to accept the document pursuant to paragraph 1, the service of the document can be remedied through the service on the addressee in accordance with the provisions of this Regulation of the document accompanied by a translation into a language provided for in paragraph 1. In that case, the date of service of the document shall be the date on which the document accompanied by the translation is served in accordance with the law of the Member State addressed. However, where according to the law of a Member State, a document has to be served within a particular period, the date to be taken into account with respect to the applicant shall be the date of the service of the initial document determined pursuant to Article 9(2).

4. Paragraphs 1, 2 and 3 shall also apply to the means of transmission and service of judicial documents provided for in Section 2.

5. For the purposes of paragraph 1, the diplomatic or consular agents, where service is effected in accordance with Article 13, or the authority or person, where service is effected in accordance with Article 14, shall inform the addressee that he may refuse to accept the document and that any document refused must be sent to those agents or to that authority or person respectively.

*Article 9*

**Date of service**

1. Without prejudice to Article 8, the date of service of a document pursuant to Article 7 shall be the date on which it is served in accordance with the law of the Member State addressed.

2. However, where according to the law of a Member State a document has to be served within a particular period, the date to be taken into account with respect to the applicant shall be that determined by the law of that Member State.

3. Paragraphs 1 and 2 shall also apply to the means of transmission and service of judicial documents provided for in Section 2.

*Article 10*

**Certificate of service and copy of the document served**

1. When the formalities concerning the service of the document have been completed, a certificate of completion of those formalities shall be drawn up in the standard form set out in Annex I and

addressed to the transmitting agency, together with, where Article 4(5) applies, a copy of the document served.

2. The certificate shall be completed in the official language or one of the official languages of the Member State of origin or in another language which the Member State of origin has indicated that it can accept. Each Member State shall indicate the official language or languages of the institutions of the European Union other than its own which is or are acceptable to it for completion of the form.

## Article 11

### Costs of service

1. The service of judicial documents coming from a Member State shall not give rise to any payment or reimbursement of taxes or costs for services rendered by the Member State addressed.

2. However, the applicant shall pay or reimburse the costs occasioned by:

(a)  recourse to a judicial officer or to a person competent under the law of the Member State addressed;

(b)  the use of a particular method of service.

Costs occasioned by recourse to a judicial officer or to a person competent under the law of the Member State addressed shall correspond to a single fixed fee laid down by that Member State in advance which respects the principles of proportionality and non-discrimination. Member States shall communicate such fixed fees to the Commission.

### Section 2

Other means of transmission and service of judicial documents

## Article 12

### Transmission by consular or diplomatic channels

Each Member State shall be free, in exceptional circumstances, to use consular or diplomatic channels to forward judicial documents, for the purpose of service, to those agencies of another Member State which are designated pursuant to Articles 2 or 3.

## Article 13

### Service by diplomatic or consular agents

1. Each Member State shall be free to effect service of judicial documents on persons residing in another Member State, without application of any compulsion, directly through its diplomatic or consular agents.

2. Any Member State may make it known, in accordance with Article 23(1), that it is opposed to such service within its territory, unless the documents are to be served on nationals of the Member State in which the documents originate.

## Article 14

### Service by postal services

Each Member State shall be free to effect service of judicial documents directly by postal services on persons residing in another Member State by registered letter with acknowledgement of receipt or equivalent.

## Article 15

### Direct service

Any person interested in a judicial proceeding may effect service of judicial documents directly through the judicial officers, officials or other competent persons of the Member State addressed, where such direct service is permitted under the law of that Member State.

European Union Materials

## CHAPTER III

## EXTRAJUDICIAL DOCUMENTS

*Article 16*

Transmission

Extrajudicial documents may be transmitted for service in another Member State in accordance with the provisions of this Regulation.

## CHAPTER IV

## FINAL PROVISIONS

*Article 17*

Implementing rules

Measures designed to amend non-essential elements of this Regulation relating to the updating or to the making of technical amendments to the standard forms set out in Annexes I and II shall be adopted in accordance with the regulatory procedure with scrutiny referred to in Article 18(2).

*Article 18*

Committee

1. The Commission shall be assisted by a committee.

2. Where reference is made to this paragraph, Article 5a(1) to (4), and Article 7 of Decision 1999/468/EC shall apply, having regard to the provisions of Article 8 thereof.

*Article 19*

Defendant not entering an appearance

1. Where a writ of summons or an equivalent document has had to be transmitted to another Member State for the purpose of service under the provisions of this Regulation and the defendant has not appeared, judgment shall not be given until it is established that:

(a)  the document was served by a method prescribed by the internal law of the Member State addressed for the service of documents in domestic actions upon persons who are within its territory;

or

(b)  the document was actually delivered to the defendant or to his residence by another method provided for by this Regulation;

and that in either of these cases the service or the delivery was effected in sufficient time to enable the defendant to defend.

2. Each Member State may make it known, in accordance with Article 23(1), that the judge, notwithstanding the provisions of paragraph 1, may give judgment even if no certificate of service or delivery has been received, if all the following conditions are fulfilled:

(a)  the document was transmitted by one of the methods provided for in this Regulation;

(b)  a period of time of not less than six months, considered adequate by the judge in the particular case, has elapsed since the date of the transmission of the document;

(c)  no certificate of any kind has been received, even though every reasonable effort has been made to obtain it through the competent authorities or bodies of the Member State addressed.

3. Notwithstanding paragraphs 1 and 2, the judge may order, in case of urgency, any provisional or protective measures.

4. When a writ of summons or an equivalent document has had to be transmitted to another Member State for the purpose of service under the provisions of this Regulation and a judgment has been entered

against a defendant who has not appeared, the judge shall have the power to relieve the defendant from the effects of the expiry of the time for appeal from the judgment if the following conditions are fulfilled:

(a)   the defendant, without any fault on his part, did not have knowledge of the document in sufficient time to defend, or knowledge of the judgment in sufficient time to appeal; and

(b)   the defendant has disclosed a prima facie defence to the action on the merits.

An application for relief may be filed only within a reasonable time after the defendant has knowledge of the judgment.

Each Member State may make it known, in accordance with Article 23(1), that such application will not be entertained if it is filed after the expiry of a time to be stated by it in that communication, but which shall in no case be less than one year following the date of the judgment.

5. Paragraph 4 shall not apply to judgments concerning the status or capacity of persons.

## Article 20

**Relationship with agreements or arrangements to which Member States are party**

1. This Regulation shall, in relation to matters to which it applies, prevail over other provisions contained in bilateral or multilateral agreements or arrangements concluded by the Member States, and in particular Article IV of the Protocol to the Brussels Convention of 1968 and the Hague Convention of 15 November 1965.

2. This Regulation shall not preclude individual Member States from maintaining or concluding agreements or arrangements to expedite further or simplify the transmission of documents, provided that they are compatible with this Regulation.

3. Member States shall send to the Commission:

(a)   a copy of the agreements or arrangements referred to in paragraph 2 concluded between the Member States as well as drafts of such agreements or arrangements which they intend to adopt;

and

(b)   any denunciation of, or amendments to, these agreements or arrangements.

## Article 21

**Legal aid**

This Regulation shall not affect the application of Article 23 of the Convention on civil procedure of 17 July 1905, Article 24 of the Convention on civil procedure of 1 March 1954 or Article 13 of the Convention on international access to justice of 25 October 1980 between the Member States party to those Conventions.

## Article 22

**Protection of information transmitted**

1. Information, including in particular personal data, transmitted under this Regulation shall be used by the receiving agency only for the purpose for which it was transmitted.

2. Receiving agencies shall ensure the confidentiality of such information, in accordance with their national law.

3. Paragraphs 1 and 2 shall not affect national laws enabling data subjects to be informed of the use made of information transmitted under this Regulation.

4. This Regulation shall be without prejudice to Directives 95/46/EC and 2002/58/EC.

## Article 23

**Communication and publication**

1. Member States shall communicate to the Commission the information referred to in Articles 2, 3, 4, 10, 11, 13, 15 and 19. Member States shall communicate to the Commission if, according to their law, a document has to be served within a particular period as referred to in Articles 8(3) and 9(2).

2. The Commission shall publish the information communicated in accordance with paragraph 1 in the Official Journal of the European Union with the exception of the addresses and other contact details of the agencies and of the central bodies and the geographical areas in which they have jurisdiction.

3. The Commission shall draw up and update regularly a manual containing the information referred to in paragraph 1, which shall be available electronically, in particular through the European Judicial Network in Civil and Commercial Matters.

*Article 24*

**Review**

No later than 1 June 2011, and every five years thereafter, the Commission shall present to the European Parliament, the Council and the European Economic and Social Committee a report on the application of this Regulation, paying special attention to the effectiveness of the agencies designated pursuant to Article 2 and to the practical application of Article 3(c) and Article 9. The report shall be accompanied if need be by proposals for adaptations of this Regulation in line with the evolution of notification systems.

*Article 25*

**Repeal**

1. Regulation (EC) No 1348/2000 shall be repealed as from the date of application of this Regulation.

2. References made to the repealed Regulation shall be construed as being made to this Regulation and should be read in accordance with the correlation table in Annex III.

*Article 26*

**Entry into force**

This Regulation shall enter into force on the 20th day following its publication in the Official Journal of the European Union.

It shall apply from 13 November 2008 with the exception of Article 23 which shall apply from 13 August 2008.

This Regulation shall be binding in its entirety and directly applicable in the Member States in accordance with the Treaty establishing the European Community.

*[Annexes I–III omitted]*

# Regulation (EC) No 593/2008 of the European Parliament and of the Council of 17 June 2008 on the law applicable to contractual obligations (Rome I)

[2008] OJ L177/6

THE EUROPEAN PARLIAMENT AND THE COUNCIL OF THE EUROPEAN UNION,

Having regard to the Treaty establishing the European Community, and in particular Article 61(c) and the second indent of Article 67(5) thereof,

Having regard to the proposal from the Commission,

Having regard to the opinion of the European Economic and Social Committee ,

Acting in accordance with the procedure laid down in Article 251 of the Treaty,

Whereas:

(1) The Community has set itself the objective of maintaining and developing an area of freedom, security and justice. For the progressive establishment of such an area, the Community is to adopt measures relating to judicial cooperation in civil matters with a cross-border impact to the extent necessary for the proper functioning of the internal market.

(2) According to Article 65, point (b) of the Treaty, these measures are to include those promoting the compatibility of the rules applicable in the Member States concerning the conflict of laws and of jurisdiction.

(3) The European Council meeting in Tampere on 15 and 16 October 1999 endorsed the principle of mutual recognition of judgments and other decisions of judicial authorities as the cornerstone of judicial cooperation in civil matters and invited the Council and the Commission to adopt a programme of measures to implement that principle.

(4) On 30 November 2000 the Council adopted a joint Commission and Council programme of measures for implementation of the principle of mutual recognition of decisions in civil and commercial matters. The programme identifies measures relating to the harmonisation of conflict-of-law rules as those facilitating the mutual recognition of judgments.

(5) The Hague Programme, adopted by the European Council on 5 November 2004, called for work to be pursued actively on the conflict-of-law rules regarding contractual obligations (Rome I).

(6) The proper functioning of the internal market creates a need, in order to improve the predictability of the outcome of litigation, certainty as to the law applicable and the free movement of judgments, for the conflict-of-law rules in the Member States to designate the same national law irrespective of the country of the court in which an action is brought.

(7) The substantive scope and the provisions of this Regulation should be consistent with Council Regulation (EC) No 44/2001 of 22 December 2000 on jurisdiction and the recognition and enforcement of judgments in civil and commercial matters (Brussels I) and Regulation (EC) No 864/2007 of the European Parliament and of the Council of 11 July 2007 on the law applicable to non-contractual obligations (Rome II).

(8) Family relationships should cover parentage, marriage, affinity and collateral relatives. The reference in Article 1(2) to relationships having comparable effects to marriage and other family relationships should be interpreted in accordance with the law of the Member State in which the court is seised.

(9) Obligations under bills of exchange, cheques and promissory notes and other negotiable instruments should also cover bills of lading to the extent that the obligations under the bill of lading arise out of its negotiable character.

(10) Obligations arising out of dealings prior to the conclusion of the contract are covered by Article 12 of Regulation (EC) No 864/2007. Such obligations should therefore be excluded from the scope of this Regulation.

(11) The parties' freedom to choose the applicable law should be one of the cornerstones of the system of conflict-of-law rules in matters of contractual obligations.

(12) An agreement between the parties to confer on one or more courts or tribunals of a Member State exclusive jurisdiction to determine disputes under the contract should be one of the factors to be taken into account in determining whether a choice of law has been clearly demonstrated.

(13) This Regulation does not preclude parties from incorporating by reference into their contract a non-State body of law or an international convention.

(14) Should the Community adopt, in an appropriate legal instrument, rules of substantive contract law, including standard terms and conditions, such instrument may provide that the parties may choose to apply those rules.

(15) Where a choice of law is made and all other elements relevant to the situation are located in a country other than the country whose law has been chosen, the choice of law should not prejudice the application of provisions of the law of that country which cannot be derogated from by agreement. This rule should apply whether or not the choice of law was accompanied by a choice of court or tribunal. Whereas no substantial change is intended as compared with Article 3(3) of the 1980 Convention on the Law Applicable to Contractual Obligations (the Rome Convention), the wording of this Regulation is aligned as far as possible with Article 14 of Regulation (EC) No 864/2007.

(16) To contribute to the general objective of this Regulation, legal certainty in the European judicial area, the conflict-of-law rules should be highly foreseeable. The courts should, however, retain a degree of discretion to determine the law that is most closely connected to the situation.

(17) As far as the applicable law in the absence of choice is concerned, the concept of 'provision of services' and 'sale of goods' should be interpreted in the same way as when applying Article 5 of Regulation (EC) No 44/2001 in so far as sale of goods and provision of services are covered by that Regulation. Although franchise and distribution contracts are contracts for services, they are the subject of specific rules.

(18) As far as the applicable law in the absence of choice is concerned, multilateral systems should be those in which trading is conducted, such as regulated markets and multilateral trading facilities as referred to in Article 4 of Directive 2004/39/EC of the European Parliament and of the Council of 21 April 2004 on markets in financial instruments, regardless of whether or not they rely on a central counterparty.

(19) Where there has been no choice of law, the applicable law should be determined in accordance with the rule specified for the particular type of contract. Where the contract cannot be categorised as being one of the specified types or where its elements fall within more than one of the specified types, it should be governed by the law of the country where the party required to effect the characteristic performance of the contract has his habitual residence. In the case of a contract consisting of a bundle of rights and obligations capable of being categorised as falling within more than one of the specified types of contract, the characteristic performance of the contract should be determined having regard to its centre of gravity.

(20) Where the contract is manifestly more closely connected with a country other than that indicated in Article 4(1) or (2), an escape clause should provide that the law of that other country is to apply. In order to determine that country, account should be taken, inter alia, of whether the contract in question has a very close relationship with another contract or contracts.

(21) In the absence of choice, where the applicable law cannot be determined either on the basis of the fact that the contract can be categorised as one of the specified types or as being the law of the country of habitual residence of the party required to effect the characteristic performance of the contract, the contract should be governed by the law of the country with which it is most closely connected. In order to determine that country, account should be taken, inter alia, of whether the contract in question has a very close relationship with another contract or contracts.

(22) As regards the interpretation of contracts for the carriage of goods, no change in substance is intended with respect to Article 4(4), third sentence, of the Rome Convention. Consequently, single-voyage charter parties and other contracts the main purpose of which is the carriage of goods should be treated as contracts for the carriage of goods. For the purposes of this Regulation, the term 'consignor'

should refer to any person who enters into a contract of carriage with the carrier and the term 'the carrier' should refer to the party to the contract who undertakes to carry the goods, whether or not he performs the carriage himself.

(23) As regards contracts concluded with parties regarded as being weaker, those parties should be protected by conflict-of-law rules that are more favourable to their interests than the general rules.

(24) With more specific reference to consumer contracts, the conflict-of-law rule should make it possible to cut the cost of settling disputes concerning what are commonly relatively small claims and to take account of the development of distance-selling techniques. Consistency with Regulation (EC) No 44/2001 requires both that there be a reference to the concept of directed activity as a condition for applying the consumer protection rule and that the concept be interpreted harmoniously in Regulation (EC) No 44/2001 and this Regulation, bearing in mind that a joint declaration by the Council and the Commission on Article 15 of Regulation (EC) No 44/2001 states that 'for Article 15(1)(c) to be applicable it is not sufficient for an undertaking to target its activities at the Member State of the consumer's residence, or at a number of Member States including that Member State; a contract must also be concluded within the framework of its activities'. The declaration also states that 'the mere fact that an Internet site is accessible is not sufficient for Article 15 to be applicable, although a factor will be that this Internet site solicits the conclusion of distance contracts and that a contract has actually been concluded at a distance, by whatever means. In this respect, the language or currency which a website uses does not constitute a relevant factor'.

(25) Consumers should be protected by such rules of the country of their habitual residence that cannot be derogated from by agreement, provided that the consumer contract has been concluded as a result of the professional pursuing his commercial or professional activities in that particular country. The same protection should be guaranteed if the professional, while not pursuing his commercial or professional activities in the country where the consumer has his habitual residence, directs his activities by any means to that country or to several countries, including that country, and the contract is concluded as a result of such activities.

(26) For the purposes of this Regulation, financial services such as investment services and activities and ancillary services provided by a professional to a consumer, as referred to in sections A and B of Annex I to Directive 2004/39/EC, and contracts for the sale of units in collective investment undertakings, whether or not covered by Council Directive 85/611/EEC of 20 December 1985 on the coordination of laws, regulations and administrative provisions relating to undertakings for collective investment in transferable securities (UCITS), should be subject to Article 6 of this Regulation. Consequently, when a reference is made to terms and conditions governing the issuance or offer to the public of transferable securities or to the subscription and redemption of units in collective investment undertakings, that reference should include all aspects binding the issuer or the offeror to the consumer, but should not include those aspects involving the provision of financial services.

(27) Various exceptions should be made to the general conflict-of-law rule for consumer contracts. Under one such exception the general rule should not apply to contracts relating to rights in rem in immovable property or tenancies of such property unless the contract relates to the right to use immovable property on a timeshare basis within the meaning of Directive 94/47/EC of the European Parliament and of the Council of 26 October 1994 on the protection of purchasers in respect of certain aspects of contracts relating to the purchase of the right to use immovable properties on a timeshare basis.

(28) It is important to ensure that rights and obligations which constitute a financial instrument are not covered by the general rule applicable to consumer contracts, as that could lead to different laws being applicable to each of the instruments issued, therefore changing their nature and preventing their fungible trading and offering. Likewise, whenever such instruments are issued or offered, the contractual relationship established between the issuer or the offeror and the consumer should not necessarily be subject to the mandatory application of the law of the country of habitual residence of the consumer, as there is a need to ensure uniformity in the terms and conditions of an issuance or an offer. The same rationale should apply with regard to the multilateral systems covered by Article 4(1) (h), in respect of which it should be ensured that the law of the country of habitual residence of the consumer will not interfere with the rules applicable to contracts concluded within those systems or with the operator of such systems.

(29) For the purposes of this Regulation, references to rights and obligations constituting the terms and conditions governing the issuance, offers to the public or public take-over bids of transferable securities and references to the subscription and redemption of units in collective investment undertakings should include the terms governing, inter alia, the allocation of securities or units, rights in the event of over-subscription, withdrawal rights and similar matters in the context of the offer as well as those matters referred to in Articles 10, 11, 12 and 13, thus ensuring that all relevant contractual aspects of an offer binding the issuer or the offeror to the consumer are governed by a single law.

(30) For the purposes of this Regulation, financial instruments and transferable securities are those instruments referred to in Article 4 of Directive 2004/39/EC.

(31) Nothing in this Regulation should prejudice the operation of a formal arrangement designated as a system under Article 2(a) of Directive 98/26/EC of the European Parliament and of the Council of 19 May 1998 on settlement finality in payment and securities settlement systems.

(32) Owing to the particular nature of contracts of carriage and insurance contracts, specific provisions should ensure an adequate level of protection of passengers and policy holders. Therefore, Article 6 should not apply in the context of those particular contracts.

(33) Where an insurance contract not covering a large risk covers more than one risk, at least one of which is situated in a Member State and at least one of which is situated in a third country, the special rules on insurance contracts in this Regulation should apply only to the risk or risks situated in the relevant Member State or Member States.

(34) The rule on individual employment contracts should not prejudice the application of the overriding mandatory provisions of the country to which a worker is posted in accordance with Directive 96/71/EC of the European Parliament and of the Council of 16 December 1996 concerning the posting of workers in the framework of the provision of services.

(35) Employees should not be deprived of the protection afforded to them by provisions which cannot be derogated from by agreement or which can only be derogated from to their benefit.

(36) As regards individual employment contracts, work carried out in another country should be regarded as temporary if the employee is expected to resume working in the country of origin after carrying out his tasks abroad. The conclusion of a new contract of employment with the original employer or an employer belonging to the same group of companies as the original employer should not preclude the employee from being regarded as carrying out his work in another country temporarily.

(37) Considerations of public interest justify giving the courts of the Member States the possibility, in exceptional circumstances, of applying exceptions based on public policy and overriding mandatory provisions. The concept of 'overriding mandatory provisions' should be distinguished from the expression 'provisions which cannot be derogated from by agreement' and should be construed more restrictively.

(38) In the context of voluntary assignment, the term 'relationship' should make it clear that Article 14(1) also applies to the property aspects of an assignment, as between assignor and assignee, in legal orders where such aspects are treated separately from the aspects under the law of obligations. However, the term 'relationship' should not be understood as relating to any relationship that may exist between assignor and assignee. In particular, it should not cover preliminary questions as regards a voluntary assignment or a contractual subrogation. The term should be strictly limited to the aspects which are directly relevant to the voluntary assignment or contractual subrogation in question.

(39) For the sake of legal certainty there should be a clear definition of habitual residence, in particular for companies and other bodies, corporate or unincorporated. Unlike Article 60(1) of Regulation (EC) No 44/2001, which establishes three criteria, the conflict-of-law rule should proceed on the basis of a single criterion; otherwise, the parties would be unable to foresee the law applicable to their situation.

(40) A situation where conflict-of-law rules are dispersed among several instruments and where there are differences between those rules should be avoided. This Regulation, however, should not exclude the possibility of inclusion of conflict-of-law rules relating to contractual obligations in provisions of Community law with regard to particular matters.

This Regulation should not prejudice the application of other instruments laying down provisions designed to contribute to the proper functioning of the internal market in so far as they cannot be applied in conjunction with the law designated by the rules of this Regulation. The application of provisions of the applicable law designated by the rules of this Regulation should not restrict the free movement of goods and services as regulated by Community instruments, such as Directive 2000/31/EC of the European Parliament and of the Council of 8 June 2000 on certain legal aspects of information society services, in particular electronic commerce, in the Internal Market (Directive on electronic commerce).

(41) Respect for international commitments entered into by the Member States means that this Regulation should not affect international conventions to which one or more Member States are parties at the time when this Regulation is adopted. To make the rules more accessible, the Commission should publish the list of the relevant conventions in the Official Journal of the European Union on the basis of information supplied by the Member States.

(42) The Commission will make a proposal to the European Parliament and to the Council concerning the procedures and conditions according to which Member States would be entitled to negotiate and conclude, on their own behalf, agreements with third countries in individual and exceptional cases, concerning sectoral matters and containing provisions on the law applicable to contractual obligations.

(43) Since the objective of this Regulation cannot be sufficiently achieved by the Member States and can therefore, by reason of the scale and effects of this Regulation, be better achieved at Community level, the Community may adopt measures, in accordance with the principle of subsidiarity as set out in Article 5 of the Treaty. In accordance with the principle of proportionality, as set out in that Article, this Regulation does not go beyond what is necessary to attain its objective.

(44) In accordance with Article 3 of the Protocol on the position of the United Kingdom and Ireland, annexed to the Treaty on European Union and to the Treaty establishing the European Community, Ireland has notified its wish to take part in the adoption and application of the present Regulation.

(45) In accordance with Articles 1 and 2 of the Protocol on the position of the United Kingdom and Ireland, annexed to the Treaty on European Union and to the Treaty establishing the European Community, and without prejudice to Article 4 of the said Protocol, the United Kingdom is not taking part in the adoption of this Regulation and is not bound by it or subject to its application.

(46) In accordance with Articles 1 and 2 of the Protocol on the position of Denmark, annexed to the Treaty on European Union and to the Treaty establishing the European Community, Denmark is not taking part in the adoption of this Regulation and is not bound by it or subject to its application,

HAVE ADOPTED THIS REGULATION:

## CHAPTER I

## SCOPE

*Article 1*

**Material scope**

1. This Regulation shall apply, in situations involving a conflict of laws, to contractual obligations in civil and commercial matters.

It shall not apply, in particular, to revenue, customs or administrative matters.

2. The following shall be excluded from the scope of this Regulation:

(a)   questions involving the status or legal capacity of natural persons, without prejudice to Article 13;

(b)   obligations arising out of family relationships and relationships deemed by the law applicable to such relationships to have comparable effects, including maintenance obligations;

(c)   obligations arising out of matrimonial property regimes, property regimes of relationships deemed by the law applicable to such relationships to have comparable effects to marriage, and wills and succession;

(d) obligations arising under bills of exchange, cheques and promissory notes and other negotiable instruments to the extent that the obligations under such other negotiable instruments arise out of their negotiable character;

(e) arbitration agreements and agreements on the choice of court;

(f) questions governed by the law of companies and other bodies, corporate or unincorporated, such as the creation, by registration or otherwise, legal capacity, internal organisation or winding-up of companies and other bodies, corporate or unincorporated, and the personal liability of officers and members as such for the obligations of the company or body;

(g) the question whether an agent is able to bind a principal, or an organ to bind a company or other body corporate or unincorporated, in relation to a third party;

(h) the constitution of trusts and the relationship between settlors, trustees and beneficiaries;

(i) obligations arising out of dealings prior to the conclusion of a contract;

(j) insurance contracts arising out of operations carried out by organisations other than undertakings referred to in Article 2 of Directive 2002/83/EC of the European Parliament and of the Council of 5 November 2002 concerning life assurance the object of which is to provide benefits for employed or self-employed persons belonging to an undertaking or group of undertakings, or to a trade or group of trades, in the event of death or survival or of discontinuance or curtailment of activity, or of sickness related to work or accidents at work.

3. This Regulation shall not apply to evidence and procedure, without prejudice to Article 18.

4. In this Regulation, the term 'Member State' shall mean Member States to which this Regulation applies. However, in Article 3(4) and Article 7 the term shall mean all the Member States.

*Article 2*

**Universal application**

Any law specified by this Regulation shall be applied whether or not it is the law of a Member State.

## CHAPTER II

## UNIFORM RULES

*Article 3*

**Freedom of choice**

1. A contract shall be governed by the law chosen by the parties. The choice shall be made expressly or clearly demonstrated by the terms of the contract or the circumstances of the case. By their choice the parties can select the law applicable to the whole or to part only of the contract.

2. The parties may at any time agree to subject the contract to a law other than that which previously governed it, whether as a result of an earlier choice made under this Article or of other provisions of this Regulation. Any change in the law to be applied that is made after the conclusion of the contract shall not prejudice its formal validity under Article 11 or adversely affect the rights of third parties.

3. Where all other elements relevant to the situation at the time of the choice are located in a country other than the country whose law has been chosen, the choice of the parties shall not prejudice the application of provisions of the law of that other country which cannot be derogated from by agreement.

4. Where all other elements relevant to the situation at the time of the choice are located in one or more Member States, the parties' choice of applicable law other than that of a Member State shall not prejudice the application of provisions of Community law, where appropriate as implemented in the Member State of the forum, which cannot be derogated from by agreement.

5. The existence and validity of the consent of the parties as to the choice of the applicable law shall be determined in accordance with the provisions of Articles 10, 11 and 13.

European Union Materials

*Article 4*

**Applicable law in the absence of choice**

1. To the extent that the law applicable to the contract has not been chosen in accordance with Article 3 and without prejudice to Articles 5 to 8, the law governing the contract shall be determined as follows:

(a)  a contract for the sale of goods shall be governed by the law of the country where the seller has his habitual residence;

(b)  a contract for the provision of services shall be governed by the law of the country where the service provider has his habitual residence;

(c)  a contract relating to a right in rem in immovable property or to a tenancy of immovable property shall be governed by the law of the country where the property is situated;

(d)  notwithstanding point (c), a tenancy of immovable property concluded for temporary private use for a period of no more than six consecutive months shall be governed by the law of the country where the landlord has his habitual residence, provided that the tenant is a natural person and has his habitual residence in the same country;

(e)  a franchise contract shall be governed by the law of the country where the franchisee has his habitual residence;

(f)  a distribution contract shall be governed by the law of the country where the distributor has his habitual residence;

(g)  a contract for the sale of goods by auction shall be governed by the law of the country where the auction takes place, if such a place can be determined;

(h)  a contract concluded within a multilateral system which brings together or facilitates the bringing together of multiple third-party buying and selling interests in financial instruments, as defined by Article 4(1), point (17) of Directive 2004/39/EC, in accordance with non-discretionary rules and governed by a single law, shall be governed by that law.

2. Where the contract is not covered by paragraph 1 or where the elements of the contract would be covered by more than one of points (a) to (h) of paragraph 1, the contract shall be governed by the law of the country where the party required to effect the characteristic performance of the contract has his habitual residence.

3. Where it is clear from all the circumstances of the case that the contract is manifestly more closely connected with a country other than that indicated in paragraphs 1 or 2, the law of that other country shall apply.

4. Where the law applicable cannot be determined pursuant to paragraphs 1 or 2, the contract shall be governed by the law of the country with which it is most closely connected.

*Article 5*

**Contracts of carriage**

1. To the extent that the law applicable to a contract for the carriage of goods has not been chosen in accordance with Article 3, the law applicable shall be the law of the country of habitual residence of the carrier, provided that the place of receipt or the place of delivery or the habitual residence of the consignor is also situated in that country. If those requirements are not met, the law of the country where the place of delivery as agreed by the parties is situated shall apply.

2. To the extent that the law applicable to a contract for the carriage of passengers has not been chosen by the parties in accordance with the second subparagraph, the law applicable shall be the law of the country where the passenger has his habitual residence, provided that either the place of departure or the place of destination is situated in that country. If these requirements are not met, the law of the country where the carrier has his habitual residence shall apply.

The parties may choose as the law applicable to a contract for the carriage of passengers in accordance with Article 3 only the law of the country where:

(a)  the passenger has his habitual residence;

or

(b)  the carrier has his habitual residence;

or

(c)  the carrier has his place of central administration;

or

(d)  the place of departure is situated;

or

(e)  the place of destination is situated.

3.  Where it is clear from all the circumstances of the case that the contract, in the absence of a choice of law, is manifestly more closely connected with a country other than that indicated in paragraphs 1 or 2, the law of that other country shall apply.

*Article 6*

**Consumer contracts**

1.  Without prejudice to Articles 5 and 7, a contract concluded by a natural person for a purpose which can be regarded as being outside his trade or profession (the consumer) with another person acting in the exercise of his trade or profession (the professional) shall be governed by the law of the country where the consumer has his habitual residence, provided that the professional:

(a)  pursues his commercial or professional activities in the country where the consumer has his habitual residence,

or

(b)  by any means, directs such activities to that country or to several countries including that country,

and the contract falls within the scope of such activities.

2.  Notwithstanding paragraph 1, the parties may choose the law applicable to a contract which fulfils the requirements of paragraph 1, in accordance with Article 3. Such a choice may not, however, have the result of depriving the consumer of the protection afforded to him by provisions that cannot be derogated from by agreement by virtue of the law which, in the absence of choice, would have been applicable on the basis of paragraph 1.

3.  If the requirements in points (a) or (b) of paragraph 1 are not fulfilled, the law applicable to a contract between a consumer and a professional shall be determined pursuant to Articles 3 and 4.

4.  Paragraphs 1 and 2 shall not apply to:

(a)  a contract for the supply of services where the services are to be supplied to the consumer exclusively in a country other than that in which he has his habitual residence;

(b)  a contract of carriage other than a contract relating to package travel within the meaning of Council Directive 90/314/EEC of 13 June 1990 on package travel, package holidays and package tours;

(c)  a contract relating to a right in rem in immovable property or a tenancy of immovable property other than a contract relating to the right to use immovable properties on a timeshare basis within the meaning of Directive 94/47/EC;

(d)  rights and obligations which constitute a financial instrument and rights and obligations constituting the terms and conditions governing the issuance or offer to the public and public take-over bids of transferable securities, and the subscription and redemption of units in collective investment undertakings in so far as these activities do not constitute provision of a financial service;

(e)  a contract concluded within the type of system falling within the scope of Article 4(1)(h).

*Article 7*

**Insurance contracts**

1. This Article shall apply to contracts referred to in paragraph 2, whether or not the risk covered is situated in a Member State, and to all other insurance contracts covering risks situated inside the territory of the Member States. It shall not apply to reinsurance contracts.

2. An insurance contract covering a large risk as defined in Article 5(d) of the First Council Directive 73/239/EEC of 24 July 1973 on the coordination of laws, regulations and administrative provisions relating to the taking-up and pursuit of the business of direct insurance other than life assurance shall be governed by the law chosen by the parties in accordance with Article 3 of this Regulation.

To the extent that the applicable law has not been chosen by the parties, the insurance contract shall be governed by the law of the country where the insurer has his habitual residence. Where it is clear from all the circumstances of the case that the contract is manifestly more closely connected with another country, the law of that other country shall apply.

3. In the case of an insurance contract other than a contract falling within paragraph 2, only the following laws may be chosen by the parties in accordance with Article 3:

(a)   the law of any Member State where the risk is situated at the time of conclusion of the contract;

(b)   the law of the country where the policy holder has his habitual residence;

(c)   in the case of life assurance, the law of the Member State of which the policy holder is a national;

(d)   for insurance contracts covering risks limited to events occurring in one Member State other than the Member State where the risk is situated, the law of that Member State;

(e)   where the policy holder of a contract falling under this paragraph pursues a commercial or industrial activity or a liberal profession and the insurance contract covers two or more risks which relate to those activities and are situated in different Member States, the law of any of the Member States concerned or the law of the country of habitual residence of the policy holder.

Where, in the cases set out in points (a), (b) or (e), the Member States referred to grant greater freedom of choice of the law applicable to the insurance contract, the parties may take advantage of that freedom.

To the extent that the law applicable has not been chosen by the parties in accordance with this paragraph, such a contract shall be governed by the law of the Member State in which the risk is situated at the time of conclusion of the contract.

4. The following additional rules shall apply to insurance contracts covering risks for which a Member State imposes an obligation to take out insurance:

(a)   the insurance contract shall not satisfy the obligation to take out insurance unless it complies with the specific provisions relating to that insurance laid down by the Member State that imposes the obligation. Where the law of the Member State in which the risk is situated and the law of the Member State imposing the obligation to take out insurance contradict each other, the latter shall prevail;

(b)   by way of derogation from paragraphs 2 and 3, a Member State may lay down that the insurance contract shall be governed by the law of the Member State that imposes the obligation to take out insurance.

5. For the purposes of paragraph 3, third subparagraph, and paragraph 4, where the contract covers risks situated in more than one Member State, the contract shall be considered as constituting several contracts each relating to only one Member State.

6. For the purposes of this Article, the country in which the risk is situated shall be determined in accordance with Article 2(d) of the Second Council Directive 88/357/EEC of 22 June 1988 on the coordination of laws, regulations and administrative provisions relating to direct insurance other than life assurance and laying down provisions to facilitate the effective exercise of freedom to provide services and, in the case of life assurance, the country in which the risk is situated shall be the country of the commitment within the meaning of Article 1(1)(g) of Directive 2002/83/EC.

*Article 8*

**Individual employment contracts**

1. An individual employment contract shall be governed by the law chosen by the parties in accordance with Article 3. Such a choice of law may not, however, have the result of depriving the employee of the protection afforded to him by provisions that cannot be derogated from by agreement under the law that, in the absence of choice, would have been applicable pursuant to paragraphs 2, 3 and 4 of this Article.

2. To the extent that the law applicable to the individual employment contract has not been chosen by the parties, the contract shall be governed by the law of the country in which or, failing that, from which the employee habitually carries out his work in performance of the contract. The country where the work is habitually carried out shall not be deemed to have changed if he is temporarily employed in another country.

3. Where the law applicable cannot be determined pursuant to paragraph 2, the contract shall be governed by the law of the country where the place of business through which the employee was engaged is situated.

4. Where it appears from the circumstances as a whole that the contract is more closely connected with a country other than that indicated in paragraphs 2 or 3, the law of that other country shall apply.

*Article 9*

**Overriding mandatory provisions**

1. Overriding mandatory provisions are provisions the respect for which is regarded as crucial by a country for safeguarding its public interests, such as its political, social or economic organisation, to such an extent that they are applicable to any situation falling within their scope, irrespective of the law otherwise applicable to the contract under this Regulation.

2. Nothing in this Regulation shall restrict the application of the overriding mandatory provisions of the law of the forum.

3. Effect may be given to the overriding mandatory provisions of the law of the country where the obligations arising out of the contract have to be or have been performed, in so far as those overriding mandatory provisions render the performance of the contract unlawful. In considering whether to give effect to those provisions, regard shall be had to their nature and purpose and to the consequences of their application or non-application.

*Article 10*

**Consent and material validity**

1. The existence and validity of a contract, or of any term of a contract, shall be determined by the law which would govern it under this Regulation if the contract or term were valid.

2. Nevertheless, a party, in order to establish that he did not consent, may rely upon the law of the country in which he has his habitual residence if it appears from the circumstances that it would not be reasonable to determine the effect of his conduct in accordance with the law specified in paragraph 1.

*Article 11*

**Formal validity**

1. A contract concluded between persons who, or whose agents, are in the same country at the time of its conclusion is formally valid if it satisfies the formal requirements of the law which governs it in substance under this Regulation or of the law of the country where it is concluded.

2. A contract concluded between persons who, or whose agents, are in different countries at the time of its conclusion is formally valid if it satisfies the formal requirements of the law which governs it in substance under this Regulation, or of the law of either of the countries where either of the parties or their agent is present at the time of conclusion, or of the law of the country where either of the parties had his habitual residence at that time.

3. A unilateral act intended to have legal effect relating to an existing or contemplated contract is formally valid if it satisfies the formal requirements of the law which governs or would govern the contract in substance under this Regulation, or of the law of the country where the act was done, or of the law of the country where the person by whom it was done had his habitual residence at that time.

4. Paragraphs 1, 2 and 3 of this Article shall not apply to contracts that fall within the scope of Article 6. The form of such contracts shall be governed by the law of the country where the consumer has his habitual residence.

5. Notwithstanding paragraphs 1 to 4, a contract the subject matter of which is a right *in rem* in immovable property or a tenancy of immovable property shall be subject to the requirements of form of the law of the country where the property is situated if by that law:

(a)   those requirements are imposed irrespective of the country where the contract is concluded and irrespective of the law governing the contract; and

(b)   those requirements cannot be derogated from by agreement.

## Article 12

### Scope of the law applicable

1. The law applicable to a contract by virtue of this Regulation shall govern in particular:

(a)   interpretation;

(b)   performance;

(c)   within the limits of the powers conferred on the court by its procedural law, the consequences of a total or partial breach of obligations, including the assessment of damages in so far as it is governed by rules of law;

(d)   the various ways of extinguishing obligations, and prescription and limitation of actions;

(e)   the consequences of nullity of the contract.

2. In relation to the manner of performance and the steps to be taken in the event of defective performance, regard shall be had to the law of the country in which performance takes place.

## Article 13

### Incapacity

In a contract concluded between persons who are in the same country, a natural person who would have capacity under the law of that country may invoke his incapacity resulting from the law of another country, only if the other party to the contract was aware of that incapacity at the time of the conclusion of the contract or was not aware thereof as a result of negligence.

## Article 14

### Voluntary assignment and contractual subrogation

1. The relationship between assignor and assignee under a voluntary assignment or contractual subrogation of a claim against another person (the debtor) shall be governed by the law that applies to the contract between the assignor and assignee under this Regulation.

2. The law governing the assigned or subrogated claim shall determine its assignability, the relationship between the assignee and the debtor, the conditions under which the assignment or subrogation can be invoked against the debtor and whether the debtor's obligations have been discharged.

3. The concept of assignment in this Article includes outright transfers of claims, transfers of claims by way of security and pledges or other security rights over claims.

## Article 15

### Legal subrogation

Where a person (the creditor) has a contractual claim against another (the debtor) and a third person has a duty to satisfy the creditor, or has in fact satisfied the creditor in discharge of that duty, the law which governs the third person's duty to satisfy the creditor shall determine whether and to what extent the third person is entitled to exercise against the debtor the rights which the creditor had against the debtor under the law governing their relationship.

*Article 16*

**Multiple liability**

If a creditor has a claim against several debtors who are liable for the same claim, and one of the debtors has already satisfied the claim in whole or in part, the law governing the debtor's obligation towards the creditor also governs the debtor's right to claim recourse from the other debtors. The other debtors may rely on the defences they had against the creditor to the extent allowed by the law governing their obligations towards the creditor.

*Article 17*

**Set-off**

Where the right to set-off is not agreed by the parties, set-off shall be governed by the law applicable to the claim against which the right to set-off is asserted.

*Article 18*

**Burden of proof**

1. The law governing a contractual obligation under this Regulation shall apply to the extent that, in matters of contractual obligations, it contains rules which raise presumptions of law or determine the burden of proof.

2. A contract or an act intended to have legal effect may be proved by any mode of proof recognised by the law of the forum or by any of the laws referred to in Article 11 under which that contract or act is formally valid, provided that such mode of proof can be administered by the forum.

CHAPTER III

OTHER PROVISIONS

*Article 19*

**Habitual residence**

1. For the purposes of this Regulation, the habitual residence of companies and other bodies, corporate or unincorporated, shall be the place of central administration.

The habitual residence of a natural person acting in the course of his business activity shall be his principal place of business.

2. Where the contract is concluded in the course of the operations of a branch, agency or any other establishment, or if, under the contract, performance is the responsibility of such a branch, agency or establishment, the place where the branch, agency or any other establishment is located shall be treated as the place of habitual residence.

3. For the purposes of determining the habitual residence, the relevant point in time shall be the time of the conclusion of the contract.

*Article 20*

**Exclusion of renvoi**

The application of the law of any country specified by this Regulation means the application of the rules of law in force in that country other than its rules of private international law, unless provided otherwise in this Regulation.

*Article 21*

**Public policy of the forum**

The application of a provision of the law of any country specified by this Regulation may be refused only if such application is manifestly incompatible with the public policy (ordre public) of the forum.

*Article 22*

**States with more than one legal system**

1. Where a State comprises several territorial units, each of which has its own rules of law in respect of contractual obligations, each territorial unit shall be considered as a country for the purposes of identifying the law applicable under this Regulation.

2. A Member State where different territorial units have their own rules of law in respect of contractual obligations shall not be required to apply this Regulation to conflicts solely between the laws of such units.

*Article 23*

**Relationship with other provisions of Community law**

With the exception of Article 7, this Regulation shall not prejudice the application of provisions of Community law which, in relation to particular matters, lay down conflict-of-law rules relating to contractual obligations.

*Article 24*

**Relationship with the Rome Convention**

1. This Regulation shall replace the Rome Convention in the Member States, except as regards the territories of the Member States which fall within the territorial scope of that Convention and to which this Regulation does not apply pursuant to Article 299 of the Treaty.

2. In so far as this Regulation replaces the provisions of the Rome Convention, any reference to that Convention shall be understood as a reference to this Regulation.

*Article 25*

**Relationship with existing international conventions**

1. This Regulation shall not prejudice the application of international conventions to which one or more Member States are parties at the time when this Regulation is adopted and which lay down conflict-of-law rules relating to contractual obligations.

2. However, this Regulation shall, as between Member States, take precedence over conventions concluded exclusively between two or more of them in so far as such conventions concern matters governed by this Regulation.

*Article 26*

**List of Conventions**

1. By 17 June 2009, Member States shall notify the Commission of the conventions referred to in Article 25(1). After that date, Member States shall notify the Commission of all denunciations of such conventions.

2. Within six months of receipt of the notifications referred to in paragraph 1, the Commission shall publish in the Official Journal of the European Union:

(a)   a list of the conventions referred to in paragraph 1;

(b)   the denunciations referred to in paragraph 1.

*Article 27*

**Review clause**

1. By 17 June 2013, the Commission shall submit to the European Parliament, the Council and the European Economic and Social Committee a report on the application of this Regulation. If appropriate, the report shall be accompanied by proposals to amend this Regulation. The report shall include:

(a) a study on the law applicable to insurance contracts and an assessment of the impact of the provisions to be introduced, if any; and

(b) an evaluation on the application of Article 6, in particular as regards the coherence of Community law in the field of consumer protection.

2. By 17 June 2010, the Commission shall submit to the European Parliament, the Council and the European Economic and Social Committee a report on the question of the effectiveness of an assignment or subrogation of a claim against third parties and the priority of the assigned or subrogated claim over a right of another person. The report shall be accompanied, if appropriate, by a proposal to amend this Regulation and an assessment of the impact of the provisions to be introduced.

*Article 28*

**Application in time**

This Regulation shall apply to contracts concluded as from 17 December 2009.

CHAPTER IV

FINAL PROVISIONS

*Article 29*

**Entry into force and application**

This Regulation shall enter into force on the 20th day following its publication in the Official Journal of the European Union.

It shall apply from 17 December 2009 except for Article 26 which shall apply from 17 June 2009.

This Regulation shall be binding in its entirety and directly applicable in the Member States in accordance with the Treaty establishing the European Community.

## Commission Decision of 22 December 2008 on the request from the United Kingdom to accept Regulation (EC) No 593/2008 of the European Parliament and the Council on the law applicable to contractual obligations (Rome I) (notified under document number C (2008) 8554) (2009/26/EC)

[2009] OJ L10/22

THE COMMISSION OF THE EUROPEAN COMMUNITIES,

Having regard to the Treaty establishing the European Community, in particular to Article 11a thereof,

Whereas:

(1) On 17 June 2008, the European Parliament and the Council adopted Regulation (EC) No 593/2008 on the law applicable to contractual obligations (Rome I) (1).

(2) Pursuant to Article 1 of the Protocol on the position of the United Kingdom and Ireland, the United Kingdom did not participate in the adoption of Regulation (EC) No 593/2008.

(3) In accordance with Article 4 of that Protocol, the United Kingdom notified the Commission by letter of 24 July 2008, received by the Commission on 30 July 2008, of its intention to accept and to participate in Regulation (EC) No 593/2008.

(4) On 11 November 2008 the Commission gave a positive opinion to the Council on the request from the United Kingdom,

HAS ADOPTED THIS DECISION:

*Article 1*

Regulation (EC) No 593/2008 shall apply to the United Kingdom in accordance with Article 2.

*Article 2*

Regulation (EC) No 593/2008 shall enter into force in the United Kingdom from the date of notification of this Decision. It shall apply from 17 December 2009, except for Article 26 which shall apply from 17 June 2009.

*Article 3*

This Decision is addressed to the Member States.

# Council Regulation (EC) No 4/2009 of 18 December 2008 on jurisdiction, applicable law, recognition and enforcement of decisions and cooperation in matters relating to maintenance obligations

[2009] OJ L7/1

THE COUNCIL OF THE EUROPEAN UNION,

Having regard to the Treaty establishing the European Community, and in particular Article 61(c) and Article 67(2) thereof,

Having regard to the proposal from the Commission,

Having regard to the opinion of the European Parliament,

Having regard to the opinion of the European Economic and Social Committee,

Whereas:

(1) The Community has set itself the objective of maintaining and developing an area of freedom, security and justice, in which the free movement of persons is ensured. For the gradual establishment of such an area, the Community is to adopt, among others, measures relating to judicial cooperation in civil matters having cross-border implications, in so far as necessary for the proper functioning of the internal market.

(2) In accordance with Article 65(b) of the Treaty, these measures must aim, inter alia, to promote the compatibility of the rules applicable in the Member States concerning the conflict of laws and of jurisdiction.

(3) In this respect, the Community has among other measures already adopted Council Regulation (EC) No 44/2001 of 22 December 2000 on jurisdiction and the recognition and enforcement of judgments in civil and commercial matters, Council Decision 2001/470/EC of 28 May 2001 establishing a European Judicial Network in civil and commercial matters, Council Regulation (EC) No 1206/2001 of 28 May 2001 on cooperation between the courts of the Member States in the taking of evidence in civil or commercial matters, Council Directive 2003/8/EC of 27 January 2003 to improve access to justice in cross-border disputes by establishing minimum common rules relating to legal aid for such disputes, Council Regulation (EC) No 2201/2003 of 27 November 2003 on jurisdiction and the recognition and enforcement of judgments in matrimonial matters and in matters of parental responsibility, Regulation (EC) No 805/2004 of the European Parliament and of the Council of 21 April 2004 creating a European Enforcement Order for uncontested claims, and Regulation (EC) No 1393/2007 of the European Parliament and of the Council of 13 November 2007 on the service in the Member States of judicial and extrajudicial documents in civil or commercial matters (service of documents).

(4) The European Council in Tampere on 15 and 16 October 1999 invited the Council and the Commission to establish special common procedural rules to simplify and accelerate the settlement of cross-border disputes concerning, inter alia, maintenance claims. It also called for the abolition of intermediate measures required for the recognition and enforcement in the requested State of a decision given in another Member State, particularly a decision relating to a maintenance claim.

(5) A programme of measures for the enforcement of the principle of mutual recognition of decisions in civil and commercial matters, common to the Commission and to the Council, was adopted on 30 November 2000. That programme provides for the abolition of the exequatur procedure for maintenance claims in order to boost the effectiveness of the means by which maintenance creditors safeguard their rights.

(6) The European Council meeting in Brussels on 4 and 5 November 2004 adopted a new programme called 'The Hague Programme: strengthening freedom, security and justice in the European Union' (hereinafter referred to as The Hague Programme).

(7) At its meeting on 2 and 3 June 2005, the Council adopted a Council and Commission Action Plan which implements The Hague Programme in concrete actions and which mentions the necessity of adopting proposals on maintenance obligations.

(8) In the framework of The Hague Conference on Private International Law, the Community and its Member States took part in negotiations which led to the adoption on 23 November 2007 of the Convention on the International Recovery of Child Support and other Forms of Family Maintenance (hereinafter referred to as the 2007 Hague Convention) and the Protocol on the Law Applicable to Maintenance Obligations (hereinafter referred to as the 2007 Hague Protocol). Both those instruments should therefore be taken into account in this Regulation.

(9) A maintenance creditor should be able to obtain easily, in a Member State, a decision which will be automatically enforceable in another Member State without further formalities.

(10) In order to achieve this goal, it is advisable to create a Community instrument in matters relating to maintenance obligations bringing together provisions on jurisdiction, conflict of laws, recognition and enforceability, enforcement, legal aid and cooperation between Central Authorities.

(11) The scope of this Regulation should cover all maintenance obligations arising from a family relationship, parentage, marriage or affinity, in order to guarantee equal treatment of all maintenance creditors. For the purposes of this Regulation, the term 'maintenance obligation' should be interpreted autonomously.

(12) In order to take account of the various ways of resolving maintenance obligation issues in the Member States, this Regulation should apply both to court decisions and to decisions given by administrative authorities, provided that the latter offer guarantees with regard to, in particular, their impartiality and the right of all parties to be heard. Those authorities should therefore apply all the rules of this Regulation.

(13) For the reasons set out above, this Regulation should also ensure the recognition and enforcement of court settlements and authentic instruments without affecting the right of either party to such a settlement or instrument to challenge the settlement or instrument before the courts of the Member State of origin.

(14) It should be provided in this Regulation that for the purposes of an application for the recognition and enforcement of a decision relating to maintenance obligations the term 'creditor' includes public bodies which are entitled to act in place of a person to whom maintenance is owed or to claim reimbursement of benefits provided to the creditor in place of maintenance. Where a public body acts in this capacity, it should be entitled to the same services and the same legal aid as a creditor.

(15) In order to preserve the interests of maintenance creditors and to promote the proper administration of justice within the European Union, the rules on jurisdiction as they result from Regulation (EC) No 44/2001 should be adapted. The circumstance that the defendant is habitually resident in a third State should no longer entail the non-application of Community rules on jurisdiction, and there should no longer be any referral to national law. This Regulation should therefore determine the cases in which a court in a Member State may exercise subsidiary jurisdiction.

(16) In order to remedy, in particular, situations of denial of justice this Regulation should provide a forum necessitatis allowing a court of a Member State, on an exceptional basis, to hear a case which is closely connected with a third State. Such an exceptional basis may be deemed to exist when proceedings prove impossible in the third State in question, for example because of civil war, or when an applicant cannot reasonably be expected to initiate or conduct proceedings in that State. Jurisdiction based on the forum necessitatis should, however, be exercised only if the dispute has a sufficient connection with the Member State of the court seised, for instance the nationality of one of the parties.

(17) An additional rule of jurisdiction should provide that, except under specific conditions, proceedings to modify an existing maintenance decision or to have a new decision given can be brought by the debtor only in the State in which the creditor was habitually resident at the time the decision was given and in which he remains habitually resident. To ensure proper symmetry between the 2007 Hague Convention and this Regulation, this rule should also apply as regards decisions given in a third State which is party to the said Convention in so far as that Convention is in force between that State and the Community and covers the same maintenance obligations in that State and in the Community.

(18)  For the purposes of this Regulation, it should be provided that in Ireland the concept of 'domicile' replaces the concept of 'nationality' which is also the case in the United Kingdom, subject to this Regulation being applicable in the latter Member State in accordance with Article 4 of the Protocol on the position of the United Kingdom and Ireland annexed to the Treaty on European Union and the Treaty establishing the European Community.

(19)  In order to increase legal certainty, predictability and the autonomy of the parties, this Regulation should enable the parties to choose the competent court by agreement on the basis of specific connecting factors. To protect the weaker party, such a choice of court should not be allowed in the case of maintenance obligations towards a child under the age of 18.

(20)  It should be provided in this Regulation that, for Member States bound by the 2007 Hague Protocol, the rules on conflict of laws in respect of maintenance obligations will be those set out in that Protocol. To that end, a provision referring to the said Protocol should be inserted. The 2007 Hague Protocol will be concluded by the Community in time to enable this Regulation to apply. To take account of a scenario in which the 2007 Hague Protocol does not apply to all the Member States a distinction for the purposes of recognition, enforceability and enforcement of decisions needs to be made in this Regulation between the Member States bound by the 2007 Hague Protocol and those not bound by it.

(21)  It needs to be made clear in this Regulation that these rules on conflict of laws determine only the law applicable to maintenance obligations and do not determine the law applicable to the establishment of the family relationships on which the maintenance obligations are based. The establishment of family relationships continues to be covered by the national law of the Member States, including their rules of private international law.

(22)  In order to ensure swift and efficient recovery of a maintenance obligation and to prevent delaying actions, decisions in matters relating to maintenance obligations given in a Member State should in principle be provisionally enforceable. This Regulation should therefore provide that the court of origin should be able to declare the decision provisionally enforceable even if the national law does not provide for enforceability by operation of law and even if an appeal has been or could still be lodged against the decision under national law.

(23)  To limit the costs of proceedings subject to this Regulation, the greatest possible use of modern communications technologies, particularly for hearing parties, would be helpful.

(24)  The guarantees provided by the application of rules on conflict of laws should provide the justification for having decisions relating to maintenance obligations given in a Member State bound by the 2007 Hague Protocol recognised and regarded as enforceable in all the other Member States without any procedure being necessary and without any form of control on the substance in the Member State of enforcement.

(25)  Recognition in a Member State of a decision relating to maintenance obligations has as its only object to allow the recovery of the maintenance claim determined in the decision. It does not imply the recognition by that Member State of the family relationship, parentage, marriage or affinity underlying the maintenance obligations which gave rise to the decision.

(26)  For decisions on maintenance obligations given in a Member State not bound by the 2007 Hague Protocol, there should be provision in this Regulation for a procedure for recognition and declaration of enforceability. That procedure should be modelled on the procedure and the grounds for refusing recognition set out in Regulation (EC) No 44/2001. To accelerate proceedings and enable the creditor to recover his claim quickly, the court seised should be required to give its decision within a set time, unless there are exceptional circumstances.

(27)  It would also be appropriate to limit as far as possible the formal enforcement requirements likely to increase the costs to be borne by the maintenance creditor. To that end, this Regulation should provide that a maintenance creditor ought not to be required to have a postal address or an authorised representative in the Member State of enforcement, without this otherwise affecting the internal organisation of the Member States in matters relating to enforcement proceedings.

(28)  In order to limit the costs of enforcement proceedings, no translation should be required unless enforcement is contested, and without prejudice to the rules applicable to service of documents.

(29) In order to guarantee compliance with the requirements of a fair trial, this Regulation should provide for the right of a defendant who did not enter an appearance in the court of origin of a Member State bound by the 2007 Hague Protocol to apply for a review of the decision given against him at the stage of enforcement. However, the defendant must apply for this review within a set period which should start no later than the day on which, in the enforcement proceedings, his property was first made non-disposable in whole or in part. That right to apply for a review should be an extraordinary remedy granted to the defendant in default and not affecting the application of any extraordinary remedies laid down in the law of the Member State of origin provided that those remedies are not incompatible with the right to a review under this Regulation.

(30) In order to speed up the enforcement in another Member State of a decision given in a Member State bound by the 2007 Hague Protocol it is necessary to limit the grounds of refusal or of suspension of enforcement which may be invoked by the debtor on account of the cross-border nature of the maintenance claim. This limitation should not affect the grounds of refusal or of suspension laid down in national law which are not incompatible with those listed in this Regulation, such as the debtor's discharge of his debt at the time of enforcement or the unattachable nature of certain assets.

(31) To facilitate cross-border recovery of maintenance claims, provision should be made for a system of cooperation between Central Authorities designated by the Member States. These Authorities should assist maintenance creditors and debtors in asserting their rights in another Member State by submitting applications for recognition, enforceability and enforcement of existing decisions, for the modification of such decisions or for the establishment of a decision. They should also exchange information in order to locate debtors and creditors, and identify their income and assets, as necessary. Lastly, they should cooperate with each other by exchanging general information and promoting cooperation amongst the competent authorities in their Member States.

(32) A Central Authority designated under this Regulation should bear its own costs, except in specifically determined cases, and should provide assistance for all applicants residing in its Member State. The criterion for determining a person's right to request assistance from a Central Authority should be less strict than the connecting factor of 'habitual residence' used elsewhere in this Regulation. However, the 'residence' criterion should exclude mere presence.

(33) In order to provide full assistance to maintenance creditors and debtors and to facilitate as much as possible cross-border recovery of maintenance, the Central Authorities should be able to obtain a certain amount of personal information. This Regulation should therefore oblige the Member States to ensure that their Central Authorities have access to such information through the public authorities or administrations which hold the information concerned in the course of their ordinary activities. It should however be left to each Member State to decide on the arrangements for such access. Accordingly, a Member State should be able to designate the public authorities or administrations which will be required to supply the information to the Central Authority in accordance with this Regulation, including, if appropriate, public authorities or administrations already designated in the context of other systems for access to information. Where a Member State designates public authorities or administrations, it should ensure that its Central Authority is able to access the requisite information held by those bodies as provided for in this Regulation. A Member State should also be able to allow its Central Authority to access requisite information from any other legal person which holds it and controls its processing.

(34) In the context of access to personal data and the use and transmission thereof, the requirements of Directive 95/46/EC of the European Parliament and of the Council of 24 October 1995 on the protection of individuals with regard to the processing of personal data and on the free movement of such data, as transposed into the national law of the Member States, should be complied with.

(35) For the purposes of the application of this Regulation it is however necessary to define the specific conditions of access to personal data and of the use and transmission of such data. In this context, the opinion of the European Data Protection Supervisor has been taken into consideration. Notification of the data subject should take place in accordance with national law. It should however be possible to defer the notification to prevent the debtor from transferring his assets and thus jeopardising the recovery of the maintenance claim.

(36) On account of the costs of proceedings it is appropriate to provide for a very favourable legal aid scheme, that is, full coverage of the costs relating to proceedings concerning maintenance obligations in respect of children under the age of 21 initiated via the Central Authorities. Specific rules should therefore be added to the current rules on legal aid in the European Union which exist by virtue of Directive 2003/8/EC thus setting up a special legal aid scheme for maintenance obligations. In this context, the competent authority of the requested Member State should be able, exceptionally, to recover costs from an applicant having received free legal aid and lost the case, provided that the person's financial situation so permits. This would apply, in particular, where someone well-off had acted in bad faith.

(37) In addition, for maintenance obligations other than those referred to in the preceding recital, all parties should be guaranteed the same treatment in terms of legal aid at the time of enforcement of a decision in another Member State. Accordingly, the provisions of this Regulation on continuity of legal aid should be understood as also granting such aid to a party who, while not having received legal aid in the proceedings to obtain or amend a decision in the Member State of origin, did then benefit from such aid in that State in the context of an application for enforcement of the decision. Similarly, a party who benefited from free proceedings before an administrative authority listed in Annex X should, in the Member State of enforcement, benefit from the most favourable legal aid or the most extensive exemption from costs or expenses, provided that he shows that he would have so benefited in the Member State of origin.

(38) In order to minimise the costs of translating supporting documents the court seised should only require a translation of such documents when this is necessary, without prejudice to the rights of the defence and the rules applicable concerning service of documents.

(39) To facilitate the application of this Regulation, Member States should be obliged to provide the Commission with the names and contact details of their Central Authorities and with other information. That information should be made available to practitioners and to the public through publication in the Official Journal of the European Union or through electronic access to the European Judicial Network in civil and commercial matters established by Decision 2001/470/EC. Furthermore, the use of forms provided for in this Regulation should facilitate and speed up communication between the Central Authorities and make it possible to submit applications electronically.

(40) The relationship between this Regulation and the bilateral or multilateral conventions and agreements on maintenance obligations to which the Member States are party should be specified. In this context it should be stipulated that Member States which are party to the Convention of 23 March 1962 between Sweden, Denmark, Finland, Iceland and Norway on the recovery of maintenance by the Member States may continue to apply that Convention since it contains more favourable rules on recognition and enforcement than those in this Regulation. As regards the conclusion of future bilateral agreements on maintenance obligations with third States, the procedures and conditions under which Member States would be authorised to negotiate and conclude such agreements on their own behalf should be determined in the course of discussions relating to a Commission proposal on the subject.

(41) In calculating the periods and time limits provided for in this Regulation, Regulation (EEC, Euratom) No 1182/71 of the Council of 3 June 1971 determining the rules applicable to periods, dates and time limits should apply.

(42) The measures necessary for the implementation of this Regulation should be adopted in accordance with Council Decision 1999/468/EC of 28 June 1999 laying down the procedures for the exercise of implementing powers conferred on the Commission.

(43) In particular, the Commission should be empowered to adopt any amendments to the forms provided for in this Regulation in accordance with the advisory procedure provided for in Article 3 of Decision 1999/468/EC. For the establishment of the list of the administrative authorities falling within the scope of this Regulation, and the list of authorities competent to certify the right to legal aid, the Commission should be empowered to act in accordance with the management procedure provided for in Article 4 of that Decision.

(44) This Regulation should amend Regulation (EC) No 44/2001 by replacing the provisions of that Regulation applicable to maintenance obligations. Subject to the transitional provisions of this

Regulation, Member States should, in matters relating to maintenance obligations, apply the provisions of this Regulation on jurisdiction, recognition, enforceability and enforcement of decisions and on legal aid instead of those of Regulation (EC) No 44/2001 as from the date on which this Regulation becomes applicable.

(45) Since the objectives of this Regulation, namely the introduction of a series of measures to ensure the effective recovery of maintenance claims in cross-border situations and thus to facilitate the free movement of persons within the European Union, cannot be sufficiently achieved by the Member States and can therefore, by reason of the scale and effects of this Regulation, be better achieved at Community level, the Community may adopt measures in accordance with the principle of subsidiarity as set out in Article 5 of the Treaty. In accordance with the principle of proportionality as set out in that Article this Regulation does not go beyond what is necessary to achieve those objectives.

(46) In accordance with Article 3 of the Protocol on the position of the United Kingdom and Ireland, annexed to the Treaty on European Union and to the Treaty establishing the European Community, Ireland has given notice of its wish to take part in the adoption and application of this Regulation.

(47) In accordance with Articles 1 and 2 of the Protocol on the position of the United Kingdom and Ireland, annexed to the Treaty on European Union and to the Treaty establishing the European Community, the United Kingdom is not taking part in the adoption of this Regulation and is not bound by it or subject to its application. This is, however, without prejudice to the possibility for the United Kingdom of notifying its intention of accepting this Regulation after its adoption in accordance with Article 4 of the said Protocol.

(48) In accordance with Articles 1 and 2 of the Protocol on the position of Denmark annexed to the Treaty on European Union and the Treaty establishing the European Community, Denmark is not taking part in the adoption of this Regulation and is not bound by it or subject to its application, without prejudice to the possibility for Denmark of applying the amendments made here to Regulation (EC) No 44/2001 pursuant to Article 3 of the Agreement of 19 October 2005 between the European Community and the Kingdom of Denmark on jurisdiction and the recognition and enforcement of judgments in civil and commercial matters,

HAS ADOPTED THIS REGULATION:

## CHAPTER I

## SCOPE AND DEFINITIONS

*Article 1*

### Scope of application

1. This Regulation shall apply to maintenance obligations arising from a family relationship, parentage, marriage or affinity.

2. In this Regulation, the term 'Member State' shall mean Member States to which this Regulation applies.

*Article 2*

### Definitions

1. For the purposes of this Regulation:

1. the term 'decision' shall mean a decision in matters relating to maintenance obligations given by a court of a Member State, whatever the decision may be called, including a decree, order, judgment or writ of execution, as well as a decision by an officer of the court determining the costs or expenses. For the purposes of Chapters VII and VIII, the term 'decision' shall also mean a decision in matters relating to maintenance obligations given in a third State;

2. the term 'court settlement' shall mean a settlement in matters relating to maintenance obligations which has been approved by a court or concluded before a court in the course of proceedings;

3. the term 'authentic instrument' shall mean:

(a)  a document in matters relating to maintenance obligations which has been formally drawn up or registered as an authentic instrument in the Member State of origin and the authenticity of which:

  (i)  relates to the signature and the content of the instrument,

  and

  (ii)  has been established by a public authority or other authority empowered for that purpose;

or,

(b)  an arrangement relating to maintenance obligations concluded with administrative authorities of the Member State of origin or authenticated by them;

4.  the term 'Member State of origin' shall mean the Member State in which, as the case may be, the decision has been given, the court settlement has been approved or concluded, or the authentic instrument has been established;

5.  the term 'Member State of enforcement' shall mean the Member State in which the enforcement of the decision, the court settlement or the authentic instrument is sought;

6.  the term 'requesting Member State' shall mean the Member State whose Central Authority transmits an application pursuant to Chapter VII;

7.  the term 'requested Member State' shall mean the Member State whose Central Authority receives an application pursuant to Chapter VII;

8.  the term '2007 Hague Convention Contracting State' shall mean a State which is a contracting party to the Hague Convention of 23 November 2007 on the International Recovery of Child Support and other Forms of Family Maintenance (hereinafter referred to as the 2007 Hague Convention) to the extent that the said Convention applies between the Community and that State;

9.  the term 'court of origin' shall mean the court which has given the decision to be enforced;

10.  the term 'creditor' shall mean any individual to whom maintenance is owed or is alleged to be owed;

11.  the term 'debtor' shall mean any individual who owes or who is alleged to owe maintenance.

2. For the purposes of this Regulation, the term 'court' shall include administrative authorities of the Member States with competence in matters relating to maintenance obligations provided that such authorities offer guarantees with regard to impartiality and the right of all parties to be heard and provided that their decisions under the law of the Member State where they are established:

(i)  may be made the subject of an appeal to or review by a judicial authority;

and

(ii)  have a similar force and effect as a decision of a judicial authority on the same matter.

These administrative authorities shall be listed in Annex X. That Annex shall be established and amended in accordance with the management procedure referred to in Article 73(2) at the request of the Member State in which the administrative authority concerned is established.

3. For the purposes of Articles 3, 4 and 6, the concept of 'domicile' shall replace that of 'nationality' in those Member States which use this concept as a connecting factor in family matters.

For the purposes of Article 6, parties which have their 'domicile' in different territorial units of the same Member State shall be deemed to have their common 'domicile' in that Member State.

## CHAPTER II

## JURISDICTION

*Article 3*

**General provisions**

In matters relating to maintenance obligations in Member States, jurisdiction shall lie with:

(a)  the court for the place where the defendant is habitually resident,

or

(b)   the court for the place where the creditor is habitually resident,

or

(c)   the court which, according to its own law, has jurisdiction to entertain proceedings concerning the status of a person if the matter relating to maintenance is ancillary to those proceedings, unless that jurisdiction is based solely on the nationality of one of the parties,

or

(d)   the court which, according to its own law, has jurisdiction to entertain proceedings concerning parental responsibility if the matter relating to maintenance is ancillary to those proceedings, unless that jurisdiction is based solely on the nationality of one of the parties.

### Article 4

**Choice of court**

1. The parties may agree that the following court or courts of a Member State shall have jurisdiction to settle any disputes in matters relating to a maintenance obligation which have arisen or may arise between them:

(a)   a court or the courts of a Member State in which one of the parties is habitually resident;

(b)   a court or the courts of a Member State of which one of the parties has the nationality;

(c)   in the case of maintenance obligations between spouses or former spouses:

  (i)   the court which has jurisdiction to settle their dispute in matrimonial matters;

  or

  (ii)   a court or the courts of the Member State which was the Member State of the spouses' last common habitual residence for a period of at least one year.

The conditions referred to in points (a), (b) or (c) have to be met at the time the choice of court agreement is concluded or at the time the court is seised.

The jurisdiction conferred by agreement shall be exclusive unless the parties have agreed otherwise.

2. A choice of court agreement shall be in writing. Any communication by electronic means which provides a durable record of the agreement shall be equivalent to 'writing'.

3. This Article shall not apply to a dispute relating to a maintenance obligation towards a child under the age of 18.

4. If the parties have agreed to attribute exclusive jurisdiction to a court or courts of a State party to the Convention on jurisdiction and the recognition and enforcement of judgments in civil and commercial matters, signed on 30 October 2007 in Lugano (hereinafter referred to as the Lugano Convention), where that State is not a Member State, the said Convention shall apply except in the case of the disputes referred to in paragraph 3.

### Article 5

**Jurisdiction based on the appearance of the defendant**

Apart from jurisdiction derived from other provisions of this Regulation, a court of a Member State before which a defendant enters an appearance shall have jurisdiction. This rule shall not apply where appearance was entered to contest the jurisdiction.

### Article 6

**Subsidiary jurisdiction**

Where no court of a Member State has jurisdiction pursuant to Articles 3, 4 and 5 and no court of a State party to the Lugano Convention which is not a Member State has jurisdiction pursuant to the provisions of that Convention, the courts of the Member State of the common nationality of the parties shall have jurisdiction.

European Union Materials

## Article 7

**Forum necessitatis**

Where no court of a Member State has jurisdiction pursuant to Articles 3, 4, 5 and 6, the courts of a Member State may, on an exceptional basis, hear the case if proceedings cannot reasonably be brought or conducted or would be impossible in a third State with which the dispute is closely connected.

The dispute must have a sufficient connection with the Member State of the court seised.

## Article 8

**Limit on proceedings**

1. Where a decision is given in a Member State or a 2007 Hague Convention Contracting State where the creditor is habitually resident, proceedings to modify the decision or to have a new decision given cannot be brought by the debtor in any other Member State as long as the creditor remains habitually resident in the State in which the decision was given.

2. Paragraph 1 shall not apply:

(a) where the parties have agreed in accordance with Article 4 to the jurisdiction of the courts of that other Member State;

(b) where the creditor submits to the jurisdiction of the courts of that other Member State pursuant to Article 5;

(c) where the competent authority in the 2007 Hague Convention Contracting State of origin cannot, or refuses to, exercise jurisdiction to modify the decision or give a new decision; or

(d) where the decision given in the 2007 Hague Convention Contracting State of origin cannot be recognised or declared enforceable in the Member State where proceedings to modify the decision or to have a new decision given are contemplated.

## Article 9

**Seising of a court**

For the purposes of this Chapter, a court shall be deemed to be seised:

(a) at the time when the document instituting the proceedings or an equivalent document is lodged with the court, provided that the claimant has not subsequently failed to take the steps he was required to take to have service effected on the defendant; or

(b) if the document has to be served before being lodged with the court, at the time when it is received by the authority responsible for service, provided that the claimant has not subsequently failed to take the steps he was required to take to have the document lodged with the court.

## Article 10

**Examination as to jurisdiction**

Where a court of a Member State is seised of a case over which it has no jurisdiction under this Regulation it shall declare of its own motion that it has no jurisdiction.

## Article 11

**Examination as to admissibility**

1. Where a defendant habitually resident in a State other than the Member State where the action was brought does not enter an appearance, the court with jurisdiction shall stay the proceedings so long as it is not shown that the defendant has been able to receive the document instituting the proceedings or an equivalent document in sufficient time to enable him to arrange for his defence, or that all necessary steps have been taken to this end.

2. Article 19 of Regulation (EC) No 1393/2007 shall apply instead of the provisions of paragraph 1 of this Article if the document instituting the proceedings or an equivalent document had to be transmitted from one Member State to another pursuant to that Regulation.

3. Where the provisions of Regulation (EC) No 1393/2007 are not applicable, Article 15 of the Hague Convention of 15 November 1965 on the service abroad of judicial and extrajudicial documents in civil or commercial matters shall apply if the document instituting the proceedings or an equivalent document had to be transmitted abroad pursuant to that Convention.

*Article 12*

*Lis pendens*

1. Where proceedings involving the same cause of action and between the same parties are brought in the courts of different Member States, any court other than the court first seised shall of its own motion stay its proceedings until such time as the jurisdiction of the court first seised is established.

2. Where the jurisdiction of the court first seised is established, any court other than the court first seised shall decline jurisdiction in favour of that court.

*Article 13*

Related actions

1. Where related actions are pending in the courts of different Member States, any court other than the court first seised may stay its proceedings.

2. Where these actions are pending at first instance, any court other than the court first seised may also, on the application of one of the parties, decline jurisdiction if the court first seised has jurisdiction over the actions in question and its law permits the consolidation thereof.

3. For the purposes of this Article, actions are deemed to be related where they are so closely connected that it is expedient to hear and determine them together to avoid the risk of irreconcilable judgments resulting from separate proceedings.

*Article 14*

Provisional, including protective, measures

Application may be made to the courts of a Member State for such provisional, including protective, measures as may be available under the law of that State, even if, under this Regulation, the courts of another Member State have jurisdiction as to the substance of the matter.

CHAPTER III

APPLICABLE LAW

*Article 15*

Determination of the applicable law

The law applicable to maintenance obligations shall be determined in accordance with the Hague Protocol of 23 November 2007 on the law applicable to maintenance obligations (hereinafter referred to as the 2007 Hague Protocol) in the Member States bound by that instrument.

CHAPTER IV

RECOGNITION, ENFORCEABILITY AND ENFORCEMENT OF DECISIONS

*Article 16*

Scope of application of this Chapter

1. This Chapter shall govern the recognition, enforceability and enforcement of decisions falling within the scope of this Regulation.

2. Section 1 shall apply to decisions given in a Member State bound by the 2007 Hague Protocol.

3. Section 2 shall apply to decisions given in a Member State not bound by the 2007 Hague Protocol.

4. Section 3 shall apply to all decisions.

SECTION 1

## Decisions given in a Member State bound by the 2007 Hague Protocol

*Article 17*

### Abolition of exequatur

1. A decision given in a Member State bound by the 2007 Hague Protocol shall be recognised in another Member State without any special procedure being required and without any possibility of opposing its recognition.

2. A decision given in a Member State bound by the 2007 Hague Protocol which is enforceable in that State shall be enforceable in another Member State without the need for a declaration of enforceability.

*Article 18*

### Protective measures

An enforceable decision shall carry with it by operation of law the power to proceed to any protective measures which exist under the law of the Member State of enforcement.

*Article 19*

### Right to apply for a review

1. A defendant who did not enter an appearance in the Member State of origin shall have the right to apply for a review of the decision before the competent court of that Member State where:

(a)  he was not served with the document instituting the proceedings or an equivalent document in sufficient time and in such a way as to enable him to arrange for his defence; or

(b)  he was prevented from contesting the maintenance claim by reason of force majeure or due to extraordinary circumstances without any fault on his part;

unless he failed to challenge the decision when it was possible for him to do so.

2. The time limit for applying for a review shall run from the day the defendant was effectively acquainted with the contents of the decision and was able to react, at the latest from the date of the first enforcement measure having the effect of making his property non-disposable in whole or in part. The defendant shall react promptly, in any event within 45 days. No extension may be granted on account of distance.

3. If the court rejects the application for a review referred to in paragraph 1 on the basis that none of the grounds for a review set out in that paragraph apply, the decision shall remain in force.

If the court decides that a review is justified for one of the reasons laid down in paragraph 1, the decision shall be null and void. However, the creditor shall not lose the benefits of the interruption of prescription or limitation periods, or the right to claim retroactive maintenance acquired in the initial proceedings.

*Article 20*

### Documents for the purposes of enforcement

1. For the purposes of enforcement of a decision in another Member State, the claimant shall provide the competent enforcement authorities with:

(a)  a copy of the decision which satisfies the conditions necessary to establish its authenticity;

(b)  the extract from the decision issued by the court of origin using the form set out in Annex I;

(c)  where appropriate, a document showing the amount of any arrears and the date such amount was calculated;

(d)  where necessary, a transliteration or a translation of the content of the form referred to in point (b) into the official language of the Member State of enforcement or, where there are several official languages in that Member State, into the official language or one of the official languages of court proceedings of the place where the application is made, in accordance with the law of that Member State, or into another language that the Member State concerned has indicated it can accept. Each Member State may indicate the official language or languages of the institutions of the European Union other than its own which it can accept for the completion of the form.

2. The competent authorities of the Member State of enforcement may not require the claimant to provide a translation of the decision. However, a translation may be required if the enforcement of the decision is challenged.

3. Any translation under this Article must be done by a person qualified to do translations in one of the Member States.

## Article 21

### Refusal or suspension of enforcement

1. The grounds of refusal or suspension of enforcement under the law of the Member State of enforcement shall apply in so far as they are not incompatible with the application of paragraphs 2 and 3.

2. The competent authority in the Member State of enforcement shall, on application by the debtor, refuse, either wholly or in part, the enforcement of the decision of the court of origin if the right to enforce the decision of the court of origin is extinguished by the effect of prescription or the limitation of action, either under the law of the Member State of origin or under the law of the Member State of enforcement, whichever provides for the longer limitation period.

Furthermore, the competent authority in the Member State of enforcement may, on application by the debtor, refuse, either wholly or in part, the enforcement of the decision of the court of origin if it is irreconcilable with a decision given in the Member State of enforcement or with a decision given in another Member State or in a third State which fulfils the conditions necessary for its recognition in the Member State of enforcement.

A decision which has the effect of modifying an earlier decision on maintenance on the basis of changed circumstances shall not be considered an irreconcilable decision within the meaning of the second subparagraph.

3. The competent authority in the Member State of enforcement may, on application by the debtor, suspend, either wholly or in part, the enforcement of the decision of the court of origin if the competent court of the Member State of origin has been seised of an application for a review of the decision of the court of origin pursuant to Article 19.

Furthermore, the competent authority of the Member State of enforcement shall, on application by the debtor, suspend the enforcement of the decision of the court of origin where the enforceability of that decision is suspended in the Member State of origin.

## Article 22

### No effect on the existence of family relationships

The recognition and enforcement of a decision on maintenance under this Regulation shall not in any way imply the recognition of the family relationship, parentage, marriage or affinity underlying the maintenance obligation which gave rise to the decision.

## SECTION 2

## Decisions given in a Member State not bound by the 2007 Hague Protocol

## Article 23

### Recognition

1. A decision given in a Member State not bound by the 2007 Hague Protocol shall be recognised in the other Member States without any special procedure being required.

2. Any interested party who raises the recognition of a decision as the principal issue in a dispute may, in accordance with the procedures provided for in this Section, apply for a decision that the decision be recognised.

3. If the outcome of proceedings in a court of a Member State depends on the determination of an incidental question of recognition, that court shall have jurisdiction over that question.

## Article 24

### Grounds of refusal of recognition

A decision shall not be recognised:

(a) if such recognition is manifestly contrary to public policy in the Member State in which recognition is sought. The test of public policy may not be applied to the rules relating to jurisdiction;

(b) where it was given in default of appearance, if the defendant was not served with the document which instituted the proceedings or with an equivalent document in sufficient time and in such a way as to enable him to arrange for his defence, unless the defendant failed to commence proceedings to challenge the decision when it was possible for him to do so;

(c) if it is irreconcilable with a decision given in a dispute between the same parties in the Member State in which recognition is sought;

(d) if it is irreconcilable with an earlier decision given in another Member State or in a third State in a dispute involving the same cause of action and between the same parties, provided that the earlier decision fulfils the conditions necessary for its recognition in the Member State in which recognition is sought.

A decision which has the effect of modifying an earlier decision on maintenance on the basis of changed circumstances shall not be considered an irreconcilable decision within the meaning of points (c) or (d).

## Article 25

### Staying of recognition proceedings

A court of a Member State in which recognition is sought of a decision given in a Member State not bound by the 2007 Hague Protocol shall stay the proceedings if the enforceability of the decision is suspended in the Member State of origin by reason of an appeal.

## Article 26

### Enforceability

A decision given in a Member State not bound by the 2007 Hague Protocol and enforceable in that State shall be enforceable in another Member State when, on the application of any interested party, it has been declared enforceable there.

## Article 27

### Jurisdiction of local courts

1. The application for a declaration of enforceability shall be submitted to the court or competent authority of the Member State of enforcement notified by that Member State to the Commission in accordance with Article 71.

2. The local jurisdiction shall be determined by reference to the place of habitual residence of the party against whom enforcement is sought, or to the place of enforcement.

## Article 28

### Procedure

1. The application for a declaration of enforceability shall be accompanied by the following documents:

(a) a copy of the decision which satisfies the conditions necessary to establish its authenticity;

European Union Materials

(b) an extract from the decision issued by the court of origin using the form set out in Annex II, without prejudice to Article 29;

(c) where necessary, a transliteration or a translation of the content of the form referred to in point (b) into the official language of the Member State of enforcement or, where there are several official languages in that Member State, into the official language or one of the official languages of court proceedings of the place where the application is made, in accordance with the law of that Member State, or into another language that the Member State concerned has indicated it can accept. Each Member State may indicate the official language or languages of the institutions of the European Union other than its own which it can accept for the completion of the form.

2. The court or competent authority seised of the application may not require the claimant to provide a translation of the decision. However, a translation may be required in connection with an appeal under Articles 32 or 33.

3. Any translation under this Article must be done by a person qualified to do translations in one of the Member States.

### Article 29

**Non-production of the extract**

1. If the extract referred to in Article 28(1)(b) is not produced, the competent court or authority may specify a time for its production or accept an equivalent document or, if it considers that it has sufficient information before it, dispense with its production.

2. In the situation referred to in paragraph 1, if the competent court or authority so requires, a translation of the documents shall be produced. The translation shall be done by a person qualified to do translations in one of the Member States.

### Article 30

**Declaration of enforceability**

The decision shall be declared enforceable without any review under Article 24 immediately on completion of the formalities in Article 28 and at the latest within 30 days of the completion of those formalities, except where exceptional circumstances make this impossible. The party against whom enforcement is sought shall not at this stage of the proceedings be entitled to make any submissions on the application.

### Article 31

**Notice of the decision on the application for a declaration**

1. The decision on the application for a declaration of enforceability shall forthwith be brought to the notice of the applicant in accordance with the procedure laid down by the law of the Member State of enforcement.

2. The declaration of enforceability shall be served on the party against whom enforcement is sought, accompanied by the decision, if not already served on that party.

### Article 32

**Appeal against the decision on the application for a declaration**

1. The decision on the application for a declaration of enforceability may be appealed against by either party.

2. The appeal shall be lodged with the court notified by the Member State concerned to the Commission in accordance with Article 71.

3. The appeal shall be dealt with in accordance with the rules governing procedure in contradictory matters.

4. If the party against whom enforcement is sought fails to appear before the appellate court in proceedings concerning an appeal brought by the applicant, Article 11 shall apply even where the party against whom enforcement is sought is not habitually resident in any of the Member States.

5. An appeal against the declaration of enforceability shall be lodged within 30 days of service thereof. If the party against whom enforcement is sought has his habitual residence in a Member State other than that in which the declaration of enforceability was given, the time for appealing shall be 45 days and shall run from the date of service, either on him in person or at his residence. No extension may be granted on account of distance.

## Article 33

**Proceedings to contest the decision given on appeal**

The decision given on appeal may be contested only by the procedure notified by the Member State concerned to the Commission in accordance with Article 71.

## Article 34

**Refusal or revocation of a declaration of enforceability**

1. The court with which an appeal is lodged under Articles 32 or 33 shall refuse or revoke a declaration of enforceability only on one of the grounds specified in Article 24.

2. Subject to Article 32(4), the court seised of an appeal under Article 32 shall give its decision within 90 days from the date it was seised, except where exceptional circumstances make this impossible.

3. The court seised of an appeal under Article 33 shall give its decision without delay.

## Article 35

**Staying of proceedings**

The court with which an appeal is lodged under Articles 32 or 33 shall, on the application of the party against whom enforcement is sought, stay the proceedings if the enforceability of the decision is suspended in the Member State of origin by reason of an appeal.

## Article 36

**Provisional, including protective measures**

1. When a decision must be recognised in accordance with this Section, nothing shall prevent the applicant from availing himself of provisional, including protective, measures in accordance with the law of the Member State of enforcement without a declaration of enforceability under Article 30 being required.

2. The declaration of enforceability shall carry with it by operation of law the power to proceed to any protective measures.

3. During the time specified for an appeal pursuant to Article 32(5) against the declaration of enforceability and until any such appeal has been determined, no measures of enforcement may be taken other than protective measures against the property of the party against whom enforcement is sought.

## Article 37

**Partial enforceability**

1. Where a decision has been given in respect of several matters and the declaration of enforceability cannot be given for all of them, the competent court or authority shall give it for one or more of them.

2. An applicant may request a declaration of enforceability limited to parts of a decision.

## Article 38

**No charge, duty or fee**

In proceedings for the issue of a declaration of enforceability, no charge, duty or fee calculated by reference to the value of the matter at issue may be levied in the Member State of enforcement.

SECTION 3

## Common provisions

*Article 39*

### Provisional enforceability

The court of origin may declare the decision provisionally enforceable, notwithstanding any appeal, even if national law does not provide for enforceability by operation of law.

*Article 40*

### Invoking a recognised decision

1. A party who wishes to invoke in another Member State a decision recognised within the meaning of Article 17(1) or recognised pursuant to Section 2 shall produce a copy of the decision which satisfies the conditions necessary to establish its authenticity.

2. If necessary, the court before which the recognised decision is invoked may ask the party invoking the recognised decision to produce an extract issued by the court of origin using the form set out in Annex I or in Annex II, as the case may be.

The court of origin shall also issue such an extract at the request of any interested party.

3. Where necessary, the party invoking the recognised decision shall provide a transliteration or a translation of the content of the form referred to in paragraph 2 into the official language of the Member State concerned or, where there are several official languages in that Member State, into the official language or one of the official languages of court proceedings of the place where the recognised decision is invoked, in accordance with the law of that Member State, or into another language that the Member State concerned has indicated it can accept. Each Member State may indicate the official language or languages of the institutions of the European Union other than its own which it can accept for the completion of the form.

4. Any translation under this Article must be done by a person qualified to do translations in one of the Member States.

*Article 41*

### Proceedings and conditions for enforcement

1. Subject to the provisions of this Regulation, the procedure for the enforcement of decisions given in another Member State shall be governed by the law of the Member State of enforcement. A decision given in a Member State which is enforceable in the Member State of enforcement shall be enforced there under the same conditions as a decision given in that Member State of enforcement.

2. The party seeking the enforcement of a decision given in another Member State shall not be required to have a postal address or an authorised representative in the Member State of enforcement, without prejudice to persons with competence in matters relating to enforcement proceedings.

*Article 42*

### No review as to substance

Under no circumstances may a decision given in a Member State be reviewed as to its substance in the Member State in which recognition, enforceability or enforcement is sought.

*Article 43*

### No precedence for the recovery of costs

Recovery of any costs incurred in the application of this Regulation shall not take precedence over the recovery of maintenance.

CHAPTER V

## ACCESS TO JUSTICE

*Article 44*

### Right to legal aid

1. Parties who are involved in a dispute covered by this Regulation shall have effective access to justice in another Member State, including enforcement and appeal or review procedures, in accordance with the conditions laid down in this Chapter.

In cases covered by Chapter VII, effective access to justice shall be provided by the requested Member State to any applicant who is resident in the requesting Member State.

2. To ensure such effective access, Member States shall provide legal aid in accordance with this Chapter, unless paragraph 3 applies.

3. In cases covered by Chapter VII, a Member State shall not be obliged to provide legal aid if and to the extent that the procedures of that Member State enable the parties to make the case without the need for legal aid, and the Central Authority provides such services as are necessary free of charge.

4. Entitlements to legal aid shall not be less than those available in equivalent domestic cases.

5. No security, bond or deposit, however described, shall be required to guarantee the payment of costs and expenses in proceedings concerning maintenance obligations.

*Article 45*

### Content of legal aid

Legal aid granted under this Chapter shall mean the assistance necessary to enable parties to know and assert their rights and to ensure that their applications, lodged through the Central Authorities or directly with the competent authorities, are fully and effectively dealt with. It shall cover as necessary the following:

(a)  pre-litigation advice with a view to reaching a settlement prior to bringing judicial proceedings;

(b)  legal assistance in bringing a case before an authority or a court and representation in court;

(c)  exemption from or assistance with the costs of proceedings and the fees to persons mandated to perform acts during the proceedings;

(d)  in Member States in which an unsuccessful party is liable for the costs of the opposing party, if the recipient of legal aid loses the case, the costs incurred by the opposing party, if such costs would have been covered had the recipient been habitually resident in the Member State of the court seised;

(e)  interpretation;

(f)  translation of the documents required by the court or by the competent authority and presented by the recipient of legal aid which are necessary for the resolution of the case;

(g)  travel costs to be borne by the recipient of legal aid where the physical presence of the persons concerned with the presentation of the recipient's case is required in court by the law or by the court of the Member State concerned and the court decides that the persons concerned cannot be heard to the satisfaction of the court by any other means.

*Article 46*

### Free legal aid for applications through Central Authorities concerning maintenance to children

1. The requested Member State shall provide free legal aid in respect of all applications by a creditor under Article 56 concerning maintenance obligations arising from a parent-child relationship towards a person under the age of 21.

2. Notwithstanding paragraph 1, the competent authority of the requested Member State may, in relation to applications other than those under Article 56(1)(a) and (b), refuse free legal aid if it considers that, on the merits, the application or any appeal or review is manifestly unfounded.

*Article 47*

**Cases not covered by Article 46**

1. Subject to Articles 44 and 45, in cases not covered by Article 46, legal aid may be granted in accordance with national law, particularly as regards the conditions for the means test or the merits test.

2. Notwithstanding paragraph 1, a party who, in the Member State of origin, has benefited from complete or partial legal aid or exemption from costs or expenses, shall be entitled, in any proceedings for recognition, enforceability or enforcement, to benefit from the most favourable legal aid or the most extensive exemption from costs or expenses provided for by the law of the Member State of enforcement.

3. Notwithstanding paragraph 1, a party who, in the Member State of origin, has benefited from free proceedings before an administrative authority listed in Annex X, shall be entitled, in any proceedings for recognition, enforceability or enforcement, to benefit from legal aid in accordance with paragraph 2. To that end, he shall present a statement from the competent authority in the Member State of origin to the effect that he fulfils the financial requirements to qualify for the grant of complete or partial legal aid or exemption from costs or expenses.

Competent authorities for the purposes of this paragraph shall be listed in Annex XI. That Annex shall be established and amended in accordance with the management procedure referred to in Article 73(2).

## CHAPTER VI

## COURT SETTLEMENTS AND AUTHENTIC INSTRUMENTS

*Article 48*

**Application of this Regulation to court settlements and authentic instruments**

1. Court settlements and authentic instruments which are enforceable in the Member State of origin shall be recognised in another Member State and be enforceable there in the same way as decisions, in accordance with Chapter IV.

2. The provisions of this Regulation shall apply as necessary to court settlements and authentic instruments.

3. The competent authority of the Member State of origin shall issue, at the request of any interested party, an extract from the court settlement or the authentic instrument using the forms set out in Annexes I and II or in Annexes III and IV as the case may be.

## CHAPTER VII

## COOPERATION BETWEEN CENTRAL AUTHORITIES

*Article 49*

**Designation of Central Authorities**

1. Each Member State shall designate a Central Authority to discharge the duties which are imposed by this Regulation on such an authority.

2. Federal Member States, Member States with more than one system of law or Member States having autonomous territorial units shall be free to appoint more than one Central Authority and shall specify the territorial or personal extent of their functions. Where a Member State has appointed more than one Central Authority, it shall designate the Central Authority to which any communication may be addressed for transmission to the appropriate Central Authority within that Member State. If a communication is sent to a Central Authority which is not competent, the latter shall be responsible for forwarding it to the competent Central Authority and for informing the sender accordingly.

3. The designation of the Central Authority or Central Authorities, their contact details, and where appropriate the extent of their functions as specified in paragraph 2, shall be communicated by each Member State to the Commission in accordance with Article 71.

*Article 50*

**General functions of Central Authorities**

1. Central Authorities shall:

(a) cooperate with each other, including by exchanging information, and promote cooperation amongst the competent authorities in their Member States to achieve the purposes of this Regulation;

(b) seek as far as possible solutions to difficulties which arise in the application of this Regulation.

2. Central Authorities shall take measures to facilitate the application of this Regulation and to strengthen their cooperation. For this purpose the European Judicial Network in civil and commercial matters established by Decision 2001/470/EC shall be used.

*Article 51*

**Specific functions of Central Authorities**

1. Central Authorities shall provide assistance in relation to applications under Article 56 and shall in particular:

(a) transmit and receive such applications;

(b) initiate or facilitate the institution of proceedings in respect of such applications.

2. In relation to such applications Central Authorities shall take all appropriate measures:

(a) where the circumstances require, to provide or facilitate the provision of legal aid;

(b) to help locate the debtor or the creditor, in particular pursuant to Articles 61, 62 and 63;

(c) to help obtain relevant information concerning the income and, if necessary, other financial circumstances of the debtor or creditor, including the location of assets, in particular pursuant to Articles 61, 62 and 63;

(d) to encourage amicable solutions with a view to obtaining voluntary payment of maintenance, where suitable by use of mediation, conciliation or similar processes;

(e) to facilitate the ongoing enforcement of maintenance decisions, including any arrears;

(f) to facilitate the collection and expeditious transfer of maintenance payments;

(g) to facilitate the obtaining of documentary or other evidence, without prejudice to Regulation (EC) No 1206/2001;

(h) to provide assistance in establishing parentage where necessary for the recovery of maintenance;

(i) to initiate or facilitate the institution of proceedings to obtain any necessary provisional measures which are territorial in nature and the purpose of which is to secure the outcome of a pending maintenance application;

(j) to facilitate the service of documents, without prejudice to Regulation (EC) No 1393/2007.

3. The functions of the Central Authority under this Article may, to the extent permitted under the law of the Member State concerned, be performed by public bodies, or other bodies subject to the supervision of the competent authorities of that Member State. The designation of any such public bodies or other bodies, as well as their contact details and the extent of their functions, shall be communicated by each Member State to the Commission in accordance with Article 71.

4. Nothing in this Article or in Article 53 shall impose an obligation on a Central Authority to exercise powers that can be exercised only by judicial authorities under the law of the requested Member State.

*Article 52*

**Power of attorney**

The Central Authority of the requested Member State may require a power of attorney from the applicant only if it acts on his behalf in judicial proceedings or before other authorities, or in order to designate a representative so to act.

*Article 53*

**Requests for specific measures**

1. A Central Authority may make a request, supported by reasons, to another Central Authority to take appropriate specific measures under points (b), (c), (g), (h), (i) and (j) of Article 51(2) when no application under Article 56 is pending. The requested Central Authority shall take such measures as are appropriate if satisfied that they are necessary to assist a potential applicant in making an application under Article 56 or in determining whether such an application should be initiated.

2. Where a request for measures under Article 51(2)(b) and (c) is made, the requested Central Authority shall seek the information requested, if necessary pursuant to Article 61. However, the information referred to in points (b), (c) and (d) of Article 61(2) may be sought only when the creditor produces a copy of the decision, court settlement or authentic instrument to be enforced, accompanied by the extract provided for in Articles 20, 28 or 48, as appropriate.

The requested Central Authority shall communicate the information obtained to the requesting Central Authority. Where that information was obtained pursuant to Article 61, this communication shall specify only the address of the potential defendant in the requested Member State. In the case of a request with a view to recognition, declaration of enforceability or enforcement, the communication shall, in addition, specify merely whether the debtor has income or assets in that State.

If the requested Central Authority is not able to provide the information requested it shall inform the requesting Central Authority without delay and specify the grounds for this impossibility.

3. A Central Authority may also take specific measures at the request of another Central Authority in relation to a case having an international element concerning the recovery of maintenance pending in the requesting Member State.

4. For requests under this Article, the Central Authorities shall use the form set out in Annex V.

*Article 54*

**Central Authority costs**

1. Each Central Authority shall bear its own costs in applying this Regulation.

2. Central Authorities may not impose any charge on an applicant for the provision of their services under this Regulation save for exceptional costs arising from a request for a specific measure under Article 53.

For the purposes of this paragraph, costs relating to locating the debtor shall not be regarded as exceptional.

3. The requested Central Authority may not recover the costs of the services referred to in paragraph 2 without the prior consent of the applicant to the provision of those services at such cost.

*Article 55*

**Application through Central Authorities**

An application under this Chapter shall be made through the Central Authority of the Member State in which the applicant resides to the Central Authority of the requested Member State.

*Article 56*

**Available applications**

1. A creditor seeking to recover maintenance under this Regulation may make applications for the following:

(a) recognition or recognition and declaration of enforceability of a decision;

(b) enforcement of a decision given or recognised in the requested Member State;

(c) establishment of a decision in the requested Member State where there is no existing decision, including where necessary the establishment of parentage;

(d) establishment of a decision in the requested Member State where the recognition and declaration

European Union Materials

of enforceability of a decision given in a State other than the requested Member State is not possible;

(e)  modification of a decision given in the requested Member State;

(f)  modification of a decision given in a State other than the requested Member State.

2. A debtor against whom there is an existing maintenance decision may make applications for the following:

(a)  recognition of a decision leading to the suspension, or limiting the enforcement, of a previous decision in the requested Member State;

(b)  modification of a decision given in the requested Member State;

(c)  modification of a decision given in a State other than the requested Member State.

3. For applications under this Article, the assistance and representation referred to in Article 45(b) shall be provided by the Central Authority of the requested Member State directly or through public authorities or other bodies or persons.

4. Save as otherwise provided in this Regulation, the applications referred to in paragraphs 1 and 2 shall be determined under the law of the requested Member State and shall be subject to the rules of jurisdiction applicable in that Member State.

*Article 57*

**Application contents**

1. An application under Article 56 shall be made using the form set out in Annex VI or in Annex VII.

2. An application under Article 56 shall as a minimum include:

(a)  a statement of the nature of the application or applications;

(b)  the name and contact details, including the address, and date of birth of the applicant;

(c)  the name and, if known, address and date of birth of the defendant;

(d)  the name and the date of birth of any person for whom maintenance is sought;

(e)  the grounds upon which the application is based;

(f)  in an application by a creditor, information concerning where the maintenance payment should be sent or electronically transmitted;

(g)  the name and contact details of the person or unit from the Central Authority of the requesting Member State responsible for processing the application.

3. For the purposes of paragraph 2(b), the applicant's personal address may be replaced by another address in cases of family violence, if the national law of the requested Member State does not require the applicant to supply his or her personal address for the purposes of proceedings to be brought.

4. As appropriate, and to the extent known, the application shall in addition in particular include:

(a)  the financial circumstances of the creditor;

(b)  the financial circumstances of the debtor, including the name and address of the employer of the debtor and the nature and location of the assets of the debtor;

(c)  any other information that may assist with the location of the defendant.

5. The application shall be accompanied by any necessary supporting information or documentation including, where appropriate, documentation concerning the entitlement of the applicant to legal aid. Applications under Article 56(1)(a) and (b) and under Article 56(2)(a) shall be accompanied, as appropriate, only by the documents listed in Articles 20, 28 and 48, or in Article 25 of the 2007 Hague Convention.

*Article 58*

**Transmission, receipt and processing of applications and cases through Central Authorities**

1. The Central Authority of the requesting Member State shall assist the applicant in ensuring that the application is accompanied by all the information and documents known by it to be necessary for consideration of the application.

2. The Central Authority of the requesting Member State shall, when satisfied that the application complies with the requirements of this Regulation, transmit the application to the Central Authority of the requested Member State.

3. The requested Central Authority shall, within 30 days from the date of receipt of the application, acknowledge receipt using the form set out in Annex VIII, and inform the Central Authority of the requesting Member State what initial steps have been or will be taken to deal with the application, and may request any further necessary documents and information. Within the same 30-day period, the requested Central Authority shall provide to the requesting Central Authority the name and contact details of the person or unit responsible for responding to inquiries regarding the progress of the application.

4. Within 60 days from the date of acknowledgement, the requested Central Authority shall inform the requesting Central Authority of the status of the application.

5. Requesting and requested Central Authorities shall keep each other informed of:

(a)  the person or unit responsible for a particular case;

(b)  the progress of the case;

and shall provide timely responses to enquiries.

6. Central Authorities shall process a case as quickly as a proper consideration of the issues will allow.

7. Central Authorities shall employ the most rapid and efficient means of communication at their disposal.

8. A requested Central Authority may refuse to process an application only if it is manifest that the requirements of this Regulation are not fulfilled. In such a case, that Central Authority shall promptly inform the requesting Central Authority of its reasons for refusal using the form set out in Annex IX.

9. The requested Central Authority may not reject an application solely on the basis that additional documents or information are needed. However, the requested Central Authority may ask the requesting Central Authority to provide these additional documents or this information. If the requesting Central Authority does not do so within 90 days or a longer period specified by the requested Central Authority, the requested Central Authority may decide that it will no longer process the application. In this case, it shall promptly notify the requesting Central Authority using the form set out in Annex IX.

*Article 59*

**Languages**

1. The request or application form shall be completed in the official language of the requested Member State or, if there are several official languages in that Member State, in the official language or one of the official languages of the place of the Central Authority concerned, or in any other official language of the institutions of the European Union which that Member State has indicated it can accept, unless the Central Authority of that Member State dispenses with translation.

2. The documents accompanying the request or application form shall not be translated into the language determined in accordance with paragraph 1 unless a translation is necessary in order to provide the assistance requested, without prejudice to Articles 20, 28, 40 and 66.

3. Any other communication between Central Authorities shall be in the language determined in accordance with paragraph 1 unless the Central Authorities agree otherwise.

*Article 60*

**Meetings**

1. In order to facilitate the application of this Regulation, Central Authorities shall meet regularly.

2. These meetings shall be convened in compliance with Decision 2001/470/EC.

*Article 61*

**Access to information for Central Authorities**

1. Under the conditions laid down in this Chapter and by way of exception to Article 51(4), the requested Central Authority shall use all appropriate and reasonable means to obtain the information referred to in paragraph 2 necessary to facilitate, in a given case, the establishment, the modification, the recognition, the declaration of enforceability or the enforcement of a decision.

The public authorities or administrations which, in the course of their ordinary activities, hold, within the requested State, the information referred to in paragraph 2 and which control the processing thereof within the meaning of Directive 95/46/EC shall, subject to limitations justified on grounds of national security or public safety, provide the information to the requested Central Authority at its request in cases where the requested Central Authority does not have direct access to it.

Member States may designate the public authorities or administrations able to provide the requested Central Authority with the information referred to in paragraph 2. Where a Member State makes such a designation, it shall ensure that its choice of authorities and administrations permits its Central Authority to have access, in accordance with this Article, to the information requested.

Any other legal person which holds within the requested Member State the information referred to in paragraph 2 and controls the processing thereof within the meaning of Directive 95/46/EC shall provide the information to the requested Central Authority at the latter's request if it is authorised to do so by the law of the requested Member State.

The requested Central Authority shall, as necessary, transmit the information thus obtained to the requesting Central Authority.

2. The information referred to in this Article shall be the information already held by the authorities, administrations or persons referred to in paragraph 1. It shall be adequate, relevant and not excessive and shall relate to:

(a)  the address of the debtor or of the creditor;

(b)  the debtor's income;

(c)  the identification of the debtor's employer and/or of the debtor's bank account(s);

(d)  the debtor's assets.

For the purpose of obtaining or modifying a decision, only the information listed in point (a) may be requested by the requested Central Authority.

For the purpose of having a decision recognised, declared enforceable or enforced, all the information listed in the first subparagraph may be requested by the requested Central Authority. However, the information listed in point (d) may be requested only if the information listed in points (b) and (c) is insufficient to allow enforcement of the decision.

*Article 62*

**Transmission and use of information**

1. The Central Authorities shall, within their Member State, transmit the information referred to in Article 61(2) to the competent courts, the competent authorities responsible for service of documents and the competent authorities responsible for enforcement of a decision, as the case may be.

2. Any authority or court to which information has been transmitted pursuant to Article 61 may use this only to facilitate the recovery of maintenance claims.

Except for information merely indicating the existence of an address, income or assets in the requested Member State, the information referred to in Article 61(2) may not be disclosed to the person having applied to the requesting Central Authority, subject to the application of procedural rules before a court.

3. Any authority processing information transmitted to it pursuant to Article 61 may not store such information beyond the period necessary for the purposes for which it was transmitted.

4. Any authority processing information communicated to it pursuant to Article 61 shall ensure the confidentiality of such information, in accordance with its national law.

*Article 63*

### Notification of the data subject

1. Notification of the data subject of the communication of all or part of the information collected on him shall take place in accordance with the national law of the requested Member State.

2. Where there is a risk that it may prejudice the effective recovery of the maintenance claim, such notification may be deferred for a period which shall not exceed 90 days from the date on which the information was provided to the requested Central Authority.

## CHAPTER VIII

## PUBLIC BODIES

*Article 64*

### Public bodies as applicants

1. For the purposes of an application for recognition and declaration of enforceability of decisions or for the purposes of enforcement of decisions, the term 'creditor' shall include a public body acting in place of an individual to whom maintenance is owed or one to which reimbursement is owed for benefits provided in place of maintenance.

2. The right of a public body to act in place of an individual to whom maintenance is owed or to seek reimbursement of benefits provided to the creditor in place of maintenance shall be governed by the law to which the body is subject.

3. A public body may seek recognition and a declaration of enforceability or claim enforcement of:

(a) a decision given against a debtor on the application of a public body which claims payment of benefits provided in place of maintenance;

(b) a decision given between a creditor and a debtor to the extent of the benefits provided to the creditor in place of maintenance.

4. The public body seeking recognition and a declaration of enforceability or claiming enforcement of a decision shall upon request provide any document necessary to establish its right under paragraph 2 and to establish that benefits have been provided to the creditor.

## CHAPTER IX

## GENERAL AND FINAL PROVISIONS

*Article 65*

### Legalisation or other similar formality

No legalisation or other similar formality shall be required in the context of this Regulation.

*Article 66*

### Translation of supporting documents

Without prejudice to Articles 20, 28 and 40, the court seised may require the parties to provide a translation of supporting documents which are not in the language of proceedings only if it deems a translation necessary in order to give a decision or to respect the rights of the defence.

## Article 67

**Recovery of costs**

Without prejudice to Article 54, the competent authority of the requested Member State may recover costs from an unsuccessful party having received free legal aid pursuant to Article 46, on an exceptional basis and if his financial circumstances so allow.

## Article 68

**Relations with other Community instruments**

1. Subject to Article 75(2), this Regulation shall modify Regulation (EC) No 44/2001 by replacing the provisions of that Regulation applicable to matters relating to maintenance obligations.

2. This Regulation shall replace, in matters relating to maintenance obligations, Regulation (EC) No 805/2004, except with regard to European Enforcement Orders on maintenance obligations issued in a Member State not bound by the 2007 Hague Protocol.

3. In matters relating to maintenance obligations, this Regulation shall be without prejudice to the application of Directive 2003/8/EC, subject to Chapter V.

4. This Regulation shall be without prejudice to the application of Directive 95/46/EC.

## Article 69

**Relations with existing international conventions and agreements**

1. This Regulation shall not affect the application of bilateral or multilateral conventions and agreements to which one or more Member States are party at the time of adoption of this Regulation and which concern matters governed by this Regulation, without prejudice to the obligations of Member States under Article 307 of the Treaty.

2. Notwithstanding paragraph 1, and without prejudice to paragraph 3, this Regulation shall, in relations between Member States, take precedence over the conventions and agreements which concern matters governed by this Regulation and to which Member States are party.

3. This Regulation shall not preclude the application of the Convention of 23 March 1962 between Sweden, Denmark, Finland, Iceland and Norway on the recovery of maintenance by the Member States which are party thereto, since, with regard to the recognition, enforceability and enforcement of decisions, that Convention provides for:

(a) simplified and more expeditious procedures for the enforcement of decisions relating to maintenance obligations, and

(b) legal aid which is more favourable than that provided for in Chapter V of this Regulation.

However, the application of the said Convention may not have the effect of depriving the defendant of his protection under Articles 19 and 21 of this Regulation.

## Article 70

**Information made available to the public**

The Member States shall provide within the framework of the European Judicial Network in civil and commercial matters established by Decision 2001/470/EC the following information with a view to making it available to the public:

(a) a description of the national laws and procedures concerning maintenance obligations;

(b) a description of the measures taken to meet the obligations under Article 51;

(c) a description of how effective access to justice is guaranteed, as required under Article 44, and

(d) a description of national enforcement rules and procedures, including information on any limitations on enforcement, in particular debtor protection rules and limitation or prescription periods.

Member States shall keep this information permanently updated.

*Article 71*

[Information on contact details and language]

1. By 18 September 2010, the Member States shall communicate to the Commission:

(a)  the names and contact details of the courts or authorities with competence to deal with applications for a declaration of enforceability in accordance with Article 27(1) and with appeals against decisions on such applications in accordance with Article 32(2);

(b)  the redress procedures referred to in Article 33;

(c)  the review procedure for the purposes of Article 19 and the names and contact details of the courts having jurisdiction;

(d)  the names and contact details of their Central Authorities and, where appropriate, the extent of their functions, in accordance with Article 49(3);

(e)  the names and contact details of the public bodies or other bodies and, where appropriate, the extent of their functions, in accordance with Article 51(3);

(f)  the names and contact details of the authorities with competence in matters of enforcement for the purposes of Article 21;

(g)  the languages accepted for translations of the documents referred to in Articles 20, 28 and 40;

(h)  the languages accepted by their Central Authorities for communication with other Central Authorities referred to in Article 59.

The Member States shall apprise the Commission of any subsequent changes to this information.

2. The Commission shall publish the information communicated in accordance with paragraph 1 in the Official Journal of the European Union, with the exception of the addresses and other contact details of the courts and authorities referred to in points (a), (c) and (f).

3. The Commission shall make all information communicated in accordance with paragraph 1 publicly available through any other appropriate means, in particular through the European Judicial Network in civil and commercial matters established by Decision 2001/470/EC.

*Article 72*

**Amendments to the forms**

Any amendment to the forms provided for in this Regulation shall be adopted in accordance with the advisory procedure referred to in Article 73(3).

*Article 73*

**Committee**

1. The Commission shall be assisted by the committee established by Article 70 of Regulation (EC) No 2201/2003.

2. Where reference is made to this paragraph, Articles 4 and 7 of Decision 1999/468/EC shall apply. The period laid down in Article 4(3) of Decision 1999/468/EC shall be set at three months.

3. Where reference is made to this paragraph, Articles 3 and 7 of Decision 1999/468/EC shall apply.

*Article 74*

**Review clause**

By five years from the date of application determined in the third subparagraph of Article 76 at the latest, the Commission shall submit to the European Parliament, the Council and the European Economic and Social Committee a report on the application of this Regulation, including an evaluation of the practical experiences relating to the cooperation between Central Authorities, in particular regarding those Authorities' access to the information held by public authorities and administrations, and an evaluation of the functioning of the procedure for recognition, declaration of enforceability and enforcement applicable to decisions given in a Member State not bound by the 2007 Hague Protocol. If necessary the report shall be accompanied by proposals for adaptation.

European Union Materials

*Article 75*

**Transitional provisions**

[1. This Regulation shall apply only to proceedings instituted, to court settlements approved or concluded, and to authentic instruments established as from its date of application, subject to paragraphs 2 and 3.

2. Sections 2 and 3 of Chapter IV shall apply:

(a)   to decisions given in the Member States before the date of application of this Regulation for which recognition and the declaration of enforceability are requested as from that date;

(b)   to decisions given as from the date of application of this Regulation following proceedings begun before that date,

in so far as those decisions fall with the scope of Regulation (EC) No 44/2001 for the purposes of recognition and enforcement.]

Regulation (EC) No 44/2001 shall continue to apply to procedures for recognition and enforcement under way on the date of application of this Regulation.

The first and second subparagraphs shall apply mutatis mutandis to court settlements approved or concluded and to authentic instruments established in the Member States.

3. Chapter VII on cooperation between Central Authorities shall apply to requests and applications received by the Central Authority as from the date of application of this Regulation.

*Article 76*

**Entry into force**

This Regulation shall enter into force on the 20th day following its publication in the Official Journal of the European Union.

Articles 2(2), 47(3), 71, 72 and 73 shall apply from 18 September 2010.

Except for the provisions referred to in the second paragraph, this Regulation shall apply from 18 June 2011, subject to the 2007 Hague Protocol being applicable in the Community by that date. Failing that, this Regulation shall apply from the date of application of that Protocol in the Community.

This Regulation shall be binding in its entirety and directly applicable in the Member States in accordance with the Treaty establishing the European Community.

*[Annexes I–IX omitted]*

## Commission Decision of 8 June 2009 on the intention of the United Kingdom to accept Council Regulation (EC) No 4/2009 on jurisdiction, applicable law, recognition and enforcement of decisions and cooperation in matters relating to maintenance obligations (notified under document number C(2009) 4427) (2009/451/EC)

[2009] OJ L149/73

THE COMMISSION OF THE EUROPEAN COMMUNITIES,

Having regard to the Treaty establishing the European Community, in particular to Article 11a thereof,

Having regard to the letter from the United Kingdom to the Council and the Commission of 15 January 2009,

Whereas:

(1) On 18 December 2008, the Council adopted Regulation (EC) No 4/2009 on jurisdiction, applicable law, recognition and enforcement of decisions and cooperation in matters relating to maintenance obligations.

(2) Pursuant to Article 1 of the Protocol on the position of the United Kingdom and Ireland, annexed to the Treaty on European Union and to the Treaty establishing the European Community, the United Kingdom did not participate in the adoption of Regulation (EC) No 4/2009.

(3) In accordance with Article 4 of that Protocol, the United Kingdom notified the Council and the Commission by letter of 15 January 2009, received by the Commission on 17 January 2009, of its intention to accept Regulation (EC) No 4/2009.

(4) On 21 April 2009 the Commission gave a positive opinion to the Council on the United Kingdom's intention to accept Regulation (EC) No 4/2009,

HAS ADOPTED THIS DECISION:

*Article 1*

Regulation (EC) No 4/2009 shall apply to the United Kingdom in accordance with Article 2.

*Article 2*

Regulation (EC) No 4/2009 shall enter into force in the United Kingdom on 1 July 2009.

Article 2(2), Article 47(3) and Articles 71, 72 and 73 of the Regulation shall apply from 18 September 2010.

The other provisions of the Regulation shall apply from 18 June 2011, subject to the 2007 Hague Protocol on the law applicable to maintenance obligations being applicable in the Community by that date. Failing that, the Regulation shall apply from the date of application of that Protocol in the Community.

*Article 3*

This Decision is addressed to the Member States.

# Regulation (EU) No 1215/2012 of the European Parliament and of the Council of 12 December 2012 on jurisdiction and the recognition and enforcement of judgments in civil and commercial matters (recast)

[2012] OJ L351/1

THE EUROPEAN PARLIAMENT AND THE COUNCIL OF THE EUROPEAN UNION,

Having regard to the Treaty on the Functioning of the European Union, and in particular Article 67(4) and points (a), (c) and (e) of Article 81(2) thereof,

Having regard to the proposal from the European Commission,

After transmission of the draft legislative act to the national parliaments,

Having regard to the opinion of the European Economic and Social Committee ,

Acting in accordance with the ordinary legislative procedure,

Whereas:

(1) On 21 April 2009, the Commission adopted a report on the application of Council Regulation (EC) No 44/2001 of 22 December 2000 on jurisdiction and the recognition and enforcement of judgments in civil and commercial matters. The report concluded that, in general, the operation of that Regulation is satisfactory, but that it is desirable to improve the application of certain of its provisions, to further facilitate the free circulation of judgments and to further enhance access to justice. Since a number of amendments are to be made to that Regulation it should, in the interests of clarity, be recast.

(2) At its meeting in Brussels on 10 and 11 December 2009, the European Council adopted a new multiannual programme entitled 'The Stockholm Programme – an open and secure Europe serving and protecting citizens'. In the Stockholm Programme the European Council considered that the process of abolishing all intermediate measures (the exequatur) should be continued during the period covered by that Programme. At the same time the abolition of the exequatur should also be accompanied by a series of safeguards.

(3) The Union has set itself the objective of maintaining and developing an area of freedom, security and justice, inter alia, by facilitating access to justice, in particular through the principle of mutual recognition of judicial and extra-judicial decisions in civil matters. For the gradual establishment of such an area, the Union is to adopt measures relating to judicial cooperation in civil matters having cross-border implications, particularly when necessary for the proper functioning of the internal market.

(4) Certain differences between national rules governing jurisdiction and recognition of judgments hamper the sound operation of the internal market. Provisions to unify the rules of conflict of jurisdiction in civil and commercial matters, and to ensure rapid and simple recognition and enforcement of judgments given in a Member State, are essential.

(5) Such provisions fall within the area of judicial cooperation in civil matters within the meaning of Article 81 of the Treaty on the Functioning of the European Union (TFEU).

(6) In order to attain the objective of free circulation of judgments in civil and commercial matters, it is necessary and appropriate that the rules governing jurisdiction and the recognition and enforcement of judgments be governed by a legal instrument of the Union which is binding and directly applicable.

(7) On 27 September 1968, the then Member States of the European Communities, acting under Article 220, fourth indent, of the Treaty establishing the European Economic Community, concluded the Brussels Convention on Jurisdiction and the Enforcement of Judgments in Civil and Commercial Matters, subsequently amended by conventions on the accession to that Convention of new Member States ('the 1968 Brussels Convention'). On 16 September 1988, the then Member States of the European Communities and certain EFTA States concluded the Lugano Convention on Jurisdiction

and the Enforcement of Judgments in Civil and Commercial Matters ('the 1988 Lugano Convention'), which is a parallel convention to the 1968 Brussels Convention. The 1988 Lugano Convention became applicable to Poland on 1 February 2000.

(8) On 22 December 2000, the Council adopted Regulation (EC) No 44/2001, which replaces the 1968 Brussels Convention with regard to the territories of the Member States covered by the TFEU, as between the Member States except Denmark. By Council Decision 2006/325/EC, the Community concluded an agreement with Denmark ensuring the application of the provisions of Regulation (EC) No 44/2001 in Denmark. The 1988 Lugano Convention was revised by the Convention on Jurisdiction and the Recognition and Enforcement of Judgments in Civil and Commercial Matters, signed at Lugano on 30 October 2007 by the Community, Denmark, Iceland, Norway and Switzerland ('the 2007 Lugano Convention').

(9) The 1968 Brussels Convention continues to apply to the territories of the Member States which fall within the territorial scope of that Convention and which are excluded from this Regulation pursuant to Article 355 of the TFEU.

(10) The scope of this Regulation should cover all the main civil and commercial matters apart from certain well-defined matters, in particular maintenance obligations, which should be excluded from the scope of this Regulation following the adoption of Council Regulation (EC) No 4/2009 of 18 December 2008 on jurisdiction, applicable law, recognition and enforcement of decisions and cooperation in matters relating to maintenance obligations.

(11) For the purposes of this Regulation, courts or tribunals of the Member States should include courts or tribunals common to several Member States, such as the Benelux Court of Justice when it exercises jurisdiction on matters falling within the scope of this Regulation. Therefore, judgments given by such courts should be recognised and enforced in accordance with this Regulation.

(12) This Regulation should not apply to arbitration. Nothing in this Regulation should prevent the courts of a Member State, when seised of an action in a matter in respect of which the parties have entered into an arbitration agreement, from referring the parties to arbitration, from staying or dismissing the proceedings, or from examining whether the arbitration agreement is null and void, inoperative or incapable of being performed, in accordance with their national law.

A ruling given by a court of a Member State as to whether or not an arbitration agreement is null and void, inoperative or incapable of being performed should not be subject to the rules of recognition and enforcement laid down in this Regulation, regardless of whether the court decided on this as a principal issue or as an incidental question.

On the other hand, where a court of a Member State, exercising jurisdiction under this Regulation or under national law, has determined that an arbitration agreement is null and void, inoperative or incapable of being performed, this should not preclude that court's judgment on the substance of the matter from being recognised or, as the case may be, enforced in accordance with this Regulation. This should be without prejudice to the competence of the courts of the Member States to decide on the recognition and enforcement of arbitral awards in accordance with the Convention on the Recognition and Enforcement of Foreign Arbitral Awards, done at New York on 10 June 1958 ('the 1958 New York Convention'), which takes precedence over this Regulation.

This Regulation should not apply to any action or ancillary proceedings relating to, in particular, the establishment of an arbitral tribunal, the powers of arbitrators, the conduct of an arbitration procedure or any other aspects of such a procedure, nor to any action or judgment concerning the annulment, review, appeal, recognition or enforcement of an arbitral award.

(13) There must be a connection between proceedings to which this Regulation applies and the territory of the Member States. Accordingly, common rules of jurisdiction should, in principle, apply when the defendant is domiciled in a Member State.

(14) A defendant not domiciled in a Member State should in general be subject to the national rules of jurisdiction applicable in the territory of the Member State of the court seised.

However, in order to ensure the protection of consumers and employees, to safeguard the jurisdiction of the courts of the Member States in situations where they have exclusive jurisdiction and to respect the autonomy of the parties, certain rules of jurisdiction in this Regulation should apply regardless of the defendant's domicile.

(15)  The rules of jurisdiction should be highly predictable and founded on the principle that jurisdiction is generally based on the defendant's domicile. Jurisdiction should always be available on this ground save in a few well-defined situations in which the subject-matter of the dispute or the autonomy of the parties warrants a different connecting factor. The domicile of a legal person must be defined autonomously so as to make the common rules more transparent and avoid conflicts of jurisdiction.

(16)  In addition to the defendant's domicile, there should be alternative grounds of jurisdiction based on a close connection between the court and the action or in order to facilitate the sound administration of justice. The existence of a close connection should ensure legal certainty and avoid the possibility of the defendant being sued in a court of a Member State which he could not reasonably have foreseen. This is important, particularly in disputes concerning non-contractual obligations arising out of violations of privacy and rights relating to personality, including defamation.

(17)  The owner of a cultural object as defined in Article 1(1) of Council Directive 93/7/EEC of 15 March 1993 on the return of cultural objects unlawfully removed from the territory of a Member State should be able under this Regulation to initiate proceedings as regards a civil claim for the recovery, based on ownership, of such a cultural object in the courts for the place where the cultural object is situated at the time the court is seised. Such proceedings should be without prejudice to proceedings initiated under Directive 93/7/EEC.

(18)  In relation to insurance, consumer and employment contracts, the weaker party should be protected by rules of jurisdiction more favourable to his interests than the general rules.

(19)  The autonomy of the parties to a contract, other than an insurance, consumer or employment contract, where only limited autonomy to determine the courts having jurisdiction is allowed, should be respected subject to the exclusive grounds of jurisdiction laid down in this Regulation.

(20)  Where a question arises as to whether a choice-of-court agreement in favour of a court or the courts of a Member State is null and void as to its substantive validity, that question should be decided in accordance with the law of the Member State of the court or courts designated in the agreement, including the conflict-of-laws rules of that Member State.

(21)  In the interests of the harmonious administration of justice it is necessary to minimise the possibility of concurrent proceedings and to ensure that irreconcilable judgments will not be given in different Member States. There should be a clear and effective mechanism for resolving cases of *lis pendens* and related actions, and for obviating problems flowing from national differences as to the determination of the time when a case is regarded as pending. For the purposes of this Regulation, that time should be defined autonomously.

(22)  However, in order to enhance the effectiveness of exclusive choice-of-court agreements and to avoid abusive litigation tactics, it is necessary to provide for an exception to the general *lis pendens* rule in order to deal satisfactorily with a particular situation in which concurrent proceedings may arise. This is the situation where a court not designated in an exclusive choice-of-court agreement has been seised of proceedings and the designated court is seised subsequently of proceedings involving the same cause of action and between the same parties. In such a case, the court first seised should be required to stay its proceedings as soon as the designated court has been seised and until such time as the latter court declares that it has no jurisdiction under the exclusive choice-of-court agreement. This is to ensure that, in such a situation, the designated court has priority to decide on the validity of the agreement and on the extent to which the agreement applies to the dispute pending before it. The designated court should be able to proceed irrespective of whether the non-designated court has already decided on the stay of proceedings.

This exception should not cover situations where the parties have entered into conflicting exclusive choice-of-court agreements or where a court designated in an exclusive choice-of-court agreement has been seised first. In such cases, the general *lis pendens* rule of this Regulation should apply.

(23)  This Regulation should provide for a flexible mechanism allowing the courts of the Member States to take into account proceedings pending before the courts of third States, considering in particular

whether a judgment of a third State will be capable of recognition and enforcement in the Member State concerned under the law of that Member State and the proper administration of justice.

(24) When taking into account the proper administration of justice, the court of the Member State concerned should assess all the circumstances of the case before it. Such circumstances may include connections between the facts of the case and the parties and the third State concerned, the stage to which the proceedings in the third State have progressed by the time proceedings are initiated in the court of the Member State and whether or not the court of the third State can be expected to give a judgment within a reasonable time.

That assessment may also include consideration of the question whether the court of the third State has exclusive jurisdiction in the particular case in circumstances where a court of a Member State would have exclusive jurisdiction.

(25) The notion of provisional, including protective, measures should include, for example, protective orders aimed at obtaining information or preserving evidence as referred to in Articles 6 and 7 of Directive 2004/48/EC of the European Parliament and of the Council of 29 April 2004 on the enforcement of intellectual property rights. It should not include measures which are not of a protective nature, such as measures ordering the hearing of a witness. This should be without prejudice to the application of Council Regulation (EC) No 1206/2001 of 28 May 2001 on cooperation between the courts of the Member States in the taking of evidence in civil or commercial matters.

(26) Mutual trust in the administration of justice in the Union justifies the principle that judgments given in a Member State should be recognised in all Member States without the need for any special procedure. In addition, the aim of making cross-border litigation less time-consuming and costly justifies the abolition of the declaration of enforceability prior to enforcement in the Member State addressed. As a result, a judgment given by the courts of a Member State should be treated as if it had been given in the Member State addressed.

(27) For the purposes of the free circulation of judgments, a judgment given in a Member State should be recognised and enforced in another Member State even if it is given against a person not domiciled in a Member State.

(28) Where a judgment contains a measure or order which is not known in the law of the Member State addressed, that measure or order, including any right indicated therein, should, to the extent possible, be adapted to one which, under the law of that Member State, has equivalent effects attached to it and pursues similar aims. How, and by whom, the adaptation is to be carried out should be determined by each Member State.

(29) The direct enforcement in the Member State addressed of a judgment given in another Member State without a declaration of enforceability should not jeopardise respect for the rights of the defence. Therefore, the person against whom enforcement is sought should be able to apply for refusal of the recognition or enforcement of a judgment if he considers one of the grounds for refusal of recognition to be present. This should include the ground that he had not had the opportunity to arrange for his defence where the judgment was given in default of appearance in a civil action linked to criminal proceedings. It should also include the grounds which could be invoked on the basis of an agreement between the Member State addressed and a third State concluded pursuant to Article 59 of the 1968 Brussels Convention.

(30) A party challenging the enforcement of a judgment given in another Member State should, to the extent possible and in accordance with the legal system of the Member State addressed, be able to invoke, in the same procedure, in addition to the grounds for refusal provided for in this Regulation, the grounds for refusal available under national law and within the time-limits laid down in that law.

The recognition of a judgment should, however, be refused only if one or more of the grounds for refusal provided for in this Regulation are present.

(31) Pending a challenge to the enforcement of a judgment, it should be possible for the courts in the Member State addressed, during the entire proceedings relating to such a challenge, including any appeal, to allow the enforcement to proceed subject to a limitation of the enforcement or to the provision of security.

(32) In order to inform the person against whom enforcement is sought of the enforcement of a judgment given in another Member State, the certificate established under this Regulation, if necessary accompanied by the judgment, should be served on that person in reasonable time before the first enforcement measure. In this context, the first enforcement measure should mean the first enforcement measure after such service.

(33) Where provisional, including protective, measures are ordered by a court having jurisdiction as to the substance of the matter, their free circulation should be ensured under this Regulation. However, provisional, including protective, measures which were ordered by such a court without the defendant being summoned to appear should not be recognised and enforced under this Regulation unless the judgment containing the measure is served on the defendant prior to enforcement. This should not preclude the recognition and enforcement of such measures under national law. Where provisional, including protective, measures are ordered by a court of a Member State not having jurisdiction as to the substance of the matter, the effect of such measures should be confined, under this Regulation, to the territory of that Member State.

(34) Continuity between the 1968 Brussels Convention, Regulation (EC) No 44/2001 and this Regulation should be ensured, and transitional provisions should be laid down to that end. The same need for continuity applies as regards the interpretation by the Court of Justice of the European Union of the 1968 Brussels Convention and of the Regulations replacing it.

(35) Respect for international commitments entered into by the Member States means that this Regulation should not affect conventions relating to specific matters to which the Member States are parties.

(36) Without prejudice to the obligations of the Member States under the Treaties, this Regulation should not affect the application of bilateral conventions and agreements between a third State and a Member State concluded before the date of entry into force of Regulation (EC) No 44/2001 which concern matters governed by this Regulation.

(37) In order to ensure that the certificates to be used in connection with the recognition or enforcement of judgments, authentic instruments and court settlements under this Regulation are kept up-to-date, the power to adopt acts in accordance with Article 290 of the TFEU should be delegated to the Commission in respect of amendments to Annexes I and II to this Regulation. It is of particular importance that the Commission carry out appropriate consultations during its preparatory work, including at expert level. The Commission, when preparing and drawing up delegated acts, should ensure a simultaneous, timely and appropriate transmission of relevant documents to the European Parliament and to the Council.

(38) This Regulation respects fundamental rights and observes the principles recognised in the Charter of Fundamental Rights of the European Union, in particular the right to an effective remedy and to a fair trial guaranteed in Article 47 of the Charter.

(39) Since the objective of this Regulation cannot be sufficiently achieved by the Member States and can be better achieved at Union level, the Union may adopt measures in accordance with the principle of subsidiarity as set out in Article 5 of the Treaty on European Union (TEU). In accordance with the principle of proportionality, as set out in that Article, this Regulation does not go beyond what is necessary in order to achieve that objective.

(40) The United Kingdom and Ireland, in accordance with Article 3 of the Protocol on the position of the United Kingdom and Ireland, annexed to the TEU and to the then Treaty establishing the European Community, took part in the adoption and application of Regulation (EC) No 44/2001. In accordance with Article 3 of Protocol No 21 on the position of the United Kingdom and Ireland in respect of the area of freedom, security and justice, annexed to the TEU and to the TFEU, the United Kingdom and Ireland have notified their wish to take part in the adoption and application of this Regulation.

(41) In accordance with Articles 1 and 2 of Protocol No 22 on the position of Denmark annexed to the TEU and to the TFEU, Denmark is not taking part in the adoption of this Regulation and is not bound by it or subject to its application, without prejudice to the possibility for Denmark of applying the amendments to Regulation (EC) No 44/2001 pursuant to Article 3 of the Agreement of 19 October 2005

between the European Community and the Kingdom of Denmark on jurisdiction and the recognition and enforcement of judgments in civil and commercial matters ,

HAVE ADOPTED THIS REGULATION:

## CHAPTER I

## SCOPE AND DEFINITIONS

*Article 1*

1. This Regulation shall apply in civil and commercial matters whatever the nature of the court or tribunal. It shall not extend, in particular, to revenue, customs or administrative matters or to the liability of the State for acts and omissions in the exercise of State authority (*acta iure imperii*).

2. This Regulation shall not apply to:

(a)  the status or legal capacity of natural persons, rights in property arising out of a matrimonial relationship or out of a relationship deemed by the law applicable to such relationship to have comparable effects to marriage;

(b)  bankruptcy, proceedings relating to the winding-up of insolvent companies or other legal persons, judicial arrangements, compositions and analogous proceedings;

(c)  social security;

(d)  arbitration;

(e)  maintenance obligations arising from a family relationship, parentage, marriage or affinity;

(f)  wills and succession, including maintenance obligations arising by reason of death.

*Article 2*

For the purposes of this Regulation:

(a)  'judgment' means any judgment given by a court or tribunal of a Member State, whatever the judgment may be called, including a decree, order, decision or writ of execution, as well as a decision on the determination of costs or expenses by an officer of the court.

For the purposes of Chapter III, 'judgment' includes provisional, including protective, measures ordered by a court or tribunal which by virtue of this Regulation has jurisdiction as to the substance of the matter. It does not include a provisional, including protective, measure which is ordered by such a court or tribunal without the defendant being summoned to appear, unless the judgment containing the measure is served on the defendant prior to enforcement;

(b)  'court settlement' means a settlement which has been approved by a court of a Member State or concluded before a court of a Member State in the course of proceedings;

(c)  'authentic instrument' means a document which has been formally drawn up or registered as an authentic instrument in the Member State of origin and the authenticity of which:

(i)  relates to the signature and the content of the instrument; and

(ii)  has been established by a public authority or other authority empowered for that purpose;

(d)  'Member State of origin' means the Member State in which, as the case may be, the judgment has been given, the court settlement has been approved or concluded, or the authentic instrument has been formally drawn up or registered;

(e)  'Member State addressed' means the Member State in which the recognition of the judgment is invoked or in which the enforcement of the judgment, the court settlement or the authentic instrument is sought;

(f)  'court of origin' means the court which has given the judgment the recognition of which is invoked or the enforcement of which is sought.

*Article 3*

For the purposes of this Regulation, 'court' includes the following authorities to the extent that they have jurisdiction in matters falling within the scope of this Regulation:

(a) in Hungary, in summary proceedings concerning orders to pay (fizetési meghagyásos eljárás), the notary (közjegyző);

(b) in Sweden, in summary proceedings concerning orders to pay (betalningsföreläggande) and assistance (handräckning), the Enforcement Authority (Kronofogdemyndigheten).

## CHAPTER II

## JURISDICTION

### SECTION 1

**General provisions**

*Article 4*

1. Subject to this Regulation, persons domiciled in a Member State shall, whatever their nationality, be sued in the courts of that Member State.

2. Persons who are not nationals of the Member State in which they are domiciled shall be governed by the rules of jurisdiction applicable to nationals of that Member State.

*Article 5*

1. Persons domiciled in a Member State may be sued in the courts of another Member State only by virtue of the rules set out in Sections 2 to 7 of this Chapter.

2. In particular, the rules of national jurisdiction of which the Member States are to notify the Commission pursuant to point (a) of Article 76(1) shall not be applicable as against the persons referred to in paragraph 1.

*Article 6*

1. If the defendant is not domiciled in a Member State, the jurisdiction of the courts of each Member State shall, subject to Article 18(1), Article 21(2) and Articles 24 and 25, be determined by the law of that Member State.

2. As against such a defendant, any person domiciled in a Member State may, whatever his nationality, avail himself in that Member State of the rules of jurisdiction there in force, and in particular those of which the Member States are to notify the Commission pursuant to point (a) of Article 76(1), in the same way as nationals of that Member State.

### SECTION 2

**Special jurisdiction**

*Article 7*

A person domiciled in a Member State may be sued in another Member State:

(1)

    (a) in matters relating to a contract, in the courts for the place of performance of the obligation in question;

    (b) for the purpose of this provision and unless otherwise agreed, the place of performance of the obligation in question shall be:

    — in the case of the sale of goods, the place in a Member State where, under the contract, the goods were delivered or should have been delivered,

— in the case of the provision of services, the place in a Member State where, under the contract, the services were provided or should have been provided;

(c) if point (b) does not apply then point (a) applies;

(2) in matters relating to tort, delict or quasi-delict, in the courts for the place where the harmful event occurred or may occur;

(3) as regards a civil claim for damages or restitution which is based on an act giving rise to criminal proceedings, in the court seised of those proceedings, to the extent that that court has jurisdiction under its own law to entertain civil proceedings;

(4) as regards a civil claim for the recovery, based on ownership, of a cultural object as defined in point 1 of Article 1 of Directive 93/7/EEC initiated by the person claiming the right to recover such an object, in the courts for the place where the cultural object is situated at the time when the court is seised;

(5) as regards a dispute arising out of the operations of a branch, agency or other establishment, in the courts for the place where the branch, agency or other establishment is situated;

(6) as regards a dispute brought against a settlor, trustee or beneficiary of a trust created by the operation of a statute, or by a written instrument, or created orally and evidenced in writing, in the courts of the Member State in which the trust is domiciled;

(7) as regards a dispute concerning the payment of remuneration claimed in respect of the salvage of a cargo or freight, in the court under the authority of which the cargo or freight in question:

(a) has been arrested to secure such payment; or

(b) could have been so arrested, but bail or other security has been given;

provided that this provision shall apply only if it is claimed that the defendant has an interest in the cargo or freight or had such an interest at the time of salvage.

## Article 8

A person domiciled in a Member State may also be sued:

(1) where he is one of a number of defendants, in the courts for the place where any one of them is domiciled, provided the claims are so closely connected that it is expedient to hear and determine them together to avoid the risk of irreconcilable judgments resulting from separate proceedings;

(2) as a third party in an action on a warranty or guarantee or in any other third-party proceedings, in the court seised of the original proceedings, unless these were instituted solely with the object of removing him from the jurisdiction of the court which would be competent in his case;

(3) on a counter-claim arising from the same contract or facts on which the original claim was based, in the court in which the original claim is pending;

(4) in matters relating to a contract, if the action may be combined with an action against the same defendant in matters relating to rights *in rem* in immovable property, in the court of the Member State in which the property is situated.

## Article 9

Where by virtue of this Regulation a court of a Member State has jurisdiction in actions relating to liability from the use or operation of a ship, that court, or any other court substituted for this purpose by the internal law of that Member State, shall also have jurisdiction over claims for limitation of such liability.

SECTION 3

## Jurisdiction in matters relating to insurance

*Article 10*

In matters relating to insurance, jurisdiction shall be determined by this Section, without prejudice to Article 6 and point 5 of Article 7.

*Article 11*

1. An insurer domiciled in a Member State may be sued:

(a)  in the courts of the Member State in which he is domiciled;

(b)  in another Member State, in the case of actions brought by the policyholder, the insured or a beneficiary, in the courts for the place where the claimant is domiciled; or

(c)  if he is a co-insurer, in the courts of a Member State in which proceedings are brought against the leading insurer.

2. An insurer who is not domiciled in a Member State but has a branch, agency or other establishment in one of the Member States shall, in disputes arising out of the operations of the branch, agency or establishment, be deemed to be domiciled in that Member State.

*Article 12*

In respect of liability insurance or insurance of immovable property, the insurer may in addition be sued in the courts for the place where the harmful event occurred. The same applies if movable and immovable property are covered by the same insurance policy and both are adversely affected by the same contingency.

*Article 13*

1. In respect of liability insurance, the insurer may also, if the law of the court permits it, be joined in proceedings which the injured party has brought against the insured.

2. Articles 10, 11 and 12 shall apply to actions brought by the injured party directly against the insurer, where such direct actions are permitted.

3. If the law governing such direct actions provides that the policyholder or the insured may be joined as a party to the action, the same court shall have jurisdiction over them.

*Article 14*

1. Without prejudice to Article 13(3), an insurer may bring proceedings only in the courts of the Member State in which the defendant is domiciled, irrespective of whether he is the policyholder, the insured or a beneficiary.

2. The provisions of this Section shall not affect the right to bring a counter-claim in the court in which, in accordance with this Section, the original claim is pending.

*Article 15*

The provisions of this Section may be departed from only by an agreement:

(1)  which is entered into after the dispute has arisen;

(2)  which allows the policyholder, the insured or a beneficiary to bring proceedings in courts other than those indicated in this Section;

(3)  which is concluded between a policyholder and an insurer, both of whom are at the time of conclusion of the contract domiciled or habitually resident in the same Member State, and which has the effect of conferring jurisdiction on the courts of that Member State even if the harmful event were to occur abroad, provided that such an agreement is not contrary to the law of that Member State;

(4) which is concluded with a policyholder who is not domiciled in a Member State, except in so far as the insurance is compulsory or relates to immovable property in a Member State; or

(5) which relates to a contract of insurance in so far as it covers one or more of the risks set out in Article 16.

*Article 16*

The following are the risks referred to in point 5 of Article 15:

(1) any loss of or damage to:

    (a) seagoing ships, installations situated offshore or on the high seas, or aircraft, arising from perils which relate to their use for commercial purposes;

    (b) goods in transit other than passengers' baggage where the transit consists of or includes carriage by such ships or aircraft;

(2) any liability, other than for bodily injury to passengers or loss of or damage to their baggage:

    (a) arising out of the use or operation of ships, installations or aircraft as referred to in point 1(a) in so far as, in respect of the latter, the law of the Member State in which such aircraft are registered does not prohibit agreements on jurisdiction regarding insurance of such risks;

    (b) for loss or damage caused by goods in transit as described in point 1(b);

(3) any financial loss connected with the use or operation of ships, installations or aircraft as referred to in point 1(a), in particular loss of freight or charter-hire;

(4) any risk or interest connected with any of those referred to in points 1 to 3;

(5) notwithstanding points 1 to 4, all 'large risks' as defined in Directive 2009/138/EC of the European Parliament and of the Council of 25 November 2009 on the taking-up and pursuit of the business of Insurance and Reinsurance (Solvency II).

## SECTION 4

### Jurisdiction over consumer contracts

*Article 17*

1. In matters relating to a contract concluded by a person, the consumer, for a purpose which can be regarded as being outside his trade or profession, jurisdiction shall be determined by this Section, without prejudice to Article 6 and point 5 of Article 7, if:

(a) it is a contract for the sale of goods on instalment credit terms;

(b) it is a contract for a loan repayable by instalments, or for any other form of credit, made to finance the sale of goods; or

(c) in all other cases, the contract has been concluded with a person who pursues commercial or professional activities in the Member State of the consumer's domicile or, by any means, directs such activities to that Member State or to several States including that Member State, and the contract falls within the scope of such activities.

2. Where a consumer enters into a contract with a party who is not domiciled in a Member State but has a branch, agency or other establishment in one of the Member States, that party shall, in disputes arising out of the operations of the branch, agency or establishment, be deemed to be domiciled in that Member State.

3. This Section shall not apply to a contract of transport other than a contract which, for an inclusive price, provides for a combination of travel and accommodation.

*Article 18*

1. A consumer may bring proceedings against the other party to a contract either in the courts of the Member State in which that party is domiciled or, regardless of the domicile of the other party, in the courts for the place where the consumer is domiciled.

2. Proceedings may be brought against a consumer by the other party to the contract only in the courts of the Member State in which the consumer is domiciled.

3. This Article shall not affect the right to bring a counter-claim in the court in which, in accordance with this Section, the original claim is pending.

## Article 19

The provisions of this Section may be departed from only by an agreement:

(1)  which is entered into after the dispute has arisen;

(2)  which allows the consumer to bring proceedings in courts other than those indicated in this Section; or

(3)  which is entered into by the consumer and the other party to the contract, both of whom are at the time of conclusion of the contract domiciled or habitually resident in the same Member State, and which confers jurisdiction on the courts of that Member State, provided that such an agreement is not contrary to the law of that Member State.

## SECTION 5

### Jurisdiction over individual contracts of employment

## Article 20

1. In matters relating to individual contracts of employment, jurisdiction shall be determined by this Section, without prejudice to Article 6, point 5 of Article 7 and, in the case of proceedings brought against an employer, point 1 of Article 8.

2. Where an employee enters into an individual contract of employment with an employer who is not domiciled in a Member State but has a branch, agency or other establishment in one of the Member States, the employer shall, in disputes arising out of the operations of the branch, agency or establishment, be deemed to be domiciled in that Member State.

## Article 21

1. An employer domiciled in a Member State may be sued:

(a)  in the courts of the Member State in which he is domiciled; or

(b)  in another Member State:

   (i)   in the courts for the place where or from where the employee habitually carries out his work or in the courts for the last place where he did so; or

   (ii)  if the employee does not or did not habitually carry out his work in any one country, in the courts for the place where the business which engaged the employee is or was situated.

2. An employer not domiciled in a Member State may be sued in a court of a Member State in accordance with point (b) of paragraph 1.

## Article 22

1. An employer may bring proceedings only in the courts of the Member State in which the employee is domiciled.

2. The provisions of this Section shall not affect the right to bring a counter-claim in the court in which, in accordance with this Section, the original claim is pending.

## Article 23

The provisions of this Section may be departed from only by an agreement:

(1)  which is entered into after the dispute has arisen; or

(2)  which allows the employee to bring proceedings in courts other than those indicated in this Section.

SECTION 6

## Exclusive jurisdiction

*Article 24*

The following courts of a Member State shall have exclusive jurisdiction, regardless of the domicile of the parties:

(1) in proceedings which have as their object rights *in rem* in immovable property or tenancies of immovable property, the courts of the Member State in which the property is situated.

However, in proceedings which have as their object tenancies of immovable property concluded for temporary private use for a maximum period of six consecutive months, the courts of the Member State in which the defendant is domiciled shall also have jurisdiction, provided that the tenant is a natural person and that the landlord and the tenant are domiciled in the same Member State;

(2) in proceedings which have as their object the validity of the constitution, the nullity or the dissolution of companies or other legal persons or associations of natural or legal persons, or the validity of the decisions of their organs, the courts of the Member State in which the company, legal person or association has its seat. In order to determine that seat, the court shall apply its rules of private international law;

(3) in proceedings which have as their object the validity of entries in public registers, the courts of the Member State in which the register is kept;

(4) in proceedings concerned with the registration or validity of patents, trade marks, designs, or other similar rights required to be deposited or registered, irrespective of whether the issue is raised by way of an action or as a defence, the courts of the Member State in which the deposit or registration has been applied for, has taken place or is under the terms of an instrument of the Union or an international convention deemed to have taken place.

Without prejudice to the jurisdiction of the European Patent Office under the Convention on the Grant of European Patents, signed at Munich on 5 October 1973, the courts of each Member State shall have exclusive jurisdiction in proceedings concerned with the registration or validity of any European patent granted for that Member State;

(5) in proceedings concerned with the enforcement of judgments, the courts of the Member State in which the judgment has been or is to be enforced.

SECTION 7

## Prorogation of jurisdiction

*Article 25*

1. If the parties, regardless of their domicile, have agreed that a court or the courts of a Member State are to have jurisdiction to settle any disputes which have arisen or which may arise in connection with a particular legal relationship, that court or those courts shall have jurisdiction, unless the agreement is null and void as to its substantive validity under the law of that Member State. Such jurisdiction shall be exclusive unless the parties have agreed otherwise. The agreement conferring jurisdiction shall be either:

(a) in writing or evidenced in writing;

(b) in a form which accords with practices which the parties have established between themselves; or

(c) in international trade or commerce, in a form which accords with a usage of which the parties are or ought to have been aware and which in such trade or commerce is widely known to, and regularly observed by, parties to contracts of the type involved in the particular trade or commerce concerned.

2. Any communication by electronic means which provides a durable record of the agreement shall be equivalent to 'writing'.

3. The court or courts of a Member State on which a trust instrument has conferred jurisdiction shall have exclusive jurisdiction in any proceedings brought against a settlor, trustee or beneficiary, if relations between those persons or their rights or obligations under the trust are involved.

4. Agreements or provisions of a trust instrument conferring jurisdiction shall have no legal force if they are contrary to Articles 15, 19 or 23, or if the courts whose jurisdiction they purport to exclude have exclusive jurisdiction by virtue of Article 24.

5. An agreement conferring jurisdiction which forms part of a contract shall be treated as an agreement independent of the other terms of the contract.

The validity of the agreement conferring jurisdiction cannot be contested solely on the ground that the contract is not valid.

## Article 26

1. Apart from jurisdiction derived from other provisions of this Regulation, a court of a Member State before which a defendant enters an appearance shall have jurisdiction. This rule shall not apply where appearance was entered to contest the jurisdiction, or where another court has exclusive jurisdiction by virtue of Article 24.

2. In matters referred to in Sections 3, 4 or 5 where the policyholder, the insured, a beneficiary of the insurance contract, the injured party, the consumer or the employee is the defendant, the court shall, before assuming jurisdiction under paragraph 1, ensure that the defendant is informed of his right to contest the jurisdiction of the court and of the consequences of entering or not entering an appearance.

## SECTION 8

## Examination as to jurisdiction and admissibility

## Article 27

Where a court of a Member State is seised of a claim which is principally concerned with a matter over which the courts of another Member State have exclusive jurisdiction by virtue of Article 24, it shall declare of its own motion that it has no jurisdiction.

## Article 28

1. Where a defendant domiciled in one Member State is sued in a court of another Member State and does not enter an appearance, the court shall declare of its own motion that it has no jurisdiction unless its jurisdiction is derived from the provisions of this Regulation.

2. The court shall stay the proceedings so long as it is not shown that the defendant has been able to receive the document instituting the proceedings or an equivalent document in sufficient time to enable him to arrange for his defence, or that all necessary steps have been taken to this end.

3. Article 19 of Regulation (EC) No 1393/2007 of the European Parliament and of the Council of 13 November 2007 on the service in the Member States of judicial and extrajudicial documents in civil or commercial matters (service of documents) shall apply instead of paragraph 2 of this Article if the document instituting the proceedings or an equivalent document had to be transmitted from one Member State to another pursuant to that Regulation.

4. Where Regulation (EC) No 1393/2007 is not applicable, Article 15 of the Hague Convention of 15 November 1965 on the Service Abroad of Judicial and Extrajudicial Documents in Civil or Commercial Matters shall apply if the document instituting the proceedings or an equivalent document had to be transmitted abroad pursuant to that Convention.

SECTION 9

## *Lis pendens* — related actions

*Article 29*

1. Without prejudice to Article 31(2), where proceedings involving the same cause of action and between the same parties are brought in the courts of different Member States, any court other than the court first seised shall of its own motion stay its proceedings until such time as the jurisdiction of the court first seised is established.

2. In cases referred to in paragraph 1, upon request by a court seised of the dispute, any other court seised shall without delay inform the former court of the date when it was seised in accordance with Article 32.

3. Where the jurisdiction of the court first seised is established, any court other than the court first seised shall decline jurisdiction in favour of that court.

*Article 30*

1. Where related actions are pending in the courts of different Member States, any court other than the court first seised may stay its proceedings.

2. Where the action in the court first seised is pending at first instance, any other court may also, on the application of one of the parties, decline jurisdiction if the court first seised has jurisdiction over the actions in question and its law permits the consolidation thereof.

3. For the purposes of this Article, actions are deemed to be related where they are so closely connected that it is expedient to hear and determine them together to avoid the risk of irreconcilable judgments resulting from separate proceedings.

*Article 31*

1. Where actions come within the exclusive jurisdiction of several courts, any court other than the court first seised shall decline jurisdiction in favour of that court.

2. Without prejudice to Article 26, where a court of a Member State on which an agreement as referred to in Article 25 confers exclusive jurisdiction is seised, any court of another Member State shall stay the proceedings until such time as the court seised on the basis of the agreement declares that it has no jurisdiction under the agreement.

3. Where the court designated in the agreement has established jurisdiction in accordance with the agreement, any court of another Member State shall decline jurisdiction in favour of that court.

4. Paragraphs 2 and 3 shall not apply to matters referred to in Sections 3, 4 or 5 where the policyholder, the insured, a beneficiary of the insurance contract, the injured party, the consumer or the employee is the claimant and the agreement is not valid under a provision contained within those Sections.

*Article 32*

1. For the purposes of this Section, a court shall be deemed to be seised:

(a) at the time when the document instituting the proceedings or an equivalent document is lodged with the court, provided that the claimant has not subsequently failed to take the steps he was required to take to have service effected on the defendant; or

(b) if the document has to be served before being lodged with the court, at the time when it is received by the authority responsible for service, provided that the claimant has not subsequently failed to take the steps he was required to take to have the document lodged with the court.

The authority responsible for service referred to in point (b) shall be the first authority receiving the documents to be served.

2. The court, or the authority responsible for service, referred to in paragraph 1, shall note, respectively, the date of the lodging of the document instituting the proceedings or the equivalent document, or the date of receipt of the documents to be served.

*Article 33*

1. Where jurisdiction is based on Article 4 or on Articles 7, 8 or 9 and proceedings are pending before a court of a third State at the time when a court in a Member State is seised of an action involving the same cause of action and between the same parties as the proceedings in the court of the third State, the court of the Member State may stay the proceedings if:

(a) it is expected that the court of the third State will give a judgment capable of recognition and, where applicable, of enforcement in that Member State; and

(b) the court of the Member State is satisfied that a stay is necessary for the proper administration of justice.

2. The court of the Member State may continue the proceedings at any time if:

(a) the proceedings in the court of the third State are themselves stayed or discontinued;

(b) it appears to the court of the Member State that the proceedings in the court of the third State are unlikely to be concluded within a reasonable time; or

(c) the continuation of the proceedings is required for the proper administration of justice.

3. The court of the Member State shall dismiss the proceedings if the proceedings in the court of the third State are concluded and have resulted in a judgment capable of recognition and, where applicable, of enforcement in that Member State.

4. The court of the Member State shall apply this Article on the application of one of the parties or, where possible under national law, of its own motion.

*Article 34*

1. Where jurisdiction is based on Article 4 or on Articles 7, 8 or 9 and an action is pending before a court of a third State at the time when a court in a Member State is seised of an action which is related to the action in the court of the third State, the court of the Member State may stay the proceedings if:

(a) it is expedient to hear and determine the related actions together to avoid the risk of irreconcilable judgments resulting from separate proceedings;

(b) it is expected that the court of the third State will give a judgment capable of recognition and, where applicable, of enforcement in that Member State; and

(c) the court of the Member State is satisfied that a stay is necessary for the proper administration of justice.

2. The court of the Member State may continue the proceedings at any time if:

(a) it appears to the court of the Member State that there is no longer a risk of irreconcilable judgments;

(b) the proceedings in the court of the third State are themselves stayed or discontinued;

(c) it appears to the court of the Member State that the proceedings in the court of the third State are unlikely to be concluded within a reasonable time; or

(d) the continuation of the proceedings is required for the proper administration of justice.

3. The court of the Member State may dismiss the proceedings if the proceedings in the court of the third State are concluded and have resulted in a judgment capable of recognition and, where applicable, of enforcement in that Member State.

4. The court of the Member State shall apply this Article on the application of one of the parties or, where possible under national law, of its own motion.

SECTION 10

**Provisional, including protective, measures**

*Article 35*

Application may be made to the courts of a Member State for such provisional, including protective, measures as may be available under the law of that Member State, even if the courts of another Member State have jurisdiction as to the substance of the matter.

## CHAPTER III

## RECOGNITION AND ENFORCEMENT

### SECTION 1

### Recognition

*Article 36*

1. A judgment given in a Member State shall be recognised in the other Member States without any special procedure being required.

2. Any interested party may, in accordance with the procedure provided for in Subsection 2 of Section 3, apply for a decision that there are no grounds for refusal of recognition as referred to in Article 45.

3. If the outcome of proceedings in a court of a Member State depends on the determination of an incidental question of refusal of recognition, that court shall have jurisdiction over that question.

*Article 37*

1. A party who wishes to invoke in a Member State a judgment given in another Member State shall produce:

(a)   a copy of the judgment which satisfies the conditions necessary to establish its authenticity; and

(b)   the certificate issued pursuant to Article 53.

2. The court or authority before which a judgment given in another Member State is invoked may, where necessary, require the party invoking it to provide, in accordance with Article 57, a translation or a transliteration of the contents of the certificate referred to in point (b) of paragraph 1. The court or authority may require the party to provide a translation of the judgment instead of a translation of the contents of the certificate if it is unable to proceed without such a translation.

*Article 38*

The court or authority before which a judgment given in another Member State is invoked may suspend the proceedings, in whole or in part, if:

(a)   the judgment is challenged in the Member State of origin; or

(b)   an application has been submitted for a decision that there are no grounds for refusal of recognition as referred to in Article 45 or for a decision that the recognition is to be refused on the basis of one of those grounds.

### SECTION 2

### Enforcement

*Article 39*

A judgment given in a Member State which is enforceable in that Member State shall be enforceable in the other Member States without any declaration of enforceability being required.

*Article 40*

An enforceable judgment shall carry with it by operation of law the power to proceed to any protective measures which exist under the law of the Member State addressed.

*Article 41*

1. Subject to the provisions of this Section, the procedure for the enforcement of judgments given in another Member State shall be governed by the law of the Member State addressed. A judgment given in a Member State which is enforceable in the Member State addressed shall be enforced there under the same conditions as a judgment given in the Member State addressed.

2. Notwithstanding paragraph 1, the grounds for refusal or of suspension of enforcement under the law of the Member State addressed shall apply in so far as they are not incompatible with the grounds referred to in Article 45.

3. The party seeking the enforcement of a judgment given in another Member State shall not be required to have a postal address in the Member State addressed. Nor shall that party be required to have an authorised representative in the Member State addressed unless such a representative is mandatory irrespective of the nationality or the domicile of the parties.

## Article 42

1. For the purposes of enforcement in a Member State of a judgment given in another Member State, the applicant shall provide the competent enforcement authority with:

(a)  a copy of the judgment which satisfies the conditions necessary to establish its authenticity; and

(b)  the certificate issued pursuant to Article 53, certifying that the judgment is enforceable and containing an extract of the judgment as well as, where appropriate, relevant information on the recoverable costs of the proceedings and the calculation of interest.

2. For the purposes of enforcement in a Member State of a judgment given in another Member State ordering a provisional, including a protective, measure, the applicant shall provide the competent enforcement authority with:

(a)  a copy of the judgment which satisfies the conditions necessary to establish its authenticity;

(b)  the certificate issued pursuant to Article 53, containing a description of the measure and certifying that:

(i)   the court has jurisdiction as to the substance of the matter;

(ii)  the judgment is enforceable in the Member State of origin; and

(c)  where the measure was ordered without the defendant being summoned to appear, proof of service of the judgment.

3. The competent enforcement authority may, where necessary, require the applicant to provide, in accordance with Article 57, a translation or a transliteration of the contents of the certificate.

4. The competent enforcement authority may require the applicant to provide a translation of the judgment only if it is unable to proceed without such a translation.

## Article 43

1. Where enforcement is sought of a judgment given in another Member State, the certificate issued pursuant to Article 53 shall be served on the person against whom the enforcement is sought prior to the first enforcement measure. The certificate shall be accompanied by the judgment, if not already served on that person.

2. Where the person against whom enforcement is sought is domiciled in a Member State other than the Member State of origin, he may request a translation of the judgment in order to contest the enforcement if the judgment is not written in or accompanied by a translation into either of the following languages:

(a)  a language which he understands; or

(b)  the official language of the Member State in which he is domiciled or, where there are several official languages in that Member State, the official language or one of the official languages of the place where he is domiciled.

Where a translation of the judgment is requested under the first subparagraph, no measures of enforcement may be taken other than protective measures until that translation has been provided to the person against whom enforcement is sought.

This paragraph shall not apply if the judgment has already been served on the person against whom enforcement is sought in one of the languages referred to in the first subparagraph or is accompanied by a translation into one of those languages.

3. This Article shall not apply to the enforcement of a protective measure in a judgment or where the person seeking enforcement proceeds to protective measures in accordance with Article 40.

### Article 44

1. In the event of an application for refusal of enforcement of a judgment pursuant to Subsection 2 of Section 3, the court in the Member State addressed may, on the application of the person against whom enforcement is sought:

(a)  limit the enforcement proceedings to protective measures;

(b)  make enforcement conditional on the provision of such security as it shall determine; or

(c)  suspend, either wholly or in part, the enforcement proceedings.

2. The competent authority in the Member State addressed shall, on the application of the person against whom enforcement is sought, suspend the enforcement proceedings where the enforceability of the judgment is suspended in the Member State of origin.

## SECTION 3

### Refusal of recognition and enforcement

## SUBSECTION 1

### Refusal of recognition

### Article 45

1. On the application of any interested party, the recognition of a judgment shall be refused:

(a)  if such recognition is manifestly contrary to public policy (ordre public) in the Member State addressed;

(b)  where the judgment was given in default of appearance, if the defendant was not served with the document which instituted the proceedings or with an equivalent document in sufficient time and in such a way as to enable him to arrange for his defence, unless the defendant failed to commence proceedings to challenge the judgment when it was possible for him to do so;

(c)  if the judgment is irreconcilable with a judgment given between the same parties in the Member State addressed;

(d)  if the judgment is irreconcilable with an earlier judgment given in another Member State or in a third State involving the same cause of action and between the same parties, provided that the earlier judgment fulfils the conditions necessary for its recognition in the Member State addressed; or

(e)  if the judgment conflicts with:

(i)  Sections 3, 4 or 5 of Chapter II where the policyholder, the insured, a beneficiary of the insurance contract, the injured party, the consumer or the employee was the defendant; or

(ii)  Section 6 of Chapter II.

2. In its examination of the grounds of jurisdiction referred to in point (e) of paragraph 1, the court to which the application was submitted shall be bound by the findings of fact on which the court of origin based its jurisdiction.

3. Without prejudice to point (e) of paragraph 1, the jurisdiction of the court of origin may not be reviewed. The test of public policy referred to in point (a) of paragraph 1 may not be applied to the rules relating to jurisdiction.

4. The application for refusal of recognition shall be made in accordance with the procedures provided for in Subsection 2 and, where appropriate, Section 4.

SUBSECTION 2

## Refusal of enforcement

*Article 46*

On the application of the person against whom enforcement is sought, the enforcement of a judgment shall be refused where one of the grounds referred to in Article 45 is found to exist.

*Article 47*

1. The application for refusal of enforcement shall be submitted to the court which the Member State concerned has communicated to the Commission pursuant to point (a) of Article 75 as the court to which the application is to be submitted.

2. The procedure for refusal of enforcement shall, in so far as it is not covered by this Regulation, be governed by the law of the Member State addressed.

3. The applicant shall provide the court with a copy of the judgment and, where necessary, a translation or transliteration of it.

The court may dispense with the production of the documents referred to in the first subparagraph if it already possesses them or if it considers it unreasonable to require the applicant to provide them. In the latter case, the court may require the other party to provide those documents.

4. The party seeking the refusal of enforcement of a judgment given in another Member State shall not be required to have a postal address in the Member State addressed. Nor shall that party be required to have an authorised representative in the Member State addressed unless such a representative is mandatory irrespective of the nationality or the domicile of the parties.

*Article 48*

The court shall decide on the application for refusal of enforcement without delay.

*Article 49*

1. The decision on the application for refusal of enforcement may be appealed against by either party.

2. The appeal is to be lodged with the court which the Member State concerned has communicated to the Commission pursuant to point (b) of Article 75 as the court with which such an appeal is to be lodged.

*Article 50*

The decision given on the appeal may only be contested by an appeal where the courts with which any further appeal is to be lodged have been communicated by the Member State concerned to the Commission pursuant to point (c) of Article 75.

*Article 51*

1. The court to which an application for refusal of enforcement is submitted or the court which hears an appeal lodged under Article 49 or Article 50 may stay the proceedings if an ordinary appeal has been lodged against the judgment in the Member State of origin or if the time for such an appeal has not yet expired. In the latter case, the court may specify the time within which such an appeal is to be lodged.

2. Where the judgment was given in Ireland, Cyprus or the United Kingdom, any form of appeal available in the Member State of origin shall be treated as an ordinary appeal for the purposes of paragraph 1.

## SECTION 4

### Common provisions

*Article 52*

Under no circumstances may a judgment given in a Member State be reviewed as to its substance in the Member State addressed.

*Article 53*

The court of origin shall, at the request of any interested party, issue the certificate using the form set out in Annex I.

*Article 54*

1. If a judgment contains a measure or an order which is not known in the law of the Member State addressed, that measure or order shall, to the extent possible, be adapted to a measure or an order known in the law of that Member State which has equivalent effects attached to it and which pursues similar aims and interests.

Such adaptation shall not result in effects going beyond those provided for in the law of the Member State of origin.

2. Any party may challenge the adaptation of the measure or order before a court.

3. If necessary, the party invoking the judgment or seeking its enforcement may be required to provide a translation or a transliteration of the judgment.

*Article 55*

A judgment given in a Member State which orders a payment by way of a penalty shall be enforceable in the Member State addressed only if the amount of the payment has been finally determined by the court of origin.

*Article 56*

No security, bond or deposit, however described, shall be required of a party who in one Member State applies for the enforcement of a judgment given in another Member State on the ground that he is a foreign national or that he is not domiciled or resident in the Member State addressed.

*Article 57*

1. When a translation or a transliteration is required under this Regulation, such translation or transliteration shall be into the official language of the Member State concerned or, where there are several official languages in that Member State, into the official language or one of the official languages of court proceedings of the place where a judgment given in another Member State is invoked or an application is made, in accordance with the law of that Member State.

2. For the purposes of the forms referred to in Articles 53 and 60, translations or transliterations may also be into any other official language or languages of the institutions of the Union that the Member State concerned has indicated it can accept.

3. Any translation made under this Regulation shall be done by a person qualified to do translations in one of the Member States.

## CHAPTER IV

## AUTHENTIC INSTRUMENTS AND COURT SETTLEMENTS

*Article 58*

1. An authentic instrument which is enforceable in the Member State of origin shall be enforceable in the other Member States without any declaration of enforceability being required. Enforcement of the

authentic instrument may be refused only if such enforcement is manifestly contrary to public policy (ordre public) in the Member State addressed.

The provisions of Section 2, Subsection 2 of Section 3, and Section 4 of Chapter III shall apply as appropriate to authentic instruments.

2. The authentic instrument produced must satisfy the conditions necessary to establish its authenticity in the Member State of origin.

*Article 59*

A court settlement which is enforceable in the Member State of origin shall be enforced in the other Member States under the same conditions as authentic instruments.

*Article 60*

The competent authority or court of the Member State of origin shall, at the request of any interested party, issue the certificate using the form set out in Annex II containing a summary of the enforceable obligation recorded in the authentic instrument or of the agreement between the parties recorded in the court settlement.

## CHAPTER V

## GENERAL PROVISIONS

*Article 61*

No legalisation or other similar formality shall be required for documents issued in a Member State in the context of this Regulation.

*Article 62*

1. In order to determine whether a party is domiciled in the Member State whose courts are seised of a matter, the court shall apply its internal law.

2. If a party is not domiciled in the Member State whose courts are seised of the matter, then, in order to determine whether the party is domiciled in another Member State, the court shall apply the law of that Member State.

*Article 63*

1. For the purposes of this Regulation, a company or other legal person or association of natural or legal persons is domiciled at the place where it has its:

(a)   statutory seat;

(b)   central administration; or

(c)   principal place of business.

2. For the purposes of Ireland, Cyprus and the United Kingdom, 'statutory seat' means the registered office or, where there is no such office anywhere, the place of incorporation or, where there is no such place anywhere, the place under the law of which the formation took place.

3. In order to determine whether a trust is domiciled in the Member State whose courts are seised of the matter, the court shall apply its rules of private international law.

*Article 64*

Without prejudice to any more favourable provisions of national laws, persons domiciled in a Member State who are being prosecuted in the criminal courts of another Member State of which they are not nationals for an offence which was not intentionally committed may be defended by persons qualified to do so, even if they do not appear in person. However, the court seised of the matter may order appearance in person; in the case of failure to appear, a judgment given in the civil action without the person concerned having had the opportunity to arrange for his defence need not be recognised or enforced in the other Member States.

*Article 65*

1. The jurisdiction specified in point 2 of Article 8 and Article 13 in actions on a warranty or guarantee or in any other third-party proceedings may be resorted to in the Member States included in the list established by the Commission pursuant to point (b) of Article 76(1) and Article 76(2) only in so far as permitted under national law. A person domiciled in another Member State may be invited to join the proceedings before the courts of those Member States pursuant to the rules on third-party notice referred to in that list.

2. Judgments given in a Member State by virtue of point 2 of Article 8 or Article 13 shall be recognised and enforced in accordance with Chapter III in any other Member State. Any effects which judgments given in the Member States included in the list referred to in paragraph 1 may have, in accordance with the law of those Member States, on third parties by application of paragraph 1 shall be recognised in all Member States.

3. The Member States included in the list referred to in paragraph 1 shall, within the framework of the European Judicial Network in civil and commercial matters established by Council Decision 2001/470/EC ('the European Judicial Network') provide information on how to determine, in accordance with their national law, the effects of the judgments referred to in the second sentence of paragraph 2.

## CHAPTER VI

## TRANSITIONAL PROVISIONS

*Article 66*

1. This Regulation shall apply only to legal proceedings instituted, to authentic instruments formally drawn up or registered and to court settlements approved or concluded on or after 10 January 2015.

2. Notwithstanding Article 80, Regulation (EC) No 44/2001 shall continue to apply to judgments given in legal proceedings instituted, to authentic instruments formally drawn up or registered and to court settlements approved or concluded before 10 January 2015 which fall within the scope of that Regulation.

## CHAPTER VII

## RELATIONSHIP WITH OTHER INSTRUMENTS

*Article 67*

This Regulation shall not prejudice the application of provisions governing jurisdiction and the recognition and enforcement of judgments in specific matters which are contained in instruments of the Union or in national legislation harmonised pursuant to such instruments.

*Article 68*

1. This Regulation shall, as between the Member States, supersede the 1968 Brussels Convention, except as regards the territories of the Member States which fall within the territorial scope of that Convention and which are excluded from this Regulation pursuant to Article 355 of the TFEU.

2. In so far as this Regulation replaces the provisions of the 1968 Brussels Convention between the Member States, any reference to that Convention shall be understood as a reference to this Regulation.

*Article 69*

Subject to Articles 70 and 71, this Regulation shall, as between the Member States, supersede the conventions that cover the same matters as those to which this Regulation applies. In particular, the conventions included in the list established by the Commission pursuant to point (c) of Article 76(1) and Article 76(2) shall be superseded.

*Article 70*

1. The conventions referred to in Article 69 shall continue to have effect in relation to matters to which this Regulation does not apply.

2. They shall continue to have effect in respect of judgments given, authentic instruments formally drawn up or registered and court settlements approved or concluded before the date of entry into force of Regulation (EC) No 44/2001.

*Article 71*

1. This Regulation shall not affect any conventions to which the Member States are parties and which, in relation to particular matters, govern jurisdiction or the recognition or enforcement of judgments.

2. With a view to its uniform interpretation, paragraph 1 shall be applied in the following manner:

(a) this Regulation shall not prevent a court of a Member State which is party to a convention on a particular matter from assuming jurisdiction in accordance with that convention, even where the defendant is domiciled in another Member State which is not party to that convention. The court hearing the action shall, in any event, apply Article 28 of this Regulation;

(b) judgments given in a Member State by a court in the exercise of jurisdiction provided for in a convention on a particular matter shall be recognised and enforced in the other Member States in accordance with this Regulation.

Where a convention on a particular matter to which both the Member State of origin and the Member State addressed are parties lays down conditions for the recognition or enforcement of judgments, those conditions shall apply. In any event, the provisions of this Regulation on recognition and enforcement of judgments may be applied.

*[Article 71a*

1. For the purposes of this Regulation, a court common to several Member States as specified in paragraph 2 (a 'common court') shall be deemed to be a court of a Member State when, pursuant to the instrument establishing it, such a common court exercises jurisdiction in matters falling within the scope of this Regulation.

2. For the purposes of this Regulation, each of the following courts shall be a common court:

(a) the Unified Patent Court established by the Agreement on a Unified Patent Court signed on 19 February 2013 (the 'UPC Agreement'); and

(b) the Benelux Court of Justice established by the Treaty of 31 March 1965 concerning the establishment and statute of a Benelux Court of Justice (the 'Benelux Court of Justice Treaty').]

*[Article 71b*

The jurisdiction of a common court shall be determined as follows:

(1) a common court shall have jurisdiction where, under this Regulation, the courts of a Member State party to the instrument establishing the common court would have jurisdiction in a matter governed by that instrument;

(2) where the defendant is not domiciled in a Member State, and this Regulation does not otherwise confer jurisdiction over him, Chapter II shall apply as appropriate regardless of the defendant's domicile.

Application may be made to a common court for provisional, including protective, measures even if the courts of a third State have jurisdiction as to the substance of the matter;

(3) where a common court has jurisdiction over a defendant under point 2 in a dispute relating to an infringement of a European patent giving rise to damage within the Union, that court may also exercise jurisdiction in relation to damage arising outside the Union from such an infringement.

Such jurisdiction may only be established if property belonging to the defendant is located in any Member State party to the instrument establishing the common court and the dispute has a sufficient connection with any such Member State.]

[*Article 71c*

1. Articles 29 to 32 shall apply where proceedings are brought in a common court and in a court of a Member State not party to the instrument establishing the common court.

2. Articles 29 to 32 shall apply where, during the transitional period referred to in Article 83 of the UPC Agreement, proceedings are brought in the Unified Patent Court and in a court of a Member State party to the UPC Agreement.]

[*Article 71d*

This Regulation shall apply to the recognition and enforcement of:

(a) judgments given by a common court which are to be recognised and enforced in a Member State not party to the instrument establishing the common court; and

(b) judgments given by the courts of a Member State not party to the instrument establishing the common court which are to be recognised and enforced in a Member State party to that instrument.

However, where recognition and enforcement of a judgment given by a common court is sought in a Member State party to the instrument establishing the common court, any rules of that instrument on recognition and enforcement shall apply instead of the rules of this Regulation.]

*Article 72*

This Regulation shall not affect agreements by which Member States, prior to the entry into force of Regulation (EC) No 44/2001, undertook pursuant to Article 59 of the 1968 Brussels Convention not to recognise judgments given, in particular in other Contracting States to that Convention, against defendants domiciled or habitually resident in a third State where, in cases provided for in Article 4 of that Convention, the judgment could only be founded on a ground of jurisdiction specified in the second paragraph of Article 3 of that Convention.

*Article 73*

1. This Regulation shall not affect the application of the 2007 Lugano Convention.

2. This Regulation shall not affect the application of the 1958 New York Convention.

3. This Regulation shall not affect the application of bilateral conventions and agreements between a third State and a Member State concluded before the date of entry into force of Regulation (EC) No 44/2001 which concern matters governed by this Regulation.

CHAPTER VIII

**FINAL PROVISIONS**

*Article 74*

The Member States shall provide, within the framework of the European Judicial Network and with a view to making the information available to the public, a description of national rules and procedures concerning enforcement, including authorities competent for enforcement, and information on any limitations on enforcement, in particular debtor protection rules and limitation or prescription periods.

The Member States shall keep this information permanently updated.

*Article 75*

By 10 January 2014, the Member States shall communicate to the Commission:

(a) the courts to which the application for refusal of enforcement is to be submitted pursuant to Article 47(1);

(b) the courts with which an appeal against the decision on the application for refusal of enforcement is to be lodged pursuant to Article 49(2);

(c) the courts with which any further appeal is to be lodged pursuant to Article 50; and

(d)   the languages accepted for translations of the forms as referred to in Article 57(2).

The Commission shall make the information publicly available through any appropriate means, in particular through the European Judicial Network.

## Article 76

1. The Member States shall notify the Commission of:

(a)   the rules of jurisdiction referred to in Articles 5(2) and 6(2);

(b)   the rules on third-party notice referred to in Article 65; and

(c)   the conventions referred to in Article 69.

2. The Commission shall, on the basis of the notifications by the Member States referred to in paragraph 1, establish the corresponding lists.

3. The Member States shall notify the Commission of any subsequent amendments required to be made to those lists. The Commission shall amend those lists accordingly.

4. The Commission shall publish the lists and any subsequent amendments made to them in the Official Journal of the European Union.

5. The Commission shall make all information notified pursuant to paragraphs 1 and 3 publicly available through any other appropriate means, in particular through the European Judicial Network.

## Article 77

The Commission shall be empowered to adopt delegated acts in accordance with Article 78 concerning the amendment of Annexes I and II.

## Article 78

1. The power to adopt delegated acts is conferred on the Commission subject to the conditions laid down in this Article.

2. The power to adopt delegated acts referred to in Article 77 shall be conferred on the Commission for an indeterminate period of time from 9 January 2013.

3. The delegation of power referred to in Article 77 may be revoked at any time by the European Parliament or by the Council. A decision to revoke shall put an end to the delegation of the power specified in that decision. It shall take effect the day following the publication of the decision in the Official Journal of the European Union or at a later date specified therein. It shall not affect the validity of any delegated acts already in force.

4. As soon as it adopts a delegated act, the Commission shall notify it simultaneously to the European Parliament and to the Council.

5. A delegated act adopted pursuant to Article 77 shall enter into force only if no objection has been expressed either by the European Parliament or the Council within a period of two months of notification of that act to the European Parliament and the Council or if, before the expiry of that period, the European Parliament and the Council have both informed the Commission that they will not object. That period shall be extended by two months at the initiative of the European Parliament or of the Council.

## Article 79

By 11 January 2022 the Commission shall present a report to the European Parliament, to the Council and to the European Economic and Social Committee on the application of this Regulation. That report shall include an evaluation of the possible need for a further extension of the rules on jurisdiction to defendants not domiciled in a Member State, taking into account the operation of this Regulation and possible developments at international level. Where appropriate, the report shall be accompanied by a proposal for amendment of this Regulation.

*Article 80*

This Regulation shall repeal Regulation (EC) No 44/2001. References to the repealed Regulation shall be construed as references to this Regulation and shall be read in accordance with the correlation table set out in Annex III.

*Article 81*

This Regulation shall enter into force on the twentieth day following that of its publication in the Official Journal of the European Union.

It shall apply from 10 January 2015, with the exception of Articles 75 and 76, which shall apply from 10 January 2014.

This Regulation shall be binding in its entirety and directly applicable in the Member States in accordance with the Treaties.

*[Annexes I–III omitted]*

# Regulation (EU) No 606/2013 of the European Parliament and of The Council of 12 June 2013 on mutual recognition of protection measures in civil matters

[2013] OJ L181/4

THE EUROPEAN PARLIAMENT AND THE COUNCIL OF THE EUROPEAN UNION,

Having regard to the Treaty on the Functioning of the European Union, and in particular points (a), (e) and (f) of Article 81(2) thereof,

Having regard to the proposal from the European Commission,

After transmission of the draft legislative act to the national parliaments,

After consulting the European Economic and Social Committee,

Having regard to the opinion of the Committee of the Regions,

Acting in accordance with the ordinary legislative procedure,

Whereas:

(1) The Union has set itself the objective of maintaining and developing an area of freedom, security and justice in which the free movement of persons is ensured and access to justice is facilitated, in particular through the principle of mutual recognition of judicial and extrajudicial decisions in civil matters. For the gradual establishment of such an area, the Union is to adopt measures relating to judicial cooperation in civil matters having cross-border implications, particularly when necessary for the proper functioning of the internal market.

(2) Article 81(1) of the Treaty on the Functioning of the European Union (TFEU) provides that judicial cooperation in civil matters having cross-border implications is to be based on the principle of mutual recognition of judgments and of decisions in extrajudicial cases.

(3) In a common area of justice without internal borders, provisions to ensure rapid and simple recognition and, where applicable, enforcement in another Member State of protection measures ordered in a Member State are essential to ensure that the protection afforded to a natural person in one Member State is maintained and continued in any other Member State to which that person travels or moves. It is necessary to ensure that the legitimate exercise by citizens of the Union of their right to move and reside freely within the territory of Member States, in accordance with Article 3(2) of the Treaty on European Union (TEU) and Article 21 TFEU, does not result in a loss of that protection.

(4) Mutual trust in the administration of justice in the Union and the aim of ensuring quicker and less costly circulation of protection measures within the Union justify the principle according to which protection measures ordered in one Member State are recognised in all other Member States without any special procedure being required. As a result, a protection measure ordered in one Member State ('Member State of origin') should be treated as if it had been ordered in the Member State where its recognition is sought ('Member State addressed').

(5) In order to attain the objective of free movement of protection measures, it is necessary and appropriate that the rules governing the recognition and, where applicable, enforcement of protection measures be governed by a legal instrument of the Union which is binding and directly applicable.

(6) This Regulation should apply to protection measures ordered with a view to protecting a person where there exist serious grounds for considering that that person's life, physical or psychological integrity, personal liberty, security or sexual integrity is at risk, for example so as to prevent any form of gender-based violence or violence in close relationships such as physical violence, harassment, sexual aggression, stalking, intimidation or other forms of indirect coercion. It is important to underline that this Regulation applies to all victims, regardless of whether they are victims of gender-based violence.

(7) Directive 2012/29/EU of the European Parliament and of the Council of 25 October 2012 establishing minimum standards on the rights, support and protection of victims of crime ensures that victims of crime receive appropriate information and support.

(8) This Regulation complements Directive 2012/29/EU. The fact that a person is the object of a protection measure ordered in civil matters does not necessarily preclude that person from being defined as a 'victim' under that Directive.

(9) The scope of this Regulation is within the field of judicial cooperation in civil matters within the meaning of Article 81 TFEU. This Regulation applies only to protection measures ordered in civil matters. Protection measures adopted in criminal matters are covered by Directive 2011/99/EU of the European Parliament and of the Council of 13 December 2011 on the European Protection Order.

(10) The notion of civil matters should be interpreted autonomously, in accordance with the principles of Union law. The civil, administrative or criminal nature of the authority ordering a protection measure should not be determinative for the purpose of assessing the civil character of a protection measure.

(11) This Regulation should not interfere with the functioning of Council Regulation (EC) No 2201/2003 of 27 November 2003 concerning jurisdiction and the recognition and enforcement of judgments in matrimonial matters and the matters of parental responsibility ('Brussels IIa Regulation'). Decisions taken under the Brussels IIa Regulation should continue to be recognised and enforced under that Regulation.

(12) This Regulation takes account of the different legal traditions of the Member States and does not interfere with the national systems for ordering protection measures. This Regulation does not oblige the Member States to modify their national systems so as to enable protection measures to be ordered in civil matters, or to introduce protection measures in civil matters for the application of this Regulation.

(13) In order to take account of the various types of authorities which order protection measures in civil matters in the Member States, and unlike in other areas of judicial cooperation, this Regulation should apply to decisions of both judicial authorities and administrative authorities provided that the latter offer guarantees with regard, in particular, to their impartiality and to the right of the parties to judicial review. In no event should police authorities be considered as issuing authorities within the meaning of this Regulation.

(14) Based on the principle of mutual recognition, protection measures ordered in civil matters in the Member State of origin should be recognised in the Member State addressed as protection measures in civil matters in accordance with this Regulation.

(15) According to the principle of mutual recognition, the recognition corresponds to the duration of the protection measure. However, taking into account the diversity of protection measures under the laws of the Member States, in particular in terms of their duration, and the fact that this Regulation will typically apply in urgent situations, the effects of recognition under this Regulation should, by way of exception, be limited to a period of 12 months from the issuing of the certificate provided for by this Regulation, irrespective of whether the protection measure itself (be it provisional, time-limited or indefinite in nature) has a longer duration.

(16) In cases where the duration of a protection measure is greater than 12 months, the limitation of the effects of recognition under this Regulation should be without prejudice to the right of the protected person to invoke that protection measure under any other available legal act of the Union providing for recognition or to apply for a national protection measure in the Member State addressed.

(17) The limitation of the effects of recognition is exceptional due to the special nature of the subject matter of this Regulation and should not serve as a precedent for other instruments in civil and commercial matters.

(18) This Regulation should deal only with the recognition of the obligation imposed by the protection measure. It should not regulate the procedures for implementation or enforcement of the protection measure, nor should it cover any potential sanctions that might be imposed if the obligation ordered by the protection measure is infringed in the Member State addressed. Those matters are left to the law of that Member State. However, in accordance with the general principles of Union law and particularly the principle of mutual recognition, Member States are to ensure that protection measures recognised under this Regulation can take effect in the Member State addressed.

(19) Protection measures covered by this Regulation should afford protection to the protected person at his or her place of residence or place of work, or at another place which that person visits on a regular basis, such as the residence of close relatives or the school or educational establishment attended by his or her child. Irrespective of whether the place in question or the extent of the area covered by the protection measure is described in the protection measure by one or more specific addresses or by reference to a circumscribed area which the person causing the risk may not approach or enter, respectively (or a combination of the two), the recognition of the obligation imposed by the protection measure relates to the purpose which the place serves for the protected person rather than to the specific address.

(20) In the light of the foregoing and provided that the nature and the essential elements of the protection measure are maintained, the competent authority of the Member State addressed should be allowed to adjust the factual elements of the protection measure where such adjustment is necessary in order for the recognition of the protection measure to be effective in practical terms in the Member State addressed. Factual elements include the address, the general location or the minimum distance the person causing the risk must keep from the protected person, the address or the general location. However, the type and the civil nature of the protection measure may not be affected by such adjustment.

(21) In order to facilitate any adjustment of a protection measure, the certificate should indicate whether the address specified in the protection measure constitutes the place of residence, the place of work or a place that the protected person visits on a regular basis. Furthermore, if relevant, the circumscribed area (approximate radius from the specific address) to which the obligation imposed by the protection measure on the person causing the risk applies should also be indicated in the certificate.

(22) In order to facilitate the free movement of protection measures within the Union, this Regulation should introduce a uniform model of certificate and provide for the establishment of a multilingual standard form for that purpose. The issuing authority should issue the certificate upon request by the protected person.

(23) Free text fields in the multilingual standard form for the certificate should be as limited as possible, so that translation or transliteration may be provided in most cases without imposing any costs on the protected person by making use of the standard form in the relevant language. Any costs for necessary translation that goes beyond the text of the multilingual standard form are to be allocated as provided under the law of the Member State of origin.

(24) Where a certificate contains free text, the competent authority of the Member State addressed should determine whether any translation or transliteration is required. This should not preclude the protected person or the issuing authority of the Member State of origin from providing a translation or transliteration on their own initiative.

(25) To ensure respect for the rights of defence of the person causing the risk, where the protection measure was ordered in default of appearance or under a procedure that does not provide for prior notice to that person ('ex-parte proceeding'), the issue of the certificate should only be possible if that person has had the opportunity to arrange for his or her defence against the protection measure. However, with a view to avoiding circumvention and taking into account the typical urgency of cases necessitating protection measures, it should not be required that the period for raising such defence has expired before a certificate may be issued. The certificate should be issued as soon as the protection measure is enforceable in the Member State of origin.

(26) Having regard to the objectives of simplicity and speed, this Regulation provides for simple and quick methods to be used for bringing procedural steps to the notice of the person causing the risk. Those specific methods of notification should apply only for the purposes of this Regulation due to the special nature of its subject matter, should not serve as a precedent for other instruments in civil and commercial matters and should not affect any obligations of a Member State concerning the service abroad of judicial and extrajudicial documents in civil matters arising from a bilateral or multilateral convention concluded between that Member State and a third country.

(27) When the certificate is brought to the notice of the person causing the risk and also when any adjustment is made to any factual elements of a protection measure in the Member State addressed, due regard should be paid to the interest of the protected person in not having his or her whereabouts

or other contact details disclosed. Such details should not be disclosed to the person causing the risk unless such disclosure is necessary for compliance with, or the enforcement of, the protection measure.

(28) The issuing of the certificate should not be subject to appeal.

(29) The certificate should be rectified where, due to an obvious error or inaccuracy, such as a typing error or an error of transcription or copying, the certificate does not correctly reflect the protection measure, or should be withdrawn if it was clearly wrongly granted, for example where it was used for a measure that falls outside the scope of this Regulation or where it was issued in breach of the requirements for its issuing.

(30) The issuing authority of the Member State of origin should, upon request, assist the protected person in obtaining information on the authorities of the Member State addressed before which the protection measure is to be invoked or enforcement is to be sought.

(31) The harmonious functioning of justice requires that irreconcilable decisions should not be delivered in two Member States. To that end, this Regulation should provide for a ground for refusal of recognition or enforcement of the protection measure in cases of irreconcilability with a judgment given or recognised in the Member State addressed.

(32) Public interest considerations may, in exceptional circumstances, justify a refusal by the court of the Member State addressed to recognise or enforce a protection measure where its application would be manifestly incompatible with the public policy of that Member State. However, the court should not be able to apply the public-policy exception in order to refuse recognition or enforcement of a protection measure when to do so would be contrary to the rights set out in the Charter of Fundamental Rights of the European Union, and in particular Article 21 thereof.

(33) In the event of suspension or withdrawal of the protection measure or withdrawal of the certificate in the Member State of origin, the competent authority of the Member State addressed should, upon submission of the relevant certificate, suspend or withdraw the effects of recognition and, where applicable, the enforcement of the protection measure.

(34) A protected person should have effective access to justice in other Member States. To ensure such effective access in procedures covered by this Regulation, legal aid is to be provided in accordance with Council Directive 2003/8/EC of 27 January 2003 to improve access to justice in cross-border disputes by establishing minimum common rules relating to legal aid for such disputes.

(35) In order to facilitate the application of this Regulation, Member States should be required to provide certain information regarding their national rules and procedures concerning protection measures in civil matters within the framework of the European Judicial Network in civil and commercial matters established by Council Decision 2001/470/EC. Access to the information provided by the Member States should be made available through the European e-Justice Portal.

(36) In order to ensure uniform conditions for the implementation of this Regulation, implementing powers should be conferred on the Commission with regard to the establishment and subsequent amendment of the forms provided for in this Regulation. Those powers should be exercised in accordance with Regulation (EU) No 182/2011 of the European Parliament and of the Council of 16 February 2011 laying down the rules and general principles concerning mechanisms for control by Member States of the Commission's exercise of implementing powers.

(37) The examination procedure should be used for the adoption of implementing acts establishing and subsequently amending the forms provided for in this Regulation.

(38) This Regulation respects the fundamental rights and observes the principles recognised in the Charter of Fundamental Rights of the European Union. In particular, it seeks to ensure the rights of the defence and fair trial, as established in Articles 47 and 48 thereof. This Regulation should be applied according to those rights and principles.

(39) Since the objective of this Regulation, namely to establish rules for a simple and rapid mechanism for the recognition of protection measures ordered in a Member State in civil matters, cannot be sufficiently achieved by the Member States and can therefore be better achieved at Union level, the Union may adopt measures, in accordance with the principle of subsidiarity as set out in Article 5 TEU.

In accordance with the principle of proportionality, as set out in that Article, this Regulation does not go beyond what is necessary in order to achieve that objective.

(40) In accordance with Article 3 of Protocol No 21 on the position of the United Kingdom and Ireland in respect of the Area of Freedom, Security and Justice, annexed to the TEU and to the TFEU, those Member States have notified their wish to take part in the adoption and application of this Regulation.

(41) In accordance with Articles 1 and 2 of Protocol No 22 on the position of Denmark, annexed to the TEU and to the TFEU, Denmark is not taking part in the adoption of this Regulation and is not bound by it or subject to its application.

(42) The European Data Protection Supervisor delivered an opinion on 17 October 2011, based on Article 41(2) of Regulation (EC) No 45/2001 of the European Parliament and of the Council of 18 December 2000 on the protection of individuals with regard to the processing of personal data by the Community institutions and bodies and on the free movement of such data,

HAVE ADOPTED THIS REGULATION:

## CHAPTER I

## SUBJECT MATTER, SCOPE AND DEFINITIONS

### Article 1

**Subject matter**

This Regulation establishes rules for a simple and rapid mechanism for the recognition of protection measures ordered in a Member State in civil matters.

### Article 2

**Scope**

1. This Regulation shall apply to protection measures in civil matters ordered by an issuing authority within the meaning of point (4) of Article 3.

2. This Regulation shall apply to cross-border cases. For the purposes of this Regulation, a case shall be deemed to be a cross-border case where the recognition of a protection measure ordered in one Member State is sought in another Member State.

3. This Regulation shall not apply to protection measures falling within the scope of Regulation (EC) No 2201/2003.

### Article 3

**Definitions**

For the purposes of this Regulation, the following definitions shall apply:

(1) 'protection measure' means any decision, whatever it may be called, ordered by the issuing authority of the Member State of origin in accordance with its national law and imposing one or more of the following obligations on the person causing the risk with a view to protecting another person, when the latter person's physical or psychological integrity may be at risk:

(a) a prohibition or regulation on entering the place where the protected person resides, works, or regularly visits or stays;

(b) a prohibition or regulation of contact, in any form, with the protected person, including by telephone, electronic or ordinary mail, fax or any other means;

(c) a prohibition or regulation on approaching the protected person closer than a prescribed distance;

(2) 'protected person' means a natural person who is the object of the protection afforded by a protection measure;

(3) 'person causing the risk' means a natural person on whom one or more of the obligations referred to in point (1) have been imposed;

(4) 'issuing authority' means any judicial authority, or any other authority designated by a Member State as having competence in the matters falling within the scope of this Regulation, provided that such other authority offers guarantees to the parties with regard to impartiality, and that its decisions in relation to the protection measure may, under the law of the Member State in which it operates, be made subject to review by a judicial authority and have similar force and effects to those of a decision of a judicial authority on the same matter;

(5) 'Member State of origin' means the Member State in which the protection measure is ordered;

(6) 'Member State addressed' means the Member State in which the recognition and, where applicable, the enforcement of the protection measure is sought.

## CHAPTER II

## RECOGNITION AND ENFORCEMENT OF PROTECTION MEASURES

*Article 4*

**Recognition and enforcement**

1. A protection measure ordered in a Member State shall be recognised in the other Member States without any special procedure being required and shall be enforceable without a declaration of enforceability being required.

2. A protected person who wishes to invoke in the Member State addressed a protection measure ordered in the Member State of origin shall provide the competent authority of the Member State addressed with:

(a) a copy of the protection measure which satisfies the conditions necessary to establish its authenticity;

(b) the certificate issued in the Member State of origin pursuant to Article 5; and

(c) where necessary, a transliteration and/or a translation of the certificate in accordance with Article 16.

3. The certificate shall take effect only within the limits of the enforceability of the protection measure.

4. Irrespective of whether the protection measure has a longer duration, the effects of recognition pursuant to paragraph 1 shall be limited to a period of 12 months, starting from the date of the issuing of the certificate.

5. The procedure for the enforcement of protection measures shall be governed by the law of the Member State addressed.

*Article 5*

**Certificate**

1. The issuing authority of the Member State of origin shall, upon request by the protected person, issue the certificate using the multilingual standard form established in accordance with Article 19 and containing the information provided for in Article 7.

2. No appeal shall lie against the issuing of the certificate.

3. Upon request by the protected person, the issuing authority of the Member State of origin shall provide the protected person with a transliteration and/or a translation of the certificate by making use of the multilingual standard form established in accordance with Article 19.

*Article 6*

**Requirements for the issuing of the certificate**

1. The certificate may only be issued if the protection measure has been brought to the notice of the person causing the risk in accordance with the law of the Member State of origin.

2. Where the protection measure was ordered in default of appearance, the certificate may only be issued if the person causing the risk had been served with the document which instituted the proceeding

or an equivalent document or, where relevant, had been otherwise informed of the initiation of the proceeding in accordance with the law of the Member State of origin in sufficient time and in such a way as to enable that person to arrange for his or her defence.

3. Where the protection measure was ordered under a procedure that does not provide for prior notice to be given to the person causing the risk ('ex-parte proceeding'), the certificate may only be issued if that person had the right to challenge the protection measure under the law of the Member State of origin.

## Article 7

### Contents of the certificate

The certificate shall contain the following information:

(a)  the name and address/contact details of the issuing authority;

(b)  the reference number of the file;

(c)  the date of issue of the certificate;

(d)  details concerning the protected person: name, date and place of birth, where available, and an address to be used for notification purposes, preceded by a conspicuous warning that that address may be disclosed to the person causing the risk;

(e)  details concerning the person causing the risk: name, date and place of birth, where available, and address to be used for notification purposes;

(f)  all information necessary for enforcement of the protection measure, including, where applicable, the type of the measure and the obligation imposed by it on the person causing the risk and specifying the function of the place and/or the circumscribed area which that person is prohibited from approaching or entering, respectively;

(g)  the duration of the protection measure;

(h)  the duration of the effects of recognition pursuant to Article 4(4);

(i)  a declaration that the requirements laid down in Article 6 have been met;

(j)  information on the rights granted under Articles 9 and 13;

(k)  for ease of reference, the full title of this Regulation.

## Article 8

### Notification of the certificate to the person causing the risk

1. The issuing authority of the Member State of origin shall bring to the notice of the person causing the risk the certificate and the fact that the issuing of the certificate results in the recognition and, where applicable, in the enforceability of the protection measure in all Member States pursuant to Article 4.

2. Where the person causing the risk resides in the Member State of origin, the notification shall be effected in accordance with the law of that Member State. Where the person causing the risk resides in a Member State other than the Member State of origin or in a third country, the notification shall be effected by registered letter with acknowledgment of receipt or equivalent.

Situations in which the address of the person causing the risk is not known or in which that person refuses to accept receipt of the notification shall be governed by the law of the Member State of origin.

3. The whereabouts or other contact details of the protected person shall not be disclosed to the person causing the risk unless their disclosure is necessary for compliance with, or the enforcement of, the protection measure.

## Article 9

### Rectification or withdrawal of the certificate

1. Without prejudice to Article 5(2) and upon request by the protected person or the person causing the risk to the issuing authority of the Member State of origin or on that authority's own initiative, the certificate shall be:

(a)  rectified where, due to a clerical error, there is a discrepancy between the protection measure and the certificate; or

(b)  withdrawn where it was clearly wrongly granted, having regard to the requirements laid down in Article 6 and the scope of this Regulation.

2. The procedure, including any appeal, with regard to the rectification or withdrawal of the certificate shall be governed by the law of the Member State of origin.

*Article 10*

**Assistance to the protected person**

Upon request by the protected person, the issuing authority of the Member State of origin shall assist that person in obtaining information, as made available in accordance with Articles 17 and 18, concerning the authorities of the Member State addressed before which the protection measure is to be invoked or enforcement is to be sought.

*Article 11*

**Adjustment of the protection measure**

1. The competent authority of the Member State addressed shall, where and to the extent necessary, adjust the factual elements of the protection measure in order to give effect to the protection measure in that Member State.

2. The procedure for the adjustment of the protection measure shall be governed by the law of the Member State addressed.

3. The adjustment of the protection measure shall be brought to the notice of the person causing the risk.

4. Where the person causing the risk resides in the Member State addressed, the notification shall be effected in accordance with the law of that Member State. Where the person causing the risk resides in a Member State other than the Member State addressed or in a third country, the notification shall be effected by registered letter with acknowledgment of receipt or equivalent.

Situations in which the address of the person causing the risk is not known or in which that person refuses to accept receipt of the notification shall be governed by the law of the Member State addressed.

5. An appeal against the adjustment of the protection measure may be lodged by the protected person or the person causing the risk. The appeal procedure shall be governed by the law of the Member State addressed. However, the lodging of an appeal shall not have suspensive effect.

*Article 12*

**No review as to substance**

Under no circumstances may a protection measure ordered in the Member State of origin be reviewed as to its substance in the Member State addressed.

*Article 13*

**Refusal of recognition or enforcement**

1. The recognition and, where applicable, the enforcement of the protection measure shall be refused, upon application by the person causing the risk, to the extent such recognition is:

(a)  manifestly contrary to public policy in the Member State addressed; or

(b)  irreconcilable with a judgment given or recognised in the Member State addressed.

2. The application for refusal of recognition or enforcement shall be submitted to the court of the Member State addressed as communicated by that Member State to the Commission in accordance with point (a)(iv) of Article 18(1).

3. The recognition of the protection measure may not be refused on the ground that the law of the Member State addressed does not allow for such a measure based on the same facts.

*Article 14*

**Suspension or withdrawal of recognition or enforcement**

1. In the event of suspension or withdrawal of the protection measure in the Member State of origin, suspension or limitation of its enforceability, or withdrawal of the certificate in accordance with point (b) of Article 9(1), the issuing authority of the Member State of origin shall, upon request by the protected person or the person causing the risk, issue a certificate indicating that suspension, limitation or withdrawal using the multilingual standard form established in accordance with Article 19.

2. Upon submission by the protected person or the person causing the risk of the certificate issued in accordance with paragraph 1, the competent authority of the Member State addressed shall suspend or withdraw the effects of the recognition and, where applicable, the enforcement of the protection measure.

## CHAPTER III

## GENERAL AND FINAL PROVISIONS

*Article 15*

**Legalisation and other similar formalities**

No legalisation or other similar formality shall be required for documents issued in a Member State in the context of this Regulation.

*Article 16*

**Transliteration or translation**

1. Any transliteration or translation required under this Regulation shall be into the official language or one of the official languages of the Member State addressed or into any other official language of the institutions of the Union which that Member State has indicated it can accept.

2. Subject to Article 5(3), any translation under this Regulation shall be done by a person qualified to do translations in one of the Member States.

*Article 17*

**Information made available to the public**

The Member States shall provide, within the framework of the European Judicial Network in civil and commercial matters established by Decision 2001/470/EC and with a view to making the information available to the public, a description of the national rules and procedures concerning protection measures in civil matters, including information on the type of authorities which are competent in the matters falling within the scope of this Regulation.

The Member States shall keep that information updated.

*Article 18*

**Communication of information by the Member States**

1. By 11 July 2014, Member States shall communicate to the Commission the following information:

(a) the type of authorities which are competent in the matters falling within the scope of this Regulation, specifying, where applicable:

   (i) the authorities which are competent to order protection measures and issue certificates in accordance with Article 5;

   (ii) the authorities before which a protection measure ordered in another Member State is to be invoked and/or which are competent to enforce such a measure;

   (iii) the authorities which are competent to effect the adjustment of protection measures in accordance with Article 11(1);

   (iv) the courts to which the application for refusal of recognition and, where applicable, enforcement is to be submitted in accordance with Article 13;

(b)   the language or languages accepted for translations as referred to in Article 16(1).

2. The Commission shall make the information referred to in paragraph 1 available to the public through any appropriate means, in particular through the website of the European Judicial Network in civil and commercial matters.

## Article 19

### Establishment and subsequent amendment of the forms

The Commission shall adopt implementing acts establishing and subsequently amending the forms referred to in Articles 5 and 14. Those implementing acts shall be adopted in accordance with the examination procedure referred to in Article 20.

## Article 20

### Committee procedure

1. The Commission shall be assisted by a committee. That committee shall be a committee within the meaning of Regulation (EU) No 182/2011.

2. Where reference is made to this paragraph, Article 5 of Regulation (EU) No 182/2011 shall apply.

## Article 21

### Review

By 11 January 2020, the Commission shall submit to the European Parliament, the Council and the European Economic and Social Committee a report on the application of this Regulation. If necessary, the report shall be accompanied by proposals for amendments.

## Article 22

### Entry into force

This Regulation shall enter into force on the twentieth day following that of its publication in the Official Journal of the European Union.

It shall apply from 11 January 2015.

This Regulation shall apply to protection measures ordered on or after 11 January 2015, irrespective of when proceedings have been instituted.

This Regulation shall be binding in its entirety and directly applicable in the Member States in accordance with the Treaties.

# Council Directive 93/13/EEC of 5 April 1993 on unfair terms in consumer contracts

[1993] OJ L95/29

THE COUNCIL OF THE EUROPEAN COMMUNITIES,

. . .

Whereas there is a risk that, in certain cases, the consumer may be deprived of protection under this Directive by designating the law of a non-Member country as the law applicable to the contract; whereas provisions should therefore be included in this Directive designed to avert this risk;

. . .

HAS ADOPTED THIS DIRECTIVE:

### Article 1

1. The purpose of this Directive is to approximate the laws, regulations and administrative provisions of the Member States relating to unfair terms in contracts concluded between a seller or supplier and a consumer.

2. The contractual terms which reflect mandatory statutory or regulatory provisions and the provisions or principles of international conventions to which the Member States or the Community are party, particularly in the transport area, shall not be subject to the provisions of this Directive.

### Article 2

For the purposes of this Directive:

(a) 'unfair terms' means the contractual terms defined in Article 3;

(b) 'consumer' means any natural person who, in contracts covered by this Directive, is acting for purposes which are outside his trade, business or profession;

(c) 'seller or supplier' means any natural or legal person who, in contracts covered by this Directive, is acting for purposes relating to his trade, business or profession, whether publicly owned or privately owned.

### Article 3

1. A contractual term which has not been individually negotiated shall be regarded as unfair if, contrary to the requirement of good faith, it causes a significant imbalance in the parties' rights and obligations arising under the contract, to the detriment of the consumer.

2. A term shall always be regarded as not individually negotiated where it has been drafted in advance and the consumer has therefore not been able to influence the substance of the term, particularly in the context of a pre-formulated standard contract.

The fact that certain aspects of a term or one specific term have been individually negotiated shall not exclude the application of this Article to the rest of a contract if an overall assessment of the contract indicates that it is nevertheless a pre-formulated standard contract.

Where any seller or supplier claims that a standard term has been individually negotiated, the burden of proof in this respect shall be incumbent on him.

3. The Annex shall contain an indicative and non-exhaustive list of the terms which may be regarded as unfair.

. . .

### Article 6

1. Member States shall lay down that unfair terms used in a contract concluded with a consumer by a

seller or supplier shall, as provided for under their national law, not be binding on the consumer and that the contract shall continue to bind the parties upon those terms if it is capable of continuing in existence without the unfair terms.

2. Member States shall take the necessary measures to ensure that the consumer does not lose the protection granted by this Directive by virtue of the choice of the law of a non-Member country as the law applicable to the contract if the latter has a close connection with the territory of the Member States.

. . .

## ANNEX

### TERMS REFERRED TO IN ARTICLE 3(3)

1. Terms which have the object or effect of:

. . .

(b) inappropriately excluding or limiting the legal rights of the consumer vis-à-vis the seller or supplier or another party in the event of total or partial non-performance or inadequate performance by the seller or supplier of any of the contractual obligations, including the option of offsetting a debt owed to the seller or supplier against any claim which the consumer may have against him;

. . .

(q) excluding or hindering the consumer's right to take legal action or exercise any other legal remedy, particularly by requiring the consumer to take disputes exclusively to arbitration not covered by legal provisions, unduly restricting the evidence available to him or imposing on him a burden of proof which, according to the applicable law, should lie with another party to the contract.

. . .

# Council Directive 2003/8/EC of 27 January 2003 to improve access to justice in cross-border disputes by establishing minimum common rules relating to legal aid for such disputes

[2003] OJ L26/41

THE COUNCIL OF THE EUROPEAN UNION,

Having regard to the Treaty establishing the European Community, and in particular Articles 61(c) and 67 thereof,

Having regard to the proposal from the Commission,

Having regard to the opinion of the European Parliament,

Having regard to the opinion of the Economic and Social Committee,

Whereas:

(1) The European Union has set itself the objective of maintaining and developing an area of freedom, security and justice in which the free movement of persons is ensured. For the gradual establishment of such an area, the Community is to adopt, among others, the measures relating to judicial cooperation in civil matters having cross-border implications and needed for the proper functioning of the internal market.

(2) According to Article 65(c) of the Treaty, these measures are to include measures eliminating obstacles to the good functioning of civil proceedings, if necessary by promoting the compatibility of the rules on civil procedure applicable in the Member States.

(3) The Tampere European Council on 15 and 16 October 1999 called on the Council to establish minimum standards ensuring an adequate level of legal aid in cross-border cases throughout the Union.

(4) All Member States are contracting parties to the European Convention for the Protection of Human Rights and Fundamental Freedom of 4 November 1950. The matters referred to in this Directive shall be dealt with in compliance with that Convention and in particular the respect of the principle of equality of both parties in a dispute.

(5) This Directive seeks to promote the application of legal aid in cross-border disputes for persons who lack sufficient resources where aid is necessary to secure effective access to justice. The generally recognised right to access to justice is also reaffirmed by Article 47 of the Charter of Fundamental Rights of the European Union.

(6) Neither the lack of resources of a litigant, whether acting as claimant or as defendant, nor the difficulties flowing from a dispute's cross-border dimension should be allowed to hamper effective access to justice.

(7) Since the objectives of this Directive cannot be sufficiently achieved by the Member States acting alone and can therefore be better achieved at Community level, the Community may adopt measures, in accordance with the principle of subsidiarity as set out in Article 5 of the Treaty. In accordance with the principle of proportionality, as set out in that Article, this Directive does not go beyond what is necessary in order to achieve those objectives.

(8) The main purpose of this Directive is to guarantee an adequate level of legal aid in cross-border disputes by laying down certain minimum common standards relating to legal aid in such disputes. A Council directive is the most suitable legislative instrument for this purpose.

(9) This Directive applies in cross-border disputes, to civil and commercial matters.

(10) All persons involved in a civil or commercial dispute within the scope of this Directive must be able to assert their rights in the courts even if their personal financial situation makes it impossible for them to bear the costs of the proceedings. Legal aid is regarded as appropriate when it allows the recipient effective access to justice under the conditions laid down in this Directive.

(11) Legal aid should cover pre-litigation advice with a view to reaching a settlement prior to bringing legal proceedings, legal assistance in bringing a case before a court and representation in court and assistance with or exemption from the cost of proceedings.

(12) It shall be left to the law of the Member State in which the court is sitting or where enforcement is sought whether the costs of proceedings may include the costs of the opponent imposed on the recipient of legal aid.

(13) All Union citizens, wherever they are domiciled or habitually resident in the territory of a Member State, must be eligible for legal aid in cross-border disputes if they meet the conditions provided for by this Directive. The same applies to third-country nationals who habitually and lawfully reside in a Member State.

(14) Member States should be left free to define the threshold above which a person would be presumed able to bear the costs of proceedings, in the conditions defined in this Directive. Such thresholds are to be defined in the light of various objective factors such as income, capital or family situation.

(15) The objective of this Directive could not, however, be attained if legal aid applicants did not have the possibility of proving that they cannot bear the costs of proceedings even if their resources exceed the threshold defined by the Member State where the court is sitting. When making the assessment of whether legal aid is to be granted on this basis, the authorities in the Member State where the court is sitting may take into account information as to the fact that the applicant satisfies criteria in respect of financial eligibility in the Member State of domicile or habitual residence.

(16) The possibility in the instant case of resorting to other mechanisms to ensure effective access to justice is not a form of legal aid. But it can warrant a presumption that the person concerned can bear the costs of the procedure despite his/her unfavourable financial situation.

(17) Member States should be allowed to reject applications for legal aid in respect of manifestly unfounded actions or on grounds related to the merits of the case in so far as pre-litigation advice is offered and access to justice is guaranteed. When taking a decision on the merits of an application, Member States may reject legal aid applications when the applicant is claiming damage to his or her reputation, but has suffered no material or financial loss or the application concerns a claim arising directly out of the applicant's trade or self-employed profession.

(18) The complexity of and differences between the legal systems of the Member States and the costs inherent in the cross-border dimension of a dispute should not preclude access to justice. Legal aid should accordingly cover costs directly connected with the cross-border dimension of a dispute.

(19) When considering if the physical presence of a person in court is required, the courts of a Member State should take into consideration the full advantage of the possibilities offered by Council Regulation (EC) No 1206/2001 of 28 May 2001 on cooperation between the courts of the Member States in the taking of evidence in civil or commercial matters .

(20) If legal aid is granted, it must cover the entire proceeding, including expenses incurred in having a judgment enforced; the recipient should continue receiving this aid if an appeal is brought either against or by the recipient in so far as the conditions relating to the financial resources and the substance of the dispute remain fulfilled.

(21) Legal aid is to be granted on the same terms both for conventional legal proceedings and for out-of-court procedures such as mediation, where recourse to them is required by the law, or ordered by the court.

(22) Legal aid should also be granted for the enforcement of authentic instruments in another Member State under the conditions defined in this Directive.

(23) Since legal aid is given by the Member State in which the court is sitting or where enforcement is sought, except pre-litigation assistance if the legal aid applicant is not domiciled or habitually resident in the Member State where the court is sitting, that Member State must apply its own legislation, in compliance with the principles of this Directive.

(24) It is appropriate that legal aid is granted or refused by the competent authority of the Member State in which the court is sitting or where a judgment is to be enforced. This is the case both when that court is trying the case in substance and when it first has to decide whether it has jurisdiction.

(25) Judicial cooperation in civil matters should be organised between Member States to encourage information for the public and professional circles and to simplify and accelerate the transmission of legal aid applications between Member States.

(26) The notification and transmission mechanisms provided for by this Directive are inspired directly by those of the European Agreement on the transmission of applications for legal aid, signed in Strasbourg on 27 January 1977, hereinafter referred to as '1977 Agreement'. A time limit, not provided for by the 1977 Agreement, is set for the transmission of legal aid applications. A relatively short time limit contributes to the smooth operation of justice.

(27) The information transmitted pursuant to this Directive should enjoy protection. Since Directive 95/46/EC of the European Parliament and of the Council of 24 October 1995 on the protection of individuals with regard to the processing of personal data and on the free movement of such data, and Directive 97/66/EC of the European Parliament and of the Council of 15 December 1997 concerning the processing of personal data and the protection of privacy in the telecommunications sector, are applicable, there is no need for specific provisions on data protection in this Directive.

(28) The establishment of a standard form for legal aid applications and for the transmission of legal aid applications in the event of cross-border litigation will make the procedures easier and faster.

(29) Moreover, these application forms, as well as national application forms, should be made available on a European level through the information system of the European Judicial Network, established in accordance with Decision 2001/470/EC.

(30) The measures necessary for the implementation of this Directive should be adopted in accordance with Council Decision 1999/468/EC of 28 June 1999 laying down the procedures for the exercise of implementing powers conferred on the Commission.

(31) It should be specified that the establishment of minimum standards in cross-border disputes does not prevent Member States from making provision for more favourable arrangements for legal aid applicants and recipients.

(32) The 1977 Agreement and the additional Protocol to the European Agreement on the transmission of applications for legal aid, signed in Moscow in 2001, remain applicable to relations between Member States and third countries that are parties to the 1977 Agreement or the Protocol. But this Directive takes precedence over provisions contained in the 1977 Agreement and the Protocol in relations between Member States.

(33) The United Kingdom and Ireland have given notice of their wish to participate in the adoption of this Directive in accordance with Article 3 of the Protocol on the position of the United Kingdom and Ireland annexed to the Treaty on European Union and to the Treaty establishing the European Community.

(34) In accordance with Articles 1 and 2 of the Protocol on the position of Denmark annexed to the Treaty on European Union and to the Treaty establishing the European Community, Denmark is not taking part in the adoption of this Directive and is not bound by it or subject to its application,

HAS ADOPTED THIS DIRECTIVE:

## CHAPTER I

## SCOPE AND DEFINITIONS

### Article 1

### Aims and scope

1. The purpose of this Directive is to improve access to justice in cross-border disputes by establishing minimum common rules relating to legal aid in such disputes.

2. It shall apply, in cross-border disputes, to civil and commercial matters whatever the nature of the court or tribunal. It shall not extend, in particular, to revenue, customs or administrative matters.

3. In this Directive, 'Member State' shall mean Member States with the exception of Denmark.

*Article 2*

**Cross-border disputes**

1. For the purposes of this Directive, a cross-border dispute is one where the party applying for legal aid in the context of this Directive is domiciled or habitually resident in a Member State other than the Member State where the court is sitting or where the decision is to be enforced.

2. The Member State in which a party is domiciled shall be determined in accordance with Article 59 of Council Regulation (EC) No 44/2001 of 22 December 2000 on jurisdiction and the recognition and enforcement of judgments in civil and commercial matters.

3. The relevant moment to determine if there is a cross-border dispute is the time when the application is submitted, in accordance with this Directive.

## CHAPTER II

## RIGHT TO LEGAL AID

*Article 3*

**Right to legal aid**

1. Natural persons involved in a dispute covered by this Directive shall be entitled to receive appropriate legal aid in order to ensure their effective access to justice in accordance with the conditions laid down in this Directive.

2. Legal aid is considered to be appropriate when it guarantees:

(a)  pre-litigation advice with a view to reaching a settlement prior to bringing legal proceedings;

(b)  legal assistance and representation in court, and exemption from, or assistance with, the cost of proceedings of the recipient, including the costs referred to in Article 7 and the fees to persons mandated by the court to perform acts during the proceedings.

In Member States in which a losing party is liable for the costs of the opposing party, if the recipient loses the case, the legal aid shall cover the costs incurred by the opposing party, if it would have covered such costs had the recipient been domiciled or habitually resident in the Member State in which the court is sitting.

3. Member States need not provide legal assistance or representation in the courts or tribunals in proceedings especially designed to enable litigants to make their case in person, except when the courts or any other competent authority otherwise decide in order to ensure equality of parties or in view of the complexity of the case.

4. Member States may request that legal aid recipients pay reasonable contributions towards the costs of proceedings taking into account the conditions referred to in Article 5.

5. Member States may provide that the competent authority may decide that recipients of legal aid must refund it in whole or in part if their financial situation has substantially improved or if the decision to grant legal aid had been taken on the basis of inaccurate information given by the recipient.

*Article 4*

**Non-discrimination**

Member States shall grant legal aid without discrimination to Union citizens and third-country nationals residing lawfully in a Member State.

## CHAPTER III

## CONDITIONS AND EXTENT OF LEGAL AID

*Article 5*

**Conditions relating to financial resources**

1. Member States shall grant legal aid to persons referred to in Article 3(1) who are partly or totally

unable to meet the costs of proceedings referred to in Article 3(2) as a result of their economic situation, in order to ensure their effective access to justice.

2. The economic situation of a person shall be assessed by the competent authority of the Member State in which the court is sitting, in the light of various objective factors such as income, capital or family situation, including an assessment of the resources of persons who are financially dependant on the applicant.

3. Member States may define thresholds above which legal aid applicants are deemed partly or totally able to bear the costs of proceedings set out in Article 3(2). These thresholds shall be defined on the basis of the criteria defined in paragraph 2 of this Article.

4. Thresholds defined according to paragraph 3 of this Article may not prevent legal aid applicants who are above the thresholds from being granted legal aid if they prove that they are unable to pay the cost of the proceedings referred to in Article 3(2) as a result of differences in the cost of living between the Member States of domicile or habitual residence and of the forum.

5. Legal aid does not need to be granted to applicants in so far as they enjoy, in the instant case, effective access to other mechanisms that cover the cost of proceedings referred to in Article 3(2).

## Article 6

### Conditions relating to the substance of disputes

1. Member States may provide that legal aid applications for actions which appear to be manifestly unfounded may be rejected by the competent authorities.

2. If pre-litigation advice is offered, the benefit of further legal aid may be refused or cancelled on grounds related to the merits of the case in so far as access to justice is guaranteed.

3. When taking a decision on the merits of an application and without prejudice to Article 5, Member States shall consider the importance of the individual case to the applicant but may also take into account the nature of the case when the applicant is claiming damage to his or her reputation but has suffered no material or financial loss or when the application concerns a claim arising directly out of the applicant's trade or self-employed profession.

## Article 7

### Costs related to the cross-border nature of the dispute

Legal aid granted in the Member State in which the court is sitting shall cover the following costs directly related to the cross-border nature of the dispute:

(a) interpretation;

(b) translation of the documents required by the court or by the competent authority and presented by the recipient which are necessary for the resolution of the case; and

(c) travel costs to be borne by the applicant where the physical presence of the persons concerned with the presentation of the applicant's case is required in court by the law or by the court of that Member State and the court decides that the persons concerned cannot be heard to the satisfaction of the court by any other means.

## Article 8

### Costs covered by the Member State of the domicile or habitual residence

The Member State in which the legal aid applicant is domiciled or habitually resident shall provide legal aid, as referred to in Article 3(2), necessary to cover:

(a) costs relating to the assistance of a local lawyer or any other person entitled by the law to give legal advice, incurred in that Member State until the application for legal aid has been received, in accordance with this Directive, in the Member State where the court is sitting;

(b) the translation of the application and of the necessary supporting documents when the application is submitted to the authorities in that Member State.

*Article 9*

**Continuity of legal aid**

1. Legal aid shall continue to be granted totally or partially to recipients to cover expenses incurred in having a judgment enforced in the Member State where the court is sitting.

2. A recipient who in the Member State where the court is sitting has received legal aid shall receive legal aid provided for by the law of the Member State where recognition or enforcement is sought.

3. Legal aid shall continue to be available if an appeal is brought either against or by the recipient, subject to Articles 5 and 6.

4. Member States may make provision for the re-examination of the application at any stage in the proceedings on the grounds set out in Articles 3(3) and (5), 5 and 6, including proceedings referred to in paragraphs 1 to 3 of this Article.

*Article 10*

**Extrajudicial procedures**

Legal aid shall also be extended to extrajudicial procedures, under the conditions defined in this Directive, if the law requires the parties to use them, or if the parties to the dispute are ordered by the court to have recourse to them.

*Article 11*

**Authentic instruments**

Legal aid shall be granted for the enforcement of authentic instruments in another Member State under the conditions defined in this Directive.

## CHAPTER IV

## PROCEDURE

*Article 12*

**Authority granting legal aid**

Legal aid shall be granted or refused by the competent authority of the Member State in which the court is sitting, without prejudice to Article 8.

*Article 13*

**Introduction and transmission of legal aid applications**

1. Legal aid applications may be submitted to either:

(a)  the competent authority of the Member State in which the applicant is domiciled or habitually resident (transmitting authority); or

(b)  the competent authority of the Member State in which the court is sitting or where the decision is to be enforced (receiving authority).

2. Legal aid applications shall be completed in, and supporting documents translated into:

(a)  the official language or one of the languages of the Member State of the competent receiving authority which corresponds to one of the languages of the Community institutions; or

(b)  another language which that Member State has indicated it can accept in accordance with Article 14(3).

3. The competent transmitting authorities may decide to refuse to transmit an application if it is manifestly:

(a)  unfounded; or

(b)  outside the scope of this Directive.

The conditions referred to in Article 15(2) and (3) apply to such decisions.

4. The competent transmitting authority shall assist the applicant in ensuring that the application is accompanied by all the supporting documents known by it to be required to enable the application to be determined. It shall also assist the applicant in providing any necessary translation of the supporting documents, in accordance with Article 8(b).

The competent transmitting authority shall transmit the application to the competent receiving authority in the other Member State within 15 days of the receipt of the application duly completed in one of the languages referred to in paragraph 2, and the supporting documents, translated, where necessary, into one of those languages.

5. Documents transmitted under this Directive shall be exempt from legalisation or any equivalent formality.

6. The Member States may not charge for services rendered in accordance with paragraph 4. Member States in which the legal aid applicant is domiciled or habitually resident may lay down that the applicant must repay the costs of translation borne by the competent transmitting authority if the application for legal aid is rejected by the competent authority.

## Article 14

### Competent authorities and language

1. Member States shall designate the authority or authorities competent to send (transmitting authorities) and receive (receiving authorities) the application.

2. Each Member State shall provide the Commission with the following information:

— the names and addresses of the competent receiving or transmitting authorities referred to in paragraph 1,

— the geographical areas in which they have jurisdiction,

— the means by which they are available to receive applications, and

— the languages that may be used for the completion of the application.

3. Member States shall notify the Commission of the official language or languages of the Community institutions other than their own which is or are acceptable to the competent receiving authority for completion of the legal aid applications to be received, in accordance with this Directive.

4. Member States shall communicate to the Commission the information referred to in paragraphs 2 and 3 before 30 November 2004. Any subsequent modification of such information shall be notified to the Commission no later than two months before the modification enters into force in that Member State.

5. The information referred to in paragraphs 2 and 3 shall be published in the Official Journal of the European Communities.

## Article 15

### Processing of applications

1. The national authorities empowered to rule on legal aid applications shall ensure that the applicant is fully informed of the processing of the application.

2. Where applications are totally or partially rejected, the reasons for rejection shall be given.

3. Member States shall make provision for review of or appeals against decisions rejecting legal aid applications. Member States may exempt cases where the request for legal aid is rejected by a court or tribunal against whose decision on the subject of the case there is no judicial remedy under national law or by a court of appeal.

4. When the appeals against a decision refusing or cancelling legal aid by virtue of Article 6 are of an administrative nature, they shall always be ultimately subject to judicial review.

*Article 16*

**Standard form**

1. To facilitate transmission, a standard form for legal aid applications and for the transmission of such applications shall be established in accordance with the procedure set out in Article 17(2).

2. The standard form for the transmission of legal aid applications shall be established at the latest by 30 May 2003.

The standard form for legal aid applications shall be established at the latest by 30 November 2004.

## CHAPTER V

## FINAL PROVISIONS

*Article 17*

**Committee**

1. The Commission shall be assisted by a Committee.

2. Where reference is made to this paragraph, Articles 3 and 7 of Decision 1999/468/EC shall apply.

3. The Committee shall adopt its Rules of Procedure.

*Article 18*

**Information**

The competent national authorities shall cooperate to provide the general public and professional circles with information on the various systems of legal aid, in particular via the European Judicial Network, established in accordance with Decision 2001/470/EC.

*Article 19*

**More favourable provisions**

This Directive shall not prevent the Member States from making provision for more favourable arrangements for legal aid applicants and recipients.

*Article 20*

**Relation with other instruments**

This Directive shall, as between the Member States, and in relation to matters to which it applies, take precedence over provisions contained in bilateral and multilateral agreements concluded by Member States including:

(a)  the European Agreement on the transmission of applications for legal aid, signed in Strasbourg on 27 January 1977, as amended by the additional Protocol to the European Agreement on the transmission of applications for legal aid, signed in Moscow in 2001;

(b)  the Hague Convention of 25 October 1980 on International Access to Justice.

*Article 21*

**Transposition into national law**

1. Member States shall bring into force the laws, regulations and administrative provisions necessary to comply with this Directive no later than 30 November 2004 with the exception of Article 3(2)(a) where the transposition of this Directive into national law shall take place no later than 30 May 2006. They shall forthwith inform the Commission thereof.

When Member States adopt these measures, they shall contain a reference to this Directive or shall be accompanied by such a reference on the occasion of their official publication. The methods of making such a reference shall be laid down by Member States.

2. Member States shall communicate to the Commission the text of the main provisions of national law which they adopt in the field covered by this Directive.

*Article 22*

**Entry into force**

This Directive shall enter into force on the date of its publication in the Official Journal of the European Communities.

*Article 23*

**Addressees**

This Directive is addressed to the Member States in accordance with the Treaty establishing the European Community.

# Directive 2008/52/EC of the European Parliament and of the Council of 21 May 2008 on certain aspects of mediation in civil and commercial matters

[2008] OJ L136/3

THE EUROPEAN PARLIAMENT AND THE COUNCIL OF THE EUROPEAN UNION,

Having regard to the Treaty establishing the European Community, and in particular Article 61(c) and the second indent of Article 67(5) thereof,

Having regard to the proposal from the Commission,

Having regard to the Opinion of the European Economic and Social Committee,

Acting in accordance with the procedure laid down in Article 251 of the Treaty,

Whereas:

(1) The Community has set itself the objective of maintaining and developing an area of freedom, security and justice, in which the free movement of persons is ensured. To that end, the Community has to adopt, inter alia, measures in the field of judicial cooperation in civil matters that are necessary for the proper functioning of the internal market.

(2) The principle of access to justice is fundamental and, with a view to facilitating better access to justice, the European Council at its meeting in Tampere on 15 and 16 October 1999 called for alternative, extra-judicial procedures to be created by the Member States.

(3) In May 2000 the Council adopted Conclusions on alternative methods of settling disputes under civil and commercial law, stating that the establishment of basic principles in this area is an essential step towards enabling the appropriate development and operation of extrajudicial procedures for the settlement of disputes in civil and commercial matters so as to simplify and improve access to justice.

(4) In April 2002 the Commission presented a Green Paper on alternative dispute resolution in civil and commercial law, taking stock of the existing situation as concerns alternative dispute resolution methods in the European Union and initiating widespread consultations with Member States and interested parties on possible measures to promote the use of mediation.

(5) The objective of securing better access to justice, as part of the policy of the European Union to establish an area of freedom, security and justice, should encompass access to judicial as well as extrajudicial dispute resolution methods. This Directive should contribute to the proper functioning of the internal market, in particular as concerns the availability of mediation services.

(6) Mediation can provide a cost-effective and quick extrajudicial resolution of disputes in civil and commercial matters through processes tailored to the needs of the parties. Agreements resulting from mediation are more likely to be complied with voluntarily and are more likely to preserve an amicable and sustainable relationship between the parties. These benefits become even more pronounced in situations displaying cross-border elements.

(7) In order to promote further the use of mediation and ensure that parties having recourse to mediation can rely on a predictable legal framework, it is necessary to introduce framework legislation addressing, in particular, key aspects of civil procedure.

(8) The provisions of this Directive should apply only to mediation in cross-border disputes, but nothing should prevent Member States from applying such provisions also to internal mediation processes.

(9) This Directive should not in any way prevent the use of modern communication technologies in the mediation process.

(10) This Directive should apply to processes whereby two or more parties to a cross-border dispute attempt by themselves, on a voluntary basis, to reach an amicable agreement on the settlement of their

dispute with the assistance of a mediator. It should apply in civil and commercial matters. However, it should not apply to rights and obligations on which the parties are not free to decide themselves under the relevant applicable law. Such rights and obligations are particularly frequent in family law and employment law.

(11) This Directive should not apply to pre-contractual negotiations or to processes of an adjudicatory nature such as certain judicial conciliation schemes, consumer complaint schemes, arbitration and expert determination or to processes administered by persons or bodies issuing a formal recommendation, whether or not it be legally binding as to the resolution of the dispute.

(12) This Directive should apply to cases where a court refers parties to mediation or in which national law prescribes mediation. Furthermore, in so far as a judge may act as a mediator under national law, this Directive should also apply to mediation conducted by a judge who is not responsible for any judicial proceedings relating to the matter or matters in dispute. This Directive should not, however, extend to attempts made by the court or judge seised to settle a dispute in the context of judicial proceedings concerning the dispute in question or to cases in which the court or judge seised requests assistance or advice from a competent person.

(13) The mediation provided for in this Directive should be a voluntary process in the sense that the parties are themselves in charge of the process and may organise it as they wish and terminate it at any time. However, it should be possible under national law for the courts to set time-limits for a mediation process. Moreover, the courts should be able to draw the parties' attention to the possibility of mediation whenever this is appropriate.

(14) Nothing in this Directive should prejudice national legislation making the use of mediation compulsory or subject to incentives or sanctions provided that such legislation does not prevent parties from exercising their right of access to the judicial system. Nor should anything in this Directive prejudice existing self-regulating mediation systems in so far as these deal with aspects which are not covered by this Directive.

(15) In order to provide legal certainty, this Directive should indicate which date should be relevant for determining whether or not a dispute which the parties attempt to settle through mediation is a cross-border dispute. In the absence of a written agreement, the parties should be deemed to agree to use mediation at the point in time when they take specific action to start the mediation process.

(16) To ensure the necessary mutual trust with respect to confidentiality, effect on limitation and prescription periods, and recognition and enforcement of agreements resulting from mediation, Member States should encourage, by any means they consider appropriate, the training of mediators and the introduction of effective quality control mechanisms concerning the provision of mediation services.

(17) Member States should define such mechanisms, which may include having recourse to market-based solutions, and should not be required to provide any funding in that respect. The mechanisms should aim at preserving the flexibility of the mediation process and the autonomy of the parties, and at ensuring that mediation is conducted in an effective, impartial and competent way. Mediators should be made aware of the existence of the European Code of Conduct for Mediators which should also be made available to the general public on the Internet.

(18) In the field of consumer protection, the Commission has adopted a Recommendation establishing minimum quality criteria which out-of-court bodies involved in the consensual resolution of consumer disputes should offer to their users. Any mediators or organisations coming within the scope of that Recommendation should be encouraged to respect its principles. In order to facilitate the dissemination of information concerning such bodies, the Commission should set up a database of out-of-court schemes which Member States consider as respecting the principles of that Recommendation.

(19) Mediation should not be regarded as a poorer alternative to judicial proceedings in the sense that compliance with agreements resulting from mediation would depend on the good will of the parties. Member States should therefore ensure that the parties to a written agreement resulting from mediation can have the content of their agreement made enforceable. It should only be possible for a Member State to refuse to make an agreement enforceable if the content is contrary to its law, including

its private international law, or if its law does not provide for the enforceability of the content of the specific agreement. This could be the case if the obligation specified in the agreement was by its nature unenforceable.

(20) The content of an agreement resulting from mediation which has been made enforceable in a Member State should be recognised and declared enforceable in the other Member States in accordance with applicable Community or national law. This could, for example, be on the basis of Council Regulation (EC) No 44/2001 of 22 December 2000 on jurisdiction and the recognition and enforcement of judgments in civil and commercial matters or Council Regulation (EC) No 2201/2003 of 27 November 2003 concerning jurisdiction and the recognition and enforcement of judgments in matrimonial matters and the matters of parental responsibility.

(21) Regulation (EC) No 2201/2003 specifically provides that, in order to be enforceable in another Member State, agreements between the parties have to be enforceable in the Member State in which they were concluded. Consequently, if the content of an agreement resulting from mediation in a family law matter is not enforceable in the Member State where the agreement was concluded and where the request for enforceability is made, this Directive should not encourage the parties to circumvent the law of that Member State by having their agreement made enforceable in another Member State.

(22) This Directive should not affect the rules in the Member States concerning enforcement of agreements resulting from mediation.

(23) Confidentiality in the mediation process is important and this Directive should therefore provide for a minimum degree of compatibility of civil procedural rules with regard to how to protect the confidentiality of mediation in any subsequent civil and commercial judicial proceedings or arbitration.

(24) In order to encourage the parties to use mediation, Member States should ensure that their rules on limitation and prescription periods do not prevent the parties from going to court or to arbitration if their mediation attempt fails. Member States should make sure that this result is achieved even though this Directive does not harmonise national rules on limitation and prescription periods. Provisions on limitation and prescription periods in international agreements as implemented in the Member States, for instance in the area of transport law, should not be affected by this Directive.

(25) Member States should encourage the provision of information to the general public on how to contact mediators and organisations providing mediation services. They should also encourage legal practitioners to inform their clients of the possibility of mediation.

(26) In accordance with point 34 of the Interinstitutional agreement on better law-making, Member States are encouraged to draw up, for themselves and in the interests of the Community, their own tables illustrating, as far as possible, the correlation between this Directive and the transposition measures, and to make them public.

(27) This Directive seeks to promote the fundamental rights, and takes into account the principles, recognised in particular by the Charter of Fundamental Rights of the European Union.

(28) Since the objective of this Directive cannot be sufficiently achieved by the Member States and can therefore, by reason of the scale or effects of the action, be better achieved at Community level, the Community may adopt measures in accordance with the principle of subsidiarity as set out in Article 5 of the Treaty. In accordance with the principle of proportionality, as set out in that Article, this Directive does not go beyond what is necessary in order to achieve that objective.

(29) In accordance with Article 3 of the Protocol on the position of the United Kingdom and Ireland, annexed to the Treaty on European Union and to the Treaty establishing the European Community, the United Kingdom and Ireland have given notice of their wish to take part in the adoption and application of this Directive.

(30) In accordance with Articles 1 and 2 of the Protocol on the position of Denmark, annexed to the Treaty on European Union and to the Treaty establishing the European Community, Denmark does not take part in the adoption of this Directive and is not bound by it or subject to its application,

HAVE ADOPTED THIS DIRECTIVE:

## Article 1

**Objective and scope**

1. The objective of this Directive is to facilitate access to alternative dispute resolution and to promote the amicable settlement of disputes by encouraging the use of mediation and by ensuring a balanced relationship between mediation and judicial proceedings.

2. This Directive shall apply, in cross-border disputes, to civil and commercial matters except as regards rights and obligations which are not at the parties' disposal under the relevant applicable law. It shall not extend, in particular, to revenue, customs or administrative matters or to the liability of the State for acts and omissions in the exercise of State authority (acta iure imperii).

3. In this Directive, the term 'Member State' shall mean Member States with the exception of Denmark.

## Article 2

**Cross-border disputes**

1. For the purposes of this Directive a cross-border dispute shall be one in which at least one of the parties is domiciled or habitually resident in a Member State other than that of any other party on the date on which:

(a)   the parties agree to use mediation after the dispute has arisen;

(b)   mediation is ordered by a court;

(c)   an obligation to use mediation arises under national law; or

(d)   for the purposes of Article 5 an invitation is made to the parties.

2. Notwithstanding paragraph 1, for the purposes of Articles 7 and 8 a cross-border dispute shall also be one in which judicial proceedings or arbitration following mediation between the parties are initiated in a Member State other than that in which the parties were domiciled or habitually resident on the date referred to in paragraph 1(a), (b) or (c).

3. For the purposes of paragraphs 1 and 2, domicile shall be determined in accordance with Articles 59 and 60 of Regulation (EC) No 44/2001.

## Article 3

**Definitions**

For the purposes of this Directive the following definitions shall apply:

(a)   'Mediation' means a structured process, however named or referred to, whereby two or more parties to a dispute attempt by themselves, on a voluntary basis, to reach an agreement on the settlement of their dispute with the assistance of a mediator. This process may be initiated by the parties or suggested or ordered by a court or prescribed by the law of a Member State.

It includes mediation conducted by a judge who is not responsible for any judicial proceedings concerning the dispute in question. It excludes attempts made by the court or the judge seised to settle a dispute in the course of judicial proceedings concerning the dispute in question.

(b)   'Mediator' means any third person who is asked to conduct a mediation in an effective, impartial and competent way, regardless of the denomination or profession of that third person in the Member State concerned and of the way in which the third person has been appointed or requested to conduct the mediation.

## Article 4

**Ensuring the quality of mediation**

1. Member States shall encourage, by any means which they consider appropriate, the development of, and adherence to, voluntary codes of conduct by mediators and organisations providing mediation services, as well as other effective quality control mechanisms concerning the provision of mediation services.

2. Member States shall encourage the initial and further training of mediators in order to ensure that the mediation is conducted in an effective, impartial and competent way in relation to the parties.

## Article 5

### Recourse to mediation

1. A court before which an action is brought may, when appropriate and having regard to all the circumstances of the case, invite the parties to use mediation in order to settle the dispute. The court may also invite the parties to attend an information session on the use of mediation if such sessions are held and are easily available.

2. This Directive is without prejudice to national legislation making the use of mediation compulsory or subject to incentives or sanctions, whether before or after judicial proceedings have started, provided that such legislation does not prevent the parties from exercising their right of access to the judicial system.

## Article 6

### Enforceability of agreements resulting from mediation

1. Member States shall ensure that it is possible for the parties, or for one of them with the explicit consent of the others, to request that the content of a written agreement resulting from mediation be made enforceable. The content of such an agreement shall be made enforceable unless, in the case in question, either the content of that agreement is contrary to the law of the Member State where the request is made or the law of that Member State does not provide for its enforceability.

2. The content of the agreement may be made enforceable by a court or other competent authority in a judgment or decision or in an authentic instrument in accordance with the law of the Member State where the request is made.

3. Member States shall inform the Commission of the courts or other authorities competent to receive requests in accordance with paragraphs 1 and 2.

4. Nothing in this Article shall affect the rules applicable to the recognition and enforcement in another Member State of an agreement made enforceable in accordance with paragraph 1.

## Article 7

### Confidentiality of mediation

1. Given that mediation is intended to take place in a manner which respects confidentiality, Member States shall ensure that, unless the parties agree otherwise, neither mediators nor those involved in the administration of the mediation process shall be compelled to give evidence in civil and commercial judicial proceedings or arbitration regarding information arising out of or in connection with a mediation process, except:

(a) where this is necessary for overriding considerations of public policy of the Member State concerned, in particular when required to ensure the protection of the best interests of children or to prevent harm to the physical or psychological integrity of a person; or

(b) where disclosure of the content of the agreement resulting from mediation is necessary in order to implement or enforce that agreement.

2. Nothing in paragraph 1 shall preclude Member States from enacting stricter measures to protect the confidentiality of mediation.

## Article 8

### Effect of mediation on limitation and prescription periods

1. Member States shall ensure that parties who choose mediation in an attempt to settle a dispute are not subsequently prevented from initiating judicial proceedings or arbitration in relation to that dispute by the expiry of limitation or prescription periods during the mediation process.

2. Paragraph 1 shall be without prejudice to provisions on limitation or prescription periods in international agreements to which Member States are party.

*Article 9*

**Information for the general public**

Member States shall encourage, by any means which they consider appropriate, the availability to the general public, in particular on the Internet, of information on how to contact mediators and organisations providing mediation services.

*Article 10*

**Information on competent courts and authorities**

The Commission shall make publicly available, by any appropriate means, information on the competent courts or authorities communicated by the Member States pursuant to Article 6(3).

*Article 11*

**Review**

Not later than 21 May 2016, the Commission shall submit to the European Parliament, the Council and the European Economic and Social Committee a report on the application of this Directive. The report shall consider the development of mediation throughout the European Union and the impact of this Directive in the Member States. If necessary, the report shall be accompanied by proposals to adapt this Directive.

*Article 12*

**Transposition**

1. Member States shall bring into force the laws, regulations, and administrative provisions necessary to comply with this Directive before 21 May 2011, with the exception of Article 10, for which the date of compliance shall be 21 November 2010 at the latest. They shall forthwith inform the Commission thereof.

When they are adopted by Member States, these measures shall contain a reference to this Directive or shall be accompanied by such reference on the occasion of their official publication. The methods of making such reference shall be laid down by Member States.

2. Member States shall communicate to the Commission the text of the main provisions of national law which they adopt in the field covered by this Directive.

*Article 13*

**Entry into force**

This Directive shall enter into force on the 20th day following its publication in the Official Journal of the European Union.

*Article 14*

**Addressees**

This Directive is addressed to the Member States.

# Council Decision of 28 May 2001 establishing a European Judicial Network in civil and commercial matters (2001/470/EC)

[2001] OJ L174/25

THE COUNCIL OF THE EUROPEAN UNION,

Having regard to the Treaty establishing the European Community, and in particular Articles 61(c) and (d), 66 and 67(1) thereof,

Having regard to the proposal from the Commission,

Having regard to the opinion of the European Parliament,

Having regard to the opinion of the Economic and Social Committee,

Whereas:

(1) The European Union has set itself the objective of maintaining and developing the European Union as an area of freedom, security and justice, in which the free movement of persons is assured.

(2) The gradual establishment of this area and the sound operation of the internal market entails the need to improve, simplify and expedite effective judicial cooperation between the Member States in civil and commercial matters.

(3) The action plan of the Council and the Commission on how best to implement the provisions of the Treaty of Amsterdam on an area of freedom, security and justice which was adopted by the Council on 3 December 1998 and approved by the European Council on 11 and 12 December 1998 acknowledges that reinforcement of judicial cooperation in civil matters represents a fundamental stage in the creation of a European judicial area which will bring tangible benefits for every European Union citizen.

(4) One of the measures provided for in paragraph 40 of the action plan is to examine the possibility of extending the concept of the European Judicial Network in criminal matters to embrace civil proceedings.

(5) The conclusions of the special European Council held at Tampere on 15 and 16 October 1999 recommend the establishment of an easily accessible information system, to be maintained and updated by a Network of competent national authorities.

(6) In order to improve, simplify and expedite effective judicial cooperation between the Member States in civil and commercial matters, it is necessary to establish at Community level a network cooperation structure — the European Judicial Network in civil and commercial matters.

(7) This is a subject falling within the ambit of Articles 65 and 66 of the Treaty, and the measures are to be adopted in accordance with Article 67.

(8) To ensure the attainment of the objectives of the European Judicial Network in civil and commercial matters, the rules governing its establishment should be laid down in a mandatory instrument of Community law.

(9) The objectives of the proposed action, namely to improve effective judicial cooperation between the Member States and effective access to justice for persons engaging in cross-border litigation cannot be sufficiently achieved by the Member States and can therefore by reason of the scale or effects of the action be better achieved at Community level, the Community may adopt measures in accordance with the principle of subsidiarity as set out in Article 5 of the Treaty. In accordance with the principle of proportionality as set out in that Article, this Decision does not go beyond what is necessary in order to achieve those objectives.

(10) The European Judicial Network in civil and commercial matters established by this Decision seeks to facilitate judicial cooperation between the Member States in civil and commercial matters both in areas to which existing instruments apply and in those where no instrument is currently applicable.

(11) In certain specific areas, Community or international instruments relating to judicial cooperation in civil and commercial matters already provide for cooperation mechanisms. The European Judicial Network in civil and commercial matters does not set out to replace these mechanisms, and it must operate in full compliance with them. This Decision will consequently be without prejudice to Community or international instruments relating to judicial cooperation in civil or commercial matters.

(12) The European Judicial Network in civil and commercial matters should be established in stages on the basis of the closest cooperation between the Commission and the Member States. It should be able to take advantage of modern communication and information technologies.

(13) To attain its objectives, the European Judicial Network in civil and commercial matters needs to be supported by contact points designated by the Member States and to be sure of the participation of their authorities with specific responsibilities for judicial cooperation in civil and commercial matters. Contacts between them and periodic meetings are essential to the operation of the Network.

(14) It is essential that efforts to establish an area of freedom, security and justice produce tangible benefits for persons engaging in cross-border litigation. It is accordingly necessary for the European Judicial Network in civil and commercial matters to promote access to justice. To this end, using the information supplied and updated by the contact points, the Network should progressively establish an information system that is accessible to the public, both the general public and specialists.

(15) This Decision does not preclude the provision of other information than that which is provided for herein, within the European Judicial Network in civil and commercial matters and to the public. The enumeration in Title III is accordingly not to be regarded as exhaustive.

(16) Processing of information and data should take place in compliance with Directive 95/46/EC of the European Parliament and of the Council of 24 October 1995 on the protection of individuals with regard to the processing of personal data and of the free movement of such data and Directive 97/66/EC of the European Parliament and of the Council of 15 December 1997 concerning the processing of personal data and the protection of privacy in the telecommunications sector.

(17) To ensure that the European Judicial Network in civil and commercial matters remains an effective instrument, incorporates the best practice in judicial cooperation and internal operation and meets the public's expectations, provision should be made for periodic evaluations and for proposals for such changes as may be found necessary.

(18) The United Kingdom and Ireland, in accordance with Article 3 of the Protocol on the position of the United Kingdom and Ireland annexed to the Treaty on European Union and to the Treaty establishing the European Community, have given notice of their wish to take part in the adoption and application of this Decision.

(19) Denmark, in accordance with Articles 1 and 2 of the Protocol on the position of Denmark, annexed to the Treaty on European Union and to the Treaty establishing the European Community, is not participating in the adoption of this Decision and is therefore not bound by it nor subject to its application,

HAS ADOPTED THIS DECISION:

## TITLE I

## PRINCIPLES OF THE EUROPEAN JUDICIAL NETWORK IN CIVIL AND COMMERCIAL MATTERS

*Article 1*

Establishment

1. A European Judicial Network in civil and commercial matters ('the Network') is hereby established among the Member States.

2. In this Decision, the term 'Member State' shall mean Member States with the exception of Denmark.

*Article 2*

**Composition**

1. The Network shall be composed of:

(a) contact points designated by the Member States, in accordance with paragraph 2;

(b) central bodies and central authorities provided for in Community instruments, instruments of international law to which the Member States are parties or rules of domestic law in the area of judicial cooperation in civil and commercial matters;

[(c) the liaison magistrates to whom Joint Action 96/277/JHA of 22 April 1996 concerning a framework for the exchange of liaison magistrates to improve judicial cooperation between the Member States of the European Union applies, where they have responsibilities in judicial cooperation in civil and commercial matters;

(d) any other appropriate judicial or administrative authority with responsibilities for judicial cooperation in civil and commercial matters whose membership of the Network is considered to be useful by the Member State to which it belongs;

[(e) professional associations representing, at national level in the Member States, legal practitioners directly involved in the application of Community and international instruments concerning judicial cooperation in civil and commercial matters.]

2. Each Member State shall designate a contact point. Each Member State may, however, designate a limited number of other contact points if they consider this necessary on the basis of the existence of separate legal systems, the domestic distribution of jurisdiction, the tasks to be entrusted to the contact points or in order to associate judicial bodies that frequently deal with cross-border litigation directly with the activities of the contact points.

Where a Member State designates several contact points, it shall ensure that appropriate coordination mechanisms apply between them.

[If the contact point designated under this paragraph is not a judge, the Member State concerned shall provide for effective liaison with the national judiciary. To facilitate this, a Member State may designate a judge to support this function. This judge shall be a member of the Network.]

[2a. Member States shall ensure that the contact points have sufficient and appropriate facilities in terms of staff, resources and modern means of communication to adequately fulfil their tasks as contact points.]

3. The Member States shall identify the authorities mentioned at points (b) and (c) of paragraph 1.

4. The Member States shall designate the authorities mentioned at point (d) of paragraph 1.

[4a. Member States shall determine the professional associations referred to in paragraph 1(e). To that end, they shall obtain the agreement of the professional associations concerned on their participation in the Network.

Where there is more than one association representing a legal profession in a Member State, it shall be the responsibility of that Member State to provide for appropriate representation of that profession on the Network.]

[5. The Member States shall notify the Commission, in accordance with Article 20, of the names and full addresses of the authorities referred to in paragraphs 1 and 2 of this Article, specifying:]

(a) the communication facilities available to them;

(b) their knowledge of languages; and

[(c) where appropriate, their specific functions in the Network, including, where there is more than one contact point, their specific responsibilities.]

*Article 3*

**Tasks and activities of the Network**

1. The Network shall be responsible for:

(a) facilitating judicial cooperation between the Member States in civil and commercial matters, including devising, progressively establishing and updating an information system for the members of the Network;

[(b) facilitating effective access to justice, through measures providing information on the working of Community and international instruments concerning judicial cooperation in civil and commercial matters.]

2. Without prejudice to other Community or international instruments relating to judicial cooperation in civil or commercial matters, the Network shall develop its activities for the following purposes in particular:

(a) the smooth operation of procedures having a cross-border impact and the facilitation of requests for judicial cooperation between the Member States, in particular where no Community or international instrument is applicable;

[(b) the effective and practical application of Community instruments or conventions in force between two or more Member States.

In particular where the law of another Member State is applicable, the courts or authorities responsible for the matter may apply to the Network for information on the content of that law;

(c) the establishment, maintenance and promotion of an information system for the public on judicial cooperation in civil and commercial matters in the European Union, on relevant Community and international instruments and on the domestic law of the Member States, with particular reference to access to justice.]

The main source of information shall be the Network's website containing up-to-date information in all the official languages of the institutions of the Union.

*Article 4*

**Modus operandi of the Network**

The Network shall accomplish its tasks in particular by the following means:

1. it shall facilitate appropriate contacts between the authorities of the Member States mentioned in Article 2(1) for the accomplishment of the tasks provided for by Article 3;

2. it shall organise periodic meetings of the contact points and of the members of the Network in accordance with the rules laid down in Title II;

3. it shall draw up and keep updated the information on judicial cooperation in civil and commercial matters and the legal systems of the Member States referred to in Title III, in accordance with the rules laid down in that Title.

*Article 5*

**Contact points**

1. The contact points shall be at the disposal of the authorities referred to in Article 2(1)(b) to (d) for the accomplishment of the tasks provided for by Article 3.

The contact points shall also be at the disposal of the local judicial authorities in their own Member State for the same purposes, in accordance with rules to be determined by each Member State.

[2. In particular, the contact points shall:

(a) ensure that the local judicial authorities receive general information concerning the Community and international instruments relating to judicial cooperation in civil and commercial matters. In particular, they shall ensure that the Network, including the website of the Network, is better known to the local judicial authorities;

(b) supply the other contact points, the authorities mentioned in Article 2(1)(b) to (d) and the local judicial authorities in their own Member State with all the information needed for sound judicial cooperation between the Member States in accordance with Article 3, in order to assist them in preparing operable requests for judicial cooperation and in establishing the most appropriate direct contacts;

(c) supply any information to facilitate the application of the law of another Member State that is applicable under a Community or international instrument. To this end, the contact point to which such a request is addressed may draw on the support of any of the other authorities in its Member State referred to in Article 2 in order to supply the information requested. The information contained in the reply shall not be binding on the contact point, the authorities consulted or the authority which made the request;

(d) seek solutions to difficulties arising on the occasion of a request for judicial cooperation, without prejudice to paragraph 4 of this Article and to Article 6;

(e) facilitate coordination of the processing of requests for judicial cooperation in the relevant Member State, in particular where several requests from the judicial authorities in that Member State fall to be executed in another Member State;

(f) contribute to generally informing the public, through the Network's website, on judicial cooperation in civil and commercial matters in the European Union, on relevant Community and international instruments and on the domestic law of the Member States, with particular reference to access to justice;

(g) collaborate in the organisation of, and participate in, the meetings referred to in Article 9;

(h) assist with the preparation and updating of the information referred to in Title III, and in particular with the information system for the public, in accordance with the rules laid down in that Title;

(i) ensure coordination between members of the Network at national level;

(j) draw up a two-yearly report on their activities, including, where appropriate, best practice in the Network, submit it at a meeting of the members of the Network, and draw specific attention to possible improvements in the Network.]

3. Where a contact point receives a request for information from another member of the Network to which it is unable to respond, it shall forward it to the contact point or the member of the Network which is best able to respond to it. The contact point shall remain available for any such assistance as may be useful for subsequent contacts.

4. In areas where Community or international instruments governing judicial cooperation already provide for the designation of authorities responsible for facilitating judicial cooperation, contact points shall address requesters to such authorities.

[*Article 5a*

**Professional associations**

1. In order to contribute to the accomplishment of the tasks provided for by Article 3, the contact points shall have appropriate contacts with the professional associations mentioned in Article 2(1)(e), in accordance with rules to be determined by each Member State.

2. In particular, the contacts referred to in paragraph 1 may include the following activities:

(a) exchange of experience and information as regards the effective and practical application of Community and international instruments;

(b) collaboration in the preparation and updating of the information sheets referred to in Article 15;

(c) participation of the professional associations in relevant meetings.

3. Professional associations shall not request information relating to individual cases from contact points.]

*Article 6*

**Relevant authorities for the purposes of Community or international instruments relating to judicial cooperation in civil and commercial matters**

1. The involvement of relevant authorities provided for by Community or international instruments relating to judicial cooperation in civil and commercial matters in the Network shall be without prejudice to the powers conferred on them by the instrument providing for their designation.

Contacts within the Network shall be without prejudice to regular or occasional contacts between these authorities.

2. In each Member State the authorities provided for by Community or international instruments relating to judicial cooperation in civil and commercial matters and the contact points of the Network shall engage in regular exchanges of views and contacts to ensure that their respective experience is disseminated as widely as possible.

[To this end, each Member State shall ensure, in accordance with the procedures to be determined by it, that the contact point(s) and competent authorities have the means to meet on a regular basis.]

3. The contact points of the Network shall be at the disposal of the authorities provided for by Community or international instruments relating to judicial cooperation in civil and commercial matters and shall assist them in all practicable ways.

*Article 7*

**Language knowledge of the contact points**

[To facilitate the practical operation of the Network, each Member State shall ensure that the contact points have adequate knowledge of an official language of the institutions of the Union other than their own, given that they need to be able to communicate with the contact points in other Member States.]

Member States shall facilitate and encourage specialised language training for contact point staff and promote exchanges of staff between contact points in the Member States.

[*Article 8*

**Processing of requests for judicial cooperation**

1. The contact points shall respond to all requests submitted to them without delay and at the latest within fifteen days of receipt thereof. If a contact point cannot reply to a request within that time limit, it shall inform the maker of the request briefly of this fact, indicating how much time it considers that it will need to reply, but this period shall not, as a rule, exceed thirty days.

2. In order to respond as efficiently and rapidly as possible to the requests referred to in paragraph 1, the contact points shall use the most appropriate technological facilities made available to them by the Member States.

3. The Commission shall keep a secure, limited-access electronic register of the requests for judicial cooperation and replies referred to in Article 5(2)(b), (c), (d) and (e). The contact points shall ensure that the information necessary for the establishment and operation of this register is supplied regularly to the Commission.

4. The Commission shall supply the contact points with information on the statistics relating to the judicial cooperation requests and replies referred to in paragraph 3 at least once every six months.]

TITLE II

**MEETINGS WITHIN THE NETWORK**

[*Article 9*

**Meetings of the contact points**

1. The contact points of the Network shall meet at least once every six months, in accordance with Article 12.

2. Each Member State shall be represented at those meetings by one or more contact points, who may be accompanied by other members of the Network, but there shall be no more than six representatives per Member State.]

*Article 10*

**Purpose of periodic meetings of contact points**

1. The purpose of the periodic meetings of contact points shall be to:

(a) enable the contact points to get to know each other and exchange experience, in particular as regards the operation of the Network;

(b) provide a platform for discussion of practical and legal problems encountered by the Member States in the course of judicial cooperation, with particular reference to the application of measures adopted by the European Community;

(c) identify best practices in judicial cooperation in civil and commercial matters and ensure that relevant information is disseminated within the Network;

(d) exchange data and views, in particular on the structure, organisation and content of and access to the available information mentioned in Title III;

(e) draw up guidelines for progressively establishing the practical information sheets provided for by Article 15, in particular as regards the subject matter to be covered and the form of such information sheets;

(f) identify specific initiatives other than those referred to in Title III which pursue comparable objectives.

2. The Member States shall ensure that experience in the operation of specific cooperation mechanisms provided for by Community or international instruments is shared at meetings of the contact points.

*Article 11*

**Meetings of members of the Network**

1. Meetings open to all members of the Network shall be held to enable them to get to know each other and exchange experience, to provide a platform for discussion of practical and legal problems met and to deal with specific questions.

Meetings can also be held on specific issues.

2. Meetings shall be convened, where appropriate, in accordance with Article 12.

3. The Commission, in close cooperation with the Presidency of the Council and with the Member States, shall fix for each meeting the maximum number of participants.

[*Article 11a*

**Participation of observers in Network meetings**

1. Without prejudice to Article 1(2), Denmark may be represented at the meetings referred to in Articles 9 and 11.

2. Accession countries and candidate countries may be invited to attend these meetings as observers. Third countries that are party to international agreements on judicial cooperation in civil and commercial matters concluded by the Community may also be invited to attend certain Network meetings as observers.

3. Each observer State may be represented at the meetings by one or more persons, but under no circumstances may there be more than three representatives per State.]

*Article 12*

**Organisation and proceedings of meetings of the Network**

1. The Commission, in close cooperation with the Presidency of the Council and with the Member States, shall convene the meetings provided for by Articles 9 and 11. It shall chair them and provide secretarial services.

2. Before each meeting the Commission shall prepare the draft agenda in agreement with the Presidency of the Council and in consultation with the Member States via their respective contact points.

3. The contact points shall be notified of the agenda prior to the meeting. They may ask for changes to be made or for additional items to be entered.

4. After each meeting the Commission shall prepare a record, which shall be notified to the contact points.

5. Meetings of the contact points and of members of the Network may take place in any Member State.

[*Article 12a*

**Relations with other networks and international organisations**

1. The Network shall maintain relations and share experience and best practice with the other European networks that share its objectives, such as the European Judicial Network in criminal matters. The Network shall also maintain relations with the European Judicial Training Network with a view to promoting, where appropriate and without prejudice to national practices, training sessions on judicial cooperation in civil and commercial matters for the benefit of the local judicial authorities of the Member States.

2. The Network shall maintain relations with the European Consumer Centres Network (ECC-Net). In particular, in order to supply any general information on the working of Community and international instruments to facilitate consumer access to justice, the contact points of the Network shall be at the disposal of the members of ECC-Net.

3. In order to meet its responsibilities under Article 3 concerning international instruments on judicial cooperation in civil and commercial matters, the Network shall maintain contact and exchanges of experience with the other judicial cooperation networks established between third countries and with international organisations that promote international judicial cooperation.

4. The Commission, in close cooperation with the Presidency of the Council and the Member States, shall be responsible for implementing the provisions of this Article.]

[TITLE III

**INFORMATION AVAILABLE WITHIN THE NETWORK AND INFORMATION PROVIDED TO THE PUBLIC**]

*Article 13*

**Information disseminated within the Network**

1. The information disseminated within the network shall include:

(a) the information referred to in Article 2(5);

(b) any further information deemed useful by the contact points for the proper functioning of the Network;

[(c) the information referred to in Article 8.]

2. For the purpose of paragraph 1, the Commission shall progressively establish a secure limited-access electronic information exchange-system in consultation with the contact points.

[*Article 13a*

**Provision of general information to the public**

The Network shall contribute towards providing the public with general information, using the most appropriate technological facilities to inform it about the content and working of Community or international instruments on judicial cooperation in civil and commercial matters.

To that end, and without prejudice to the provisions of Article 18, the contact points shall promote to the public the information system referred to in Article 14.]

*Article 14*

**Information system for the public**

1. An Internet-based information system for the public, including the dedicated website for the Network, shall be progressively established in accordance with Articles 17 and 18.

2. The information system shall comprise the following elements:

(a) Community instruments in force or in preparation relating to judicial cooperation in civil and commercial matters;

(b)  national measures for the domestic implementation of the instruments in force referred to in point (a);

(c)  international instruments in force relating to judicial cooperation in civil and commercial matters to which the Member States are parties, and declarations and reservations made in connection with such instruments;

(d)  the relevant elements of Community case-law in the area of judicial cooperation in civil and commercial matters;

(e)  the information sheets provided for by Article 15.

3. For the purposes of access to the information mentioned in paragraph 2(a) to (d), the Network should, where appropriate, in its site, make use of links to other sites where the original information is to be found.

4. The site dedicated to the Network shall likewise facilitate access to comparable public information initiatives in related matters and to sites containing information relating to the legal systems of the Member States.

*Article 15*

**Information sheets**

1. The information sheets shall be devoted by way of priority to questions relating to access to justice in the Member States and shall include information on the procedures for bringing cases in the courts and for obtaining legal aid, without prejudice to other Community initiatives, to which the Network shall have the fullest regard.

2. Information sheets shall be of a practical and concise nature. They shall be written in easily comprehensible language and contain practical information for the public. They shall progressively be produced on at least the following subjects:

(a)  principles of the legal system and judicial organisation of the Member States;

(b)  procedures for bringing cases to court, with particular reference to small claims, and subsequent court procedures, including appeal possibilities and procedures;

(c)  conditions and procedures for obtaining legal aid, including descriptions of the tasks of non-governmental organisations active in this field, account being taken of work already done in the Dialogue with Citizens;

(d)  national rules governing the service of documents;

(e)  rules and procedures for the enforcement of judgments given in other Member States;

(f)  possibilities and procedures for obtaining interim relief measures, with particular reference to seizures of assets for the purposes of enforcement;

(g)  alternative dispute-settlement possibilities, with an indication of the national information and advice centres of the Community-wide Network for the Extra-Judicial Settlement of Consumer Disputes;

(h)  organisation and operation of the legal professions.

3. The information sheets shall, where appropriate, include elements of the relevant case-law of the Member States.

4. The information sheets may provide more detailed information for the specialists.

*Article 16*

**Updating of information**

All information distributed within the Network and to the public under Articles 13 to 15 shall be updated regularly.

*Article 17*

**Role of the Commission in the public information system**

The Commission shall:

1.  be responsible for managing the information system for the public;

2.  construct, in consultation with the contact points, a dedicated website for the Network on its Internet site;

3.  provide information on relevant aspects of Community law and procedures, including Community case-law, in accordance with Article 14;

4.

(a) ensure that the format of the information sheets is consistent and that they include all information considered necessary by the Network;

[(b) arrange for the translations into the official languages of the institutions of the Union of information on the relevant aspects of Community law and procedures, including Community case-law, and of the information system's general pages and the information sheets referred to in Article 15, and install them on the Network's dedicated website.]

*Article 18*

**Role of contact points in the public information system**

Contact points shall ensure that

1.  the appropriate information needed to create and operate the information system is supplied to the Commission;

2.  the information installed in the system is accurate;

3.  the Commission is notified forthwith of any updates as soon as an item of information requires changing;

4.  the information sheets relating to their respective Member States are [ . . .] established, according to the guidelines referred to in Article 10(1)(e);

5.  the broadest possible dissemination of the information sheets installed on the site dedicated to the Network is arranged in their Member State.

TITLE IV

**FINAL PROVISIONS**

[*Article 19*

**Reporting**

No later than 1 January 2014, and every three years thereafter, the Commission shall present to the European Parliament, the Council and the European Economic and Social Committee a report on the activities of the Network. This report shall be accompanied, if appropriate, by proposals aimed at adapting this Decision and shall include information on the Network's activities aimed at making progress with the design, development and implementation of European e-justice, particularly from the point of view of facilitating access to justice.]

[*Article 20*

**Notification**

No later than 1 July 2010, the Member States shall notify the Commission of the information referred to in Article 2(5).]

*Article 21*

**Date of application**

This Decision shall apply from 1 December 2002, except for Articles 2 and 20 which shall apply from the date of notification of the Decision to the Member States to which it is addressed.

This Decision is addressed to the Member States in accordance with the Treaty establishing the European Community.

# Council Decision of 20 September 2005 on the signing, on behalf of the Community, of the Agreement between the European Community and the Kingdom of Denmark on jurisdiction and the recognition and enforcement of judgments in civil and commercial matters (2005/790/EC)

[2005] OJ L299/61

THE COUNCIL OF THE EUROPEAN UNION,

Having regard to the Treaty establishing the European Community, and in particular Article 61(c) thereof, in conjunction with the first sentence of the first subparagraph of Article 300(2) thereof,

Having regard to the proposal from the Commission,

Whereas:

(1) In accordance with Articles 1 and 2 of the Protocol on the position of Denmark annexed to the Treaty on European Union and the Treaty establishing the European Community, Denmark is not bound by the provisions of Council Regulation (EC) No 44/2001 of 22 December 2000 on jurisdiction and the recognition and enforcement of judgments in civil and commercial matters, nor subject to their application.

(2) By Decision of 8 May 2003, the Council authorised exceptionally the Commission to negotiate an agreement between the European Community and the Kingdom of Denmark extending to Denmark the provisions of the abovementioned Regulation.

(3) The Commission has negotiated such agreement, on behalf of the Community, with the Kingdom of Denmark.

(4) The United Kingdom and Ireland, in accordance with Article 3 of the Protocol on the position of the United Kingdom and Ireland annexed to the Treaty on European Union and the Treaty establishing the European Community, are taking part in the adoption and application of this Decision.

(5) In accordance with Articles 1 and 2 of the abovementioned Protocol on the position of Denmark, Denmark is not taking part in the adoption of this Decision and is not bound by it or subject to its application.

(6) The Agreement, initialled at Brussels on 17 January 2005, should be signed,

HAS DECIDED AS FOLLOWS:

*Article 1*

The signing of the Agreement between the European Community and the Kingdom of Denmark on jurisdiction and the recognition and enforcement of judgments in civil and commercial matters is hereby approved on behalf of the Community, subject to the Council Decision concerning the conclusion of the said Agreement.

The text of the Agreement is attached to this Decision.

*Article 2*

The President of the Council is hereby authorised to designate the person(s) empowered to sign the Agreement on behalf of the Community subject to its conclusion.

## Agreement between the European Community and the Kingdom of Denmark on jurisdiction and the recognition and enforcement of judgments in civil and commercial matters

[2005] OJ L299/62

THE EUROPEAN COMMUNITY, hereinafter referred to as 'the Community',

of the one part, and

THE KINGDOM OF DENMARK, hereinafter referred to as 'Denmark',

of the other part,

DESIRING to unify the rules of conflict of jurisdiction in civil and commercial matters and to simplify the formalities with a view to rapid and simple recognition and enforcement of judgments within the Community,

WHEREAS on 27 September 1968 the Member States, acting under Article 293, fourth indent, of the Treaty establishing the European Community, concluded the Brussels Convention on Jurisdiction and the Enforcement of Judgments in Civil and Commercial Matters (the Brussels Convention), as amended by Conventions on the Accession of the new Member States to that Convention. On 16 September 1988 the Member States and the EFTA States concluded the Convention on Jurisdiction and the Enforcement of Judgments in Civil and Commercial Matters (the Lugano Convention), which is a parallel Convention to the Brussels Convention,

WHEREAS the main content of the Brussels Convention has been taken over in Council Regulation (EC) No 44/2001 of 22 December 2000 on jurisdiction and the recognition and enforcement of judgments in civil and commercial matters (the Brussels I Regulation),

REFERRING to the Protocol on the position of Denmark annexed to the Treaty on European Union and to the Treaty establishing the European Community (the Protocol on the position of Denmark) pursuant to which the Brussels I Regulation shall not be binding upon or applicable in Denmark,

STRESSING that a solution to the unsatisfactory legal situation arising from differences in applicable rules on jurisdiction, recognition and enforcement of judgments within the Community must be found,

DESIRING that the provisions of the Brussels I Regulation, future amendments thereto and the implementing measures relating to it should under international law apply to the relations between the Community and Denmark being a Member State with a special position with respect to Title IV of the Treaty establishing the European Community,

STRESSING that continuity between the Brussels Convention and this Agreement should be ensured, and that transitional provisions as in the Brussels I Regulation should be applied to this Agreement as well. The same need for continuity applies as regards the interpretation of the Brussels Convention by the Court of Justice of the European Communities and the 1971 Protocol should remain applicable also to cases already pending when this Agreement enters into force,

STRESSING that the Brussels Convention also continues to apply to the territories of the Member States which fall within the territorial scope of that Convention and which are excluded from this Agreement,

STRESSING the importance of proper coordination between the Community and Denmark with regard to the negotiation and conclusion of international agreements that may affect or alter the scope of the Brussels I Regulation,

STRESSING that Denmark should seek to join international agreements entered into by the Community where Danish participation in such agreements is relevant for the coherent application of the Brussels I Regulation and this Agreement,

STATING that the Court of Justice of the European Communities should have jurisdiction in order to secure the uniform application and interpretation of this Agreement including the provisions of the Brussels I Regulation and any implementing Community measures forming part of this Agreement,

REFERRING to the jurisdiction conferred to the Court of Justice of the European Communities pursuant to Article 68(1) of the Treaty establishing the European Community to give rulings on preliminary questions relating to the validity and interpretation of acts of the institutions of the Community based on Title IV of the Treaty, including the validity and interpretation of this Agreement, and to the circumstance that this provision shall not be binding upon or applicable in Denmark, as results from the Protocol on the position of Denmark,

CONSIDERING that the Court of Justice of the European Communities should have jurisdiction under the same conditions to give preliminary rulings on questions concerning the validity and interpretation of this Agreement which are raised by a Danish court or tribunal, and that Danish courts and tribunals should therefore request preliminary rulings under the same conditions as courts and tribunals of other Member States in respect of the interpretation of the Brussels I Regulation and its implementing measures,

REFERRING to the provision that, pursuant to Article 68(3) of the Treaty establishing the European Community, the Council of the European Union, the European Commission and the Member States may request the Court of Justice of the European Communities to give a ruling on the interpretation of acts of the institutions of the Community based on Title IV of the Treaty, including the interpretation of this Agreement, and the circumstance that this provision shall not be binding upon or applicable in Denmark, as results from the Protocol on the position of Denmark,

CONSIDERING that Denmark should, under the same conditions as other Member States in respect of the Brussels I Regulation and its implementing measures, be accorded the possibility to request the Court of Justice of the European Communities to give rulings on questions relating to the interpretation of this Agreement,

STRESSING that under Danish law the courts in Denmark should, when interpreting this Agreement including the provisions of the Brussels I Regulation and any implementing Community measures forming part of this Agreement, take due account of the rulings contained in the case law of the Court of Justice of the European Communities and of the courts of the Member States of the European Communities in respect of provisions of the Brussels Convention, the Brussels I Regulation and any implementing Community measures,

CONSIDERING that it should be possible to request the Court of Justice of the European Communities to rule on questions relating to compliance with obligations under this Agreement pursuant to the provisions of the Treaty establishing the European Community governing proceedings before the Court,

WHEREAS, by virtue of Article 300(7) of the Treaty establishing the European Community, this Agreement binds Member States; it is therefore appropriate that Denmark, in the case of non-compliance by a Member State, should be able to seize the Commission as guardian of the Treaty,

HAVE AGREED AS FOLLOWS:

*Article 1*

**Aim**

1. The aim of this Agreement is to apply the provisions of the Brussels I Regulation and its implementing measures to the relations between the Community and Denmark, in accordance with Article 2(1) of this Agreement.

2. It is the objective of the Contracting Parties to arrive at a uniform application and interpretation of the provisions of the Brussels I Regulation and its implementing measures in all Member States.

3. The provisions of Articles 3(1), 4(1) and 5(1) of this Agreement result from the Protocol on the position of Denmark.

*Article 2*

**Jurisdiction and the recognition and enforcement of judgments in civil and commercial matters**

1. The provisions of the Brussels I Regulation, which is annexed to this Agreement and forms part thereof, together with its implementing measures adopted pursuant to Article 74(2) of the Regulation and, in respect of implementing measures adopted after the entry into force of this Agreement, implemented by Denmark as referred to in Article 4 of this Agreement, and the measures adopted pursuant to Article 74(1) of the Regulation, shall under international law apply to the relations between the Community and Denmark.

2. However, for the purposes of this Agreement, the application of the provisions of that Regulation shall be modified as follows:

(a)   Article 1(3) shall not apply.

(b)   Article 50 shall be supplemented by the following paragraph (as paragraph 2):

'2. However, an applicant who requests the enforcement of a decision given by an administrative authority in Denmark in respect of a maintenance order may, in the Member State addressed, claim the benefits referred to in the first paragraph if he presents a statement from the Danish Ministry of Justice to the effect that he fulfils the financial requirements to qualify for the grant of complete or partial legal aid or exemption from costs or expenses.'

(c)   Article 62 shall be supplemented by the following paragraph (as paragraph 2):

'2. In matters relating to maintenance, the expression "court" includes the Danish administrative authorities.'

(d)   Article 64 shall apply to seagoing ships registered in Denmark as well as in Greece and Portugal.

(e)   The date of entry into force of this Agreement shall apply instead of the date of entry into force of the Regulation as referred to in Articles 70(2), 72 and 76 thereof.

(f)   The transitional provisions of this Agreement shall apply instead of Article 66 of the Regulation.

(g)   In Annex I the following shall be added: 'in Denmark: Article 246(2) and (3) of the Administration of Justice Act (lov om rettens pleje)'.

(h)   In Annex II the following shall be added: 'in Denmark, the "byret"'.

(i)   In Annex III the following shall be added: 'in Denmark, the "landsret"'.

(j)   In Annex IV the following shall be added: 'in Denmark, an appeal to the "Højesteret" with leave from the "Procesbevillingsnævnet"'.

*Article 3*

**Amendments to the Brussels I Regulation**

1. Denmark shall not take part in the adoption of amendments to the Brussels I Regulation and no such amendments shall be binding upon or applicable in Denmark.

2. Whenever amendments to the Regulation are adopted Denmark shall notify the Commission of its decision whether or not to implement the content of such amendments. Notification shall be given at the time of the adoption of the amendments or within 30 days thereafter.

3. If Denmark decides that it will implement the content of the amendments the notification shall indicate whether implementation can take place administratively or requires parliamentary approval.

4. If the notification indicates that implementation can take place administratively the notification shall, moreover, state that all necessary administrative measures enter into force on the date of entry into force of the amendments to the Regulation or have entered into force on the date of the notification, whichever date is the latest.

5. If the notification indicates that implementation requires parliamentary approval in Denmark, the following rules shall apply:

(a)   Legislative measures in Denmark shall enter into force on the date of entry into force of the amendments to the Regulation or within 6 months after the notification, whichever date is the latest;

European Union Materials

(b) Denmark shall notify the Commission of the date upon which the implementing legislative measures enter into force.

6. A Danish notification that the content of the amendments has been implemented in Denmark, in accordance with paragraphs 4 and 5, creates mutual obligations under international law between Denmark and the Community. The amendments to the Regulation shall then constitute amendments to this Agreement and shall be considered annexed hereto.

7. In cases where:

(a) Denmark notifies its decision not to implement the content of the amendments; or

(b) Denmark does not make a notification within the 30-day time-limit set out in paragraph 2; or

(c) Legislative measures in Denmark do not enter into force within the time-limits set out in paragraph 5,

this Agreement shall be considered terminated unless the parties decide otherwise within 90 days or, in the situation referred to under (c), legislative measures in Denmark enter into force within the same period. Termination shall take effect three months after the expiry of the 90-day period.

8. Legal proceedings instituted and documents formally drawn up or registered as authentic instruments before the date of termination of the Agreement as set out in paragraph 7 are not affected hereby.

## Article 4

### Implementing measures

1. Denmark shall not take part in the adoption of opinions by the Committee referred to in Article 75 of the Brussels I Regulation. Implementing measures adopted pursuant to Article 74(2) of that Regulation shall not be binding upon and shall not be applicable in Denmark.

2. Whenever implementing measures are adopted pursuant to Article 74(2) of the Regulation, the implementing measures shall be communicated to Denmark. Denmark shall notify the Commission of its decision whether or not to implement the content of the implementing measures. Notification shall be given upon receipt of the implementing measures or within 30 days thereafter.

3. The notification shall state that all necessary administrative measures in Denmark enter into force on the date of entry into force of the implementing measures or have entered into force on the date of the notification, whichever date is the latest.

4. A Danish notification that the content of the implementing measures has been implemented in Denmark creates mutual obligations under international law between Denmark and the Community. The implementing measures will then form part of this Agreement.

5. In cases where:

(a) Denmark notifies its decision not to implement the content of the implementing measures; or

(b) Denmark does not make a notification within the 30-day time-limit set out in paragraph 2,

this Agreement shall be considered terminated unless the parties decide otherwise within 90 days. Termination shall take effect three months after the expiry of the 90-day period.

6. Legal proceedings instituted and documents formally drawn up or registered as authentic instruments before the date of termination of the Agreement as set out in paragraph 5 are not affected hereby.

7. If in exceptional cases the implementation requires parliamentary approval in Denmark, the Danish notification under paragraph 2 shall indicate this and the provisions of Article 3(5) to (8) shall apply.

8. Denmark shall notify the Commission of texts amending the items set out in Article 2(2)(g) to (j) of this Agreement. The Commission shall adapt Article 2(2)(g) to (j) accordingly.

## Article 5

### International agreements which affect the Brussels I Regulation

1. International agreements entered into by the Community based on the rules of the Brussels I Regulation shall not be binding upon and shall not be applicable in Denmark.

2. Denmark will abstain from entering into international agreements which may affect or alter the

scope of the Brussels I Regulation as annexed to this Agreement unless it is done in agreement with the Community and satisfactory arrangements have been made with regard to the relationship between this Agreement and the international agreement in question.

3. When negotiating international agreements that may affect or alter the scope of the Brussels I Regulation as annexed to this Agreement, Denmark will coordinate its position with the Community and will abstain from any actions that would jeopardise the objectives of a Community position within its sphere of competence in such negotiations.

### Article 6

**Jurisdiction of the Court of Justice of the European Communities in relation to the interpretation of the Agreement**

1. Where a question on the validity or interpretation of this Agreement is raised in a case pending before a Danish court or tribunal, that court or tribunal shall request the Court of Justice to give a ruling thereon whenever under the same circumstances a court or tribunal of another Member State of the European Union would be required to do so in respect of the Brussels I Regulation and its implementing measures referred to in Article 2(1) of this Agreement.

2. Under Danish law, the courts in Denmark shall, when interpreting this Agreement, take due account of the rulings contained in the case law of the Court of Justice in respect of provisions of the Brussels Convention, the Brussels I Regulation and any implementing Community measures.

3. Denmark may, like the Council, the Commission and any Member State, request the Court of Justice to give a ruling on a question of interpretation of this Agreement. The ruling given by the Court of Justice in response to such a request shall not apply to judgments of courts or tribunals of the Member States which have become res judicata.

4. Denmark shall be entitled to submit observations to the Court of Justice in cases where a question has been referred to it by a court or tribunal of a Member State for a preliminary ruling concerning the interpretation of any provision referred to in Article 2(1).

5. The Protocol on the Statute of the Court of Justice of the European Communities and its Rules of Procedure shall apply.

6. If the provisions of the Treaty establishing the European Community regarding rulings by the Court of Justice are amended with consequences for rulings in respect of the Brussels I Regulation, Denmark may notify the Commission of its decision not to apply the amendments in respect of this Agreement. Notification shall be given at the time of the entry into force of the amendments or within 60 days thereafter.

In such a case this Agreement shall be considered terminated. Termination shall take effect three months after the notification.

7. Legal proceedings instituted and documents formally drawn up or registered as authentic instruments before the date of termination of the Agreement as set out in paragraph 6 are not affected hereby.

### Article 7

**Jurisdiction of the Court of Justice of the European Communities in relation to compliance with the Agreement**

1. The Commission may bring before the Court of Justice cases against Denmark concerning non-compliance with any obligation under this Agreement.

2. Denmark may bring a complaint before the Commission as to the non-compliance by a Member State of its obligations under this Agreement.

3. The relevant provisions of the Treaty establishing the European Community governing proceedings before the Court of Justice as well as the Protocol on the Statute of the Court of Justice of the European Communities and its Rules of Procedure shall apply.

*Article 8*

**Territorial application**

1. This Agreement shall apply to the territories referred to in Article 299 of the Treaty establishing the European Community.

2. If the Community decides to extend the application of the Brussels I Regulation to territories currently governed by the Brussels Convention, the Community and Denmark shall cooperate in order to ensure that such an application also extends to Denmark.

*Article 9*

**Transitional provisions**

1. This Agreement shall apply only to legal proceedings instituted and to documents formally drawn up or registered as authentic instruments after the entry into force thereof.

2. However, if the proceedings in the Member State of origin were instituted before the entry into force of this Agreement, judgments given after that date shall be recognised and enforced in accordance with this Agreement,

(a) if the proceedings in the Member State of origin were instituted after the entry into force of the Brussels or the Lugano Convention both in the Member State of origin and in the Member State addressed;

(b) in all other cases, if jurisdiction was founded upon rules which accorded with those provided for either in this Agreement or in a convention concluded between the Member State of origin and the Member State addressed which was in force when the proceedings were instituted.

*Article 10*

**Relationship to the Brussels I Regulation**

1. This Agreement shall not prejudice the application by the Member States of the Community other than Denmark of the Brussels I Regulation.

2. However, this Agreement shall in any event be applied:

(a) in matters of jurisdiction, where the defendant is domiciled in Denmark, or where Article 22 or 23 of the Regulation, applicable to the relations between the Community and Denmark by virtue of Article 2 of this Agreement, confer jurisdiction on the courts of Denmark;

(b) in relation to a lis pendens or to related actions as provided for in Articles 27 and 28 of the Brussels I Regulation, applicable to the relations between the Community and Denmark by virtue of Article 2 of this Agreement, when proceedings are instituted in a Member State other than Denmark and in Denmark;

(c) in matters of recognition and enforcement, where Denmark is either the State of origin or the State addressed.

*Article 11*

**Termination of the agreement**

1. This Agreement shall terminate if Denmark informs the other Member States that it no longer wishes to avail itself of the provisions of Part I of the Protocol on the position of Denmark, in accordance with Article 7 of that Protocol.

2. This Agreement may be terminated by either Contracting Party giving notice to the other Contracting Party. Termination shall be effective six months after the date of such notice.

3. Legal proceedings instituted and documents formally drawn up or registered as authentic instruments before the date of termination of the Agreement as set out in paragraph 1 or 2 are not affected hereby.

*Article 12*

### Entry into force

1. The Agreement shall be adopted by the Contracting Parties in accordance with their respective procedures.

2. The Agreement shall enter into force on the first day of the sixth month following the notification by the Contracting Parties of the completion of their respective procedures required for this purpose.

*Article 13*

### Authenticity of texts

This Agreement is drawn up in duplicate in the Czech, Danish, Dutch, English, Estonian, Finnish, French, German, Greek, Hungarian, Italian, Latvian, Lithuanian, Maltese, Polish, Portuguese, Slovene, Slovak, Spanish and Swedish languages, each of these texts being equally authentic.

# Council Decision of 27 April 2006 concerning the conclusion of the Agreement between the European Community and the Kingdom of Denmark on jurisdiction and the recognition and enforcement of judgments in civil and commercial matters (2006/325/EC)

[2006] OJ L120/22

THE COUNCIL OF THE EUROPEAN UNION,

Having regard to the Treaty establishing the European Community, and in particular Article 61(c) thereof, in conjunction with the first sentence of the first subparagraph of Article 300(2) and the first subparagraph of Article 300(3) thereof,

Having regard to the proposal from the Commission,

Having regard to the opinion of the European Parliament,

Whereas:

(1) In accordance with Articles 1 and 2 of the Protocol on the position of Denmark annexed to the Treaty on European Union and the Treaty establishing the European Community, Denmark is not bound by the provisions of Council Regulation (EC) No 44/2001 of 22 December 2000 on jurisdiction and the recognition and enforcement of judgments in civil and commercial matters, nor subject to their application.

(2) The Commission has negotiated an Agreement between the European Community and the Kingdom of Denmark extending to Denmark the provisions of Regulation (EC) No 44/2001.

(3) The Agreement was signed, on behalf of the European Community, on 19 October 2005, subject to its possible conclusion at a later date, in accordance with Council Decision 2005/790/EC of 20 September 2005.

(4) In accordance with Article 3 of the Protocol on the position of the United Kingdom and Ireland annexed to the Treaty on European Union and the Treaty establishing the European Community, the United Kingdom and Ireland are taking part in the adoption and application of this Decision.

(5) In accordance with Articles 1 and 2 of the Protocol on the position of Denmark, Denmark is not taking part in the adoption of this Decision and is not bound by it or subject to its application.

(6) The Agreement should be approved,

HAS DECIDED AS FOLLOWS:

European Union Materials

*Article 1*

The Agreement between the European Community and the Kingdom of Denmark on jurisdiction and the recognition and enforcement of judgments in civil and commercial matters is hereby approved on behalf of the Community.

*[Article 1a*

1. For the purpose of applying Article 5(2) of the Agreement, the Commission shall assess, before taking a decision expressing the Community's agreement, whether the international agreement envisaged by Denmark would not render the Agreement ineffective and would not undermine the proper functioning of the system established by its rules.

2. The Commission shall take a reasoned decision within 90 days of being informed by Denmark of Denmark's intention to enter into the international agreement in question.

If the international agreement in question meets the conditions referred to in paragraph 1, the decision by the Commission shall express the Community's agreement within the meaning of Article 5(2) of the Agreement.]

*[Article 1b*

The Commission shall inform the Member States of the international agreements which Denmark has been authorised to conclude in accordance with Article 1a.]

*Article 2*

The President of the Council is hereby authorised to designate the person empowered to make the notification provided for in Article 12(2) of the Agreement.

# Agreement between the European Community and the Kingdom of Denmark on jurisdiction and the recognition and enforcement of judgments in civil and commercial matters

[2013] OJ L79/4

According to Article 3(2) of the Agreement of 19 October 2005 between the European Community and the Kingdom of Denmark on jurisdiction and the recognition and enforcement of judgments in civil and commercial matters (hereafter the Agreement), concluded by Council Decision 2006/325/EC, whenever amendments to Council Regulation (EC) No 44/2001 of 22 December 2000 on jurisdiction and the recognition and enforcement of judgments in civil and commercial matters are adopted, Denmark shall notify the Commission of its decision whether or not to implement the content of such amendments.

Regulation (EU) No 1215/2012 of the European Parliament and of the Council of 12 December 2012 on jurisdiction and the recognition and enforcement of judgments in civil and commercial matters was adopted on 12 December 2012.

In accordance with Article 3(2) of the Agreement, Denmark has by letter of 20 December 2012 notified the Commission of its decision to implement the contents of Regulation (EU) No 1215/2012. This means that the provisions of Regulation (EU) No 1215/2012 will be applied to relations between the Union and Denmark.

In accordance with Article 3(6) of the Agreement, the Danish notification creates mutual obligations between Denmark and the Community. Thus, Regulation (EU) No 1215/2012 constitutes an amendment to the Agreement and is considered annexed thereto.

With reference to Article 3(3) and (4) of the Agreement, implementation of Regulation (EU) No 1215/2012 in Denmark can take place by amending existing legislation by the decision of Danish Parliament. In accordance with Article 3(5)(b) of the Agreement, Denmark shall notify the Commission of the date upon which such implementing legislative measures enter into force.

## Agreement between the European Union and the Kingdom of Denmark on jurisdiction and the recognition and enforcement of judgments in civil and commercial matters

[2014] OJ L240/1

According to Article 3(2) of the Agreement of 19 October 2005 between the European Community and the Kingdom of Denmark on jurisdiction and the recognition and enforcement of judgments in civil and commercial matters (hereafter the Agreement), concluded by Council Decision 2006/325/EC, whenever amendments to Council Regulation (EC) No 44/2001 of 22 December 2000 on jurisdiction and the recognition and enforcement of judgments in civil and commercial matters are adopted, Denmark shall notify the Commission of its decision whether or not to implement the content of such amendments.

Regulation (EU) No 542/2014 of the European Parliament and of the Council amending Regulation (EU) No 1215/2012 as regards the rules to be applied with respect to the Unified Patent Court and the Benelux Court of Justice was adopted on 15 May 2014.

In accordance with Article 3(2) of the Agreement, Denmark has by letter of 2 June 2014 notified the Commission of its decision to implement the contents of Regulation (EU) No 542/2014. This means that the provisions of Regulation (EU) No 542/2014 will be applied to relations between the European Union and Denmark.

In accordance with Article 3(6) of the Agreement, the Danish notification that the content of the amendments has been implemented in Denmark creates mutual obligations between Denmark and the European Union. Thus, Regulation (EU) No 542/2014 constitutes an amendment to the Agreement and is considered annexed thereto.

With reference to Article 3(3) and (4) of the Agreement, implementation of Regulation (EU) No 542/2014 in Denmark can take place administratively. The necessary administrative measures entered into force on 18 June.

# Council Decision of 20 September 2005 on the signing, on behalf of the Community, of the Agreement between the European Community and the Kingdom of Denmark on the service of judicial and extrajudicial documents in civil or commercial matters (2005/794/EC)

[2005] OJ L300/53

THE COUNCIL OF THE EUROPEAN UNION,

Having regard to the Treaty establishing the European Community, and in particular Article 61(c) thereof, in conjunction with the first sentence of the first subparagraph of Article 300(2) thereof,

Having regard to the proposal from the Commission,

Whereas:

(1) In accordance with Articles 1 and 2 of the Protocol on the position of Denmark annexed to the Treaty on European Union and the Treaty establishing the European Community, Denmark is not bound by the provisions of Council Regulation (EC) No 1348/2000 of 29 May 2000 on the service in the Member States of judicial and extrajudicial documents in civil or commercial matters, nor subject to their application.

(2) By Decision of 8 May 2003, the Council authorised exceptionally the Commission to negotiate an agreement between the European Community and the Kingdom of Denmark extending to Denmark the provisions of the abovementioned Regulation.

(3) The Commission has negotiated such agreement, on behalf of the Community, with the Kingdom of Denmark.

(4) The United Kingdom and Ireland, in accordance with Article 3 of the Protocol on the position of the United Kingdom and Ireland annexed to the Treaty on European Union and the Treaty establishing the European Community, are taking part in the adoption and application of this Decision.

(5) In accordance with Articles 1 and 2 of the abovementioned Protocol on the position of Denmark, Denmark is not taking part in the adoption of this Decision and is not bound by it or subject to its application.

(6) The Agreement, initialled at Brussels on 17 January 2005, should be signed,

HAS DECIDED AS FOLLOWS:

*Article 1*

The signing of the Agreement between the European Community and the Kingdom of Denmark on the service of judicial and extrajudicial documents in civil or commercial matters is hereby approved on behalf of the Community, subject to the Council Decision concerning the conclusion of the said Agreement.

The text of the Agreement is attached to this Decision.

*Article 2*

The President of the Council is hereby authorised to designate the person(s) empowered to sign the Agreement on behalf of the Community subject to its conclusion.

# Agreement between the European Community and the Kingdom of Denmark on the service of judicial and extrajudicial documents in civil or commercial matters

[2005] OJ L300/55

THE EUROPEAN COMMUNITY, hereinafter referred to as 'the Community',

of the one part, and

THE KINGDOM OF DENMARK, hereinafter referred to as 'Denmark',

of the other part,

DESIRING to improve and expedite transmission between Denmark and the other Member States of the Community of judicial and extrajudicial documents in civil or commercial matters,

CONSIDERING that transmission for this purpose is to be made directly between local bodies designated by the Contracting Parties,

CONSIDERING that speed in transmission warrants the use of all appropriate means, provided that certain conditions as to the legibility and reliability of the documents received are observed,

CONSIDERING that security in transmission requires that the document to be transmitted be accompanied by a pre-printed form, to be completed in the language of the place where the service is to be effected, or in another language accepted by the receiving Member State,

CONSIDERING that to secure the effectiveness of this Agreement, the possibility of refusing service of documents should be confined to exceptional situations,

WHEREAS the Convention on the service in the Member States of the European Union of judicial and extrajudicial documents in civil or commercial matters drawn up by the Council of the European Union by Act of 26 May 1997 (1) has not entered into force and that continuity in the results of the negotiations for conclusion of the Convention should be ensured,

WHEREAS the main content of that Convention has been taken over in Council Regulation (EC) No 1348/2000 of 29 May 2000 on the service in the Member States of judicial and extrajudicial documents in civil or commercial matters (2) (the Regulation on the service of documents),

REFERRING to the Protocol on the position of Denmark annexed to the Treaty on European Union and to the Treaty establishing the European Community (the Protocol on the position of Denmark) pursuant to which the Regulation on the service of documents shall not be binding upon or applicable in Denmark,

DESIRING that the provisions of the Regulation on the service of documents, future amendments hereto and the implementing measures relating to it should under international law apply to the relations between the Community and Denmark being a Member State with a special position with respect to Title IV of the Treaty establishing the European Community,

STRESSING the importance of proper coordination between the Community and Denmark with regard to the negotiation and conclusion of international agreements that may affect or alter the scope of the Regulation on the service of documents,

STRESSING that Denmark should seek to join international agreements entered into by the Community where Danish participation in such agreements is relevant for the coherent application of the Regulation on the service of documents and this Agreement,

STATING that the Court of Justice of the European Communities should have jurisdiction in order to secure the uniform application and interpretation of this Agreement including the provisions of the Regulation on the service of documents and any implementing Community measures forming part of this Agreement,

REFERRING to the jurisdiction conferred to the Court of Justice of the European Communities pursuant to Article 68(1) of the Treaty establishing the European Community to give rulings on preliminary questions relating to the validity and interpretation of acts of the institutions of the Community based on Title IV of the Treaty, including the validity and interpretation of this Agreement, and to the circumstance that this provision shall not be binding upon or applicable in Denmark, as results from the Protocol on the position of Denmark,

CONSIDERING that the Court of Justice of the European Communities should have jurisdiction under the same conditions to give preliminary rulings on questions concerning the validity and interpretation of this Agreement which are raised by a Danish court or tribunal, and that Danish courts and tribunals should therefore request preliminary rulings under the same conditions as courts and tribunals of other Member States in respect of the interpretation of the Regulation on the service of documents and its implementing measures,

REFERRING to the provision that, pursuant to Article 68(3) of the Treaty establishing the European Community, the Council of the European Union, the European Commission and the Member States may request the Court of Justice of the European Communities to give a ruling on the interpretation of acts of the institutions of the Community based on Title IV of the Treaty, including the interpretation of this Agreement, and the circumstance that this provision shall not be binding upon or applicable in Denmark, as results from the Protocol on the position of Denmark,

CONSIDERING that Denmark should, under the same conditions as other Member States in respect of the Regulation on the service of documents and its implementing measures, be accorded the possibility to request the Court of Justice of the European Communities to give rulings on questions relating to the interpretation of this Agreement,

STRESSING that under Danish law the courts in Denmark should — when interpreting this Agreement including the provisions of the Regulation on the service of documents and any implementing Community measures forming part of this Agreement — take due account of the rulings contained in the case law of the Court of Justice of the European Communities and of the courts of the Member States of the European Communities in respect of provisions of the Regulation on the service of documents and any implementing Community measures,

CONSIDERING that it should be possible to request the Court of Justice of the European Communities to rule on questions relating to compliance with obligations under this Agreement pursuant to the provisions of the Treaty establishing the European Community governing proceedings before the Court,

WHEREAS, by virtue of Article 300(7) of the Treaty establishing the European Community, this Agreement binds Member States; it is therefore appropriate that Denmark, in the case of non-compliance by a Member State, should be able to seize the Commission as guardian of the Treaty,

HAVE AGREED AS FOLLOWS:

*Article 1*

**Aim**

1. The aim of this Agreement is to apply the provisions of the Regulation on the service of documents and its implementing measures to the relations between the Community and Denmark, in accordance with Article 2(1) of this Agreement.

2. It is the objective of the Contracting Parties to arrive at a uniform application and interpretation of the provisions of the Regulation on the service of documents and its implementing measures in all Member States.

3. The provisions of Articles 3(1), 4(1) and 5(1) of this Agreement result from the Protocol on the position of Denmark.

*Article 2*

**Cooperation on the service of documents**

1. The provisions of the Regulation on the service of documents, which is annexed to this Agreement and forms part thereof, together with its implementing measures adopted pursuant to Article 17 of the Regulation and — in respect of implementing measures adopted after the entry into force

of this Agreement — implemented by Denmark as referred to in Article 4 of this Agreement, and the information communicated by Member States under Article 23 of the Regulation, shall under international law apply to the relations between the Community and Denmark.

2. The date of entry into force of this Agreement shall apply instead of the date referred to in Article 25 of the Regulation.

## Article 3

### Amendments to the Regulation on the service of documents

1. Denmark shall not take part in the adoption of amendments to the Regulation on the service of documents and no such amendments shall be binding upon or applicable in Denmark.

2. Whenever amendments to the Regulation are adopted Denmark shall notify the Commission of its decision whether or not to implement the content of such amendments. Notification shall be given at the time of the adoption of the amendments or within 30 days thereafter.

3. If Denmark decides that it will implement the content of the amendments the notification shall indicate whether implementation can take place administratively or requires parliamentary approval.

4. If the notification indicates that implementation can take place administratively the notification shall, moreover, state that all necessary administrative measures enter into force on the date of entry into force of the amendments to the Regulation or have entered into force on the date of the notification, whichever date is the latest.

5. If the notification indicates that implementation requires parliamentary approval in Denmark, the following rules shall apply:

(a) legislative measures in Denmark shall enter into force on the date of entry into force of the amendments to the Regulation or within 6 months after the notification, whichever date is the latest;

(b) Denmark shall notify the Commission of the date upon which the implementing legislative measures enter into force.

6. A Danish notification that the content of the amendments have been implemented in Denmark, in accordance with paragraph 4 and 5, creates mutual obligations under international law between Denmark and the Community. The amendments to the Regulation shall then constitute amendments to this Agreement and shall be considered annexed hereto.

7. In cases where:

(a) Denmark notifies its decision not to implement the content of the amendments; or

(b) Denmark does not make a notification within the 30-day time limit set out in paragraph 2; or

(c) legislative measures in Denmark do not enter into force within the time limits set out in paragraph 5,

this Agreement shall be considered terminated unless the parties decide otherwise within 90 days or, in the situation referred to under (c), legislative measures in Denmark enter into force within the same period. Termination shall take effect three months after the expiry of the 90-day period.

8. Requests that have been transmitted before the date of termination of the Agreement as set out in paragraph 7 are not affected hereby.

## Article 4

### Implementing measures

1. Denmark shall not take part in the adoption of opinions by the Committee referred to in Article 18 of the Regulation on the service of documents. Implementing measures adopted pursuant to Article 17 of that Regulation shall not be binding upon and shall not be applicable in Denmark.

2. Whenever implementing measures are adopted pursuant to Article 17 of the Regulation, the implementing measures shall be communicated to Denmark. Denmark shall notify the Commission of its decision whether or not to implement the content of the implementing measures. Notification shall be given upon receipt of the implementing measures or within 30 days thereafter.

3. The notification shall state that all necessary administrative measures in Denmark enter into force on the date of entry into force of the implementing measures or have entered into force on the date of the notification, whichever date is the latest.

4. A Danish notification that the content of the implementing measures has been implemented in Denmark creates mutual obligations under international law between Denmark and the Community. The implementing measures will then form part of this Agreement.

5. In cases where:

(a)   Denmark notifies its decision not to implement the content of the implementing measures; or

(b)   Denmark does not make a notification within the 30-day time limit set out in paragraph 2,

this Agreement shall be considered terminated unless the parties decide otherwise within 90 days. Termination shall take effect three months after the expiry of the 90-day period.

6. Requests that have been transmitted before the date of termination of the Agreement as set out in paragraph 5 are not affected hereby.

7. If in exceptional cases the implementation requires parliamentary approval in Denmark, the Danish notification under paragraph 2 shall indicate this and the provisions of Article 3(5) to (8), shall apply.

8. Denmark shall communicate to the Commission the information referred to in Articles 2, 3, 4, 9, 10, 13, 14, 15, 17(a) and 19 of the Regulation on the service of documents. The Commission shall publish this information together with the relevant information concerning the other Member States. The manual and the glossary drawn up pursuant to Article 17 of that Regulation shall include also the relevant information on Denmark.

## Article 5

**International agreements which affect the Regulation on the service of documents**

1. International agreements entered into by the Community when exercising its external competence based on the rules of the Regulation on the service of documents shall not be binding upon and shall not be applicable in Denmark.

2. Denmark will abstain from entering into international agreements which may affect or alter the scope of the Regulation on the service of documents as annexed to this Agreement unless it is done in agreement with the Community and satisfactory arrangements have been made with regard to the relationship between this Agreement and the international agreement in question.

3. When negotiating international agreements that may affect or alter the scope of the Regulation on the service of documents as annexed to this Agreement, Denmark will coordinate its position with the Community and will abstain from any actions that would jeopardise the objectives of a coordinated position of the Community within its sphere of competence in such negotiations.

## Article 6

**Jurisdiction of the Court of Justice of the European Communities in relation to the interpretation of the Agreement**

1. Where a question on the validity or interpretation of this Agreement is raised in a case pending before a Danish court or tribunal, that court or tribunal shall request the Court of Justice to give a ruling thereon whenever under the same circumstances a court or tribunal of another Member State of the European Union would be required to do so in respect of the Regulation on the service of documents and its implementing measures referred to in Article 2(1) of this Agreement.

2. Under Danish law, the courts in Denmark shall, when interpreting this Agreement, take due account of the rulings contained in the case law of the Court of Justice in respect of provisions of the Regulation on the service of documents and any implementing Community measures.

3. Denmark may, like the Council, the Commission and any Member State, request the Court of Justice to give a ruling on a question of interpretation of this Agreement. The ruling given by the Court of Justice in response to such a request shall not apply to judgments of courts or tribunals of the Member States which have become res judicata.

4. Denmark shall be entitled to submit observations to the Court of Justice in cases where a question has been referred to it by a court or tribunal of a Member State for a preliminary ruling concerning the interpretation of any provision referred to in Article 2(1).

5. The Protocol on the Statute of the Court of Justice of the European Communities and its Rules of Procedure shall apply.

6. If the provisions of the Treaty establishing the European Community regarding rulings by the Court of Justice are amended with consequences for rulings in respect of the Regulation on the service of documents, Denmark may notify the Commission of its decision not to apply the amendments under this Agreement. Notification shall be given at the time of the entry into force of the amendments or within 60 days thereafter.

In such a case this Agreement shall be considered terminated. Termination shall take effect three months after the notification.

7. Requests that have been transmitted before the date of termination of the Agreement as set out in paragraph 6 are not affected hereby.

### Article 7

**Jurisdiction of the Court of Justice of the European Communities in relation to compliance with the Agreement**

1. The Commission may bring before the Court of Justice cases against Denmark concerning non-compliance with any obligation under this Agreement.

2. Denmark may bring a complaint before the Commission as to the non-compliance by a Member State of its obligations under this Agreement.

3. The relevant provisions of the Treaty establishing the European Community governing proceedings before the Court of Justice as well as the Protocol on the Statute of the Court of Justice of the European Communities and its Rules of Procedure shall apply.

### Article 8

**Territorial application**

This Agreement shall apply to the territories referred to in Article 299 of the Treaty establishing the European Community.

### Article 9

**Termination of the Agreement**

1. This Agreement shall terminate if Denmark informs the other Member States that it no longer wishes to avail itself of the provisions of Part I of the Protocol on the position of Denmark, in accordance with Article 7 of that Protocol.

2. This Agreement may be terminated by either Contracting Party giving notice to the other Contracting Party. Termination shall be effective six months after the date of such notice.

3. Requests that have been transmitted before the date of termination of the Agreement as set out in paragraph 1 or 2 are not affected hereby.

### Article 10

**Entry into force**

1. The Agreement shall be adopted by the Contracting Parties in accordance with their respective procedures.

2. The Agreement shall enter into force on the first day of the sixth month following the notification by the Contracting Parties of the completion of their respective procedures required for this purpose.

### Article 11

**Authenticity of texts**

This Agreement is drawn up in duplicate in the Czech, Danish, Dutch, English, Estonian, Finnish,

French, German, Greek, Hungarian, Italian, Latvian, Lithuanian, Maltese, Polish, Portuguese, Slovene, Slovak, Spanish and Swedish languages, each of these texts being equally authentic.

# Council Decision of 27 April 2006 concerning the conclusion of the Agreement between the European Community and the Kingdom of Denmark on the service of judicial and extrajudicial documents in civil or commercial matters (2006/326/EC)

[2006] OJ L120/23

THE COUNCIL OF THE EUROPEAN UNION,

Having regard to the Treaty establishing the European Community, and in particular Article 61(c) thereof, in conjunction with the first sentence of the first subparagraph of Article 300(2) and the first subparagraph of Article 300(3) thereof,

Having regard to the proposal from the Commission,

Having regard to the opinion of the European Parliament,

Whereas:

(1) In accordance with Articles 1 and 2 of the Protocol on the position of Denmark annexed to the Treaty on European Union and the Treaty establishing the European Community, Denmark is not bound by the provisions of Council Regulation (EC) No 1348/2000 of 29 May 2000 on the service in the Member States of judicial and extrajudicial documents in civil or commercial matters, nor subject to their application.

(2) The Commission has negotiated an Agreement between the European Community and the Kingdom of Denmark extending to Denmark the provisions of Regulation (EC) No 1348/2000.

(3) The Agreement was signed, on behalf of the European Community, on 19 October 2005, subject to its possible conclusion at a later date, in accordance with Council Decision 2005/794/EC of 20 September 2005.

(4) In accordance with Article 3 of the Protocol on the position of the United Kingdom and Ireland annexed to the Treaty on European Union and the Treaty establishing the European Community, the United Kingdom and Ireland are taking part in the adoption and application of this Decision.

(5) In accordance with Articles 1 and 2 of the Protocol on the position of Denmark, Denmark is not taking part in the adoption of this Decision and is not bound by it or subject to its application.

(6) The Agreement should be approved,

HAS DECIDED AS FOLLOWS:

### Article 1

The Agreement between the European Community and the Kingdom of Denmark on the service of judicial and extrajudicial documents in civil or commercial matters is hereby approved on behalf of the Community.

### [Article 1a

1. For the purpose of applying Article 5(2) of the Agreement, the Commission shall assess, before taking a decision expressing the Community's agreement, whether the international agreement envisaged by Denmark would not render the Agreement ineffective and would not undermine the proper functioning of the system established by its rules.

2. The Commission shall take a reasoned decision within 90 days of being informed by Denmark of Denmark's intention to enter into the international agreement in question.

If the international agreement in question meets the conditions referred to in paragraph 1, the decision by the Commission shall express the Community's agreement within the meaning of Article 5(2) of the Agreement.]

[*Article 1b*

The Commission shall inform the Member States of the international agreements which Denmark has been authorised to conclude in accordance with Article 1a.]

*Article 2*

The President of the Council is hereby authorised to designate the person empowered to make the notification provided for in Article 10(2) of the Agreement.

# Agreement between the European Community and the Kingdom of Denmark on the service of judicial and extrajudicial documents in civil or commercial matters

[2008] OJ L331/21

According to Article 3(2) of the Agreement between the European Community and the Kingdom of Denmark on the service of judicial and extrajudicial documents in civil or commercial matters, concluded by Council Decision 2006/326/EC (hereafter 'the Agreement'), whenever amendments to Council Regulation (EC) No 1348/2000 are adopted, Denmark shall notify to the Commission of its decision whether or not to implement the content of such amendments.

Regulation (EC) No 1393/2007 of the European Parliament and of the Council on the service in the Member States of judicial and extrajudicial documents in civil or commercial matters (service of documents), and repealing Council Regulation (EC) No 1348/2000 was adopted on 13 November 2007.

In accordance with Article 3(2) of the Agreement, Denmark has by letter of 20 November 2007 notified the Commission of its decision to implement the contents of Regulation (EC) No 1393/2007. In accordance with Article 3(6) of the Agreement, the Danish notification creates mutual obligations between Denmark and the Community. Thus, Regulation (EC) No 1393/2007 constitutes amendment to the Agreement and is considered annexed thereto.

In accordance with Article 3(4) of the Agreement, the necessary administrative measures will take effect on the date of entry into force of Regulation (EC) No 1393/2007.

# Council Decision of 15 October 2007 on the signing, on behalf of the Community, of the Convention on jurisdiction and the recognition and enforcement of judgments in civil and commercial matters (2007/712/EC)

[2007] OJ L339/1

THE COUNCIL OF THE EUROPEAN UNION,

Having regard to the Treaty establishing the European Community, and in particular Article 61(c) thereof, in conjunction with the first subparagraph of Article 300(2) thereof,

Having regard to the proposal from the Commission,

Whereas:

(1) On 16 September 1988, the Member States of the European Communities signed an international agreement with the Republic of Iceland, the Kingdom of Norway and the Swiss Confederation on jurisdiction and the enforcement of judgments in civil and commercial matters (the Lugano Convention), thereby extending to Iceland, Norway and Switzerland the application of the rules of the Convention of 27 September 1968 on the same subject matter (the Brussels Convention).

(2) Negotiations on a revision of the Brussels Convention and the Lugano Convention were undertaken during the years 1998-1999 within the framework of an ad hoc Working Party enlarged with Switzerland, Norway and Iceland. These negotiations led to the adoption of a text of a draft convention prepared by the Working Party, which was confirmed by the Council at its meeting on 27 and 28 May 1999.

(3) Subsequent negotiations within the Council on the basis of this text led to the adoption of Council Regulation (EC) No 44/2001 of 22 December 2000 on jurisdiction and the recognition and enforcement of judgments in civil and commercial matters, which modernised the rules of the Brussels Convention and made the system of recognition and enforcement swifter and more efficient.

(4) In the light of the parallelism between the Brussels and the Lugano Convention regimes on jurisdiction and on recognition and enforcement of judgments in civil and commercial matters, the rules of the Lugano Convention should be aligned with the rules of Regulation (EC) No 44/2001 in order to achieve the same level of circulation of judgments between the EU Member States and the EFTA States concerned.

(5) In accordance with the Protocol on the position of Denmark annexed to the Treaty on European Union and to the Treaty establishing the European Community, Denmark does not take part in the application of measures pursuant to Title IV of the Treaty establishing the European Community. In order for the rules of the Lugano Convention to apply to Denmark, Denmark should therefore participate as a Contracting Party to a new convention covering the same subject matter.

(6) By Decision of 27 September 2002, the Council authorised the Commission to negotiate with a view to the adoption of a new Lugano Convention on jurisdiction and the recognition and enforcement of judgments in civil and commercial matters.

(7) The Commission has negotiated such a convention, on behalf of the Community, with Iceland, Norway, Switzerland and Denmark.

(8) In accordance with Article 3 of the Protocol on the position of the United Kingdom and Ireland annexed to the Treaty on European Union and to the Treaty establishing the European Community, the United Kingdom and Ireland are taking part in the adoption and application of this Decision.

(9) In accordance with Articles 1 and 2 of the Protocol on the position of Denmark, Denmark does not take part in the adoption of this Decision and is not bound by it or subject to its application.

(10) The Convention, initialled at Brussels on 28 March 2007, should be signed,

HAS DECIDED AS FOLLOWS:

*Article 1*

The signing of the Convention on jurisdiction and the recognition and enforcement of judgments in civil and commercial matters, which will replace the Lugano Convention of 16 September 1988, is hereby approved on behalf of the Community, subject to the conclusion of the said Convention.

The text of the Convention is attached to this Decision.

*Article 2*

The President of the Council is hereby authorised to designate the person(s) empowered to sign, on behalf of the Community, the Convention on jurisdiction and the recognition and enforcement of judgments in civil and commercial matters.

# Convention on jurisdiction and the recognition and enforcement of judgments in civil and commercial matters

[2007] OJ L339/3

PREAMBLE

THE HIGH CONTRACTING PARTIES TO THIS CONVENTION,

DETERMINED to strengthen in their territories the legal protection of persons therein established,

CONSIDERING that it is necessary for this purpose to determine the international jurisdiction of the courts, to facilitate recognition, and to introduce an expeditious procedure for securing the enforcement of judgments, authentic instruments and court settlements,

AWARE of the links between them, which have been sanctioned in the economic field by the free trade agreements concluded between the European Community and certain States members of the European Free Trade Association,

TAKING INTO ACCOUNT:

— the Brussels Convention of 27 September 1968 on jurisdiction and the enforcement of judgments in civil and commercial matters, as amended by the Accession Conventions under the successive enlargements of the European Union,

— the Lugano Convention of 16 September 1988 on jurisdiction and the enforcement of judgments in civil and commercial matters, which extends the application of the rules of the 1968 Brussels Convention to certain States members of the European Free Trade Association,

— Council Regulation (EC) No 44/2001 of 22 December 2000 on jurisdiction and the recognition and enforcement of judgments in civil and commercial matters, which has replaced the abovementioned Brussels Convention,

— the Agreement between the European Community and the Kingdom of Denmark on jurisdiction and the recognition and enforcement of judgments in civil and commercial matters, signed at Brussels on 19 October 2005,

PERSUADED that the extension of the principles laid down in Regulation (EC) No 44/2001 to the Contracting Parties to this instrument will strengthen legal and economic cooperation,

DESIRING to ensure as uniform an interpretation as possible of this instrument,

HAVE in this spirit DECIDED to conclude this Convention, and

HAVE AGREED AS FOLLOWS:

# TITLE I

## SCOPE

*Article 1*

1. This Convention shall apply in civil and commercial matters whatever the nature of the court or tribunal. It shall not extend, in particular, to revenue, customs or administrative matters.

2. The Convention shall not apply to:

(a) the status or legal capacity of natural persons, rights in property arising out of a matrimonial relationship, wills and succession;

(b) bankruptcy, proceedings relating to the winding-up of insolvent companies or other legal persons, judicial arrangements, compositions and analogous proceedings;

(c) social security;

(d) arbitration.

3. In this Convention, the term 'State bound by this Convention' shall mean any State that is a Contracting Party to this Convention or a Member State of the European Community. It may also mean the European Community.

# TITLE II

## JURISDICTION

### SECTION 1

**General provisions**

*Article 2*

1. Subject to the provisions of this Convention, persons domiciled in a State bound by this Convention shall, whatever their nationality, be sued in the courts of that State.

2. Persons who are not nationals of the State bound by this Convention in which they are domiciled shall be governed by the rules of jurisdiction applicable to nationals of that State.

*Article 3*

1. Persons domiciled in a State bound by this Convention may be sued in the courts of another State bound by this Convention only by virtue of the rules set out in Sections 2 to 7 of this Title.

2. In particular the rules of national jurisdiction set out in Annex I shall not be applicable as against them.

*Article 4*

1. If the defendant is not domiciled in a State bound by this Convention, the jurisdiction of the courts of each State bound by this Convention shall, subject to the provisions of Articles 22 and 23, be determined by the law of that State.

2. As against such a defendant, any person domiciled in a State bound by this Convention may, whatever his nationality, avail himself in that State of the rules of jurisdiction there in force, and in particular those specified in Annex I, in the same way as the nationals of that State.

### SECTION 2

**Special jurisdiction**

*Article 5*

A person domiciled in a State bound by this Convention may, in another State bound by this Convention, be sued:

1. (a) in matters relating to a contract, in the courts for the place of performance of the obligation in question;

   (b) for the purpose of this provision and unless otherwise agreed, the place of performance of the obligation in question shall be:

   — in the case of the sale of goods, the place in a State bound by this Convention where, under the contract, the goods were delivered or should have been delivered;

   — in the case of the provision of services, the place in a State bound by this Convention where, under the contract, the services were provided or should have been provided.

   (c) if (b) does not apply then subparagraph (a) applies;

2. in matters relating to maintenance:

   (a) in the courts for the place where the maintenance creditor is domiciled or habitually resident; or

   (b) in the court which, according to its own law, has jurisdiction to entertain proceedings concerning the status of a person if the matter relating to maintenance is ancillary to those proceedings, unless that jurisdiction is based solely on the nationality of one of the parties; or

   (c) in the court which, according to its own law, has jurisdiction to entertain proceedings concerning parental responsibility, if the matter relating to maintenance is ancillary to those proceedings, unless that jurisdiction is based solely on the nationality of one of the parties;

3. in matters relating to tort, delict or quasi-delict, in the courts for the place where the harmful event occurred or may occur;

4. as regards a civil claim for damages or restitution which is based on an act giving rise to criminal proceedings, in the court seised of those proceedings, to the extent that that court has jurisdiction under its own law to entertain civil proceedings;

5. as regards a dispute arising out of the operations of a branch, agency or other establishment, in the courts for the place in which the branch, agency or other establishment is situated;

6. as settlor, trustee or beneficiary of a trust created by the operation of a statute, or by a written instrument, or created orally and evidenced in writing, in the courts of the State bound by this Convention in which the trust is domiciled;

7. as regards a dispute concerning the payment of remuneration claimed in respect of the salvage of a cargo or freight, in the court under the authority of which the cargo or freight in question:

   (a) has been arrested to secure such payment; or

   (b) could have been so arrested, but bail or other security has been given;

provided that this provision shall apply only if it is claimed that the defendant has an interest in the cargo or freight or had such an interest at the time of salvage.

*Article 6*

A person domiciled in a State bound by this Convention may also be sued:

1. where he is one of a number of defendants, in the courts for the place where any one of them is domiciled, provided the claims are so closely connected that it is expedient to hear and determine them together to avoid the risk of irreconcilable judgments resulting from separate proceedings;

2. as a third party in an action on a warranty or guarantee, or in any other third party proceedings, in the court seised of the original proceedings, unless these were instituted solely with the object of removing him from the jurisdiction of the court which would be competent in his case;

3. on a counter-claim arising from the same contract or facts on which the original claim was based, in the court in which the original claim is pending;

4. in matters relating to a contract, if the action may be combined with an action against the same defendant in matters relating to rights *in rem* in immovable property, in the court of the State bound by this Convention in which the property is situated.

*Article 7*

Where by virtue of this Convention a court of a State bound by this Convention has jurisdiction in actions relating to liability from the use or operation of a ship, that court, or any other court substituted for this purpose by the internal law of that State, shall also have jurisdiction over claims for limitation of such liability.

## SECTION 3

### Jurisdiction in matters relating to insurance

*Article 8*

In matters relating to insurance, jurisdiction shall be determined by this Section, without prejudice to Articles 4 and 5(5).

*Article 9*

1. An insurer domiciled in a State bound by this Convention may be sued:

(a) in the courts of the State where he is domiciled; or

(b) in another State bound by this Convention, in the case of actions brought by the policyholder, the insured or a beneficiary, in the courts for the place where the plaintiff is domiciled; or

(c) if he is a co-insurer, in the courts of a State bound by this Convention in which proceedings are brought against the leading insurer.

2. An insurer who is not domiciled in a State bound by this Convention but has a branch, agency or other establishment in one of the States bound by this Convention shall, in disputes arising out of the operations of the branch, agency or establishment, be deemed to be domiciled in that State.

*Article 10*

In respect of liability insurance or insurance of immovable property, the insurer may in addition be sued in the courts for the place where the harmful event occurred. The same applies if movable and immovable property are covered by the same insurance policy and both are adversely affected by the same contingency.

*Article 11*

1. In respect of liability insurance, the insurer may also, if the law of the court permits it, be joined in proceedings which the injured party has brought against the insured.

2. Articles 8, 9 and 10 shall apply to actions brought by the injured party directly against the insurer, where such direct actions are permitted.

3. If the law governing such direct actions provides that the policyholder or the insured may be joined as a party to the action, the same court shall have jurisdiction over them.

*Article 12*

1. Without prejudice to Article 11(3), an insurer may bring proceedings only in the courts of the State bound by this Convention in which the defendant is domiciled, irrespective of whether he is the policyholder, the insured or a beneficiary.

2. The provisions of this Section shall not affect the right to bring a counter-claim in the court in which, in accordance with this Section, the original claim is pending.

*Article 13*

The provisions of this Section may be departed from only by an agreement:

1. which is entered into after the dispute has arisen; or

2. which allows the policyholder, the insured or a beneficiary to bring proceedings in courts other than those indicated in this Section; or

3.  which is concluded between a policyholder and an insurer, both of whom are at the time of conclusion of the contract domiciled or habitually resident in the same State bound by this Convention, and which has the effect of conferring jurisdiction on the courts of that State even if the harmful event were to occur abroad, provided that such an agreement is not contrary to the law of that State; or

4.  which is concluded with a policyholder who is not domiciled in a State bound by this Convention, except insofar as the insurance is compulsory or relates to immovable property in a State bound by this Convention; or

5.  which relates to a contract of insurance insofar as it covers one or more of the risks set out in Article 14.

*Article 14*

The following are the risks referred to in Article 13(5):

1.  any loss of or damage to:
    (a)  seagoing ships, installations situated offshore or on the high seas, or aircraft, arising from perils which relate to their use for commercial purposes;
    (b)  goods in transit, other than passengers' baggage, where the transit consists of or includes carriage by such ships or aircraft;

2.  any liability, other than for bodily injury to passengers or loss of or damage to their baggage:
    (a)  arising out of the use or operation of ships, installations or aircraft as referred to in point 1(a) insofar as, in respect of the latter, the law of the State bound by this Convention in which such aircraft are registered does not prohibit agreements on jurisdiction regarding insurance of such risks;
    (b)  for loss or damage caused by goods in transit as described in point 1(b);

3.  any financial loss connected with the use or operation of ships, installations or aircraft as referred to in point 1(a), in particular loss of freight or charter-hire;

4.  any risk or interest connected with any of those referred to in points 1 to 3;

5.  notwithstanding points 1 to 4, all large risks.

## SECTION 4

### Jurisdiction over consumer contracts

*Article 15*

1. In matters relating to a contract concluded by a person, the consumer, for a purpose which can be regarded as being outside his trade or profession, jurisdiction shall be determined by this Section, without prejudice to Articles 4 and 5(5), if:

(a)  it is a contract for the sale of goods on instalment credit terms; or

(b)  it is a contract for a loan repayable by instalments, or for any other form of credit, made to finance the sale of goods; or

(c)  in all other cases, the contract has been concluded with a person who pursues commercial or professional activities in the State bound by this Convention of the consumer's domicile or, by any means, directs such activities to that State or to several States including that State, and the contract falls within the scope of such activities.

2. Where a consumer enters into a contract with a party who is not domiciled in the State bound by this Convention but has a branch, agency or other establishment in one of the States bound by this Convention, that party shall, in disputes arising out of the operations of the branch, agency or establishment, be deemed to be domiciled in that State.

3. This section shall not apply to a contract of transport other than a contract which, for an inclusive price, provides for a combination of travel and accommodation.

*Article 16*

1. A consumer may bring proceedings against the other party to a contract either in the courts of the State bound by this Convention in which that party is domiciled or in the courts for the place where the consumer is domiciled.

2. Proceedings may be brought against a consumer by the other party to the contract only in the courts of the State bound by this Convention in which the consumer is domiciled.

3. This Article shall not affect the right to bring a counter-claim in the court in which, in accordance with this Section, the original claim is pending.

*Article 17*

The provisions of this Section may be departed from only by an agreement:

1.   which is entered into after the dispute has arisen; or

2.   which allows the consumer to bring proceedings in courts other than those indicated in this Section; or

3.   which is entered into by the consumer and the other party to the contract, both of whom are at the time of conclusion of the contract domiciled or habitually resident in the same State bound by this Convention, and which confers jurisdiction on the courts of that State, provided that such an agreement is not contrary to the law of that State.

## SECTION 5

### Jurisdiction over individual contracts of employment

*Article 18*

1. In matters relating to individual contracts of employment, jurisdiction shall be determined by this Section, without prejudice to Articles 4 and 5(5).

2. Where an employee enters into an individual contract of employment with an employer who is not domiciled in a State bound by this Convention but has a branch, agency or other establishment in one of the States bound by this Convention, the employer shall, in disputes arising out of the operations of the branch, agency or establishment, be deemed to be domiciled in that State.

*Article 19*

An employer domiciled in a State bound by this Convention may be sued:

1.   in the courts of the State where he is domiciled; or

2.   in another State bound by this Convention:

   (a)   in the courts for the place where the employee habitually carries out his work or in the courts for the last place where he did so; or

   (b)   if the employee does not or did not habitually carry out his work in any one country, in the courts for the place where the business which engaged the employee is or was situated.

*Article 20*

1. An employer may bring proceedings only in the courts of the State bound by this Convention in which the employee is domiciled.

2. The provisions of this Section shall not affect the right to bring a counter-claim in the court in which, in accordance with this Section, the original claim is pending.

*Article 21*

The provisions of this Section may be departed from only by an agreement on jurisdiction:

1.   which is entered into after the dispute has arisen; or

2.   which allows the employee to bring proceedings in courts other than those indicated in this Section.

## SECTION 6

### Exclusive jurisdiction

*Article 22*

The following courts shall have exclusive jurisdiction, regardless of domicile:

1.   in proceedings which have as their object rights *in rem* in immovable property or tenancies of immovable property, the courts of the State bound by this Convention in which the property is situated.

However, in proceedings which have as their object tenancies of immovable property concluded for temporary private use for a maximum period of six consecutive months, the courts of the State bound by this Convention in which the defendant is domiciled shall also have jurisdiction, provided that the tenant is a natural person and that the landlord and the tenant are domiciled in the same State bound by this Convention;

2.   in proceedings which have as their object the validity of the constitution, the nullity or the dissolution of companies or other legal persons or associations of natural or legal persons, or of the validity of the decisions of their organs, the courts of the State bound by this Convention in which the company, legal person or association has its seat. In order to determine that seat, the court shall apply its rules of private international law;

3.   in proceedings which have as their object the validity of entries in public registers, the courts of the State bound by this Convention in which the register is kept;

4.   in proceedings concerned with the registration or validity of patents, trade marks, designs, or other similar rights required to be deposited or registered, irrespective of whether the issue is raised by way of an action or as a defence, the courts of the State bound by this Convention in which the deposit or registration has been applied for, has taken place or is, under the terms of a Community instrument or an international convention, deemed to have taken place.

Without prejudice to the jurisdiction of the European Patent Office under the Convention on the grant of European patents, signed at Munich on 5 October 1973, the courts of each State bound by this Convention shall have exclusive jurisdiction, regardless of domicile, in proceedings concerned with the registration or validity of any European patent granted for that State irrespective of whether the issue is raised by way of an action or as a defence;

5.   in proceedings concerned with the enforcement of judgments, the courts of the State bound by this Convention in which the judgment has been or is to be enforced.

## SECTION 7

### Prorogation of jurisdiction

*Article 23*

1. If the parties, one or more of whom is domiciled in a State bound by this Convention, have agreed that a court or the courts of a State bound by this Convention are to have jurisdiction to settle any disputes which have arisen or which may arise in connection with a particular legal relationship, that court or those courts shall have jurisdiction. Such jurisdiction shall be exclusive unless the parties have agreed otherwise. Such an agreement conferring jurisdiction shall be either:

(a)  in writing or evidenced in writing; or

(b)  in a form which accords with practices which the parties have established between themselves; or

(c)  in international trade or commerce, in a form which accords with a usage of which the parties are or ought to have been aware and which in such trade or commerce is widely known to, and regularly observed by, parties to contracts of the type involved in the particular trade or commerce concerned.

2. Any communication by electronic means which provides a durable record of the agreement shall be equivalent to 'writing'.

3. Where such an agreement is concluded by parties, none of whom is domiciled in a State bound by this Convention, the courts of other States bound by this Convention shall have no jurisdiction over their disputes unless the court or courts chosen have declined jurisdiction.

4. The court or courts of a State bound by this Convention on which a trust instrument has conferred jurisdiction shall have exclusive jurisdiction in any proceedings brought against a settlor, trustee or beneficiary, if relations between these persons or their rights or obligations under the trust are involved.

5. Agreements or provisions of a trust instrument conferring jurisdiction shall have no legal force if they are contrary to the provisions of Articles 13, 17 or 21, or if the courts whose jurisdiction they purport to exclude have exclusive jurisdiction by virtue of Article 22.

*Article 24*

Apart from jurisdiction derived from other provisions of this Convention, a court of a State bound by this Convention before which a defendant enters an appearance shall have jurisdiction. This rule shall not apply where appearance was entered to contest the jurisdiction, or where another court has exclusive jurisdiction by virtue of Article 22.

## SECTION 8

### Examination as to jurisdiction and admissibility

*Article 25*

Where a court of a State bound by this Convention is seised of a claim which is principally concerned with a matter over which the courts of another State bound by this Convention have exclusive jurisdiction by virtue of Article 22, it shall declare of its own motion that it has no jurisdiction.

*Article 26*

1. Where a defendant domiciled in one State bound by this Convention is sued in a court of another State bound by this Convention and does not enter an appearance, the court shall declare of its own motion that it has no jurisdiction unless its jurisdiction is derived from the provisions of this Convention.

2. The court shall stay the proceedings so long as it is not shown that the defendant has been able to receive the document instituting the proceedings or an equivalent document in sufficient time to enable him to arrange for his defence, or that all necessary steps have been taken to this end.

3. Instead of the provisions of paragraph 2, Article 15 of the Hague Convention of 15 November 1965 on the Service Abroad of Judicial and Extrajudicial Documents in Civil and Commercial matters shall apply if the document instituting the proceedings or an equivalent document had to be transmitted pursuant to that Convention.

4. Member States of the European Community bound by Council Regulation (EC) No 1348/2000 of 29 May 2000 or by the Agreement between the European Community and the Kingdom of Denmark on the service of judicial and extrajudicial documents in civil or commercial matters, signed at Brussels on 19 October 2005, shall apply in their mutual relations the provision in Article 19 of that Regulation if the document instituting the proceedings or an equivalent document had to be transmitted pursuant to that Regulation or that Agreement.

SECTION 9

## *Lis pendens* — related actions

*Article 27*

1. Where proceedings involving the same cause of action and between the same parties are brought in the courts of different States bound by this Convention, any court other than the court first seised shall of its own motion stay its proceedings until such time as the jurisdiction of the court first seised is established.

2. Where the jurisdiction of the court first seised is established, any court other than the court first seised shall decline jurisdiction in favour of that court.

*Article 28*

1. Where related actions are pending in the courts of different States bound by this Convention, any court other than the court first seised may stay its proceedings.

2. Where these actions are pending at first instance, any court other than the court first seised may also, on the application of one of the parties, decline jurisdiction if the court first seised has jurisdiction over the actions in question and its law permits the consolidation thereof.

3. For the purposes of this Article, actions are deemed to be related where they are so closely connected that it is expedient to hear and determine them together to avoid the risk of irreconcilable judgments resulting from separate proceedings.

*Article 29*

Where actions come within the exclusive jurisdiction of several courts, any court other than the court first seised shall decline jurisdiction in favour of that court.

*Article 30*

For the purposes of this Section, a court shall be deemed to be seised:

1. at the time when the document instituting the proceedings or an equivalent document is lodged with the court, provided that the plaintiff has not subsequently failed to take the steps he was required to take to have service effected on the defendant; or

2. if the document has to be served before being lodged with the court at the time when it is received by the authority responsible for service, provided that the plaintiff has not subsequently failed to take the steps he was required to take to have the document lodged with the court.

SECTION 10

## Provisional, including protective, measures

*Article 31*

Application may be made to the courts of a State bound by this Convention for such provisional, including protective, measures as may be available under the law of that State, even if, under this Convention, the courts of another State bound by this Convention have jurisdiction as to the substance of the matter.

TITLE III

## RECOGNITION AND ENFORCEMENT

*Article 32*

For the purposes of this Convention, 'judgment' means any judgment given by a court or tribunal of a State bound by this Convention, whatever the judgment may be called, including a decree, order, decision or writ of execution, as well as the determination of costs or expenses by an officer of the court.

## SECTION 1

### Recognition

*Article 33*

1. A judgment given in a State bound by this Convention shall be recognised in the other States bound by this Convention without any special procedure being required.

2. Any interested party who raises the recognition of a judgment as the principal issue in a dispute may, in accordance with the procedures provided for in Sections 2 and 3 of this Title, apply for a decision that the judgment be recognised.

3. If the outcome of proceedings in a court of a State bound by this Convention depends on the determination of an incidental question of recognition that court shall have jurisdiction over that question.

*Article 34*

A judgment shall not be recognised:

1. if such recognition is manifestly contrary to public policy in the State in which recognition is sought;

2. where it was given in default of appearance, if the defendant was not served with the document which instituted the proceedings or with an equivalent document in sufficient time and in such a way as to enable him to arrange for his defence, unless the defendant failed to commence proceedings to challenge the judgment when it was possible for him to do so;

3. if it is irreconcilable with a judgment given in a dispute between the same parties in the State in which recognition is sought;

4. if it is irreconcilable with an earlier judgment given in another State bound by this Convention or in a third State involving the same cause of action and between the same parties, provided that the earlier judgment fulfils the conditions necessary for its recognition in the State addressed.

*Article 35*

1. Moreover, a judgment shall not be recognised if it conflicts with Sections 3, 4 or 6 of Title II, or in a case provided for in Article 68. A judgment may furthermore be refused recognition in any case provided for in Article 64(3) or 67(4).

2. In its examination of the grounds of jurisdiction referred to in the foregoing paragraph, the court or authority applied to shall be bound by the findings of fact on which the court of the State of origin based its jurisdiction.

3. Subject to the provisions of paragraph 1, the jurisdiction of the court of the State of origin may not be reviewed. The test of public policy referred to in Article 34(1) may not be applied to the rules relating to jurisdiction.

*Article 36*

Under no circumstances may a foreign judgment be reviewed as to its substance.

*Article 37*

1. A court of a State bound by this Convention in which recognition is sought of a judgment given in another State bound by this Convention may stay the proceedings if an ordinary appeal against the judgment has been lodged.

2. A court of a State bound by this Convention in which recognition is sought of a judgment given in Ireland or the United Kingdom may stay the proceedings if enforcement is suspended in the State of origin, by reason of an appeal.

SECTION 2

## Enforcement

*Article 38*

1. A judgment given in a State bound by this Convention and enforceable in that State shall be enforced in another State bound by this Convention when, on the application of any interested party, it has been declared enforceable there.

2. However, in the United Kingdom, such a judgment shall be enforced in England and Wales, in Scotland, or in Northern Ireland when, on the application of any interested party, it has been registered for enforcement in that part of the United Kingdom.

*Article 39*

1. The application shall be submitted to the court or competent authority indicated in the list in Annex II.

2. The local jurisdiction shall be determined by reference to the place of domicile of the party against whom enforcement is sought, or to the place of enforcement.

*Article 40*

1. The procedure for making the application shall be governed by the law of the State in which enforcement is sought.

2. The applicant must give an address for service of process within the area of jurisdiction of the court applied to. However, if the law of the State in which enforcement is sought does not provide for the furnishing of such an address, the applicant shall appoint a representative ad litem.

3. The documents referred to in Article 53 shall be attached to the application.

*Article 41*

The judgment shall be declared enforceable immediately on completion of the formalities in Article 53 without any review under Articles 34 and 35. The party against whom enforcement is sought shall not at this stage of the proceedings be entitled to make any submissions on the application.

*Article 42*

1. The decision on the application for a declaration of enforceability shall forthwith be brought to the notice of the applicant in accordance with the procedure laid down by the law of the State in which enforcement is sought.

2. The declaration of enforceability shall be served on the party against whom enforcement is sought, accompanied by the judgment, if not already served on that party.

*Article 43*

1. The decision on the application for a declaration of enforceability may be appealed against by either party.

2. The appeal is to be lodged with the court indicated in the list in Annex III.

3. The appeal shall be dealt with in accordance with the rules governing procedure in contradictory matters.

4. If the party against whom enforcement is sought fails to appear before the appellate court in proceedings concerning an appeal brought by the applicant, Article 26(2) to (4) shall apply even where the party against whom enforcement is sought is not domiciled in any of the States bound by this Convention.

5. An appeal against the declaration of enforceability is to be lodged within one month of service thereof. If the party against whom enforcement is sought is domiciled in a State bound by this Convention other than that in which the declaration of enforceability was given, the time for appealing shall be

two months and shall run from the date of service, either on him in person or at his residence. No extension of time may be granted on account of distance.

## Article 44

The judgment given on the appeal may be contested only by the appeal referred to in Annex IV.

## Article 45

1. The court with which an appeal is lodged under Article 43 or Article 44 shall refuse or revoke a declaration of enforceability only on one of the grounds specified in Articles 34 and 35. It shall give its decision without delay.

2. Under no circumstances may the foreign judgment be reviewed as to its substance.

## Article 46

1. The court with which an appeal is lodged under Article 43 or Article 44 may, on the application of the party against whom enforcement is sought, stay the proceedings if an ordinary appeal has been lodged against the judgment in the State of origin or if the time for such an appeal has not yet expired; in the latter case, the court may specify the time within which such an appeal is to be lodged.

2. Where the judgment was given in Ireland or the United Kingdom, any form of appeal available in the State of origin shall be treated as an ordinary appeal for the purposes of paragraph 1.

3. The court may also make enforcement conditional on the provision of such security as it shall determine.

## Article 47

1. When a judgment must be recognised in accordance with this Convention, nothing shall prevent the applicant from availing himself of provisional, including protective, measures in accordance with the law of the State requested without a declaration of enforceability under Article 41 being required.

2. The declaration of enforceability shall carry with it the power to proceed to any protective measures.

3. During the time specified for an appeal pursuant to Article 43(5) against the declaration of enforceability and until any such appeal has been determined, no measures of enforcement may be taken other than protective measures against the property of the party against whom enforcement is sought.

## Article 48

1. Where a foreign judgment has been given in respect of several matters and the declaration of enforceability cannot be given for all of them, the court or competent authority shall give it for one or more of them.

2. An applicant may request a declaration of enforceability limited to parts of a judgment.

## Article 49

A foreign judgment which orders a periodic payment by way of a penalty shall be enforceable in the State in which enforcement is sought only if the amount of the payment has been finally determined by the courts of the State of origin.

## Article 50

1. An applicant who in the State of origin has benefited from complete or partial legal aid or exemption from costs or expenses shall be entitled, in the procedure provided for in this Section, to benefit from the most favourable legal aid or the most extensive exemption from costs or expenses provided for by the law of the State addressed.

2. However, an applicant who requests the enforcement of a decision given by an administrative authority in Denmark, in Iceland or in Norway in respect of maintenance may, in the State addressed, claim the benefits referred to in paragraph 1 if he presents a statement from the Danish, Icelandic, or

Norwegian Ministry of Justice to the effect that he fulfils the economic requirements to qualify for the grant of complete or partial legal aid or exemption from costs or expenses.

*Article 51*

No security, bond or deposit, however described, shall be required of a party who in one State bound by this Convention, applies for enforcement of a judgment given in another State bound by this Convention on the ground that he is a foreign national or that he is not domiciled or resident in the State in which enforcement is sought.

*Article 52*

In proceedings for the issue of a declaration of enforceability, no charge, duty or fee calculated by reference to the value of the matter at issue may be levied in the State in which enforcement is sought.

## SECTION 3

## Common provisions

*Article 53*

1. A party seeking recognition or applying for a declaration of enforceability shall produce a copy of the judgment which satisfies the conditions necessary to establish its authenticity.

2. A party applying for a declaration of enforceability shall also produce the certificate referred to in Article 54, without prejudice to Article 55.

*Article 54*

The court or competent authority of a State bound by this Convention where a judgment was given shall issue, at the request of any interested party, a certificate using the standard form in Annex V to this Convention.

*Article 55*

1. If the certificate referred to in Article 54 is not produced, the court or competent authority may specify a time for its production or accept an equivalent document or, if it considers that it has sufficient information before it, dispense with its production.

2. If the court or competent authority so requires, a translation of the documents shall be produced. The translation shall be certified by a person qualified to do so in one of the States bound by this Convention.

*Article 56*

No legalisation or other similar formality shall be required in respect of the documents referred to in Article 53 or Article 55(2), or in respect of a document appointing a representative ad litem.

## TITLE IV

## AUTHENTIC INSTRUMENTS AND COURT SETTLEMENTS

*Article 57*

1. A document which has been formally drawn up or registered as an authentic instrument and is enforceable in one State bound by this Convention shall, in another State bound by this Convention, be declared enforceable there, on application made in accordance with the procedures provided for in Article 38, et seq. The court with which an appeal is lodged under Article 43 or Article 44 shall refuse or revoke a declaration of enforceability only if enforcement of the instrument is manifestly contrary to public policy in the State addressed.

2. Arrangements relating to maintenance obligations concluded with administrative authorities or authenticated by them shall also be regarded as authentic instruments within the meaning of paragraph 1.

3. The instrument produced must satisfy the conditions necessary to establish its authenticity in the State of origin.

4. Section 3 of Title III shall apply as appropriate. The competent authority of a State bound by this Convention where an authentic instrument was drawn up or registered shall issue, at the request of any interested party, a certificate using the standard form in Annex VI to this Convention.

*Article 58*

A settlement which has been approved by a court in the course of proceedings and is enforceable in the State bound by this Convention in which it was concluded shall be enforceable in the State addressed under the same conditions as authentic instruments. The court or competent authority of a State bound by this Convention where a court settlement was approved shall issue, at the request of any interested party, a certificate using the standard form in Annex V to this Convention.

## TITLE V

## GENERAL PROVISIONS

*Article 59*

1. In order to determine whether a party is domiciled in the State bound by this Convention whose courts are seised of a matter, the court shall apply its internal law.

2. If a party is not domiciled in the State whose courts are seised of the matter, then, in order to determine whether the party is domiciled in another State bound by this Convention, the court shall apply the law of that State.

*Article 60*

1. For the purposes of this Convention, a company or other legal person or association of natural or legal persons is domiciled at the place where it has its:

(a)   statutory seat;

or

(b)   central administration;

or

(c)   principal place of business.

2. For the purposes of the United Kingdom and Ireland 'statutory seat' means the registered office or, where there is no such office anywhere, the place of incorporation or, where there is no such place anywhere, the place under the law of which the formation took place.

3. In order to determine whether a trust is domiciled in the State bound by this Convention whose courts are seised of the matter, the court shall apply its rules of private international law.

*Article 61*

Without prejudice to any more favourable provisions of national laws, persons domiciled in a State bound by this Convention who are being prosecuted in the criminal courts of another State bound by this Convention of which they are not nationals for an offence which was not intentionally committed may be defended by persons qualified to do so, even if they do not appear in person. However, the court seised of the matter may order appearance in person; in the case of failure to appear, a judgment given in the civil action without the person concerned having had the opportunity to arrange for his defence need not be recognised or enforced in the other States bound by this Convention.

*Article 62*

For the purposes of this Convention, the expression 'court' shall include any authorities designated by a State bound by this Convention as having jurisdiction in the matters falling within the scope of this Convention.

## TITLE VI

## TRANSITIONAL PROVISIONS

*Article 63*

1. This Convention shall apply only to legal proceedings instituted and to documents formally drawn up or registered as authentic instruments after its entry into force in the State of origin and, where recognition or enforcement of a judgment or authentic instruments is sought, in the State addressed.

2. However, if the proceedings in the State of origin were instituted before the entry into force of this Convention, judgments given after that date shall be recognised and enforced in accordance with Title III:

(a) if the proceedings in the State of origin were instituted after the entry into force of the Lugano Convention of 16 September 1988 both in the State of origin and in the State addressed;

(b) in all other cases, if jurisdiction was founded upon rules which accorded with those provided for either in Title II or in a convention concluded between the State of origin and the State addressed which was in force when the proceedings were instituted.

## TITLE VII

## RELATIONSHIP TO COUNCIL REGULATION (EC) No 44/2001 AND OTHER INSTRUMENTS

*Article 64*

1. This Convention shall not prejudice the application by the Member States of the European Community of the Council Regulation (EC) No 44/2001 on jurisdiction and the recognition and enforcement of judgments in civil and commercial matters, as well as any amendments thereof, of the Convention on Jurisdiction and the Enforcement of Judgments in Civil and Commercial Matters, signed at Brussels on 27 September 1968, and of the Protocol on interpretation of that Convention by the Court of Justice of the European Communities, signed at Luxembourg on 3 June 1971, as amended by the Conventions of Accession to the said Convention and the said Protocol by the States acceding to the European Communities, as well as of the Agreement between the European Community and the Kingdom of Denmark on jurisdiction and the recognition and enforcement of judgments in civil and commercial matters, signed at Brussels on 19 October 2005.

2. However, this Convention shall in any event be applied:

(a) in matters of jurisdiction, where the defendant is domiciled in the territory of a State where this Convention but not an instrument referred to in paragraph 1 of this Article applies, or where Articles 22 or 23 of this Convention confer jurisdiction on the courts of such a State;

(b) in relation to *lis pendens* or to related actions as provided for in Articles 27 and 28, when proceedings are instituted in a State where the Convention but not an instrument referred to in paragraph 1 of this Article applies and in a State where this Convention as well as an instrument referred to in paragraph 1 of this Article apply;

(c) in matters of recognition and enforcement, where either the State of origin or the State addressed is not applying an instrument referred to in paragraph 1 of this Article.

3. In addition to the grounds provided for in Title III, recognition or enforcement may be refused if the ground of jurisdiction on which the judgment has been based differs from that resulting from this Convention and recognition or enforcement is sought against a party who is domiciled in a State

where this Convention but not an instrument referred to in paragraph 1 of this Article applies, unless the judgment may otherwise be recognised or enforced under any rule of law in the State addressed.

### Article 65

Subject to the provisions of Articles 63(2), 66 and 67, this Convention shall, as between the States bound by this Convention, supersede the conventions concluded between two or more of them that cover the same matters as those to which this Convention applies. In particular, the conventions mentioned in Annex VII shall be superseded.

### Article 66

1. The conventions referred to in Article 65 shall continue to have effect in relation to matters to which this Convention does not apply.

2. They shall continue to have effect in respect of judgments given and documents formally drawn up or registered as authentic instruments before the entry into force of this Convention.

### Article 67

1. This Convention shall not affect any conventions by which the Contracting Parties and/or the States bound by this Convention are bound and which in relation to particular matters, govern jurisdiction or the recognition or enforcement of judgments. Without prejudice to obligations resulting from other agreements between certain Contracting Parties, this Convention shall not prevent Contracting Parties from entering into such conventions.

2. This Convention shall not prevent a court of a State bound by this Convention and by a convention on a particular matter from assuming jurisdiction in accordance with that convention, even where the defendant is domiciled in another State bound by this Convention which is not a party to that convention. The court hearing the action shall, in any event, apply Article 26 of this Convention.

3. Judgments given in a State bound by this Convention by a court in the exercise of jurisdiction provided for in a convention on a particular matter shall be recognised and enforced in the other States bound by this Convention in accordance with Title III of this Convention.

4. In addition to the grounds provided for in Title III, recognition or enforcement may be refused if the State addressed is not bound by the convention on a particular matter and the person against whom recognition or enforcement is sought is domiciled in that State, or, if the State addressed is a Member State of the European Community and in respect of conventions which would have to be concluded by the European Community, in any of its Member States, unless the judgment may otherwise be recognised or enforced under any rule of law in the State addressed.

5. Where a convention on a particular matter to which both the State of origin and the State addressed are parties lays down conditions for the recognition or enforcement of judgments, those conditions shall apply. In any event, the provisions of this Convention which concern the procedures for recognition and enforcement of judgments may be applied.

### Article 68

1. This Convention shall not affect agreements by which States bound by this Convention undertook, prior to the entry into force of this Convention, not to recognise judgments given in other States bound by this Convention against defendants domiciled or habitually resident in a third State where, in cases provided for in Article 4, the judgment could only be founded on a ground of jurisdiction as specified in Article 3(2). Without prejudice to obligations resulting from other agreements between certain Contracting Parties, this Convention shall not prevent Contracting Parties from entering into such conventions.

2. However, a Contracting Party may not assume an obligation towards a third State not to recognise a judgment given in another State bound by this Convention by a court basing its jurisdiction on the presence within that State of property belonging to the defendant, or the seizure by the plaintiff of property situated there:

(a) if the action is brought to assert or declare proprietary or possessory rights in that property, seeks to obtain authority to dispose of it, or arises from another issue relating to such property; or

(b) if the property constitutes the security for a debt which is the subject-matter of the action.

## TITLE VIII

## FINAL PROVISIONS

*Article 69*

1. The Convention shall be open for signature by the European Community, Denmark, and States which, at the time of the opening for signature, are Members of the European Free Trade Association.

2. This Convention shall be subject to ratification by the Signatories. The instruments of ratification shall be deposited with the Swiss Federal Council, which shall act as Depositary of this Convention.

3. At the time of the ratification, the Contracting Parties may submit declarations in accordance with Articles I, II and III of Protocol 1.

4. The Convention shall enter into force on the first day of the sixth month following the date on which the European Community and a Member of the European Free Trade Association deposit their instruments of ratification.

5. The Convention shall enter into force in relation to any other Party on the first day of the third month following the deposit of its instrument of ratification.

6. Without prejudice to Article 3(3) of Protocol 2, this Convention shall replace the Convention on jurisdiction and the enforcement of judgments in civil and commercial matters done at Lugano on 16 September 1988 as of the date of its entry into force in accordance with paragraphs 4 and 5 above. Any reference to the 1988 Lugano Convention in other instruments shall be understood as a reference to this Convention.

7. Insofar as the relations between the Member States of the European Community and the non-European territories referred to in Article 70(1)(b) are concerned, this Convention shall replace the Convention on Jurisdiction and the Enforcement of Judgments in Civil and Commercial Matters, signed at Brussels on 27 September 1968, and of the Protocol on interpretation of that Convention by the Court of Justice of the European Communities, signed at Luxembourg on 3 June 1971, as amended by the Conventions of Accession to the said Convention and the said Protocol by the States acceding to the European Communities, as of the date of the entry into force of this Convention with respect to these territories in accordance with Article 73(2).

*Article 70*

1. After entering into force this Convention shall be open for accession by:

(a) the States which, after the opening of this Convention for signature, become Members of the European Free Trade Association, under the conditions laid down in Article 71;

(b) Member States of the European Community acting on behalf of certain non-European territories that are part of the territory of that Member State or for whose external relations that Member State is responsible, under the conditions laid down in Article 71;

(c) any other State, under the conditions laid down in Article 72.

2. States referred to in paragraph 1, which wish to become a Contracting Party to this Convention, shall address their application to the Depositary. The application, including the information referred to in Articles 71 and 72 shall be accompanied by a translation into English and French.

*Article 71*

1. Any State referred to in Article 70(1)(a) and (b) wishing to become a Contracting Party to this Convention:

(a) shall communicate the information required for the application of this Convention;

(b) may submit declarations in accordance with Articles I and III of Protocol 1.

European Union Materials

2. The Depositary shall transmit any information received pursuant to paragraph 1 to the other Contracting Parties prior to the deposit of the instrument of accession by the State concerned.

## Article 72

1. Any State referred to in Article 70(1)(c) wishing to become a Contracting Party to this Convention:

(a)  shall communicate the information required for the application of this Convention;

(b)  may submit declarations in accordance with Articles I and III of Protocol 1; and

(c)  shall provide the Depositary with information on, in particular:

(1)  their judicial system, including information on the appointment and independence of judges;

(2)  their internal law concerning civil procedure and enforcement of judgments; and

(3)  their private international law relating to civil procedure.

2. The Depositary shall transmit any information received pursuant to paragraph 1 to the other Contracting Parties prior to inviting the State concerned to accede in accordance with paragraph 3 of this Article.

3. Without prejudice to paragraph 4, the Depositary shall invite the State concerned to accede only if it has obtained the unanimous agreement of the Contracting Parties. The Contracting Parties shall endeavour to give their consent at the latest within one year after the invitation by the Depositary.

4. The Convention shall enter into force only in relations between the acceding State and the Contracting Parties which have not made any objections to the accession before the first day of the third month following the deposit of the instrument of accession.

## Article 73

1. The instruments of accession shall be deposited with the Depositary.

2. In respect of an acceding State referred to in Article 70, the Convention shall enter into force on the first day of the third month following the deposit of its instrument of accession. As of that moment, the acceding State shall be considered a Contracting Party to the Convention.

3. Any Contracting Party may submit to the Depositary a text of this Convention in the language or languages of the Contracting Party concerned, which shall be authentic if so agreed by the Contracting Parties in accordance with Article 4 of Protocol 2.

## Article 74

1. This Convention is concluded for an unlimited period.

2. Any Contracting Party may, at any time, denounce the Convention by sending a notification to the Depositary.

3. The denunciation shall take effect at the end of the calendar year following the expiry of a period of six months from the date of receipt by the Depositary of the notification of denunciation.

## Article 75

The following are annexed to this Convention:

— a Protocol 1, on certain questions of jurisdiction, procedure and enforcement,

— a Protocol 2, on the uniform interpretation of this Convention and on the Standing Committee,

— a Protocol 3, on the application of Article 67 of this Convention,

— Annexes I through IV and Annex VII, with information related to the application of this Convention,

— Annexes V and VI, containing the certificates referred to in Articles 54, 58 and 57 of this Convention,

— Annex VIII, containing the authentic languages referred to in Article 79 of this Convention, and

— Annex IX, concerning the application of Article II of Protocol 1.

These Protocols and Annexes shall form an integral part of this Convention.

*Article 76*

Without prejudice to Article 77, any Contracting Party may request the revision of this Convention. To that end, the Depositary shall convene the Standing Committee as laid down in Article 4 of Protocol 2.

*Article 77*

1. The Contracting Parties shall communicate to the Depositary the text of any provisions of the laws which amend the lists set out in Annexes I through IV as well as any deletions in or additions to the list set out in Annex VII and the date of their entry into force. Such communication shall be made within reasonable time before the entry into force and be accompanied by a translation into English and French. The Depositary shall adapt the Annexes concerned accordingly, after having consulted the Standing Committee in accordance with Article 4 of Protocol 2. For that purpose, the Contracting Parties shall provide a translation of the adaptations into their languages.

2. Any amendment of Annexes V through VI and VIII through IX to this Convention shall be adopted by the Standing Committee in accordance with Article 4 of Protocol 2.

*Article 78*

1. The Depositary shall notify the Contracting Parties of:

(a)  the deposit of each instrument of ratification or accession;

(b)  the dates of entry into force of this Convention in respect of the Contracting Parties;

(c)  any declaration received pursuant to Articles I to IV of Protocol 1;

(d)  any communication made pursuant to Article 74(2), Article 77(1) and paragraph 4 of Protocol 3.

2. The notifications will be accompanied by translations into English and French.

*Article 79*

This Convention, drawn up in a single original in the languages listed in Annex VIII, all texts being equally authentic, shall be deposited in the Swiss Federal Archives. The Swiss Federal Council shall transmit a certified copy to each Contracting Party.

# Protocol 1 on certain questions of jurisdiction, procedure and enforcement

THE HIGH CONTRACTING PARTIES HAVE AGREED AS FOLLOWS:

*Article I*

1. Judicial and extrajudicial documents drawn up in one State bound by this Convention which have to be served on persons in another State bound by this Convention shall be transmitted in accordance with the procedures laid down in the conventions and agreements applicable between these States.

2. Unless the Contracting Party on whose territory service is to take place objects by declaration to the Depositary, such documents may also be sent by the appropriate public officers of the State in which the document has been drawn up directly to the appropriate public officers of the State in which the addressee is to be found. In this case the officer of the State of origin shall send a copy of the document to the officer of the State applied to who is competent to forward it to the addressee. The document

shall be forwarded in the manner specified by the law of the State applied to. The forwarding shall be recorded by a certificate sent directly to the officer of the State of origin.

3. Member States of the European Community bound by Council Regulation (EC) No 1348/2000 of 29 May 2000 or by the Agreement between the European Community and the Kingdom of Denmark on the service of judicial and extrajudicial documents in civil or commercial matters, signed at Brussels on 19 October 2005, shall apply in their mutual relations that Regulation and that Agreement.

## Article II

1. The jurisdiction specified in Articles 6(2) and 11 in actions on a warranty or guarantee or in any other third party proceedings may not be fully resorted to in the States bound by this Convention referred to in Annex IX. Any person domiciled in another State bound by this Convention may be sued in the courts of these States pursuant to the rules referred to in Annex IX.

2. At the time of ratification the European Community may declare that proceedings referred to in Articles 6(2) and 11 may not be resorted to in some other Member States and provide information on the rules that shall apply.

3. Judgments given in the other States bound by this Convention by virtue of Article 6(2) or Article 11 shall be recognised and enforced in the States mentioned in paragraphs 1 and 2 in accordance with Title III. Any effects which judgments given in these States may have on third parties by application of the provisions in paragraphs 1 and 2 shall also be recognised in the other States bound by this Convention.

## Article III

1. Switzerland reserves the right to declare upon ratification that it will not apply the following part of the provision in Article 34(2):

'unless the defendant failed to commence proceedings to challenge the judgment when it was possible for him to do so'.

If Switzerland makes such declaration, the other Contracting Parties shall apply the same reservation in respect of judgments rendered by the courts of Switzerland.

2. Contracting Parties may, in respect of judgments rendered in an acceding State referred to in Article 70(1)(c), by declaration reserve:

(a)   the right mentioned in paragraph 1; and

(b)   the right of an authority mentioned in Article 39, notwithstanding the provisions of Article 41, to examine of its own motion whether any of the grounds for refusal of recognition and enforcement of a judgment is present or not.

3. If a Contracting Party has made such a reservation towards an acceding State as referred to in paragraph 2, this acceding State may by declaration reserve the same right in respect of judgments rendered by the courts of that Contracting Party.

4. Except for the reservation mentioned in paragraph 1, the declarations are valid for periods of five years and are renewable at the end of such periods. The Contracting Party shall notify a renewal of a declaration referred to under paragraph 2 not later than six months prior to the end of such period. An acceding State may only renew its declaration made under paragraph 3 after renewal of the respective declaration under paragraph 2.

## Article IV

The declarations referred to in this Protocol may be withdrawn at any time by notification to the Depositary. The notification shall be accompanied by a translation into English and French. The Contracting Parties provide for translations into their languages. Any such withdrawal shall take effect as of the first day of the third month following that notification.

# Protocol 2 on the uniform interpretation of the Convention and on the Standing Committee

PREAMBLE

THE HIGH CONTRACTING PARTIES,

HAVING REGARD to Article 75 of this Convention,

CONSIDERING the substantial link between this Convention, the 1988 Lugano Convention, and the instruments referred to in Article 64(1) of this Convention,

CONSIDERING that the Court of Justice of the European Communities has jurisdiction to give rulings on the interpretation of the provisions of the instruments referred to in Article 64(1) of this Convention,

CONSIDERING that this Convention becomes part of Community rules and that therefore the Court of Justice of the European Communities has jurisdiction to give rulings on the interpretation of the provisions of this Convention as regards the application by the courts of the Member States of the European Community,

BEING AWARE of the rulings delivered by the Court of Justice of the European Communities on the interpretation of the instruments referred to in Article 64(1) of this Convention up to the time of signature of this Convention, and of the rulings delivered by the courts of the Contracting Parties to the 1988 Lugano Convention on the latter Convention up to the time of signature of this Convention,

CONSIDERING that the parallel revision of both the 1988 Lugano and Brussels Conventions, which led to the conclusion of a revised text for these Conventions, was substantially based on the above mentioned rulings on the 1968 Brussels and the 1988 Lugano Conventions,

CONSIDERING that the revised text of the Brussels Convention has been incorporated, after the entry into force of the Amsterdam Treaty, into Regulation (EC) No 44/2001,

CONSIDERING that this revised text also constituted the basis for the text of this Convention,

DESIRING to prevent, in full deference to the independence of the courts, divergent interpretations and to arrive at an interpretation as uniform as possible of the provisions of this Convention and of those of the Regulation (EC) No 44/2001 which are substantially reproduced in this Convention and of other instruments referred to in Article 64(1) of this Convention,

HAVE AGREED AS FOLLOWS:

*Article 1*

1. Any court applying and interpreting this Convention shall pay due account to the principles laid down by any relevant decision concerning the provision(s) concerned or any similar provision(s) of the 1988 Lugano Convention and the instruments referred to in Article 64(1) of the Convention rendered by the courts of the States bound by this Convention and by the Court of Justice of the European Communities.

2. For the courts of Member States of the European Community, the obligation laid down in paragraph 1 shall apply without prejudice to their obligations in relation to the Court of Justice of the European Communities resulting from the Treaty establishing the European Community or from the Agreement between the European Community and the Kingdom of Denmark on jurisdiction and the recognition and enforcement of judgments in civil and commercial matters, signed at Brussels on 19 October 2005.

*Article 2*

Any State bound by this Convention and which is not a Member State of the European Community is entitled to submit statements of case or written observations, in accordance with Article 23 of the Protocol on the Statute of the Court of Justice of the European Communities, where a court or tribunal of a Member State of the European Community refers to the Court of Justice for a preliminary ruling

European Union Materials

a question on the interpretation of this Convention or of the instruments referred to in Article 64(1) of this Convention.

## Article 3

1. The Commission of the European Communities shall set up a system of exchange of information concerning relevant judgments delivered pursuant to this Convention as well as relevant judgments under the 1988 Lugano Convention and the instruments referred to in Article 64(1) of this Convention. This system shall be accessible to the public and contain judgments delivered by the courts of last instance and of the Court of Justice of the European Communities as well as judgments of particular importance which have become final and have been delivered pursuant to this Convention, the 1988 Lugano Convention, and the instruments referred to in Article 64(1) of this Convention. The judgments shall be classified and provided with an abstract.

The system shall comprise the transmission to the Commission by the competent authorities of the States bound by this Convention of judgments as referred to above delivered by the courts of these States.

2. A selection of cases of particular interest for the proper functioning of the Convention will be made by the Registrar of the Court of Justice of the European Communities, who shall present the selected case law at the meeting of experts in accordance with Article 5 of this Protocol.

3. Until the European Communities have set up the system pursuant to paragraph 1, the Court of Justice of the European Communities shall maintain the system for the exchange of information established by Protocol 2 of the 1988 Lugano Convention for judgments delivered under this Convention and the 1988 Lugano Convention.

## Article 4

1. A Standing Committee shall be set up, composed of the representatives of the Contracting Parties.

2. At the request of a Contracting Party, the Depositary of the Convention shall convene meetings of the Committee for the purpose of:

— a consultation on the relationship between this Convention and other international instruments,

— a consultation on the application of Article 67, including intended accessions to instruments on particular matters according to Article 67(1), and proposed legislation according to Protocol 3,

— the consideration of the accession of new States. In particular, the Committee may ask acceding States referred to in Article 70(1)(c) questions about their judicial systems and the implementation of the Convention. The Committee may also consider possible adaptations to the Convention necessary for its application in the acceding States,

— the acceptance of new authentic language versions pursuant to Article 73(3) of this Convention and the necessary amendments to Annex VIII,

— a consultation on a revision of the Convention pursuant to Article 76,

— a consultation on amendments to Annexes I through IV and Annex VII pursuant to Article 77(1),

— the adoption of amendments to Annexes V and VI pursuant to Article 77(2),

— a withdrawal of the reservations and declarations made by the Contracting Parties pursuant to Protocol 1 and necessary amendments to Annex IX.

3. The Committee shall establish the procedural rules concerning its functioning and decision-making. These rules shall provide for the possibility to consult and decide by written procedure.

## Article 5

1. The Depositary may convene, whenever necessary, a meeting of experts to exchange views on the functioning of the Convention, in particular on the development of the case-law and new legislation that may influence the application of the Convention.

2. This meeting shall be composed of experts of the Contracting Parties, of the States bound by this Convention, of the Court of Justice of the European Communities, and of the European Free Trade Association. It shall be open to any other experts whose presence is deemed appropriate.

3. Any problems arising on the functioning of the Convention may be referred to the Standing Committee referred to in Article 4 of this Protocol for further action.

# Protocol 3 on the application of Article 67 of the Convention

THE HIGH CONTRACTING PARTIES HAVE AGREED AS FOLLOWS:

1. For the purposes of the Convention, provisions which, in relation to particular matters, govern jurisdiction or the recognition or enforcement of judgments and which are or will be contained in acts of the institutions of the European Communities shall be treated in the same way as the conventions referred to in Article 67(1).

2. If one of the Contracting Parties is of the opinion that a provision contained in a proposed act of the institutions of the European Communities is incompatible with the Convention, the Contracting Parties shall promptly consider amending the Convention pursuant to Article 76, without prejudice to the procedure established by Protocol 2.

3. Where a Contracting Party or several Parties together incorporate some or all of the provisions contained in acts of the institutions of the European Community referred to in paragraph 1 into national law, then these provisions of national law shall be treated in the same way as the conventions referred to in Article 67(1).

4. The Contracting Parties shall communicate to the Depositary the text of the provisions mentioned in paragraph 3. Such communication shall be accompanied by a translation into English and French.

*[Annexes I–VII omitted]*

ANNEX VIII

The languages referred to in Article 79 of the Convention are Bulgarian, Czech, Danish, Dutch, English, Estonian, Finnish, French, German, Greek, Hungarian, Icelandic, Irish, Italian, Latvian, Lithuanian, Maltese, Norwegian, Polish, Portuguese, Romanian, Slovak, Slovenian, Spanish and Swedish.

ANNEX IX

The States and the rules referred to in Article II of Protocol 1 are the following:

— Germany: Articles 68, 72, 73 and 74 of the code of civil procedure (Zivilprozeßordnung) concerning third-party notices,

— Austria: Article 21 of the code of civil procedure (Zivilprozeßordnung) concerning third-party notices,

— Hungary: Articles 58 to 60 of the Code of Civil Procedure (Polgári perrendtartás) concerning third-party notices,

— Switzerland, with respect to those cantons whose applicable code of civil procedure does not provide for the jurisdiction referred to in Articles 6(2) and 11 of the Convention: the appropriate provisions concerning third-party notices (litis denuntiatio) of the applicable code of civil procedure.

European Union Materials

# Council Decision of 27 November 2008 concerning the conclusion of the Convention on jurisdiction and the recognition and enforcement of judgments in civil and commercial matters (2009/430/EC)

[2009] OJ L147/1

THE COUNCIL OF THE EUROPEAN UNION,

Having regard to the Treaty establishing the European Community, and in particular Article 61(c) thereof, in conjunction with the first subparagraph of Article 300(2) and the second subparagraph of Article 300(3) thereof,

Having regard to the proposal from the Commission,

Having regard to the assent of the European Parliament,

Whereas:

(1) On 16 September 1988, the Member States of the European Communities signed an international agreement with the Republic of Iceland, the Kingdom of Norway and the Swiss Confederation on jurisdiction and the enforcement of judgments in civil and commercial matters (the Lugano Convention), thereby extending to Iceland, Norway, and Switzerland the application of the rules of the Convention of 27 September 1968 on the same subject matter (the Brussels Convention).

(2) Negotiations concerning a revision of the Brussels Convention and the Lugano Convention were undertaken during the years 1998-1999 within the framework of an ad hoc Working Party enlarged with Iceland, Norway and Switzerland. These negotiations led to the adoption of a text of a draft convention prepared by the Working Party, which was confirmed by the Council at its meeting on 27 and 28 May 1999.

(3) Subsequent negotiations within the Council on the basis of this text led to the adoption of Council Regulation (EC) No 44/2001 of 22 December 2000 on jurisdiction and the recognition and enforcement of judgments in civil and commercial matters, which modernised the rules of the Brussels Convention and made the system of recognition and enforcement swifter and more efficient.

(4) In the light of the parallelism between the Brussels and the Lugano Convention regimes on jurisdiction and on recognition and enforcement of judgments in civil and commercial matters, the rules of the Lugano Convention should be aligned with the rules of Regulation (EC) No 44/2001 in order to achieve the same level of circulation of judgments between the EU Member States and the EFTA States concerned.

(5) In accordance with the Protocol on the position of Denmark, annexed to the Treaty on European Union and to the Treaty establishing the European Community, Denmark does not take part in the application of measures pursuant to Title IV of the Treaty establishing the European Community. In order for the rules of the Lugano Convention to apply to Denmark, Denmark should therefore participate as a Contracting Party to a new convention covering the same subject matter.

(6) By Decision of 27 September 2002, the Council authorised the Commission to negotiate with a view to the adoption of a new Lugano Convention on jurisdiction and the recognition and enforcement of judgments in civil and commercial matters.

(7) The Commission negotiated such a convention, on behalf of the Community, with Iceland, Norway, Switzerland and Denmark. This Convention was signed, on behalf of the Community, on 30 October 2007 in accordance with Council Decision 2007/712/EC, subject to its conclusion at a later date.

(8) At the time of the adoption of Decision 2007/712/EC the Council agreed to examine in the framework of the discussions on the conclusion of the new Lugano Convention the possibility of making a declaration in accordance with Article II(2) of Protocol 1 to the Convention. The Community should make such a declaration at the time of conclusion of the Convention.

(9) During the negotiations of the Convention the Community committed itself to making a declaration, at the time of ratification of the Convention, to the effect that when amending Regulation (EC) No 44/2001 the Community would clarify the scope of Article 22(4) of the said Regulation with a view to taking into account the relevant case law of the Court of Justice of the European Communities with respect to proceedings concerned with the registration or validity of intellectual property rights, thereby ensuring its parallelism with Article 22(4) of the Convention. In this context, regard should be had to the results of the evaluation of the application of Regulation (EC) No 44/2001.

(10) In accordance with Article 3 of the Protocol on the position of the United Kingdom and Ireland, annexed to the Treaty on European Union and to the Treaty establishing the European Community, the United Kingdom and Ireland are taking part in the adoption and application of this Decision.

(11) In accordance with Articles 1 and 2 of the Protocol on the position of Denmark, Denmark does not take part in the adoption of this Decision and is not bound by it or subject to its application.

(12) The Convention should now be concluded,

HAS DECIDED AS FOLLOWS:

*Article 1*

The conclusion of the Convention on jurisdiction and the recognition and enforcement of judgments in civil and commercial matters, which will replace the Lugano Convention of 16 September 1988, is hereby approved on behalf of the Community.

When depositing its instrument of ratification, the Community shall make the declarations set out in Annexes I and II to this Decision.

The text of the Convention is attached to this Decision.

*Article 2*

The President of the Council is hereby authorised to designate the person(s) empowered to deposit on behalf of the Community the instrument of ratification in accordance with Article 69(2) of the Convention.

## ANNEX I

### Declaration by the European Community

'The European Community hereby declares that, when amending Council Regulation (EC) No 44/2001 on jurisdiction, recognition and enforcement of judgments in civil and commercial matters, it intends to clarify the scope of Article 22(4) of the said Regulation with a view to taking into account the relevant case law of the Court of Justice of the European Communities with respect to proceedings concerned with the registration or validity of intellectual property rights, thereby ensuring its parallelism with Article 22(4) of the Convention while taking into account the results of the evaluation of the application of Regulation (EC) No 44/2001.'

## ANNEX II

### Declaration by the European Community in accordance with Article II(2) of Protocol 1 to the Convention

'The European Community declares that proceedings referred to in Articles 6(2) and 11 may not be resorted to in the following Member States: Estonia, Latvia, Lithuania, Poland and Slovenia in addition to the three already mentioned in Annex IX to the Convention.

In accordance with Article 77(2) of the Convention the Standing Committee set up by Article 4 of Protocol 2 to the Convention should therefore as soon as the Convention enters into force be requested to amend Annex IX to the Convention as follows:

### "ANNEX IX

The States and the rules referred to in Article II of Protocol 1 are the following:

— Germany: Articles 68, 72, 73 and 74 of the code of civil procedure (Zivilprozessordnung) concerning third-party notices,

— Estonia: Article 214(3) and (4) and Article 216 of the Code of Civil Procedure (tsiviilkohtumenetluse seadustik) concerning third-party notices,

— Latvia: Articles 78, 79, 80 and 81 of the Civil Procedure Law (Civilprocesa likums) concerning third-party notices,

— Lithuania: Article 47 of the Code of Civil Procedure (Civilinio proceso kodeksas),

— Hungary: Articles 58 to 60 of the Code of Civil Procedure (Polgári perrendtartás) concerning third-party notices,

— Austria: Article 21 of the code of civil procedure (Zivilprozessordnung) concerning third-party notices,

— Poland: Articles 84 and 85 of the Code of Civil Procedure (Kodeks postępowania cywilnego) concerning third-party notices (przypozwanie),

— Slovenia: Article 204 of the Civil Procedure Act (Zakon o pravdnem postopku) concerning third-party notices,

— Switzerland, with respect to those cantons whose applicable code of civil procedure does not provide for the jurisdiction referred to in Articles 6(2) and 11 of the Convention: the appropriate provisions concerning third-party notices (litis denuntiatio) of the applicable code of civil procedure."

# Council Decision of 26 February 2009 on the signing on behalf of the European Community of the Convention on Choice of Court Agreements (2009/397/EC)

[2009] OJ L133/1

THE COUNCIL OF THE EUROPEAN UNION,

Having regard to the Treaty establishing the European Community, and in particular Article 61(c) in conjunction with the first sentence of the second paragraph of Article 300 thereof,

Having regard to the proposal from the Commission,

Whereas:

(1) The Community is working towards the establishment of a common judicial area based on the principle of mutual recognition of judicial decisions.

(2) The Convention on Choice of Court Agreements concluded on 30 June 2005 under The Hague Conference on Private International Law, (hereinafter referred to as the Convention) makes a valuable contribution to promoting party autonomy in international commercial transactions and increasing the predictability of judicial solutions in such transactions.

(3) The Convention affects Community secondary legislation on jurisdiction based on choice by the parties and the recognition and enforcement of the resulting judgments, in particular Council Regulation (EC) 44/2001 of 22 December 2000 on jurisdiction and the recognition and enforcement of judgments in civil and commercial matters.

(4) The Community has exclusive competence in all matters governed by the Convention.

(5) Article 30 of the Convention allows the Community to sign, accept, approve or accede to the Convention.

(6) The United Kingdom and Ireland are taking part in the adoption and application of this Decision.

(7) In accordance with Articles 1 and 2 of the Protocol on the position of Denmark annexed to the Treaty on European Union and the Treaty establishing the European Community, Denmark is not taking part in the adoption of this Decision and is not bound by it nor subject to its application.

(8) The Convention should be signed and the attached declaration be approved,

HAS DECIDED AS FOLLOWS:

*Article 1*

The signing of the Convention on Choice of Court Agreements concluded at The Hague on 30 June 2005 is hereby approved on behalf of the European Community, subject to the conclusion of the Convention at a later date.

The text of the Convention is attached to this Decision as Annex I.

*Article 2*

The President of the Council is hereby authorised to designate the person(s) empowered to sign the Convention on behalf of the Community and to make the declaration set out in Annex II to this Decision.

*Article 3*

This Decision shall be published in the Official Journal of the European Union.

ANNEX 1

## Convention on Choice of Court Agreements

The States Parties to the present Convention,

Desiring to promote international trade and investment through enhanced judicial cooperation,

Believing that such cooperation can be enhanced by uniform rules on jurisdiction and on recognition and enforcement of foreign judgments in civil or commercial matters,

Believing that such enhanced cooperation requires in particular an international legal regime that provides certainty and ensures the effectiveness of exclusive choice of court agreements between parties to commercial transactions and that governs the recognition and enforcement of judgments resulting from proceedings based on such agreements,

Have resolved to conclude this Convention and have agreed upon the following provisions:

## CHAPTER I

## SCOPE AND DEFINITIONS

*Article 1*

### Scope

1. This Convention shall apply in international cases to exclusive choice of court agreements concluded in civil or commercial matters.

2. For the purposes of Chapter II, a case is international unless the parties are resident in the same Contracting State and the relationship of the parties and all other elements relevant to the dispute, regardless of the location of the chosen court, are connected only with that State.

3. For the purposes of Chapter III, a case is international where recognition or enforcement of a foreign judgment is sought.

*Article 2*

### Exclusions from scope

1. This Convention shall not apply to exclusive choice of court agreements:
(a) to which a natural person acting primarily for personal, family or household purposes (a consumer) is a party;
(b) relating to contracts of employment, including collective agreements.

2. This Convention shall not apply to the following matters:
(a) the status and legal capacity of natural persons;
(b) maintenance obligations;
(c) other family law matters, including matrimonial property regimes and other rights or obligations arising out of marriage or similar relationships;
(d) wills and succession;
(e) insolvency, composition and analogous matters;
(f) the carriage of passengers and goods;
(g) marine pollution, limitation of liability for maritime claims, general average, and emergency towage and salvage;
(h) anti-trust (competition) matters;
(i) liability for nuclear damage;
(j) claims for personal injury brought by or on behalf of natural persons;
(k) tort or delict claims for damage to tangible property that do not arise from a contractual relationship;

(l)   rights in rem in immovable property, and tenancies of immovable property;

(m)  the validity, nullity, or dissolution of legal persons, and the validity of decisions of their organs;

(n)   the validity of intellectual property rights other than copyright and related rights;

(o)   infringement of intellectual property rights other than copyright and related rights, except where infringement proceedings are brought for breach of a contract between the parties relating to such rights, or could have been brought for breach of that contract;

(p)   the validity of entries in public registers.

3. Notwithstanding paragraph 2, proceedings are not excluded from the scope of this Convention where a matter excluded under that paragraph arises merely as a preliminary question and not as an object of the proceedings. In particular, the mere fact that a matter excluded under paragraph 2 arises by way of defence does not exclude proceedings from the Convention, if that matter is not an object of the proceedings.

4. This Convention shall not apply to arbitration and related proceedings.

5. Proceedings are not excluded from the scope of this Convention by the mere fact that a State, including a government, a governmental agency or any person acting for a State, is a party thereto.

6. Nothing in this Convention shall affect privileges and immunities of States or of international organisations, in respect of themselves and of their property.

*Article 3*

**Exclusive choice of court agreements**

For the purposes of this Convention:

(a)   'exclusive choice of court agreement' means an agreement concluded by two or more parties that meets the requirements of paragraph (c) and designates, for the purpose of deciding disputes which have arisen or may arise in connection with a particular legal relationship, the courts of one Contracting State or one or more specific courts of one Contracting State to the exclusion of the jurisdiction of any other courts;

(b)   a choice of court agreement which designates the courts of one Contracting State or one or more specific courts of one Contracting State shall be deemed to be exclusive unless the parties have expressly provided otherwise;

(c)   an exclusive choice of court agreement must be concluded or documented:

   (i)   in writing; or

   (ii)  by any other means of communication which renders information accessible so as to be usable for subsequent reference;

(d)   an exclusive choice of court agreement that forms part of a contract shall be treated as an agreement independent of the other terms of the contract. The validity of the exclusive choice of court agreement cannot be contested solely on the ground that the contract is not valid.

*Article 4*

**Other definitions**

1. In this Convention, 'judgment' means any decision on the merits given by a court, whatever it may be called, including a decree or order, and a determination of costs or expenses by the court (including an officer of the court), provided that the determination relates to a decision on the merits which may be recognised or enforced under this Convention. An interim measure of protection is not a judgment.

2. For the purposes of this Convention, an entity or person other than a natural person shall be considered to be resident in the State:

(a)   where it has its statutory seat;

(b)   under whose law it was incorporated or formed;

(c)   where it has its central administration; or

(d)   where it has its principal place of business.

## CHAPTER II

## JURISDICTION

*Article 5*

**Jurisdiction of the chosen court**

1. The court or courts of a Contracting State designated in an exclusive choice of court agreement shall have jurisdiction to decide a dispute to which the agreement applies, unless the agreement is null and void under the law of that State.

2. A court that has jurisdiction under paragraph 1 shall not decline to exercise jurisdiction on the ground that the dispute should be decided in a court of another State.

3. The preceding paragraphs shall not affect rules:

(a) on jurisdiction related to subject matter or to the value of the claim;

(b) on the internal allocation of jurisdiction among the courts of a Contracting State. However, where the chosen court has discretion as to whether to transfer a case, due consideration should be given to the choice of the parties.

*Article 6*

**Obligations of a court not chosen**

A court of a Contracting State other than that of the chosen court shall suspend or dismiss proceedings to which an exclusive choice of court agreement applies unless:

(a) the agreement is null and void under the law of the State of the chosen court;

(b) a party lacked the capacity to conclude the agreement under the law of the State of the court seised;

(c) giving effect to the agreement would lead to a manifest injustice or would be manifestly contrary to the public policy of the State of the court seised;

(d) for exceptional reasons beyond the control of the parties, the agreement cannot reasonably be performed; or

(e) the chosen court has decided not to hear the case.

*Article 7*

**Interim measures of protection**

Interim measures of protection are not governed by this Convention. This Convention neither requires nor precludes the grant, refusal or termination of interim measures of protection by a court of a Contracting State and does not affect whether or not a party may request or a court should grant, refuse or terminate such measures.

## CHAPTER III

## RECOGNITION AND ENFORCEMENT

*Article 8*

**Recognition and enforcement**

1. A judgment given by a court of a Contracting State designated in an exclusive choice of court agreement shall be recognised and enforced in other Contracting States in accordance with this Chapter. Recognition or enforcement may be refused only on the grounds specified in this Convention.

2. Without prejudice to such review as is necessary for the application of the provisions of this Chapter, there shall be no review of the merits of the judgment given by the court of origin. The court addressed shall be bound by the findings of fact on which the court of origin based its jurisdiction, unless the judgment was given by default.

3. A judgment shall be recognised only if it has effect in the State of origin, and shall be enforced only if it is enforceable in the State of origin.

4. Recognition or enforcement may be postponed or refused if the judgment is the subject of review in the State of origin or if the time limit for seeking ordinary review has not expired. A refusal does not prevent a subsequent application for recognition or enforcement of the judgment.

5. This Article shall also apply to a judgment given by a court of a Contracting State pursuant to a transfer of the case from the chosen court in that Contracting State as permitted by Article 5(3). However, where the chosen court had discretion as to whether to transfer the case to another court, recognition or enforcement of the judgment may be refused against a party who objected to the transfer in a timely manner in the State of origin.

## Article 9

### Refusal of recognition or enforcement

Recognition or enforcement may be refused if:

(a)  the agreement was null and void under the law of the State of the chosen court, unless the chosen court has determined that the agreement is valid;

(b)  a party lacked the capacity to conclude the agreement under the law of the requested State;

(c)  the document which instituted the proceedings or an equivalent document, including the essential elements of the claim:

  (i)  was not notified to the defendant in sufficient time and in such a way as to enable him to arrange for his defence, unless the defendant entered an appearance and presented his case without contesting notification in the court of origin, provided that the law of the State of origin permitted notification to be contested; or

  (ii)  was notified to the defendant in the requested State in a manner that is incompatible with fundamental principles of the requested State concerning service of documents;

(d)  the judgment was obtained by fraud in connection with a matter of procedure;

(e)  recognition or enforcement would be manifestly incompatible with the public policy of the requested State, including situations where the specific proceedings leading to the judgment were incompatible with fundamental principles of procedural fairness of that State;

(f)  the judgment is inconsistent with a judgment given in the requested State in a dispute between the same parties; or

(g)  the judgment is inconsistent with an earlier judgment given in another State between the same parties on the same cause of action, provided that the earlier judgment fulfils the conditions necessary for its recognition in the requested State.

## Article 10

### Preliminary questions

1. Where a matter excluded under Article 2(2), or under Article 21, arose as a preliminary question, the ruling on that question shall not be recognised or enforced under this Convention.

2. Recognition or enforcement of a judgment may be refused if, and to the extent that, the judgment was based on a ruling on a matter excluded under Article 2(2).

3. However, in the case of a ruling on the validity of an intellectual property right other than copyright or a related right, recognition or enforcement of a judgment may be refused or postponed under the preceding paragraph only where:

(a)  that ruling is inconsistent with a judgment or a decision of a competent authority on that matter given in the State under the law of which the intellectual property right arose; or

(b)  proceedings concerning the validity of the intellectual property right are pending in that State.

4. Recognition or enforcement of a judgment may be refused if, and to the extent that, the judgment was based on a ruling on a matter excluded pursuant to a declaration made by the requested State under Article 21.

*Article 11*

**Damages**

1. Recognition or enforcement of a judgment may be refused if, and to the extent that, the judgment awards damages, including exemplary or punitive damages, that do not compensate a party for actual loss or harm suffered.

2. The court addressed shall take into account whether and to what extent the damages awarded by the court of origin serve to cover costs and expenses relating to the proceedings.

*Article 12*

**Judicial settlements (transactions judiciaires)**

Judicial settlements (transactions judiciaires) which a court of a Contracting State designated in an exclusive choice of court agreement has approved, or which have been concluded before that court in the course of proceedings, and which are enforceable in the same manner as a judgment in the State of origin, shall be enforced under this Convention in the same manner as a judgment.

*Article 13*

**Documents to be produced**

1. The party seeking recognition or applying for enforcement shall produce:

(a)   a complete and certified copy of the judgment;

(b)   the exclusive choice of court agreement, a certified copy thereof, or other evidence of its existence;

(c)   if the judgment was given by default, the original or a certified copy of a document establishing that the document which instituted the proceedings or an equivalent document was notified to the defaulting party;

(d)   any documents necessary to establish that the judgment has effect or, where applicable, is enforceable in the State of origin;

(e)   in the case referred to in Article 12, a certificate of a court of the State of origin that the judicial settlement or a part of it is enforceable in the same manner as a judgment in the State of origin.

2. If the terms of the judgment do not permit the court addressed to verify whether the conditions of this Chapter have been complied with, that court may require any necessary documents.

3. An application for recognition or enforcement may be accompanied by a document, issued by a court (including an officer of the court) of the State of origin, in the form recommended and published by the Hague Conference on Private International Law.

4. If the documents referred to in this Article are not in an official language of the requested State, they shall be accompanied by a certified translation into an official language, unless the law of the requested State provides otherwise.

*Article 14*

**Procedure**

The procedure for recognition, declaration of enforceability or registration for enforcement, and the enforcement of the judgment, are governed by the law of the requested State unless this Convention provides otherwise. The court addressed shall act expeditiously.

*Article 15*

**Severability**

Recognition or enforcement of a severable part of a judgment shall be granted where recognition or enforcement of that part is applied for, or only part of the judgment is capable of being recognised or enforced under this Convention.

## CHAPTER IV

## GENERAL CLAUSES

*Article 16*

**Transitional provisions**

1. This Convention shall apply to exclusive choice of court agreements concluded after its entry into force for the State of the chosen court.

2. This Convention shall not apply to proceedings instituted before its entry into force for the State of the court seised.

*Article 17*

**Contracts of insurance and reinsurance**

1. Proceedings under a contract of insurance or reinsurance are not excluded from the scope of this Convention on the ground that the contract of insurance or reinsurance relates to a matter to which this Convention does not apply.

2. Recognition and enforcement of a judgment in respect of liability under the terms of a contract of insurance or reinsurance may not be limited or refused on the ground that the liability under that contract includes liability to indemnify the insured or reinsured in respect of:

(a)    a matter to which this Convention does not apply; or

(b)    an award of damages to which Article 11 might apply.

*Article 18*

**No legalisation**

All documents forwarded or delivered under this Convention shall be exempt from legalisation or any analogous formality, including an Apostille.

*Article 19*

**Declarations limiting jurisdiction**

A State may declare that its courts may refuse to determine disputes to which an exclusive choice of court agreement applies if, except for the location of the chosen court, there is no connection between that State and the parties or the dispute.

*Article 20*

**Declarations limiting recognition and enforcement**

A State may declare that its courts may refuse to recognise or enforce a judgment given by a court of another Contracting State if the parties were resident in the requested State, and the relationship of the parties and all other elements relevant to the dispute, other than the location of the chosen court, were connected only with the requested State.

*Article 21*

**Declarations with respect to specific matters**

1. Where a State has a strong interest in not applying this Convention to a specific matter, that State may declare that it will not apply the Convention to that matter. The State making such a declaration

shall ensure that the declaration is no broader than necessary and that the specific matter excluded is clearly and precisely defined.

2. With regard to that matter, the Convention shall not apply:

(a) in the Contracting State that made the declaration;

(b) in other Contracting States, where an exclusive choice of court agreement designates the courts, or one or more specific courts, of the State that made the declaration.

## Article 22

**Reciprocal declarations on non-exclusive choice of court agreements**

1. A Contracting State may declare that its courts will recognise and enforce judgments given by courts of other Contracting States designated in a choice of court agreement concluded by two or more parties that meets the requirements of Article 3(c), and designates, for the purpose of deciding disputes which have arisen or may arise in connection with a particular legal relationship, a court or courts of one or more Contracting States (a non-exclusive choice of court agreement).

2. Where recognition or enforcement of a judgment given in a Contracting State that has made such a declaration is sought in another Contracting State that has made such a declaration, the judgment shall be recognised and enforced under this Convention, if:

(a) the court of origin was designated in a non-exclusive choice of court agreement;

(b) there exists neither a judgment given by any other court before which proceedings could be brought in accordance with the non-exclusive choice of court agreement, nor a proceeding pending between the same parties in any other such court on the same cause of action; and

(c) the court of origin was the court first seised.

## Article 23

**Uniform interpretation**

In the interpretation of this Convention, regard shall be had to its international character and to the need to promote uniformity in its application.

## Article 24

**Review of operation of the Convention**

The Secretary General of the Hague Conference on Private International Law shall at regular intervals make arrangements for:

(a) review of the operation of this Convention, including any declarations; and

(b) consideration of whether any amendments to this Convention are desirable.

## Article 25

**Non-unified legal systems**

1. In relation to a Contracting State in which two or more systems of law apply in different territorial units with regard to any matter dealt with in this Convention:

(a) any reference to the law or procedure of a State shall be construed as referring, where appropriate, to the law or procedure in force in the relevant territorial unit;

(b) any reference to residence in a State shall be construed as referring, where appropriate, to residence in the relevant territorial unit;

(c) any reference to the court or courts of a State shall be construed as referring, where appropriate, to the court or courts in the relevant territorial unit;

(d) any reference to a connection with a State shall be construed as referring, where appropriate, to a connection with the relevant territorial unit.

2. Notwithstanding the preceding paragraph, a Contracting State with two or more territorial units in which different systems of law apply shall not be bound to apply this Convention to situations which involve solely such different territorial units.

3. A court in a territorial unit of a Contracting State with two or more territorial units in which different systems of law apply shall not be bound to recognise or enforce a judgment from another Contracting State solely because the judgment has been recognised or enforced in another territorial unit of the same Contracting State under this Convention.

4. This Article shall not apply to a Regional Economic Integration Organisation.

*Article 26*

**Relationship with other international instruments**

1. This Convention shall be interpreted so far as possible to be compatible with other treaties in force for Contracting States, whether concluded before or after this Convention.

2. This Convention shall not affect the application by a Contracting State of a treaty, whether concluded before or after this Convention, in cases where none of the parties is resident in a Contracting State that is not a Party to the treaty.

3. This Convention shall not affect the application by a Contracting State of a treaty that was concluded before this Convention entered into force for that Contracting State, if applying this Convention would be inconsistent with the obligations of that Contracting State to any non-Contracting State. This paragraph shall also apply to treaties that revise or replace a treaty concluded before this Convention entered into force for that Contracting State, except to the extent that the revision or replacement creates new inconsistencies with this Convention.

4. This Convention shall not affect the application by a Contracting State of a treaty, whether concluded before or after this Convention, for the purposes of obtaining recognition or enforcement of a judgment given by a court of a Contracting State that is also a Party to that treaty. However, the judgment shall not be recognised or enforced to a lesser extent than under this Convention.

5. This Convention shall not affect the application by a Contracting State of a treaty which, in relation to a specific matter, governs jurisdiction or the recognition or enforcement of judgments, even if concluded after this Convention and even if all States concerned are Parties to this Convention.

This paragraph shall apply only if the Contracting State has made a declaration in respect of the treaty under this paragraph. In the case of such a declaration, other Contracting States shall not be obliged to apply this Convention to that specific matter to the extent of any inconsistency, where an exclusive choice of court agreement designates the courts, or one or more specific courts, of the Contracting State that made the declaration.

6. This Convention shall not affect the application of the rules of a Regional Economic Integration Organisation that is a Party to this Convention, whether adopted before or after this Convention:

(a) where none of the parties is resident in a Contracting State that is not a Member State of the Regional Economic Integration Organisation;

(b) as concerns the recognition or enforcement of judgments as between Member States of the Regional Economic Integration Organisation.

## CHAPTER V

## FINAL CLAUSES

*Article 27*

**Signature, ratification, acceptance, approval or accession**

1. This Convention is open for signature by all States.

2. This Convention is subject to ratification, acceptance or approval by the signatory States.

3. This Convention is open for accession by all States.

4. Instruments of ratification, acceptance, approval or accession shall be deposited with the Ministry of Foreign Affairs of the Kingdom of the Netherlands, depositary of the Convention.

## Article 28

### Declarations with respect to non-unified legal systems

1. If a State has two or more territorial units in which different systems of law apply in relation to matters dealt with in this Convention, it may at the time of signature, ratification, acceptance, approval or accession declare that the Convention shall extend to all its territorial units or only to one or more of them and may modify this declaration by submitting another declaration at any time.

2. A declaration shall be notified to the depositary and shall state expressly the territorial units to which the Convention applies.

3. If a State makes no declaration under this Article, the Convention shall extend to all territorial units of that State.

4. This Article shall not apply to a Regional Economic Integration Organisation.

## Article 29

### Regional Economic Integration Organisations

1. A Regional Economic Integration Organisation which is constituted solely by sovereign States and has competence over some or all of the matters governed by this Convention may similarly sign, accept, approve or accede to this Convention. The Regional Economic Integration Organisation shall in that case have the rights and obligations of a Contracting State, to the extent that the Organisation has competence over matters governed by this Convention.

2. The Regional Economic Integration Organisation shall, at the time of signature, acceptance, approval or accession, notify the depositary in writing of the matters governed by this Convention in respect of which competence has been transferred to that Organisation by its Member States. The Organisation shall promptly notify the depositary in writing of any changes to its competence as specified in the most recent notice given under this paragraph.

3. For the purposes of the entry into force of this Convention, any instrument deposited by a Regional Economic Integration Organisation shall not be counted unless the Regional Economic Integration Organisation declares in accordance with Article 30 that its Member States will not be Parties to this Convention.

4. Any reference to a 'Contracting State' or 'State' in this Convention shall apply equally, where appropriate, to a Regional Economic Integration Organisation that is a Party to it.

## Article 30

### Accession by a Regional Economic Integration Organisation without its Member States

1. At the time of signature, acceptance, approval or accession, a Regional Economic Integration Organisation may declare that it exercises competence over all the matters governed by this Convention and that its Member States will not be Parties to this Convention but shall be bound by virtue of the signature, acceptance, approval or accession of the Organisation.

2. In the event that a declaration is made by a Regional Economic Integration Organisation in accordance with paragraph 1, any reference to a 'Contracting State' or 'State' in this Convention shall apply equally, where appropriate, to the Member States of the Organisation.

## Article 31

### Entry into force

1. This Convention shall enter into force on the first day of the month following the expiration of three months after the deposit of the second instrument of ratification, acceptance, approval or accession referred to in Article 27.

2. Thereafter this Convention shall enter into force:

European Union Materials

(a) for each State or Regional Economic Integration Organisation subsequently ratifying, accepting, approving or acceding to it, on the first day of the month following the expiration of three months after the deposit of its instrument of ratification, acceptance, approval or accession;

(b) for a territorial unit to which this Convention has been extended in accordance with Article 28(1), on the first day of the month following the expiration of three months after the notification of the declaration referred to in that Article.

## Article 32

### Declarations

1. Declarations referred to in Articles 19, 20, 21, 22 and 26 may be made upon signature, ratification, acceptance, approval or accession or at any time thereafter, and may be modified or withdrawn at any time.

2. Declarations, modifications and withdrawals shall be notified to the depositary.

3. A declaration made at the time of signature, ratification, acceptance, approval or accession shall take effect simultaneously with the entry into force of this Convention for the State concerned.

4. A declaration made at a subsequent time, and any modification or withdrawal of a declaration, shall take effect on the first day of the month following the expiration of three months after the date on which the notification is received by the depositary.

5. A declaration under Articles 19, 20, 21 and 26 shall not apply to exclusive choice of court agreements concluded before it takes effect.

## Article 33

### Denunciation

1. This Convention may be denounced by notification in writing to the depositary. The denunciation may be limited to certain territorial units of a non-unified legal system to which this Convention applies.

2. The denunciation shall take effect on the first day of the month following the expiration of 12 months after the date on which the notification is received by the depositary. Where a longer period for the denunciation to take effect is specified in the notification, the denunciation shall take effect upon the expiration of such longer period after the date on which the notification is received by the depositary.

## Article 34

### Notifications by the depositary

The depositary shall notify the Members of the Hague Conference on Private International Law, and other States and Regional Economic Integration Organisations which have signed, ratified, accepted, approved or acceded in accordance with Articles 27, 29 and 30 of the following:

(a) the signatures, ratifications, acceptances, approvals and accessions referred to in Articles 27, 29 and 30;

(b) the date on which this Convention enters into force in accordance with Article 31;

(c) the notifications, declarations, modifications and withdrawals of declarations referred to in Articles 19, 20, 21, 22, 26, 28, 29 and 30;

(d) the denunciations referred to in Article 33.

In witness whereof the undersigned, being duly authorised thereto, have signed this Convention.

Done at The Hague, on 30 June 2005, in the English and French languages, both texts being equally authentic, in a single copy which shall be deposited in the archives of the Government of the Kingdom of the Netherlands, and of which a certified copy shall be sent, through diplomatic channels, to each of the Member States of the Hague Conference on Private International Law as of the date of its Twentieth Session and to each State which participated in that Session.

ANNEX II

### Declaration by the European Community in accordance with Article 30 of the Convention on Choice of Court Agreements

The European Community declares, in accordance with Article 30 of the Convention on Choice of Court Agreements, that it exercises competence over all the matters governed by this Convention. Its Member States will not sign, ratify, accept or approve the Convention, but shall be bound by the Convention by virtue of its conclusion by the European Community.

For the purpose of this declaration, the term 'European Community' does not include Denmark by virtue of Articles 1 and 2 of the Protocol on the position of Denmark annexed to the Treaty on European Union and the Treaty establishing the European Community.

## Council Decision of 4 December 2014 on the approval, on behalf of the European Union, of the Hague Convention of 30 June 2005 on Choice of Court Agreements (2014/887/EU)

[2014] OJ L353/5

THE COUNCIL OF THE EUROPEAN UNION,

Having regard to the Treaty on the Functioning of the European Union, and in particular Article 81(2), in conjunction with point (a) of the second subparagraph of Article 218(6) thereof,

Having regard to the proposal from the European Commission,

Having regard to the consent of the European Parliament,

Whereas:

(1) The European Union is working towards the establishment of a common judicial area based on the principle of mutual recognition of judicial decisions.

(2) The Convention on Choice of Court Agreements concluded on 30 June 2005 under the auspices of the Hague Conference on Private International Law ('the Convention') makes a valuable contribution to promoting party autonomy in international commercial transactions and to increasing the predictability of judicial solutions in such transactions. In particular, the Convention ensures the necessary legal certainty for the parties that their choice of court agreement will be respected and that a judgment given by the chosen court will be capable of recognition and enforcement in international cases.

(3) Article 29 of the Convention allows Regional Economic Integration Organisations such as the European Union to sign, accept, approve or accede to the Convention. The Union signed the Convention on 1 April 2009, subject to its conclusion at a later date, in accordance with Council Decision 2009/397/EC.

(4) The Convention affects Union secondary legislation relating to jurisdiction based on the choice of the parties and to the recognition and enforcement of the resulting judgments, in particular Council Regulation (EC) No 44/2001, which is to be replaced as of 10 January 2015 by Regulation (EU) No 1215/2012 of the European Parliament and of the Council.

(5) With the adoption of Regulation (EU) No 1215/2012 the Union paved the way for the approval of the Convention, on behalf of the Union, by ensuring coherence between the rules of the Union on the choice of court in civil and commercial matters and the rules of the Convention.

(6) When signing the Convention, the Union declared under Article 30 of the Convention that it exercises competence over all the matters governed by the Convention. Consequently, the Member States shall be bound by the Convention by virtue of its approval by the Union.

(7) The Union should, when approving the Convention, in addition make the declaration allowed under Article 21 excluding from the scope of the Convention insurance contracts in general, subject to certain well-defined exceptions. The objective of the declaration is to preserve the protective jurisdiction rules available to the policyholder, the insured party or a beneficiary in matters relating to insurance under Regulation (EC) No 44/2001. The exclusion should be limited to what is necessary to protect the interests of the weaker parties in insurance contracts. It should therefore not cover reinsurance contracts nor contracts relating to large risks. The Union should at the same time make a unilateral declaration stating that it may, at a later stage in light of the experience acquired in the application of the Convention, reassess the need to maintain its declaration under Article 21.

(8) The United Kingdom and Ireland are bound by Regulation (EC) No 44/2001 and are therefore taking part in the adoption and application of this Decision.

(9) In accordance with Articles 1 and 2 of Protocol No 22 on the position of Denmark, annexed to the Treaty on European Union and to the Treaty on the Functioning of the European Union, Denmark is not taking part in the adoption of this Decision and is not bound by it or subject to its application,

HAS ADOPTED THIS DECISION:

*Article 1*

The Hague Convention of 30 June 2005 on Choice of Court Agreements ('the Convention') is hereby approved on behalf of the European Union.

*Article 2*

The President of the Council is hereby authorised to designate the person(s) empowered to deposit, on behalf of the Union, the instrument of approval provided for in Article 27(4) of the Convention.

The deposit of the instrument of approval referred to in the first subparagraph shall take place within one month of 5 June 2015.

*Article 3*

1. When depositing the instrument of approval provided for in Article 27(4) of the Convention, the Union shall, in accordance with Article 21 of the Convention, make a declaration relating to insurance contracts.

The text of that declaration is attached as Annex I to this Decision.

2. When depositing the instrument of approval provided for in Article 27(4) of the Convention, the Union shall make a unilateral declaration.

The text of that declaration is attached as Annex II to this Decision.

*Article 4*

This Decision shall enter into force on the date of its adoption.

ANNEX I

**Declaration by the European Union at the time of approval of the Hague Convention of 30 June 2005 on Choice of Court Agreements ('the Convention') in accordance with Article 21 thereof**

The objective of this declaration which excludes certain types of insurance contracts from the scope of the Convention is to protect certain policyholders, insured parties and beneficiaries who, according to internal EU law, receive special protection.

1. The European Union declares, in accordance with Article 21 of the Convention, that it will not apply the Convention to insurance contracts, except as provided for in paragraph 2 below.

2. The European Union will apply the Convention to insurance contracts in the following cases:

(a)  where the contract is a reinsurance contract;

(b)  where the choice of court agreement is entered into after the dispute has arisen;

(c) where, without prejudice to Article 1(2) of the Convention, the choice of court agreement is concluded between a policyholder and an insurer, both of whom are, at the time of the conclusion of the contract of insurance, domiciled or habitually resident in the same Contracting State, and that agreement has the effect of conferring jurisdiction on the courts of that State, even if the harmful event were to occur abroad, provided that such an agreement is not contrary to the law of that State;

(d) where the choice of court agreement relates to a contract of insurance which covers one or more of the following risks considered to be large risks:

(i) any loss or damage arising from perils which relate to their use for commercial purposes, of, or to:

(a) seagoing ships, installations situated offshore or on the high seas or river, canal and lake vessels;

(b) aircraft;

(c) railway rolling stock;

(ii) any loss of or damage to goods in transit or baggage other than passengers' baggage, irrespective of the form of transport;

(iii) any liability, other than for bodily injury to passengers or loss of or damage to their baggage, arising out of the use or operation of:

(a) ships, installations or vessels as referred to in point (i)(a);

(b) aircraft, in so far as the law of the Contracting State in which such aircraft are registered does not prohibit choice of court agreements regarding the insurance of such risks;

(c) railway rolling stock;

(iv) any liability, other than for bodily injury to passengers or loss of or damage to their baggage, for loss or damage caused by goods in transit or baggage as referred to in point (ii);

(v) any financial loss connected with the use or operation of ships, installations, vessels, aircraft or railway rolling stock as referred to in point (i), in particular loss of freight or charter-hire;

(vi) any risk or interest connected with any of the risks referred to in points (i) to (v);

(vii) any credit risk or suretyship risk where the policy holder is engaged professionally in an industrial or commercial activity or in one of the liberal professions and the risk relates to such activity;

(viii) any other risks where the policy holder carries on a business of a size which exceeds the limits of at least two of the following criteria:

(a) a balance-sheet total of EUR 6,2 million;

(b) a net turnover of EUR 12,8 million;

(c) an average number of 250 employees during the financial year.

## ANNEX II

**Unilateral declaration by the European Union at the time of the approval of the Hague Convention of 30 June 2005 on Choice of Court Agreements ('the Convention')**

The European Union makes the following unilateral declaration:

'The European Union declares that it may, at a later stage in the light of the experience acquired in the application of the Convention, reassess the need to maintain its declaration under Article 21 of the Convention.'

# Council Decision of 31 March 2011 on the signing, on behalf of the European Union, of the Hague Convention of 23 November 2007 on the International Recovery of Child Support and Other Forms of Family Maintenance (2011/220/EU)

[2011] OJ L93/9

THE COUNCIL OF THE EUROPEAN UNION,

Having regard to the Treaty on the Functioning of the European Union, and in particular the first subparagraph of Article 81(3), in conjunction with Article 218(5) thereof,

Having regard to the proposal from the European Commission,

Whereas:

(1) The Union is working towards the establishment of a common judicial area based on the principle of mutual recognition of decisions.

(2) The Hague Convention of 23 November 2007 on the International Recovery of Child Support and Other Forms of Family Maintenance ('the Convention') constitutes a good basis for a worldwide system of administrative cooperation and for recognition and enforcement of maintenance decisions and maintenance arrangements, providing for free legal assistance in virtually all child support cases and for a streamlined procedure for recognition and enforcement.

(3) Article 59 of the Convention allows Regional Economic Integration Organisations such as the Union to sign, accept, approve or accede to the Convention.

(4) Matters governed by the Convention are also dealt with in Council Regulation (EC) No 4/2009 of 18 December 2008 on jurisdiction, applicable law, recognition and enforcement of decisions and cooperation in matters relating to maintenance obligations. The Union should decide, in this particular case, to sign the Convention alone and to exercise competence over all the matters governed by it.

(5) All appropriate declarations and reservations should be made by the Union at the time of the approval of the Convention.

(6) In accordance with Article 3 of Protocol (No 21) on the position of the United Kingdom and Ireland in respect of the Area of Freedom, Security and Justice, annexed to the Treaty on European Union and to the Treaty on the Functioning of the European Union, the United Kingdom and Ireland are taking part in the adoption and application of this Decision.

(7) In accordance with Articles 1 and 2 of Protocol (No 22) on the position of Denmark, annexed to the Treaty on European Union and to the Treaty on the Functioning of the European Union, Denmark is not taking part in the adoption of this Decision and is not bound by it or subject to its application,

HAS ADOPTED THIS DECISION:

*Article 1*

The signing of the Hague Convention of 23 November 2007 on the International Recovery of Child Support and Other Forms of Family Maintenance ('the Convention') is hereby approved on behalf of the European Union .

*Article 2*

The President of the Council is hereby authorised to designate the person(s) empowered to sign the Convention on behalf of the Union.

*Article 3*

This Decision shall enter into force on the day of its adoption.

## Council Decision of 9 June 2011 on the approval, on behalf of the European Union, of the Hague Convention of 23 November 2007 on the International Recovery of Child Support and Other Forms of Family Maintenance (2011/432/EU)

THE COUNCIL OF THE EUROPEAN UNION,

Having regard to the Treaty on the Functioning of the European Union, and in particular the first subparagraph of Article 81(3), in conjunction with point (b) of the second subparagraph of Article 218(6) and the first sentence of the second subparagraph of Article 218(8) thereof,

Having regard to the proposal from the European Commission,

Having regard to the opinion of the European Parliament ,

Whereas:

(1) The Union is working towards the establishment of a common judicial area based on the principle of mutual recognition of decisions.

(2) The Hague Convention of 23 November 2007 on the International Recovery of Child Support and Other Forms of Family Maintenance ('the Convention') constitutes a good basis for a worldwide system of administrative cooperation and for recognition and enforcement of maintenance decisions and maintenance arrangements, providing for free legal assistance in virtually all child support cases and for a streamlined procedure for recognition and enforcement.

(3) Article 59 of the Convention allows Regional Economic Integration Organisations such as the Union to sign, accept, approve or accede to the Convention.

(4) Matters governed by the Convention are also dealt with in Council Regulation (EC) No 4/2009 of 18 December 2008 on jurisdiction, applicable law, recognition and enforcement of decisions and cooperation in matters relating to maintenance obligations. As agreed when Council Decision 2011/220/EU on the signing of the Convention was adopted, the Union should approve the Convention alone and exercise its competence over all the matters governed by it. Consequently, the Member States should be bound by the Convention by virtue of its approval by the Union.

(5) When approving the Convention, the Union should therefore make the declaration of competence pursuant to Article 59(3) of the Convention.

(6) Moreover, the Union should, when approving the Convention, make all the appropriate reservations and declarations allowed under Articles 62 and 63 respectively of the Convention that it deems necessary.

(7) In this respect, the Union should declare, pursuant to Article 2(3) of the Convention, that it will extend the application of Chapters II and III of the Convention to spousal support. It should at the same time make a unilateral declaration in which it undertakes to examine, at a later stage, the possibility of further extending the scope of application.

(8) The Union should make the reservation provided for in Article 44(3) of the Convention concerning the languages accepted in communications between Central Authorities. Member States that wish the Union to make that reservation with regard to them should notify the Commission thereof in advance, indicating the content of the reservation to be made.

(9) The Union should make the declarations provided for in point (g) of Article 11(1) and Article 44(1) and (2) of the Convention. Member States that wish the Union to make such declarations with regard to them should notify the Commission thereof in advance, indicating the content of the declarations to be made.

(10) A Member State that subsequently needs to withdraw the reservation regarding it set out in Annex II or to modify or withdraw the declaration regarding it set out in Annex III or to add a declaration regarding it in Annex III should inform the Council and the Commission thereof. On that basis, the Union should notify the depositary accordingly.

(11) Member States should inform the Commission of the Central Authorities designated in accordance with Article 4(3) of the Convention and should notify the Commission of the information concerning laws, procedures and services referred to in Article 57 of the Convention. The Commission should forward that information to the Permanent Bureau of the Hague Conference on Private International Law ('the Permanent Bureau') at the time when the Union deposits its instrument of approval, as required by the Convention.

(12) When notifying the Commission of the relevant information on their Central Authorities and on their laws, procedures and services, Member States should use the Country Profile Form recommended and published by the Hague Conference on Private International Law, if possible, in electronic format.

(13) A Member State that subsequently needs to modify the information on its Central Authority or on its laws, procedures and services should inform the Permanent Bureau thereof directly and at the same time notify the Commission of the change.

(14) In accordance with Article 3 of Protocol (No 21) on the position of the United Kingdom and Ireland in respect of the Area of Freedom, Security and Justice, annexed to the Treaty on European Union and to the Treaty on the Functioning of the European Union, the United Kingdom and Ireland are taking part in the adoption and application of this Decision.

(15) In accordance with Articles 1 and 2 of Protocol (No 22) on the position of Denmark, annexed to the Treaty on European Union and to the Treaty on the Functioning of the European Union, Denmark is not taking part in the adoption of this Decision and is not bound by it or subject to its application,

HAS ADOPTED THIS DECISION:

### Article 1

The Hague Convention of 23 November 2007 on the International Recovery of Child Support and Other Forms of Family Maintenance ('the Convention') is hereby approved on behalf of the European Union.

The text of the Convention is attached to this Decision.

### Article 2

The President of the Council is hereby authorised to designate the person(s) empowered to deposit, on behalf of the Union, the instrument referred to in Article 58(2) of the Convention.

### Article 3

When depositing the instrument referred to in Article 58(2) of the Convention, the Union shall make the declaration of competence pursuant to Article 59(3) of the Convention.

The text of that declaration is attached as part A of Annex I to this Decision.

### Article 4

1. When depositing the instrument referred to in Article 58(2) of the Convention, the Union shall declare, pursuant to Article 2(3) of the Convention, that it will extend the application of Chapters II and III of the Convention to spousal support.

The text of that declaration is attached as part B of Annex I to this Decision.

2. When depositing the instrument referred to in Article 58(2) of the Convention, the Union shall make the unilateral declaration the text of which is attached as Annex IV to this Decision.

### Article 5

When depositing the instrument referred to in Article 58(2) of the Convention, the Union shall make the reservation provided for in Article 44(3) of the Convention concerning the Member States that object to the use of either English or French in communications between Central Authorities.

The text of that reservation is attached as Annex II to this Decision.

*Article 6*

When depositing the instrument referred to in Article 58(2) of the Convention, the Union shall make the declarations provided for in point (g) of Article 11(1) of the Convention concerning the information or documents required by the Member States and in Article 44(1) of the Convention concerning the languages accepted by the Member States other than their official languages, and the declaration provided for in Article 44(2) of the Convention.

The text of those declarations is attached as Annex III to this Decision.

*Article 7*

1. Member States shall notify the Commission, no later than 10 December 2012, of:

(a) the contact details of the Central Authorities designated in accordance with Article 4(3) of the Convention; and

(b) the information concerning laws, procedures and services referred to in Article 57 of the Convention.

2. When forwarding the information set out in paragraph 1 to the Commission, Member States shall use the Country Profile Form recommended and published by the Hague Conference on Private International Law, if possible, in electronic format.

3. The Commission shall forward the individual Country Profile Forms completed by the Member States to the Permanent Bureau of the Hague Conference on Private International Law ('the Permanent Bureau') at the time when the Union deposits the instrument referred to in Article 58(2) of the Convention.

*Article 8*

A Member State that wishes to withdraw the reservation regarding it set out in Annex II or to modify or withdraw the declaration regarding it set out in Annex III or to add a declaration regarding it in Annex III shall inform the Council and the Commission of the desired withdrawal, modification or addition.

The Union shall subsequently notify the depositary accordingly pursuant to Article 63(2) of the Convention.

*Article 9*

A Member State that wishes to modify the information given in its Country Profile Form after the initial forwarding of that form by the Commission shall inform the Permanent Bureau directly thereof or shall make the necessary change directly, if the electronic format of the Country Profile Form is being used. It shall inform the Commission at the same time.

*Article 10*

This Decision shall enter into force on the day of its adoption.

ANNEX I

**European Union declarations at the time of the approval of the Hague Convention of 23 November 2007 on the International Recovery of Child Support and Other Forms of Family Maintenance ('the Convention') in accordance with Article 63 thereof**

**A. DECLARATION REFERRED TO IN ARTICLE 59(3) OF THE CONVENTION CONCERNING THE COMPETENCE OF THE EUROPEAN UNION OVER THE MATTERS GOVERNED BY THE CONVENTION**

1. The European Union declares that it exercises competence over all the matters governed by the Convention. The Member States shall be bound by the Convention by virtue of its approval by the European Union.

2. The current Members of the European Union are the Kingdom of Belgium, the Republic of Bulgaria, the Czech Republic, the Kingdom of Denmark, the Federal Republic of Germany, the Republic of

Estonia, Ireland, the Hellenic Republic, the Kingdom of Spain, the French Republic, the Italian Republic, the Republic of Cyprus, the Republic of Latvia, the Republic of Lithuania, the Grand-Duchy of Luxembourg, the Republic of Hungary, Malta, the Kingdom of the Netherlands, the Republic of Austria, the Republic of Poland, the Portuguese Republic, Romania, the Republic of Slovenia, the Slovak Republic, the Republic of Finland, the Kingdom of Sweden and the United Kingdom of Great Britain and Northern Ireland.

3. However, this declaration does not apply to the Kingdom of Denmark, in accordance with Articles 1 and 2 of Protocol (No 22) on the position of Denmark, annexed to the Treaty on European Union and to the Treaty on the Functioning of the European Union.

4. This declaration is not applicable to territories of the Member States to which the Treaty on the Functioning of the European Union does not apply (see Article 355 of that Treaty) and is without prejudice to such acts or positions as may be adopted pursuant to the Convention by the Member States concerned on behalf of and in the interests of those territories.

5. The application of the Convention in cooperation between Central Authorities will be the responsibility of the Central Authorities of each individual Member State of the European Union. Accordingly, whenever a Central Authority of a Contracting State needs to contact a Central Authority of a Member State of the European Union it should contact the Central Authority concerned directly. The Member States of the European Union, if they deem it appropriate, will also attend all the Special Commissions likely to be tasked with following up the application of the Convention.

## B. DECLARATION REFERRED TO IN ARTICLE 2(3) OF THE CONVENTION

The European Union declares that it will extend the application of Chapters II and III of the Convention to spousal support.

*[Annexes II–III omitted]*

## ANNEX IV

### Unilateral declaration by the European Union at the time of the approval of the Hague Convention of 23 November 2007 on the International Recovery of Child Support and Other Forms of Family Maintenance

The European Union makes the following unilateral declaration:

'The European Union wishes to underline the great importance it attaches to the 2007 Hague Convention on the International Recovery of Child Support and Other Forms of Family Maintenance. The Union recognises that extending the application of the Convention to all maintenance obligations arising from a family relationship, parentage, marriage or affinity is likely to increase considerably its effectiveness, allowing all maintenance creditors to benefit from the system of administrative cooperation established by the Convention.

It is in this spirit that the European Union intends to extend the application of Chapters II and III of the Convention to spousal support when the Convention enters into force with regard to the Union.

Furthermore, the European Union undertakes, within 7 years, in the light of experience acquired and possible declarations of extension made by other Contracting States, to examine the possibility of extending the application of the Convention as a whole to all maintenance obligations arising from a family relationship, parentage, marriage or affinity.'

## Convention on the International Recovery of Child Support and Other Forms of Family Maintenance

(Concluded 23 November 2007)

THE STATES SIGNATORY TO THE PRESENT CONVENTION,

DESIRING TO improve cooperation among States for the international recovery of child support and other forms of family maintenance,

AWARE OF the need for procedures which produce results and are accessible, prompt, efficient, cost-effective, responsive and fair,

WISHING TO build upon the best features of existing Hague Conventions and other international instruments, in particular the United Nations Convention on the Recovery Abroad of Maintenance of 20 June 1956,

SEEKING TO take advantage of advances in technologies and to create a flexible system which can continue to evolve as needs change and further advances in technology create new opportunities,

RECALLING that, in accordance with Articles 3 and 27 of the United Nations Convention on the Rights of the Child of 20 November 1989,

— in all actions concerning children the best interests of the child shall be a primary consideration,

— every child has a right to a standard of living adequate for the child's physical, mental, spiritual, moral and social development,

— the parent(s) or others responsible for the child have the primary responsibility to secure, within their abilities and financial capacities, the conditions of living necessary for the child's development, and

— States Parties should take all appropriate measures, including the conclusion of international agreements, to secure the recovery of maintenance for the child from the parent(s) or other responsible persons, in particular where such persons live in a State different from that of the child,

HAVE RESOLVED TO CONCLUDE THIS CONVENTION AND HAVE AGREED UPON THE FOLLOWING PROVISIONS:

## CHAPTER I

## OBJECT, SCOPE AND DEFINITIONS

*Article 1*

Object

The object of the present Convention is to ensure the effective international recovery of child support and other forms of family maintenance, in particular by:

(a) establishing a comprehensive system of cooperation between the authorities of the Contracting States;

(b) making available applications for the establishment of maintenance decisions;

(c) providing for the recognition and enforcement of maintenance decisions; and

(d) requiring effective measures for the prompt enforcement of maintenance decisions.

*Article 2*

Scope

(1) This Convention shall apply:

(a) to maintenance obligations arising from a parent-child relationship towards a person under the age of 21 years;

(b) to recognition and enforcement or enforcement of a decision for spousal support when the application is made with a claim within the scope of subparagraph a); and

(c) with the exception of Chapters II and III, to spousal support.

(2) Any Contracting State may reserve, in accordance with Article 62, the right to limit the application of the Convention under subparagraph 1 a), to persons who have not attained the age of 18 years. A Contracting State which makes this reservation shall not be entitled to claim the application of the Convention to persons of the age excluded by its reservation.

(3) Any Contracting State may declare in accordance with Article 63 that it will extend the application of the whole or any part of the Convention to any maintenance obligation arising from a family relationship, parentage, marriage or affinity, including in particular obligations in respect of vulnerable persons. Any such declaration shall give rise to obligations between two Contracting States only in so far as their declarations cover the same maintenance obligations and parts of the Convention.

(4) The provisions of this Convention shall apply to children regardless of the marital status of the parents.

*Article 3*

**Definitions**

For the purposes of this Convention:

(a) 'creditor' means an individual to whom maintenance is owed or is alleged to be owed;

(b) 'debtor' means an individual who owes or who is alleged to owe maintenance;

(c) 'legal assistance' means the assistance necessary to enable applicants to know and assert their rights and to ensure that applications are fully and effectively dealt with in the requested State. The means of providing such assistance may include as necessary legal advice, assistance in bringing a case before an authority, legal representation and exemption from costs of proceedings;

(d) 'agreement in writing' means an agreement recorded in any medium, the information contained in which is accessible so as to be usable for subsequent reference;

(e) 'maintenance arrangement' means an agreement in writing relating to the payment of maintenance which:

(i) has been formally drawn up or registered as an authentic instrument by a competent authority; or

(ii) has been authenticated by, or concluded, registered or filed with a competent authority;

and may be the subject of review and modification by a competent authority;

(f) 'vulnerable person' means a person who, by reason of an impairment or insufficiency of his or her personal faculties, is not able to support him or herself.

CHAPTER II

**ADMINISTRATIVE CO-OPERATION**

*Article 4*

**Designation of Central Authorities**

(1) A Contracting State shall designate a Central Authority to discharge the duties that are imposed by the Convention on such an authority.

(2) Federal States, States with more than one system of law or States having autonomous territorial units shall be free to appoint more than one Central Authority and shall specify the territorial or personal extent of their functions. Where a State has appointed more than one Central Authority, it shall designate the Central Authority to which any communication may be addressed for transmission to the appropriate Central Authority within that State.

(3) The designation of the Central Authority or Central Authorities, their contact details, and where appropriate the extent of their functions as specified in paragraph 2, shall be communicated by a Contracting State to the Permanent Bureau of the Hague Conference on Private International Law at the time when the instrument of ratification or accession is deposited or when a declaration is submitted in accordance with Article 61. Contracting States shall promptly inform the Permanent Bureau of any changes.

## Article 5

### General functions of Central Authorities

Central Authorities shall:

(a)   cooperate with each other and promote cooperation amongst the competent authorities in their States to achieve the purposes of the Convention;

(b)   seek as far as possible solutions to difficulties which arise in the application of the Convention.

## Article 6

### Specific functions of Central Authorities

(1) Central Authorities shall provide assistance in relation to applications under Chapter III. In particular they shall:

(a)   transmit and receive such applications;

(b)   initiate or facilitate the institution of proceedings in respect of such applications.

(2)   In relation to such applications they shall take all appropriate measures:

(a)   where the circumstances require, to provide or facilitate the provision of legal assistance;

(b)   to help locate the debtor or the creditor;

(c)   to help obtain relevant information concerning the income and, if necessary, other financial circumstances of the debtor or creditor, including the location of assets;

(d)   to encourage amicable solutions with a view to obtaining voluntary payment of maintenance, where suitable by use of mediation, conciliation or similar processes;

(e)   to facilitate the ongoing enforcement of maintenance decisions, including any arrears;

(f)   to facilitate the collection and expeditious transfer of maintenance payments;

(g)   to facilitate the obtaining of documentary or other evidence;

(h)   to provide assistance in establishing parentage where necessary for the recovery of maintenance;

(i)   to initiate or facilitate the institution of proceedings to obtain any necessary provisional measures that are territorial in nature and the purpose of which is to secure the outcome of a pending maintenance application;

(j)   to facilitate service of documents.

(3) The functions of the Central Authority under this Article may, to the extent permitted under the law of its State, be performed by public bodies, or other bodies subject to the supervision of the competent authorities of that State. The designation of any such public bodies or other bodies, as well as their contact details and the extent of their functions, shall be communicated by a Contracting State to the Permanent Bureau of the Hague Conference on Private International Law. Contracting States shall promptly inform the Permanent Bureau of any changes.

(4) Nothing in this Article or Article 7 shall be interpreted as imposing an obligation on a Central Authority to exercise powers that can be exercised only by judicial authorities under the law of the requested State.

## Article 7

### Requests for specific measures

(1) A Central Authority may make a request, supported by reasons, to another Central Authority to take appropriate specific measures under Article 6(2)(b), (c), (g), (h), (i) and (j) when no application

under Article 10 is pending. The requested Central Authority shall take such measures as are appropriate if satisfied that they are necessary to assist a potential applicant in making an application under Article 10 or in determining whether such an application should be initiated.

(2) A Central Authority may also take specific measures on the request of another Central Authority in relation to a case having an international element concerning the recovery of maintenance pending in the requesting State.

### Article 8

**Central Authority costs**

(1) Each Central Authority shall bear its own costs in applying this Convention.

(2) Central Authorities may not impose any charge on an applicant for the provision of their services under the Convention save for exceptional costs arising from a request for a specific measure under Article 7.

(3) The requested Central Authority may not recover the costs of the services referred to in paragraph 2 without the prior consent of the applicant to the provision of those services at such cost.

## CHAPTER III

## APPLICATIONS THROUGH CENTRAL AUTHORITIES

### Article 9

**Application through Central Authorities**

An application under this Chapter shall be made through the Central Authority of the Contracting State in which the applicant resides to the Central Authority of the requested State. For the purpose of this provision, residence excludes mere presence.

### Article 10

**Available applications**

(1) The following categories of application shall be available to a creditor in a requesting State seeking to recover maintenance under this Convention:

(a) recognition or recognition and enforcement of a decision;

(b) enforcement of a decision made or recognised in the requested State;

(c) establishment of a decision in the requested State where there is no existing decision, including where necessary the establishment of parentage;

(d) establishment of a decision in the requested State where recognition and enforcement of a decision is not possible, or is refused, because of the lack of a basis for recognition and enforcement under Article 20, or on the grounds specified in Article 22(b) or (e);

(e) modification of a decision made in the requested State;

(f) modification of a decision made in a State other than the requested State.

(2) The following categories of application shall be available to a debtor in a requesting State against whom there is an existing maintenance decision:

(a) recognition of a decision, or an equivalent procedure leading to the suspension, or limiting the enforcement, of a previous decision in the requested State;

(b) modification of a decision made in the requested State;

(c) modification of a decision made in a State other than the requested State.

(3) Save as otherwise provided in this Convention, the applications in paragraphs 1 and 2 shall be determined under the law of the requested State, and applications in paragraphs 1(c) to (f) and 2(b) and (c) shall be subject to the jurisdictional rules applicable in the requested State.

*Article 11*

**Application contents**

(1) All applications under Article 10 shall as a minimum include:

(a) a statement of the nature of the application or applications;

(b) the name and contact details, including the address and date of birth of the applicant;

(c) the name and, if known, address and date of birth of the respondent;

(d) the name and date of birth of any person for whom maintenance is sought;

(e) the grounds upon which the application is based;

(f) in an application by a creditor, information concerning where the maintenance payment should be sent or electronically transmitted;

(g) save in an application under Article 10(1)(a) and (2)(a), any information or document specified by declaration in accordance with Article 63 by the requested State;

(h) the name and contact details of the person or unit from the Central Authority of the requesting State responsible for processing the application.

(2) As appropriate, and to the extent known, the application shall in addition in particular include:

(a) the financial circumstances of the creditor;

(b) the financial circumstances of the debtor, including the name and address of the employer of the debtor and the nature and location of the assets of the debtor;

(c) any other information that may assist with the location of the respondent.

(3) The application shall be accompanied by any necessary supporting information or documentation including documentation concerning the entitlement of the applicant to free legal assistance. In the case of applications under Article 10(1)(a) and (2)(a), the application shall be accompanied only by the documents listed in Article 25.

(4) An application under Article 10 may be made in the form recommended and published by the Hague Conference on Private International Law.

*Article 12*

**Transmission, receipt and processing of applications and cases through Central Authorities**

(1) The Central Authority of the requesting State shall assist the applicant in ensuring that the application is accompanied by all the information and documents known by it to be necessary for consideration of the application.

(2) The Central Authority of the requesting State shall, when satisfied that the application complies with the requirements of the Convention, transmit the application on behalf of and with the consent of the applicant to the Central Authority of the requested State. The application shall be accompanied by the transmittal form set out in Annex 1. The Central Authority of the requesting State shall, when requested by the Central Authority of the requested State, provide a complete copy certified by the competent authority in the State of origin of any document specified under Articles 16(3), 25(1)(a), (b) and (d) and (3)(b) and 30(3).

(3) The requested Central Authority shall, within 6 weeks from the date of receipt of the application, acknowledge receipt in the form set out in Annex 2, and inform the Central Authority of the requesting State what initial steps have been or will be taken to deal with the application, and may request any further necessary documents and information. Within the same 6-week period, the requested Central Authority shall provide to the requesting Central Authority the name and contact details of the person or unit responsible for responding to inquiries regarding the progress of the application.

(4) Within 3 months after the acknowledgement, the requested Central Authority shall inform the requesting Central Authority of the status of the application.

(5) Requesting and requested Central Authorities shall keep each other informed of:

(a) the person or unit responsible for a particular case;

(b)   the progress of the case;

and shall provide timely responses to enquiries.

(6)   Central Authorities shall process a case as quickly as a proper consideration of the issues will allow.

(7)   Central Authorities shall employ the most rapid and efficient means of communication at their disposal.

(8)   A requested Central Authority may refuse to process an application only if it is manifest that the requirements of the Convention are not fulfilled. In such case, that Central Authority shall promptly inform the requesting Central Authority of its reasons for refusal.

(9)   The requested Central Authority may not reject an application solely on the basis that additional documents or information are needed. However, the requested Central Authority may ask the requesting Central Authority to provide these additional documents or information. If the requesting Central Authority does not do so within 3 months or a longer period specified by the requested Central Authority, the requested Central Authority may decide that it will no longer process the application. In this case, it shall inform the requesting Central Authority of this decision.

*Article 13*

**Means of communication**

Any application made through Central Authorities of the Contracting States in accordance with this Chapter, and any document or information appended thereto or provided by a Central Authority, may not be challenged by the respondent by reason only of the medium or means of communication employed between the Central Authorities concerned.

*Article 14*

**Effective access to procedures**

(1)   The requested State shall provide applicants with effective access to procedures, including enforcement and appeal procedures, arising from applications under this Chapter.

(2)   To provide such effective access, the requested State shall provide free legal assistance in accordance with Articles 14 to 17 unless paragraph 3 applies.

(3)   The requested State shall not be obliged to provide such free legal assistance if and to the extent that the procedures of that State enable the applicant to make the case without the need for such assistance, and the Central Authority provides such services as are necessary free of charge.

(4)   Entitlements to free legal assistance shall not be less than those available in equivalent domestic cases.

(5)   No security, bond or deposit, however described, shall be required to guarantee the payment of costs and expenses in proceedings under the Convention.

*Article 15*

**Free legal assistance for child support applications**

(1)   The requested State shall provide free legal assistance in respect of all applications by a creditor under this Chapter concerning maintenance obligations arising from a parent-child relationship towards a person under the age of 21 years.

(2)   Notwithstanding paragraph 1, the requested State may, in relation to applications other than those under Article 10(1)(a) and (b) and the cases covered by Article 20(4), refuse free legal assistance if it considers that, on the merits, the application or any appeal is manifestly unfounded.

*Article 16*

**Declaration to permit use of child-centred means test**

(1)   Notwithstanding Article 15(1), a State may declare, in accordance with Article 63, that it will provide free legal assistance in respect of applications other than under Article 10(1)(a) and (b) and the cases covered by Article 20(4), subject to a test based on an assessment of the means of the child.

(2) A State shall, at the time of making such a declaration, provide information to the Permanent Bureau of the Hague Conference on Private International Law concerning the manner in which the assessment of the child's means will be carried out, including the financial criteria which would need to be met to satisfy the test.

(3) An application referred to in paragraph 1, addressed to a State which has made the declaration referred to in that paragraph, shall include a formal attestation by the applicant stating that the child's means meet the criteria referred to in paragraph 2. The requested State may only request further evidence of the child's means if it has reasonable grounds to believe that the information provided by the applicant is inaccurate.

(4) If the most favourable legal assistance provided for by the law of the requested State in respect of applications under this Chapter concerning maintenance obligations arising from a parent-child relationship towards a child is more favourable than that provided for under paragraphs 1 to 3, the most favourable legal assistance shall be provided.

*Article 17*

**Applications not qualifying under Article 15 or Article 16**

In the case of all applications under this Convention other than those under Article 15 or Article 16:

(a) the provision of free legal assistance may be made subject to a means or a merits test;

(b) an applicant, who in the State of origin has benefited from free legal assistance, shall be entitled, in any proceedings for recognition or enforcement, to benefit, at least to the same extent, from free legal assistance as provided for by the law of the State addressed under the same circumstances.

## CHAPTER IV

## RESTRICTIONS ON BRINGING PROCEEDINGS

*Article 18*

**Limit on proceedings**

(1) Where a decision is made in a Contracting State where the creditor is habitually resident, proceedings to modify the decision or to make a new decision cannot be brought by the debtor in any other Contracting State as long as the creditor remains habitually resident in the State where the decision was made.

(2) Paragraph 1 shall not apply:

(a) where, except in disputes relating to maintenance obligations in respect of children, there is agreement in writing between the parties to the jurisdiction of that other Contracting State;

(b) where the creditor submits to the jurisdiction of that other Contracting State either expressly or by defending on the merits of the case without objecting to the jurisdiction at the first available opportunity;

(c) where the competent authority in the State of origin cannot, or refuses to, exercise jurisdiction to modify the decision or make a new decision; or

(d) where the decision made in the State of origin cannot be recognised or declared enforceable in the Contracting State where proceedings to modify the decision or make a new decision are contemplated.

## CHAPTER V

## RECOGNITION AND ENFORCEMENT

*Article 19*

### Scope of the Chapter

(1) This Chapter shall apply to a decision rendered by a judicial or administrative authority in respect of a maintenance obligation. The term 'decision' also includes a settlement or agreement concluded before or approved by such an authority. A decision may include automatic adjustment by indexation and a requirement to pay arrears, retroactive maintenance or interest and a determination of costs or expenses.

(2) If a decision does not relate solely to a maintenance obligation, the effect of this Chapter is limited to the parts of the decision which concern maintenance obligations.

(3) For the purpose of paragraph 1, 'administrative authority' means a public body whose decisions, under the law of the State where it is established:

(a)  may be made the subject of an appeal to or review by a judicial authority; and

(b)  have a similar force and effect to a decision of a judicial authority on the same matter.

(4) This Chapter also applies to maintenance arrangements in accordance with Article 30.

(5) The provisions of this Chapter shall apply to a request for recognition and enforcement made directly to a competent authority of the State addressed in accordance with Article 37.

*Article 20*

### Bases for recognition and enforcement

(1) A decision made in one Contracting State ('the State of origin') shall be recognised and enforced in other Contracting States if:

(a)  the respondent was habitually resident in the State of origin at the time proceedings were instituted;

(b)  the respondent has submitted to the jurisdiction either expressly or by defending on the merits of the case without objecting to the jurisdiction at the first available opportunity;

(c)  the creditor was habitually resident in the State of origin at the time proceedings were instituted;

(d)  the child for whom maintenance was ordered was habitually resident in the State of origin at the time proceedings were instituted, provided that the respondent has lived with the child in that State or has resided in that State and provided support for the child there;

(e)  except in disputes relating to maintenance obligations in respect of children, there has been agreement to the jurisdiction in writing by the parties; or

(f)  the decision was made by an authority exercising jurisdiction on a matter of personal status or parental responsibility, unless that jurisdiction was based solely on the nationality of one of the parties.

(2) A Contracting State may make a reservation, in accordance with Article 62, in respect of paragraph 1(c), (e) or (f).

(3) A Contracting State making a reservation under paragraph 2 shall recognise and enforce a decision if its law would in similar factual circumstances confer or would have conferred jurisdiction on its authorities to make such a decision.

(4) A Contracting State shall, if recognition of a decision is not possible as a result of a reservation under paragraph 2, and if the debtor is habitually resident in that State, take all appropriate measures to establish a decision for the benefit of the creditor. The preceding sentence shall not apply to direct requests for recognition and enforcement under Article 19(5) or to claims for support referred to in Article 2(1)(b).

(5) A decision in favour of a child under the age of 18 years which cannot be recognised by virtue only of a reservation in respect of paragraph 1(c), (e) or (f) shall be accepted as establishing the eligibility of that child for maintenance in the State addressed.

(6) A decision shall be recognised only if it has effect in the State of origin, and shall be enforced only if it is enforceable in the State of origin.

## Article 21

**Severability and partial recognition and enforcement**

(1) If the State addressed is unable to recognise or enforce the whole of the decision, it shall recognise or enforce any severable part of the decision which can be so recognised or enforced.

(2) Partial recognition or enforcement of a decision can always be applied for.

## Article 22

**Grounds for refusing recognition and enforcement**

Recognition and enforcement of a decision may be refused if:

(a) recognition and enforcement of the decision is manifestly incompatible with the public policy ('ordre public') of the State addressed;

(b) the decision was obtained by fraud in connection with a matter of procedure;

(c) proceedings between the same parties and having the same purpose are pending before an authority of the State addressed and those proceedings were the first to be instituted;

(d) the decision is incompatible with a decision rendered between the same parties and having the same purpose, either in the State addressed or in another State, provided that this latter decision fulfils the conditions necessary for its recognition and enforcement in the State addressed;

(e) in a case where the respondent has neither appeared nor was represented in proceedings in the State of origin:

(i) when the law of the State of origin provides for notice of proceedings, the respondent did not have proper notice of the proceedings and an opportunity to be heard; or

(ii) when the law of the State of origin does not provide for notice of the proceedings, the respondent did not have proper notice of the decision and an opportunity to challenge or appeal it on fact and law; or

(f) the decision was made in violation of Article 18.

## Article 23

**Procedure on an application for recognition and enforcement**

(1) Subject to the provisions of the Convention, the procedures for recognition and enforcement shall be governed by the law of the State addressed.

(2) Where an application for recognition and enforcement of a decision has been made through Central Authorities in accordance with Chapter III, the requested Central Authority shall promptly either:

(a) refer the application to the competent authority which shall without delay declare the decision enforceable or register the decision for enforcement; or

(b) if it is the competent authority take such steps itself.

(3) Where the request is made directly to a competent authority in the State addressed in accordance with Article 19(5), that authority shall without delay declare the decision enforceable or register the decision for enforcement.

(4) A declaration or registration may be refused only on the ground set out in Article 22(a). At this stage neither the applicant nor the respondent is entitled to make any submissions.

(5) The applicant and the respondent shall be promptly notified of the declaration or registration, made under paragraphs 2 and 3, or the refusal thereof in accordance with paragraph 4, and may bring a challenge or appeal on fact and on a point of law.

(6) A challenge or an appeal is to be lodged within 30 days of notification under paragraph 5. If the contesting party is not resident in the Contracting State in which the declaration or registration was made or refused, the challenge or appeal shall be lodged within 60 days of notification.

(7) A challenge or appeal may be founded only on the following:

(a)  the grounds for refusing recognition and enforcement set out in Article 22;

(b)  the bases for recognition and enforcement under Article 20;

(c)  the authenticity or integrity of any document transmitted in accordance with Article 25(1)(a), (b) or (d) or (3)(b).

(8) A challenge or an appeal by a respondent may also be founded on the fulfilment of the debt to the extent that the recognition and enforcement relates to payments that fell due in the past.

(9) The applicant and the respondent shall be promptly notified of the decision following the challenge or the appeal.

(10) A further appeal, if permitted by the law of the State addressed, shall not have the effect of staying the enforcement of the decision unless there are exceptional circumstances.

(11) In taking any decision on recognition and enforcement, including any appeal, the competent authority shall act expeditiously.

## *Article 24*

### Alternative procedure on an application for recognition and enforcement

(1) Notwithstanding Article 23(2) to (11), a State may declare, in accordance with Article 63, that it will apply the procedure for recognition and enforcement set out in this Article.

(2) Where an application for recognition and enforcement of a decision has been made through Central Authorities in accordance with Chapter III, the requested Central Authority shall promptly either:

(a)  refer the application to the competent authority which shall decide on the application for recognition and enforcement; or

(b)  if it is the competent authority, take such a decision itself.

(3) A decision on recognition and enforcement shall be given by the competent authority after the respondent has been duly and promptly notified of the proceedings and both parties have been given an adequate opportunity to be heard.

(4) The competent authority may review the grounds for refusing recognition and enforcement set out in Article 22(a), (c) and (d) of its own motion. It may review any grounds listed in Articles 20, 22 and 23(7)(c) if raised by the respondent or if concerns relating to those grounds arise from the face of the documents submitted in accordance with Article 25.

(5) A refusal of recognition and enforcement may also be founded on the fulfilment of the debt to the extent that the recognition and enforcement relates to payments that fell due in the past.

(6) Any appeal, if permitted by the law of the State addressed, shall not have the effect of staying the enforcement of the decision unless there are exceptional circumstances.

(7) In taking any decision on recognition and enforcement, including any appeal, the competent authority shall act expeditiously.

## *Article 25*

### Documents

(1) An application for recognition and enforcement under Article 23 or Article 24 shall be accompanied by the following:

(a)  a complete text of the decision;

(b)  a document stating that the decision is enforceable in the State of origin and, in the case of a decision by an administrative authority, a document stating that the requirements of Article 19(3) are met unless that State has specified in accordance with Article 57 that decisions of its administrative authorities always meet those requirements;

(c)  if the respondent did not appear and was not represented in the proceedings in the State of origin, a document or documents attesting, as appropriate, either that the respondent had proper notice of the proceedings and an opportunity to be heard, or that the respondent had proper notice of the decision and the opportunity to challenge or appeal it on fact and law;

(d)  where necessary, a document showing the amount of any arrears and the date such amount was calculated;

(e)  where necessary, in the case of a decision providing for automatic adjustment by indexation, a document providing the information necessary to make the appropriate calculations;

(f)  where necessary, documentation showing the extent to which the applicant received free legal assistance in the State of origin.

(2) Upon a challenge or appeal under Article 23(7)(c) or upon request by the competent authority in the State addressed, a complete copy of the document concerned, certified by the competent authority in the State of origin, shall be provided promptly:

(a)  by the Central Authority of the requesting State, where the application has been made in accordance with Chapter III;

(b)  by the applicant, where the request has been made directly to a competent authority of the State addressed.

(3) A Contracting State may specify in accordance with Article 57:

(a)  that a complete copy of the decision certified by the competent authority in the State of origin must accompany the application;

(b)  circumstances in which it will accept, in lieu of a complete text of the decision, an abstract or extract of the decision drawn up by the competent authority of the State of origin, which may be made in the form recommended and published by the Hague Conference on Private International Law; or

(c)  that it does not require a document stating that the requirements of Article 19(3) are met.

## Article 26

### Procedure on an application for recognition

This Chapter shall apply mutatis mutandis to an application for recognition of a decision, save that the requirement of enforceability is replaced by the requirement that the decision has effect in the State of origin.

## Article 27

### Findings of fact

Any competent authority of the State addressed shall be bound by the findings of fact on which the authority of the State of origin based its jurisdiction.

## Article 28

### No review of the merits

There shall be no review by any competent authority of the State addressed of the merits of a decision.

## Article 29

### Physical presence of the child or the applicant not required

The physical presence of the child or the applicant shall not be required in any proceedings in the State addressed under this Chapter.

## Article 30

### Maintenance arrangements

(1) A maintenance arrangement made in a Contracting State shall be entitled to recognition and enforcement as a decision under this Chapter provided that it is enforceable as a decision in the State of origin.

European Union Materials

(2) For the purpose of Article 10(1)(a) and (b) and (2)(a), the term 'decision' includes a maintenance arrangement.

(3) An application for recognition and enforcement of a maintenance arrangement shall be accompanied by the following:

(a) a complete text of the maintenance arrangement; and

(b) a document stating that the particular maintenance arrangement is enforceable as a decision in the State of origin.

(4) Recognition and enforcement of a maintenance arrangement may be refused if:

(a) the recognition and enforcement is manifestly incompatible with the public policy of the State addressed;

(b) the maintenance arrangement was obtained by fraud or falsification;

(c) the maintenance arrangement is incompatible with a decision rendered between the same parties and having the same purpose, either in the State addressed or in another State, provided that this latter decision fulfils the conditions necessary for its recognition and enforcement in the State addressed.

(5) The provisions of this Chapter, with the exception of Articles 20, 22, 23(7) and 25(1) and (3), shall apply mutatis mutandis to the recognition and enforcement of a maintenance arrangement save that:

(a) a declaration or registration in accordance with Article 23(2) and (3) may be refused only on the ground set out in paragraph 4(a);

(b) a challenge or appeal as referred to in Article 23(6) may be founded only on the following:

(i) the grounds for refusing recognition and enforcement set out in paragraph 4;

(ii) the authenticity or integrity of any document transmitted in accordance with paragraph 3;

(c) as regards the procedure under Article 24(4), the competent authority may review of its own motion the ground for refusing recognition and enforcement set out in paragraph 4(a) of this Article. It may review all grounds listed in paragraph 4 of this Article and the authenticity or integrity of any document transmitted in accordance with paragraph 3 if raised by the respondent or if concerns relating to those grounds arise from the face of those documents.

(6) Proceedings for recognition and enforcement of a maintenance arrangement shall be suspended if a challenge concerning the arrangement is pending before a competent authority of a Contracting State.

(7) A State may declare, in accordance with Article 63, that applications for recognition and enforcement of a maintenance arrangement shall only be made through Central Authorities.

(8) A Contracting State may, in accordance with Article 62, reserve the right not to recognise and enforce a maintenance arrangement.

## Article 31

### Decisions produced by the combined effect of provisional and confirmation orders

Where a decision is produced by the combined effect of a provisional order made in one State and an order by an authority in another State ('the confirming State') confirming the provisional order:

(a) each of those States shall be deemed for the purposes of this Chapter to be a State of origin;

(b) the requirements of Article 22(e) shall be met if the respondent had proper notice of the proceedings in the confirming State and an opportunity to oppose the confirmation of the provisional order;

(c) the requirement of Article 20(6) that a decision be enforceable in the State of origin shall be met if the decision is enforceable in the confirming State; and

(d) Article 18 shall not prevent proceedings for the modification of the decision being commenced in either State.

## CHAPTER VI

## ENFORCEMENT BY THE STATE ADDRESSED

*Article 32*

**Enforcement under internal law**

(1) Subject to the provisions of this Chapter, enforcement shall take place in accordance with the law of the State addressed.

(2) Enforcement shall be prompt.

(3) In the case of applications through Central Authorities, where a decision has been declared enforceable or registered for enforcement under Chapter V, enforcement shall proceed without the need for further action by the applicant.

(4) Effect shall be given to any rules applicable in the State of origin of the decision relating to the duration of the maintenance obligation.

(5) Any limitation on the period for which arrears may be enforced shall be determined either by the law of the State of origin of the decision or by the law of the State addressed, whichever provides for the longer limitation period.

*Article 33*

**Non-discrimination**

The State addressed shall provide at least the same range of enforcement methods for cases under the Convention as are available in domestic cases.

*Article 34*

**Enforcement measures**

(1) Contracting States shall make available in internal law effective measures to enforce decisions under this Convention.

(2) Such measures may include:

(a)   wage withholding;

(b)   garnishment from bank accounts and other sources;

(c)   deductions from social security payments;

(d)   lien on or forced sale of property;

(e)   tax refund withholding;

(f)   withholding or attachment of pension benefits;

(g)   credit bureau reporting;

(h)   denial, suspension or revocation of various licences (for example, driving licences);

(i)   the use of mediation, conciliation or similar processes to bring about voluntary compliance.

*Article 35*

**Transfer of funds**

(1) Contracting States are encouraged to promote, including by means of international agreements, the use of the most cost-effective and efficient methods available to transfer funds payable as maintenance.

(2) A Contracting State, under whose law the transfer of funds is restricted, shall accord the highest priority to the transfer of funds payable under this Convention.

# CHAPTER VII

## PUBLIC BODIES

*Article 36*

### Public bodies as applicants

(1) For the purposes of applications for recognition and enforcement under Article 10(1)(a) and (b) and cases covered by Article 20(4), 'creditor' includes a public body acting in place of an individual to whom maintenance is owed or one to which reimbursement is owed for benefits provided in place of maintenance.

(2) The right of a public body to act in place of an individual to whom maintenance is owed or to seek reimbursement of benefits provided to the creditor in place of maintenance shall be governed by the law to which the body is subject.

(3) A public body may seek recognition or claim enforcement of:

(a) a decision rendered against a debtor on the application of a public body which claims payment of benefits provided in place of maintenance;

(b) a decision rendered between a creditor and debtor to the extent of the benefits provided to the creditor in place of maintenance.

(4) The public body seeking recognition or claiming enforcement of a decision shall upon request furnish any document necessary to establish its right under paragraph 2 and that benefits have been provided to the creditor.

# CHAPTER VIII

## GENERAL PROVISIONS

*Article 37*

### Direct requests to competent authorities

(1) The Convention shall not exclude the possibility of recourse to such procedures as may be available under the internal law of a Contracting State allowing a person (an applicant) to seise directly a competent authority of that State in a matter governed by the Convention including, subject to Article 18, for the purpose of having a maintenance decision established or modified.

(2) Articles 14(5) and 17(b) and the provisions of Chapters V, VI, VII and this Chapter, with the exception of Articles 40(2), 42, 43(3), 44(3), 45 and 55, shall apply in relation to a request for recognition and enforcement made directly to a competent authority in a Contracting State.

(3) For the purpose of paragraph 2, Article 2(1)(a) shall apply to a decision granting maintenance to a vulnerable person over the age specified in that subparagraph where such decision was rendered before the person reached that age and provided for maintenance beyond that age by reason of the impairment.

*Article 38*

### Protection of personal data

Personal data gathered or transmitted under the Convention shall be used only for the purposes for which they were gathered or transmitted.

*Article 39*

### Confidentiality

Any authority processing information shall ensure its confidentiality in accordance with the law of its State.

*Article 40*

Non-disclosure of information

(1) An authority shall not disclose or confirm information gathered or transmitted in application of this Convention if it determines that to do so could jeopardise the health, safety or liberty of a person.

(2) A determination to this effect made by one Central Authority shall be taken into account by another Central Authority, in particular in cases of family violence.

(3) Nothing in this Article shall impede the gathering and transmitting of information by and between authorities in so far as necessary to carry out the obligations under the Convention.

*Article 41*

No legalisation

No legalisation or similar formality may be required in the context of this Convention.

*Article 42*

Power of attorney

The Central Authority of the requested State may require a power of attorney from the applicant only if it acts on his or her behalf in judicial proceedings or before other authorities, or in order to designate a representative so to act.

*Article 43*

Recovery of costs

(1) Recovery of any costs incurred in the application of this Convention shall not take precedence over the recovery of maintenance.

(2) A State may recover costs from an unsuccessful party.

(3) For the purposes of an application under Article 10(1)(b) to recover costs from an unsuccessful party in accordance with paragraph 2, the term 'creditor' in Article 10(1) shall include a State.

(4) This Article shall be without prejudice to Article 8.

*Article 44*

Language requirements

(1) Any application and related documents shall be in the original language, and shall be accompanied by a translation into an official language of the requested State or another language which the requested State has indicated, by way of declaration in accordance with Article 63, it will accept, unless the competent authority of that State dispenses with translation.

(2) A Contracting State which has more than one official language and cannot, for reasons of internal law, accept for the whole of its territory documents in one of those languages shall, by declaration in accordance with Article 63, specify the language in which such documents or translations thereof shall be drawn up for submission in the specified parts of its territory.

(3) Unless otherwise agreed by the Central Authorities, any other communications between such Authorities shall be in an official language of the requested State or in either English or French. However, a Contracting State may, by making a reservation in accordance with Article 62, object to the use of either English or French.

*Article 45*

Means and costs of translation

(1) In the case of applications under Chapter III, the Central Authorities may agree in an individual case or generally that the translation into an official language of the requested State may be made in the requested State from the original language or from any other agreed language. If there is no agreement and it is not possible for the requesting Central Authority to comply with the requirements of Article

44(1) and (2), then the application and related documents may be transmitted with translation into English or French for further translation into an official language of the requested State.

(2) The cost of translation arising from the application of paragraph 1 shall be borne by the requesting State unless otherwise agreed by Central Authorities of the States concerned.

(3) Notwithstanding Article 8, the requesting Central Authority may charge an applicant for the costs of translation of an application and related documents, except in so far as those costs may be covered by its system of legal assistance.

*Article 46*

**Non-unified legal systems — interpretation**

(1) In relation to a State in which two or more systems of law or sets of rules of law with regard to any matter dealt with in this Convention apply in different territorial units:

(a) any reference to the law or procedure of a State shall be construed as referring, where appropriate, to the law or procedure in force in the relevant territorial unit;

(b) any reference to a decision established, recognised, recognised and enforced, enforced or modified in that State shall be construed as referring, where appropriate, to a decision established, recognised, recognised and enforced, enforced or modified in the relevant territorial unit;

(c) any reference to a judicial or administrative authority in that State shall be construed as referring, where appropriate, to a judicial or administrative authority in the relevant territorial unit;

(d) any reference to competent authorities, public bodies, and other bodies of that State, other than Central Authorities, shall be construed as referring, where appropriate, to those authorised to act in the relevant territorial unit;

(e) any reference to residence or habitual residence in that State shall be construed as referring, where appropriate, to residence or habitual residence in the relevant territorial unit;

(f) any reference to location of assets in that State shall be construed as referring, where appropriate, to the location of assets in the relevant territorial unit;

(g) any reference to a reciprocity arrangement in force in a State shall be construed as referring, where appropriate, to a reciprocity arrangement in force in the relevant territorial unit;

(h) any reference to free legal assistance in that State shall be construed as referring, where appropriate, to free legal assistance in the relevant territorial unit;

(i) any reference to a maintenance arrangement made in a State shall be construed as referring, where appropriate, to a maintenance arrangement made in the relevant territorial unit;

(j) any reference to recovery of costs by a State shall be construed as referring, where appropriate, to the recovery of costs by the relevant territorial unit.

(2) This Article shall not apply to a Regional Economic Integration Organisation.

*Article 47*

**Non-unified legal systems — substantive rules**

(1) A Contracting State with two or more territorial units in which different systems of law apply shall not be bound to apply this Convention to situations which involve solely such different territorial units.

(2) A competent authority in a territorial unit of a Contracting State with two or more territorial units in which different systems of law apply shall not be bound to recognise or enforce a decision from another Contracting State solely because the decision has been recognised or enforced in another territorial unit of the same Contracting State under this Convention.

(3) This Article shall not apply to a Regional Economic Integration Organisation.

*Article 48*

**Coordination with prior Hague Maintenance Conventions**

In relations between the Contracting States, this Convention replaces, subject to Article 56(2), the Hague Convention of 2 October 1973 on the Recognition and Enforcement of Decisions Relating to Maintenance Obligations and the Hague Convention of 15 April 1958 concerning the recognition and enforcement of decisions relating to maintenance obligations towards children in so far as their scope of application as between such States coincides with the scope of application of this Convention.

*Article 49*

**Coordination with the 1956 New York Convention**

In relations between the Contracting States, this Convention replaces the United Nations Convention on the Recovery Abroad of Maintenance of 20 June 1956, in so far as its scope of application as between such States coincides with the scope of application of this Convention.

*Article 50*

**Relationship with prior Hague Conventions on service of documents and taking of evidence**

This Convention does not affect the Hague Convention of 1 March 1954 on civil procedure, the Hague Convention of 15 November 1965 on the Service Abroad of Judicial and Extrajudicial Documents in Civil or Commercial Matters and the Hague Convention of 18 March 1970 on the Taking of Evidence Abroad in Civil or Commercial Matters.

*Article 51*

**Coordination of instruments and supplementary agreements**

(1) This Convention does not affect any international instrument concluded before this Convention to which Contracting States are Parties and which contains provisions on matters governed by this Convention.

(2) Any Contracting State may conclude with one or more Contracting States agreements, which contain provisions on matters governed by the Convention, with a view to improving the application of the Convention between or among themselves, provided that such agreements are consistent with the objects and purpose of the Convention and do not affect, in the relationship of such States with other Contracting States, the application of the provisions of the Convention. The States which have concluded such an agreement shall transmit a copy to the depositary of the Convention.

(3) Paragraphs 1 and 2 shall also apply to reciprocity arrangements and to uniform laws based on special ties between the States concerned.

(4) This Convention shall not affect the application of instruments of a Regional Economic Integration Organisation that is a Party to this Convention, adopted after the conclusion of the Convention, on matters governed by the Convention provided that such instruments do not affect, in the relationship of Member States of the Regional Economic Integration Organisation with other Contracting States, the application of the provisions of the Convention. As concerns the recognition or enforcement of decisions as between Member States of the Regional Economic Integration Organisation, the Convention shall not affect the rules of the Regional Economic Integration Organisation, whether adopted before or after the conclusion of the Convention.

*Article 52*

**Most effective rule**

(1) This Convention shall not prevent the application of an agreement, arrangement or international instrument in force between the requesting State and the requested State, or a reciprocity arrangement in force in the requested State that provides for:

(a)  broader bases for recognition of maintenance decisions, without prejudice to Article 22(f) of the Convention;

(b) simplified, more expeditious procedures on an application for recognition or recognition and enforcement of maintenance decisions;

(c) more beneficial legal assistance than that provided for under Articles 14 to 17; or

(d) procedures permitting an applicant from a requesting State to make a request directly to the Central Authority of the requested State.

(2) This Convention shall not prevent the application of a law in force in the requested State that provides for more effective rules as referred to in paragraph 1(a) to (c). However, as regards simplified, more expeditious procedures referred to in paragraph 1(b), they must be compatible with the protection offered to the parties under Articles 23 and 24, in particular as regards the rights of the parties to be duly notified of the proceedings and be given adequate opportunity to be heard and as regards the effects of any challenge or appeal.

## Article 53

### Uniform interpretation

In the interpretation of this Convention, regard shall be had to its international character and to the need to promote uniformity in its application.

## Article 54

### Review of practical operation of the Convention

(1) The Secretary General of the Hague Conference on Private International Law shall at regular intervals convene a Special Commission in order to review the practical operation of the Convention and to encourage the development of good practices under the Convention.

(2) For the purpose of such review, Contracting States shall cooperate with the Permanent Bureau of the Hague Conference on Private International Law in the gathering of information, including statistics and case law, concerning the practical operation of the Convention.

## Article 55

### Amendment of forms

(1) The forms annexed to this Convention may be amended by a decision of a Special Commission convened by the Secretary General of the Hague Conference on Private International Law to which all Contracting States and all Members shall be invited. Notice of the proposal to amend the forms shall be included in the agenda for the meeting.

(2) Amendments adopted by the Contracting States present at the Special Commission shall come into force for all Contracting States on the first day of the seventh calendar month after the date of their communication by the depositary to all Contracting States.

(3) During the period provided for in paragraph 2 any Contracting State may by notification in writing to the depositary make a reservation, in accordance with Article 62, with respect to the amendment. The State making such reservation shall, until the reservation is withdrawn, be treated as a State not Party to the present Convention with respect to that amendment.

## Article 56

### Transitional provisions

(1) The Convention shall apply in every case where:

(a) a request pursuant to Article 7 or an application pursuant to Chapter III has been received by the Central Authority of the requested State after the Convention has entered into force between the requesting State and the requested State;

(b) a direct request for recognition and enforcement has been received by the competent authority of the State addressed after the Convention has entered into force between the State of origin and the State addressed.

(2) With regard to the recognition and enforcement of decisions between Contracting States to this Convention that are also Parties to either of the Hague Maintenance Conventions mentioned in Article 48, if the conditions for the recognition and enforcement under this Convention prevent the recognition and enforcement of a decision given in the State of origin before the entry into force of this Convention for that State, that would otherwise have been recognised and enforced under the terms of the Convention that was in effect at the time the decision was rendered, the conditions of that Convention shall apply.

(3) The State addressed shall not be bound under this Convention to enforce a decision or a maintenance arrangement, in respect of payments falling due prior to the entry into force of the Convention between the State of origin and the State addressed, except for maintenance obligations arising from a parent-child relationship towards a person under the age of 21 years.

*Article 57*

**Provision of information concerning laws, procedures and services**

(1) A Contracting State, by the time its instrument of ratification or accession is deposited or a declaration is submitted in accordance with Article 61 of the Convention, shall provide the Permanent Bureau of the Hague Conference on Private International Law with:

(a) a description of its laws and procedures concerning maintenance obligations;

(b) a description of the measures it will take to meet the obligations under Article 6;

(c) a description of how it will provide applicants with effective access to procedures, as required under Article 14;

(d) a description of its enforcement rules and procedures, including any limitations on enforcement, in particular debtor protection rules and limitation periods;

(e) any specification referred to in Article 25(1)(b) and (3).

(2) Contracting States may, in fulfilling their obligations under paragraph 1, utilise a country profile form recommended and published by the Hague Conference on Private International Law.

(3) Information shall be kept up to date by the Contracting States.

## CHAPTER IX

## FINAL PROVISIONS

*Article 58*

**Signature, ratification and accession**

(1) The Convention shall be open for signature by the States which were Members of the Hague Conference on Private International Law at the time of its Twenty-First Session and by the other States which participated in that Session.

(2) It shall be ratified, accepted or approved and the instruments of ratification, acceptance or approval shall be deposited with the Ministry of Foreign Affairs of the Kingdom of the Netherlands, depositary of the Convention.

(3) Any other State or Regional Economic Integration Organisation may accede to the Convention after it has entered into force in accordance with Article 60(1).

(4) The instrument of accession shall be deposited with the depositary.

(5) Such accession shall have effect only as regards the relations between the acceding State and those Contracting States which have not raised an objection to its accession in the 12 months after the date of the notification referred to in Article 65. Such an objection may also be raised by States at the time when they ratify, accept or approve the Convention after an accession. Any such objection shall be notified to the depositary.

*Article 59*

**Regional Economic Integration Organisations**

(1) A Regional Economic Integration Organisation which is constituted solely by sovereign States and has competence over some or all of the matters governed by this Convention may similarly sign, accept, approve or accede to this Convention. The Regional Economic Integration Organisation shall in that case have the rights and obligations of a Contracting State, to the extent that the Organisation has competence over matters governed by the Convention.

(2) The Regional Economic Integration Organisation shall, at the time of signature, acceptance, approval or accession, notify the depositary in writing of the matters governed by this Convention in respect of which competence has been transferred to that Organisation by its Member States. The Organisation shall promptly notify the depositary in writing of any changes to its competence as specified in the most recent notice given under this paragraph.

(3) At the time of signature, acceptance, approval or accession, a Regional Economic Integration Organisation may declare in accordance with Article 63 that it exercises competence over all the matters governed by this Convention and that the Member States which have transferred competence to the Regional Economic Integration Organisation in respect of the matter in question shall be bound by this Convention by virtue of the signature, acceptance, approval or accession of the Organisation.

(4) For the purposes of the entry into force of this Convention, any instrument deposited by a Regional Economic Integration Organisation shall not be counted unless the Regional Economic Integration Organisation makes a declaration in accordance with paragraph 3.

(5) Any reference to a 'Contracting State' or 'State' in this Convention shall apply equally to a Regional Economic Integration Organisation that is a Party to it, where appropriate. In the event that a declaration is made by a Regional Economic Integration Organisation in accordance with paragraph 3, any reference to a 'Contracting State' or 'State' in this Convention shall apply equally to the relevant Member States of the Organisation, where appropriate.

*Article 60*

**Entry into force**

(1) The Convention shall enter into force on the first day of the month following the expiration of 3 months after the deposit of the second instrument of ratification, acceptance or approval referred to in Article 58.

(2) Thereafter the Convention shall enter into force:

(a) for each State or Regional Economic Integration Organisation referred to in Article 59(1) subsequently ratifying, accepting or approving it, on the first day of the month following the expiration of 3 months after the deposit of its instrument of ratification, acceptance or approval;

(b) for each State or Regional Economic Integration Organisation referred to in Article 58(3) on the day after the end of the period during which objections may be raised in accordance with Article 58(5);

(c) for a territorial unit to which the Convention has been extended in accordance with Article 61, on the first day of the month following the expiration of 3 months after the notification referred to in that Article.

*Article 61*

**Declarations with respect to non-unified legal systems**

(1) If a State has two or more territorial units in which different systems of law are applicable in relation to matters dealt with in the Convention, it may at the time of signature, ratification, acceptance, approval or accession declare in accordance with Article 63 that this Convention shall extend to all its territorial units or only to one or more of them and may modify this declaration by submitting another declaration at any time.

(2) Any such declaration shall be notified to the depositary and shall state expressly the territorial units to which the Convention applies.

(3) If a State makes no declaration under this Article, the Convention shall extend to all territorial units of that State.

(4) This Article shall not apply to a Regional Economic Integration Organisation.

## Article 62

**Reservations**

(1) Any Contracting State may, not later than the time of ratification, acceptance, approval or accession, or at the time of making a declaration in terms of Article 61, make one or more of the reservations provided for in Articles 2(2), 20(2), 30(8), 44(3) and 55(3). No other reservation shall be permitted.

(2) Any State may at any time withdraw a reservation it has made. The withdrawal shall be notified to the depositary.

(3) The reservation shall cease to have effect on the first day of the third calendar month after the notification referred to in paragraph 2.

(4) Reservations under this Article shall have no reciprocal effect with the exception of the reservation provided for in Article 2(2).

## Article 63

**Declarations**

(1) Declarations referred to in Articles 2(3), 11(1)(g), 16(1), 24(1), 30(7), 44(1) and (2), 59(3) and 61(1), may be made upon signature, ratification, acceptance, approval or accession or at any time thereafter, and may be modified or withdrawn at any time.

(2) Declarations, modifications and withdrawals shall be notified to the depositary.

(3) A declaration made at the time of signature, ratification, acceptance, approval or accession shall take effect simultaneously with the entry into force of this Convention for the State concerned.

(4) A declaration made at a subsequent time, and any modification or withdrawal of a declaration, shall take effect on the first day of the month following the expiration of 3 months after the date on which the notification is received by the depositary.

## Article 64

**Denunciation**

(1) A Contracting State to the Convention may denounce it by a notification in writing addressed to the depositary. The denunciation may be limited to certain territorial units of a multi-unit State to which the Convention applies.

(2) The denunciation shall take effect on the first day of the month following the expiration of 12 months after the date on which the notification is received by the depositary. Where a longer period for the denunciation to take effect is specified in the notification, the denunciation shall take effect upon the expiration of such longer period after the date on which the notification is received by the depositary.

## Article 65

**Notification**

The depositary shall notify the Members of the Hague Conference on Private International Law, and other States and Regional Economic Integration Organisations which have signed, ratified, accepted, approved or acceded in accordance with Articles 58 and 59 of the following:

(a) the signatures, ratifications, acceptances and approvals referred to in Articles 58 and 59;

(b) the accessions and objections raised to accessions referred to in Articles 58(3) and (5) and 59;

(c) the date on which the Convention enters into force in accordance with Article 60;

(d) the declarations referred to in Articles 2(3), 11(1) g), 16(1), 24(1), 30(7), 44(1) and (2), 59(3) and 61(1);

(e) the agreements referred to in Article 51(2);

(f)   the reservations referred to in Articles 2(2), 20(2), 30(8), 44(3) and 55(3), and the withdrawals referred to in Article 62(2);

(g)   the denunciations referred to in Article 64.

In witness whereof the undersigned, being duly authorised thereto, have signed this Convention.

Done at The Hague, on the twenty-third day of November in the year two thousand and seven, in the English and French languages, both texts being equally authentic, in a single copy which shall be deposited in the archives of the Government of the Kingdom of the Netherlands, and of which a certified copy shall be sent, through diplomatic channels, to each of the Members of the Hague Conference on Private International Law at the date of its Twenty-First Session and to each of the other States which have participated in that Session.

*[Annexes I–II omitted]*

# Colonial Probates Act
# 1892 ch 6

### 1  Application of Act by Order in Council

Her Majesty the Queen may, on being satisfied that the legislature of any British possession has made adequate provision for the recognition in that possession of probates and letters of administration granted by the courts of the United Kingdom, direct by Order in Council that this Act shall, subject to any exceptions and modifications specified in the Order, apply to that possession, and thereupon, while the Order is in force, this Act shall apply accordingly.

[1A

This Act shall apply in relation to the Hong Kong Special Administrative Region of the People's Republic of China as it applied, immediately before 1st July 1997, to Hong Kong; and the Colonial Probates Act Application Order 1965 shall, in relation to that Region, continue in force accordingly.]

### 2  Sealing in United Kingdom of colonial probates and letters of administration

(1)  Where a court of probate in a British possession to which this Act applies has granted probate or letters of administration in respect of the estate of a deceased person [then (subject to section [109 of the Senior Courts Act 1981], section 42 of the Probate and Legacy Duties Act 1808 and section 99A of the Probates and Letters of Administration Act (Ireland) 1857)], the probate or letters so granted may, on being produced to, and a copy thereof deposited with, a court of probate in the United Kingdom, be sealed with the seal of that court, and, thereupon, shall be of the like force and effect, and have the same operation in the United Kingdom, as if granted by that court.

(2)  Provided that the court shall, before sealing a probate or letters of administration under this section, be satisfied—

(a)  [. . .]

(b)  in the case of letters of administration, that security has been given in a sum sufficient in amount to cover the property (if any) in the United Kingdom to which letters of administration relate;

and may require such evidence, if any, as it thinks fit as to the domicile of the deceased person.

(3)  The court may also, if it thinks fit, on the application of any creditor, require, before sealing, that adequate security be given for the payment of debts due from the estate to creditors residing in the United Kingdom.

(4)  For the purposes of this section, a duplicate of any probate or letters of administration sealed with the seal of the court granting the same, or a copy thereof certified as correct by or under the authority of the court granting the same, shall have the same effect as the original.

(5)  Rules of court may be made for regulating the procedure and practice, including fees and costs, in courts of the United Kingdom, on and incidental to an application for sealing a probate or letters of administration granted in a British possession to which this Act applies. [. . .]

### 3  Application of Act to British courts in foreign countries

This Act shall extend to authorise the sealing in the United Kingdom of any probate or letters of administration granted by a British court in a foreign country, in like manner as it authorises the sealing of a probate or letters of administration granted in a British possession to which this Act applies, and the provisions of this Act shall apply accordingly with the necessary modifications.

### 4  Orders in Council

(1)  Every Order in Council made under this Act shall be laid before both Houses of Parliament [. . .]

(2)  Her Majesty the Queen in Council may revoke or alter any Order in Council previously made under this Act.

(3) Where it appears to Her Majesty in Council that the legislature of part of a British possession has power to make the provision requisite for bringing this Act into operation in that part, it shall be lawful for Her Majesty to direct by Order in Council that this Act shall apply to that part as if it were a separate British possession, and thereupon, while the Order is in force, this Act shall apply accordingly.

### 5  Application of Acts to probates, etc already granted

This Act when applied by an Order in Council to a British possession shall, subject to the provisions of the Order, apply to probates and letters of administration granted in that possession either before or after the passing of this Act.

### 6  Definitions

In this Act—

The expression "court of probate" means any court or authority, by whatever name designated, having jurisdiction in matters of probate, and in Scotland means the sheriff court of the county of Edinburgh:

The expression "probate" and "letters of administration" include confirmation in Scotland, and any instrument having in a British possession the same effect which under English law is given to probate and letters of administration respectively:

[. . .]

The expression "British court in a foreign country" means any British court having jurisdiction out of the Queen's dominions in pursuance of an Order in Council, whether made under any Act or otherwise.

. . .

# Administration of Justice Act
# 1920 ch 81

PART II

**9 Enforcement in the United Kingdom of judgments obtained in superior courts in other British dominions**

(1) Where a judgment has been obtained in a superior court in any part of His Majesty's dominions outside the United Kingdom to which this Part of this Act extends, the judgment creditor may apply to the High Court in England or [Northern Ireland] or to the Court of Session in Scotland, at any time within twelve months after the date of the judgment, or such longer period as may be allowed by the court, to have the judgment registered in the court, and on any such application the court may, if in all the circumstances of the case they think it just and convenient that the judgment should be enforced in the United Kingdom, and subject to the provisions of this section, order the judgment to be registered accordingly.

(2) No judgment shall be ordered to be registered under this section if—

(a)   the original court acted without jurisdiction; or

(b)   the judgment debtor, being a person who was neither carrying on business nor ordinarily resident within the jurisdiction of the original court, did not voluntarily appear or otherwise submit or agree to submit to the jurisdiction of that court; or

(c)   the judgment debtor, being the defendant in the proceedings, was not duly served with the process of the original court and did not appear, notwithstanding that he was ordinarily resident or was carrying on business within the jurisdiction of that court or agreed to submit to the jurisdiction of that court; or

(d)   the judgment was obtained by fraud; or

(e)   the judgment debtor satisfies the registering court either that an appeal is pending, or that he is entitled and intends to appeal, against the judgment; or

(f)   the judgment was in respect of a cause of action which for reasons of public policy or for some other similar reason could not have been entertained by the registering court.

(3) Where a judgment is registered under this section—

(a)   the judgment shall, as from the date of registration, be of the same force and effect, and proceedings may be taken thereon, as if it had been a judgment originally obtained or entered up on the date of registration in the registering court;

(b)   the registering court shall have the same control and jurisdiction over the judgment as it has over similar judgments given by itself, but in so far only as relates to execution under this section;

(c)   the reasonable costs of and incidental to the registration of the judgment (including the costs of obtaining a certified copy thereof from the original court and of the application for registration) shall be recoverable in like manner as if they were sums payable under the judgment.

(4) Rules of court shall provide—

(a)   for service on the judgment debtor of notice of the registration of a judgment under this section; and

(b)   for enabling the registering court on an application by the judgment debtor to set aside the registration of a judgment under this section on such terms as the court thinks fit; and

(c)   for suspending the execution of a judgment registered under this section until the expiration of the period during which the judgment debtor may apply to have the registration set aside.

(5) In any action brought in any court in the United Kingdom on any judgment which might be ordered to be registered under this section, the plaintiff shall not be entitled to recover any costs of the action unless an application to register the judgment under this section has previously been refused or unless the court otherwise orders.

[10 **Issue of certificates of judgments obtained in the United Kingdom**

(1) Where—

(a) a judgment has been obtained in the High Court in England or Northern Ireland, or in the Court of Session in Scotland, against any person; and

(b) the judgment creditor wishes to secure the enforcement of the judgment in a part of Her Majesty's dominions outside the United Kingdom to which this Part of this Act extends,

the court shall, on an application made by the judgment creditor, issue to him a certified copy of the judgment.

(2) The reference in the preceding subsection to Her Majesty's dominions shall be construed as if that subsection had come into force in its present form at the commencement of this Act.]

11 **Power to make rules**

Provision may be made by rules of court for regulating the practice and procedure (including scales of fees and evidence), in respect of proceedings of any kind under this Part of this Act.

12 **Interpretation**

(1) In this Part of this Act, unless the context otherwise requires—

The expression "judgment" means any judgment or order given or made by a court in any civil proceedings, whether before or after the passing of this Act, whereby any sum of money is made payable, and includes an award in proceedings on an arbitration if the award has, in pursuance of the law in force in the place where it was made, become enforceable in the same manner as a judgment given by a court in that place:

The expression "original court" in relation to any judgment means the court by which the judgment was given:

The expression "registering court" in relation to any judgment means the court by which the judgment was registered:

The expression "judgment creditor" means the person by whom the judgment was obtained, and includes the successors and assigns of that person:

The expression "judgment debtor" means the person against whom the judgment was given, and includes any person against whom the judgment is enforceable in the place where it was given.

(2) Subject to rules of court, any of the powers conferred by this Part of this Act on any court may be exercised by a judge of the court.

13 **Power to apply Part II of Act to territories under His Majesty's protection**

His Majesty may by Order in Council declare that this Part of this Act shall apply to any territory which is under His Majesty's protection, or in respect of which a mandate is being exercised by the Government of any part of His Majesty's dominions, as if that territory were part of His Majesty's dominions, and on the making of any such Order this Part of this Act shall, subject to the provisions of the Order, have effect accordingly.

14 **Extent of Part II of Act**

(1) Where His Majesty is satisfied that reciprocal provisions have been made by the legislature of any part of His Majesty's dominions outside the United Kingdom for the enforcement within that part of His dominions of judgments obtained in the High Court in England, the Court of Session in Scotland, and the [High Court in Northern Ireland], His Majesty may by Order in Council declare that this Part

of this Act shall extend to that part of His dominions, and on any such Order being made this Part of this Act shall extend accordingly.

(2)  An Order in Council under this section may be varied or revoked by a subsequent Order.

[(3)  Her Majesty may by Order in Council under this section consolidate any Orders in Council under this section which are in force when the consolidating Order is made.]

# Maintenance Orders (Facilities for Enforcement) Act 1920 ch 33

UK Statutes

**1 Enforcement in England and Ireland of maintenance orders made in His Majesty's dominions outside the United Kingdom**

(1) Where a maintenance order has, whether before or after the passing of this Act, been made against any person by any court in any part of His Majesty's dominions outside the United Kingdom to which this Act extends, and a certified copy of the order has been transmitted by the governor of that part of His Majesty's dominions to the [Lord Chancellor], the [Lord Chancellor] shall send a copy of the order to the prescribed officer of a court in England or Ireland for registration; and on receipt thereof the order shall be registered in the prescribed manner, and shall, from the date of such registration, be of the same force and effect, and, subject to the provisions of this Act, all proceedings may be taken on such order as if it had been an order originally obtained in the court in which it is so registered, and that court shall have power to enforce the order accordingly.

(2) The Court in which an order is to be so registered as aforesaid shall, if the court by which the order was made was a court of superior jurisdiction, be the [Family Division] of the High Court, or in Ireland the King's Bench Division (Matrimonial) of the High Court of Justice in Ireland, and, if the court was not a court of superior jurisdiction, be [the family court or, in Northern Ireland,] a court of summary jurisdiction.

**2 Transmission of maintenance orders made in England or Ireland**

Where a court in England or Ireland has, whether before or after the commencement of this Act, made a maintenance order against any person, and it is proved to that court that the person against whom the order was made is resident in some part of His Majesty's dominions outside the United Kingdom to which this Act extends, the court shall send to the [Lord Chancellor] for transmission to the governor of that part of His Majesty's dominions a certified copy of the order.

**3 Power to make provisional orders of maintenance against persons resident in His Majesty's dominions outside the United Kingdom**

(1) Where an application is made to [the family court, or in Northern Ireland to a court of summary jurisdiction,] for a maintenance order against any person, and it is proved that that person is resident in a part of His Majesty's dominions outside the United Kingdom to which this Act extends, the court may, in the absence of that person, if after hearing the evidence it is satisfied of the justice of the application, make any such order as it might have made if [that person had been [habitually] resident in England and Wales, has received reasonable notice of the date of the hearing of the application and] had failed to appear at the hearing, but in such case the order shall be provisional only, and shall have no effect unless and until confirmed by a competent court in such part of His Majesty's dominions as aforesaid.

(2) The evidence of any witness who is examined on any such application shall be put into writing, and such deposition shall be read over to and signed by him.

(3) Where such an order is made, the court shall send to the [Lord Chancellor] for transmission to the governor of the part of His Majesty's dominions in which the person against whom the order is made is alleged to reside the depositions so taken and a certified copy of the order, together with a statement of the grounds on which the making of the order might have been opposed if the person against whom the order is made had been [habitually] [resident in England and Wales, had received reasonable notice of the date of the hearing] and had appeared at the hearing, and such information as the court possesses for facilitating the identification of that person, and ascertaining his whereabouts.

(4) Where any such provisional order has come before a court in a part of His Majesty's dominions outside the United Kingdom to which this Act extends for confirmation, and the order has by that court been remitted to the court [. . .] which made the order for the purpose of taking further evidence, that court or[, in Northern Ireland,] any other court of summary jurisdiction [. . .] shall, after giving

the prescribed notice, proceed to take the evidence in like manner and subject to the like conditions as the evidence in support of the original application.

If upon the hearing of such evidence it appears to the court that the order ought not to have been made, the court may [revoke] the order, but in any other case the depositions shall be sent to the [Lord Chancellor] and dealt with in like manner as the original depositions.

(5) The confirmation of an order made under this section shall not affect any power of [the family court, or] a court of summary jurisdiction [in Northern Ireland,] to vary or [revoke] that order:

Provided that on the making of a varying or [revoking] order the court shall send a certified copy thereof to the [Lord Chancellor] for transmission to the governor of the part of His Majesty's dominions in which the original order was confirmed, and that in the case of an order varying the original order the order shall not have any effect unless and until confirmed in like manner as the original order.

(6) The applicant shall have the same right of appeal, if any, against a refusal to make a provisional order as he would have had against a refusal to make the order had [the person against whom the order is sought to be made been [habitually] resident in England and Wales and received reasonable notice of the date of the hearing of the application].

[(7) [. . .]

(8) In this section "revoke" includes discharge.]

#### 4 Power of court of summary jurisdiction to confirm maintenance order made out of the United Kingdom

(1) Where a maintenance order has been made by a court in a part of His Majesty's dominions outside the United Kingdom to which this Act extends, and the order is provisional only and has no effect unless and until confirmed by [the family court or by] a court of summary jurisdiction in [. . .] Ireland, and a certified copy of the order, together with the depositions of witnesses and a statement of the grounds on which the order might have been opposed has been transmitted to the [Lord Chancellor], and it appears to the [Lord Chancellor] that the person against whom the order was made is resident in England or Ireland, the [Lord Chancellor] may send the said documents [to the family court if it appears to the Lord Chancellor that the person is resident in England and Wales or] to the prescribed officer of a court of summary jurisdiction [in Northern Ireland if it appears to the Lord Chancellor that the person is resident in Northern Ireland], with a requisition that a [notice be served on the person informing him that he may attend a hearing at the time and place specified in the notice] to show cause why that order should not be confirmed, and upon receipt of such documents and requisition the court shall [cause such a notice] to be served upon such person.

[(2) A notice required to be served under this section may be served by post.]

(3) At the hearing it shall be open to the person on whom the [notice] was served to [oppose the confirmation of the order on any grounds on which he might have opposed the making of the order in the original proceedings had he been a party to them, but on no other grounds], and the certificate from the court which made the provisional order stating the grounds on which the making of the order might have been opposed if the person against whom the order was made had been a party to the proceedings shall be conclusive evidence that those grounds are grounds on which objection may be taken.

(4) If at the hearing the person served with the [notice] does not appear or, on appearing, fails to satisfy the court that the order ought not to be confirmed, the court may confirm the order either without modification or with such modifications as to the court after hearing the evidence may seem just.

(5) If the person [served with the notice] appears at the hearing and satisfies the court that for the purpose of [establishing any grounds on which he opposes the confirmation of the order] it is necessary to remit the case to the court which made the provisional order for the taking of any further evidence, the court may so remit the case and adjourn the proceedings for the purpose.

[(5A) Where [the family] court confirms a provisional order under this section, it [may] at the same time exercise one of its powers under subsection (5B).

(5B) The powers of the court are—

(a) the power to order that payments under the order be made directly to [the family court];

(b) the power to order that payments under the order be made to [the family court] by such method of payment falling within section [1(5) of the Maintenance Enforcement Act 1991] (standing order, etc) as may be specified;

(c) the power to make an attachment of earnings order under the Attachment of Earnings Act 1971 to secure payments under the order.

(5C) In deciding [whether to exercise any of its] powers under subsection (5B) [. . .] the court shall have regard to any representations made by the person liable to make payments under the order.

(5D) [Subsection (6) of section 1 of the Maintenance Enforcement Act 1991] (power of court to require debtor to open account) shall apply for the purposes of subsection (5B) as it applies for the purposes of that section but as if for paragraph (a) there were substituted—

"(a) the court proposes to exercise its power under paragraph (b) of section 4(5B) of the Maintenance Orders (Facilities for Enforcement) Act 1920, and".]

[(6) [. . .] Where a provisional order has been confirmed under this section, it may be varied or revoked in like manner as if it had originally been made by the confirming court.

(6A) [. . .]

(6B) Where on an application for variation or revocation the confirming court is satisfied that it is necessary to remit the case to the court which made the order for the purpose of taking any further evidence, the court may so remit the case and adjourn the proceedings for the purpose.]

(7) Where an order has been so confirmed, the person bound thereby shall have the same right of appeal, if any, against the confirmation of the order as he would have had against the making of the order had the order been an order made by the court confirming the order.

[**4A Variation and revocation of maintenance orders**]

[(1) This section applies to—

(a) any maintenance order made by virtue of section 3 of this Act which has been confirmed as mentioned in that section; and

(b) any maintenance order which has been confirmed under section 4 of this Act.

(2) Where the respondent to an application for the variation or revocation of a maintenance order to which this section applies is residing in a part of Her Majesty's dominions outside the United Kingdom to which this Act extends, [the family court] shall have jurisdiction to hear the application (where it would not have such jurisdiction apart from this subsection) if that court would have had jurisdiction to hear it had the respondent been [habitually resident] in England and Wales.

. . .

(4) Where—

(a) the respondent to an application for the variation or revocation of a maintenance order to which this section applies does not appear at the time and place appointed for the hearing of the application by [the family court], and

(b) the court is satisfied that the respondent is residing in a part of Her Majesty's dominions outside the United Kingdom to which this Act extends,

the court may proceed to hear and determine the application at the time and place appointed for the hearing or for any adjourned hearing in like manner as if the respondent had appeared at that time and place.

. . .

(6) In this section "revocation" includes discharge.]

**5 Power of [Lord Chancellor] to make regulations for facilitating communications between courts**

The [Lord Chancellor] may make regulations as to the manner in which a case can be remitted by a court authorised to confirm a provisional order to the court which made the provisional order, and generally for facilitating communications between such courts.

**6 Mode of enforcing orders**

(1) A court [. . .] in which an order has been registered under this Act or by which an order has been confirmed under this Act, and the officers of such court, shall take all such steps for enforcing the order as may be prescribed.

[(2) Every such order registered in or confirmed by the family court is enforceable as if it were an order made by the family court and as if that court had had jurisdiction to make it.]

(3) A warrant of distress [, control] or commitment issued by [the family court or] a court of summary jurisdiction for the purpose of enforcing any order so registered or confirmed may be executed in any part of the United Kingdom in the same manner as if the warrant had been originally issued or subsequently endorsed by a court of summary jurisdiction having jurisdiction in the place where the warrant is executed.

[(4) For the purposes of its execution under subsection (3) in England and Wales, a warrant of distress has effect as a warrant of control.

(5) For the purposes of its execution under subsection (3) elsewhere than in England and Wales, a warrant of control has effect as a warrant of distress.]

**7 Application of Summary Jurisdiction Acts**

[(1)] The Summary Jurisdiction Acts shall apply to proceedings before courts of summary jurisdiction under this Act in like manner as they apply to proceedings under those Acts [. . .].

[(2) Without prejudice to the generality of the power to make rules under section 144 of the Magistrates' Courts Act 1980 (magistrates' courts rules), for the purpose of giving effect to this Act such rules [For the purpose of giving effect to this Act rules of court] may make, in relation to any proceedings brought under or by virtue of this Act, any provision which—

(a)   falls within subsection (2) of section 93 of the Children Act 1989, and

(b)   may be made in relation to relevant proceedings under that section.]

**8 Proof of documents signed by officers of court**

Any document purporting to be signed by a judge or officer of a court outside the United Kingdom shall, until the contrary is proved, be deemed to have been so signed without proof of the signature or judicial or official character of the person appearing to have signed it, and the officer of a court by whom a document is signed shall, until the contrary is proved, be deemed to have been the proper officer of the court to sign the document.

**9 Depositions to be evidence**

Depositions taken in a court in a part of His Majesty's dominions outside the United Kingdom to which this Act extends for the purposes of this Act, may be received in evidence in proceedings before courts of summary jurisdiction[, or the family court,] under this Act.

**10 Interpretation**

For the purposes of this Act, the expression "maintenance order" means an order other than an order of affiliation for the periodical payment of sums of money towards the maintenance of the wife or other dependants of the person against whom the order is made, and the expression "dependants" means such persons as that person is, according to the law in force in the part of His Majesty's dominions in which the maintenance order was made, liable to maintain; the expression "certified copy" in relation to an order of a court means a copy of the order certified by the proper officer of the court to be a true copy, and the expression "prescribed" means prescribed by rules of court.

. . .

## 12  Extent of Act

(1)  Where His Majesty is satisfied that reciprocal provisions have been made by the legislature of any part of His Majesty's dominions outside the United Kingdom for the enforcement within that part of maintenance orders made by courts within England and Ireland, His Majesty may by Order in Council extend this Act to that part, and thereupon that part shall become a part of His Majesty's dominions to which this Act extends.

(2)  His Majesty may by Order in Council extend this Act to any British protectorate, and where so extended this Act shall apply as if any such protectorate was a part of His Majesty's dominions to which this Act extends.

# Foreign Judgments (Reciprocal Enforcement) Act 1933 ch 13

PART I

## Registration of Foreign Judgments

### 1 Power to extend Part I of Act to foreign countries giving reciprocal treatment

[(1) If, in the case of any foreign country, Her Majesty is satisfied that, in the event of the benefits conferred by this Part of this Act being extended to, or to any particular class of, judgments given in the courts of that country or in any particular class of those courts, substantial reciprocity of treatment will be assured as regards the enforcement in that country of similar judgments given in similar courts of the United Kingdom, She may by Order in Council direct—

(a)  that this Part of this Act shall extend to that country;

(b)  that such courts of that country as are specified in the Order shall be recognised courts of that country for the purposes of this Part of this Act; and

(c)  that judgments of any such recognised court, or such judgments of any class so specified, shall, if within subsection (2) of this section, be judgments to which this Part of this Act applies.

(2)  Subject to subsection (2A) of this section, a judgment of a recognised court is within this subsection if it satisfies the following conditions, namely—

(a)  it is either final and conclusive as between the judgment debtor and the judgment creditor or requires the former to make an interim payment to the latter; and

(b)  there is payable under it a sum of money, not being a sum payable in respect of taxes or other charges of a like nature or in respect of a fine or other penalty; and

(c)  it is given after the coming into force of the Order in Council which made that court a recognised court.

(2A)  The following judgments of a recognised court are not within subsection (2) of this section—

(a)  a judgment given by that court on appeal from a court which is not a recognised court;

(b)  a judgment or other instrument which is regarded for the purposes of its enforcement as a judgment of that court but which was given or made in another country;

(c)  a judgment given by that court in proceedings founded on a judgment of a court in another country and having as their object the enforcement of that judgment.]

(3)  For the purposes of this section, a judgment shall be deemed to be final and conclusive notwithstanding that an appeal may be pending against it, or that it may still be subject to appeal, in the courts of the country of the original court.

(4)  His Majesty may by a subsequent Order in Council vary or revoke any Order previously made under this section.

[(5)  Any Order in Council made under this section before its amendment by the Civil Jurisdiction and Judgments Act 1982 which deems any court of a foreign country to be a superior court of that country for the purposes of this Part of this Act shall (without prejudice to subsection (4) of this section) have effect from the time of that amendment as if it provided for that court to be a recognised court of that country for those purposes, and for any final and conclusive judgment of that court, if within subsection (2) of this section, to be a judgment to which this Part of this Act applies.]

### 2 Application for, and effect of, registration of foreign judgment

(1)  A person, being a judgment creditor under a judgment to which this Part of this Act applies, may apply to the High Court at any time within six years after the date of the judgment, or, where there

have been proceedings by way of appeal against the judgment, after the date of the last judgment given in those proceedings, to have the judgment registered in the High Court, and on any such application the court shall, subject to proof of the prescribed matters and to the other provisions of this Act, order the judgment to be registered:

Provided that a judgment shall not be registered if at the date of the application—

(a) it has been wholly satisfied; or

(b) it could not be enforced by execution in the country of the original court.

(2) Subject to the provisions of this Act with respect to the setting aside of registration—

(a) a registered judgment shall, for the purposes of execution, be of the same force and effect; and

(b) proceedings may be taken on a registered judgment; and

(c) the sum for which a judgment is registered shall carry interest; and

(d) the registering court shall have the same control over the execution of a registered judgment;

as if the judgment had been a judgment originally given in the registering court and entered on the date of registration:

Provided that execution shall not issue on the judgment so long as, under this Part of the Act and the Rules of Court made thereunder, it is competent for any party to make an application to have the registration of the judgment set aside, or, where such an application is made, until after the application has been finally determined.

(3) [. . .]

(4) If at the date of the application for registration the judgment of the original court has been partly satisfied, the judgment shall not be registered in respect of the whole sum payable under the judgment of the original court, but only in respect of the balance remaining payable at that date.

(5) If, on an application for the registration of a judgment, it appears to the registering court that the judgment is in respect of different matters and that some, but not all, of the provisions of the judgment are such that if those provisions had been contained in separate judgments those judgments could properly have been registered, the judgment may be registered in respect of the provisions aforesaid but not in respect of any other provisions contained therein.

(6) In addition to the sum of money payable under the judgment of the original court, including any interest which by the law of the country of the original court becomes due under the judgment up to the time of registration, the judgment shall be registered for the reasonable costs of and incidental to registration, including the costs of obtaining a certified copy of the judgment from the original court.

### 3 Rules of court

(1) The power to make [Civil Procedure Rules], shall, subject to the provisions of this section, include power to make rules for the following purposes—

(a) For making provision with respect to the giving of security for costs by persons applying for the registration of judgments;

(b) For prescribing the matters to be proved on an application for the registration of a judgment and for regulating the mode of proving those matters;

(c) For providing for the service on the judgment debtor of notice of the registration of a judgment;

(d) For making provision with respect to the fixing of the period within which an application may be made to have the registration of the judgment set aside and with respect to the extension of the period so fixed;

(e) For prescribing the method by which any question arising under this Act whether a foreign judgment can be enforced by execution in the country of the original court, or what interest is payable under a foreign judgment under the law of the original court, is to be determined;

(f) For prescribing any matter which under this Part of this Act is to be prescribed.

(2) Rules made for the purposes of this Part of this Act shall be expressed to have, and shall have, effect subject to any such provisions contained in Order in Council made under section one of this

Act as are declared by the said Orders to be necessary for giving effect to agreements made between His Majesty and foreign countries in relation to matters with respect to which there is power to make rules of court for the purposes of this Part of this Act.

## 4 Cases in which registered judgments must, or may, be set aside

(1) On an application in that behalf duly made by any party against whom a registered judgment may be enforced, the registration of the judgment—

(a) shall be set aside if the registering court is satisfied—

   (i) that the judgment is not a judgment to which this Part of this Act applies or was registered in contravention of the foregoing provisions of this Act; or

   (ii) that the courts of the country of the original court had no jurisdiction in the circumstances of the case; or

   (iii) that the judgment debtor, being the defendant in the proceedings in the original court, did not (notwithstanding that process may have been duly served on him in accordance with the law of the country of the original court) receive notice of those proceedings in sufficient time to enable him to defend the proceedings and did not appear; or

   (iv) that the judgment was obtained by fraud; or

   (v) that the enforcement of the judgment would be contrary to public policy in the country of the registering court; or

   (vi) that the rights under the judgment are not vested in the person by whom the application for registration was made;

(b) may be set aside if the registering court is satisfied that the matter in dispute in the proceedings in the original court had previously to the date of the judgment in the original court been the subject of a final and conclusive judgment by a court having jurisdiction in the matter.

(2) For the purposes of this section the courts of the country of the original court shall, subject to the provisions of subsection (3) of this section, be deemed to have had jurisdiction—

(a) in the case of a judgment given in an action in personam—

   (i) if the judgment debtor, being a defendant in the original court, submitted to the jurisdiction of that court by voluntarily appearing in the proceedings [. . .]); or

   (ii) if the judgment debtor was plaintiff in, or counter-claimed in, the proceedings in the original court; or

   (iii) if the judgment debtor, being a defendant in the original court, had before the commencement of the proceedings agreed, in respect of the subject matter of the proceedings, to submit to the jurisdiction of that court or of the courts of the country of that court; or

   (iv) if the judgment debtor, being a defendant in the original court, was at the time when the proceedings were instituted resident in, or being a body corporate had its principal place of business in, the country of that court; or

   (v) if the judgment debtor, being a defendant in the original court, had an office or place of business in the country of that court and the proceedings in that court were in respect of a transaction effected through or at that office or place;

(b) in the case of a judgment given in an action of which the subject matter was immovable property or in an action in rem of which the subject matter was movable property, if the property in question was at the time of the proceedings in the original court situate in the country of that court;

(c) in the case of a judgment given in an action other than any such action as is mentioned in paragraph (a) or paragraph (b) of this subsection, if the jurisdiction of the original court is recognised by the law of the registering court.

(3) Notwithstanding anything in subsection (2) of this section, the courts of the country of the original court shall not be deemed to have had jurisdiction—

(a)   if the subject matter of the proceedings was immovable property outside the country of the original court; or

(b)   [. . .]

(c)   if the judgment debtor, being a defendant in the original proceedings, was a person who under the rules of public international law was entitled to immunity from the jurisdiction of the courts of the country of the original court and did not submit to the jurisdiction of that court.

### 5   Powers of registering court on application to set aside registration

(1) If, on an application to set aside the registration of a judgment, the applicant satisfies the registering court either that an appeal is pending, or that he is entitled and intends to appeal, against the judgment, the court, if it thinks fit, may, on such terms as it may think just, either set aside the registration or adjourn the application to set aside the registration until after the expiration of such period as appears to the court to be reasonably sufficient to enable the applicant to take the necessary steps to have the appeal disposed of by the competent tribunal.

(2) Where the registration of a judgment is set aside under the last foregoing subsection, or solely for the reason that the judgment was not at the date of the application for registration enforceable by execution in the country of the original court, the setting aside of the registration shall not prejudice a further application to register the judgment when the appeal has been disposed of or if and when the judgment becomes enforceable by execution in that country, as the case may be.

(3) Where the registration of a judgment is set aside solely for the reason that the judgment, notwithstanding that it had at the date of the application for registration been partly satisfied, was registered for the whole sum payable thereunder, the registering court shall, on the application of the judgment creditor, order judgment to be registered for the balance remaining payable at that date.

### 6   Foreign judgments which can be registered not to be enforceable otherwise

No proceedings for the recovery of a sum payable under a foreign judgment, being a judgment to which this Part of this Act applies, other than proceedings by way of registration of the judgment, shall be entertained by any court in the United Kingdom.

### 7   Power to apply Part I of Act to British dominions, protectorates and mandated territories

(1) His Majesty may by Order in Council direct that this Part of this Act shall apply to His Majesty's dominions outside the United Kingdom and to judgments obtained in the courts of the said dominions as it applies to foreign countries and judgments obtained in the courts of foreign countries, and in the event of His Majesty so directing, this Act shall have effect accordingly and Part II of the Administration of Justice Act 1920, shall cease to have effect except in relation to those parts of the said dominions to which it extends at the date of the Order.

(2) If at any time after His Majesty has directed as aforesaid an Order in Council is made under section one of this Act extending Part I of this Act to any part of His Majesty's dominions to which the said Part II extends as aforesaid, the said Part II shall cease to have effect in relation to that part of His Majesty's dominions.

(3) References in this section to His Majesty's dominions outside the United Kingdom shall be construed as including references to any territories which are under His Majesty's protection and to any territories in respect of which a mandate under the League of Nations has been accepted by His Majesty.

## PART II

## Miscellaneous and General

### 8   General effect of certain foreign judgments

(1) Subject to the provisions of this section, a judgment to which Part I of this Act applies or would have applied if a sum of money had been payable thereunder, whether it can be registered or not, and

whether, if it can be registered, it is registered or not, shall be recognised in any court in the United Kingdom as conclusive between the parties thereto in all proceedings founded on the same cause of action and may be relied on by way of defence or counterclaim in any such proceedings.

(2) This section shall not apply in the case of any judgment—

(a) where the judgment has been registered and the registration thereof has been set aside on some ground other than—

    (i) that a sum of money was not payable under the judgment; or

    (ii) that the judgment had been wholly or partly satisfied; or

    (iii) that at the date of the application the judgment could not be enforced by execution in the country of the original court; or

(b) where the judgment has not been registered, it is shown (whether it could have been registered or not) that if it had been registered the registration thereof would have been set aside on an application for that purpose on some ground other than one of the grounds specified in paragraph (a) of this subsection.

(3) Nothing in this section shall be taken to prevent any court in the United Kingdom recognising any judgment as conclusive of any matter of law or fact decided therein if that judgment would have been so recognised before the passing of this Act.

### 9 Power to make foreign judgments unenforceable in United Kingdom if no reciprocity

(1) If it appears to His Majesty that the treatment in respect of recognition and enforcement accorded by the courts of any foreign country to judgments given in the [. . .] courts of the United Kingdom is substantially less favourable than that accorded by the courts of the United Kingdom to judgments of the [. . .] courts of that country, His Majesty may by Order in Council apply this section to that country.

(2) Except in so far as His Majesty may by Order in Council under this section otherwise direct, no proceedings shall be entertained in any court in the United Kingdom for the recovery of any sum alleged to be payable under a judgment given in a court of a country to which this section applies.

(3) His Majesty may by a subsequent Order in Council vary or revoke any Order previously made under this section.

### [10 Provision for issue of copies of, and certificates in connection with, UK judgments

(1) Rules may make provision for enabling any judgment creditor wishing to secure the enforcement in a foreign country to which Part I of this Act extends of a judgment to which this subsection applies, to obtain, subject to any conditions specified in the rules—

(a) a copy of the judgment; and

(b) a certificate giving particulars relating to the judgment and the proceedings in which it was given.

(2) Subsection (1) applies to any judgment given by a court or tribunal in the United Kingdom under which a sum of money is payable, not being a sum payable in respect of taxes or other charges of a like nature or in respect of a fine or other penalty.

(3) In this section "rules"—

(a) in relation to judgments given by a court, means rules of court;

(b) in relation to judgments given by any other tribunal, means rules or regulations made by the authority having power to make rules or regulations regulating the procedure of that tribunal.]

. . .

### 11 Interpretation

(1) In this Act, unless the context otherwise requires, the following expressions have the meanings hereby assigned to them respectively, that is to say—

    "Appeal" includes any proceeding by way of discharging or setting aside a judgment or an application for a new trial or a stay of execution;

"Country of the original court" means the country in which the original court is situated;

["Court", except in section 10 of this Act, includes a tribunal;]

"Judgment" means a judgment or order given or made by a court in any civil proceedings, or a judgment or order given or made by a court in any criminal proceedings for the payment of a sum of money in respect of compensation or damages to an injured party;

"Judgment creditor" means the person in whose favour the judgment was given and includes any person in whom the rights under the judgment have become vested by succession or assignment or otherwise;

"Judgment debtor" means the person against whom the judgment was given, and includes any person against whom the judgment is enforceable under the law of the original court;

[. . .]

"Original court" in relation to any judgment means the court by which the judgment was given;

"Prescribed" means prescribed by rules of court;

"Registration" means registration under Part I of this Act, and the expressions "register" and "registered" shall be construed accordingly;

"Registering court" in relation to any judgment means the court to which an application to register the judgment is made.

(2)  For the purposes of this Act, the expression "action in personam" shall not be deemed to include any matrimonial cause or any proceedings in connection with any of the following matters, that is to say, matrimonial matters, administration of the estates of deceased persons, bankruptcy, winding up of companies, lunacy, or guardianship of infants.

. . .

# Maintenance Orders Act
# 1950 ch 37

## PART II

### Enforcement

### 16 Application of Part II

(1) Any order to which this section applies (in this Part of this Act referred to as a maintenance order) made by a court in any part of the United Kingdom may, if registered in accordance with the provisions of this Part of this Act in a court in another part of the United Kingdom, be enforced in accordance with those provisions in that other part of the United Kingdom.

(2) This section applies to the following orders, that is to say—

(a) an order for alimony, maintenance or other payments made or deemed to be made by a court in England under any of the following enactments—

   [(i) sections 15 to 17, 19 to 22, 30, 34 and 35 of the Matrimonial Causes Act 1965 and sections 22, 23(1), (2) and (4) and 27 of the Matrimonial Causes Act 1973] [and section 14 or 17 of the Matrimonial and Family Proceedings Act 1984];

   [(ii) Part I of the Domestic Proceedings and Magistrates' Courts Act 1978];

   [(iii) Schedule 1 to the Children Act 1989;]

   (iv) [. . .];

   (v) [paragraph 23 of Schedule 2 to the Children Act 1989;]

   [(vi) section 18 of the Supplementary Benefits Act 1976;]

   . . .

   [(viii) [section 106 of the Social Security Administration Act 1992;]

   [(ix) Part 1, 8 or 9 of Schedule 5 to the Civil Partnership Act 2004, Schedule 6 to that Act or paragraph 5 or 9 of Schedule 7 to that Act;]

(b) a decree for payment of aliment granted by a court in Scotland, including—

   (i) an order for the payment of an annual or periodical allowance under section two of the Divorce (Scotland) Act 1938 or [an order for the payment of a periodical allowance [or a capital sum] under section 26 of the Succession (Scotland) Act 1964 or section 5 of the Divorce (Scotland) Act 1976] [or section 29 of the Matrimonial and Family Proceedings Act 1984] [or an order for financial provision in the form of a monetary payment under section 8 of the Family Law (Scotland) Act 1985];

   (ii) an order for the payment of weekly or periodical sums under subsection (2) of section three or subsection (4) of section five of the Guardianship of Infants Act 1925;

   (iii) an order for the payment of sums in respect of aliment under subsection (3) of section one of the Illegitimate Children (Scotland) Act 1930;

   (iv) a decree for payment of aliment under section forty-four of the National Assistance Act 1948, or under section twenty-six of the Children Act 1948; and

   (v) [. . .] an order under section forty-three of the National Assistance Act 1948;

   [(vi) a contribution order under section 80 of, or a decree or an order made under section 81 of, the Social Work (Scotland) Act 1968;]

   [(vii) an order for the payment of weekly or other periodical sums under subsection (3) of section 11 of the Guardianship Act 1973;]

   [(viii) an order made on an application under [section 18 or section 19(8)] of the Supplementary

Benefits Act 1976;]

[(ix) an order made on an application under [section 106 of the Social Security Administration Act 1992];]

[(x) an order made on an application under Schedule 11 to the Civil Partnership Act 2004;]

(c) an order for alimony, maintenance or other payments made by a court in Northern Ireland under or by virtue of any of the following enactments—

(i) subsection (2) of section seventeen, subsections (2) to (7) of section nineteen, subsection (2) of section twenty, section twenty-two or subsection (1) of section twenty-eight of the Matrimonial Causes Act (Northern Ireland) 1939;

[(ii) Schedule 1 to the Children (Northern Ireland) Order 1995;]

(iii) [. . .];

[(iv) [Article 41 of the Children (Northern Ireland) Order 1995] or Article 101 of the Health and Personal Social Services (Northern Ireland) Order 1972];

[(v) any enactment of the Parliament of Northern Ireland containing provisions corresponding with section 22(1), 34 or 35 of the Matrimonial Causes Act 1965, with section 22, 23(1), (2) or (4) or 27 of the Matrimonial Causes Act 1973, [. . .];]

[(vi) Article 23 or 24 of the Supplementary Benefits (Northern Ireland) Order 1977;]

[(vii) the Domestic Proceedings (Northern Ireland) Order 1980;]

[(viii) any enactment applying in Northern Ireland and corresponding to [section 106 of the Social Security Administration Act 1992];]

[(ix) Article 18 or 21 of the Matrimonial and Family Proceedings (Northern Ireland) Order 1989;]

[(x) Part 1, 7 or 8 of Schedule 15 to the Civil Partnership Act 2004, Schedule 16 to that Act or paragraph 5 or 9 of Schedule 17 to that Act].

(3) For the purposes of this section, any order made before the commencement of the Matrimonial Causes Act (Northern Ireland) 1939, being an order which, if that Act had been in force, could have been made under or by virtue of any provision of that Act, shall be deemed to be an order made by virtue of that provision.

### 17 Procedure for registration of maintenance orders

(1) An application for the registration of a maintenance order under this Part of this Act shall be made in the prescribed manner to the appropriate authority, that is to say—

(a) [. . .]

(b) where the maintenance order was made by a court of summary jurisdiction in Northern Ireland, a resident magistrate acting for the same petty sessions district as the court which made the order;

(c) in every other case, the prescribed officer of the court which made the order.

(2) If upon application made as aforesaid by or on behalf of the person entitled to payments under a maintenance order it appears that the person liable to make those payments resides in another part of the United Kingdom, and that it is convenient that the order should be enforceable there, the appropriate authority shall cause a certified copy of the order to be sent to the prescribed officer of a court in that part of the United Kingdom in accordance with the provisions of the next following subsection.

(3) The court to whose officer the certified copy of a maintenance order is sent under this section shall be—

(a) where the maintenance order was made by a superior court, the [Senior Courts], the Court of Session or the [Court of Judicature], as the case may be;

(b) in any other case[—

(i) where the defendant appears to be in England and Wales, the family court;

(ii) where the defendant appears to be in Northern Ireland, a court of summary jurisdiction

UK Statutes

acting for the place in which the defendant appears to be;

   (iii) where the defendant appears to be in Scotland, the sheriff court within the jurisdiction of which the defendant appears to be].

(4) Where the prescribed officer of any court receives a certified copy of a maintenance order sent to him under this section, he shall cause the order to be registered in that court in the prescribed manner, and shall give notice of the registration in the prescribed manner to the prescribed officer of the court which made the order.

(5) The officer to whom any notice is given under the last foregoing subsection shall cause particulars of the notice to be registered in his court in the prescribed manner.

(6) Where the sums payable under a maintenance order, being an order [made by the family court or a court of summary jurisdiction in Northern Ireland], are payable to or through an officer of any court, that officer shall, if the person entitled to the payments so requests, make an application on behalf of that person for the registration of the order under this Part of this Act; but the person at whose request the application is made shall have the same liability for costs properly incurred in or about the application as if the application had been made by him.

(7) An order which is for the time being registered under this Part of this Act in any court shall not be registered thereunder in any other court.

## 18 Enforcement of registered orders

(1) Subject to the provisions of this section, a maintenance order registered under this Part of this Act in a court in any part of the United Kingdom may be enforced in that part of the United Kingdom in all respects as if it had been made by that court and as if that court had had jurisdiction to make it; and proceedings for or with respect to the enforcement of any such order may be taken accordingly.

[(1A) A maintenance order registered under this Part of this Act in [the family court or] a court of summary jurisdiction in [. . .] Northern Ireland shall not carry interest; but where a maintenance order so registered is registered in the High Court under [. . .] section 36 of the Civil Jurisdiction and Judgments Act 1982, this subsection shall not prevent any sum for whose payment the order provides from carrying interest in accordance with [. . .] section 11A of the Maintenance and Affiliation Orders Act (Northern Ireland) 1966.

(1B) A maintenance order made in Scotland which is registered under this Part of this Act in the [Senior Courts or the Court of Judicature] shall, if interest is by the law of Scotland recoverable under the order, carry the like interest in accordance with subsection (1) of this section.]

. . .

[(3A) Notwithstanding subsection (1) above, no court in England in which a maintenance order is registered under this Part of this Act shall enforce that order [to the extent that it is for the time being registered] in another court in England under Part I of the Maintenance Orders Act 1958.]

. . .

(6) Except as provided by this section, no proceedings shall be taken for or with respect to the enforcement of a maintenance order which is for the time being registered in any court under this Part of this Act.

## 19 Functions of collecting officer, etc

(1) Where a maintenance order made in England [by the family court or in] Northern Ireland by a court of summary jurisdiction is registered in any court under this Part of this Act, any provision of the court by virtue of which sums payable thereunder are required to be paid through or to any [court or] officer or person on behalf of the person entitled thereto shall be of no effect so long as the order is so registered.

. . .

(4) Where by virtue of the provisions of this section or any order made thereunder payments under a maintenance order cease to be or become payable through or to any [court or] officer or person, the person liable to make the payments shall, until he is given the prescribed notice to that effect, be deemed

to comply with the maintenance order if he makes payments in accordance with the maintenance order and any order under this section of which he has received such notice.

. . .

## 20 Arrears under registered maintenance orders

(1) Where application is made for the registration of a maintenance order under this Part of this Act, the applicant may lodge with the appropriate authority—

(a) if the payments under the order are required to be made to or through [a court or] an officer of any court, a certificate in the prescribed form, signed by [an officer of that court or (as the case may be)] that officer, as to the amount of any arrears due under the order;

(b) in any other case, a statutory declaration or affidavit as to the amount of those arrears;

and if a certified copy of the maintenance order is sent to the prescribed officer of any court in pursuance of the application, the certificate, declaration or affidavit shall also be sent to that officer.

(2) In any proceedings for or with respect to the enforcement of a maintenance order which is for the time being registered in any court under this Part of this Act, a certificate, declaration or affidavit sent under this section to the appropriate officer of that court shall be evidence, and in Scotland sufficient evidence, of the facts stated therein.

(3) Where a maintenance order made by a court in England or Northern Ireland is registered in a court in Scotland, a person shall not be entitled, except with the leave of the last-mentioned court, to enforce, whether by diligence or otherwise, the payment of any arrears accrued and due under the order before the commencement of this Act; and on any application for leave to enforce the payment of any such arrears, the court may refuse leave, or may grant leave subject to such restrictions and conditions (including conditions as to the allowing of time for payment or the making of payment by instalments) as the court thinks proper, or may remit the payment of such arrears or of any part thereof.

## 21 Discharge and variation of maintenance orders registered in superior courts

(1) The registration of a maintenance order in a superior court under this Part of this Act shall not confer on that court any power to vary or discharge the order, or affect any jurisdiction of the court in which the order was made to vary or discharge the order.

(2) Where a maintenance order made in Scotland is for the time being—

[(a) registered under this Part of this Act in a superior court and not registered under Part I of the Maintenance Orders Act 1958 [or under section 36 of the Civil Jurisdiction and Judgments Act 1982], or

(b) registered in a court in England under that Part of that Act [of 1958] by virtue of section 1(2) of that Act [of 1958],]

. . .

the person liable to make payments under the order may, upon application made to that court in the prescribed manner, adduce before that court any evidence upon which he would be entitled to rely in any proceedings brought before the court by which the order was made for the variation or discharge of the order.

(3) A court before which evidence is adduced in accordance with the foregoing subsection shall cause a transcript or summary of that evidence, signed by the deponent, to be sent to the prescribed officer of the court by which the order was made; and in any proceedings before the last-mentioned court for the variation or discharge of the order, the transcript or summary shall be evidence of the facts stated therein.

## 22 Discharge and variation of maintenance orders registered in summary or sheriff courts

(1) [Subject to subsection (1ZA),] where a maintenance order is for the time being registered under this Part of this Act in [the family court, a court of summary jurisdiction in Northern Ireland or a] sheriff court, that court may, upon application made in the prescribed manner by or on behalf of the person liable to make [periodical] payments under the order or the person entitled to those payments,

by order make such variation as the court thinks fit in the rate of the payments under the maintenance order; but no such variation shall impose on the person liable to make payments under the maintenance order a liability to make payments in excess of the maximum rate (if any) authorised by the law for the time being in force in the part of the United Kingdom in which the maintenance order was made.

[(1ZA) The power under subsection (1) to vary the rate of payments may not be exercised where paragraph 9(2) of Schedule 6 to the Civil Jurisdiction and Judgments (Maintenance) Regulations 2011 applies (restriction on modifying maintenance decision where creditor remains habitually resident in the part of the United Kingdom in which the decision was made).]

[(1A) The family court may exercise the same powers in relation to an order registered in the family court under this Part of this Act as are exercisable by the family court under section 1 of the Maintenance Enforcement Act 1991 in relation to a qualifying periodical maintenance order (within the meaning of that section) which has been made by the family court, including the power under subsection (7) of that section to revoke, suspend, revive or vary any means of payment order (within the meaning of that subsection) made by virtue of this subsection.]

. . .

(2)  For the purposes of subsection (1) of this section, a court in any part of the United Kingdom may take notice of the law in force in any other part of the United Kingdom.

(3)  Section fifteen of this Act shall apply to the service of process for the purposes of this section as it applies to the service of process in proceedings begun in a court having jurisdiction by virtue of Part I of this Act.

(4)  Except as provided by subsection (1) of this section, no variation shall be made in the rate of the payments under a maintenance order which is for the time being registered under this Part of this Act in [the family court, a court of summary jurisdiction in Northern Ireland or a] sheriff court, but without prejudice to any power of the court which made the order to discharge it or vary it otherwise than in respect of the rate of the payments thereunder.

(5)  Where a maintenance order is for the time being registered under this Part of this Act in [the family court, a court of summary jurisdiction in Northern Ireland or a] sheriff court—

(a)   the person entitled to payments under the order or the person liable to make payments under the order may, upon application made in the prescribed manner to the court by which the order was made, or in which the order is registered, as the case may be, adduce in the prescribed manner before the court in which the application is made any evidence on which he would be entitled to rely in proceedings for the variation or discharge of the order;

(b)   the court in which the application is made shall cause a transcript or summary of that evidence, signed by the deponent, to be sent to the prescribed officer of the court in which the order is registered or of the court by which the order was made, as the case may be; and in any proceedings for the variation or discharge of the order the transcript or summary shall be evidence of the facts stated therein.

[23  Notice of variation, etc

(1)  Where a maintenance order registered under this Part of this Act is discharged or varied by any court, the prescribed officer of that court shall give notice of the discharge or variation in the prescribed manner—

(a)   to the prescribed officer of any court in which the order is registered; and

(b)   if the order was made by another court, to the prescribed officer of that court.

(2)  Any officer to whom a notice is given under this section shall cause particulars of the notice to be registered in his court in the prescribed manner.]

24  Cancellation of registration

(1)  At any time while a maintenance order is registered under this Part of this Act in any court, an application for the cancellation of the registration may be made in the prescribed manner to the prescribed officer of that court by or on behalf of the person entitled to payments under the order;

and upon any such application that officer shall (unless proceedings for the variation of the order are pending in that court), cancel the registration, and thereupon the order shall cease to be registered in that court.

(2) Where, after a maintenance order has been registered under this Part of this Act in [the family court, a court of summary jurisdiction in Northern Ireland] or a sheriff court in Scotland, it appears to the appropriate authority (as defined by section seventeen of this Act), upon application made in the prescribed manner by or on behalf of the person liable to make payments under the order, that the person has ceased to reside in England, Northern Ireland or Scotland, as the case may be, the appropriate authority may cause a notice to that effect to be sent to the prescribed officer [of any court] in which the order is registered; and where such a notice is sent the prescribed officer shall cancel the registration of the maintenance order, and thereupon the order shall cease to be registered in that court.

(3) Where the prescribed officer of any court cancels the registration of a maintenance order under this section, he shall give notice of the cancellation in the prescribed manner

[(a) to the prescribed officer of the court by which the order was made; and

(b) to the prescribed officer of any court in which it is registered under Part I of the Maintenance Orders Act 1958 [or section 36 of the Civil Jurisdiction and Judgments Act 1982].]

[(3A) On receipt of a notice under subsection (3) above—

(a) any such officer as is mentioned in paragraph (a) of that subsection shall cause particulars of the notice to be registered in his court in the prescribed manner; and

(b) any such officer as is mentioned in paragraph (b) of that subsection shall cause particulars of the notice to be registered in his court in the prescribed manner and shall cancel the registration of the order.]

(4) Except as provided by subsection (5) of this section, the cancellation of the registration of a maintenance order shall not affect anything done in relation to the maintenance order while it was registered.

(5) On the cancellation of the registration of a maintenance order, any order made in relation thereto under subsection (2) of section nineteen of this Act shall cease to have effect; but until the person liable to make payments under the maintenance order receives the prescribed notice of the cancellation, he shall be deemed to comply with the maintenance order if he makes payments in accordance with any order under the said subsection (2) which was in force immediately before the cancellation.

[(5A) On the cancellation of the registration of a maintenance order registered in [the family] court in England and Wales, any order—

(a) made in relation thereto by virtue of the powers conferred by [. . .] section 22(1A) [. . .] of this Act, and

(b) requiring payment to [the family court] (whether or not by any method of payment falling within section [1(5) of the Maintenance Enforcement Act 1991]),

shall cease to have effect; but until the person liable to make payments under the maintenance order receives the prescribed notice of the cancellation, he shall be deemed to comply with the maintenance order if he makes payments in accordance with any such order which was in force immediately before the cancellation.]

. . .

25 **Rules as to procedure of courts of summary jurisdiction**

. . .

# Marriage (Enabling) Act
## 1960 ch 29

**1 Certain marriages not to be void.**

(1)  No marriage hereafter contracted (whether in or out of Great Britain) between a man and a woman who is the sister, aunt or niece of a former wife of his (whether living or not), or was formerly the wife of his brother, uncle or nephew (whether living or not), shall by reason of that relationship be void or voidable under any enactment or rule of law applying in Great Britain as a marriage between persons within the prohibited degrees of affinity.

(2)  In the foregoing subsection words of kinship apply equally to kin of the whole and of the half blood.

(3)  This section does not validate a marriage, if either party to it is at the time of the marriage domiciled in a country outside Great Britain, and under the law of that country there cannot be a valid marriage between the parties.

(4)  [. . .]

# Wills Act
# 1963 ch 44

### 1 General rule as to formal validity

A will shall be treated as properly executed if its execution conformed to the internal law in force in the territory where it was executed, or in the territory where, at the time of its execution or of the testator's death, he was domiciled or had his habitual residence, or in a state of which, at either of those times, he was a national.

### 2 Additional rules

(1) Without prejudice to the preceding section, the following shall be treated as properly executed—

(a)  a will executed on board a vessel or aircraft of any description, if the execution of the will conformed to the internal law in force in the territory with which, having regard to its registration (if any) and other relevant circumstances, the vessel or aircraft may be taken to have been most closely connected;

(b)  a will so far as it disposes of immovable property, if its execution conformed to the internal law in force in the territory where the property was situated;

(c)  a will so far as it revokes a will which under this Act would be treated as properly executed or revokes a provision which under this Act would be treated as comprised in a properly executed will, if the execution of the later will conformed to any law by reference to which the revoked will or provision would be so treated;

(d)  a will so far as it exercises a power of appointment, if the execution of the will conformed to the law governing the essential validity of the power.

(2) A will so far as it exercises a power of appointment shall not be treated as improperly executed by reason only that its execution was not in accordance with any formal requirements contained in the instrument creating the power.

### 3 Certain requirements to be treated as formal

Where (whether in pursuance of this Act or not) a law in force outside the United Kingdom falls to be applied in relation to a will, any requirement of that law whereby special formalities are to be observed by testators answering a particular description, or witnesses to the execution of a will are to possess certain qualifications, shall be treated, notwithstanding any rule of that law to the contrary, as a formal requirement only.

### 4 Construction of wills

The construction of a will shall not be altered by reason of any change in the testator's domicile after the execution of the will.

### 5 [...]

### 6 Interpretation

(1) In this Act—

"internal law" in relation to any territory or state means the law which would apply in a case where no question of the law in force in any other territory or state arose;

"state" means a territory or group of territories having its own law of nationality;

"will" includes any testamentary instrument or act, and "testator" shall be construed accordingly.

(2) Where under this Act the internal law in force in any territory or state is to be applied in the case of a will, but there are in force in that territory or state two or more systems of internal law relating to the formal validity of wills, the system to be applied shall be ascertained as follows—

(a) if there is in force throughout the territory or state a rule indicating which of those systems can properly be applied in the case in question, that rule shall be followed; or

(b) if there is no such rule, the system shall be that with which the testator was most closely connected at the relevant time, and for this purpose the relevant time is the time of the testator's death where the matter is to be determined by reference to circumstances prevailing at his death, and the time of execution of the will in any other case.

(3) In determining for the purposes of this Act whether or not the execution of a will conformed to a particular law, regard shall be had to the formal requirements of that law at the time of execution, but this shall not prevent account being taken of an alteration of law affecting wills executed at that time if the alteration enables the will to be treated as properly executed.

# Administration of Estates Act
# 1971 ch 25

## Reciprocal recognition of grants

### 1 Recognition in England and Wales of Scottish confirmations and Northern Irish grants of representation

(1) Where a person dies domiciled in Scotland—

(a) a confirmation granted in respect of all or part of his estate and noting his Scottish domicile, and

(b) a certificate of confirmation noting his Scottish domicile and relating to one or more items of his estate,

shall, without being resealed, be treated for the purposes of the law of England and Wales as a grant of representation (in accordance with subsection (2) below) to the executors named in the confirmation or certificate in respect of the property of the deceased of which according to the terms of the confirmation they are executors or, as the case may be, in respect of the item or items of property specified in the certificate of confirmation.

(2) Where by virtue of subsection (1) above a confirmation or certificate of confirmation is treated for the purposes of the law of England and Wales as a grant of representation to the executors named therein then, subject to subsections (3) and (5) below, the grant shall be treated—

(a) as a grant of probate where it appears from the confirmation or certificate that the executors so named are executors nominate; and

(b) in any other case, as a grant of letters of administration.

(3) Section 7 of the Administration of Estates Act 1925 (executor of executor represents original testator) shall not, by virtue of subsection (2)(a) above, apply on the death of an executor named in a confirmation or certificate of confirmation.

(4) Subject to subsection (5) below, where a person dies domiciled in Northern Ireland a grant of probate of his will or letters of administration in respect of his estate (or any part of it) made by the High Court in Northern Ireland and noting his domicile there shall, without being resealed, be treated for the purposes of the law of England and Wales as if it had been originally made by the High Court in England and Wales.

(5) Notwithstanding anything in the preceding provisions of this section, a person who is a personal representative according to the law of England and Wales by virtue only of those provisions may not be required, under section 25 of the Administration of Estates Act 1925, to deliver up his grant to the High Court.

(6) This section applies in relation to confirmations, probates and letters of administration granted before as well as after the commencement of this Act, and in relation to a confirmation, probate or letters of administration granted before the commencement of this Act, this section shall have effect as if it had come into force immediately before the grant was made.

(7) In this section "confirmation" includes an additional confirmation, and the term "executors", where used in relation to a confirmation or certificate of confirmation, shall be construed according to the law of Scotland.

. . .

### 4 Evidence of grants

(1) In England and Wales and in Northern Ireland—

(a) a document purporting to be a confirmation, additional confirmation or certificate of confirmation given under the seal of office of any commissariat in Scotland shall, except where the contrary is proved, be taken to be such a confirmation, additional confirmation or certificate of confirmation without further proof; and

(b) a document purporting to be a duplicate of such a confirmation or additional confirmation and to be given under such a seal shall be receivable in evidence in like manner and for the like purposes as the confirmation or additional confirmation of which it purports to be a duplicate.

(2) In England and Wales and in Scotland—

(a) a document purporting to be a grant of probate or of letters of administration issued under the seal of the High Court in Northern Ireland or of the principal or district probate registry there shall, except where the contrary is proved, be taken to be such a grant without further proof; and

(b) a document purporting to be a copy of such a grant and to be sealed with such a seal shall be receivable in evidence in like manner and for the like purposes as the grant of which it purports to be a copy.

(3) In Scotland and in Northern Ireland—

(a) a document purporting to be a grant of probate or of letters of administration issued under the seal of the High Court in England and Wales or of the principal or a district probate registry there shall, except where the contrary is proved, be taken to be such a grant without further proof; and

(b) a document purporting to be a copy of such a grant and to be sealed with such a seal shall be receivable in evidence in like manner and for the like purposes as the grant of which it purports to be a copy.

### 5 Property outside Scotland of which deceased was trustee

(1) A confirmation or additional confirmation granted in respect of property situated in Scotland of a person who died domiciled there, which notes that domicile, may contain or have appended thereto and signed by the sheriff clerk a note or statement of property in England and Wales or in Northern Ireland held by the deceased in trust, being a note or statement which has been set forth in any inventory recorded in the books of the court of which the sheriff clerk is clerk.

(2) Section 1 or, as the case may be, section 2 of this Act shall apply in relation to property specified in such a note or statement as is mentioned in subsection (1) above as it applies in relation to property specified in the confirmation or additional confirmation concerned.

. . .

### Miscellaneous and supplemental

### 11 Sealing of Commonwealth and Colonial grants

(1) The following provisions of section 2 of the Colonial Probates Act 1892, that is to say—

(a) subsection (2)(b) (which makes it a condition precedent to sealing in the United Kingdom letters of administration granted in certain overseas countries and territories that a sufficient security has been given to cover property in the United Kingdom); and

(b) subsection (3) (power of the court in the United Kingdom to require that adequate security is given for the payment of debts due to creditors residing in the United Kingdom);

shall not apply to the sealing of letters of administration by the High Court in England and Wales under that section, and the following provisions of this section shall apply instead.

(2) A person to whom letters of administration have been granted in a country or territory to which the said Act of 1892 applies shall on their being sealed by the High Court in England and Wales under the said section 2 have the like duties with respect to the estate of the deceased which is situated in England and Wales and the debts of the deceased which fall to be paid there as are imposed by section 25(a) and (b) of the Administration of Estates Act 1925 on a person to whom a grant of administration has been made by that court.

(3) As a condition of sealing letters of administration granted in any such country or territory, the High Court in England and Wales may, in cases to which [section 120 of the [Senior Courts Act 1981]] (power to require administrators to produce sureties) applies and subject to the following provisions of

this section and subject to and in accordance with probate rules [. . .] require one or more sureties, in such amount as the court thinks fit, to guarantee that they will make good, within any limit imposed by the court on the total liability of the surety or sureties, any loss which any person interested in the administration of the estate of the deceased in England and Wales may suffer in consequence of a breach by the administrator of his duties in administering it there.

(4) A guarantee given in pursuance of any such requirement shall enure for the benefit of every person interested in the administration of the estate in England and Wales as if contained in a contract under seal made by the surety or sureties with every such person and, where there are two or more sureties, as if they had bound themselves jointly or severally.

(5) No action shall be brought on any such guarantee without the leave of the High Court.

(6) Stamp duty shall not be chargeable on any such guarantee.

(7) Subsections (2) to (6) above apply to the sealing by the High Court in England and Wales of letters of administration granted by a British court in a foreign country as they apply to the sealing of letters of administration granted in a country or territory to which the Colonial Probates Act 1892 applies.

(8) In this section—

"letters of administration" and "British court in a foreign country" have the same meaning as in the Colonial Probates Act 1892; and

["probate rules" means rules of court made under section 127 of the [Senior Courts Act 1981]].

# Civil Evidence Act
## 1972 ch 30

### 4 Evidence of foreign law.

(1) It is hereby declared that in civil proceedings a person who is suitably qualified to do so on account of his knowledge or experience is competent to give expert evidence as to the law of any country or territory outside the United Kingdom, or of any part of the United Kingdom other than England and Wales, irrespective of whether he has acted or is entitled to act as a legal practitioner there.

(2) Where any question as to the law of any country or territory outside the United Kingdom, or of any part of the United Kingdom other than England and Wales, with respect to any matter has been determined (whether before or after the passing of this Act) in any such proceedings as are mentioned in subsection (4) below, then in any civil proceedings (not being proceedings before a court which can take judicial notice of the law of that country, territory or part with respect to that matter)—

(a) any finding made or decision given on that question in the first-mentioned proceedings shall, if reported or recorded in citable form, be admissible in evidence for the purpose of proving the law of that country, territory or part with respect to that matter; and

(b) if that finding or decision, as so reported or recorded, is adduced for that purpose, the law of that country, territory or part with respect to that matter shall be taken to be in accordance with that finding or decision unless the contrary is proved:

Provided that paragraph (b) above shall not apply in the case of a finding or decision which conflicts with another finding or decision on the same question adduced by virtue of this subsection in the same proceedings.

(3) Except with the leave of the court, a party to any civil proceedings shall not be permitted to adduce any such finding or decision as is mentioned in subsection (2) above by virtue of that subsection unless he has in accordance with rules of court given to every other party to the proceedings notice that he intends to do so.

(4) The proceedings referred to in subsection (2) above are the following, whether civil or criminal, namely—

(a) proceedings at first instance in any of the following courts, namely the High Court, the Crown Court, a court of quarter sessions, the Court of Chancery of the county palatine of Lancaster and the Court of Chancery of the county palatine of Durham;

(b) appeals arising out of any such proceedings as are mentioned in paragraph (a) above;

(c) proceedings before the Judicial Committee of the Privy Council on appeal (whether to Her Majesty in Council or to the Judicial Committee as such) from any decision of any court outside the United Kingdom.

(5) For the purposes of this section a finding or decision on any such question as is mentioned in subsection (2) above shall be taken to be reported or recorded in citable form if, but only if, it is reported or recorded in writing in a report, transcript or other document which, if that question had been a question as to the law of England and Wales, could be cited as an authority in legal proceedings in England and Wales.

### 5 Interpretation, application to arbitrations etc. and savings.

[(1) In this Act "civil proceedings" means civil proceedings, before any tribunal, in relation to which the strict rules of evidence apply, whether as a matter of law or by agreement of the parties; and references to "the court" shall be construed accordingly.]

[(2) The rules of court made for the purposes of the application of sections 2 and 4 of this Act to proceedings in the High Court apply, except in so far as their application is excluded by agreement, to proceedings before tribunals other than the ordinary courts of law, subject to such modifications as may be appropriate.

Any question arising as to what modifications are appropriate shall be determined, in default of agreement, by the tribunal.]

(3) Nothing in this Act shall prejudice—

(a) any power of a court, in any civil proceedings, to exclude evidence (whether by preventing questions from being put or otherwise) at its discretion; or

(b) the operation of any agreement (whenever made) between the parties to any civil proceedings as to the evidence which is to be admissible (whether generally or for any particular purpose) in those proceedings.

# Maintenance Orders (Reciprocal Enforcement) Act 1972 ch 18

PART I

## Reciprocal Enforcement of Maintenance Orders made in United Kingdom or Reciprocating Country

*Designation of reciprocating countries*

### 1 Orders in Council designating reciprocating countries

(1) Her Majesty, if satisfied that, in the event of the benefits conferred by this Part of this Act being applied to, or to particular classes of, maintenance orders made by the courts of any country or territory outside the United Kingdom, similar benefits will in that country or territory be applied to, or to those classes of, maintenance orders made by the courts of the United Kingdom, may by Order in Council designate that country or territory as a reciprocating country for the purposes of this Part of this Act; and, subject to subsection (2) below, in this Part of this Act "reciprocating country" means a country or territory that is for the time being so designated.

(2) A country or territory may be designated under subsection (1) above as a reciprocating country either as regards maintenance orders generally, or as regards maintenance orders other than those of any specified class, or as regards maintenance orders of one or more specified classes only; and a country or territory which is for the time being so designated otherwise than as regards maintenance orders generally shall for the purposes of this Part of this Act be taken to be a reciprocating country only as regards maintenance orders of the class to which the designation extends.

*Orders made by Courts in the United Kingdom*

### 2 Transmission of maintenance order made in United Kingdom for enforcement in reciprocating country

(1) Subject to subsection (2) below, where the payer under a maintenance order made, whether before or after the commencement of this Part of this Act, by a court in the United Kingdom is residing [or has assets] in a reciprocating country, the payee under the order may apply for the order to be sent to that country for enforcement.

(2) Subsection (1) above shall not have effect in relation to a provisional order or to an order made by virtue of a provision of Part II of this Act.

(3) Every application under this section shall be made in the prescribed manner to the prescribed officer of the court which made the maintenance order to which the application relates.

(4) If, on an application duly made under this section to the prescribed officer of a court in the United Kingdom, that officer is satisfied that the payer under the maintenance order to which the application relates is residing [or has assets] in a reciprocating country, the following documents, that is to say—

(a) a certified copy of the maintenance order;

(b) a certificate signed by that officer certifying that the order is enforceable in the United Kingdom;

(c) a certificate of arrears so signed;

(d) a statement giving such information as the officer possesses as to the whereabouts of the payer [and the nature and location of his assets in that country];

(e) a statement giving such information as the officer possesses for facilitating the identification of the payer; and

(f) where available, a photograph of the payer;

shall be sent by that officer to the Secretary of State with a view to their being transmitted by the

Secretary of State to the responsible authority in the reciprocating country if he is satisfied that the statement relating to the whereabouts of the payer [and the nature and location of his assets in that country] gives sufficient information to justify that being done.

(5) Nothing in this section shall be taken as affecting any jurisdiction of a court in the United Kingdom with respect to a maintenance order to which this section applies, and any such order may be enforced, varied or revoked accordingly.

### 3 Power of [. . .] court to make provisional maintenance order against person residing in reciprocating country

[(1) Where an application is made to [the family court] for a maintenance order against a person residing in a reciprocating country and the court would have jurisdiction to determine the application under the Domestic Proceedings and Magistrates' Courts Act 1978 or the Children Act 1989 if that person—

(a)   were [habitually resident] in England and Wales, and

(b)   received reasonable notice of the date of the hearing of the application,

the court shall (subject to subsection (2) below) have jurisdiction to determine the application.]

(2)   A maintenance order made by virtue of this section shall be a provisional order.

(3)   [. . .]

[(4)   No enactment (or provision made under an enactment) requiring or enabling—

[(za) a court to transfer proceedings from the family court to the High Court,]

. . .

shall apply in relation to an application to which subsection (1) above applies.]

(5)   Where a court makes a maintenance order which is by virtue of this section a provisional order, the following documents, that is to say—

(a)   a certified copy of the maintenance order;

(b)   a document, authenticated in the prescribed manner, setting out or summarising the evidence given in the proceedings;

(c)   a certificate signed by the prescribed officer of the court certifying that the grounds stated in the certificate are the grounds on which the making of the order might have been opposed by the payer under the order;

(d)   a statement giving such information as was available to the court as to the whereabouts of the payer;

(e)   a statement giving such information as the officer possesses for facilitating the identification of the payer; and

(f)   where available, a photograph of the payer;

shall be sent by that officer to the Secretary of State with a view to their being transmitted by the Secretary of State to the responsible authority in the reciprocating country in which the payer is residing if he is satisfied that the statement relating to the whereabouts of the payer gives sufficient information to justify that being done.

(6)   A maintenance order made by virtue of this section which has been confirmed by a competent court in a reciprocating country shall be treated for all purposes as if the [. . .] court which made the order had made it in the form in which it was confirmed and as if the order had never been a provisional order, and subject to section 5 of this Act, any such order may be enforced, varied or revoked accordingly.

. . .

### 4 Power of sheriff to make provisional maintenance order against person residing in reciprocating country

[(1) In any action where the sheriff has jurisdiction by virtue of [the Maintenance Regulation and

Schedule 6 to the Civil Jurisdiction and Judgments (Maintenance) Regulations 2011] and the defender resides in a reciprocating country, any maintenance order granted by the sheriff shall be a provisional order.]

(2) [. . .]

(3) [. . .]

(4) In any action [referred to in] subsection (1) above—

(a)   it shall not be necessary for the pursuer to obtain a warrant for the citation of any person, and the action may commence and proceed without such citation;

(b)   no decree shall be granted in favour of the pursuer unless the grounds of action have been substantiated by sufficient evidence, and section 36(3) of the Sheriff Courts (Scotland) Act 1971 shall not apply in relation to any such action which is a summary cause.

(5)   No enactment empowering the sheriff to remit an action to the Court of Session shall apply in relation to proceedings [referred to in] subsection (1) above.

(6)   Section 3(5) and (6) of this Act shall apply for the purposes of this section as they apply for the purposes of that section, with the substitution, for references to [a court that are references to the family court or] a magistrates' court, of reference to the sheriff.

[(7)   In this section, "the Maintenance Regulation" means Council Regulation (EC) No 4/2009 including as applied in relation to Denmark by virtue of the Agreement made on 19th October 2005 between the European Community and the Kingdom of Denmark.]

### 5 Variation and revocation of maintenance order made in United Kingdom

(1) This section applies to a maintenance order a certified copy of which has been sent to a reciprocating country in pursuance of section 2 of this Act and to a maintenance order made by virtue of section 3 or 4 thereof which has been confirmed by a competent court in such a country.

(2) A court in the United Kingdom having power to vary a maintenance order to which this section applies shall have power to vary that order by a provisional order.

(3) Where the court hearing an application for the variation of a maintenance order to which this section applies proposes to vary it by increasing the rate of the payments under the order then, unless either—

(a)   both the payer and the payee under the order appear in the proceedings, or

(b)   the applicant appears and the appropriate process has been duly served on the other party,

the order varying the order shall be a provisional order.

[. . .]

(4) Where a court in the United Kingdom makes a provisional order varying a maintenance order to which this section applies, the prescribed officer of the court shall send in the prescribed manner to the court in a reciprocating country having power to confirm the provisional order a certified copy of the provisional order together with a document, authenticated in the prescribed manner, setting out or summarising the evidence given in the proceedings.

(5) Where a certified copy of a provisional order made by a court in a reciprocating country, being an order varying or revoking a maintenance order, to which this section applies, together with a document, duly authenticated, setting out or summarising the evidence given in the proceedings in which the provisional order was made, is received by the court in the United Kingdom which made the maintenance order, that court may confirm or refuse to confirm the provisional order and, if that order is an order varying the maintenance order, confirm it either without alteration or with such alterations as it thinks reasonable.

(6) For the purpose of determining whether a provisional order should be confirmed under subsection (5) above, the court shall proceed as if an application for the variation or revocation, as the case may be, of the maintenance order in question, had been made to it.

(7) Where a maintenance order to which this section applies has been varied by an order (including a provisional order which has been confirmed) made by a court in the United Kingdom or by a

competent court in a reciprocating country, the maintenance order shall, as from [the date on which under the provisions of the order the variation is to take effect], have effect as varied by that order and, where that order was a provisional order, as if that order had been made in the form in which it was confirmed, and as if it had never been a provisional order.

(8) Where a maintenance order to which this section applies has been revoked by an order made by a court in the United Kingdom or by a competent court in a reciprocating country, including a provisional order made by the last-mentioned court which has been confirmed by a court in the United Kingdom, the maintenance order shall, as from [the date on which under the provisions of the order the revocation is to take effect], be deemed to have ceased to have effect except as respects any arrears due under the maintenance order at that date.

(9) Where before a maintenance order made by virtue of section 3 or 4 of this Act is confirmed a document, duly authenticated, setting out or summarising evidence taken in a reciprocating country for the purpose of proceedings relating to the confirmation of the order is received by the court in the United Kingdom which made the order, or that court, in compliance with a request made to it by a court in such a country, takes the evidence of a person residing in the United Kingdom for the purpose of such proceedings, the court in the United Kingdom which made the order shall consider that evidence and if, having done so, it appears to it that the order ought not to have been made—

(a) it shall, in such manner as may be prescribed, give to the person on whose application the maintenance order was made an opportunity to consider that evidence, to make representations with respect to it and to adduce further evidence; and

(b) after considering all the evidence and any representations made by that person, it may revoke the maintenance order.

. . .

### Orders made by Courts in reciprocating countries

#### 6 Registration in United Kingdom court of maintenance order made in reciprocating country

(1) This section applies to a maintenance order made, whether before or after the commencement of this Part of this Act, by a court in a reciprocating country, including such an order made by such a court which has been confirmed by a court in another reciprocating country but excluding a provisional order which has not been confirmed.

(2) Where a certified copy of an order to which this section applies is received by the Secretary of State from the responsible authority in a reciprocating country, and it appears to the Secretary of State that the payer under the order is residing [or has assets] in the United Kingdom, he shall send the copy of the order to the prescribed officer of the appropriate court.

(3) Where the prescribed officer of the appropriate court receives from the Secretary of State a certified copy of an order to which this section applies, he shall, subject to subsection (4) below, register the order in the prescribed manner in that court.

(4) Before registering an order under this section an officer of a court shall take such steps as he thinks fit for the purpose of ascertaining whether the payer under the order is residing [or has assets] within the jurisdiction of the court, and if after taking those steps he is satisfied that the payer is not [residing and has no assets within the jurisdiction of the court] he shall return the certified copy of the order to the Secretary of State with a statement giving such information as he possesses as to the whereabouts of the payer [and the nature and location of his assets].

#### 7 Confirmation by United Kingdom court of provisional maintenance order made in reciprocating country

(1) This section applies to a maintenance order made, whether before or after the commencement of this Part of this Act, by a court in a reciprocating country being a provisional order.

(2) Where a certified copy of an order to which this section applies together with—

(a) a document, duly authenticated, setting out or summarising the evidence given in the proceedings in which the order was made; and

(b)  a statement of the grounds on which the making of the order might have been opposed by the payer under the order,

is received by the Secretary of State from the responsible authority in a reciprocating country, and it appears to the Secretary of State that the payer under the order is residing in the United Kingdom, he shall send the copy of the order and documents which accompanied it to the prescribed officer of the appropriate court, and that court shall—

(i)  if the payer under the order establishes [any grounds on which he might have opposed the making of the order] in the proceedings in which the order was made, refuse to confirm the order; and

(ii)  in any other case, confirm the order either without alteration or with such alterations as it thinks reasonable.

(3)  In any proceedings for the confirmation under this section of a provisional order, the statement received from the court which made the order of the grounds on which the making of the order might have been opposed by the payer under the order shall be conclusive evidence that the payer might have [opposed the making of the order on any of those grounds].

. . .

(5)  The prescribed officer of a court having power under this section to confirm a provisional order shall, if the court confirms the order, register the order in the prescribed manner in that court, and shall, if the court refuses to confirm the order, return the certified copy of the order and the documents which accompanied it to the Secretary of State.

[(5A)  Where [the family court] confirms a provisional order under this section, it [may] at the same time exercise one of its powers under subsection (5B) below.

(5B)  The powers of the court are—

(a)  the power to order that payments under the order be made directly to [the court];

(b)  the power to order that payments under the order be made to [the court] by such method of payment falling within section [1(5) of the Maintenance Enforcement Act 1991] (standing order, etc) as may be specified;

(c)  the power to make an attachment of earnings order under the Attachment of Earnings Act 1971 to secure payments under the order.

(5C)  In deciding [whether to exercise any of its] powers under subsection (5B) above [. . .], the court shall have regard to any representations made by the payer under the order.

(5D)  [Subsection (6) of section 1 of the Maintenance Enforcement Act 1991] (power of court to require debtor to open account) shall apply for the purposes of subsection (5B) above as it applies for the purposes of that section but as if for paragraph (a) there were substituted—

(a)  the court proposes to exercise its power under paragraph (b) of section 7(5B) of the Maintenance Orders (Reciprocal Enforcement) Act 1972, and.]

(6)  If [notice of] the proceedings for the confirmation of the provisional order cannot be duly served on the payer under that order the officer by whom the certified copy of the order was received shall return that copy and the documents which accompanied it to the Secretary of State with a statement giving such information as he possesses as to the whereabouts of the payer.

. . .

## 8 Enforcement of maintenance order registered in United Kingdom court

(1)  Subject to subsection (2) below, a registered order may be enforced in the United Kingdom as if it had been made by the registering court and as if that court had had jurisdiction to make it; and proceedings for or with respect to the enforcement of any such order may be taken accordingly.

(2)  Subsection (1) above does not apply to an order which is for the time being registered [. . .] in the High Court of Justice in Northern Ireland under Part II of the Maintenance and Affiliation Orders Act (Northern Ireland) 1966.

(3)  Any person for the time being under an obligation to make payments in pursuance of [an order

registered in a court in Northern Ireland] shall give notice of any change of address to the [clerk of that] court, and any person failing without reasonable excuse to give such a notice shall be liable on summary conviction to a fine not exceeding [level 2 on the standard scale].

[...]

(6) In any proceedings for or with respect to the enforcement of an order which is for the time being registered in any court under this Part of this Act a certificate of arrears sent to the prescribed officer of the court shall be evidence of the facts stated therein.

(7) Subject to subsection (8) below, sums of money payable under a registered order shall be payable in accordance with the order as from [the date on which they are required to be paid under the provisions of the order].

(8) The court having power under section 7 of this Act to confirm a provisional order may, if it decides to confirm the order, direct that the sums of money payable under it shall be deemed to have been payable in accordance with the order as from [the date on which they are required to be paid under the provisions of the order or such later date] as it may specify; and subject to any such direction, a maintenance order registered under the said section 7 shall be treated as if it had been made in the form in which it was confirmed and as if it had never been a provisional order.

. . .

### 9 Variation and revocation of maintenance order registered in United Kingdom court

(1) Subject to the provisions of this section, the registering court—

(a) shall have the like power, on an application made by the payer or payee under a registered order, to vary or revoke the order as if it had been made by the registering court and as if that court had had jurisdiction to make it; and

(b) shall have power to vary or revoke a registered order by a provisional order.

. . .

[(1A) The powers conferred by subsection (1) above are not exercisable in relation to so much of a registered order as provides for the payment of a lump sum.

(1B) The registering court shall not vary or revoke a registered order if neither the payer nor the payee under the order is resident in the United Kingdom.]

(2) The registering court shall not vary a registered order otherwise than by a provisional order unless—

(a) both the payer and the payee under the registered order are for the time being residing in the United Kingdom; or

(b) the application is made by the payee under the registered order; or

(c) the variation consists of a reduction in the rate of the payments under the registered order and is made solely on the ground that there has been a change in the financial circumstances of the payer since the registered order was made or, in the case of an order registered under section 7 of this Act, since the registered order was confirmed, and the courts in the reciprocating country in which the maintenance order in question was made do not have power, according to the law in force in that country, to confirm provisional orders varying maintenance orders.

(3) The registering court shall not revoke a registered order otherwise than by a provisional order unless both the payer and the payee under the registered order are for the time being residing in the United Kingdom.

(4) On an application for the revocation of a registered order the registering court shall, unless both the payer and the payee under the registered order are for the time being residing in the United Kingdom, apply the law applied by the reciprocating country in which the registered order was made; but where by virtue of this subsection the registering court is required to apply that law, that court may make a provisional order if it has reason to believe that the ground on which the application is made is a ground on which the order could be revoked according to the law applied by the reciprocating country, notwithstanding that it has not been established that it is such a ground.

(5) Where the registering court makes a provisional order varying or revoking a registered order the

prescribed officer of the court shall send in the prescribed manner to the court in the reciprocating country which made the registered order a certified copy of the provisional order together with a document, authenticated in the prescribed manner, setting out or summarising the evidence given in the proceedings.

(6) Where a certified copy of a provisional order made by a court in a reciprocating country, being an order varying a registered order, together with a document, duly authenticated, setting out or summarising the evidence given in the proceedings in which the provisional order was made, is received by the registering court, that court may confirm the order either without alteration or with such alterations as it thinks reasonable or refuse to confirm the order.

(7) For the purpose of determining whether a provisional order should be confirmed under subsection (6) above the court shall proceed as if an application for the variation of the registered order had been made to it.

(8) Where a registered order has been varied by an order (including a provisional order which has been confirmed) made by a court in the United Kingdom or by a competent court in a reciprocating country, the registered order shall, as from [the date on which under the provisions of the order the variation is to take effect], have effect as varied by that order and, where that order was a provisional order, as if that order had been made in the form in which it was confirmed and as if it had never been a provisional order.

(9) Where a registered order has been revoked by an order made by a court in the United Kingdom or by a competent court in a reciprocating country, including a provisional order made by the first-mentioned court which has been confirmed by a competent court in a reciprocating country, the registered order shall, as from [the date on which under the provisions of the order the revocation is to take effect], be deemed to have ceased to have effect except as respects any arrears due under the registered order at that date.

(10) The prescribed officer of the registering court shall register in the prescribed manner any order varying a registered order other than a provisional order which is not confirmed.

. . .

## 10 Cancellation of registration and transfer of order

(1) Where—

(a)  a registered order is revoked by an order made by the registering court; or

(b)  a registered order is revoked by a provisional order made by that court which has been confirmed by a court in a reciprocating country and notice of the confirmation is received by the registering court; or

(c)  a registered order is revoked by an order made by a court in such a country and notice of the revocation is received by the registering court,

the prescribed officer of the registering court shall cancel the registration; but any arrears due under the registered order at the date when its registration is cancelled by virtue of this subsection shall continue to be recoverable as if the registration had not been cancelled.

(2) Where the prescribed officer of the registering court is of opinion that the payer under a registered order [is not residing within the jurisdiction of that court and has no assets within that jurisdiction against which the order can be effectively enforced], he shall cancel the registration of the order and, subject to subsection (3) below, shall send the certified copy of the order to the Secretary of State.

. . .

(5) Where the certified copy of an order is received by the Secretary of State under this section and it appears to him that the payer under the order is [residing or has assets] in the United Kingdom, he shall transfer the order to the appropriate court by sending the certified copy of the order together with the related documents to the prescribed officer of the appropriate court and, subject to subsection (6) below, that officer shall register the order in the prescribed manner in that court.

(6) Before registering an order in pursuance of subsection (4) or (5) above an officer of a court shall take such steps as he thinks fit for the purpose of ascertaining whether the payer is residing [or has

assets] within the jurisdiction of the court, and if after taking those steps he is satisfied that the payer is not [residing and has no assets within the jurisdiction of the court] he shall send the certified copy of the order to the Secretary of State.

(7) The officer of a court who is required by any of the foregoing provisions of this section to send to the Secretary of State or to the prescribed officer of another court the certified copy of an order shall send with that copy—

(a)  a certificate of arrears signed by him;

(b)  a statement giving such information as he possesses as to the whereabouts of the payer [and the nature and location of his assets]; and

(c)  any relevant documents in his possession relating to the case.

. . .

**11  Steps to be taken by Secretary of State where payer under certain orders is not residing in the United Kingdom**

(1) If [at any time] it appears to the Secretary of State that the payer under a maintenance order, a certified copy of which has been received by him from a reciprocating country, is not residing [and has no assets in the United Kingdom,] he shall send to the responsible authority in that country or, if having regard to all the circumstances he thinks it proper to do so, to the responsible authority in another reciprocating country—

(a)  the certified copy of the order in question and a certified copy of any order varying that order;

(b)  if the order has at any time been a registered order, a certificate of arrears signed by the prescribed officer;

(c)  a statement giving such information as the Secretary of State possesses as to the whereabouts of the payer [and the nature and location of his assets]; and

(d)  any other relevant documents in his possession relating to the case.

(2) Where the documents mentioned in subsection (1) above are sent to the responsible authority in a reciprocating country other than that in which the order in question was made, the Secretary of State shall inform the responsible authority in the reciprocating country in which that order was made of what he has done.

*Appeals*

**12  Appeals**

(1) No appeal shall lie from a provisional order made in pursuance of any provision of this Part of this Act by a court in the United Kingdom.

(2) Where in pursuance of any such provision any such court confirms or refuses to confirm a provisional order made by a court in a reciprocating country, whether a maintenance order or an order varying or revoking a maintenance order, the payer or payee under the maintenance order shall have the like right of appeal (if any) from the confirmation of, or refusal to confirm, the provisional order as he would have if that order were not a provisional order and the court which confirmed or refused to confirm it had made or, as the case may be, refused to make it.

(3) Where in pursuance of any such provision any such court makes, or refuses to make, an order varying or revoking a maintenance order made by a court in a reciprocating country, then, subject to subsection (1) above, the payer or payee under the maintenance order shall have the like right of appeal (if any) from that order or from the refusal to make it as he would have if the maintenance order had been made by the first-mentioned court.

(4) Nothing in this section (except subsection (1)) shall be construed as affecting any right of appeal conferred by any other enactment.

*Evidence*

### 13 Admissibility of evidence given in reciprocating country

(1) A statement contained in—

(a) a document, duly authenticated, which purports to set out or summarise evidence given in proceedings in a court in a reciprocating country; or

(b) a document, duly authenticated, which purports to set out or summarise evidence taken in such a country for the purpose of proceedings in a court in the United Kingdom under this Part of this Act, whether in response to a request made by such a court or otherwise; or

(c) a document, duly authenticated, which purports to have been received in evidence in proceedings in a court in such a country or to be a copy of a document so received,

shall in any proceedings in a court in the United Kingdom relating to a maintenance order to which this Part of this Act applies be admissible as evidence of any fact stated therein to the same extent as oral evidence of that fact is admissible in those proceedings.

(2) A document purporting to set out or summarise evidence given as mentioned in subsection (1) (a) above, or taken as mentioned in subsection (1)(b) above, shall be deemed to be duly authenticated for the purposes of that subsection if the document purports to be certified by the judge, magistrate or other person before whom the evidence was given, or, as the case may be, by whom it was taken, to be the original document containing or recording, or, as the case may be, summarising, that evidence or a true copy of that document.

(3) A document purporting to have been received in evidence as mentioned in subsection (1)(c) above, or to be a copy of a document so received, shall be deemed to be duly authenticated for the purposes of that subsection if the document purports to be certified by a judge, magistrate or officer of the court in question to have been, or to be a true copy of a document which has been, so received.

(4) It shall not be necessary in any such proceedings to prove the signature or official position of the person appearing to have given such a certificate.

(5) Nothing in this section shall prejudice the admission in evidence of any document which is admissible in evidence apart from this section.

### 14 Obtaining of evidence needed for purpose of certain proceedings

(1) Where for the purpose of any proceedings in a court in a reciprocating country relating to a maintenance order to which this Part of this Act applies a request is made by or on behalf of that court for the taking in the United Kingdom of the evidence of a person residing therein relating to matters specified in the request, such court in the United Kingdom as may be prescribed shall have power to take that evidence and, after giving notice of the time and place at which the evidence is to be taken to such persons and in such manner as it thinks fit, shall take the evidence in such manner as may be prescribed.

Evidence taken in compliance with such a request shall be sent in the prescribed manner by the prescribed officer of the court to the court in the reciprocating country by or on behalf of which the request was made.

(2) Where any person, not being the payer or the payee under the maintenance order to which the proceedings in question relate, is required by virtue of this section to give evidence before a court in the United Kingdom, the court may order that there shall be paid—

(a) if the court is a court in England, Wales or Scotland, out of moneys provided by Parliament;

. . .

(5) A court in the United Kingdom may for the purpose of any proceedings in that court under this Part of this Act relating to a maintenance order to which this Part of this Act applies request a court in a reciprocating country to take or provide evidence relating to such matters as may be specified in the request and may remit the case to that court for that purpose.

(6) [...]

### 15 Order, etc made abroad need not be proved

For the purposes of this Part of this Act, unless the contrary is shown—

(a) any order made by a court in a reciprocating country purporting to bear the seal of that court or to be signed by any person in his capacity as a judge, magistrate or officer of the court, shall be deemed without further proof to have been duly sealed or, as the case may be, to have been signed by that person;

(b) the person by whom the order was signed shall be deemed without further proof to have been a judge, magistrate or officer, as the case may be, of that court when he signed it and, in the case of an officer, to have been authorised to sign it; and

(c) a document purporting to be a certified copy of an order made by a court in a reciprocating country shall be deemed without further proof to be such a copy.

## *Supplemental*

### 16 Payment of sums under orders made abroad: conversion of currency

(1) Payment of sums due under a registered order shall, while the order is registered in a court in England, Wales or Northern Ireland, be made in such manner and to such person as may be prescribed.

(2) Where the sums required to be paid under a registered order are expressed in a currency other than the currency of the United Kingdom, then, as from the relevant date, the order shall be treated as if it were an order requiring the payment of such sums in the currency of the United Kingdom as, on the basis of the rate of exchange prevailing at that date, are equivalent to the sums so required to be paid.

(3) Where the sum specified in any statement, being a statement of the amount of any arrears due under a maintenance order made by a court in a reciprocating country, is expressed in a currency other than the currency of the United Kingdom, that sum shall be deemed to be such sum in the currency of the United Kingdom as, on the basis of the rate of exchange prevailing at the relevant date, is equivalent to the sum so specified.

(4) For the purposes of this section a written certificate purporting to be signed by an officer of any bank in the United Kingdom certifying that a specified rate of exchange prevailed between currencies at a specified date and that at such rate a specified sum in the currency of the United Kingdom is equivalent to a specified sum in another specified currency shall be evidence of the rate of exchange so prevailing on that date and of the equivalent sums in terms of the respective currencies.

(5) In this section "the relevant date" means—

(a) in relation to a registered order or to a statement of arrears due under a maintenance order made by a court in a reciprocating country, the date on which the order first becomes a registered order or (if earlier) the date on which it is confirmed by a court in the United Kingdom;

(b) in relation to a registered order which has been varied, the date on which the last order varying that order is registered in a court in the United Kingdom or (if earlier) the date on which the last order varying that order is confirmed by such a court.

. . .

### 17 Proceedings in [the family court in England and Wales or in magistrates' courts in Northern Ireland]

[. . .]

. . .

[(5A) Where the respondent to an application for the variation or revocation of—

(a) a maintenance order made by [the family court], being an order to which section 5 of this Act applies; or

(b) a registered order which is registered in [the family court],

is residing in a reciprocating country, [the family court] shall have jurisdiction to hear the application (where it would not have such jurisdiction apart from this subsection) if it would have had jurisdiction to hear it had the respondent been [habitually resident] in England and Wales.]

. . .

(7) Where the [respondent] to [an application] for the variation or revocation—

(a) of a maintenance order made by [the family court in England and Wales or a magistrates' court in Northern Ireland], being an order to which section 5 of this Act applies; or

(b) of a registered order registered in [the family court in England and Wales or a magistrates' court in Northern Ireland],

does not appear at the time and place appointed for the hearing of [the application], but the court is satisfied that the [respondent] is residing in a reciprocating country, the court may proceed to hear and determine [the application] at the time and place appointed for the hearing or for any adjourned hearing in like manner as if the [respondent] had appeared at that time and place.

. . .

**[18  Rules of court]**

[(A1)  Rules of court may make provision with respect to the matters that would be mentioned in any of paragraphs (b), (c), (e) and (f) of subsection (1) if references in those paragraphs to a magistrates' court, or to magistrates' courts, were references to the family court.]

(1) [The matters referred to in subsections (A1) and (2) are—]

(a) the circumstances in which anything authorised or required by this Part of this Act to be done by, to or before a magistrates' court acting [in a particular [petty sessions district]] or by, to or before an officer of that court may be done by, to or before a magistrates' court acting [in such other [petty sessions district]] as the rules may provide or by, to or before an officer of that court;

(b) the orders made, or other things done, by a magistrates' court, or an officer of such a court, under this Part of this Act, or by a court in a reciprocating country, notice of which is to be given to such persons as the rules may provide and the manner in which such notice shall be given;

(c) the cases and manner in which courts in reciprocating countries are to be informed of orders made, or other things done, by a magistrates' court under this Part of this Act;

(d) the cases and manner in which a justices' clerk may take evidence needed for the purpose of proceedings in a court in a reciprocating country relating to a maintenance order to which this Part of this Act applies;

(e) the circumstances and manner in which cases may be remitted by magistrates' courts to courts in reciprocating countries;

(f) the circumstances and manner in which magistrates' courts may for the purposes of this Part of this Act communicate with courts in reciprocating countries.

[(1A)  For the purpose of giving effect to this Part of this Act, [rules of court] may make, in relation to any proceedings brought under or by virtue of this Part of this Act, any provision not covered by subsection [(A1)] above which—

(a) falls within subsection (2) of section 93 of the Children Act 1989, and

(b) may be made in relation to relevant proceedings under that section.]

. . .

**21  Interpretation of Part I**

(1) In this Part of this Act—

"affiliation order" means an order (however described) adjudging, finding or declaring a person to be the father of a child, whether or not it also provides for the maintenance of the child;

"the appropriate court"[—

(a)] in relation to a person residing [or having assets] in England and [Wales means the family court;

. . .

"certificate of arrears", in relation to a maintenance order, means a certificate certifying that the sum specified in the certificate is to the best of the information or belief of the officer giving the certificate the amount of the arrears due under the order at the date of the certificate or, as the case may be, that to the best of his information or belief there are no arrears due thereunder at that date;

"certified copy", in relation to an order of a court, means a copy of the order certified by the proper officer of the court to be a true copy;

"court" includes any tribunal or person having power to make, confirm, enforce, vary or revoke a maintenance order;

[. . .]

"maintenance order" means an order (however described) of any of the following descriptions, that is to say—

(a) an order (including an affiliation order or order consequent upon an affiliation order) which provides for the [payment of a lump sum or the making of periodical payments] towards the maintenance of any person, being a person whom the person liable to make payments under the order is, according to the law applied in the place where the order was made, liable to maintain; and

[(aa) an order which has been made in Scotland, on or after the granting of a decree of divorce, for the payment of a periodical allowance by one party to the marriage to the other party;]

(b) an affiliation order or order consequent upon an affiliation order, being an order which provides for the payment by a person adjudged, found or declared to be a child's father of expenses incidental to the child's birth or, where the child has died, of his funeral expenses,

and, in the case of a maintenance order which has been varied, means that order as varied;

"order", as respects Scotland, includes any interlocutor, and any decree or provision contained in an interlocutor;

"payee", in relation to a maintenance order, means the person entitled to the payments for which the order provides;

"payer", in relation to a maintenance order, means the person liable to make payments under the order;

. . .

"provisional order" means (according to the context)—

(a) an order made by a court in the United Kingdom which is provisional only and has no effect unless and until confirmed, with or without alteration, by a competent court in a reciprocating country; or

(b) an order made by a court in a reciprocating country which is provisional only and has no effect unless and until confirmed, with or without alteration, by a court in the United Kingdom having power under this Part of this Act to confirm it;

"reciprocating country" has the meaning assigned to it by section 1 of this Act;

"registered order" means a maintenance order which is for the time being registered in a court in the United Kingdom under this Part of this Act;

"registering court", in relation to a registered order, means the court in which that order is for the time being registered under this Part of this Act;

"the responsible authority", in relation to a reciprocating country, means any person who in that country has functions similar to those of the Secretary of State under this Part of this Act;

["revoke" and "revocation" include discharge].

(2) For the purposes of this Part of this Act an order shall be taken to be a maintenance order so far (but only so far) as it relates to the [payment of a lump sum or the making of periodical payments] as mentioned in paragraph (a) of the definition of "maintenance order" in subsection (1) above or to the payment by a person adjudged, found or declared to be a child's father of any such expenses as are mentioned in paragraph (b) of that definition.

(3) Any reference in this Part of this Act to the payment of money for the maintenance of a child shall be construed as including a reference to the payment of money for the child's education.

*Amendments, repeals and transitional provisions*

...

### 23 Maintenance order registered in High Court under the Maintenance Orders etc Act 1920

(1) Where a country or territory, being a country or territory to which at the commencement of section 1 of this Act the Maintenance Orders (Facilities for Enforcement) Act 1920 extended, becomes a reciprocating country, then, if immediately before the Order in Council made under section 12 of that Act extending that Act to that country or territory was revoked any maintenance order made by a court in that country or territory was registered in the High Court [or the High Court of Justice in Northern Ireland] under section 1 of that Act, [subsection (1A) applies in relation to the order].

[(1A) Where the order was at that time registered in the High Court, that court may, on an application by the payer or the payee under the order or of its own motion, transfer the order to the family court, with a view to the order being registered in the family court under this Part of this Act; and where the order was at that time registered in the High Court of Justice in Northern Ireland, that court] may, on an application by the payer or the payee under the order or of its own motion, transfer the order to such magistrates' court [in Northern Ireland] as having regard to the place where the payer is residing and to all the circumstances it thinks most appropriate, with a view to the order being registered in that [magistrates] court under this Part of this Act.

[(1B) Where the High Court transfers an order to the family court under this section it shall—

(a) cause a certified copy of the order to be sent to an officer of the family court, and

(b) cancel the registration of the order in the High Court.]

...

(3) The [[. . .] officer] of the court who receives a certified copy of an order sent to him under this section shall register the order in the prescribed manner in that court.

(4) On registering a maintenance order in [a] court by virtue of this section the [officer registering it] shall, if the order is registered in that court under Part I of the Maintenance Orders Act 1958, cancel that registration.

(5) [. . .]

[(6) In this section "appropriate officer" [, in relation to a magistrates' court in Northern Ireland, means the clerk of the court].]

### 24 Application of Part I to certain orders and proceedings under the Maintenance Orders etc Act 1920

Where Her Majesty proposes by an Order in Council under section 1 of this Act to designate as a reciprocating country a country or territory to which at the commencement of that section the Maintenance Orders (Facilities for Enforcement) Act 1920 extended, that Order in Council may contain such provisions as Her Majesty considers expedient for the purpose of securing—

(a) that the provisions of this Part of this Act apply, subject to such modifications as may be specified in the Order, to maintenance orders, or maintenance orders of a specified class—

(i) made by a court in England, Wales or Northern Ireland against a person residing [or having assets] in that country or territory, or

(ii) made by a court in that country or territory against a person residing [or having assets] in England, Wales or Northern Ireland,

being orders to which immediately before the date of the coming into operation of the Order in Council the said Act of 1920 applied, except any order which immediately before that date is registered in the High Court or the High Court of Justice in Northern Ireland under section 1 of that Act;

(b) that any maintenance order, or maintenance order of a specified class, made by a court in that country or territory which has been confirmed by a court in England, Wales or Northern Ireland under section 4 of the said Act of 1920 and is in force immediately before that date is registered under section 7 of this Act;

(c) that any proceedings brought under or by virtue of a provision of the said Act of 1920 in a court in England, Wales or Northern Ireland which are pending at that date, being proceedings affecting a person resident in that country or territory, are continued as if they had been brought under or by virtue of the corresponding provision of this Part of this Act.

## PART II

## Reciprocal Enforcement of Claims for the Recovery of Maintenance

*Convention countries*

### 25 Convention countries

(1) Her Majesty may by Order in Council declare that any country or territory specified in the Order, being a country or territory outside the United Kingdom to which the Maintenance Convention extends, is a convention country for the purposes of this Part of this Act.

(2) In this section "the Maintenance Convention" means the United Nations Convention on the Recovery Abroad of Maintenance done at New York on 20th June 1956.

*Application by person in the United Kingdom for recovery, etc of maintenance in convention country*

### 26 Application by person in United Kingdom for recovery, etc of maintenance in convention country

(1) Where a person in the United Kingdom ("the applicant") claims to be entitled to recover in a convention country maintenance from another person, and that other person is for the time being subject to the jurisdiction of that country, the applicant may apply to the Secretary of State, in accordance with the provisions of this section, to have his claim for the recovery of maintenance from that other person transmitted to that country.

(2) Where the applicant seeks to vary any provision made in a convention country for the payment by any other person of maintenance to the applicant, and that other person is for the time being subject to the jurisdiction of that country, the applicant may apply to the Secretary of State, in accordance with the provisions of this section, to have his application for the variation of that provision transmitted to that country.

(3) An application to the Secretary of State under subsection (1) or (2) above shall be made through the appropriate officer, and that officer shall assist the applicant in completing an application which will comply with the requirements of the law applied by the convention country and shall send the application to the Secretary of State, together with such other documents, if any, as are required by that law.

(4) On receiving an application from the appropriate officer the Secretary of State shall transmit it, together with any accompanying documents, to the appropriate authority in the convention country, unless he is satisfied that the application is not made in good faith or that it does not comply with the requirements of the law applied by that country.

(5) The Secretary of State may request the appropriate officer to obtain from the court of which he is an officer such information relating to the application as may be specified in the request, and it shall be the duty of the court to furnish the Secretary of State with the information he requires.

[(6) The appropriate officer for the purposes of this section is—

(a) where the applicant is residing in England and Wales, [an officer of the family court];

. . .

*Application by person in convention country for recovery of maintenance in England, Wales or Northern Ireland*

**[27A  Applications for recovery of maintenance in England and Wales]**

[(1) This section applies to any application which—

(a)  is received by the Lord Chancellor from the appropriate authority in a convention country, and

(b)  is an application by a person in that country for the recovery of maintenance from another person who is for the time being residing in England and Wales.

(2) Subject to sections 27B to 28B of this Act, an application to which this section applies shall be treated for the purposes of any enactment as if it were an application for a maintenance order under the relevant Act, made at the time when the application was received by the Lord Chancellor. [This subsection does not confer jurisdiction on a court in England and Wales that it would not otherwise have.]

(3) In the case of an application for maintenance for a child (or children) alone, the relevant Act is the Children Act 1989.

(4) In any other case, the relevant Act is the Domestic Proceedings and Magistrates' Courts Act 1978.

(5) In subsection (3) above, "child" means the same as in Schedule 1 to the Children Act 1989.]

**[27B  Sending application to the [family]**

[(1) On receipt of an application to which section 27A of this Act applies, the Lord Chancellor shall send it, together with any accompanying documents, to the [family court].

(2) [If] notice of the hearing of the application by [the family court] cannot be duly served on the respondent, the [family] court shall return the application and the accompanying documents to the Lord Chancellor with a statement giving such information as [the family court] possesses as to the whereabouts of the respondent.

(3) If the application is returned to the Lord Chancellor under subsection (2) above, then, unless he is satisfied that the respondent is not residing in the United Kingdom, he shall deal with it in accordance with subsection (1) above or section [28D(1)] of this Act or send it to the Secretary of State to be dealt with in accordance with section 31 of this Act (as the circumstances of the case require).

[. . .]

**[27C  Applications to which section 27A applies: general]**

[(1) This section applies where [the family] court makes an order on an application to which section 27A of this Act applies.

(2) [. . .]

(3) The court [may], at the same time that it makes the order, exercise one of its powers under subsection (4) below.

(4) Those powers are—

(a)  the power to order that payments under the order be made directly to [the court];

(b)  the power to order that payments under the order be made to [the court] by such method of payment falling within section [1(5) of the Maintenance Enforcement Act 1991] (standing order, etc) as may be specified;

(c)  the power to make an attachment of earnings order under the Attachment of Earnings Act 1971 to secure payments under the order.

(5) In deciding [whether to exercise any of its] powers under subsection (4) above [. . .], the court shall have regard to any representations made by the person liable to make payments under the order.

(6) [Subsection (6) of section 1 of the Maintenance Enforcement Act 1991] (power of court to require debtor to open account) shall apply for the purposes of subsection (4) above as it applies for the purposes of that section, but as if for paragraph (a) there were substituted—

"(a) the court proposes to exercise its power under paragraph (b) of section 27C(4) of the Maintenance Orders (Reciprocal Enforcement) Act 1972, and".

(7) The [. . .] court shall register the order in the prescribed manner [. . .].]

### [28 Applications by spouses under the Domestic Proceedings and Magistrates' Courts Act 1978]

[(1) [On] hearing an application which by virtue of section 27A of this Act is to be treated as if it were an application for a maintenance order under the Domestic Proceedings and Magistrates' Courts Act 1978[, the family court] may make any order on the application which it has power to make under section 2 or 19(1) of that Act.

(2) Part I of that Act shall apply in relation to such an application, and to any order made on such an application, with the following modifications—

(a)   sections 6 to 8, 16 to 18, 20ZA, 25[, 26] and 28(2) shall be omitted,

(b)   [. . .] and

(c)   section 32(2) shall be omitted.

(3) Subsections (1) and (2) above do not apply where section 28A of this Act applies.]

### [28A Applications by former spouses under the Domestic Proceedings and Magistrates' Courts Act 1978]

[(1) This section applies where in the case of any application which by virtue of section 27A of this Act is to be treated as if it were an application for a maintenance order under the Domestic Proceedings and Magistrates' Courts Act 1978 ("the 1978 Act")—

(a)   the applicant and respondent were formerly married,

(b)   their marriage was dissolved or annulled in a country or territory outside the United Kingdom by a divorce or annulment which is recognised as valid by the law of England and Wales,

(c)   an order for the payment of maintenance for the benefit of the applicant or a child of the family has, by reason of the divorce or annulment, been made by a court in a convention country, and

(d)   where the order for the payment of maintenance was made by a court of a different country from that in which the divorce or annulment was obtained, either the applicant or the respondent was resident in the convention country whose court made that order at the time that order was applied for.

(2) [The family court shall have jurisdiction to hear the application] notwithstanding the dissolution or annulment of the marriage.

(3) If the [family court] is satisfied that the respondent has failed to comply with the provisions of any order such as is mentioned in subsection (1)(c) above, it may (subject to subsections (4) and (5) below) make any order which it has power to make under section 2 or 19(1) of the 1978 Act.

(4) The court shall not make an order for the making of periodical payments for the benefit of the applicant or any child of the family unless the order made in the convention country provides for the making of periodical payments for the benefit of the applicant or, as the case may be, that child.

(5) The court shall not make an order for the payment of a lump sum for the benefit of the applicant or any child of the family unless the order made in the convention country provides for the payment of a lump sum to the applicant or, as the case may be, to that child.

(6) Part I of the 1978 Act shall apply in relation to the application, and to any order made on the application, with the following modifications—

(a)   section 1 shall be omitted,

(b)   for the reference in section 2(1) to any ground mentioned in section 1 of that Act there shall be substituted a reference to non-compliance with any such order as is mentioned in subsection (1)(c) of this section,

(c)   for the references in section 3(2) and (3) to the occurrence of the conduct which is alleged as the ground of the application there shall be substituted references to the breakdown of the marriage,

(d) the reference in section 4(2) to the subsequent dissolution or annulment of the marriage of the parties affected by the order shall be omitted,

(e) sections 6 to 8, 16 to 18, 20ZA [25, 26 and 28] shall be omitted,

(f) [. . .] and

(g) section 32(2) shall be omitted.

(7) A divorce or annulment obtained in a country or territory outside the United Kingdom shall be presumed for the purposes of this section to be one the validity of which is recognised by the law of England and Wales, unless the contrary is proved by the respondent.

(8) In this section, "child of the family" has the meaning given in section 88 of the 1978 Act.]

. . .

*Transfer, enforcement, variation and revocation of registered orders*

### 32 Transfer of orders

(1) Where the prescribed officer of the registering court is of opinion that the payer under a registered order has ceased to reside within the jurisdiction of that court, then, unless he is of opinion that the payer has ceased to reside in the United Kingdom, he shall, subject to subsection (2) below, send a certified copy of the order and the related documents to the Secretary of State, and if he is of opinion that the payer has ceased to reside in the United Kingdom he shall send a notice to that effect to the Secretary of State.

. . .

(3) Where a certified copy of an order is received by the Secretary of State under this section and it appears to him that the payer under the order is still residing in the United Kingdom, he shall transfer the order to the appropriate court by sending the copy of the order and the related documents to the prescribed officer of the appropriate court and, subject to subsection (4) below, that officer shall register the order in the prescribed manner in that court.

(4) Before registering an order in pursuance of subsection (2) or (3) above an officer of a court shall take such steps as he thinks fit for the purpose of ascertaining whether the payer under the order is residing within the jurisdiction of the court, and if after taking those steps he is satisfied that the payer is not so residing shall return the certified copy of the order and the related documents to the officer of the court or the Secretary of State, as the case may be, from whom he received them, together with a statement giving such information as he possesses as to the whereabouts of the payer.

(5) Where a certified copy of an order is received by the Secretary of State under this section and it appears to him that the payer under the order has ceased to reside in the United Kingdom he shall return the copy of the order and the related documents to the registering court.

(6) An officer of a court on registering an order in the court in pursuance of subsection (2) or (3) above shall give notice of the registration in the prescribed manner to the prescribed officer of the court in which immediately before its registration under this section the order was registered.

(7) The officer to whom notice is given under subsection (6) above shall on receiving the notice cancel the registration of the order in that court.

. . .

(8) In this section—

"the appropriate court",[—

(a)] in relation to a person residing in England and [Wales, means the family court;

. . .

"certificate of arrears" and "certified copy" have the same meanings respectively as in Part I of this Act;

"payer", in relation to a registered order, means the person liable to make payments under the order; and

"related documents" means—

    (a)  the application on which the order was made;

    (b)  a certificate of arrears signed by the prescribed officer of the registering court;

    (c)  a statement giving such information as he possesses as to the whereabouts of the payer; and

    (d)  any relevant documents in his possession relating to the case.

. . .

### 33 Enforcement of orders

(1) Subject to subsection (2) below, a registered order which is registered in a court other than the court by which the order was made may be enforced as if it had been made by the registering court and as if that court had had jurisdiction to make it; and proceedings for or with respect to the enforcement of any such order may be taken in accordance with this subsection but not otherwise.

. . .

(5) In any proceedings for or with respect to the enforcement of an order which is for the time being registered in any court under this Part of this Act a certificate of arrears sent under section 32 of this Act to the prescribed officer of the court shall be evidence of the facts stated therein.

(6) Part II of the Maintenance Orders Act 1950 (enforcement of certain orders throughout the United Kingdom) shall not apply to a registered order.

. . .

### 34 Variation and revocation of orders

(1) [Subject to [. . .] section 34A of this Act] where a registered order is registered in a court other than the court by which the order was made, the registering court shall have the like power to vary or revoke the order as if it had been made by the registering court and as if that court had had jurisdiction to make it; and no court other than the registering court shall have power to vary or revoke a registered order.

(2) Where the registering court revokes a registered order it shall cancel the registration.

(3) Where the Secretary of State receives from the appropriate authority in a convention country an application by a person in that country for the variation of a registered order, he [shall—

(a)  if the registering court is the family court, send the application together with any documents accompanying it to that court;

. . .

(4) Where a court in a part of the United Kingdom makes, or refuses to make, an order varying or revoking a registered order made by a court in another part thereof, any person shall have the like right of appeal (if any) against the order or refusal as he would have if the registered order had been made by the first-mentioned court.

. . .

### [34A Variation of orders by [the family court]

[(1) The provisions of this section shall have effect in relation to a registered order which is registered in [the family court] (whether or not the court made the order) in place of the following enactments, that is to say—

[(a)  section 1(3A) of the Maintenance Enforcement Act 1991;]

(b)  section 20ZA of the Domestic Proceedings and Magistrates' Courts Act 1978; and

(c)  paragraph 6A of Schedule 1 to the Children Act 1989.

(2) The power of [the family court] to vary a registered order shall include power, if the court is satisfied that payment has not been made in accordance with the order, to exercise one of its powers under subsection (3) below.

(3) The powers of the court are—

(a)  the power to order that payments under the order be made directly to [the court];

(b)  the power to order that payments under the order be made to [the court] by such method of payment falling within section [1(5) of the Maintenance Enforcement Act 1991] (standing order, etc) as may be specified;

(c)  the power to make an attachment of earnings order under the Attachment of Earnings Act 1971 to secure payments under the order.

[. . .]

(9)  In deciding, for the purposes of [subsection (2)] above, [whether to exercise any of its] powers under subsection (3) above [. . .], the court shall have regard to any representations made by the debtor [or the creditor].

(10)  [Subsection (6) of section 1 of the Maintenance Enforcement Act 1991] (power of court to require debtor to open account) shall apply for the purposes of subsection (3) above as it applies for the purposes of that section but as if for paragraph (a) there were substituted—

> "(a)  the court proposes to exercise its power under paragraph (b) of section 34A(3) of the Maintenance Orders (Reciprocal Enforcement) Act 1972, and".

(11)  In this section "creditor" and "debtor" have the same meaning as they have in [section 1 of the Maintenance Enforcement Act 1991].]

. . .

**[35  Further provisions with respect to variation etc of orders by [the family court]**

[(1)  Subsection (1A) applies in relation to an application for the variation or revocation of a registered order registered in [the family court] ("the registering court") made—

(a)  by the person against whom or on whose application the registered order was made, and

(b)  in circumstances where the person by or against whom the application is made is residing outside England and Wales.

(1A)  The registering court has jurisdiction to hear the application even though—

(a)  a party to the application is residing outside England and Wales [. . .],

(b)  [. . .].

(1B)  But if the application or part of it relates to a matter where jurisdiction falls to be determined by reference to the jurisdictional requirements of the Maintenance Regulation and Schedule 6 to the Civil Jurisdiction and Judgments (Maintenance) Regulations 2011, the registering court may not entertain the application or that part of it unless it has jurisdiction to do so by virtue of that Regulation and that Schedule.]

(2)  None of the powers of the court [. . .] under section 34A of this Act shall be exercisable in relation to such an application.

(3)  Where the respondent to an application for the variation or revocation of a registered order which is registered in [the family court] does not appear at the time and place appointed for the hearing of the application, but the court is satisfied—

(a)  that the respondent is residing outside England and Wales, and

(b)  that the prescribed notice of the making of the application and of the time and place appointed for the hearing has been given to the respondent in the prescribed manner,

the court may proceed to hear and determine the application at the time and place appointed for the hearing or for any adjourned hearing in like manner as if the respondent had appeared at that time and place.]

[(4)  In subsection (1B) "the Maintenance Regulation" means Council Regulation (EC) No 4/2009 including as applied in relation to Denmark by virtue of the Agreement made on 19th October 2005 between the European Community and the Kingdom of Denmark.]

. . .

*Supplemental*

### 36 Admissibility of evidence given in convention country

[(A1) A statement contained in a document mentioned in subsection (1) shall—

(a) in any proceedings in the family court arising out of an application to which section 27A(1) of this Act applies or an application made by any person for the variation or revocation of a registered order, or

(b) in proceedings on appeal from proceedings within paragraph (a),

be admissible as evidence of any fact stated to the same extent as oral evidence of that fact is admissible in those proceedings.]

(1) [The documents referred to in subsections (A1) and (1A) are—]

(a) a document, duly authenticated, which purports to set out or summarise evidence given in proceedings in a court in a convention country; [. . .]

(b) a document, duly authenticated, which purports to set out or summarise evidence taken in such a country for the purpose of proceedings in a court in the United Kingdom under this Part of this Act, whether in response to a request made on behalf of such a court or otherwise; [. . .]

(c) a document, duly authenticated, which purports to have been received in evidence in proceedings in a court in such a country, or to be a copy of a document so received.

. . .

(2) A document purporting to set out or summarise evidence given as mentioned in subsection (1)(a) above, or taken as mentioned in subsection (1)(b) above, shall be deemed to be duly authenticated for the purposes of that subsection if the document purports to be certified by the judge, magistrate or other person before whom the evidence was given or, as the case may be, by whom it was taken, to be the original document containing or recording, or, as the case may be, summarising, that evidence or a true copy of that document.

(3) A document purporting to have been received in evidence as mentioned in subsection (1)(c) above, or to be a copy of a document so received, shall be deemed to be duly authenticated for the purposes of that subsection if the document purports to be certified by a judge, magistrate or officer of the court in question to have been, or to be a true copy of a document which has been, so received.

(4) It shall not be necessary in any such proceedings to prove the signature or official position of the person appearing to have given such a certificate.

(5) Nothing in this section shall prejudice the admission in evidence of any document which is admissible in evidence apart from this section.

### 37 Obtaining of evidence for purpose of proceedings in United Kingdom court

(1) A court in the United Kingdom may for the purpose of any proceedings in that court under this Part of this Act arising out of an application received by the Secretary of State from a convention country request the Secretary of State to make to the appropriate authority or court in the convention country a request for the taking in that country of the evidence of a person residing therein relating to matters connected with the application.

(2) A request made by a court under this section shall—

(a) give details of the application in question;

(b) state the name and address of the person whose evidence is to be taken; and

(c) specify the matters relating to which the evidence of that person is required.

(3) If the Secretary of State is satisfied that a request made to him under this section contains sufficient information to enable the evidence of the person named in the request relating to the matters specified therein to be taken by a court or person in the convention country, he shall transmit the request to the appropriate authority or court in that country.

**38  Taking of evidence at request of court in convention country**

(1)  Where a request is made to the Secretary of State by or on behalf of a court in a convention country to obtain the evidence of a person residing in the United Kingdom relating to matters connected with an application to which section 26 of this Act applies, the Secretary of State shall request such court, or such officer of a court, as he may determine to take the evidence of that person relating to such matters connected with that application as may be specified in the request.

(2)  The court by which or officer by whom a request under subsection (1) above is received from the Secretary of State shall have power to take the evidence and, after giving notice of the time and place at which the evidence is to be taken to such persons and in such manner as it or he thinks fit, shall take the evidence of the person named in the request relating to the matters specified therein in such manner as may be prescribed; and the evidence so taken shall be sent in the prescribed manner by the prescribed officer to the court in the convention country by or on behalf of which the request referred to in subsection (1) above was made.

(3)  Where any person, not being the person by whom the application mentioned in subsection (1) above was made, is required by virtue of this section to give evidence before a court in the United Kingdom, the court may order that there shall be paid—

(a)  if the court is a court in England, Wales or Scotland, out of moneys provided by Parliament;

. . .

such sums as appear to the court reasonably sufficient to compensate that person for the expense, trouble or loss of time properly incurred in or incidental to his attendance.

. . .

**[38A  Rules of court]**

[(1)  [Rules of court] may make provision with respect to the orders made or other things done by [the family court or] a magistrates' court, or an officer of such a court, by virtue of this Part of this Act, notice of which is to be given to such persons as the rules may provide and the manner in which such notice shall be given.

(2)  For the purpose of giving effect to this Part of this Act, [rules of court] may make, in relation to any proceedings brought under or by virtue of this Part of this Act, any provision not covered by subsection (1) above which—

(a)  falls within subsection (2) of section 93 of the Children Act 1989, and

(b)  may be made in relation to relevant proceedings under that section.

. . .

**39  Interpretation of Part II**

In this Part of this Act—

[. . .]

["maintenance order" has the same meaning as in Part I of this Act;]

"prescribed" has the same meaning as in Part I of this Act;

"registered order" means an order which is for the time being registered in a court in the United Kingdom under this Part of this Act;

"registering court", in relation to a registered order, means the court in which that order is for the time being registered under this Part of this Act.

["revoke" and "revocation" include discharge.]

PART III

## Miscellaneous and Supplemental

*Further provisions relating to enforcement of maintenance orders and to applications for recovery of maintenance*

### 40 Power to apply Act to maintenance orders and applications for recovery of maintenance made in certain countries

Where Her Majesty is satisfied—

(a) that arrangements have been or will be made in a country or territory outside the United Kingdom to ensure that maintenance orders made by courts in the United Kingdom [. . .] can be enforced in that country or territory or that applications by persons in the United Kingdom for the recovery of maintenance from persons in that country or territory can be entertained by courts in that country or territory; and

(b) that in the interest of reciprocity it is desirable to ensure that maintenance orders made by courts in that country or territory [. . .] can be enforced in the United Kingdom or, as the case may be, that applications by persons in that country or territory for the recovery of maintenance from persons in the United Kingdom can be entertained by courts in the United Kingdom,

Her Majesty may by Order in Council make provision for applying the provisions of this Act, with such exceptions, adaptations and modifications as may be specified in the Order, to such orders or applications as are referred to in paragraphs (a) and (b) above and to maintenance and other orders made in connection with such applications by courts in the United Kingdom or in that country or territory.

*Provisions with respect to certain orders of magistrates' courts*

[. . .]

### 42 Provisional order for maintenance of party to marriage made by [. . .] court to cease to have effect on remarriage of party

(1) Where a [. . .] court has, by virtue of section 3 of this Act, made a provisional maintenance order consisting of, or including, a provision such as is mentioned in [section 2(1)(a) of the Domestic Proceedings and Magistrates' Courts Act 1978 (making of periodical payments by husband or wife)] [or Article 4(1)(a) of the Domestic Proceedings (Northern Ireland) Order 1980] and the order has been confirmed by a competent court in a reciprocating country, then, if after the making of that order the marriage of the parties of the proceedings in which the order was made is dissolved or annulled but the order continues in force, that order or, as the case may be, that provision thereof shall cease to have effect on the remarriage of the party in whose favour it was made, except in relation to any arrears due under it on the date of such remarriage and shall not be capable of being revived.

(2) For the avoidance of doubt it is hereby declared that references in this section to remarriage include references to a marriage which is by law void or voidable.

(3) [. . .]

*Supplemental provisions*

. . .

### 44 Exclusion of certain enactments relating to evidence

(1) Section 20 of the Family Law Reform Act 1969 (power of court hearing certain proceedings to require use of blood tests to determine paternity) and any corresponding enactment of the Parliament of Northern Ireland shall not apply to any proceedings under this Act, but the foregoing provision is without prejudice to the power of a court to allow the report of any person who has carried out such tests to be given in evidence in those proceedings.

(2) [The Evidence (Proceedings in Other Jurisdictions) Act 1975] shall not apply to the taking of evidence in the United Kingdom for the taking of which section 14 or section 38 of this Act provides.

### 45  Orders in Council

(1)  An Order in Council under section 1, section 25 or section 40 of this Act may be varied or revoked by a subsequent Order in Council thereunder, and an Order made by virtue of this section may contain such incidental, consequential and transitional provisions as Her Majesty considers expedient for the purposes of that section.

(2)  An Order in Council made under the said section 1 or the said section 40 shall be subject to annulment in pursuance of a resolution of either House of Parliament.

### 46  Financial provisions

There shall be paid out of moneys provided by Parliament—

(a)  any sums ordered by a court under section 14(2) or 38(3) of this Act to be paid out of moneys so provided; and

(b)  any increase attributable to the provisions of this Act in the sums payable under the Legal Aid and Advice Act 1949 or the Legal Aid (Scotland) Act 1967 out of moneys so provided.

### 47  Interpretation: general

. . .

(2)  References in this Act to a part of the United Kingdom are references to England and Wales, to Scotland, or to Northern Ireland.

. . .

(4)  Any reference in this Act to any other enactment is a reference thereto as amended, and includes a reference thereto as extended or applied, by or under any other enactment.

. . .

UK Statutes

# Domicile and Matrimonial Proceedings Act 1973 ch 45

PART I

## Domicile

### Husband and wife

**1 Abolition of wife's dependent domicile**

(1) Subject to subsection (2) below, the domicile of a married woman as at any time after the coming into force of this section shall, instead of being the same as her husband's by virtue only of marriage, be ascertained by reference to the same factors as in the case of any other individual capable of having an independent domicile.

(2) Where immediately before this section came into force a woman was married and then had her husband's domicile by dependence, she is to be treated as retaining that domicile (as a domicile of choice, if it is not also her domicile of origin) unless and until it is changed by acquisition or revival of another domicile either on or after the coming into force of this section.

(3) This section extends to England and Wales, Scotland and Northern Ireland.

[. . .]

### Minors and pupils

**3 Age at which independent domicile can be acquired**

(1) The time at which a person first becomes capable of having an independent domicile shall be when he attains the age of sixteen or marries under that age; and in the case of a person who immediately before 1st January 1974 was incapable of having an independent domicile, but had then attained the age of sixteen or been married, it shall be that date.

(2) This section extends to England and Wales and Northern Ireland (but not to Scotland).

**4 Dependent domicile of child not living with his father**

(1) Subsection (2) of this section shall have effect with respect to the dependent domicile of a child as at any time after the coming into force of this section when his father and mother are alive but living apart.

(2) The child's domicile as at that time shall be that of his mother if—

(a)   he then has his home with her and has no home with his father; or

(b)   he has at any time had her domicile by virtue of paragraph (a) above and has not since had a home with his father.

(3) As at any time after the coming into force of this section, the domicile of a child whose mother is dead shall be that which she last had before she died if at her death he had her domicile by virtue of subsection (2) above and he has not since had a home with his father.

(4) Nothing in this section prejudices any existing rule of law as to the cases in which a child's domicile is regarded as being, by dependence, that of his mother.

(5) In this section, "child" means a person incapable of having an independent domicile; [. . .]

(6) This section extends to England and Wales, Scotland and Northern Ireland.

PART II

## Jurisdiction in Matrimonial Proceedings (England and Wales)

### 5 Jurisdiction of High Court and [family court]

(1) Subsections (2) to (5) below shall have effect, subject to section 6(3) and (4) of this Act, with respect to the jurisdiction of the court to entertain [any of the following proceedings in relation to a marriage of a man and a woman]—

(a) proceedings for divorce, judicial separation or nullity of marriage; and

(b) proceedings for death to be presumed and a marriage to be dissolved in pursuance of section 19 of the Matrimonial Causes Act 1973 [. . .].

[(1A) In this Part of this Act—

["the Council Regulation" means Council Regulation (EC) No 2201/2003 of 27th November 2003 concerning jurisdiction and the recognition and enforcement of judgments in matrimonial matters and matters of parental responsibility;]

"Contracting State" means—

[(a) a party to the Council Regulation, that is to say, Belgium, Cyprus, Czech Republic, Germany, Greece, Spain, Estonia, France, Hungary, Ireland, Italy, Latvia, Lithuania, Luxembourg, Malta, Netherlands, Austria, Poland, Portugal, Slovakia, Slovenia, Finland, Sweden and the United Kingdom, and]

(b) a party which has subsequently adopted the Council Regulation; and

"the court" means the High Court [and the family court].]

[(2) The court shall have jurisdiction to entertain proceedings for divorce or judicial separation if (and only if)—

(a) the court has jurisdiction under the Council Regulation; or

(b) no court of a Contracting State has jurisdiction under the Council Regulation and either of the parties to the marriage is domiciled in England and Wales on the date when the proceedings are begun.]

[(3) The court shall have jurisdiction to entertain proceedings for nullity of marriage if (and only if)—

(a) the court has jurisdiction under the Council Regulation; or

(b) no court of a Contracting State has jurisdiction under the Council Regulation and either of the parties to the marriage—

(i) is domiciled in England and Wales on the date when the proceedings are begun; or

(ii) died before that date and either was at death domiciled in England and Wales or had been habitually resident in England and Wales throughout the period of one year ending with the date of death.]

[. . .]

(4) The court shall have jurisdiction to entertain proceedings for death to be presumed and a marriage to be dissolved if (and only if) the petitioner—

(a) is domiciled in England and Wales on the date when the proceedings are begun; or

(b) was habitually resident in England and Wales throughout the period of one year ending with that date.

(5) The court shall, at any time when proceedings are pending in respect of which it has jurisdiction by virtue of subsection (2) or (3) above (or of this subsection), also have jurisdiction to entertain other proceedings, in respect of the same marriage, for divorce, judicial separation or nullity of marriage, notwithstanding that jurisdiction would not be exercisable under subsection (2) or (3).

[(5A) Schedule A1 (jurisdiction in relation to marriage of same sex couples) has effect.]

(6) Schedule 1 to this Act shall have effect as to the cases in which matrimonial proceedings in England and Wales [[whether the proceedings are in respect of the marriage of a man and a woman or the

marriage of a same sex couple)] are to be, or may be, stayed by the court where there are concurrent proceedings elsewhere in respect of the same marriage, and as to the other matters dealt with in that Schedule; but nothing in the Schedule—

(a) requires or authorises a stay of proceedings which are pending when this section comes into force; or

(b) prejudices any power to stay proceedings which is exercisable by the court apart from the Schedule.

[(6A) Subsection (6) and Schedule 1, and any power as mentioned in subsection (6)(b), are subject to Article 19 of the Council Regulation.]

. . .

## [SCHEDULE A1

### Jurisdiction in Relation to Marriage of Same Sex Couples

*Introduction*

1

This Schedule shall have effect, subject to section 6(3) and (4), with respect to the jurisdiction of the court to entertain any of the following proceedings in relation to a marriage of a same sex couple—

(a) proceedings for divorce, judicial separation or nullity of marriage;

(b) proceedings for an order which ends a marriage on the ground that one of the couple is dead; and

(c) proceedings for a declaration of validity.

*Divorce, judicial separation or annulment*

2

(1) The court has jurisdiction to entertain proceedings for divorce or judicial separation if (and only if)—

(a) the court has jurisdiction under regulations under paragraph 5,

(b) no court has, or is recognised as having, jurisdiction under regulations under paragraph 5 and either of the married same sex couple is domiciled in England and Wales on the date when the proceedings are begun, or

(c) the following conditions are met—

    (i) the two people concerned married each other under the law of England and Wales,

    (ii) no court has, or is recognised as having, jurisdiction under regulations under paragraph 5, and

    (iii) it appears to the court to be in the interests of justice to assume jurisdiction in the case.

(2) The court has jurisdiction to entertain proceedings for nullity of marriage if (and only if)—

(a) the court has jurisdiction under regulations under paragraph 5,

(b) no court has, or is recognised as having, jurisdiction under regulations under paragraph 5 and either of the married same sex couple—

    (i) is domiciled in England and Wales on the date when the proceedings are begun, or

    (ii) died before that date and either was at death domiciled in England and Wales or had been habitually resident in England and Wales throughout the period of 1 year ending with the date of death, or

(c) the following conditions are met—

    (i) the two people concerned married each other under the law of England and Wales,

    (ii) no court has, or is recognised as having, jurisdiction under regulations under paragraph 5, and

    (iii) it appears to the court to be in the interests of justice to assume jurisdiction in the case.

(3) At any time when proceedings are pending in respect of which the court has jurisdiction by virtue of sub-paragraph (1) or (2) (or this sub-paragraph), the court also has jurisdiction to entertain other proceedings, in respect of the same marriage, for divorce, judicial separation or nullity of marriage, even though that jurisdiction would not be exercisable under subsection (1) or (2).

### Presumption of death order

3

The court has jurisdiction to entertain proceedings for an order which ends a marriage on the ground that one of the couple is dead on an application made by the other of the couple ("the applicant") if (and only if)—

(a)  at the time the application is made, the High Court does not have jurisdiction to entertain an application by the applicant under section 1 of the Presumption of Death Act 2013 for a declaration that the applicant's spouse is presumed to be dead, and

(b)  the two people concerned married each other under the law of England and Wales and it appears to the court to be in the interests of justice to assume jurisdiction in the case.

### Declaration of validity

4

The court has jurisdiction to entertain an application for a declaration of validity if (and only if)—

(a)  either of the parties to the marriage to which the application relates—

(i)  is domiciled in England and Wales on the date of the application,

(ii)  has been habitually resident in England and Wales throughout the period of 1 year ending with that date, or

(iii)  died before that date and either was at death domiciled in England and Wales or had been habitually resident in England and Wales throughout the period of 1 year ending with the date of death, or

(b)  the two people concerned married each other under the law of England and Wales and it appears to the court to be in the interests of justice to assume jurisdiction in the case.

### Power to make provision corresponding to EC Regulation 2201/2003

5

(1) The Lord Chancellor may by regulations make provision—

(a)  as to the jurisdiction of courts in England and Wales in proceedings for the divorce of, or annulment of the marriage of, a same sex couple or for judicial separation of a married same sex couple where one of the couple—

(i)  is or has been habitually resident in a member State,

(ii)  is a national of a member State, or

(iii)  is domiciled in a part of the United Kingdom or the Republic of Ireland, and

(b)  as to the recognition in England and Wales of any judgment of a court of another member State which orders the divorce of, or annulment of a marriage of, a same sex couple or the judicial separation of a married same sex couple.

(2) The regulations may in particular make provision corresponding to that made by Council Regulation (EC) No 2201/2003 of 27th November 2003 in relation to jurisdiction and the recognition and enforcement of judgments in matrimonial matters.

(3) The regulations may provide that for the purposes of the regulations "member State" means—

(a)  all member States with the exception of such member States as are specified in the regulations, or

(b)  such member States as are specified in the regulations.

(4) The regulations may make provision under sub-paragraph (1)(b) which applies even if the date of

the divorce, annulment or judicial separation is earlier than the date on which this paragraph comes into force.

(5) Regulations under this paragraph are to be made by statutory instrument.

(6) A statutory instrument containing regulations under this paragraph may not be made unless a draft of the statutory instrument containing the order or regulations has been laid before, and approved by resolution of, each House of Parliament.

*Interpretation*

**6**

In this Schedule "declaration of validity" means—

(a) a declaration as to the validity of a marriage,

(b) a declaration as to the subsistence of a marriage, or

(c) a declaration as to the validity of a divorce, annulment or judicial separation obtained outside England and Wales in respect of a marriage.]

## SCHEDULE 1

### Staying of Matrimonial Proceedings (England and Wales)

*Interpretation*

**1**

The following five paragraphs [Paragraphs 2 to 6 below] have effect for the interpretation of this Schedule.

**2**

"Matrimonial proceedings" means any proceedings so far as they are one or more of the five following kinds [(whether relating to a marriage of a man and a woman or a marriage of a same sex couple)], namely, proceedings for—

divorce,

judicial separation,

nullity of marriage,

a declaration as to the validity of a marriage of the petitioner, and

a declaration as to the subsistence of such a marriage.

**3**

(1) "Another jurisdiction" means any country outside England and Wales.

(2) "Related jurisdiction" means any of the following countries, namely, Scotland, Northern Ireland, Jersey, Guernsey and the Isle of Man (the reference to Guernsey being treated as including Alderney and Sark).

**4**

(1) References to the trial or first trial in any proceedings do not include references to the separate trial of an issue as to jurisdiction only.

(2) For purposes of this Schedule, proceedings in the court are continuing if they are pending and not stayed.

**5**

Any reference in this Schedule to proceedings in another jurisdiction is to proceedings in a court of that jurisdiction, and to any other proceedings in that jurisdiction, which are of a description prescribed for the purposes of this paragraph; and provision may be made by rules of court as to when proceedings of any description in another jurisdiction are continuing for the purposes of this Schedule.

**6**

"Prescribed" means prescribed by rules of court.

*Duty to furnish particulars of concurrent proceedings in another jurisdiction*

**7**

While matrimonial proceedings are pending in the court in respect of a marriage and the trial or first trial in those proceedings has not begun, it shall be the duty of any person who is a petitioner in the proceedings, or is a respondent and has in his answer included a prayer for relief to furnish, in such manner and to such persons and on such occasions as may be prescribed, such particulars as may be prescribed of any proceedings which—

(a)  he knows to be continuing in another jurisdiction; and

(b)  are in respect of that marriage or capable of affecting its validity or subsistence.

*Obligatory stays*

**8**

(1)  Where before the beginning of the trial or first trial or first trial in any proceedings for divorce which are continuing in the court it appears to the court on the application of a party to the marriage—

(a)  that in respect of the same marriage proceedings for divorce or nullity of marriage are continuing in a related jurisdiction; and

(b)  that the parties to the marriage have resided together after [they entered into it]; and

(c)  that the place where they resided together when the proceedings in the court were begun or, if they did not then reside together, where they last resided together before those proceedings were begun, is in that jurisdiction; and

(d)  that either of the said parties was habitually resident in that jurisdiction throughout the year ending with the date on which they last resided together before the date on which the proceedings in the court were begun,

it shall be the duty of the court, subject to paragraph 10(2) below, to order that the proceedings in the court be stayed.

(2)  References in sub-paragraph (1) above to the proceedings in the court are, in the case of proceedings which are not only proceedings for divorce, to the proceedings so far as they are proceedings for divorce.

*Discretionary stays*

**9**

(1)  Where before the beginning of the trial or first trial in any matrimonial proceedings[, other than proceedings governed by the Council Regulation,] which are continuing in the court it appears to the court—

(a)  that any proceedings in respect of the marriage in question, or capable of affecting its validity or subsistence, are continuing in another jurisdiction; and

(b)  that the balance of fairness (including convenience) as between the parties to the marriage is such that it is appropriate for the proceedings in that jurisdiction to be disposed of before further steps are taken in the proceedings in the court or in those proceedings so far as they consist of a particular kind of matrimonial proceedings,

the court may then, if it thinks fit, order that the proceedings in the court be stayed or, as the case may be, that those proceedings be stayed so far as they consist of proceedings of that kind.

(2)  In considering the balance of fairness and convenience for the purposes of sub-paragraph (1)(b) above, the court shall have regard to all factors appearing to be relevant, including the convenience

of witnesses and any delay or expense which may result from the proceedings being stayed, or not being stayed.

(3) In the case of any proceedings so far as they are proceedings for divorce, the court shall not exercise the power conferred on it by sub-paragraph (1) above while an application under paragraph 8 above in respect of the proceedings is pending.

(4) If, at any time after the beginning of the trial or first trial in any matrimonial proceedings which are pending in the court, the court declares by order that it is satisfied that a person has failed to perform the duty imposed on him in respect of the proceedings by paragraph 7 above, sub-paragraph (1) above shall have effect in relation to those proceedings and, to the other proceedings by reference to which the declaration is made, as if the words "before the beginning of the trial or first trial" were omitted; but no action shall lie in respect of the failure of a person to perform such a duty.

*Supplementary*

**10**

(1) Where an order staying any proceedings is in force in pursuance of paragraph 8 or 9 above, the court may, if it thinks fit, on the application of a party to the proceedings, discharge the order if it appears to the court that the other proceedings by reference to which the order was made are stayed or concluded, or that a party to those other proceedings has delayed unreasonably in prosecuting them.

(2) If the court discharges an order staying any proceedings and made in pursuance of paragraph 8 above, the court shall not again stay those proceedings in pursuance of that paragraph.

**11**

(1) The provisions of sub-paragraphs (2) and (3) below shall apply (subject to sub-paragraph (4)) where proceedings for divorce, judicial separation or nullity of marriage are stayed by reference to proceedings in a related jurisdiction for divorce, judicial separation of nullity of marriage; and in this paragraph—

[. . .]

"lump sum order" means such an order as is mentioned in paragraph (f) of section 23(1) of the Matrimonial Causes Act 1973 (lump sum payment for children), being an order made under section 23(1) or (2)(a) [or an order made in equivalent circumstances under Schedule 1 to the Children Act 1989 and of a kind mentioned in paragraph 1(2)(c) of that Schedule];

"the other proceedings", in relation to any stayed proceedings, means the proceedings in another jurisdiction by reference to which the stay was imposed;

"relevant order" means—

(a)  an order under section 22 of the Matrimonial Causes Act 1973 (maintenance for spouse pending suit),

(b)  such an order as is mentioned in paragraph (d) or (e) of section 23(1) of that Act (periodical payments for children) being an order made under section 23(1) or (2)(a) [or an order made in equivalent circumstances under Schedule 1 to the Children Act 1989 and of a kind mentioned in paragraph 1(2)(a) or (b) of that Schedule],

(c)  an order under section 42(1)(a) of that Act (orders for the custody and education of children) [or a section 8 order under the Children Act 1989], and

(d)  except for the purposes of sub-paragraph (3) below, any order restraining a person from removing a child out of England and Wales or out of the [care] of another person; and

"stayed" means stayed in pursuance of this Schedule.

(2) Where any proceedings are stayed, then, without prejudice to the effect of the stay apart from this paragraph—

(a)  the court shall not have power to make a relevant order or a lump sum order in connection with the stayed proceedings except in pursuance of paragraph (c) below; and

(b)  subject to paragraph (c) below, any relevant order made in connection with the stayed proceedings

UK Statutes

shall, unless the stay is previously removed or the order previously discharged, cease to have effect on the expiration of the period of three months beginning with the date on which the stay was imposed; but

(c) if the court considers that, for the purpose of dealing with circumstances needing to be dealt with urgently, it is necessary during or after that period to make a relevant order or a lump sum order in connection with the stayed proceedings or to extend or further extend the duration of a relevant order made in connection with the stayed proceedings, the court may do so and the order shall not cease to have effect by virtue of paragraph (b) above.

(3) Where any proceedings are stayed and at the time when the stay is imposed an order is in force, or at a subsequent time an order comes into force, which was made in connection with the other proceedings and provides for any of the [. . .] following matters, namely, periodical payments for a spouse of the marriage in question, periodical payments for a child, [or any provision which could be made by a section 8 order under the Children Act 1989] then, on the imposition of the stay in a case where the order is in force when the stay is imposed and on the coming into force of the order in any other case—

(a) any relevant order made in connection with the stayed proceedings shall cease to have effect in so far as it makes for a spouse or child any provision for any of those matters as respects which the same or different provision for that spouse or child is made by the other order;

(b) the court shall not have power in connection with the stayed proceedings to make a relevant order containing for a spouse or child provision for any of those matters as respects which any provision for that spouse or child is made by the other order; and

(c) if the other order contains provision for periodical payments for a child, the court shall not have power in connection with the stayed proceedings to make a lump sum order for that child.

[(3A) Where any such order as is mentioned in paragraph (e) of section 23(1) of the Matrimonial Causes Act 1973, being an order made under section 23(1) or (2)(a) of that Act, ceases to have effect by virtue of sub-paragraph (2) or (3) above, any order made under section 24A(1) of that Act which requires the proceeds of sale of property to be used for securing periodical payments under the first mentioned order shall also cease to have effect.]

(4) If any proceedings are stayed so far as they consist of matrimonial proceedings of a particular kind but are not stayed so far as they consist of matrimonial proceedings of a different kind, sub-paragraphs (2) and (3) above shall not apply to the proceedings but, without prejudice to the effect of the stay apart from this paragraph, the court shall not have power to make a relevant order or a lump sum order in connection with the proceedings so far as they are stayed; and in this sub-paragraph references to matrimonial proceedings do not include proceedings for a declaration.

[(4A) Sub-paragraph (4B) applies where—

(a) proceedings are stayed as described in [sub-paragraph (1)], and

(b) at the time when the stay is imposed, a [child arrangements] order (within the meaning of the Children Act 1989) made in connection with the stayed proceedings is in force.

(4B) While the stay applies to the proceedings, the court may not—

(a) make an enforcement order (within the meaning of the Children Act 1989) in relation to the [child arrangements] order, or

(b) as regards an enforcement order already made in relation to the [child arrangements] order, exercise its powers under paragraph 9(2) of Schedule A1 to the Children Act 1989 in relation to the enforcement order.]

(5) [Except as provided in sub-paragraph (4B),] nothing in this paragraph affects any power of the court—

(a) to vary or discharge a relevant order so far as the order is for the time being in force; or

(b) to enforce a relevant order as respects any period when it is or was in force; or

(c) to make a relevant order or a lump sum order in connection with proceedings which were but are no longer stayed.

# Matrimonial Causes Act
# 1973 ch 18

**11 Grounds on which a marriage is void**

A marriage celebrated after 31st July 1971 shall be void on the following grounds only, that is to say—

(a) that it is not a valid marriage under the provisions of [the [Marriage Acts 1949 to 1986]] (that is to say where—

    (i) the parties are within the prohibited degrees of relationship;

    (ii) either party is under the age of sixteen; or

    (iii) the parties have intermarried in disregard of certain requirements as to the formation of marriage);

(b) that at the time of the marriage either party was already lawfully married [or a civil partner];

(c) that the parties are not respectively male and female;

(d) in the case of a polygamous marriage entered into outside England and Wales, that either party was at the time of the marriage domiciled in England and Wales.

For the purposes of paragraph (d) of this subsection a marriage [is not polygamous if] at its inception neither party has any spouse additional to the other.

. . .

**14 Marriages governed by foreign law or celebrated abroad under English law**

(1) [Subject to subsection (3)] where, apart from this Act, any matter affecting the validity of a marriage would fall to be determined (in accordance with the rules of private international law) by reference to the law of a country outside England and Wales, nothing in section 11, 12 or 13(1) above shall—

(a) preclude the determination of that matter as aforesaid; or

(b) require the application to the marriage of the grounds or bar there mentioned except so far as applicable in accordance with those rules.

(2) In the case of a marriage which purports to have been celebrated under the Foreign Marriage Acts 1892 to 1947 or has taken place outside England and Wales and purports to be a marriage under common law, section 11 above is without prejudice to any ground on which the marriage may be void under those Acts or, as the case may be, by virtue of the rules governing the celebration of marriages outside England and Wales under common law.

[(3) No marriage is to be treated as valid by virtue of subsection (1) if, at the time when it purports to have been celebrated, either party was already a civil partner.]

. . .

**35 Alteration of agreements by court during lives of parties**

(1) Where a maintenance agreement is for the time being subsisting and each of the parties to the agreement is for the time being either domiciled or resident in England and Wales, then, subject to [subsections (1A) and (3)] below, either party may apply to the court [. . .] for an order under this section.

[(1A) If an application or part of an application relates to a matter where jurisdiction falls to be determined by reference to the jurisdictional requirements of the Maintenance Regulation and Schedule 6 to the Civil Jurisdiction and Judgments (Maintenance) Regulations 2011—

(a) the requirement as to domicile or residence in subsection (1) does not apply to the application or that part of it, but

(b)  the court may not entertain the application or that part of it unless it has jurisdiction to do so by virtue of that Regulation and that Schedule.]

(2)  If the court [. . .] is satisfied either—

(a)  that by reason of a change in the circumstances in the light of which any financial arrangements contained in the agreement were made or, as the case may be, financial arrangements were omitted from it (including a change foreseen by the parties when making the agreement), the agreement should be altered so as to make different, or, as the case may be, so as to contain, financial arrangements, or

(b)  that the agreement does not contain proper financial arrangements with respect to any child of the family,

then subject to [subsections] (4) and (5) below, [the court] may by order make such alterations in the agreement—

(i)  by varying or revoking any financial arrangements contained in it, or

(ii)  by inserting in it financial arrangements for the benefit of one of the parties to the agreement or of a child of the family,

as may appear to [the court] to be just having regard to all the circumstances, including, if relevant, the matters mentioned in [section 25(4)] above; and the agreement shall have effect thereafter as if any alteration made by the order had been made by agreement between the parties and for valuable consideration.

(3)  [. . .]

(4)  Where [the court] decides to alter, by order under this section, an agreement by inserting provision for the making or securing by one of the parties to the agreement of periodical payments for the maintenance of the other party or by increasing the rate of the periodical payments which the agreement provides shall be made by one of the parties for the maintenance of the other, the term for which the payments or, as the case may be, the additional payments attributable to the increase are to be made under the agreement as altered by the order shall be such term as the court may specify, subject to the following limits, that is to say—

(a)  where the payments will not be secured, the term shall be so defined as not to extend beyond the death of either of the parties to the agreement or the remarriage of[, or formation of a civil partnership by,] the party to whom the payments are to be made;

(b)  where the payments will be secured, the term shall be so defined as not to extend beyond the death or remarriage of[, or formation of a civil partnership by,] that party.

(5)  Where [the court] decides to alter, by order under this section, an agreement by inserting provision for the making or securing by one of the parties to the agreement of periodical payments for the maintenance of a child of the family or by increasing the rate of the periodical payments which the agreement provides shall be made or secured by one of the parties for the maintenance of such a child, then, in deciding the term for which under the agreement as altered by the order the payments, or as the case may be, the additional payments attributable to the increase are to be made or secured for the benefit of the child, the court shall apply the provisions of section 29(2) and (3) above as to age limits as if the order in question were a periodical payments or secured periodical payments order in favour of the child.

(6)  For the avoidance of doubt it is hereby declared that nothing in this section or in section 34 above affects any power of a court before which any proceedings between the parties to a maintenance agreement are brought under any other enactment (including a provision of this Act) to make an order containing financial arrangements or any right of either party to apply for such an order in such proceedings.

### 36  Alteration of agreements by court after death of one party

(1)  Where a maintenance agreement within the meaning of section 34 above provides for the continuation of payments under the agreement after the death of one of the parties and that party dies domiciled in England and Wales, the surviving party or the personal representatives of the deceased

party may, subject to subsections (2) and (3) below, apply to the [. . .] court for an order under section 35 above.

(2) An application under this section shall not, except with the permission of the [. . .] court, be made after the end of the period of six months from the date on which representation in regard to the estate of the deceased is first taken out.

(3) [. . .]

(4) If a maintenance agreement is altered by [the court] on an application made in pursuance of subsection (1) above, the like consequences shall ensue as if the alteration had been made immediately before the death by agreement between the parties and for valuable consideration.

(5) The provisions of this section shall not render the personal representatives of the deceased liable for having distributed any part of the estate of the deceased after the expiration of the period of six months referred to in subsection (2) above on the ground that they ought to have taken into account the possibility that [the court] might permit an application by virtue of this section to be made by the surviving party after that period; but this subsection shall not prejudice any power to recover any part of the estate so distributed arising by virtue of the making of an order in pursuance of this section.

(6) Section 31(9) above shall apply for the purposes of subsection (2) above as it applies for the purposes of subsection (6) of section 31.

(7) [. . .]

# Evidence (Proceedings in Other Jurisdictions) Act 1975 ch 34

*Evidence for civil proceedings*

**1 Application to United Kingdom court for assistance in obtaining evidence for civil proceedings in other court**

Where an application is made to the High Court, the Court of Session or the High Court of Justice in Northern Ireland for an order for evidence to be obtained in the part of the United Kingdom in which it exercises jurisdiction, and the court is satisfied—

(a) that the application is made in pursuance of a request issued by or on behalf of a court or tribunal ("the requesting court") exercising jurisdiction in any other part of the United Kingdom or in a country or territory outside the United Kingdom; and

(b) that the evidence to which the application relates is to be obtained for the purposes of civil proceedings which either have been instituted before the requesting court or whose institution before that court is contemplated,

the High Court, Court of Session or High Court of Justice in Northern Ireland, as the case may be, shall have the powers conferred on it by the following provisions of this Act.

**2 Power of United Kingdom court to give effect to application for assistance**

(1) Subject to the provisions of this section, the High Court, the Court of Session and the High Court of Justice in Northern Ireland shall each have power, on any such application as is mentioned in section 1 above, by order to make such provision for obtaining evidence in the part of the United Kingdom in which it exercises jurisdiction as may appear to the court to be appropriate for the purpose of giving effect to the request in pursuance of which the application is made; and any such order may require a person specified therein to take such steps as the court may consider appropriate for that purpose.

(2) Without prejudice to the generality of subsection (1) above but subject to the provisions of this section, an order under this section, in particular, make provision—

(a) for the examination of witnesses, either orally or in writing;

(b) for the production of documents;

(c) for the inspection, photographing, preservation, custody or detention of any property;

(d) for the taking of samples of any property and the carrying out of any experiments on or with any property;

(e) for the medical examination of any person;

(f) without prejudice to paragraph (e) above, for the taking and testing of samples of blood from any person.

(3) An order under this section shall not require any particular steps to be taken unless they are steps which can be required to be taken by way of obtaining evidence for the purposes of civil proceedings in the court making the order (whether or not proceedings of the same description as those to which the application for the order relates); but this subsection shall not preclude the making of an order requiring a person to give testimony (either orally or in writing) otherwise than on oath where this is asked for by the requesting court.

(4) An order under this section shall not require a person—

(a) to state what documents relevant to the proceedings to which the application for the order relates are or have been in his possession, custody or power; or

(b) to produce any documents other than particular documents specified in the order as being documents appearing to the court making the order to be, or to be likely to be, in his possession, custody or power.

UK Statutes

(5)  A person who, by virtue of an order under this section, is required to attend at any place shall be entitled to the like conduct money and payment for expenses and loss of time as on attendance as a witness in civil proceedings before the court making the order.

### 3  Privilege of witnesses

(1)  A person shall not be compelled by virtue of an order under section 2 above to give any evidence which he could not be compelled to give—

(a)  in civil proceedings in the part of the United Kingdom in which the court that made the order exercises jurisdiction; or

(b)  subject to subsection (2) below, in civil proceedings in the country or territory in which the requesting court exercises jurisdiction.

(2)  Subsection (1)(b) above shall not apply unless the claim of the person in question to be exempt from giving the evidence is either—

(a)  supported by a statement contained in the request (whether it is so supported unconditionally or subject to conditions that are fulfilled); or

(b)  conceded by the applicant for the order;

and where such a claim made by any person is not supported or conceded as aforesaid he may (subject to the other provisions of this section) be required to give the evidence to which the claim relates but that evidence shall not be transmitted to the requesting court if that court, on the matter being referred to it, upholds the claim.

(3)  Without prejudice to subsection (1) above, a person shall not be compelled by virtue of an order under section 2 above to give any evidence if his doing so would be prejudicial to the security of the United Kingdom; and a certificate signed by or on behalf of the Secretary of State to the effect that it would be so prejudicial for that person to do so shall be conclusive evidence of that fact.

(4)  In this section references to giving evidence include references to answering any question and to producing any document and the reference in subsection (2) above to the transmission of evidence given by a person shall be construed accordingly.

### 4  Extension of powers of High Court etc in relation to obtaining evidence for proceedings in that court

[The Attendance of Witnesses Act 1854 (which enables the Court of Session to order the issue of a warrant of citation in special form, enforceable throughout the United Kingdom, for the attendance of a witness at a trial) shall] have effect as if references to attendance at a trial included references to attendance before an examiner or commissioner appointed by the court or a judge thereof in any cause or matter in that court, including an examiner or commissioner appointed to take evidence outside the jurisdiction of the court.

[. . .]

*Evidence for international proceedings*

### 6  Power of United Kingdom court to assist in obtaining evidence for international proceedings

(1)  Her Majesty may by Order in Council direct that, subject to such exceptions, adaptations or modifications as may be specified in the Order, the provisions of sections 1 to 3 above shall have effect in relation to international proceedings of any description specified in the order.

(2)  An Order in Council under this section may direct that section 1(4) of the Perjury Act 1911 or [article 3(4) of the Perjury (Northern Ireland) Order 1979] shall have effect in relation to international proceedings to which the Order applies as it has effect in relation to a judicial proceeding in a tribunal of a foreign state.

(3)  In this section "international proceedings" means proceedings before the International Court of Justice or any other court, tribunal, commission, body or authority (whether consisting of one or more persons) which, in pursuance of any international agreement or any resolution of the General Assembly of the United Nations, exercises any jurisdiction or performs any functions of a judicial nature or by

way of arbitration, conciliation or inquiry or is appointed (whether permanently or temporarily) for the purpose of exercising any jurisdiction or performing any such functions.

*Supplementary*

### 7 Rules of court

[Civil Procedure Rules or rules of court under] section 7 of the Northern Ireland Act 1962 [may make provision]—

(a) as to the manner in which any such application as is mentioned in section 1 above is to be made;

(b) subject to the provisions of this Act, as to the circumstances in which an order can be made under section 2 above; and

(c) as to the manner in which any such reference as is mentioned in section 3(2) above is to be made;

and any such rules may include such incidental, supplementary and consequential provision as the authority making the rules, may consider necessary or expedient.

### 8 Consequential amendments and repeals

(1) The enactments mentioned in Schedule 1 to this Act shall have effect subject to the amendments there specified, being amendments consequential on the provisions of this Act.

(2) The enactments mentioned in Schedule 2 to this Act are hereby repealed to the extent specified in the third column of that Schedule.

(3) Nothing in this section shall affect—

(a) any application to any court or judge which is pending at the commencement of this Act;

(b) any certificate given for the purposes of any such application;

(c) any power to make an order on such an application; or

(d) the operation or enforcement of any order made on such an application.

(4) Subsection (3) above is without prejudice to section 38(2) of the Interpretation Act 1889 (effect of repeals).

### 9 Interpretation

(1) In this Act—

"civil proceedings", in relation to the requesting court, means proceedings in any civil or commercial matter;

"requesting court" has the meaning given in section 1 above;

"property" includes any land, chattel or other corporeal property of any description;

"request" includes any commission, order or other process issued by or on behalf of the requesting court.

(2) In relation to any application made in pursuance of a request issued by the High Court under [section 56 of the County Courts Act 1984] or the High Court of Justice in Northern Ireland under [Article 43 of the County Courts (Northern Ireland) Order 1980] the reference in section 1(b) above to proceedings instituted before the requesting court shall be construed as a reference to the relevant proceedings in the county court.

(3) Any power conferred by this Act to make an Order in Council includes power to revoke or vary any such Order by a subsequent Order in Council.

(4) Nothing in this Act shall be construed as enabling any court to make an order that is binding on the Crown or on any person in his capacity as an officer or servant of the Crown.

(5) Except so far as the context otherwise requires, any reference in this Act to any enactment is a reference to that enactment as amended or extended by or under any other enactment.

### 10 Short title, commencement and extent

(1) This Act may be cited as the Evidence (Proceedings in Other Jurisdictions) Act 1975.

(2) This Act shall come into operation of such day as Her Majesty may by Order in Council appoint.

(3) Her Majesty may by Order in Council make provision for extending any of the provisions of this Act (including section 6 or any Order in Council made thereunder), with such exceptions, adaptations or modifications as may be specified, in the Order, to any of the Channel Islands, the Isle of Man, any colony (other than a colony for whose external relations a country other than the United Kingdom is responsible) or any country or territory outside Her Majesty's dominions in which Her Majesty has jurisdiction in right of Her Majesty's Government in the United Kingdom.

. . .

# Legitimacy Act
# 1976 ch 31

## 1 Legitimacy of children of certain void marriages

(1) The child of a void marriage, whenever born, shall, subject to subsection (2) below and Schedule 1 to this Act, be treated as the legitimate child of his parents if at the time of [the insemination resulting in the birth, or where there was no such insemination, the child's conception] (or at the time of the celebration of the marriage if later) both or either of the parties reasonably believed that the marriage was valid.

[(2) This section only applies where—

(a) the father of the child was domiciled in England and Wales at the time of the birth, or if he died before the birth, was so domiciled immediately before his death, or

(b) if a woman is treated as the female parent of a child by virtue of section 42 or 43 of the Human Fertilisation and Embryology Act 2008, that female parent was domiciled in England and Wales at the time of the birth, or if she died before the birth, was so domiciled immediately before her death.]

[(3) It is hereby declared for the avoidance of doubt that subsection (1) above applies notwithstanding that the belief that the marriage was valid was due to a mistake as to law.

(4) In relation to a child born after the coming into force of section 28 of the Family Law Reform Act 1987, it shall be presumed for the purposes of subsection (1) above, unless the contrary is shown, that one of the parties to the void marriage reasonably believed at the time of the insemination resulting in the birth or, where there was no such insemination, the child's conception (or at the time of the celebration of the marriage if later) that the marriage was valid.]

[(5) Subsections (1) and (4) are to be read, in relation to the child of a void marriage which has resulted from the purported conversion of a civil partnership under section 9 of the Marriage (Same Sex Couples) Act 2013 and regulations made under that section, as if the reference to the time of the celebration of the marriage was a reference to the date of the purported conversion of the civil partnership into a marriage.]

## 2 Legitimation by subsequent marriage of [mother and father]

Subject to the following provisions of this Act, where the [mother and father] of an illegitimate person marry one another, the marriage shall, if the father of the illegitimate person is at the date of marriage domiciled in England and Wales, render that person, if living, legitimate from the date of the marriage.

## [2A Legitimation by subsequent [marriage or] civil partnership of parents

[Subject to the following provisions of this Act, where—

(a) a person ("the child") has a parent ("the female parent") by virtue of section 43 of the Human Fertilisation and Embryology Act 2008 (treatment provided to woman who agrees that second woman to be parent),

(b) at the time of the child's birth, the female parent and the child's mother are [neither married nor] civil partners of each other,

(c) the female parent and the child's mother subsequently [marry or] enter into a civil partnership, and

(d) the female parent is at the date of [the marriage or] the formation of the civil partnership domiciled in England and Wales,

[the marriage or] the civil partnership shall render the child, if living, legitimate from the date of [the marriage or] the formation of the civil partnership.]

### 3 Legitimation by extraneous law

[(1)] Subject to the following provisions of this Act, where the [mother and father] of an illegitimate person marry one another and the father of the illegitimate person is not at the time of the marriage domiciled in England and Wales but is domiciled in a country by the law of which the illegitimate person became legitimated by virtue of such subsequent marriage, that person, if living, shall in England and Wales be recognised as having been so legitimated from the date of the marriage notwithstanding that, at the time of his birth, his father was domiciled in a country the law of which did not permit legitimation by subsequent marriage.

[(2) Subject to the following provisions of this Act, where—

(a)   a person ("the child") has a parent ("the female parent") by virtue of section 43 of the Human Fertilisation and Embryology Act 2008 (treatment provided to woman who agrees that second woman to be parent),

(b)   at the time of the child's birth, the female parent and the child's mother are [neither married nor] civil partners of each other,

(c)   the female parent and the child's mother subsequently [marry or] enter into a civil partnership, and

(d)   the female parent is not at the time of [the marriage or] the formation of the civil partnership domiciled in England and Wales but is domiciled in a country by the law of which the child became legitimated by virtue of the [marriage or] civil partnership,

the child, if living, shall in England and Wales be recognised as having been so legitimated from the date of the [marriage or] formation of the civil partnership notwithstanding that, at the time of the child's birth, the female parent was domiciled in a country the law of which did not permit legitimation by subsequent [marriage or] civil partnership.]

. . .

### 10 Interpretation

(1) In this Act, except where the context otherwise requires,—

. . .

"legitimated person" means a person legitimated or recognised as legitimated—

(a)   under section 2[, 2A] or 3 above; or

(b)   under section 1 or 8 of the Legitimacy Act 1926; or

(c)   except in section 8, by a legitimation (whether or not by virtue of the subsequent marriage of his parents) recognised by the law of England and Wales and effected under the law of any other country;

and cognate expressions shall be construed accordingly;

. . .

"void marriage" means a marriage, not being voidable only, in respect of which the High Court has or had jurisdiction to grant a decree of nullity, or would have or would have had such jurisdiction if the parties were domiciled in England and Wales.

. . .

# Unfair Contract Terms Act
# 1977 ch 50[1]

## PART III

## Provisions applying to whole of United Kingdom

### *Miscellaneous*

### 26 International supply contracts

(1) The limits imposed by this Act on the extent to which a person may exclude or restrict liability by reference to a contract term do not apply to liability arising under such a contract as is described in subsection (3) below.

(2) The terms of such a contract are not subject to any requirement of reasonableness under section 3 [. . .]: and nothing in Part II of this Act shall require the incorporation of the terms of such a contract to be fair and reasonable for them to have effect.

(3) Subject to subsection (4), that description of contract is one whose characteristics are the following—

(a)  either it is a contract of sale of goods or it is one under or in pursuance of which the possession or ownership of goods passes; and

(b)  it is made by parties whose places of business (or, if they have none, habitual residences) are in the territories of different States (the Channel Islands and the Isle of Man being treated for this purpose as different States from the United Kingdom).

(4) A contract falls within subsection (3) above only if either—

(a)  the goods in question are, at the time of the conclusion of the contract, in the course of carriage, or will be carried, from the territory of one State to the territory of another; or

(b)  the acts constituting the offer and acceptance have been done in the territories of different States; or

(c)  the contract provides for the goods to be delivered to the territory of a State other than that within whose territory those acts were done.

### 27 Choice of law clauses

(1) Where the [law applicable to] a contract is the law of any part of the United Kingdom only by choice of the parties (and apart from that choice would be the law of some country outside the United Kingdom) sections 2 to 7 and 16 to 21 of this Act do not operate as part [of the law applicable to the contract].

(2) This Act has effect notwithstanding any contract term which applies or purports to apply the law of some country outside the United Kingdom, where (either or both)—

(a)  the term appears to the court, or arbitrator or arbiter to have been imposed wholly or mainly for the purpose of enabling the party imposing it to evade the operation of this Act;

[. . .]

. . .

---

[1] Reflecting the amendments made by the Consumer Rights Act 2015, expected to enter into force on 1 October 2015.

# Protection of Trading Interests Act
# 1980 ch 11

UK Statutes

### 5 Restriction on enforcement of certain overseas judgments

(1) A judgment to which this section applies shall not be registered under Part II of the Administration of Justice Act 1920 or Part I of the Foreign Judgments (Reciprocal Enforcement) Act 1933 and no court in the United Kingdom shall entertain proceedings at common law for the recovery of any sum payable under such a judgment.

(2) This section applies to any judgment given by a court of an overseas country, being—

(a) a judgment for multiple damages within the meaning of subsection (3) below;

(b) a judgment based on a provision or rule of law specified or described in an order under subsection (4) below and given after the coming into force of the order; or

(c) a judgment on a claim for contribution in respect of damages awarded by a judgment falling within paragraph (a) or (b) above.

(3) In subsection (2)(a) above a judgment for multiple damages means a judgment for an amount arrived at by doubling, trebling or otherwise multiplying a sum assessed as compensation for the loss or damage sustained by the person in whose favour the judgment is given.

(4) The Secretary of State may for the purposes of subsection (2)(b) above make an order in respect of any provision or rule of law which appears to him to be concerned with the prohibition or regulation of agreements, arrangements or practices designed to restrain, distort or restrict competition in the carrying on of business of any description or to be otherwise concerned with the promotion of such competition as aforesaid.

(5) The power of the Secretary of State to make orders under subsection (4) above shall be exercisable by statutory instrument subject to annulment in pursuance of a resolution of either House of Parliament.

(6) Subsection (2)(a) above applies to a judgement given before the date of the passing of this Act as well as to a judgment given on or after that date but this section does not affect any judgment which has been registered before that date under the provisions mentioned in subsection (1) above or in respect of which such proceedings as are there mentioned have been finally determined before that date.

### 6 Recovery of awards of multiple damages

(1) This section applies where a court of an overseas country has given a judgment for multiple damages within the meaning of section 5(3) above against—

(a) a citizen of the United Kingdom and Colonies; or

(b) a body corporate incorporated in the United Kingdom or in a territory outside the United Kingdom for whose international relations Her Majesty's Government in the United Kingdom are responsible; or

(c) a person carrying on business in the United Kingdom,

(in this section referred to as a "qualifying defendant") and an amount on account of the damages has been paid by the qualifying defendant either to the party in whose favour the judgment was given or to another party who is entitled as against the qualifying defendant to contribution in respect of the damages.

(2) Subject to subsections (3) and (4) below, the qualifying defendant shall be entitled to recover from the party in whose favour the judgment was given so much of the amount referred to in subsection (1) above as exceeds the part attributable to compensation; and that part shall be taken to be such part of the amount as bears to the whole of it the same proportion as the sum assessed by the court that gave the judgment as compensation for the loss or damage sustained by that party bears to the whole of the damages awarded to that party.

(3) Subsection (2) above does not apply where the qualifying defendant is an individual who was ordinarily resident in the overseas country at the time when the proceedings in which the judgment was given were instituted or a body corporate which had its principal place of business there at that time.

(4) Subsection (2) above does not apply where the qualifying defendant carried on business in the overseas country and the proceedings in which the judgment was given were concerned with activities exclusively carried on in that country.

(5) A court in the United Kingdom may entertain proceedings on a claim under this section notwithstanding that the person against whom the proceedings are brought is not within the jurisdiction of the court.

(6) The reference in subsection (1) above to an amount paid by the qualifying defendant includes a reference to an amount obtained by execution against his property or against the property of a company which (directly or indirectly) is wholly owned by him; and references in that subsection and subsection (2) above to the party in whose favour the judgment was given or to a party entitled to contribution include references to any person in whom the rights of any such party have become vested by succession or assignment or otherwise.

(7) This section shall, with the necessary modifications, apply also in relation to any order which is made by a tribunal or authority of an overseas country and would, if that tribunal or authority were a court, be a judgment for multiple damages within the meaning of section 5(3) above.

(8) This section does not apply to any judgment given or order made before the passing of this Act.

### 7 Enforcement of overseas judgment under provision corresponding to s. 6

(1) If it appears to Her Majesty that the law of an overseas country provides or will provide for the enforcement in that country of judgments given under section 6 above, Her Majesty may by Order in Council provide for the enforcement in the United Kingdom of [judgments of any description specified in the Order which are given under any provision of the law of that country relating to the recovery of sums paid or obtained pursuant to a judgment for multiple damages within the meaning of section 5(3) above, whether or not that provision corresponds to section 6 above].

[(1A) Such an Order in Council may, as respects judgments to which it relates—

(a)   make different provisions for different descriptions of judgment; and

(b)   impose conditions or restrictions on the enforcement of judgments of any description.]

(2)   An Order under this section may apply, with or without modification, any of the provisions of the Foreign Judgments (Reciprocal Enforcement) Act 1933.

# Senior Courts Act
# 1981 ch 54

## The High Court

*Powers*

. . .

### 37 Powers of High Court with respect to injunctions and receivers

(1) The High Court may by order (whether interlocutory or final) grant an injunction or appoint a receiver in all cases in which it appears to the court to be just and convenient to do so.

(2) Any such order may be made either unconditionally or on such terms and conditions as the court thinks just.

(3) The power of the High Court under subsection (1) to grant an interlocutory injunction restraining a party to any proceedings from removing from the jurisdiction of the High Court, or otherwise dealing with, assets located within that jurisdiction shall be exercisable in cases where that party is, as well as in cases where he is not, domiciled, resident or present within that jurisdiction.

(4) The power of the High Court to appoint a receiver by way of equitable execution shall operate in relation to all legal estates and interests in land; and that power—

(a) may be exercised in relation to an estate or interest in land whether or not a charge has been imposed on that land under section 1 of the Charging Orders Act 1979 for the purpose of enforcing the judgment, order or award in question; and

(b) shall be in addition to, and not in derogation of, any power of any court to appoint a receiver in proceedings for enforcing such a charge.

(5) Where an order under the said section 1 imposing a charge for the purpose of enforcing a judgment, order or award has been, or has effect as if, registered under section 6 of the Land Charges Act 1972, subsection (4) of the said section 6 (effect of non-registration of writs and orders registrable under that section) shall not apply to an order appointing a receiver made either—

(a) in proceedings for enforcing the charge; or

(b) by way of equitable execution of the judgment, order or award or, as the case may be, of so much of it as requires payment of moneys secured by the charge.

[(6) This section applies in relation to the family court as it applies in relation to the High Court.]

. . .

## General Provisions

*Law and equity*

### 49 Concurrent administration of law and equity

(1) Subject to the provisions of this or any other Act, every court exercising jurisdiction in England or Wales in any civil cause or matter shall continue to administer law and equity on the basis that, wherever there is any conflict or variance between the rules of equity and the rules of the common law with reference to the same matter, the rules of equity shall prevail.

(2) Every such court shall give the same effect as hitherto—

(a) to all equitable estates, titles, rights, reliefs, defences and counterclaims, and to all equitable duties and liabilities; and

(b) subject thereto, to all legal claims and demands and all estates, titles, rights, duties, obligations and liabilities existing by the common law or by any custom or created by any statute, and, subject to the provisions of this or any other Act, shall so exercise its jurisdiction in every cause or matter before it as to secure that, as far as possible, all matters in dispute between the parties are completely and finally determined, and all multiplicity of legal proceedings with respect to any of those matters is avoided.

(3) Nothing in this Act shall affect the power of the Court of Appeal or the High Court to stay any proceedings before it, where it thinks fit to do so, either of its own motion or on the application of any person, whether or not a party to the proceedings.

# Civil Jurisdiction and Judgments Act
# 1982 ch 27

## PART I

## Implementation of the Conventions

*Main implementing provisions*

### 1 Interpretation of references to the Conventions and Contracting States

(1) In this Act—

"the 1968 Convention" means the Convention on jurisdiction and the enforcement of judgments in civil and commercial matters (including the Protocol annexed to that Convention), signed at Brussels on 27th September 1968;

"the 1971 Protocol" means the Protocol on the interpretation of the 1968 Convention by the European Court, signed at Luxembourg on 3rd June 1971;

"the Accession Convention" means the Convention on the accession to the 1968 Convention and the 1971 Protocol of Denmark, the Republic of Ireland and the United Kingdom, signed at Luxembourg on 9th October 1978;

["the 1982 Accession Convention" means the Convention on the accession of the Hellenic Republic to the 1968 Convention and the 1971 Protocol, with the adjustments made to them by the Accession Convention, signed at Luxembourg on 25th October 1982;]

["the 1989 Accession Convention" means the Convention on the accession of the Kingdom of Spain and the Portuguese Republic to the 1968 Convention and the 1971 Protocol, with the adjustments made to them by the Accession Convention and the 1982 Accession Convention, signed at Donostia — San Sebastian on 26th May 1989;]

["the 1996 Accession Convention" means the Convention on the accession of the Republic of Austria, the Republic of Finland and the Kingdom of Sweden to the 1968 Convention and the 1971 Protocol, with the adjustments made to them by the Accession Convention, the 1982 Accession Convention and the 1989 Accession Convention, signed at Brussels on 29th November 1996;]

["the 2007 Hague Convention" means the Convention on the International Recovery of Child Support and other forms of Family Maintenance done at The Hague on 23 November 2007;]

[["the Brussels Conventions"] means the 1968 Convention, the 1971 Protocol, the Accession Convention, the 1982 Accession Convention[, the 1989 Accession Convention and the 1996 Accession Convention;]]

["the Lugano Convention" means the Convention on jurisdiction and the recognition and enforcement of judgments in civil and commercial matters, between the European Community and the Republic of Iceland, the Kingdom of Norway, the Swiss Confederation and the Kingdom of Denmark signed on behalf of the European Community on 30th October 2007;]

["the Maintenance Regulation" means Council Regulation (EC) No 4/2009 including as applied in relation to Denmark by virtue of the Agreement made on 19th October 2005 between the European Community and the Kingdom of Denmark;]

["the Regulation" means Regulation (EU) No 1215/2012 of the European Parliament and of the Council of 12 December 2012 on jurisdiction and the recognition and enforcement of judgments in civil and commercial matters (recast) as amended from time to time and as applied by virtue of the Agreement made on 19 October 2005 between the European Community and the Kingdom of Denmark on jurisdiction and the recognition and enforcement of judgments in civil and commercial matters (OJ No L 299, 16.11.2005, p 62; OJ No L79, 21.3.2013, p 4)].

(2) In this Act, unless the context otherwise requires—

[(a) references to, or to any provision of, the 1968 Convention or the 1971 Protocol are references to that Convention, Protocol or provision as amended by the Accession Convention, the 1982 Accession Convention[, the 1989 Accession Convention and the 1996 Accession Convention]; and]

[(aa)...]

[(b) any reference in any provision to a numbered Article without more is a reference—

    (i) to the Article so numbered of the 1968 Convention, in so far as the provision applies in relation to that Convention, and

    (ii) to the Article so numbered of the Lugano Convention, in so far as the provision applies in relation to that Convention,

and any reference to a sub-division of a numbered Article shall be construed accordingly].

[(3) [In this Act—

["2007 Hague Convention State", in any provision, in the application of that provision in relation to the 2007 Hague Convention, means a State bound by that Convention;]

"Contracting State", without more, in any provision means—

    (a) in the application of the provision in relation to the Brussels Conventions, a Brussels Contracting State; and

    (b) in the application of the provision in relation to the Lugano Convention, a [State bound by the Lugano Convention];]

["Brussels Contracting State" means a state which is one of the original parties to the 1968 Convention or one of the parties acceding to that Convention under the Accession Convention, or under the 1982 Accession Convention, or under the 1989 Accession Convention, but only with respect to any territory—

    (a) to which the Brussels Conventions apply; and

    (b) which is excluded from the scope of the Regulation pursuant to [Articles 349 and 355 of the Treaty on the Functioning of the European Union];]

["Maintenance Regulation State", in any provision, in the application of that provision in relation to the Maintenance Regulation means a Member State;]

["State bound by the Lugano Convention" in any provision, in the application of that provision in relation to the Lugano Convention has the same meaning as in Article 1(3) of that Convention;]

["Regulation State" in any provision, in the application of that provision in relation to the Regulation, means a Member State].]

[(4) Any question arising as to whether it is the Regulation, any of the Brussels Conventions, or the Lugano Convention which applies in the circumstances of a particular case shall be determined as follows—

(a) in accordance with [Article 64] of the Lugano Convention (which determines the relationship between the Brussels Conventions and the Lugano Convention); and

(b) in accordance with Article 68 of the Regulation (which determines the relationship between the Brussels Conventions and the Regulation).]

...

[4A Enforcement of judgments, other than maintenance orders, under the Lugano Convention]

[(1) Where a judgment, other than a maintenance order, is registered under the Lugano Convention, the reasonable costs or expenses of and incidental to its registration shall be recoverable as if they were sums recoverable under the judgment.

(2) A judgment other than a maintenance order registered under the Lugano Convention shall, for the purposes of its enforcement, be of the same force and effect, the registering court shall have in relation to its enforcement the same powers, and proceedings for or with respect to its enforcement

may be taken, as if the judgment had been originally given by the registering court and had (where relevant) been entered.

(3) Subsection (2) is subject to Article 47(3) of the Lugano Convention (restriction on enforcement where appeal pending or time for appeal unexpired), to section 7 (interest on registered judgments) and to any provision made by rules of court as to the manner in which and conditions subject to which a judgment registered under the Lugano Convention may be enforced.]

. . .

## [5A  Recognition and enforcement of maintenance orders under the Lugano Convention

(1) The Secretary of State's function (under Article 39 and Annex II of the Lugano Convention) of transmitting to the appropriate court an application for the recognition or enforcement in the United Kingdom of a maintenance order (made under Article 38 of the Lugano Convention) shall be discharged—

(a)  as respects England and Wales [. . .], by the Lord Chancellor;

. . .

In this subsection "the appropriate court" means the magistrates' court or sheriff court having jurisdiction in the matter in accordance with the second paragraph of Article 39 [but, if the appropriate court is a magistrates' court in England and Wales, the Lord Chancellor is to transmit the application to the family court].

(2) Such an application shall be determined in the first instance by the prescribed [officer—

(a)  of the family court if the application is transmitted to that court, or

(b)  in any other case, of] the court having jurisdiction in the matter.

(3) A maintenance order registered under the Lugano Convention shall, for the purposes of its enforcement, be of the same force and effect, the registering court shall have in relation to its enforcement the same powers, and proceedings for or with respect to its enforcement may be taken, as if the order had been made by the registering court.

(4) Subsection (3) is subject to Article 47 of the Lugano Convention (restriction on enforcement where appeal pending or time for appeal unexpired), to subsection (6) and to any provision made by rules of court as to the manner in which and conditions subject to which an order registered under the Lugano Convention may be enforced.

(5) [. . .]

In this subsection "magistrates' court maintenance order" has the same meaning as in section 150(1) of the Magistrates' Courts Act 1980.

(6) A maintenance order which by virtue of the Lugano Convention is enforceable by a magistrates' court in Northern Ireland shall, subject to the modifications of Article 98 of the Magistrates' Courts (Northern Ireland) Order 1981 specified in section 5(6A) of this Act, be enforceable as an order made by that court to which that Article applies.

. . .

## [6A  Appeals under Article 44 and Annex IV of the Lugano Convention

(1) The single further appeal on a point of law referred to in Article 44 and Annex IV of the Lugano Convention in relation to the recognition or enforcement of a judgment other than a maintenance order lies—

(a)  in England and Wales or Northern Ireland, to the Court of Appeal or to the Supreme Court in accordance with Part II of the Administration of Justice Act 1969 (appeals direct from the High Court to the Supreme Court);

. . .

(2) Paragraph (a) of subsection (1) has effect notwithstanding section 15(2) of the Administration of Justice Act 1969 (exclusion of direct appeal to the Supreme Court in cases where no appeal to that House lies from a decision of the Court of Appeal).

. . .

### 10 Allocation within UK of jurisdiction with respect to trusts and consumer contracts

(1) The provisions of this section have effect for the purpose of allocating within the United Kingdom jurisdiction in certain proceedings in respect of which the 1968 Convention [or the Lugano Convention] confers jurisdiction on the courts of the United Kingdom generally and to which section 16 does not apply.

(2) Any proceedings which by virtue of Article 5(6) (trusts) are brought in the United Kingdom shall be brought in the courts of the part of the United Kingdom in which the trust is domiciled.

(3) Any proceedings which by virtue of the first paragraph of Article 14 [of the 1968 Convention or Article 16(1) of the Lugano Convention] (consumer contracts) are brought in the United Kingdom by a consumer on the ground that he is himself domiciled there shall be brought in the courts of the part of the United Kingdom in which he is domiciled.

. . .

### [11A Proof and admissibility of certain judgments and related documents for the purposes of the Lugano Convention

(1) For the purposes of the Lugano Convention—

(a) a document, duly authenticated, which purports to be a copy of a judgment given by a court of a State bound by the Lugano Convention other than the United Kingdom shall without further proof be deemed to be a true copy, unless the contrary is shown; and

(b) a certificate obtained in accordance with Article 54 and Annex V shall be evidence, and in Scotland sufficient evidence, that the judgment is enforceable in the State of origin which is bound by the Lugano Convention.

(2) A document purporting to be a copy of a judgment given by any such court as is mentioned in subsection (1)(a) is duly authenticated for the purposes of this section if it purports—

(a) to bear the seal of that court; or

(b) to be certified by any person in his capacity as a judge or officer of that court to be a true copy of a judgment given by that court.

(3) Nothing in this section shall prejudice the admission in evidence of any document which is admissible apart from this section.]

### 12 Provision for issue of copies of, and certificates in connection with, UK judgments

Rules of court may make provision for enabling any interested party wishing to secure under the 1968 Convention [or the Lugano Convention] the recognition or enforcement in another Contracting State of a judgment given by a court in the United Kingdom to obtain, subject to any conditions specified in the rules—

(a) a copy of the judgment; and

(b) a certificate giving particulars relating to the judgment and the proceedings in which it was given.

. . .

### 15 Interpretation of Part I and consequential amendments

(1) In this Part, unless the context otherwise requires—

"judgment" has the meaning given by Article 25 [of the 1968 Convention or, as the case may be, Article 32 of the Lugano Convention];

"maintenance order" means a maintenance judgment within the meaning of the 1968 Convention [or, as the case may be, the Lugano Convention];

"payer", in relation to a maintenance order, means the person liable to make the payments for which the order provides;

"prescribed" means prescribed by rules of court.

(2) References in this Part to a judgment registered under [sections 4, 4A, 5 or 5A] include, to the extent of its registration, references to a judgment so registered to a limited extent only.

. . .

(4) The enactments specified in Part I of Schedule 12 shall have effect with the amendments specified there, being amendments consequential on this Part.

## PART II

### Jurisdiction, and Recognition and Enforcement of Judgments, within United Kingdom

### 16  Allocation within UK of jurisdiction in certain civil proceedings

(1) The provisions set out in Schedule 4 (which contains a modified version of [Chapter II of the Regulation]) shall have effect for determining, for each part of the United Kingdom, whether the courts of law of that part, or any particular court of law in that part, have or has jurisdiction in proceedings where—

[(a)  the subject-matter of the proceedings is within the scope of the Regulation as determined by Article 1 of the Regulation (whether or not the Regulation has effect in relation to the proceedings); and]

(b)  the defendant or defender is domiciled in the United Kingdom or the proceedings are of a kind mentioned in [[Article 24] of the Regulation] (exclusive jurisdiction regardless of domicile).

(2) [. . .]

(3) In determining any question as to the meaning or effect of any provision contained in Schedule 4—

(a)  regard shall be had to any relevant principles laid down by the European Court in connection with Title II of the 1968 Convention [or Chapter II of the Regulation] and to any relevant decision of that court as to the meaning or effect of any provision of that Title [or that Chapter]; and

(b)  without prejudice to the generality of paragraph (a), the reports mentioned in section 3(3) may be considered and shall, so far as relevant, be given such weight as is appropriate in the circumstances.

(4) The provisions of this section and Schedule 4 shall have effect subject to [the Regulation[, Schedule 6 to the Civil Jurisdiction and Judgments (Maintenance) Regulations 2011],] the 1968 Convention [and the Lugano Convention] and to the provisions of section 17.

(5) [. . .]

### 17  Exclusion of certain proceedings from Schedule 4

(1) Schedule 4 shall not apply to proceedings of any description listed in Schedule 5 or to proceedings in Scotland under any enactment which confers jurisdiction on a Scottish court in respect of a specific subject-matter on specific grounds.

(2) Her Majesty may by Order in Council—

(a)  add to the list in Schedule 5 any description of proceedings in any part of the United Kingdom; and

(b)  remove from that list any description of proceedings in any part of the United Kingdom (whether included in the list as originally enacted or added by virtue of this subsection).

(3) An Order in Council under subsection (2)—

(a)  may make different provisions for different descriptions of proceedings, for the same description of proceedings in different courts or for different parts of the United Kingdom; and

(b)  may contain such transitional and other incidental provisions as appear to Her Majesty to be appropriate.

(4) An Order in Council under subsection (2) shall not be made unless a draft of the Order has been laid before Parliament and approved by a resolution of each House of Parliament.

### 18  Enforcement of UK judgments in other parts of UK

(1) In relation to any judgment to which this section applies—

(a) Schedule 6 shall have effect for the purpose of enabling any money provisions contained in the judgment to be enforced in a part of the United Kingdom other than the part in which the judgment was given; and

(b) Schedule 7 shall have effect for the purpose of enabling any non-money provisions so contained to be so enforced.

(2) In this section "judgment" means any of the following (references to the giving of a judgment being construed accordingly)—

(a) any judgment or order (by whatever name called) given or made by a court of law in the United Kingdom;

(b) any judgment or order not within paragraph (a) which has been entered in England and Wales [in the High Court or the county court or in] Northern Ireland in the High Court or a county court;

(c) any document which in Scotland has been registered for execution in the Books of Council and Session or in the sheriff court books kept for any sheriffdom;

(d) any award or order made by a tribunal in any part of the United Kingdom which is enforceable in that part without an order of a court of law;

(e) an arbitration award which has become enforceable in the part of the United Kingdom in which it was given in the same manner as a judgment given by a court of law in that part;

[(f) an order made, or a warrant issued, under Part 8 of the Proceeds of Crime Act 2002 for the purposes of a civil recovery investigation [. . .] within the [meaning] given by section 341 of that Act;]

[(g) an order made, or a warrant issued, under Chapter 3 of Part 8 of the Proceeds of Crime Act 2002 for the purposes of a detained cash investigation within the meaning given by section 341 of that Act;]

and, subject to the following provisions of this section, this section applies to all such judgments.

(3) Subject to subsection (4), this section does not apply to—

(a) a judgment given in proceedings in a magistrates' court in England and Wales or Northern Ireland;

(b) a judgment given in proceedings other than civil proceedings;

[(ba)a judgment given in the exercise of jurisdiction in relation to insolvency law, within the meaning of section [426 of the Insolvency Act 1986];]

(c) a judgment given in proceedings relating to—

(i) [. . .]

(ii) [. . .]

(iii) the obtaining of title to administer the estate of a deceased person;

[(d) an order made under Part 2, 3 or 4 of the Proceeds of Crime Act 2002 (confiscation)].

(4) This section applies, whatever the nature of the proceedings in which it is made, to—

(a) a decree issued under section 13 of the Court of Exchequer (Scotland) Act 1856 (recovery of certain rentcharges and penalties by process of the Court of Session);

(b) an order which is enforceable in the same manner as a judgment of the High Court in England and Wales by virtue of section 16 of the Contempt of Court Act 1981 or section 140 of the [Senior Courts Act 1981] (which relate to fines for contempt of court and forfeiture of recognisances).

[(4A) This section does not apply as respects—

. . .

(b) the enforcement in England and Wales of orders made by the Court of Session [or by the sheriff] under or for the purposes of [the Proceeds of Crime (Scotland) Act 1995].]

(5) This section does not apply to so much of any judgment as—

(a) is an order to which section 16 of the Maintenance Orders Act 1950 applies (and is therefore an order for whose enforcement in another part of the United Kingdom provision is made by Part II of that Act);

(b)   concerns the status or legal capacity of an individual;

(c)   relates to the management of the affairs of a person not capable of managing his own affairs;

(d)   is a provisional (including protective) measure other than an order for the making of an interim payment [or an interim order made in connection with the civil recovery of proceeds of unlawful conduct];

and except where otherwise stated references to a judgment to which this section applies are to such a judgment exclusive of any such provisions.

(6) The following are within subsection (5)(b), but without prejudice to the generality of that provision—

(a)   a decree of judicial separation or of separation;

[(b)   any order which is a Part I order for the purposes of the Family Law Act 1986.]

[(6A) In subsection (5)(d), "an interim order made in connection with the civil recovery of proceeds of unlawful conduct" means any of the following made under Chapter 2 of Part 5 of the Proceeds of Crime Act 2002—

(a)   a property freezing order or prohibitory property order;

(b)   an order under section 245E or 245F of that Act (order relating to receivers in connection with property freezing order);

(c)   an interim receiving order or interim administration order;

[(d)   an order under section 255G or 255H of that Act (order relating to PPO receivers in connection with prohibitory property order)].]

(7) This section does not apply to a judgment of a court outside the United Kingdom which falls to be treated for the purposes of its enforcement as a judgment of a court of law in the United Kingdom by virtue of registration under Part II of the Administration of Justice Act 1920, Part I of the Foreign Judgments (Reciprocal Enforcement) Act 1933, Part I of the Maintenance Orders (Reciprocal Enforcement) Act 1972[, the International Recovery of Maintenance (Hague Convention 2007) Regulations 2012] or section 4 or 5 of this Act [or by virtue of the Civil Jurisdiction and Judgments (Maintenance) Regulations 2011].

(8) A judgment to which this section applies, other than a judgment within paragraph (e) of subsection (2), shall not be enforced in another part of the United Kingdom except by way of registration under Schedule 6 or 7.

## 19  Recognition of UK judgments in other parts of UK

(1) A judgment to which this section applies given in one part of the United Kingdom shall not be refused recognition in another part of the United Kingdom solely on the ground that, in relation to that judgment, the court which gave it was not a court of competent jurisdiction according to the rules of private international law in force in that other part.

(2) Subject to subsection (3), this section applies to any judgment to which section 18 applies.

(3) This section does not apply to—

(a)   the documents mentioned in paragraph (c) of the definition of "judgment" in section 18(2);

(b)   the awards and orders mentioned in paragraphs (d) and (e) of that definition;

(c)   the decrees and orders referred to in section 18(4).

UK Statutes

PART IV

## Miscellaneous Provisions

*Provisions relating to jurisdiction*

**24 Interim relief and protective measures in cases of doubtful jurisdiction**

(1) Any power of a court in England and Wales or Northern Ireland to grant interim relief pending trial or pending the determination of an appeal shall extend to a case where—

(a) the issue to be tried, or which is the subject of the appeal, relates to the jurisdiction of the court to entertain the proceedings; or

(b) the proceedings involve the reference of any matter to the European Court under the 1971 Protocol[; or

(c) the proceedings involve a reference of any matter relating to the Regulation [or the Lugano Convention] to the European Court under] [Article 267 of the Treaty on the Functioning of the European Union][; or

(d) the proceedings involve a reference of any matter relating to the Maintenance Regulation to the European Court under Article 267 of the Treaty on the Functioning of the European Union].

(2) Any power of a court in Scotland to grant protective measures pending the decision of any hearing shall apply to a case where—

(a) the subject of the proceedings includes a question as to the jurisdiction of the court to entertain them; or

(b) the proceedings involve the reference of a matter to the European Court under the 1971 Protocol[; or

(c) the proceedings involve a reference of any matter relating to the Regulation [or the Lugano Convention] to the European Court under] [Article 267 of the Treaty on the Functioning of the European Union][; or

(d) the proceedings involve a reference of any matter relating to the Maintenance Regulation to the European Court under Article 267 of the Treaty on the Functioning of the European Union].

(3) Subsections (1) and (2) shall not be construed as restricting any power to grant interim relief or protective measures which a court may have apart from this section.

**25 Interim relief in England and Wales and Northern Ireland in the absence of substantive proceedings**

(1) The High Court in England and Wales or Northern Ireland shall have power to grant interim relief where—

(a) proceedings have been or are to be commenced in a [Brussels [Contracting State or a State bound by the Lugano Convention]] [or a Regulation State] [or a Maintenance Regulation State] other than the United Kingdom or in a part of the United Kingdom other than that in which the High Court in question exercises jurisdiction; and

[(b) they are or will be proceedings whose subject-matter is either within the scope of the Regulation as determined by Article 1 of the Regulation[, within the scope of the Maintenance Regulation as determined by Article 1 of that Regulation] or within the scope of the Lugano Convention as determined by Article 1 of the Lugano Convention (whether or not the Regulation[, the Maintenance Regulation] or the Lugano Convention has effect in relation to the proceedings)].

(2) On an application for any interim relief under subsection (1) the court may refuse to grant that relief if, in the opinion of the court, the fact that the court has no jurisdiction apart from this section in relation to the subject-matter of the proceedings in question makes it inexpedient for the court to grant it.

(3) Her Majesty may by Order in Council extend the power to grant interim relief conferred by subsection (1) so as to make it exercisable in relation to proceedings of any of the following descriptions, namely—

(a) proceedings commenced or to be commenced otherwise than in a [Brussels [Contracting State or a State bound by the Lugano Convention]] [or Regulation State] [or a Maintenance Regulation State];

[(b) proceedings whose subject-matter is not within the scope [. . .] of the Regulation as determined by Article 1 of the Regulation[, the Maintenance Regulation as determined by Article 1 of that Regulation] or the Lugano Convention as determined by Article 1 of the Lugano Convention;]

(c) [. . .]

(4) An Order in Council under subsection (3)—

(a) may confer power to grant only specified descriptions of interim relief;

(b) may make different provision for different classes of proceedings, for proceedings pending in different countries or courts outside the United Kingdom or in different parts of the United Kingdom, and for other different circumstances; and

(c) may impose conditions or restrictions on the exercise of any power conferred by the Order.

(5) [. . .]

(6) Any Order in Council under subsection (3) shall be subject to annulment in pursuance of a resolution of either House of Parliament.

(7) In this section "interim relief", in relation to the High Court in England and Wales or Northern Ireland, means interim relief of any kind which that court has power to grant in proceedings relating to matters within its jurisdiction, other than—

(a) a warrant for the arrest of property; or

(b) provision for obtaining evidence.

. . .

### 30 Proceedings in England and Wales or Northern Ireland for torts to immovable property

(1) The jurisdiction of any court in England and Wales or Northern Ireland to entertain proceedings for trespass to, or any other tort affecting, immovable property shall extend to cases in which the property in question is situated outside that part of the United Kingdom unless the proceedings are principally concerned with a question of the title to, or the right to possession of, that property.

(2) Subsection (1) has effect subject to the 1968 Convention [and the Lugano Convention] [and the Regulation] and to the provisions set out in Schedule 4.

. . .

### 32 Overseas judgments given in proceedings brought in breach of agreement for settlement of disputes

(1) Subject to the following provisions of this section, a judgment given by a court of an overseas country in any proceedings shall not be recognised or enforced in the United Kingdom if—

(a) the bringing of those proceedings in that court was contrary to an agreement under which the dispute in question was to be settled otherwise than by proceedings in the courts of that country; and

(b) those proceedings were not brought in that court by, or with the agreement of, the person against whom the judgment was given; and

(c) that person did not counterclaim in the proceedings or otherwise submit to the jurisdiction of that court.

(2) Subsection (1) does not apply where the agreement referred to in paragraph (a) of that subsection was illegal, void or unenforceable or was incapable of being performed for reasons not attributable to the fault of the party bringing the proceedings in which the judgment was given.

(3) In determining whether a judgment given by a court of an overseas country should be recognised or enforced in the United Kingdom, a court in the United Kingdom shall not be bound by any decision of the overseas court relating to any of the matters mentioned in subsection (1) or (2).

UK Statutes

(4) Nothing in subsection (1) shall affect the recognition or enforcement in the United Kingdom of—

(a) a judgment which is required to be recognised or enforced there under the 1968 Convention [or the Lugano Convention] [or the Regulation] [or the Maintenance Regulation] [or the 2007 Hague Convention];

(b) a judgment to which Part I of the Foreign Judgments (Reciprocal Enforcement) Act 1933 applies by virtue of section 4 of the Carriage of Goods by Road Act 1965, section 17(4) of the Nuclear Installations Act 1965, [. . .] [regulation 8 of the Railways (Convention on International Carriage by Rail) Regulations 2005] [. . .] or [section 34(1)(a) of the Merchant Shipping Act 1995].

## 33 Certain steps not to amount to submission to jurisdiction of overseas court

(1) For the purposes of determining whether a judgment given by a court of an overseas country should be recognised or enforced in England and Wales or Northern Ireland, the person against whom the judgment was given shall not be regarded as having submitted to the jurisdiction of the court by reason only of the fact that he appeared (conditionally or otherwise) in the proceedings for all or any one or more of the following purposes, namely—

(a) to contest the jurisdiction of the court;

(b) to ask the court to dismiss or stay the proceedings on the ground that the dispute in question should be submitted to arbitration or to the determination of the courts of another country;

(c) to protect, or obtain the release of, property seized or threatened with seizure in the proceedings.

(2) Nothing in this section shall affect the recognition or enforcement in England and Wales or Northern Ireland of a judgment which is required to be recognised or enforced there under the 1968 Convention [or the Lugano Convention] [or the Regulation] [or the Maintenance Regulation] [or the 2007 Hague Convention].

## 34 Certain judgments a bar to further proceedings on the same cause of action

No proceedings may be brought by a person in England and Wales or Northern Ireland on a cause of action in respect of which a judgment has been given in his favour in proceedings between the same parties, or their privies, in a court in another part of the United Kingdom or in a court of an overseas country, unless that judgment is not enforceable or entitled to recognition in England and Wales or, as the case may be, in Northern Ireland.

. . .

## [41A Domicile of individuals for the purposes of the Lugano Convention

(1) Subject to Article 59 of the Lugano Convention (which contains provisions for determining whether a party is domiciled in a State bound by the Lugano Convention), the following provisions of this section determine, for the purposes of the Lugano Convention, whether an individual is domiciled in the United Kingdom or in a particular part of, or place in, the United Kingdom or in a state other than a State bound by the Lugano Convention.

(2) An individual is domiciled in the United Kingdom if and only if—

(a) he is resident in the United Kingdom; and

(b) the nature and circumstances of his residence indicate that he has a substantial connection with the United Kingdom.

(3) Subject to subsection (5), an individual is domiciled in a particular part of the United Kingdom if and only if—

(a) he is resident in that part; and

(b) the nature and circumstances of his residence indicate that he has a substantial connection with that part.

(4) An individual is domiciled in a particular place in the United Kingdom if and only if he—

(a) is domiciled in the part of the United Kingdom in which that place is situated; and

(b) is resident in that place.

(5) An individual who is domiciled in the United Kingdom but in whose case the requirements of subsection (3)(b) are not satisfied in relation to any particular part of the United Kingdom shall be treated as domiciled in the part of the United Kingdom in which he is resident.

(6) In the case of an individual who—

(a)   is resident in the United Kingdom, or in a particular part of the United Kingdom; and

(b)   has been so resident for the last three months or more,

the requirements of subsection (2)(b) or, as the case may be, subsection (3)(b) shall be presumed to be fulfilled unless the contrary is proved.

(7) An individual is domiciled in a state other than a State bound by the Lugano Convention if and only if—

(a)   he is resident in that state; and

(b)   the nature and circumstances of his residence indicate that he has a substantial connection with that state.]

. . .

[43A  Seat of companies or other legal persons, or of associations, for the purposes of Article 22(2) of the Lugano Convention

(1) The following provisions of this section determine where a company, or other legal person or an association of natural or legal persons, has its seat for the purposes of Article 22(2) of the Lugano Convention (which confers exclusive jurisdiction over proceedings relating to the validity of the constitution, the nullity or the dissolution of such bodies, or to the validity of the decisions of their organs).

(2) A company, legal person or association has its seat in the United Kingdom if and only if—

(a)   it was incorporated or formed under the law of a part of the United Kingdom; or

(b)   its central management and control is exercised in the United Kingdom.

(3) Subject to subsection (4), a company, legal person or association has its seat in a State bound by the Lugano Convention other than the United Kingdom if and only if—

(a)   it was incorporated or formed under the law of that state; or

(b)   its central management and control is exercised in that state.

(4) A company, legal person or association shall not be regarded as having its seat in a State bound by the Lugano Convention other than the United Kingdom if—

(a)   it has its seat in the United Kingdom by virtue of subsection (2)(a); or

(b)   it is shown that the courts of that other state would not regard it for the purposes of Article 22(2) as having its seat there.]

. . .

[44A  Persons deemed to be domiciled in the United Kingdom for certain purposes of the Lugano Convention

(1) This section applies to—

(a)   proceedings within Section 3 of Title II of the Lugano Convention (insurance contracts);

(b)   proceedings within Section 4 of Title II of the Lugano Convention (consumer contracts); and

(c)   proceedings within Section 5 of Title II of the Lugano Convention (employment contracts).

(2) A person who, for the purposes of proceedings to which this section applies arising out of the operations of a branch, agency or other establishment in the United Kingdom, is deemed for the purposes of the Lugano Convention to be domiciled in the United Kingdom by virtue of—

(a)   Article 9(2) (insurers); or

(b)   Article 15(2) (suppliers of goods, services or credit to consumers); or

(c)   Article 18(2) (employers),

shall, for the purposes of those proceedings, be treated as so domiciled and as domiciled in the part of the United Kingdom in which the branch, agency or establishment in question is situated.]

### 45  Domicile of trusts

(1) The following provisions of this section determine, for the purposes of the 1968 Convention [the Lugano Convention] and this Act, where a trust is domiciled.

(2) A trust is domiciled in the United Kingdom if and only if it is by virtue of subsection (3) domiciled in a part of the United Kingdom.

(3) A trust is domiciled in a part of the United Kingdom if and only if the system of law of that part is the system of law with which the trust has its closest and most real connection.

. . .

### 48  Matters for which rules of court may provide

(1) Rules of court may make provision for regulating the procedure to be followed in any court in connection with any provision of this Act [the Lugano Convention or the Brussels Conventions] [or the Regulation] [or the Maintenance Regulation] [or the 2007 Hague Convention].

(2) Rules of court may make provision as to the manner in which and the conditions subject to which a [certificate or judgment—

(a)  which has been registered in any court under any provision of this Act[[. . .] or the 2007 Hague Convention],

[(aa) which is enforceable in the United Kingdom under the Regulation,]

(b)  which is enforceable in the United Kingdom by virtue of Section 1 of Chapter IV of the Maintenance Regulation, or

(c)  which has been registered for the purposes of Section 2 of that Chapter,

may be enforced,] including provision for enabling the court or, in Northern Ireland the Enforcement of Judgments Office, subject to any conditions specified in the rules, to give directions about such matters.

(3) Without prejudice to the generality of subsections (1) and (2), the power to make rules of court for [the family court, the power to make rules of court for magistrates' courts in Northern Ireland,] and in Northern Ireland the power to make Judgment Enforcement Rules, shall include power to make such provision as the rule-making authority considers necessary or expedient for the purposes of the provisions of [the Lugano Convention, the Brussels Conventions][, the Regulation][, the Maintenance Regulation][, the 2007 Hague Convention] and this Act relating to maintenance proceedings and the recognition and enforcement of maintenance orders, and shall in particular include power to make provision as to any of the following matters—

(a)  authorising the service in another Contracting State[, Regulation State][, Maintenance Regulation State or 2007 Hague Convention State] of process issued by or for the purposes of [the family court or] a magistrates' court and the service and execution in England and Wales or Northern Ireland of process issued in another Contracting State[, Regulation State][, Maintenance Regulation State or 2007 Hague Convention State];

(b)  requesting courts in other parts of the United Kingdom or in other Contracting States[, Regulation States][, Maintenance Regulation States or 2007 Hague Convention States] to take evidence there for the purposes of proceedings in England and Wales or Northern Ireland;

(c)  the taking of evidence in England and Wales or Northern Ireland in response to similar requests received from such courts;

(d)  the circumstances in which and the conditions subject to which any powers conferred under paragraphs (a) to (c) are to be exercised;

(e)  the admission in evidence, subject to such conditions as may be prescribed in the rules, of statements contained in documents purporting to be made or authenticated by a court in another part of the United Kingdom or in another Contracting State[, Regulation State][, Maintenance

Regulation State or 2007 Hague Convention State], or by a judge or official of such a court, which purport—

    (i)   to set out or summarise evidence given in proceedings in that court or to be documents received in evidence in such proceedings or copies of such documents; or

    (ii)  to set out or summarise evidence taken for the purposes of proceedings in England and Wales or Northern Ireland, whether or not in response to any such request as is mentioned in paragraph (b); or

    (iii) to record information relating to the payments made under an order of that court;

(f)  the circumstances and manner in which [the family court or] a magistrates' court may or must vary or revoke a maintenance order registered in that court, cancel the registration of, or refrain from enforcing, such an order or transmit such an order for enforcement in another part of the United Kingdom;

(g)  the cases and manner in which courts in other parts of the United Kingdom or in other Contracting States[, Regulation States][, Maintenance Regulation States or 2007 Hague Convention States] are to be informed of orders made, or other things done, by or for the purposes of [the family court or] a magistrates' court;

(h)  the circumstances and manner in which [the family court or] a magistrates' court may communicate for other purposes with such courts;

    (i)   the giving of notice of such matters as may be prescribed in the rules to such persons as may be so prescribed and the manner in which such notice is to be given.

(4)  Nothing in this section shall be taken as derogating from the generality of any power to make rules of court conferred by any other enactment.

### 49 Saving for powers to stay, sist, strike out or dismiss proceedings

Nothing in this Act shall prevent any court in the United Kingdom from staying, sisting, striking out or dismissing any proceedings before it, on the ground of *forum non conveniens* or otherwise, where to do so is not inconsistent with the 1968 Convention [or, as the case may be, the Lugano Convention].

*General*

### 50 Interpretation: general

In this Act, unless the context otherwise requires—

    ["the Accession Convention", ["the 1982 Accession Convention", "the 1989 Accession Convention" and "the 1996 Accession Convention"] have the meaning given by section 1(1);]

    "Article" and references to sub-divisions of numbered Articles are to be construed in accordance with section 1(2)(b);

    "association" means an unincorporated body of persons;

    ["Brussels Contracting State" has the meaning given by section 1(3);

    "the Brussels Conventions" has the meaning given by section 1(1);]

    "Contracting State" has the meaning given by section 1(3);

    "the 1968 Convention" has the meaning given by section 1(1), and references to that Convention and to provisions of it are to be construed in accordance with section 1(2)(a);

    [. . .]

    "corporation" means a body corporate, and includes a partnership subsisting under the law of Scotland;

    "court", without more, includes a tribunal;

    "court of law", in relation to the United Kingdom, means any of the following courts, namely—

    [(a) the Supreme Court,]

    [(aa) in England and Wales, the Court of Appeal, the High Court, the Crown Court, the family court, the county court and a magistrates' court,]

(b) in [. . .] Northern Ireland, the Court of Appeal, the High Court, the Crown Court, a county court and a magistrates' court,

(c) in Scotland, the Court of Session[, the Sheriff Appeal Court] and a sheriff court;

"the Crown" is to be construed in accordance with section 51(2);

"enactment" includes an enactment comprised in Northern Ireland legislation;

["the 2007 Hague Convention" has the meaning given by section 1(1);

"2007 Hague Convention State" has the meaning given by section 1(3);]

"judgment", subject to sections 15(1) and 18(2) and to paragraph 1 of Schedules 6 and 7, means any judgment or order (by whatever name called) given or made by a court in any civil proceedings;

[. . .]

["the Lugano Convention" has the meaning given by section 1(1);]

"magistrates' court", in relation to Northern Ireland, means a court of summary jurisdiction;

["the Maintenance Regulation" has the meaning given by section 1(1);

"Maintenance Regulation State" has the meaning given by section 1(3);]

"modifications" includes additions, omissions and alterations;

"overseas country" means any country or territory outside the United Kingdom;

"part of the United Kingdom" means England and Wales, Scotland or Northern Ireland;

"the 1971 Protocol" has the meaning given by section 1(1), and references to that Protocol and to provisions of it are to be construed in accordance with section 1(2)(a);

["the Regulation" has the meaning given by section 1(1);]

["Regulation State" has the meaning given by section 1(3);]

"rules of court", in relation to any court, means rules, orders or regulations made by the authority having power to make rules, orders or regulations regulating the procedure of that court, and includes—

(a) in Scotland, Acts of Sederunt;

(b) in Northern Ireland, Judgment Enforcement Rules;

["State bound by the Lugano Convention" has the meaning given by section 1(3);]

"statutory provision" means any provision contained in an Act, or in any Northern Ireland legislation, or in—

(a) subordinate legislation (as defined in section 21(1) of the Interpretation Act 1978); or

(b) any instrument of a legislative character made under any Northern Ireland legislation;

"tribunal"—

(a) means a tribunal of any description other than a court of law;

(b) in relation to an overseas country, includes, as regards matters relating to maintenance within the meaning of the 1968 Convention, any authority having power to give, enforce, vary or revoke a maintenance order.

## 51 Application to Crown

(1) This Act binds the Crown.

(2) In this section and elsewhere in this Act references to the Crown do not include references to Her Majesty in Her private capacity or to Her Majesty in right of Her Duchy of Lancaster or to the Duke of Cornwall.

## 52 Extent

(1) This Act extends to Northern Ireland.

(2) Without prejudice to the power conferred by section 39, Her Majesty may by Order in Council direct that all or any of the provisions of this Act apart from that section shall extend, subject to such modifications as may be specified in the Order, to any of the following territories, that is to say—

(a)   the Isle of Man;

(b)   any of the Channel Islands;

[(c)  any colony].

### 53 Commencement, transitional provisions and savings

(1) This Act shall come into force in accordance with the provisions of Part I of Schedule 13.

(2) The transitional provisions and savings contained in Part II of that Schedule shall have effect in relation to the commencement of the provisions of this Act mentioned in that Part.

. . .

## [SCHEDULE 4

## Chapter II of the Regulation as Modified: Rules for Allocation of Jurisdiction within UK

*General*

1

Subject to the rules of this Schedule, persons domiciled in a part of the United Kingdom shall be sued in the courts of that part.

2

Persons domiciled in a part of the United Kingdom may be sued in the courts of another part of the United Kingdom only by virtue of rules 3 to 13 of this Schedule.

*Special jurisdiction*

3

A person domiciled in a part of the United Kingdom may, in another part of the United Kingdom, be sued—

(a)   in matters relating to a contract, in the courts for the place of performance of the obligation in question;

(b)   [. . .]

(c)   in matters relating to tort, delict or quasi-delict, in the courts for the place where the harmful event occurred or may occur;

(d)   as regards a civil claim for damages or restitution which is based on an act giving rise to criminal proceedings, in the court seised of those proceedings, to the extent that that court has jurisdiction under its own law to entertain civil proceedings;

(e)   as regards a dispute arising out of the operations of a branch, agency or other establishment, in the courts for the place in which the branch, agency or other establishment is situated;

(f)   as settlor, trustee or beneficiary of a trust created by the operation of a statute, or by a written instrument, or created orally and evidenced in writing, in the courts of the part of the United Kingdom in which the trust is domiciled;

(g)   as regards a dispute concerning the payment of remuneration claimed in respect of the salvage of a cargo or freight, in the court under the authority of which the cargo or freight in question—

  (i)   has been arrested to secure such payment; or

  (ii)  could have been so arrested, but bail or other security has been given;

provided that this provision shall apply only if it is claimed that the defendant has an interest in the cargo or freight or had such an interest at the time of salvage;

(h)  in proceedings—

    (i)   concerning a debt secured on immovable property; or

    (ii)  which are brought to assert, declare or determine proprietary or possessory rights, or rights of security, in or over movable property, or to obtain authority to dispose of movable property,

in the courts of the part of the United Kingdom in which the property is situated.

**4**

Proceedings which have as their object a decision of an organ of a company or other legal person or of an association of natural or legal persons may, without prejudice to the other provisions of this Schedule, be brought in the courts of the part of the United Kingdom in which that company, legal person or association has its seat.

**5**

A person domiciled in a part of the United Kingdom may, in another part of the United Kingdom, also be sued—

(a)  where he is one of a number of defendants, in the courts for the place where any one of them is domiciled, provided the claims are so closely connected that it is expedient to hear and determine them together to avoid the risk of irreconcilable judgments resulting from separate proceedings;

(b)  as a third party in an action on a warranty or guarantee or in any other third party proceedings, in the court seised of the original proceedings, unless these were instituted solely with the object of removing him from the jurisdiction of the court which would be competent in his case;

(c)  on a counter-claim arising from the same contract or facts on which the original claim was based, in the court in which the original claim is pending;

(d)  in matters relating to a contract, if the action may be combined with an action against the same defendant in matters relating to rights in rem in immovable property, in the court of the part of the United Kingdom in which the property is situated.

**6**

Where by virtue of this Schedule a court of a part of the United Kingdom has jurisdiction in actions relating to liability arising from the use or operation of a ship, that court, or any other court substituted for this purpose by the internal law of that part, shall also have jurisdiction over claims for limitation of such liability.

*Jurisdiction over consumer contracts*

**7**

(1) In matters relating to a contract concluded by a person, the consumer, for a purpose which can be regarded as being outside his trade or profession, jurisdiction shall be determined by this rule and rules 8 and 9, without prejudice to rule 3(e) and (h)(ii), if—

(a)  it is a contract for the sale of goods on instalment credit terms; or

(b)  it is a contract for a loan repayable by instalments, or for any other form of credit, made to finance the sale of goods; or

(c)  in all other cases, the contract has been concluded with a person who pursues commercial or professional activities in the part of the United Kingdom in which the consumer is domiciled or, by any means, directs such activities to that part or to other parts of the United Kingdom including that part, and the contract falls within the scope of such activities.

(2) This rule shall not apply to a contract of transport other than a contract which, for an inclusive price, provides for a combination of travel and accommodation, or to a contract of insurance.

**8**

(1) A consumer may bring proceedings against the other party to a contract either in the courts of the part of the United Kingdom in which that party is domiciled or in the courts of the part of the United Kingdom in which the consumer is domiciled.

(2) Proceedings may be brought against a consumer by the other party to the contract only in the courts of the part of the United Kingdom in which the consumer is domiciled.

(3) The provisions of this rule shall not affect the right to bring a counter-claim in the court in which, in accordance with this rule and rules 7 and 9, the original claim is pending.

**9**

The provisions of rules 7 and 8 may be departed from only by an agreement—

(a)   which is entered into after the dispute has arisen; or

(b)   which allows the consumer to bring proceedings in courts other than those indicated in those rules; or

(c)   which is entered into by the consumer and the other party to the contract, both of whom are at the time of conclusion of the contract domiciled or habitually resident in the same part of the United Kingdom, and which confers jurisdiction on the courts of that part, provided that such an agreement is not contrary to the law of that part.

*Jurisdiction over individual contracts of employment*

**10**

(1) In matters relating to individual contracts of employment, jurisdiction shall be determined by this rule, without prejudice to rule 3(e).

(2) An employer may be sued—

(a)   in the courts of the part of the United Kingdom in which he is domiciled; or

(b)   in the courts of the part of the United Kingdom where the employee habitually carries out his work or in the courts of that part where he last did so; or

(c)   if the employee does not or did not habitually carry out his work in any one place, in the courts of the part of the United Kingdom where the business which engaged the employee is or was situated.

(3) An employer may bring proceedings only in the courts of the part of the United Kingdom in which the employee is domiciled.

(4) The provisions of this rule shall not affect the right to bring a counter-claim in the court in which, in accordance with this rule, the original claim is pending.

(5) The provisions of this rule may be departed from only by an agreement on jurisdiction—

(a)   which is entered into after the dispute has arisen; or

(b)   which allows the employee to bring proceedings in courts other than those indicated in this rule.

*Exclusive jurisdiction*

**11**

The following courts shall have exclusive jurisdiction, regardless of domicile:—

(a)

   (i)   in proceedings which have as their object rights *in rem* in immovable property or tenancies of immovable property, the courts of the part of the United Kingdom in which the property is situated;

   (ii)   however, in proceedings which have as their object tenancies of immovable property concluded for temporary private use for a maximum period of six consecutive months, the courts of the part of the United Kingdom in which the defendant is domiciled shall also have jurisdiction, provided that the tenant is a natural person and that the landlord and the tenant are domiciled in the same part of the United Kingdom;

(b) in proceedings which have as their object the validity of the constitution, the nullity or the dissolution of companies or other legal persons or associations of natural or legal persons, the courts of the part of the United Kingdom in which the company, legal person or association has its seat;

(c) in proceedings which have as their object the validity of entries in public registers, the courts of the part of the United Kingdom in which the register is kept;

(d) in proceedings concerned with the enforcement of judgments, the courts of the part of the United Kingdom in which the judgment has been or is to be enforced.

*Prorogation of jurisdiction*

12

(1) If the parties have agreed that a court or the courts of a part of the United Kingdom are to have jurisdiction to settle any disputes which have arisen or which may arise in connection with a particular legal relationship, and, apart from this Schedule, the agreement would be effective to confer jurisdiction under the law of that part, that court or those courts shall have jurisdiction.

(2) The court or courts of a part of the United Kingdom on which a trust instrument has conferred jurisdiction shall have jurisdiction in any proceedings brought against a settlor, trustee or beneficiary, if relations between these persons or their rights or obligations under the trust are involved.

(3) Agreements or provisions of a trust instrument conferring jurisdiction shall have no legal force if they are contrary to the provisions of rule 9, or if the courts whose jurisdiction they purport to exclude have exclusive jurisdiction by virtue of rule 11.

13

(1) Apart from jurisdiction derived from other provisions of this Schedule, a court of a part of the United Kingdom before which a defendant enters an appearance shall have jurisdiction.

(2) This rule shall not apply where appearance was entered to contest the jurisdiction, or where another court has exclusive jurisdiction by virtue of rule 11.

*Examination as to jurisdiction and admissibility*

14

Where a court of a part of the United Kingdom is seised of a claim which is principally concerned with a matter over which the courts of another part of the United Kingdom have exclusive jurisdiction by virtue of rule 11, it shall declare of its own motion that it has no jurisdiction.

15

(1) Where a defendant domiciled in one part of the United Kingdom is sued in a court of another part of the United Kingdom and does not enter an appearance, the court shall declare of its own motion that it has no jurisdiction unless its jurisdiction is derived from the provisions of this Schedule.

(2) The court shall stay the proceedings so long as it is not shown that the defendant has been able to receive the document instituting the proceedings or an equivalent document in sufficient time to enable him to arrange for his defence, or that all necessary steps have been taken to this end.

*Provisional, including protective, measures*

16

Application may be made to the courts of a part of the United Kingdom for such provisional, including protective, measures as may be available under the law of that part, even if, under this Schedule, the courts of another part of the United Kingdom have jurisdiction as to the substance of the matter.]

. . .

SCHEDULE 6

**Enforcement of UK Judgments (Money Provisions)**

**Section 18**

*Preliminary*

1

In this Schedule—

"judgment" means any judgment to which section 18 applies and references to the giving of a judgment shall be construed accordingly;

"money provision" means a provision for the payment of one or more sums of money;

"prescribed" means prescribed by rules of court.

*Certificates in respect of judgments*

2

(1)  Any interested party who wishes to secure the enforcement in another part of the United Kingdom of any money provisions contained in a judgment may apply for a certificate under this Schedule.

(2)  The application shall be made in the prescribed manner to the proper officer of the original court, that is to say—

(a)  in relation to a judgment within paragraph (a) of the definition of "judgment" in section 18(2), the court by which the judgment or order was given or made;

(b)  in relation to a judgment within paragraph (b) of that definition, the court in which the judgment or order is entered;

(c)  in relation to a judgment within paragraph (c) of that definition, the court in whose books the document is registered;

(d)  in relation to a judgment within paragraph (d) of that definition, the tribunal by which the award or order was made;

(e)  in relation to a judgment within paragraph (e) of that definition, the court which gave the judgment or made the order by virtue of which the award has become enforceable as mentioned in that paragraph.

3

A certificate shall not be issued under this Schedule in respect of a judgment unless under the law of the part of the United Kingdom in which the judgment was given—

(a)  either—

(i)  the time for bringing an appeal against the judgment has expired, no such appeal having been brought within that time; or

(ii)  such an appeal having been brought within that time, that appeal has been finally disposed of; and

(b)  enforcement of the judgment is not for the time being stayed or suspended, and the time available for its enforcement has not expired.

4

(1)  Subject to paragraph 3, on an application under paragraph 2 the proper officer shall issue to the applicant a certificate in the prescribed form—

(a)  stating the sum or aggregate of the sums (including any costs or expenses) payable under the money provisions contained in the judgment, the rate of interest, if any, payable thereon and the date or time from which any such interest began to accrue;

(b) stating that the conditions specified in paragraph 3(a) and (b) are satisfied in relation to the judgment; and

(c) containing such other particulars as may be prescribed.

(2) More than one certificate may be issued under this Schedule (simultaneously or at different times) in respect of the same judgment.

*Registration of certificates*

5

(1) Where a certificate has been issued under this Schedule in any part of the United Kingdom, any interested party may, within six months from the date of its issue, apply in the prescribed manner to the proper officer of the superior court in any other part of the United Kingdom for the certificate to be registered in that court.

(2) In this paragraph "superior court" means, in relation to England and Wales or Northern Ireland, the High Court and, in relation to Scotland, the Court of Session.

(3) Where an application is duly made under this paragraph to the proper officer of a superior court, he shall register the certificate in that court in the prescribed manner.

*General effect of registration*

6

(1) A certificate registered under this Schedule shall, for the purposes of its enforcement, be of the same force and effect, the registering court shall have in relation to its enforcement the same powers, and proceedings for or with respect to its enforcement may be taken, as if the certificate had been a judgment originally given in the registering court and had (where relevant) been entered.

(2) Sub-paragraph (1) is subject to the following provisions of this Schedule and to any provision made by rules of court as to the manner in which and the conditions subject to which a certificate registered under this Schedule may be enforced.

*Costs or expenses*

7

Where a certificate is registered under this Schedule, the reasonable costs or expenses of and incidental to the obtaining of the certificate and its registration shall be recoverable as if they were costs or expenses stated in the certificate to be payable under a money provision contained in the original judgment.

*Interest*

8

(1) Subject to any provision made under sub-paragraph (2), the debt resulting, apart from paragraph 7, from the registration of the certificate shall carry interest at the rate, if any, stated in the certificate from the date or time so stated.

(2) Provision may be made by rules of court as to the manner in which and the periods by reference to which any interest payable by virtue of sub-paragraph (1) is to be calculated and paid, including provision for such interest to cease to accrue as from a prescribed date.

(3) All such sums as are recoverable by virtue of paragraph 7 carry interest as if they were the subject of an order for costs or expenses made by the registering court on the date of registration of the certificate.

(4) Except as provided by this paragraph sums payable by virtue of the registration of a certificate under this Schedule shall not carry interest.

*Stay or sisting of enforcement in certain cases*

9

Where a certificate in respect of a judgment has been registered under this Schedule, the registering court may, if it is satisfied that any person against whom it is sought to enforce the certificate is entitled and intends to apply under the law of the part of the United Kingdom in which the judgment was given for any remedy which would result in the setting aside or quashing of the judgment, stay (or, in Scotland, sist) proceedings for the enforcement of the certificate, on such terms as it thinks fit, for such period as appears to the court to be reasonably sufficient to enable the application to be disposed of.

*Cases in which registration of a certificate must or may be set aside*

**10**

Where a certificate has been registered under this Schedule, the registering court—

(a)   shall set aside the registration if, on an application made by any interested party, it is satisfied that the registration was contrary to the provisions of this Schedule;

(b)   may set aside the registration if, on an application so made, it is satisfied that the matter in dispute in the proceedings in which the judgment in question was given had previously been the subject of a judgment by another court or tribunal having jurisdiction in the matter.

SCHEDULE 7

**Enforcement of UK Judgments (Non-Money Provisions)**

**Section 18**

*Preliminary*

**1**

In this Schedule—

"judgment" means any judgment to which section 18 applies and references to the giving of a judgment shall be construed accordingly;

"non-money provision" means a provision for any relief or remedy not requiring payment of a sum of money;

"prescribed" means prescribed by rules of court.

*Certified copies of judgments*

**2**

(1)   Any interested party who wishes to secure the enforcement in another part of the United Kingdom of any non-money provisions contained in a judgment may apply for a certified copy of the judgment.

(2)   The application shall be made in the prescribed manner to the proper officer of the original court, that is to say—

(a)   in relation to a judgment within paragaph (a) of the definition of "judgment" in section 18(2), the court by which the judgment or order was given or made;

(b)   in relation to a judgment within paragraph (b) of that definition, the court in which the judgment or order is entered;

(c)   in relation to a judgment within paragraph (c) of that definition, the court in whose books the document is registered;

(d)   in relation to a judgment within paragraph (d) of that definition, the tribunal by which the award or order was made;

(e)   in relation to a judgment within paragraph (e) of that definition, the court which gave the judgment or made the order by virtue of which the award has become enforceable as mentioned in that paragraph.

**3**

A certified copy of a judgment shall not be issued under this Schedule unless under the law of the part of the United Kingdom in which the judgment was given—

UK Statutes

(a) either—

    (i) the time for bringing an appeal against the judgment has expired, no such appeal having been brought within that time; or

    (ii) such an appeal having been brought within that time, that appeal has been finally disposed of; and

(b) enforcement of the judgment is not for the time being stayed or suspended, and the time available for its enforcement has not expired.

**4**

(1) Subject to paragraph 3, on an application under paragraph 2 the proper officer shall issue to the applicant—

(a) a certified copy of the judgment (including any money provisions or excepted provisions which it may contain); and

(b) a certificate stating that the conditions specified in paragraph 3(a) and (b) are satisfied in relation to the judgment.

(2) In sub-paragraph (1)(a) "excepted provision" means any provision of a judgment which is excepted from the application of section 18 by subsection (5) of that section.

(3) There may be issued under this Schedule (simultaneously or at different times)—

(a) more than one certified copy of the same judgment; and

(b) more than one certificate in respect of the same judgment.

*Registration of judgments*

**5**

(1) Where a certified copy of a judgment has been issued under this Schedule in any part of the United Kingdom, any interested party may apply in the prescribed manner to the superior court in any other part of the United Kingdom for the judgment to be registered in that court.

(2) In this paragraph "superior court" means, in relation to England and Wales or Northern Ireland, the High Court and, in relation to Scotland, the Court of Session.

(3) An application under this paragraph for the registration of a judgment must be accompanied by—

(a) a certified copy of the judgment issued under this Schedule; and

(b) a certificate issued under paragraph 4(1)(b) in respect of the judgment not more than six months before the date of the application.

(4) Subject to sub-paragraph (5), where an application under this paragraph is duly made to a superior court, the court shall order the whole of the judgment as set out in the certified copy to be registered in that court in the prescribed manner.

(5) A judgment shall not be registered under this Schedule by the superior court in any part of the United Kingdom if compliance with the non-money provisions contained in the judgment would involve a breach of the law of that part of the United Kingdom.

*General effect of registration*

**6**

(1) The non-money provisions contained in a judgment registered under this Schedule shall, for the purposes of their enforcement, be of the same force and effect, the registering court shall have in relation to their enforcement the same powers, and proceedings for or with respect to their enforcement may be taken, as if the judgment containing them had been originally given in the registering court and had (where relevant) been entered.

(2) Sub-paragraph (1) is subject to the following provisions of this Schedule and to any provision made by rules of court as to the manner in which and the conditions subject to which the non-money provisions contained in a judgment registered under this Schedule may be enforced.

*Costs or expenses*

7

(1) Where a judgment is registered under this Schedule, the reasonable costs or expenses of and incidental to—

(a) the obtaining of the certified copy of the judgment and of the necessary certificate under paragraph 4(1)(b) in respect of it; and

(b) the registration of the judgment,

shall be recoverable as if on the date of registration there had also been registered in the registering court a certificate under Schedule 6 in respect of the judgment and as if those costs or expenses were costs or expenses stated in that certificate to be payable under a money provision contained in the judgment.

(2) All such sums as are recoverable by virtue of sub-paragraph (1) shall carry interest as if they were the subject of an order for costs or expenses made by the registering court on the date of registration of the judgment.

*Stay or sisting of enforcement in certain cases*

8

Where a judgment has been registered under this Schedule, the registering court may, if it is satisfied that any person against whom it is sought to enforce the judgment is entitled and intends to apply under the law of the part of the United Kingdom in which the judgment was given for any remedy which would result in the setting aside or quashing of the judgment, stay (or, in Scotland, sist) proceedings for the enforcement of the judgment, on such terms as it thinks fit, for such period as appears to the court to be reasonably sufficient to enable the application to be disposed of.

*Cases in which registered judgment must or may be set aside*

9

Where a judgment has been registered under this Schedule, the registering court—

(a) shall set aside the registration if, on an application made by any interested party, it is satisfied that the registration was contrary to the provisions of this Schedule;

(b) may set aside the registration if, on an application so made, it is satisfied that the matter in dispute in the proceedings in which the judgment was given had previously been the subject of a judgment by another court or tribunal having jurisdiction in the matter.

UK Statutes

# Foreign Limitation Periods Act
## 1984 ch 16

UK Statutes

### 1 Application of foreign limitation law

(1) Subject to the following provisions of this Act, where in any action or proceedings in a court in England and Wales the law of any other country falls (in accordance with rules of private international law applicable by any such court) to be taken into account in the determination of any matter—

(a) the law of that other country relating to limitation shall apply in respect of that matter for the purposes of the action or proceedings[, subject to section 1A]; and

(b) except where that matter falls within subsection (2) below, the law of England and Wales relating to limitation shall not so apply.

(2) A matter falls within this subsection if it is a matter in the determination of which both the law of England and Wales and the law of some other country fall to be taken into account.

(3) The law of England and Wales shall determine for the purposes of any law applicable by virtue of subsection (1)(a) above whether, and the time at which, proceedings have been commenced in respect of any matter; and, accordingly, section 35 of the Limitation Act 1980 (new claims in pending proceedings) shall apply in relation to time limits applicable by virtue of subsection (1)(a) above as it applies in relation to time limits under that Act.

(4) A court in England and Wales, in exercising in pursuance of subsection (1)(a) above any discretion conferred by the law of any other country, shall so far as practicable exercise that discretion in the manner in which it is exercised in comparable cases by the courts of that other country.

(5) In this section "law", in relation to any country, shall not include rules of private international law applicable by the courts of that country or, in the case of England and Wales, this Act.

### [1A Extension of limitation periods because of mediation of certain cross-border disputes

(1) In this section—

(a) "Mediation Directive" means Directive 2008/52/EC of the European Parliament and of the Council of 21 May 2008 on certain aspects of mediation in civil and commercial matters,

(b) "mediation" has the meaning given by article 3(a) of the Mediation Directive,

(c) "mediator" has the meaning given by article 3(b) of the Mediation Directive, and

(d) "relevant dispute" means a dispute to which article 8(1) of the Mediation Directive applies (certain cross-border disputes).

(2) Subsection (3) applies where—

(a) a limitation period prescribed by any law applicable by virtue of section 1(1)(a) relates to the subject of the whole or part of a relevant dispute,

(b) a mediation in relation to the relevant dispute starts before the period expires, and

(c) if not extended by this section, the period would expire before the mediation ends or less than eight weeks after it ends.

(3) For the purposes of initiating judicial proceedings or arbitration, the limitation period expires instead at the end of eight weeks after the mediation ends (subject to subsection (4)).

(4) If a limitation period has been extended by this section, subsections (2) and (3) apply to the extended limitation period as they apply to a limitation period mentioned in subsection (2)(a).

(5) For the purposes of this section, mediation starts on the date of the agreement to mediate that is entered into by the parties and the mediator.

(6) For the purposes of this section, a mediation ends on the date of the first of these to occur—

(a) the parties reach an agreement in resolution of the relevant dispute,

(b)  a party completes the notification of the other parties that it has withdrawn from the mediation,

(c)  a party to whom a qualifying request is made fails to give a response reaching the other parties within 14 days of the request,

(d)  after the parties are notified that the mediator's appointment has ended (by death, resignation or otherwise), they fail to agree within 14 days to seek to appoint a replacement mediator,

(e)  the mediation otherwise comes to an end pursuant to the terms of the agreement to mediate.

(7)  For the purpose of subsection (6), a qualifying request is a request by a party that another (A) confirm to all parties that A is continuing with the mediation.

(8)  In the case of any relevant dispute, references in this section to a mediation are references to the mediation so far as it relates to that dispute, and references to a party are to be read accordingly.

(9)  This section is without prejudice to any enactment which has effect for the purposes of provisions—

(a)  relating to limitation or prescription periods and

(b)  contained in an international agreement to which the United Kingdom is a party.]

## 2  Exceptions to section 1

(1)  In any case in which the application of section 1 above would to any extent conflict (whether under subsection (2) below or otherwise) with public policy, that section shall not apply to the extent that its application would so conflict.

(2)  The application of section 1 above in relation to any action or proceedings shall conflict with public policy to the extent that its application would cause undue hardship to a person who is, or might be made, a party to the action or proceedings.

(3)  Where, under a law applicable by virtue of section 1(1)(a) above for the purposes of any action or proceedings, a limitation period is or may be extended or interrupted in respect of the absence of a party to the action or proceedings from any specified jurisdiction or country, so much of that law as provides for the extension or interruption shall be disregarded for those purposes.

(4)  [. . .]

## 3  Foreign judgments on limitation points

Where a court in any country outside England and Wales has determined any matter wholly or partly by reference to the law of that or any other country (including England and Wales) relating to limitation, then, for the purposes of the law relating to the effect to be given in England and Wales to that determination, that court shall, to the extent that it has so determined the matter, be deemed to have determined it on its merits.

## 4  Meaning of law relating to limitation

(1)  Subject to subsection (3) below, references in this Act to the law of any country (including England and Wales) relating to limitation shall, in relation to any matter, be construed as references to so much of the relevant law of that country as (in any manner) makes provision with respect to a limitation period applicable to the bringing of proceedings in respect of that matter in the courts of that country and shall include—

(a)  references to so much of that law as relates to, and to the effect of, the application, extension, reduction or interruption of that period; and

(b)  a reference, where under that law there is no limitation period which is so applicable, to the rule that such proceedings may be brought within an indefinite period.

(2)  In subsection (1) above "relevant law", in relation to any country, means the procedural and substantive law applicable, apart from any rules of private international law, by the courts of that country.

(3)  References in this Act to the law of England and Wales relating to limitation shall not include the rules by virtue of which a court may, in the exercise of any discretion, refuse equitable relief on the grounds of acquiescence or otherwise; but, in applying those rules to a case in relation to which the law

of any country outside England and Wales is applicable by virtue of section 1(1)(*a*) above (not being a law that provides for a limitation period that has expired), a court in England and Wales shall have regard, in particular, to the provisions of the law that is so applicable.

[. . .]

## 6 Application to Crown

(1) This Act applies in relation to any action or proceedings by or against the Crown as it applies in relation to actions and proceedings to which the Crown is not a party.

(2) For the purposes of this section references to an action or proceedings by or against the Crown include references to—

(a) any action or proceedings by or against Her Majesty in right of the Duchy of Lancaster;

(b) any action or proceedings by or against any Government department or any officer of the Crown as such or any person acting on behalf of the Crown;

(c) any action or proceedings by or against the Duke of Cornwall.

## 7 Short title, commencement, transitional provision and extent

(1) This Act may be cited as the Foreign Limitation Periods Act 1984.

(2) This Act shall come into force on such day as the Lord Chancellor may by order made by statutory instrument appoint.

(3) Nothing in this Act shall—

(a) affect any action, proceedings or arbitration commenced in England and Wales before the day appointed under subsection (2) above; or

(b) apply in relation to any matter if the limitation period which, apart from this Act, would have been applied in respect of that matter in England and Wales expired before that day.

(4) This Act extends to England and Wales only.

[8 Disapplication of sections 1, 2 and 4 where [the law applicable to limitation is determined by other instruments

(1) Where in proceedings in England and Wales the law of a country other than England and Wales falls to be taken into account by virtue of any choice of law rule contained in [the Rome I Regulation or] the Rome II Regulation, sections 1, 2 and 4 above shall not apply in respect of that matter.

[(1A) In subsection (1) the "Rome I Regulation" means Regulation (EC) No 593/2008 of the European Parliament and of the Council on the law applicable to contractual obligations, including that Regulation as applied by regulation 5 of the Law Applicable to Contractual Obligations (England and Wales and Northern Ireland) Regulations 2009 (conflicts solely between the laws of different parts of the United Kingdom or between one or more parts of the United Kingdom and Gibraltar).]

(2) In subsection (1) the "Rome II Regulation" means Regulation (EC) No 864/2007 of the European Parliament and of the Council on the law applicable to non-contractual obligations, including that Regulation as applied by regulation 6 of the Law Applicable to Non-Contractual Obligations (England and Wales and Northern Ireland) Regulations 2008 (conflicts solely between the laws of different parts of the United Kingdom or between one or more parts of the United Kingdom and Gibraltar).]

# Matrimonial and Family Proceedings Act
# 1984 ch 42

PART III

## Financial Relief in England and Wales after Overseas Divorce etc

*Applications for financial relief*

**12 Applications for financial relief after overseas divorce etc**

(1) Where—

(a) a marriage has been dissolved or annulled, or the parties to a marriage have been legally separated, by means of judicial or other proceedings in an overseas country, and

(b) the divorce, annulment or legal separation is entitled to be recognised as valid in England and Wales,

either party to the marriage may apply to the court in the manner prescribed by rules of court for an order for financial relief under this Part of this Act.

(2) If after a marriage has been dissolved or annulled in an overseas country one of the parties to the marriage [forms a subsequent marriage or civil partnership,] that party shall not be entitled to make an application in relation to that marriage.

[(3) The reference in subsection (2) above to the forming of a subsequent marriage or civil partnership includes a reference to the forming of a marriage or civil partnership which is by law void or voidable.]

(4) In this Part of this Act except sections 19, 23, and 24 "order for financial relief" means an order under section 17 or 22 below of a description referred to in that section.

**13 Leave of the court required for applications for financial relief**

(1) No application for an order for financial relief shall be made under this Part of this Act unless the leave of the court has been obtained in accordance with rules of court; and the court shall not grant leave unless it considers that there is substantial ground for the making of an application for such an order.

(2) The court may grant leave under this section notwithstanding that an order has been made by a court in a country outside England and Wales requiring the other party to the marriage to make any payment or transfer any property to the applicant or a child of the family.

(3) Leave under this section may be granted subject to such conditions as the court thinks fit.

**14 Interim orders for maintenance**

(1) Where leave is granted under section 13 above for the making of an application for an order for financial relief and it appears to the court that the applicant or any child of the family is in immediate need of financial assistance, the court may make an interim order for maintenance, that is to say, an order requiring the other party to the marriage to make to the applicant or to the child such periodical payments, and for such term, being a term beginning not earlier than the date of the grant of leave and ending with the date of the determination of the application for an order for financial relief, as the court thinks reasonable.

(2) If it appears to the court that the court has jurisdiction to entertain the application for an order for financial relief by reason only of paragraph (c) of section 15(1) below the court shall not make an interim order under this section.

(3) An interim order under subsection (1) above may be made subject to such conditions as the court thinks fit.

### 15 Jurisdiction of the court

(1) Subject to [subsections (1A) and (2)] below, the court shall have jurisdiction to entertain an application for an order for financial relief if any of the following jurisdictional requirements are satisfied, that is to say—

(a) either of the parties to the marriage was domiciled in England and Wales on the date of the application for leave under section 13 above or was so domiciled on the date on which the divorce, annulment or legal separation obtained in the overseas country took effect in that country; or

(b) either of the parties to the marriage was habitually resident in England and Wales throughout the period of one year ending with the date of the application for leave or was so resident throughout the period of one year ending with the date on which the divorce, annulment or legal separation obtained in the overseas country took effect in that country; or

(c) either or both of the parties to the marriage had at the date of the application for leave a beneficial interest in possession in a dwelling-house situated in England or Wales which was at some time during the marriage a matrimonial home of the parties to the marriage.

[(1A) If an application or part of an application relates to a matter where jurisdiction falls to be determined by reference to the jurisdictional requirements of the Maintenance Regulation and Schedule 6 to the Civil Jurisdiction and Judgments (Maintenance) Regulations 2011, those requirements are to determine whether the court has jurisdiction to entertain the application or that part of it.]

(2) Where the jurisdiction of the court to entertain proceedings under this Part of this Act would fall to be determined by reference to the jurisdictional requirements imposed by virtue of Part I of the Civil Jurisdiction and Judgments Act 1982 (implementation of certain European conventions) [. . .] then—

(a) satisfaction of the requirements of subsection (1) above shall not obviate the need to satisfy the requirements imposed by virtue of [. . .] Part I of that Act; and

(b) satisfaction of the requirements imposed by virtue of [. . .] Part I of that Act shall obviate the need to satisfy the requirements of subsection (1) above;

and the court shall entertain or not entertain the proceedings accordingly.

[(3) In this section, "the Maintenance Regulation" means Council Regulation (EC) No 4/2009 including as applied in relation to Denmark by virtue of the Agreement made on 19th October 2005 between the European Community and the Kingdom of Denmark.]

### 16 Duty of the court to consider whether England and Wales is appropriate venue for application

(1) [Subject to subsection (3),] before making an order for financial relief the court shall consider whether in all the circumstances of the case it would be appropriate for such an order to be made by a court in England and Wales, and if the court is not satisfied that it would be appropriate, the court shall dismiss the application.

(2) The court shall in particular have regard to the following matters—

(a) the connection which the parties to the marriage have with England and Wales;

(b) the connection which those parties have with the country in which the marriage was dissolved or annulled or in which they were legally separated;

(c) the connection which those parties have with any other country outside England and Wales;

(d) any financial benefit which the applicant or a child of the family has received, or is likely to receive, in consequence of the divorce, annulment or legal separation, by virtue of any agreement or the operation of the law of a country outside England and Wales;

(e) in a case where an order has been made by a court in a country outside England and Wales requiring the other party to the marriage to make any payment or transfer any property for the benefit of the applicant or a child of the family, the financial relief given by the order and the extent to which the order has been complied with or is likely to be complied with;

(f) any right which the applicant has, or has had, to apply for financial relief from the other party to the marriage under the law of any country outside England and Wales and if the applicant has omitted to exercise that right the reason for that omission;

(g)  the availability in England and Wales of any property in respect of which an order under this Part of this Act in favour of the applicant could be made;

(h)  the extent to which any order made under this Part of this Act is likely to be enforceable;

(i)  the length of time which has elapsed since the date of the divorce, annulment or legal separation.

[(3)  If the court has jurisdiction in relation to the application or part of it by virtue of the Maintenance Regulation and Schedule 6 to the Civil Jurisdiction and Judgments (Maintenance) Regulations 2011, the court may not dismiss the application or that part of it on the ground mentioned in subsection (1) if to do so would be inconsistent with the jurisdictional requirements of that Regulation and that Schedule.

(4)  In this section, "the Maintenance Regulation" means Council Regulation (EC) No 4/2009 including as applied in relation to Denmark by virtue of the Agreement made on 19th October 2005 between the European Community and the Kingdom of Denmark.]

*Orders for financial provision and property adjustment*

**17  Orders for financial provision and property adjustment**

[(1)  Subject to section 20 below, on an application by a party to a marriage for an order for financial relief under this section, the court may—

(a)  make any one or more of the orders which it could make under Part II of the 1973 Act if a decree of divorce, a decree of nullity of marriage or a decree of judicial separation in respect of the marriage had been granted in England and Wales, that is to say—

(i)  any order mentioned in section 23(1) of the 1973 Act (financial provision orders); and

(ii)  any order mentioned in section 24(1) of that Act (property adjustment orders);

[(a)  make one or more orders each of which would, within the meaning of Part II of the 1973 Act, be a financial provision order in favour of a party to the marriage or a child of the family or a property adjustment order in relation to the marriage;] and

(b)  if the marriage has been dissolved or annulled, make one or more orders each of which would, within the meaning of that Part of that Act, be a pension sharing order in relation to the marriage;

[(c)  if the marriage has been dissolved or annulled, make an order which would, within the meaning of that Part of that Act, be a pension compensation sharing order in relation to the marriage].]

(2)  Subject to section 20 below, where the court makes a secured periodical payments order, an order for the payment of a lump sum or a property adjustment order under subsection (1) above, then, on making that order or at any time thereafter, the court may make any order mentioned in section 24A(1) of the 1973 Act (orders for sale of property) which the court would have power to make if the order under subsection (1) above had been made under Part II of the 1973 Act.

**18  Matters to which the court is to have regard in exercising its powers under s 17**

(1)  In deciding whether to exercise its powers under section 17 above and, if so, in what manner the court shall act in accordance with this section.

(2)  The court shall have regard to all the circumstances of the case, first consideration being given to the welfare while a minor of any child of the family who has not attained the age of eighteen.

(3)  As regards the exercise of those powers in relation to a party to the marriage, the court shall in particular have regard to the matters mentioned in section 25(2)(a) to (h) of the 1973 Act and shall be under duties corresponding with those imposed by section 25A(1) and (2) of the 1973 Act where it decides to exercise under section 17 above powers corresponding with the powers referred to in those subsections.

[(3A)  The matters to which the court is to have regard under subsection (3) above—

(a)  so far as relating to paragraph (a) of section 25(2) of the 1973 Act, include any benefits under a pension arrangement which a party to the marriage has or is likely to have [and any PPF compensation to which a party to the marriage is or is likely to be entitled,] (whether or not in the foreseeable future), and

(b) so far as relating to paragraph (h) of that provision, include[—

    (i)] any benefits under a pension arrangement which, by reason of the dissolution or annulment of the marriage, a party to the marriage will lose the chance of acquiring[,] and

    (ii) any PPF compensation which, by reason of the dissolution or annulment of the marriage, a party to the marriage will lose the chance of acquiring entitlement to].

(4) As regards the exercise of those powers in relation to a child of the family, the court shall in particular have regard to the matters mentioned in section 25(3)(a) to (e) of the 1973 Act.

(5) As regards the exercise of those powers against a party to the marriage in favour of a child of the family who is not the child of that party, the court shall also have regard to the matters mentioned in section 25(4)(a) to (c) of the 1973 Act.

(6) Where an order has been made by a court outside England and Wales for the making of payments or the transfer of property by a party to the marriage, the court in considering in accordance with this section the financial resources of the other party to the marriage or a child of the family shall have regard to the extent to which that order has been complied with or is likely to be complied with.

[(7) In this section—

(a) "pension arrangement" has the meaning given by section 25D(3) of the 1973 Act, and

(b) references to benefits under a pension arrangement include any benefits by way of pension, whether under a pension arrangement or not[, and

[(c) "PPF compensation" means compensation payable under—

    (i) Chapter 3 of Part 2 of the Pensions Act 2004 (pension protection) or any regulations or order made under it,

    (ii) Chapter 1 of Part 3 of the Pensions Act 2008 (pension compensation sharing) or any regulations or order made under it, or

    (iii) any provision corresponding to the provisions mentioned in sub-paragraph (i) or (ii) in force in Northern Ireland]].]

### 19 Consent orders for financial provision or property adjustment

(1) Notwithstanding anything in section 18 above, on an application for a consent order for financial relief the court may, unless it has reason to think that there are other circumstances into which it ought to inquire, make an order in the terms agreed on the basis only of the prescribed information furnished with the application.

(2) Subsection (1) above applies to an application for a consent order varying or discharging an order for financial relief as it applies to an application for an order for financial relief.

(3) In this section—

"consent order", in relation to an application for an order, means an order in the terms applied for to which the respondent agrees;

"order for financial relief" means an order under section 17 above; and

"prescribed" means prescribed by rules of court.

### 20 Restriction of powers of court where jurisdiction depends on matrimonial home in England or Wales

(1) Where the court has jurisdiction to entertain an application for an order for financial relief by reason only of the situation in England or Wales of a dwelling-house which was a matrimonial home of the parties, the court may make under section 17 above any one or more of the following orders (but no other)—

(a) an order that either party to the marriage shall pay to the other such lump sum as may be specified in the order;

(b) an order that a party to the marriage shall pay to such person as may be so specified for the benefit of a child of the family, or to such a child, such lump sum as may be so specified;

(c) an order that a party to the marriage shall transfer to the other party, to any child of the family or to such person as may be so specified for the benefit of such a child, the interest of the first-mentioned party in the dwelling-house, or such part of that interest as may be so specified;

(d) an order that a settlement of the interest of a party to the marriage in the dwelling-house, or such part of that interest as may be so specified, be made to the satisfaction of the court for the benefit of the other party to the marriage and of the children of the family or either or any of them;

(e) an order varying for the benefit of the parties to the marriage and of the children of the family or either or any of them any ante-nuptial or post-nuptial settlement (including such a settlement made by will or codicil) made on the parties to the marriage so far as that settlement relates to an interest in the dwelling-house;

(f) an order extinguishing or reducing the interest of either of the parties to the marriage under any such settlement so far as that interest is an interest in the dwelling-house;

(g) an order for the sale of the interest of a party to the marriage in the dwelling-house.

(2) Where, in the circumstances mentioned in subsection (1) above, the court makes an order for the payment of a lump sum by a party to the marriage, the amount of the lump sum shall not exceed, or where more than one such order is made the total amount of the lump sums shall not exceed in aggregate, the following amount, that is to say—

(a) if the interest of that party in the dwelling-house is sold in pursuance of an order made under subsection (1)(g) above, the amount of the proceeds of the sale of that interest after deducting therefrom any costs incurred in the sale thereof;

(b) if the interest of that party is not so sold, the amount which in the opinion of the court represents the value of that interest.

(3) Where the interest of a party to the marriage in the dwelling-house is held jointly or in common with any other person or persons—

(a) the reference in subsection (1)(g) above to the interest of a party to the marriage shall be construed as including a reference to the interest of that other person, or the interest of those other persons, in the dwelling-house, and

(b) the reference in subsection (2)(a) above to the amount of the proceeds of a sale ordered under subsection (1)(g) above shall be construed as a reference to that part of those proceeds which is attributable to the interest of that party to the marriage in the dwelling-house.

## 21 Application to orders under ss 14 and 17 of certain provisions of Part II of Matrimonial Causes Act 1973

[(1)] The following provisions of Part II of the 1973 Act (financial relief for parties to marriage and children of family) shall apply in relation to an order . . . under section 14 or 17 above as they apply in relation to a like order . . . under that Part of that Act, that is to say—

(a) section 23(3) (provisions as to lump sums);

(b) section 24A(2), (4), (5) and (6) (provisions as to orders for sale);

[(ba) section 24B(3) to (5) (provisions about pension sharing orders in relation to divorce and nullity);

(bb) section 24C (duty to stay pension sharing orders);

(bc) section 24D (apportionment of pension sharing charges);]

[(bca) section 24E(3) to (10) (provisions about pension compensation orders in relation to divorce and nullity);

(bcb) section 24F (duty to stay pension compensation sharing orders);

(bcc) section 24G (apportionment of pension compensation sharing charges);]

[(bd) section 25B(3) to (7B) (power, by financial provision order, to attach payments under a pension arrangement, or to require the exercise of a right of commutation under such an arrangement);

(be) section 25C (extension of lump sum powers in relation to death benefits under a pension arrangement);]

[(bf) section 25E(2) to (10) (the Pension Protection Fund);]

[(bg) section 25F (power, by financial provision order, to attach pension compensation payments, or to require the exercise of a right of commutation of pension compensation);]

(c)   section 28(1) and (2) (duration of continuing financial provision orders in favour of party to marriage);

(d)   section 29 (duration of continuing financial provision orders in favour of children, and age limit on making certain orders in their favour);

(e)   section 30 (direction for settlement of instrument for securing payments or effecting property adjustment), except paragraph (b);

(f)   section 31 variation, discharge etc of certain orders for financial relief), except subsection (2)(e) and subsection (4);

(g)   section 32 (payment of certain arrears unenforceable without the leave of the court);

(h)   section 33 (orders for repayment of sums paid under certain orders);

  (i)   section 38 (orders for repayment of sums paid after cessation of order by reason of remarriage);

(j)   section 39 (settlements etc made in compliance with a property adjustment order may be avoided on bankruptcy of settlor); and

(k)   section 40 (payments etc under order made in favour of person suffering from mental disorder);

[(l)   section 40A (appeals relating to pension sharing orders which have taken effect)];

[(m) section 40B (appeals relating to pension compensation sharing orders which have taken effect)].

[(2) Subsection (1)(bd)[, (be) and (bg)] above shall not apply where the court has jurisdiction to entertain an application for an order for financial relief by reason only of the situation in England or Wales of a dwelling-house which was a matrimonial home of the parties.

(3) Section 25D(1) of the 1973 Act (effect of transfers on orders relating to rights under a pension arrangement) shall apply in relation to an order made under section 17 above by virtue of subsection (1)(bd) or (be) above as it applies in relation to an order made under section 23 [section 22A or 23] of that Act by virtue of section 25B or 25C of the 1973 Act.

(4) The Lord Chancellor may by regulations make for the purposes of this Part of this Act provision corresponding to any provision which may be made by him under subsections (2) to (2B) of section 25D of the 1973 Act [or under subsections (1) to (3) of section 25G of that Act].

(5) Power to make regulations under this section shall be exercisable by statutory instrument which shall be subject to annulment in pursuance of a resolution of either House of Parliament.]

*Orders for transfer of tenancies*

**[22 Powers of court in relation to certain tenancies of dwelling-houses]**

[(1) This section applies if—

(a)   an application is made by a party to a marriage for an order for financial relief; and

(b)   one of the parties is entitled, either in his own right or jointly with the other party, to occupy a dwelling-house situated in England or Wales by virtue of a tenancy which is a relevant tenancy within the meaning of Schedule 7 to the Family Law Act 1996 (certain statutory tenancies).

(2) The court may make in relation to that dwelling-house any order which it could make under Part II of that Schedule [if a decree of divorce, a decree of nullity of marriage or a decree of judicial separation has been granted] in England and Wales in respect of the marriage.

(3) The provisions of paragraphs 10, 11 and 14(1) in Part III of that Schedule apply in relation to any order under this section as they apply to any order under Part II of that Schedule.]

*Avoidance of transactions intended to prevent or reduce financial relief*

### 23 Avoidance of transactions intended to defeat applications for financial relief

(1) For the purposes of this section "financial relief" means relief under section 14 or 17 above and any reference to defeating a claim by a party to a marriage for financial relief from being granted is a reference to preventing financial relief from being granted or reducing the amount of relief which might be granted, or frustrating or impeding the enforcement of any order which might be or has been made under either of those provisions at the instance of that party.

(2) Where leave is granted under section 13 above for the making by a party to a marriage of an application for an order for financial relief under section 17 above, the court may, on an application by that party—

(a) if it is satisfied that the other party to the marriage is, with the intention of defeating the claim for financial relief, about to make any disposition or to transfer out of the jurisdiction or otherwise deal with any property, make such order as it thinks fit for restraining the other party from so doing or otherwise for protecting the claim;

(b) if it is satisfied that the other party has, with that intention, made a reviewable disposition and that if the disposition were set aside financial relief or different financial relief would be granted to the applicant, make an order setting aside the disposition.

(3) Where an order for financial relief under section 14 or 17 above has been made by the court at the instance of a party to a marriage, then, on an application made by that party, the court may, if it is satisfied that the other party to the marriage has, with the intention of defeating the claim for financial relief, made a reviewable disposition, make an order setting aside the disposition.

(4) Where the court has jurisdiction to entertain the application for an order for financial relief by reason only of paragraph (c) of section 15(1) above, it shall not make any order under subsection (2) or (3) above in respect of any property other than the dwelling-house concerned.

(5) Where the court makes an order under subsection (2)(b) or (3) above setting aside a disposition it shall give such consequential directions as it thinks fit for giving effect to the order (including directions requiring the making of any payments or the disposal of any property).

(6) Any disposition made by the other party to the marriage (whether before or after the commencement of the application) is a reviewable disposition for the purposes of subsections (2)(b) and (3) above unless it was made for valuable consideration (other than marriage) to a person who, at the time of the disposition, acted in relation to it in good faith and without notice of any intention on the part of the other party to defeat the applicant's claim for financial relief.

(7) Where an application is made under subsection (2) or (3) above with respect to a disposition which took place less than three years before the date of the application or with respect to a disposition or other dealing with property which is about to take place and the court is satisfied—

(a) in a case falling within subsection(2)(a) or (b) above, that the disposition or other dealing would (apart from this section) have the consequence, or

(b) in a case falling within subsection (3) above, that the disposition has had the consequence,

of defeating a claim by the applicant for financial relief, it shall be presumed, unless the contrary is shown, that the person who disposed of or is about to dispose of or deal with the property did so or, as the case may be, is about to do so, with the intention of defeating the applicant's claim for financial relief.

(8) In this section "disposition" does not include any provision contained in a will or codicil but, with that exception, includes any conveyance, assurance or gift of property of any description, whether made by an instrument or otherwise.

(9) The preceding provisions of this section are without prejudice to any power of the High Court to grant injunctions under section 37 of the [Senior Courts Act 1981].

### 24 Prevention of transactions intended to defeat prospective applications for financial relief

(1) Where, on an application by a party to a marriage, it appears to the court—

UK Statutes

(a)  that the marriage has been dissolved or annulled, or that the parties to the marriage have been legally separated, by means of judicial or other proceedings in an overseas country; and

(b)  that the applicant intends to apply for leave to make an application for an order for financial relief under section 17 above as soon as he or she has been habitually resident in England and Wales for a period of one year; and

(c)  that the other party to the marriage is, with the intention of defeating a claim for financial relief, about to make any disposition or to transfer out of the jurisdiction or otherwise deal with any property,

the court may make such order as it thinks fit for restraining the other party from taking such action as is mentioned in paragraph (c) above.

(2)  For the purposes of an application under subsection (1) above—

(a)  the reference to defeating a claim for financial relief shall be construed in accordance with subsection (1) of section 23 above (omitting the reference to any order which has been made); and

(b)  subsections (7) and (8) of section 23 above shall apply for the purposes of an application under that section.

(3)  The preceding provisions of this section are without prejudice to any power of the High Court to grant injunctions under section 37 of the [Senior Courts Act 1981].

. . .

*Interpretation*

**27  Interpretation of Part III**

In this Part of this Act—

"the 1973 Act" means the Matrimonial Causes Act 1973;

"child of the family" has the meaning as in section 52(1) of the 1973 Act;

"the court" means the High Court or [the family court];

"dwelling-house" includes any building or part thereof which is occupied as a dwelling, and any yard, garden, garage or outhouse belonging to the dwelling-house and occupied therewith;

"order for financial relief" has the meaning given by section 12(4) above;

"overseas country" means a country or territory outside the British Islands;

"possession" includes receipt of, or the right to receive, rents and profits;

"property adjustment order" means such an order as is specified in section 24(1)(a), (b), (c) or (d) of the 1973 Act;

"rent" does not include mortgage interest;

"secured periodical payments order" means such an order as is specified in section 23(1)(b) or (e) of the 1973 Act.

# Child Abduction and Custody Act
# 1985 ch 60

PART I

## International Child Abduction

### 1 The Hague Convention

(1) In this Part of this Act "the Convention" means the Convention on the Civil Aspects of International Child Abduction which was signed at The Hague on 25th October 1980.

(2) Subject to the provisions of this Part of this Act, the provisions of that Convention set out in Schedule 1 to this Act shall have the force of law in the United Kingdom.

[(3) But—

(a) those provisions of the Convention;

(b) this Part of this Act; and

(c) rules of court under section 10 of this Act,

are subject to Article 60 of the Council Regulation (by virtue of which the Regulation takes precedence over the Convention, in so far as it concerns matters governed by the Regulation).

(4) "The Council Regulation" means Council Regulation (EC) No 2201/2003 of 27th November 2003 concerning jurisdiction and the recognition and enforcement of judgments in matrimonial matters and matters of parental responsibility.]

### 2 Contracting States

(1) For the purposes of the Convention as it has effect under this Part of this Act the Contracting States other than the United Kingdom shall be those for the time being specified by an Order in Council under this section.

(2) An Order in Council under this section shall specify the date of the coming into force of the Convention as between the United Kingdom and any State specified in the Order; and, except where the Order otherwise provides, the Convention shall apply as between the United Kingdom and that State only in relation to wrongful removals or retentions occurring on or after that date.

(3) Where the Convention applies, or applies only, to a particular territory or particular territories specified in a declaration made by a Contracting State under Article 39 or 40 of the Convention references to that State in subsections (1) and (2) above shall be construed as references to that territory or those territories.

### 3 Control Authorities

(1) Subject to subsection (2) below, the functions under the Convention of a Central Authority shall be discharged—

(a) in England and Wales [. . .] by the Lord Chancellor;

. . .

(2) Any application made under the Convention by or on behalf of a person outside the United Kingdom may be addressed to the Lord Chancellor as the Central Authority in the United Kingdom.

[(3) Where any such application relates to a function to be discharged under subsection (1) above by an authority ("the responsible authority") other than the authority to which the application is addressed, the authority to which the application is addressed shall transmit it to the responsible authority.]

### 4 Judicial authorities

The courts having jurisdiction to entertain applications under the Convention shall be—

(a)  in England and Wales or in Northern Ireland the High Court; and

(b)  in Scotland the Court of Session.

### 5 Interim powers

Where an application has been made to a court in the United Kingdom under the Convention, the court may, at any time before the application is determined, give such interim directions as it thinks fit for the purpose of securing the welfare of the child concerned or of preventing changes in the circumstances relevant to the determination of the application.

### 6 Reports

Where the Lord Chancellor[, the Department of Justice in Northern Ireland] or the Secretary of State is requested to provide information relating to a child under Article 7(d) of the Convention he may—

(a)  request a local authority or [an officer of the Service] [or a Welsh family proceedings officer] to make a report to him in writing with respect to any matter which appears to him to be relevant;

(b)  request the Department of Health and Social Services for Northern Ireland to arrange for a suitably qualified person to make such a report to him;

(c)  request any court to which a written report relating to the child has been made to send him a copy of the report;

and such a request shall be duly complied with.

### 7  Proof of documents and evidence

(1)  For the purposes of Article 14 of the Convention a decision or determination of a judicial or administrative authority outside the United Kingdom may be proved by a duly authenticated copy of the decision or determination; and any document purporting to be such a copy shall be deemed to be a true copy unless the contrary is shown.

(2)  For the purposes of subsection (1) above a copy is duly authenticated if it bears the seal, or is signed by a judge or officer, of the authority in question.

(3)  For the purposes of Articles 14 and 30 of the Convention any such document as is mentioned in Article 8 of the Convention, or a certified copy of any such document, shall be sufficient evidence of anything stated in it.

### 8  Declarations by United Kingdom courts

The High Court or Court of Session may, on an application made for the purposes of Article 15 of the Convention by any person appearing to the court to have an interest in the matter, make a declaration or declarator that the removal of any child from, or his retention outside, the United Kingdom was wrongful within the meaning of Article 3 of the Convention.

### 9  Suspension of court's powers in cases of wrongful removal

The reference in Article 16 of the Convention to deciding on the merits of rights of custody shall be construed as a reference to—

(a)  making, varying or revoking a custody order, or [a supervision order under section 31 of the Children Act 1989] or [Article 50 of the Children (Northern Ireland) Order 1995];

[(aa) enforcing under section 29 of the Family Law Act 1986 a custody order within the meaning of Chapter V of Part I of that Act;]

(b)  registering or enforcing a decision under Part II of this Act;

[(ba) registering or enforcing a decision under the Convention on Jurisdiction, Applicable Law, Recognition, Enforcement and Co-Operation in respect of Parental Responsibility and Measures for the Protection of Children that was signed at The Hague on 19 October 1996 ("the 1996 Convention"), except where provisions of the 1996 Convention are invoked in accordance with Article 50 of the 1996 Convention;]

(c)  [. . .]

. . .

(e) [. . .]

## 10 Rules of court

(1) An authority having power to make rules of court may make such provision for giving effect to this Part of this Act as appears to that authority to be necessary or expedient.

(2) Without prejudice to the generality of subsection (1) above, rules of court may make provision—

(a) with respect to the procedure on applications for the return of a child and with respect to the documents and information to be furnished and the notices to be given in connection with any such application;

(b) for the transfer of any such application between the appropriate courts in the different parts of the United Kingdom;

(c) for the giving of notices by or to a court for the purposes of the provisions of Article 16 of the Convention and section 9 above and generally as respects proceedings to which those provisions apply;

(d) for enabling a person who wishes to make an application under the Convention in a Contracting State other than the United Kingdom to obtain from any court in the United Kingdom an authenticated copy of any decision of that court relating to the child to whom the application is to relate.

## 11 Cost of applications

The United Kingdom having made such a reservation as is mentioned in the third paragraph of Article 26 of the Convention, the costs mentioned in that paragraph shall not be borne by any Minister or other authority in the United Kingdom except so far as they fall to be so borne [by virtue of—

[(a) the provision of any civil legal services (within the meaning of Part 1 of the Legal Aid, Sentencing and Punishment of Offenders Act 2012) under arrangements made for the purposes of that Part of that Act,] or

. . .

## PART II

### Recognition and Enforcement of Custody Decisions

### 12 The European Convention

(1) In this Part of this Act "the Convention" means the European Convention on Recognition and Enforcement of Decisions concerning Custody of Children and on the Restoration of Custody of Children which was signed in Luxembourg on 20th May 1980.

(2) Subject to the provisions of this Part of this Act, the provisions of that Convention set out in Schedule 2 to this Act (which includes Articles 9 and 10 as they have effect in consequence of a reservation made by the United Kingdom under Article 17) shall have the force of law in the United Kingdom.

[(3) But—

(a) those provisions of the Convention;

(b) this Part of this Act; and

(c) rules of court under section 24 of this Act,

are subject to Article 60 of the Council Regulation (by virtue of which the Regulation takes precedence over the Convention, in so far as it concerns matters governed by the Regulation).

(4) "The Council Regulation" means Council Regulation (EC) No 2201/2003 of 27th November 2003 concerning jurisdiction and the recognition and enforcement of judgments in matrimonial matters and matters of parental responsibility.]

UK Statutes

### 13 Contracting States

(1) For the purposes of the Convention as it has effect under this Part of this Act the Contracting States other than the United Kingdom shall be those for the time being specified by an Order in Council under this section.

(2) An Order in Council under this section shall specify the date of the coming into force of the Convention as between the United Kingdom and any State specified in the Order.

(3) Where the Convention applies, or applies only, to a particular territory or particular territories specified by a Contracting State under Article 24 or 25 of the Convention references to that State in subsections (1) and (2) above shall be construed as references to that territory or those territories.

### 14 Central Authorities

(1) Subject to subsection (2) below, the functions under the Convention of a Central Authority shall be discharged—

(a)  in England and Wales [. . .] by the Lord Chancellor;

. . .

(2) Any application made under the Convention by or on behalf of a person outside the United Kingdom may be addressed to the Lord Chancellor as the Central Authority in the United Kingdom.

[(3) Where any such application relates to a function to be discharged under subsection (1) above by an authority ("the responsible authority") other than the authority to which the application is addressed, the authority to which the application is addressed shall transmit it to the responsible authority.]

### 15 Recognition of decisions

(1) Articles 7 and 12 of the Convention shall have effect in accordance with this section.

(2) A decision to which either of those Articles applies which was made in a Contracting State other than the United Kingdom shall be recognised in each part of the United Kingdom as if made by a court having jurisdiction to make it in that part but—

(a)  the appropriate court in any part of the United Kingdom may, on the application of any person appearing to it to have an interest in the matter, declare on any of the grounds specified in Article 9 or 10 of the Convention that the decision is not to be recognised in any part of the United Kingdom; and

(b)  the decision shall not be enforceable in any part of the United Kingdom unless registered in the appropriate court under section 16 below.

(3) The references in Article 9(1)(c) of the Convention to the removal of the child are to his improper removal within the meaning of the Convention.

### 16 Registration of decisions

(1) A person on whom any rights are conferred by a decision relating to custody made by an authority in a Contracting State other than the United Kingdom may make an application for the registration of the decision in an appropriate court in the United Kingdom.

(2) The Central Authority in the United Kingdom shall assist such a person in making such an application if a request for such assistance is made by him or on his behalf by the Central Authority of the Contracting State in question.

(3) An application under subsection (1) above or a request under subsection (2) above shall be treated as a request for enforcement for the purposes of Articles 10 and 13 of the Convention.

(4) The High Court or Court of Session shall refuse to register a decision if—

(a)  the court is of the opinion that on any of the grounds specified in Article 9 or 10 of the Convention the decision should not be recognised in any part of the United Kingdom;

(b)  the court is of the opinion that the decision is not enforceable in the Contracting State where it was made and is not a decision to which Article 12 of the Convention applies; or

(c)  an application in respect of the child under Part I of this Act is pending.

[(5) Where an authority mentioned in subsection (1) of section 14 above is requested to assist in making an application under this section to the appropriate court in a part of the United Kingdom ("the relevant part of the United Kingdom") other than the part in relation to which the authority has functions under that subsection, the authority shall transmit the request to the authority which has functions under that subsection in relation to the relevant part of the United Kingdom.]

(6) In this section "decision relating to custody" has the same meaning as in the Convention.

### 17 Variation and revocation of registered decisions

(1) Where a decision which has been registered under section 16 above is varied or revoked by an authority in the Contracting State in which it was made, the person on whose behalf the application for registration of the decision was made shall notify the court in which the decision is registered of the variation or revocation.

(2) Where a court is notified under subsection (1) above of the revocation of a decision, it shall—

(a)   cancel the registration, and

(b)   notify such persons as may be prescribed by rules of court of the cancellation.

(3) Where a court is notified under subsection (1) above of the variation of a decision, it shall—

(a)   notify such persons as may be prescribed by rules of court of the variation; and

(b)   subject to any conditions which may be so prescribed, vary the registration.

(4) The court in which a decision is registered under section 16 above may also, on the application of any person appearing to the court to have an interest in the matter, cancel or vary the registration if it is satisfied that the decision has been revoked or, as the case may be, varied by an authority in the Contracting State in which it was made.

### 18 Enforcement of decisions

Where a decision relating to custody has been registered under section 16 above, the court in which it is registered shall have the same powers for the purpose of enforcing the decision as if it had been made by that court; and proceedings for or with respect to enforcement may be taken accordingly.

### 19 Interim powers

Where an application has been made to a court for the registration of a decision under section 16 above or for the enforcement of such a decision, the court may, at any time before the application is determined, give such interim directions as it thinks fit for the purpose of securing the welfare of the child concerned or of preventing changes in the circumstances relevant to the determination of the application or, in the case of an application for registration, to the determination of any subsequent application for the enforcement of the decision.

### 20 Suspension of court's powers

(1) Where it appears to any court in which such proceedings as are mentioned in subsection (2) below are pending in respect of a child that—

(a)   an application has been made for the registration of a decision in respect of the child under section 16 above (other than a decision mentioned in subsection (3) below) or that such a decision is registered; and

(b)   the decision was made in proceedings commenced before the proceedings which are pending,

the powers of the court with respect to the child in those proceedings shall be restricted as mentioned in subsection (2) below unless, in the case of an application for registration, the application is refused.

(2) Where subsection (1) above applies the court shall not—

(a)   in the case of custody proceedings, make, vary or revoke any custody order, or [a supervision order under section 31 of the Children Act 1989] or [Article 50 of the Children (Northern Ireland) Order 1995];

[(aa) in the case of proceedings under section 29 of the Family Law Act 1986 for the enforcement of a custody order within the meaning of Chapter V of Part I of that Act, enforce that order;] [or]

(b), (c)  [. . .]

. . .

(e)  [. . .]

[(2A)  Where it appears to the Secretary of State—

(a)  that an application has been made for the registration of a decision in respect of a child under section 16 above (other than a decision mentioned in subsection (3) below); or

(b)  that such a decision is registered,

the Secretary of State shall not make, vary or revoke any custody order in respect of the child unless, in the case of an application for registration, the application is refused.]

(3)  The decision referred to in subsection (1) [or (2A)] above is a decision which is only a decision relating to custody within the meaning of section 16 of this Act by virtue of being a decision relating to rights of access.

(4)  Paragraph (b) of Article 10(2) of the Convention shall be construed as referring to custody proceedings within the meaning of this Act.

(5)  This section shall apply to a children's hearing [. . .] as it does to a court.

. . .

### 21  Reports

Where the Lord Chancellor[, the Department of Justice in Northern Ireland] or the Secretary of State is requested to make enquiries about a child under Article 15(1)(b) of the Convention he may—

(a)  request a local authority or [an officer of the Service] [or a Welsh family proceedings officer] to make a report to him in writing with respect to any matter relating to the child concerned which appears to him to be relevant;

(b)  request the Department of Health and Social Services for Northern Ireland to arrange for a suitably qualified person to make such a report to him;

(c)  request any court to which a written report relating to the child has been made to send him a copy of the report;

and any such request shall be duly complied with.

### 22  Proof of documents and evidence

(1)  In any proceedings under this Part of this Act a decision of an authority outside the United Kingdom may be proved by a duly authenticated copy of the decision; and any document purporting to be such a copy shall be deemed to be a true copy unless the contrary is shown.

(2)  For the purposes of subsection (1) above a copy is duly authenticated if it bears the seal, or is signed by a judge or officer, of the authority in question.

(3)  In any proceedings under this Part of this Act any such document as is mentioned in Article 13 of the Convention, or a certified copy of any such document, shall be sufficient evidence of anything stated in it.

### 23  Decisions of United Kingdom courts

(1)  Where a person on whom any rights are conferred by a decision relating to custody made by a court in the United Kingdom makes an application to the Lord Chancellor[, the Department of Justice in Northern Ireland] or the Secretary of State under Article 4 of the Convention with a view to securing its recognition or enforcement in another Contracting State, the Lord Chancellor[, the Department of Justice in Northern Ireland] or the Secretary of State may require the court which made the decision to furnish him with all or any of the documents referred to in Article 13(1)(b), (c) and (d) of the Convention.

(2) Where in any custody proceedings a court in the United Kingdom makes a decision relating to a child who has been removed from the United Kingdom, the court may also, on an application made by any person for the purposes of Article 12 of the Convention, declare the removal to have been unlawful if it is satisfied that the applicant has an interest in the matter and that the child has been taken from or sent or kept out of the United Kingdom without the consent of the person (or, if more than one, all the persons) having the right to determine the child's place of residence under the law of the part of the United Kingdom in which the child was habitually resident.

(3) In this section "decision relating to custody" has the same meaning as in the Convention.

### 24 Rules of court

(1) An authority having power to make rules of court may make such provision for giving effect to this Part of this Act as appears to that authority to be necessary or expedient.

(2) Without prejudice to the generality of subsection (1) above, rules of court may make provision—

(a) with respect to the procedure on applications to a court under any provision of this Part of this Act and with respect to the documents and information to be furnished and the notices to be given in connection with any such application;

(b) for the transfer of any such application between the appropriate courts in the different parts of the United Kingdom;

(c) for the giving of directions requiring the disclosure of information about any child who is the subject of proceedings under this Part of this Act and for safeguarding its welfare.

## PART III

## Supplementary

### [24A Power to order disclosure of child's whereabouts

(1) Where—

(a) in proceedings for the return of a child under Part I of this Act; or

(b) on an application for the recognition, registration or enforcement of a decision in respect of a child under Part II of this Act,

there is not available to the court adequate information as to where the child is, the court may order any person who it has reason to believe may have relevant information to disclose it to the court.

(2) A person shall not be excused from complying with an order under subsection (1) above by reason that to do so may incriminate him or his spouse [or civil partner] of an offence; but a statement or admission made in compliance with such an order shall not be admissible in evidence against either of them in proceedings for any offence other than perjury.]

### 25 Termination of existing custody orders, etc

(1) Where—

(a) an order is made for the return of a child under Part I of this Act; or

(b) a decision with respect to a child (other than a decision mentioned in subsection (2) below) is registered under section 16 of this Act,

any custody order relating to him shall cease to have effect.

(2) The decision referred to in subsection (1)(b) above is a decision which is only a decision relating to custody within the meaning of section 16 of this Act by virtue of being a decision relating to rights of access.

[. . .]

### 26 Expenses

There shall be paid out of money provided by Parliament—

(a)   any expenses incurred by the Lord Chancellor or the Secretary of State by virtue of this Act; and

(b)   any increase attributable to this Act in the sums so payable under any other Act.

### 27 Interpretation

(1) In this Act "custody order" means [(unless the contrary intention appears)] any such order or authorisation as is mentioned in Schedule 3 to this Act and "custody proceedings" means proceedings in which an order within paragraphs 1, 2, 5, 6, 8 or 9 of that Schedule may be [made, varied or revoked].

(2) For the purposes of this Act "part of the United Kingdom" means England and Wales, Scotland or Northern Ireland and "the appropriate court", in relation to England and Wales or Northern Ireland means the High Court and, in relation to Scotland, the Court of Session.

(3) In this Act "local authority" means—

(a)   in relation to England and Wales, the council of a non-metropolitan county, a metropolitan district, a London borough or the Common Council of the City of London;

. . .

[(4) In this Act a decision relating to rights of access in England and Wales [or Scotland] [or Northern Ireland] means a decision as to the contact which a child may, or may not, have with any person.]

[(5) In this Act "officer of the Service" has the same meaning as in the Criminal Justice and Court Services Act 2000.]

[(5A) In this Act "Welsh family proceedings officer" has the meaning given by section 35 of the Children Act 2004.]

### 28 Applications as respects British Islands and colonies

(1) Her Majesty may by Order in Council direct that any of the provisions of this Act specified in the Order shall extend, subject to such modifications as may be specified in the Order, to—

(a)   the Isle of Man,

(b)   any of the Channel Islands, and

(c)   any colony.

(2) Her Majesty may by Order in Council direct that this Act shall have effect in the United Kingdom as if any reference in this Act, or in any amendment made by this Act, to any order which may be made, or any proceedings which may be brought or any other thing which may be done in, or in any part of, the United Kingdom included a reference to any corresponding order which may be made or, as the case may be, proceedings which may be brought or other thing which may be done in any of the territories mentioned in subsection (1) above.

(3) An Order in Council under this section may make such consequential, incidental and supplementary provision as Her Majesty considers appropriate.

(4) An Order in Council under this section shall be subject to annulment in pursuance of a resolution of either House of Parliament.

### 29 Short title, commencement and extent

(1) This Act may be cited as the Child Abduction and Custody Act 1985.

(2) This Act shall come into force on such day as may be appointed by an order made by statutory instrument by the Lord Chancellor and the Lord Advocate; and different days may be so appointed for different provisions.

(3) This Act extends to Northern Ireland.

SCHEDULE 1

## Convention on the Civil Aspects of International Child Abduction

*Chapter I—Scope of the Convention*

### Article 3

The removal or the retention of a child is to be considered wrongful where—

(a) it is in breach of rights of custody attributed to a person, an institution or any other body, either jointly or alone, under the law of the State in which the child was habitually resident immediately before the removal or retention; and

(b) at the time of removal or retention those rights were actually exercised, either jointly or alone, or would have been so exercised but for the removal or retention.

The rights of custody mentioned in sub-paragraph (a) above may arise in particular by operation of law or by reason of a judicial or administrative decision, or by reason of an agreement having legal effect under the law of that State.

### Article 4

The Convention shall apply to any child who was habitually resident in a Contracting State immediately before any breach of custody or access rights. The Convention shall cease to apply when the child attains the age of sixteen years.

### Article 5

For the purposes of this Convention—

(a) "rights of custody" shall include rights relating to the care of the person of the child and, in particular, the right to determine the child's place of residence;

(b) "rights of access" shall include the right to take a child for a limited period of time to a place other than the child's habitual residence.

*Chapter II—Central Authorities*

### Article 7

Central Authorities shall co-operate with each other and promote co-operation amongst the competent authorities in their respective States to secure the prompt return of children and to achieve the other objects of this Convention.

In particular, either directly or through any intermediary, they shall take all appropriate measures—

(a) to discover the whereabouts of a child who has been wrongfully removed or retained;

(b) to prevent further harm to the child or prejudice to interested parties by taking or causing to be taken provisional measures;

(c) to secure the voluntary return of the child or to bring about an amicable resolution of the issues;

(d) to exchange, where desirable, information relating to the social background of the child;

(e) to provide information of a general character as to the law of their State in connection with the application of the Convention;

(f) to initiate or facilitate the institution of judicial or administrative proceedings with a view to obtaining the return of the child and, in a proper case, to make arrangements for organising or securing the effective exercise of rights of access;

(g) where the circumstances so require, to provide or facilitate the provision of legal aid and advice, including the participation of legal counsel and advisers;

(h) to provide such administrative arrangements as may be necessary and appropriate to secure the safe return of the child;

(i) to keep each other informed with respect to the operation of this Convention and, as far as possible, to eliminate any obstacles to its application.

UK Statutes

*Chapter III—Return of Children*

### Article 8

Any person, institution or other body claiming that a child has been removed or retained in breach of custody rights may apply either to the Central Authority of the child's habitual residence or to the Central Authority of any other Contracting State for assistance in securing the return of the child.

The application shall contain—

(a) information concerning the identity of the applicant, of the child and of the person alleged to have removed or retained the child;

(b) where available, the date of birth of the child;

(c) the grounds on which the applicant's claim for return of the child is based;

(d) all available information relating to the whereabouts of the child and the identity of the person with whom the child is presumed to be.

The application may be accompanied or supplemented by—

(e) an authenticated copy of any relevant decision or agreement;

(f) a certificate or an affidavit emanating from a Central Authority, or other competent authority of the State of the child's habitual residence, or from a qualified person, concerning the relevant law of that State;

(g) any other relevant document.

### Article 9

If the Central Authority which receives an application referred to in Article 8 has reason to believe that the child is in another Contracting State, it shall directly and without delay transmit the application to the Central Authority of that Contracting State and inform the requesting Central Authority, or the applicant, as the case may be.

### Article 10

The Central Authority of the State where the child is shall take or cause to be taken all appropriate measures in order to obtain the voluntary return of the child.

### Article 11

The judicial or administrative authorities of Contracting States shall act expeditiously in proceedings for the return of children.

If the judicial or administrative authority concerned has not reached a decision within six weeks from the date of commencement of the proceedings, the applicant or the Central Authority of the requested State, on its own initiative or if asked by the Central Authority of the requesting State, shall have the right to request a statement of the reasons for the delay. If a reply is received by the Central Authority of the requested State, that Authority shall transmit the reply to the Central Authority of the requesting State, or to the applicant, as the case may be.

### Article 12

Where a child has been wrongfully removed or retained in terms of Article 3 and, at the date of the commencement of the proceedings before the judicial or administrative authority of the Contracting State where the child is, a period of less than one year has elapsed from the date of the wrongful removal or retention, the authority concerned shall order the return of the child forthwith.

The judicial or administrative authority, even where the proceedings have been commenced after the expiration of the period of one year referred to in the preceding paragraph, shall also order the return of the child, unless it is demonstrated that the child is now settled in its new environment.

Where the judicial or administrative authority in the requested state has reason to believe that the child has been taken to another State, it may stay the proceedings or dismiss the application for the return of the child.

### Article 13

Notwithstanding the provisions of the preceding Article, the judicial or administrative authority of the requested State is not bound to order the return of the child if the person, institution or other body which opposes its return establishes that—

(a)  the person, institution or other body having the care of the person of the child was not actually exercising the custody rights at the time of removal or retention, or had consented to or subsequently acquiesced in the removal or retention; or

(b)  there is a grave risk that his or her return would expose the child to physical or psychological harm or otherwise place the child in an intolerable situation.

The judicial or administrative authority may also refuse to order the return of the child if it finds that the child objects to being returned and has attained an age and degree of maturity at which it is appropriate to take account of its views.

In considering the circumstances referred to in this Article, the judicial and administrative authorities shall take into account the information relating to the social background of the child provided by the Central Authority or other competent authority of the child's habitual residence.

### Article 14

In ascertaining whether there has been a wrongful removal or retention within the meaning of Article 3, the judicial or administrative authorities of the requested State may take notice directly of the law of, and of judicial or administrative decisions, formally recognised or not in the State of the habitual residence of the child, without recourse to the specific procedures for the proof of that law or for the recognition of foreign decisions which would otherwise be applicable.

### Article 15

The judicial or administrative authorities of a Contracting State may, prior to the making of an order for the return of the child, request that the applicant obtain from the authorities of the State of the habitual residence of the child a decision or other determination that the removal or retention was wrongful within the meaning of Article 3 of the Convention, where such a decision or determination may be obtained in that State. The Central Authorities of the Contracting States shall so far as practicable assist applicants to obtain such a decision or determination.

### Article 16

After receiving notice of a wrongful removal or retention of a child in the sense of Article 3, the judicial or administrative authorities of the Contracting State to which the child has been removed or in which it has been retained shall not decide on the merits of rights of custody until it has been determined that the child is not to be returned under this Convention or unless an application under this Convention is not lodged within a reasonable time following receipt of the notice.

### Article 17

The sole fact that a decision relating to custody has been given in or is entitled to recognition in the requested State shall not be a ground for refusing to return a child under this Convention, but the judicial or administrative authorities of the requested State may take account of the reasons for that decision in applying this Convention.

### Article 18

The provisions of this Chapter do not limit the power of a judicial or administrative authority to order the return of the child at any time.

### Article 19

A decision under this Convention concerning the return of the child shall not be taken to be a determination on the merits of any custody issue.

UK Statutes

## Chapter IV—Rights of Access

### Article 21

An application to make arrangements for organising or securing the effective exercise of rights of access may be presented to the Central Authorities of the Contracting States in the same way as an application for the return of a child.

The Central Authorities are bound by the obligations of co-operation which are set forth in Article 7 to promote the peaceful enjoyment of access rights and the fulfilment of any conditions to which the exercise of those rights may be subject. The Central Authorities shall take steps to remove, as far as possible, all obstacles to the exercise of such rights. The Central Authorities, either directly or through intermediaries, may initiate or assist in the institution of proceedings with a view to organising or protecting these rights and securing respect for the conditions to which the exercise of these rights may be subject.

## Chapter V—General Provisions

### Article 22

No security , bond or deposit, however described, shall be required to guarantee the payment of costs and expenses in the judicial or administrative proceedings falling within the scope of this Convention.

### Article 24

Any application, communication or other document sent to the Central Authority of the requested State shall be in the original language, and shall be accompanied by a translation into the official language or one of the official languages of the requested State or, where that is not feasible, a translation into French or English.

### Article 26

Each Central Authority shall bear its own costs in applying this Convention.

Central Authorities and other public services of Contracting States shall not impose any charges in relation to applications submitted under this Convention. In particular, they may not require any payment from the applicant towards the costs and expenses of the proceedings or, where applicable, those arising from the participation of legal counsel or advisers. However, they may require the payment of the expenses incurred or to be incurred in implementing the return of the child.

However, a Contracting State may, by making a reservation in accordance with Article 42, declare that it shall not be bound to assume any costs referred to in the preceding paragraph resulting from the participation of legal counsel or advisers or from court proceedings, except insofar as those costs may be covered by its system of legal aid and advice.

Upon ordering the return of a child or issuing an order concerning rights of access under this Convention, the judicial or administrative authorities may, where appropriate, direct the person who removed or retained the child, or who prevented the exercise of rights of access, to pay necessary expenses incurred by or on behalf of the applicant, including travel expenses, any costs incurred or payments made for locating the child, the costs of legal representation of the applicant, and those of returning the child.

### Article 27

When it is manifest that the requirements of this Convention are not fulfilled or that the application is otherwise not well founded, a Central Authority is not bound to accept the application. In that case, the Central Authority shall forthwith inform the applicant or the Central Authority through which the application was submitted, as the case may be, of its reasons.

### Article 28

A Central Authority may require that the application be accompanied by a written authorisation empowering it to act on behalf of the applicant, or to designate a representative so to act.

### Article 29

This Convention shall not preclude any person, institution or body who claims that there has been a breach of custody or access rights within the meaning of Article 3 or 21 from applying directly to the judicial or administrative authorities of a Contracting State, whether or not under the provisions of this Convention.

### Article 30

Any application submitted to the Central Authorities or directly to the judicial or administrative authorities of a Contracting State in accordance with the terms of this Convention, together with documents and any other information appended thereto or provided by a Central Authority, shall be admissible in the courts or administrative authorities of the Contracting States.

### Article 31

In relation to a State which in matters of custody of children has two or more systems of law applicable in different territorial units—

(a) any reference to habitual residence in that State shall be construed as referring to habitual residence in a territorial unit of that State;

(b) any reference to the law of the State of habitual residence shall be construed as referring to the law of the territorial unit in that State where the child habitually resides.

### Article 32

In relation to a State which in matters of custody of children has two or more systems of law applicable to different categories of persons, any reference to the law of that State shall be construed as referring to the legal system specified by the law of that State.

## SCHEDULE 2

## European Convention on Recognition and Enforcement of Decisions Concerning Custody of Children

### Article 1

For the purposes of this Convention:

(a) "child" means a person of any nationality, so long as he is under 16 years of age and has not the right to decide on his own place of residence under the law of his habitual residence, the law of his nationality or the internal law of the State addressed;

(b) "authority" means a judicial or administrative authority;

(c) "decision relating to custody" means a decision of an authority in so far as it relates to the care of the person of the child, including the right to decide on the place of his residence, or to the right of access to him;

(d) "improper removal" means the removal of a child across an international frontier in breach of a decision relating to his custody which has been given in a Contracting State and which is enforceable in such a State; "improper removal" also includes:

    (i) the failure to return a child across an international frontier at the end of a period of the exercise of the right of access to this child or at the end of any other temporary stay in a territory other than that where the custody is exercised;

    (ii) a removal which is subsequently declared unlawful within the meaning of Article 12.

### Article 4

(1) Any person who has obtained in a Contracting State a decision relating to the custody of a child and who wishes to have that decision recognised or enforced in another Contracting State may submit an application for this purpose to the central authority in any Contracting State.

(2) The application shall be accompanied by the documents mentioned in Article 13.

(3) The central authority receiving the application, if it is not the central authority in the State addressed, shall send the documents directly and without delay to that central authority.

(4) The central authority receiving the application may refuse to intervene where it is manifestly clear that the conditions laid down by this Convention are not satisfied.

(5) The central authority receiving the application shall keep the applicant informed without delay of the progress of his application.

### Article 5

(1) The central authority in the State addressed shall take or cause to be taken without delay all steps which it considers to be appropriate, if necessary by instituting proceedings before its competent authorities, in order:

(a)   to discover the whereabouts of the child;

(b)   to avoid, in particular by any necessary provisional measures, prejudice to the interests of the child or of the applicant;

(c)   to secure the recognition or enforcement of the decision;

(d)   to secure the delivery of the child to the applicant where enforcement is granted;

(e)   to inform the requesting authority of the measures taken and their results.

(2) Where the central authority in the State addressed has reason to believe that the child is in the territory of another Contracting State it shall send the documents directly and without delay to the central authority of that State.

(3) With the exception of the cost of repatriation, each Contracting State undertakes not to claim any payment from an applicant in respect of any measures taken under paragraph (1) of this Article by the central authority of that State on the applicant's behalf, including the costs of proceedings and, where applicable, the costs incurred by the assistance of a lawyer.

(4) If recognition or enforcement is refused, and if the central authority of the State addressed considers that it should comply with a request by the applicant to bring in that State proceedings concerning the substance of the case, that authority shall use its best endeavours to secure the representation of the applicant in the proceedings under conditions no less favourable than those available to a person who is resident in and a national of that State and for this purpose it may, in particular, institute proceedings before its competent authorities.

### Article 7

A decision relating to custody given in a Contracting State shall be recognised and, where it is enforceable in the State of origin, made enforceable in every other Contracting State.

### Article 9

(1) [*Recognition and enforcement may be refused*] if:

(a)   in the case of a decision given in the absence of the defendant or his legal representative, the defendant was not duly served with the document which instituted the proceedings or an equivalent document in sufficient time to enable him to arrange his defence; but such a failure to effect service cannot constitute a ground for refusing recognition or enforcement where service was not effected because the defendant had concealed his whereabouts from the person who instituted the proceedings in the State of origin;

(b)   in the case of a decision given in the absence of the defendant or his legal representative, the competence of the authority giving the decision was not founded:

(i)    on the habitual residence of the defendant; or

(ii)   on the last common habitual residence of the child's parents, at least one parent being still habitually resident there, or

(iii)  on the habitual residence of the child;

(c)   the decision is incompatible with a decision relating to custody which became enforceable in the

State addressed before the removal of the child, unless the child has had his habitual residence in the territory of the requesting State for one year before his removal.

(3) In no circumstances may the foreign decision be reviewed as to its substance.

## Article 10

(1) [*Recognition and enforcement may also be refused*] on any of the following grounds:

(a) if it is found that the effects of the decision are manifestly incompatible with the fundamental principles of the law relating to the family and children in the State addressed;

(b) if it is found that by reason of a change in the circumstances including the passage of time but not including a mere change in the residence of the child after an improper removal, the effects of the original decision are manifestly no longer in accordance with the welfare of the child;

(c) if at the time when the proceedings were instituted in the State of origin:

   (i)   the child was a national of the State addressed or was habitually resident there and no such connection existed with the State of origin;

   (ii)  the child was a national both of the State of origin and of the State addressed and was habitually resident in the State addressed;

(d) if the decision is incompatible with a decision given in the State addressed or enforceable in that State after being given in a third State, pursuant to proceedings begun before the submission of the request for recognition or enforcement, and if the refusal is in accordance with the welfare of the child.

(2) Proceedings for recognition or enforcement may be adjourned on any of the following grounds:

(a) if an ordinary form of review of the original decision has been commenced;

(b) if proceedings relating to the custody of the child, commenced before the proceedings in the State of origin were instituted, are pending in the State addressed;

(c) if another decision concerning the custody of the child is the subject of proceedings for enforcement or of any other proceedings concerning the recognition of the decision.

## Article 11

(1) Decisions on rights of access and provisions of decisions relating to custody which deal with the rights of access shall be recognised and enforced subject to the same conditions as other decisions relating to custody.

(2) However, the competent authority of the State addressed may fix the conditions for the implementation and exercise of the right of access taking into account, in particular, undertakings given by the parties on this matter.

(3) Where no decision on the right of access has been taken or where recognition or enforcement of the decision relating to custody is refused, the central authority of the State addressed may apply to its competent authorities for a decision on the right of access if the person claiming a right of access so requests.

## Article 12

Where, at the time of the removal of a child across an international frontier, there is no enforceable decision given in a Contracting State relating to his custody, the provisions of this Convention shall apply to any subsequent decision, relating to the custody of that child and declaring the removal to be unlawful, given in a Contracting State at the request of any interested person.

## Article 13

(1) A request for recognition or enforcement in another Contracting State of a decision relating to custody shall be accompanied by:

(a) a document authorising the central authority of the State addressed to act on behalf of the applicant or to designate another representative for that purpose;

(b)   a copy of the decision which satisfies the necessary conditions of authenticity;

(c)   in the case of a decision given in the absence of the defendant or his legal representative, a document which establishes that the defendant was duly served with the document which instituted the proceedings or an equivalent document;

(d)   if applicable, any document which establishes that, in accordance with the law of the State of origin, the decision is enforceable;

(e)   if possible, a statement indicating the whereabouts or likely whereabouts of the child in the State addressed;

(f)   proposals as to how the custody of the child should be restored.

### Article 15

(1) Before reaching a decision under paragraph (1)(b) of Article 10, the authority concerned in the State addressed:

(a)   shall ascertain the child's views unless this is impracticable having regard in particular to his age and understanding; and

(b)   may request that any appropriate enquiries be carried out.

(2) The cost of enquiries in any Contracting State shall be met by the authorities of the State where they are carried out.

Requests for enquiries and the results of enquiries may be sent to the authority concerned through the central authorities.

### Article 26

(1) In relation to a State which has in matters of custody two or more systems of law of territorial application:

(a)   reference to the law of a person's habitual residence or to the law of a person's nationality shall be construed as referring to the system of law determined by the rules in force in that State or, if there are no such rules, to the system of law with which the person concerned is most closely connected;

(b)   reference to the State of origin or to the State addressed shall be construed as referring, as the case may be, to the territorial unit where the decision was given or to the territorial unit where recognition or enforcement of the decision or restoration of custody is requested.

(2) Paragraph (1)(a) of this Article also applies *mutatis mutandis* to States which have in matters of custody two or more systems of law of personal application.

### SCHEDULE 3

### Custody Orders

### Part I

*England and Wales*

[1

The following are the orders referred to in section 27(1) of this Act—

(a)   a care order under the Children Act 1989 (as defined by section 31(11) of that Act, read with section 105(1) and Schedule 14);

[(b)   a child arrangements order (as defined by section 8 of the Act of 1989) if the arrangements regulated by the order consist of, or include, arrangements relating to either or both of the following—

(i)    with whom a child is to live, or

(ii)   when a child is to live with any person;]

[(bb)     a special guardianship order (within the meaning of the Act of 1989); and]

(c)   any order made by a court in England and Wales under any of the following enactments—

   (i)    section 9(1), 10(1)(a) or 11(a) of the Guardianship of Minors Act 1971;

   (ii)   section 42(1) or (2) or 43(1) of the Matrimonial Causes Act 1973;

   (iii)  section 2(2)(b), 4(b) or (5) of the Guardianship Act 1973 as applied by section 34(5) of the Children Act 1975;

   (iv)   section 8(2)(a), 10(1) or 19(1)(ii) of the Domestic Proceedings and Magistrates Courts Act 1978;

   (v)    [. . .] .]

**2**

An order made by the High Court in the exercise of its jurisdiction relating to wardship so far as it gives the care and control of a child to any person.

**3**

[. . .]

**4**

An authorisation given by the Secretary of State under section 26(2) of the Children and Young Persons Act 1969 (except where the relevant order, within the meaning of that section, was made by virtue of the court which made it being satisfied that the child was guilty of an offence).

. . .

UK Statutes

# Family Law Act
# 1986 ch 55

PART I

**Child Custody**

**Chapter I**

*Preliminary*

**1 Orders to which Part I applies**

(1) Subject to the following provisions of this section, in this Part ["Part I order"] means—

[(a) a section 8 order made by a court in England and Wales under the Children Act 1989, other than an order varying or discharging such an order;]

[(aa) a special guardianship order made by a court in England and Wales under the Children Act 1989;

(ab) an order made under section 26 of the Adoption and Children Act 2002 (contact), other than an order varying or revoking such an order;]

[(ac) an order made under section 51A of the Adoption and Children Act 2002 (post-adoption contact), other than an order varying or revoking such an order;]

(b) an order made by a court of civil jurisdiction in Scotland under any enactment or rule of law with respect to the [residence, custody, care or control of a child, contact with or], access to a child or the education or upbringing of a child, excluding—

    (i) an order committing the care of a child to a local authority or placing a child under the supervision of a local authority;

    (ii) [. . .]

    (iii) [. . .]

    (iv) an order [giving parental responsibilities and parental rights in relation to] a child made in the course of proceedings for the adoption of the child (other than an order made following the making of a direction under section 53(1) of the Children Act 1975);

    (v) an order made under the Education (Scotland) Act 1980;

    (vi) an order made under Part II or III of the Social Work (Scotland) Act 1968;

    (vii) an order made under the Child Abduction and Custody Act 1985;

    (viii) an order for the delivery of a child or other order for the enforcement of a [Part I order];

    (ix) an order relating to the [guardianship] of a child;

    [(x) an adoption order (as defined in section 28(1) of the Adoption and Children (Scotland) Act 2007 (asp 4);

    (xi) a permanence order (as defined in subsection (2) of section 80 of that Act) which includes provision such as is mentioned in paragraph (c) of that subsection;]

[(c) an Article 8 order made by a court in Northern Ireland under the Children (Northern Ireland) Order 1995, other than an order varying or discharging such an order;]

[(d) an order made by a court in England and Wales in the exercise of the inherent jurisdiction of the High Court with respect to children—

    (i) so far as it gives care of a child to any person or provides for contact with, or the education of, a child; but

    (ii) excluding an order varying or revoking such an order;

[(e) an order made by the High Court in Northern Ireland in the exercise of its inherent jurisdiction with respect to children—

  (i) so far as it gives care of a child to any person or provides for contact with, or the education of, a child; but

  (ii) excluding an order varying or discharging such an order;]]

. . .

[(3) In this Part, "Part I order"—

(a) includes any order which would have been a custody order by virtue of this section in any form in which it was in force at any time before its amendment by the Children Act 1989 [or the Children (Northern Ireland) Order 1995, as the case may be]; and

(b) (subject to sections 32 and 40 of this Act) excludes any order which would have been excluded from being a custody order by virtue of this section in any such form.]

[(3A) In subsection (1)(b)(xi) "permanence order" includes a deemed permanence order having effect by virtue of article 13(1), 14(2), 17(1) or 19(2) of the Adoption and Children (Scotland) Act 2007 (Commencement No 4, Transitional and Savings Provisions) Order 2009.]

(6) Provision may be made by act of sederunt prescribing, in relation to orders within subsection (1) (b) above, what constitutes an application for the purposes of this Part.

## Chapter II

*Jurisdiction of Courts in England and Wales*

[2 Jurisdiction: general

[(1) A court in England and Wales shall not make a section 1(1)(a) order with respect to a child unless—

(a) it has jurisdiction under the Council Regulation [or the Hague Convention], or

(b) [neither the Council Regulation nor the Hague Convention applies] but—

  (i) the question of making the order arises in or in connection with matrimonial proceedings [or civil partnership proceedings] and the condition in section 2A of this Act is satisfied, or

  (ii) the condition in section 3 of this Act is satisfied].

[(2A) A court in England and Wales shall not have jurisdiction to make a special guardianship order under the Children Act 1989 unless the condition in section 3 of this Act is satisfied.

(2B) A court in England and Wales shall not have jurisdiction to make an order under section 26 of the Adoption and Children Act 2002 unless the condition in section 3 of this Act is satisfied.]

[(2C) A court in England and Wales shall not have jurisdiction to make an order under section 51A of the Adoption and Children Act 2002 unless—

(a) it has jurisdiction under the Council Regulation or the Hague Convention, or

(b) neither the Council Regulation nor the Hague Convention applies but the condition in section 3 of this Act is satisfied.]

[(3) A court in England and Wales shall not make a section 1(1)(d) order unless—

(a) it has jurisdiction under the Council Regulation [or the Hague Convention], or

(b) [neither the Council Regulation nor the Hague Convention applies] but—

  (i) the condition in section 3 of this Act is satisfied, or

  (ii) the child concerned is present in England and Wales on the relevant date and the court considers that the immediate exercise of its powers is necessary for his protection].]

**[2A Jurisdiction in or in connection with matrimonial proceedings [or civil partnership proceedings]**

[(1) The condition referred to in section 2(1) of this Act is that the . . . proceedings are proceedings in respect of the marriage [or civil partnership] of the parents of the child concerned and—

(a) the proceedings—

    (i)   are proceedings for divorce or nullity of marriage[, or dissolution or annulment of a civil partnership], and

    (ii)  are continuing;

(b) the proceedings—

    (i)   are proceedings for judicial separation [or legal separation of civil partners],

    (ii)  are continuing,

and the jurisdiction of the court is not excluded by subsection (2) below; or

(c) the proceedings have been dismissed after the beginning of the trial but—

    (i)   the section 1(1)(a) order is being made forthwith, or

    (ii)  the application for the order was made on or before the dismissal.

[(2) For the purposes of subsection (1)(b) above, the jurisdiction of the court is excluded if—

(a) after the grant of a decree of judicial separation, on the relevant date, proceedings for divorce or nullity in respect of the marriage, or

(b) after the making of a separation order, on the relevant date, proceedings for dissolution or annulment in respect of the civil partnership,

are continuing in Scotland or Northern Ireland.]

(3) Subsection (2) above shall not apply if the court in which the other proceedings there referred to are continuing has made—

(a) an order under section 13(6) or [19A(4)] of this Act (not being an order made by virtue of section 13(6)(a)(i)), or

(b) an order under section 14(2) or 22(2) of this Act which is recorded as being made for the purpose of enabling Part I proceedings to be taken in England and Wales with respect to the child concerned.

(4) Where a court—

(a) has jurisdiction to make a section 1(1)(a) order [by virtue of section 2(1)(b)(i) of this Act], but

(b) considers that it would be more appropriate for Part I matters relating to the child to be determined outside England and Wales,

the court may by order direct that, while the order under this subsection is in force, no section 1(1)(a) order shall be made by any court [by virtue of section 2(1)(b)(i) of this Act].]

**3 Habitual residence or presence of child**

(1) The condition referred to in [section 2(1)(b)(ii)] of this Act is that on the relevant date the child concerned—

(a) is habitually resident in England and Wales, or

(b) is present in England and Wales and is not habitually resident in any part of the United Kingdom,

and, in either case, the jurisdiction of the court is not excluded by subsection (2) below.

(2) For the purposes of subsection (1) above, the jurisdiction of the court is excluded if, on the relevant date, [matrimonial proceedings] [or civil partnership proceedings] are continuing in a court in Scotland or Northern Ireland in respect of the marriage [or civil partnership] of the parents of the child concerned.

(3) Subsection (2) above shall not apply if the court in which the other proceedings there referred to are continuing has made—

UK Statutes

(a) an order under section 13(6) or [19A(4)] of this Act (not being an order made by virtue of section 13(6)(a)(i), or

(b) an order under section 14(2) or 22(2) of this Act which is recorded as made for the purpose of enabling [Part I proceedings with respect to] the child concerned to be taken in England and Wales,

and that order is in force.

[. . .]

### 5 Power of court to refuse application or stay proceedings

(1) A court in England and Wales which has jurisdiction to make a [Part I order] may refuse an application for the order in any case where the matter in question has already been determined in proceedings outside England and Wales.

(2) Where, at any stage of the proceedings on an application made to a court in England and Wales for a [Part I order], or for the variation of a [Part I order], [. . .] it appears to the court—

(a) that proceedings with respect to the matters to which the application relates are continuing outside England and Wales, [. . .]

(b) that it would be more appropriate for those matters to be determined in proceedings to be taken outside England and Wales, [. . .

(c) that it should exercise its powers under Article 15 of the Council Regulation (transfer to a court better placed to hear the case),] [or

(d) that it should exercise its powers under Article 8 of the Hague Convention (request to authority in another Contracting State to assume jurisdiction),]

the court may stay the proceedings on the application [or (as the case may be) exercise its powers under Article 15] [of the Council Regulation or Article 8 of the Hague Convention].

[(2A) If the proceedings on the application are proceedings in which [an] activity direction has been made under section 11A of the Children Act 1989 (or an enforcement order has been made under section 11J of that Act), the court may when granting a stay under or by virtue of subsection (2) also suspend [the] activity direction (or the enforcement order).]

(3) The court may remove a stay granted [by virtue of subsection (2)(a) or (b) above] if it appears to the court that there has been unreasonable delay in the taking or prosecution of the other proceedings referred to in that subsection, or that those proceedings are stayed, sisted or concluded.

[(3A) The court may remove a stay granted under Article 15 of the Council Regulation only in accordance with that Article.]

[(3AA) The court may remove a stay granted in order for it to exercise its powers under Article 8 of the Hague Convention, and withdraw any request made by it to an authority in another Contracting State to assume jurisdiction, if—

(a) the authority in the other Contracting State does not assume jurisdiction within the period for which the court granted the stay, or

(b) the parties do not, within the period specified by the court, request the authority in the other Contracting State to assume jurisdiction.]

[(3B) If the stay removed under subsection (3)[, (3A) or (3AA)] is a stay in relation to which the court suspended [an] activity direction made under section 11A of the Children Act 1989 (or an enforcement order made under section 11J of that Act), the court may when removing the stay under subsection (3) or (3A) also bring the suspension to an end.]

(4) Nothing in this section [so far as it relates to proceedings not governed by the Council Regulation] shall affect any power exercisable apart from this section to refuse an application or to grant or remove a stay.

**6 Duration and variation of [Part I orders]**

(1) If a [Part I order] made by a court in Scotland or Northern Ireland (or a variation of such an order) comes into force with respect to a child at a time when a [Part I order] made by a court in England and Wales has effect with respect to him, the latter order shall cease to have effect so far as it makes provision for any matter for which the same or different provision is made by (or by the variation of) the order made by the court in Scotland or Northern Ireland.

(2) Where by virtue of subsection (1) above a [Part I order] has ceased to have effect so far as it makes provision for any matter, a court in England and Wales shall not have jurisdiction to vary that order so as to make provision for that matter.

[(3) A court in England and Wales shall not have jurisdiction to vary a Part I order if, on the relevant date, matrimonial proceedings [or civil partnership proceedings] are continuing in Scotland or Northern Ireland in respect of the marriage [or civil partnership] of the parents of the child concerned.

[(3A) Subsection (3) shall not apply if—

(a) the Part 1 order was made in or in connection with proceedings—

    (i) for divorce or nullity in England and Wales in respect of the marriage of the parents of the child concerned; or

    (ii) for dissolution or annulment in England and Wales in respect of the civil partnership of the parents of the child concerned; and

(b) those proceedings are continuing.

(3B) Subsection (3) shall not apply if—

(a) the Part 1 order was made in or in connection with proceedings—

    (i) for judicial separation in England and Wales; or

    (ii) for a separation order in England and Wales; and

(b) those proceedings are continuing; and

(c) as the case may be, the decree of judicial separation has not yet been granted or the separation order has not yet been made.]]

(4) Subsection (3) above shall not apply if the court in which the proceedings there referred to are continuing has made—

(a) an order under section 13(6) or [19A(4)] of this Act (not being an order made by virtue of section 13(6)(a)(i)), or

(b) an order under section 14(2) or 22(2) of this Act which is recorded as made for the purpose of enabling proceedings with respect to the custody of the child concerned to be taken in England and Wales,

and that order is in force.

(5) Subsection (3) above shall not apply in the case of a [variation of a section 1(1)(d) order if the child concerned] is present in England and Wales on the relevant date and the court considers that the immediate exercise of its powers is necessary for his protection.

[(5A) Subsection (7) below applies where a Part I order which is a child arrangements order (within the meaning of section 8(1) of the Children Act 1989) ceases by virtue of subsection (1) above to name a person as someone with whom a child is to live.]

[(6) Subsection (7) below [also] applies where a Part I order which is—

(a) [. . .]

(b) an order made in the exercise of the High Court's inherent jurisdiction with respect to children by virtue of which a person has care of a child, or

(c) an order—

    (i) of a kind mentioned in section 1(3)(a) of this Act,

    (ii) under which a person is entitled to the actual possession of a child,

UK Statutes

ceases to have effect in relation to that person by virtue of subsection (1) above.

(7) Where this subsection applies, any family assistance order made under section 16 of the Children Act 1989 with respect to the child shall also cease to have effect.

(8) For the purposes of subsection (7) above the reference to a family assistance order under section 16 of the Children Act 1989 shall be deemed to include a reference to an order for the supervision of a child made under—

(a)   section 7(4) of the Family Law Reform Act 1969,

(b)   section 44 of the Matrimonial Causes Act 1973,

(c)   section 2(2)(a) of the Guardianship Act 1973,

(d)   section 34(5) or 36(3)(b) of the Children Act 1975, or

(e)   section 9 of the Domestic Proceedings and Magistrates' Courts Act 1978;

but this subsection shall cease to have effect once all such orders for the supervision of children have ceased to have effect in accordance with Schedule 14 to the Children Act 1989.]

[7  **Interpretation of Chapter II**]

[In this Chapter—

(a)   "child" means a person who has not attained the age of eighteen;

[(aa)"civil partnership proceedings" means proceedings for the dissolution or annulment of a civil partnership or for legal separation of the civil partners;]

(b)   "matrimonial proceedings" means proceedings for divorce, nullity of marriage or judicial separation;

(c)   "the relevant date" means, in relation to the making or variation of an order—

   (i)   where an application is made for an order to be made or varied, the date of the application (or first application, if two or more are determined together), and

   (ii)   where no such application is made, the date on which the court is considering whether to make or, as the case may be, vary the order; and

(d)   "section 1(1)(a) order" and "section 1(1)(d) order" mean orders falling within section 1(1)(a) and (d) of this Act respectively.]

. . .

## Chapter V

*Recognition and Enforcement*

### 25  Recognition of [Part I orders]: general

(1) Where a [Part I order] made by a court in any part of the United Kingdom is in force with respect to a child who has not attained the age of sixteen, then, subject to subsection (2) below, the order shall be recognised in any other part of the United Kingdom as having the same effect in that other part as if it had been made by the appropriate court in that other part and as if that court had had jurisdiction to make it.

(2) Where a [Part I order] includes provision as to the means by which rights conferred by the order are to be enforced, subsection (1) above shall not apply to that provision.

(3) A court in a part of the United Kingdom in which a [Part I order] is recognised in accordance with subsection (1) above shall not enforce the order unless it has been registered in that part of the United Kingdom under section 27 of this Act and proceedings for enforcement are taken in accordance with section 29 of this Act.

. . .

UK Statutes

### 27 Registration

(1) Any person on whom any rights are conferred by a [Part I order] may apply to the court which made it for the order to be registered in another part of the United Kingdom under this section.

(2) An application under this section shall be made in the prescribed manner and shall contain the prescribed information and be accompanied by such documents as may be prescribed.

(3) On receiving an application under this section the court which made the [Part I order] shall, unless it appears to the court that the order is no longer in force, cause the following documents to be sent to the appropriate court in the part of the United Kingdom specified in the application, namely—

(a) a certified copy of the order, and

(b) where the order has been varied, prescribed particulars of any variation which is in force, and

(c) a copy of the application and of any accompanying documents.

(4) Where the prescribed officer of the appropriate court receives a certified copy of a [Part I order] under subsection (3) above, he shall forthwith cause the order, together with particulars of any variation, to be registered in that court in the prescribed manner.

(5) An order shall not be registered under this section in respect of a child who has attained the age of sixteen, and the registration of an order in respect of a child who has not attained the age of sixteen shall cease to have effect on the attainment by the child of that age.

### 28 Cancellation and variation of registration

(1) A court which revokes, recalls or varies an order registered under section 27 of this Act shall cause notice of the revocation, recall or variation to be given in the prescribed manner to the prescribed officer of the court in which it is registered and, on receiving the notice, the prescribed officer—

(a) in the case of the revocation or recall of the order, shall cancel the registration, and

(b) in the case of the variation of the order, shall cause particulars of the variation to be registered in the prescribed manner.

(2) Where—

(a) an order registered under section 27 of this Act ceases (in whole or in part) to have effect in the part of the United Kingdom in which it was made, otherwise than because of its revocation, recall or variation,

...

the court in which the order is registered may, of its own motion or on the application of any person who appears to the court to have an interest in the matter, cancel the registration (or, if the order has ceased to have effect in part, cancel the registration so far as it relates to the provisions which have ceased to have effect).

### 29 Enforcement

(1) Where a [Part I order] has been registered under section 27 of this Act, the court in which it is registered shall have the same powers for the purpose of enforcing the order [(including, where an order with respect to contact is registered in England and Wales, the powers under section 110 of the Children Act 1989)] as it would have if it had itself made the order and had jurisdiction to make it; and proceedings for or with respect to enforcement may be taken accordingly.

(2) Where an application has been made to any court for the enforcement of an order registered in that court under section 27 of this Act, the court may, at any time before the application is determined, give such interim directions as it thinks fit for the purpose of securing the welfare of the child concerned or of preventing changes in the circumstances relevant to the determination of the application.

(3) The references in subsection (1) above to a [Part I order] do not include references to any provision of the order as to the means by which rights conferred by the order are to be enforced.

### 30 Staying or sisting of enforcement proceedings

(1) Where in accordance with section 29 of this Act proceedings are taken in any court for the enforcement of an order registered in that court, any person who appears to the court to have an interest in the matter may apply for the proceedings to be stayed or sisted on the ground that he has taken or intends to take other proceedings (in the United Kingdom or elsewhere) as a result of which the order may cease to have effect, or may have a different effect, in the part of the United Kingdom in which it is registered.

[(1A) No application may be made under subsection (1) for proceedings to be stayed or sisted if the proceedings are proceedings on an application for an order under section 11O(2) of the Children Act 1989.]

(2) If after considering an application under subsection (1) above the court considers that the proceedings for enforcement should be stayed or sisted in order that other proceedings may be taken or concluded, it shall stay or sist the proceedings for enforcement accordingly.

(3) The court may remove a stay or recall a sist granted in accordance with subsection (2) above if it appears to the court—

(a)  that there has been unreasonable delay in the taking or prosecution of the other proceedings referred to in that subsection, or

(b)  that those other proceedings are concluded and that the registered order, or a relevant part of it, is still in force.

(4) Nothing in this section shall affect any power exercisable apart from this section to grant, remove or recall a stay or sist.

### 31 Dismissal of enforcement proceedings

(1) Where in accordance with section 29 of this Act proceedings are taken in any court for the enforcement of an order registered in that court, any person who appears to the court to have an interest in the matter may apply for those proceedings to be dismissed on the ground that the order has (in whole or in part) ceased to have effect in the part of the United Kingdom in which it was made.

[(1A) No application may be made under subsection (1) for proceedings to be dismissed if the proceedings are proceedings on an application for an order under section 11O(2) of the Children Act 1989.]

. . .

(3) If, after considering an application under subsection (1) or (2) above, the court is satisfied that the registered order has ceased to have effect, it shall dismiss the proceedings for enforcement (or, if it is satisfied that the order has ceased to have effect in part, it shall dismiss the proceedings so far as they relate to the enforcement of provisions which have ceased to have effect).

### 32 Interpretation of Chapter V

(1) In this Chapter—

"the appropriate court", in relation to England and Wales or Northern Ireland, means the High Court and, in relation to Scotland, means the Court of Session;

["Part I order"] includes (except where the context otherwise requires) any order within section 1(3) of this Act which, on the assumptions mentioned in subsection (3) below—

(a)  could have been made notwithstanding the provisions of this Part;

(b)  would have been a [Part I order] for the purposes of this Part; and

(c)  would not have ceased to have effect by virtue of section 6, 15 or 23 of this Act.

(2) In the application of this Chapter to Scotland, ["Part I order"] also includes (except where the context otherwise requires) any order within section 1(3) of this Act which, on the assumptions mentioned in subsection (3) below—

(a)  would have been a [Part I order] for the purposes of this Part; and

(b)  would not have ceased to have effect by virtue of section 6 or 23 of this Act, and which, but for the provisions of this Part, would be recognised in Scotland under any rule of law.

(3) The said assumptions are—

(a) that this Part had been in force at all material times; and

(b) that any reference in section 1 of this Act to any enactment included a reference to any corresponding enactment previously in force.

## Chapter VI

*Miscellaneous and Supplemental*

### 33 Power to order disclosure of child's whereabouts

(1) Where in proceedings for or relating to a [Part I order] in respect of a child there is not available to the court adequate information as to where the child is, the court may order any person who it has reason to believe may have relevant information to disclose it to the court.

(2) A person shall not be excused from complying with an order under subsection (1) above by reason that to do so may incriminate him or his spouse [or civil partner] of an offence; but a statement or admission made in compliance with such an order shall not be admissible in evidence against either of them in proceedings for any offence other than perjury.

. . .

### 34 Power to order recovery of child

(1) Where—

(a) a person is required by a [Part I order], or an order for the enforcement of a [Part I order], to give up a child to another person ("the person concerned"), and

(b) the court which made the order imposing the requirement is satisfied that the child has not been given up in accordance with the order,

the court may make an order authorising an officer of the court or a constable to take charge of the child and deliver him to the person concerned.

(2) The authority conferred by subsection (1) above includes authority—

(a) to enter and search any premises where the person acting in pursuance of the order has reason to believe the child may be found, and

(b) to use such force as may be necessary to give effect to the purpose of the order.

(3) Where by virtue of—

[(a) section 14 of the Children Act 1989,]

. . .

a [Part I order] (or a provision of a [Part I order]) may be enforced as if it were an order requiring a person to give up a child to another person, subsection (1) above shall apply as if the [Part I order] had included such a requirement.

(4) This section is without prejudice to any power conferred on a court by or under any other enactment or rule of law.

. . .

### 36 Effect of orders restricting removal

(1) This section applies to any order made by a court in the United Kingdom prohibiting the removal of a child from the United Kingdom or from any specified part of it.

(2) An order to which this section applies shall have effect in each part of the United Kingdom other than the part in which it was made—

(a) as if it had been made by the appropriate court in that other part, and

(b) in the case of an order which has the effect of prohibiting the child's removal to that other part, as if it had included a prohibition on his further removal to any place except one to which he could be removed consistently with the order.

(3) The references in subsections (1) and (2) above to prohibitions on a child's removal include references to prohibitions subject to exceptions; and in a case where removal is prohibited except with the consent of the court, nothing in subsection (2) above shall be construed as affecting the identity of the court whose consent is required.

(4) In this section "child" means a person who has not attained the age of sixteen; and this section shall cease to apply to an order relating to a child when he attains the age of sixteen.

### 37 Surrender of passports

(1) Where there is in force an order prohibiting or otherwise restricting the removal of a child from the United Kingdom or from any specified part of it, the court by which the order was in fact made, or by which it is treated under section 36 of this Act as having been made, may require any person to surrender any United Kingdom passport which has been issued to, or contains particulars of, the child.

(2) In this section "United Kingdom passport" means a current passport issued by the Government of the United Kingdom.

### 38 Automatic restriction on removal of wards of court

(1) The rule of law which (without any order of the court) restricts the removal of a ward of court from the jurisdiction of the court shall, in a case to which this section applies, have effect subject to the modifications in subsection (3) below.

(2) This section applies in relation to a ward of court if—

(a)  proceedings for divorce, nullity or judicial separation in respect of the marriage of his parents are continuing in a court in another part of the United Kingdom (that is to say, in a part of the United Kingdom outside the jurisdiction of the court of which he is a ward), or

[(aa) proceedings for dissolution or annulment or legal separation in respect of the civil partnership of his parents are continuing in a court in another part of the United Kingdom (that is to say, in a part of the United Kingdom outside the jurisdiction of the court of which he is a ward), or]

(b)  he is habitually resident in another part of the United Kingdom,

except where that other part is Scotland and he has attained the age of sixteen.

(3) Where this section applies, the rule referred to in subsection (1) above shall not prevent—

(a)  the removal of the ward of court, without the consent of any court, to the other part of the United Kingdom mentioned in subsection (2) above, or

(b)  his removal to any other place with the consent of either the appropriate court in that other part of the United Kingdom or the court mentioned in subsection [(2)(a) or (aa) above].

### 39 Duty to furnish particulars of other proceedings

Parties to proceedings for or relating to a [Part I order] shall, to such extent and in such manner as may be prescribed, give particulars of other proceedings known to them which relate to the child concerned (including proceedings instituted abroad and proceedings which are no longer continuing).

### 40 Interpretation of Chapter VI

(1) In this Chapter—

"the appropriate court" has the same meaning as in Chapter V;

["Part I order"] includes (except where the context otherwise requires) any such order as is mentioned in section 32(1) of this Act.

. . .

### 41 Habitual residence after removal without consent, etc

(1) Where a child who—

UK Statutes

(a)  has not attained the age of sixteen, and

(b)  is habitually resident in a part of the United Kingdom,

becomes habitually resident outside that part of the United Kingdom in consequence of circumstances of the kind specified in subsection (2) below, he shall be treated for the purposes of this Part as continuing to be habitually resident in that part of the United Kingdom for the period of one year beginning with the date on which those circumstances arise.

(2)  The circumstances referred to in subsection (1) above exist where the child is removed from or retained outside, or himself leaves or remains outside, the part of the United Kingdom in which he was habitually resident before his change of residence—

(a)  without the agreement of the person or all the persons having, under the law of that part of the United Kingdom, the right to determine where he is to reside, or

(b)  in contravention of an order made by a court in any part of the United Kingdom.

(3)  A child shall cease to be treated by virtue of subsection (1) above as habitually resident in a part of the United Kingdom if, during the period there mentioned—

(a)  he attains the age of sixteen, or

(b)  he becomes habitually resident outside that part of the United Kingdom with the agreement of the person or persons mentioned in subsection (2)(a) above and not in contravention of an order made by a court in any part of the United Kingdom.

**42  General interpretation of Part I**

(1)  In this Part—

"certified copy", in relation to an order of any court, means a copy certified by the prescribed officer of the court to be a true copy of the order or of the official record of the order;

["parental responsibilities" and "parental rights" have the meanings respectively given by sections 1(3) and 2(4) of the Children (Scotland) Act 1995;]

"part of the United Kingdom" means England and Wales, Scotland or Northern Ireland;

"prescribed" means prescribed by rules of court or act of sederunt;

["the Council Regulation" means Council Regulation (EC) No 2201/2003 of 27th November 2003 concerning jurisdiction and the recognition and enforcement of judgments in matrimonial matters and matters of parental responsibility];

["the Hague Convention" means the Convention on Jurisdiction, Applicable Law, Recognition, Enforcement and Co-Operation in respect of Parental Responsibility and Measures for the Protection of Children that was signed at The Hague on 19 October 1996].

(2)  For the purposes of this Part proceedings in England and Wales or in Northern Ireland for divorce, nullity or judicial separation in respect of the marriage of the parents of a child shall, unless they have been dismissed, be treated as continuing until the child concerned attains the age of eighteen (whether or not a decree has been granted and whether or not, in the case of a decree of divorce or nullity of marriage, that decree has been made absolute).

[(2A)  For the purposes of this Part proceedings in England and Wales or in Northern Ireland for dissolution, annulment or legal separation in respect of the civil partnership of the parents of the child shall, unless they have been dismissed, be treated as continuing until the child concerned attains the age of eighteen (whether or not a dissolution, nullity or separation order has been made and whether or not, in the case of a dissolution or nullity order, that order has been made final).]

. . .

(4)  Any reference in this Part to proceedings in respect of the marriage [or civil partnership] of the parents of a child shall, in relation to a child who, although not a child of both parties to the marriage [or civil partnership], is a child of the family of those parties, be construed as a reference to proceedings in respect of that marriage [or civil partnership]; and for this purpose "child of the family"—

(a)  if the proceedings are in England and Wales, means any child who has been treated by both parties as a child of their family, except a child who [is placed with those parties as foster parents] by a local authority or a voluntary organisation;

. . .

[(4A) Any reference in this Part to proceedings in respect of the civil partnership of the parents of a child shall, in relation to a child who, although not a child of the civil partners, is a child of the family of the civil partners, be construed as a reference to proceedings in respect of that civil partnership; and for this purpose "child of the family" has the meaning given in paragraphs (a) to (c) of subsection (4) (but substituting references to the civil partners for references to the parties to the marriage).]

(5) References in this Part to [Part I orders] include (except where the context otherwise requires) references to [Part I orders] as varied.

(6) For the purposes of this Part each of the following orders shall be treated as varying the [Part I order] to which it relates—

(a) an order which provides for a person [to be allowed contact with or] to be given access to a child who is the subject of a [Part I order], or which makes provision for the education of such a child,

[. . .]

[(7) In this Part—

(a) references to Part I proceedings in respect of a child are references to any proceedings for a Part I order or an order corresponding to a Part I order and include, in relation to proceedings outside the United Kingdom, references to proceedings before a tribunal or other authority having power under the law having effect there to determine Part I matters; and

(b) references to Part I matters are references to matters that might be determined by a Part I order or an order corresponding to a Part I order.]

**43 Application of Part I to dependent territories**

(1) Her Majesty may by Order in Council make provision corresponding to or applying any of the foregoing provisions of this Part, with such modifications as appear to Her Majesty to be appropriate, for the purpose of regulating—

(a) in any dependent territory;

(b) as between any dependent territory and any part of the United Kingdom; or

(c) as between any dependent territory and any other such territory,

the jurisdiction of courts to make [Part I orders], or orders corresponding to [Part I orders], and the recognition and enforcement of such orders.

(2) In subsection (1) above "dependent territory" means any of the following territories—

(a) the Isle of Man,

(b) any of the Channel Islands, and

(c) any colony.

(3) An Order in Council under subsection (1) above may contain such consequential, incidental and supplementary provisions as appear to Her Majesty to be necessary or expedient.

(4) An Order in Council under subsection (1)(b) above which makes provision affecting the law of any part of the United Kingdom shall be subject to annulment in pursuance of a resolution of either House of Parliament.

PART II

## Recognition of Divorces, Annulments and Legal Separations

*Divorces, annulments and judicial separations granted in the British Islands*

**44 Recognition in United Kingdom of divorces, annulments and judicial separations granted in the British Islands**

(1) Subject to section 52(4) and (5)(a) of this Act, no divorce or annulment obtained in any part of the British Islands shall be regarded as effective in any part of the United Kingdom unless granted by a court of civil jurisdiction.

(2) Subject to section 51 of this Act, the validity of any divorce, annulment or judicial separation granted by a court of civil jurisdiction in any part of the British Islands shall be recognised throughout the United Kingdom.

*Overseas divorces, annulments and legal separations*

**45 Recognition in the United Kingdom of overseas divorces, annulments and legal separations**

[(1) Subject to subsection (2) of this section and] to sections 51 and 52 of this Act, the validity of a divorce, annulment or legal separation obtained in a country outside the British Islands (in this Part referred to as an overseas divorce, annulment or legal separation) shall be recognised in the United Kingdom if, and only if, it is entitled to recognition—

(a)   by virtue of sections 46 to 49 of this Act, or

(b)   by virtue of any enactment other than this Part.

[(2) Subsection (1) and the following provisions of this Part do not apply to an overseas divorce, annulment or legal separation as regards which provision as to recognition is made by [Articles 21 to 27, 41(1) and 42(1)] of the Council Regulation.]

**46 Grounds for recognition**

(1) The validity of an overseas divorce, annulment or legal separation obtained by means of proceedings shall be recognised if—

(a)   the divorce, annulment or legal separation is effective under the law of the country in which it was obtained; and

(b)   at the relevant date either party to the marriage—

    (i)   was habitually resident in the country in which the divorce, annulment or legal separation was obtained; or

    (ii)   was domiciled in that country; or

    (iii)   was a national of that country.

(2) The validity of an overseas divorce, annulment or legal separation obtained otherwise than by means of proceedings shall be recognised if—

(a)   the divorce, annulment or legal separation is effective under the law of the country in which it was obtained;

(b)   at the relevant date—

    (i)   each party to the marriage was domiciled in that country; or

    (ii)   either party to the marriage was domiciled in that country and the other party was domiciled in a country under whose law the divorce, annulment or legal separation is recognised as valid; and

(c)   neither party to the marriage was habitually resident in the United Kingdom throughout the period of one year immediately preceding that date.

(3) In this section "the relevant date" means—

(a) in the case of an overseas divorce, annulment or legal separation obtained by means of proceedings, the date of the commencement of the proceedings;

(b) in the case of an overseas divorce, annulment or legal separation obtained otherwise than by means of proceedings, the date on which it was obtained.

(4) Where in the case of an overseas annulment, the relevant date fell after the death of either party to the marriage, any reference in subsection (1) or (2) above to that date shall be construed in relation to that party as a reference to the date of death.

(5) For the purpose of this section, a party to a marriage shall be treated as domiciled in a country if he was domiciled in that country either according to the law of that country in family matters or according to the law of the part of the United Kingdom in which the question of recognition arises.

### 47 Cross-proceedings and divorces following legal separations

(1) Where there have been cross-proceedings, the validity of an overseas divorce, annulment or legal separation obtained either in the original proceedings or in the cross-proceedings shall be recognised if—

(a) the requirements of section 46(1)(b)(i), (ii) or (iii) of this Act are satisfied in relation to the date of the commencement either of the original proceedings or of the cross-proceedings, and

(b) the validity of the divorce, annulment or legal separation is otherwise entitled to recognition by virtue of the provisions of this Part.

(2) Where a legal separation, the validity of which is entitled to recognition by virtue of the provisions of section 46 of this Act or of subsection (1) above is converted, in the country in which it was obtained, into a divorce which is effective under the law of that country, the validity of the divorce shall be recognised whether or not it would itself be entitled to recognition by virtue of those provisions.

### 48 Proof of facts relevant to recognition

(1) For the purpose of deciding whether an overseas divorce, annulment or legal separation obtained by means of proceedings is entitled to recognition by virtue of section 46 and 47 of this Act, any finding of fact made (whether expressly or by implication) in the proceedings and on the basis of which jurisdiction was assumed in the proceedings shall—

(a) if both parties to the marriage took part in the proceedings, be conclusive evidence of the fact found; and

(b) in any other case, be sufficient proof of that fact unless the contrary is shown.

(2) In this section "finding of fact" includes a finding that either party to the marriage—

(a) was habitually resident in the country in which the divorce, annulment or legal separation was obtained; or

(b) was under the law of that country domiciled there; or

(c) was a national of that country.

(3) For the purposes of subsection (1)(a) above, a party to the marriage who has appeared in judicial proceedings shall be treated as having taken part in them.

### *Supplemental*

### 49 Modifications of Part II in relation to countries comprising territories having different systems of law

(1) In relation to a country comprising territories in which different systems of law are in force in matters of divorce, annulment or legal separation, the provisions of this Part mentioned in subsections (2) to (5) below shall have effect subject to the modifications there specified.

(2) In the case of a divorce, annulment or legal separation the recognition of the validity of which depends on whether the requirements of subsection (1)(b)(i) or (ii) of section 46 of this Act are satisfied, that section and, in the case of a legal separation, section 47(2) of this Act shall have effect as if each territory were a separate country.

(3) In the case of a divorce, annulment or legal separation the recognition of the validity of which depends on whether the requirements of subsection (1)(b)(iii) of section 46 of this Act are satisfied—

(a)  that section shall have effect as if for paragraph (a) of subsection (1) there were substituted the following paragraph—

"(a)  the divorce, annulment or legal separation is effective throughout the country in which it was obtained;"; and

(b)  in the case of a legal separation, section 47(2) of this Act shall have effect as if for the words "is effective under the law of that country" there were substituted the words "is effective throughout the country".

(4) In the case of a divorce, annulment or legal separation the recognition of the validity of which depends on whether the requirements of subsection (2)(b) of section 46 of this Act are satisfied, that section and section 52(3) and (4) of this Act and, in the case of a legal separation, section 47(2) of this Act shall have effect as if each territory were a separate country.

(5) Paragraphs (a) and (b) of section 48(2) of this Act shall each have effect as if each territory were a separate country.

### 50 Non-recognition of divorce or annulment in another jurisdiction no bar to remarriage

Where, in any part of the United Kingdom—

(a)  a divorce or annulment has been granted by a court of civil jurisdiction, or

(b)  the validity of a divorce or annulment is recognised by virtue of this Part,

the fact that the divorce or annulment would not be recognised elsewhere shall not preclude either party to the marriage from [forming a subsequent marriage or civil partnership in that part of the United Kingdom or cause the subsequent marriage or civil partnership of either party (wherever it takes place) to be treated as invalid in that part].

### 51 Refusal of recognition

(1) Subject to section 52 of this Act, recognition of the validity of—

(a)  a divorce, annulment or judicial separation granted by a court of civil jurisdiction in any part of the British Islands, or

(b)  an overseas divorce, annulment or legal separation,

may be refused in any part of the United Kingdom if the divorce, annulment or separation was granted or obtained at a time when it was irreconcilable with a decision determining the question of the subsistence or validity of the marriage of the parties previously given (whether before or after the commencement of this Part) by a court of civil jurisdiction in that part of the United Kingdom or by a court elsewhere and recognised or entitled to be recognised in that part of the United Kingdom.

(2) Subject to section 52 of this Act, recognition of the validity of—

(a)  a divorce or judicial separation granted by a court of civil jurisdiction in any part of the British Islands, or

(b)  an overseas divorce or legal separation,

may be refused in any part of the United Kingdom if the divorce or separation was granted or obtained at a time when, according to the law of that part of the United Kingdom (including its rules of private international law and the provisions of this Part), there was no subsisting marriage between the parties.

(3) Subject to section 52 of this Act, recognition by virtue of section 45 of this Act of the validity of an overseas divorce, annulment or legal separation may be refused if—

(a)  in the case of a divorce, annulment or legal separation obtained by means of proceedings, it was obtained—

(i)  without such steps having been taken for giving notice of the proceedings to a party to the marriage as, having regard to the nature of the proceedings and all the circumstances, should reasonably have been taken; or

(ii)   without a party to the marriage having been given (for any reason other than lack of notice) such opportunity to take part in the proceedings as, having regard to those matters, he should reasonably have been given; or

(b)   in the case of a divorce, annulment or legal separation obtained otherwise than by means of proceedings—

(i)   there is no official document certifying that the divorce, annulment or legal separation is effective under the law of the country in which it was obtained; or

(ii)   where either party to the marriage was domiciled in another country at the relevant date, there is no official document certifying that the divorce, annulment or legal separation is recognised as valid under the law of that other country; or

(c)   in either case, recognition of the divorce, annulment or legal separation would be manifestly contrary to public policy.

(4)  In this section—

"official", in relation to a document certifying that a divorce, annulment or legal separation is effective, or is recognised as valid, under the law of any country, means issued by a person or body appointed or recognised for the purpose under that law;

"the relevant date" has the same meaning as in section 46 of this Act;

and subsection (5) of that section shall apply for the purposes of this section as it applies for the purposes of that section.

(5)  Nothing in this Part shall be construed as requiring the recognition of any finding of fault made in any proceedings for divorce, annulment or separation or of any maintenance, custody or other ancillary order made in any such proceedings.

### 52  Provisions as to divorces, annulments etc obtained before commencement of Part II

(1)  The provisions of this Part shall apply—

(a)   to a divorce, annulment or judicial separation granted by a court of civil jurisdiction in the British Islands before the date of the commencement of this Part, and

(b)   to an overseas divorce, annulment or legal separation obtained before that date,

as well as to one granted or obtained on or after that date.

(2)  In the case of such a divorce, annulment or separation as is mentioned in subsection (1)(*a*) or (*b*) above, the provisions of this Part shall require or, as the case may be, preclude the recognition of its validity in relation to any time before that date as well as in relation to any subsequent time, but those provisions shall not—

(a)   affect any property to which any person became entitled before that date, or

(b)   affect the recognition of the validity of the divorce, annulment or separation if that matter has been decided by any competent court in the British Islands before that date.

(3)  Subsections (1) and (2) above shall apply in relation to any divorce or judicial separation granted by a court of civil jurisdiction in the British Islands before the date of the commencement of this Part whether granted before or after the commencement of section 1 of the Recognition of Divorces and Legal Separations Act 1971.

(4)  The validity of any divorce, annulment or legal separation mentioned in subsection (5) below shall be recognised in the United Kingdom whether or not it is entitled to recognition by virtue of any of the foregoing provisions of this Part.

(5)  The divorces, annulments and legal separations referred to in subsection (4) above are—

(a)   a divorce which was obtained in the British Islands before 1st January 1974 and was recognised as valid under rules of law applicable before that date;

(b)   an overseas divorce which was recognised as valid under the Recognition of Divorces and Legal Separations Act 1971 and was not affected by section 16(2) of the Domicile and Matrimonial

Proceedings Act 1973 (proceedings otherwise than in a court of law where both parties resident in United Kingdom);

(c)   a divorce of which the decree was registered under section 1 of the Indian and Colonial Divorce Jurisdiction Act 1926;

(d)   a divorce or annulment which was recognised as valid under section 4 of the Matrimonial Causes (War Marriages) Act 1944; and

(e)   an overseas legal separation which was recognised as valid under the Recognition of Divorces and Legal Separations Act 1971.

[. . .]

### 54  Interpretation of Part II

(1)  In this Part—

"annulment" includes any decree or declarator of nullity of marriage, however expressed;

["the Council Regulation" means Council Regulation (EC) No 2201/2003 of 27th November 2003 concerning jurisdiction and the recognition and enforcement of judgments in matrimonial matters and matters of parental responsibility;]

"part of the United Kingdom" means England and Wales, Scotland or Northern Ireland;

"proceedings" means judicial or other proceedings.

(2)  In this Part "country" includes a colony or other dependent territory of the United Kingdom but for the purposes of this Part a person shall be treated as a national of such a territory only if it has a law of citizenship or nationality separate from that of the United Kingdom and he is a citizen or national of that territory under that law.

## Part III

*Declarations of Status*

### 55  Declarations as to marital status

(1)  Subject to the following provisions of this section, any person may apply to [the High Court or [the family court]] for one or more of the following declarations in relation to a marriage specified in the application, that is to say—

(a)   a declaration that the marriage was at its inception a valid marriage;

(b)   a declaration that the marriage subsisted on a date specified in the application;

(c)   a declaration that the marriage did not subsist on a date so specified;

(d)   a declaration that the validity of a divorce, annulment or legal separation obtained in any country outside England and Wales in respect of the marriage is entitled to recognition in England and Wales;

(e)   a declaration that the validity of a divorce, annulment or legal separation so obtained in respect of the marriage is not entitled to recognition in England and Wales.

(2)  A court shall have jurisdiction to entertain an application under subsection (1) above if, and only if, either of the parties to the marriage to which the application relates—

(a)   is domiciled in England and Wales on the date of the application, or

(b)   has been habitually resident in England and Wales throughout the period of one year ending with that date, or

(c)   died before that date and either—

  (i)   was at death domiciled in England and Wales, or

  (ii)  had been habitually resident in England and Wales throughout the period of one year ending with the date of death.

UK Statutes

(3) Where an application under subsection (1) above is made [to a court] by any person other than a party to the marriage to which the application relates, the court shall refuse to hear the application if it considers that the applicant does not have a sufficient interest in the determination of that application.

[**55A Declarations of parentage**

(1) Subject to the following provisions of this section, any person may apply to the High Court [or the family court] for a declaration as to whether or not a person named in the application is or was the parent of another person so named.

(2) A court shall have jurisdiction to entertain an application under subsection (1) above if, and only if, either of the persons named in it for the purposes of that subsection—

(a)   is domiciled in England and Wales on the date of the application, or

(b)   has been habitually resident in England and Wales throughout the period of one year ending with that date, or

(c)   died before that date and either—

(i)    was at death domiciled in England and Wales, or

(ii)   had been habitually resident in England and Wales throughout the period of one year ending with the date of death.

(3) Except in a case falling within subsection (4) below, the court shall refuse to hear an application under subsection (1) above unless it considers that the applicant has a sufficient personal interest in the determination of the application (but this is subject to section 27 of the Child Support Act 1991).

(4) The excepted cases are where the declaration sought is as to whether or not—

(a)   the applicant is the parent of a named person;

(b)   a named person is the parent of the applicant; or

(c)   a named person is the other parent of a named child of the applicant.

(5) Where an application under subsection (1) above is made and one of the persons named in it for the purposes of that subsection is a child, the court may refuse to hear the application if it considers that the determination of the application would not be in the best interests of the child.

(6) Where a court refuses to hear an application under subsection (1) above it may order that the applicant may not apply again for the same declaration without leave of the court.

(7) Where a declaration is made by a court on an application under subsection (1) above, the prescribed officer of the court shall notify the Registrar General, in such a manner and within such period as may be prescribed, of the making of that declaration.]

[**56 Declarations of parentage, legitimacy or legitimation**]

[(1) Any person may apply to [the High Court or [the family court]] for a declaration—

(a)   . . .

(b)   that he is the legitimate child of his parents.

(2) Any person may apply to [the High Court or [the family court]] for one (or for one or, in the alternative, the other) of the following declarations, that is to say—

(a)   a declaration that he has become a legitimated person;

(b)   a declaration that he has not become a legitimated person.

(3) A court shall have jurisdiction to entertain an application under this section if, the applicant—

(a)   is domiciled in England and Wales on the date of the application; or

(b)   has been habitually resident in England and Wales throughout the period of one year ending with that date.

(4) Where a declaration is made [by a court] on an application under subsection (1) above, the prescribed officer of the court shall notify the Registrar General, in such a manner and within such period as may be prescribed, of the making of that declaration.

(5) In this section "legitimated person" means a person legitimated or recognised as legitimated—

(a) under section 2[, 2A] or 3 of the Legitimacy Act 1976;

(b) under section 1 or 8 of the Legitimacy Act 1926; or

(c) by a legitimation (whether or not by virtue of the subsequent marriage of his parents) recognised by the law of England and Wales and effected under the law of another country.]

### 57 Declarations as to adoptions effected overseas

(1) Any person whose status as an adopted child of any person depends on whether he has been adopted by that person by either—

[(a) a Convention adoption, or an overseas adoption, within the meaning of the Adoption and Children Act 2002, or]

(b) an adoption recognised by the law of England and Wales and effected under the law of any country outside the British Islands,

may apply to [the High Court or [the family court]] for one (or for one or, in the alternative, the other) of the declarations mentioned in subsection (2) below.

(2) The said declarations are—

(a) a declaration that the applicant is for the purposes of section 39 of the Adoption Act 1976 [or section 67 of the Adoption and Children Act 2002] the adopted child of that person;

(b) a declaration that the applicant is not for the purposes of that section the adopted child of that person.

(3) A court shall have jurisdiction to entertain an application under subsection (1) above if, and only if, the applicant—

(a) is domiciled in England and Wales on the date of the application, or

(b) has been habitually resident in England and Wales throughout the period of one year ending with that date.

(4) . . .

### 58 General provisions as to the making and effect of declarations

(1) Where on an application [to a court] for a declaration under this Part the truth of the proposition to be declared is proved to the satisfaction of the court, the court shall make that declaration unless to do so would manifestly be contrary to public policy.

(2) Any declaration made under this Part shall be binding on Her Majesty and all other persons.

(3) [A] court, on the dismissal of an application for a declaration under this Part, shall not have power to make any declaration for which an application has not been made.

(4) No declaration which may be applied for under this Part may be made otherwise than under this Part by any court.

(5) No declaration may be made by any court, whether under this Part or otherwise—

(a) that a marriage was at its inception void;

(b) . . ..

(6) Nothing in this section shall affect the powers of any court to grant a decree of nullity of marriage.

. . .

UK Statutes

# Marriage (Prohibited Degrees of Relationship) Act 1986 ch 16

1 **Marriage between certain persons related by affinity not to be void**

(1) A marriage solemnized after the commencement of this Act between a man and a woman who is the daughter or grand-daughter of a former spouse of his (whether the former spouse is living or not) or who is the former spouse of his father or grand-father (whether his father or grandfather is living or not) shall not be void by reason only of that relationship if both the parties have attained the age of twenty-one at the time of the marriage and the younger party has not at any time before attaining the age of eighteen been a child of the family in relation to the other party.

(2) A marriage solemnized after the commencement of this Act between a man and a woman who is the grandmother of a former spouse of his (whether the former spouse is living or not) or is a former spouse of his grandson (whether his grandson is living or not) shall not be void by reason only of that relationship.

(3) [. . .]

(4) [. . .]

(5) In this section "child of the family" in relation to any person, means a child who has lived in the same household as that person and been treated by that person as a child of his family.

(6) The Marriage Act 1949 shall have effect subject to the amendments specified in the Schedule to this Act, being amendments consequential on the preceding provisions of this section.

(7) Where, apart from this Act, any matter affecting the validity of a marriage would fall to be determined (in accordance with the rules of private international law) by reference to the law of a country outside England and Wales nothing in this Act shall preclude the determination of that matter in accordance with that law.

(8) Nothing in this section shall affect any marriage solemnized before the commencement of this Act.

# Recognition of Trusts Act
# 1987 ch 14

## 1 Applicable law and recognition of trusts

(1) The provisions of the Convention set out in the Schedule to this Act shall have the force of law in the United Kingdom.

(2) Those provisions shall, so far as applicable, have effect not only in relation to the trusts described in Articles 2 and 3 of the Convention but also in relation to any other trusts of property arising under the law of any part of the United Kingdom or by virtue of a judicial decision whether in the United Kingdom or elsewhere.

(3) In accordance with Articles 15 and 16 such provisions of the law as are there mentioned shall, to the extent there specified, apply to the exclusion of the other provisions of the Convention.

(4) In Article 17 the reference to a State includes a reference to any country or territory (whether or not a party to the Convention and whether or not forming part of the United Kingdom) which has its own system of law.

(5) Article 22 shall not be construed as affecting the law to be applied in relation to anything done or omitted before the coming into force of this Act.

## 2 Extent

(1) This Act extends to Northern Ireland.

(2) Her Majesty may by Order in Council direct that this Act shall also form part of the law of the Isle of Man, any of the Channel Islands or any colony.

(3) An Order in Council under subsection (2) above may modify this Act in its application to any of the territories there mentioned and may contain such supplementary provisions as Her Majesty considers appropriate.

(4) An Order in Council under subsection (2) above shall be subject to annulment in pursuance of a resolution of either House of Parliament.

## 3 Short title, commencement and application to the Crown

(1) This Act may be cited as the Recognition of Trusts Act 1987.

(2) This Act shall come into force on such date as the Lord Chancellor and the Lord Advocate may appoint by an order made by statutory instrument.

(3) This Act binds the Crown.

## SCHEDULE

### Convention on the Law Applicable to Trusts and on Their Recognition

### Section 1

### Chapter I

*Scope*

### Article 1

This Convention specifies the law applicable to trusts and governs their recognition.

### Article 2

For the purposes of this Convention, the term "trust" refers to the legal relationship created— inter vivos or on death— by a person, the settlor, when assets have been placed under the control of a trustee for the benefit of a beneficiary or for a specified purpose.

A trust has the following characteristics—

(a) the assets constitute a separate fund and are not a part of the trustee's own estate;

(b) title to the trust assets stands in the name of the trustee or in the name of another person on behalf of the trustee;

(c) the trustee has the power and the duty, in respect of which he is accountable, to manage, employ or dispose of the assets in accordance with the terms of the trust and the special duties imposed upon him by law.

The reservation by the settlor of certain rights and powers, and the fact that the trustee may himself have rights as a beneficiary, are not necessarily inconsistent with the existence of a trust.

### Article 3

The Convention applies only to trusts created voluntarily and evidenced in writing.

### Article 4

The Convention does not apply to preliminary issues relating to the validity of wills or of other acts by virtue of which assets are transferred to the trustee.

### Article 5

The Convention does not apply to the extent that the law specified by Chapter II does not provide for trusts or the category of trusts involved.

## Chapter II

*Applicable Law*

### Article 6

A trust shall be governed by the law chosen by the settlor. The choice must be express or be implied in the terms of the instrument creating or the writing evidencing the trust, interpreted, if necessary, in the light of the circumstances of the case.

Where the law chosen under the previous paragraph does not provide for trusts or the category of trust involved, the choice shall not be effective and the law specified in Article 7 shall apply.

### Article 7

Where no applicable law has been chosen, a trust shall be governed by the law with which it is most closely connected.

In ascertaining the law with which a trust is most closely connected reference shall be made in particular to—

(a) the place of administration of the trust designated by the settlor;

(b) the situs of the assets of the trust;

(c) the place of residence or business of the trustee;

(d) the objects of the trust and the places where they are to be fulfilled.

### Article 8

The law specified by Article 6 or 7 shall govern the validity of the trust, its construction, its effects and the administration of the trust. In particular that law shall govern—

(a) the appointment, resignation and removal of trustees, the capacity to act as a trustee, and the devolution of the office of trustee;

(b)   the rights and duties of trustees among themselves;

(c)   the right of trustees to delegate in whole or in part the discharge of their duties or the exercise of their powers;

(d)   the power of trustees to administer or to dispose of trust assets, to create security interests in the trust assets, or to acquire new assets;

(e)   the powers of investment of trustees;

(f)   restrictions upon the duration of the trust, and upon the power to accumulate the income of the trust;

(g)   the relationships between the trustees and the beneficiaries including the personal liability of the trustees to the beneficiaries;

(h)   the variation or termination of the trust;

  (i)   the distribution of the trust assets;

(j)   the duty of trustees to account for their administration.

### Article 9

In applying this Chapter a severable aspect of the trust, particularly matters of administration, may be governed by a different law.

### Article 10

The law applicable to the validity of the trust shall determine whether that law or the law governing a severable aspect of the trust may be replaced by another law.

## Chapter III

*Recognition*

### Article 11

A trust created in accordance with the law specified by the preceding Chapter shall be recognised as a trust.

Such recognition shall imply, as a minimum, that the trust property constitutes a separate fund, that the trustee may sue and be sued in his capacity as trustee, and that he may appear or act in this capacity before a notary or any person acting in an official capacity.

In so far as the law applicable to the trust requires or provides, such recognition shall imply in particular—

(a)   that personal creditors of the trustee shall have no recourse against the trust assets;

(b)   that the trust assets shall not form part of the trustee's estate upon his insolvency or bankruptcy;

(c)   that the trust assets shall not form part of the matrimonial property of the trustee or his spouse nor part of the trustee's estate upon his death;

(d)   that the trust assets may be recovered when the trustee, in breach of trust, has mingled trust assets with his own property or has alienated trust assets. However, the rights and obligations of any third party holder of the assets shall remain subject to the law determined by the choice of law rules of the forum.

### Article 12

Where the trustee desires to register assets, movable or immovable, or documents of title to them, he shall be entitled, in so far as this is not prohibited by or inconsistent with the law of the State where registration is sought, to do so in his capacity as trustee or in such other way that the existence of the trust is disclosed.

UK Statutes

### Article 14

The Convention shall not prevent the application of rules of law more favourable to the recognition of trusts.

## Chapter IV

*General Clauses*

### Article 15

The Convention does not prevent the application of provisions of the law designated by the conflicts rules of the forum, in so far as those provisions cannot be derogated from by voluntary act, relating in particular to the following matters—

(a) the protection of minors and incapable parties;

(b) the personal and proprietary effects of marriage;

(c) succession rights, testate and intestate, especially the indefeasible shares of spouses and relatives;

(d) the transfer of title property and security interests in property;

(e) the protection of creditors in matters of insolvency;

(f) the protection, in other respects, of third parties acting in good faith.

If recognition of a trust is prevented by application of the preceding paragraph, the court shall try to give effect to the objects of the trust by other means.

### Article 16

The Convention does not prevent the application of those provisions of the law of the forum which must be applied even to international situations, irrespective of rules of conflict of laws.

### Article 17

In the Convention the word "law" means the rules of law in force in a State other than its rules of conflict of laws.

### Article 18

The provisions of the Convention may be disregarded when their application would be manifestly incompatible with public policy.

### Article 22

The Convention applies to trusts regardless of the date on which they were created.

# Foreign Corporations Act
# 1991 ch 44

### 1  Recognition of corporate status of certain foreign corporations

(1)  If at any time—

(a)  any question arises whether a body which purports to have or, as the case may be, which appears to have lost corporate status under the laws of a territory which is not at that time a recognised State should or should not be regarded as having legal personality as a body corporate under the law of any part of the United Kingdom, and

(b)  it appears that the laws of that territory are at that time applied by a settled court system in that territory,

that question and any other material question relating to the body shall be determined (and account shall be taken of those laws) as if that territory were a recognised State.

(2)  For the purposes of subsection (1) above—

(a)  "a recognised State" is a territory which is recognised by Her Majesty's Government in the United Kingdom as a State;

(b)  the laws of a territory which is so recognised shall be taken to include the laws of any part of the territory which are acknowledged by the federal or other central government of the territory as a whole; and

(c)  a material question is a question (whether as to capacity, constitution or otherwise) which, in the case of a body corporate, falls to be determined by reference to the laws of the territory under which the body is incorporated.

(3)  Any registration or other thing done at a time before the coming into force of this section shall be regarded as valid if it would have been valid at that time, had subsections (1) and (2) above then been in force.

UK Statutes

# Private International Law (Miscellaneous Provisions) Act 1995 ch 42

## PART II

### Validity of Marriages under a Law which permits Polygamy

#### 5 Validity in English law of potentially polygamous marriages

(1) A marriage entered into outside England and Wales between parties neither of whom is already married is not void under the law of England and Wales on the ground that it is entered into under a law which permits polygamy and that either party is domiciled in England and Wales.

(2) This section does not affect the determination of the validity of a marriage by reference to the law of another country to the extent that it falls to be so determined in accordance with the rules of private international law.

#### 6 Application of section 5 to prior marriages

(1) Section 5 above shall be deemed to apply, and always to have applied, to any marriage entered into before commencement which is not excluded by subsection (2) or (3) below.

(2) That section does not apply to a marriage a party to which has (before commencement) entered into a later marriage which either—

(a) is valid apart from this section but would be void if section 5 above applied to the earlier marriage; or

(b) is valid by virtue of this section.

(3) That section does not apply to a marriage which has been annulled before commencement, whether by a decree granted in England and Wales or by an annulment obtained elsewhere and recognised in England and Wales at commencement.

(4) An annulment of a marriage resulting from legal proceedings begun before commencement shall be treated for the purposes of subsection (3) above as having taken effect before that time.

(5) For the purposes of subsections (3) and (4) above a marriage which has been declared to be invalid by a court of competent jurisdiction in any proceedings concerning either the validity of the marriage or any right dependent on its validity shall be treated as having been annulled.

(6) Nothing in section 5 above, in its application to marriages entered into before commencement—

(a) gives or affects any entitlement to an interest—

    (i) under the will or codicil of, or on the intestacy of, a person who died before commencement; or

    (ii) under a settlement or other disposition of property made before that time (otherwise than by will or codicil);

(b) gives or affects any entitlement to a benefit, allowance, pension or other payment—

    (i) payable before, or in respect of a period before, commencement; or

    (ii) payable in respect of the death of a person before that time;

(c) affects tax in respect of a period or event before commencement; or

(d) affects the succession to any dignity or title of honour.

(7) In this section "commencement" means the commencement of this Part.

. . .

PART III

## Choice of Law in Tort and Delict

### 9 Purpose of Part III

(1) The rules in this Part apply for choosing the law (in this Part referred to as "the applicable law") to be used for determining issues relating to tort or (for the purposes of the law of Scotland) delict.

(2) The characterisation for the purposes of private international law of issues arising in a claim as issues relating to tort or delict is a matter for the courts of the forum.

(3) The rules in this Part do not apply in relation to issues arising in any claim excluded from the operation of this Part by section 13 below.

(4) The applicable law shall be used for determining the issues arising in a claim, including in particular the question whether an actionable tort or delict has occurred.

(5) The applicable law to be used for determining the issues arising in a claim shall exclude any choice of law rules forming part of the law of the country or countries concerned.

(6) For the avoidance of doubt (and without prejudice to the operation of section 14 below) this Part applies in relation to events occurring in the forum as it applies in relation to events occurring in any other country.

(7) In this Part as it extends to any country within the United Kingdom, "the forum" means England and Wales, Scotland or Northern Ireland, as the case may be.

(8) In this Part "delict" includes quasi-delict.

### 10 Abolition of certain common law rules

The rules of the common law, in so far as they—

(a) require actionability under both the law of the forum and the law of another country for the purpose of determining whether a tort or delict is actionable; or

(b) allow (as an exception from the rules falling within paragraph (a) above) for the law of a single country to be applied for the purpose of determining the issues, or any of the issues, arising in the case in question,

are hereby abolished so far as they apply to any claim in tort or delict which is not excluded from the operation of this Part by section 13 below.

### 11 Choice of applicable law: the general rule

(1) The general rule is that the applicable law is the law of the country in which the events constituting the tort or delict in question occur.

(2) Where elements of those events occur in different countries, the applicable law under the general rule is to be taken as being—

(a) for a cause of action in respect of personal injury caused to an individual or death resulting from personal injury, the law of the country where the individual was when he sustained the injury;

(b) for a cause of action in respect of damage to property, the law of the country where the property was when it was damaged; and

(c) in any other case, the law of the country in which the most significant element or elements of those events occurred.

(3) In this section "personal injury" includes disease or any impairment of physical or mental condition.

### 12 Choice of applicable law: displacement of general rule

(1) If it appears, in all the circumstances, from a comparison of—

(a) the significance of the factors which connect a tort or delict with the country whose law would be the applicable law under the general rule; and

(b) the significance of any factors connecting the tort or delict with another country, that it is substantially more appropriate for the applicable law for determining the issues arising in the case, or any of those issues, to be the law of the other country, the general rule is displaced and the applicable law for determining those issues or that issue (as the case may be) is the law of that other country.

(2) The factors that may be taken into account as connecting a tort or delict with a country for the purposes of this section include, in particular, factors relating to the parties, to any of the events which constitute the tort or delict in question or to any of the circumstances or consequences of those events.

## 13  Exclusion of defamation claims from Part III

(1) Nothing in this Part applies to affect the determination of issues arising in any defamation claim.

(2) For the purposes of this section "defamation claim" means—

(a)  any claim under the law of any part of the United Kingdom for libel or slander or for slander of title, slander of goods or other malicious falsehood and any claim under the law of Scotland for verbal injury; and

(b)  any claim under the law of any other country corresponding to or otherwise in the nature of a claim mentioned in paragraph (a) above.

## 14  Transitional provision and savings

(1) Nothing in this Part applies to acts or omissions giving rise to a claim which occur before the commencement of this Part.

(2) Nothing in this Part affects any rules of law (including rules of private international law) except those abolished by section 10 above.

(3) Without prejudice to the generality of subsection (2) above, nothing in this Part—

(a)  authorises the application of the law of a country outside the forum as the applicable law for determining issues arising in any claim in so far as to do so—

(i)  would conflict with principles of public policy; or

(ii)  would give effect to such a penal, revenue or other public law as would not otherwise be enforceable under the law of the forum; or

(b)  affects any rules of evidence, pleading or practice or authorises questions of procedure in any proceedings to be determined otherwise than in accordance with the law of the forum.

(4) This Part has effect without prejudice to the operation of any rule of law which either has effect notwithstanding the rules of private international law applicable in the particular circumstances or modifies the rules of private international law that would otherwise be so applicable.

## 15  Crown application

(1) This Part applies in relation to claims by or against the Crown as it applies in relation to claims to which the Crown is not a party.

(2) In subsection (1) above a reference to the Crown does not include a reference to Her Majesty in Her private capacity or to Her Majesty in right of Her Duchy of Lancaster or to the Duke of Cornwall.

(3) Without prejudice to the generality of section 14(2) above, nothing in this section affects any rule of law as to whether proceedings of any description may be brought against the Crown.

## [15A  Disapplication of Part III where the rules in the Rome II Regulation apply

(1) Nothing in this Part applies to affect the determination of issues relating to tort which fall to be determined under the Rome II Regulation.

(2) In subsection (1) the "Rome II Regulation" means Regulation (EC) No 864/2007 of the European Parliament and of the Council on the law applicable to non-contractual obligations , including that Regulation as applied by regulation 6 of the Law Applicable to Non-Contractual Obligations (England

and Wales and Northern Ireland) Regulations 2008 (conflicts solely between the laws of different parts of the United Kingdom or between one or more parts of the United Kingdom and Gibraltar).

(3) This section extends to England and Wales and Northern Ireland only.]

. . .

# Employment Rights Act
## 1996 ch 18

**204  Law governing employment**

(1)  For the purposes of this Act it is immaterial whether the law which (apart from this Act) governs any person's employment is the law of the United Kingdom, or of a part of the United Kingdom, or not.

. . .

# Late Payment of Commercial Debts (Interest) Act
## 1998 ch 20

**12 Conflict of laws**

(1) This Act does not have effect in relation to a contract governed by the law of a part of the United Kingdom by choice of the parties if—

(a) there is no significant connection between the contract and that part of the United Kingdom; and

(b) but for that choice, the applicable law would be a foreign law.

(2) This Act has effect in relation to a contract governed by a foreign law by choice of the parties if—

(a) but for that choice, the applicable law would be the law of a part of the United Kingdom; and

(b) there is no significant connection between the contract and any country other than that part of the United Kingdom.

(3) In this section—

"contract" means a contract falling within section 2(1); and

"foreign law" means the law of a country outside the United Kingdom.

UK Statutes

# Adoption (Intercountry Aspects) Act
# 1999 ch 18

*Implementation of Convention*

## 1 Regulations giving effect to Convention

(1) Subject to the provisions of this Act, regulations made by the Secretary of State may make provision for giving effect to the Convention on Protection of Children and Co-operation in respect of Intercountry Adoption, concluded at the Hague on 29th May 1993 ("the Convention").

(2) The text of the Convention (so far as material) is set out in Schedule 1 to this Act.

(3) Regulations under this section may—

(a)    apply, with or without modifications, any provision of the enactments relating to adoption;

(b)    provide that any person who contravenes or fails to comply with any provision of the regulations is to be guilty of an offence and liable on summary conviction to imprisonment for a term not exceeding three months, or a fine not exceeding level 5 on the standard scale, or both;

(c)    make different provision for different purposes or areas; and

(d)    make such incidental, supplementary, consequential or transitional provision as appears to the Secretary of State to be expedient.

(4) Regulations under this section shall be made by statutory instrument which shall be subject to annulment in pursuance of a resolution of either House of Parliament.

(5) Subject to subsection (6), any power to make subordinate legislation under or for the purposes of the enactments relating to adoption includes power to do so with a view to giving effect to the provisions of the Convention.

(6) Subsection (5) does not apply in relation to any power which is exercisable by the National Assembly for Wales.

. . .

## 2 Central Authorities and accredited bodies

(1) The functions under the Convention of the Central Authority are to be discharged—

(a)    separately in relation to England and Scotland by the Secretary of State; and

(b)    in relation to Wales by the National Assembly for Wales.

(2) A communication may be sent to the Central Authority in relation to any part of Great Britain by sending it (for forwarding if necessary) to the Central Authority in relation to England.

[(2A)  [A registered adoption society] is an accredited body for the purposes of the Convention if, in accordance with the conditions of the registration, the [society] may provide facilities in respect of Convention adoptions and adoptions effected by Convention adoption orders.]

[(2B)  A registered adoption service is an accredited body for the purposes of the Convention if, in accordance with the conditions of its registration, the service may provide facilities in respect of Convention adoptions and adoptions effected by Convention adoption orders.]

(3) An approved adoption society is an accredited body for the purposes of the Convention if the approval extends to the provision of facilities in respect of Convention adoptions and adoptions effected by Convention adoption orders.

(4) The functions under Article 9(a) to (c) of the Convention are to be discharged by local authorities and accredited bodies on behalf of the Central Authority.

[(5)  In this section, "registered adoption society" has the same meaning as in section 2 of the Adoption and Children Act 2002 (basic definitions); and expressions used in this section in its application to England and Wales which are also used in that Act have the same meanings as in that Act.]

[(6) In this section in its application to Scotland, "registered adoption service" means an adoption service provided as mentioned in section 2(11)(b) of the Regulation of Care (Scotland) Act 2001 (asp 8) and registered under Part 1 of that Act; and "registration" shall be construed accordingly.]

*Convention adoptions*

3 [...]

### 4 Effect of Convention adoptions in England and Wales

(1) In subsection (1) of section 38 of the 1976 Act (meaning of "adoption" for purposes of provisions relating to status of adopted children), after paragraph (c) there shall be inserted—

"(cc)which is a Convention adoption;".

(2) In subsection (2) of section 39 of that Act (status conferred by adoption), for "subsection (3)" there shall be substituted "subsections (3) and (3A)".

(3) After subsection (3) of that section there shall be inserted—

"(3A) Where, in the case of a Convention adoption, the High Court is satisfied, on an application under this subsection—

(a)  that under the law of the country in which the adoption was effected the adoption is not a full adoption;

(b)  that the consents referred to in Article 4(c) and (d) of the Convention have not been given for a full adoption, or that the United Kingdom is not the receiving State (within the meaning of Article 2 of the Convention); and

(c)  that it would be more favourable to the adopted child for a direction to be given under this subsection,

the Court may direct that subsection (2) shall not apply, or shall not apply to such extent as may be specified in the direction.

In this subsection "full adoption" means an adoption by virtue of which the adopted child falls to be treated in law as if he were not the child of any person other than the adopters or adopter.

(3B) The following provisions of the Family Law Act 1986—

(a)  section 59 (provisions relating to the Attorney General); and

(b)  section 60 (supplementary provision as to declarations), shall apply in relation to, and to an application for, a direction under subsection (3A) as they apply in relation to, and to an application for, a declaration under Part III of that Act."

5 [...]

6 [...]

. . .

### 17 Savings for adoptions etc under 1965 Convention

(1) In relation to—

(a)  a 1965 Convention adoption order or an application for such an order; or

(b)  a 1965 Convention adoption,

the 1976 and 1978 Acts shall have effect without the amendments made by sections 3 to 6 and 8 and Schedule 2 to this Act and the associated repeals made by Schedule 3 to this Act.

(2) In subsection (1) in its application to the 1976 or 1978 Act—

"1965 Convention adoption order" has the meaning which "Convention adoption order" has in that Act as it has effect without the amendments and repeals mentioned in that subsection;

"1965 Convention adoption" has the meaning which "regulated adoption" has in that Act as it so has effect.

...

SCHEDULE 1

**Convention on Protection of Children and Co-operation in Respect of Intercountry Adoption**

*Section 1*

The States signatory to the present Convention.

Recognizing that the child, for the full and harmonious development of his or her personality, should grow up in a family environment, in an atmosphere of happiness, love and understanding,

Recalling that each State should take, as a matter of priority, appropriate measures to enable the child to remain in the care of his or her family of origin,

Recognizing that intercountry adoption may offer the advantage of a permanent family to a child for whom a suitable family cannot be found in his or her State of origin,

Convinced of the necessity to take measures to ensure that intercountry adoptions are made in the best interests of the child and with respect for his or her fundamental rights, and to prevent the abduction, the sale of, or traffic in children,

Desiring to establish common provisions to this effect, taking into account the principles set forth in international instruments, in particular the United Nations Convention on the Rights of the Child, of 20 November 1989, and the United Nations Declaration on Social and Legal Principles relating to the Protection and Welfare of Children, with Special Reference to Foster Placement and Adoption Nationally and Internationally (General Assembly Resolution 41/85, of 3 December 1986),

Have agreed upon the following provisions—

**Chapter I**

*Scope of the Convention*

**Article 1**

The objects of the present Convention are—

(a)   to establish safeguards to ensure that intercountry adoptions take place in the best interests of the child and with respect for his or her fundamental rights as recognised in international law;

(b)   to establish a system of co-operation amongst Contracting States to ensure that those safeguards are respected and thereby prevent the abduction, the sale of, or traffic in children;

(c)   to secure the recognition in Contracting States of adoptions made in accordance with the Convention.

**Article 2**

1 The Convention shall apply where a child habitually resident in one Contracting State ("the State of origin") has been, is being, or is to be moved to another Contracting State ("the receiving State") either after his or her adoption in the State of origin by spouses or a person habitually resident in the receiving State, or for the purposes of such an adoption in the receiving State or in the State of origin.

2 The Convention covers only adoptions which create a permanent parent-child relationship.

**Article 3**

The Convention ceases to apply if the agreements mentioned in Article 17, sub-paragraph (c), have not been given before the child attains the age of eighteen years.

## Chapter II

*Requirements for Intercountry Adoptions*

### Article 4

An adoption within the scope of the Convention shall take place only if the competent authorities of the State of origin—

(a) have established that the child is adoptable;

(b) have determined, after possibilities for placement of the child within the State of origin have been given due consideration, that an intercountry adoption is in the child's best interests;

(c) have ensured that—

    (i) the persons, institutions and authorities whose consent is necessary for adoption, have been counselled as may be necessary and duly informed of the effects of their consent, in particular whether or not an adoption will result in the termination of the legal relationship between the child and his or her family of origin,

    (ii) such persons, institutions and authorities have given their consent freely, in the required legal form, and expressed or evidenced in writing,

    (iii) the consents have not been induced by payment or compensation of any kind and have not been withdrawn, and

    (iv) the consent of the mother, where required, has been given only after the birth of the child; and

(d) have ensured, having regard to the age and degree of maturity of the child, that—

    (i) he or she has been counselled and duly informed of the effects of the adoption and of his or her consent to the adoption, where such consent is required,

    (ii) consideration has been given to the child's wishes and opinions,

    (iii) the child's consent to the adoption, where such consent is required, has been given freely, in the required legal form, and expressed or evidenced in writing, and

    (iv) such consent has not been induced by payment or compensation of any kind.

### Article 5

An adoption within the scope of the Convention shall take place only if the competent authorities of the receiving State—

(a) have determined that the prospective adoptive parents are eligible and suited to adopt;

(b) have ensured that the prospective adoptive parents have been counselled as may be necessary; and

(c) have determined that the child is or will be authorised to enter and reside permanently in that State.

## Chapter III

*Central Authorities and Accredited Bodies*

### Article 6

1 A Contracting State shall designate a Central Authority to discharge the duties which are imposed by the Convention upon such authorities.

2 Federal States, States with more than one system of law or States having autonomous territorial units shall be free to appoint more than one Central Authority and to specify the territorial or personal extent of their functions. Where a State has appointed more than one Central Authority, it shall designate the Central Authority to which any communication may be addressed for transmission to the appropriate Central Authority within that State.

### Article 7

1 Central Authorities shall co-operate with each other and promote co-operation amongst the competent authorities in their States to protect children and to achieve the other objects of the Convention.

2 They shall take directly all appropriate measures to—

(a)  provide information as to the laws of their States concerning adoption and other general information, such as statistics and standard forms;

(b)  keep one another informed about the operation of the Convention and, as far as possible, eliminate any obstacles to its application.

### Article 8

Central Authorities shall take, directly or through public authorities, all appropriate measures to prevent improper financial or other gain in connection with an adoption and to deter all practices contrary to the objects of the Convention.

### Article 9

Central Authorities shall take, directly or through public authorities or other bodies duly accredited in their State, all appropriate measures, in particular to—

(a)  collect, preserve and exchange information about the situation of the child and the prospective adoptive parents, so far as is necessary to complete the adoption;

(b)  facilitate, follow and expedite proceedings with a view to obtaining the adoption;

(c)  promote the development of adoption counselling and post-adoption services in their States;

(d)  provide each other with general evaluation reports about experience with intercountry adoption;

(e)  reply, in so far as is permitted by the law of their State, to justified requests from other Central Authorities or public authorities for information about a particular adoption situation.

### Article 10

Accreditation shall only be granted to and maintained by bodies demonstrating their competence to carry out properly the tasks with which they may be entrusted.

### Article 11

An accredited body shall—

(a)  pursue only non-profit objectives according to such conditions and within such limits as may be established by the competent authorities of the State of accreditation;

(b)  be directed and staffed by persons qualified by their ethical standards and by training or experience to work in the field of intercountry adoption; and

(c)  be subject to supervision by competent authorities of that State as to its composition, operation and financial situation.

### Article 12

A body accredited in one Contracting State may act in another Contracting State only if the competent authorities of both States have authorised it to do so.

### Article 13

The designation of the Central Authorities and, where appropriate, the extent of their functions, as well as the names and addresses of the accredited bodies shall be communicated by each Contracting State to the Permanent Bureau of the Hague Conference on Private International Law.

UK Statutes

## Chapter IV

*Procedural Requirements in Intercountry Adoption*

### Article 14

Persons habitually resident in a Contracting State, who wish to adopt a child habitually resident in another Contracting State, shall apply to the Central Authority in the State of their habitual residence.

### Article 15

1 If the Central Authority of the receiving State is satisfied that the applicants are eligible and suited to adopt, it shall prepare a report including information about their identity, eligibility and suitability to adopt, background, family and medical history, social environment, reasons for adoption, ability to undertake an intercountry adoption, as well as the characteristics of the children for whom they would be qualified to care.

2 It shall transmit the report to the Central Authority of the State of origin.

### Article 16

1 If the Central Authority of the State of origin is satisfied that the child is adoptable, it shall—

(a) prepare a report including information about his or her identity, adoptability, background, social environment, family history, medical history including that of the child's family, and any special needs of the child;

(b) give due consideration to the child's upbringing and to his or her ethnic, religious and cultural background;

(c) ensure that consents have been obtained in accordance with Article 4; and

(d) determine, on the basis in particular of the reports relating to the child and the prospective adoptive parents, whether the envisaged placement is in the best interests of the child.

2 It shall transmit to the Central Authority of the receiving State its report on the child, proof that the necessary consents have been obtained and the reasons for its determination on the placement, taking care not to reveal the identity of the mother and the father if, in the State of origin, these identities may not be disclosed.

### Article 17

Any decision in the State of origin that a child should be entrusted to prospective adoptive parents may only be made if—

(a) the Central Authority of that State has ensured that the prospective adoptive parents agree;

(b) the Central Authority of the receiving State has approved such decision, where such approval is required by the law of that State or by the Central Authority of the State of origin;

(c) the Central Authorities of both States have agreed that the adoption may proceed; and

(d) it has been determined, in accordance with Article 5, that the prospective adoptive parents are eligible and suited to adopt and that the child is or will be authorised to enter and reside permanently in the receiving State.

### Article 18

The Central Authorities of both States shall take all necessary steps to obtain permission for the child to leave the State of origin and to enter and reside permanently in the receiving State.

### Article 19

1 The transfer of the child to the receiving State may only be carried out if the requirements of Article 17 have been satisfied.

2 The Central Authorities of both States shall ensure that this transfer takes place in secure and appropriate circumstances and, if possible, in the company of the adoptive or prospective adoptive parents.

3 If the transfer of the child does not take place, the reports referred to in Articles 15 and 16 are to be sent back to the authorities who forwarded them.

### Article 20

The Central Authorities shall keep each other informed about the adoption process and the measures taken to complete it, as well as about the progress of the placement if a probationary period is required.

### Article 21

1 Where the adoption is to take place after the transfer of the child to the receiving State and it appears to the Central Authority of that State that the continued placement of the child with the prospective adoptive parents is not in the child's best interests, such Central Authority shall take the measures necessary to protect the child, in particular—

(a) to cause the child to be withdrawn from the prospective adoptive parents and to arrange temporary care;

(b) in consultation with the Central Authority of the State of origin, to arrange without delay a new placement of the child with a view to adoption or, if this is not appropriate, to arrange alternative long-term care; an adoption shall not take place until the Central Authority of the State of origin has been duly informed concerning the new prospective adoptive parents;

(c) as a last resort, to arrange the return of the child, if his or her interests so require.

2 Having regard in particular to the age and degree of maturity of the child, he or she shall be consulted and, where appropriate, his or her consent obtained in relation to measures to be taken under this Article.

### Article 22

1 The functions of a Central Authority under this Chapter may be performed by public authorities or by bodies accredited under Chapter III, to the extent permitted by the law of its State.

2 Any Contracting State may declare to the depositary of the Convention that the functions of the Central Authority under Articles 15 to 21 may be performed in that State, to the extent permitted by the law and subject to the supervision of the competent authorities of that State, also by bodies or persons who—

(a) meet the requirements of integrity, professional competence, experience and accountability of that State; and

(b) are qualified by their ethical standards and by training or experience to work in the field of intercountry adoption.

3 A Contracting State which makes the declaration provided for in paragraph 2 shall keep the Permanent Bureau of the Hague Conference on Private International Law informed of the names and addresses of these bodies and persons.

4 Any Contracting State may declare to the depositary of the Convention that adoptions of children habitually resident in its territory may only take place if the functions of the Central Authorities are performed in accordance with paragraph 1.

5 Notwithstanding any declaration made under paragraph 2, the reports provided for in Articles 15 and 16 shall, in every case, be prepared under the responsibility of the Central Authority or other authorities or bodies in accordance with paragraph 1.

## Chapter V

### *Recognition and Effects of the Adoption*

### Article 23

1 An adoption certified by the competent authority of the State of the adoption as having been made in accordance with the Convention shall be recognised by operation of law in the other Contracting

States. The certificate shall specify when and by whom the agreements under Article 17, sub-paragraph c, were given.

2 Each Contracting State shall, at the time of signature, ratification, acceptance, approval or accession, notify the depositary of the Convention of the identity and the functions of the authority or the authorities which, in that State, are competent to make the certification. It shall also notify the depositary of any modification in the designation of these authorities.

### Article 24

The recognition of an adoption may be refused in a contracting State only if the adoption is manifestly contrary to its public policy, taking into account the best interests of the child.

### Article 25

Any Contracting State may declare to the depositary of the convention that it will not be bound under this Convention to recognise adoptions made in accordance with an agreement concluded by application of Article 39, paragraph 2.

### Article 26

1 The recognition of an adoption includes recognition of—

(a)  the legal parent-child relationship between the child and his or her adoptive parents;

(b)  parental responsibility of the adoptive parents for the child;

(c)  the termination of a pre-existing legal relationship between the child and his or her mother and father, if the adoption has this effect in the Contracting State where it was made.

2 In the case of an adoption having the effect of terminating a pre-existing legal parent-child relationship, the child shall enjoy in the receiving State, and in any other Contracting State where the adoption is recognised, rights equivalent to those resulting from adoptions having this effect in each such State.

3 The preceding paragraphs shall not prejudice the application of any provision more favourable for the child, in force in the Contracting State which recognises the adoption.

### *Article 27*

1 Where an adoption granted in the State of origin does not have the effect of terminating a pre-existing legal parent-child relationship, it may, in the receiving State which recognises the adoption under the Convention, be converted into an adoption having such an effect—

(a)  if the law of the receiving State so permits; and

(b)  if the consents referred to in Article 4, sub-paragraphs c and d, have been or are given for the purpose of such an adoption.

2 Article 23 applies to the decision converting the adoption.

## Chapter VI

### *General Provisions*

### Article 28

The Convention does not affect any law of a State of origin which requires that the adoption of a child habitually resident within that State take place in that State or which prohibits the child's placement in, or transfer to, the receiving State prior to adoption.

### Article 29

There shall be no contact between the prospective adoptive parents and the child's parents or any other person who has care of the child until the requirements of Article 4, sub-paragraphs a to c, and Article 5, sub-paragraph a, have been met, unless the adoption takes place within a family or unless the contact is in compliance with the conditions established by the competent authority of the State of origin.

Article 30

1 The competent authorities of a Contracting State shall ensure that information held by them concerning the child's origin, in particular information concerning the identity of his or her parents, as well as the medical history, is preserved.

2 They shall ensure that the child or his or her representative has access to such information, under appropriate guidance, in so far as is permitted by the law of that State.

Article 31

Without prejudice to Article 30, personal data gathered or transmitted under the Convention, especially data referred to in Articles 15 and 16, shall be used only for the purposes for which they were gathered or transmitted.

Article 32

1 No one shall derive improper financial or other gain from an activity related to an intercountry adoption.

2 Only costs and expenses, including reasonable professional fees of persons involved in the adoption, may be charged or paid.

3 The directors, administrators and employees of bodies involved in an adoption shall not receive remuneration which is unreasonably high in relation to services rendered.

Article 33

A competent authority which finds that any provision of the Convention has not been respected or that there is a serious risk that it may not be respected, shall immediately inform the Central Authority of its State. This Central Authority shall be responsible for ensuring that appropriate measures are taken.

Article 34

If the competent authority of the State of destination of a document so requests, a translation certified as being in conformity with the original must be furnished. Unless otherwise provided, the costs of such translation are to be borne by the prospective adoptive parents.

Article 35

The competent authorities of the contracting States shall act expeditiously in the process of adoption.

Article 36

In relation to a State which has two or more systems of law with regard to adoption applicable in different territorial units—

(a)  any reference to habitual residence in that State shall be construed as referring to habitual residence in a territorial unit of that State;

(b)  any reference to the law of that State shall be construed as referring to the law in force in the relevant territorial unit;

(c)  any reference to the competent authorities or to the public authorities of that State shall be construed as referring to those authorised to act in the relevant territorial unit;

(d)  any reference to the accredited bodies of that State shall be construed as referring to bodies accredited in the relevant territorial unit.

Article 37

In relation to a State which with regard to adoption has two or more systems of law applicable to different categories of persons, any reference to the law of that State shall be construed as referring to the legal system specified by the law of that State.

UK Statutes

### Article 38

A State within which different territorial units have their own rules of law in respect of adoption shall not be bound to apply the Convention where a State with a unified system of law would not be bound to do so.

### Article 39

1 The convention does not affect any international instrument to which Contracting States are Parties and which contains provisions on matters governed by the Convention, unless a contrary declaration is made by the States parties to such instrument.

2 Any Contracting State may enter into agreements with one or more other Contracting States, with a view to improving the application of the Convention in their mutual relations. These agreements may derogate only from the provisions of Articles 14 to 16 and 18 to 21. The States which have concluded such an agreement shall transmit a copy to the depositary of the Convention.

### Article 40

No reservation to the Convention shall be permitted.

### Article 41

The Convention shall apply in every case where an application pursuant to Article 14 has been received after the Convention has entered into force in the receiving State and the State of origin.

### Article 42

The Secretary General of the Hague Conference on Private International Law shall at regular intervals convene a Special Commission in order to review the practical operation of the Convention.

. . .

# Adoption and Children Act
# 2002 ch 38

CHAPTER 6

## Adoptions with a Foreign Element

*Bringing children into and out of the United Kingdom*

### 83 Restriction on bringing children in

(1) This section applies where a person who is habitually resident in the British Islands (the "British resident")—

(a) brings, or causes another to bring, a child who is habitually resident outside the British Islands into the United Kingdom for the purpose of adoption by the British resident, or

(b) at any time brings, or causes another to bring, into the United Kingdom a child adopted by the British resident under an external adoption effected within the period of [twelve] months ending with that time.

The references to adoption, or to a child adopted, by the British resident include a reference to adoption, or to a child adopted, by the British resident and another person.

(2) But this section does not apply if the child is intended to be adopted under a Convention adoption order.

(3) An external adoption means an adoption, other than a Convention adoption, of a child effected under the law of any country or territory outside the British Islands, whether or not the adoption is—

(a) an adoption within the meaning of Chapter 4, or

(b) a full adoption (within the meaning of section 88(3)).

(4) Regulations may require a person intending to bring, or to cause another to bring, a child into the United Kingdom in circumstances where this section applies—

(a) to apply to an adoption agency (including a Scottish or Northern Irish adoption agency) in the prescribed manner for an assessment of his suitability to adopt the child, and

(b) to give the agency any information it may require for the purpose of the assessment.

(5) Regulations may require prescribed conditions to be met in respect of a child brought into the United Kingdom in circumstances where this section applies.

(6) In relation to a child brought into the United Kingdom for adoption in circumstances where this section applies, regulations may—

(a) provide for any provision of Chapter 3 to apply with modifications or not to apply,

(b) if notice of intention to adopt has been given, impose functions in respect of the child on the local authority to which the notice was given.

(7) If a person brings, or causes another to bring, a child into the United Kingdom at any time in circumstances where this section applies, he is guilty of an offence if—

(a) he has not complied with any requirement imposed by virtue of subsection (4), or

(b) any condition required to be met by virtue of subsection (5) is not met,

before that time, or before any later time which may be prescribed.

(8) A person guilty of an offence under this section is liable—

(a) on summary conviction to imprisonment for a term not exceeding six months, or a fine not exceeding the statutory maximum, or both,

(b) on conviction on indictment, to imprisonment for a term not exceeding twelve months, or a fine, or both.

(9) In this section, "prescribed" means prescribed by regulations and "regulations" means regulations made by the Secretary of State, after consultation with the Assembly.

### 84 Giving parental responsibility prior to adoption abroad

(1) The High Court may, on an application by persons who the court is satisfied intend to adopt a child under the law of a country or territory outside the British Islands, make an order giving parental responsibility for the child to them.

(2) An order under this section may not give parental responsibility to persons who the court is satisfied meet those requirements as to domicile, or habitual residence, in England and Wales which have to be met if an adoption order is to be made in favour of those persons.

(3) An order under this section may not be made unless any requirements prescribed by regulations are satisfied.

(4) An application for an order under this section may not be made unless at all times during the preceding ten weeks the child's home was with the applicant or, in the case of an application by two people, both of them.

(5) Section 46(2) to (4) has effect in relation to an order under this section as it has effect in relation to adoption orders.

(6) Regulations may provide for any provision of this Act which refers to adoption orders to apply, with or without modifications, to orders under this section.

(7) In this section, "regulations" means regulations made by the Secretary of State, after consultation with the Assembly.

### 85 Restriction on taking children out

(1) A child who—

(a) is a Commonwealth citizen, or

(b) is habitually resident in the United Kingdom,

must not be removed from the United Kingdom to a place outside the British Islands for the purpose of adoption unless the condition in subsection (2) is met.

(2) The condition is that—

(a) the prospective adopters have parental responsibility for the child by virtue of an order under section 84, or

(b) the child is removed under the authority of an order under [section 59 of the Adoption and Children (Scotland) Act 2007 (asp 4)] or Article 57 of the Adoption (Northern Ireland) Order 1987 (SI 1987/2203 (NI 22)).

(3) Removing a child from the United Kingdom includes arranging to do so; and the circumstances in which a person arranges to remove a child from the United Kingdom include those where he—

(a) enters into an arrangement for the purpose of facilitating such a removal of the child,

(b) initiates or takes part in any negotiations of which the purpose is the conclusion of an arrangement within paragraph (a), or

(c) causes another person to take any step mentioned in paragraph (a) or (b).

An arrangement includes an agreement (whether or not enforceable).

(4) A person who removes a child from the United Kingdom in contravention of subsection (1) is guilty of an offence.

(5) A person is not guilty of an offence under subsection (4) of causing a person to take any step mentioned in paragraph (a) or (b) of subsection (3) unless it is proved that he knew or had reason to suspect that the step taken would contravene subsection (1).

But this subsection only applies if sufficient evidence is adduced to raise an issue as to whether the person had the knowledge or reason mentioned.

(6) A person guilty of an offence under this section is liable—

(a) on summary conviction to imprisonment for a term not exceeding six months, or a fine not exceeding the statutory maximum, or both,

(b) on conviction on indictment, to imprisonment for a term not exceeding twelve months, or a fine, or both.

(7) In any proceedings under this section—

(a) a report by a British consular officer or a deposition made before a British consular officer and authenticated under the signature of that officer is admissible, upon proof that the officer or the deponent cannot be found in the United Kingdom, as evidence of the matters stated in it, and

(b) it is not necessary to prove the signature or official character of the person who appears to have signed any such report or deposition.

## 86 Power to modify sections 83 and 85

(1) Regulations may provide for section 83 not to apply if—

(a) the adopters or (as the case may be) prospective adopters are natural parents, natural relatives or guardians of the child in question (or one of them is), or

(b) the British resident in question is a partner of a parent of the child,

and any prescribed conditions are met.

(2) Regulations may provide for section 85(1) to apply with modifications, or not to apply, if—

(a) the prospective adopters are parents, relatives or guardians of the child in question (or one of them is), or

(b) the prospective adopter is a partner of a parent of the child,

and any prescribed conditions are met.

(3) On the occasion of the first exercise of the power to make regulations under this section—

(a) the statutory instrument containing the regulations is not to be made unless a draft of the instrument has been laid before, and approved by a resolution of, each House of Parliament, and

(b) accordingly section 140(2) does not apply to the instrument.

(4) In this section, "prescribed" means prescribed by regulations and "regulations" means regulations made by the Secretary of State after consultation with the Assembly.

*Overseas adoptions*

## 87 Overseas adoptions

(1) In this Act, "overseas adoption"—

(a) means an adoption of a description specified in an order made by the Secretary of State, being a description of adoptions effected under the law of any country or territory outside the British Islands, but

(b) does not include a Convention adoption.

(2) Regulations may prescribe the requirements that ought to be met by an adoption of any description effected after the commencement of the regulations for it to be an overseas adoption for the purposes of this Act.

(3) At any time when such regulations have effect, the Secretary of State must exercise his powers under this section so as to secure that subsequently effected adoptions of any description are not overseas adoptions for the purposes of this Act if he considers that they are not likely within a reasonable time to meet the prescribed requirements.

(4) In this section references to this Act include the Adoption Act 1976 (c 36).

(5) An order under this section may contain provision as to the manner in which evidence of any overseas adoption may be given.

(6) In this section—

"adoption" means an adoption of a child or of a person who was a child at the time the adoption was applied for,

"regulations" means regulations made by the Secretary of State after consultation with the Assembly.

*Miscellaneous*

### 88 Modification of section 67 for Hague Convention adoptions

(1) If the High Court is satisfied, on an application under this section, that each of the following conditions is met in the case of a Convention adoption, it may direct that section 67(3) does not apply, or does not apply to any extent specified in the direction.

(2) The conditions are—

(a) that under the law of the country in which the adoption was effected, the adoption is not a full adoption,

(b) that the consents referred to in Article 4(c) and (d) of the Convention have not been given for a full adoption or that the United Kingdom is not the receiving State (within the meaning of Article 2 of the Convention),

(c) that it would be more favourable to the adopted child for a direction to be given under subsection (1).

(3) A full adoption is an adoption by virtue of which the child is to be treated in law as not being the child of any person other than the adopters or adopter.

(4) In relation to a direction under this section and an application for it, sections 59 and 60 of the Family Law Act 1986 (c 55) (declarations under Part 3 of that Act as to marital status) apply as they apply in relation to a direction under that Part and an application for such a direction.

### 89 Annulment etc of overseas or Hague Convention adoptions

(1) The High Court may, on an application under this subsection, by order annul a Convention adoption or Convention adoption order on the ground that the adoption is contrary to public policy.

(2) The High Court may, on an application under this subsection—

(a) by order provide for an overseas adoption or a determination under section 91 to cease to be valid on the ground that the adoption or determination is contrary to public policy or that the authority which purported to authorise the adoption or make the determination was not competent to entertain the case, or

(b) decide the extent, if any, to which a determination under section 91 has been affected by a subsequent determination under that section.

(3) The High Court may, in any proceedings in that court, decide that an overseas adoption or a determination under section 91 is to be treated, for the purposes of those proceedings, as invalid on either of the grounds mentioned in subsection (2)(a).

(4) Subject to the preceding provisions, the validity of a Convention adoption, Convention adoption order or overseas adoption or a determination under section 91 cannot be called in question in proceedings in any court in England and Wales.

### 90 Section 89: supplementary

(1) Any application for an order under section 89 or a decision under subsection (2)(b) or (3) of that section must be made in the prescribed manner and within any prescribed period.

"Prescribed" means prescribed by rules.

(2) No application may be made under section 89(1) in respect of an adoption unless immediately before the application is made—

(a) the person adopted, or

(b) the adopters or adopter,

habitually reside in England and Wales.

(3) In deciding in pursuance of section 89 whether such an authority as is mentioned in section 91 was competent to entertain a particular case, a court is bound by any finding of fact made by the authority and stated by the authority to be so made for the purpose of determining whether the authority was competent to entertain the case.

### 91 Overseas determinations and orders

(1) Subsection (2) applies where any authority of a Convention country (other than the United Kingdom) or of the Channel Islands, the Isle of Man or any British overseas territory has power under the law of that country or territory—

(a) to authorise, or review the authorisation of, an adoption order made in that country or territory, or

(b) to give or review a decision revoking or annulling such an order or a Convention adoption.

(2) If the authority makes a determination in the exercise of that power, the determination is to have effect for the purpose of effecting, confirming or terminating the adoption in question or, as the case may be, confirming its termination.

(3) Subsection (2) is subject to section 89 and to any subsequent determination having effect under that subsection

UK Statutes

# Civil Partnership Act
# 2004 ch 33

PART 5

## Civil Partnership Formed or Dissolved Abroad etc

### Chapter 1

*Registration Outside UK under Order in Council*

#### 210 Registration at British consulates etc

(1) Her Majesty may by Order in Council make provision for two people to register as civil partners of each other—

(a)   in prescribed countries or territories outside the United Kingdom, and

(b)   in the presence of [a registration officer],

in cases where the officer is satisfied that the conditions in subsection (2) are met.

(2) The conditions are that—

(a)   at least one of the proposed civil partners is a United Kingdom national,

(b)   the proposed civil partners would have been eligible to register as civil partners of each other in such part of the United Kingdom as is determined in accordance with the Order,

(c)   the authorities of the country or territory in which it is proposed that they register as civil partners will not object to the registration, and

(d)   insufficient facilities exist for them to enter into an overseas relationship under the law of that country or territory.

(3) [A registration officer] is not required to allow two people to register as civil partners of each other if in his opinion the formation of a civil partnership between them would be inconsistent with international law or the comity of nations.

(4) An Order in Council under this section may make provision for appeals against a refusal, in reliance on subsection (3), to allow two people to register as civil partners of each other.

(5) An Order in Council under this section may provide that two people who register as civil partners of each other under such an Order are to be treated for the purposes of sections 221(1)(c)(i) and (2)(c)(i), 222(c), 224(b), 225(1)(c)(i) and (3)(c)(i), 229(1)(c)(i) and (2)(c)(i), 230(c) and 232(b) and section 1(3)(c)(i) of the Presumption of Death (Scotland) Act 1977 (c 27) as if they had done so in the part of the United Kingdom determined as mentioned in subsection (2)(b).

[(6) "Registration officer" means—

(a)   a consular officer in the service of Her Majesty's government in the United Kingdom, or

(b)   in the case of registration in a country [or territory] in which Her Majesty's government in the United Kingdom has for the time being no consular representative, a person authorised by the Secretary of State in respect of registration of civil partnerships in that country [or territory].]

#### 211 Registration by armed forces personnel

(1) Her Majesty may by Order in Council make provision for two people to register as civil partners of each other—

(a)   in prescribed countries or territories outside the United Kingdom, and

(b)   in the presence of an officer appointed by virtue of the Registration of Births, Deaths and Marriages (Special Provisions) Act 1957 (c 58),

in cases where the officer is satisfied that the conditions in subsection (2) are met.

UK Statutes

(2) The conditions are that—

(a) at least one of the proposed civil partners—

   (i) is a member of a part of Her Majesty's forces serving in the country or territory,

   (ii) is employed in the country or territory in such other capacity as may be prescribed, or

   (iii) is a child of a person falling within sub-paragraph (i) or (ii) and has his home with that person in that country or territory,

(b) the proposed civil partners would have been eligible to register as civil partners of each other in such part of the United Kingdom as is determined in accordance with the Order, and

(c) such other requirements as may be prescribed are complied with.

(3) In determining for the purposes of subsection (2) whether one person is the child of another, a person who is or was treated by another as a child of the family in relation to—

(a) a marriage to which the other is or was a party, or

(b) a civil partnership in which the other is or was a civil partner,

is to be regarded as the other's child.

(4) An Order in Council under this section may provide that two people who register as civil partners of each other under such an Order are to be treated for the purposes of section 221(1)(c)(i) and (2)(c)(i), 222(c), 224(b), 225(1)(c)(i) and (3)(c)(i), 229(1)(c)(i) and (2)(c)(i), 230(c) and 232(b) and section 1(3)(c)(i) of the Presumption of Death (Scotland) Act 1977 (c 27) as if they had done so in the part of the United Kingdom determined in accordance with subsection (2)(b).

(5) Any references in this section—

(a) to a country or territory outside the United Kingdom,

(b) to forces serving in such a country or territory, and

(c) to persons employed in such a country or territory,

include references to ships which are for the time being in the waters of a country or territory outside the United Kingdom, to forces serving in any such ship and to persons employed in any such ship.

## Chapter 2

*Overseas Relationships Treated as Civil Partnerships*

### 212 Meaning of "overseas relationship"

(1) For the purposes of this Act an overseas relationship is a relationship which—

(a) is either a specified relationship or a relationship which meets the general conditions, and

(b) is registered (whether before or after the passing of this Act) with a responsible authority in a country or territory outside the United Kingdom, by two people—

   (i) who under the relevant law are of the same sex at the time when they do so, and

   (ii) neither of whom is already a civil partner or lawfully married.

[(1A) But, for the purposes of the application of this Act to England and Wales, marriage is not an overseas relationship.]

(2) In this Chapter, "the relevant law" means the law of the country or territory where the relationship is registered (including its rules of private international law).

### 213 Specified relationships

(1) A specified relationship is a relationship which is specified for the purposes of section 212 by Schedule 20.

(2) The [Secretary of State] may by order amend Schedule 20 by—

(a) adding a relationship,

(b) amending the description of a relationship, or

(c)   omitting a relationship.

(3) No order may be made under this section without the consent of the Scottish Ministers and the Department of Finance and Personnel.

(4) The power to make an order under this section is exercisable by statutory instrument.

(5) An order which contains any provision (whether alone or with other provisions) amending Schedule 20 by—

(a)   amending the description of a relationship, or

(b)   omitting a relationship,

may not be made unless a draft of the statutory instrument containing the order is laid before, and approved by a resolution of, each House of Parliament.

(6) A statutory instrument containing any other order under this section is subject to annulment in pursuance of a resolution of either House of Parliament.

### 214  The general conditions

The general conditions are that, under the relevant law—

(a)   the relationship may not be entered into if either of the parties is already a party to a relationship of that kind or lawfully married,

(b)   the relationship is of indeterminate duration, and

(c)   the effect of entering into it is that the parties are—

　　(i)   treated as a couple either generally or for specified purposes, or

　　(ii)   treated as married.

### 215  Overseas relationships treated as civil partnerships: the general rule

(1) Two people are to be treated as having formed a civil partnership as a result of having registered an overseas relationship if, under the relevant law, they—

(a)   had capacity to enter into the relationship, and

(b)   met all requirements necessary to ensure the formal validity of the relationship.

(2) Subject to subsection (3), the time when they are to be treated as having formed the civil partnership is the time when the overseas relationship is registered (under the relevant law) as having been entered into.

(3) If the overseas relationship is registered (under the relevant law) as having been entered into before this section comes into force, the time when they are to be treated as having formed a civil partnership is the time when this section comes into force.

(4) But if—

(a)   before this section comes into force, a dissolution or annulment of the overseas relationship was obtained outside the United Kingdom, and

(b)   the dissolution or annulment would be recognised under Chapter 3 if the overseas relationship had been treated as a civil partnership at the time of the dissolution or annulment,

subsection (3) does not apply and subsections (1) and (2) have effect subject to subsection (5).

(5) The overseas relationship is not to be treated as having been a civil partnership for the purposes of any provisions except—

(a)   Schedules 7, 11 and 17 (financial relief in United Kingdom after dissolution or annulment obtained outside the United Kingdom);

(b)   such provisions as are specified (with or without modifications) in an order under section 259;

(c)   Chapter 3 (so far as necessary for the purposes of paragraphs (a) and (b)).

(6) This section is subject to sections 216, 217 and 218.

### 216 The same-sex requirement

(1) Two people are not to be treated as having formed a civil partnership as a result of having registered an overseas relationship if, at the critical time, they were not of the same sex under United Kingdom law.

(2) But if a full gender recognition certificate is issued under the 2004 Act to a person who has registered an overseas relationship which is within subsection (4), after the issue of the certificate the relationship is no longer prevented from being treated as a civil partnership on the ground that, at the critical time, the parties were not of the same sex.

(3) However, subsection (2) does not apply to an overseas relationship which is within subsection (4) if either of the parties has formed a subsequent civil partnership or lawful marriage.

(4) An overseas relationship is within this subsection if (and only if), at the time mentioned in section 215(2)—

(a)   one of the parties ("A") was regarded under the relevant law as having changed gender (but was not regarded under United Kingdom law as having done so), and

(b)   the other party was (under United Kingdom law) of the gender to which A had changed under the relevant law.

(5) In this section—

"the critical time" means the time determined in accordance with section 215(2) or (as the case may be) (3);

"the 2004 Act" means the Gender Recognition Act 2004 (c 7);

"United Kingdom law" means any enactment or rule of law applying in England and Wales, Scotland and Northern Ireland.

(6) Nothing in this section prevents the exercise of any enforceable [EU] right.

### 217 Person domiciled in a part of the United Kingdom

(1) Subsection (2) applies if an overseas relationship has been registered by a person who was at the time mentioned in section 215(2) domiciled in England and Wales.

(2) The two people concerned are not to be treated as having formed a civil partnership if, at the time mentioned in section 215(2)—

(a)   either of them was under 16, or

(b)   they would have been within prohibited degrees of relationship under Part 1 of Schedule 1 if they had been registering as civil partners of each other in England and Wales.

(3) Subsection (4) applies if an overseas relationship has been registered by a person who at the time mentioned in section 215(2) was domiciled in Scotland.

(4) The two people concerned are not to be treated as having formed a civil partnership if, at the time mentioned in section 215(2), they were not eligible by virtue of paragraph (b), (c) or (e) of section 86(1) to register in Scotland as civil partners of each other.

(5) Subsection (6) applies if an overseas relationship has been registered by a person who at the time mentioned in section 215(2) was domiciled in Northern Ireland.

(6) The two people concerned are not to be treated as having formed a civil partnership if, at the time mentioned in section 215(2)—

(a)   either of them was under 16, or

(b)   they would have been within prohibited degrees of relationship under Schedule 12 if they had been registering as civil partners of each other in Northern Ireland.

### 218 The public policy exception

Two people are not to be treated as having formed a civil partnership as a result of having entered into an overseas relationship if it would be manifestly contrary to public policy to recognise the capacity, under the relevant law, of one or both of them to enter into the relationship.

## Chapter 3

## Dissolution etc: Jurisdiction and Recognition

*Introduction*

### 219 Power to make provision corresponding to EC Regulation 2201/2003

(1) The Lord Chancellor may by regulations make provision—

(a) as to the jurisdiction of courts in England and Wales [. . .] in proceedings for the dissolution or annulment of a civil partnership or for legal separation of the civil partners in cases where a civil partner—

(i)   is or has been habitually resident in a member State,

(ii)  is a national of a member State, or

(iii) is domiciled in a part of the United Kingdom or the Republic of Ireland, and

(b) as to the recognition in England and Wales [. . .] of any judgment of a court of another member State which orders the dissolution or annulment of a civil partnership or the legal separation of the civil partners.

. . .

(3) The regulations may in particular make provision corresponding to that made by Council Regulation (EC) No 2201/2003 of 27th November 2003 in relation to jurisdiction and the recognition and enforcement of judgments in matrimonial matters.

(4) The regulations may provide that for the purposes of this Part and the regulations "member State" means—

(a) all member States with the exception of such member States as are specified in the regulations, or

(b) such member States as are specified in the regulations.

(5) The regulations may make provision under subsections (1)(b)[, (1A)(b)] and (2)(b) which applies even if the date of the dissolution, annulment or legal separation is earlier than the date on which this section comes into force.

(6) Regulations under subsection (1) are to be made by statutory instrument and may only be made if a draft has been laid before and approved by resolution of each House of Parliament.

. . .

(8) In this Part "section 219 regulations" means regulations made under this section.

*Jurisdiction of courts in England and Wales*

### 220 Meaning of "the court"

In sections 221 to 224 "the court" means—

(a)  the High Court, or

[(b) the family court].

### 221 Proceedings for dissolution, separation or nullity order

(1) The court has jurisdiction to entertain proceedings for a dissolution order or a separation order if (and only if)—

(a)  the court has jurisdiction under section 219 regulations,

(b)  no court has, or is recognised as having, jurisdiction under section 219 regulations and either civil partner is domiciled in England and Wales on the date when the proceedings are begun, or

(c)  the following conditions are met—

(i)   the two people concerned registered as civil partners of each other in England or Wales,

(ii)  no court has, or is recognised as having, jurisdiction under section 219 regulations, and

(iii) it appears to the court to be in the interests of justice to assume jurisdiction in the case.

UK Statutes

(2) The court has jurisdiction to entertain proceedings for a nullity order if (and only if)—

(a) the court has jurisdiction under section 219 regulations,

(b) no court has, or is recognised as having, jurisdiction under section 219 regulations and either civil partner—

    (i) is domiciled in England and Wales on the date when the proceedings are begun, or

    (ii) died before that date and either was at death domiciled in England and Wales or had been habitually resident in England and Wales throughout the period of 1 year ending with the date of death, or

(c) the following conditions are met—

    (i) the two people concerned registered as civil partners of each other in England or Wales,

    (ii) no court has, or is recognised as having, jurisdiction under section 219 regulations, and

    (iii) it appears to the court to be in the interests of justice to assume jurisdiction in the case.

(3) At any time when proceedings are pending in respect of which the court has jurisdiction by virtue of subsection (1) or (2) (or this subsection), the court also has jurisdiction to entertain other proceedings, in respect of the same civil partnership, for a dissolution, separation or nullity order, even though that jurisdiction would not be exercisable under subsection (1) or (2).

### 222 Proceedings for presumption of death order

The court has jurisdiction to entertain proceedings for a presumption of death order [on an application made by a civil partner] if (and only if)—

[(ba) at the time the application is made, the High Court does not have jurisdiction to entertain an application by that civil partner under section 1 of the Presumption of Death Act 2013 for a declaration that the other civil partner is presumed to be dead, and]

(c) the two people concerned registered as civil partners of each other in England and Wales and it appears to the court to be in the interests of justice to assume jurisdiction in the case.

### 223 Proceedings for dissolution, nullity or separation order: supplementary

(1) Rules of court may make provision in relation to civil partnerships corresponding to the provision made in relation to marriages by Schedule 1 to the Domicile and Matrimonial Proceedings Act 1973 (c 45).

(2) The rules may in particular make provision—

(a) for the provision of information by applicants and respondents in proceedings for dissolution, nullity or separation orders where proceedings relating to the same civil partnership are continuing in another jurisdiction, and

(b) for proceedings before the court to be stayed by the court where there are concurrent proceedings elsewhere in respect of the same civil partnership.

### 224 Applications for declarations as to validity etc

The court has jurisdiction to entertain an application under section 58 if (and only if)—

(a) either of the civil partners in the civil partnership to which the application relates—

    (i) is domiciled in England and Wales on the date of the application,

    (ii) has been habitually resident in England and Wales throughout the period of 1 year ending with that date, or

    (iii) died before that date and either was at death domiciled in England and Wales or had been habitually resident in England and Wales throughout the period of 1 year ending with the date of death, or

(b) the two people concerned registered as civil partners of each other in England and Wales and it appears to the court to be in the interests of justice to assume jurisdiction in the case.

. . .

*Recognition of dissolution, annulment and separation*

### 233 Effect of dissolution, annulment or separation obtained in the UK

(1) No dissolution or annulment of a civil partnership obtained in one part of the United Kingdom is effective in any part of the United Kingdom unless obtained from a court of civil jurisdiction.

(2) Subject to subsections (3) and (4), the validity of a dissolution or annulment of a civil partnership or a legal separation of civil partners which has been obtained from a court of civil jurisdiction in one part of the United Kingdom is to be recognised throughout the United Kingdom.

(3) Recognition of the validity of a dissolution, annulment or legal separation obtained from a court of civil jurisdiction in one part of the United Kingdom may be refused in any other part if the dissolution, annulment or separation was obtained at a time when it was irreconcilable with a decision determining the question of the subsistence or validity of the civil partnership—

(a)  previously given by a court of civil jurisdiction in the other part, or

(b)  previously given by a court elsewhere and recognised or entitled to be recognised in the other part.

(4) Recognition of the validity of a dissolution or legal separation obtained from a court of civil jurisdiction in one part of the United Kingdom may be refused in any other part if the dissolution or separation was obtained at a time when, according to the law of the other part, there was no subsisting civil partnership.

### 234 Recognition in the UK of overseas dissolution, annulment or separation

(1) Subject to subsection (2), the validity of an overseas dissolution, annulment or legal separation is to be recognised in the United Kingdom if, and only if, it is entitled to recognition by virtue of sections 235 to 237.

(2) This section and sections 235 to 237 do not apply to an overseas dissolution, annulment or legal separation as regards which provision as to recognition is made by section 219 regulations.

(3) For the purposes of subsections (1) and (2) and sections 235 to 237, an overseas dissolution, annulment or legal separation is a dissolution or annulment of a civil partnership or a legal separation of civil partners which has been obtained outside the United Kingdom (whether before or after this section comes into force).

### 235 Grounds for recognition

(1) The validity of an overseas dissolution, annulment or legal separation obtained by means of proceedings is to be recognised if—

(a)  the dissolution, annulment or legal separation is effective under the law of the country in which it was obtained, and

(b)  at the relevant date either civil partner—

    (i)  was habitually resident in the country in which the dissolution, annulment or legal separation was obtained,

    (ii)  was domiciled in that country, or

    (iii)  was a national of that country.

(2) The validity of an overseas dissolution, annulment or legal separation obtained otherwise than by means of proceedings is to be recognised if—

(a)  the dissolution, annulment or legal separation is effective under the law of the country in which it was obtained,

(b)  at the relevant date—

    (i)  each civil partner was domiciled in that country, or

    (ii)  either civil partner was domiciled in that country and the other was domiciled in a country under whose law the dissolution, annulment or legal separation is recognised as valid, and

(c) neither civil partner was habitually resident in the United Kingdom throughout the period of 1 year immediately preceding that date.

(3) In this section "the relevant date" means—

(a) in the case of an overseas dissolution, annulment or legal separation obtained by means of proceedings, the date of the commencement of the proceedings;

(b) in the case of an overseas dissolution, annulment or legal separation obtained otherwise than by means of proceedings, the date on which it was obtained.

(4) Where in the case of an overseas annulment the relevant date fell after the death of either civil partner, any reference in subsection (1) or (2) to that date is to be read in relation to that civil partner as a reference to the date of death.

### 236 Refusal of recognition

(1) Recognition of the validity of an overseas dissolution, annulment or legal separation may be refused in any part of the United Kingdom if the dissolution, annulment or separation was obtained at a time when it was irreconcilable with a decision determining the question of the subsistence or validity of the civil partnership—

(a) previously given by a court of civil jurisdiction in that part of the United Kingdom, or

(b) previously given by a court elsewhere and recognised or entitled to be recognised in that part of the United Kingdom.

(2) Recognition of the validity of an overseas dissolution or legal separation may be refused in any part of the United Kingdom if the dissolution or separation was obtained at a time when, according to the law of that part of the United Kingdom, there was no subsisting civil partnership.

(3) Recognition of the validity of an overseas dissolution, annulment or legal separation may be refused if—

(a) in the case of a dissolution, annulment or legal separation obtained by means of proceedings, it was obtained—

   (i) without such steps having been taken for giving notice of the proceedings to a civil partner as, having regard to the nature of the proceedings and all the circumstances, should reasonably have been taken, or

   (ii) without a civil partner having been given (for any reason other than lack of notice) such opportunity to take part in the proceedings as, having regard to those matters, he should reasonably have been given, or

(b) in the case of a dissolution, annulment or legal separation obtained otherwise than by means of proceedings—

   (i) there is no official document certifying that the dissolution, annulment or legal separation is effective under the law of the country in which it was obtained, or

   (ii) where either civil partner was domiciled in another country at the relevant date, there is no official document certifying that the dissolution, annulment or legal separation is recognised as valid under the law of that other country, or

(c) in either case, recognition of the dissolution, annulment or legal separation would be manifestly contrary to public policy.

(4) In this section—

"official", in relation to a document certifying that a dissolution, annulment or legal separation is effective, or is recognised as valid, under the law of any country, means issued by a person or body appointed or recognised for the purpose under that law;

"the relevant date" has the same meaning as in section 235.

### 237 Supplementary provisions relating to recognition of dissolution etc

(1) For the purposes of sections 235 and 236, a civil partner is to be treated as domiciled in a country if he was domiciled in that country—

(a)   according to the law of that country in family matters, or

(b)   according to the law of the part of the United Kingdom in which the question of recognition arises.

(2) The Lord Chancellor[, the Department of Justice in Northern Ireland] or the Scottish Ministers may by regulations make provision—

(a)   applying sections 235 and 236 and subsection (1) with modifications in relation to any country whose territories have different systems of law in force in matters of dissolution, annulment or legal separation;

(b)   applying sections 235 and 236 with modifications in relation to—

    (i)   an overseas dissolution, annulment or legal separation in the case of an overseas relationship (or an apparent or alleged overseas relationship);

    (ii)   any case where a civil partner is domiciled in a country or territory whose law does not recognise legal relationships between two people of the same sex;

(c)   with respect to recognition of the validity of an overseas dissolution, annulment or legal separation in cases where there are cross-proceedings;

(d)   with respect to cases where a legal separation is converted under the law of the country or territory in which it is obtained into a dissolution which is effective under the law of that country or territory;

(e)   with respect to proof of findings of fact made in proceedings in any country or territory outside the United Kingdom.

(3) The power [of the Lord Chancellor or the Scottish Ministers] to make regulations under subsection (2) is exercisable by statutory instrument.

(4) A statutory instrument containing such regulations—

(a)   if made by the Lord Chancellor, is subject to annulment in pursuance of a resolution of either House of Parliament;

. . .

(5) In this section (except subsection (4)) and sections 233 to 236 and 238—

    "annulment" includes any order annulling a civil partnership, however expressed;

    "part of the United Kingdom" means England and Wales, Scotland or Northern Ireland;

    "proceedings" means judicial or other proceedings.

(6) Nothing in this Chapter is to be read as requiring the recognition of any finding of fault made in proceedings for dissolution, annulment or legal separation or of any maintenance, custody or other ancillary order made in any such proceedings.

## 238  Non-recognition elsewhere of dissolution or annulment

(1) This section applies where, in any part of the United Kingdom—

(a)   a dissolution or annulment of a civil partnership has been granted by a court of civil jurisdiction, or

(b)   the validity of a dissolution or annulment of a civil partnership is recognised by virtue of this Chapter.

(2) The fact that the dissolution or annulment would not be recognised outside the United Kingdom does not—

(a)   preclude either party from forming a subsequent civil partnership or marriage in that part of the United Kingdom, or

(b)   cause the subsequent civil partnership or marriage of either party (wherever it takes place) to be treated as invalid in that part.

## Chapter 4

*Miscellaneous and Supplementary*

### 239 Commanding officers' certificates for Part 2 purposes

(1) Her Majesty may by Order in Council make provision in relation to cases where—

(a) two people wish to register as civil partners of each other in England and Wales (under Chapter 1 of Part 2), and

(b) one of them ("A") is [an officer, seaman or marine borne on the books of one of Her Majesty's ships at sea] and the other is resident in England and Wales,

for the issue [to A, by the captain or other officer in command of the ship,] of a certificate of no impediment.

(2) The Order may provide for the issue of the certificate to be subject to the giving of such notice and the making of such declarations as may be prescribed.

(3) A certificate of no impediment is a certificate that no legal impediment to the formation of the civil partnership has been shown to the . . . officer issuing the certificate to exist.

(4) [. . .]

### 240 Certificates of no impediment to overseas relationships

(1) Her Majesty may by Order in Council make provision for the issue of certificates of no impediment to—

(a) United Kingdom nationals, and

(b) such other persons falling within subsection (2) as may be prescribed,

who wish to enter into overseas relationships in prescribed countries or territories outside the United Kingdom with persons who are not United Kingdom nationals and who do not fall within subsection (2).

(2) A person falls within this subsection if under any enactment for the time being in force in any country mentioned in Schedule 3 to the British Nationality Act 1981 (c 61) (Commonwealth countries) that person is a citizen of that country.

(3) A certificate of no impediment is a certificate that, after proper notices have been given, no legal impediment to the recipient entering into the overseas relationship has been shown to the person issuing the certificate to exist.

### 241 Transmission of certificates of registration of overseas relationships

(1) Her Majesty may by Order in Council provide—

(a) for the transmission to the Registrar General, by such persons or in such manner as may be prescribed, of certificates of the registration of overseas relationships entered into by United Kingdom nationals in prescribed countries or territories outside the United Kingdom,

(b) for the issue by the Registrar General of a certified copy of such a certificate received by him, and

(c) for such certified copies to be received in evidence.

(2) "The Registrar General" means—

(a) in relation to England and Wales, the Registrar General for England and Wales,

(b) in relation to Scotland, the Registrar General of Births, Deaths and Marriages for Scotland, and

(c) in relation to Northern Ireland, the Registrar General for Northern Ireland.

### 242 Power to make provision relating to certain Commonwealth forces

(1) This section applies if it appears to Her Majesty that any law in force in Canada, the Commonwealth of Australia or New Zealand (or in a territory of either of the former two countries) makes, in relation to forces raised there, provision similar to that made by section 211 (registration by armed forces personnel).

(2) Her Majesty may by Order in Council make provision for securing that the law in question has effect as part of the law of the United Kingdom.

### 243 Fees

(1) The power to make an order under section 34(1) (fees) includes power to make an order prescribing fees in respect of anything which, by virtue of an Order in Council under this Part, is required to be done by registration authorities in England and Wales or by or on behalf of the Registrar General for England and Wales.

(2) Regulations made by the Registrar General of Births, Deaths and Marriages for Scotland may prescribe fees in respect of anything which, by virtue of an Order in Council under this Part, is required to be done by him or on his behalf.

(3) Subsections (3) and (4) of section 126 apply to regulations made under subsection (2) as they apply to regulations under Part 3.

(4) The power to make an order under section 157(1) includes power to make an order prescribing fees in respect of anything which, by virtue of an Order in Council under this Part, is required to be done by or on behalf of the Registrar General for Northern Ireland.

### 244 Orders in Council: supplementary

(1) An Order in Council under section 210, 211, 239, 240, 241 or 242 may make—

(a)   different provision for different cases, and

(b)   such supplementary, incidental, consequential, transitional, transitory or saving provision as appears to Her Majesty to be appropriate.

(2) The provision that may be made by virtue of subsection (1)(b) includes in particular provision corresponding to or applying with modifications any provision made by or under—

(a)   this Act, or

(b)   any Act relating to marriage outside the United Kingdom.

(3) A statutory instrument containing an Order in Council under section 210, 211, 239, 240, 241 or 242 is subject to annulment in pursuance of a resolution of either House of Parliament.

(4) Subsection (3) applies whether or not the Order also contains other provisions made by Order in Council under—

the Foreign Marriage Act 1892 (c 23),

section 3 of the Foreign Marriage Act 1947 (c 33), or

section 39 of the Marriage Act 1949 (c 76).

(5) In sections 210, 211, 239, 240 and 241 "prescribed" means prescribed by an Order in Council under the section in question.

### 245 Interpretation

(1) In this Part "United Kingdom national" means a person who is—

(a)   a British citizen, a British overseas territories citizen, a British Overseas citizen or a British National (Overseas),

(b)   a British subject under the British Nationality Act 1981 (c 61), or

(c)   a British protected person, within the meaning of that Act.

(2) In this Part "Her Majesty's forces" has the same meaning as in the [Armed Forces Act 2006].

# Mental Capacity Act
# 2005 ch 9

PART III

## Miscellaneous and general

*Private international law*

### 63 International protection of adults

Schedule 3—

(a)  gives effect in England and Wales to the Convention on the International Protection of Adults signed at the Hague on 13th January 2000 (Cm 5881) (in so far as this Act does not otherwise do so), and

(b)  makes related provision as to the private international law of England and Wales.

SCHEDULE 3

## International Protection of Adults

*Section 63*

PART 1

## Preliminary

*Introduction*

1

This Part applies for the purposes of this Schedule.

*The Convention*

2

(1)  "Convention" means the Convention referred to in section 63.

(2)  "Convention country" means a country in which the Convention is in force.

(3)  A reference to an Article or Chapter is to an Article or Chapter of the Convention.

(4)  An expression which appears in this Schedule and in the Convention is to be construed in accordance with the Convention.

*Countries, territories and nationals*

3

(1)  "Country" includes a territory which has its own system of law.

(2)  Where a country has more than one territory with its own system of law, a reference to the country, in relation to one of its nationals, is to the territory with which the national has the closer, or the closest, connection.

*Adults with incapacity*

4

[(1)] "Adult" means [(subject to sub-paragraph (2)] a person who—

(a)  as a result of an impairment or insufficiency of his personal faculties, cannot protect his interests, and

(b)  has reached 16.

[(2)  But "adult" does not include a child to whom either of the following applies—

(a)  the Convention on Jurisdiction, Applicable Law, Recognition, Enforcement and Co-Operation in respect of Parental Responsibility and Measures for the Protection of Children that was signed at The Hague on 19 October 1996;

(b)  Council Regulation (EC) No 2201/2003 concerning jurisdiction and the recognition and enforcement of judgments in matrimonial matters and the matters of parental responsibility.]

*Protective measures*

5

(1)  "Protective measure" means a measure directed to the protection of the person or property of an adult; and it may deal in particular with any of the following—

(a)  the determination of incapacity and the institution of a protective regime,

(b)  placing the adult under the protection of an appropriate authority,

(c)  guardianship, curatorship or any corresponding system,

(d)  the designation and functions of a person having charge of the adult's person or property, or representing or otherwise helping him,

(e)  placing the adult in a place where protection can be provided,

(f)  administering, conserving or disposing of the adult's property,

(g)  authorising a specific intervention for the protection of the person or property of the adult.

(2)  Where a measure of like effect to a protective measure has been taken in relation to a person before he reaches 16, this Schedule applies to the measure in so far as it has effect in relation to him once he has reached 16.

*Central Authority*

6

(1)  Any function under the Convention of a Central Authority is exercisable in England and Wales by the Lord Chancellor.

(2)  A communication may be sent to the Central Authority in relation to England and Wales by sending it to the Lord Chancellor.

PART 2

**Jurisdiction of Competent Authority**

*Scope of jurisdiction*

7

(1)  The court may exercise its functions under this Act (in so far as it cannot otherwise do so) in relation to—

(a)  an adult habitually resident in England and Wales,

(b)  an adult's property in England and Wales,

(c)  an adult present in England and Wales or who has property there, if the matter is urgent, or

(d)  an adult present in England and Wales, if a protective measure which is temporary and limited in its effect to England and Wales is proposed in relation to him.

(2)  An adult present in England and Wales is to be treated for the purposes of this paragraph as habitually resident there if—

(a)   his habitual residence cannot be ascertained,

(b)   he is a refugee, or

(c)   he has been displaced as a result of disturbance in the country of his habitual residence.

**8**

(1) The court may also exercise its functions under this Act (in so far as it cannot otherwise do so) in relation to an adult if sub-paragraph (2) or (3) applies in relation to him.

(2) This sub-paragraph applies in relation to an adult if—

(a)   he is a British citizen,

(b)   he has a closer connection with England and Wales than with Scotland or Northern Ireland, and

(c)   Article 7 has, in relation to the matter concerned, been complied with.

(3) This sub-paragraph applies in relation to an adult if the Lord Chancellor, having consulted such persons as he considers appropriate, agrees to a request under Article 8 in relation to the adult.

*Exercise of jurisdiction*

**9**

(1) This paragraph applies where jurisdiction is exercisable under this Schedule in connection with a matter which involves a Convention country other than England and Wales.

(2) Any Article on which the jurisdiction is based applies in relation to the matter in so far as it involves the other country (and the court must, accordingly, comply with any duty conferred on it as a result).

(3) Article 12 also applies, so far as its provisions allow, in relation to the matter in so far as it involves the other country.

**10**

A reference in this Schedule to the exercise of jurisdiction under this Schedule is to the exercise of functions under this Act as a result of this Part of this Schedule.

## PART 3

## Applicable Law

*Applicable law*

**11**

In exercising jurisdiction under this Schedule, the court may, if it thinks that the matter has a substantial connection with a country other than England and Wales, apply the law of that other country.

**12**

Where a protective measure is taken in one country but implemented in another, the conditions of implementation are governed by the law of the other country.

*Lasting powers of attorney, etc*

**13**

(1) If the donor of a lasting power is habitually resident in England and Wales at the time of granting the power, the law applicable to the existence, extent, modification or extinction of the power is—

(a)   the law of England and Wales, or

(b)   if he specifies in writing the law of a connected country for the purpose, that law.

(2) If he is habitually resident in another country at that time, but England and Wales is a connected country, the law applicable in that respect is—

(a)   the law of the other country, or

(b) if he specifies in writing the law of England and Wales for the purpose, that law.

(3) A country is connected, in relation to the donor, if it is a country—

(a) of which he is a national,

(b) in which he was habitually resident, or

(c) in which he has property.

(4) Where this paragraph applies as a result of sub-paragraph (3)(c), it applies only in relation to the property which the donor has in the connected country.

(5) The law applicable to the manner of the exercise of a lasting power is the law of the country where it is exercised.

(6) In this Part of this Schedule, "lasting power" means—

(a) a lasting power of attorney (see section 9),

(b) an enduring power of attorney within the meaning of Schedule 4, or

(c) any other power of like effect.

**14**

(1) Where a lasting power is not exercised in a manner sufficient to guarantee the protection of the person or property of the donor, the court, in exercising jurisdiction under this Schedule, may disapply or modify the power.

(2) Where, in accordance with this Part of this Schedule, the law applicable to the power is, in one or more respects, that of a country other than England and Wales, the court must, so far as possible, have regard to the law of the other country in that respect (or those respects).

**15**

Regulations may provide for Schedule 1 (lasting powers of attorney: formalities) to apply with modifications in relation to a lasting power which comes within paragraph 13(6)(c) above.

*Protection of third parties*

**16**

(1) This paragraph applies where a person (a "representative") in purported exercise of an authority to act on behalf of an adult enters into a transaction with a third party.

(2) The validity of the transaction may not be questioned in proceedings, nor may the third party be held liable, merely because—

(a) where the representative and third party are in England and Wales when entering into the transaction, sub-paragraph (3) applies;

(b) where they are in another country at that time, sub-paragraph (4) applies.

(3) This sub-paragraph applies if—

(a) the law applicable to the authority in one or more respects is, as a result of this Schedule, the law of a country other than England and Wales, and

(b) the representative is not entitled to exercise the authority in that respect (or those respects) under the law of that other country.

(4) This sub-paragraph applies if—

(a) the law applicable to the authority in one or more respects is, as a result of this Part of this Schedule, the law of England and Wales, and

(b) the representative is not entitled to exercise the authority in that respect (or those respects) under that law.

(5) This paragraph does not apply if the third party knew or ought to have known that the applicable law was—

(a) in a case within sub-paragraph (3), the law of the other country;

(b)  in a case within sub-paragraph (4), the law of England and Wales.

*Mandatory rules*

17

Where the court is entitled to exercise jurisdiction under this Schedule, the mandatory provisions of the law of England and Wales apply, regardless of any system of law which would otherwise apply in relation to the matter.

*Public policy*

18

Nothing in this Part of this Schedule requires or enables the application in England and Wales of a provision of the law of another country if its application would be manifestly contrary to public policy.

PART 4

**Recognition and Enforcement**

*Recognition*

19

(1)  A protective measure taken in relation to an adult under the law of a country other than England and Wales is to be recognised in England and Wales if it was taken on the ground that the adult is habitually resident in the other country.

(2)  A protective measure taken in relation to an adult under the law of a Convention country other than England and Wales is to be recognised in England and Wales if it was taken on a ground mentioned in Chapter 2 (jurisdiction).

(3)  But the court may disapply this paragraph in relation to a measure if it thinks that—

(a)  the case in which the measure was taken was not urgent,

(b)  the adult was not given an opportunity to be heard, and

(c)  that omission amounted to a breach of natural justice.

(4)  It may also disapply this paragraph in relation to a measure if it thinks that—

(a)  recognition of the measure would be manifestly contrary to public policy,

(b)  the measure would be inconsistent with a mandatory provision of the law of England and Wales, or

(c)  the measure is inconsistent with one subsequently taken, or recognised, in England and Wales in relation to the adult.

(5)  And the court may disapply this paragraph in relation to a measure taken under the law of a Convention country in a matter to which Article 33 applies, if the court thinks that that Article has not been complied with in connection with that matter.

20

(1)  An interested person may apply to the court for a declaration as to whether a protective measure taken under the law of a country other than England and Wales is to be recognised in England and Wales.

(2)  No permission is required for an application to the court under this paragraph.

21

For the purposes of paragraphs 19 and 20, any finding of fact relied on when the measure was taken is conclusive.

*Enforcement*

**22**

(1) An interested person may apply to the court for a declaration as to whether a protective measure taken under the law of, and enforceable in, a country other than England and Wales is enforceable, or to be registered, in England and Wales in accordance with Court of Protection Rules.

(2) The court must make the declaration if—

(a)   the measure comes within sub-paragraph (1) or (2) of paragraph 19, and

(b)   the paragraph is not disapplied in relation to it as a result of sub-paragraph (3), (4) or (5).

(3) A measure to which a declaration under this paragraph relates is enforceable in England and Wales as if it were a measure of like effect taken by the court.

*Measures taken in relation to those aged under 16*

**23**

(1) This paragraph applies where—

(a)   provision giving effect to, or otherwise deriving from, the Convention in a country other than England and Wales applies in relation to a person who has not reached 16, and

(b)   a measure is taken in relation to that person in reliance on that provision.

(2) This Part of this Schedule applies in relation to that measure as it applies in relation to a protective measure taken in relation to an adult under the law of a Convention country other than England and Wales.

*Supplementary*

**24**

The court may not review the merits of a measure taken outside England and Wales except to establish whether the measure complies with this Schedule in so far as it is, as a result of this Schedule, required to do so.

**25**

Court of Protection Rules may make provision about an application under paragraph 20 or 22.

PART 5

**Co-operation**

*Proposal for cross-border placement*

**26**

(1) This paragraph applies where a public authority proposes to place an adult in an establishment in a Convention country other than England and Wales.

(2) The public authority must consult an appropriate authority in that other country about the proposed placement and, for that purpose, must send it—

(a)   a report on the adult, and

(b)   a statement of its reasons for the proposed placement.

(3) If the appropriate authority in the other country opposes the proposed placement within a reasonable time, the public authority may not proceed with it.

**27**

A proposal received by a public authority under Article 33 in relation to an adult is to proceed unless the authority opposes it within a reasonable time.

*Adult in danger etc*

**28**

(1) This paragraph applies if a public authority is told that an adult—

(a)  who is in serious danger, and

(b)  in relation to whom the public authority has taken, or is considering taking, protective measures,

is, or has become resident, in a Convention country other than England and Wales.

(2) The public authority must tell an appropriate authority in that other country about—

(a)  the danger, and

(b)  the measures taken or under consideration.

**29**

A public authority may not request from, or send to, an appropriate authority in a Convention country information in accordance with Chapter 5 (co-operation) in relation to an adult if it thinks that doing so—

(a)  would be likely to endanger the adult or his property, or

(b)  would amount to a serious threat to the liberty or life of a member of the adult's family.

## PART 6

## General

*Certificates*

**30**

A certificate given under Article 38 by an authority in a Convention country other than England and Wales is, unless the contrary is shown, proof of the matters contained in it.

*Powers to make further provision as to private international law*

**31**

Her Majesty may by Order in Council confer on the Lord Chancellor, the court or another public authority functions for enabling the Convention to be given effect in England and Wales.

**32**

(1) Regulations may make provision—

(a)  giving further effect to the Convention, or

(b)  otherwise about the private international law of England and Wales in relation to the protection of adults.

(2) The regulations may—

(a)  confer functions on the court or another public authority;

(b)  amend this Schedule;

(c)  provide for this Schedule to apply with specified modifications;

(d)  make provision about countries other than Convention countries.

*Exceptions*

**33**

Nothing in this Schedule applies, and no provision made under paragraph 32 is to apply, to any matter to which the Convention, as a result of Article 4, does not apply.

*Regulations and orders*

34

A reference in this Schedule to regulations or an order (other than an Order in Council) is to regulations or an order made for the purposes of this Schedule by the Lord Chancellor.

*Commencement*

35

The following provisions of this Schedule have effect only if the Convention is in force in accordance with Article 57—

(a)  paragraph 8,

(b)  paragraph 9,

(c)  paragraph 19(2) and (5),

(d)  Part 5,

(e)  paragraph 30.

# Companies Act
# 2006 ch 46

PART 34

## Overseas Companies

*Introductory*

**1044  Overseas companies**

In the Companies Acts an "overseas company" means a company incorporated outside the United Kingdom.

**1045  Company contracts and execution of documents by companies**

(1) The Secretary of State may make provision by regulations applying sections 43 to 52 (formalities of doing business and other matters) to overseas companies, subject to such exceptions, adaptations or modifications as may be specified in the regulations.

(2) Regulations under this section are subject to negative resolution procedure.

. . .

**1052  Company charges**

(1) The Secretary of State may by regulations make provision about the registration of specified charges over property in the United Kingdom of a registered overseas company.

(2) The power in subsection (1) includes power to make provision about—

(a)  a registered overseas company that—

　(i)   has particulars registered in more than one part of the United Kingdom;

　(ii)  has property in more than one part of the United Kingdom;

(b)  the circumstances in which property is to be regarded, for the purposes of the regulations, as being, or not being, in the United Kingdom or in a particular part of the United Kingdom;

(c)  the keeping by a registered overseas company of records and registers about specified charges and their inspection;

(d)  the consequences of a failure to register a charge in accordance with the regulations;

(e)  the circumstances in which a registered overseas company ceases to be subject to the regulations.

(3) The regulations may for this purpose apply, with or without modifications, any of the provisions of Part 25 (company charges).

(4) The regulations may modify any reference in an enactment to Part 25, or to a particular provision of that Part, so as to include a reference to the regulations or to a specified provision of the regulations.

(5) Regulations under this section are subject to negative resolution procedure.

(6) In this section—

"registered overseas company" means an overseas company that has registered particulars under section 1046(1), and

"specified" means specified in the regulations.

. . .

*Service addresses*

### 1139 Service of documents on company

(1) A document may be served on a company registered under this Act by leaving it at, or sending it by post to, the company's registered office.

(2) A document may be served on an overseas company whose particulars are registered under section 1046—

(a) by leaving it at, or sending it by post to, the registered address of any person resident in the United Kingdom who is authorised to accept service of documents on the company's behalf, or

(b) if there is no such person, or if any such person refuses service or service cannot for any other reason be effected, by leaving it at or sending by post to any place of business of the company in the United Kingdom.

(3) For the purposes of this section a person's "registered address" means any address for the time being shown as a current address in relation to that person in the part of the register available for public inspection.

(4) Where a company registered in Scotland or Northern Ireland carries on business in England and Wales, the process of any court in England and Wales may be served on the company by leaving it at, or sending it by post to, the company's principal place of business in England and Wales, addressed to the manager or other head officer in England and Wales of the company.

Where process is served on a company under this subsection, the person issuing out the process must send a copy of it by post to the company's registered office.

(5) Further provision as to service and other matters is made in the company communications provisions (see section 1143).

### 1140 Service of documents on directors, secretaries and others

(1) A document may be served on a person to whom this section applies by leaving it at, or sending it by post to, the person's registered address.

(2) This section applies to—

(a) a director or secretary of a company;

(b) in the case of an overseas company whose particulars are registered under section 1046, a person holding any such position as may be specified for the purposes of this section by regulations under that section;

(c) a person appointed in relation to a company as—

(i) a judicial factor (in Scotland),

(ii) [an interim manager] appointed under [section 76 of the Charities Act 2011] [or section 33 of Charities Act (Northern Ireland) 2008], or

(iii) a manager appointed under section 47 of the Companies (Audit, Investigations and Community Enterprise) Act 2004 (c 27).

(3) This section applies whatever the purpose of the document in question.

It is not restricted to service for purposes arising out of or in connection with the appointment or position mentioned in subsection (2) or in connection with the company concerned.

(4) For the purposes of this section a person's "registered address" means any address for the time being shown as a current address in relation to that person in the part of the register available for public inspection.

(5) If notice of a change of that address is given to the registrar, a person may validly serve a document at the address previously registered until the end of the period of 14 days beginning with the date on which notice of the change is registered.

(6) Service may not be effected by virtue of this section at an address—

(a) if notice has been registered of the termination of the appointment in relation to which the address was registered and the address is not a registered address of the person concerned in relation to any other appointment;

(b)   in the case of a person holding any such position as is mentioned in subsection (2)(b), if the overseas company has ceased to have any connection with the United Kingdom by virtue of which it is required to register particulars under section 1046.

(7) Further provision as to service and other matters is made in the company communications provisions (see section 1143).

(8) Nothing in this section shall be read as affecting any enactment or rule of law under which permission is required for service out of the jurisdiction.

### 1141  Service addresses

(1) In the Companies Acts a "service address", in relation to a person, means an address at which documents may be effectively served on that person.

(2) The Secretary of State may by regulations specify conditions with which a service address must comply.

(3) Regulations under this section are subject to negative resolution procedure.

### 1142  Requirement to give service address

Any obligation under the Companies Acts to give a person's address is, unless otherwise expressly provided, to give a service address for that person.

UK Statutes

# Defamation Act
## 2013 ch 26

*Jurisdiction*

**9 Action against a person not domiciled in the UK or a Member State etc**

(1) This section applies to an action for defamation against a person who is not domiciled—

(a)  in the United Kingdom;

(b)  in another Member State; or

(c)  in a state which is for the time being a contracting party to the Lugano Convention.

(2) A court does not have jurisdiction to hear and determine an action to which this section applies unless the court is satisfied that, of all the places in which the statement complained of has been published, England and Wales is clearly the most appropriate place in which to bring an action in respect of the statement.

(3) The references in subsection (2) to the statement complained of include references to any statement which conveys the same, or substantially the same, imputation as the statement complained of.

(4) For the purposes of this section—

(a)  a person is domiciled in the United Kingdom or in another Member State if the person is domiciled there for the purposes of the Brussels Regulation;

(b)  a person is domiciled in a state which is a contracting party to the Lugano Convention if the person is domiciled in the state for the purposes of that Convention.

(5) In this section—

"the Brussels Regulation" means [Regulation (EU) No 1215/2012 of the European Parliament and of the Council of 12 December 2012 on jurisdiction and the recognition and enforcement of judgments in civil and commercial matters (recast), as amended from time to time and as applied by virtue of the Agreement made on 19 October 2005 between the European Community and the Kingdom of Denmark on jurisdiction and the recognition and enforcement of judgments in civil and commercial matters (OJ No L 299, 16.11.2005, p 62; OJ No L79, 21.3.2013, p 4)];

"the Lugano Convention" means the Convention on jurisdiction and the recognition and enforcement of judgments in civil and commercial matters, between the European Community and the Republic of Iceland, the Kingdom of Norway, the Swiss Confederation and the Kingdom of Denmark signed on behalf of the European Community on 30th October 2007.

UK Statutes

# Marriage (Same Sex Couples) Act
# 2013 ch 30

PART 1

## Marriage of Same Sex Couples in England and Wales

*Other provisions relating to marriages of same sex couples*

. . .

### 10 Extra-territorial matters

(1) A marriage under—

(a)   the law of any part of the United Kingdom (other than England and Wales), or

(b)   the law of any country or territory outside the United Kingdom,

is not prevented from being recognised under the law of England and Wales only because it is the marriage of a same sex couple.

(2) For the purposes of this section it is irrelevant whether the law of a particular part of the United Kingdom, or a particular country or territory outside the United Kingdom—

(a)   already provides for marriage of same sex couples at the time when this section comes into force, or

(b)   provides for marriage of same sex couples from a later time.

(3) Schedule 2 (extra-territorial matters) has effect.

*Effect of extension of marriage*

### 11 Effect of extension of marriage

(1) In the law of England and Wales, marriage has the same effect in relation to same sex couples as it has in relation to opposite sex couples.

(2) The law of England and Wales (including all England and Wales legislation whenever passed or made) has effect in accordance with subsection (1).

(3) Schedule 3 (interpretation of legislation) has effect.

(4) Schedule 4 (effect of extension of marriage: further provision) has effect.

(5) For provision about limitations on the effects of subsections (1) and (2) and Schedule 3, see Part 7 of Schedule 4.

(6) Subsections (1) and (2) and Schedule 3 do not have any effect in relation to—

(a)   Measures and Canons of the Church of England (whenever passed or made),

(b)   subordinate legislation (whenever made) made under a Measure or Canon of the Church of England, or

(c)   other ecclesiastical law (whether or not contained in England and Wales legislation, and, if contained in England and Wales legislation, whenever passed or made).

(7) In Schedules 3 and 4—

"existing England and Wales legislation" means—

(a)   in the case of England and Wales legislation that is primary legislation, legislation passed before the end of the Session in which this Act is passed (excluding this Act), or

(b)   in the case of England and Wales legislation that is subordinate legislation, legislation made on or before the day on which this Act is passed (excluding legislation made under this Act);

"new England and Wales legislation" means—

  (a) in the case of England and Wales legislation that is primary legislation, legislation passed after the end of the Session in which this Act is passed, or

  (b) in the case of England and Wales legislation that is subordinate legislation, legislation made after the day on which this Act is passed.

. . .

## PART 2

*Other provisions relating to marriage and civil partnership*

. . .

### 13 Marriage overseas

(1) Schedule 6 (marriage overseas) has effect.

(2) The Foreign Marriage Act 1892 is repealed.

. . .

## SCHEDULE 6

### Marriage Overseas

## PART 1

### Consular Marriage Under UK Law

*Provision for consular marriage*

1

(1) Her Majesty may by Order in Council make provision for two people to marry each other—

(a) in prescribed countries or territories outside the United Kingdom, and

(b) in the presence of a registration officer,

in cases where the officer is satisfied that the conditions in sub-paragraph (2) are met.

(2) The conditions are that—

(a) at least one of the people proposing to marry is a United Kingdom national,

(b) the people proposing to marry would have been eligible to marry each other in such part of the United Kingdom as is determined in accordance with the Order,

(c) the authorities of the country or territory in which it is proposed that they marry will not object to the marriage, and

(d) insufficient facilities exist for them to enter into a marriage under the law of that country or territory.

*Refusal by registration officer*

2

(1) A registration officer is not required to allow two people to marry each other if the registration officer's opinion is that a marriage between them would be inconsistent with international law or the comity of nations.

(2) An Order in Council under this Part of this Schedule may make provision for appeals against a refusal, in reliance on sub-paragraph (1), to allow two people to marry each other.

*No religious service*

3

No religious service is to be used at the solemnization of a consular marriage.

*Treatment of marriage as taking place in part of UK for certain purposes*

**4**

An Order in Council under this Part of this Schedule may provide that two people who marry in a consular marriage are to be treated for prescribed purposes as if they had married in the relevant part of the United Kingdom.

*Validity of consular marriage*

**5**

A consular marriage is valid in law as if the marriage had been solemnized in the relevant part of the United Kingdom with a due observance of all forms required by the law of the relevant part of the United Kingdom.

*Interpretation*

**6**

In this Part of this Schedule—

"consular marriage" means a marriage solemnized in accordance with the provisions of this Part of this Schedule and any Order in Council made under it;

"registration officer" means—

(a)   a consular officer in the service of Her Majesty's government in the United Kingdom, or

(b)   in the case of registration in a country or territory in which Her Majesty's government in the United Kingdom has for the time being no consular representative, a person authorised by the Secretary of State in respect of the solemnization of marriages in that country or territory;

"relevant part of the United Kingdom", in relation to a consular marriage, means the part of the United Kingdom determined in accordance with paragraph 1(2)(b) for the purposes of the marriage.

## PART 2

### Marriage Under Foreign Law: Certificates of No Impediment

*Provision for certificates of no impediment*

**7**

(1)  Her Majesty may by Order in Council make provision for the issue of certificates of no impediment to—

(a)   United Kingdom nationals, and

(b)   such other persons as may be prescribed,

who wish to marry in prescribed countries or territories outside the United Kingdom.

(2)  A certificate of no impediment is a certificate that no legal impediment to the recipient entering into the marriage has been shown to the person issuing the certificate to exist.

## PART 3

### Marriage of Forces Personnel Under UK Law

*Provision for marriage of armed forces personnel*

**8**

(1)  Her Majesty may by Order in Council make provision for—

(a)   a man and a woman to marry each other in any country or territory outside the United Kingdom, and

(b)   for a same sex couple to marry in prescribed countries or territories outside the United Kingdom,

UK Statutes

in the presence of an authorised person, in cases where the authorised person is satisfied that the conditions in sub-paragraph (2) are met.

(2) The conditions are that—

(a) at least one of the people proposing to marry is—

    (i) a member of Her Majesty's forces serving in the country or territory in which it is proposed that they marry,

    (ii) a relevant civilian who is employed in that country or territory, or

    (iii) a child of a person falling within sub-paragraph (i) or (ii) whose home is with that person in that country or territory, and

(b) the people proposing to marry would have been eligible to marry each other in such part of the United Kingdom as is determined in accordance with the Order.

(3) In a case where one person ("P") treats, or has treated, another person ("C"), as a child of the family in relation to—

(a) a marriage to which P is or was a party, or

(b) a civil partnership to which P is or was a party,

C is to be regarded for the purposes of sub-paragraph (2)(a)(iii) as the child of P.

*Religious services at forces marriages of same sex couples*

**9**

(1) An Order in Council under this Part of this Schedule may make provision about the solemnization of forces marriages of same sex couples according to religious rites and usages.

(2) An Order in Council may, in particular, make provision—

(a) prohibiting the solemnization of such marriages according to particular religious rites or usages; or

(b) permitting the solemnization of such marriages according to particular religious rites or usages.

(3) Sub-paragraph (2)(b) is subject to sub-paragraphs (4) and (5).

(4) An Order in Council may not make provision allowing the solemnization of forces marriages of same sex couples according to the rites of the Church of England or Church in Wales.

(5) If an Order in Council makes provision allowing the solemnization of forces marriages of same sex couples according to particular religious rites or usages (other than those of the Church of England or Church in Wales), the Order in Council must also make provision to secure that such a marriage may not be solemnized according to those rites or usages unless the relevant governing authority has given written consent to marriages of same sex couples.

(6) The person or persons who are the relevant governing body for that purpose are to be determined in accordance with provision made by an Order in Council under this Part of this Schedule.

(7) This paragraph does not affect the provision that may be made about the solemnization of forces marriages of opposite sex couples according to religious rites and usages.

(8) If section 8 applies, the Lord Chancellor may, by order, make such relevant amending provision as the Lord Chancellor considers appropriate to allow for the solemnization of forces marriages of same sex couples according to the rites of the Church in Wales.

(9) For that purpose "relevant amending provision" means—

(a) provision amending sub-paragraphs (4) and (5) by omitting the words "or Church in Wales";

(b) provision amending any Order in Council made under this Part of this Schedule;

(c) provision amending any other UK legislation (including legislation contained in this Part of this Schedule).

(10) In making an order under sub-paragraph (8), the Lord Chancellor must have regard to the terms of the resolution of the Governing Body of the Church in Wales referred to in section 8(1).

*Treatment of marriage as taking place in part of UK for certain purposes*

**10**

An Order in Council under this Part of this Schedule may provide that two people who marry in a forces marriage are to be treated for prescribed purposes as if they had married in the relevant part of the United Kingdom.

*Validity of forces marriage*

**11**

A forces marriage is valid in law as if the marriage had been solemnized in the relevant part of the United Kingdom with a due observance of all forms required by the law of the relevant part of the United Kingdom.

*Interpretation*

**12**

(1) In this Part of this Schedule—

(a)  a reference to a country or territory includes a reference to the waters of a country or territory;

(b)  a reference to Her Majesty's forces serving in a country or territory includes a reference to such forces serving in a ship in the waters of a country or territory;

(c)  a reference to a relevant civilian employed in a country or territory includes a reference to such a civilian employed in a ship in the waters of a country or territory.

(2) In this Part of this Schedule—

"authorised person", in relation to a marriage in a country or territory outside the United Kingdom, means—

(a)  a chaplain serving in any of Her Majesty's forces in that country or territory, or

(b)  a person authorised by the commanding officer of any of Her Majesty's forces in that country or territory to conduct that marriage or marriages generally;

"commanding officer" has the same meaning as in the Armed Forces Act 2006;

"forces marriage" means a marriage solemnized in accordance with the provisions of this Part of this Schedule and any Order in Council made under it;

"Her Majesty's forces" has the same meaning as in the Armed Forces Act 2006;

"relevant civilian" means a civilian subject to service discipline (within the meaning of the Armed Forces Act 2006) who is of a prescribed description;

"relevant part of the United Kingdom", in relation to a forces marriage, means the part of the United Kingdom determined in accordance with paragraph 8(2)(b) for the purposes of the marriage.

## PART 4

**General Provisions**

*Parliamentary scrutiny*

**13**

(1)  No recommendation is to be made to Her Majesty in Council to make an Order in Council under this Schedule unless a draft of the statutory instrument containing the Order in Council has been laid before, and approved by resolution of, each House of Parliament.

(2)  In the case of an Order in Council containing provision which would (if contained in an Act of the Scottish Parliament) be within the legislative competence of that Parliament, no recommendation is to be made to Her Majesty under this paragraph unless the Scottish Ministers have been consulted.

*Particular kinds of provision*

14

(1) An Order in Council under this Schedule may—

(a) make different provision for different purposes,

(b) make transitional, transitory or saving provision, or

(c) make consequential provision.

(2) An Order in Council under this Schedule may make provision corresponding to, or applying (with or without modifications), any UK legislation.

(3) An Order in Council under this Schedule may amend, repeal or revoke UK legislation.

*Interpretation*

15

In this Schedule—

"prescribed" means prescribed by an Order in Council made under this Schedule;

"United Kingdom national" means a person who is—

(a) a British citizen, a British overseas territories citizen, a British Overseas citizen or a British National (Overseas),

(b) a British subject under the British Nationality Act 1981, or

(c) a British protected person, within the meaning of that Act.

# Consumer Rights Act
## 2015 ch 15[1]

### 2 Key definitions

(1) These definitions apply in this Part (as well as the definitions in section 59).

(2) "Trader" means a person acting for purposes relating to that person's trade, business, craft or profession, whether acting personally or through another person acting in the trader's name or on the trader's behalf.

(3) "Consumer" means an individual acting for purposes that are wholly or mainly outside that individual's trade, business, craft or profession.

(4) A trader claiming that an individual was not acting for purposes wholly or mainly outside the individual's trade, business, craft or profession must prove it.

(5) For the purposes of Chapter 2, except to the extent mentioned in subsection (6), a person is not a consumer in relation to a sales contract if—

(a)   the goods are second hand goods sold at public auction, and

(b)   individuals have the opportunity of attending the sale in person.

(6) A person is a consumer in relation to such a contract for the purposes of—

(a)   sections 11(4) and (5), 12, 28 and 29, and

(b)   the other provisions of Chapter 2 as they apply in relation to those sections.

(7) "Business" includes the activities of any government department or local or public authority.

(8) "Goods" means any tangible moveable items, but that includes water, gas and electricity if and only if they are put up for supply in a limited volume or set quantity.

(9) "Digital content" means data which are produced and supplied in digital form.

. . .

### 5 Sales contracts

(1)   A contract is a sales contract if under it—

(a)   the trader transfers or agrees to transfer ownership of goods to the consumer, and

(b)   the consumer pays or agrees to pay the price.

(2) A contract is a sales contract (whether or not it would be one under subsection (1)) if under the contract—

(a)   goods are to be manufactured or produced and the trader agrees to supply them to the consumer,

(b)   on being supplied, the goods will be owned by the consumer, and

(c)   the consumer pays or agrees to pay the price.

(3) A sales contract may be conditional (see section 3(5)), but in this Part "conditional sales contract" means a sales contract under which—

(a)   the price for the goods or part of it is payable by instalments, and

(b)   the trader retains ownership of the goods until the conditions specified in the contract (for the payment of instalments or otherwise) are met;

and it makes no difference whether or not the consumer possesses the goods.

. . .

[1] The Act is expected to enter into force on 1 October 2015.

### 32 Contracts applying law of non-EEA State

(1) If—

(a) the law of a country or territory other than an EEA State is chosen by the parties to be applicable to a sales contract, but

(b) the sales contract has a close connection with the United Kingdom,

this Chapter, except the provisions in subsection (2), applies despite that choice.

(2) The exceptions are—

(a) sections 11(4) and (5) and 12;

(b) sections 28 and 29;

(c) section 31(1)(d), (j) and (k).

(3) For cases where those provisions apply, or where the law applicable has not been chosen or the law of an EEA State is chosen, see Regulation (EC) No 593/2008 of the European Parliament and of the Council of 17 June 2008 on the law applicable to contractual obligations.

. . .

## PART 2

## Unfair Terms

*What Contracts and Notices are Covered by this Part?*

### 61 Contracts and notices covered by this Part

(1) This Part applies to a contract between a trader and a consumer.

(2) This does not include a contract of employment or apprenticeship.

(3) A contract to which this Part applies is referred to in this Part as a "consumer contract".

(4) This Part applies to a notice to the extent that it—

(a) relates to rights or obligations as between a trader and a consumer, or

(b) purports to exclude or restrict a trader's liability to a consumer.

(5) This does not include a notice relating to rights, obligations or liabilities as between an employer and an employee.

(6) It does not matter for the purposes of subsection (4) whether the notice is expressed to apply to a consumer, as long as it is reasonable to assume it is intended to be seen or heard by a consumer.

(7) A notice to which this Part applies is referred to in this Part as a "consumer notice".

(8) In this section "notice" includes an announcement, whether or not in writing, and any other communication or purported communication.

. . .

### 74 Contracts applying law of non-EEA State

(1) If—

(a) the law of a country or territory other than an EEA State is chosen by the parties to be applicable to a consumer contract, but

(b) the consumer contract has a close connection with the United Kingdom,

this Part applies despite that choice.

(2) For cases where the law applicable has not been chosen or the law of an EEA State is chosen, see Regulation (EC) No 593/2008 of the European Parliament and of the Council of 17 June 2008 on the law applicable to contractual obligations.

. . .

## 76 Interpretation of Part 2

(1) In this Part—

"consumer contract" has the meaning given by section 61(3);

"consumer notice" has the meaning given by section 61(7);

"transparent" is to be construed in accordance with sections 64(3) and 68(2).

(2) The following have the same meanings in this Part as they have in Part 1—

"trader" (see section 2(2));

"consumer" (see section 2(3));

"goods" (see section 2(8));

"digital content" (see section 2(9)).

(3) Section 2(4) (trader who claims an individual is not a consumer must prove it) applies in relation to this Part as it applies in relation to Part 1.

# Civil Jurisdiction and Judgments Act 1982 (Interim Relief) Order 1997

SI 1997/302

1. This Order may be cited as the Civil Jurisdiction and Judgments Act 1982 (Interim Relief) Order 1997 and shall come into force on 1st April 1997.

2. The High Court in England and Wales or Northern Ireland shall have power to grant interim relief under section 25(1) of the Civil Jurisdiction and Judgments Act 1982 in relation to proceedings of the following descriptions, namely—

(a) proceedings commenced or to be commenced otherwise than in a Brussels [Contracting State, a State bound by the Lugano Convention or a] [or Regulation State];

[(b) proceedings whose subject-matter is not within the scope of the Regulation as determined by Article 1 of the Regulation.]

# Unfair Terms in Consumer Contracts Regulations 1999

SI 1999/2083 (as amended)

. . .

## Interpretation

3.—(1) In these Regulations—

. . .

"consumer" means any natural person who, in contracts covered by these Regulations, is acting for purposes which are outside his trade, business or profession;

"court" in relation to England and Wales and Northern Ireland means a county court or the High Court, and in relation to Scotland, the Sheriff or the Court of Session;

. . .

"Member State" means a State which is a contracting party to the EEA Agreement;

. . .

"seller or supplier" means any natural or legal person who, in contracts covered by these Regulations, is acting for purposes relating to his trade, business or profession, whether publicly owned or privately owned;

"unfair terms" means the contractual terms referred to in regulation 5.

. . .

[(1A) The references—

(a) in regulation 4(1) to a seller or a supplier, and

(b) in regulation 8(1) to a seller or supplier,

include references to a distance supplier and to an intermediary.]

[(1B) In paragraph (1A) and regulation 5(6)—

"distance supplier" means—

(a) a supplier under a distance contract within the meaning of the Financial Services (Distance Marketing) Regulations 2004, or

(b) a supplier of unsolicited financial services within regulation 15 of those Regulations; and

"intermediary" has the same meaning as in those Regulations.]

## Terms to which these Regulations apply

4.—(1) These Regulations apply in relation to unfair terms in contracts concluded between a seller or a supplier and a consumer.

(2) These Regulations do not apply to contractual terms which reflect—

(a) mandatory statutory or regulatory provisions (including such provisions under the law of any Member State or in [EU] legislation having effect in the United Kingdom without further enactment);

(b) the provisions or principles of international conventions to which the Member States or the [European Union] are party.

## Unfair terms

5.—(1) A contractual term which has not been individually negotiated shall be regarded as unfair if, contrary to the requirement of good faith, it causes a significant imbalance in the parties' rights and obligations arising under the contract, to the detriment of the consumer.

(2) A term shall always be regarded as not having been individually negotiated where it has been drafted in advance and the consumer has therefore not been able to influence the substance of the term.

(3) Notwithstanding that a specific term or certain aspects of it in a contract has been individually negotiated, these Regulations shall apply to the rest of a contract if an overall assessment of it indicates that it is a pre-formulated standard contract.

(4) It shall be for any seller or supplier who claims that a term was individually negotiated to show that it was.

(5) Schedule 2 to these Regulations contains an indicative and non-exhaustive list of the terms which may be regarded as unfair.

. . .

### Effect of unfair term

8.—(1) An unfair term in a contract concluded with a consumer by a seller or supplier shall not be binding on the consumer.

(2) The contract shall continue to bind the parties if it is capable of continuing in existence without the unfair term.

[(3) This regulation does not apply to anything that is governed by Article 6 of Regulation (EU) No 181/2011 of the European Parliament and of the Council of 16 February 2011 concerning the rights of passengers in bus and coach transport and amending Regulation (EC) No 2006/2004.]

### Choice of law clauses

9. These Regulations shall apply notwithstanding any contract term which applies or purports to apply the law of a non-Member State, if the contract has a close connection with the territory of the Member States.

. . .

### SCHEDULE 2

### INDICATIVE AND NON-EXHAUSTIVE LIST OF TERMS WHICH MAY BE REGARDED AS UNFAIR

1. Terms which have the object or effect of—

   . . .

(b) inappropriately excluding or limiting the legal rights of the consumer vis-à-vis the seller or supplier or another party in the event of total or partial non-performance or inadequate performance by the seller or supplier of any of the contractual obligations, including the option of offsetting a debt owed to the seller or supplier against any claim which the consumer may have against him;

   . . .

(q) excluding or hindering the consumer's right to take legal action or exercise any other legal remedy, particularly by requiring the consumer to take disputes exclusively to arbitration not covered by legal provisions, unduly restricting the evidence available to him or imposing on him a burden of proof which, according to the applicable law, should lie with another party to the contract.

   . . .

# Civil Jurisdiction and Judgments (Authentic Instruments and Court Settlements) Order 2001

SI 2001/3928

1.—(1) This Order may be cited as the Civil Jurisdiction and Judgments (Authentic Instruments and Court Settlements) Order 2001 and shall come into force on 1st March 2002.

(2) In this Order—

"the Act" means the Civil Jurisdiction and Judgments Act 1982;

["the Regulation" means Regulation (EU) No 1215/2012 of the European Parliament and of the Council of 12 December 2012 on jurisdiction and the recognition and enforcement of judgments in civil and commercial matters (recast) as amended from time to time and as applied by virtue of the Agreement made on 19 October 2005 between the European Community and the Kingdom of Denmark on jurisdiction and the recognition and enforcement of judgments in civil and commercial matters;]

["Regulation State" in any provision, in the application of that provision in relation to the Regulation, means a Member State;]

"the 2001 Order" means the Civil Jurisdiction and Judgments Order 2001.

(3) In this Order—

(a) references to authentic instruments and court settlements are references to those instruments and settlements referred to in Chapter IV of the Regulation; and

(b) references to judgments [. . .] are references to judgments and maintenance orders to which the Regulation applies.

2.—(1) Subject to the modifications specified in paragraphs (2) and (3), paragraphs 1 to 6 of Schedule 1 to the 2001 Order shall apply, as appropriate, to authentic instruments and court settlements which—

(a) do not concern maintenance as if they were judgments,

[. . .]

(2) In the application of paragraph 2(2) of Schedule 1 to the 2001 Order to authentic instruments and court settlements, for the words "as if the judgment had been originally given" there shall be substituted "as if it was a judgment which had been originally given".

(3) In the application of paragraph 3(3) of Schedule 1 to the 2001 Order to authentic instruments and court settlements, for the words "as if the order had been originally made" there shall be substituted the words "as if it was an order which had been originally made".

(4) Paragraph 8 of Schedule 1 to the 2001 Order shall apply to authentic instruments as if they were judgments and in its application—

(a) for sub-paragraph (1)(b) there shall be substituted the following—

"(b) a certificate obtained in accordance with [Articles 58 and 60 and Annex II] shall be evidence, and in Scotland sufficient evidence, that the authentic instrument is enforceable in the Regulation State of origin."; and

(b) for sub-paragraph (2) there shall be substituted the following—

"(2) A document purporting to be a copy of an authentic instrument [. . .] enforceable [. . .] in a Regulation State other than the United Kingdom is duly authenticated for the purposes of this paragraph if it purports to be certified to be a true copy of such an instrument by a person duly authorised in that Regulation State to do so.".

(5) Paragraph 8 of Schedule 1 to the 2001 Order shall apply to court settlements as if they were judgments and in its application for "Article [53]" there shall be substituted "Article [60]".

3. The disapplication of section 18 of the Act (enforcement of United Kingdom judgments in other parts of the United Kingdom) by section 18(7) will extend to authentic instruments and court settlements enforceable in a Regulation State outside the United Kingdom which will fall to be treated for the purposes of their enforcement as judgments of a court of law in the United Kingdom by virtue of [enforcement] under the Regulation.

4. Section 48(5) of the Act (matters for which rules of court may provide) will apply to authentic instruments and court settlements as if they were judgments [. . .] to which the Regulation applies.

# Civil Jurisdiction and Judgments Order 2001

SI 2001/3929

Citation and commencement

1. This Order may be cited as the Civil Jurisdiction and Judgments Order 2001 and shall come into force—

(a) as to articles 1 and 2, paragraphs 1(a), 1(b)(ii) and 17 of Schedule 2 and, so far as it relates to those paragraphs, article 4, on 25th January 2002; and

(b) as to the remainder of this Order, on 1st March 2002.

Interpretation

2.—(1) In this Order—

"the Act" means the Civil Jurisdiction and Judgments Act 1982;

["the 2005 Agreement" means the Agreement made on 19th October 2005 between the European Community and the Kingdom of Denmark on jurisdiction and the recognition and enforcement of judgments in civil and commercial matters;]

["the Regulation" means Regulation (EU) No 1215/2012 of the European Parliament and of the Council of 12 December 2012 on jurisdiction and the recognition and enforcement of judgments in civil and commercial matters (recast) as amended from time to time and as applied by virtue of the Agreement made on 19 October 2005 between the European Community and the Kingdom of Denmark on jurisdiction and the recognition and enforcement of judgments in civil and commercial matters;]

["Regulation State" in any provision, in the application of that provision in relation to the Regulation, means a Member State].

. . .

The Regulation

3. Schedule 1 to this Order (which applies certain provisions of the Act with modifications for the purposes of the Regulation) shall have effect.

The 2005 Agreement

[3A. The Regulation shall have effect as regards Denmark in accordance with the 2005 Agreement.]

. . .

## SCHEDULE 1

## THE REGULATION

Interpretation

1.—(1) In this Schedule—

"court", without more, includes a tribunal;

"judgment" has the meaning given by [Article 2] of the Regulation;

. . .

"maintenance order" means a maintenance judgment within the meaning of the Regulation;

"part of the United Kingdom" means England and Wales, Scotland or Northern Ireland;

"payer", in relation to a maintenance order, means the person liable to make the payments for which the order provides;

"prescribed" means prescribed by rules of court.

(2) In this Schedule, any reference to a numbered Article or Annex is a reference to the Article or Annex so numbered in the Regulation, and any reference to a sub-division of a numbered Article shall be construed accordingly.

. . .

### Enforcement of judgments other than maintenance orders (section 4)

2.—(1) Where a judgment is [enforced] under the Regulation, the reasonable costs or expenses of and incidental to its registration shall be recoverable as if they were sums recoverable under the judgment.

[(2) A judgment to be enforced under the Regulation shall for the purposes of its enforcement be of the same force and effect, the enforcing court shall have in relation to its enforcement the same powers, and proceedings for or with respect to its enforcement may be taken, as if the judgment had been originally given by the enforcing court.]

. . .

(3) Sub-paragraph (2) is subject to [Articles 41(2) and 46], to paragraph 5 and to any provision made by rules of court as to the manner in which and conditions subject to which a judgment registered under the Regulation may be enforced.

. . .

### Appeals under [Article 50 and 75(c)] (section 6)

4.—(1) The single further appeal on a point of law referred to under [Article 50 and 75(c)] in relation to the recognition or enforcement of a judgment [. . .] lies—

(a) in England and Wales or Northern Ireland, to the Court of Appeal or to the House of Lords in accordance with Part II of the Administration of Justice Act 1969(14) (appeals direct from the High Court to the House of Lords);

. . .

(2) Paragraph (a) of sub-paragraph (1) has effect notwithstanding section 15(2) of the Administration of Justice Act 1969(15) (exclusion of direct appeal to the House of Lords in cases where no appeal to that House lies from a decision of the Court of Appeal).

[. . .]

### Interest on [. . .] judgments (section 7)

5.—[(1) Subject to sub-paragraph (2) and rules of court as to the payment of interest under this paragraph, where a person applying for enforcement of a judgment under the Regulation shows that—

(a) the judgment provides for the payment of a sum of money; and

(b) in accordance with the law of the Regulation State in which the judgment was given and the terms of the judgment, interest on that sum is recoverable at a particular rate and from a particular date or time,

the debt resulting from enforcement of the judgment is to carry interest at that rate and from that date or time.]

(2) Costs or expenses recoverable by virtue of paragraph 2(1) shall carry interest as if they were the subject of an order for the payment of costs or expenses made by the [enforcing] court on the date of [enforcement].

[. . .]

(4) [Debts under judgments enforced] under the Regulation shall carry interest only as provided by this paragraph.

[. . .]

**Allocation within United Kingdom of jurisdiction with respect to trusts and consumer contracts (section 10)**

7.—(1) The provisions of this paragraph have effect for the purpose of allocating within the United Kingdom jurisdiction in certain proceedings in respect of which the Regulation confers jurisdiction on the courts of the United Kingdom generally and to which section 16 of the Act does not apply.

(2) Any proceedings which by virtue of [Article 7(6)] (trusts) are brought in the United Kingdom shall be brought in the courts of the part of the United Kingdom in which the trust is domiciled.

(3) Any proceedings which by virtue of the [Article 18(1)] (consumer contracts) are brought in the United Kingdom by a consumer on the ground that he is himself domiciled there shall be brought in the courts of the part of the United Kingdom in which he is domiciled.

**Proof and admissibility of certain judgments and related documents (section 11)**

8.—(1) For the purposes of the Regulation—

(a) a document, duly authenticated, which purports to be a copy of a judgment given by a court of a Regulation State other than the United Kingdom shall without further proof be deemed to be a true copy, unless the contrary is shown; and

(b) a certificate obtained in accordance with [Article 53 and Annex I] shall be evidence, and in Scotland sufficient evidence, that the judgment is enforceable in the Regulation State of origin.

(2) A document purporting to be a copy of a judgment given by any such court as is mentioned in sub-paragraph (1)(a) is duly authenticated for the purposes of this paragraph if it purports—

(a) to bear the seal of that court; or

(b) to be certified by any person in his capacity as a judge or officer of that court to be a true copy of a judgment given by that court.

(3) Nothing in this paragraph shall prejudice the admission in evidence of any document which is admissible apart from this paragraph.

**Domicile of individuals (section 41)**

9.—(1) Subject to [Article 62] (which contains provisions for determining whether a party is domiciled in a Regulation State), the following provisions of this paragraph determine, for the purposes of the Regulation, whether an individual is domiciled in the United Kingdom or in a particular part of, or place in, the United Kingdom or in a state other than a Regulation State.

(2) An individual is domiciled in the United Kingdom if and only if—

(a) he is resident in the United Kingdom; and

(b) the nature and circumstances of his residence indicate that he has a substantial connection with the United Kingdom.

(3) Subject to sub-paragraph (5), an individual is domiciled in a particular part of the United Kingdom if and only if—

(a) he is resident in that part; and

(b) the nature and circumstances of his residence indicate that he has a substantial connection with that part.

(4) An individual is domiciled in a particular place in the United Kingdom if and only if he—

(a) is domiciled in the part of the United Kingdom in which that place is situated; and

(b) is resident in that place.

(5) An individual who is domiciled in the United Kingdom but in whose case the requirements of sub-paragraph (3)(b) are not satisfied in relation to any particular part of the United Kingdom shall be treated as domiciled in the part of the United Kingdom in which he is resident.

(6) In the case of an individual who—

(a) is resident in the United Kingdom, or in a particular part of the United Kingdom; and

(b)   has been so resident for the last three months or more,

the requirements of sub-paragraph (2)(b) or, as the case may be, sub-paragraph (3)(b) shall be presumed to be fulfilled unless the contrary is proved.

(7) An individual is domiciled in a state other than a Regulation State if and only if—

(a)   he is resident in that state; and

(b)   the nature and circumstances of his residence indicate that he has a substantial connection with that state.

**Seat of company, or other legal person or association for purposes of [Article 24(2)] (section 43)**

10.—(1) The following provisions of this paragraph determine where a company, legal person or association has its seat for the purposes of [Article 24(2)] (which confers exclusive jurisdiction over proceedings relating to the formation or dissolution of such bodies, or to the decisions of their organs).

(2) A company, legal person or association has its seat in the United Kingdom if and only if—

(a)   it was incorporated or formed under the law of a part of the United Kingdom; or

(b)   its central management and control is exercised in the United Kingdom.

(3) Subject to sub-paragraph (4), a company, legal person or association has its seat in a Regulation State other than the United Kingdom if and only if—

(a)   it was incorporated or formed under the law of that state; or

(b)   its central management and control is exercised in that state.

(4) A company, legal person or association shall not be regarded as having its seat in a Regulation State other than the United Kingdom if -

(a)   it has its seat in the United Kingdom by virtue of sub-paragraph (2)(a); or

(b)   it is shown that the courts of that other state would not regard it for the purposes of [Article 24(2)] as having its seat there.

**Persons deemed to be domiciled in the United Kingdom for certain purposes (section 44)**

11.—(1) This paragraph applies to

(a)   proceedings within Section 3 of Chapter II of the Regulation (insurance contracts),

(b)   proceedings within Section 4 of Chapter II of the Regulation (consumer contracts), and

(c)   proceedings within Section 5 of Chapter II of the Regulation (employment contracts).

(2) A person who, for the purposes of proceedings to which this paragraph applies arising out of the operations of a branch, agency or other establishment in the United Kingdom, is deemed for the purposes of the Regulation to be domiciled in the United Kingdom by virtue of—

(a)   [Article 11(2)] (insurers); or

(b)   [Article 17(2)] (suppliers of goods, services or credit to consumers), or

(c)   [Article 20(2)] (employers),

shall, for the purposes of those proceedings, be treated as so domiciled and as domiciled in the part of the United Kingdom in which the branch, agency or establishment in question is situated.

**Domicile of trusts (section 45)**

12.—(1) The following provisions of this paragraph determine for the purposes of the Regulation where a trust is domiciled.

(2) A trust is domiciled in the United Kingdom if and only if it is by virtue of sub-paragraph (3) domiciled in a part of the United Kingdom.

(3) A trust is domiciled in a part of the United Kingdom if and only if the system of law of that part is the system of law with which the trust has its closest and most real connection.

. . .

# Adoptions with a Foreign Element Regulations 2005

SI 2005/392

PART 1

**GENERAL**

**Citation, commencement and application**

1.—(1) These Regulations may be cited as the Adoptions with a Foreign Element Regulations 2005 and shall come into force on 30th December 2005.

(2) These Regulations apply to England and Wales.

**Interpretation**

2. In these Regulations—

"the Act" means the Adoption and Children Act 2002;

"adoption support services" has the meaning given in section 2(6)(a) of the Act and any regulations made under section 2(6)(b) of the Act;

"adoptive family" has the same meaning as in regulation 31(2)(a) of the Agencies Regulations or corresponding Welsh provision;

"adoption panel" means a panel established in accordance with regulation 3 of the Agencies Regulations or corresponding Welsh provision;

"the Agencies Regulations" means the Adoption Agencies Regulations 2005;

"child's case record" has the same meaning as in regulation 12 of the Agencies Regulations or corresponding Welsh provision;

"CA of the receiving State" means, in relation to a Convention country other than the United Kingdom, the Central Authority of the receiving State;

"CA of the State of origin" means, in relation to a Convention country other than the United Kingdom, the Central Authority of the State of origin;

"Convention adoption" is given a meaning by virtue of section 66(1)(c) of the Act;

"Convention country" has the same meaning as in section 144(1) of the Act;

"Convention list" means—

(a) in relation to a relevant Central Authority, a list of children notified to that Authority in accordance with regulation 40; or

(b) in relation to any other Central Authority within the British Islands, a list of children notified to that Authority in accordance with provisions, which correspond to regulation 40.

"corresponding Welsh provision" in relation to a Part or a regulation of the Agencies Regulations means the provision of regulations made by the Assembly under section 9 of the Act which corresponds to that Part or regulation;

"prospective adopter's case record" has the same meaning as in [regulation 23(1)] of the Agencies Regulations or corresponding Welsh provision;

"prospective adopter's report" has the same meaning as in [regulation 30(2)] of the Agencies Regulations or corresponding Welsh provisions;

"receiving State" has the same meaning as in Article 2 of the Convention;

"relevant Central Authority" means—

(c) in Chapter 1 of Part 3, in relation to a prospective adopter who is habitually resident in—

(i)   England, the Secretary of State; and

(ii)  Wales, the National Assembly for Wales; and

(d)  in Chapter 2 of Part 3 in relation to a local authority in—

(i)   England, the Secretary of State; and

(ii)  Wales, the National Assembly for Wales;

"relevant local authority" means in relation to a prospective adopter—

(a)  the local authority within whose area he has his home; or

(b)  in the case where he no longer has a home in England or Wales, the local authority for the area in which he last had his home;

"relevant foreign authority" means a person, outside the British Islands performing functions in the country in which the child is, or in which the prospective adopter is, habitually resident which correspond to the functions of an adoption agency or to the functions of the Secretary of State in respect of adoptions with a foreign element;

"State of origin" has the same meaning as in Article 2 of the Convention.

## PART 2

## BRINGING CHILDREN INTO AND OUT OF THE UNITED KINGDOM

## CHAPTER 1

## BRINGING CHILDREN INTO THE UNITED KINGDOM

**Requirements applicable in respect of bringing or causing a child to be brought into the United Kingdom**

3. A person intending to bring, or to cause another to bring, a child into the United Kingdom in circumstances where section 83(1) of the Act applies must—

(a)  apply in writing to an adoption agency for an assessment of his suitability to adopt a child; and

(b)  give the adoption agency any information it may require for the purpose of the assessment.

Conditions applicable in respect of a child brought into the United Kingdom

4.—(1) This regulation prescribes the conditions for the purposes of section 83(5) of the Act in respect of a child brought into the United Kingdom in circumstances where section 83 applies.

(2) Prior to the child's entry into the United Kingdom, the prospective adopter must—

(a)  receive in writing, notification from the Secretary of State that she has issued a certificate confirming to the relevant foreign authority—

(i)   that the person has been assessed and approved as eligible and suitable to be an adoptive parent in accordance with Part 4 of the Agencies Regulations or corresponding Welsh provision; and

(ii)  that if entry clearance and leave to enter and remain, as may be necessary, is granted and not revoked or curtailed, and an adoption order is made or an overseas adoption is effected, the child will be authorised to enter and reside permanently in the United Kingdom;

(b)  before visiting the child in the State of origin—

(i)   notify the adoption agency of the details of the child to be adopted;

(ii)  provide the adoption agency with any information and reports received from the relevant foreign authority; and

(iii) [discuss with the adoption agency the] proposed adoption and information received from the relevant foreign authority;

(c)  visit the child in the State of origin (and where the prospective adopters are a couple each of them); and

(d) after that visit—

    (i) confirm in writing to the adoption agency that he has done so and wishes to proceed with the adoption;

    (ii) provide the adoption agency with any additional reports and information received on or after that visit; and

    (iii) notify the adoption agency of his expected date of entry into the United Kingdom with the child.

(3) The prospective adopter must accompany the child on entering the United Kingdom unless, in the case of a couple, the adoption agency and the relevant foreign authority have agreed that it is necessary for only one of them to do so.

(4) Except where an overseas adoption is or is to be effected, the prospective adopter must within the period of 14 days beginning with the date on which the child is brought into the United Kingdom give notice to the relevant local authority—

(a) of the child's arrival in the United Kingdom; and

(b) of his intention—

    (i) to apply for an adoption order in accordance with section 44(2) of the Act; or

    (ii) not to give the child a home.

(5) In a case where a prospective adopter has given notice in accordance with paragraph (4) and subsequently moves his home into the area of another local authority, he must within 14 days of that move confirm in writing to that authority, the child's entry into the United Kingdom and that notice of his intention—

(a) to apply for an adoption order in accordance with section 44(2) of the Act has been given to another local authority; or

(b) not to give the child a home,

has been given.

### Functions imposed on the local authority

5.—(1) Where notice of intention to adopt has been given to the local authority, that authority must—

(a) if it has not already done so, set up a case record in respect of the child and place on it any information received from the—

    (i) relevant foreign authority;

    (ii) adoption agency, if it is not the local authority;

    (iii) prospective adopter;

    (iv) entry clearance officer; and

    (v) Secretary of State, or as the case may be, the Assembly;

(b) send the prospective adopter's general practitioner written notification of the arrival in England or Wales of the child and send with that notification a written report of the child's health history and current state of health, so far as is known;

(c) send to the [clinical commissioning group] or Local Health Board (Wales), in whose area the prospective adopter has his home, [and to the National Health Service Commissioning Board if the prospective adopter's home is in England,] written notification of the arrival in England or Wales of the child;

[. . .]

(e) ensure that the child and the prospective adopter are visited within one week of receipt of the notice of intention to adopt and thereafter not less than once a week until the review referred to in sub-paragraph (f) and thereafter at such frequency as the authority may decide;

(f) carry out a review of the child's case not more than 4 weeks after receipt of the notice of intention to adopt and—

    (i)    visit and, if necessary, review not more than 3 months after that initial review; and

    (ii)   thereafter not more than 6 months after the date of the previous visit,

unless the child no longer has his home with the prospective adopter or an adoption order is made;

(g)   when carrying out a review consider—

    (i)    the child's needs, welfare and development, and whether any changes need to be made to meet his needs or assist his development;

    (ii)   the arrangements for the provision of adoption support services and whether there should be any re-assessment of the need for those services; and

    (iii)  the need for further visits and reviews; and

(h)   ensure that—

    (i)    advice is given as to the child's needs, welfare and development;

    (ii)   written reports are made of all visits and reviews of the case and placed on the child's case record; and

    (iii)  on such visits, where appropriate, advice is given as to the availability of adoption support services.

(2) Part 7 of the Agencies Regulations or corresponding Welsh provision (case records) shall apply to the case record set up in respect of the child as a consequence of this regulation as if that record had been set up under the Agencies Regulations or corresponding Welsh provision.

(3) In a case where the prospective adopter fails to make an application under section 50 or 51 of the Act within two years of the receipt by a local authority of the notice of intention to adopt the local authority must review the case.

(4) For the purposes of the review referred to in paragraph (3), the local authority must consider—

(a)   the child's needs, welfare and development, and whether any changes need to be made to meet his needs or assist his development;

(b)   the arrangements, if any, in relation to the exercise of parental responsibility for the child;

(c)   the terms upon which leave to enter the United Kingdom is granted and the immigration status of the child;

(d)   the arrangements for the provision of adoption support services for the adoptive family and whether there should be any re-assessment of the need for those services; and

(e)   in conjunction with the appropriate agencies, the arrangements for meeting the child's health care and educational needs.

(5) In a case where the local authority to which notice of intention to adopt is given ("the original authority") is notified by the prospective adopter that he intends to move or has moved his home into the area of another local authority, the original authority must notify the local authority into whose area the prospective adopter intends to move or has moved, within 14 days of receiving information in respect of that move, of—

(a)   the name, sex, date and place of birth of child;

(b)   the prospective adopter's name, sex and date of birth;

(c)   the date on which the child entered the United Kingdom;

(d)   where the original authority received notification of intention to adopt, the date of receipt of such notification whether an application for an adoption order has been made and the stage of those proceedings; and

(e)   any other relevant information.

### Application of Chapter 3 of the Act

6. In the case of a child brought into the United Kingdom for adoption in circumstances where section 83 of the Act applies—

(a)   the modifications in regulations 7 to 9 apply;

(b)   section 36(2) and (5) (restrictions on removal) and section 39(3)(a) (partners of parents) of the Act shall not apply.

### Change of name and removal from the United Kingdom

7. Section 28(2) of the Act (further consequences of placement) shall apply as if from the words "is placed" to "then", there is substituted "enters the United Kingdom in the circumstances where section 83(1)(a) of this Act applies".

### Return of the child

8.—(1) Section 35 of the Act (return of child) shall apply with the following modifications.

(2) Subsections (1), (2) and (3) shall apply as if in each place where—

(a)   the words "is placed for adoption by an adoption agency" occur there were substituted "enters the United Kingdom in circumstances where section 83(1) applies";

(b)   the words "the agency" occur there were substituted the words "the local authority"; and

(c)   the words "any parent or guardian of the child" occur there were substituted "the Secretary of State or, as the case may be, the Assembly".

(3) Subsection (5) shall apply as if for the words "an adoption agency" or "the agency" there were substituted the words "the local authority".

### Child to live with adopters before application

9.—(1) In a case where the requirements imposed by section 83(4) of the Act have been complied with and the conditions required by section 83(5) of the Act have been met, section 42 shall apply as if—

(a)   subsection (3) is omitted; and

(b)   in subsection (5) the words from "three years" to "preceding" there were substituted "six months".

(2) In a case where the requirements imposed by section 83(4) of the Act have not been complied with or the conditions required by section 83(5) have not been met, section 42 shall apply as if—

(a)   subsection (3) is omitted; and

(b)   in subsection (5) the words from "three years" to "preceding" there were substituted "twelve months".

## CHAPTER 2

## TAKING CHILDREN OUT OF THE UNITED KINGDOM

### Requirements applicable in respect of giving parental responsibility prior to adoption abroad

10. The prescribed requirements for the purposes of section 84(3) of the Act (requirements to be satisfied prior to the making of an order) are that—

(a)   in the case of a child placed by an adoption agency, that agency has—

(i)   confirmed to the court that it has complied with the requirements imposed in accordance with Part 3 of the Agencies Regulations or corresponding Welsh provision;

(ii)   submitted to the court—

(aa) the reports and information referred to in [regulation 17(2D) and (3), as appropriate] of the Agencies Regulations or corresponding Welsh provision;

(bb) the recommendations made by the adoption panel in accordance with regulations 18 (placing child for adoption)[, where applicable,] and 33 (proposed placement) of the Agencies Regulations or corresponding Welsh provision;

(cc) the adoption placement report prepared in accordance with regulation 31(2)(d) of the Agencies Regulations or corresponding Welsh provision;

(dd) the reports of and information obtained in respect of the visits and reviews referred to in regulation 36 of the Agencies Regulations or corresponding Welsh provision; and

UK Statutory Instruments

(ee) the report referred to in section 43 of the Act as modified by regulation 11;

(b) in the case of a child placed by an adoption agency the relevant foreign authority has—

    (i) confirmed in writing to that agency that the prospective adopter has been counselled and the legal implications of adoption have been explained to him;

    (ii) prepared a report on the suitability of the prospective adopter to be an adoptive parent;

    (iii) determined and confirmed in writing to that agency that he is eligible and suitable to adopt in the country or territory in which the adoption is to be effected; and

    (iv) confirmed in writing to that agency that the child is or will be authorised to enter and reside permanently in that foreign country or territory; and

(c) in the case of a child placed by an adoption agency the prospective adopter has confirmed in writing to the adoption agency that he will accompany the child on taking him out of the United Kingdom and entering the country or territory where the adoption is to be effected, or in the case of a couple, the agency and relevant foreign authority have confirmed that it is necessary for only one of them to do so.

### Application of the Act in respect of orders under section 84

11.—(1) The following provisions of the Act which refer to adoption orders shall apply to orders under section 84 as if in each place where the words "adoption order" appear there were substituted "order under section 84"—

(a) section 1(7)(a) (coming to a decision relating to adoption of a child);

(b) section 18(4) (placement for adoption by agencies);

(c) section 21(4)(b) (placement orders);

(d) section 22(5)(a) and (b) (application for placement orders);

(e) section 24(4) (revoking placement orders);

(f) section 28(1) (further consequences of placement);

(g) section 29(4)(a) and (5)(a) (further consequences of placement orders);

(h) section 32(5) (recovery by parent etc. where child placed and consent withdrawn);

    (i) section 42(7) (sufficient opportunity for adoption agency to see the child);

(j) section 43 (reports where child placed by agency);

(k) section 44(2) (notice of intention to adopt);

(l) section 47(1) to (5), (8) and (9) (conditions for making orders);

(m) section 48(1) (restrictions on making applications);

(n) section 50(1) and (2) (adoption by a couple);

(o) section 51(1) to (4) (adoption by one person);

(p) section 52(1) to (4) (parental etc. consent);

(q) section 53(5) (contribution towards maintenance); and

(r) section 141(3) and (4)(c) (rules of procedure).

(2) Section 35(5) of the Act (return of child in other cases) shall apply to orders under section 84 of that Act as if in paragraph (b) of that subsection—

(a) for the first reference to "adoption order" there were substituted "order under section 84(1)"; and

(b) the words in brackets were omitted.

PART 3

ADOPTIONS UNDER THE CONVENTION

CHAPTER 1

REQUIREMENTS, PROCEDURE, RECOGNITION AND EFFECT OF ADOPTIONS WHERE THE UNITED KINGDOM IS THE RECEIVING STATE

**Application of Chapter 1**

12. The provisions in this Chapter shall apply where a couple or a person, habitually resident in the British Islands, wishes to adopt a child who is habitually resident in a Convention country outside the British Islands in accordance with the Convention.

Requirements applicable in respect of eligibility and suitability

13.—(1) A couple or a person who wishes to adopt a child habitually resident in a Convention country outside the British Islands shall—

[(a) in the case of an adoption agency in Wales, apply in writing to the adoption agency for a determination of eligibility and an assessment of their suitability to adopt, and give the agency any information it may require for the purposes of the assessment, or

(b) in the case of an adoption agency in England, notify the agency that they want to adopt a child, and give the agency any information it may require for the purposes of the pre-assessment process set out in Part 4 of the Agencies Regulations].

[(2) An adoption agency in Wales may not consider an application under paragraph (1)(a), and an adoption agency in England may not proceed with the pre-assessment process referred to in paragraph (1)(b), unless at the date of that application or notification (as the case may be)—]

(a) in the case of an application by a couple, they have both—

   (i) attained the age of 21 years; and

   (ii) been habitually resident in a part of the British Islands for a period of not less than one year ending with the date of application; and

(b) in the case of an application by one person, he has—

   (i) attained the age of 21 years; and

   (ii) been habitually resident in a part of the British Islands for a period of not less than one year ending with the date of application.

**Counselling and information**

14.—(1) An adoption agency must provide a counselling service in accordance with [regulation 24(1) (a)] of the Agencies Regulations or corresponding Welsh provision and must—

(a) explain to the prospective adopter the procedure in relation to, and the legal implications of, adopting a child from the State of origin from which the prospective adopter wishes to adopt in accordance with the Convention; and

(b) provide him with written information about the matters referred to in sub-paragraph (a).

(2) Paragraph (1) does not apply if the adoption agency is satisfied that the requirements set out in that paragraph have been carried out in respect of the prospective adopter by another agency.

**Procedure in respect of carrying out an assessment**

15.—[(1) Where the adoption agency is satisfied that that the requirements in regulation 14 have been met the agency must consider the suitability of the prospective adopter in accordance with Part 4 of the Agencies Regulations.][1]

[1] This paragraph applies to England only. The text of Regulation 15(1)–(2), as originally adopted, applies in Wales.

(3) The adoption agency must place on the prospective adopter's case record any information obtained as a consequence of this Chapter.

(4) The adoption agency must include in the prospective adopter's report—

(a) the State of origin from which the prospective adopter wishes to adopt a child;

(b) confirmation that the prospective adopter is eligible to adopt a child under the law of that State;

(c) any additional information obtained as a consequence of the requirements of that State; and

(d) the agency's assessment of the prospective adopter's suitability to adopt a child who is habitually resident in that State.

(5) The references to information in [regulations 30(2) and 30A(2)] of the Agencies Regulations or corresponding Welsh provisions shall include information obtained by the adoption agency or adoption panel as a consequence of this regulation.

### Adoption agency decision and notification

16. The adoption agency must make a decision about whether the prospective adopter is suitable to adopt a child in accordance with [regulation 30B] of the Agencies Regulations and regulations made under section 45 of the Act, or corresponding Welsh provisions.

### Review and termination of approval

17. The adoption agency must review the approval of each prospective adopter in accordance with [regulation 30D] of the Agencies Regulations or corresponding Welsh provision unless the agency has received written notification from the relevant Central Authority that the agreement under Article 17(c) of the Convention has been made.

### Procedure following decision as to suitability to adopt

18.—(1) Where an adoption agency has made a decision that the prospective adopter is suitable to adopt a child in accordance with regulation 16, it must send to the relevant Central Authority—

(a) written confirmation of the decision and any recommendation the agency may make in relation to the number of children the prospective adopter may be suitable to adopt, their age range, sex, likely needs and background;

(b) the enhanced criminal record certificate obtained under [regulation 25] of the Agencies Regulations or corresponding Welsh provision;

(c) all the documents and information which were passed to the adoption panel in accordance with [regulations 30(6) or (7)] of the Agencies Regulations or corresponding Welsh provision;

(d) the record of the proceedings of the adoption panel, its recommendation and the reasons for its recommendation; and

(e) any other information relating to the case as the relevant Central Authority or the CA of the State of origin may require.

(2) If the relevant Central Authority is satisfied that the adoption agency has complied with the duties and procedures imposed by the Agencies Regulations or corresponding Welsh provision, and that all the relevant information has been supplied by that agency, the Authority must send to the CA of the State of origin—

(a) the prospective adopter's report prepared in accordance with [regulation 30] of the Agencies Regulations or corresponding Welsh provision;

[. . .]

(c) a copy of the adoption agency's decision and the adoption panel's recommendation;

(d) any other information that the CA of the State of origin may require; [. . .]

[(da)    if the prospective adopter applied to the appropriate Minister for a review under section 12 of the Adoption and Children Act 2002, the record of the proceedings of the panel, its recommendation and the reasons for its recommendation; and]

(e)  a certificate in the form set out in Schedule 1 confirming that the—

  (i)   prospective adopter is eligible to adopt;

  (ii)  prospective adopter has been assessed in accordance with this Chapter;

  (iii) prospective adopter has been approved as suitable to adopt a child; and

  (iv)  child will be authorised to enter and reside permanently in the United Kingdom if entry clearance, and leave to enter or remain as may be necessary, is granted and not revoked or curtailed and a Convention adoption order or Convention adoption is made.

(3)  The relevant Central Authority must notify the adoption agency and the prospective adopter in writing that the certificate and the documents referred to in paragraph (2) have been sent to the CA of the State of origin.

**Procedure following receipt of the Article 16 Information from the CA of the State of origin**

19.—(1)  Where the relevant Central Authority receives from the CA of the State of origin, the Article 16 Information relating to the child whom the CA of the State of origin considers should be placed for adoption with the prospective adopter, the relevant Central Authority must send that Information to the adoption agency.

(2)  The adoption agency must consider the Article 16 Information and—

(a)  send that Information to the prospective adopter;

(b)  [discuss with the prospective adopter]—

  (i)   that Information;

  (ii)  the proposed placement;

  (iii) the availability of adoption support services; and

(c)  if appropriate, offer a counselling service and further information as required.

[(3)  Where—

(a)  the procedure in paragraph (2) has been followed; and

(b)  the prospective adopter has confirmed in writing to the adoption agency that he wishes to proceed to adopt the child,

the agency must notify the relevant Central Authority in writing that the requirements specified in sub-paragraphs (a) and (b) have been satisfied and at the same time it must confirm that it is content for the adoption to proceed.]

(4)  Where the relevant Central Authority has received notification from the adoption agency under paragraph (3), the relevant Central Authority shall—

(a)  notify the CA of the State of origin that—

  (i)   the prospective adopter wishes to proceed to adopt the child;

  (ii)  it is prepared to agree with the CA of the State of origin that the adoption may proceed; and

(b)  confirm to the CA of the State of origin that—

  (i)   in the case where the requirements specified in section 1(5A) of the British Nationality Act 1981 are met that the child will be authorised to enter and reside permanently in the United Kingdom; or

  (ii)  in any other case, if entry clearance and leave to enter and remain, as may be necessary, is granted and not revoked or curtailed and a Convention adoption order or a Convention adoption is made, the child will be authorised to enter and reside permanently in the United Kingdom.

(5)  The relevant Central Authority must inform the adoption agency and the prospective adopter when the agreement under Article 17(c) of the Convention has been made.

(6)  For the purposes of this regulation and regulation 20 "the Article 16 Information" means—

(a)  the report referred to in Article 16(1) of the Convention including information about the child's identity, adoptability, background, social environment, family history, medical history including that of the child's family and any special needs of the child;

(b) proof of confirmation that the consents of the persons, institutions and authorities whose consents are necessary for adoption have been obtained in accordance with Article 4 of the Convention; and

(c) the reasons for the CA of the State of origin's determination on the placement.

### Procedure where proposed adoption is not to proceed

20.—(1) If, at any stage before the agreement under Article 17(c) of the Convention is made, the CA of the State of origin notifies the relevant Central Authority that it has decided the proposed placement should not proceed—

(a) the relevant Central Authority must inform the adoption agency of the CA of the State of origin's decision;

(b) the agency must then inform the prospective adopter and return the Article 16 Information to the relevant Central Authority; and

(c) the relevant Central Authority must then return those documents to the CA of the State of origin.

(2) Where at any stage before the adoption agency receives notification of the agreement under Article 17(c) of the Convention the approval of the prospective adopter is reviewed under [regulation 30D] of the Agencies Regulations or corresponding Welsh provision, and as a consequence, the agency determines that the prospective adopter is no longer suitable to adopt a child—

(a) the agency must inform the relevant Central Authority and return the documents referred to in regulation 19(1);

(b) the relevant Central Authority must notify the CA of the State of origin and return those documents.

(3) If, at any stage before [before any Convention adoption is made and before the child's entry into the United Kingdom], the prospective adopter notifies the adoption agency that he does not wish to proceed with the adoption of the child—

(a) that agency must inform the relevant Central Authority and return the documents to that Authority; and

(b) the relevant Central Authority must notify the CA of the State of origin of the prospective adopter's decision and return the documents to the CA of the State of origin.

### Applicable requirements in respect of prospective adopter entering the United Kingdom with a child

21. Following any agreement under Article 17(c) of the Convention, the prospective adopter must—

(a) notify the adoption agency of his expected date of entry into the United Kingdom with the child;

(b) confirm to the adoption agency when the child is placed with him by the competent authority in the State of origin; and

(c) accompany the child on entering the United Kingdom unless, in the case of a couple, the adoption agency and the CA of the State of origin have agreed that it is necessary for only one of them to do so.

### Applicable requirements in respect of an adoption agency before the child enters the United Kingdom

22. Where the adoption agency is informed by the relevant Central Authority that the agreement under Article 17(c) of the Convention has been made and the adoption may proceed, before the child enters the United Kingdom that agency must—

(a) send the prospective adopter's general practitioner written notification of the proposed placement and send with that notification a written report of the child's health history and current state of health, so far as it is known; [and]

(b) send the local authority (if that authority is not the adoption agency) and the [clinical commissioning group] or Local Health Board (Wales), in whose area the prospective adopter has his home, [and to the National Health Service Commissioning Board if the prospective adopter's home is in England,] written notification of the proposed arrival of the child into England or Wales [and, where the child is of compulsory school age, include in the notification to the local authority information about the child's educational history and whether the child has been or is likely to be assessed for special educational needs under the Education Act 1996] [or the Children and Families Act 2014]

[. . .]

23. Regulations 24 to 27 apply where—

(a) following the agreement between the relevant Central Authority and the CA of the State of origin under Article 17(c) of the Convention that the adoption may proceed, no Convention adoption is made, or applied for, in the State of origin; and

(b) the child is placed with the prospective adopter in the State of origin who then returns to England or Wales with that child.

**Applicable requirements in respect of prospective adopter following child's entry into the United Kingdom**

24.—(1) A prospective adopter must within the period of 14 days beginning with the date on which the child enters the United Kingdom give notice to the relevant local authority—

(a) of the child's arrival in the United Kingdom; and

(b) of his intention—

    (i) to apply for an adoption order in accordance with section 44(2) of the Act; or

    (ii) not to give the child a home.

(2) In a case where a prospective adopter has given notice in accordance with paragraph (1) and he subsequently moves his home into the area of another local authority, he must within 14 days of that move confirm to that authority in writing the child's entry into the United Kingdom and that notice of his intention—

(a) to apply for an adoption order in accordance with section 44(2) of the Act has been given to another local authority; or

(b) not to give the child a home,

has been given.

**Functions imposed on the local authority following the child's entry into the United Kingdom**

25.—(1) Where notice is given to a local authority in accordance with regulation 24, the functions imposed on the local authority by virtue of regulation 5 shall apply subject to the modifications in paragraph (2).

(2) Paragraph (1) of regulation 5 shall apply as if—

(a) in sub-paragraph (a)—

    (i) in head (i) for the words "relevant foreign authority" there is substituted "CA of the State of origin and competent foreign authority";

    (ii) in head (v) there is substituted "the relevant Central Authority"; and

(b) sub-paragraphs (b) to (d) were omitted.

**Prospective adopter unable to proceed with adoption]**

[26.—(1) Where the prospective adopter gives notice to the relevant local authority that he does not wish to proceed with the adoption and no longer wishes to give the child a home, he must return the child to that authority not later than the end of the period of seven days beginning with the date on which notice was given.

UK Statutory Instruments

(2) Where a relevant local authority have received a notice in accordance with paragraph (1), that authority must give notice to the relevant Central Authority of the decision of the prospective adopter not to proceed with the adoption.]

### Withdrawal of child from prospective adopter

27.—(1) Where the relevant local authority are of the opinion that the continued placement of the child is not in the child's best interests—

(a) that authority must give notice to the prospective adopter of their opinion and request the return of the child to them; and

(b) subject to paragraph (3), the prospective adopter must, not later than the end of the period of seven days beginning with the date on which notice was given, return the child to that authority.

(2) Where the relevant local authority has given notice under paragraph (1), that authority must at the same time notify the relevant Central Authority that they have requested the return of the child.

(3) Where notice is given under paragraph (1) but—

(a) an application for a Convention adoption order was made prior to the giving of that notice; and

(b) the application has not been disposed of,

the prospective adopter is not required by virtue of paragraph (1) to return the child unless the court so orders.

(4) This regulation does not affect the exercise by any local authority or other person of any power conferred by any enactment or the exercise of any power of arrest.

### Breakdown of placement

28.—(1) This regulation applies where—

(a) notification is given by the prospective adopter under regulation 26 (unable to proceed with adoption);

(b) the child is withdrawn from the prospective adopter under regulation 27 (withdrawal of child from prospective adopter);

(c) an application for a Convention adoption order is refused;

(d) a Convention adoption which is subject to a probationary period cannot be made; or

(e) a Convention adoption order or a Convention adoption is annulled pursuant to section 89(1) of the Act.

(2) Where the relevant local authority are satisfied that it would be in the child's best interests to be placed for adoption with another prospective adopter habitually resident in the United Kingdom they must take the necessary measures to identify a suitable adoptive parent for that child.

(3) Where the relevant local authority have identified and approved another prospective adopter who is eligible, and has been assessed as suitable, to adopt in accordance with these Regulations—

(a) that authority must notify the relevant Central Authority in writing that—

　　(i) another prospective adopter has been identified; and

　　(ii) the provisions in regulations 14, 15 and 16 have been complied with; and

(b) the requirements specified in regulations 18 and 19 have been complied with.

(4) Where the relevant Central Authority has been notified in accordance with paragraph (3)(a)—

(a) it shall inform the CA of the State of origin of the proposed placement; and

(b) it shall agree the placement with the CA of the State of origin in accordance with the provisions in this Chapter.

(5) Subject to paragraph (2), where the relevant local authority is not satisfied it would be in the child's best interests to be placed for adoption with another prospective adopter in England or Wales, it must liaise with the relevant Central Authority to arrange for the return of the child to his State of origin.

(6) Before coming to any decision under this regulation, the relevant local authority must have

regard to the wishes and feelings of the child, having regard to his age and understanding, and where appropriate, obtain his consent in relation to measures to be taken under this regulation.

### Convention adoptions subject to a probationary period

29.—(1) This regulation applies where—

(a) the child has been placed with the prospective adopters by the competent authority in the State of origin and a Convention adoption has been applied for by the prospective adopters in the State of origin but the child's placement with the prospective adopter is subject to a probationary period before the Convention adoption is made; and

(b) the prospective adopter returns to England or Wales with the child before that probationary period is completed and the Convention adoption is made in the State of origin.

(2) The relevant local authority must, if requested by the competent authority of the State of origin, submit a report about the placement to that authority and such a report must be prepared within such timescales and contain such information as the competent authority may reasonably require.

### Report of local authority investigation

30. The report of the investigation which a local authority must submit to the court in accordance with section 44(5) of the Act must include—

(a) confirmation that the Certificate of eligibility and approval has been sent to the CA of the State of origin in accordance with regulation 18;

(b) the date on which the agreement under Article 17(c) of the Convention was made; and

(c) details of the reports of the visits and reviews made in accordance with regulation 5 as modified by regulation 25.

### Convention adoption order

31. An adoption order shall not be made as a Convention adoption order unless—

(a) in the case of—

    (i) an application by a couple, both members of the couple have been habitually resident in any part of the British Islands for a period of not less than one year ending with the date of the application; or

    (ii) an application by one person, the applicant has been habitually resident in any part of the British Islands for a period of not less than one year ending with the date of the application;

(b) the child to be adopted was, on the date on which the agreement under Article 17(c) of the Convention was made, habitually resident in a Convention country outside the British Islands; and

(c) in a case where one member of a couple (in the case of an application by a couple) or the applicant (in the case of an application by one person) is not a British citizen, the Home Office has confirmed that the child is authorised to enter and reside permanently in the United Kingdom.

### Requirements following a Convention adoption order or Convention adoption

32.—(1) Where the relevant Central Authority receives a copy of a Convention adoption order made by a court in England or Wales that Authority must issue a certificate in the form set out in Schedule 2 certifying that the adoption has been made in accordance with the Convention.

(2) A copy of the certificate issued under paragraph (1) must be sent to the—

(a) CA of the State of origin;

(b) adoptive parent; and

(c) adoption agency and, if different, the relevant local authority.

(3) Where a Convention adoption is made and the relevant Central Authority receives a certificate under Article 23 of the Convention in respect of that Convention adoption, the relevant Central Authority must send a copy of that certificate to the—

(a)   adoptive parent; and

(b)   adoption agency and, if different, the relevant local authority.

### Refusal of a court in England or Wales to make a Convention adoption order

33.   Where an application for a Convention adoption order is refused by the court or is withdrawn, the prospective adopter must return the child to the relevant local authority within the period determined by the court.

Annulment of a Convention adoption order or a Convention adoption

34.   Where a Convention adoption order or a Convention adoption is annulled under section 89(1) of the Act and the relevant Central Authority receives a copy of the order from the court, it must forward a copy of that order to the CA of the State of origin.

## CHAPTER 2

## REQUIREMENTS, PROCEDURE, RECOGNITION AND EFFECT OF ADOPTIONS IN ENGLAND AND WALES WHERE THE UNITED KINGDOM IS THE STATE OF ORIGIN

### Application of Chapter 2

35.   The provisions in this Chapter shall apply where a couple or a person habitually resident in a Convention country outside the British Islands, wishes to adopt a child who is habitually resident in the British Islands in accordance with the Convention.

### Counselling and information for the child

36.—(1) Where an adoption agency is considering whether a child is suitable for an adoption in accordance with the Convention, it must provide a counselling service for and information to that child in accordance with regulation 13 of the Agencies Regulations or corresponding Welsh provision and it must—

(a)   explain to the child in an appropriate manner the procedure in relation to, and the legal implications of, adoption under the Convention for that child by a prospective adopter habitually resident in the receiving State; and

(b)   provide him with written information about the matters referred to in sub-paragraph (a).

(2) Paragraph (1) does not apply if the adoption agency is satisfied that the requirements set out in that paragraph have been carried out in respect of the prospective adopter by another agency.

### Counselling and information for the parent or guardian of the child etc.

37.—(1) An adoption agency must provide a counselling service and information in accordance with regulation 14 of the Agencies Regulations or corresponding Welsh provision for the parent or guardian of the child and, where regulation 14(4) of the Agencies Regulations or corresponding Welsh provision applies, for the father.

(2) The adoption agency must also—

(a)   explain to the parent or guardian, and, where regulation 14(4) of the Agencies Regulations or corresponding Welsh provision applies, the father the procedure in relation to, and the legal implications of, adoption under the Convention by a prospective adopter in a receiving State; and

(b)   provide him with written information about the matters referred to in sub-paragraph (a).

(3) Paragraphs (1) and (2) do not apply if the adoption agency is satisfied that the requirements set out in that paragraph have been carried out in respect of the prospective adopter by another agency.

### Requirements in respect of the child's permanence report and information for the adoption panel

38.—(1) The child's permanence report which the adoption agency is required to prepare in accordance with regulation 17 of the Agencies Regulations or corresponding Welsh provision must include—

(a)   a summary of the possibilities for placement of the child within the United Kingdom; and

(b)   an assessment of whether an adoption by a person in a particular receiving State is in the child's best interests.

(2) [In a case falling within regulation 17(2C) of the Agencies Regulations or the corresponding Welsh provision, the] adoption agency must send—

(a)   if received, the Article 15 Report; and

(b)   their observations on that Report,

together with the reports and information referred to in regulation [17(2D)] of the Agencies Regulations or corresponding Welsh provision to the adoption panel.

[(3)  In a case falling within regulation 17(2) of the Agencies Regulations or the corresponding Welsh provision, the adoption agency must consider—

(a)   if received, the Article 15 Report; and

(b)   their observations on that Report together with the reports and information referred to in regulation 17(2D) of the Agencies Regulations or the corresponding Welsh provision

in deciding whether the child should be placed for adoption in accordance with the Convention.]

### Recommendation of adoption panel

39. Where an adoption panel make a recommendation in accordance with regulation 18(1) of the Agencies Regulations or corresponding Welsh provision it must consider and take into account the Article 15 Report, if available, and the observations thereon together with the information passed to it as a consequence of regulation 38.

### Adoption agency decision and notification

40. Where the adoption agency decides in accordance with regulation 19 of the Agencies Regulations or corresponding Welsh provision that the child should be placed for an adoption in accordance with the Convention it must notify the relevant Central Authority of—

(a)   the name, sex and age of the child;

(b)   the reasons why they consider that the child may be suitable for such an adoption;

(c)   whether a prospective adopter has been identified and, if so, provide any relevant information; and

(d)   any other information that Authority may require.

### Convention list

41.—(1)  The relevant Central Authority is to maintain a Convention list of children who are notified to that Authority under regulation 40 and shall make the contents of that list available for consultation by other Authorities within the British Islands.

(2)  Where an adoption agency—

(a)   places for adoption a child whose details have been notified to the relevant Central Authority under regulation 40; or

(b)   determines that an adoption in accordance with the Convention is no longer in the best interests of the child,

it must notify the relevant Central Authority accordingly and that Authority must remove the details relating to that child from the Convention list.

### Receipt of the Article 15 Report from the CA of the receiving State

42.—(1)  This regulation applies where—

(a)   the relevant Central Authority receives a report from the CA of the receiving State which has been prepared for the purposes of Article 15 of the Convention ("the Article 15 Report");

(b) the Article 15 Report relates to a prospective adopter who is habitually resident in that receiving State; and

(c) the prospective adopter named in the Article 15 Report wishes to adopt a child who is habitually resident in the British Islands.

(2) Subject to paragraph (3), if the relevant Central Authority is satisfied the prospective adopter meets the following requirements—

(a) the age requirements as specified in section 50 of the Act in the case of adoption by a couple, or section 51 of the Act in the case of adoption by one person; and

(b) in the case of a couple, both are, or in the case of adoption by one person, that person is habitually resident in a Convention country outside the British Islands,

that Authority must consult the Convention list and may, if the Authority considers it appropriate, consult any Convention list maintained by another Central Authority within the British Islands.

(3) Where a prospective adopter has already been identified in relation to a proposed adoption of a particular child and the relevant Central Authority is satisfied that prospective adopter meets the requirements referred to in paragraph (2)(a) and (b), that Authority—

(a) need not consult the Convention list; and

(b) must send the Article 15 Report to the local authority which referred the child's details to the Authority.

(4) The relevant Central Authority may pass a copy of the Article 15 Report to any other Central Authority within the British Islands for the purposes of enabling that Authority to consult its Convention list.

(5) Where the relevant Central Authority identifies a child on the Convention list who may be suitable for adoption by the prospective adopter, that Authority must send the Article 15 Report to the local authority which referred the child's details to that Authority.

### Proposed placement and referral to adoption panel

43.—(1) Where the adoption agency is considering whether a proposed placement should proceed in accordance with the procedure provided for in regulation 31 of the Agencies Regulations or corresponding Welsh provision it must take into account the Article 15 Report.

(2) Where the adoption agency refers the proposal to place the child with the particular prospective adopter to the adoption panel in accordance with regulation 31 of the Agencies Regulations or corresponding Welsh provision, it must also send the Article 15 Report to the panel.

### Consideration by adoption panel

44. The adoption panel must take into account when considering what recommendation to make in accordance with regulation 32(1) of the Agencies Regulations or corresponding Welsh provision the Article 15 Report and any other information passed to it as a consequence of the provisions in this Chapter.

### Adoption agency's decision in relation to the proposed placement

45.—(1) Regulation 33 of the Agencies Regulations or corresponding Welsh provision shall apply as if paragraph (3) of that regulation or corresponding Welsh provision was omitted.

(2) As soon as possible after the agency makes its decision, it must notify the relevant Central Authority of its decision.

(3) If the proposed placement is not to proceed—

(a) the adoption agency must return the Article 15 Report and any other documents or information sent to it by the relevant Central Authority to that Authority; and

(b) the relevant Central Authority must then send that Report, any such documents or such information to the CA of the receiving State.

**Preparation of the Article 16 Information**

46.—(1) If the adoption agency decides that the proposed placement should proceed, it must prepare a report for the purposes of Article 16(1) of the Convention which must include—

(a) the information about the child which is specified in Schedule 1 to the Agencies Regulations or corresponding Welsh provision; and

(b) the reasons for their decision.

(2) The adoption agency must send the following to the relevant Central Authority—

(a) the report referred to in paragraph (1);

(b) details of any placement order or other orders, if any, made by the courts; and

(c) confirmation that the parent or guardian consents to the proposed adoption.

(3) The relevant Central Authority must then send the documents referred to in paragraph (2) to the CA of the receiving State.

**Requirements to be met before the child is placed for adoption with prospective adopter**

47.—(1) The relevant Central Authority may notify the CA of the receiving State that it is prepared to agree that the adoption may proceed provided that CA has confirmed that—

(a) the prospective adopter has agreed to adopt the child and has received such counselling as may be necessary;

(b) the prospective adopter has confirmed that he will accompany the child to the receiving State, unless in the case of a couple, the adoption agency and the CA of the receiving State have agreed that it is only necessary for one of them to do so;

(c) it is content for the adoption to proceed;

(d) in the case where a Convention adoption is to be effected, it has explained to the prospective adopter the need to make an application under section 84(1) of the Act; and

(e) the child is or will be authorised to enter and reside permanently in the Convention country if a Convention adoption is effected or a Convention adoption order is made.

(2) The relevant Central Authority may not make an agreement under Article 17(c) of the Convention with the CA of the receiving State unless—

(a) confirmation has been received in respect of the matters referred to in paragraph (1); and

(b) the adoption agency has confirmed to the relevant Central Authority that—

(i) it has met the prospective adopter and explained the requirement to make an application for an order under section 84 of the Act before the child can be removed from the United Kingdom;

(ii) the prospective adopter has visited the child; and

(iii) the prospective adopter is content for the adoption to proceed.

(3) An adoption agency may not place a child for adoption unless the agreement under Article 17(c) of the Convention has been made and the relevant Central Authority must advise that agency when that agreement has been made.

(4) In this regulation, the reference to "prospective adopter" means in the case of a couple, both of them.

**Requirements in respect of giving parental responsibility prior to a proposed Convention adoption**

48. In the case of a proposed Convention adoption, the prescribed requirements for the purposes of section 84(3) of the Act (requirements to be satisfied prior to making an order) are—

(a) the competent authorities of the receiving State have—

(i) prepared a report for the purposes of Article 15 of the Convention;

(ii) determined and confirmed in writing that the prospective adoptive parent is eligible and suitable to adopt;

    (iii) ensured and confirmed in writing that the prospective adoptive parent has been counselled as may be necessary; and

    (iv) determined and confirmed in writing that the child is or will be authorised to enter and reside permanently in that State;

(b) the report required for the purposes of Article 16(1) of the Convention has been prepared by the adoption agency;

(c) the adoption agency confirms in writing that it has complied with the requirements imposed upon it under Part 3 of the Agencies Regulations or corresponding Welsh provision and this Chapter;

(d) the adoption agency has obtained and made available to the court—

    (i) the reports and information referred to in [regulation 17(2D) of the Agencies Regulations or corresponding Welsh provision;

    (ii) the recommendation made by the adoption panel in accordance with regulations 18[, where applicable,] and 33 of the Agencies Regulations or corresponding Welsh provisions; and

    (iii) the adoption placement report prepared in accordance with regulation 31(2) of the Agencies Regulations or corresponding Welsh provision;

(e) the adoption agency includes in their report submitted to the court in accordance with section 43(a) or 44(5) of the Act as modified respectively by regulation 11, details of any reviews and visits carried out as consequence of Part 6 of the Agencies Regulations or corresponding Welsh provision; and

(f) the prospective adopter has confirmed in writing that he will accompany the child on taking the child out of the United Kingdom to travel to the receiving State or in the case of a couple the agency and competent foreign authority have confirmed that it is necessary for only one of them to do so.

### Local authority report

49. In the case of a proposed application for a Convention adoption order, the report which a local authority must submit to the court in accordance with section 43(a) or 44(5) of the Act must include a copy of the—

(a) Article 15 Report;

(b) report prepared for the purposes of Article 16(1); and

(c) written confirmation of the agreement under Article 17(c) of the Convention.

### Convention adoption order

50. An adoption order shall not be made as a Convention adoption order unless—

(a) in the case of—

    (i) an application by a couple, both members of the couple have been habitually resident in a Convention country outside the British Islands for a period of not less than one year ending with the date of the application; or

       (aa) an application by one person, the applicant has been habitually resident in a Convention country outside the British Islands for a period of not less than one year ending with the date of the application;

(b) the child to be adopted was, on the date on which the agreement under Article 17(c) of the Convention was made, habitually resident in any part of the British Islands; and

(c) the competent authority has confirmed that the child is authorised to enter and remain permanently in the Convention country in which the applicant is habitually resident.

### Requirements following a Convention adoption order or Convention adoption

51.—(1) Where the relevant Central Authority receives a copy of a Convention adoption order made by a court in England or Wales, that Authority must issue a certificate in the form set out in Schedule 2 certifying that the adoption has been made in accordance with the Convention.

(2) A copy of the certificate must be sent to the—

(a) CA of the receiving State; and

(b) the relevant local authority.

(3) Where a Convention adoption is made and the Central Authority receives a certificate under Article 23 in respect of that Convention adoption, the relevant Central Authority must send a copy of that certificate to the relevant local authority.

## CHAPTER 3

## MISCELLANEOUS PROVISIONS

### Application, with or without modifications, of the Act

52.—(1) Subject to the modifications provided for in this Chapter, the provisions of the Act shall apply to adoptions within the scope of the Convention so far as the nature of the provision permits and unless the contrary intention is shown.

### Change of name and removal from the United Kingdom

53. In a case falling within Chapter 1 of this Part, section 28(2) of the Act shall apply as if—

(a) at the end of paragraph (a), "or" was omitted;

(b) at the end of paragraph (b) there were inserted "or (c) a child is placed by a competent foreign authority for the purposes of an adoption under the Convention,"; and

(c) at the end of subsection (2) there were inserted "or the competent foreign authority consents to a change of surname.".

### Removal of children

54.—(1) In a case falling within Chapter 1 of this Part, sections 36 to 40 of the Act shall not apply.

(2) In a case falling within Chapter 2 of this Part—

(a) section 36 of the Act shall apply, as if—

    (i) for the words "an adoption order" in paragraphs (a) and (c) in subsection (1) there were substituted "a Convention adoption order"; and

    (ii) subsection (2) was omitted; and

(b) section 39 of the Act shall apply as if subsection (3)(a) was omitted.

### Modifications of the Act in respect of orders under section 84 where child is to be adopted under the Convention

55. The modifications set out in regulation 11 shall apply in the case where a couple or person habitually resident in a Convention country outside the British Islands intend to adopt a child who is habitually resident in England or Wales in accordance with the Convention.

### Child to live with adopters before application for a Convention adoption order

56. Section 42 of the Act shall apply as if—

(a) subsections (1)(b) and (3) to (6) were omitted; and

(b) in subsection (2) from the word "If" to the end of paragraph (b) there were substituted "In the case of an adoption under the Convention,".

### Notice of intention to adopt

57. Section 44 of the Act shall apply as if subsection (3) was omitted.

UK Statutory Instruments

**Application for Convention adoption order**

58. Section 49 of the Act shall apply as if—

(a)  in subsection (1), the words from "but only" to the end were omitted;

(b)  subsections (2) and (3) were omitted.

**Offences**

59. Any person who contravenes or fails to comply with—

[(a)  regulation 24 (requirements in respect of prospective adopter following child's entry into the United Kingdom);

(b)  regulation 26(1) (return of child to relevant local authority where prospective adopter does not wish to proceed);

(c)  regulation 27(1)(b) (return of child to relevant local authority on request of local authority or by order of court); or

(d)  regulation 33 (refusal of a court in England or Wales to make a Convention adoption order)]

is guilty of an offence and liable on summary conviction to imprisonment for a term not exceeding three months, or a fine not exceeding level 5 on the standard scale, or both.

*[Schedules 1–2 omitted]*

# Civil Partnership (Jurisdiction and Recognition of Judgments) Regulations 2005

SI 2005/3334

### Citation and commencement

1. These Regulations may be cited as the Civil Partnership (Jurisdiction and Recognition of Judgments) Regulations 2005 and shall come into force on 5 December 2005.

### Extent

2.—(1) Except as provided by this regulation, these Regulations extend to England and Wales and Northern Ireland.

(2) Regulations 4 and 11(1) extend to England and Wales only.

(3) Regulations 5 and 11(2) extend to Northern Ireland only.

### Application

3.—(1) These Regulations apply to proceedings for the dissolution or annulment of an overseas relationship entitled to be treated as a civil partnership, or the legal separation of the same, as they apply to proceedings for the dissolution or annulment of a civil partnership or the legal separation of civil partners.

(2) Regulations 7 and 8, in respect of recognition and non-recognition of a judgment, apply to all judgments even if the date of the judgment is earlier than the date on which section 219 of the Civil Partnership Act 2004 and these Regulations come into force.

## PART 1

## Jurisdiction

### Jurisdiction: England and Wales

4. The courts in England and Wales shall have jurisdiction in relation to proceedings for the dissolution or annulment of a civil partnership or for the legal separation of civil partners where—

(a)  both civil partners are habitually resident in England and Wales;

(b)  both civil partners were last habitually resident in England and Wales and one of the civil partners continues to reside there;

(c)  the respondent is habitually resident in England and Wales;

(d)  the petitioner is habitually resident in England and Wales and has resided there for at least one year immediately preceding the presentation of the petition; or

(e)  the petitioner is domiciled and habitually resident in England and Wales and has resided there for at least six months immediately preceding the presentation of the petition.

. . .

## PART 2

## Recognition and Refusal of Recognition of Judgments

### Definitions for Part 2

6.—(1) In this Part "judgment" means an order for the dissolution or annulment of a civil partnership or the legal separation of civil partners, pronounced by a court of a Member State, however termed by that State.

(2) A "court of a Member State" referred to in paragraph (1) means all the authorities, whether judicial or administrative, in Member States with jurisdiction in those matters falling within the scope of these Regulations.

(3) The "Member States" referred to in paragraph (1) are any of the following States—Belgium, Cyprus, Czech Republic, Denmark, Germany, Greece, Spain, Estonia, France, Hungary, Ireland, Italy, Latvia, Lithuania, Luxembourg, Malta, Netherlands, Austria, Poland, Portugal, Slovakia, Slovenia, Finland and Sweden.

### Recognition of a judgment

7.—(1) Where a judgment is (or has been) given in respect of a civil partnership, that judgment shall, without any special formalities, be recognised in England and Wales or Northern Ireland.

(2) Any interested party may, in accordance with the procedure set out in rules, apply for a judgment to be, or not to be, recognised.

(3) Where the recognition of a judgment is raised as an incidental issue in proceedings before the court, that court may determine the issue.

### Refusal of recognition of a judgment

8.—(1) Recognition of the validity of a judgment may be refused in England and Wales or Northern Ireland if the judgment was obtained at a time when it was irreconcilable with a decision determining the question of the subsistence or validity of the civil partnership—

(a) previously given by a court of civil jurisdiction in that part of the United Kingdom, or

(b) previously given by a court elsewhere and recognised or entitled to be recognised in that part of the United Kingdom.

(2) Recognition of the validity of a judgment may be refused in England and Wales or Northern Ireland if the judgment was obtained at a time when, according to the law of that part of the United Kingdom, there was no subsisting civil partnership.

(3) Recognition of the validity of a judgment may be refused if—

(a) in the case of a judgment obtained by means of proceedings, it was obtained—

  (i) without such steps having been taken for giving notice of the proceedings to a civil partner as, having regard to the nature of the proceedings and all the circumstances, should reasonably have been taken, or

  (ii) without a civil partner having been given (for any reason other than lack of notice) such opportunity to take part in the proceedings as, having regard to those matters, he should reasonably have been given, or

(b) in the case of a judgment obtained otherwise than by means of proceedings—

  (i) there is no official document certifying the judgment is effective under the law of the country in which it was obtained, or

  (ii) where either civil partner was domiciled in another country at the relevant date, there is no official document certifying that the judgment is recognised as valid under the law of that other country, or

(c) in either case, recognition of the judgment would be manifestly contrary to public policy.

(4) In this regulation—

"official", in relation to a document certifying that a judgment is effective, or is recognised as valid, under the law of any country, means issued by a person or body appointed or recognised for the purpose under that law;

"the relevant date" means—

(a) in the case of a judgment obtained by means of proceedings, the date of the commencement of the proceedings;

(b) in the case of a judgment obtained otherwise than by means of proceedings, the date on which it was obtained.

### Jurisdiction and review

9. The court may not review the jurisdiction of the court which issued the judgment.

10. A judgment may not be reviewed as to its substance.

### Differences in applicable law

11.—(1) The recognition of a judgment in England and Wales may not be refused because the law of England and Wales would not allow dissolution, annulment or legal separation on the same facts.

. . .

### Stay of proceedings

12. Where recognition is sought of a judgment given in a Member State and an appeal against that judgment has been lodged in a Member State, the court may stay the proceedings.

# Overseas Companies (Execution of Documents and Registration of Charges) Regulations 2009

SI 2009/1917

## PART 1

## INTRODUCTION

### Citation and commencement

1.—(1) These Regulations may be cited as the Overseas Companies (Execution of Documents and Registration of Charges) Regulations 2009.

(2) These Regulations come into force on 1st October 2009.

### Interpretation

2. In these Regulations—

"certified copy" means a copy certified as a correct copy;

"establishment" means—

(a) a branch within the meaning of the Eleventh Company Law Directive (89/666/EEC)(2), or

(b) a place of business that is not such a branch, and

"UK establishment" means an establishment in the United Kingdom.

## PART 2

## EXECUTION OF DOCUMENTS ETC

### Application of Part

3. This Part applies to all overseas companies.

### Formalities of doing business under the law of England and Wales and Northern Ireland

4. Sections 43, 44 and 46 of the Companies Act 2006 apply to overseas companies, modified so that they read as follows—

### "Company contracts

43.—(1) Under the law of England and Wales or Northern Ireland a contract may be made—

(a) by an overseas company, by writing under its common seal or in any manner permitted by the laws of the territory in which the company is incorporated for the execution of documents by such a company, and

(b) on behalf of an overseas company, by any person who, in accordance with the laws of the territory in which the company is incorporated, is acting under the authority (express or implied) of that company.

(2) Any formalities required by law in the case of a contract made by an individual also apply, unless a contrary intention appears, to a contract made by or on behalf of an overseas company.

### Execution of documents

44.—(1) Under the law of England and Wales or Northern Ireland a document is executed by an overseas company—

(a) by the affixing of its common seal, or

UK Statutory Instruments

(b) if it is executed in any manner permitted by the laws of the territory in which the company is incorporated for the execution of documents by such a company.

(2) A document which—

(a) is signed by a person who, in accordance with the laws of the territory in which an overseas company is incorporated, is acting under the authority (express or implied) of the company, and

(b) is expressed (in whatever form of words) to be executed by the company,

has the same effect in relation to that company as it would have in relation to a company incorporated in England and Wales or Northern Ireland if executed under the common seal of a company so incorporated.

(3) In favour of a purchaser a document is deemed to have been duly executed by an overseas company if it purports to be signed in accordance with subsection (2).

A "purchaser" means a purchaser in good faith for valuable consideration and includes a lessee, mortgagee or other person who for valuable consideration acquires an interest in property.

(4) Where a document is to be signed by a person on behalf of more than one overseas company, it is not duly signed by that person for the purposes of this section unless he signs it separately in each capacity.

(5) References in this section to a document being (or purporting to be) signed by a person who, in accordance with the laws of the territory in which an overseas company is incorporated, is acting under the authority (express or implied) of the company are to be read, in a case where that person is a firm, as references to its being (or purporting to be) signed by an individual authorised by the firm to sign on its behalf.

(6) This section applies to a document that is (or purports to be) executed by an overseas company in the name of or on behalf of another person whether or not that person is also an overseas company.

**Execution of deeds**

46.—(1) A document is validly executed by an overseas company as a deed for the purposes of section 1(2)(b) of the Law of Property (Miscellaneous Provisions) Act 1989 (c.34) and for the purposes of the law of Northern Ireland if, and only if—

(a) it is duly executed by the company, and

(b) it is delivered as a deed.

(2) For the purposes of subsection (1)(b) a document is presumed to be delivered upon its being executed, unless a contrary intention is proved.".

**Formalities of doing business under the law of Scotland**

5. Section 48 of the Companies Act 2006 applies to overseas companies, modified so that it reads as follows—

**"Execution of documents by overseas companies**

48.—(1) The following provision forms part of the law of Scotland only.

(2) For the purposes of any enactment—

(a) providing for a document to be executed by a company by affixing its common seal, or

(b) referring (in whatever terms) to a document so executed,

a document signed or subscribed by or on behalf of an overseas company in accordance with the provisions of the Requirements of Writing (Scotland) Act 1995 (c.7) has effect as if so executed.".

**Other matters**

6. Section 51 of the Companies Act 2006 applies to overseas companies, modified so that it reads as follows—

**"Pre-incorporation contracts, deeds and obligations**

51.—(1) A contract that purports to be made by or on behalf of an overseas company at a time when the company has not been formed has effect, subject to any agreement to the contrary, as one made with the person purporting to act for the company or as agent for it, and he is personally liable on the contract accordingly.

(2) Subsection (1) applies—

(a)   to the making of a deed under the law of England and Wales or Northern Ireland, and

(b)   to the undertaking of an obligation under the law of Scotland,

as it applies to the making of a contract.".

. . .

# Parental Responsibility and Measures for the Protection of Children (International Obligations) (England and Wales and Northern Ireland) Regulations 2010

SI 2010/1898

### Citation, commencement and extent

1.—(1) These Regulations may be cited as the Parental Responsibility and Measures for the Protection of Children (International Obligations) (England and Wales and Northern Ireland) Regulations 2010.

(2) These Regulations come into force on the day on which the Convention enters into force for the United Kingdom, which date will be notified in the London, Edinburgh and Belfast Gazettes.

(3) These Regulations extend to England and Wales and Northern Ireland.

### Interpretation

2. In these Regulations—

"Central Authority" has the meaning given by regulation 9(1);

"Contracting State" means a state party to the Convention;

"the Convention" means the Convention on Jurisdiction, Applicable Law, Recognition, Enforcement and Co-Operation in respect of Parental Responsibility and Measures for the Protection of Children that was signed at The Hague on 19 October 1996;

"the Council Regulation" means Council Regulation (EC) No. 2201/2003 concerning jurisdiction and the recognition and enforcement of judgments in matrimonial matters and the matters of parental responsibility;

. . .

"local authority" means—

(a)  in relation to England, the council of a county, a metropolitan district, the Council of the Isles of Scilly, a London borough or the Common Council of the City of London, and

(b)  in relation to Wales, the council of a county or a county borough;

"member State" means a member State of the European Union which is bound by the Council Regulation;

. . .

"public authority" means a body whose functions are wholly or mainly of a public nature;

"Welsh family proceedings officer" has the meaning given by section 35 of the Children Act 2004.

UK Statutory Instruments

### Power of court to remove stay under Article 8

3.—(1) This regulation applies where—

(a)  a court has exercised its power under Article 8 of the Convention to request an authority of another Contracting State to assume jurisdiction in relation to an application,

(b)  the court has stayed proceedings on the application, and

(c)  Part 1 of the Family Law Act 1986 does not apply in relation to the application.

(2) The court may remove a stay granted in order for it to exercise its powers under Article 8 of the Convention, and withdraw any request made by it under that Article to an authority in another Contracting State to assume jurisdiction, if—

(a)  the authority in the other Contracting State does not assume jurisdiction within the period for which the court granted the stay, or

(b) the parties do not, within the period specified by the court, request the authority in the other Contracting State to assume jurisdiction.

### Local authorities and Northern Ireland authorities: application to court to make request under Article 9

4.—(1) This regulation applies where—

(a) . . .

  (i) a local authority in England and Wales wishes to make an application in respect of a child under section 31 of the Children Act 1989 (care and supervision orders), . . ., and

(b) the authorities of another Contracting State have jurisdiction in respect of the child under the Convention.

(2) The local authority . . . must make an application to the High Court, requesting the court to exercise its power under Article 9 of the Convention (request to competent authority of the Contracting State of the habitual residence of the child for authorisation to exercise jurisdiction).

### Local authorities: application for interim care order or supervision order

5.—(1) This regulation applies where—

(a) a local authority in England and Wales thinks that the conditions in section 31(2)(a) and (b) of the Children Act 1989 (threshold for care and supervision orders) apply in relation to a child, and

(b) one of the following applies in relation to the child—

  (i) Article 11 of the Convention (measures of protection in cases of urgency),

  (ii) Article 12 of the Convention (measures of a provisional character), or

  (iii) Article 20 of the Council Regulation (provisional and protective measures).

(2) Where this regulation applies, section 38 of the Children Act 1989 (interim orders) has effect as if—

(a) for subsection (1)(a) and (b) there were substituted—

"(a) a local authority makes an application for an interim care order or interim supervision order in relation to a child, and

(b) one of the following applies in relation to the child—

  (i) Article 11 of the Convention on Jurisdiction, Applicable Law, Recognition, Enforcement and Co-Operation in respect of Parental Responsibility and Measures for the Protection of Children that was signed at The Hague on 19 October 1996 (measures of protection in cases of urgency) ("the Convention"),

  (ii) Article 12 of the Convention (measures of a provisional character), or

  (iii) Article 20 of Council Regulation (EC) No. 2201/2003 concerning jurisdiction and the recognition and enforcement of judgments in matrimonial matters and the matters of parental responsibility (provisional and protective measures) ("the Council Regulation");",

(b) subsection (3) were omitted,

(c) in subsection (4)(b) the words "in the same proceedings" were omitted, and

(d) for subsection (4)(c) to (e) there were substituted—

"(c) in a case which falls within subsection (1)(b)(i) or (ii), when—

  (i) the authorities in another Contracting State with jurisdiction under the Convention have taken the measures required by the situation, or

  (ii) measures taken by the authorities of another State are recognised in England and Wales;

(d) in a case which falls within subsection (1)(b)(iii), when the court of the member State with jurisdiction under the Council Regulation has taken the measures it considers appropriate.".

(3) Where this regulation applies—

(a) section 31 of the Children Act 1989 (care and supervision orders) has effect as if, in section 31(3A), after "care order" there were inserted the words ", other than an interim care order,"

(b)   section 31A of that Act (care plans) has effect as if subsection (5) were omitted, and

(c)   section 41 of that Act (representation of child's interests) has effect as if in subsection (6) there were included a reference to an application for an interim care order or interim supervision order by virtue of this regulation.

. . .

### Application of Article 15

7. The reference to Chapter II of the Convention in Article 15(1) of the Convention is to be read as including a reference to Chapter II of the Council Regulation.

### Judicial authorities

8.—(1) The High Court has jurisdiction to entertain an application under Article 24 of the Convention for recognition, or non-recognition, of a measure taken in another Contracting State.

(2) But where the recognition or non-recognition of a measure is raised as an incidental question in another court, that court may determine the issue.

(3) The High Court is also to have jurisdiction—

(a)   to register a measure taken in another Contracting State for enforcement under Article 26 of the Convention, and

(b)   to entertain an application for a declaration—

   (i)   that a person has, or does not have, parental responsibility for a child by virtue of Article 16 of the Convention, or

   (ii)   as to the extent of a person's parental responsibility for a child by virtue of that Article.

### Central authorities

9.—(1) The functions under the Convention of a Central Authority are to be discharged—

(a)   in England, by the Lord Chancellor,

(b)   in Wales, by the Welsh Ministers, and

(c)   in Northern Ireland, by the Department of Justice,

and a reference in these Regulations to a "Central Authority" means any of the Lord Chancellor, the Welsh Ministers or the Department of Justice in so far as they have functions under this regulation.

(2) If a person outside the United Kingdom does not know to which Central Authority in the United Kingdom a communication should be addressed, the person may address it to the Lord Chancellor.

### Requests for information by Central Authority where request received under Article 31(c)

10.—(1) Paragraphs (2), (3) and (4) apply if a Central Authority receives a request for assistance under Article 31(c) of the Convention (either directly or via another Central Authority in the United Kingdom).

(2) The Lord Chancellor may request information about the whereabouts of a child from—

(a)   a local authority in England, or

(b)   the Secretary of State.

(3) The Welsh Ministers may request information about the whereabouts of a child from—

(a)   a local authority in Wales,

(b)   a Local Health Board (within the meaning given by section 11 of the National Health Service (Wales) Act 2006), or

(c)   an NHS Trust (within the meaning given by section 18 of that Act).

. . .

(5) A person . . . who receives a request for information under this regulation must comply with the request as soon as reasonably practicable (but this is subject to paragraph (6)).

UK Statutory Instruments

(6) Nothing in this regulation requires a person to disclose information if—

(a)   Article 37 of the Convention applies, or

(b)   the disclosure would constitute contempt of court or a criminal offence.

(7) If a person who receives a request under this regulation thinks that it is desirable, in responding to the request, to refer to information the disclosure of which would constitute contempt of court, the person must notify the court.

(8) If a person who receives a request under this regulation thinks that it is desirable, in responding to the request, to refer to information the disclosure of which would constitute a criminal offence unless the disclosure were authorised by a court, the person must notify the court.

### Requests for information under Council Regulation

11.—(1) This regulation applies if the designated Central Authority in England and Wales under Article 53 of the Council Regulation receives a request for information from another member State under Article 55(a)(i) of the Council Regulation.

(2) The designated Central Authority in England and Wales may request information about the whereabouts of a child from—

(a)   a local authority in England,

(b)   a local authority in Wales,

(c)   the Secretary of State,

(d)   an officer of the Children and Family Court Advisory and Support Service,

(e)   a Welsh family proceedings officer,

(f)   a Local Health Board (within the meaning given by section 11 of the National Health Service (Wales) Act 2006), or

(g)   an NHS Trust (within the meaning given by section 18 of that Act).

(3) The designated Central Authority in England and Wales may request a report on the situation of a child from—

(a)   a local authority in England,

(b)   a local authority in Wales,

(c)   an officer of the Children and Family Court Advisory and Support Service, or

(d)   a Welsh family proceedings officer.

(4) A person who receives a request for information under this regulation must comply with the request as soon as reasonably practicable (but this is subject to paragraph (5)).

(5) Nothing in this regulation requires a person to disclose information if the disclosure would constitute contempt of court or a criminal offence.

(6) If a person who receives a request under this regulation thinks that it is desirable, in responding to the request, to refer to information the disclosure of which would constitute contempt of court, the person must notify the court.

(7) If a person who receives a request under this regulation thinks that it is desirable, in responding to the request, to refer to information the disclosure of which would constitute a criminal offence unless the disclosure were authorised by a court, the person must notify the court.

### Power to request report on child's situation

12.—(1) This regulation applies where a Central Authority thinks it appropriate to provide a report on the situation of a child under Article 32(a) of the Convention.

(2) The Lord Chancellor may request a written report on the situation of the child from—

(a)   a local authority in England, or

(b)   an officer of the Children and Family Court Advisory and Support Service.

(3) The Welsh Ministers may request a written report on the situation of the child from—

(a)    a local authority in Wales, or

(b)    a Welsh family proceedings officer.

. . .

(5) A person in England and Wales or any public authority . . . who receives a request for a report under this regulation must comply with the request as soon as reasonably practicable (but this is subject to paragraph (6)).

(6) Nothing in this regulation requires a person to disclose information if—

(a)    Article 37 of the Convention applies, or

(b)    the disclosure would constitute contempt of court or a criminal offence.

(7) If a person who receives a request under this regulation thinks that it is desirable, in responding to the request, to refer to information the disclosure of which would constitute contempt of court, the person must notify the court.

(8) If a person who receives a request under this regulation thinks that it is desirable, in responding to the request, to refer to information the disclosure of which would constitute a criminal offence unless the disclosure were authorised by a court, the person must notify the court.

### Local authorities and Northern Ireland authorities: requirement to provide a report

13.—(1) This regulation applies if a local authority in England and Wales . . . is contemplating—

(a)    placing a child in another Contracting State, within the meaning given by Article 33 of the Convention, or

(b)    placing a child in another member State, within the meaning given by Article 56 of the Council Regulation.

(2) Either the court or the local authority . . ., whichever has jurisdiction under Articles 5 to 10 of the Convention or Articles 8 to 14 of the Council Regulation, as the case may be ("the authority")—

(a)    must provide a report to the Central Authority, or other competent authority, of the other Contracting State in accordance with Article 33(1) of the Convention, if the authority is exercising jurisdiction under the Convention, or

(b)    must consult the Central Authority, or other competent authority, of the other member State in accordance with Article 56 of the Council Regulation, if the authority is exercising jurisdiction under the Council Regulation.

### Power to respond to a request under Article 34

14. A public authority in England and Wales or Northern Ireland may provide information in response to a request communicated to it by the Central Authority under Article 34 of the Convention.

. . .

### Services under Article 35

16.—(1) The Secretary of State may charge a reasonable fee in respect of the provision of a service under Article 35 (1) or (2) of the Convention.

(2) The Welsh Ministers may charge a reasonable fee in respect of the provision of a service under Article 35(1) or (2) of the Convention.

. . .

(4) A request under Article 35(2) of the Convention is to be made—

(a)    if the parent making the request resides in England and Wales, to the local authority in whose area the parent resides, . . .

(5) A local authority in England may charge a reasonable fee in respect of the provision of a service under Article 35(1) or (2) of the Convention.

(6) A local authority in Wales may charge a reasonable fee in respect of the provision of a service under Article 35(1) or (2) of the Convention.

(7)  A fee is "reasonable" for the purposes of this regulation if the income from fees of that kind equates as nearly as possible to the costs of providing the service to which the fees relate (including a reasonable share of expenditure which is referable only partly or only indirectly to the provision of that service).

. . .

# Civil Jurisdiction and Judgments (Maintenance) (Rules of Court) Regulations 2011

SI 2011/1215

### Authentic instruments and court settlements

7.—(1) Section 48 of the Civil Jurisdiction and Judgments Act 1982 (matters for which rules of court may provide) applies in relation to authentic instruments and court settlements as if they were maintenance decisions to which the Maintenance Regulation applies.

(2) The reference in paragraph (1) to authentic instruments and court settlements is to those authentic instruments and court settlements which are to be recognised and enforceable in the same way as maintenance decisions by virtue of Article 48 of the Maintenance Regulation.

(3) In this regulation—

"the Maintenance Regulation" means Council Regulation (EC) No 4/2009 including as applied in relation to Denmark by virtue of the Agreement made on 19th October 2005 between the European Community and the Kingdom of Denmark;

"authentic instrument" and "court settlement" have the meanings given in Article 2 of the Maintenance Regulation.

UK Statutory Instruments

# Civil Jurisdiction and Judgments (Maintenance) Regulations 2011

SI 2011/1484 (as amended)

### Citation, commencement and extent

1.—(1) These Regulations may be cited as the Civil Jurisdiction and Judgments (Maintenance) Regulations 2011, and shall come into force on 18th June 2011.

(2) These Regulations extend to England and Wales, Scotland and Northern Ireland.[1]

(3) An amendment, repeal or revocation made by these Regulations has the same extent as the enactment amended, repealed or revoked.

### Interpretation

2. In these Regulations—

"the Act" means the Civil Jurisdiction and Judgments Act 1982(3);

"the Order" means the Civil Jurisdiction and Judgments Order 2001;

"the Maintenance Regulation" means Council Regulation (EC) No 4/2009 including as applied in relation to Denmark by virtue of the Agreement made on 19th October 2005 between the European Community and the Kingdom of Denmark;

"Maintenance Regulation State" in any provision, in the application of that provision in relation to the Maintenance Regulation, refers to any of the Member States.

### The Maintenance Regulation

3. Schedule 1 (which contains provisions relating to the enforcement of maintenance decisions pursuant to the Maintenance Regulation) has effect.

. . .

### Provisions relating to authentic instruments and court settlements

5. Schedule 3 (which contains provisions relating to authentic instruments and court settlements) has effect.

. . .

### Allocation of jurisdiction within the United Kingdom

8. Schedule 6 (which contains rules for the allocation of jurisdiction within the United Kingdom in relation to maintenance) has effect.

. . .

### Review

10.—(1) Before the end of each review period, the Secretary of State must—

(a)  carry out a review of the provisions of these Regulations,

(b)  set out the conclusions of the review in a report, and

(c)  publish the report.

(2) The review shall relate to the operation of these Regulations as they affect England and Wales only.

(3) In carrying out the review the Secretary of State must, so far as is reasonable, have regard to how the Maintenance Regulation has been given effect in other Member States.

[1]Note: Provisions and wording concerning Scotland or Northern Ireland only are not reproduced below, unless necessary to maintain the sense of the provision.

(4) The report must in particular—

(a)   set out the objectives intended to be achieved by the provisions of these Regulations,

(b)   assess the extent to which those objectives are achieved, and

(c)   assess whether those objectives remain appropriate, and, if so, the extent to which they could be achieved in a manner that imposes less regulation.

(5) "Review period" means—

(a)   the period of five years beginning with the day on which these Regulations come into force, and

(b)   subject to paragraph (6), each successive period of five years.

(6) If a report under this regulation is published before the last day of the review period to which it relates, the following review period is to begin with the day on which that report is published.

## SCHEDULE 1

## THE MAINTENANCE REGULATION

## PART 1

### Introductory

#### Interpretation

1.—(1)  In this Schedule—

"court" includes a tribunal, and any administrative authority which is a court for the purposes of the Maintenance Regulation by virtue of Article 2(2) of that Regulation;

"debtor", in relation to a maintenance decision, means the person liable, or alleged to be liable, to make the payments for which that decision provides;

"maintenance decision" has the meaning given to "decision" by Article 2 of the Maintenance Regulation.

(2) In this Schedule—

(a)   any reference to a numbered Article is a reference to the Article so numbered in the Maintenance Regulation and any reference to a sub-division of a numbered Article shall be construed accordingly;

(b)   references to a registered decision include, to the extent of its registration, references to a decision so registered to a limited extent only.

(3) Anything authorised or required by the Maintenance Regulation or by this Schedule to be done by, to or before a particular magistrates' court may be done by, to or before any magistrates' court acting for the same local justice area . . . as that court.

#### Central Authorities

2.—(1)  The following are designated as Central Authorities under Article 49 of the Maintenance Regulation—

(a)   in relation to England and Wales, the Lord Chancellor . . .

(2) If a person outside the United Kingdom does not know to which Central Authority in the United Kingdom a communication should be addressed, the person may address it to the Lord Chancellor.

## PART 2

## Recognition and enforcement of maintenance decisions made by courts in Maintenance Regulation States other than Denmark

### Application of Part 2

3. This Part shall apply to maintenance decisions made by courts in Maintenance Regulation States other than Denmark.

### Enforcement of maintenance decisions

4.—(1) Subject to sub-paragraph (2), where a maintenance decision falls to be enforced in the United Kingdom under Section 1 of Chapter IV of the Maintenance Regulation, the court to which an application for enforcement is to be made is—

(a)   in England and Wales, [the family court] . . .

(2) An application for enforcement is to be transmitted to [the family court] . . . designated for these purposes by rules of court ("the enforcing court")—

(a)   in England and Wales, by the Lord Chancellor . . .

(3) Jurisdiction in relation to applications for enforcement of such maintenance decisions lies with the courts for the part of the United Kingdom in which—

(a)   the person against whom enforcement is sought is resident,

(b)   assets belonging to that person and which are susceptible to enforcement are situated or held, or

(c)   any other matter relevant to enforcement arises.

(4) For the purposes of the enforcement of a maintenance decision—

(a)   the decision shall be of the same force and effect,

(b)   the enforcing court shall have in relation to its enforcement the same powers, and

(c)   proceedings for or with respect to its enforcement may be taken,

as if the decision had originally been made by the enforcing court.

(5) Sub-paragraph (4) is subject to sub-paragraphs (6) and (7).

(6) (a) A maintenance decision which is enforceable in England and Wales by virtue of Section 1 of Chapter IV of the Maintenance Regulation and these Regulations shall be enforceable in [the family court] in the same manner as a maintenance order made by that court [. . .]

(b)   In this sub-paragraph "maintenance order" has the meaning given by [section 1(10) of the Maintenance Enforcement Act 1991].

. . .

(8) Sub-paragraph (4) is also subject to—

(a)   Article 21 (application by debtor for refusal or suspension of enforcement);

(b)   paragraph 8 below;

(c)   any provision made by rules of court as to the procedure for the enforcement of maintenance decisions given in another Maintenance Regulation State.

(9) (a) The debtor under a maintenance decision which is or has been the subject of enforcement proceedings in England and Wales . . . by virtue of Section 1 of Chapter IV of the Maintenance Regulation and these Regulations must give notice of any change of address to the designated officer . . . of the court in which enforcement proceedings have been, or are being, taken.

(b)   A person who without reasonable excuse fails to comply with this sub-paragraph shall be guilty of an offence and liable on summary conviction to a fine not exceeding level 2 on the standard scale.

(10) An application for refusal or suspension of enforcement under Article 21(2) or (3) of the Maintenance Regulation shall be made—

(a)   in England and Wales . . ., to a magistrates' court by way of complaint . . .

UK Statutory Instruments

PART 3

## Recognition and enforcement of maintenance decisions made by courts in Denmark etc

### Application of Part 3

5. This Part applies in relation to—

(a) maintenance decisions made by courts in Denmark, and

(b) maintenance decisions to which Sections 2 and 3 of Chapter IV of the Maintenance Regulation apply by virtue of Article 75(2)(a) or (b).

### Recognition and enforcement of maintenance orders

6.—(1) Subject to sub-paragraph (2), the court to which an application for registration of a maintenance decision under Section 2 of Chapter IV of the Maintenance Regulation is to be made is—

(a) in England and Wales, [the family court] . . .

(2) An application for registration is to be transmitted to the [family court] . . . designated for these purposes by rules of court ("the registering court")—

(a) in England and Wales, by the Lord Chancellor . . .

(3) Where an application for registration of a maintenance decision is transmitted to a court—

(a) the decision may be registered for enforcement by the court, and

(b) if so registered, the decision shall be treated as having been declared enforceable for the purposes of Section 2 of Chapter IV of the Maintenance Regulation.

(4) (a) An application for registration shall be determined in the first instance by the prescribed officer of the registering court.

(b) In this sub-paragraph, "prescribed" means prescribed by rules of court.

(5) For the purposes of the enforcement of a registered maintenance decision—

(a) the decision shall be of the same force and effect,

(b) the registering court shall have in relation to its enforcement the same powers, and

(c) proceedings for or with respect to its enforcement may be taken,

as if the decision had originally been made by the registering court.

(6) Sub-paragraph (5) is subject to sub-paragraphs (7) and (8).

(7)

(a) A maintenance decision which is enforceable in England and Wales by virtue of Section 2 of Chapter IV of the Maintenance Regulation and these Regulations shall be enforceable in [the family court] in England and Wales in the same manner as a maintenance order made by that court [. . .]

(b) In this sub-paragraph "maintenance order" has the meaning given by [section 1(10) of the Maintenance Enforcement Act 1991].

. . .

(9) Sub-paragraph (5) is also subject to—

(a) Article 36(3) (restriction on enforcement where appeal pending or time for appeal unexpired);

(b) paragraph 8 below;

(c) any provision made by rules of court as to the procedure for the enforcement of maintenance decisions registered under the Maintenance Regulation and these Regulations.

(10)

(a) The debtor under a maintenance decision registered in accordance with this paragraph in [the family court] in England and Wales . . . must give notice of any change of address to the designated officer . . .

(b) A person who without reasonable excuse fails to comply with this sub-paragraph shall be guilty of an offence and liable on summary conviction to a fine not exceeding level 2 on the standard scale.

**Proceedings to contest decisions given on appeal in connection with applications for registration**

7. An appeal under Article 33 may only be on a point of law and lies—

(a) in England and Wales, to [the family court] in accordance with section 111A of the Magistrates' Courts Act 1980 . . .

## PART 4

## Recognition and enforcement of maintenance decisions – general

**Interest on judgments**

8.—(1) Subject to sub-paragraphs (2) and (3) and rules of court as to the payment of interest under this paragraph, where a person applying for registration or enforcement of a maintenance decision shows that—

(a) the decision provides for the payment of a sum of money, and

(b) in accordance with the law of the Maintenance Regulation State in which the maintenance decision was given and the terms of the decision, interest on that sum is recoverable at a particular rate and from a particular date or time,

the debt resulting from registration or enforcement of the decision is to carry interest at that rate and from that date or time.

(2) In the case of an application for registration of a maintenance decision, interest is not recoverable unless the rate of interest and the date or time referred to in sub-paragraph (1)(b) are registered with the decision.

(3) (a) Interest on arrears of sums payable under a maintenance decision which falls to be enforced in [the family court] . . . by virtue of the Maintenance Regulation and these Regulations shall not be recoverable in that court.

. . .

(4) Except as mentioned in sub-paragraph (3), debts under maintenance decisions enforceable in the United Kingdom by virtue of the Maintenance Regulation shall carry interest only as provided by this paragraph.

**Currency of payments under maintenance decisions**

9.—(1) Sums payable under a maintenance decision enforceable in the United Kingdom by virtue of the Maintenance Regulation, including any arrears so payable, shall be paid in sterling where an order is made on an application for enforcement in England and Wales . . .

(2) Where the maintenance decision is expressed in any other currency, the amount shall be converted on the basis of the exchange rate prevailing on the date on which the application for enforcement or registration of the decision was received by a Central Authority in the United Kingdom for transmission to a court.

(3) For the purposes of this paragraph, a written certificate purporting to be signed by an officer of any bank in the United Kingdom and stating the exchange rate prevailing on a specified date shall be evidence of the facts stated . . .

**Proof and admissibility of certain maintenance decisions and related documents**

10.—(1) For the purposes of proceedings relating to the Maintenance Regulation—

(a) a document, duly authenticated, which purports to be a copy of a maintenance decision given by a court in a Maintenance Regulation State shall without further proof be deemed to be a true copy, unless the contrary is shown; and

(b)  an extract from a maintenance decision issued by a court in a Maintenance Regulation State in accordance with Article 20 or Article 28 (as the case may be) shall be evidence that that decision is enforceable there.

(2) A document purporting to be a copy of a maintenance decision given by a court mentioned in sub-paragraph (1)(a) is duly authenticated for the purposes of this paragraph if it purports—

(a)  to bear the seal of that court; or

(b)  to be certified by any person in his capacity as a judge or officer of that court to be a true copy of a maintenance decision given by that court.

(3) Nothing in this paragraph shall prejudice the admission in evidence of any document which is admissible apart from this paragraph.

## PART 5

**Establishment and Modification of Maintenance Under the Maintenance Regulation]**

[11.—(1) This paragraph applies to an application submitted under Article 56 for establishment or modification of a decision to the Lord Chancellor, in relation to England and Wales . . .

(2) Upon receipt of an application submitted under Article 56 for establishment or modification of a decision in England and Wales, the Lord Chancellor shall send that application to the court officer of the family court in the Designated Family Judge area in which the respondent is residing.

(3) Upon receipt of the application under sub-paragraph (2), the court officer of that court shall decide—

(a)  whether the courts of England and Wales have jurisdiction to determine the application by virtue of the Maintenance Regulation and Schedule 6 to these Regulations; and

(b)  if so, whether the family court has power to make the decision or modification sought under the law in force in England and Wales.

(4) Where the court officer decides under sub-paragraph (3)(a) that the courts of England and Wales do not have jurisdiction to determine the application, the court officer shall return the application to the Lord Chancellor with a written explanation of the reasons for that decision.

. . .

(6) Subject to sub-paragraph (7), if the court officer decides under sub-paragraph (3)(b) that the family court has power to make the decision or modification sought, the designated officer shall issue the application and serve it on the respondent.

(7) If the respondent does not reside in the Designated Family Judge area to which the application has been sent, the court officer shall—

(a)  if satisfied that the respondent is residing within another Designated Family Judge area, send the application to the court officer of the family court in that other area and inform the Lord Chancellor that it has been so sent; or

(b)  if unable to establish where the respondent is residing, return the application to the Lord Chancellor.

(8) A court officer who receives an application by virtue of sub-paragraph (7)(a) shall proceed under sub-paragraph (6) as if that court officer had decided that the family court has power to make the decision or modification sought.

(9) Where the court officer has determined in accordance with sub-paragraph (3)(b) that the family court has power to make the decision or modification sought, the application shall be treated for the purpose of establishment or modification of a decision under the Maintenance Regulation as an application under the law in force in England and Wales.

. . .

(11) In this paragraph—

"respondent" means the person who is alleged in an application for establishment of a decision under Article 56 to owe maintenance, or where the application is for modification of a decision, the person against whom the modification is sought;

and a reference to an application is a reference to an application together with any documents which accompany it.]

. . .

## SCHEDULE 3

## PROVISIONS RELATING TO AUTHENTIC INSTRUMENTS AND COURT SETTLEMENTS

1. References in this Schedule to authentic instruments and court settlements are references to those authentic instruments and court settlements (as defined in Article 2 of the Maintenance Regulation) which are to be recognised and enforceable in the same way as maintenance decisions by virtue of Article 48 of that Regulation.

2.—(1) In relation to an authentic instrument or court settlement which is enforceable in the Maintenance Regulation State of origin, Schedule 1 applies, subject to the modifications in sub-paragraphs (2), (3) and (4), as if that authentic instrument or court settlement was a maintenance decision given by a court in that Maintenance Regulation State.

(2) Paragraphs 4(4) and 6(5) of Schedule 1 apply in relation to authentic instruments and court settlements as if, for the words "as if the decision had been originally made" there were substituted "as if it was a decision which had originally been made".

(3) Paragraph 10 of Schedule 1 applies to authentic instruments as if—

(a)   in sub-paragraph (1)(a), for the words "given by a court" there were substituted "drawn up by, registered by, authenticated by or concluded before a competent authority";

(b)   for sub-paragraph (1)(b) there were substituted—

"(b) an extract from an authentic instrument issued by a competent authority in a Maintenance Regulation State in accordance with Article 48 shall be evidence that that instrument is enforceable there.";

(c)   for sub-paragraph (2) there were substituted—

"(2) A document purporting to be a copy of an authentic instrument drawn up by, registered by, authenticated by or concluded before a competent authority in a Maintenance Regulation State is duly authenticated for the purposes of this paragraph if it purports to be certified to be a true copy of such an instrument by a person duly authorised in that State to do so."

(4) Paragraph 10(1)(b) of Schedule 1 applies to court settlements as if, for the words "Article 20 or Article 28 (as the case may be)" there were substituted "Article 48".

3. Section 18(7) of the Act (disapplication of section 18) has effect to disapply section 18 in relation to an authentic instrument or court settlement to which Article 48 applies.

. . .

## SCHEDULE 6

## ALLOCATION WITHIN THE UNITED KINGDOM OF JURISDICTION RELATING TO MAINTENANCE MATTERS

1. The provisions of this Schedule have effect for determining, as between the parts of the United Kingdom, whether the courts of a particular part of the United Kingdom, or any particular court in that part, have or has jurisdiction in proceedings where the subject-matter of the proceedings is within the scope of the Maintenance Regulation as determined by Article 1 of that Regulation.

2. In this Schedule, a reference to an Article by number alone is a reference to the Article so numbered in the Maintenance Regulation.

3. The provisions of Chapter II of the Maintenance Regulation apply to the determination of jurisdiction

in the circumstances mentioned in paragraph 1, subject to the modifications specified in the following provisions of this Schedule.

4. Article 3 applies as if—

(a) the references in Article 3(a) and (b) to the court for the place where the defendant or the creditor is habitually resident were references to the court for the part of the United Kingdom in which the defendant, or the creditor, as the case may be, is habitually resident;

(b) the references to a person's nationality were references to a person's domicile.

5. Article 4(1) to (3) applies as if—

(a) for "Member State", wherever it occurs, there were substituted "part of the United Kingdom";

(b) the reference to a person's nationality was a reference to a person's domicile.

6. Article 5 applies as if—

(a) after "this Regulation" there were inserted "as modified by Schedule 6 to the Civil Jurisdiction and Judgments (Maintenance) Regulations 2011";

(b) for "Member State" there were substituted "part of the United Kingdom".

7. Where Article 6, as read with the second paragraph of Article 2(3), indicates that the courts of the United Kingdom have jurisdiction under the Maintenance Regulation, and the parties are domiciled in different parts of the United Kingdom, the courts of either part may exercise jurisdiction (subject to Article 12 as it has effect by virtue of this Schedule).

8. Article 7 applies as if for the second sentence there were substituted—

"The dispute must have a sufficient connection with the part of the United Kingdom in which the court seised is located.".

9.—(1) Sub-paragraphs (2) and (3) have effect in addition to Article 8.

(2) Where a decision is given in a part of the United Kingdom where the creditor is habitually resident, proceedings to modify the decision or to have a new decision given cannot be brought by the debtor in any other part of the United Kingdom as long as the creditor remains habitually resident in the part of the United Kingdom in which the decision was given.

(3) Sub-paragraph (2) does not apply where—

(a) the parties have agreed that the courts of that other part of the United Kingdom are to have jurisdiction in accordance with Article 4 as applied by paragraph 5 of this Schedule, or

(b) the creditor submits to the jurisdiction of the courts of that other part of the United Kingdom pursuant to Article 5 as applied by paragraph 6 of this Schedule.

10. Article 9 does not apply.

11.—(1) Sub-paragraphs (2) and (3) have effect instead of Articles 10 and 11.

(2) Where a defendant habitually resident in one part of the United Kingdom is sued in a court of another part of the United Kingdom and does not enter an appearance, the court will declare of its own initiative that it has no jurisdiction unless its jurisdiction is derived from the provisions of this Schedule.

(3) The court will stay the proceedings so long as it is not shown that the defendant has been able to receive the document instituting the proceedings or an equivalent document in sufficient time to enable him to arrange for his defence, or that all necessary steps have been taken to this end.

12. Article 12 applies as if after "different Member States" there were inserted "or different parts of the United Kingdom".

13. Article 13 applies as if after "different Member States" there were inserted "or different parts of the United Kingdom".

14. Article 14 applies as if—

(a) for "a Member State" there were substituted "a part of the United Kingdom";

(b) after "another Member State" there were inserted "or another part of the United Kingdom".

15. Notwithstanding the preceding provisions of this Schedule, the exercise of jurisdiction in any proceedings in a court in the United Kingdom is subject to—

(a)   the Maintenance Regulation;

(b)   the Convention on jurisdiction and the recognition and enforcement of judgments in civil and commercial matters, between the European Community and the Republic of Iceland, the Kingdom of Norway, the Swiss Confederation and the Kingdom of Denmark signed on behalf of the European Community on 30th October 2007;

(c)   the Convention on jurisdiction and the enforcement of judgments in civil and commercial matters signed at Brussels on the 27th September 1968; and

(d)   the Convention on jurisdiction and the enforcement of judgments in civil and commercial matters concluded at Lugano on the 16th September 1988.

16. This Schedule does not apply to—

(a)   matters in relation to which—

    (i)   the [Secretary of State] has jurisdiction to make a maintenance calculation by virtue of section 44 of the Child Support Act 1991;

. . .

(b)   proceedings for, or otherwise relating to, an order under any of the following provisions—

    (i)   paragraph 23 of Schedule 2 to the Children Act 1989 (contribution orders);

    (ii)   section 106 of the Social Security Administration Act 1992 (recovery of expenditure on benefit from person liable for maintenance);

. . .

# International Recovery of Maintenance (Hague Convention 2007 etc) Regulations 2012

SI 2012/2814

### Citation, commencement and extent

1.—(1) These Regulations may be cited as the International Recovery of Maintenance (Hague Convention 2007 etc) Regulations 2012, and, subject as follows, shall come into force on the day on which the Convention enters into force in respect of the European Union, which day will be notified in the London, Edinburgh and Belfast Gazettes.

(2) Regulations 1, 2, 3 and 9, and Schedule 5 come into force on 7th December 2012.

(3) Regulation 6 and Schedule 2 come into force on 1st April 2013, except in so far as they apply to the enforcement of a maintenance decision registered under the Convention.

2.—(1) Subject as follows, these Regulations extend only to England and Wales.

(2) Regulations 1 to 3, 4(2), 6, 7 and 10 and Schedules 2 and 3 also extend to Scotland.

(3) Regulations 1 to 3, 4(2), 7 and 10 and Schedule 3 also extend to Northern Ireland.

(4) Any amendment, repeal or revocation made by these Regulations has the same extent as the enactment to which it relates.

### Interpretation

3. In these Regulations—

"the Convention" means the Convention on the International Recovery of Child Support and other forms of Family Maintenance done at The Hague on 23rd November 2007; and

"the Maintenance Regulation" means Council Regulation (EC) No 4/2009 on jurisdiction, applicable law, recognition and enforcement of decisions and cooperation in matters relating to maintenance obligations, including as applied in relation to Denmark by virtue of the Agreement made on 19th October 2005 between the European Community and the Kingdom of Denmark.

### Central Authority for England and Wales

4.—(1) The Lord Chancellor is designated under Article 4 of the Convention as the Central Authority in relation to England and Wales.

(2) If a person outside the United Kingdom does not know to which Central Authority in the United Kingdom a communication should be addressed, the person may address it to the Lord Chancellor.

### The Convention

5. Schedule 1 (which contains provisions relating to the establishment, modification, recognition and enforcement in England and Wales pursuant to the Convention of maintenance decisions made in States bound by the Convention which are not European Union Member States) has effect.

. . .

## SCHEDULE 1

### RECOGNITION AND ENFORCEMENT OF NON-EU MAINTENANCE DECISIONS, AND ESTABLISHMENT AND MODIFICATION OF MAINTENANCE OBLIGATIONS UNDER THE CONVENTION

### Interpretation

1.—(1) In this Schedule—

UK Statutory Instruments

"Contracting State" means a State bound by the Convention other than an EU Member State;

"court", in relation to a maintenance decision given in a Contracting State, includes a tribunal, and any administrative authority (within the meaning of Article 19(3)) with competence to make a decision in respect of a maintenance obligation;

"maintenance decision" means a decision, or part of a decision, made by a court in a Contracting State, to which Chapter V of the Convention applies by virtue of Article 19(1).

(2) In this Schedule, any reference to a numbered Article is a reference to the Article so numbered in the Convention and any reference to a sub-division of a numbered Article shall be construed accordingly.

[. . .]

Recognition and enforcement of maintenance decisions made by courts in Contracting States

2.—(1) Subject to sub-paragraph (2), the court in England and Wales to which an application for registration of a maintenance decision under the Convention is to be made is [the family court].

(2) An application for registration is to be transmitted by the Lord Chancellor to [the family court] ("the registering court").

(3) Jurisdiction in relation to applications for registration of maintenance decisions lies with the courts of England and Wales if—

(a) the person against whom enforcement is sought is resident in England and Wales, or

(b) assets belonging to that person and which are susceptible to enforcement are situated or held in England and Wales.

(4) An application for registration shall be determined in the first instance by the prescribed officer of the registering court.

In this sub-paragraph and in sub-paragraph (5), "prescribed" means prescribed by rules of court.

(5) The decision of the prescribed officer may be appealed to the registering court in accordance with rules of court.

(6) For the purposes of the enforcement of a maintenance decision registered under the Convention in the registering court—

(a) the decision shall be of the same force and effect,

(b) the registering court shall have in relation to its enforcement the same powers, and

(c) proceedings for or with respect to its enforcement may be taken,

as if the decision had originally been made by the registering court.

(7) Sub-paragraph (6) is subject to sub-paragraph (8).

(8) A maintenance decision which is so registered shall be enforceable in [the family court] in England and Wales in the same manner as a maintenance order made by that court [. . .].

In this sub-paragraph "maintenance order" has the meaning given by [section 1(10) of the Maintenance Enforcement Act 1991].

(9) Sub-paragraph (6) is also subject to—

(a) paragraph 3;

(b) any provision made by rules of court as to the procedure for the enforcement of maintenance decisions registered in accordance with this paragraph.

(10) The debtor under a maintenance decision registered in accordance with this paragraph in [the family court] must give notice of any change of address to the [court officer of the family court in the Designated Family Judge area in which the maintenance decision is registered].

In this sub-paragraph, "debtor" has the meaning given by Article 3.

(11) A person who without reasonable excuse fails to comply with sub-paragraph (10) shall be guilty of an offence and liable on summary conviction to a fine not exceeding level 2 on the standard scale.

### Interest on judgments

3.—(1) Subject to [sub-paragraph (2)] and rules of court as to the payment of interest under this paragraph, where a person applying for registration of a maintenance decision shows that—

(a) the decision provides for the payment of money, and

(b) in accordance with the law of the Contracting State in which the maintenance decision was given and the terms of the decision, interest on that sum is recoverable at a particular rate and from a particular date or time,

the debt resulting from registration of the decision is to carry interest at that rate and from that date or time.

(2) Interest is not recoverable under sub-paragraph (1) unless the rate of interest and the date or time referred to in sub-paragraph (1)(b) are registered with the decision.

[. . .]

### Currency of payments under a maintenance decision

4.—(1) Sums payable under a maintenance decision registered in England and Wales under the Convention, including any arrears so payable, shall be paid in sterling.

(2) Where the maintenance decision is expressed in any other currency, the amounts shall be converted on the basis of the exchange rate prevailing on the date on which the application for registration was received by the Lord Chancellor for transmission to a court.

(3) For the purposes of this paragraph, a written certificate purporting to be signed by an officer of any bank in England and Wales and stating the exchange rate prevailing on a specified date shall be evidence of the facts stated.

### Proof and admissibility of certain maintenance decisions and related documents

5.—(1) For the purposes of proceedings relating to the Convention a document, duly authenticated, which purports to be a copy of a maintenance decision given by a court in a Contracting State shall without further proof be deemed to be a true copy, unless the contrary is shown.

(2) A document purporting to be a copy of a maintenance decision given by a court in a Contracting State is duly authenticated for the purposes of this paragraph if it purports—

(a) to bear the seal of that court; or

(b) to be certified by any person in that person's capacity as a judge or officer of that court to be a true copy of a maintenance decision given by that court.

(3) Nothing in this paragraph shall prejudice the admission in evidence of any document which is admissible apart from this paragraph.

### Maintenance arrangements

6.—(1) References in this paragraph to maintenance arrangements are to those maintenance arrangements (as defined in Article 3(e)) which are to be recognised and enforceable in the same way as maintenance decisions by virtue of Article 30.

(2) In relation to a maintenance arrangement which is enforceable as a maintenance decision in the Contracting State of origin, this Schedule applies, subject to the modifications in sub-paragraphs (3), (4) and (5), as if that maintenance arrangement was a maintenance decision given by a court of that State.

(3) Paragraph 2 applies to maintenance arrangements as if—

(a) in sub-paragraph (6), for "as if the decision had originally" there were substituted "as if it were a decision which had originally";

(b) after sub-paragraph (9)(b) there were inserted—

"(c) Article 30(6) (restriction on enforcement where there is a challenge to a maintenance arrangement in the Contracting State of origin).".

UK Statutory Instruments

(4) Paragraph 3 applies to maintenance arrangements as if in sub-paragraph (1)(b), for the word "given" there were substituted "concluded".

(5) Paragraph 5 applies to maintenance arrangements as if—

(a) in sub-paragraph (1), for "given by a court" there were substituted "formally drawn up or registered as an authentic instrument by, or authenticated by, or concluded, registered or filed with a competent authority";

(b) for sub-paragraph (2) there were substituted—

"(2) A document purporting to be a copy of a maintenance arrangement drawn up or registered as an authentic instrument by, or authenticated by, or concluded, registered or filed with a competent authority in a Contracting State is duly authenticated for the purposes of this paragraph if it purports to be certified to be a true copy of such an arrangement by a person duly authorised in that State to do so.".

(6) Section 18 of the Civil Jurisdiction and Judgments Act 1982 does not apply to maintenance arrangements.

### Applications for establishment or modification of maintenance in England and Wales

7.—(1) Upon receipt of an application submitted under Article 10 for establishment or modification of a decision, the Lord Chancellor shall send that application to [the court officer of the family court in the Designated Family Judge area] in which the respondent is residing.

(2) Upon receipt of the application under sub-paragraph (1), the [court officer] shall decide—

(a) whether the courts of England and Wales have jurisdiction to determine the application by virtue of the Maintenance Regulation and Schedule 6 to the Civil Jurisdiction and Judgments (Maintenance) Regulations 2011; and

[(b) if so, whether the family court has the power to make the decision or modification sought under the law in force in England and Wales].

(3) Where the [court officer] decides under sub-paragraph (2)(a) that the courts of England and Wales do not have jurisdiction to determine the application, the [court officer] shall return the application to the Lord Chancellor with a written explanation of the reasons for that decision.

(4) [. . .]

(5) Subject to sub-paragraph (6), if the [court officer] decides under sub-paragraph (2)(b) that the [family court] has power to make the decision or modification sought, the [court officer] shall issue the application and serve it on the respondent.

(6) If the respondent does not reside in [the Designated Family Judge area to which the application has been sent, the court officer] shall—

(a) if satisfied that the respondent is residing within [another Designated Family Judge area], send the application to the [court officer of the family court] acting in that other area and inform the Lord Chancellor that it has been so sent; or

(b) if unable to establish where the respondent is residing, return the application to the Lord Chancellor.

(7) A [court officer] who receives an application by virtue of sub-paragraph (6)(a) shall proceed under sub-paragraph (5) as if that [court officer] had decided that the [family court] has power to make the decision or modification sought.

(8) Where the [court officer] has determined in accordance with sub-paragraph (2)(b) that [the family court] has power to make the decision or modification sought, the application shall be treated for the purpose of establishment or modification of a decision under the [law in force in England and Wales].

(9)  In this paragraph—

"respondent" means the person who is alleged in an application for establishment of a decision under Article 10 to owe maintenance, or where the application is for modification of a decision, the applicant for the original decision; and

a reference to an application is a reference to an application together with any documents which accompany it.

. . .

# Marriage (Same Sex Couples) (Jurisdiction and Recognition of Judgments) Regulations 2014

SI 2014/543

## PART 1

### Introductory

**Citation, commencement and extent**

1.—(1) These Regulations may be cited as the Marriage (Same Sex Couples) (Jurisdiction and Recognition of Judgments) Regulations 2014 and shall come into force on 13th March 2014.

(2) These Regulations extend to England and Wales only.

## PART 2

### Jurisdiction

**Jurisdiction**

2. The court has jurisdiction in proceedings for the divorce of, or annulment of the marriage of, a same sex couple or for the judicial separation of a married same sex couple where—

(a) both spouses are habitually resident in England and Wales;

(b) both spouses were last habitually resident in England and Wales and one of the spouses continues to reside there;

(c) the respondent is habitually resident in England and Wales;

(d) the petitioner is habitually resident in England and Wales and has resided there for at least one year immediately preceding the presentation of the petition;

(e) the petitioner is domiciled and habitually resident in England and Wales and has resided there for at least six months immediately preceding the presentation of the petition; or

(f) both spouses are domiciled in England and Wales.

## PART 3

### Recognition and Refusal of Recognition of Judgments

**Interpretation and application of Part 3**

3.—(1) In this Part—

(a) "judgment" means a judgment of a court of a member State which orders the divorce of, or annulment of the marriage of, a same sex couple or the judicial separation of a married same sex couple;

(b) "member State" means a member State of the European Union other than the United Kingdom.

(2) A "court of a member State" referred to in paragraph (1)(a) means any authority, whether judicial or administrative, in a member State with jurisdiction in those matters falling within the scope of these Regulations.

(3) This Part applies to all judgments even if the date of the judgment is earlier than the date on which paragraph 5 of Schedule A1 to the Domicile and Matrimonial Proceedings Act 1973 and these Regulations come into force.

### Recognition of a judgment

4.—(1) Where a judgment is (or has been) given in respect of a marriage of a same sex couple, that judgment shall, without any special formalities, be recognised.

(2) Any interested party may, in accordance with the procedure set out in the Family Procedure Rules 2010, apply to the court for a judgment to be, or not to be, recognised.

(3) Where the recognition of a judgment is raised as an incidental issue in proceedings before the court, that court may determine the issue.

### Refusal of recognition of a judgment

5.—(1) The court shall refuse to recognise the validity of a judgment if the judgment was obtained at a time when it was irreconcilable with a decision determining the question of the subsistence or validity of the marriage—

(a) previously given in proceedings between the same parties by a court of civil jurisdiction in England and Wales, or

(b) previously given in proceedings between the same parties by a court elsewhere, but only if that decision was capable of being recognised or was entitled to be recognised in England and Wales at the time it was obtained.

(2) The court shall refuse to recognise the validity of a judgment if the judgment was obtained at a time when the law of England and Wales did not recognise marriages of same sex couples.

(3) Paragraph (2) does not prevent the recognition of a judgment if, at the time the judgment was obtained, the marriage would have been treated as a subsisting civil partnership according to the law of England and Wales.

(4) The court shall refuse to recognise the validity of a judgment if—

(a) in the case of a judgment obtained by means of proceedings, it was obtained—

   (i) without such steps having been taken for giving notice of the proceedings to a spouse as, having regard to the nature of the proceedings and all the circumstances, should reasonably have been taken, or

   (ii) without a spouse having been given (for any reason other than lack of notice) such opportunity to take part in the proceedings as, having regard to those matters, he or she should reasonably have been given; or

(b) in the case of a judgment obtained otherwise than by means of proceedings—

   (i) there is no official document certifying that the judgment is effective under the law of the country in which it was obtained, or

   (ii) where either spouse was domiciled in another country at the relevant date, there is no official document certifying that the judgment is recognised as valid under the law of that other country; or

(c) in either case, recognition of the judgment would be manifestly contrary to public policy.

(5) In this regulation—

"official", in relation to a document certifying that a judgment is effective, or is recognised as valid, under the law of any country, means issued by a person or body appointed or recognised for the purpose under that law;

"the relevant date" means—

   (a) in the case of a judgment obtained by means of proceedings, the date of the commencement of the proceedings;

   (b) in the case of a judgment obtained otherwise than by means of proceedings, the date on which it was obtained.

### Jurisdiction and review

6. The court may not review the jurisdiction of the court which issued the judgment.

7.  A judgment may not be reviewed as to its substance.

### Differences in applicable law

8.  The court may not refuse to recognise a judgment because the law of England and Wales would not allow divorce, annulment or judicial separation on the same facts.

### Stay of proceedings

9.  Where recognition is sought of a judgment given in a member State and an appeal against that judgment has been lodged in that member State, the court may stay the proceedings.

# Consular Marriages and Marriages under Foreign Law (No. 2) Order 2014

SI 2014/3265

## PART 1

### Introductory

1.—(1) This Order may be cited as the Consular Marriages and Marriages under Foreign Law (No. 2) Order 2014 and comes into force on the day after the day on which it is made.

(2) In this Order—

"the Act" means the Marriage (Same Sex Couples) Act 2013;

"registration officer" has the same meaning as in paragraph 6 of Schedule 6 to the Act.

(3) Part 2 does not extend to Northern Ireland.

## PART 2

### Consular marriages

#### Countries or territories in which consular marriages may take place

2.—(1) The marriage of two people may, in accordance with the following provisions of the Order, take place in the presence of a registration officer in a country or territory referred to in paragraph (2), where the registration officer is satisfied that the conditions specified in paragraph 1(2) of Schedule 6 to the Act are met.

(2) A consular marriage may take place in those countries or territories outside the United Kingdom which have notified the Secretary of State in writing that there is no objection to such marriages taking place in that country or territory and which have not subsequently revoked that notice.

#### Relevant part of the United Kingdom

3. For the purposes of paragraph 1(2)(b) of Schedule 6 to the Act and this Order, the relevant part of the United Kingdom is the part jointly elected by the parties under article 4(4)(a).

#### Notice of intended marriage

4.—(1) Before any marriage can be solemnized under this Order, one of the parties to the proposed marriage must give notice to a registration officer of the parties' intention to marry.

(2) The notice of intention to marry must be given to the registration officer within whose consular district both of the parties have had their residence for the period of seven days ending on the day on which the notice is given.

(3) The notice of intention to marry must contain the following details of each of the parties to the proposed marriage—

(a) forenames;

(b) surname;

(c) nationality;

(d) date of birth;

(e) sex;

(f) address;

(g) marital condition;

(4) The notice of intention to marry must also contain the following details—

(a) the part of the United Kingdom, which must be either England and Wales or Scotland, which the parties have jointly elected as the relevant part of the United Kingdom for the purposes of the marriage; and

(b) the date on which the notice was given.

(5) The registration officer must retain every notice of intended marriage and must display a true copy of the notice, and the contact details of the person to whom any notice of objection to the proposed marriage should be sent, in a conspicuous place in the consular district of the registration officer for the period of 14 days ending on the day on which the solemnization of the marriage to which the notice relates may take place.

### Consent to marriage

5.—(1) Where either party to the proposed marriage is under the age of 18 and the relevant part of the United Kingdom is England and Wales then the same consent is required as would be required in respect of a marriage solemnized in England and Wales on the authority of a certificate issued by a superintendent registrar under Part 3 of the Marriage Act 1949.

(2) The Secretary of State may dispense with the requirement to obtain consent if satisfied that it cannot be obtained because of the absence, inaccessibility or disability of the person whose consent is so required.

(3) On a request in person of any person whose consent is required, the registration officer must produce the notice given under article 4(1).

(4) Such person may forbid the solemnization of the marriage referred to in the notice at any time before the marriage has been solemnized by writing the word "forbidden" on the notice, together with the person's name and address and capacity to forbid the marriage.

(5) If a person forbids the proposed marriage to which the notice relates in accordance with paragraph (4), the notice is void and the proposed marriage cannot be solemnized under that notice.

### Objection to marriage

6.—(1) Any person may enter an objection to a proposed marriage, including by electronic means, by giving notice of the objection in writing to the registration officer to whom the notice of the proposed marriage was given under article 4.

(2) An objection must be signed by the person making it, or on that person's behalf, and must include the person's name, address and ground of objection.

(3) An objection entered by electronic means need not contain the signature of the person making it but must contain a statement from that person that it originates from them.

(4) If an objection is entered in accordance with paragraphs (1) to (3) in respect of a proposed marriage, the registration officer must give notice in writing of the objection to the person who gave notice of the proposed marriage under article 4, and the marriage may not be solemnized until either the objection has been withdrawn by the person who made it, or the registration officer is satisfied that the objection should not obstruct the solemnization of the marriage.

(5) The registration officer must notify in writing the person who gave notice of the proposed marriage if any objection entered in respect of the proposed marriage under paragraph (1) is withdrawn.

(6) The registration officer must notify in writing the person who has entered the objection and the person who gave notice of the proposed marriage of any decision that the objection should not obstruct the solemnization of the marriage.

### Expiry of notice

7.—(1) A marriage cannot be solemnized on a day unless a notice under article 4(1) relating to that marriage has been given within the period of three months before that day.

(2) If an objection has been made under article 6, paragraph (1) is to have effect as if it prohibited

a marriage from being solemnized on a day which is after the end of the period of three months beginning with—

(a) where the objection is withdrawn, the day on which the registration officer gives notice of the withdrawal of the objection under article 6(5);

(b) where the registration officer decides that the objection should not obstruct the solemnization of the marriage, the day on which the registration officer gives notice of that decision under article 6(6).

### Oath before marriage

8. Before a marriage is solemnized under this Order, each of the parties entering into the marriage must appear before a registration officer and sign, in a book kept by a registration officer for the purpose, a declaration—

(a) that he or she believes—

    (i) where the relevant part of the United Kingdom is England and Wales, that there is no impediment to the marriage such that the marriage would be void under section 1 of the Marriage Act 1949 or other lawful hindrance;

    (ii) where the relevant part of the United Kingdom is Scotland, that there is no impediment to the marriage such that the marriage would be void under section 2 of the Marriage (Scotland) Act 1977 (marriage of related persons) or other lawful hindrance;

(b) that both of the parties have for a period of 21 days ending on the day on which the declaration is made had their usual residence within the consular district of the registration officer; and

(c) where either party is under the age of 18 and the relevant part of the United Kingdom is England and Wales—

    (i) that any consent to the marriage which is required in respect of that party has been obtained;

    (ii) that the necessity of obtaining any such consent in respect of that party has been dispensed with; or

    (iii) that the party is either a widow or a widower or surviving civil partner or that there is no person having authority to give any such consent.

### Solemnization of marriage

9.—(1) After the 14 day period in article 4(5) has elapsed, if no impediment to the marriage has been shown to the registration officer to whom the notice of the proposed marriage was given under article 4 and the conditions in paragraph 1(2) of the Act are fulfilled, the marriage may be solemnized.

(2) Every marriage must be solemnized in consular premises, with open doors, in the presence of two or more witnesses, none of whom may be the registration officer in whose presence the marriage is solemnized.

(3) Where it would otherwise not be stated or indicated in the course of the ceremony that neither of the parties knows of any lawful impediment to their marriage, then, in some part of the ceremony and in the presence of the registration officer and witnesses, each of the parties is to declare "I solemnly declare that I know not of any lawful impediment why I A.B. (or C.D.) may not be joined in matrimony to C.D. (or A.B.)."

(4) As an alternative to the declaration set out in paragraph (3) the persons contracting the marriage may make the requisite declaration either—

(a) by saying "I declare that I know of no legal reason why I (name) may not be joined in marriage to (name)"; or

(b) by replying "I am" to the question put to them successively "Are you (name) free lawfully to marry (name)?".

(5) Where it would otherwise not be stated by each of the parties in the course of the ceremony that they take the other person as husband or wife then, in some part of the ceremony and in the presence of the registration officer and witnesses, each of the parties is to say to the other "I call upon these

persons here present to witness that I A.B. (or C.D.) take thee C.D. (or A.B.) to be my lawful wedded wife (or husband)."

(6) As an alternative to the words of the contract set out in paragraph (5) the persons to be married may say to each other "I (name) take you (or thee) (name) to be my wedded wife (or husband)."

(7) A certificate of the Secretary of State as to any place being, or being part of, consular premises is conclusive.

### Register of marriages

10.—(1) A registration officer for the consular district, nominated by the Secretary of State for these purposes, must maintain a register and therein register the details provided in accordance with article 4(3) of every marriage solemnized in the consular district in accordance with this Order.

(2) The entry in the register of every marriage must be signed by the registration officer solemnizing the marriage, by both the parties married and by two witnesses to the marriage.

(3) Every nominated registration officer must, at such times as are determined by the Secretary of State, send to the Registrar General for England and Wales a copy of all the entries of marriages in the register kept by the registration officer entered since such details were last sent, and if there has been no such entry, confirmation of that fact.

(4) Where the Registrar General for England and Wales receives a copy of an entry of marriage in the register under paragraph (3) in relation to which the parties elected Scotland as the relevant part of the United Kingdom for the purposes of the marriage, the Registrar General for England and Wales must send a certified copy of the entry to the Registrar General for Scotland.

(5) Any person shall be entitled, upon payment of a fee, to obtain from the Registrar General for England and Wales or the Registrar General for Scotland, as the case may be, a certified copy of an entry of marriage in the register received under paragraph (3) or (4).

(6) The fee payable under paragraph (5) shall be the same fee as is for the time being charged by that Registrar General for the provision of a certified copy of, and any necessary search for, an entry in the records in his custody of marriages performed in England and Wales or Scotland, as the case may be.

### Conclusive proof of marriages

11. After a marriage has been solemnized in accordance with this Order it shall not be necessary to prove—

(a)  that the parties fulfilled any requirement of residence imposed;

(b)  that any necessary consent was obtained;

(c)  that the registration officer had authority to solemnize the marriage;

(d)  that the solemnization took place within consular premises;

and no evidence to prove the contrary shall be given in any legal proceedings touching on the validity of the marriage.

### Power to dispense with provisions

12.—(1) If the Secretary of State is satisfied there are good reasons why the requirement as to residence or notice in paragraph (2) or (as the case may be) (5) of article 4 cannot be complied with and is satisfied that the proposed marriage is not clandestine, the Secretary of State may authorise the registration officer to dispense with the requirement.

(2) The Secretary of State must notify the registration officer in writing of the decision to authorise dispensing with the requirement and provide a statement of reasons for the decision.

(3) If the Secretary of State authorises the registration officer to dispense with any requirements in accordance with paragraph (1), the registration officer must record the good reasons referred to in paragraph (1).

**Appeal against refusal by registration officer**

13.—(1) If a registration officer does not allow two people to marry in reliance on paragraph 2(1) of Schedule 6 to the Act, either person may appeal in writing to the Secretary of State within 28 days of the decision of the registration officer.

(2) In considering an appeal under paragraph (1), the Secretary of State's decision is final.

PART 3

## Marriage under Foreign Law

**Application for a certificate of no impediment to the superintendent registrar**

14.—(1) Any United Kingdom national (N) (if resident in England and Wales) who wishes to be married in a country or territory outside the United Kingdom which is not included in Schedule 3 to the British Nationality Act 1981 where the law of that country or territory requires N to obtain a certificate of no impediment to be issued by the domestic authorities in the United Kingdom may make an application for such a certificate to the superintendent registrar in England and Wales.

(2) An application under paragraph (1) must be made to the superintendent registrar of the registration district in which N is resident and has resided in for no less than the period immediately preceding the application as would be required in order to give notice of marriage in England and Wales.

(3) An application under paragraph (1) must be accompanied by—

(a) a notice, which must be dated and signed by N, containing the following details in relation to each of the parties to the proposed marriage—

    (i) forenames;

    (ii) surname;

    (iii) nationality;

    (iv) date of birth;

    (v) sex;

    (vi) address;

    (vii) marital condition;

    (viii) occupation;

(b) a declaration signed by N that—

    (i) N is resident and has resided in the registration district in which notice is given for no less than the same period immediately preceding the giving of the notice as would be required if the marriage were to be solemnized in England and Wales;

    (ii) if N, not being a widower or widow or surviving civil partner, is under the age of eighteen years, that the consent of the persons whose consent to the marriage is required by law has been obtained, or that there is no person having authority to give that consent, as the case may be;

    (iii) N believes there to be no impediment to the marriage such that the marriage would be void under section 1 of the Marriage Act 1949 or otherwise.

**Issuing a certificate of no impediment by the superintendent registrar**

15.—(1) The superintendent registrar must retain every notice and declaration made under article 15 and display a copy of the notice in a conspicuous place for the same period preceding the issuing of the certificate of no impediment as would be required if the marriage were to be solemnized in England and Wales.

(2) The superintendent registrar must, upon payment of a fee, issue a certificate of no impediment unless the superintendent registrar considers there is reason to believe there would be an impediment to the marriage if it were to take place in England and Wales.

(3) The fee payable under paragraph (2) shall be the same fee as is for the time being payable for an entry in the marriage notice book under section 27(6) of the Marriage Act 1949.

### Application for a consular certificate of no impediment

16.—(1) Any United Kingdom national (N) who wishes to enter into a marriage in a country or territory outside the United Kingdom which requires a consular certificate of no impediment to be issued may apply for a certificate of no impediment to the registration officer nominated by the Secretary of State for the purposes of this article in respect of the country or territory in which the marriage is to be registered.

(2) An application under paragraph (1) must be accompanied by—

(a)  a notice, which must be signed and dated by N, containing the following details in relation to each of parties to the proposed marriage—

    (i)  forenames;

    (ii)  surname;

    (iii)  nationality;

    (iv)  date of birth;

    (v)  sex;

    (vi)  address;

    (vii)  marital condition;

(b)  a declaration signed by N that—

    (i)  N has been resident in the country or territory in which the notice is being given for a period of at least three days immediately preceding the giving of the notice;

    (ii)  if N, not being a widower or widow or surviving civil partner, is under the age of eighteen years, that the consent of the persons whose consent to the marriage is required by law has been obtained, or that there is no person having authority to give that consent, as the case may be;

    (iii)  N believes there to be no impediment to the marriage such that the marriage would be void under section 1 of the Marriage Act 1949, section 2 of the Marriage (Scotland) Act 1977, article 18 of the Family Law (Miscellaneous Provisions) (Northern Ireland) Order 1984 or otherwise.

(3) The notice detailed in paragraph (2)(a) and the declaration detailed in paragraph (2)(b) must be signed in the presence of any person authorised to witness the signature in the country or territory in which the marriage is to be registered or the registration officer responsible for the consular district in which the marriage is to be registered.

(4) A person witnessing the signature under paragraph (3) must also sign and date the notice and declaration with a statement that they have witnessed the signature.

### Issuing a consular certificate of no impediment

17.—(1) The registration officer must retain every notice and declaration made under article 17 and must display a true copy of the notice in a conspicuous place in the consular district of the registration officer for a period of seven consecutive days preceding the issuing of a certificate of no impediment.

(2) A registration officer may request any further information from N which the registration officer considers to be relevant to the decision whether to issue a certificate of no impediment.

(3) Where an application is made in accordance with article 14, the registration officer must issue a certificate of no impediment unless the registration officer considers there is reason to believe that there would be an impediment to the marriage taking place if it were to take place in England and Wales, Scotland or Northern Ireland.

. . .

# Civil Jurisdiction and Judgments (Protection Measures) Regulations 2014

SI 2014/3298

1.—(1) These Regulations may be cited as the Civil Jurisdiction and Judgments (Protection Measures) Regulations 2014.

(2) An amendment made by these Regulations has the same extent as the enactment amended.

(3) Otherwise, these Regulations extend to England and Wales and to Northern Ireland.

(4) These Regulations come into force on 11th January 2015 . . .

## Interpretation

2. In these Regulations—

"incoming protection measure" means a protection measure that has been ordered in a Member State of the European Union other than the United Kingdom or Denmark;

"protection measure" has the meaning given by Article 3 of the Protection Measures Regulation;

"Protection Measures Regulation" means Regulation (EU) No 606/2013 of the European Parliament and of the Council of 12 June 2013 on mutual recognition of protection measures in civil matters.

## Jurisdiction in relation to incoming protection measures

3.—(1) The courts specified in paragraph (2) have jurisdiction for the purposes of—

(a) enforcement of an incoming protection measure under Article 4 of the Protection Measures Regulation;

(b) adjustment of a factual element of an incoming protection measure under Article 11 of the Protection Measures Regulation;

(c) refusal of recognition or enforcement of an incoming protection measure under Article 13 of the Protection Measures Regulation; and

(d) suspension or withdrawal of the effects of recognition or enforcement under Article 14(2) of the Protection Measures Regulation.

(2) The courts are—

(a) in England and Wales, the family court, the county court and the High Court . . .

. . .

## Enforcement of incoming protection measures

4. For the purposes of the enforcement of an incoming protection measure by a court specified by regulation 3(2) ("the enforcing court")—

(a) the incoming protection measure has the same force and effect,

(b) the enforcing court has the same powers, and

(c) proceedings for or with respect to enforcement may be taken,

as if the incoming protection measure were a protection measure ordered by the enforcing court.

# Civil Procedure Rules 1998

SI 1998/3132[1]


## PART 2 – APPLICATION AND INTERPRETATION OF THE RULES

*Interpretation*

**2.3**

(1) In these Rules—

> . . .

> 'claimant' means a person who makes a claim;

> . . .

> 'defendant' means a person against whom a claim is made;

> . . .

> 'jurisdiction' means, unless the context requires otherwise, England and Wales and any part of the territorial waters of the United Kingdom adjoining England and Wales;

. . .


## PART 6 – SERVICE OF DOCUMENTS

### I    SCOPE OF THIS PART AND INTERPRETATION

. . .

*Interpretation*

**6.2**

In this Part—

> . . .

(c)  'claim' includes petition and any application made before action or to commence proceedings and 'claim form', 'claimant' and 'defendant' are to be construed accordingly;

> . . .


### II   SERVICE OF THE CLAIM FORM IN THE JURISDICTION OR IN SPECIFIED CIRCUMSTANCES WITHIN THE EEA

*Methods of service*

**6.3**

(1) A claim form may (subject to Section IV of this Part and the rules in this Section relating to service out of the jurisdiction on solicitors, European Lawyers and parties) be served by any of the following methods—

(a)  personal service in accordance with rule 6.5;

(b)  first class post, document exchange or other service which provides for delivery on the next business day, in accordance with Practice Direction 6A;

---

[1] Version shown reflects 81st Update in the Civil Procedure (Amendment No 4) Rules 2015, SI 2015/1569. Amendments not marked.

(c)   leaving it at a place specified in rule 6.7, 6.8, 6.9 or 6.10;

(d)   fax or other means of electronic communication in accordance with Practice Direction 6A; or

(e)   any method authorised by the court under rule 6.15.

(2) A company may be served—

(a)   by any method permitted under this Part; or

(b)   by any of the methods of service permitted under the Companies Act 20062.

(3) A limited liability partnership may be served—

(a)   by any method permitted under this Part; or

(b)   by any of the methods of service permitted under the Companies Act 2006 as applied with modification by regulations made under the Limited Liability Partnerships Act 2000.

. . .

*Personal service*

**6.5**

(1) Where required by another Part, any other enactment, a practice direction or a court order, a claim form must be served personally.

(2) In other cases, a claim form may be served personally except—

(a)   where rule 6.7 applies; or

(b)   in any proceedings against the Crown.

(Part 54 contains provisions about judicial review claims and Part 66 contains provisions about Crown proceedings.)

(3) A claim form is served personally on—

(a)   an individual by leaving it with that individual;

(b)   a company or other corporation by leaving it with a person holding a senior position within the company or corporation; or

(c)   a partnership (where partners are being sued in the name of their firm) by leaving it with—

   (i)   a partner; or

   (ii)   a person who, at the time of service, has the control or management of the partnership business at its principal place of business.

(Practice Direction 6A sets out the meaning of 'senior position'.)

*Where to serve the claim form – general provisions*

**6.6**

(1) The claim form must be served within the jurisdiction except where rule 6.7(2), 6.7(3) or 6.11 applies or as provided by Section IV of this Part.

(2) The claimant must include in the claim form an address at which the defendant may be served. That address must include a full postcode or its equivalent in any EEA state (if applicable), unless the court orders otherwise.

(Paragraph 2.4 of Practice Direction 16 contains provisions about postcodes.)

(3) Paragraph (2) does not apply where an order made by the court under rule 6.15 (service by an alternative method or at an alternative place) specifies the place or method of service of the claim form.

. . .

**6.8**

Subject to rules 6.5(1) and 6.7 and the provisions of Section IV of this Part, and except where any other rule or practice direction makes different provision—

(a)   the defendant may be served with the claim form at an address at which the defendant resides or carries on business within the UK or any other EEA state and which the defendant has given for the purpose of being served with the proceedings; or

(b)   in any claim by a tenant against a landlord, the claim form may be served at an address given by the landlord under section 48 of the Landlord and Tenant Act 19875.

(For Production Centre Claims see paragraph 2.3(7A) of Practice Direction 7C; for Money Claims Online see paragraph 4(6) of Practice Direction 7E; and for Possession Claims Online see paragraph 5.1(4) of Practice Direction 55B.)

(For service out of the jurisdiction see rules 6.40 to 6.47.)

*Service of the claim form where the defendant does not give an address at which the defendant may be served*

**6.9**

(1)   This rule applies where—

(a)   rule 6.5(1) (personal service);

(b)   rule 6.7 (service of claim form on solicitor or European Lawyer); and

(c)   rule 6.8 (defendant gives address at which the defendant may be served), do not apply and the claimant does not wish to effect personal service under rule 6.5(2).

(2)   Subject to paragraphs (3) to (6), the claim form must be served on the defendant at the place shown in the following table.

(For service out of the jurisdiction see rules 6.40 to 6.47.)

| Nature of defendant to be served | Place of service |
| --- | --- |
| 1. Individual | Usual or last known residence. |
| 2. Individual being sued in the name of a business | Usual or last known residence of the individual; or principal or last known place of business. |
| 3. Individual being sued in the business name of a partnership | Usual or last known residence of the individual; or principal or last known place of business of the partnership. |
| 4. Limited liability partnership | Principal office of the partnership; or any place of business of the partnership within the jurisdiction which has a real connection with the claim. |
| 5. Corporation (other than a company) incorporated in England and Wales | Principal office of the corporation; or any place within the jurisdiction where the corporation carries on its activities and which has a real connection with the claim. |
| 6. Company registered in England and Wales | Principal office of the company; or any place of business of the company within the jurisdiction which has a real connection with the claim. |
| 7. Any other company or corporation | Any place within the jurisdiction where the corporation carries on its activities; or any place of business of the company within the jurisdiction. |

(3)   Where a claimant has reason to believe that the address of the defendant referred to in entries 1, 2 or 3 in the table in paragraph (2) is an address at which the defendant no longer resides or carries on business, the claimant must take reasonable steps to ascertain the address of the defendant's current residence or place of business ('current address').

(4)   Where, having taken the reasonable steps required by paragraph (3), the claimant—

(a)   ascertains the defendant's current address, the claim form must be served at that address; or

(b)   is unable to ascertain the defendant's current address, the claimant must consider whether there is—

(i)   an alternative place where; or

(ii)   an alternative method by which,

service may be effected.

(5) If, under paragraph (4)(b), there is such a place where or a method by which service may be effected, the claimant must make an application under rule 6.15.

(6) Where paragraph (3) applies, the claimant may serve on the defendant's usual or last known address in accordance with the table in paragraph (2) where the claimant—

(a)   cannot ascertain the defendant's current residence or place of business; and

(b)   cannot ascertain an alternative place or an alternative method under paragraph (4)(b).

. . .

*Service of the claim form by contractually agreed method*

**6.11**

(1) Where—

(a)   a contract contains a term providing that, in the event of a claim being started in relation to the contract, the claim form may be served by a method or at a place specified in the contract; and

(b)   a claim solely in respect of that contract is started,

the claim form may, subject to paragraph (2), be served on the defendant by the method or at the place specified in the contract.

(2) Where in accordance with the contract the claim form is to be served out of the jurisdiction, it may be served—

(a)   if permission to serve it out of the jurisdiction has been granted under rule 6.36; or

(b)   without permission under rule 6.32 or 6.33.

*Service of the claim form relating to a contract on an agent of a principal who is out of the jurisdiction*

**6.12**

(1) The court may, on application, permit a claim form relating to a contract to be served on the defendant's agent where—

(a)   the defendant is out of the jurisdiction;

(b)   the contract to which the claim relates was entered into within the jurisdiction with or through the defendant's agent; and

(c)   at the time of the application either the agent's authority has not been terminated or the agent is still in business relations with the defendant.

(2) An application under this rule—

(a)   must be supported by evidence setting out—

   (i)    details of the contract and that it was entered into within the jurisdiction or through an agent who is within the jurisdiction;

   (ii)   that the principal for whom the agent is acting was, at the time the contract was entered into and is at the time of the application, out of the jurisdiction; and

   (iii)  why service out of the jurisdiction cannot be effected; and

(b)   may be made without notice.

(3) An order under this rule must state the period within which the defendant must respond to the particulars of claim.

(4) Where the court makes an order under this rule—

(a)   a copy of the application notice and the order must be served with the claim form on the agent; and

(b) unless the court orders otherwise, the claimant must send to the defendant a copy of the application notice, the order and the claim form.

(5) This rule does not exclude the court's power under rule 6.15 (service by an alternative method or at an alternative place).

. . .

*Service of the claim form by an alternative method or at an alternative place*

**6.15**

(1) Where it appears to the court that there is a good reason to authorise service by a method or at a place not otherwise permitted by this Part, the court may make an order permitting service by an alternative method or at an alternative place.

(2) On an application under this rule, the court may order that steps already taken to bring the claim form to the attention of the defendant by an alternative method or at an alternative place is good service.

(3) An application for an order under this rule—

(a) must be supported by evidence; and

(b) may be made without notice.

(4) An order under this rule must specify—

(a) the method or place of service;

(b) the date on which the claim form is deemed served; and

(c) the period for—

  (i) filing an acknowledgment of service;

  (ii) filing an admission; or

  (iii) filing a defence.

*Power of court to dispense with service of the claim form*

**6.16**

(1) The court may dispense with service of a claim form in exceptional circumstances.

(2) An application for an order to dispense with service may be made at any time and—

(a) must be supported by evidence; and

(b) may be made without notice.

. . .

# IV SERVICE OF THE CLAIM FORM AND OTHER DOCUMENTS OUT OF THE JURISDICTION

*Scope of this Section*

**6.30**

This Section contains rules about—

(a) service of the claim form and other documents out of the jurisdiction;

(b) when the permission of the court is required and how to obtain that permission; and

(c) the procedure for service.

('Jurisdiction' is defined in rule 2.3(1).)

*Interpretation*

**6.31**

(1) For the purposes of this Section—

(a) 'the Hague Convention' means the Convention on the service abroad of judicial and extrajudicial documents in civil or commercial matters signed at the Hague on 15 November 1965[7];

(b) 'the 1982 Act' means the Civil Jurisdiction and Judgments Act 1982[8];

(c) 'Civil Procedure Convention' means the Brussels and Lugano Conventions (as defined in section 1(1) of the 1982 Act) and any other Convention (including the Hague Convention) entered into by the United Kingdom regarding service out of the jurisdiction;

(d) 'the Judgments Regulation' means Regulation (EU) No. 1215/2012 of the European Parliament and of the Council of 12 December 2012 on jurisdiction and the recognition and enforcement of judgments in civil and commercial matters (recast)[9], as amended from time to time and as applied pursuant to the Agreement made on 19 October 2005 between the European Community and the Kingdom of Denmark on jurisdiction and the recognition and enforcement of judgments in civil and commercial matters[10];

(For application of the recast Judgments Regulation to Denmark, see also the Official Journal of the European Union at OJ L79, 21.3.2013. p 4)

(e) 'the Service Regulation' means Regulation (EC) No. 1393/2007 of the European Parliament and of the Council of 13 November 2007 on the service in the Member States of judicial and extrajudicial documents in civil or commercial matters (service of documents)[11], and repealing Council Regulation (EC) No. 1348/2000[12], as amended from time to time and as applied by the Agreement made on 19 October 2005 between the European Community and the Kingdom of Denmark on the service of judicial and extrajudicial documents on civil and commercial matters[13];

(f) 'Commonwealth State' means a state listed in Schedule 3 to the British Nationality Act 1981[14];

(g) 'Contracting State' has the meaning given by section 1(3) of the 1982 Act;

(h) 'Convention territory' means the territory or territories of any Contracting State to which the Brussels or Lugano Conventions (as defined in section 1(1) of the 1982 Act) apply; and

(i) 'domicile' is to be determined—

    (i) in relation to a Convention territory, in accordance with sections 41 to 46 of the 1982 Act; and

    (ii) in relation to a Member State, in accordance with the Judgments Regulation and paragraphs 9 to 12 of Schedule 1 to the Civil Jurisdiction and Judgments Order 2001[15].

(j) 'the Lugano Convention' means the Convention on jurisdiction and the recognition and enforcement of judgments in civil and commercial matters, between the European Community and the Republic of Iceland, the Kingdom of Norway, the Swiss Confederation and the Kingdom of Denmark and signed by the European Community on 30th October 2007.

*Service of the claim form where the permission of the court is not required – Scotland and Northern Ireland*

**6.32**

(1) The claimant may serve the claim form on a defendant in Scotland or Northern Ireland where each claim made against the defendant to be served and included in the claim form is a claim which the court has power to determine under the 1982 Act and—

(a) no proceedings between the parties concerning the same claim are pending in the courts of any other part of the United Kingdom; and

(b)

    (i) the defendant is domiciled in the United Kingdom;

    (ii) the proceedings are within paragraph 11 of Schedule 4 to the 1982 Act; or

    (iii) the defendant is a party to an agreement conferring jurisdiction, within paragraph 12 of Schedule 4 to the 1982 Act.

(2) The claimant may serve the claim form on a defendant in Scotland or Northern Ireland where each claim made against the defendant to be served and included in the claim form is a claim which the court has power to determine under any enactment other than the 1982 Act notwithstanding that—

(a)   the person against whom the claim is made is not within the jurisdiction; or

(b)   the facts giving rise to the claim did not occur within the jurisdiction.

*Service of the claim form where the permission of the court is not required – out of the United Kingdom*

**6.33**

(1) The claimant may serve the claim form on the defendant out of the United Kingdom where each claim against the defendant to be served and included in the claim form is a claim which the court has power to determine under the 1982 Act or the Lugano Convention and—

(a)   no proceedings between the parties concerning the same claim are pending in the courts of any other part of the United Kingdom or any other Convention territory; and

(b)

  (i)    the defendant is domiciled in the United Kingdom or in any Convention territory;

  (ii)   the proceedings are within article 16 of Schedule 1 to the 1982 Act or article 22 of the Lugano Convention; or

  (iii)  the defendant is a party to an agreement conferring jurisdiction, within article 17 of Schedule 1 to the 1982 Act or article 23 of the Lugano Convention.

(2) The claimant may serve the claim form on a defendant out of the United Kingdom where each claim made against the defendant to be served and included in the claim form is a claim which the court has power to determine under the Judgments Regulation and—

(a)   subject to paragraph (2A) no proceedings between the parties concerning the same claim are pending in the courts of any other part of the United Kingdom or any other Member State; and

(b)

  (i)    the defendant is domiciled in the United Kingdom or in any Member State;

  (ii)   the defendant is not a consumer, but is a party to a consumer contract within article 17 of the Judgments Regulation;

  (iii)  the defendant is an employer and a party to a contract of employment within article 20 of the Judgments Regulation;

  (iv)  the proceedings are within article 24 of the Judgments Regulation; or

  (v)   the defendant is a party to an agreement conferring jurisdiction within article 25 of the Judgments Regulation.

(2A)   Paragraph (2)(a) does not apply if the jurisdiction conferred by the agreement referred to in paragraph (2)(b)(v) is exclusive.

(3) The claimant may serve the claim form on a defendant out of the United Kingdom where each claim made against the defendant to be served and included in the claim form is a claim which the court has power to determine other than under the 1982 Act or the Lugano Convention or the Judgments Regulation, notwithstanding that—

(a)   the person against whom the claim is made is not within the jurisdiction; or

(b)   the facts giving rise to the claim did not occur within the jurisdiction.

*Notice of statement of grounds where the permission of the court is not required for service*

**6.34**

(1) Where the claimant intends to serve a claim form on a defendant under rule 6.32 or 6.33, the claimant must—

(a) file with the claim form a notice containing a statement of the grounds on which the claimant is entitled to serve the claim form out of the jurisdiction; and

(b) serve a copy of that notice with the claim form.

(2) Where the claimant fails to file with the claim form a copy of the notice referred to in paragraph (1)(a), the claim form may only be served—

(a) once the claimant files the notice; or

(b) if the court gives permission.

*Period for responding to the claim form where permission was not required for service*

**6.35**

(1) This rule sets out the period for—

(a) filing an acknowledgment of service;

(b) filing an admission; or

(c) filing a defence,

where a claim form has been served out of the jurisdiction under rule 6.32 or 6.33.

(Part 10 contains rules about acknowledgments of service, Part 14 contains rules about admissions and Part 15 contains rules about defences.)

### *Service of the claim form on a defendant in Scotland or Northern Ireland*

(2) Where the claimant serves on a defendant in Scotland or Northern Ireland under rule 6.32, the period—

(a) for filing an acknowledgment of service or admission is 21 days after service of the particulars of claim; or

(b) for filing a defence is—

    (i) 21 days after service of the particulars of claim; or

    (ii) where the defendant files an acknowledgment of service, 35 days after service of the particulars of claim.

(Part 7 provides that particulars of claim must be contained in or served with the claim form or served separately on the defendant within 14 days after service of the claim form.)

### *Service of the claim form on a defendant in a Convention territory within Europe or a Member State*

(3) Where the claimant serves the claim form on a defendant in a Convention territory within Europe or a Member State under rule 6.33, the period—

(a) for filing an acknowledgment of service or admission, is 21 days after service of the particulars of claim; or

(b) for filing a defence is—

    (i) 21 days after service of the particulars of claim; or

    (ii) where the defendant files an acknowledgment of service, 35 days after service of the particulars of claim.

### *Service of the claim form on a defendant in a Convention territory outside Europe*

(4) Where the claimant serves the claim form on a defendant in a Convention territory outside Europe under rule 6.33, the period—

(a) for filing an acknowledgment of service or admission, is 31 days after service of the particulars of claim; or

(b) for filing a defence is—

    (i)   31 days after service of the particulars of claim; or

    (ii)  where the defendant files an acknowledgment of service, 45 days after service of the particulars of claim.

### Service on a defendant elsewhere

(5) Where the claimant serves the claim form under rule 6.33 in a country not referred to in paragraph (3) or (4), the period for responding to the claim form is set out in Practice Direction 6B.

### Service of the claim form where the permission of the court is required
**6.36**

In any proceedings to which rule 6.32 or 6.33 does not apply, the claimant may serve a claim form out of the jurisdiction with the permission of the court if any of the grounds set out in paragraph 3.1 of Practice Direction 6B apply.

### Application for permission to serve the claim form out of the jurisdiction
**6.37**

(1) An application for permission under rule 6.36 must set out—

(a)   which ground in paragraph 3.1 of Practice Direction 6B is relied on;

(b)   that the claimant believes that the claim has a reasonable prospect of success; and

(c)   the defendant's address or, if not known, in what place the defendant is, or is likely, to be found.

(2) Where the application is made in respect of a claim referred to in paragraph 3.1(3) of Practice Direction 6B, the application must also state the grounds on which the claimant believes that there is between the claimant and the defendant a real issue which it is reasonable for the court to try.

(3) The court will not give permission unless satisfied that England and Wales is the proper place in which to bring the claim.

(4) In particular, where—

(a)   the application is for permission to serve a claim form in Scotland or Northern Ireland; and

(b)   it appears to the court that the claimant may also be entitled to a remedy in Scotland or Northern Ireland, the court, in deciding whether to give permission, will—

    (i)   compare the cost and convenience of proceeding there or in the jurisdiction; and

    (ii)  (where relevant) have regard to the powers and jurisdiction of the Sheriff court in Scotland or the county courts or courts of summary jurisdiction in Northern Ireland.

(5) Where the court gives permission to serve a claim form out of the jurisdiction—

(a)   it will specify the periods within which the defendant may—

    (i)   file an acknowledgment of service;

    (ii)  file or serve an admission;

    (iii) file a defence; or

    (iv) file any other response or document required by a rule in another Part, any other enactment or a practice direction; and

(b)   it may—

    (i)   give directions about the method of service; and

    (ii)  give permission for other documents in the proceedings to be served out of the jurisdiction.

(The periods referred to in paragraphs (5)(a)(i), (ii) and (iii) are those specified in the Table in Practice Direction 6B.)

*Service of documents other than the claim form – permission*

**6.38**

(1) Unless paragraph (2) or (3) applies, where the permission of the court is required for the claimant to serve the claim form out of the jurisdiction, the claimant must obtain permission to serve any other document in the proceedings out of the jurisdiction.

(2) Where—

(a) the court gives permission for a claim form to be served on a defendant out of the jurisdiction; and

(b) the claim form states that particulars of claim are to follow,

the permission of the court is not required to serve the particulars of claim.

(3) The permission of the court is not required if a party has given an address for service in Scotland or Northern Ireland.

*Service of application notice on a non-party to the proceedings*

**6.39**

(1) Where an application notice is to be served out of the jurisdiction on a person who is not a party to the proceedings rules 6.35 and 6.37(5)(a)(i), (ii) and (iii) do not apply.

(2) Where an application is served out of the jurisdiction on a person who is not a party to the proceedings, that person may make an application to the court under Part 11 as if that person were a defendant, but rule 11(2) does not apply.

(Part 11 contains provisions about disputing the court's jurisdiction.)

*Methods of service – general provisions*

**6.40**

(1) This rule contains general provisions about the method of service of a claim form or other document on a party out of the jurisdiction.

**Where service is to be effected on a party in Scotland or Northern Ireland**

(2) Where a party serves a claim form or other document on a party in Scotland or Northern Ireland, it must be served by a method permitted by Section II (and references to 'jurisdiction' in that Section are modified accordingly) or Section III of this Part and rule 6.23(4) applies.

**Where service is to be effected on a party out of the United Kingdom**

(3) Where a party wishes to serve a claim form or other document on a party out of the United Kingdom, it may be served—

(a) by any method provided for by—

    (i) rule 6.41 (service in accordance with the Service Regulation);

    (ii) rule 6.42 (service through foreign governments, judicial authorities and British Consular authorities); or

    (iii) rule 6.44 (service of claim form or other document on a State);

(b) by any method permitted by a Civil Procedure Convention or Treaty; or

(c) by any other method permitted by the law of the country in which it is to be served.

(4) Nothing in paragraph (3) or in any court order authorises or requires any person to do anything which is contrary to the law of the country where the claim form or other document is to be served.

(The texts of the Civil Procedure Treaties which the United Kingdom has entered into may be found on the Foreign and Commonwealth Office website at http://www.fco.gov.uk/en/publications-and-documents/treaties/lists-treaties/bilateral-civil-procedure.)

*Service in accordance with the Service Regulation*

**6.41**

(1) This rule applies where a party wishes to serve the claim form or other document in accordance with the Service Regulation.

(2) The party must file—

(a)   the claim form or other document;

(b)   any translation; and

(c)   any other documents required by the Service Regulation.

(3) When a party files the documents referred to in paragraph (2), the court officer will forward the relevant documents to the Senior Master.

(4) Rule 6.47 does not apply to this rule.

(The Service Regulation is annexed to Practice Direction 6B.)

(Article 20(1) of the Service Regulation provides that the Regulation prevails over other provisions contained in any other agreement or arrangement concluded by Member States. The Regulation does not apply to service in EEA states that are not member states of the EU.)

*Service through foreign governments, judicial authorities and British Consular authorities*

**6.42**

(1) Where a party wishes to serve a claim form or any other document in any country which is a party to a Civil Procedure Convention or Treaty providing for service in that country, it may be served—

(a)   through the authority designated under the Hague Convention or any other Civil Procedure Convention or Treaty (where relevant) in respect of that country; or

(b)   if the law of that country permits—

  (i)   through the judicial authorities of that country, or

  (ii)   through a British Consular authority in that country (subject to any provisions of the applicable convention about the nationality of persons who may be served by such a method).

(2) Where a party wishes to serve a claim form or any other document in any country with respect to which there is no Civil Procedure Convention or Treaty providing for service in that country, the claim form or other document may be served, if the law of that country so permits—

(a)   through the government of that country, where that government is willing to serve it; or

(b)   through a British Consular authority in that country.

(3) Where a party wishes to serve the claim form or other document in—

(a)   any Commonwealth State which is not a party to the Hague Convention or is such a party but HM Government has not declared acceptance of its accession to the Convention;

(b)   the Isle of Man or the Channel Islands; or

(c)   any British overseas territory,

the methods of service permitted by paragraphs (1)(b) and (2) are not available and the party or the party's agent must effect service direct, unless Practice Direction 6B provides otherwise.

(A list of British overseas territories is reproduced in paragraph 5.2 of Practice Direction 6B.)

*Procedure where service is to be through foreign governments, judicial authorities and British Consular authorities*

**6.43**

(1) This rule applies where a party wishes to serve a claim form or any other document under rule 6.42(1) or 6.42(2).

(2) Where this rule applies, that party must file—

Rules of Procedure

(a) a request for service of the claim form or other document specifying one or more of the methods in rule 6.42(1) or 6.42(2);

(b) a copy of the claim form or other document;

(c) any other documents or copies of documents required by Practice Direction 6B; and

(d) any translation required under rule 6.45.

(3) Where a party files the documents specified in paragraph (2), the court officer will—

(a) seal the copy of the claim form or other document; and

(b) forward the documents to the Senior Master.

(4) The Senior Master will send documents forwarded under this rule—

(a) where the claim form or other document is being served through the authority designated under the Hague Convention or any other Civil Procedure Convention or Treaty, to that authority; or

(b) in any other case, to the Foreign and Commonwealth Office with a request that it arranges for the claim form or other document to be served.

(5) An official certificate which—

(a) states that the method requested under paragraph (2)(a) has been performed and the date of such performance;

(b) states, where more than one method is requested under paragraph (2)(a), which method was used; and

(c) is made by—

(i) a British Consular authority in the country where the method requested under paragraph (2)(a) was performed;

(ii) the government or judicial authorities in that country; or

(iii) the authority designated in respect of that country under the a Civil Procedure Convention or Treaty,

is evidence of the facts stated in the certificate.

(6) A document purporting to be an official certificate under paragraph (5) is to be treated as such a certificate, unless it is proved not to be.

*Service of claim form or other document on a State*

**6.44**

(1) This rule applies where a party wishes to serve the claim form or other document on a State.

(2) In this rule, 'State' has the meaning given by section 14 of the State Immunity Act 197816.

(3) The party must file in the Central Office of the Royal Courts of Justice—

(a) a request for service to be arranged by the Foreign and Commonwealth Office;

(b) a copy of the claim form or other document; and

(c) any translation required under rule 6.45.

(4) The Senior Master will send the documents filed under this rule to the Foreign and Commonwealth Office with a request that it arranges for them to be served.

(5) An official certificate by the Foreign and Commonwealth Office stating that a claim form or other document has been duly served on a specified date in accordance with a request made under this rule is evidence of that fact.

(6) A document purporting to be such a certificate is to be treated as such a certificate, unless it is proved not to be.

(7) Where—

(a) section 12(6) of the State Immunity Act 1978 applies; and

(b) the State has agreed to a method of service other than through the Foreign and Commonwealth Office,

the claim form or other document may be served either by the method agreed or in accordance with this rule.

(Section 12(6) of the State Immunity Act 1978 provides that section 12(1) enables the service of a claim form or other document in a manner to which the State has agreed.)

## Translation of claim form or other document

**6.45**

(1) Except where paragraph (4) or (5) applies, every copy of the claim form or other document filed under rule 6.43 (service through foreign governments, judicial authorities etc.) or 6.44 (service of claim form or other document on a State) must be accompanied by a translation of the claim form or other document.

(2) The translation must be—

(a) in the official language of the country in which it is to be served; or

(b) if there is more than one official language of that country, in any official language which is appropriate to the place in the country where the claim form or other document is to be served.

(3) Every translation filed under this rule must be accompanied by a statement by the person making it that it is a correct translation, and the statement must include that person's name, address and qualifications for making the translation.

(4) A party is not required to file a translation of a claim form or other document filed under rule 6.43 (service through foreign governments, judicial authorities etc.) where the claim form or other document is to be served—

(a) in a country of which English is an official language; or

(b) on a British citizen (within the meaning of the British Nationality Act 198117),

unless a Civil Procedure Convention or Treaty requires a translation.

(5) A party is not required to file a translation of a claim form or other document filed under rule 6.44 (service of claim form or other document on a State) where English is an official language of the State in which the claim form or other document is to be served.

(The Service Regulation contains provisions about the translation of documents.)

## Undertaking to be responsible for expenses

**6.46**

Every request for service filed under rule 6.43 (service through foreign governments, judicial authorities etc.) or rule 6.44 (service of claim form or other document on a State) must contain an undertaking by the person making the request—

(a) to be responsible for all expenses incurred by the Foreign and Commonwealth Office or foreign judicial authority; and

(b) to pay those expenses to the Foreign and Commonwealth Office or foreign judicial authority on being informed of the amount.

## Proof of service before obtaining judgment

**6.47**

Where

(a) a hearing is fixed when the claim form is issued;

(b) the claim form is served on a defendant out of the jurisdiction; and

(c) that defendant does not appear at the hearing,

the claimant may not obtain judgment against the defendant until the claimant files written evidence that the claim form has been duly served in accordance with this Part.

## V   SERVICE OF DOCUMENTS FROM FOREIGN COURTS OR TRIBUNALS

### Scope of this Section

**6.48**

This Section—

(a)  applies to the service in England and Wales of any document in connection with civil or commercial proceedings in a foreign court or tribunal; but

(b)  does not apply where the Service Regulation (which has the same meaning as in rule 6.31(e)) applies.

### Interpretation

**6.49**

In this Section—

(a)  'convention country' means a country in relation to which there is a Civil Procedure Convention (which has the same meaning as in rule 6.31(c));

(b)  'foreign court or tribunal' means a court or tribunal in a country outside of the United Kingdom; and

(c)  'process server' means—

    (i)   a process server appointed by the Lord Chancellor to serve documents to which this Section applies, or

    (ii)  the process server's agent.

### Request for service

**6.50**

The Senior Master will serve a document to which this Section applies upon receipt of—

(a)  a written request for service—

    (i)   where the foreign court or tribunal is in a convention country, from a consular or other authority of that country; or

    (ii)  from the Secretary of State for Foreign and Commonwealth Affairs, with a recommendation that service should be effected;

(b)  a translation of that request into English;

(c)  two copies of the document to be served; and

(d)  unless the foreign court or tribunal certifies that the person to be served understands the language of the document, two copies of a translation of it into English.

### Method of service

**6.51**

The Senior Master will determine the method of service.

### After service

**6.52**

(1)  Where service of a document has been effected by a process server, the process server must—

(a)  send to the Senior Master a copy of the document, and

    (i)   proof of service; or

(ii)   a statement why the document could not be served; and

(b)   if the Senior Master directs, specify the costs incurred in serving or attempting to serve the document.

(2) The Senior Master will send to the person who requested service—

(a)   a certificate, sealed with the seal of the Senior Courts for use out of the jurisdiction, stating—

(i)   when and how the document was served or the reason why it has not been served; and

(ii)   where appropriate, an amount certified by a costs judge to be the costs of serving or attempting to serve the document; and

(b)   a copy of the document.

## PRACTICE DIRECTION 6B – SERVICE OUT OF THE JURISDICTION

*Scope of this Practice Direction*

**1.1**

This Practice Direction supplements Section IV (service of the claim form and other documents out of the jurisdiction) of Part 6.

(Practice Direction 6A contains relevant provisions supplementing rule 6.40 in relation to the method of service on a party in Scotland or Northern Ireland.)

*Service out of the jurisdiction where permission of the court is not required*

**2.1**

Where rule 6.34 applies, the claimant must file practice form N510 when filing the claim form.

*Service out of the jurisdiction where permission is required*

**3.1**

The claimant may serve a claim form out of the jurisdiction with the permission of the court under rule 6.36 where—

### General grounds

(1)  A claim is made for a remedy against a person domiciled within the jurisdiction.

(2)  A claim is made for an injunction ordering the defendant to do or refrain from doing an act within the jurisdiction.

(3)  A claim is made against a person ('the defendant') on whom the claim form has been or will be served (otherwise than in reliance on this paragraph) and—

(a)   there is between the claimant and the defendant a real issue which it is reasonable for the court to try; and

(b)   the claimant wishes to serve the claim form on another person who is a necessary or proper party to that claim.

(4)  A claim is an additional claim under Part 20 and the person to be served is a necessary or proper party to the claim or additional claim.

(4A)  A claim is made against the defendant in reliance on one or more of paragraphs (2), (6) to (16), (19) or (21) and a further claim is made against the same defendant which arises out of the same or closely connected facts.

### Claims for interim remedies

(5)  A claim is made for an interim remedy under section 25(1) of the Civil Jurisdiction and Judgments Act 1982.

### Claims in relation to contracts

(6) A claim is made in respect of a contract where the contract—

(a) was made within the jurisdiction;

(b) was made by or through an agent trading or residing within the jurisdiction;

(c) is governed by English law; or

(d) contains a term to the effect that the court shall have jurisdiction to determine any claim in respect of the contract.

(7) A claim is made in respect of a breach of contract committed within the jurisdiction.

(8) A claim is made for a declaration that no contract exists where, if the contract was found to exist, it would comply with the conditions set out in paragraph (6).

### Claims in tort

(9) A claim is made in tort where

(a) damage was sustained, or will be sustained, within the jurisdiction; or

(b) damage which has been or will be sustained results from an act committed, or likely to be committed, within the jurisdiction.

### Enforcement

(10) A claim is made to enforce any judgment or arbitral award.

### Claims about property within the jurisdiction

(11) The subject matter of the claim relates wholly or principally to property within the jurisdiction, provided that nothing under this paragraph shall render justiciable the title to or the right to possession of immovable property outside England and Wales.

### Claims about trusts etc.

(12) A claim is made in respect of a trust which is created by the operation of a statute, or by a written instrument, or created orally and evidenced in writing, and which is governed by the law of England and Wales.

(12A) A claim is made in respect of a trust which is created by the operation of a statute, or by a written instrument, or created orally and evidenced in writing, and which provides that jurisdiction in respect of such a claim shall be conferred upon the courts of England and Wales.

(13) A claim is made for a remedy which might be obtained in proceedings for the administration of the estate of a person who died domiciled within the jurisdiction or whose estate includes assets within the jurisdiction.

(14) A probate claim or a claim for the rectification of a will.

(15) A claim is made against the defendant as constructive trustee, or as trustee of a resulting trust, where the claim arises out of acts committed or events occurring within the jurisdiction or relates to assets within the jurisdiction.

(16) A claim is made for restitution where:

(a) the defendant's alleged liability arises out of acts committed within the jurisdiction; or

(b) the enrichment is obtained within the jurisdiction; or

(c) the claim is governed by the law of England and Wales.

### Claims by HM Revenue and Customs

(17) A claim is made by the Commissioners for H.M. Revenue and Customs relating to duties or taxes against a defendant not domiciled in Scotland or Northern Ireland.

### Claim for costs order in favour of or against third parties

(18) A claim is made by a party to proceedings for an order that the court exercise its power under section 51 of the Senior Courts Act 1981 to make a costs order in favour of or against a person who is not a party to those proceedings.

(Rule 46.2 sets out the procedure where the court is considering whether to exercise its discretion to make a costs order in favour of or against a non-party.)

### Admiralty claims

(19) A claim is—

(a) in the nature of salvage and any part of the services took place within the jurisdiction; or

(b) to enforce a claim under section 153, 154,175 or 176A of the Merchant Shipping Act 1995.

### Claims under various enactments

(20) A claim is made—

(a) under an enactment which allows proceedings to be brought and those proceedings are not covered by any of the other grounds referred to in this paragraph; or

(b) under the Directive of the Council of the European Communities dated 15 March 1976 No. 76/308/EEC, where service is to be effected in a Member State of the European Union.

### Claims for breach of confidence and misuse of private information

(21) A claim is made for breach of confidence or misuse of private information where:

(a) detriment was suffered, or will be suffered, within the jurisdiction; or

(b) detriment which has been, or will be, suffered results from an act committed, or likely to be committed, within the jurisdiction.

### Documents to be filed under rule 6.43(2)(c)

**4.1**

A party must provide the following documents for each party to be served out of the jurisdiction—

(1) a copy of the particulars of claim if not already contained in or served with the claim form and any other relevant documents;

(2) a duplicate of the claim form, a duplicate of the particulars of claim (if not already contained in or served with the claim form), copies of any documents accompanying the claim form and copies of any other relevant documents;

(3) forms for responding to the claim; and

(4) any translation required under rule 6.45 in duplicate.

**4.2**

Some countries require legalisation of the document to be served and some require a formal letter of request which must be signed by the Senior Master. Any queries on this should be addressed to the Foreign Process Section (Room E02) at the Royal Courts of Justice.

### Service in a Commonwealth State or British overseas territory

**5.1**

The judicial authorities of certain Commonwealth States which are not a party to the Hague Convention require service to be in accordance with rule 6.42(1)(b)(i) and not 6.42(3). A list of such countries can be obtained from the Foreign Process Section (Room E02) at the Royal Courts of Justice.

**5.2**

The list of British overseas territories is contained in Schedule 6 to the British Nationality Act 1981. For ease of reference, these are—

(a) Anguilla;

(b) Bermuda;

(c) British Antarctic Territory;

(d) British Indian Ocean Territory;

(e) British Virgin Islands;

(f) Cayman Islands;

(g) Falkland Islands;

(h) Gibraltar;

(i) Montserrat;

(j) Pitcairn, Henderson, Ducie and Oeno;

(k) St. Helena and Dependencies;

(l) South Georgia and the South Sandwich Islands;

(m) Sovereign Base Areas of Akrotiri and Dhekelia; and

(n) Turks and Caicos Islands.

*Period for responding to a claim form*

**6.1**

Where rule 6.35(5) applies, the periods within which the defendant must—

(1) file an acknowledgment of service;

(2) file or serve an admission; or

(3) file a defence,

will be calculated in accordance with paragraph 6.3, 6.4 or 6.5.

**6.2**

Where the court grants permission to serve a claim form out of the jurisdiction the court will determine in accordance with paragraph 6.3, 6.4 or 6.5 the periods within which the defendant must—

(1) file an acknowledgment of service;

(2) file or serve an admission; or

(3) file a defence.

(Rule 6.37(5)(a) provides that when giving permission to serve a claim form out of the jurisdiction the court will specify the period within which the defendant may respond to the claim form.)

**6.3**

The period for filing an acknowledgment of service under Part 10 or for filing or serving an admission under Part 14 is the number of days listed in the Table after service of the particulars of claim.

**6.4**

The period for filing a defence under Part 15 is—

(1) the number of days listed in the Table after service of the particulars of claim; or

(2) where the defendant has filed an acknowledgment of service, the number of days listed in the Table plus an additional 14 days after the service of the particulars of claim.

**6.5**

Under the State Immunity Act 1978, where a State is served, the period permitted under paragraphs 6.3 and 6.4 for filing an acknowledgment of service or defence or for filing or serving an admission does not begin to run until 2 months after the date on which the State is served.

**6.6**

Where particulars of claim are served out of the jurisdiction any statement as to the period for responding to the claim contained in any of the forms required by rule 7.8 to accompany the particulars of claim must specify the period prescribed under rule 6.35 or by the order permitting service out of the jurisdiction under rule 6.37(5).

*Period for responding to an application notice*

**7.1**

Where an application notice is served out of the jurisdiction, the period for responding is 7 days less than the number of days listed in the Table.

*Further information*

**7.2**

Further information concerning service out of the jurisdiction can be obtained from the Foreign Process Section, Room E02, Royal Courts of Justice, Strand, London WC2A 2LL (telephone 020 7947 6691).

*[Table omitted]*

## PART 11 – DISPUTING THE COURT'S JURISDICTION

*Procedure for disputing the court's jurisdiction*

**11**

(1) A defendant who wishes to—

(a)   dispute the court's jurisdiction to try the claim; or

(b)   argue that the court should not exercise its jurisdiction

may apply to the court for an order declaring that it has no such jurisdiction or should not exercise any jurisdiction which it may have.

(2) A defendant who wishes to make such an application must first file an acknowledgment of service in accordance with Part 10.

(3) A defendant who files an acknowledgment of service does not, by doing so, lose any right that he may have to dispute the court's jurisdiction.

(4) An application under this rule must—

(a)   be made within 14 days after filing an acknowledgment of service; and

(b)   be supported by evidence.

(5) If the defendant—

(a)   files an acknowledgment of service; and

(b)   does not make such an application within the period specified in paragraph (4),

he is to be treated as having accepted that the court has jurisdiction to try the claim.

(6) An order containing a declaration that the court has no jurisdiction or will not exercise its jurisdiction may also make further provision including—

(a)   setting aside the claim form;

(b)   setting aside service of the claim form;

(c)   discharging any order made before the claim was commenced or before the claim form was served; and

(d)   staying the proceedings.

(7) If on an application under this rule the court does not make a declaration—

(a)   the acknowledgment of service shall cease to have effect;

Rules of Procedure

(b) the defendant may file a further acknowledgment of service within 14 days or such other period as the court may direct; and

(c) the court shall give directions as to the filing and service of the defence in a claim under Part 7 or the filing of evidence in a claim under Part 8 in the event that a further acknowledgment of service is filed.

(8) If the defendant files a further acknowledgment of service in accordance with paragraph (7)(b) he shall be treated as having accepted that the court has jurisdiction to try the claim.

(9) If a defendant makes an application under this rule, he must file and serve his written evidence in support with the application notice, but he need not before the hearing of the application file—

(a) in a Part 7 claim, a defence; or

(b) in a Part 8 claim, any other written evidence.

. . .

## PART 34 – WITNESSES, DEPOSITIONS AND EVIDENCE FOR FOREIGN COURTS

### I   WITNESSES AND DEPOSITIONS

*Where a person to be examined is out of the jurisdiction – letter of request*
34.13

(1) This rule applies where a party wishes to take a deposition from a person who is—

(a) out of the jurisdiction; and

(b) not in a Regulation State within the meaning of Section III of this Part.

(1A) The High Court may order the issue of a letter of request to the judicial authorities of the country in which the proposed deponent is.

(2) A letter of request is a request to a judicial authority to take the evidence of that person, or arrange for it to be taken.

(3) The High Court may make an order under this rule in relation to county court proceedings.

(4) If the government of a country allows a person appointed by the High Court to examine a person in that country, the High Court may make an order appointing a special examiner for that purpose.

(5) A person may be examined under this rule on oath or affirmation or in accordance with any procedure permitted in the country in which the examination is to take place.

(6) If the High Court makes an order for the issue of a letter of request, the party who sought the order must file—

(a) the following documents and, except where paragraph (7) applies, a translation of them—

(i) a draft letter of request;

(ii) a statement of the issues relevant to the proceedings;

(iii) a list of questions or the subject matter of questions to be put to the person to be examined; and

(b) an undertaking to be responsible for the Secretary of State's expenses.

(7) There is no need to file a translation if—

(a) English is one of the official languages of the country where the examination is to take place; or

(b) a practice direction has specified that country as a country where no translation is necessary.

. . .

## II EVIDENCE FOR FOREIGN COURTS

*Scope and interpretation*

**34.16**

(1) This Section applies to an application for an order under the 1975 Act for evidence to be obtained, other than an application made as a result of a request by a court in another Regulation State.

(2) In this Section—

(a) 'the 1975 Act' means the Evidence (Proceedings in Other Jurisdictions) Act 1975; and

(b) 'Regulation State' has the same meaning as in Section III of this Part.

Application for order

**34.17**

An application for an order under the 1975 Act for evidence to be obtained—

(a) must be—

    (i) made to the High Court;

    (ii) supported by written evidence; and

    (iii) accompanied by the request as a result of which the application is made, and where appropriate, a translation of the request into English; and

(b) may be made without notice.

*Examination*

**34.18**

(1) The court may order an examination to be taken before—

(a) any fit and proper person nominated by the person applying for the order;

(b) an examiner of the court; or

(c) any other person whom the court considers suitable.

(2) Unless the court orders otherwise—

(a) the examination will be taken as provided by rule 34.9; and

(b) rule 34.10 applies.

(3) The court may make an order under rule 34.14 for payment of the fees and expenses of the examination.

*Dealing with deposition*

**34.19**

(1) The examiner must send the deposition of the witness to the Senior Master unless the court orders otherwise.

(2) The Senior Master will—

(a) give a certificate sealed with the seal of the Senior Courts for use out of the jurisdiction identifying the following documents—

    (i) the request;

    (ii) the order of the court for examination; and

    (iii) the deposition of the witness; and

(b) send the certificate and the documents referred to in paragraph (a) to—

    (i) the Secretary of State; or

    (ii) where the request was sent to the Senior Master by another person in accordance with a Civil Procedure Convention, to that other person, for transmission to the court or tribunal requesting the examination.

### Claim to privilege

**34.20**

(1) This rule applies where—

(a) a witness claims to be exempt from giving evidence on the ground specified in section 3(1)(b) of the 1975 Act; and

(b) That claim is not supported or conceded as referred to in section 3(2) of that Act.

(2) The examiner may require the witness to give the evidence which he claims to be exempt from giving.

(3) Where the examiner does not require the witness to give that evidence, the court may order the witness to do so.

(4) An application for an order under paragraph (3) may be made by the person who obtained the order under section 2 of the 1975 Act.

(5) Where such evidence is taken—

(a) it must be contained in a document separate from the remainder of the deposition;

(b) the examiner will send to the Senior Master—

    (i) the deposition; and

    (ii) a signed statement setting out the claim to be exempt and the ground on which it was made;

(6) On receipt of the statement referred to in paragraph (5)(b)(ii), the Senior Master will—

(a) retain the document containing the part of the witness's evidence to which the claim to be exempt relates; and

(b) send the statement and a request to determine that claim to the foreign court or tribunal together with the documents referred to in rule 34.17.

(7) The Senior Master will—

(a) if the claim to be exempt is rejected by the foreign court or tribunal, send the document referred to in paragraph (5)(a) to that court or tribunal;

(b) if the claim is upheld, send the document to the witness; and

(c) in either case, notify the witness and person who obtained the order under section 2 of the foreign court or tribunal's decision.

### Order under 1975 Act as applied by Patents Act 1977

**34.21**

Where an order is made for the examination of witnesses under section 1 of the 1975 Act as applied by section 92 of the Patents Act 1977 the court may permit an officer of the European Patent Office to—

(a) attend the examination and examine the witnesses; or

(b) request the court or the examiner before whom the examination takes place to put specified questions to them.

### III TAKING OF EVIDENCE – MEMBER STATES OF THE EUROPEAN UNION

### Interpretation

**34.22**

In this Section—

(a) 'designated court' has the meaning given in Practice Direction 34A;

(b) 'Regulation State' has the same meaning as 'Member State' in the Taking of Evidence Regulation, that is all Member States except Denmark;

(c) 'the Taking of Evidence Regulation' means Council Regulation (EC) No. 1206/2001 of 28 May 2001 on co-operation between the courts of the Member States in the taking of evidence in civil and commercial matters.

### *Where a person to be examined is in another Regulation State*

**34.23**

(1) Subject to rule 34.13A, this rule applies where a party wishes to take a deposition from a person who is in another Regulation State–

(a)   outside the jurisdiction; and

(b)   in a Regulation State.

(2) The court may order the issue of a request to a designated court ('the requested court') in the Regulation State in which the proposed deponent is.

(3) If the court makes an order for the issue of a request, the party who sought the order must file—

(a)   a draft Form A as set out in the annex to the Taking of Evidence Regulation (request for the taking of evidence);

(b)   except where paragraph (4) applies, a translation of the form;

(c)   an undertaking to be responsible for costs sought by the requested court in relation to—

  (i)   fees paid to experts and interpreters; and

  (ii)   where requested by that party, the use of special procedures or communications technology; and

(d)   an undertaking to be responsible for the court's expenses.

(4) There is no need to file a translation if—

(a)   English is one of the official languages of the Regulation State where the examination is to take place; or

(b)   the Regulation State has indicated, in accordance with the Taking of Evidence Regulation, that English is a language which it will accept.

(5) Where article 17 of the Taking of Evidence Regulation (direct taking of evidence by the requested court) allows evidence to be taken directly in another Regulation State, the court may make an order for the submission of a request in accordance with that article.

(6) If the court makes an order for the submission of a request under paragraph (5), the party who sought the order must file—

(a)   a draft Form I as set out in the annex to the Taking of Evidence Regulation (request for direct taking of evidence);

(b)   except where paragraph (4) applies, a translation of the form; and

(c)   an undertaking to be responsible for the court's expenses.

### *Evidence for courts of other Regulation States*

**34.24**

(1) This rule applies where a court in another Regulation State ('the requesting court') issues a request for evidence to be taken from a person who is in the jurisdiction.

(2) An application for an order for evidence to be taken—

(a)   must be made to a designated court;

(b)   must be accompanied by—

  (i)   the form of request for the taking of evidence as a result of which the application is made; and

  (ii)   where appropriate, a translation of the form of request; and

(c)   may be made without notice.

(3) Rule 34.18(1) and (2) apply.

(4) The examiner must send—

(a) the deposition to the court for transmission to the requesting court; and

(b) a copy of the deposition to the person who obtained the order for evidence to be taken.

## PRACTICE DIRECTION 34A – DEPOSITIONS AND COURT ATTENDANCE BY WITNESSES

DEPOSITIONS

. . .

*Depositions to be taken abroad for use as evidence in proceedings before courts in England and Wales (where the Taking of Evidence Regulation does not apply)*

**5.1**

Where a party wishes to take a deposition from a person outside the jurisdiction, the High Court may order the issue of a letter of request to the judicial authorities of the country in which the proposed deponent is18.

**5.2**

An application for an order referred to in paragraph 5.1 should be made by application notice in accordance with Part 23.

**5.3**

The documents which a party applying for an order for the issue of a letter of request must file with his application notice are set out in rule 34.13(6). They are as follows:

(1) a draft letter of request in the form set out in Annex A to this practice direction,

(2) a statement of the issues relevant to the proceedings,

(3) a list of questions or the subject matter of questions to be put to the proposed deponent,

(4) a translation of the documents in (1), (2) and (3) above, unless the proposed deponent is in a country of which English is an official language, and

(5) an undertaking to be responsible for the expenses of the Secretary of State.

In addition to the documents listed above the party applying for the order must file a draft order.

**5.4**

The above documents should be filed with the Masters' Secretary in Room E214, Royal Courts of Justice, Strand, London WC2A 2LL.

**5.5**

The application will be dealt with by the Senior Master of the Queen's Bench Division of the High Court who will, if appropriate, sign the letter of request.

**5.6**

Attention is drawn to the provisions of rule 23.10 (application to vary or discharge an order made without notice).

**5.7**

If parties are in doubt as to whether a translation under paragraph 5.3(4) above is required, they should seek guidance from the Foreign Process Section of the Masters' Secretary's Department.

**5.8**

A special examiner appointed under rule 34.13(4) may be the British Consul or the Consul-General or his deputy in the country where the evidence is to be taken if:

(1)   there is in respect of that country a Civil Procedure Convention providing for the taking of evidence in that country for the assistance of proceedings in the High Court or other court in this country, or

(2)   with the consent of the Secretary of State.

**5.9**

The provisions of paragraphs 4.1 to 4.12 above apply to the depositions referred to in this paragraph.

Depositions to be taken in England and Wales for use as evidence in proceedings before courts abroad pursuant to letters of request (where the Taking of Evidence Regulation does not apply)

**6.1**

Section II of Part 34 relating to obtaining evidence for foreign courts applies to letters of request and should be read in conjunction with this part of the practice direction.

**6.2**

The Evidence (Proceedings in Other Jurisdictions) Act 1975 applies to these depositions.

**6.3**

The written evidence supporting an application under rule 34.17 (which should be made by application notice – see Part 23) must include or exhibit—

(1)   a statement of the issues relevant to the proceedings;

(2)   a list of questions or the subject matter of questions to be put to the proposed deponent;

(3)   a draft order; and

(4)   a translation of the documents in (1) and (2) into English, if necessary.

**6.4**

(1)   The Senior Master will send to the Treasury Solicitor any request—

(a)   forwarded by the Secretary of State with a recommendation that effect should be given to the request without requiring an application to be made; or

(b)   received by him in pursuance of a Civil Procedure Convention providing for the taking of evidence of any person in England and Wales to assist a court or tribunal in a foreign country where no person is named in the document as the applicant.

(2)   In relation to such a request, the Treasury Solicitor may, with the consent of the Treasury—

(a)   apply for an order under the 1975 Act; and

(b)   take such other steps as are necessary to give effect to the request.

**6.5**

The order for the deponent to attend and be examined together with the evidence upon which the order was made must be served on the deponent.

**6.6**

Attention is drawn to the provisions of rule 23.10 (application to vary or discharge an order made without notice).

6.7

Arrangements for the examination to take place at a specified time and place before an examiner of the court or such other person as the court may appoint shall be made by the applicant for the order and approved by the Senior Master.

6.8

The provisions of paragraph 4.2 to 4.12 apply to the depositions referred to in this paragraph, except that the examiner must send the deposition to the Senior Master.

(For further information about evidence see Part 32 and Practice Direction 32.)

## TAKING OF EVIDENCE BETWEEN EU MEMBER STATES

### Taking of Evidence Regulation

7.1

Where evidence is to be taken—

(a) from a person in another Member State of the European Union for use as evidence in proceedings before courts in England and Wales; or

(b) from a person in England and Wales for use as evidence in proceedings before a court in another Member State,

Council Regulation (EC) No 1206/2001 of 28 May 2001 on co-operation between the courts of the Member States in the taking of evidence in civil or commercial matters ('the Taking of Evidence Regulation') applies.

7.2

The Taking of Evidence Regulation is annexed to this practice direction as Annex B.

7.3

The Taking of Evidence Regulation does not apply to Denmark. In relation to Denmark, therefore, rule 34.13 and Section II of Part 34 will continue to apply.

(Article 21(1) of the Taking of Evidence Regulation provides that the Regulation prevails over other provisions contained in bilateral or multilateral agreements or arrangements concluded by the Member States and in particular the Hague Convention of 1 March 1954 on Civil Procedure and the Hague Convention of 18 March 1970 on the Taking of Evidence Abroad in Civil or Commercial Matters)

Originally published in the official languages of the European Community in the Official Journal of the European Communities by the Office for Official Publications of the European Communities.

### Meaning of 'designated court'

8.1

In accordance with the Taking of Evidence Regulation, each Regulation State has prepared a list of courts competent to take evidence in accordance with the Regulation indicating the territorial and, where appropriate, special jurisdiction of those courts.

8.2

Where Part 34, Section III refers to a 'designated court' in relation to another Regulation State, the reference is to the court, referred to in the list of competent courts of that State, which is appropriate to the application in hand.

**8.3**

Where the reference is to the 'designated court' in England and Wales, the reference is to the appropriate competent court in the jurisdiction. The designated courts for England and Wales are listed in Annex C to this practice direction.

*Central Body*

**9.1**

The Taking of Evidence Regulation stipulates that each Regulation State must nominate a Central Body responsible for—

(a)   supplying information to courts;

(b)   seeking solutions to any difficulties which may arise in respect of a request; and

(c)   forwarding, in exceptional cases, at the request of a requesting court, a request to the competent court.

**9.2**

The United Kingdom has nominated the Senior Master, Queen's Bench Division, to be the Central Body for England and Wales.

**9.3**

The Senior Master, as Central Body, has been designated responsible for taking decisions on requests pursuant to Article 17 of the Regulation. Article 17 allows a court to submit a request to the Central Body or a designated competent authority in another Regulation State to take evidence directly in that State.

*Evidence to be taken in another Regulation State for use in England and Wales*

**10.1**

Where a person wishes to take a deposition from a person in another Regulation State, the court where the proceedings are taking place may order the issue of a request to the designated court in the Regulation State ( Rule 34.23(2)). The form of request is prescribed as Form A in the Taking of Evidence Regulation.

**10.2**

An application to the court for an order under rule 34.23(2) should be made by application notice in accordance with Part 23.

**10.3**

Rule 34.23(3) provides that the party applying for the order must file a draft form of request in the prescribed form. Where completion of the form requires attachments or documents to accompany the form, these must also be filed.

**10.4**

If the court grants an order under rule 34.23 (2), it will send the form of request directly to the designated court.

**10.5**

Where the taking of evidence requires the use of an expert, the designated court may require a deposit in advance towards the costs of that expert. The party who obtained the order is responsible for the payment of any such deposit which should be deposited with the court for onward transmission. Under the provisions of the Taking of Evidence Regulation, the designated court is not required to execute the request until such payment is received.

10.6

Article 17 permits the court where proceedings are taking place to take evidence directly from a deponent in another Regulation State if the conditions of the article are satisfied. Direct taking of evidence can only take place if evidence is given voluntarily without the need for coercive measures. Rule 34.23(5) provides for the court to make an order for the submission of a request to take evidence directly. The form of request is Form I annexed to the Taking of Evidence Regulation and rule 34.23(6) makes provision for a draft of this form to be filed by the party seeking the order. An application for an order under rule 34.23(5) should be by application notice in accordance with Part 23.

10.7

Attention is drawn to the provisions of rule 23.10 (application to vary or discharge an order made without notice).

*Evidence to be taken in England and Wales for use in another Regulation State*

11.1

Where a designated court in England and Wales receives a request to take evidence from a court in a Regulation State, the court will send the request to the Treasury Solicitor.

11.2

On receipt of the request, the Treasury Solicitor may, with the consent of the Treasury, apply for an order under rule 34.24.

11.3

An application to the court for an order must be accompanied by the Form of request to take evidence and any accompanying documents, translated if required under paragraph 11.4.

11.4

The United Kingdom has indicated that, in addition to English, it will accept French as a language in which documents may be submitted. Where the form or request and any accompanying documents are received in French they will be translated into English by the Treasury Solicitor.

11.5

The order for the deponent to attend and be examined together with the evidence on which the order was made must be served on the deponent.

11.6

Arrangements for the examination to take place at a specified time and place shall be made by the Treasury Solicitor and approved by the court.

11.7

The court shall send details of the arrangements for the examination to such of

(a)   the parties and, if any, their representatives; or

(b)   the representatives of the foreign court,

who have indicated, in accordance with the Taking of Evidence Regulation, that they wish to be present at the examination.

11.8

The provisions of paragraph 4.3 to 4.12 apply to the depositions referred to in this paragraph.

**Annex A Draft Letter of Request (where the Taking of Evidence Regulation does not apply)**

To the Competent Judicial Authority of

in the

of

I [name] Senior Master of the Queen's Bench Division of the Senior Courts of England and Wales respectfully request the assistance of your court with regard to the following matters.

1

A claim is now pending in the

Division of the High Court of Justice in England and Wales entitled as follows [set out full title and claim number] in which [name] of [address] is the claimant and [name] of [address] is the defendant.

2

The names and addresses of the representatives or agents of [set out names and addresses of representatives of the parties].

3

The claim by the claimant is for:-

(a)  [set out the nature of the claim]

(b)  [the relief sought, and]

(c)  [a summary of the facts.]

4

It is necessary for the purposes of justice and for the due determination of the matters in dispute between the parties that you cause the following witnesses, who are resident within your jurisdiction, to be examined. The names and addresses of the witnesses are as follows:

5

The witnesses should be examined on oath or if that is not possible within your laws or is impossible of performance by reason of the internal practice and procedure of your court or by reason of practical difficulties, they should be examined in accordance with whatever procedure your laws provide for in these matters.

6

Either/

The witnesses should be examined in accordance with the list of questions annexed hereto.

Or/

The witnesses should be examined regarding [set out full details of evidence sought]

N.B. Where the witness is required to produce documents, these should be clearly identified.

7

I would ask that you cause me, or the agents of the parties (if appointed), to be informed of the date and place where the examination is to take place.

8

Finally, I request that you will cause the evidence of the said witnesses to be reduced into writing and all documents produced on such examinations to be duly marked for identification and that you will further be pleased to authenticate such examinations by the seal of your court or in such other way as is in accordance with your procedure and return the written evidence and documents produced to me addressed as follows:

Senior Master of the Queen's Bench Division
Royal Courts of Justice
Strand

London WC2A 2LL

England

[*Annexes B–C omitted*]

## PART 74 – ENFORCEMENT OF JUDGMENTS IN DIFFERENT JURISDICTIONS

*Scope of this Part and interpretation*

**74.1**

(1) Section I of this Part applies to the enforcement in England and Wales of judgments of foreign courts.

(2) Section II applies to the enforcement in foreign countries of judgments of the High Court and of the County Court.

(3) Section III applies to the enforcement of United Kingdom judgments in other parts of the United Kingdom.

(4) Section IV applies to the enforcement in England and Wales of European Community judgments and Euratom inspection orders.

(4A) Section V applies to—

(a) the certification of judgments and court settlements in England and Wales as European Enforcement Orders; and

(b) the enforcement in England and Wales of judgments, court settlements and authentic instruments certified as European Enforcement Orders by other Member States.

(4B) Section VI applies to—

(a) the certification in England and Wales of outgoing protection measures; and

(b) the enforcement in England and Wales of certified protection measures from Member States of the European Union other than the United Kingdom or Denmark.

(5) In this Part—

(a) 'the 1920 Act' means the Administration of Justice Act 1920;

(b) 'the 1933 Act' means the Foreign Judgments (Reciprocal Enforcement) Act 1933;

(c) 'the 1982 Act' means the Civil Jurisdiction and Judgments Act 1982;

(d) 'the Judgments Regulation' means Regulation (EU) No. 1215/2012 of the European Parliament and of the Council of 12 December 2012 on jurisdiction and the recognition and enforcement of judgments in civil and commercial matters (recast), as amended from time to time and as applied pursuant to the Agreement made on 19 October 2005 between the European Community and the Kingdom of Denmark on jurisdiction and the recognition and enforcement of judgments in civil and commercial matters;

(For application of the recast Judgments Regulation to Denmark, see also the Official Journal of the European Union at OJ L79, 21.3.2013. p4)

(e) 'the EEO Regulation' means Council Regulation (EC) No 805/2004 creating a European Enforcement Order for uncontested claims;

(f) 'the Lugano Convention' means the Convention on jurisdiction and the recognition and enforcement of judgments in civil and commercial matters, between the European Community and the Republic of Iceland, the Kingdom of Norway, the Swiss Confederation and the Kingdom of Denmark and signed by the European Community on 30th October 2007.

# I ENFORCEMENT IN ENGLAND AND WALES OF JUDGMENTS OF FOREIGN COURTS

*Interpretation*

**74.2**

(1) In this Section—

(a) 'Contracting State' has the meaning given in section 1(3) of the 1982 Act;

(b) 'Regulation State' means a Member State;

(c) 'judgment' means, subject to any other enactment, any judgment given by a foreign court or tribunal, whatever the judgment may be called, and includes

  (i) a decree;

  (ii) an order;

  (iii) a decision;

  (iv) a writ of execution or a writ of control; and

  (v) the determination of costs by an officer of the court;

(d) 'State of origin', in relation to any judgment, means the State in which that judgment was given; and

(e) 'writ of control' is to be construed in accordance with section 62(4) of the Tribunals, Courts and Enforcement Act 2007;

(f) 'writ of execution' includes—

  (i) a writ of possession;

  (ii) a writ of delivery;

  (iii) a writ of sequestration;

  (iv) a writ of fieri facias de bonis ecclesiasticis,

and any further writ in favour of any such writs, but does not include a writ of control.

(2) For the purposes of this Section, 'domicile' is to be determined—

(a) in an application under the 1982 Act or the Lugano Convention, in accordance with sections 41 to 46 that Act;

(b) in an application under the Judgments Regulation, in accordance with paragraphs 9 to 12 of Schedule 1 to the Civil Jurisdiction and Judgments Order 2001.

*Applications for registration*

**74.3**

(1) This Section provides rules about applications under—

(a) section 9 of the 1920 Act, in respect of judgments to which Part II of that Act applies;

(b) section 2 of the 1933 Act, in respect of judgments to which Part I of that Act applies;

(c) section 4 of the 1982 Act; and

(d) the Lugano Convention,

for the registration of foreign judgments for enforcement in England and Wales.

(2) Applications—

(a) must be made to the High Court; and

(b) may be made without notice.

*Enforcement under the Judgments Regulation*

**74.3A**

(1) This Section also provides rules about—

(a) the enforcement of foreign judgments in England and Wales under the Judgments Regulation; and

(b) applications for the refusal of recognition and enforcement under the Judgments Regulation.

*Evidence in support*

**74.4**

(1) An application for registration of a judgment under the 1920, 1933 or 1982 Act must be supported by written evidence exhibiting—

(a) the judgment or a verified or certified or otherwise authenticated copy of it; and

(b) where the judgment is not in English, a translation of it into English—

    (i) certified by a notary public or other qualified person; or

    (ii) accompanied by written evidence confirming that the translation is accurate.

(2) The written evidence in support of the application must state—

(a) the name of the judgment creditor and his address for service within the jurisdiction;

(b) the name of the judgment debtor and his address or place of business, if known;

(c) the grounds on which the judgment creditor is entitled to enforce the judgment;

(d) in the case of a money judgment, the amount in respect of which it remains unsatisfied; and

(e) where interest is recoverable on the judgment under the law of the State of origin—

    (i) the amount of interest which has accrued up to the date of the application, or

    (ii) the rate of interest, the date from which it is recoverable, and the date on which it ceases to accrue.

(3) Written evidence in support of an application under the 1920 Act must also state that the judgment is not a judgment—

(a) which under section 9 of that Act may not be ordered to be registered; or

(b) to which section 5 of the Protection of Trading Interests Act 1980 applies7.

(4) Written evidence in support of an application under the 1933 Act must also—

(a) state that the judgment is a money judgment;

(b) confirm that it can be enforced by execution in the State of origin;

(c) confirm that the registration could not be set aside under section 4 of that Act;

(d) confirm that the judgment is not a judgment to which section 5 of the Protection of Trading Interests Act 1980 applies;

(e) where the judgment contains different provisions, some but not all of which can be registered for enforcement, set out those provisions in respect of which it is sought to register the judgment; and

(f) be accompanied by any further evidence as to—

    (i) the enforceability of the judgment in the State of origin, and

    (ii) the law of that State under which any interest has become due under the judgment,

which may be required under the relevant Order in Council extending Part I of the 1933 Act to that State.

(5) Written evidence in support of an application under the 1982 Act must also exhibit—

(a) documents which show that, under the law of the State of origin, the judgment is enforceable on the judgment debtor and has been served;

(b)   in the case of a judgment in default, a document which establishes that the party in default was served with the document instituting the proceedings or with an equivalent document; and

(c)   where appropriate, a document showing that the judgment creditor is in receipt of legal aid in the State of origin.

(6) An application for registration under the Lugano Convention must, in addition to the evidence required by that Convention, be supported by the evidence required by paragraphs (1)(b) and (2)(e) of this rule.

*Procedure for enforcing judgments under the Judgments Regulation*

**74.4A**

A person seeking the enforcement of a judgment which is enforceable under the Judgments Regulation must, except in a case falling within article 43(3) of the Regulation (protective measures), provide the documents required by article 42 of the Regulation.

*Security for costs*

**74.5**

(1) Subject to paragraphs (2) and (3), section II of Part 25 applies to an application for security for the costs of—

(a)   the application for registration;

(b)   any proceedings brought to set aside the registration;

(c)   any appeal against the granting of the registration; and

(d)   any application relating to the recognition or enforcement of a judgment pursuant to the Judgments Regulation,

as if the judgment creditor were a claimant.

(2) A judgment creditor making an application under the 1982 Act or the Lugano Convention, the Judgments Regulation may not be required to give security solely on the ground that he is resident out of the jurisdiction.

(3) Paragraph (1) does not apply to an application under the 1933 Act where the relevant Order in Council otherwise provides.

*Registration orders*

**74.6**

(1) An order granting permission to register a judgment ('a registration order') must be drawn up by the judgment creditor and served on the judgment debtor—

(a)   by delivering it to the judgment debtor personally;

(b)   by any of the methods of service permitted under the Companies Act 2006; or

(c)   in such other manner as the court may direct.

(2) Permission is not required to serve a registration order out of the jurisdiction, and rules 6.40, 6.42, 6.43 and 6.46 apply to such an order as they apply to a claim form.

(3) A registration order must state—

(a)   full particulars of the judgment registered;

(b)   the name of the judgment creditor and his address for service within the jurisdiction;

(c)   the right of the judgment debtor—

(i)    in the case of registration following an application under the 1920 or the 1933 Act, to apply to have the registration set aside;

(ii)   in the case of registration following an application under the 1982 Act or the Lugano Convention, to appeal against the registration order;

(d) the period within which such an application or appeal may be made; and

(e) that no measures of enforcement will be taken before the end of that period, other than measures ordered by the court to preserve the property of the judgment debtor.

## Applications to set aside registration

**74.7**

(1) An application to set aside registration under the 1920 or the 1933 Act must be made within the period set out in the registration order.

(2) The court may extend that period; but an application for such an extension must be made before the end of the period as originally fixed or as subsequently extended.

(3) The court hearing the application may order any issue between the judgment creditor and the judgment debtor to be tried.

## Refusal of recognition or enforcement under the Judgments Regulation

**74.7A**

(1) An application under article 45 or 46 of the Judgments Regulation that the court should refuse to recognise or enforce a judgment must be made—

(a) in accordance with Part 23; and

(b) to the court in which the judgment is being enforced or, if the judgment debtor is not aware of any proceedings relating to enforcement, the High Court.

(2) An appeal against a decision granting or refusing an application for refusal of recognition or enforcement of a judgment under the Judgments Regulation must be made in accordance with Part 52, subject to the following provisions of this rule.

(3) Permission is not required to—

(a) appeal; or

(b) put in evidence.

(4) Unless the court orders otherwise, the judgment debtor must, as soon as practicable, serve copies of any order made under article 45 or 46 or in any appeal under article 49 on—

(a) all other parties to the proceedings and any other person affected by the order;

(b) any court in which proceedings relating to enforcement of the judgment are pending in England and Wales; and

(c) any enforcement agent or enforcement officer (as defined in rule 83.1(2)) instructed by the judgment creditor,

and any such order will not have effect on any person until it has been served.

(5) The court may require the judgment creditor to disclose to the judgment debtor the court or courts in which any proceedings relating to enforcement of the judgment are pending in England and Wales.

## Relief against enforcement under the Judgments Regulation

**74.7B**

(1) An application for relief under article 44 of the Judgments Regulation must be made—

(a) in accordance with Part 23; and

(b) to the court in which the judgment is being enforced or, if the judgment debtor is not aware of any proceedings relating to enforcement, the High Court.

(2) The judgment debtor must, as soon as practicable, serve copies of any order made under article 44 on—

(a) all other parties to the proceedings and any other person affected by the order;

(b)   any court in which proceedings relating to enforcement of the judgment are pending in England and Wales; and

(c)   any enforcement agent or enforcement officer (as defined in rule 83.1(2)) instructed by the judgment creditor,

and any such order will not have effect on any person until it has been served.

*Suspension of proceedings in which a judgment is invoked under the Judgments Regulation*
**74.7C**

(1) The court may suspend proceedings under article 38 of the Judgments Regulation either on its own initiative or on the application of any party.

(2) An application for suspension of proceedings under article 38 of the Judgments Regulation must be made—

(a)   in accordance with Part 23; and

(b)   to the court in which the judgment is invoked.

(3) The judgment debtor must, as soon as practicable, serve copies of any order made under article 38 on—

(a)   all other parties to the proceedings and any other person affected by the order;

(b)   any court in which proceedings relating to enforcement of the judgment are pending in England and Wales; and

(c)   any enforcement agent or enforcement officer (as defined in rule 83.1(2)) instructed by the judgment creditor,

and any such order will not have effect on any person until it has been served.

*Appeals*
**74.8**

(1) An appeal against the granting or the refusal of registration under the 1982 Act or the Lugano Convention must be made in accordance with Part 52, subject to the following provisions of this rule.

(2) Permission is not required—

(a)   to appeal; or

(b)   to put in evidence.

(3) If—

(a)   the judgment debtor is not domiciled within a Contracting State, and

(b)   an application to extend the time for appealing is made within two months of service of the registration order

the court may extend the period for filing an appellant's notice against the order granting registration, but not on grounds of distance.

(4) The appellant's notice must be served—

(a)   where the appeal is against the granting of registration, within—

   (i)   one month; or

   (ii)   where service is to be effected on a party not domiciled within the jurisdiction, two months

of service of the registration order;

(b)   where the appeal is against the refusal of registration, within one month of the decision on the application for registration.

*Enforcement*

**74.9**

(1) In relation to enforcement of a judgment to which the Judgments Regulation applies, the judgment creditor must comply with article 43 of the Regulation.

(2) In relation to a judgment to which the Judgments Regulation does not apply, no steps may be taken to enforce the judgment—

(a) before the end of the period specified in accordance with rule 74.6(3)(d), or that period as extended by the court; or

(b) where there is an application under rule 74.7 or an appeal under rule 74.3, until the application or appeal has been determined.

(3) Any party wishing to enforce a judgment to which the Judgments Regulation does not apply must file evidence of the service on the judgment debtor of—

(a) the registration order; and

(b) any other relevant order of the court.

(4) Nothing in this rule prevents the court from making orders to preserve the property of the judgment debtor pending final determination of any issue relating to the enforcement of the judgment.

*Recognition*

**74.10**

(1) Registration of a judgment serves as a decision that the judgment is recognised for the purposes of the 1982 Act and the Lugano Convention.

(2) An application for recognition of a judgment is governed by the same rules as an application for registration of a judgment under the 1982 Act and the Lugano Convention, except that rule 74.4(5) (a) and (c) does not apply.

*Authentic instruments and court settlements*

**74.11**

The rules governing the registration of judgments under the 1982 Act and the Lugano Convention and applications for the refusal of recognition or enforcement or suspension of any judgments under the Judgments Regulation apply as appropriate and with any necessary modifications for the enforcement of—

(a) authentic instruments which are subject to—

    (i) article 50 of Schedule 3C to the 1982 Act;

    (ii) article 57 of the Lugano Convention; and

    (iii) article 58 of the Judgments Regulation; and

(b) court settlements which are subject to—

    (i) article 51 of Schedule 1 to the 1982 Act;

    (ii) article 58 of the Lugano Convention; and

    (iii) articles 59 and 60 of the Judgments Regulation.

Adaptation of certain orders in foreign judgments subject to the Judgments Regulation

**74.11A**

(1) In this rule, an "adaptation order" means an order for the adaptation of a legal remedy which is contained in a foreign judgment but is unknown under the law of England and Wales pursuant to article 54 of the Judgments Regulation.

(2) The court may make an adaptation order on its own initiative or on an application by any party.

(3) In accordance with article 54(1) of the Judgments Regulation, an adaptation order may only result in a remedy whose legal effects are equivalent to those contained in the judgment and which does not produce such effects extending beyond those provided for under the law of England and Wales.

(4) An application for an adaptation order or a challenge under article 54(2) of the Judgments Regulation to the adaptation of any measure without an adaptation order must be made—

(a)   to the High Court; and

(b)   in accordance with Part 23.

## II   ENFORCEMENT IN FOREIGN COUNTRIES OF JUDGMENTS OF THE HIGH COURT AND THE COUNTY COURT

*Application for a certified copy of a judgment*

**74.12**

(1)  This Section applies to applications—

(a)   to the High Court under section 10 of the 1920 Act;

(b)   to the High Court or to the County Court under section 10 of the 1933 Act;

(c)   to the High Court or to the County Court under section 12 of the 1982 Act; or

(d)   to the High Court or to the County Court under article 53 of the Judgments Regulation or under article 54 of the Lugano Convention.

(2)  A judgment creditor who wishes to enforce in a foreign country a judgment obtained in the High Court or in the County Court—

(a)   must apply for a certified copy of the judgment; and

(b)   if applying under article 53 of the Judgments Regulation, must apply to the court which gave the judgment by filing a draft of the certificate in the form in Annex I to the Judgments Regulation.

(3)  The application may be made without notice.

*Evidence in support*

**74.13**

(1)  The application must be supported by written evidence exhibiting copies of—

(a)   the claim form in the proceedings in which judgment was given;

(b)   evidence that it was served on the defendant;

(c)   the statements of case; and

(d)   where relevant, a document showing that for those proceedings the applicant was an assisted person or an LSC funded client, as defined in rule 43.2(1)(h) and (i).

(2)  The written evidence must—

(a)   identify the grounds on which the judgment was obtained;

(b)   state whether the defendant objected to the jurisdiction and, if he did, the grounds of his objection;

(c)   show that the judgment—

(i)   has been served in accordance with Part 6 and rule 40.4, and

(ii)   is not subject to a stay of execution;

(d)   state—

(i)   the date on which the time for appealing expired or will expire;

(ii)   whether an appeal notice has been filed;

(iii)   the status of any application for permission to appeal; and

(iv)   whether an appeal is pending;

(e)   state whether the judgment provides for the payment of a sum of money, and if so, the amount in respect of which it remains unsatisfied;

(f)   state whether interest is recoverable on the judgment, and if so, either—

    (i)   the amount of interest which has accrued up to the date of the application, or

    (ii)   the rate of interest, the date from which it is recoverable, and the date on which it ceases to accrue.

## III   ENFORCEMENT OF UNITED KINGDOM JUDGMENTS IN OTHER PARTS OF THE UNITED KINGDOM

*Interpretation*

74.14

In this Section—

(a)   'money provision' means a provision for the payment of one or more sums of money in a judgment whose enforcement is governed by section 18 of, and Schedule 6 to, the 1982 Act; and

(b)   'non-money provision' means a provision for any relief or remedy not requiring payment of a sum of money in a judgment whose enforcement is governed by section 18 of, and Schedule 7 to, the 1982 Act.

*Registration of money judgments in the High Court*

74.15

(1) This rule applies to applications to the High Court under paragraph 5 of Schedule 6 to the 1982 Act for the registration of a certificate for the enforcement of the money provisions of a judgment—

(a)   which has been given by a court in another part of the United Kingdom, and

(b)   to which section 18 of that Act applies.

(2) The certificate must within six months of the date of its issue be filed in the Central Office of the Senior Courts, together with a copy certified by written evidence to be a true copy.

*Registration of non-money judgments in the High Court*

74.16

(1) This rule applies to applications to the High Court under paragraph 5 of Schedule 7 to the 1982 Act for the registration for enforcement of the non-money provisions of a judgment—

(a)   which has been given by a court in another part of the United Kingdom, and

(b)   to which section 18 of that Act applies.

(2) An application under paragraph (1) may be made without notice.

(3) An application under paragraph (1) must be accompanied

(a)   by a certified copy of the judgment issued under Schedule 7 to the 1982 Act; and

(b)   by a certificate, issued not more than six months before the date of the application, stating that the conditions set out in paragraph 3 of Schedule 7 are satisfied in relation to the judgment.

(4) Rule 74.6 applies to judgments registered under Schedule 7 to the 1982 Act as it applies to judgments registered under section 4 of that Act.

(5) Rule 74.7 applies to applications to set aside the registration of a judgment under paragraph 9 of Schedule 7 to the 1982 Act as it applies to applications to set aside registrations under the 1920 and 1933 Acts.

*Certificates of High Court and County Court money judgments*

**74.17**

(1) This rule applies to applications under paragraph 2 of Schedule 6 to the 1982 Act for a certificate to enable the money provisions of a judgment of the High Court or of the County Court to be enforced in another part of the United Kingdom.

(2) The judgment creditor may apply for a certificate by filing at the court where the judgment was given or has been entered written evidence stating—

(a)  the name and address of the judgment creditor and, if known, of the judgment debtor;

(b)  the sums payable and unsatisfied under the money provisions of the judgment;

(c)  where interest is recoverable on the judgment, either—

  (i)   the amount of interest which has accrued up to the date of the application, or

  (ii)  the rate of interest, the date from which it is recoverable, and the date on which it ceases to accrue;

(d)  that the judgment is not stayed;

(e)  the date on which the time for appealing expired or will expire;

(f)  whether an appeal notice has been filed;

(g)  the status of any application for permission to appeal; and

(h)  whether an appeal is pending.

*Certified copies of High Court and County Court non-money judgments*

**74.18**

(1) This rule applies to applications under paragraph 2 of Schedule 7 to the 1982 Act for a certified copy of a judgment of the High Court or of the County Court to which section 18 of the Act applies and which contains non-money provisions for enforcement in another part of the United Kingdom.

(2) An application under paragraph (1) may be made without notice.

(3) The applicant may apply for a certified copy of a judgment by filing at the court where the judgment was given or has been entered written evidence stating—

(a)  full particulars of the judgment;

(b)  the name and address of the judgment creditor and, if known, of the judgment debtor;

(c)  that the judgment is not stayed;

(d)  the date on which the time for appealing expired or will expire;

(e)  whether an appeal notice has been filed;

(f)  the status of any application for permission to appeal; and

(g)  whether an appeal is pending.

## IV  ENFORCEMENT IN ENGLAND AND WALES OF EUROPEAN COMMUNITY JUDGMENTS

*Interpretation*

**74.19**

In this Section—

(a)  'Community judgment' means any judgment, decision or order which is enforceable under—

  (i)   article 280 or 299 of the Treaty on the Functioning of the European Union;

  (ii)  article 18 or 164 of the Euratom Treaty;

  (iii) omitted;

      (iv)   article 86 of Council Regulation (EC) 207/2009 of 26 February 2009 on the Community trade mark;

      (v)   article 71 of Council Regulation (EC) 6/2002 of 12 December 2001 on Community designs;

      (vi)   article 36a or 36b of Regulation (EC) 1060/2009 on credit rating agencies; or

      (vii)   article 65 or 66 of Regulation (EU) 648/2012 on OTC derivatives, central counterparties and trade repositories;

(b)   'Euratom inspection order' means an order made by the President of the European Court, or a decision of the Commission of the European Union, under article 81 of the Euratom Treaty;

(c)   'European Court' means the Court of Justice of the European Union;

(d)   'order for enforcement' means an order under the authority of the Secretary of State that the Community judgment to which it is appended is to be registered for enforcement in the United Kingdom.

*Application for registration of a Community judgment*

**74.20**

An application to the High Court for the registration of a Community judgment may be made without notice.

*Evidence in support*

**74.21**

(1) An application for registration must be supported by written evidence exhibiting—

(a)   the Community judgment and the order for its enforcement, or an authenticated copy; and

(b)   where the judgment is not in English, a translation of it into English—

      (i)   certified by a notary public or other qualified person; or

      (ii)   accompanied by written evidence confirming that the translation is accurate.

(2) Where the application is for registration of a Community judgment which is a money judgment, the evidence must state—

(a)   the name of the judgment creditor and his address for service within the jurisdiction;

(b)   the name of the judgment debtor and his address or place of business, if known;

(c)   the amount in respect of which the judgment is unsatisfied; and

(d)   that the European Court has not suspended enforcement of the judgment.

*Registration orders*

**74.22**

(1) A copy of the order granting permission to register a Community judgment ('the registration order') must be served on every person against whom the judgment was given.

(2) The registration order must state the name and address for service of the person who applied for registration, and must exhibit—

(a)   a copy of the registered Community judgment; and

(b)   a copy of the order for its enforcement.

(3) In the case of a Community judgment which is a money judgment, the registration order must also state the right of the judgment debtor to apply within 28 days for the variation or cancellation of the registration under rule 74.23.

*Application to vary or cancel registration*

**74.23**

(1) An application to vary or cancel the registration of a Community judgment which is a money judgment on the ground that at the date of registration the judgment had been partly or wholly satisfied must be made within 28 days of the date on which the registration order was served on the judgment debtor.

(2) The application must be supported by written evidence.

*Enforcement*

**74.24**

No steps may be taken to enforce a Community judgment which is a money judgment—

(a)   before the end of the period specified in accordance with rule 74.23(1); or

(b)   where an application is made under that rule, until it has been determined.

*Application for registration of suspension order*

**74.25**

(1) Where the European Court has made an order that the enforcement of a registered Community judgment should be suspended, an application for the registration of that order in the High Court is made by filing a copy of the order in the Central Office of the Senior Courts.

(2) The application may be made without notice.

*Registration and enforcement of a Euratom inspection order*

**74.26**

(1) Rules 74.20, 74.21(1), and 74.22(1) and (2), which apply to the registration of a Community judgment, also apply to the registration of a Euratom inspection order but with the necessary modifications.

(2) An application under article 6 of the European Communities (Enforcement of Community Judgments) Order 19728 to give effect to a Euratom inspection order may be made on written evidence, and—

(a)   where the matter is urgent, without notice;

(b)   otherwise, by claim form.

## V  EUROPEAN ENFORCEMENT ORDERS

*Interpretation*

**74.27**

(1) In this Section—

(a)   'European Enforcement Order' has the meaning given in the EEO Regulation;

(b)   'EEO' means European Enforcement Order;

(c)   'judgment', 'authentic instrument', 'member state of origin', 'member state of enforcement', and 'court of origin' have the meanings given by Article 4 of the EEO Regulation; and

(d)   'Regulation State' has the same meaning as 'Member State' in the EEO Regulation, that is all Member States except Denmark.

### Certification of Judgments of the Courts of England and Wales

**74.28**

An application for an EEO certificate must be made by filing the relevant practice form in accordance with Article 6 of the EEO Regulation.

### Applications for a certificate of lack or limitation of enforceability

**74.29**

An application under Article 6(2) of the EEO Regulation for a certificate indicating the lack or limitation of enforceability of an EEO certificate must be made to the court of origin by application in accordance with Part 23.

### Applications for rectification or withdrawal

**74.30**

An application under Article 10 of the EEO Regulation for rectification or withdrawal of an EEO certificate must be made to the court of origin and may be made by application in accordance with Part 23.

### Enforcement of European Enforcement Orders in England and Wales

**74.31**

(1) A person seeking to enforce an EEO in England and Wales must lodge at the court in which enforcement proceedings are to be brought the documents required by Article 20 of the EEO Regulation.

(2) Where a person applies to enforce an EEO expressed in a foreign currency, the application must contain a certificate of the sterling equivalent of the judgment sum at the close of business on the date nearest preceding the date of the application.

(Part 70 contains further rules about enforcement.)

### Refusal of enforcement

**74.32**

(1) An application under Article 21 of the EEO Regulation that the court should refuse to enforce an EEO must be made by application in accordance with Part 23 to the court in which the EEO is being enforced.

(2) The judgment debtor must, as soon as practicable, serve copies of any order made under Article 21(1) on—

(a) all other parties to the proceedings and any other person affected by the order ('the affected persons'); and

(b) any court in which enforcement proceedings are pending in England and Wales ('the relevant courts').

(3) Upon service of the order on the affected persons, all enforcement proceedings under the EEO in the relevant courts will cease.

### Stay of or limitation on enforcement

**74.33**

(1) Where an EEO certificate has been lodged and the judgment debtor applies to stay or limit the enforcement proceedings under Article 23 of the EEO Regulation, such application must be made in accordance with Part 23 to the court in which the EEO is being enforced.

(2) The judgment debtor shall, as soon as practicable, serve a copy of any order made under the Article on—

(a) all other parties to the proceedings and any other person affected by the order; and

(b)   any court in which enforcement proceedings are pending in England and Wales;

and the order will not have effect on any person until it has been served in accordance with this rule and they have received it.

## VI  RECOGNITION AND ENFORCEMENT OF PROTECTION MEASURES

*Interpretation*

74.34

In this Section—

(a)   "Article 5 certificate" means a certificate issued under Article 5 of the Protection Measures Regulation;

(b)   "Article 8 notice" means the notification required by Article 8 of the Protection Measures Regulation;

(c)   "Article 11 notice" means the notification required by Article 11 of the Protection Measures Regulation;

(d)   "Article 14 certificate" means a certificate issued under Article 14 of the Protection Measures Regulation;

(e)   "incoming protection measure" means a protection measure that has been ordered in a Member State of the European Union other than the United Kingdom or Denmark;

(f)   "outgoing protection measure" means any protection measure included in any of—

   (i)    an injunction issued for the purpose mentioned in section 3(3)(a) of the Protection from Harassment Act 19979;

   (ii)   any other injunction or order of the County Court;

   (iii)  an undertaking accepted by the County Court;

   (iv)  in proceedings to which these Rules apply—

   (aa) any other injunction or order of the High Court;

   (bb) an undertaking accepted by the High Court;

(g)   "person causing the risk" has the meaning given to it in the Protection Measures Regulation;

(h)   "protected person" has the meaning given to it in the Protection Measures Regulation;

(i)   "protection measure" has the meaning given to it in the Protection Measures Regulation;

(j)   "Protection Measures Regulation" means Regulation (EU) No 606/2013 of the European Parliament and of the Council of 12th June 2013 on mutual recognition of protection measures in civil matters.

*Procedure for applications in this Section*

74.35

Subject to the rules in this Section, applications under the Protection Measures Regulation to the County Court or to the High Court must be made in accordance with Part 23.

## OUTGOING PROTECTION MEASURES

*Application for an Article 5 certificate*

74.36

(1)  A protected person may apply for an Article 5 certificate—

(a)   at the time of application for an injunction or other order containing an outgoing protection measure; or

(b)   at any time after such application, provided—

    (i)   the order or undertaking containing the outgoing protection measure has not yet been made or accepted as the case may be; or

    (ii)  the outgoing protection measure is still in force.

(2) An application for an Article 5 certificate may be made without notice.

### *The court to which an application for an Article 5 certificate must be made*

**74.37**

An application for an Article 5 certificate must be made—

(a)  where the outgoing protection measure has not yet been ordered or accepted—

    (i)   to the County Court if the proceedings relating to the outgoing protection measure are before the County Court; or

    (ii)  to the High Court if the proceedings relating to the outgoing protection measure are before the High Court; or

(b)  where the outgoing protection measure has been ordered or accepted—

    (i)   to the County Court if that court made the order or accepted the undertaking as the case may be; or

    (ii)  to the High Court if that court made the order or accepted the undertaking as the case may be.

### *When a request for a translation of an Article 5 certificate may be made*

**74.38**

A protected person may request a translation of an Article 5 certificate—

(a)  at the time of application for the Article 5 certificate; or

(b)  at any time after such application, provided the Article 5 certificate—

    (i)   has not yet been issued; or

    (ii)  if issued, is still in force.

### *The court to which a request for a translation of an Article 5 certificate must be made*

**74.39**

A request for a translation of an Article 5 certificate must be made—

(a)  if the certificate has not yet been issued, to—

    (i)   the County Court if the application for the certificate is before the County Court;

    (ii)  the High Court if the application for the certificate is before the High Court;

(b)  if the certificate has been issued, to—

    (i)   the Count Court if the County Court issued it;

    (ii)  the High Court if the High Court issued it.

### *Service requirements under Article 6*

**74.40**

(1) Where the outgoing protection measure is included in an order, the court may only issue an Article 5 certificate if satisfied that the order has been served on the person causing the risk in accordance with the requirements specified in rule 81.5, unless the court has dispensed with service of the order in accordance with the requirements specified in rule 81.8.

(2) Where the protected person is responsible for serving the order on the person causing the risk, any application for an Article 5 certificate must be accompanied by a certificate of service.

*Notification of the certificate under Article 8*

**74.41**

(1)   Subject to paragraph (2), Article 8 notice must be given to the person causing the risk by serving it in accordance with Section III of Part 6 and the rules in that Section shall apply to service of the notice as they apply to any other document to be served.

(2)   If the person causing the risk resides in a Member State of the European Union other than the United Kingdom or in a country outside the European Union, Article 8 notice must be given by sending it by registered letter with acknowledgement of receipt or confirmation of delivery or equivalent to the last known place of residence of that person.

*Rectification of an Article 5 certificate*

**74.42**

(1)   An application pursuant to Article 9 of the Protection Measures Regulation for rectification of an Article 5 certificate must be made to—

(a)   the County Court if the County Court issued the certificate;

(b)   the High Court if the High Court issued the certificate.

(2)   An application for such rectification may be made by—

(a)   the protected person; or

(b)   the person causing the risk.

(3)   An Article 5 certificate may be rectified pursuant to Article 9(1)(a) of the Protection Measures Regulation by the court—

(a)   on application under this rule; or

(b)   on its own initiative.

*Withdrawal of an Article 5 certificate*

**74.43**

(1)   An application pursuant to Article 9 of the Protection Measures Regulation for withdrawal of an Article 5 certificate must be made to—

(a)   the County Court if the County Court issued the certificate;

(b)   the High Court if the High Court issued the certificate.

(2)   An application for such withdrawal may be made by—

(a)   the protected person; or

(b)   the person causing the risk.

(3)   An Article 5 certificate may be withdrawn pursuant to Article 9(1)(b) of the Protection Measures Regulation by the court—

(a)   on application under this rule; or

(b)   on its own initiative.

*When an application for an Article 14 certificate may be made*

**74.44**

A protected person or person causing the risk may apply for an Article 14 certificate—

(a)   at the time of application to vary or set aside the order containing the outgoing protection measure, or for acceptance of a variation or setting aside of the undertaking containing the outgoing protection measure, as the case may be;

(b)   at any time after the order containing the outgoing protection measure has been varied or set aside or a variation or setting aside of the undertaking containing the outgoing protection measure has been accepted, as the case may be;

Rules of Procedure

(c) at any time after an Article 5 certificate has been withdrawn under Article 9 of the Protection Measures Regulation; or

(d) on, or at any time after, the making of an order staying or suspending enforcement of the order or undertaking containing the outgoing protection measure.

*The court to which an application for an Article 14 certificate must be made*

**74.45**

An application for an Article 14 certificate must be made—

(a) if the order containing the outgoing protection measure has not yet been varied or set aside or a variation or setting aside of the undertaking containing the protection measure has not yet been accepted, as the case may be, to—

  (i) the County Court if the application for such variation or setting aside is before the County Court; or

  (ii) the High Court if the application for such variation or setting aside is before the High Court; or

(b) if there has been an application under Article 9 of the Protection Measures Regulation for withdrawal of the Article 5 certificate, and that application has not yet been decided, to—

  (i) the County Court if the application for such withdrawal is before the County Court; or

  (ii) the High Court if the application for such withdrawal is before the High Court; or

(c) if the order containing the outgoing protection measure has been varied or set aside, or a variation or setting aside of the undertaking containing the outgoing protection measure has been accepted, to—

  (i) the County Court if the County Court ordered or accepted such variation or setting aside, as the case may be; or

  (ii) the High Court if the High Court ordered or accepted such variation or setting aside, as the case may be; or

(d) if an Article 5 certificate has been withdrawn under Article 9, to—

  (i) the County Court if the County Court ordered such withdrawal;

  (ii) the High Court if the High Court ordered such withdrawal; or

(e) where enforcement of the order has been stayed or suspended, to—

  (i) the County Court if the County Court made the order for the stay or suspension; or

  (ii) the High Court if the High Court made the order for the stay or suspension.

INCOMING PROTECTION MEASURES

*Application for adjustment under Article 11*

**74.46**

A protected person may apply to the court under Article 11 of the Protection Measures Regulation to adjust the factual elements of an incoming protection measure.

*Notification of the adjustment under Article 11*

**74.47**

(1) Subject to paragraph (2), Article 11 notice must be given to the person causing the risk by serving it in accordance with Section III of Part 6 and the rules in that Section apply to service of the notice as they apply to any other document to be served.

(2) If the person causing the risk resides in a Member State of the European Union other than the United Kingdom or in a country outside the European Union, Article 11 notice must be given by

sending it by registered letter with acknowledgment of receipt or other confirmation of delivery or equivalent to the last known place of residence of that person.

### *Enforcement of an incoming protection measure*

**74.48**

Section II of Part 81 applies to applications in relation to a breach of an incoming protection measure as if the incoming protection measure had been ordered by the County Court.

### *Application for refusal of recognition or enforcement under Article 13*

**74.49**

A person causing the risk may apply to the court under Article 13 of the Protection Measures Regulation for refusal of recognition or enforcement of an incoming protection measure.

### *Application under Article 14(2)*

**74.50**

(1)  This rule applies where an Article 14 certificate has been issued in a Member State of the European Union other than the United Kingdom or Denmark.

(2)  A protected person or person causing the risk may apply to the court to stay, suspend or withdraw the effects of recognition or, where applicable, the enforcement of the protection measure.

(3)  An application under this rule must include a copy of the Article 14 certificate issued in the other Member State.

(4)  On an application under this rule, the court must make such orders or give such directions as may be necessary to give effect to the Article 14 certificate.

## PRACTICE DIRECTION 74A – ENFORCEMENT OF JUDGMENTS IN DIFFERENT JURISDICTIONS

**1**

This practice direction is divided into two sections—

(1)  Section I – Provisions about the enforcement of judgments

(2)  Section II – The Merchant Shipping (Liner Conferences) Act 1982

## SECTION I ENFORCEMENT OF JUDGMENTS

### *Meaning of 'judgment'*

**2**

In rule 74.2(1)(c), the definition of 'judgment' is 'subject to any other enactment'. Such provisions include—

(1)  section 9(1) of the 1920 Act, which limits enforcement under that Act to judgments of superior courts;

(2)  section 1(1) of the 1933 Act, which limits enforcement under that Act to judgments of those courts specified in the relevant Order in Council;

(3)  section 1(2) of the 1933 Act, which limits enforcement under that Act to money judgments.

### *Registers*

**3**

There will be kept in the Central Office of the Senior Courts at the Royal Courts of Justice, under the direction of the Senior Master—

(1) registers of foreign judgments ordered by the High Court to be enforced following applications under—

  (a) section 9 of the 1920 Act;

  (b) section 2 of the 1933 Act;

  (c) section 4 of the 1982 Act;

  (d) (omitted)

  (e) the Lugano Convention.

(2) registers of certificates issued for the enforcement in foreign countries of High Court judgments under the 1920, 1933 and 1982 Acts, and under article 53 of the Judgments Regulation and article 54 of the Lugano Convention;

(3) a register of certificates filed in the Central Office of the High Court under rule 74.15(2) for the enforcement of money judgments given by the courts of Scotland or Northern Ireland;

(4) a register of certificates issued under rule 74.16(3) for the enforcement of non-money judgments given by the courts of Scotland or Northern Ireland;

(5) registers of certificates issued under rules 74.17 and 74.18 for the enforcement of High Court judgments in Scotland or Northern Ireland under Schedule 6 or Schedule 7 to the 1982 Act; and

(6) a register of Community judgments and Euratom inspection orders ordered to be registered under article 3 of the European Communities (Enforcement of Community Judgments) Order 1972.

Enforcement of foreign judgments pursuant to the Judgments Regulation and registration of other judgments for enforcement

**4.1**

Enforcement under rule 74.3A of foreign judgments pursuant to the Judgments Regulation (for which registration is no longer required), and applications for—

(1) foreign judgments under rule 74.3;

(2) judgments of courts in Scotland or Northern Ireland under rule 74.15 or 74.16; and

(3) European Community judgments under rule 74.20,

are assigned to the Queen's Bench Division and may be heard by a Master.

*Making an application*

**4.2**

An application under rule 74.12 for a certified copy of a High Court or county court judgment for enforcement abroad must be made—

(1) in the case of a judgment given in the Chancery Division or the Queen's Bench Division of the High Court, to a Master, Registrar or district judge;

(2) in the case of a judgment given in the Family Division of the High Court, to a district judge of that Division;

(3) in the case of a county court judgment, to a district judge.

**4.3**

An application under rule 74.17 or 74.18 for a certificate or a certified copy of a High Court or county court judgment for enforcement in Scotland or Northern Ireland must be made—

(1) in the case of a judgment given in the Chancery Division or the Queen's Bench Division of the High Court, to a Master, Registrar or district judge;

(2) in the case of a judgment given in the Family Division of the High Court, to a district judge of that Division;

(3) in the case of a county court judgment, to a district judge.

**4.4**

The following applications must be made under Part 23—

(1)   applications under rule 74.3 for the registration of a judgment;

(2)   applications under rule 74.7 to set aside the registration of a judgment;

(2A) applications under rules 74.7A for refusal of recognition of a judgment under the Judgments Regulation;

(2B) applications under rule 74.7B for relief against enforcement under article 44 of the Judgments Regulation;

(2C) applications under rule 74.7C for suspension of proceedings under article 38 of the Judgments Regulation;

(2D) applications under rule 74.11A for an adaptation order under article 54 of the Judgments Regulation;

(3)   applications under rule 74.12 for a certified copy of a judgment;

(4)   applications under section III for a certificate for enforcement of a judgment;

(5)   applications under rule 74.20 for the registration of a Community judgment;

(6)   applications under rule 74.23 to vary or cancel the registration of a Community judgment; and

(7)   applications under rule 74.25 for the registration of an order of the European Court that the enforcement of a registered Community judgment should be suspended.

*Applications under the 1920 Act or 1933 Act*

**5**

Foreign judgments are enforceable in England and Wales under the 1920 or 1933 Act where there is an agreement on the reciprocal enforcement of judgments between the United Kingdom and the country in which the judgment was given. Such an agreement may contain particular provisions governing the enforcement of judgments (for example limiting the categories of judgments which are enforceable, or the courts whose judgments are enforceable). Any such specific limitations will be listed in the Order in Council giving effect in the United Kingdom to the agreement in question, and the rules in Section I of Part 74 will take effect subject to such limitations.

*Procedure for enforcement of a judgment under the Judgments Regulation: rule 74.4(6)*

**6.1**

Where a judgment is to be enforced in a Regulation State, the Judgments Regulation applies.

[. . .]

**6.3**

The Judgments Regulation may be found on the EU legislation website at http://eur-lex.europa.eu. The form for a certificate under the Judgments Regulation may be found at Annex I to the Regulation.

**6.4**

Section 2, subsection 2 of Section 3 and Section 4 of Chapter III of the Judgments Regulation (in particular articles 41, 42, 43 and 53 and Annex I) set out the documents which the judgment creditor must provide to the court for the purposes of enforcement. Completion of the certificate in the form of Annex I requires confirmation whether Article 43.1 has been complied with.

**6.5**

The Judgments Regulation is supplemented by the Civil Jurisdiction and Judgments Order 2001, SI 2001 No. 3929. The Order also makes amendments, in respect of that Regulation, to the Civil Jurisdiction and Judgments Act 1982.

*Evidence in support of an application under the Lugano Convention: rule 74(4)*

**6A.1**

Where a judgment is to be recognised or enforced in a Contracting State which is a State bound by the Lugano Convention, that Convention applies.

**6A.2**

As a consequence of article 38(2) of the Lugano Convention the provisions of Title III of that Convention relating to declaring judgments enforceable are the equivalent, in the United Kingdom, of provisions relating to registering judgments for enforcement.

**6A.3**

Title III of, and Annex V to, the Lugano Convention are annexed to this Practice Direction. They were originally published in the official languages of the European Community in the Official Journal of the European Communities by the Office for Official Publications of the European Communities.

**6A.4**

Sections 2 and 3 of Title III of the Lugano Convention (in particular articles 40, 53, 54 and annex V) set out the evidence needed in support of an application.

**6A.5**

The Civil Jurisdiction and Judgments (England and Wales and Northern Ireland) Regulations 2009 make amendments to the Civil Jurisdiction and Judgments Act 1982 in respect of the Lugano Convention.

*Rule 74.7A – Applications for refusal of recognition or enforcement under the Judgments Regulation*

**6B.1**

An application must be accompanied by a copy of the judgment, any other documents relied upon and any necessary translations, and be supported by written evidence showing why the court should find that one of the grounds referred to in article 45 of the Judgments Regulation exists.

*Rule 74.7C – Applications for suspension of proceedings in which a judgment is invoked under article 38 of the Judgments Regulation*

**6C.1**

An application for suspension of proceedings on either of the grounds set out in article 38(a) or (b) of the Judgments Regulation must be accompanied by a copy of the judgment, any other documents relied upon and any necessary translations, and be supported by written evidence of the challenge referred to in article 38(a) or application referred to in article 38(b) as the case may be.

**6C.2**

Where the application is granted, the court must send a sealed copy of the judgment to the person making the application. The applicant must serve a sealed copy of that order as provided in rule 74.7C(3). Where the application is refused, the court must give reasons for the refusal and may give further directions.

*Rule 74.12 – Applications for certificates of judgments of the courts of England and Wales under article 53 of the Judgments Regulation*

**6D.1**

An application under article 53 of the Judgments Regulation for a certificate of a High Court or County Court judgment for enforcement in another Regulation State must be made as indicated in paragraph 4.2 and must be accompanied by a draft certificate in the form in Annex I to the Judgments Regulation.

**6D.2**

Where the application is granted, the court must send a sealed copy of the judgment to the person making the application. Where the application is refused, the court must give reasons for the refusal and may give further directions.

*Certified copies of judgments issued under rule 74.12*

**7.1**

In an application by a judgment creditor under rule 74.12 for the enforcement abroad of a High Court judgment, the certified copy of the judgment will be an office copy, and will be accompanied by a certificate signed by a judge. The judgment and certificate will be sealed with the Seal of the Senior Courts.

**7.2**

In an application by a judgment creditor under rule 74.12 for the enforcement abroad of a County Court judgment, the certified copy will be a sealed copy, and will be accompanied by a certificate signed by a judge.

**7.3**

In applications under the 1920, 1933 or 1982 Acts, the certificate will be in Form 110, and will have annexed to it a copy of the claim form by which the proceedings were begun.

**7.4**

In an application under the Judgments Regulation, the certificate will be in the form of Annex V to the Regulation.

**7.5**

In an application under the Lugano Convention, the certificate will be in the form of Annex V to the Convention.

*Certificates under section III of Part 74*

**8.1**

A certificate of a money judgment of a court in Scotland or Northern Ireland must be filed for enforcement under rule 74.15(2) in the Action Department of the Central Office of the Senior Courts, Royal Courts of Justice, Strand, London WC2A 2LL. The copy will be sealed by a court officer before being returned to the applicant.

**8.2**

A certificate issued under rule 74.17 for the enforcement in Scotland or Northern Ireland of a money judgment of the High Court or of a county court will be in Form 111.

**8.3**

In an application by a judgment creditor under rule 74.18 for the enforcement in Scotland or Northern Ireland of a non-money judgment of the High Court or of a county court, the certified copy of the judgment will be a sealed copy to which will be annexed a certificate in Form 112.

*Material additional to section IV of Part 74*

**9.1**

Enforcement of Community judgments and of Euratom inspection orders is governed by the European Communities (Enforcement of Community Judgments) Order 1972, SI 1972 No. 1590.

Rules of Procedure

**9.2**

The Treaty establishing the European Community is the Treaty establishing the European Economic Community (Rome, 1957); relevant amendments are made by the Treaty of Amsterdam (1997, Cm. 3780).

**9.3**

The text of the Protocol of 3 June 1971 on the interpretation by the European Court of the Convention of 27 September 1968 on Jurisdiction and the Enforcement of Judgments in Civil and Commercial Matters is set out in Schedule 2 to the Civil Jurisdiction and Judgments Act 1982.

**9.4**

The text of the Protocol of 19 December 1988 on the interpretation by the European Court of the Convention of 19 June 1980 on the Law applicable to Contractual Obligations is set out in Schedule 3 to the Contracts (Applicable Law) Act 1990. After the commencement on 17 December 2009 of EC Regulation 593/2008 ('the Rome I Regulation') this Convention and Protocol will only apply to contracts concluded before that date.

. . .

## PRACTICE DIRECTION 74B – EUROPEAN ENFORCEMENT ORDERS

*Council Regulation*

**1.1**

Certification and enforcement of European Enforcement Orders is governed by Council Regulation (EC) No 805/2004 creating a European Enforcement Order for uncontested claims.

**1.2**

The EEO Regulation can be found on the European legislation website. It was originally published in the official languages of the European Community in the Official Journal of the European Communities by the Office for Official Publications of the European Communities.

**1.3**

Section V of Part 74 sets out the procedure for enforcement under the EEO Regulation. A claim that does not meet the requirements of the EEO Regulation, or which the judgment creditor does not wish to enforce using the EEO Regulation, may be enforceable using another method of enforcement.

*Rule 74.28 – Certification of Judgments of the Courts of England and Wales*

**2.1**

An application under rule 74.28 for a certificate of a High Court or County Court judgment for enforcement in another Regulation State must be made using Form N219 or Form N219A—

(1) in the case of a judgment given in the Chancery or Queen's Bench Division of the High Court, or in a district registry, to a Master, Registrar or District Judge; or

(2) in the case of a County Court judgment, to a District Judge.

**2.2**

Where the application is granted, the court will send the EEO certificate and a sealed copy of the judgment to the person making the application. Where the court refuses the application, the court will give reasons for the refusal and may give further directions.

## Rule 74.29 – Applications for a certificate of lack of enforceability

**3.1**

An application must be supported by written evidence in support of the grounds on which the judgment has ceased to be enforceable or its enforceability has been suspended or limited.

## Rule 74.30 – Application for rectification or withdrawal

**4.1**

An application must be supported by written evidence in support of the grounds on which it is contended that the EEO should be rectified or withdrawn.

## Rule 74.31 – Enforcement of European Enforcement Orders in England and Wales

**5.1**

When an EEO is lodged at the court in which enforcement proceedings are to be brought, it will be assigned a case number.

**5.2**

A copy of a document will satisfy the conditions necessary to establish its authenticity if it is an official copy of the court of origin.

**5.3**

If judgment is set aside in the court of origin, the judgment creditor must notify all courts in which enforcement proceedings are pending in England and Wales under the EEO as soon as reasonably practicable after the order is served on the judgment creditor. Notification may be by any means available including fax, e-mail, post or telephone.

## Rule 74.32 – An application for refusal of enforcement

**6.1**

An application must be accompanied by an official copy of the earlier judgment, any other documents relied upon and any translations required by the EEO Regulation and supported by written evidence showing—

(1)   why the earlier judgment is irreconcilable with the judgment which the judgment creditor is seeking to enforce; and

(2)   why the irreconcilability was not, and could not have been, raised as an objection in the proceedings in the court of origin.

## Rule 74.33 – Stay or limitation of enforcement

**7.1**

Unless the court orders otherwise, an application must be accompanied by evidence of the application in the court of origin, including—

(1)   the application (or equivalent foreign process) or a copy of the application (or equivalent foreign process) certified by an appropriate officer of the court of origin; and

(2)   where that document is not in English, a translation of it into English—

    (a)   certified by a notary public or person qualified to certify a translation in the Member State of the court of origin under Article 20(2)(c) of the EEO Regulation; or

    (b)   accompanied by written evidence confirming that the translation is accurate.

**7.2**

The written evidence in support of the application must state—

(1) that an application has been brought in the member state of origin;

(2) the nature of that application; and

(3) the date on which the application was filed, the state of the proceedings and the date by which it is believed that the application will be determined.

*[Annex omitted]*

## PART 78 – EUROPEAN PROCEDURES

*Scope of this Part and interpretation*

**78.1**

(1) Section I contains rules about European orders for payment made under Regulation (EC) No 1896/2006 of the European Parliament and of the Council of 12 December 2006 creating a European order for payment procedure1.

(2) Section II contains rules about the European small claims procedure under Regulation (EC) No 861/2007 of the European Parliament and of the Council of 11 July 2007 establishing a European small claims procedure2.

(2A) Section III contains rules about mediated cross-border disputes that are subject to Directive 2008/52/EC of the European Parliament and of the Council of 21 May 2008 on certain aspects of mediation in civil and commercial matters.

(3) In this Part—

(a) unless otherwise stated, a reference to an Annex is to an Annex to Practice Direction 78; and

(b) 'Service Regulation' means Regulation (EC) 1393/2007 on service, within the same meaning as rule 6.31(e).

(4) Except where—

(a) the EOP Regulation (which has the same meaning as in rule 78.2(2)(a));

(b) the ESCP Regulation (which has the same meaning as in rule 78.12(2)(a)); or

(c) the Service Regulation

makes different provisions about the certification or verification of translations, every translation required by this Part or such Regulation must be accompanied by a statement by the person making it that it is a correct translation. The statement must include that person's name, address and qualifications for making the translation.

## I    EUROPEAN ORDER FOR PAYMENT PROCEDURE

*Scope of this Section and interpretation*

**78.2**

(1) This Section applies to applications for European orders for payment and other related proceedings under Regulation (EC) No 1896/2006 of the European Parliament and of the Council of 12 December 2006 creating a European order for payment procedure.

(2) In this Section—

(a) 'EOP Regulation' means Regulation (EC) No 1896/2006 of the European Parliament and of the Council of 12 December 2006 creating a European order for payment procedure. A copy of the EOP Regulation can be found at Annex 1;

(b) 'court of origin' has the meaning given by article 5(4) of the EOP Regulation;

(c) 'EOP' means a European order for payment;

(d) 'EOP application' means an application for an EOP;

(e) 'EOP application form A' means the Application for a European order for payment form A, annexed to the EOP Regulation at Annex I to that Regulation;

(f) 'European order for payment' means an order for payment made by a court under article 12(1) of the EOP Regulation;

(g) 'Member State' has the meaning given by article 2(3) of the EOP Regulation;

(h) 'Member State of origin' has the meaning given by article 5(1) of the EOP Regulation;

(i) 'statement of opposition' means a statement of opposition filed in accordance with article 16 of the EOP Regulation.

## EOP applications made to a court in England and Wales
### Application for a European Order for Payment
**78.3**

Where a declaration provided by the claimant under article 7(3) of the EOP Regulation contains any deliberate false statement, rule 32.14 applies as if the EOP application form A were verified by a statement of truth.

(An EOP application is made in accordance with the EOP Regulation and in particular article 7 of that Regulation.)

### Withdrawal of EOP application
**78.4**

(1) At any stage before a statement of opposition is filed, the claimant may notify the court that the claimant no longer wishes to proceed with the claim.

(2) Where the claimant notifies the court in accordance with paragraph (1)—

(a) the court will notify the defendant that the application has been withdrawn; and

(b) no order as to costs will be made.

Transfer of proceedings where an EOP application has been opposed

**78.5**

(1) Where a statement of opposition is filed in accordance with article 16 of the EOP Regulation and the claimant has not opposed the transfer of the matter—

(a) the EOP application will be treated as if it had been started as a claim under Part 7 and the EOP application form A will be treated as a Part 7 claim form including particulars of claim; and

(b) thereafter, these Rules apply with necessary modifications and subject to this rule and rules 78.6 and 78.7.

(2) When the court notifies the claimant in accordance with article 17(3) of the EOP Regulation the court will also—

(a) notify the claimant—

(i) that the EOP application form A is now treated as a Part 7 claim form including particulars of claim; and

(ii) of the time within which the defendant must respond under rule 78.6; and

(b) notify the defendant—

(i) that a statement of opposition has been received;

(ii) that the application will not continue under Part 78;

(iii) that the application has been transferred under article 17 of the EOP Regulation;

(iv) that the EOP application form A is now treated as a Part 7 claim form including particulars of claim; and

(v) of the time within which the defendant must respond under rule 78.6.

Filing of acknowledgment of service and defence where an EOP application is transferred under article 17 of the EOP Regulation

**78.6**

(1) The defendant must file a defence within 30 days of the date of the notice issued by the court under rule 78.5(2)(b).

(2) If the defendant wishes to dispute the court's jurisdiction, the defendant must instead—

(a) file an acknowledgment of service within the period specified in paragraph (1); and

(b) make an application under Part 11 within the period specified in that Part.

(3) Where this rule applies, the following rules do not apply—

(a) rule 10.1(3);

(b) rule 10.3; and

(c) rule 15.4(1).

### Default judgment

**78.7**

(1) If—

(a) the defendant fails to file an acknowledgment of service within the period specified in rule 78.6(2)(a); and

(b) does not within that period—

(i) file a defence in accordance with Part 15 (except rule 15.4(1)) and rule 78.6(1); or

(ii) file an admission in accordance with Part 14,

the claimant may obtain default judgment if Part 12 allows it.

(2) Where this rule applies, rule 10.2 does not apply.

### Review in exceptional cases

**78.8**

An application for a review under article 20 of the EOP Regulation must be made in accordance with Part 23.

### Enforcement of EOPS in England and Wales

### Enforcement of European orders for payment

**78.9**

(1) A person seeking to enforce an EOP in England and Wales must file at the court in which enforcement proceedings are to be brought the documents required by article 21 of the EOP Regulation.

(2) Where a person applies to enforce an EOP expressed in a foreign currency, the application must contain a certificate of the sterling equivalent of the judgment sum at the close of business on the date nearest preceding the date of the application.

(Parts 70 to 74 contain further rules about enforcement.)

### Refusal of enforcement

**78.10**

(1) An application under article 22 of the EOP Regulation that the court should refuse to enforce an EOP must be made in accordance with Part 23 to the court in which the EOP is being enforced.

(2) The judgment debtor must, as soon as practicable, serve copies of any order made under article 22 on—

(a) all other parties to the proceedings and any other person affected by the order ('the affected persons'); and

(b) any court in which enforcement proceedings of the EOP are pending in England and Wales ('the relevant courts').

(3) Upon service of the order on the affected persons, all enforcement proceedings of the EOP in the relevant courts will cease.

## *Stay of or limitation on enforcement*

**78.11**

(1) Where the defendant has sought a review and also applies for a stay of or limitation on enforcement in accordance with article 23 of the EOP Regulation, such application must be made in accordance with Part 23 to the court in which the EOP is being enforced.

(2) The defendant must, as soon as practicable, serve a copy of any order made under article 23 on—

(a) all other parties to the proceedings and any other person affected by the order; and

(b) any court in which enforcement proceedings are pending in England and Wales,

and the order will not have effect on any person until it has been served in accordance with this rule and they have received it.

## II   EUROPEAN SMALL CLAIMS PROCEDURE

## *Scope of this Section and interpretation*

**78.12**

(1) This Section applies to the European small claims procedure under Regulation (EC) No 861/2007 of the European Parliament and of the Council of 11 July 2007 establishing a European small claims procedure.

(2) In this Section—

(a) 'ESCP Regulation' means Regulation (EC) No 861/2007 of the European Parliament and of the Council of 11 July 2007 establishing a European small claims procedure. A copy of the ESCP Regulation can be found at Annex 2;

(b) 'defendant's response' means the response to the ESCP claim form;

(c) 'ESCP' means the European small claims procedure established by the ESCP Regulation;

(d) 'ESCP claim form' means the claim form completed and filed in the ESCP;

(e) 'ESCP counterclaim' has the meaning given to counterclaim by recital 16 of the ESCP Regulation;

(f) 'ESCP judgment' means a judgment given in the ESCP;

(g) 'Member State' has the meaning given by article 2(3) of the ESCP Regulation;

(h) 'Member State of enforcement' is the Member State in which the ESCP judgment is to be enforced;

  (i) 'Member State of judgment' is the Member State in which the ESCP judgment is given.

ESCP claims made in a court in England and Wales

## *Filing an ESCP claim form*

**78.13**

Where a declaration provided by the claimant in the ESCP claim form contains any deliberate false statement, rule 32.14 applies as if the ESCP claim form were verified by a statement of truth.

(An ESCP claim form is completed and filed in accordance with the ESCP Regulation, in particular article 4(1), and in accordance with this paragraph.)

## *Allocation of ESCP claims*

**78.14**

(1) ESCP claims are treated as if they were allocated to the small claims track.

(2) Part 27 applies, except rule 27.14.

### Transfer of proceedings where the claim is outside the scope of the ESCP Regulation – article 4(3) of the ESCP Regulation

**78.15**

(1) Where the court identifies that the claim is outside the scope of the ESCP Regulation, the court will notify the claimant of this in a transfer of proceedings notice.

(2) If the claimant wishes to withdraw the claim, the claimant must notify the court of this within 21 days of the date of the transfer of proceedings notice.

(3) Where the claimant has notified the court in accordance with paragraph (2), the claim is automatically withdrawn.

(4) Where the claimant has not notified the court in accordance with paragraph (2) and the claim is instead to be transferred under article 4(3) of the ESCP Regulation—

(a) the claim will be treated as if it had been started as a claim under Part 7 and the ESCP claim form will be treated as a Part 7 claim form including particulars of claim; and

(b) thereafter, these Rules apply with necessary modifications and subject to this rule,

and the court will notify the claimant of the transfer and its effect.

### Defendant's response

**78.16**

Where a declaration provided by the defendant in the defendant's response contains any deliberate false statement, rule 32.14 applies as if the defendant's response were verified by a statement of truth.

(The defendant's response is made in accordance with the ESCP Regulation and in particular article 5(3) of the ESCP Regulation.)

### Transfer of proceedings where the defendant claims that the non-monetary claim exceeds the limit set in article 2(1) of the ESCP Regulation – article 5(5) of the ESCP Regulation

**78.17**

(1) This rule applies where, under article 5(5) of the ESCP Regulation, the defendant claims that the value of a non-monetary claim exceeds the limit in article 2(1) of the ESCP Regulation.

(2) When the court dispatches the defendant's response to the claimant, it will—

(a) notify the claimant that the court is considering whether the claim is outside the scope of the ESCP Regulation in a consideration of transfer notice; and

(b) send a copy of the notice to the defendant.

(3) If the claimant wishes to withdraw the claim in the event that the court decides that the claim is outside the scope of the ESCP Regulation the claimant must notify the court and the defendant of this within 21 days of the date of the consideration of transfer notice.

(4) The court will notify the defendant as well as the claimant of its decision whether the claim is outside the scope of the ESCP Regulation.

(Article 5(5) of the ESCP Regulation provides that the court shall decide within 30 days of dispatching the defendant's response to the claimant, whether the claim is within the scope of the ESCP Regulation.)

(5) If the court decides that the claim is outside the scope of the ESCP Regulation and the claimant has notified the court and defendant in accordance with paragraph (3), the claim is automatically withdrawn.

(6) If the court decides that the claim is outside the scope of the ESCP Regulation and the claimant has not notified the court and defendant in accordance with paragraph (3)—

(a) the claim will be treated as if it had been started as a claim under Part 7 and the ESCP claim form will be treated as a Part 7 claim form including particulars of claim;

(b)   the defendant's response will be treated as a defence; and

(c)   thereafter, these Rules apply with necessary modifications and subject to this rule,

and the court will notify the parties.

(7) This rule applies to an ESCP counterclaim as if the counterclaim were an ESCP claim.

*Transfer of proceedings where the ESCP counterclaim exceeds the limit set in article 2(1) of the ESCP Regulation – article 5(7) of the ESCP Regulation*

**78.18**

(1) Where the ESCP counterclaim exceeds the limit set in article 2(1) of the ESCP Regulation, the court will—

(a)   notify the defendant of this in a transfer of proceedings notice; and

(b)   send a copy of the notice to the claimant,

when the court dispatches the defendant's response to the claimant.

(2) If the defendant wishes to withdraw the ESCP counterclaim, the defendant must notify the court and the claimant of this within 21 days of the date of the transfer of proceedings notice.

(3) If the defendant notifies the court and claimant under paragraph (2), the ESCP counterclaim is automatically withdrawn.

(4) If the defendant does not notify the court and claimant in accordance with paragraph (2)—

(a)   the claim will be treated as if it had been started as a claim under Part 7 and the ESCP claim form will be treated as a Part 7 claim form including particulars of claim;

(b)   the defendant's response and ESCP counterclaim are to be treated as the defence and counterclaim; and

(c)   thereafter, these Rules apply with necessary modifications and subject to this rule,

and the court will notify the parties.

*Review of judgment*

**78.19**

An application for a review under article 18 of the ESCP Regulation must be made in accordance with Part 23.

*Enforcement of ESCP judgments in England and Wales*

*Enforcement of an ESCP judgment*

**78.20**

(1) A person seeking to enforce an ESCP judgment in England and Wales must file at the court in which enforcement proceedings are to be brought the documents required by article 21 of the ESCP Regulation.

(2) Where a person applies to enforce an ESCP judgment expressed in a foreign currency, the application must contain a certificate of the sterling equivalent of the judgment sum at the close of business on the date nearest preceding the date of the application.

(Parts 70 to 74 contain further rules about enforcement.)

*Refusal of enforcement*

**78.21**

(1) An application under article 22 of the ESCP Regulation that the court should refuse to enforce an ESCP judgment must be made in accordance with Part 23 to the court in which the ESCP judgment is being enforced.

(2) The judgment debtor must, as soon as practicable, serve copies of any order made under article 22 on—

(a) all other parties to the proceedings and any other person affected by the order ('the affected persons'); and

(b) any court in which enforcement proceedings are pending in England and Wales ('the relevant courts').

(3) Upon service of the order on the affected persons, all enforcement proceedings of the ESCP judgment in the relevant courts will cease.

*Stay of or limitation on enforcement*

**78.22**

(1) An application by the defendant under article 23 of the ESCP Regulation must be made in accordance with Part 23 to the court in which the ESCP judgment is being enforced.

(2) The defendant must, as soon as practicable, serve a copy of any order made under article 23 on—

(a) all other parties to the proceedings and any other person affected by the order; and

(b) any court in which enforcement proceedings are pending in England and Wales,

and the order will not have effect on any person until it has been served in accordance with this rule and they have received it.

## III  MEDIATION DIRECTIVE

*Scope of this Section and interpretation*

**78.23**

(1) This Section applies to mediated cross-border disputes that are subject to Directive 2008/52/EC of the European Parliament and of the Council of 21 May 2008 on certain aspects of mediation in civil and commercial matters.

(2) In this Section—

'Mediation Directive' means Directive 2008/52/EC of the European Parliament and of the Council of 21 May 2008 on certain aspects of mediation in civil and commercial matters. A copy of the Directive can be found at Annex 3;

'cross-border dispute' has the meaning given by article 2 of the Mediation Directive;

'mediation' has the meaning given by article 3(a) of the Mediation Directive;

'mediation administrator' means a person involved in the administration of the mediation process;

'mediation evidence' means evidence arising out of or in connection with a mediation process;

'mediation settlement' means the content of a written agreement resulting from mediation of a relevant dispute;

'mediation settlement agreement' means a written agreement resulting from mediation of a relevant dispute;

'mediation settlement enforcement order' means an order made under rule 78.24(5);

'mediator' has the meaning given by article 3(b) of the Mediation Directive; and

'relevant dispute' means a cross-border dispute that is subject to the Mediation Directive.

*Making a mediation settlement enforceable (mediation settlement enforcement orders)*

**78.24**

(1) Where the parties, or one of them with the explicit consent of the others, wish to apply for a mediation settlement to be made enforceable, the parties or party may apply—

(a) where there are existing proceedings in England and Wales, by an application made in accordance with Part 23; or

(b) where there are no existing proceedings in England and Wales, by the Part 8 procedure as modified by this rule and Practice Direction 78 – European Procedures.

(2) Where rule 78.24(1)(b) applies, rules 8.3 to 8.8 will not apply.

(3) The mediation settlement agreement must be annexed to the application notice or claim form when it is filed.

(4) Except to the extent that paragraph (7) applies, the parties must file any evidence of explicit consent to the application under paragraph (1) when the parties file the application or claim form.

(5) Subject to paragraph (6), where an application is made under paragraph (1), the court will make an order making the mediation settlement enforceable.

(6) The court will not make an order under paragraph (5) unless the court has evidence that each of the parties to the mediation settlement agreement has given explicit consent to the application for the order.

(7) Where a party to the mediation settlement agreement—

(a) has agreed in the mediation settlement agreement that a mediation settlement enforcement order should be made in respect of that mediation settlement;

(b) is a party to the application under paragraph (1); or

(c) has written to the court consenting to the application for the mediation settlement enforcement order,

that party is deemed to have given explicit consent to the application for the mediation settlement enforcement order.

(8) An application under paragraph (1) will be dealt with without a hearing, unless the court otherwise directs.

*Mediation settlement enforcement orders: foreign currency*

**78.25**

(1) Where a person applies to enforce a mediation settlement enforcement order which is expressed in a foreign currency, the application must contain a certificate of the sterling equivalent of the sum remaining due under the order at the close of business on the day before the date of the application.

(Parts 70 to 74 contain further rules about enforcement.)

*Mediation evidence: disclosure or inspection*

**78.26**

(1) Where a person seeks disclosure or inspection of mediation evidence that is in the control of a mediator or mediation administrator, that person must apply—

(a) where there are existing proceedings in England and Wales, by an application made in accordance with Part 23; and

(b) where there are no existing proceedings in England and Wales, by the Part 8 procedure.

(2) Where the application is made—

(a) under paragraph (1)(a), the mediator or mediation administrator who has control of the mediation evidence must be named as a respondent to the application and must be served with a copy of the application notice; and

(b) under paragraph (1)(b), the mediator or mediation administrator who has control of the mediation evidence must be made a party to the claim.

(3) Evidence in support of the application under paragraph (1)(a) or (1)(b) must include evidence that—

(a) all parties to the mediation agree to the disclosure or inspection of the mediation evidence;

(b) disclosure or inspection of the mediation evidence is necessary for overriding considerations of public policy, in accordance with article 7(1)(a) of the Mediation Directive; or

(c) disclosure or inspection of the mediation settlement is necessary to implement or enforce the mediation settlement agreement.

(4) This rule does not apply to proceedings in England and Wales that have been allocated to the small claims track.

(5) Where this rule applies, Parts 31 to 34 apply to the extent they are consistent with this rule.

*Mediation evidence: witnesses and depositions*

78.27

(1) This rule applies where a party wishes to obtain mediation evidence from a mediator or mediation administrator by—

(a) a witness summons;

(b) cross-examination with permission of the court under rule 32.7 or 33.4;

(c) an order under rule 34.8 (evidence by deposition);

(d) an order under rule 34.10 (enforcing attendance of witness);

(e) an order under rule 34.11(4) (deponent's evidence to be given orally); or

(f) an order under rule 34.13(1A) (order for the issue of a letter of request).

(2) When applying for a witness summons, permission under rule 32.7 or 33.4 or an order under rule 34.8, 34.10, 34.11(4) or 34.13(1A), the party must provide the court with evidence that—

(a) all parties to the mediation agree to the obtaining of the mediation evidence;

(b) obtaining the mediation evidence is necessary for overriding considerations of public policy, in accordance with article 7(1)(a) of the Mediation Directive; or

(c) the disclosure or inspection of the mediation settlement is necessary to implement or enforce the mediation settlement agreement.

(3) When considering a request for a witness summons, permission under rule 32.7 or 33.4 or an order under rule 34.8, 34.10, 34.11(4) or 34.13(1A), the court may invite any person, whether or not a party, to make representations.

(4) This rule does not apply to proceedings in England and Wales that have been allocated to the small claims track.

(5) Where this rule applies, Parts 31 to 34 apply to the extent they are consistent with this rule.

*Mediation evidence: small claims*

78.28

Where a party wishes to rely on mediation evidence in proceedings that are allocated to the small claims track, that party must inform the court immediately.

## PRACTICE DIRECTION 78 – EUROPEAN PROCEDURES

*EOP Regulation and application of the Civil Procedure Rules*

1.1

EOP applications are primarily governed by the EOP Regulation. Where the EOP Regulation is silent, the Civil Procedure Rules apply with necessary modifications.

*Rule 78.3 – Application for a European order for payment*

2.1

An EOP application form A must be—

(1) completed in English or accompanied by a translation into English; and

(2) filed at court in person or by post.

**2.2**

An EOP application made to the High Court will be assigned to the Queen's Bench Division, but that will not prevent the application being transferred where appropriate.

*Filing documents at court other than the EOP application form A*

**3**

Documents other than the EOP application form A that are filed at or sent to the court in the EOP proceedings, including statements of opposition, may be filed, in addition to by post or in person, by—

(1) fax; or

(2) other electronic means where the facilities are available.

*Service*

**4**

Where the EOP Regulation is silent on service, the Service Regulation and the Civil Procedure Rules apply as appropriate.

*Article 9 of the EOP Regulation – completion or rectification of the EOP application form A*

**5.1**

Article 9 of the EOP Regulation makes provision for the completion or rectification of the EOP application form A within a specified time.

**5.2**

The time specified for the purposes of article 9 will normally be within 30 days of the date of the request by the court to complete or rectify the EOP application form A (using form B annexed to the EOP Regulation).

*Applications under Part 23*

**6.1**

Where an application is made under Section I of Part 78, there will not normally be an oral hearing.

**6.2**

Where an oral hearing is to be held, it will normally take place by telephone or video conference.

*Rule 78.9 – Enforcement of European orders for payment*

**7.1**

When an EOP is filed at the High Court, or in the County Court hearing centre in which enforcement proceedings are to be brought, it will be assigned a case number.

**7.2**

A copy of a document will satisfy the conditions necessary to establish its authenticity if it is an official copy of the court of origin.

**7.3**

If judgment is set aside in the court of origin, the judgment creditor must notify all courts in which enforcement proceedings are pending in England and Wales under the EOP as soon as reasonably practicable after the order is served on the judgment creditor. Notification may be by any means available including fax, e-mail, post or telephone.

## Rule 78.10 – An application for refusal of enforcement

**8.1**

An application must be accompanied by an official copy of the earlier judgment, any other documents relied upon and any translations required by the EOP Regulation.

**8.2**

Where the applicant relies on article 22(1) of the EOP Regulation, the application must be supported by written evidence showing—

(1) why the earlier judgment is irreconcilable with the judgment which the claimant is seeking to enforce; and

(2) why the irreconcilability was not, and could not have been, raised as an objection in the proceedings in the court of origin.

**8.3**

Where the applicant relies on article 22(2), the application must be supported by written evidence of the extent to which the defendant has paid the claimant the amount awarded in the EOP.

## Rule 78.11 – Stay of or limitation on enforcement

**9.1**

Unless the court orders otherwise, an application must be accompanied by evidence of the review application in the court of origin, including—

(1) the review application or a copy of the review application certified by an appropriate officer of the court of origin; and

(2) where that document is not in English, a translation of it into English.

**9.2**

The written evidence in support of the application must state—

(1) that a review application has been brought in the Member State of origin;

(2) the nature of that review application; and

(3) the date on which the review application was filed, the stage the application has reached and the date by which it is believed that the application will be determined.

## ESCP Regulation and application of the Civil Procedure Rules

**10**

Claims under the ESCP are primarily governed by the ESCP Regulation. Where the ESCP Regulation is silent, the Civil Procedure Rules apply with necessary modifications. In particular, Part 52 applies to any appeals.

## Rule 78.13 – Filing an ESCP claim form

**11**

An ESCP claim form must be filed at court in person or by post.

## Article 4(4) of the ESCP Regulation – inadequate or insufficient information

**12.1**

Article 4(4) of the ESCP Regulation makes provision for—

(1)   the completion or rectification of the claim form;

(2)   the supply of supplementary information or documents; or

(3)   the withdrawal of the claim,

within a specified time.

### 12.2

The time specified for the purposes of article 4(4) is within 30 days of the date of the request by the court to complete or rectify the claim form (using Form B annexed to the ESCP Regulation).

### *Rule 78.14 – Allocation of ESCP claims*

### 13.1

Rule 78.14(1) provides that ESCP claims are treated as if they were allocated to the small claims track. However, rule 78.14(2) disapplies rule 27.14 on costs because recital 29 to the ESCP Regulation contains different provisions on costs.

### 13.2

Rule 26.6(1) (scope of the small claims track) is also disapplied because article 2(1) of the ESCP Regulation has a different financial limit.

### *Filing documents at court other than the ESCP claim form*

### 14

Documents other than the ESCP claim form that are filed at or sent to the court in the ESCP proceedings, including the defendant's response, may be filed, in addition to by post or in person, by—

(1)   fax; or

(2)   other electronic means where the facilities are available.

### *Service*

### 15

Where the ESCP Regulation is silent on service, the Service Regulation and the Civil Procedure Rules apply as appropriate.

### *Rule 78.17 – Transfer of proceedings where the defendant claims that the non-monetary claim exceeds the limit set in article 2(1) of the ESCP Regulation – article 5(5) of the ESCP Regulation*

### 16.1

Rule 78.17(7) applies to counterclaims as if the counterclaim were an ESCP claim because the second paragraph of article 5(7) of the ESCP Regulation applies certain provisions about claims in the ESCP Regulation, including article 5(5), to ESCP counterclaims.

### 16.2

Attention is also drawn to the first paragraph of article 5(7) of the ESCP Regulation (transfer of claim and counterclaim in certain circumstances).

### *Oral hearing under article 8 of the ESCP Regulation*

### 17.1

Attention is drawn to article 5(1) of the ESCP Regulation, which sets out limitations on when oral hearings may be held.

Rules of Procedure

17.2

Where an oral hearing is to be held, it will normally take place by telephone or video conference.

*Applications under Part 23*

18.1

Where an application is made under Section II of Part 78 there will not normally be an oral hearing.

18.2

Where an oral hearing is to be held, it will normally take place by telephone or video conference.

*Rule 78.20 – Enforcement of an ESCP judgment*

19.1

When an ESCP judgment is filed at the High Court, or in the County Court hearing centre in which enforcement proceedings are to be brought, it will be assigned a case number.

19.2

A copy of a document will satisfy the conditions necessary to establish its authenticity if it is an official copy of the courts of the Member State of judgment.

19.3

If judgment is set aside in the Member State of judgment, the judgment creditor must notify all courts in which proceedings are pending in England and Wales to enforce the ESCP judgment as soon as reasonably practicable after the order is served on the judgment creditor. Notification may be by any means available including fax, e-mail, post or telephone.

*Rule 78.21 – Application for refusal of enforcement*

20.1

An application must be accompanied by an official copy of the earlier judgment, any other documents relied upon and any translations required by the ESCP Regulation.

20.2

The application must be supported by written evidence showing—

(1) why the earlier judgment is irreconcilable with the judgment which the claimant is seeking to enforce; and

(2) why the irreconcilability was not, and could not have been, raised as an objection in the proceedings in the Member State of judgment.

*Rule 78.22 – Stay of or limitation on enforcement – application following application for review or where the judgment has been challenged*

21.1

This paragraph applies where a defendant makes an application under article 23 of the ESCP Regulation in circumstances where—

(1) an application for review has been made under article 18 ('review application'); or

(2) the defendant has challenged the judgment.

21.2

Unless the court orders otherwise, the application under article 23 must be accompanied by evidence of the review application or challenge in the Member State of judgment. This must include a copy of the document initiating the review application or challenge or a copy of the review application or challenge, certified by an appropriate officer of the court in the Member State of judgment.

**21.3**

Where a document is not in English, it must be accompanied by a translation of it into English.

**21.4**

The written evidence in support of the application must state—

(1)  that a review application or challenge has been brought in the Member State of judgment;

(2)  the nature of that review application or challenge; and

(3)  the date on which the review application or challenge was filed, the state of the proceedings and the date by which it is believed that the application or challenge will be determined.

*Rule 78.24 Making a mediation settlement enforceable (mediation settlement enforcement orders)*

**22.1**

Where an application for a mediation settlement enforcement order is made under rule 78.24(1)(a) in accordance with Part 23, a copy of the application notice, mediation settlement agreement and evidence of explicit consent must be served on all parties to the mediation settlement agreement who are not also parties to the application.

**22.2**

Where an application for a mediation settlement enforcement order is made under rule 78.24(1)(b) by the Part 8 procedure—

(1)  the claim form may be issued without naming a defendant; and

(2)  a copy of the claim form, mediation settlement agreement and evidence of explicit consent must be served on all parties to the mediation settlement agreement who are not also parties to the application.

**22.3**

No document relating to an application for a mediation settlement enforcement order may be inspected by a person who is not a party to the proceedings under rule 5.4C without the permission of the court.

**22.4**

Where the application is supported by evidence of explicit consent to the application by a party to the mediation settlement agreement, the evidence must be in English or accompanied by a translation into English.

**22.5**

Where a party to the mediation settlement agreement writes to the court consenting to the making of the mediation settlement enforcement order, the correspondence must be in English or accompanied by a translation into English.

**22.6**

Where the parties to pending proceedings agree to apply for a mediation settlement enforcement order, they must inform the court immediately.

*[Annexes omitted]*

# Court of Protection Rules

SI 2007/1744[1]

## PART 3 – INTERPRETATION AND GENERAL PROVISIONS

6. In these Rules—

"the Act" means the Mental Capacity Act 2005;

"applicant" means a person who makes, or who seeks permission to make, an application to the court;

"application form" means the document that is to be used to begin proceedings in accordance with Part 9 of these Rules or any other provision of these Rules or the practice directions which requires the use of an application form;

"application notice" means the document that is to be used to make an application in accordance with Part 10 of these Rules or any other provision of these Rules or the practice directions which requires the use of an application notice;

. . .

"child" means a person under 18;

"court" means the Court of Protection;

. . .

"P" means any person (other than a protected party) who lacks or, so far as consistent with the context, is alleged to lack capacity to make a decision or decisions in relation to any matter that is the subject of an application to the court and references to a person who lacks capacity are to be construed in accordance with the Act;

. . .

"protected party" means a party or an intended party (other than P or a child) who lacks capacity to conduct the proceedings;

. . .

"respondent" means a person who is named as a respondent in the application form or notice, as the case may be;

## PART 6 – SERVICE OF DOCUMENTS

. . .

### *Service out of the jurisdiction*

**Scope and interpretation**

**39.**—(1) This rule and rules 39A to 39H make provision about—

(a) service of application forms and other documents out of the jurisdiction; and

(b) the procedure for service.

(2) In this rule and rules 39A to 39H—

"application form" includes an application notice;

"Commonwealth State" means a State listed in Schedule 3 to the British Nationality Act 1981;

"jurisdiction" means, unless the context otherwise requires, England and Wales and any part of the territorial waters of the United Kingdom adjoining England and Wales;

[1] Version shown reflects the amendments made by the Court of Protection (Amendment) Rules 2015 (SI 2015/548). Amendments not marked.

"Member State" means a Member State of the European Union;

"the Service Convention" means the Convention on the service abroad of judicial and extra-judicial documents in civil or commercial matters signed at the Hague on November 15, 1965;

"Service Convention country" means a country, not being a Member State, which is a party to the Service Convention; and

"the Service Regulation" means Regulation (EC) No. 1393/2007 of the European Parliament and of the Council of 13 November 2007 on the service in the Member States of judicial and extra-judicial documents in civil and commercial matters (service of documents) and repealing Council Regulation (EC) No. 1348/2000(2).

(3) In rules 39A to 39H, a reference to service by a party includes service by a person who is not a party where service by such a person is required under these Rules.

### Service of application form and other documents out of the jurisdiction

39A.—(1) Subject to paragraph (2), any document to be served for the purposes of these Rules may be served out of the jurisdiction without the permission of the court.

(2) An application form may not be served out of the jurisdiction unless the court has power to determine the application to which it relates under the Act.

### Period for acknowledging service or responding to application where application is served out of the jurisdiction

39B.—(1) This rule applies where, under these Rules, a party is required to file—

(a)  an acknowledgment of service; or

(b)  an answer to an application,

and sets out the time period for doing so where the application is served out of the jurisdiction.

(2) Where the applicant serves an application on a respondent in—

(a)  Scotland or Northern Ireland; or

(b)  a Member State or Service Convention country within Europe,

the period for filing an acknowledgment of service or an answer to an application is 21 days after service of the application.

(3) Where the applicant serves an application on a respondent in a Service Convention country outside Europe, the period for filing an acknowledgment of service or an answer to an application is 31 days after service of the application.

(4) Where the applicant serves an application on a respondent in a country not referred to in paragraphs (2) and (3), the period for filing an acknowledgment of service or an answer to an application is set out in Practice Direction 6B.

### Method of service – general provisions

39C.—(1) This rule contains general provisions about the method of service of an application form or other document on a party out of the jurisdiction.

*Where service is to be effected on a party in Scotland or Northern Ireland*

(2) Where a party serves an application form or other document on a party in Scotland or Northern Ireland, it must be served by a method permitted by this Part.

*Where service is to be effected out of the United Kingdom*

(3) Where an application form or other document is to be served on a person out of the United Kingdom, it may be served by any method—

(a)  provided for by—

    (i)   rule 39D (service in accordance with the Service Regulation); or

    (ii)   rule 39E (service through foreign governments, judicial authorities and British Consular authorities); or

(b)   permitted by the law of the country in which it is to be served.

(4) Nothing in paragraph (3) or in any court order authorises or requires any person to do anything which is contrary to the law of the country where the application form or other document is to be served.

### Service in accordance with the Service Regulation

**39D.**—(1) This rule applies where an application form or other document is to be served on a person out of the United Kingdom in accordance with the Service Regulation.

(2) The person wishing to serve must file—

(a)   the application form or other document;

(b)   any translation; and

(c)   any other documents required by the Service Regulation.

(3) When the person wishing to serve files the documents referred to in paragraph (2), the court officer must—

(a)   seal, or otherwise authenticate with the stamp of the court, the copy of the application form; and

(b)   forward the documents to the Senior Master of the Queen's Bench Division.

(4) In addition to the documents referred to in paragraph (2), the person wishing to serve may, if of the view that this would assist in ensuring effective service, file a photograph of the person to be served.

(The Service Regulation is annexed to Practice Direction 6B.)

(Rule 39E makes provision for service on a person in a Service Convention country.)

### Service through foreign governments, judicial authorities and British Consular authorities

**39E.**—(1) Where an application form or other document is to be served on a person in a Service Convention country, it may be served—

(a)   through the authority designated under the Service Convention in respect of that country; or

(b)   if the law of that country permits, through—

    (i)   the judicial authorities of that country; or

    (ii)   a British Consular authority in that country.

(2) Where an application form or other document is to be served on a person in a country which is not a Service Convention country, it may be served, if the law of that country so permits, through—

(a)   the government of that country, where that government is willing to serve it; or

(b)   a British Consular authority in that country.

(3) Where an application form or other document is to be served in—

(a)   any Commonwealth State which is not a Service Convention country;

(b)   the Isle of Man or the Channel Islands; or

(c)   any British Overseas Territory,

the methods of service permitted by paragraphs (1)(b) and (2) are not available and the person wishing to serve, or that person's agent, must effect service direct unless Practice Direction 6B provides otherwise.

(4) This rule does not apply where service is to be effected in accordance with the Service Regulation.

(Rule 39D makes provision for service on a party in a Member State in accordance with the Service Regulation.)

(A list of British Overseas Territories is reproduced in Practice Direction 6B.)

**Procedure where service is to be through foreign governments, judicial authorities and British Consular authorities**

39F.—(1) This rule applies where an application form or other document is to be served under rule 39E(1) or (2).

(2) Where this rule applies, the person wishing to serve must file—

(a) a request for service of the application form or other document, by specifying one or more of the methods in rule 39E(1) or (2);

(b) a copy of the application form or other document;

(c) any other documents or copies of documents required by Practice Direction 6B; and

(d) any translation required under rule 39G.

(3) When the person wishing to serve files the documents specified in paragraph (2), the court officer must—

(a) seal, or otherwise authenticate with the stamp of the court, the copy of the application form; and

(b) forward the documents to the Senior Master of the Queen's Bench Division.

(4) The Senior Master shall send documents forwarded under this rule—

(a) where the application form or other document is being served through the authority designated under the Service Convention, to that authority; or

(b) in any other case, to the Foreign and Commonwealth Office with a request that it arranges for the application form or other document to be served.

(5) An official certificate which—

(a) states that the method requested under paragraph (2)(a) has been performed and the date of such performance;

(b) states, where more than one method is requested under paragraph (2)(a), which method was used; and

(c) is made by—

    (i) a British Consular authority in the country where the method requested under paragraph (2)(a) was performed;

    (ii) the government or judicial authorities in that country; or

    (iii) the authority designated in respect of that country under the Service Convention,

is evidence of the facts stated in the certificate.

(6) A document purporting to be an official certificate under paragraph (5) is to be treated as such a certificate unless it is proved not to be.

**Translation of application form or other document**

39G.—(1) Except where paragraphs (4) and (5) apply, every copy of the application form or other document filed under rule 39E (service through foreign governments, judicial authorities and British Consular authorities) must be accompanied by a translation of the application form or other document.

(2) The translation must be—

(a) in the official language of the country in which it is to be served; or

(b) if there is more than one official language of that country, in any official language which is appropriate to the place in the country where the application form or other document is to be served.

(3) Every translation filed under this rule must be accompanied by a statement by the person making it that it is a correct translation, and the statement must include that person's name, address and qualifications for making the translation.

(4) The applicant is not required to file a translation of the application form or other document filed under rule 39E where it is to be served in a country of which English is an official language.

(5) The applicant is not required to file a translation of the application form or other document filed under rule 39E where—

(a)  the person on whom the document is to be served is able to read and understand English; and

(b)  service of the document is to be effected directly on that person.

(This rule does not apply to service in accordance with the Service Regulation, which contains its own provisions about the translation of documents.)

### Undertaking to be responsible for expenses of the Foreign and Commonwealth Office

**39H.** Every request for service under rule 39F (procedure where service is to be through foreign governments, judicial authorities, etc.) must contain an undertaking by the person making the request—

(a)  to be responsible for all expenses incurred by the Foreign and Commonwealth Office or foreign judicial authority; and

(b)  to pay those expenses to the Foreign and Commonwealth Office or foreign judicial authority on being informed of the amount.

## PRACTICE DIRECTION 6B – SERVICE OUT OF THE JURISDICTION

### Scope of this Practice Direction

**1.1** This Practice Direction supplements rules 39 to 39H (service out of thejurisdiction) of Part 6.

### Documents to be filed under rule 39F(2)(c)

**2.1** A party must provide the following documents for each party to be served out of the jurisdiction—

(1)  a copy of the application form and any other relevant documents;

(2)  a duplicate of the application form, copies of any documents accompanying the application and copies of any other relevant documents;

(3)  forms for responding to the application; and

(4)  any translation required under rule 39G in duplicate.

**2.2** Some countries require legalisation of the document to be served and some require a formal letter of request which must be signed by the Senior Master. Any queries on this should be addressed to the Foreign Process Section (Room E02) at the Royal Courts of Justice.

### Service in a Commonwealth State or British overseas territory

**3.1** The judicial authorities of certain Commonwealth States which are not a party to the Hague Convention require service to be in accordance with rule 39E(1)(b)(i) and not 39E(3). A list of such countries can be obtained from the Foreign Process Section (Room E02) at the Royal Courts of Justice.

**3.2** The list of British overseas territories is contained in Schedule 6 to the British Nationality Act 1981. For ease of reference, these are –

(a)  Anguilla;

(b)  Bermuda;

(c)  British Antarctic Territory;

(d)  British Indian Ocean Territory;

(e)  British Virgin Islands;

(f)  Cayman Islands;

(g)  Falkland Islands;

(h)  Gibraltar;

(i)  Montserrat;

(j)  Pitcairn, Henderson, Ducie and Oeno;

(k)  St. Helena and Dependencies;

(l) South Georgia and the South Sandwich Islands;

(m) Sovereign Base Areas of Akrotiri and Dhekelia; and

(n) Turks and Caicos Islands.

**Period for responding to an application**

4.1 Where rule 39B(4) applies, the periods within which the respondent must file an acknowledgment of service or an answer to the application is the number of days listed in the Table after service of the application.

4.2 Where an application is served out of the jurisdiction any statement as to the period for responding to the application contained in any of the forms required by the Court of Protection Rules to accompany the application must specify the period prescribed under rule 39B.

**Period for responding to a document other than an application**

5.1 Where a document other than an application is served out of the jurisdiction, the period for responding is 7 days less than the number of days listed in the Table.

**Further information**

5.2 Further information concerning service out of the jurisdiction can be obtainedfrom the Foreign Process Section, Room E02, Royal Courts of Justice, Strand, London WC2A 2LL (telephone 020 7947 6691).

*[Table and Annex omitted]*

## PART 12 – DEALING WITH APPLICATIONS

. . .

*Disputing the jurisdiction of the court*

**Procedure for disputing the court's jurisdiction**

87.—(1) A person who wishes to—

(a) dispute the court's jurisdiction to hear an application; or

(b) argue that the court should not exercise its jurisdiction,

may apply to the court at any time for an order declaring that it has no such jurisdiction or should not exercise any jurisdiction that it may have.

(2) An application under this rule must be—

(a) made by using the form specified in the relevant practice direction; and

(b) supported by evidence.

(3) An order containing a declaration that the court has no jurisdiction or will not exercise its jurisdiction may also make further provision, including—

(a) setting aside the application;

(b) discharging any order made;

(c) staying the proceedings; and

(d) discharging any litigation friend, accredited legal representative or representative.

## PRACTICE DIRECTION 12B – PROCEDURE FOR DISPUTING THE COURT'S JURISDICTION

**Disputing the jurisdiction of the court – generally**

1. A person who wishes to:

(a) dispute the court's jurisdiction to hear an application; or

(b) argue that the court should not exercise such jurisdiction as it may have, may apply to the court for an order to that effect.

3. Where a person who has been served with or notified of an application form wishes to dispute the court's jurisdiction, he must state this in the acknowledgment of service or notification (as the case may be), using form COP5 filed in accordance with rule 72.

4. In any other case (with the exception of those cases provided for in paragraphs 5 to 7), a person who wishes to dispute the court's jurisdiction must do so by filing an application notice using form COP9 in accordance with Part 10.

### Disputing the jurisdiction of the court – where P has or regains capacity

5. Where P has or regains capacity in relation to the matter or matters to which the application relates, an application may be made to the court for the proceedings to come to an end.

6. Applications in such circumstances may only be made by the following persons:

(a) P;

(b) his litigation friend; or

(c) any other person who is a party to the proceedings.

7. The application must be made by filing an application notice using form COP9 in accordance with Part 10. The application must be served on all other parties to the proceedings.

# Family Procedure Rules

SI 2010/2955[1]

## PART 2—APPLICATION AND INTERPRETATION OF RULES

*Interpretation*

**2.3**

(1)  In these rules—

. . .

'the 1980 Hague Convention' means the Convention on the Civil Aspects of International Child Abduction which was signed at The Hague on 25 October 1980;

'the 1984 Act' means the Matrimonial and Family Proceedings Act 1984;

'the 1986 Act' means the Family Law Act 1986;

'the1989 Act' means the Children Act 1989;

. . .

'the 1996 Hague Convention' means the Convention on Jurisdiction, Applicable Law, Recognition, Enforcement and Co-Operation in Respect of Parental Responsibility and Measures for the Protection of Children;

'the 2002 Act' means the Adoption and Children Act 2002;

'the 2004 Act' means the Civil Partnership Act 2004;

'the 2005 Act' means the Mental Capacity Act 2005;

'the 2007 Hague Convention' means the Convention on the International Recovery of Child Support and other forms of Family Maintenance done at The Hague on 23 November 2007;

. . .

'adoption proceedings' means proceedings for an adoption order under the 2002 Act;

. . .

'child' means a person under the age of 18 years who is the subject of the proceedings; except that—

(a)  in adoption proceedings, it also includes a person who has attained the age of 18 years before the proceedings are concluded; and

(b)  in proceedings brought under the Council Regulation, the 1980 Hague Convention or the European Convention, it means a person under the age of 16 years who is the subject of the proceedings;

. . .

'the Council Regulation' means Council Regulation (EC) No 2201/2003 of 27 November 2003 on jurisdiction and the recognition and enforcement of judgments in matrimonial matters and in matters of parental responsibility;

. . .

'the European Convention' means the European Convention on Recognition and Enforcement of Decisions concerning Custody of Children and on the Restoration of Custody of Children which was signed in Luxembourg on 20 May 1980;

Rules of Procedure

[1]Version shown reflects the changes made by the Family Procedure (Amendment No 2) Rules 2015, SI 2015/1420. Amendments not marked.

. . .

'incoming protection measure' means a protection measure that has been ordered in a Member State of the European Union other than the United Kingdom or Denmark;

. . .

'jurisdiction' means, unless the context requires otherwise, England and Wales and any part of the territorial waters of the United Kingdom adjoining England and Wales;

. . .

'the Maintenance Regulation' means Council Regulation (EC) No 4/200925 of 18th December 2008 on jurisdiction, applicable law, recognition and enforcement of decisions and co-operation in matters relating to maintenance obligations,including as applied in relation to Denmark by virtue of the Agreement made on 19th October 2005 between the European Community and the Kingdom of Denmark;

. . .

'protection measure' has the meaning given to it in the Protection Measures Regulation;

'Protection Measures Regulation' means the Regulation (EU) No 606/2013 of the European Parliament and of the Council of 12th June 2013 on mutual recognition of protection measures in civil matters;

. . .

'section 84 order' means an order made by the High Court under section 84 of the 2002 Act giving parental responsibility prior to adoption abroad;

'section 89 order' means an order made by the High Court under section 89 of the 2002 Act—

(a)  annulling a Convention adoption or Convention adoption order;

(b)  providing for an overseas adoption or determination under section 91 of the 2002 Act to cease to be valid; or

(c)  deciding the extent, if any, to which a determination under section 91 of the 2002 Act has been affected by a subsequent determination under that section;

. . .

'the Service Regulation' means Regulation(EC) No. 1393/2007 of the European Parliament and of the Council of 13 November2007 on the service in the Member States of judicial and extra judicial documents in civil or commercial matters (service of documents), and repealing Council Regulation (EC) No. 1348/2000, as amended from time to time and as applied by the Agreement made on 19 October 2005 between the European Community and the Kingdom of Denmark on the service of judicial and extra judicial documents in civil and commercial matters;

. . .

## PART 6—SERVICE

## II SERVICE OF THE APPLICATION FOR A MATRIMONIAL ORDER OR CIVIL PARTNERSHIP ORDER IN THE JURISDICTION

*Interpretation*

**6.3**

In this Chapter, unless the context otherwise requires, a reference to an application—

(a)  is a reference to an application for a matrimonial or civil partnership order; and

(b)  includes an application by a respondent as referred to in rule 7.4.

(Part 7 deals with applications in matrimonial or civil partnership proceedings.)

*Methods of service*

**6.4**

An application may be served by any of the following methods—

(a)   personal service in accordance with rule 6.7;

(b)   first class post, or other service which provides for delivery on the next business day, in accordance with Practice Direction 6A; or

(c)   where rule 6.11 applies, document exchange.

. . .

*Personal service*

**6.7**

An application is served personally on a respondent by leaving it with that respondent.

. . .

*Where to serve the application—general provisions*

**6.10**

(1) The application must be served within the jurisdiction except as provided for by Chapter 4 of this Part (service out of the jurisdiction).

(2) The applicant must include in the application an address at which the respondent may be served.

(3) Paragraph (2) does not apply where an order made by the court under rule 6.19 (service by an alternative method or at an alternative place) specifies the place or method of service of the application.

. . .

*Service of the application where the respondent gives an address at which the respondent may be served*

**6.12**

Subject to rule 6.13, the respondent may be served with the application at an address within the jurisdiction which the respondent has given for the purpose of being served with the proceedings.

*Service of the application where the respondent does not give an address at which the respondent may be served*

**6.13**

(1) This rule applies where—

(a)   rule 6.11 (service of application on solicitor); and

(b)   rule 6.12 (respondent gives address at which respondent may be served),

do not apply and the applicant does not wish the application to be served personally under rule 6.7.

(2) Subject to paragraphs (3) to (5) the application must be served on the respondent at his usual or last known address.

(3) Where the applicant has reason to believe that the respondent no longer resides at his usual or last known address, the applicant must take reasonable steps to ascertain the current address of the respondent.

(4) Where, having taken the reasonable steps required by paragraph (3), the applicant—

(a)   ascertains the respondent's current address, the application must be served at that address; or

(b)   is unable to ascertain the respondent's current address, the applicant must consider whether there is—

   (i)   an alternative place where; or

(ii)  an alternative method by which,

service may be effected.

(5) If, under paragraph (4)(b), there is such a place where or a method by which service could be effected, the applicant must make an application under rule 6.19.

. . .

*Service of the application by an alternative method or at an alternative place*

**6.19**

(1) Where it appears to the court that there is a good reason to authorise service by a method or at a place not otherwise permitted by this Part, the court may direct that service is effected by an alternative method or at an alternative place.

(2) On an application under this rule, the court may direct that steps already taken to bring the application form to the attention of the respondent by an alternative method or at an alternative place is good service.

(3) A direction under this rule must specify—

(a)  the method or place of service;

(b)  the date on which the application form is deemed served; and

(c)  the period for filing an acknowledgment of service or answer.

*Power of the court to dispense with service of the application*

**6.20**

(1) The court may dispense with service of the application where it is impracticable to serve the application by any method provided for by this Part.

(2) An application for an order to dispense with service may be made at any time and must be supported by evidence.

(3) The court may require the applicant to attend when it decides the application.

. . .

## IV  SERVICE OUT OF THE JURISDICTION

*Scope and interpretation*

**6.40**

(1) This Chapter contains rules about—

(a)  service of application forms and other documents out of the jurisdiction; and

(b)  the procedure for service.

('Jurisdiction' is defined in rule 2.3.)

(2) In this Chapter—

'application form' includes an application notice;

'Commonwealth State' means a State listed in Schedule 3 to the British Nationality Act 1981[4]; and

'the Hague Convention' means the Convention on the service abroad of judicial and extra-judicial documents in civil or commercial matters signed at the Hague on November 15, 1965.

*Permission to serve not required*

**6.41**

Any document to be served for the purposes of these rules may be served out of the jurisdiction without the permission of the court.

*Period for acknowledging service or responding to application where application is served out of the jurisdiction*

**6.42**

(1) This rule applies where, under these rules, a party is required to file—

(a)  an acknowledgment of service; or

(b)  an answer to an application,

and sets out the time period for doing so where the application is served out of the jurisdiction.

(2) Where the applicant serves an application on a respondent in—

(a)  Scotland or Northern Ireland; or

(b)  a Member State or Hague Convention country within Europe,

the period for filing an acknowledgment of service or an answer to an application is 21 days after service of the application.

(3) Where the applicant serves an application on a respondent in a Hague Convention country outside Europe, the period for filing an acknowledgment of service or an answer to an application is 31 days after service of the application.

(4) Where the applicant serves an application on a respondent in a country not referred to in paragraphs (2) and (3), the period for filing an acknowledgment of service or an answer to an application is set out in Practice Direction 6B.

*Method of service—general provisions*

**6.43**

(1) This rule contains general provisions about the method of service of an application for a matrimonial or civil partnership order, or other document, on a party out of the jurisdiction.

*Where service is to be effected on a party in Scotland or Northern Ireland*

(2) Where a party serves an application form or other document on a party in Scotland or Northern Ireland, it must be served by a method permitted by Chapter 2 (and references to 'jurisdiction' in that Chapter are modified accordingly) or Chapter 3 of this Part and rule 6.26(5) applies.

*Where service is to be effected on a respondent out of the United Kingdom*

(3) Where the applicant wishes to serve an application form, or other document, on a respondent out of the United Kingdom, it may be served by any method—

(a)  provided for by—

    (i)  rule 6.44 (service in accordance with the Service Regulation);

    (ii)  rule 6.45 (service through foreign governments, judicial authorities and British Consular authorities); or

(b)  permitted by the law of the country in which it is to be served.

(4) Nothing in paragraph (3) or in any court order authorises or requires any person to do anything which is contrary to the law of the country where the application form, or other document, is to be served.

*Service in accordance with the Service Regulation*

**6.44**

(1) This rule applies where the applicant wishes to serve the application form, or other document, in accordance with the Service Regulation.

(2) The applicant must file—

(a)  the application form or other document;

(b) any translation; and

(c) any other documents required by the Service Regulation.

(3) When the applicant files the documents referred to in paragraph (2), the court officer will—

(a) seal, or otherwise authenticate with the stamp of the court, the copy of the application form; and

(b) forward the documents to the Senior Master of the Queen's Bench Division.

(4) In addition to the documents referred to in paragraph (2), the applicant may file a photograph of the person to be served if the applicant considers that it would assist in ensuring effective service.

(The Service Regulation is annexed to Practice Direction 6B.)

(Article 20(1) of the Service Regulation provides that the Regulation prevails over other provisions contained in any other agreement or arrangement concluded by Member States.)

*Service through foreign governments, judicial authorities and British Consular authorities*

**6.45**

(1) Where the applicant wishes to serve an application form, or other document, on a respondent in any country which is a party to the Hague Convention, it may be served—

(a) through the authority designated under the Hague Convention in respect of that country; or

(b) if the law of that country permits—

    (i) through the judicial authorities of that country; or

    (ii) through a British Consular authority in that country.

(2) Where the applicant wishes to serve an application form, or other document, on a respondent in any country which is not a party to the Hague Convention, it may be served, if the law of that country so permits—

(a) through the government of that country, where that government is willing to serve it; or

(b) through a British Consular authority in that country.

(3) Where the applicant wishes to serve an application form, or other document, in—

(a) any Commonwealth State which is not a party to the Hague Convention;

(b) the Isle of Man or the Channel Islands; or

(c) any British Overseas Territory,

the methods of service permitted by paragraphs (1)(b) and (2) are not available and the applicant or the applicant's agent must effect service on a respondent in accordance with rule 6.43 unless Practice Direction 6B provides otherwise.

(4) This rule does not apply where service is to be effected in accordance with the Service Regulation.

(A list of British overseas territories is reproduced in Practice Direction 6B.)

*Procedure where service is to be through foreign governments, judicial authorities and British Consular authorities*

**6.46**

(1) This rule applies where the applicant wishes to serve an application form, or other document, under rule 6.45(1) or (2).

(2) Where this rule applies, the applicant must file—

(a) a request for service of the application form, or other document, by specifying one or more of the methods in rule6.45(1) or (2);

(b) a copy of the application form or other document;

(c) any other documents or copies of documents required by Practice Direction 6B; and

(d) any translation required under rule 6.47.

(3) When the applicant files the documents specified in paragraph (2), the court officer will—

(a)  seal, or otherwise authenticate with the stamp of the court, the copy of the application form or other document; and

(b)  forward the documents to the Senior Master of the Queen's Bench Division.

(4)  The Senior Master will send documents forwarded under this rule—

(a)  where the application form, or other document, is being served through the authority designated under the Hague Convention, to that authority; or

(b)  in any other case, to the Foreign and Commonwealth Office with a request that it arranges for the application form or other document to be served.

(5)  An official certificate which—

(a)  states that the method requested under paragraph (2)(a) has been performed and the date of such performance;

(b)  states, where more than one method is requested under paragraph (2)(a), which method was used; and

(c)  is made by—

  (i)  a British Consular authority in the country where the method requested under paragraph (2)(a) was performed;

  (ii)  the government or judicial authorities in that country; or

  (iii)  the authority designated in respect of that country under the Hague Convention,

is evidence of the facts stated in the certificate.

(6)  A document purporting to be an official certificate under paragraph (5) is to be treated as such a certificate, unless it is proved not to be.

## *Translation of application form or other document*

**6.47**

(1)  Except where paragraphs (4) and (5) apply, every copy of the application form, or other document, filed under rule 6.45 (service through foreign governments, judicial authorities and British Consular authorities) must be accompanied by a translation of the application form or other document.

(2)  The translation must be—

(a)  in the official language of the country in which it is to be served; or

(b)  if there is more than one official language of that country, in any official language which is appropriate to the place in the country where the application form or other document is to be served.

(3)  Every translation filed under this rule must be accompanied by a statement by the person making it that it is a correct translation, and the statement must include that person's name, address and qualifications for making the translation.

(4)  The applicant is not required to file a translation of the application form, or other document, filed under rule 6.45 where it is to be served in a country of which English is an official language.

(5)  The applicant is not required to file a translation of the application form or other document filed under rule 6.45 where—

(a)  the person on whom the document is to be served is able to read and understand English; and

(b)  service of the document is to be effected directly on that person.

(This rule does not apply to service in accordance with the Service Regulation which contains its own provisions about the translation of documents.)

*Undertaking to be responsible for expenses of the Foreign and Commonwealth Office*

**6.48**

Every request for service filed under rule 6.46 (procedure where service is to be through foreign governments, judicial authorities etc) must contain an undertaking by the person making the request—

(a) to be responsible for all expenses incurred by the Foreign and Commonwealth Office or foreign judicial authority; and

(b) to pay those expenses to the Foreign and Commonwealth Office or foreign judicial authority on being informed of the amount.

## PRACTICE DIRECTION 6B—SERVICE OUT OF THE JURISDICTION

*Scope of this Practice Direction*

**1.1**

This Practice Direction supplements Chapter 4 (service out of the jurisdiction) of Part 6.

(Practice Direction 6A contains relevant provisions supplementing rule 6.43(2) in relation to the method of service on a party in Scotland or Northern Ireland.)

*Service in other Member States of the European Union*

**2.1**

Where service is to be effected in another Member of State of the European Union, the Service Regulation applies.

**2.2**

The Service Regulation is Regulation (EC) No. 1393/2007 of the European Parliament and of the Council of 13 November 2007 on the service in the Member States of judicial and extrajudicial documents in civil or commercial matters (service of documents), and repealing Council Regulation (EC) No. 1348/2000, as amended from time to time and as applied by the Agreement made on 19 October 2005 between the European Community and the Kingdom of Denmark on the service of judicial and extrajudicial documents in civil and commercial matters.

**2.3**

The Service Regulation is annexed to this Practice Direction.

(Article 20(1) of the Service Regulation provides that the Regulation prevails over other provisions contained in bilateral or multilateral agreements or arrangements concluded by the Member of States and in particular Article IV of the protocol to the Brussels Convention of 1968 and the Hague Convention of 15 November 1965)

*Documents to be filed under rule 6.46(2)*

**3.1**

A duplicate of—

(a) the application form or other document to be served under rule 6.45(1) or (2);

(b) any documents accompanying the application or other document referred to in paragraph (a); and

(c) any translation required by rule 6.47;

must be provided for each party to be served out of the jurisdiction, together with forms for responding to the application.

**3.2**

Some countries require legalisation of the document to be served and some require a formal letter of request which must be signed by the Senior Master. Any queries on this should be addressed to the Foreign Process Section (Room E02) at the Royal Courts of Justice.

*Service in a Commonwealth State or British Overseas Territory*

**4.1**

The judicial authorities of certain Commonwealth States which are not a party to the Hague Convention require service to be in accordance with rule 6.45(1)(b)(i) and not 6.45(3). A list of such countries can be obtained from the Foreign Process Section (Room E02) at the Royal Courts of Justice.

**4.2**

The list of British overseas territories is contained in Schedule 6 to the British Nationality Act 1981. For ease of reference these are—

(a)　Anguilla;

(b)　Bermuda;

(c)　British Antarctic Territory;

(d)　British Indian Ocean Territory;

(e)　Cayman Islands;

(f)　Falkland Islands;

(g)　Gibraltar;

(h)　Montserrat;

(i)　Pitcairn, Henderson, Ducie and Oeno Islands;

(j)　St. Helena, Ascension and Tristan da Cunha;

(k)　South Georgia and the South Sandwich Islands;

(l)　Sovereign Base Areas of Akrotiri and Dhekelia;

(m)　Turks and Caicos Islands;

(n)　Virgin Islands.

*Period for responding to an application form*

**5.1**

Where rule 6.42 applies, the period within which the respondent must file an acknowledgment of service or an answer to the application is the number of days listed in the Table after service of the application.

**5.2**

Where an application is served out of the jurisdiction any statement as to the period for responding to the claim contained in any of the forms required by the Family Procedure Rules to accompany the application must specify the period prescribed under rule 6.42.

*Service of application notices and orders*

**6.1**

The provisions of Chapter 4 of Part 6 (special provisions about service out of the jurisdiction) also apply to service out of the jurisdiction of an application notice or order.

6.2

Where an application notice is to be served out of the jurisdiction in accordance with Chapter 4 of Part 6 the court must have regard to the country in which the application notice is to be served in setting the date for the hearing of the application and giving any direction about service of the respondent's evidence.

*Period for responding to an application notice*

7.1

Where an application notice or order is served out of the jurisdiction, the period for responding is 7 days less than the number of days listed in the Table.

*Further information*

8.1

Further information concerning service out of the jurisdiction can be obtained from the Foreign Process Section, Room E02, Royal Courts of Justice, Strand, London WC2A 2LL (telephone 020 7947 6691).

*[Table and Annex omitted]*

## PART 12—PROCEEDINGS RELATING TO CHILDREN EXCEPT PARENTAL ORDER PROCEEDINGS AND PROCEEDINGS FOR APPLICATIONS IN ADOPTION, PLACEMENT AND RELATED PROCEEDINGS

II  GENERAL RULES

. . .

*Notice of proceedings to person with foreign parental responsibility*

12.4

(1) This rule applies where a child is subject to proceedings to which this Part applies and—

(a)  a person holds or is believed to hold parental responsibility for the child under the law of another State which subsists in accordance with Article 16 of the 1996 Hague Convention following the child becoming habitually resident in a territorial unit of the United Kingdom; and

(b)  that person is not otherwise required to be joined as a respondent under rule 12.3.

(2) The applicant shall give notice of the proceedings to any person to whom the applicant believes paragraph (1) applies in any case in which a person whom the applicant believed to have parental responsibility under the 1989 Act would be a respondent to those proceedings in accordance with rule 12.3.

(3) The applicant and every respondent to the proceedings shall provide such details as they possess as to the identity and whereabouts of any person they believe to hold parental responsibility for the child in accordance with paragraph (1) to the court officer, upon making, or responding to the application as appropriate.

(4) Where the existence of a person who is believed to have parental responsibility for the child in accordance with paragraph (1) only becomes apparent to a party at a later date during the proceedings, that party must notify the court officer of those details at the earliest opportunity.

(5) Where a person to whom paragraph (1) applies receives notice of proceedings, that person may apply to the court to be joined as a party using the Part 18 procedure.

. . .

VI PROCEEDINGS UNDER THE 1980 HAGUE CONVENTION, THE EUROPEAN CONVENTION, THE COUNCIL REGULATION, AND THE 1996 HAGUE CONVENTION

*Scope*

**12.43**

This Chapter applies to—

(a)  children proceedings under the 1980 Hague Convention or the European Convention; and

(b)  applications relating to the Council Regulation or the 1996 Hague Convention in respect of children.

SECTION 1

**Proceedings under the 1980 Hague Convention or the European Convention**

*Interpretation*

**12.44**

(1)  In this section—

'the 1985 Act' means the Child Abduction and Custody Act 1985;

'Central Authority' means, in relation to England and Wales, the Lord Chancellor;

'Contracting State' has the meaning given in—

(a)  section 2 of the 1985 Act in relation to the 1980 Hague Convention; and

(b)  section 13 of the 1985 Act in relation to the European Convention; and

'decision relating to custody' has the same meaning as in the European Convention.

('the 1980 Hague Convention' and the 'the European Convention' are defined in rule 2.3)

*Where to start proceedings*

12.45 Every application under the 1980 Hague Convention or the European Convention must be—

(a)  made in the High Court and issued in the principal registry; and

(b)  heard by a Judge of the High Court unless the application is;

(i)  to join a respondent; or

(ii)  to dispense with service or extend the time for acknowledging service.

*Evidence in support of application*

12.46 Where the party making an application under this section does not produce the documents referred to in Practice Direction 12F, the court may—

(a)  fix a time within which the documents are to be produced;

(b)  accept equivalent documents; or

(c)  dispense with production of the documents if the court considers it has sufficient information.

*Without-notice applications*

**12.47**

(1)  This rule applies to applications—

(a)  commencing or in proceedings under this section;

(b)  for interim directions under section 5 or 19 of the 1985 Act;

(c)  for the disclosure of information about the child and for safeguarding the child's welfare, under rule 12.57;

(d) for the disclosure of relevant information as to where the child is, under section 24A of the 1985 Act; or

(e) for a collection order, location order or passport order.

(2) Applications under this rule may be made without notice, in which case the applicant must file the application—

(a) where the application is made by telephone, the next business day after the making of the application; or

(b) in any other case, at the time when the application is made.

(3) Where an order is made without notice, the applicant must serve a copy of the order on the other parties as soon as practicable after the making of the order, unless the court otherwise directs.

(4) Where the court refuses to make an order on an application without notice, it may direct that the application is made on notice.

(5) Where any hearing takes place outside the hours during which the court office is usually open—

(a) if the hearing takes place by telephone, the applicant's solicitors will, if practicable, arrange for the hearing to be recorded; and

(b) in all other cases, the court or court officer will take a note of the proceedings.

(Practice Direction 12E (Urgent Business) provides further details of the procedure for out of hours applications. See also Practice Direction 12D (Inherent Jurisdiction (including Wardship Proceedings)).)

*Directions*

**12.48**

(1) As soon as practicable after an application to which this section applies has been made, the court may give directions as to the following matters, among others—

(a) whether service of the application may be dispensed with;

(b) whether the proceedings should be transferred to another court under rule 12.54;

(c) expedition of the proceedings or any part of the proceedings (and any direction for expedition may specify a date by which the court must issue its final judgment in the proceedings or a specified part of the proceedings);

(d) the steps to be taken in the proceedings and the time by which each step is to be taken;

(e) whether the child or any other person should be made a party to the proceedings;

(f) if the child is not made a party to the proceedings, the manner in which the child's wishes and feelings are to be ascertained, having regard to the child's age and maturity and in particular whether an officer of the Service or a Welsh family proceedings officer should report to the court for that purpose;

(g) where the child is made a party to the proceedings, the appointment of a children's guardian for that child unless a children's guardian has already been appointed;

(h) the attendance of the child or any other person before the court;

(i) the appointment of a litigation friend for a child or for any protected party, unless a litigation friend has already been appointed;

(j) the service of documents;

(k) the filing of evidence including expert evidence; and

(l) whether the parties and their representatives should meet at any stage of the proceedings and the purpose of such a meeting.

(Rule 16.2 provides for when the court may make the child a party to the proceedings and rule 16.4 for the appointment of a children's guardian for the child who is made a party. Rule 16.5 (without prejudice to rule 16.6) requires a child who is a party to the proceedings but not the subject of those proceedings to have a litigation friend.)

(2) Directions of a court which are in force immediately prior to the transfer of proceedings to another court under rule 12.54 will continue to apply following the transfer subject to—

(a) any changes of terminology which are required to apply those directions to the court to which the proceedings are transferred; and

(b) any variation or revocation of the directions.

(3) The court or court officer will—

(a) take a note of the giving, variation or revocation of directions under this rule; and

(b) as soon as practicable serve a copy of the directions order on every party.

*Answer*

**12.49**

(1) Subject to paragraph (2) and to any directions given under rule 12.48, a respondent must file and serve on the parties an answer to the application within 7 days beginning with the date on which the application is served.

(2) The court may direct a longer period for service where the respondent has been made a party solely on one of the following grounds—

(a) a decision relating to custody has been made in the respondent's favour; or

(b) the respondent appears to the court to have sufficient interest in the welfare of the child.

Filing and serving written evidence

**12.50**

(1) The respondent to an application to which this section applies may file and serve with the answer a statement verified by a statement of truth, together with any further evidence on which the respondent intends to rely.

(2) The applicant may, within 7 days beginning with the date on which the respondent's evidence was served under paragraph (1), file and serve a statement in reply verified by a statement of truth, together with any further evidence on which the applicant intends to rely.

*Adjournment*

**12.51** The court will not adjourn the hearing of an application to which this section applies for more than 21 days at at any one time.

## Stay of proceedings upon notification of wrongful removal etc

**12.52**

(1) In this rule and in rule 12.53—

(a) 'relevant authority' means—

    (i) the High Court;

    (ii) the family court;

    (iii) [. . .]

    (iv) the Court of Session;

    (v) a sheriff court;

    (vi) a children's hearing within the meaning of section 93 of the Children (Scotland) Act 1995;

    (vii) the High Court in Northern Ireland;

    (viii) a county court in Northern Ireland;

    (ix) a court of summary jurisdiction in Northern Ireland;

    (x) the Royal Court of Jersey;

    (xi) a court of summary jurisdiction in Jersey;

(xii) the High Court of Justice of the Isle of Man;

(xiii) a court of summary jurisdiction in the Isle of Man; or

(xiv) the Secretary of State; and

(b) 'rights of custody' has the same meaning as in the 1980 Hague Convention.

(2) Where a party to proceedings under the 1980 Hague Convention knows that an application relating to the merits of rights of custody is pending in or before a relevant authority, that party must file within the proceedings under the 1980 Hague Convention a concise statement of the nature of that application, including the relevant authority in or before which it is pending.

(3) On receipt of a statement filed in accordance with paragraph (2) above, a court officer will notify the relevant authority in or before which the application is pending and will subsequently notify the relevant authority of the result of the proceedings.

(4) On receipt by the relevant authority of a notification under paragraph (3) from the High Court or equivalent notification from the Court of Session, the High Court in Northern Ireland or the High Court of Justice of the Isle of Man—

(a) all further proceedings in the action will be stayed unless and until the proceedings under the 1980 Hague Convention in the High Court, Court of Session, the High Court in Northern Ireland or the High Court of Justice of the Isle of Man are dismissed; and

(b) the parties to the action will be notified by the court officer of the stay and dismissal.

*Stay of proceedings where application made under s.16 of the 1985 Act (registration of decisions under the European Convention)*

**12.53**

(1) A person who—

(a) is a party to—

(i) proceedings under section 16 of the 1985 Act; or

(ii) proceedings as a result of which a decision relating to custody has been registered under section 16 of the 1985 Act; and

(b) knows that an application is pending under—

(i) section 20(2) of the 1985 Act;

(ii) Article 21(2) of the Child Abduction and Custody (Jersey) Law 2005; or

(iii) section 42(2) of the Child Custody Act 1987 (an Act of Tynwald),

must file within the proceedings under section 16 of the 1985 Act a concise statement of the nature of the pending application.

(2) On receipt of a statement filed in accordance with paragraph (1) above, a court officer will notify the relevant authority in or before which the application is pending and will subsequently notify the relevant authority of the result of the proceedings.

(3) On receipt by the relevant authority of a notification under paragraph (2) from the High Court or equivalent notification from the Court of Session, the High Court in Northern Ireland or the High Court of Justice of the Isle of Man, the court officer will notify the parties to the action.

*Transfer of proceedings*

**12.54**

(1) At any stage in proceedings under the 1985 Act the court may—

(a) of its own initiative; or

(b) on the application of a party with a minimum of two days' notice;

order that the proceedings be transferred to a court listed in paragraph (4).

(2) Where the court makes an order for transfer under paragraph (1)—

(a)   the court will state its reasons on the face of the order;

(b)   a court officer will send a copy of the order, the application and the accompanying documents (if any) and any evidence to the court to which the proceedings are transferred; and

(c)   the costs of the proceedings both before and after the transfer will be at the discretion of the court to which the proceedings are transferred.

(3) Where proceedings are transferred to the High Court from a court listed in paragraph (4), a court officer will notify the parties of the transfer and the proceedings will continue as if they had been commenced in the High Court.

(4) The listed courts are the Court of Session, the High Court in Northern Ireland, the Royal Court of Jersey or the High Court of Justice of the Isle of Man.

*Revocation and variation of registered decisions*

**12.55**

(1) This rule applies to decisions which—

(a)   have been registered under section 16 of the 1985 Act; and

(b)   are subsequently varied or revoked by an authority in the Contracting State in which they were made.

(2) The court will, on cancelling the registration of a decision which has been revoked, notify—

(a)   the person appearing to the court to have care of the child;

(b)   the person on whose behalf the application for registration of the decision was made; and

(c)   any other party to the application.

(3) The court will, on being informed of the variation of a decision, notify—

(a)   the party appearing to the court to have care of the child; and

(b)   any party to the application for registration of the decision;

and any such person may apply to make representations to the court before the registration is varied.

(4) Any person appearing to the court to have an interest in the proceedings may apply for the registration of a decision for the cancellation or variation of the decision referred to in paragraph (1).

*The central index of decisions registered under the 1985 Act*

**12.56**

A central index of decisions registered under section 16 of the 1985 Act, together with any variation of those decisions made under section 17 of that Act, will be kept by the principal registry.

*Disclosure of information in proceedings under the European Convention*

**12.57**

At any stage in proceedings under the European Convention the court may, if it has reason to believe that any person may have relevant information about the child who is the subject of those proceedings, order that person to disclose such information and may for that purpose order that the person attend before it or file affidavit evidence.

SECTION 2

**Applications relating to the Council Regulation and the 1996 Hague Convention**

*Interpretation*

**12.58**

(1) In this section—

'Contracting State' means a State party to the 1996 Hague Convention;

'domestic Central Authority' means—

(a)   where the matter relates to the Council Regulation, the Lord Chancellor;

(b)   where the matter relates to the 1996 Hague Convention in England, the Lord Chancellor;

(c)   where the matter relates to the 1996 Hague Convention in Wales, the Welsh Ministers;

'judgment' has the meaning given in Article 2(4) of the Council Regulation;

'Member State' means a Member State bound by the Council Regulation or a country which has subsequently adopted the Council Regulation;

'parental responsibility' has the meaning given in—

(a)   Article 2(7) of the Council Regulation in relation to proceedings under that Regulation; and

(b)   Article 1(2) of the 1996 Hague Convention in relation to proceedings under that Convention; and

'seised' has the meaning given in Article 16 of the Council Regulation.

(2)   In rules 12.59 to 12.70, references to the court of another member State or Contracting State include authorities within the meaning of 'court' in Article 2(1) of the Council Regulation, and authorities of Contracting States which have jurisdiction to take measures directed to the protection of the person or property of the child within the meaning of the 1996 Hague Convention.

*Procedure under Article 11(6) of the Council Regulation where the court makes a non-return order under Article 13 of the 1980 Hague Convention*

**12.59**

(1)   Where the court makes an order for the non-return of a child under Article 13 of the 1980 Hague Convention, it must immediately transmit the documents referred to in Article 11(6) of the Council Regulation—

(a)   directly to the court with jurisdiction or the central authority in the Member State where the child was habitually resident immediately before the wrongful removal to, or wrongful retention in, England and Wales; or

(b)   to the domestic Central Authority for onward transmission to the court with jurisdiction or the central authority in the other Member State mentioned in sub-paragraph (a).

(2)   The documents required by paragraph(1) must be transmitted by a method which, in the case of direct transmission to the court with jurisdiction in the other Member State, ensures and, in any other case, will not prevent, their receipt by that court within one month of the date of the non-return order.

*Procedure under Article 11(7) of the Council Regulation where the court receives a non-return order made under Article 13 of the 1980 Hague Convention by a court in another Member State*

**12.60**

(1)   This rule applies where the court receives an order made by a court in another Member State for the non-return of a child.

(2)   In this rule, the order for non-return of the child and the papers transmitted with that order from the court in the other Member State are referred to as 'the non-return order'.

(3)   Where, at the time of receipt of the non-return order, the court is already seised of a question of parental responsibility in relation to the child—

(a)   the court officer shall immediately—

(i)    serve copies of the non-return order on each party to the proceedings in which a question of parental responsibility in relation to the child is at issue; and

(ii)   where the non-return order was received directly from the court or the central authority in the other Member State, transmit to the domestic Central Authority a copy of the non-return order.

(b)   the court shall immediately invite the parties to the 1980 Hague Convention proceedings to file written submissions in respect of the question of custody by a specified date, or to attend a hearing to consider the future conduct of the proceedings in the light of the non-return order.

(4)   Where, at the time of receipt of the non-return order, the court is not already seised of the question of parental responsibility in relation to the child, it shall immediately—

(a)   open a court file in respect of the child and assign a court reference to the file;

(b)   serve a copy of the non-return order on each party to the proceedings before the court in the Member State which made that order;

(c)   invite each party to file, within 3 months of notification to that party of receipt of the non-return order, submissions in the form of—

   (i)   an application for an order under—

      (aa)      the 1989 Act; or

      (bb)      (in the High Court only) an application under the inherent jurisdiction in respect of the child; or

   (ii)   where permission is required to make an application for the order in question, an application for that permission;

(d)   where the non-return order was received directly from the court or central authority in the other Member State, transmit to the domestic Central Authority a copy of the non-return order.

(5)   In a case to which paragraph (4) applies where no application is filed within the 3 month period provided for by paragraph (4)(c) the court must close its file in respect of the child.

(Enforcement of a subsequent judgment requiring the return of the child, made under Article 11(8) by a court examining custody of the child under Article 11(7), is dealt with in Part 31 below.)

### *Transfer of proceedings under Article 15 of the Council Regulation or under Article 8 of the 1996 Hague Convention*

**12.61**

(1)   Where the court is considering the transfer of proceedings to the court of another Member State or Contracting State under rules 12.62 to 12.64 it will—

(a)   fix a date for a hearing for the court to consider the question of transfer; and

(b)   give directions as to the manner in which the parties may make representations.

(2)   The court may, with the consent of all parties, deal with the question of transfer without a hearing.

(3)   Directions which are in force immediately prior to the transfer of proceedings to a court in another Member State or Contracting State under rules 12.62 to 12.64 will continue to apply until the court in that other State accepts jurisdiction in accordance with the provisions of the Council Regulation or the 1996 Hague Convention (as appropriate), subject to any variation or revocation of the directions.

(4)   The court or court officer will–

(a)   take a note of the giving, variation or revocation of directions under this rule; and

(b)   as soon as practicable serve a copy of the directions order on every party.

(5)   A register of all applications and requests for transfer of jurisdiction to or from another Member State or Contracting State will be kept by the principal registry.

### *Application by a party for transfer of the proceedings*

**12.62**

(1)   A party may apply to the court under Article 15(1) of the Council Regulation or under Article 8(1) of the 1996 Hague Convention—

(a)   to stay the proceedings or a specified part of the proceedings and to invite the parties to introduce a request before a court of another Member State or Contracting State; or

(b)  to make a request to a court of another Member State or another Contracting State to assume jurisdiction for the proceedings, or a specified part of the proceedings.

(2)  An application under paragraph (1) must be made—

(a)  to the court in which the relevant parental responsibility proceedings are pending; and

(b)  using the Part 18 procedure.

(3)  The applicant must file the application notice and serve it on the respondents—

(a)  where the application is also made under Article 11 of the Council Regulation, not less than 5 days, and

(b)  in any other case, not less than 42 days,

before the hearing of the application.

*Application by a court of another Member State or another Contracting State for transfer of the proceedings*

**12.63**

(1)  This rule applies where a court of another Member State or another Contracting State makes an application under Article 15(2)(c) of the Council Regulation or under Article 9 of the 1996 Hague Convention that the court having jurisdiction in relation to the proceedings transfer the proceedings or a specific part of the proceedings to the applicant court.

(2)  When the court receives the application, the court officer will—

(a)  as soon as practicable, notify the domestic Central Authority of the application; and

(b)  serve the application, and notice of the hearing on all other parties in England and Wales not less than 5 days before the hearing of the application.

*Exercise by the court of its own initiative of powers to seek to transfer the proceedings*

**12.64**

(1)  The court having jurisdiction in relation to the proceedings may exercise its powers of its own initiative under Article 15 of the Council Regulation or Article 8 of the 1996 Hague Convention in relation to the proceedings or a specified part of the proceedings.

(2)  Where the court proposes to exercise its powers, the court officer will give the parties not less than 5 days' notice of the hearing.

*Application to High Court to make request under Article 15 of the Council Regulation or Article 9 of the 1996 Hague Convention to request transfer of jurisdiction*

**12.65**

(1)  An application for the court to request transfer of jurisdiction in a matter concerning a child from another Member State or another Contracting State under Article 15 of the Council Regulation, or Article 9 of the 1996 Hague Convention (as the case may be) must be made to the principal registry and heard in the High Court.

(2)  An application must be made without notice to any other person and the court may give directions about joining any other party to the application.

(3)  Where there is agreement between the court and the court or competent authority to which the request under paragraph (1) is made to transfer the matter to the courts of England and Wales, the court will consider with that other court or competent authority the specific timing and conditions for the transfer.

(4)  Upon receipt of agreement to transfer jurisdiction from the court or other competent authority in the Member State, or Contracting State to which the request has been made, the court officer will serve on the applicant a notice that jurisdiction has been accepted by the courts of England and Wales.

(5) The applicant must attach the notice referred to in paragraph (3) to any subsequent application in relation to the child.

(6) Nothing in this rule requires an application with respect to a child commenced following a transfer of jurisdiction to be made to or heard in the High Court.

(7) Upon allocation, the court to which the proceedings are allocated must immediately fix a directions hearing to consider the future conduct of the case.

*Procedure where the court receives a request from the authorities of another Member State or Contracting State to assume jurisdiction in a matter concerning a child*

**12.66**

(1) Where any court other than the High Court receives a request to assume jurisdiction in a matter concerning a child from a court or other authority which has jurisdiction in another Member State or Contracting State, that court must immediately refer the request to a Judge of the High Court for a decision regarding acceptance of jurisdiction to be made.

(2) Upon the High Court agreeing to the request under paragraph (1), the court officer will notify the parties to the proceedings before the other Member State or Contracting State of that decision, and the case must be allocated as if the application had been made in England and Wales.

(3) Upon allocation, the court to which the proceedings are allocated must immediately fix a directions hearing to consider the future conduct of the case.

(4) The court officer will serve notice of the directions hearing on all parties to the proceedings in the other Member State or Contracting State no later than 5 days before the date of that hearing.

*Service of the court's order or request relating to transfer of jurisdiction under the Council Regulation or the 1996 Hague Convention*

**12.67**

The court officer will serve an order or request relating to transfer of jurisdiction on all parties, the Central Authority of the other Member State or Contracting State, and the domestic Central Authority.

*Questions as to the court's jurisdiction or whether the proceedings should be stayed*

**12.68**

(1) If at any time after issue of the application it appears to the court that under any of Articles 16 to 18 of the Council Regulation it does not or may not have jurisdiction to hear an application, or that under Article 19 of the Council Regulation or Article 13 of the 1996 Hague Convention it is or may be required to stay the proceedings or to decline jurisdiction, the court must—

(a)   stay the proceedings; and

(b)   fix a date for a hearing to determine jurisdiction or whether there should be a stay or other order.

(2) The court officer will serve notice of the hearing referred to at paragraph (1)(b) on the parties to the proceedings.

(3) The court must, in writing—

(a)   give reasons for its decision under paragraph (1); and

(b)   where it makes a finding of fact, state such finding.

(4) The court may with the consent of all the parties deal with any question as to the jurisdiction of the court, or as to whether the proceedings should be stayed, without a hearing.

*Request for consultation as to contemplated placement of child in England and Wales*

**12.69**

(1) This rule applies to a request made—

(a)   under Article 56 of the Council Regulation, by a court in another Member State; or

Rules of Procedure

(b) under Article 33 of the 1996 Hague Convention by a court in another Contracting State

for consultation on or consent to the contemplated placement of a child in England and Wales.

(2) Where the court receives a request directly from a court in another Member State or Contracting State, the court shall, as soon as practicable after receipt of the request, notify the domestic Central Authority of the request and take the appropriate action under paragraph (4).

(3) Where it appears to the court officer that no proceedings relating to the child are pending before a court in England and Wales, the court officer must inform the domestic Central Authority of that fact and forward to the Central Authority all documents relating to the request sent by the court in the other Member State or Contracting State.

(4) Where the court receives a request forwarded by the domestic Central Authority, the court must, as soon as practicable after receipt of the request, either—

(a) where proceedings relating to the child are pending before the court, fix a directions hearing; or

(b) where proceedings relating to the child are pending before another court in England and Wales, send a copy of the request to that court.

*Request made by court in England and Wales for consultation as to contemplated placement of child in another Member State or Contracting State*

**12.70**

(1) This rule applies where the court is contemplating the placement of a child in another Member State under Article 56of the Council Regulation or another Contracting State under Article 33 of the 1996 Hague Convention, and proposes to send a request for consultation with or for the consent of the central authority or other authority having jurisdiction in the other State in relation to the contemplated placement.

(2) In this rule, a reference to 'the request' includes a reference to a report prepared for purposes of Article 33 of the 1996 Hague Convention where the request is made under that Convention.

(3) Where the court sends the request directly to the central authority or other authority having jurisdiction in the other State, it shall at the same time send a copy of the request to the domestic Central Authority.

(4) The court may send the request to the domestic Central Authority for onward transmission to the central authority or other authority having jurisdiction in the other Member State.

(5) The court should give consideration to the documents which should accompany the request.

(See Chapters 1 to 3 of this Part generally, for the procedure governing applications for an order under paragraph 19(1) of Schedule 2 to the 1989 Act permitting a local authority to arrange for any child in its care to live outside England and Wales.)

(Part 14 sets out the procedure governing applications for an order under section 84 (giving parental responsibility prior to adoption abroad) of the Adoption and Children Act 2002.)

*Application for a declaration as to the extent, or existence, of parental responsibility in relation to a child under Article 16 of the 1996 Hague Convention*

**12.71**

(1) Any interested person may apply for a declaration—

(a) that a person has, or does not have, parental responsibility for a child; or

(b) as to the extent of a person's parental responsibility for a child,

where the question arises by virtue of the application of Article 16 of the 1996 Hague Convention.

(2) An application for a declaration as to the extent, or existence of a person's parental responsibility for a child by virtue of Article 16 of the 1996 Hague Convention must be made in the principal registry and heard in the High Court.

(3) An application for a declaration referred to in paragraph (1) may not be made where the question raised is otherwise capable of resolution in any other family proceedings in respect of the child.

## PRACTICE DIRECTION 12F—INTERNATIONAL CHILD ABDUCTION

### PART 1

*Introduction*

1.1

This Practice Direction explains what to do if a child has been brought to, or kept in, England and Wales without the permission of anyone who has rights of custody in respect of the child in the country where the child was habitually resident immediately before the removal or retention. It also explains what to do if a child has been taken out of, or kept out of, England and Wales[1] without the permission of a parent or someone who has rights of custody in respect of the child. These cases are called 'international child abduction cases' and are dealt with in the High Court. This Practice Direction also explains what to do if you receive legal papers claiming that you have abducted a child. You can find the legal cases which are mentioned in this Practice Direction, and other legal material, on the website http://www.bailii.org/ (British and Irish Legal Information Institute).

1.2

If you have rights of custody in respect of a child and the child has been brought to England or Wales without your permission, or has been brought here with your permission but the person your child is staying with is refusing to return the child, then you can apply to the High Court of Justice, which covers all of England and Wales, for an order for the return of the child.

1.3

How you make an application to the High Court, what evidence you need to provide and what orders you should ask the court to make are all explained in this Practice Direction.

1.4

If your child is under 16 years of age and has been brought to England or Wales from a country which is a party (a 'State party') to the 1980 Hague Convention on the Civil Aspects of International Child Abduction ('the 1980 Hague Convention') then you can make an application to the High Court for an order under that Convention for the return of your child to the State in which he or she was habitually resident immediately before being removed or being kept away. This is explained in Part 2 below.

1.5

If your child is over 16 years of age and under 18, or has been brought to England or Wales from a country which is not a State party to the 1980 Hague Convention, then you can make an application for the return of your child under the inherent jurisdiction of the High Court with respect to children. In exercising this jurisdiction over children, the High Court will make your child's welfare its paramount consideration. How to make an application under the inherent jurisdiction of the High Court with respect to children is explained in Part 3 below.

1.6

It might be necessary for you to make an urgent application to the court if you are not sure where your child is, or you think that there is a risk that the person who is keeping your child away from you might take the child out of the United Kingdom or hide them away. Part 4 below explains how to make an urgent application to the High Court for orders to protect your child until a final decision can be made about returning the child and also how to ask for help from the police and government agencies if you think your child might be taken out of the country.

*Rights of Access*

1.7

Rights of access to children (also called contact or visitation) may be enforced in England and Wales. Access orders made in other Member States of the European Union can be enforced under EU law, and the 1980 Hague Convention expects State parties to comply with orders and agreements concerning access as well as rights of custody. If you have an access order and you want to enforce it in England or Wales, you should read Part 5 below.

## PART 2

*Hague Convention Cases*

2.1

States which are party to the 1980 Hague Convention have agreed to return children who have been either wrongfully removed from, or wrongfully retained away from, the State where they were habitually resident immediately before the wrongful removal or retention. There are very limited exceptions to this obligation.

2.2

'Wrongfully removed' or 'wrongfully retained' means removed or retained in breach of rights of custody in respect of the child attributed to a person or a body or an institution. 'Rights of custody' are interpreted very widely (see paragraph 2.16 below).

2.3

The text of the 1980 Hague Convention and a list of Contracting States (that is, State parties) can be found on the website of the Hague Conference on Private International Law at http://www.hcch.net. All Member States of the European Union are State parties to the 1980 Hague Convention, and all but Denmark are bound by an EU Regulation which supplements the operation of the 1980 Hague Convention between the Member States of the EU (Council Regulation (EC) No 2201/2003, see paragraph 2.6).

2.4

In each State party there is a body called the Central Authority whose duty is to help people use the 1980 Hague Convention.

2.5

If you think that your child has been brought to, or kept in, England or Wales, and your State is a State party to the 1980 Hague Convention, then you should get in touch with your own Central Authority who will help you to send an application for the return of your child to the Central Authority for England and Wales. However, you are not obliged to contact your own Central Authority. You may contact the Central Authority for England and Wales directly, or you may simply instruct lawyers in England or Wales to make an application for you. The advantage of making your application through the Central Authority for England and Wales if you are applying from outside the United Kingdom is that you will get public funding ('legal aid') to make your application, regardless of your financial resources.

*The Central Authority for England and Wales*

2.6

The Child Abduction and Custody Act 1985 brings the 1980 Hague Convention into the law of England and Wales and identifies the Lord Chancellor as the Central Authority. His duties as the Central Authority are carried out by the International Child Abduction and Contact Unit (ICACU). ICACU also carries out the duties of the Central Authority for two other international instruments. These are the European Convention on Recognition and Enforcement of Decisions concerning Custody of Children signed at Luxembourg on 20 May 1980 (called 'the European Convention' in this Practice Direction but sometimes also referred to as 'the Luxembourg Convention') and the European Union Council Regulation (EC) No 2201/2003 of 27 November 2003 on jurisdiction and the recognition and enforcement of judgments in matrimonial matters and in matters of parental responsibility ('the Council Regulation[24]'). The Council Regulation has direct effect in the law of England and Wales.

**2.7**

ICACU is open Mondays to Fridays from 9.00 a.m. to 5.00 p.m. It is located in the Office of the Official Solicitor and Public Trustee and its contact details are as follows:

International Child Abduction and Contact Unit
81 Chancery Lane
London
WC2A 1DD
DX 0012 London Chancery Lane
Tel: + 44 (0)20 7911 7045 / 7047
Fax: + 44 (0)20 7911 7248
Email: enquiries@offsol.gsi.gov.uk

In an emergency (including out of normal working hours) contact should be made with the Royal Courts of Justice on one of the following telephone numbers:

+ 44 (0)20 7947 6000, or
+ 44 (0) 20 7947 6260

In addition, in an emergency or outside normal working hours advice on international child abduction can be sought from reunite International Child Abduction Centre on + 44 (0)1162 556 234. Outside office hours you will be directed to the 24hour emergency service. You can also see information on reunite's website http://www.reunite.org/.

*What ICACU Will Do*

**2.8**

When ICACU receives your application for the return of your child, unless you already have a legal representative in England and Wales whom you want to act for you, it will send your application to a solicitor whom it knows to be experienced in international child abduction cases and ask them to take the case for you. You will then be the solicitor's client and the solicitor will make an application for public funding to meet your legal costs. The solicitor will then apply to the High Court for an order for the return of your child.

**2.9**

You can find out more about ICACU and about the 1980 Hague Convention and the other international instruments mentioned at paragraph 2.6 on two websites: Information for parties and practitioners is available on http://www.justice.gov.uk and general information for members of the public is available on www.direct.gov.uk.

*Applying to the High Court—the Form and Content of Application*

**2.10**

An application to the High Court for an order under the 1980 Hague Convention must be made in the Principal Registry of the Family Division in Form C67. If the Council Regulation applies, then the application must be headed both 'in the matter of the Child Abduction and Custody Act 1985' and 'in the matter of Council Regulation (EC) 2201/2003'. This is to ensure that the application is handled quickly (see paragraph. 2.14 below) and to draw the court's attention to its obligations under the Council Regulation.

Rules of Procedure

2.11

The application must include—

(a)  the names and dates of birth of the children;

(b)  the names of the children's parents or guardians;

(c)  the whereabouts or suspected whereabouts of the children;

(d)  the interest of the applicant in the matter (e.g. mother, father, or person with whom the child lives and details of any order placing the child with that person);

(e)  the reasons for the application;

(f)  details of any proceedings (including proceedings not in England or Wales, and including any legal proceedings which have finished) relating to the children;

(g)  where the application is for the return of a child, the identity of the person alleged to have removed or retained the child and, if different, the identity of the person with whom the child is thought to be;

(h)  in an application to which the Council Regulation also applies, any details of measures of which you are aware that have been taken by courts or authorities to ensure the protection of the child after its return to the Member State of habitual residence.

2.12

The application should be accompanied by all relevant documents including (but not limited to)—

(a)  an authenticated copy of any relevant decision or agreement;

(b)  a certificate or an affidavit from a Central Authority, or other competent authority of the State of the child's habitual residence, or from a qualified person, concerning the relevant law of that State.

2.13

As the applicant you may also file a statement in support of the application, although usually your solicitor will make and file a statement for you on your instructions. The statement must contain and be verified by a statement of truth in the following terms:

'I make this statement knowing that it will be placed before the court, and I confirm that to the best of my knowledge and belief its contents are true.'

(Further provisions about statements of truth are contained in Part 17 of these Rules and in Practice Direction 17A.).

*The Timetable for the Case*

2.14

Proceedings to which the Council Regulation applies must be completed in 6 weeks 'except where exceptional circumstances make this impossible'. The following procedural steps are intended to ensure that applications under the 1980 Hague Convention and the Council Regulation are handled quickly—

(a)  the application must be headed both 'in the matter of the Child Abduction and Custody Act 1985' and 'in the matter of Council Regulation (EC) 2201/2003';

(b)  the court file will be marked to—

   (i)   draw attention to the nature of the application; and

   (ii)  state the date on which the 6 week period will expire (the 'hear-by date');

(c)  listing priority will, where necessary, be given to such applications;

(d)  the trial judge will expedite the transcript of the judgment and its approval and ensure that it is sent to the Central Authority without delay.

[The above is taken from the judgment of the Court of Appeal, Civil Division in Vigreux v Michel & anor [2006] EWCA Civ 630, [2006] 2 FLR 1180.]

## Applications for Declarations

### 2.15

If a child has been taken from England and Wales to another State party, the judicial or administrative authorities of that State may ask for a declaration that the removal or retention of the child was wrongful. Or it might be thought that a declaration from the High Court that a child has been wrongfully removed or retained away from the United Kingdom would be helpful in securing his return. The High Court can make such declarations under section 8 of the Child Abduction and Custody Act 1985. An application for a declaration is made in the same way as an application for a return order, the only difference being that the details of relevant legal proceedings in respect of which the declaration is sought (if any), including a copy of any order made relating to the application, should be included in the documentation.

## Rights of Custody

### 2.16

'Rights of custody' includes rights relating to the care of the person of the child and, in particular, the right to determine the child's place of residence. Rights of custody may arise by operation of law (that is, they are conferred on someone automatically by the legal system in which they are living) or by a judicial or administrative decision or as a result of an agreement having legal effect. The rights of a person, an institution or any other body are a matter for the law of the State of the child's habitual residence, but it is for the State which is being asked to return the child to decide: if those rights amount to rights of custody for the purposes of the 1980 Hague Convention; whether at the time of the removal or retention those rights were actually being exercised; and whether there has been a breach of those rights.

### 2.17

In England and Wales a father who is not married to the mother of their child does not necessarily have 'rights of custody' in respect of the child. An unmarried father in England and Wales who has parental responsibility for a child has rights of custody in respect of that child. In the case of an unmarried father without parental responsibility, the concept of rights of custody may include more than strictly legal rights and where immediately before the removal or retention of the child he was exercising parental functions over a substantial period of time as the only or main carer for the child he may have rights of custody. An unmarried father can ask ICACU or his legal representative for advice on this. It is important to remember that it will be for the State which is being asked to return the child to decide if the father's circumstances meet that State's requirements for the establishment of rights of custody.

### 2.18

Sometimes, court orders impose restrictions on the removal of children from the country in which they are living. These can be orders under the Children Act 1989 ('section 8' orders) or orders under the inherent jurisdiction of the High Court (sometimes called 'injunctions'). Any removal of a child in breach of an order imposing such a restriction would be wrongful under the 1980 Hague Convention.

### 2.19

The fact that court proceedings are in progress about a child does not of itself give rise to a prohibition on the removal of the child by a mother with sole parental responsibility from the country in which the proceedings are taking place unless:

(a)    the proceedings are Wardship proceedings in England and Wales (in which case removal would breach the rights of custody attributed to the High Court and fathers with no custody rights could rely on that breach); or

(b)    the court is actually considering the custody of the child, because then the court itself would have rights of custody.

Rules of Procedure

*Particular provisions for European Convention applications*

2.20

The European Convention provides for the mutual recognition and enforcement of decisions relating to custody and access, so if a child has been brought here or retained here in breach of a custody order, then that order can be enforced. The European Convention has now been superseded to a very great extent by the Council Regulation. If however you want to make an application under the European Convention, then you make it in the same way as is described in paragraphs 2.10 and 2.11 above, but in addition you must include a copy of the decision relating to custody (or rights of access—see paragraph 5.1 below) which you are seeking to register or enforce, or about which you are seeking a declaration by the court.

*Defending Abduction Proceedings*

2.21

If you are served with an application—whether it is under the 1980 Hague or the European Convention or the inherent jurisdiction of the High Court—you must not delay. You must obey any directions given in any order with which you have been served, and you should seek legal advice at the earliest possible opportunity, although neither you nor the child concerned will automatically be entitled to legal aid.

2.22

It is particularly important that you tell the court where the child is, because the child will not be permitted to live anywhere else without the permission of the court, or to leave England and Wales, until the proceedings are finished.

2.23

It is also particularly important that you present to the court any defence to the application which you or the child might want to make at the earliest possible opportunity, although the orders with which you will have been served are likely to tell you the time by which you will have to do this.

2.24

If the child concerned objects to any order sought in relation to them, and if the child is of an age and understanding at which the court will take account of their views, the court is likely to direct that the child is seen by an officer of the Children and Family Court Advisory and Support Service (Cafcass) or in Wales CAFCASS CYMRU. You should cooperate in this process. Children are not usually made parties to abduction cases, but in certain exceptional circumstances the court can make them parties so that they have their own separate legal representation. These are all matters about which you should seek legal advice.

(Provisions about the power of the court to join parties are contained in rule 12.3 and provisions about the joining and representation of children are contained in Part 16 of these Rules and the Practice Direction 16A (Representation of Children.).

PART 3

*Non-Convention Cases*

3.1

Applications for the return of children wrongfully removed or retained away from States which are not parties to the 1980 Hague Convention or in respect of children to whom that Convention does not apply, can be made to the High Court under its inherent jurisdiction with respect to children. Such proceedings are referred to as 'non-Convention' cases. In proceedings under the inherent jurisdiction of the High Court with respect to children, the child's welfare is the court's paramount consideration. The extent of the court's enquiry into the child's welfare will depend on the circumstances of the case; in some cases the child's welfare will be best served by a summary hearing and, if necessary, a prompt return to the State from which the child has been removed or retained. In other cases a more detailed enquiry may be necessary (see Re J (Child Returned Abroad: Convention Rights) [2005] UKHL 40; [2005] 2 FLR 802).

**3.2**

Every application for the return of a child under the inherent jurisdiction must be made in the Principal Registry of the Family Division and heard in the High Court.

Provision about the inherent jurisdiction is made at Chapter 5 of Part 12 of the Rules and in Practice Direction 12D (Inherent Jurisdiction (including Wardship) Proceedings).

### *The Form and content of the application*
**3.3**

An application for the return of a child under the inherent jurisdiction must be made in Form C66 and must include the information in paragraph 2.11 above.

**3.4**

You must file a statement in support of your application, which must exhibit all the relevant documents. The statement must contain and be verified by a statement of truth in the following terms:

'I make this statement knowing that it will be placed before the court, and I confirm that to the best of my knowledge and belief its contents are true.'

(Further provisions about statements of truth are contained in Part 17 of these Rules and Practice Direction 17A.).

### *Timetable for Non-Convention Cases*
**3.5**

While the 6 week deadline referred to in paragraph 2.14 is set out in the 1980 Hague Convention and in the Council Regulation, non-Convention child abduction cases must similarly be completed in 6 weeks except where exceptional circumstances make this impossible. Paragraph 2.14 applies to these cases as appropriate for a non-Convention case.

PART 4

**General Provisions**

### *Urgent applications, or applications out of business hours*
**4.1**

Guidance about urgent and out of hours applications is in Practice Direction 12E (Urgent Business).

### *Police assistance to prevent removal from England and Wales*
**4.2**

The Child Abduction Act 1984 sets out the circumstances in which the removal of a child from this jurisdiction is a criminal offence. The police provide the following 24 hour service to prevent the unlawful removal of a child—

(a) they inform ports directly when there is a real and imminent threat that a child is about to be removed unlawfully from the country; and

(b) they liaise with Immigration Officers at the ports in an attempt to identify children at risk of removal.

**4.3**

Where the child is under 16, it is not necessary to obtain a court order before seeking police assistance. The police do not need an order to act to protect the child. If an order has already been obtained it should however be produced to the police. Where the child is between 16 and 18, an order must be obtained restricting or restraining removal before seeking police assistance.

**4.4**

Where the child is a ward of court (see Practice Direction 12D (Inherent Jurisdiction (including Wardship) Proceedings) the court's permission is needed to remove that child from the jurisdiction. When the court has not given that permission and police assistance is sought to prevent the removal of the ward, the applicant must produce evidence that the child is a ward such as—

(a) an order confirming wardship;

(b) an injunction; or

(c) where the matter is urgent and no order has been made, a certified copy of the wardship application.

**4.5**

The application for police assistance must be made by the applicant or his legal representative to the applicant's local police station except that applications may be made to any police station—

(a) in urgent cases;

(b) where the wardship application has just been issued; or

(c) where the court has just made the order relied on.

**4.6**

The police will, if they consider it appropriate, institute the 'port alert' system (otherwise known as 'an all ports warning') to try to prevent removal from the jurisdiction where the danger of removal is—

(a) real (i.e., not being sought merely by way of insurance); and

(b) imminent (i.e. within 24 to 48 hours).

**4.7**

The request for police assistance must be accompanied by as much of the following information as possible—

(a) the child: the name, sex, date of birth, physical description, nationality and passport number; if the child has more than one nationality or passport, provide details;

(b) the person likely to remove: the name, age, physical description, nationality, passport number, relationship to the child, and whether the child is likely to assist him or her; if the person has more than one nationality or passport, provide details;

(c) person applying for a port alert: the name, relationship to the child, nationality, telephone number and (if appropriate) solicitor's or other legal representative's name and contact details; if the person has more than one nationality, provide details;

(d) likely destination;

(e) likely time of travel and port of embarkation and, if known, details of travel arrangements;

(f) grounds for port alert (as appropriate)—

    (i) suspected offence under section 1 or section 2 of the Child Abduction Act 1984;

    (ii) the child is subject to a court order.

(g) details of person to whom the child should be returned if intercepted.

**4.8**

If the police decide that the case is one in which the port-alert system should be used, the child's name will remain on the stop list for four weeks. After that time it will be removed automatically unless a further application is made.

### The Identity and Passport Service

**4.9**

Where the court makes an order prohibiting or otherwise restricting the removal of a child from the United Kingdom, or from any specified part of it, or from a specified dependent territory, the court may make an order under section 37 of the Family Law Act 1986 requiring any person to surrender any UK passport which has been issued to, or contains particulars of, the child.

**4.10**

The Identity and Passport Service ('IPS') will take action to prevent a United Kingdom passport or replacement passport being issued only where the IPS has been served with a court order expressly requiring a United Kingdom passport to be surrendered, or expressly prohibiting the issue of any further United Kingdom passport facilities to the child without the consent of the court, or the holder of such an order. Accordingly, in every case in which such an order has been made, the IPS must be served the same day if possible, or at the latest the following day, with a copy of the order. It is the responsibility of the applicant to do this. The specimen form of letter set out below should be used and a copy of the court order must be attached to the letter. Delay in sending the letter to the IPS must be kept to an absolute minimum.

"The Caveat Officer
Fraud and Intelligence Unit
Identity and Passport Service
Globe House
89 Eccleston Square
London SW1V 1PN

Dear Sir/Madam

.............v...........

Case no: .....................

This is to inform you that the court has today made an order

*prohibiting the issue of a passport/passports to [name(s)] [date of birth (if known)] of [address] without the consent of the holder of the order.

*requiring [name(s)] [date of birth (if known)] of [address] to surrender the passport(s) issued to him/her/them/the following child[ren] / or which contain(s) particulars of the following child[ren]:

Name Date of Birth

*and has granted an injunction/*made an order restraining the removal of the child[ren] from the jurisdiction.

(*Delete as appropriate)

Please add these names to your records to prevent the issue of further passport facilities for the child[ren]. I enclose a copy of the court order.

Yours faithfully

Applicant's name/Applicant's Solicitor's name"

**4.11**

Following service on the IPS of an order either expressly requiring a United Kingdom passport to be surrendered by, or expressly prohibiting the issue of any further United Kingdom passport facilities to the child, the IPS will maintain a prohibition on issuing a passport, or further passport facilities until the child's 16th birthday. The order should state that a passport must not be granted/applied for without the consent of the court or the holder of the order.

Note: These requests may also be sent to any of the regional Passport Offices.

### 4.12

Further information on communicating with the IPS where the court has made a request of, or an order against, the IPS, may be found in the Protocol: Communicating with the Identity and Passport Service in Family Proceedings of August 2003.

### 4.13

Information about other circumstances, in which the IPS will agree not to issue a passport to a child if the IPS receives an application, or an order in more general terms than set out at 4.11 above, from a person who claims to have parental responsibility for the child, is available from the IPS or at www. direct.gov.uk.

### *The Home Office*

### 4.14

Information about communicating with the Home Office, where a question of the immigration status of a party arises in family proceedings, may be found in the Protocol: Communicating with the Home Office in Family Proceedings (revised and re-issued October 2010).

### *Press Reporting*

### 4.15

When a child has been abducted and a judge considers that publicity may help in tracing the child, the judge may adjourn the case for a short period to enable representatives of the Press to attend to give the case the widest possible publicity.

### 4.16

If a Child Rescue Alert has been used concerning a child, within the UK or abroad, it will give rise to media publicity. The court should be informed that this has happened. If there are already court proceedings concerning a child, it is advisable to obtain the agreement of the court before there is publicity to trace a missing child. If the court has not given its permission for a child who is the subject of children proceedings to be identified as the subject of proceedings, to do so would be contempt of court.

### *Other Assistance*

### 4.17

The Missing Persons Bureau will be participating for the UK in the European Union wide 116 000 hotline for missing children. Parents and children can ring this number for assistance. (It is primarily intended to deal with criminal matters, for example stranger kidnapping.)

### 4.18

It may also be possible to trace a child by obtaining a court order under the inherent jurisdiction or the wardship jurisdiction of the High Court addressed to certain government departments, as set out in Practice Direction 6C.

## PART 5

*Applications about rights of access*

### 5.1

Access orders made in another Member State of the European Union (except Denmark) can be enforced in England or Wales under the Council Regulation.

### 5.2

Chapter III of the Council Regulation sets out provision for recognition and enforcement of parental responsibility orders, which include orders for custody and access (child arrangements) between Member States. Under Article 41 of the Council Regulation you can enforce an access order in your favour from another Member State directly, provided you produce the certificate given under Article 41(2) by the court which made the order. This is a quick procedure. The unsuccessful party is not allowed to oppose recognition of the order.

### 5.3

The rules on recognition and enforcement of parental responsibility orders are in Part 31. You should apply to the High Court using Form C69. Rule 31.8 covers applications for Article 41 of the Council Regulation. You can make the application without notice.

### 5.4

If the Council Regulation does not apply, and the access order was made by a State party to the European Convention, an application can be made to enforce the order under Article 11 of the European Convention. Paragraph 2.20 above gives further information about how to make the application.

### 5.5

Article 21 of the 1980 Hague Convention requires the States parties to respect rights of access. However, in the case of Re G (A Minor) (Hague Convention: Access) [1993] 1 FLR 669, the Court of Appeal took the view that Article 21 conferred no jurisdiction to determine matters relating to access, or to recognise or enforce foreign access orders (see Practice Note of 5 March 1993: Child Abduction Unit: Lord Chancellor's Department set out in the Annex to this Practice Direction). (The Child Abduction Unit is now called ICACU see paragraph 2.6.) An access order which does not fall within the Council Regulation or the (very limited) application of the European Convention may only be enforced by applying for for a child arrangements order under section 8 of the Children Act 1989.

### 5.6

This means that if, during the course of proceedings under the 1980 Hague Convention for a return order, the applicant decides to ask for access (contact) instead of the return of the child, but no agreement can be reached, a separate application for a child arrangements order will have to be made, or the court invited to make a child arrangements order without an application being made (Children Act 1989, s10(1)(b)).

## PART 6

*Child abduction cases between the United Kingdom and Pakistan*

### 6.1

A consensus was reached in January 2003 between the President of the Family Division and the Hon. Chief Justice of Pakistan as to the principles to be applied in resolving child abduction cases between the UK and Pakistan.

The Protocol setting out that consensus can be accessed at: http://www.fco.gov.uk/resources/en/pdf/2855621/3069133

## PART 14—PROCEDURE FOR APPLICATIONS IN ADOPTION, PLACEMENT AND RELATED PROCEEDINGS

*Application of this Part and interpretation*

**14.1**

. . .

(2) In this Part—

'Central Authority' means—

(a) in relation to England, the Secretary of State; and

(b) in relation to Wales, the Welsh Ministers;

'Convention adoption order' means an adoption order under the 2002 Act which, by virtue of regulations under section 1 of the Adoption (Intercountry Aspects) Act 1999 (regulations giving effect to the Convention on Protection of Children and Co-operation in Respect of Intercountry Adoption, concluded at the Hague on 29th May 1993), is made as a Convention adoption order;

. . .

'section 88 direction' means a direction given by the High Court under section 88 of the 2002 Act that section 67(3) of that Act (status conferred by adoption) does not apply or does not apply to any extent specified in the direction.

. . .

*Notice of proceedings to person with foreign parental responsibility*

**14.4**

(1) This rule applies where a child is subject to proceedings to which this Part applies and—

(a) a parent of the child holds or is believed to hold parental responsibility for the child under the law of another State which subsists in accordance with Article 16 of the 1996 Hague Convention following the child becoming habitually resident in a territorial unit of the United Kingdom; and

(b) that parent is not otherwise required to be joined as a respondent under rule 14.3.

(2) The applicant shall give notice of the proceedings to any parent to whom the applicant believes paragraph (1) applies in any case in which a person who was a parent with parental responsibility under the 1989 Act would be a respondent to the proceedings in accordance with rule 14.3.

(3) The applicant and every respondent to the proceedings shall provide such details as they possess as to the identity and whereabouts of any parent they believe to hold parental responsibility for the child in accordance with paragraph (1) to the court officer, upon making, or responding to the application as appropriate.

(4) Where the existence of such a parent only becomes apparent to a party at a later date during the proceedings, that party must notify the court officer of those details at the earliest opportunity.

(5) Where a parent to whom paragraph (1) applies receives notice of proceedings, that parent may apply to the court to be joined as a party using the Part 18 procedure.

. . .

*The first directions hearing*

**14.8**

. . .

(3) In addition to the matters referred to in paragraph (1), the court will give any of the directions listed in Practice Direction 14B in proceedings for—

(a) a Convention adoption order;

(b) a section 84 order;

(c)   a section 88 direction;

(d)   a section 89 order; or

(e)   an adoption order where section 83(1) of the 2002 Act applies (restriction on bringing children in).

. . .

## PRACTICE DIRECTION 14B—THE FIRST DIRECTIONS HEARING—ADOPTIONS WITH A FOREIGN ELEMENT

*Application*

**1.1**

This Practice Direction applies to proceedings for—

(a)   a Convention adoption order;

(b)   a section 84 order;

(c)   a section 88 direction;

(d)   a section 89 order; and

(e)   an adoption order where the child has been brought into the United Kingdom in the circumstances where section 83(1) of the Act applies.

*The first directions hearing*

**2.1**

At the first directions hearing the court will, in addition to any matters referred to in rule 14.8(1)—

(a)   consider whether the requirements of the Act and the Adoptions with a Foreign Element Regulations 2005 (SI 2005/392) appear to have been complied with and, if not, consider whether or not in a case in the family court, it is appropriate that the case should be considered by a puisne judge of the High Court sitting in the family court (who may in turn consider whether or not it is appropriate to transfer the case to the High Court); (b) consider whether all relevant documents are translated into English and, if not, fix a timetable for translating any outstanding documents;

(c)   consider whether the applicant needs to file an affidavit setting out the full details of the circumstances in which the child was brought to the United Kingdom, of the attitude of the parents to the application and confirming compliance with the requirements of The Adoptions with A Foreign Element Regulations 2005;

(d)   give directions about–

    (i)   the production of the child's passport and visa;

    (ii)   the need for an officer of the Service or a Welsh family proceedings officer and a representative of the Home Office to attend future hearings; and

    (iii)   personal service on the parents (via the Central Authority in the case of an application for a Convention Adoption Order) including information about the role of the officer of the Service or the Welsh family proceedings officer and availability of legal aid to be represented within the proceedings; and

(e)   consider fixing a further directions appointment no later than 6 weeks after the date of the first directions appointment and timetable a date by which the officer of the Service or the Welsh family proceedings officer should file an interim report in advance of that further appointment.

## PART 24—WITNESSES, DEPOSITIONS GENERALLY AND TAKING OF EVIDENCE IN MEMBER STATES OF THE EUROPEAN UNION

## I WITNESSES AND DEPOSITIONS

. . .

Rules of Procedure

*Where a person to be examined is out of the jurisdiction—letter of request*

**24.12**

(1) This rule applies where a party wishes to take a deposition from a person who is—

(a) out of the jurisdiction; and

(b) not in a Regulation State within the meaning of Chapter 2 of this Part.

(2) The High Court may order the issue of a letter of request to the judicial authorities of the country in which the proposed deponent is.

(3) A letter of request is a request to a judicial authority to take the evidence of that person, or arrange for it to be taken.

(4) The High Court may make an order under this rule in relation to family court proceedings. (5) If the government of a country allows a person appointed by the High Court to examine a person in that country, the High Court may make an order appointing a special examiner for that purpose.

(6) A person may be examined under this rule on oath or affirmation or in accordance with any procedure permitted in the country in which the examination is to take place.

(7) If the High Court makes an order for the issue of a letter of request, the party who sought the order must file—

(a) the following documents and, except where paragraph (8) applies, a translation of them—

    (i) a draft letter of request;

    (ii) a statement of the issues relevant to the proceedings; and

    (iii) a list of questions or the subject matter of questions to be put to the person to be examined; and

(b) an undertaking to be responsible for the Secretary of State's expenses.

(8) There is no need to file a translation if—

(a) English is one of the official languages of the country where the examination is to take place; or

(b) a practice direction has specified that country as a country where no translation is necessary.

(Rules 35.3 and 35.4 contain rules in relation to evidence arising out of mediation of cross-border disputes. Rule 35.4(1)(f) relates specifically to this rule.)

## II  TAKING OF EVIDENCE—MEMBER STATES OF THE EUROPEAN UNION

*Interpretation*

**24.15**

In this Chapter—

    'designated court' has the meaning given in Practice Direction 24A;

    'Regulation State' has the same meaning as 'Member State' in the Taking of Evidence Regulation, that is all Member States except Denmark;

    'the Taking of Evidence Regulation' means Council Regulation (EC) No. 1206/2001 of 28 May 2001 on co-operation between the courts of the Member States in the taking of evidence in civil or commercial matters.

*Where a person to be examined is in another Regulation State*

**24.16**

(1) This rule applies where a party wishes to take a deposition from a person who is—

(a) outside the jurisdiction; and

(b) in a Regulation State.

(2) The court may order the issue of a request to a designated court ('the requested court') in the Regulation State in which the proposed deponent is.

(3) If the court makes an order for the issue of a request, the party who sought the order must file—

(a) a draft Form A as set out in the annex to the Taking of Evidence Regulation (request for the taking of evidence);

(b) except where paragraph (4) applies, a translation of the form;

(c) an undertaking to be responsible for costs sought by the requested court in relation to—

(i) fees paid to experts and interpreters; and

(ii) where requested by that party, the use of special procedures or communications technology; and

(d) an undertaking to be responsible for the court's expenses.

(4) There is no need to file a translation if—

(a) English is one of the official languages of the Regulation State where the examination is to take place; or

(b) the Regulation State has indicated, in accordance with the Taking of Evidence Regulation, that English is a language which it will accept.

(5) Where article 17 of the Taking of Evidence Regulation (direct taking of evidence by the requested court) allows evidence to be taken directly in another Regulation State, the court may make an order for the submission of a request in accordance with that article.

(6) If the court makes an order for the submission of a request under paragraph (5), the party who sought the order must file—

(a) a draft Form I as set out in the annex to the Taking of Evidence Regulation (request for direct taking of evidence);

(b) except where paragraph (4) applies, a translation of the form; and

(c) an undertaking to be responsible for the court's expenses

## PRACTICE DIRECTION 24A—WITNESSES, DEPOSITIONS AND TAKING OF EVIDENCE IN MEMBER STATES OF THE EUROPEAN UNION

*Depositions to be taken abroad for use as evidence in proceedings before courts in England and Wales (where the Taking of Evidence Regulation does not apply)*

**5.1**

Where a party wishes to take a deposition from a person outside the jurisdiction, the High Court may order the issue of a letter of request to the judicial authorities of the country in which the proposed deponent is (see rule 24.12).

(Rule 35.4(1)(f) deals with letters of request where the Mediation Directive applies)

**5.2**

An application for an order referred to in paragraph 5.1 should be made by application notice in accordance with Part 18 (Procedure for other applications in proceedings).

**5.3**

The documents which a party applying for an order for the issue of a letter of request must file with the application notice are set out in rule 24.12(7). They are as follows—

(a) a draft letter of request in the form set out in Annex A to this practice direction;

(b) a statement of the issues relevant to the proceedings;

(c) a list of questions or the subject matter of questions to be put to the proposed deponent;

(d) a translation of the documents in (a), (b) and (c), unless the proposed deponent is in a country of which English is an official language; and

(e) an undertaking to be responsible for the expenses of the Secretary of State.

In addition to the documents listed above the party applying for the order must file a draft order.

**5.4**

The above documents should be filed with the Masters' Secretary in Room E214, Royal Courts of Justice, Strand, London WC2A 2LL.

**5.5**

The application will be dealt with by the Senior Master of the Queen's Bench Division of the Senior Courts who will, if appropriate, sign the letter of request.

**5.6**

Attention is drawn to the provisions of rule 18.11 (Application to set aside or vary order made without notice).

**5.7**

If parties are in doubt as to whether a translation under paragraph 5.3(d) is required, they should seek guidance from the Foreign Process Section of the Masters' Secretary's Department.

**5.8**

A special examiner appointed under rule 24.12(5) may be the British Consul or the Consul-General or his deputy in the country where the evidence is to be taken if—

(a) there is in respect of that country a Civil Procedure Convention providing for the taking of evidence in that country for the assistance of proceedings in the High Court or other court in this country; or

(b) the Secretary of State has consented.

**5.9**

The provisions of paragraphs 4.1 to 4.12 apply to the depositions referred to in this paragraph.

## Taking of Evidence between EU Member States

*Taking of Evidence Regulation*

**6.1**

Where evidence is to be taken from a person in another Member State of the European Union for use as evidence in proceedings before courts in England and Wales Council Regulation (EC) No 1206/2001 of 28 May 2001 on co-operation between the courts of the Member States in the taking of evidence in civil or commercial matters ('the Taking of Evidence Regulation') applies.

**6.2**

The Taking of Evidence Regulation is annexed to this practice direction as Annex B.

**6.3**

The Taking of Evidence Regulation does not apply to Denmark. In relation to Denmark, therefore, rule 24.12 will continue to apply.

(Article 21(1) of the Taking of Evidence Regulation provides that the Regulation prevails over other provisions contained in bilateral or multilateral agreements or arrangements concluded by the Member States.)

Originally published in the official languages of the European Community in the Official Journal of the European Communities by the Office for Official Publications of the European Communities.

## Meaning of 'designated court'

**7.1**

In accordance with the Taking of Evidence Regulation, each Regulation State has prepared a list of courts competent to take evidence in accordance with the Regulation indicating the territorial and, where appropriate, special jurisdiction of those courts.

**7.2**

Where Chapter 2 of this Part refers to a 'designated court' in relation to another Regulation State, the reference is to the court, referred to in the list of competent courts of that State, which is appropriate to the application in hand.

**7.3**

Where the reference is to the 'designated court' in England and Wales, the reference is to the appropriate competent court in the jurisdiction. The designated courts for England and Wales are listed in Annex C to this practice direction.

## Central Body

**8.1**

The Taking of Evidence Regulation stipulates that each Regulation State must nominate a Central Body responsible for—

(a) supplying information to courts;

(b) seeking solutions to any difficulties which may arise in respect of a request; and

(c) forwarding, in exceptional cases, at the request of a requesting court, a request to the competent court.

**8.2**

The United Kingdom has nominated the Senior Master of the Queen's Bench Division, to be the Central Body for England and Wales.

**8.3**

The Senior Master, as Central Body, has been designated responsible for taking decisions on requests pursuant to Article 17 of the Regulation. Article 17 allows a court to submit a request to the Central Body or a designated competent authority in another Regulation State to take evidence directly in that State.

## Evidence to be taken in another Regulation State for use in England and Wales

**9.1**

Where a person wishes to take a deposition from a person in another Regulation State, the court where the proceedings are taking place may order the issue of a request to the designated court in the Regulation State (rule 24.16 (2)). The form of request is prescribed as Form A in the Taking of Evidence Regulation.

Rules of Procedure

**9.2**

An application to the court for an order under rule 24.16(2) should be made by application notice in accordance with Part 18 (Procedure for other applications in proceedings).

**9.3**

Rule 24.16(3) provides that the party applying for the order must file a draft form of request in the prescribed form. Where completion of the form requires attachments or documents to accompany the form, these must also be filed.

**9.4**

If the court grants an order under rule 24.16(2), it will send the form of request directly to the designated court.

**9.5**

Where the taking of evidence requires the use of an expert, the designated court may require a deposit in advance towards the costs of that expert. The party who obtained the order is responsible for the payment of any such deposit which should be deposited with the court for onward transmission. Under the provisions of the Taking of Evidence Regulation, the designated court is not required to execute the request until such payment is received.

**9.6**

Article 17 permits the court where proceedings are taking place to take evidence directly from a deponent in another Regulation State if the conditions of the article are satisfied. Direct taking of evidence can only take place if evidence is given voluntarily without the need for coercive measures. Rule 24.16(5) provides for the court to make an order for the submission of a request to take evidence directly. The form of request is Form I annexed to the Taking of Evidence Regulation and rule 24.16(6) makes provision for a draft of this form to be filed by the party seeking the order. An application for an order under rule 24.16(5) should be by application notice in accordance with Part 18.

**9.7**

Attention is drawn to the provisions of rule 18.11 (Application to set aside or vary order made without notice).

*[Annexes A–B omitted]*

## PART 31—REGISTRATION OF ORDERS UNDER THE COUNCIL REGULATION, THE CIVIL PARTNERSHIP (JURISDICTION AND RECOGNITION OF JUDGMENTS) REGULATIONS 2005, THE MARRIAGE (SAME SEX COUPLES) (JURISDICTION AND RECOGNITION OF JUDGMENTS) REGULATIONS 2014 AND UNDER THE HAGUE CONVENTION 1996

*Scope*

**31.1**

This Part applies to proceedings for the recognition, non-recognition and registration of—

(a) judgments to which the Council Regulation applies;

(b) measures to which the 1996 Hague Convention applies; and

(c) judgments to which the Jurisdiction and Recognition of Judgments Regulations apply, and which relate to dissolution or annulment of overseas relationships entitled to be treated as a civil partnership, or legal separation of the same; and

(d) judgments to which the 2014 Regulations apply and which relate to divorce, or annulment of a marriage of a same sex couple or the judicial separation of the same

*Interpretation*

**31.2**

(1) In this Part—

(a) 'judgment' is to be construed—

    (i) in accordance with the definition in Article 2(4) of the Council Regulation where it applies;

    (ii) in accordance with regulation 6 of the Jurisdiction and Recognition of Judgments Regulations where those Regulations apply; or

    (iii) as meaning any measure taken by an authority with jurisdiction under Chapter II of the 1996 Hague Convention where that Convention applies; or

    (iv) in accordance with regulation 4(1)(a) of The Marriage (Same Sex Couples) (Jurisdiction and Recognition of Judgments) Regulations 2014 where those Regulations apply.

(b) 'the Jurisdiction and Recognition of Judgments Regulations' means the Civil Partnership (Jurisdiction and Recognition of Judgments) Regulations 2005;

(ba) 'the 2014 Regulations' means the Marriage (Same Sex Couples) (Jurisdiction and Recognition of Judgments) Regulations 2014

(c) 'Member State' means—

    (i) where registration, recognition or non-recognition is sought of a judgment under the Council Regulation, a Member State of the European Union which is bound by that Regulation or a country which has subsequently adopted it;

    (ii) where recognition is sought of a judgment to which the Jurisdiction and Recognition of Judgments Regulations apply, a Member State of the European Union to which Part II of those Regulations applies;

    (iii) where recognition is sought of a judgment to which the 2014 Regulations apply, a member State of the European Union to which Part II of those Regulations applies.

(d) 'Contracting State' means a State, other than a Member State within the meaning of (c) above, in relation to which the 1996 Hague Convention is in force as between that State and the United Kingdom; and

(e) 'parental responsibility'—

    (i) where the Council Regulation applies, has the meaning given in Article 2(7) of that Regulation; and

    (ii) where the 1996 Hague Convention applies, has the meaning given in Article 1(2) of that Convention.

(2) References in this Part to registration are to the registration of a judgment in accordance with the provisions of this Part.

*Where to start proceedings*

**31.3**

(1) Every application under this Part, except for an application under rule 31.18 for a certified copy of a judgment, or under rule 31.20 for rectification of a certificate issued under Articles 41 or 42, must be made to the principal registry.

(2) Nothing in this rule prevents the determination of an issue of recognition as an incidental question by any court in proceedings, in accordance with Article 21(4) of the Council Regulation.

(3) Notwithstanding paragraph (1), where recognition of a judgment is raised as an incidental question in proceedings under the 1996 Hague Convention, the Jurisdiction and Recognition of Judgments Regulations or the 2014 Regulations the court hearing those proceedings may determine the question of recognition.

*Application for registration, recognition or non-recognition of a judgment*

**31.4**

(1) Any interested person may apply to the court for an order that the judgment be registered, recognised or not recognised.

(2) Except for an application under rule 31.7, an application for registration, recognition or non-recognition must be—

(a)  made to a district judge of the principal registry; and

(b)  in the form, and supported by the documents and the information required by a practice direction.

*Documents—supplementary*

**31.5**

(1) Except as regards a copy of a judgment required by Article 37(1)(a) of the Council Regulation, where the person making an application under this Part does not produce the documents required by rule 31.4(2)(b) the court may—

(a)  fix a time within which the documents are to be produced;

(b)  accept equivalent documents; or

(c)  dispense with production of the documents if the court considers it has sufficient information.

(2) This rule does not apply to applications under rule 31.7.

*Directions*

**31.6**

(1) As soon as practicable after an application under this Part has been made, the court may (subject to the requirements of the Council Regulation) give such directions as it considers appropriate, including as regards the following matters—

(a)  whether service of the application may be dispensed with;

(b)  expedition of the proceedings or any part of the proceedings (and any direction for expedition may specify a date by which the court must give its decision);

(c)  the steps to be taken in the proceedings and the time by which each step is to be taken;

(d)  the service of documents; and

(e)  the filing of evidence.

(2) The court or court officer will—

(a)  record the giving, variation or revocation of directions under this rule; and

(b)  as soon as practicable serve a copy of the directions order on every party.

*Recognition and enforcement under the Council Regulation of a judgment given in another Member State relating to rights of access or under Article 11(8) for the return of the child to that State*

**31.7**

(1) This rule applies where a judgment has been given in another Member State—

(a)  relating to rights of access: or

(b)  under Article 11(8) of the Council Regulation for the return of a child to that State,

which has been certified, in accordance with Article 41(2) or 42(2) as the case may be, by the judge in the court of origin.

(2) An application for recognition or enforcement of the judgment must be—

(a)  made in writing to a district judge of the principal registry; and

(b)  accompanied by a copy of the certificate issued by the judge in the court of origin.

(3) The application may be made without notice.

(4) Rules 31.5 and 31.8 to 31.17 do not apply to an application made under this rule.

(5) Nothing in this rule shall prevent a holder of parental responsibility from seeking recognition and enforcement of a judgment in accordance with the provisions of rules 31.8 to 31.17.

*Registration for enforcement or order for non-recognition of a judgment*

**31.8**

(1) This rule applies where an application is made for an order that a judgment given in another Member State, or a Contracting State, should be registered, or should not be recognised, except where rule 31.7 applies.

(2) where the application is made for an order that the judgment should be registered—

(a) upon receipt of the application,and subject to any direction given by the court under rule 31.6, the court officer will serve the application on the person against whom registration is sought;

(b) the court will not accept submissions from either the person against whom registration is sought or any child in relation to whom the judgment was given.

(3) Where the application is for an order that the judgment should not be recognised—

(a) upon receipt of the application,and subject to any direction given by the court under rule 31.6, the court officer will serve the application on the person in whose favour judgment was given;

(b) the person in whose favour the judgment was given must file an answer to the application and serve it on the applicant—

(i) within 1 month of service of the application; or

(ii) if the applicant ishabitually resident in another Member State, within two months of service ofthe application.

(4) In cases to which the 1996 Hague Convention applies and the Council Regulation does not apply, the court may extend the time set out in sub paragraph (3)(b)(ii) on account of distance.

(5) The person in whose favour the judgment was given may request recognition or registration of the judgment in their answer, and in that event must comply with 31.4(2)(b), to the extent that such documents, information and evidence are not already contained in the application for non-recognition.

(6) If, in a case to which the Council Regulation applies, the person in whose favour the judgment was given fails to file an answer as required by paragraph (3), the court will act in accordance with the provisions of Article 18 of the Council Regulation.

(7) If, in a case to which the 1996 Hague Convention applies and the Service Regulation does not, the person in whose favour the judgment was given fails to file a answer as required by paragraph(3)—

(a) where the Hague Convention of15th November 1965 on the service abroad of judicial and extrajudicial documents in civil or commercial matters applies, the court shall apply Article15 of that Convention; and

(b) in all other cases, the court will not consider the application unless—

(i) it is proved to the satisfaction of the court that the person in whose favour judgment was given was served with the application within a reasonable period of time to arrange his or her response; or

(ii) the court is satisfied that the circumstances of the case justify proceeding with consideration of the application.

(8) In a case to which the Jurisdiction and Recognition of Judgments Regulations or the 2014 Regulations apply, if the person in whose favour judgment was given fails to file an answer as required by paragraph (3), the court will apply the Service Regulation where that regulation applies, and if it does not—

(a) where the Hague Convention of15th November 1965 on the service abroad of judicial and extrajudicial documents in civil or commercial matters applies, the court shall apply Article 15 of that Convention; and

(b)   in all other cases, the court will apply the provisions of paragraph (7)(b).

*Stay of recognition proceedings by reason of an appeal*

**31.9**

Where recognition or non-recognition of a judgment given in another Member State or Contracting State is sought, or is raised as an incidental question in other proceedings, the court may stay the proceedings—

(a)   if an ordinary appeal against the judgment has been lodged; or

(b)   if the judgment was given in the Republic of Ireland, if enforcement of the judgment is suspended there by reason of an appeal.

*Effect of refusal of application for a decision that a judgment should not be recognised*

**31.10**

Where the court refuses an application for a decision that a judgment should not be recognised, the court may—

(a)   direct that the decision to refuse the application is to be treated as a decision that the judgment be recognised; or

(b)   treat the answer under paragraph(3)(b) of rule 31.8 as an application that the judgment be registered for enforcement if paragraph (5) of that rule is complied with and order that the judgment be registered for enforcement in accordance with rule 31.11.

*Notification of the court's decision on an application for registration or non-recognition*

**31.11**

(1)   Where the court has—

(a)   made an order on an application for an order that a judgment should be registered for enforcement; or

(b)   refused an application that a judgment should not be recognised and ordered under rule 31.10 that the judgment be registered for enforcement,

the court officer will as soon as practicable take the appropriate action under paragraph (2) or (3).

(2)   If the court refuses the application for the judgment to be registered for enforcement, the court officer will serve the order on the applicant and the person against whom judgment was given in the state of origin.

(3)   If the court orders that the judgment should be registered for enforcement, the court officer will—

(a)   register the judgment in the central index of judgments kept by the principal registry;

(b)   confirm on the order that the judgment has been registered; and

(c)   serve on the parties the court's order endorsed with the court officer's confirmation that the judgment has been registered.

(4)   A sealed order of the court endorsed in accordance with paragraph (3)(b) will constitute notification that the judgment has been registered under Article 28(2) of the Council Regulation or under Article 26 of the 1996 Hague Convention, as the case may be, and in this Part 'notice of registration' means a sealed order so endorsed.

(5)   The notice of registration must state—

(a)   full particulars of the judgment registered and the order for registration;

(b)   the name of the party making the application and his address for service within the jurisdiction;

(c) the right of the person against whom judgment was given to appeal against the order for registration; and

(d) the period within which an appeal against the order for registration may be made.

*Effect of registration under rule 31.11*

**31.12**

Registration of a judgment under rule 31.11 will serve for the purpose of Article 21(3) of the Council Regulation, Article 24 of the 1996 Hague Convention, regulation 7 of the Jurisdiction and Recognition of Judgments Regulations or regulation 5 of the 2014 Regulations (as the case may be) as a decision that the judgment is recognised.

*The central index of judgments registered under rule 31.11*

**31.13**

The central index of judgments registered under rule 31.11 will be kept by the principal registry.

*Decision on recognition of a judgment only*

**31.14**

(1) Where an application is made seeking recognition of a judgment only, the provisions of rules 31.8 and 31.9 apply to that application as they do to an application for registration for enforcement.

(2) Where the court orders that the judgment should be recognised, the court officer will serve a copy of the order on each party as soon as practicable.

(3) A sealed order of the court will constitute notification that the judgment has been recognised under Article 21(3) of the Council Regulation, Article 24 of the 1996 Hague convention, regulation 7 of the Jurisdiction and Recognition of Judgments Regulations or regulation 5 of the 2014 Regulations, as the case may be. (4) The sealed order shall indicate—

(a) full particulars of the judgment recognised;

(b) the name of the party making the application and his address for service within the jurisdiction;

(c) the right of the person against whom judgment was given to appeal against the order for recognition; and

(d) the period within which an appeal against the order for recognition may be made.

*Appeal against the court's decision under rules 31.10, 31.11 or 31.14*

**31.15**

(1) An appeal against the court's decision under rules 31.10, 31.11 or 31.14 must be made to a judge of the High Court—

(a) within one month of the date of service of the notice of registration; or

(b) if the party bringing the appeal is habitually resident in another Member State, or a Contracting State, within two months of the date of service.

(2) The court may not extend time for an appeal on account of distance unless the matter is one to which the 1996 Hague Convention applies and the Council Regulation does not apply.

(3) If, in a case to which the 1996 Hague Convention applies and the Service Regulation does not, the appeal is brought by the applicant for a declaration of enforceability or registration and the respondent fails to appear—

(a) where the Hague Convention of 15th November 1965 on the service abroad of judicial and extrajudicial documents in civil or commercial matters applies, the court shall apply Article15 of that Convention; and

(b) in all other cases, the court will not consider the appeal unless—

    (i)   it is proved to the satisfaction of the court that the respondent was served with notice of the appeal within a reasonable period of time to arrange his or her response; or

    (ii)  the court is satisfied that the circumstances of the case justify proceeding with consideration of the appeal.

(4) This rule is subject to rule 31.16.

(The procedure for applications under rule 31.15 is set out in Practice Direction 30A (Appeals).)

*Stay of enforcement where appeal pending in state of origin*

**31.16**

(1) A party against whom enforcement is sought of a judgment which has been registered under rule 31.11 may apply to the court with which an appeal is lodged under rule 31.15 for the proceedings to be stayed where—

(a)   that party has lodged an ordinary appeal in the Member State or Contracting State of origin; or

(b)   the time for such an appeal has not yet expired.

(2) Where an application for a stay is filed in the circumstances described in paragraph (1)(b), the court may specify the time within which an appeal must be lodged.

*Enforcement of judgments registered under rule 31.11*

**31.17**

(1) Subject to paragraph (1A), the court will not enforce a judgment registered under rule 31.11 until after—

(a)   the expiration of any applicable period under rules 31.15 or 31.16; or

(b)   if that period has been extended by the court, the expiration of the period so extended.

(1A) The court may enforce a judgment registered under rule 31.11 before the expiration of a period referred to in paragraph (1) where urgent enforcement of the judgment is necessary to secure the welfare of the child to whom the judgment relates. (2) A party applying to the court for the enforcement of a registered judgment must produce to the court a certificate of service of—

(a)   the notice of registration of the judgment; and

(b)   any order made by the court in relation to the judgment.

(Service out of the jurisdiction, including service in accordance with the Service Regulation, is dealt with in chapter 4 of Part 6 and in Practice Direction 6B.)

*Request for a certificate or a certified copy of a judgment*

**31.18**

(1) An application for a certified copy of a judgment, or for a certificate under Articles 39, 41 or 42 of the Council Regulation, must be made to the court which made the order or judgment in respect of which certification is sought and without giving notice to any other party.

(2) The application must be made in the form, and supported by the documents and information required by a practice direction.

(3) The certified copy of the judgment will be an office copy sealed with the seal of the court and signed by a court officer. It will be issued with a certified copy of any order which has varied any of the terms of the original order. (4) Where the application is made for the purposes of applying for recognition or recognition and enforcement of the order in another Contracting State, the court must indicate on the certified copy of the judgment the grounds on which it based its jurisdiction to make the order, for the purposes of Article 23(2)(a) of the 1996 Hague Convention.

*Certificates issued in England and Wales under Articles 41 and 42 of the Council Regulation*

**31.19**

The court officer will serve—

(a) a certificate issued under Article 41 or 42; or

(b) a certificate rectified under rule 31.20,

on all parties and will transmit a copy to the Central Authority for England and Wales.

*Rectification of certificate issued under Article 41 or 42 of the Council Regulation*

**31.20**

(1) Where there is an error in a certificate issued under Article 41 or 42, an application to rectify that error must be made to the court which issued the certificate.

(2) A rectification under paragraph (1) may be made—

(a) by the court of its own initiative; or

(b) on application by—

    (i) any party to the proceedings; or

    (ii) the court or Central Authority of another Member State.

(3) An application under paragraph (2)(b) may be made without notice being served on any other party.

*Authentic instruments and agreements under Article 46 of the Council Regulation*

**31.21**

This Chapter applies to an authentic instrument and an agreement to which Article 46 of the Council Regulation applies as it applies to a judgment.

*Application for provisional, including protective measures*

**31.22**

An application for provisional, including protective, measures under Article 20 of the Council Regulation or Articles 11 or 12 of the 1996 Hague Convention may be made notwithstanding that the time for appealing against an order for registration of a judgment has not expired or that a final determination of any issue relating to enforcement of the judgment is pending.

**PRACTICE DIRECTION 31A—REGISTRATION OF ORDERS UNDER THE COUNCIL REGULATION, THE CIVIL PARTNERSHIP (JURISDICTION AND RECOGNITION OF JUDGMENTS) REGULATIONS 2005, THE MARRIAGE (SAME SEX COUPLES) (JURISDICTION AND RECOGNITION OF JUDGMENTS) REGULATIONS 2014 AND UNDER THE HAGUE CONVENTION 1996**

*Form of application*

**1.1**

An application under rule 31.4 must be made using the Part 19 procedure, except that the provisions of rules 31.8 to 31.14 and of this Practice Direction shall apply in place of rules 19.4 to 19.9.

**1.2**

Where the application is for recognition only of an order, it should be made clear that the application does not extend to registration for enforcement.

*Evidence in support of all applications for registration, recognition or non-recognition*

2.1

The requirements for information and evidence for applications differ according to whether the application is made under the Council Regulation, the Jurisdiction and Recognition of Judgments Regulations, the 2014 Regulations, or the 1996 Hague Convention.

2.2

All applications to which rule 31.4(2) applies must be supported by a statement that is sworn to be true or an affidavit, exhibiting the judgment, or a verified, certified or otherwise duly authenticated copy of the judgment. In the case of an application under the Jurisdiction and Recognition of Judgments Regulations, the 2014 Regulations or under the 1996 Hague Convention, a translation of the judgment should be supplied.

2.3

Where any other document required by this Practice Direction or by direction of the court under rule 31.5 is not in English, the applicant must supply a translation of that document into English certified by a notary public or a person qualified for the purpose, or accompanied by witness statement or affidavit confirming that the translation is accurate.

*Evidence required in support of application for registration, recognition or non-recognition of a judgment under the Council Regulation*

3.1

An application for a judgment to be registered, recognised or not recognised under the Council Regulation must be accompanied by a witness statement or an affidavit exhibiting the following documents and giving the information required by 3.2 or 3.3 below, as appropriate.

*3.2*

In the case of an application for recognition or registration—

(a) the certificate in the form set out in Annex I or Annex II of the Council Regulation, issued by the Member State in which judgment was given;

(b) in the case of a judgment given in default, the documents referred to in Article 37(2);

(c) whether the judgment provides for the payment of a sum or sums of money;

(d) whether interest is recoverable on the judgment or part of the judgment in accordance with the law of the State in which the judgment was given, and if that is the case, the rate of interest, the date from which interest is recoverable, and the date on which interest ceases to accrue;

(e) an address within the jurisdiction of the court for service of process on the party making the application and stating, in so far as is known to the applicant, the name and usual or last known address or place of business of the person against whom judgment was given; and

(f) where appropriate, whether Article 56 has been complied with, and the identity and address of the authority or authorities from whom consent has been obtained, together with evidence of that consent.

3.3

In the case of an application for an order that a judgment should not be recognised under Article 21(3)—

(a) the certificate referred to at paragraph 3.2(a);

(b) in relation to the documents identified at paragraph 3.2(b), those documents or a statement that no such service or acceptance occurred if that is the case;

(c) an address within the jurisdiction of the court for service of process on the applicant and stating, in so far as is known to the applicant, the name and usual or last known address or place of business of the person in whose favour judgment was given; and

(d) a statement of the ground or grounds under Articles 22 or 23 (as the case may be) on which it is requested that the judgment should not be recognised, the reasons why the applicant asserts that such ground or grounds is, or are, made out, and any documentary evidence on which the applicant relies.

*Evidence required in support of an application for registration, recognition or non-recognition of a judgment under the 1996 Hague Convention*

**4.1**

An application for an order for a judgment to be registered under Article 26 or not recognised under Article 24 of the 1996 Hague Convention must be accompanied by a witness statement or affidavit exhibiting the following documents and giving the information required by 4.2, 4.3 or 4.4 below as appropriate.

**4.2**

In the case of an application for registration—

(a) those documents necessary to show that the judgment is enforceable according to the law of the Contracting State in which it was given;

(b) a description of the opportunities provided by the authority which gave the judgment in question for the child to be heard, except where that judgment was given in a case of urgency;

(c) where the judgment was given in a case of urgency, a statement as to the circumstances of the urgency that led to the child not having the opportunity to be heard;

(d) details of any measures taken in the non-Contracting State of the habitual residence of the child, if applicable, specifying the nature and effect of the measure, and the date on which it was taken;

(e) in as far as not apparent from the copy of the judgment provided, a statement of the grounds on which the authority which gave the judgment based its jurisdiction, together with any documentary evidence in support of that statement;

(f) where appropriate, a statement regarding whether Article 33 of the 1996 Hague Convention has been complied with, and the identity and address of the authority or authorities from which consent has been obtained, together with evidence of that consent; and

(g) the information referred to at 3.2(c) to (e) above.

**4.3**

In the case of an application for an order that a judgment should not be recognised—

(a) a statement of the ground or grounds under Article 23 of the 1996 Hague Convention on which it is requested that the judgment be not recognised, the reasons why the applicant asserts that such ground or grounds is or are made out, and any documentary evidence on which the Applicant relies; and

(b) an address within the jurisdiction of the court for service of process on the applicant and stating, in so far as is known to the applicant, the name and usual or last known address or place of business of the person in whose favour judgment was given.

**4.4**

Where is it sought to apply for recognition only of a judgment under the 1996 Hague Convention, the provisions of paragraph 4.2 apply with the exception that the applicant is not required to produce the document referred to in subparagraph 4.2(a).

Rules of Procedure

*Evidence required in support of an application for recognition or non-recognition of a judgment under the Jurisdiction and Recognition of Judgments Regulations or the 2014 Regulations*

**5.1**

An application for recognition of a judgment under regulation 7 of the Jurisdiction and Recognition of Judgments Regulations or under regulation 4 of the 2014 Regulations or for non-recognition of a judgment under regulation 8 of the Jurisdiction and Recognition of Judgments Regulations or regulation 5 of the 2014 Regulations must be accompanied by a witness statement or affidavit exhibiting the following documents and giving the information at 5.2 or 5.3 below, as appropriate.

**5.2**

In the case of an application for recognition of a judgment—

(a) where applicable, details of any decision determining the question of the substance or validity of the civil partnership or marriage previously given by a court of civil jurisdiction in England and Wales, or by a court elsewhere;

(b) where the judgment was obtained otherwise than by means of proceedings—

    (i) an official document certifying that the judgment is effective under the law of the country in which it was obtained;

    (ii) where either civil partner or spouse was domiciled in another country from that in which the judgment was obtained at the relevant date, an official document certifying that the judgment is recognised as valid under the law of that country; or

    (iii) a verified, certified or otherwise duly authenticated copy of the document at (i) or (ii) above, as appropriate;

(c) in relation to a judgment obtained by means of proceedings and given in default, the original or a certified true copy of the document which establishes that the party who did not respond was served with the document instituting the proceedings or with an equivalent document, or any document indicating that the respondent has accepted the judgment unequivocally; and

(d) the information referred to at paragraph 3.2(c) to (e) above.

**5.3**

In the case of an application for non-recognition of a judgment—

(a) an address within the jurisdiction of the court for service of process on the applicant and stating, in so far as is known to the applicant, the name and usual or last known address or place of business of the person in whose favour judgment was given;

(b) a statement of the ground or grounds under regulation 8 of the Jurisdiction and Recognition of Judgments Regulations or regulation 5 of the 2014 Regulations on which it is requested that the judgment should not be recognised together with any documentary evidence on which the applicant relies; and

(c) where the judgment was obtained by means of proceedings, the document referred to at paragraph 5.2(c) or a statement that no such service or acceptance occurred if that is the case.

*Evidence in support of application for a certificate under Articles 39, 41 or 42 of the Council Regulation, or for a certified copy of a judgment*

**6.1**

The procedure described in the following paragraphs should be used where the application for the certified copy of the judgment or relevant certificate under the Council Regulation has not been made at the conclusion of the proceedings to which it relates.

**6.2**

An application for a certified copy of a judgment, or for a certificate under Articles 39, 41 or 42 of the Council Regulation must be made by witness statement or affidavit, containing the information and attaching the documents required under paragraph 6.3, and paragraphs 6.4, 6.5 or 6.6 below, as appropriate.

**6.3**

All applications must—

(a) provide details of the proceedings in which the judgment was obtained;

(b) attach a copy of the application by which the proceedings were begun;

(c) attach a copy of all statements of case filed in the proceedings; and

(d) state—

    (i) whether the judgment provides for the payment of a sum of money; and

    (ii) whether interest is recoverable on the judgment or part of it and if so, the rate of interest, the date from which interest is recoverable, and the date on which interest ceases to accrue.

Further, where the application relates to the Council Regulation, the applicant must attach a document showing that he or she benefitted from legal aid in the proceedings to which the judgment relates, if that is the case.

**6.4**

An application for a certified copy of the judgment and a certificate under Article 41 or 42 of the Council Regulation must—

(a) contain a statement of whether the certificate is sought under Article 41 or Article 42;

(b) attach a document evidencing the service of the application by which the proceedings were begun on all respondents, and if no such service occurred, details of all opportunities provided to each respondent to put their case before the court;

(c) provide information regarding the age of the child at the time of the judgment and the opportunities given during the proceedings, if any, for the child's wishes and feelings to be ascertained;

(d) state the full names, addresses and dates and places of birth (where available) of all persons holding parental responsibility in relation to the child or children to whom the judgment relates; and

(e) state the full names and dates of birth of each child to whom the judgment relates.

**6.5**

An application for a certified copy of the judgment and a certificate under Article 39 of the Council Regulation must—

(a) state whether the certificate sought relates to a parental responsibility matter or a matrimonial matter;

(b) in relation to a parental responsibility matter, attach evidence that the judgment has been served on the respondent;

(c) in the case of a judgment given in default, attach a document which establishes that the respondent was served with the petition or application by which the proceedings were commenced, or a document indicating that the respondent accepted the judgment unequivocally;

(d) state that the time for appealing has expired, or give the date on which it will expire, as appropriate, and state whether a notice of appeal against the judgment has been given;

(e) in relation to a matrimonial matter, give the full name, address, country and place of birth, and date of birth of each party, and the country, place and date of the marriage;

(f) in relation to a parental responsibility matter, give the full name, address, place and date of birth of each person who holds parental responsibility;

(g) as appropriate, give the name, address, and date and place of birth of the person with access rights, or to whom the child is to be returned.

**6.6**

An application for a certified copy of a judgment for the purposes of recognition and enforcement of the judgment under the 1996 Hague Convention must—

(a) provide a statement of the grounds on which the court based its jurisdiction to make the orders in question;

(b) indicate the age of the child at the time of the judgment and the measures taken, if any, for the child's wishes and feelings to be ascertained; and

(c) indicate which persons were provided with notice of the proceedings and, where such persons were served with the proceedings, attach evidence of such service.

## PART 34—RECIPROCAL ENFORCEMENT OF MAINTENANCE ORDERS

*Scope and interpretation of this Part*

**34.1**

(1) This Part contains rules about the reciprocal enforcement of maintenance orders.

(2) In this Part—

'the 1920 Act' means the Maintenance Orders (Facilities for Enforcement) Act 1920;

'the1972 Act' means the Maintenance Orders (Reciprocal Enforcement) Act 1972;

'the 1982 Act' means the Civil Jurisdiction and Judgments Act 1982;

'the 1988 Convention' means the Convention on jurisdiction and the enforcement of judgments in civil and commercial matters done at Lugano on 16th September 1988;

'the Judgments Regulation' means Council Regulation (EC) No. 44/2001 of 22nd December 2000 on jurisdiction and the recognition and enforcement of judgments in civil and commercial matters; and

'the Lugano Convention' means the Convention on jurisdiction and the recognition and enforcement of judgments in civil and commercial matters, between the European Community and the Republic of Iceland, the Kingdom of Norway, the Swiss Confederation and the Kingdom of Denmark signed on behalf of the European Community on 30th October 2007.

(3) Chapter 1 of this Part relates to the enforcement of maintenance orders in accordance with the 1920 Act.

(4) Chapter 2 of this Part relates to the enforcement of maintenance orders in accordance with Parts 1 and 2 of the 1972 Act.

(5) Chapter 3 of this Part relates to the enforcement of maintenance orders in accordance with—

(a) the 1982 Act;

(b) the Judgments Regulation;

(c) the Lugano Convention;

(d) the Maintenance Regulation; and

(e) the 2007 Hague Convention.

*Meaning of prescribed officer in the family court*

**34.2**

(1) For the purposes of the 1920 Act, the prescribed officer in relation to the family court is the court officer.

(2) For the purposes of Part 1 of the 1972 Act and section 5(2) of the 1982 Act, the prescribed officer in relation to the family court is the court officer.

(3) For the purposes of an application under Article 30 of the Maintenance Regulation for a declaration of enforceability of a maintenance order or under Article 23(2) or (3) of the 2007 Hague Convention for registration of a maintenance order, the prescribed officer in relation to the family court is the court officer.

*Registration of maintenance orders in the family court*

**34.3**

Where the family court is required by any of the enactments referred to in rule 34.1(2) or by virtue of the Maintenance Regulation or the 2007 Hague Convention to register a foreign order the court officer must—

(a) enter a memorandum of the order in the register; and

(b) state on the memorandum the statutory provision or international instrument under which the order is registered.

# I ENFORCEMENT OF MAINTENANCE ORDERS UNDER THE MAINTENANCE ORDERS (FACILITIES FOR ENFORCEMENT) ACT 1920

*Interpretation*

**34.4**

(1) In this Chapter—

'payer', in relation to a maintenance order, means the person liable to make the payments for which the order provides; and

'reciprocating country' means a country or territory to which the 1920 Act extends.

(2) In this Chapter, an expression defined in the 1920 Act has the meaning given to it in that Act.

*Confirmation of provisional orders made in a reciprocating country*

**34.5**

(1) This rule applies where, in accordance with section 4(1) of the 1920 Act, the court officer receives a provisional maintenance order.

(2) The court must fix the date, time and place for a hearing.

(3) The court officer must register the order in accordance with rule 34.3.

(4) The court officer must serve on the payer—

(a) certified copies of the provisional order and accompanying documents; and

(b) a notice—

    (i) specifying the time and date fixed for the hearing; and

    (ii) stating that the payer may attend to show cause why the order should not be confirmed.

(5) The court officer must inform—

(a) the court which made the provisional order; and

(b) the Lord Chancellor,

whether the court confirms, with or without modification, or decides not to confirm, the order.

*Payment of sums due under registered orders*

**34.6**

Where an order made by a reciprocating country is registered in the family court under section 1 of the 1920 Act, the court must order payments due to be made to the court.

(Practice Direction 34A contains further provisions relating to the payment of sums due under registered orders.)

*Collection and enforcement of sums due under registered orders*

**34.7**

(1) This rule applies to—

(a) an order made in a reciprocating county which is registered in the family court; and

(b) a provisional order made in a reciprocating country which has been confirmed by the family court where the court has ordered that payments due under the order be made to the court.

(2) The court officer must—

(a) collect the monies due under the order; and

(b) send the monies collected to—

(i) the court in the reciprocating country which made the order; or

(ii) such other person or authority as that court or the Lord Chancellor may from time to time direct.

(3) The court officer may take proceedings in that officer's own name for enforcing payment of monies due under the order.

(Rule 32.33 makes provision in relation to a court officer taking such proceedings.)

*Prescribed notice for the taking of further evidence*

**34.8**

(1) This rule applies where a court in a reciprocating country has sent a provisional order to the family court for the purpose of taking further evidence.

(2) The court officer must send a notice to the person who applied for the provisional order specifying—

(a) the further evidence required; and

(b) the time and place fixed for taking the evidence.

*Transmission of maintenance orders made in a reciprocating country to the High Court*

**34.9**

A maintenance order to be sent by the Lord Chancellor to the High Court in accordance with section 1(1) of the 1920 Act will be—

(a) sent to the senior district judge who will register it in the register kept for the purpose of the 1920 Act; and

(b) filed in the principal registry.

*Transmission of maintenance orders made in the High Court to a reciprocating country*

**34.10**

(1) This rule applies to maintenance orders made in the High Court.

(2) An application for a maintenance order to be sent to a reciprocating country under section 2 of the 1920 Act must be made in accordance with this rule.

(3) The application must be made to a district judge in the principal registry unless paragraph (4) applies.

(4) If the order was made in the course of proceedings in a district registry, the application may be made to a district judge in that district registry.

(5) The application must be—

(a) accompanied by a certified copy of the order; and

(b)  supported by a record of the sworn written evidence.

(6)  The written evidence must give—

(a)  the applicant's reason for believing that the payer resides in the reciprocating country;

(b)  such information as the applicant has as to the whereabouts of the payer; and

(c)  such other information as maybe set out in Practice Direction 34A.

### Inspection of the register in the High Court

**34.11**

(1)  A person may inspect the register and request copies of a registered order and any document filed with it if the district judge is satisfied that that person is entitled to, or liable to make, payments under a maintenance order made in—

(a)  the High Court; or

(b)  a court in a reciprocating country.

(2)  The right to inspect the register referred to in paragraph (1) may be exercised by—

(a)  a solicitor acting on behalf of the person entitled to, or liable to make, the payments referred to in that paragraph; or

(b)  with the permission of the district judge, any other person.

## II ENFORCEMENT OF MAINTENANCE ORDERS UNDER PART 1 OF THE 1972 ACT

### Interpretation

**34.12**

(1)  In this Chapter—

(a)  'reciprocating country' means a country to which Part 1 of the 1972 Act extends; and

(b)  'relevant court in the reciprocating country' means, as the case may be—

    (i)  the court which made the order which has been sent to England and Wales for confirmation;

    (ii)  the court which made the order which has been registered in a court in England and Wales;

    (iii)  the court to which an order made in England and Wales has been sent for registration; or

    (iv)  the court to which a provisional order made in England and Wales has been sent for confirmation.

(2)  In this Chapter, an expression defined in the 1972 Act has the meaning given to it in that Act.

(3)  In this Chapter, 'Hague Convention Countries' means the countries listed in Schedule 1 to the Reciprocal Enforcement of Maintenance Orders (Hague Convention Countries) Order 1993.

### Scope

**34.13**

(1)  Section 1 of this Chapter contains rules relating to the reciprocal enforcement of maintenance orders under Part 1of the 1972 Act.

(2)  Section 2 of this Chapter modifies the rules contained in Section 1 of this Chapter in their application to—

[. . .]

(b)  the Hague Convention Countries; and

(c)  the United States of America.

(3)  Section 3 of this Chapter contains a rule in relation to notification of proceedings in a Hague Convention Country or the United States of America.

Rules of Procedure

(4) Section 4 of this Chapter contains rules in relation to proceedings under Part 2 of the 1972 Act (reciprocal enforcement of claims for the recovery of maintenance).

(Practice Direction 34A sets out in full the rules for the Hague Convention Countries and the United States of America as modified by Section 2 of this Chapter.)

## SECTION 1

### Reciprocal enforcement of maintenance orders under Part 1 of the 1972 Act

*Application for transmission of maintenance order to reciprocating country*

**34.14**

An application for a maintenance order to be sent to a reciprocating country under section 2 of the 1972 Act must be made in accordance with Practice Direction 34A.

*Certification of evidence given on provisional orders*

**34.15**

A document setting out or summarising evidence is authenticated by a court in England and Wales by a certificate signed, by the judge before whom that evidence was given.

(Section 3(5)(b), 5(4) and 9(5) of the 1972 Act require a document to be authenticated by the court.)

*Confirmation of a provisional order made in a reciprocating country*

**34.16**

(1) This rule applies to proceedings for the confirmation of a provisional order made in a reciprocating country, including proceedings in the family court for the confirmation of a provisional order made in a reciprocating country varying a maintenance order to which section 5(5) or 9(6) of the 1972 Act applies.

(2) Paragraph (3) applies on receipt by the court of—

(a) a certified copy of the order; and

(b) the documents required by the1972 Act to accompany the order.

(3) On receipt of the documents referred to in paragraph (2)—

(a) the court must fix the date, time and place for a hearing or a directions appointment; and

(b) the court officer must send to the payer notice of the date, time and place fixed together with a copy of the order and accompanying documents.

(4) The date fixed for the hearing must be not less than 21 days beginning with the date on which the court officer sent the documents to the payer in accordance with paragraph (2).

(5) The court officer will send to the relevant court in the reciprocating country a certified copy of any order confirming or refusing to confirm the provisional order.

(Section 5(5) and 7 of the1972 Act provide for proceedings for the confirmation of a provisional order.)

(Rule 34.22 provides for the transmission of documents to a court in a reciprocating country.)

*Consideration of revocation of a provisional order made by the family court*

**34.17**

(1) This rule applies where—

(a) the family court has made a provisional order by virtue of section 3 of the 1972 Act;

(b) before the order is confirmed, evidence is taken by the court or received by it as set out in section 5(9) of the 1972 Act; and

(c) on consideration of the evidence the court considers that the order ought not to have been made.

(Section 5(9) of the1972 Act provides that the family court may revoke a provisional order made by it, before the order has been confirmed in a reciprocating country, if it receives new evidence.)

(2) The court officer must serve on the person who applied for the provisional order ('the applicant') a notice which must—

(a)   set out the evidence taken or received by the court;

(b)   inform the applicant that the court considers that the order ought not to have been made; and

(c)   inform the applicant that the applicant may—

(i)   make representations in relation to that evidence either orally or in writing; and

(ii)   adduce further evidence.

(3) If an applicant wishes to adduce further evidence—

(a)   the applicant must notify the court officer at the court which made the order;

(b)   the court will fix a date for the hearing of the evidence; and

(c)   the court officer will notify the applicant in writing of the date fixed.

### *Notification of variation or revocation of a maintenance order by the High Court or the family court*

**34.18**

(1) This rule applies where—

(a)   a maintenance order has been sent to a reciprocating country in pursuance of section 2 of the 1972 Act; and

(b)   the court makes an order, not being a provisional order, varying or revoking that order.

(2) The court officer must send a certified copy of the order of variation or revocation to the relevant court in the reciprocating country.

(Rule 34.22 provides for the transmission of documents to a court in a reciprocating country.)

### *Notification of confirmation, variation or revocation of a maintenance order by the family court*

**34.19**

(1) This rule applies where the family court makes an order—

(a)   not being a provisional order, revoking or varying a maintenance order to which section 5 of the 1972 Act applies;

(b)   under section 9 of the 1972 Act, revoking or varying a registered order; or

(c)   under section 7(2) of the 1972 Act, confirming an order to which section 7 of that Act applies.

(2) The court officer must send written notice of the making, variation, revocation or confirmation of the order, as appropriate,to the relevant court in the reciprocating country.

(Section 5 of the 1972 Act applies to a provisional order made by the family court in accordance with section 3 of that Act which has been confirmed by a court in a reciprocating country.)

(Rule 34.22 provides for the transmission of documents to a court in a reciprocating country.)

### *Taking of evidence for court in reciprocating country*

**34.20**

(1) This rule applies where a request is made by or on behalf of a court in a reciprocating country for the taking of evidence for the purpose of proceedings relating to a maintenance order to which Part 1 of the 1972 Act applies.

(Section 14 of the1972 Act makes provision for the taking of evidence needed for the purpose of certain proceedings.)

Rules of Procedure

(2) The High Court has power to take the evidence where—

(a)  the request for evidence relates to a maintenance order made by a superior court in the United Kingdom; and

(b)  the witness resides in England and Wales.

(3) The family court has power to take evidence where—

(a)  the request for evidence relates to a maintenance order—

    (i)  made by the family court; or

    (ii)  registered in the family court; or

(b)  the Lord Chancellor sends to the family court a request to take evidence.

(Practice Direction 34E makes further provision on this matter)

[. . .]

(6) The evidence is to be taken in accordance with Part 22.

Request for the taking of evidence by a court in a reciprocating country

**34.21**

(1) This rule applies where a request is made by the family court for the taking of evidence in a reciprocating country in accordance with section 14(5) of the 1972 Act.

(2) The request must be made in writing to the court in the reciprocating country.

(Rule 34.22 provides for the transmission of documents to a court in a reciprocating country.)

*Transmission of documents*

**34.22**

(1) This rule applies to any document, including a notice or request, which is required to be sent to a court in a reciprocating country by—

(a)  Part 1 of the 1972 Act; or

(b)  Section 1 of Chapter 2 of this Part of these rules.

(2) The document must be sent to the Lord Chancellor for transmission to the court in the reciprocating country.

*Method of payment under registered orders*

**34.23**

(1) Where an order is registered in the family court in accordance with section 6(3) of the 1972 Act, the court must order that the payment of sums due under the order be made—

(a)  to the registering court; and

(b)  at such time and place as the court officer directs.

(Section 6(3) of the 1972 Act makes provision for the registration of maintenance orders made in a reciprocating country.)

(2) Where the court orders payments to be made to the court, whether in accordance with paragraph (1) or otherwise, the court officer must send the payments—

(a)  by post to either—

    (i)  the court which made the order; or

    (ii)  such other person or authority as that court, or the Lord Chancellor, directs; or

(b)  if the court which made the order is a country or territory specified in the Practice Direction 34A—

    (i)  to the Crown Agents for Overseas Governments and Administrations for transmission to the person to whom they are due; or

    (ii)  as the Lord Chancellor directs.

(Practice Direction 34A contains further provisions relating to the payment of sums due under registered orders.)

*Enforcement of payments under registered orders*

**34.24**

(1) This rule applies where a court has ordered periodical payments under a registered maintenance order to be made to the court.

(2) The court officer must take reasonable steps to notify the payee of the means of enforcement available.

(3) Paragraph (4) applies where periodical payments due under a registered order are in arrears.

(4) The court officer, on that officer's own initiative—

(a) may; or

(b) if the sums due are more than 4 weeks in arrears, must, proceed in that officer's own name for the recovery of the sums due unless of the view that it is unreasonable to do so.

*Notification of registration and cancellation*

**34.25**

(1) The court officer must send written notice to the Lord Chancellor of the due registration of orders registered in accordance with section 6(3), 7(5), or 10(4) of the 1972 Act.

(2) The court officer must, when registering an order in accordance with section 6(3), 7(5), 9(10), 10(4) or (5) or 23(3) of the 1972 Act, send written notice to the payer stating—

(a) that the order has been registered;

(b) that payments under the order should be made to the court officer; and

(c) the hours during which and the place at which the payments should be made.

(3) The court officer must, when cancelling the registration of an order in accordance with section 10(1) of the 1972 Act, send written notice of the cancellation to the payer.

## SECTION 2

### Modification of rules in Section 1 of this Chapter

[. . .]

## SUB-SECTION 2

### Hague Convention Countries

*Application of Section 1 of this Chapter to the Hague Convention Countries*

**34.27**

(1) In relation to the Hague Convention Countries, Section 1 of this Chapter has effect as modified by this rule.

(2) A reference in this rule, and in any rule which has effect in relation to the Hague Convention Countries by virtue of this rule to—

(a) the 1972 Act is a reference to the 1972 Act as modified by Schedule 2 to the Reciprocal Enforcement of Maintenance Orders (Hague Convention Countries) Order 1993; and

(b) a section under the 1972 Act is a reference to the section so numbered in the 1972 Act as so modified.

(3) A reference to a reciprocating country in rule 34.12(1) and Section 1 of this Chapter is a reference to a Hague Convention Country.

(4) Rules 34.15 (certification of evidence given on provisional orders), 34.16 (confirmation of provisional orders), 34.19 (notification of confirmation, variation or revocation of a maintenance order by the family court) and 34.21 (request for the taking of evidence by a court in a reciprocating country) do not apply.

(5) For rule 34.17 (consideration of revocation of a provisional order made by the family court) substitute—

*'Consideration of variation or revocation of a maintenance order made by the family court*

34.17 (1) This rule applies where—

(a)   an application has been made to a the family court by a payee for the variation or revocation of an order to which section 5 of the 1972 Act applies; and

(b)   the payer resides in a Hague Convention Country.

(2) The court officer must serve on the payee, by post, a copy of any representations or evidence adduced by or on behalf of the payer.'

(6) For rule 34.18 (notification of variation or revocation of a maintenance order by the High Court or the family court) substitute—

*'Notification of variation or revocation of a maintenance order by the High Court or a county court*

34.18 (1) This rule applies if the High Court or a county court makes an order varying or revoking a maintenance order to which section 5 of the 1972 Act applies.

(2) If the time for appealing has expired without an appeal having been entered, the court officer will send to the Lord Chancellor—

(a)   the documents required by section 5(8) of the 1972 Act; and

(b)   a certificate signed by a judge stating that the order of variation or revocation is enforceable and no longer subject to the ordinary forms of review.

(3) A party who enters an appeal against the order of variation or revocation must, at the same time, give written notice to the court officer.'

(7) For rule 34.23(2) (method of payment under registered orders) substitute—

'(2) Where the court orders payment to be made to the court, the court officer must send the payments by post to the payee under the order.'

(8) For rule 34.25 (notification of registration and cancellation) substitute—

*'Notification of registration and cancellation*

34.25 The court officer must send written notice to—

(a)   the Lord Chancellor, on the due registration of an order under section 10(4) of the 1972 Act; and

(b)   the payer under the order, on—

   (i)   the registration of an order under section 10(4) of the 1972 Act; or

   (ii)   the cancellation of the registration of an order under section 10(1) of the 1972 Act.'

(9) After rule 34.25 insert—

*'General provisions as to notices*

34.25A (1) A notice to a payer of the registration of an order in the family court in accordance with section 6(3) of the 1972 Act must be in the form referred to in a practice direction.

(Section 6(8) of the 1972 Act requires notice of registration to be given to the payer.)

(2) If the court sets aside the registration of a maintenance order following an appeal under section 6(9) of the 1972 Act, the court officer must send written notice of the decision to the Lord Chancellor.

(3) A notice to a payee that the court officer has refused to register an order must be in the form referred to in a practice direction.

(Section 6(11) of the 1972 Act requires notice of refusal of registration to be given to the payee.)

(4) Where, under any provision of Part 1 of the 1972 Act, a court officer serves a notice on a payer who resides in a Hague Convention Country, the court officer must send to the Lord Chancellor a certificate of service.'.

## SUB-SECTION 3

### United States of America

*Application of Section 1 of this Chapter to the United States of America*

**34.28**

(1) In relation to the United States of America, Section 1 of this Chapter has effect as modified by this rule.

(2) A reference in this rule and in any rule which has effect in relation to the United States of America by virtue of this rule to—

(a)  the 1972 Act is a reference to the 1972 Act as modified by Schedule 1 to the Reciprocal Enforcement of Maintenance Orders (United States of America) Order 2007; and

(b)  a section under the 1972 Act is a reference to the section so numbered in the 1972 Act as so modified.

(3) A reference to a reciprocating country in rule 34.12(1) and Section 1 of this Chapter is a reference to the United States of America.

(4) Rules 34.15 (certification of evidence given on provisional orders), 34.16 (confirmation of provisional orders), 34.19 (notification of confirmation, variation or revocation of a maintenance order made by the family court) and 34.21 (request for the taking of evidence in a reciprocating country) do not apply.

(5) For rule 34.17 (consideration of revocation of a provisional order made by the family court) substitute—

*'Consideration of variation or revocation of a maintenanceorder made by the family court*

34.17 (1) This rule applies where—

(a)  an application has been made to the family court by a payee for the variation or revocation of an order to which section 5 of the 1972 Act applies; and

(b)  the payer resides in the United States of America.

(2) The court officer must serve on the payee by post a copy of any representations or evidence adduced by or on behalf of the payer.'.

(6) For rule 34.18 (notification of variation or revocation), substitute—

*'Notification of variation or revocation*

34.18 If the High Court or the family court makes an order varying or revoking a maintenance order to which section 5 of the 1972 Act applies, the court officer will send to the Lord Chancellor the documents required by section 5(7) of that Act.'.

(7) For rule 34.23(2) (method of payment under registered orders) substitute—

'(2) Where the court orders payment to be made to the court, the court officer must send the payments by post to the payee under the order.'.

(8) For rule 34.25 (notification of registration and cancellation) substitute—

*'Notification of registration and cancellation*

34.25 The court officer must send written notice to—

(a)   the Lord Chancellor, on the due registration of an order under section 10(4) of the 1972 Act; or

(b)   the payer under the order, on—

   (i)   the registration of an order under section 10(4) of the 1972 Act; or

   (ii)   the cancellation of the registration of an order under section 10(1) of that Act.'

## SECTION 3

### Proceedings in a Hague Convention Country or in the United States of America

*Notification of proceedings in a Hague Convention Country or in the United States of America*

**34.28ZA**

Practice Direction 34E applies where the court officer receives from the Lord Chancellor notice of the institution of proceedings, including notice of the substance of a claim, in a Hague Convention Country or in the United States of America in relation to the making, variation or revocation of a maintenance order.

## SECTION 4

### Reciprocal enforcement of claims for the recovery of maintenance

*Interpretation*

**34.28ZB**

In this Section—

   'convention country' means a country or territory specified in an Order in Council made under section 25 of the 1972 Act; and

   an expression defined in the 1972 Act has the meaning given to it in that Act.

*Dismissal of an application under section 27A of the 1972 Act or application for variation*

**34.28ZC**

(1)   Where the family court dismisses an application under—

(a)   section 27A of the 1972 Act (application for recovery of maintenance); or

(b)   an application by a person in a convention country for the variation of a registered order,

the court officer will send a written notice of the court's decision to the Lord Chancellor.

(2)   The notice will include a statement of the court's reasons for its decision.

*Application for recovery of maintenance in England and Wales: section 27B of the 1972 Act*

**34.28ZD**

(1)   Where the family court receives an application for the recovery of maintenance sent from the Lord Chancellor under section 27B of the 1972 Act, the court will—

(a)   fix the date, time and place for a hearing or directions appointment, allowing sufficient time for service under this rule to be effected at least 21 days before the date fixed; and

(b)   serve copies of the application and any accompanying documents, together with a notice stating the date, time and place so fixed, on the respondent.

(2)   Within 14 days of service under this rule, the respondent must file an answer to the application in the form referred to in Practice Direction 5A.

*Application under section 26(1) or (2) of the 1972 Act and certificate under section 26(3A) of the 1972 Act: registration*

**34.28ZE**

Where—

(a)   an application under section 26(1) or (2) of the 1972 Act; or

(b)   a certificate under section 26(3A) of the 1972 Act,

is required to be registered in the family court by virtue of the Recovery of Maintenance (United States of America) Order 2007, the court officer will enter a minute or memorandum of the application or certificate in the register.

*Registration of an order: sections 27C(7) and 32(3) and (6) of the 1972 Act*

**34.28ZF**

(1)   Where the family court makes an order which is required under section 27C(7) of the 1972 Act to be registered, the court officer will enter a minute or memorandum of the order in the register.

(2)   Where a court officer receives under section 32(3) of the 1972 Act a certified copy of an order, the court officer will register the order by means of a minute or memorandum in the register.

(3)   Every minute or memorandum entered under paragraph (1) or (2) will specify the section and subsection of the 1972 Act under which the order in question is registered.

(4)   Where a court officer registers an order as required by section 27C(7) or 32(3) of the 1972 Act, the court officer will send written notice to the Lord Chancellor that the order has been registered.

(5)   Where a court officer is required by section 32(6) of the 1972 Act to give notice of the registration of an order, the court officer will do this by sending written notice to the officer specified in that subsection that the order has been registered.

*Payments made to the family court*

**34.28ZG**

(1)   Where payments are made to the family court by virtue of section 27C or 34A of the 1972 Act, the court officer will send those payments by post to such person or authority as the Lord Chancellor may from time to time direct.

(2)   Subject to paragraph (3), if it appears to a court officer that any sums payable under a registered order are in arrears, the officer may proceed in the officer's own name for the recovery of those sums.

(3)   Where it appears to the officer that sums payable under the order are in arrears to an amount equal—

(a)   in the case of payments to be made monthly or less frequently, to twice the sum payable periodically; or

(b)   in any other case, to four times the sum payable periodically,

the officer will proceed in the officer's own name for the recovery of those sums, unless it appears to the officer that it is unreasonable in the circumstances to do so.

*Method of payment*

**34.28ZH**

(1)   This rule applies where the family court exercises its duties or power sunder section 27C or 34A of the 1972 Act.

(2)   Where the court orders that payments under the order are to be made by a particular means—

(a)   the court will record on the copy of the order the means of payment that the court has ordered; and

(b)   the court officer will, as soon as practicable, notify, in writing, the person liable to make the payments under the order how payments are to be made.

(3) Paragraph (4) applies where the court orders that payments be made to the court by a method of payment falling within section 1(5) of the Maintenance Enforcement Act 1991.

(4) The court officer will notify the person liable to make the payments under the order of sufficient details of the account into which the payments should be made to enable payments to be made into that account.

*Application under section 34 of the 1972 Act: variation or revocation*

**34.28ZI**

(1) This rule applies in relation to an application under section 34 of the 1972 Act for the variation or revocation of a registered order.

(2) An application which is made directly to the registering court must be filed in the form referred to in Practice Direction 5A.

(3) Where the court receives an application, either filed in accordance with paragraph (2) or sent from the Lord Chancellor under section 34(3) of the 1972 Act—

(a)  the court will set the date, time and place for a hearing or directions appointment; and

(b)  the court officer will notify the applicant of the date, time and place.

*Application under section 35 of the 1972 Act: variation or revocation*

**34.28ZJ**

(1) This rule applies in relation to an application under section 35 of the 1972 Act for the variation or revocation of a registered order.

(2) Notice under section 35(3)(b) of the 1972 Act of the time and place appointed for the hearing of the application will be in the form specified in Practice Direction 34D.

(3) The court officer will send the notice by post to the Lord Chancellor for onward transmission to the appropriate authority in the convention country in which the respondent is residing.

(4) The time appointed for the hearing of the application will not be less than six weeks later than the date on which the notice is sent to the Lord Chancellor.

*Request under section 38(1) of the 1972 Act to the family court*

**34.28ZK**

(1) This rule applies where the family court receives from the Lord Chancellor a request under section 38(1) of the 1972 Act (taking evidence at the request of a court in a convention country) to take the evidence of any person.

(2) Subject to paragraph (3)—

(a)  the evidence will be taken in the same manner as if the person concerned were a witness in family proceedings;

(b)  any oral evidence so taken will be put into writing and read to the person who gave it, who must sign the document; and

(c)  the judge who takes any such evidence of any person will certify at the foot of the document setting out the evidence of, or produced in evidence by, that person that such evidence was taken, or document received in evidence, as the case may be, by that judge.

(3) Where the request referred to in section 38(2) of the 1972 Act includes a request that the evidence be taken in a particular manner, the court by which the evidence is taken will, so far as circumstances permit, comply with that request.

*Request under section 38(1) of the 1972 Act to the officer of the court*

**34.28ZL**

(1) This rule applies where an officer of the court receives from the Lord Chancellor a request under section 38(1) of the 1972 Act to take the evidence of any person.

(2) Subject to paragraph (3)—

(a) the person whose evidence is to be taken will be examined on oath by or before a justices' clerk or any other court officer determined by the Lord Chancellor;

(b) any oral evidence will be put into writing and read to the person who gave it, who must sign the document; and

(c) the justices' clerk or other officer will certify at the foot of the document setting out the evidence of, or produced by, that person, that such evidence was taken, or document received in evidence, as the case may be, by that justices' clerk or other officer.

(3) Where the request referred to in section 38(1) of the 1972 Act includes a request that the evidence be taken in a particular manner, the justices' clerk or other officer by whom the evidence is taken will, so far as circumstances permit, comply with that request.

(4) For the purposes of this rule, the justices' clerk or other officer has the same power to administer oaths as a single justice of the peace.

*Onward transmission of documents*

**34.28ZM**

Any document mentioned in rule 34.28ZK(2)(c) or rule 34.28ZL(2)(c) will be sent to the Lord Chancellor for onward transmission to the appropriate authority in the convention country in which the request referred to in section 38(1) of the 1972 Act originated.

## III ENFORCEMENT OF MAINTENANCE ORDERS UNDER THE CIVIL JURISDICTION AND JUDGMENTS ACT 1982, THE JUDGMENTS REGULATION, THE MAINTENANCE REGULATION, THE 2007 HAGUE CONVENTION AND THE LUGANO CONVENTION

*Application of this Chapter*

**34.28A**

(1) In this Chapter—

(a) references to a maintenance order include—

    (I) a decision, a court settlement or an authentic instrument within the meaning of Article 2 of the Maintenance Regulation where that Regulation applies;

    (II) a maintenance decision to which Chapter V of the 2007 Hague Convention applies by virtue of Article 19(1) of that Convention;

    (III) a maintenance arrangement (as defined in Article 3(e) of the 2007 Hague Convention) which is to be recognised and enforceable in the same way as a maintenance decision by virtue of Article 30 of that Convention;

(b) references to the Hague Protocol are to the Protocol on the Law Applicable to Maintenance Obligations done at The Hague on 23 November 2007;

(c) 'the 1968 Convention' has the meaning given in the 1982 Act.

(2) In relation to the Maintenance Regulation—

(a) Section 1 applies to maintenance orders to which Sections 2 and 3 of Chapter IV of the Maintenance Regulation apply (decisions given in a Member State which does not apply the rules of the Hague Protocol, that is, Denmark, and decisions to which Sections 2 and 3 of Chapter IV of that Regulation apply by virtue of Article 75(2)(a) or(b));

(2) Section 2 applies to all maintenance orders made in a magistrates' court in England and Wales for which reciprocal enforcement is sought in any Member State of the European Union, including Denmark.

## SECTION 1

### Registration and Enforcement in a Magistrates' Court of Maintenance Orders made in a Contracting State to the 1968 Convention, a Contracting State to the 1988 Convention, a Regulation State, a State bound by the 2007 Hague Convention other than a Member State of the European Union or a State bound by the Lugano Convention

*Interpretation*

**34.29**

In this Section—

(a) an expression defined in the1982 Act has the meaning given to it in that Act, subject to paragraph (b); and

(b) 'Regulation State' means a Member State of the European Union which does not apply the rules of the Hague Protocol, or, where registration is sought for a maintenance order to which Article 75(2)(a) or (b) of the Maintenance Regulation applies, the Member State of the European Union from which the order originated.

*Registration of maintenance orders*

**34.30**

[ . . .]

(2) This rule and Practice Direction 34E apply where the family court receives—

(a) an application under Article 31 of the 1968 Convention for the enforcement of a maintenance order made in a Contracting State other than the United Kingdom;

(b) an application under Article 31 of the 1988 Convention for the enforcement of a maintenance order made in a State bound by the 1988 Convention other than a Member State of the European Union;

(c) an application under Article 26 of the Maintenance Regulation for a declaration of enforceability of a maintenance order made in a Regulation State other than the United Kingdom;

(d) an application under Article 38 of the Lugano Convention for the enforcement of a maintenance order made in a State bound by the Lugano Convention other than a Member State of the European Union; or

(e) an application under Article 23 of the 2007 Hague Convention for registration of a maintenance order made in a State bound by that Convention other than a Member State of the European Union.

[ . . .]

(6) Except where Practice Direction 34E provides otherwise, the court must register the order unless—

(a) in the case of an application under Article 31 of the 1968 Convention, Articles 27 or 28 of that Convention apply;

(b) in the case of an application under Article 31 of the 1988 Convention, Articles 27 or 28 of that Convention apply; and

(c) in the case of an application under Article 23(2) or (3) of the 2007 Hague Convention, Article 22(a) of that Convention applies.

(7) If the court refuses to register an order to which this rule relates the court officer must notify the applicant.

(8) If the court registers an order the court officer must send written notice of that fact to—

(a)   the Lord Chancellor;

(b)   the payer; and

(c)   the applicant.

*Appeal from a decision relating to registration*

**34.31**

(1) This rule applies to an appeal under—

(a)   Article 36 or Article 40 of the 1968 Convention;

(b)   Article 36 or Article 40 of the 1988 Convention;

(c)   Article 32 of the Maintenance Regulation;

(d)   Article 43 of the Lugano Convention; or

(e)   Article 23(5) of the 2007 Hague Convention.

(2) The appeal must be to the family court.

(Practice Direction 34E makes provision in relation to such cases.)

*Payment of sums due under a registered order*

**34.32**

(1) an order is registered in accordance with section 5(3) of the 1982 Act, Article 38 of the Judgments Regulation, Article 38 of the Lugano Convention or Article 23 of the 2007 Hague Convention or declared enforceable under Article 26 of the Maintenance Regulation by virtue of registration, the court may order that payment of sums due under the order be made to the court, at such time and place as directed.

(2) Where the court orders payments to be made to the court, whether in accordance with paragraph (1) or otherwise, the court officer must send the payments by post either—

(a)   to the court which made the order; or

(b)   to such other person or authority as that court, or the Lord Chancellor, directs.

(Practice Direction 34A contains further provisions relating to the payment of sums due under registered orders.)

*Enforcement of payments under registered orders*

**34.33**

(1) This rule applies where a court has ordered periodical payments under a registered maintenance order to be made to the family court.

(2) The court officer must take reasonable steps to notify the payee of the means of enforcement available.

(3) Paragraph (4) applies where periodical payments due under a registered order are in arrears.

(4) The court officer, on that officer's own initiative—

(a)   may; or

(b)   if the sums due are more than 4 weeks in arrears, must,

proceed in that officer's own name for the recovery of the sums due unless of the view that it is unreasonable to do so.

*Variation and revocation of registered orders*

**34.34**

(1) This rule applies where the court officer for a registering court receives notice that a registered maintenance order has been varied or revoked by a competent court in a Contracting State to the 1968 Convention, a Contracting State to the 1988 Convention (other than a Member State of the

European Union), a Regulation State or a State bound by the Lugano Convention or by the2007 Hague Convention, other than a Member State of the European Union.

(2) The court officer for the registering court must—

(a) register the order of variation or revocation; and

(b) send notice of the registration by post to the payer and payee under the order.

(3) Where the court officer for a registering court receives notice that a maintenance order registered in that court by virtue of the provisions of the Judgments Regulation has been varied or revoked by a competent court in another Member State of the European Union, the court officer must—

(a) note against the entry in the register that the original order so registered has been varied or revoked, as the case may be; and

(b) send notice of the noting of the variation or revocation, as the case may be, by post to the payer and payee under the order.

*Registered order: payer residing in a different Designated Family Judge area*

**34.35**

Practice Direction 34E makes provision for cases where a court officer in the Designated Family Judge area where an order is registered considers that the payer is residing in a different Designated Family Judge area.

*Cancellation of registered orders*

**34.36**

(1) Where the court officer for the registering court—

(a) has no reason to send papers to another Designated Family Judge area under Practice Direction 34E; and

(b) considers that the payer under the registered order is not residing within the Designated Family Judge area where the order is registered,

the court officer will cancel the registration of the order.

(2) The court officer must—

(a) give notice of cancellation to the payee; and

(b) send the information and documents relating to the registration and the other documents referred to in rule 34.35(2) to the Lord Chancellor.

*Directions as to stays, documents and translations*

**34.36A**

At any stage in proceedings for registration of a maintenance order under this Section of this Chapter, the court may give directions about the conduct of the proceedings, including—

(a) staying of proceedings in accordance with—

    (i) Article 30 or 38 of the 1968 Convention,

    (ii) Article 30 or 38 of the 1988 Convention,

    (iii) Article 37 or 46 of the Lugano Convention,

    (iv) Article 25 or 35 of the Maintenance Regulation, or

    (v) Article 30(6) of the 2007 Hague Convention;

(b) the provision of documents in accordance with—

    (i) Article 48 of the 1968 Convention,

    (ii) Article 48 of the 1988 Convention,

    (iii) Article 55 of the Lugano Convention,

   (iv)  Article 29 of the Maintenance Regulation, or

   (v)  Article 25 or 30 of the 2007 Hague Convention;

(c)  the provision of translations in accordance with—

   (i)   Article 48 of the 1968 Convention,

   (ii)  Article 48 of the 1988 Convention,

   (iii)  Article 55 of the Lugano Convention,

   (iv)  Article 28 of the Maintenance Regulation, or

   (v)  in relation to an application under this Section relating to the 2007 Hague Convention, without prejudice to Article 44 of that Convention.

*International Maintenance Obligations; Communication with the Central Authority for England and Wales*

**34.36B**

(1) Where the Lord Chancellor requests information or a document from the court officer for the relevant court for the purposes of Article 58 of the Maintenance Regulation, or Article 12 or 25(2) of the 2007 Hague Convention, the court officer shall provide the requested information or document to the Lord Chancellor forthwith.

(2) In this rule, 'relevant court' means the court at which an application under Article 56 of the Maintenance Regulation or Article 10 of the 2007 Hague Convention has been filed.

[The Lord Chancellor is the Central Authority for the 2007 Hague Convention and the Maintenance Regulation]

*The Maintenance Regulation: applications for enforcement or for refusal or suspension of enforcement*

**34.36C**

Practice Direction 34E makes provision regarding—

(a)  an application for enforcement of a maintenance decision to which section 1 of Chapter IV of the Maintenance Regulation applies; and

(b)  an application by a debtor under Article 21 of the Maintenance Regulation for refusal or suspension of enforcement.

## SECTION 2

## Reciprocal enforcement in a Contracting State or a Member State of the European Union of Orders of a court in England and Wales

[ . . .]

*Admissibility of Documents*

**34.38**

(1) This rule applies to a document, referred to in paragraph (2) and authenticated in accordance with paragraph (3), which comprises, records or summarises evidence given in, or information relating to, proceedings in a court in another part of the UK, another Contracting State to the 1968 Convention or the 1988 Convention, Member State of the European Union or State bound by the Lugano Convention, or by the 2007 Hague Convention, and any reference in this rule to 'the court', without more, is a reference to that court.

(2) The documents referred to at paragraph (1) are documents which purport to—

(a)  set out or summarise evidence given to the court;

(b)  have been received in evidence to the court;

(c) set out or summarise evidence taken in the court for the purpose of proceedings in a court in England and Wales to which the 1982 Act, the Judgments Regulation, the Maintenance Regulation or the 2007 Hague Convention applies; or

(d) record information relating to payments made under an order of the court.

(3) A document to which paragraph (1) applies shall, in any proceedings in the family court relating to a maintenance order to which the 1982 Act, the Judgments Regulation, the Maintenance Regulation or the 2007 Hague Convention applies, be admissible as evidence of any fact stated in it to the same extent as oral evidence of that fact is admissible in those proceedings.

(4) A document to which paragraph (1) applies shall be deemed to be authenticated—

(a) in relation to the documents listed at paragraph 2(a) or (c), if the document purports to be—

  (i) certified by the judge or official before whom the evidence was given or taken; or

  (ii) the original document recording or summarising the evidence, or a true copy of that document;

(b) in relation to a document listed at paragraph (2)(b), if the document purports to be certified by a judge or official of the court to be, or to be a true copy of, the document received in evidence; and

(c) in relation to the document listed at paragraph (2)(d), if the document purports to be certified by a judge or official of the court as a true record of the payments made under the order.

(5) It shall not be necessary in any proceedings in which evidence is to be received under this rule to prove the signature or official position of the person appearing to have given the certificate referred to in paragraph (4).

(6) Nothing in this rule shall prejudice the admission in evidence of any document which is admissible in evidence apart from this rule.

(7) Any request by the family court for the taking or providing of evidence by a court in a State listed in paragraph (8) for the purposes of proceedings to which an instrument listed in that paragraph applies, or by a court in another part of the United Kingdom, shall be communicated in writing to the court in question.

(8) The States and instruments referred to in paragraph (7) are—

(a) a Contracting State to the 1968 Convention;

(b) a Contracting State to the 1988 Convention;

(c) a State bound by the Lugano Convention;

(d) Denmark, in relation to proceedings to which the Maintenance Regulation applies;

(e) a State bound by the 2007 Hague Convention,

but this paragraph and paragraph (7) do not apply where the State in question is a Member State of the European Union to which the Taking of Evidence Regulation (as defined in rule 24.15) applies.

(Chapter 2 of Part 24 makes provision for taking of evidence by a court in another Member State of the European Union).

*Enforcement of orders of the family court*

**34.39**

(1) A person who wishes to enforce a maintenance order obtained in the family court in a State to which paragraph (2) applies must apply for a certified copy of the order and, where required by Practice Direction 34A, a certificate giving particulars relating to the judgment and proceedings in which it was given.

(2) The States referred to in paragraph (1) are—

(a) a Contracting State to the 1968 Convention;

(b) a Contracting State to the 1988 Convention (other than a Member State of the European Union);

(c) a Member State of the European Union;

(d)   a State bound by the Lugano Convention (other than a Member State of the European Union); or

(e)   a State bound by the 2007 Hague Convention (other than a Member State of the European Union).

(3) An application under this rule must be made in writing to the court officer and must specify—

(a)   the names of the parties to the proceedings;

(b)   the date, or approximate date, of the proceedings in which the maintenance order was made and the nature of those proceedings;

(c)   the State in which the application for recognition or enforcement has been made or is to be made; and

(d)   the postal address of the applicant.

(4) The court officer must, on receipt of the application, send a copy of the order to the applicant certified in accordance with practice direction 34A, together with a copy of any certificate required by that practice direction applies, a completed extract from the decision in the form of Annex II to that Regulation.

(5) Paragraph (6) applies where—

(a)   a maintenance order is registered in the family court; and

(b)   a person wishes to obtain a certificate giving details of any payments made or arrears accrued under the order while it has been registered, for the purposes of an application made or to be made in connection with that order in—

  (i)    another Contracting State to the 1968 Convention;

  (ii)   another Contracting State to the 1988 Convention (other than a Member State of the European Union);

  (iii)  another Member State of the European Union;

  (iv)   another State bound by the Lugano Convention (other than a Member State of the European Union);

  (v)    another part of the United Kingdom; or

  (vi)   another State bound by the 2007 Hague Convention (other than a Member State of the European Union).

(6) The person wishing to obtain the certificate referred to in paragraph (5) may make a written application to the court officer for the registering court.

(7) On receipt of an application under paragraph (6) the court officer must send to the applicant a certificate giving the information requested.

(Rule 74.12 (application for certified copy of a judgment) and 74.13 (evidence in support) of the CPR apply in relation to the application for a certified copy of a judgment obtained in the High Court or a county court.)

## *Enforcement of orders of the High Court or the family court*

**34.40**

(1) This rule applies where a person wishes to enforce a maintenance order obtained in the High Court or the family court (including the principal registry when treated as a divorce county court or, where the enforcement application relates to a civil partnership matter and the Maintenance Regulation, a civil partnership proceedings county court) in a Member State of the European Union or a State bound by the 2007 Hague Convention (other than a Member State of the European Union).

(2) Subject to the requirements of Practice Direction 34A, rules 74.12 (application for a certified copy of a judgment) and 74.13 (evidence in support) of the CPR apply in relation to—

(a)   an application under Article 40(2) of the Maintenance Regulation for a certified copy of a judgment and an extract relating to that judgment in the form of Annex II to that Regulation;

(b)   an application for a certified copy of a judgment and a certificate giving particulars relating to the judgment and the proceedings in which it was given.

## PRACTICE DIRECTION 34A—RECIPROCAL ENFORCEMENT OF MAINTENANCE ORDERS

*Noting Record of Means of Payment*

1.1

Where the family court orders payments under a maintenance order to which Part 34 applies to be made in a particular way, the court must record that on a copy of the order.

1.2

If the court orders payment to be made to the court by a method referred to in section 1(5) of the Maintenance Enforcement Act 1991, the court may vary the method of payment on the application of an interested party and where it does so the court must record the variation on a copy of the order.

(Section 1(5) refers to payment by standing order or other methods which require transfer between accounts of a specific amount on a specific date during the period for which the authority to make the payment is in force.)

*Notification by court officer*

2.1

The court officer must, as soon as practicable, notify in writing the person liable to make the payments of the method by which they must be made.

2.2

If the court orders payment to be made to the court by a method referred to in section 1(5) of the Maintenance Enforcement Act 1991 the court officer must inform the person liable to make the payments of the number and location of the account to which the payments must be made.

2.3

If, on application, the court varies the method of payment, the court officer will notify all parties of the result of the application, in writing and as soon as possible.

*Applications under section 2 of the 1920 Act*

3.1

This paragraph refers to an application for the transmission of a maintenance order to a reciprocating country under section 2 of the 1920 Act in accordance with rule 34.10.

3.2

The applicant's written evidence must include such information as may be required by the law of the reciprocating country for the purpose of enforcement of the order.

3.3

If, in accordance with section 2 of the 1920 Act, the court sends a maintenance order to the Lord Chancellor for transmission to a reciprocating country, it shall record the fact in the court records.

## Applications under section 2 of the 1972 Act (rule 34.14)

*Introduction*

4.1

An application for a maintenance order to be sent to a reciprocating country under section 2 of the 1972 Act is made by lodging specified documents with the court. The documents to be lodged vary according to which country it is intended that the maintenance order is be sent and the requirements are set out in this paragraph.

*General provision*

**4.2**

The general requirement is that the following documents should be lodged with the court—

(a) an affidavit by the applicant stating—

    (i) the reason that the applicant has for believing that the payer under the maintenance order is residing in the reciprocating country; and

    (ii) the amount of any arrears due to the applicant under the order, the date to which those arrears have been calculated and the date on which the next payment under the order falls due;

(b) a certified copy of the maintenance order;

(c) a statement giving such information as the applicant has as to the whereabouts of the payer;

(d) a statement giving such information as the applicant has for facilitating the identification of the payer, (including, if known to the applicant, the name and address of any employer of the payer, his occupation and the date and place of issue of any passport of the payer); and

(e) if available to the applicant, a photograph of the payer.

[. . .]

*Hague Convention Country*

**4.5**

If the country to which it is intended to send the maintenance order is a Hague Convention country (as defined in rule 34.12), then the following changes to the general requirements apply.

**4.6**

In addition to the matters stated in that paragraph, the affidavit referred to in paragraph 4.2(a) must also state whether the time for appealing against the maintenance order has expired and whether an appeal is pending.

**4.7**

The applicant must lodge the following documents with the court in addition to those set out in paragraph 4.2—

(a) a statement as to whether or not the payer appeared in the proceedings in which the maintenance order was made;

(b) if the payer did not so appear—

    (i) the original of a document which establishes that notice of the institution of proceedings, including notice of the substance of the claim, was served on the payer; or

    (ii) a copy of such a document certified by the applicant or the applicant's solicitor to be a true copy;

(c) a document which establishes that notice of the order was sent to the payer;

(d) a written statement as to whether or not the payee received legal aid in the proceedings in which the order was made, or in connection with the application under section 2 of the 1972 Act; and

(e) if the payee did receive legal aid, a copy certified by the applicant or the applicant's solicitor to be a true copy of the legal aid certificate.

## United States of America

**4.8**

If the country to which it is intended to send the maintenance order is a specified State of the United States of America, then the following changes to the general requirements apply.

**4.9**

There is no requirement to lodge a statement giving information as to the whereabouts of the payer since this information must be contained in the affidavit as mentioned in paragraph 4.10.

**4.10**

In addition to the matters stated in that paragraph, the affidavit referred to in paragraph 4.2(a) must also state—

(a)   the address of the payee;

(b)   such information as is known as to the whereabouts of the payer; and

(c)   a description, so far as is known, of the nature and location of any assets of the payer available for execution.

**4.11**

The applicant must lodge three certified copies of the maintenance order.

. . .

## Notification to the Lord Chancellor

**5.1**

Where, in accordance with Part 1 of the 1972 Act, the family court registers a maintenance order sent to it from a Hague Convention Country, the court officer must send written notice of the registration to the Lord Chancellor.

## Notification of means of enforcement

**6.1**

The court officer of the family court must take reasonable steps to notify the person to whom payments are due under a registered order of the means of enforcement available in respect of it.

## Certified copies of orders issued under rules 34.39 and 34.40

**7.1**

In an application under rule 34.39 or 34.40 by a person wishing to enforce abroad a maintenance order, the certified copy of the order will be a sealed copy and will be accompanied by a certificate signed by the court officer.

**7.2**

In an application under the 1982 Act, the certificate signed by the court officer must state that it is a true copy of the order concerned and must give particulars of the proceedings in which it was made.

**7.3**

In an application under the Judgments Regulation, the certificate will be in the form of Annex V to the Regulation.

**7.4**

In an application under the Lugano Convention, the certificate will be in the form of Annex V to the Convention.

**7.5**

In an application under the Maintenance Regulation, the certificate will be in the form of Annex II to that Regulation.

**7.6**

In an application under the 2007 Hague Convention, the certificate will be comprised of the following Article 11 forms duly completed by the court officer—

(a)  the Abstract of a Decision;

(b)  the Statement of Enforceability; and

(c)  the Statement of Proper Notice.

**7.7**

In an application under the 2007 Hague Convention, the certificate will additionally state the jurisdictional basis upon which the order was made, with reference to the jurisdictional criteria in Article 20(1) of that Convention to be applied by the State in which recognition and/or enforcement is to be sought.

*Countries and Territories in which Sums are Payable through Crown Agents for Overseas Governments and Territories (rule 34.23)*

**8.1**

Gibraltar, Barbados, Bermuda, Ghana, Kenya, Fiji, Hong Kong, Singapore, Turks and Caicos Islands, United Republic of Tanzania (except Zanzibar), Anguilla, Falkland Islands and Dependencies, St Helena.

PART 1 OF THE 1972 ACT—MODIFIED RULES

**9.1**

The annexes to this Practice Direction set out rules 34.14 to 34.25 as they are modified—

(a)  in relation to the Republic of Ireland, by rule 34.26 (Annex 1) (but see the note in that Annex regarding the ongoing relevance of those rules following revocation of rule 34.26);

(b)  in relation to the Hague Convention Countries, by rule 34.27 (Annex 2); and

(c)  in relation to Specified States of the United States of America, by rule 34.28 (Annex3).

**9.2**

The statutory references in the annexes are construed in accordance with rule 34.26(2), 34.27(2) or 34.28(2) as the case may be.

*[Annexes 1–3 omitted]*

**PRACTICE DIRECTION 34C—APPLICATIONS FOR RECOGNITION AND ENFORCEMENT TO OR FROM EUROPEAN UNION MEMBER STATES**

*Introduction*

**1.1**

The Maintenance Regulation (Council Regulation (EC) No 4/2009 of 18 December 2008 on jurisdiction, applicable law, recognition and enforcement of decisions and cooperation in matters relating to maintenance obligations) ('the Maintenance Regulation') applies across the European Union from 18 June 2011. It applies to all cases for recognition and enforcement in or from a European Union Member State from that date. The domestic legislation facilitating the application of the Maintenance Regulation is the Civil Jurisdiction and Judgments (Maintenance) Regulations 2011 ('the CJJMR').

Rules of Procedure

1.2

The Member States of the European Union are: Austria, Belgium, Bulgaria, Cyprus, Czech Republic, Denmark, Estonia, Finland, France, Germany, Greece, Hungary, Ireland, Italy, Latvia, Lithuania, Luxembourg, Malta, The Netherlands, Poland, Portugal, Romania, Slovakia, Slovenia, Spain, Sweden, and the United Kingdom.

*Relationship between the Maintenance Regulation and other international instruments*

2.1

The Maintenance Regulation replaces the relevant provisions of Regulation (EC) No 44/2001 of 22 December 2000 on jurisdiction and the recognition and enforcement of judgments in civil and commercial matters (known as 'Brussels I'), subject to the transitional provisions of Article 75. It will also take precedence over any other international conventions and agreements concerning matters which the Maintenance Regulation governs as regards relations between Member States. In particular (and subject to the relevant transitional provisions (discussed below)), the Maintenance Regulation must be applied between Member States instead of the following—

(a) The Convention on the Recognition and Enforcement of Decisions Relating to Maintenance Obligations done at The Hague on 2 October 1973 ('the 1973 Convention');

(b) the arrangements for reciprocal enforcement of maintenance between the United Kingdom and the Republic of Ireland reflected in the Reciprocal Enforcement of Maintenance Orders (Republic of Ireland) Order 1993 ('the Republic of Ireland Order');

(c) as regards Malta, the provisions of the Maintenance Orders (Reciprocal Enforcement) Act 1972 Part 1 ('the 1972 Act');

(d) the United Nations Convention on the Recovery Abroad of Maintenance done at New York on 20th June 1956 ('the 1956 New York Convention') (applied in England and Wales by Part II of the Maintenance Orders (Reciprocal Enforcement) Act 1972) (this Convention is concerned with the reciprocal treatment of applications for maintenance rather than reciprocal enforcement of orders, but is included here for clarity).

*Application of the Maintenance Regulation rules to recognition, registration and enforcement in England and Wales of an order from another Member State*

3.1

For an application for enforcement of a maintenance order from another European Union Member State which applies the 2007 Hague Protocol on the Law Applicable to Maintenance Orders (all other Member States except Denmark), the court will apply the rules in Sections 1 and 3 of Chapter IV of the Maintenance Regulation. Orders from such Member States are not subject to registration and benefit from direct enforceability in the family court in the same manner as an order for maintenance which had been made in proceedings in England and Wales. Rule 34.36C of the Family Procedure Rules 2010 and Practice Direction 34E make provision for such cases.

3.2

For an application from another European Union Member State which does not apply the 2007 Hague Protocol on the Law Applicable to Maintenance Orders (namely Denmark), the court will apply the rules in Sections 2 and 3 of Chapter IV of the Maintenance Regulation. These orders do require registration before they can be enforced and Section 1 of Chapter 3 of Part 34 of the Family Procedure Rules 2010 applies to these cases.

*Application of the Maintenance Regulation to recognition and enforcement of a maintenance order from England and Wales in another Member State*

4.1

Where recognition and enforcement of an England and Wales maintenance order is sought in another European Union Member State, the courts and authorities of that Member State will apply Sections 2 and 3 of Chapter IV of the Maintenance Regulation, because the United Kingdom is not a State Party to the 2007 Hague Protocol (and consequently courts and authorities of the United Kingdom are not bound to apply 'applicable law' rules to the initial decision). Section 2 of Chapter 3 of Part 34 of the Family Procedure Rules 2010 applies to those decisions.

*Transitional cases*

**5.1**

The Maintenance Regulation makes specific provision for transitional cases in Article 75. The general rule is provided by Article 75(1), whereby the Regulation applies only to proceedings instituted after its date of application (18 June 2011) However, special rules apply in relation to applications from another European Union Member State for recognition or recognition and enforcement—

(a)　Where the maintenance decision was given in any Member State prior to 18 June 2011, but recognition and enforcement are sought after that date, the court will apply the rules of Sections 2 and 3 of Chapter IV.

(b)　Where the maintenance decision was given in any Member State after 18 June 2011 but the proceedings for that decision were commenced prior to that date, the court will also apply the rules of Sections 2 and 3 of Chapter IV.

(c)　Where there is an application in progress on 18 June 2011 for recognition and enforcement under Council Regulation (EC) No 44/2001 (Brussels I) relating to a maintenance decision from a Member State, the court will apply the rules of Chapter III of Brussels I.

**5.2**

It will therefore be seen that, for transitional cases (a) and (b) above, Section 1 of Chapter IV will not be used, regardless of whether the Member State in question applies the 2007 Hague Protocol—the arrangements are the same for all Member States.

**5.3**

As stated in paragraph 2.1 above, the Maintenance Regulation will apply as between Member States instead of other existing international agreements dealing with the same matters. The provisions of 5.1 (a) and (b) above apply in all cases. Where relations in maintenance matters between the United Kingdom and another Member State were governed by Brussels I prior to the application of the Maintenance Regulation, the transitional arrangements in paragraph 5.1 (c) above will apply, and transitional arrangements regarding rules of court for such cases are made in rule 38 of the Family Procedure (Amendment) Rules 2011.

**5.4**

Where maintenance matters between the United Kingdom and another Member State were governed by the 1973 Convention or the Republic of Ireland Order prior to 18 June 2011, the following provision is made for transitional cases—

(a)　As regards cases governed by the 1973 Convention, the references in the Hague Convention Countries Order to those Member States which are party to that Convention have been revoked. However, those Member States continue to be treated under that Order as Hague Convention Countries for transitional purposes under the CJJMR, including those proceedings for establishment, variation, or revocation of a maintenance order, or for registration of a maintenance order, which are continuing on 18 June 2011. In those circumstances, the rules at Part 34, Chapter 2, Section 2 sub-section 2 of the Family Procedure Rules 2010 will continue to apply to those proceedings.

(b)　In relation to cases concerning the Republic of Ireland, the Republic of Ireland Order has been revoked[8]. Transitional provision is made by paragraph 28 of Schedule 7 to the CJJMR. Again, this includes provision for proceedings for establishment of maintenance, variation or revocation of an order, or for registration of an order, which are continuing on 18 June 2011. The Family

Procedure Rules 2010 have been amended so that Part 34, Chapter 2, Section 2 sub-section 1 has been revoked. Provision is made for the application of those rules in transitional cases in the Family Procedure (Amendment) Rules 2011 at rule 38. Annex 1 to Practice Direction 34A (which sets out rules 34.14 to 34.25 as modified by Part 34, Chapter 2, section 2 subsection 1 prior to its revocation) should therefore be applied in accordance with the provision in rule 38 of those Amendment Rules.

**5.5**

No specific provision is currently made in domestic law for transitional provision relating to Malta or in relation to the 1956 New York Convention as it relates to applications from European Union Member States. The position is directly governed by Article 75(1) of the Maintenance Regulation. Where proceedings have been instituted by virtue of the 1956 New York Convention or the operation of Part I of the 1972 Act on or prior to 18 June 2011 and are continuing on that date, those proceedings are not affected by Maintenance Regulation rules. Such proceedings would include applications for variation and revocation of orders as well as for establishment of a maintenance order. However, recognition and enforcement in another Member State of any resulting order would occur in accordance with the Maintenance Regulation (and the transitional provisions of Article 75(2) should be considered). Enforcement in England and Wales of orders registered under either part of the 1972 Act on or prior to 18 June 2011 will not be affected by the Maintenance Regulation.

## PART 35—MEDIATION DIRECTIVE

*Scope and Interpretation*

**35.1**

(1) This Part applies to mediated cross-border disputes that are subject to Directive 2008/52/EC of the European Parliament and of the Council of 21 May 2008 on certain aspects of mediation in civil and commercial matters ('the Mediation Directive').

(2) In this Part—

'cross-border dispute' has the meaning given by article 2 of the Mediation Directive;

'mediation' has the meaning given by article 3(a) of the Mediation Directive;

'mediation administrator' means a person involved in the administration of the mediation process;

'mediation evidence' means evidence regarding information arising out of or in connection with a mediation process;

'mediator' has the meaning given by article 3(b) of the Mediation Directive; and

'relevant dispute' means a cross-border dispute that is subject to the Mediation Directive.

*Relevant disputes: applications for consent orders in respect of financial remedies*

**35.2**

(1) This rule applies in relation to proceedings for a financial remedy where the applicant, with the explicit consent of the respondent, wishes to make an application that the content of a written agreement resulting from mediation of a relevant dispute be made enforceable by being made the subject of a consent order.

(2) The court will not include in a consent order any matter which is contrary to the law of England and Wales or which is not enforceable under that law.

(3) The applicant must file two copies of a draft of the order in the terms sought.

(4) Subject to paragraph (5), the application must be supported by evidence of the explicit consent of the respondent.

(5) Where the respondent has written to the court consenting to the making of the order sought, the respondent is deemed to have given explicit consent to the order and paragraph (4) does not apply.

(6) Paragraphs (1)(b) and (2) to (6) of rule 9.26 apply to an application to which this rule applies.

*Mediation evidence: disclosure and inspection*

**35.3**

(1) Where a party to proceedings seeks disclosure or inspection of mediation evidence that is in the control of a mediator or mediation administrator, that party must first obtain the court's permission to seek the disclosure or inspection, by an application made in accordance with Part 18.

(2) The mediator or mediation administrator who has control of the mediation evidence must be named as a respondent to the application and must be served with a copy of the application notice.

(3) Evidence in support of the application must include evidence that—

(a)  all parties to the mediation agree to the disclosure or inspection of the mediation evidence;

(b)  disclosure or inspection of the mediation evidence is necessary for overriding considerations of public policy, in accordance with article 7(1)(a) of the Mediation Directive; or

(c)  the disclosure of the content of an agreement resulting from mediation is necessary to implement or enforce that agreement.

(4) Where this rule applies, Parts 21 to 24 apply to the extent they are consistent with this rule.

*Mediation evidence: witnesses and depositions*

**35.4**

(1) This rule applies where a party wishes to obtain mediation evidence from a mediator or mediation administrator by—

(a)  a witness summons;

(b)  cross-examination with permission of the court under rule 22.8 or 23.4;

(c)  an order under rule 24.7 (evidence by deposition);

(d)  an order under rule 24.9 (enforcing attendance of witness);

(e)  an order under rule 24.10(4) (deponent's evidence to be given orally); or

(f)  an order under rule 24.12 (order for the issue of a letter of request).

(2) When applying for a witness summons, permission under rule 22.8 or 23.4 or order under rule 24.7, 24.9, 24.10(4) or 24.12, the party must provide the court with evidence that—

(a)  all parties to the mediation agree to the obtaining of the mediation evidence;

(b)  obtaining the mediation evidence is necessary for overriding considerations of public policy in accordance with article 7(1)(a) of the Mediation Directive; or

(c)  the disclosure of the content of an agreement resulting from mediation is necessary to implement or enforce that agreement.

(3) When considering a request for a witness summons, permission under rule 22.8 or 23.4 or order under rule 24.7, 24.9, 24.10(4) or 24.12, the court may invite any person, whether or not a party, to make representations.

(4) Where this rule applies, Parts 21 to 24 apply to the extent they are consistent with this rule.

## PART 38—RECOGNITION AND ENFORCEMENT OF PROTECTION MEASURES

*Scope and interpretation*

**38.1**

(1) This Part contains rules about the mutual recognition and enforcement of protection measures between England and Wales and Member States of the European Union other than the United Kingdom and Denmark.

(2) In this Part—

'Article 5 certificate' means a certificate issued under Article 5 of the Protection Measures Regulation;

'Article 8 notice' means the notification required by Article 8 of the Protection Measures Regulation;

'Article 11 notice' means the notification required by Article 11 of the Protection Measures Regulation;

'Article 14 certificate' means a certificate issued under Article 14 of the Protection Measures Regulation;

'outgoing protection measure' means any protection measure included in any of—

(a) a non-molestation order made under section 42 of the 1996 Act;

(b) an occupation order made under any of sections 33, 35, 36, 37 or 38 of the 1996 Act;

(c) an undertaking accepted by the court under section 46 of the 1996 Act;

(d) an order that has been varied under section 49 of the 1996 Act;

(e) a forced marriage protection order made under section 63A of the 1996 Act;

(f) an undertaking accepted by the court under section 63E of the 1996 Act;

(g) an order that has been varied under section 63G of the 1996 Act;

(h) any other order of the family court or the High Court in family proceedings; or

(i) any other undertaking accepted by the family court or the High Court in family proceedings;

'person causing the risk' has the meaning given to it in the Protection Measures Regulation; and

'protected person' has the meaning given to it in the Protection Measures Regulation.

## II CERTIFICATES FOR OUTGOING PROTECTION MEASURES

*Application for an Article 5 certificate*

**38.2**

(1) A protected person may apply for an Article 5 certificate—

(a) at the time of application for an order containing an outgoing protection measure; or

(b) at any time after such application, provided either—

(i) the order or the undertaking containing the outgoing protection measure has not yet been made or accepted, as the case may be; or

(ii) the outgoing protection measure is still in force.

*The court to which an application for an Article 5 certificate must be made*

**38.3**

An application for an Article 5 certificate must be made—

(a) where the outgoing protection measure has not yet been ordered or accepted—

(i) to the family court if the proceedings relating to the outgoing protection measure are before the family court;

(ii) to the High Court if the proceedings relating to the outgoing protection measure are before the High Court;

(b) where the outgoing protection measure has been ordered or accepted—

(i) to the family court if that court made the order or accepted the undertaking as the case may be, unless there are proceedings relating to that order or undertaking before the High Court, in which case the application must be made to the High Court;

(ii) to the High Court if that court made the order or accepted the undertaking as the case may be, unless there are proceedings relating to that order or undertaking before the family court, in which case the application must be made to the family court.

## *When a request for a translation of an Article 5 certificate may be made*

**38.4**

A protected person may request a translation of an Article 5 certificate—

(a) at the time of the application for the Article 5 certificate; or

(b) at any time after such application, provided the Article 5 certificate—

    (i) has not yet been issued; or

    (ii) if issued, is still in force.

## *The court to which a request for translation of an Article 5 certificate must be made*

**38.5**

A request for a translation of an Article 5 certificate must be made—

(a) if the certificate has not yet been issued, to—

    (i) the family court, if the application for the certificate is before the family court; or

    (ii) the High Court, if the application for the certificate is before the High Court; or

(b) if the certificate has been issued, to—

    (i) the family court, if the family court issued it;

    (ii) the High Court, if the High Court issued it.

## *Service requirements under Article 6*

**38.6**

(1) Where the outgoing protection measure is included in an order, the court may only issue an Article 5 certificate if satisfied that the order has been served upon the person causing the risk in accordance with the requirements specified in rule 37.5, unless the court has dispensed with service of the order in accordance with the requirements specified in rule 37.8.

(2) Where the protected person is responsible for serving the order on the person causing the risk, any application for an Article 5 certificate must be accompanied by a certificate of service.

## *Notification of the certificate under Article 8*

**38.7**

(1) Subject to paragraph (2), the court officer must give Article 8 notice to the person causing the risk by serving it in accordance with Chapter 3 of Part 6 and the rules in that Chapter shall apply to service of the notice as they apply to any other document served by a court officer.

(2) If the person causing the risk resides in a Member State of the European Union other than the United Kingdom or in a country outside the European Union, the court officer must give Article 8 notice by sending it by registered letter with acknowledgement of receipt or confirmation of delivery or equivalent to the last known place of residence of that person.

## *Rectification of an Article 5 certificate*

**38.8**

(1) An application pursuant to Article 9 of the Protection Measures Regulation for rectification of an Article 5 certificate must be made to—

(a) the family court if the family court issued the certificate;

(b) the High Court if the High Court issued the certificate.

(2) An application for such rectification may be made by—

(a)  the protected person; or

(b)  the person causing the risk.

(3) An Article 5 certificate may be rectified pursuant to Article 9(1)(a) of the Protection Measures Regulation by the court—

(a)  on application under this rule; or

(b)  on its own initiative.

## Withdrawal of an Article 5 certificate

**38.9**

(1) An application pursuant to Article 9 of the Protection Measures Regulation for withdrawal of an Article 5 certificate must be made to—

(a)  the family court if the family court issued the certificate; or

(b)  the High Court if the High Court issued the certificate.

(2) An application for such withdrawal may be made by—

(a)  the protected person; or

(b)  the person causing the risk.

(3) An Article 5 certificate may be withdrawn pursuant to Article 9(1)(b) of the Protection Measures Regulation by the court—

(a)  on application under this rule; or

(b)  on its own initiative.

## When an application for an Article 14 certificate may be made

**38.10**

A protected person or person causing the risk may apply for an Article 14 certificate—

(a)  at the time of application for variation or discharge of the order containing the outgoing protection measure, or for acceptance of a variation or discharge of the undertaking containing the outgoing protection measure, as the case may be;

(b)  at any time after the variation or discharge of the order containing the outgoing protection measure has been ordered or the variation or discharge of the undertaking containing the outgoing protection measure has been accepted, as the case may be;

(c)  at the time of application under Article 9 of the Protection Measures Regulation for withdrawal of an Article 5 certificate;

(d)  at any time after an Article 5 certificate has been withdrawn under Article 9 of the Protection Measures Regulation;

(e)  at the time of application for an order staying or suspending enforcement of the order or undertaking containing the outgoing protection measure; or

(f)  any time after, the making of an order staying or suspending enforcement of the order or undertaking containing the outgoing protection measure.

## The court to which an application for an Article 14 certificate must be made

**38.11**

An application for an Article 14 certificate must be made—

(a)  if the order containing the outgoing protection measure has not yet been varied or discharged or a variation or discharge of the undertaking containing the protection measure has not yet been accepted, as the case may be, to—

(i)   the family court if the application for such variation or discharge is before the family court; or

(ii)  the High Court if the application for such variation or discharge is before the High Court;

(b)  if there has been an application under Article 9 of the Protection Measures Regulation for withdrawal of the Article 5 certificate, and that application has not yet been decided, to—

(i)   the family court if the application for such withdrawal is before the family court; or

(ii)  the High Court if the application for such withdrawal is before the High Court;

(c)  if the order containing the outgoing protection measure has been varied or discharged or the variation or discharge of the undertaking containing the outgoing protection measure has been accepted, as the case may be, to—

(i)   the family court if the family court ordered or accepted such variation or discharge, as the case may be; or

(ii)  the High Court if the High Court ordered or accepted such variation or discharge, as the case may be;

(d)  if an Article 5 certificate has been withdrawn under Article 9, to—

(i)   the family court if the family court ordered such withdrawal; or

(ii)  the High Court if the High Court ordered such withdrawal;

(e)  where enforcement of the order has been stayed or suspended, to—

(i)   the family court if the family court made the order for the stay or suspension; or

(ii)  the High Court if the High Court made the order for the stay or suspension.

## III   INCOMING PROTECTION MEASURES

*Application for adjustment under Article 11*

**38.12**

A protected person may apply to the court under Article 11 of the Protection Measures Regulation to adjust the factual elements of an incoming protection measure.

*Notification of the adjustment under Article 11*

**38.13**

(1) Subject to paragraph (2), the court officer must give Article 11 notice to the person causing the risk by serving it in accordance with Chapter 3 of Part 6 and the rules in that Chapter apply to service of the notice as they apply to any other document to be served by a court officer.

(2) If the person causing the risk resides in a Member State of the European Union other than the United Kingdom or in a country outside the European Union, the court officer must give Article 11 notice by sending it by registered letter with acknowledgment of receipt or other confirmation of delivery or equivalent to the last known place of residence of that person.

*Application for refusal of recognition or enforcement under Article 13*

**38.14**

An application by a person causing the risk for refusal of recognition or enforcement under Article 13 of the Protection Measures Regulation must be made to—

(a)  the family court if—

(i)   there are proceedings relating to the same protection measure before the family court; or

(ii)  proceedings relating to the same protection measure were dealt with by the family court;

(b)  the High Court if—

(i)   there are proceedings relating to the same protection measure before the High Court; or

(ii) proceedings relating to the same protection measure were dealt with by the High Court; or

(c) the family court, unless, applying rule 5.4, the application should be made to the High Court.

*Application under Article 14(2)*

**38.15**

(1) This rule applies where an Article 14 certificate has been issued in a Member State of the European Union other than the United Kingdom or Denmark.

(2) A protected person or person causing the risk may apply to the court to stay, suspend or withdraw the effects of recognition or, where applicable, the enforcement of the protection measure.

(3) An application under this rule must include a copy of the Article 14 certificate issued in the other Member State.

(4) On an application under this rule, the court must make such orders or give such directions as may be necessary to give effect to the Article 14 certificate.

## PRACTICE DIRECTION 38A—RECOGNITION AND ENFORCEMENT OF PROTECTION MEASURES

*The Protection Measures Regulation*

**1.1**

The Protection Measures Regulation is an EU law which helps a person who has a "protection measure" obtained in one Member State to have it recognised and enforced in any other EU Member State (except Denmark). The protection can continue in the other Member State for the length of time the "protection measure" has been ordered, except it cannot continue for longer than twelve months.

**1.2**

The Protection Measures Regulation applies across the United Kingdom. Part 38 and this Practice Direction apply in England and Wales only. If you need information about Scotland you should contact the Scottish Government. If you need information about Northern Ireland you should contact the Northern Ireland Department for Justice.

**1.3**

A "protection measure" is a decision that says the "person causing the risk" must comply with one or more of the three kinds of obligation set out below, to protect another person, the "protected person", from physical or psychological harm.

The obligations are:—

a ban or controls on entering the place where the protected person lives or works, or regularly visits or stays;

a ban or controls on contact, in any form, with the protected person, including by telephone, post, e-mail, text or social media or any other means;

a ban or controls on approaching the protected person closer than a stated distance.

**1.4**

A "protected person" is the individual who is protected by the obligation in the protection measure. A "person causing the risk" is the individual on whom the obligation has been imposed.

**1.5**

In England and Wales in family proceedings a protection measure as set out at paragraph 1.3 above may be included in an order made or undertaking accepted by the family court or the High Court. In this Practice Direction, references to orders made include undertakings accepted.

**1.6**

Rule 38.1 sets out which orders made in family proceedings in England and Wales could contain a protection measure. In the Protection Measures Regulation, in the Article 5 and Article 14 certificates and in this practice direction the meanings of words are as follows. The family court or the High Court is the "issuing authority" for the protection measure when it makes the order. The EU Member State where the protection measure is ordered is the "Member State of origin". The EU Member State where the protected person can take the protection measure to get it recognised and, where applicable, enforced, is the "Member State addressed".

**1.7**

If the protected person wants to take a protection measure ordered in England and Wales to another EU Member State (except Denmark) to get it recognised and enforced there, it is called an "outgoing protection measure". If the protected person is bringing a protection measure from another EU Member State (not from Denmark and not from Scotland or Northern Ireland) to England and Wales to get it recognised and enforced in England and Wales, it is called an "incoming protection measure". To get a protection measure recognised and enforced here or in another Member State (except Denmark) it must have a certificate under Article 5 of the Protection Measures Regulation to go with it.

## Outgoing protection measures

### Application for an Article 5 certificate

**2.1**

A protected person who wants an outgoing protection measure to be recognised and enforceable in another Member State (except Denmark) can apply under Chapter 2 of Part 38 for an Article 5 certificate. The protected person can apply either at the same time as they are applying for the order which contains a protection measure, or later before the order is made or, provided the order containing the protection measure is still in force, at any time after the order is made.

**2.2**

The protected person must apply to the court where the proceedings about the order are under way or took place. This will be either the family court or the High Court. At the same time as applying for the certificate, or later, the protected person can ask the court where the proceedings are under way or took place for a translation of the certificate into another EU official language.

**2.3**

When the protected person applies for an Article 5 certificate they must provide the court with the case number, their full name, date and place of birth and an address to be used for notification purposes. If you are the protected person, you can decide what address to provide and it does not have to be your own home address. THE ADDRESS YOU PROVIDE WILL NOT BE DISCLOSED TO THE PERSON CAUSING THE RISK UNLESS IT IS NECESSARY FOR THE PERSON CAUSING THE RISK TO KNOW IT, TO COMPLY WITH THE PROTECTION MEASURE (see paragraph 2.6 below). If the protected person knows the information, they should provide the court with the following details of the person causing the risk: full name, date and place of birth and an address to be used for notification purposes.

**2.4**

Before it can issue the Article 5 certificate, the court needs to know that the order containing the protection measure has been made known to ("served on") the person causing the risk. How the court knows depends on when the protected person applies for the certificate. The protected person who is applying for the Article 5 certificate before the order containing the protection measure has been made should use the appropriate form. If the protected person is acting in person and the order is a domestic violence or forced marriage protection order, they can ask the court under rule 10.6(2) or rule 11.7(4), whichever applies, to serve any order made on the person causing the risk. When the court makes and then serves the order and at the same time issues the certificate, the court knows that the person causing the risk has been told about the order.

**2.5**

If the protected person is applying for a certificate after the order containing the protection measure has been made, the protected person should apply using the appropriate form and provide the certified copy of the order. If the protected person or their legal representative was required to provide a copy of the order made to the person causing the risk, then the protected person must provide a certificate of service with the application for the Article 5 certificate. If the protected person is acting in person and the order is a domestic violence or forced marriage protection order, they can ask the court under rule 10.6(2) or rule 11.7(4), whichever applies, to serve the order on the person causing the risk. If the court has served the order, the protected person does not have to provide a certificate of service.

### Notification of the Article 5 certificate

**2.6**

When the Article 5 certificate has been issued to the protected person, the court officer will notify the person causing the risk of the certificate in accordance with rule 38.7 (Article 8 notice) and provide them with a copy of the Article 5 certificate. The court officer will not tell the person causing the risk the address or contact details of the protected person unless the person causing the risk needs to have this information to comply with the protection measure or the information must be disclosed to get the protection measure enforced. For example, if the person causing the risk must stay away from a specific address, they need to know the address.

**2.7**

The Article 8 notice will also explain to the person causing the risk that the issue of the Article 5 certificate means the protection measure can now be recognised and is enforceable in other Member States of the European Union (except Denmark). It will explain that if the person causing the risk breaches the protection measure they could be punished under the law of the Member State where enforcement is requested.

### "Rectification" of the Article 5 certificate

**2.8**

The protected person or the person causing the risk can apply for "rectification" of the Article 5 certificate. "Rectification" means the correction of a clerical error in which the certificate does not have the same information as the protection measure. The protected person or person causing the risk can apply for rectification under rule 38.8 using the appropriate form to the court which issued the certificate. In addition, if the court notices such a clerical error in an Article 5 certificate, the court will provide to the protected person and to the person causing the risk a corrected certificate on its own initiative.

### Withdrawal of the Article 5 certificate

**2.9**

The protected person or the person causing the risk can apply under rule 38.9 using the appropriate form to the court which issued the Article 5 certificate for it to be withdrawn if it has clearly been wrongly granted under the Protection Measures Regulation. For example, an Article 5 certificate is wrongly granted if the person causing the risk did not know about the protection measure as required by Article 6. The court can also withdraw the Article 5 certificate on its own initiative (without an application) if it has clearly been wrongly granted. If the Article 5 certificate is withdrawn the protection measure cannot be recognised or enforced in any other Member State, including the Member State addressed. The court officer will notify both the protected person and the person causing the risk that the Article 5 certificate has been withdrawn.

### 2.10

When under Article 10 of the Protection Measures Regulation the protected person asks the court (as the issuing authority) for assistance to obtain information about the authorities in the Member State addressed which can adjust or enforce the protection measure, the court officer will signpost the protected person to the information on the EU website of the European Judicial Network in civil and commercial matters provided by EU Member States (except Denmark).

*Changes to protection measure or withdrawal of Article 5 certificate—Article 14 certificate*

### 2.11

If the family court or High Court discharges or stays a protection measure, or makes an order such as a variation that effectively suspends or limits its enforceability, the protected person or person causing the risk can apply for a certificate to be issued under Article 14(1) of the Protection Measures Regulation. Such a certificate can also be applied for if the Article 5 certificate is withdrawn (see paragraph 2.9 above). The application must be made in accordance with rules 38.10 and 38.11. At the same time as applying for the Article 14 certificate, or later, the protected person or the person causing the risk can ask the court where the proceedings are under way or took place for a translation of the Article 14 certificate into another EU official language.

### 2.12

When applying for an Article 14 certificate, the protected person or the person causing the risk must use the appropriate form and should provide the following documents if available: a certified copy of the court order which included the protection measure, a copy of the Article 5 certificate, a copy of the court order which varied, stayed, suspended or discharged all or part of the order including the protection measure, or the notification of the withdrawal of the Article 5 certificate by the court. The application can also be made if the protected person or the person causing the risk does not have all the documents listed. The applicant should provide the case number so that the court can locate the orders.

### 2.13

When the Article 14 certificate has been issued to the protected person or the person causing the risk the court will notify the other party. The applicant who has received an Article 14 certificate should send it to the court or other authority in the Member State addressed where the outgoing protection measure has been invoked or enforced so as to stop recognition and enforcement of the protection measure.

*Incoming protection measures*

### 3.1

An incoming protection measure for which an Article 5 certificate has been issued in another Member State, is automatically recognised by the court in England and Wales. This section sets out actions the protected person can take in relation to an incoming protection measure, and the points at which the incoming protection measure and Article 5 certificate must be provided to the court. The applications set out below can be made to the family court, the county court and sometimes to the Family Division of the High Court (see rule 5.4 of the Family Procedure Rules 2010). This practice direction and the Family Procedure Rules apply to the family court and Family Division of the High Court only. Applications to the county court are covered by the Civil Procedure Rules.

### 3.2

The protected person and the person causing the risk can make applications in relation to incoming protection measures using the procedure in Part 18 (or Part 19 if applicable) of the Family Procedure Rules. There is more information in Practice Directions 18A and 19A. These Practice Directions set out the documents the applicant must provide with the application, in addition to any requirements

Rules of Procedure

set out in this Practice Direction. When making an application the protected person or the person causing the risk must also provide a copy of the order containing the incoming protection measure and the Article 5 certificate issued in the Member State of origin. (Explanations of the terms used in the Protection Measures Regulation and the certificates are set out in section 1 above.)

*Adjustment of "factual elements" in the protection measure*

3.3

The protected person can apply to the court for the adjustment of "factual elements" in the incoming protection measure to make it effective in England and Wales. "Factual elements" can, for example, include the address or location the person causing the risk must stay away from, such as the location where the protected person lived or worked in the Member State of origin, or the minimum distance the person causing the risk must keep away from the protected person. To make the protection measure work in England and Wales the protected person can apply for the protection measure to be adjusted to show an address in England or Wales. ANY ADDRESS OR LOCATION IN THE ADJUSTED PROTECTION MEASURE WILL BE DISCLOSED TO THE PERSON CAUSING THE RISK, BECAUSE THE ADJUSTMENT MUST BE NOTIFIED TO THE PERSON CAUSING THE RISK.

3.4

The protected person can apply to the court under rule 38.12 using the appropriate form for an adjustment to the factual elements to be made. If you are the protected person, you will need to provide an address for notification. You can decide what address to provide and it does not have to be your own home address. IF YOU ARE THE PROTECTED PERSON, AND THE ADDRESS YOU PROVIDE IS ALSO IN THE ADJUSTED PROTECTION MEASURE, THAT ADDRESS WILL BE DISCLOSED TO THE PERSON CAUSING THE RISK, BECAUSE THE PERSON CAUSING THE RISK MUST BE NOTIFIED OF THE ADJUSTMENT TO BE ABLE TO COMPLY WITH IT. When the court adjusts the facts in the protection measure the court officer must notify the person causing the risk of the adjustment in accordance with rule 38.13 (Article 11 notice). A protected person may choose not to apply for an adjustment of a protection measure that contains a specific address or location, and may choose to apply only for adjustments of the factual elements of a protection measure that do not contain such information.

*Enforcement of the protection measure*

3.5

If the protected person has an incoming protection measure accompanied by an Article 5 certificate from the Member State of origin and they believe the person causing the risk has disobeyed the protection measure, the protected person can apply to the court under rule 10.11 for the issue of a civil warrant for the arrest of the person causing the risk. IF YOU ARE THE PROTECTED PERSON AND YOU BELIEVE THE PERSON CAUSING THE RISK HAS COMMITTED A CRIMINAL OFFENCE UNDER THE LAW OF ENGLAND AND WALES YOU SHOULD CONTACT THE POLICE. If this has happened, the person causing the risk may be subject to criminal punishment under the law of England and Wales.

3.6

Incoming protection measures can be enforced by the family court and the High Court in England and Wales as if they had been ordered by those courts. IF YOU ARE THE PERSON CAUSING THE RISK AND YOU DISOBEY THE PROTECTION MEASURE, YOU MAY BE HELD TO BE IN CONTEMPT OF COURT IN ENGLAND AND WALES AND YOU MAY BE IMPRISONED OR FINED. Part 10 and Part 37 of the FPR provide more information.

*Application for refusal to recognise or enforce the protection measure*

**3.7**

The person causing the risk can apply under rule 38.14 using the appropriate form for the court to refuse to recognise an incoming protection measure or to refuse to enforce it against them. Under the Protection Measures Regulation, the court will only refuse to recognise or enforce the protection measure when to do so would be "manifestly contrary to public policy" or if recognition of the incoming protection measure is "irreconcilable" with a judgment that has been given or recognised in the United Kingdom.

*Suspension or withdrawal of recognition or enforcement*

**3.8**

When a protection measure from another Member State has been suspended, limited or withdrawn in the Member State of origin or an Article 5 certificate has been withdrawn there, and an Article 14 certificate has been issued to confirm this, the protected person or the person causing the risk can apply under rule 38.15 using the appropriate form to the court in England and Wales which dealt or is dealing with the incoming protection measure to ask the court to stay, suspend or withdraw the effects of recognition or enforcement. The applicant must provide a copy of the Article 14 certificate. When the court has made orders or given directions to give effect to the Article 14 certificate the court officer will inform the other party.

*Appeals*

**4.1**

All decisions made by the court in England and Wales under the Protection Measures Regulation are subject to ordinary appeal procedures. In most cases permission to appeal will be required, but there is no need to get permission to appeal a decision made by lay justices. (The issue of an Article 5 certificate is separate and cannot be appealed.) Either the protected person or the person causing the risk can seek permission to appeal using the Part 30 procedure.

Rules of Procedure

# Alphabetical Index

Administration of Estates Act 1971, **321**

Administration of Justice Act 1920, **295**

Adoption (Intercountry Aspects) Act 1999, **465**

Adoption and Children Act 2002, **475**

Adoptions with a Foreign Element Regulations SI 2005/392, **527**

Brussels I Regulation (recast), **139**

Brussels IIa Regulation, **13**

Child Abduction and Custody Act 1985, **411**

Civil Evidence Act 1972, **325**

Civil Jurisdiction and Judgments (Authentic Instruments and Court Settlements) Order SI 2001/3928, **521**

Civil Jurisdiction and Judgments (Maintenance) (Rules of Court) Regulations SI 2011/1215, **561**

Civil Jurisdiction and Judgments (Maintenance) Regulations SI 2011/1484, **563**

Civil Jurisdiction and Judgments (Protection Measures) Regulations SI 2014/3298, **589**

Civil Jurisdiction and Judgments Act 1982, **375**

Civil Jurisdiction and Judgments Act 1982 (Interim Relief) Order SI 1997/302, **517**

Civil Jurisdiction and Judgments Order SI 2001/3929, **523**

Civil Partnership (Jurisdiction and Recognition of Judgments) Regulations SI 2005/3334, **547**

Civil Partnership Act 2004, **481**

Civil Procedure Rules SI 1998/3132, **591**

Colonial Probates Act 1892, **293**

Companies Act 2006, **501**

Consular Marriages and Marriages under Foreign Law (No. 2) Order SI 2014/3265, **583**

Consumer Rights Act 2015, **513**

Court of Protection Rules SI 2007/1744, **659**

Defamation Act 2013, **505**

Domicile and Matrimonial Proceedings Act 1973, **351**

EC-Denmark Agreement (jurisdiction and judgments),
Agreement, **206**
Amending Agreement (2013), **213**
Amending Agreement (2014), **214**
Decision 2005/790/EC (signature), **205**
Decision 2006/325/EC (conclusion), **212**

EC-Denmark Agreement (service),
Agreement, **216**
Amending Agreement, **222**
Decision 2005/794/EC (signature), **215**
Decision 2006/326/EC (conclusion), **221**

Employment Rights Act 1996, **461**

European Enforcement Order for uncontested claims (Council Regulation (EC) No 805/2004), **37**

European Judicial Network in civil and commercial matters (Council Decision 2001/470/EC), **193**

European order for payment procedure (Regulation (EC) No 1896/2006), **49**

European Small Claims Procedure (Regulation (EC) No 861/2007), **61**

Evidence (Proceedings in Other Jurisdictions) Act 1975, **363**

Family Law Act 1986, **429**

Family Procedure Rules SI 2010/2955, **667**

Foreign Corporations Act 1991, **455**

Foreign Judgments (Reciprocal Enforcement) Act 1933, **305**

Foreign Limitation Periods Act 1984, **399**

Hague Choice of Court Convention,
Convention (Annex I to Decision 2009/397/EC) 252
Decision 2009/397/EC (signature), **251**
Decision 2014/887/EU (approval), **262**

Hague Convention on the International Recovery of Child Support and Other Forms of Family Maintenance,
Convention, **270**
Decision 2011/220/EU (signature), **265**
Decision 2011/432/EU (approval), **266**

International Recovery of Maintenance (Hague Convention etc) Regulations SI 2012/2814, **573**

Jurisdiction and the recognition and enforcement of judgments in civil and commercial matters (Brussels I (recast)) (Regulation (EU) No 1215/2012), **139**

Jurisdiction and the recognition and enforcement of judgments in matrimonial matters and the matters of parental responsibility (Brussels IIa) (Council Regulation (EC) No 2201/2003), **13**

Jurisdiction, applicable law, recognition and enforcement of decisions and cooperation in matters relating to maintenance obligations (Regulation (EC) No 4/2009), **111**

Late Payment of Commercial Debts (Interest) Act 1998, **463**

Law applicable to contractual obligations (Rome I) (Regulation (EC) No 593/2008), **95**

Law applicable to non-contractual obligations (Rome II) (Regulation (EC) No 864/2007), **73**

Legal aid, establishing minimum common rules for cross-border disputes (Council Directive 2003/8/EC), **177**

Legitimacy Act 1976, **367**

Lugano Convention (jurisdiction and judgments),
Convention and Protocols, **224**
Decision 2007/712/EC (signature), **223**
Decision 2009/430/EC (conclusion), **247**

Maintenance Orders (Facilities for Enforcement) Act
1920, **299**

Maintenance Orders (Reciprocal Enforcement) Act
1972, **327**

Maintenance Orders Act 1950, **311**

Marriage (Enabling) Act 1960, **317**

Marriage (Prohibited Degrees of Relationship) Act
1986, **449**

Marriage (Same Sex Couples) (Jurisdiction and Recognition of Judgments) Regulations SI 2014/543,
**579**

Marriage (Same Sex Couples) Act 2013, **507**

Matrimonial and Family Proceedings Act 1984, **403**

Matrimonial Causes Act 1973, **359**

Mediation in civil and commercial matters (Directive
2008/52/EC), **187**

Mental Capacity Act 2005, **493**

Mutual recognition of protection measures in civil
matters (Regulation (EU) No 606/2013), **165**

Overseas Companies (Execution of Documents and
Registration of Charges) Regulations SI
2009/1917, **551**

Parental Responsibility and Measures for the Protection of Children (International Obligations)
(England and Wales and Northern Ireland)
Regulations SI 2010/1898, **555**

Private International Law (Miscellaneous Provisions)
Act 1995, **457**

Protection of Trading Interests Act 1980, **371**

Recognition of Trusts Act 1987, **451**

Rome I Regulation, **95**

Rome II Regulation, **73**

Senior Courts Act 1981, **373**

Service in the Member States of judicial and extrajudicial documents in civil or commercial matters
(Regulation (EC) No 1393/2007), **85**

Taking of evidence in civil or commercial matters
(Council Regulation (EC) No 1206/2001), **3**

Treaty on the Functioning of the European Union, **1**

Unfair Contract Terms Act 1977, **369**

Unfair terms in consumer contracts (Council Directive 93/13/EEC), **175**

Unfair Terms in Consumer Contracts Regulations SI
1999/2083, **519**

Wills Act 1963, **319**